Natural
Resource and
Environmental
Economics

Natural Resource and Environmental Economics

Second Edition

ROGER PERMAN
YUE MA
JAMES McGILVRAY
MICHAEL COMMON

LONGMAN

Pearson Education Limited
Edinburgh Gate
Harlow
Essex CM20 2JE
England
and Associated Companies throughout the world

Published in the United States of America by Pearson Education Inc., New York

Visit us on the world wide web at:
http://www.awl-he.com

First published 1996
Third impression 1998
Second edition 1999

ISBN 0 582 36876 6

British Library Cataloguing-in-Publication Data
A catalogue record for this book is available from the British Library

Library of Congress Cataloging-in-Publication Data
A catalogue record for this book is available from the Library of Congress

Set in 10/12pt Baskerville
Typeset by 32
Printed in Great Britain by Henry Ling Ltd.,
at the Dorset Press, Dorchester, Dorset

Contents

Preface to the second edition

There are two main reasons for producing a new edition of a textbook. First, the subject may have moved on; this has certainly been true in the area of natural resource and environmental economics. Second, experience in using the text may suggest areas for improvement. In spite of the favourable reception of the first edition of this book, we soon came to feel it could be substantially improved upon.

Addison Wesley Longman obtained several critical reviews of the first edition, and of our intended changes. This was very helpful. We were encouraged by the convergence between opinion among the reviewers and our own assessments, and most of the recommendations made have been acted upon. We believe that the text has been improved as a result. Our thanks go to all those who participated in that review exercise.

Some of the main changes that have taken place between the first and second editions are as follows. We have given a more extended exposition of concepts of sustainability, and have given this idea a central role in the organisation of the text. There is a new chapter on forest resources, allowing us to deal with the multiple use of renewable resources. Biodiversity is discussed in this chapter, and in several other places. In our discussions of resource exploitation, the distinction between sustainable and optimal/efficient programmes is made more carefully. The Lagrange multiplier method for solving constrained optimisation problems and the Maximum Principle of dynamic optimisation have been more fully explained and illustrated, as has the intuition for these particular techniques.

Our treatment of pollution is now organised around a targets/instruments distinction, and a more complete account of the associated theory and practical experience is provided. The relevant theory for the case where damage is related to the pollution stock is dealt with more comprehensively. More attention has also been given to the spatial dimension of pollution abatement programmes. We have somewhat changed our emphasis in the chapter on international pollution problems, focusing mainly on the coordination problems arising in a world of many sovereign nations.

There is a more comprehensive treatment of environmental valuation, which pays more attention to the practical difficulties involved, and to the criticisms that have been made of the economic approach to environmental decision making. Given the importance that irreversibility, risk and uncertainty have for environmental decision making, we have devoted a new chapter to these matters. This allows us to deal more fully with such matters as option and quasi-option values, and to discuss project appraisal at some length.

Our discussion of the theory of environmental accounting, in the final chapter, is now more firmly grounded in the capital theoretic analysis of resource depletion set out in earlier chapters. We have explicitly addressed the issue of the relationship of that theory to the question of measuring sustainable income. In this respect, we are particularly grateful to Jack Pezzey for writing an Appendix to Chapter 17, and for giving comments on drafts of the relevant parts of the chapter itself.

The task of preparing a second edition was made difficult by the death of our colleague, Professor Jim McGilvray. The task facing Yue Ma and Roger Perman appeared a little less daunting when Mick Common accepted their invitation to participate. All three of us are convinced that Jim would welcome the changes and extensions in the new edition, and would certainly feel that it retains the essential qualities of the first edition.

Once again, many thanks to our wives – Val Perman, Hong Lin and Branwen Common – for bearing many of the costs associated with the preparation of a textbook. We are also grateful to Alison McGilvray for her support and encouragement throughout this project. We are indebted to all those who have been involved in the editing and production of this text, whose efforts have made the task of writing a second edition much less onerous than it could have been. We are especially indebted to Chris Harrison at Addison Wesley Longman for his excellence in commissioning and providing general support for the text.

ROGER PERMAN
YUE MA
MICHAEL COMMON

December 1998

A personal note

Just before the completion of the first edition of this book, one of its authors – Professor James McGilvray – died suddenly. Our sadness at the loss of a friend and colleague is softened by the memories we shall retain of Jim.

Among these, we recall the pleasure and intellectual stimulus obtained in collaborating with Jim in the process of writing this book. For this reason, the book will always retain a special significance for us.

The preface which follows was written by Jim a few days before his tragic death.

ROGER PERMAN
YUE MA

Preface to the first edition

Classes in environmental and/or in natural resource economics are commonly offered at graduate level, typically in a Master's course in environmental studies, and delivered to students from a wide range of academic disciplines, or as third or fourth year electives in undergraduate degree courses in economics or business. This diversity of background training and skills amongst the students of environmental economics poses a considerable challenge to those lecturing on the subject, as well as to authors of textbooks in this field – as we have discovered to our cost on both counts! However, it is in response to this challenge that the present text has evolved, based on several years of teaching very distinct cohorts of graduate and undergraduate students. Although there are now a number of contemporary textbooks on environmental and natural resource economics, the range of choice of texts suitable for a full semester class is relatively limited, and in our view leaves many unsatisfied customers. While we do not claim that this text will satisfy all those customers, we believe it is a distinct contribution to the menu of available texts. In particular, we have sought to establish the subject-matter on firm and explicit microeconomic foundations, and thus provide a degree of rigour which we believe to be appropriate to a modern up-to-date text at the present stage of development of the subject. Although in this respect the book is directed principally at graduate or undergraduate economics students, welfare theoretic axioms and results which underpin the text are developed from basic principles, and with careful reading should be accessible to non-economists.

A supporting reason for a more rigorous approach is the rapidly growing use of environmental criteria in appraising and evaluating investment projects, particularly public sector infrastructure projects (or mixed public–private sector projects) which may have significant environmental effects. Cost–benefit analysis is the established technique of evaluation for projects of this type, and will remain so. However, there is now much greater emphasis on the identification and inclusion of environmental costs and benefits in the overall cost–benefit appraisal. It is desirable that those with an interest in the outcomes of such assessments – and not simply the economists who undertake the calculations – have an understanding of the theoretical foundations and methods of application of the cost–benefit approach. Given the uncertainties and imprecision involved in attempting to value environmental costs and benefits, wider understanding of basic principles on the part of those involved can hopefully inform and enhance the process of environmental assessment and decision-making.

Gratitude as well as prudence prompts a heartfelt thanks to our wives – Val Perman, Hong Lin and Alison McGilvray – who patiently bore many externalities of the type discussed in this book. Various colleagues provided helpful advice and comments on aspects of the book; in particular we would like to thank Darryl Holden (Economics Department, Strathclyde University) and Sue Scott (Economic and Social Research Institute, Dublin). Chris Harrison of Longman provided support and encouragement throughout, and editorial staff at Longman have been prompt and efficient in executing the various stages of conversion from what used to be called manuscript (diskscript?) to the hard copy in hand.

ROGER PERMAN
YUE MA
JAMES McGILVRAY
November 1995

Acknowledgements

It is impossible to fully acknowledge our debt to the many individuals who have developed, and fostered awareness of, the discipline of natural resource and environmental economics. We hope that this debt becomes clear to the reader of this text. What will not be evident to the reader is the debt which the authors owe to those teachers who have cultivated our interests in this area of study.

Wherever the authors have drawn heavily on expositions, in written or other form, of particular individuals or organisations, care was taken to ensure that proper acknowledgement was made at the appropriate places in the text. As noted in the Preface to the Second Edition, Jack Pezzey wrote the first of the appendices to Chapter 17.

We are grateful to the following copyright holders for permission to reproduce copyright material.

Table 3.3 from *The Globe*, No. 13, June 1993 (Atkinson & Pearce, 1993) reproduced with permission from CSERGE, University College London; Figure 8.13 from *Scarcity and Growth Reconsidered* in V.K. Smith (ed), (Brown & Field, 1979), John Hopkins University Press/Resources for the Future, Inc., Baltimore, Maryland; Table 12.5 from *Oxford Review of Economic Policy* **6**(1), (Tietenberg, 1990); Figure 13.3 from EUR report 16523 reproduced by permission of the Publishers, the Office for Official Publications of the European Communities © European Communities; Figure 17.1 from Data from Environmental Indicators: OECD Core Set, Copyright OECD, 1995; Tables 17.1 and 17.2 from *Environmental Measures*, Environmental Challenge Group; Figure 17.3 from Measuring Sustainable Development, New Economic Foundation (Jackson & Marks, 1994).; Extracts on p. 372 from 'Global warming won't cost the earth' (F.C. Ind, 1995), *The Independent*.

While every effort has been made to trace the owners of copyright material, in a few cases this has proved impossible and we take this opportunity to offer our apologies to any copyright holders whose rights we may have unwittingly infringed.

Notation

As far as possible, in using letters or symbols to denote variables or other quantities of interest, we have tried to use each character consistently to refer to one variable or quantity. This has not always been possible or desirable, however, because of the large number of variables used in the book. In the following listing, we state the meaning that is usually attached to each letter or symbol used in this way. On the few occasions where a symbol is used in two ways, this is also indicated. Where usage differs from those given below, this is made clear in the text.

A	=	Pollution stock (or ambient pollution level)
B	=	Gross benefit of an activity
C	=	Consumption flow *or* total cost of production of a good
D	=	Damage flow
E	=	An index of environmental pressure
e	=	Natural exponent
F	=	Reduction in pollution stock brought about by clean-up
G	=	Total extraction cost of a resource *or* biological growth of a resource
H	=	Renewable resource harvest rate
I	=	Investment flow
i	=	Market rate of interest
K	=	Capital stock (human-made)
L	=	Labour service flow
M	=	Emissions (pollution) flow
MP_K	=	Marginal product of capital
MP_L	=	Marginal product of labour
MP_R	=	Marginal product of resource
MU	=	Marginal utility

MU_X = Marginal utility of good X
NB = Net benefit of an activity
P = Unit price of resource (usually upper case for gross and lower case for net)
Q = Aggregate output flow
R = Resource extraction or use flow
r = Consumption rate of interest
S = Resource stock
T = Terminal time of a planning period
t = A period or instant of time
U = Utility flow
V = Environmental clean-up expenditure
W = Social welfare flow
Z = Pollution abatement flow
δ = Social rate of return on capital
α = Pollution stock decay rate
ρ = Rate of utility time preference (utility discount rate)

The Greek characters λ, μ, χ and ω are used for shadow prices deriving from optimisation problems.

The symbols X and Y are used in a variety of different ways in the text, depending on the context in question.

Mathematical notation

Where we are considering a function of a single variable such as

$$Y = Y(X)$$

then we write the first derivative in one of the following four ways:

$$\frac{dY}{dX} = \frac{dY(X)}{dX} = Y'(X) = Y_X$$

Each of these denotes the first derivative of Y with respect to X. In any particular exposition, we choose the form that seems best to convey meaning.

Where we are considering a function of several variables such as the following function of two variables:

$$Z = Z(P, Q)$$

we write first partial derivatives in one of the following ways:

$$\frac{\partial Z}{\partial P} = \frac{\partial Z(P, Q)}{\partial P} = Z_P$$

each of which is the partial derivative of Z with respect to the variable P.

We frequently use derivatives of variables with respect to time. For example, in the case of the variable S being a function of time, t, the derivative is written in one of the following forms:

$$\frac{\mathrm{d}S}{\mathrm{d}t} = \frac{\mathrm{d}S(t)}{\mathrm{d}t} = \dot{S}$$

Our most common usage is that of dot notation, as in the last term in the equalities above.

The text provides extensive discussion of the ethical basis of economics, and comparison of the conventional utilitarian ethic with rival frameworks. We demonstrate how results and conclusions of resource and environmental economics analysis depend upon the ethical framework adopted.

Applied welfare economics is used as an organising principle for the book, with relevant theory being explained early in the text. A careful distinction is drawn throughout the text between the concepts of efficiency and optimality.

The long run is given proper attention, particularly in two chapters on sustainability, explaining the nature of the problem by drawing on the natural sciences, and elucidating and comparing rival concepts. A second way in which the long run enters is through the analysis of natural resource exploitation within the framework of growth theory.

Other important features of the book are:

- a presentation of the theory and practice of environmental accounting;
- a chapter devoted to the use of environmental-augmented input–output analysis;
- a focus on environmental policy that gives proper recognition to the design of policy in circumstances of uncertainty, irreversibility, and the constraint of a safe minimum standard of conservation;
- analysis of pollution and pollution control, emphasising the important case of stock pollutants – pollutants where damage is related to the concentration or stock level of the pollutant in the air, ground or water;
- a chapter on forestry as a problem involving multiple uses of an environmental resource.

We have gone to some trouble to use, as far as is possible, consistent notation throughout the book. A list of the main symbols used and their usual meanings is given on p. xix. However, given the range of material covered it has not been possible to maintain a one-to-one correspondence between symbols and referents throughout the book. Some symbols do have different meanings in different places. Wherever there is the possibility of confusion we have made explicit what the symbols used mean at that point in the text.

Contents

The coverage of the text is structured as follows. The first two chapters provide the background to the study of resource and environmental economics, first by briefly putting the field in its context in the history of economics, and secondly by discussing the dependence of economic activity on the natural environment in terms of the sustainability problem. The third chapter considers alternative concepts of what sustainability involves.

Chapters 4 to 6 cover the foundations for the economic analysis of natural resources and the environment, dealing with the theory of welfare economics and the way in which that theory is applied to policy questions. Chapters 7 to 10 then look at the exploitation of non-renewable and renewable natural resources: Chapter 10 covers the multiple use of forest resources. Chapters 11 to 13 are concerned with environmental pollution, working through the setting of standards for control, the choice of instrument for control, and the problems that arise when damage crosses national frontiers.

Chapters 14 and 15 largely use the focus of the wilderness development/conservation decision to explore environmental valuation and the implications of irreversibility and imperfect future knowledge. Chapter 16 covers the use of input–output and applied general equilibrium models for environmental analysis. Finally, Chapter 17 returns to the question of sustainability in the context of the theory and practice of environmental accounting.

Given the nature of the subject matter, it is impossible to deal with it in a totally linear way, and our treatment involves some topics and ideas appearing at several points in the book. Examples are the Hartwick rule, which appears in Chapters 3, 7 and 17; the Safe Minimum Standard, which appears when we discuss renewable resource exploitation, pollution control, and the implications of uncertainty for decision making; and biodiversity loss and conservation, which appears at a number of points, and is, of course, intimately linked to resource exploitation and pollution, and a matter about which there is much uncertainty. We have tried to flag these connections across chapters in a useful way.

It is our judgement that most readers will find that the levels of difficulty and abstraction will generally increase as they work through the book. This is intentional. We have nowhere set out to be more difficult than we judge necessary, but we have tried to ease the path for the reader.

Mode of study

Because we believe that resource and environmental problems are inextricably linked and need to be studied together, it is our hope that this text will be used for a full course of study involving the material in all 17 chapters. However, we are aware that this would be time consuming and may not fit with all institutional structures. We therefore offer the following suggestions as to how the text might be used for somewhat shorter courses. In all cases, courses could be further shortened for students with a strong economics background by treating Chapters 4 and 5, and possibly 6, as revision material. We do not recommend that this material be completely dropped for any course.

A: Resource economics course

1 An introduction to natural resource and environmental economics
2 The origins of the sustainability problem
3 Concepts of sustainability
4 Ethics and the environment
5 Welfare economics: efficiency and optimality
6 Market failure and public policy
7 The efficient and optimal use of environmental resources
8 The theory of optimal resource extraction: non-renewable resources
9 The theory of optimal resource extraction: renewable resources
10 Forest resources
17 Accounting for the environment

B: Environmental economics course

1 An introduction to natural resource and environmental economics
2 The origins of the sustainability problem
3 Concepts of sustainability
4 Ethics and the environment
5 Welfare economics: efficiency and optimality
6 Market failure and public policy
10 Forest resources
11 Pollution control: targets
12 Pollution control: instruments
13 International environmental problems
14 Valuing the environment
15 Irreversibility, risk and uncertainty
17 Accounting for the environment

C: Environmental policy course

1 An introduction to natural resource and environmental economics
2 The origins of the sustainability problem
3 Concepts of sustainability
4 Ethics and the environment
5 Welfare economics: efficiency and optimality
6 Market failure and public policy
11 Pollution control: targets
12 Pollution control: instruments
13 International environmental problems
14 Valuing the environment

Suggestions for study

Further reading

It is not possible to include in any single text of reasonable length all the material that one might conceivably wish for in an introduction to resource and environmental economics. Furthermore, the reader will inevitably find some topics of particular interest that he or she wishes to study at greater depth. To facilitate the selection of directions for additional study, each chapter concludes with suggestions for further reading. Unless otherwise indicated, each item of recommended further reading is presented at a technical level accessible to readers of this text. We have also indicated, where appropriate, sources of empirical data that the reader may find useful for purposes of further study or research.

Use of the internet

A vast collection of useful data and information is available to the environmental and resource economist from the internet. Most of this can be downloaded without charge or without needing subscription. In addition, there are many mailing lists in which problems and information can be sent to all those who enrol on a list. We strongly recommend that you take advantage of this electronic resource. Some advice on useful web sites, the address of a web site maintained by the authors of this text which provides links to those sites, and information on how to subscribe to mailing lists is given in the section 'Sources of environmental information on the internet' towards the end of this book.

Discussion questions and problems

Each chapter of the book contains a small number of discussion questions and problems that the reader is strongly recommended to work through. Suggested answers are not provided in the text, but will be made available through the web pages that accompany this text.

The use of appendices in this textbook

Several of the chapters make use of appendices to provide complete derivations or explanations of results discussed in the main part of the relevant chapter. It is, we would conjecture, common practice for this to be taken as a signal that the material is of lesser importance, or is excessively complicated, and can easily be ignored. This is not the signal that we wish to send out!

Our use of appendices serves a distinct purpose: they are designed to facilitate a relatively quick reading of chapters. By putting technically difficult sections in an appendix, the reader may omit these on first reading, obtain an overview of the main arguments of the chapter, and then return to the material which is more demanding for study at a second reading. It is strongly recommended that every appendix is used in this way. However, no section of this book requires that the material in any appendix be fully mastered.

CHAPTER 1

An introduction to natural resource and environmental economics

Contemplation of the world's disappearing supplies of minerals, forests, and other exhaustible assets has led to demands for regulation of their exploitation. The feeling that these products are now too cheap for the good of future generations, that they are being selfishly exploited at too rapid a rate, and that in consequence of their excessive cheapness they are being produced and consumed wastefully has given rise to the conservation movement.

Hotelling (1931)

Introduction

The three themes that run through this book are efficiency, optimality and sustainability. In this chapter we briefly explain these themes, and then look at the emergence of the modern field of study which is the economic analysis of natural resources and the environment. We then identify some of the key features of that field of study. As we proceed we indicate where, later in the book, the matters raised here are discussed more fully.

Three themes

The concepts of efficiency and optimality are used in specific ways in economic analysis. We will be discussing this at some length in Chapter 5. However, a brief intuitive account here will be useful. One way of thinking about efficiency is in terms of missed opportunities. If resource use is wasteful in some way then opportunities are being squandered; eliminating that waste (or inefficiency) can bring net benefits to some groups of people. An example is energy inefficiency. It is often argued that much energy is produced or used inefficiently, and that if different techniques were employed significant resource savings could be gained at no loss in terms of final output.

This kind of argument usually refers to some kind of technical or physical inefficiency. But of greater interest to economists are allocative inefficiencies. Even where resources are used in technically efficient ways, net benefits are sometimes squandered. For example, suppose that electricity can be generated by the burning of either some heavily polluting fossil fuel or a less polluting alternative fuel. Because of lower prices of the former fuel, it is chosen by profit-maximising electricity producers. However, the pollution results in damages which necessitate expenditure on health care and clean-up operations. These expenditures may exceed the cost saving that electricity producers obtain from using the cheaper fuel.

If they do there is an inefficiency that results from resource allocation choices even where there are no technical inefficiencies. Society as a whole would obtain positive net benefits if the less polluting fuel were used. We show throughout the book that such inefficiencies will be pervasive in the use of natural and environmental resources in pure market economies. A substantial part of environmental economics is concerned with how economies might avoid inefficiencies in the allocation and use of natural and environmental resources.

The second concept – optimality – is related to efficiency, but is nevertheless conceptually distinct from it. To understand the idea of optimality we need to have in mind:

(1) a group of people taken to be the relevant 'society';
(2) some overall objective that this society has, and in terms of which we can measure the extent to which some resource use decision is desirable from that society's point of view.

Then a resource use choice is socially optimal if it maximises that objective given any relevant constraints that may be operating.

As we shall see (particularly in Chapter 5), the reason why efficiency and optimality are related is that it turns out to be the case that a resource allocation cannot be optimal unless it is efficient. That is, efficiency is a necessary condition for optimality. This should be intuitively obvious: if society squanders opportunities, then it cannot be maximising its objective (whatever that might be). However, efficiency is not a sufficient condition for optimality; in other words, even if a resource allocation is efficient, it may not be socially optimal. This arises because there will almost always be a multiplicity of different efficient resource allocations, but only one of those will be 'best' from a social point of view. Not surprisingly, the idea of optimality also plays a large role in environmental economics analysis.

The third theme is sustainability. For the moment we can say that sustainability involves taking care of posterity. Why this is something that we need to consider in the context of resource and environmental economics is something that we will discuss in the next chapter. Exactly what 'taking care of posterity' might mean is discussed in Chapter 3. Now on first thinking about this, one might feel that given optimality, a concept such as sustainability is redundant. After all, if an allocation of resources is socially optimal, then surely it must also be sustainable? If sustainability matters, then presumably it would enter into the list of society's objectives and be taken care of in achieving optimality. Things are not quite so straightforward. The pursuit of optimality as usually considered in economics will not necessarily take adequate care of posterity. If taking care of posterity is seen as a moral obligation, then the pursuit of optimality will need to be constrained by a sustainability requirement.

The emergence of resource and environmental economics

We now briefly examine the development of resource and environmental economics from the time of the industrial revolution in Europe to its modern form.

Classical economics: the contributions of Smith, Malthus, Ricardo and Mill to the development of natural resource economics

While the emergence of natural resource and environmental economics as a distinct sub-discipline has been a relatively recent event, concern with the substance of natural resource and environmental issues has much earlier antecedents. It is evident, for example, in the writings of the classical economists, for whom it was a major concern. The label 'classical' identifies a number of economists writing in the eighteenth and nineteenth centuries, a period during which the industrial revolution was taking place (at least in much of Europe and North America) and agricultural productivity was growing rapidly. A recurring theme of political–economic debate concerned the appropriate institutional arrangements for the development of trade and growth.

These issues are central to the work of Adam Smith (1723–1790). Smith was the first writer to systematise the argument for the importance of markets in allocating resources, although his emphasis was placed on what we would now call the dynamic effects of markets. His major work *An Inquiry into the Nature and Causes of the Wealth of Nations* (1776), contains the famous statement of the role of the 'invisible hand':

But it is only for the sake of profit that any man employs a capital in the support of industry; and he will always, therefore, endeavour to employ it in the support of that industry of which the produce is likely to be of the greatest value, or to exchange for the greatest quantity, either of money or of other goods.

As every individual, therefore, endeavours as much as he can both to employ his capital in the support of domestic industry, and so to direct that industry that its produce may be of the greatest value; every individual necessarily labours to render the annual revenue of the society as great as he can. He generally, indeed, neither intends to promote the public interest, nor knows how much he is promoting it. ... he is, in this as in many other cases, led by an invisible hand to promote an end which was no part of his intention ...

... By pursuing his own interest he frequently promotes that of society more effectively than when he really intends to promote it.

Smith (1776), Book IV, Chapter 2, page 477

This belief in the efficacy of the market mechanism is a fundamental organising principle of the policy prescriptions of modern economics, including resource and environmental economics, as will be seen in our account of it in the rest of the book.

A central interest of the classical economists was the question of what determined standards of living and economic growth. Natural resources were seen as important determinants of national wealth and growth. A strand running through classical political economy concerns the prospects for living standards in the long term for an economy subject to constraints on the supply of land. Land (sometimes used to refer to natural resources in general) was viewed as limited in its availability. When to this were added the assumptions that land was a necessary input to production and that it exhibited diminishing returns, the early classical economists came to the conclusion that economic progress would be a transient feature of history, and the inevitability of an eventual stationary state, in which the prospects for the living standard of the majority of people were bleak.

This thesis is most strongly associated with Thomas Malthus (1766–1834), who argued it most forcefully in his *Essay on the Principle of Population* (1798), giving rise to the practice of calling those who now question the feasibility of continuing long-run economic growth as 'neo-Malthusian'. For Malthus, a fixed land quantity, an assumed tendency for continual positive population growth, and diminishing returns in agriculture implied a tendency for output per capita to fall over time. There was, according to Malthus, a long-run tendency for the living standards of the mass to be driven down to a subsistence level. At the subsistence wage level, conditions would permit reproducibility of the population at an unchanging level, and the economy would attain a steady state.

This notion of a steady state was formalised and extended by David Ricardo (1772–1823), particularly in his *Principles of Political Economy and Taxation* (1817). Malthus's assumption of a fixed stock of land was replaced by a conception in which land was available in parcels of varying quality. Agricultural output could be expanded by increasing the intensive margin (exploiting a given parcel of land more intensively) or by increasing the extensive margin (bringing previously uncultivated land into productive use). However, in either case, returns to the land input were taken to be diminishing. Economic development then proceeds in such a way that the 'economic surplus' is appropriated increasingly in the form of rent, the return to land, and development again converges toward a Malthusian stationary state.

In the writings of John Stuart Mill (1806–1873) (see in particular Mill (1857)) one finds a full statement of classical economics at its culmination. Mill's work utilises the idea of diminishing returns, but recognises the countervailing influence of the growth of knowledge and technical progress in agriculture and in production more generally. Writing in Britain when output per person was apparently rising, not falling, he placed less emphasis on diminishing returns, reflecting the relaxation of the constraints of the extensive margin as colonial exploitation opened up new tranches of land, as fossil fuels were increasingly exploited, and as innovation rapidly increased agricultural productivity. The concept of a stationary state was not abandoned, but it was thought to be one in which a relatively high level of material prosperity would be attained.

Foreshadowing later developments in environmental economics, and the thinking of conservationists, Mill adopted a broader view of the roles played by natural resources than his predecessors. In addition to agricultural and extractive uses of land, Mill saw it as a source of amenity values (such as the intrinsic beauty of countryside) that would become of increasing relative importance as material conditions improved. We discuss this in Chapter 15.

Mill's views are clearly revealed in the following extracts from his major work:

> I cannot ... regard the stationary state of capital and wealth with the unaffected aversion so generally manifested towards it by political economists of the old school ... I confess that I am not charmed with the ideal of life held out by those who think that the normal state of human beings is that of struggling to get on; that the trampling, crushing, elbowing and treading on each other's heels which form the existing type of social life, are the most desirable lot of human kind, or anything but the disagreeable symptoms of one of the phases of industrial progress. ... Those who do not accept the present very early stage of human improvement as its ultimate type may be excused for being comparatively indifferent to the kind of economic progress which excites the congratulations of ordinary politicians: the mere increase of production ... It is only in the backward countries of the world that increased production is still an important object; in those most advanced, what is needed is a better distribution ... There is room in the world, no doubt, and even in old countries, for a great increase in population, supposing the arts of life to go on improving, and capital to increase. But even if innocuous, I confess I see very little reason for desiring it. The density of population necessary to enable mankind to obtain, in the greatest degree, all of the advantages both of cooperation and of social intercourse, has, in all the most populous countries, been attained. A population may be too crowded, though all be amply supplied with food and raiment. It is not good for man to be kept perforce at all times in the presence of his species ... Nor is there much satisfaction in contemplating the world with nothing left to the spontaneous activity of nature: with every rood of land brought into cultivation, which is capable of growing food for human beings; every flowery waste or natural pasture ploughed up, all quadrupeds or birds which are not domesticated for man's use exterminated as his rivals for food, every hedgerow or superfluous tree rooted out, and scarcely a place left where a wild shrub or flower could grow without being eradicated as a weed in the name of improved agriculture. If the earth must lose that great portion of its pleasantness which it owes to things that the unlimited increase of wealth and population would extirpate from it, for the mere purpose of enabling it to support a larger, but not a happier or better population, I sincerely hope, for the sake of posterity, that they will be content to be stationary long before necessity compels them to it.

> Mill (1857), Book IV

Neoclassical economics: marginal theory and value

A series of major works published in the 1870s began the replacement of classical economics by what subsequently became known as 'neoclassical economics'. One outcome of this was a change in the manner in which value was explained. Classical economics saw value as arising from the labour power embodied (directly and indirectly) in output, a view which found its fullest embodiment in the work of Karl Marx. Neoclassical economists explained value as being determined in exchange, so reflecting preferences and costs of production. The concepts of price and value ceased to be distinct. Moreover, previous notions of absolute scarcity were replaced by a relative concept of scarcity. This change in emphasis paved the way for the development of welfare economics, to be discussed shortly.

At the methodological level, the technique of marginal analysis was adopted, allowing earlier notions of diminishing returns to be given a formal basis in terms of diminishing marginal productivity in the context of an explicit production function. Jevons (1835–1882) and Menger (1840–1921) formalised the theory of consumer preferences in terms of utility and demand theory. The evolution of neoclassical economic analysis led to an emphasis on the structure of economic activity, and its efficiency, rather than on the aggregate level of economic activity. Concern with the prospects for continuing economic growth receded, perhaps reflecting the apparent inevitability of growth in Western Europe at this time. Leon Walras (1834–1910) developed neoclassical General Equilibrium Theory, and in so doing provided a rigorous foundation for the concepts of efficiency and optimality that we employ extensively in this text. Alfred Marshall (1842–1924) (see *Principles of Economics*, 1890) was responsible for elaboration of the partial equilibrium supply and demand based analysis of price determination so familiar to students of modern microeconomics. A substantial part of modern environmental economics continues to use these techniques as tools of exposition.

We remarked earlier that concern with the level (and the growth) of economic activity had been largely ignored in the period during which neoclassical economics was being developed. Economic depression in the industrialised economies in the inter-war years provided the backcloth against which John Maynard Keynes (1883–1946) developed his theory of income and output determination. The Keynesian agenda switched attention to aggregate supply and demand, and the reasons why market economies may fail to achieve optimal aggregate levels of activity, experiencing prolonged periods of underuse of available inputs to production.

This direction of theoretical development, while undoubtedly of importance, has little of intrinsic interest to environmental economics *per se*. However, Keynesian 'macroeconomics', as opposed to the microeconomics of neoclassical economics, was of indirect importance in stimulating a resurgence of interest in growth theory in the middle of the twentieth century, and the development of a neoclassical theory of economic growth. What is noticeable in early neoclassical growth models is the absence of

land, or any natural resources, from the production function used in such models. Classical limits to growth arguments, based on a fixed land input, did not have any place in early neoclassical growth modelling.

The introduction of natural resources into neoclassical models of economic growth occurred in the 1970s, when neoclassical economists first systematically investigated the efficient and optimal depletion of resources. This body of work, and the developments that have followed from it, is natural resource economics. The models of efficient and optimal exploitation of natural resources that we present and discuss in Chapters 7, 8 and 9 are based on the writings of those authors. We will also have call to look at such models in Chapter 17, where we discuss the theory of accounting for the environment as it relates to the question of sustainability.

Welfare economics

The final development in mainstream economic theory that needs to be briefly addressed here is the development of a rigorous theory of welfare economics. Welfare economics, as you will see in Chapters 4, 5 and 6, attempts to provide a framework in which normative judgements can be made about alternative configurations of economic activity. In particular, it attempts to identify circumstances under which it can be claimed that one allocation of resources is better (in some sense) than another.

Not surprisingly, it turns out to be the case that such rankings are only possible if one is prepared to accept some ethical criterion. The most commonly used ethical criterion adopted by classical and neoclassical economists derives from the utilitarian moral philosophy, developed by David Hume, Jeremy Bentham and John Stuart Mill. We explore this ethical structure in some depth in Chapter 4. Suffice to say now that utilitarianism suggests that social welfare consists of some weighted average of the total utility levels enjoyed by all individuals in the society.

Economists have attempted to find a method of ranking different states of the world which does not require the use of a social welfare function, makes little use of ethical principles, but is nevertheless useful in making prescriptions about resource allocation. The notion of economic efficiency, also known as allocative efficiency or Pareto optimality (because it was developed by Vilfredo Pareto (1897)) is what they have come up with. These ideas are examined at length in Chapter 5. It can be shown that, given certain rather stringent conditions, an economy organised as a competitive market economy will attain a state of economic efficiency. This is the modern, and rigorous, version of Adam Smith's story about the benign influence of the invisible hand.

Where the conditions do not hold markets do not attain efficiency in allocation, and a state of 'market failure' is said to exist. One manifestation of market failure is the phenomenon of 'externalities'. These are situations where, because of the structure of property rights, markets do not regulate all of the relationships between economic agents – individuals and firms. Market failure and the means for its correction will be discussed in Chapter 6. The problem of environmental pollution, discussed in detail in Chapters 11 and 12, entered economics as a particular example of the general class of externalities. Important early work in the analysis of externalities and market failure is to be found in Marshall (1890). The first systematic analysis of pollution as an externality is to be found in Pigou (1920, pages 159–161). The technique of cost–benefit analysis discussed in Chapter 6 emerged in the 1950s and 1960s as a practical vehicle for applied welfare economics and policy advice. It has had a profound influence on the development of environmental economics, as we shall see in Chapters 14 and 15 especially.

Ecological economics

Ecological economics is a new interdisciplinary field. Its distinguishing characteristic is that it treats the economic system as part of the larger system that is planet earth. It starts, that is, from the recognition that the economic and environmental systems are interdependent, and studies the joint economy–environment system in the light of developments in the natural sciences, particularly thermodynamics and ecology, over the last two centuries. We shall discuss these matters in the next chapter which has the title 'The origins of the sustainability problem', as it is the interdependence of economic and natural systems that gives rise to the sustainability problem.

Box 1.1 summarises a paper written in 1966 which uses vivid metaphors to indicate the change in ways of thinking that the author, Kenneth Boulding, sees as necessary in the light of modern understandings of the laws of nature. As we have seen, the dependence of economic activity on the material base which is the natural environment was a central concern of classical economics, but not of neoclassical economics. Boulding was one of a few scholars, including some economists, who continued, during the ascendancy of neoclassical economics, to insist on the central importance of studying economics in a way which takes on board what is known about the laws of nature as they affect the material basis for economic activity. In the 1980s a number of economists and natural scientists, mainly but not exclusively from ecology, came to the conclusion that if progress was to be made in understanding and addressing environmental problems it was necessary to study them in an interdisciplinary way, which they decided to call 'ecological economics'. The first issue of a journal with that title appeared in 1989.

Ecology is the study of the distribution and abundance of animals and plants. A central focus is an ecosystem, which is an interacting set of plant and animal populations and their abiotic, non-living, environment. The Greek word *oikos* is the common root for the *eco* in both economics and ecology. *Oikos* means ment. If consumption is deferred to a later period, the increment to future consumption that follows from such investment will exceed the initial consumption quantity deferred. The size of the pay-off to deferred consumption is the rate of return to investment.

Environmental resource stocks similarly have rates of return associated with their deferred use. The relations between rates of return to capital as normally understood in economics and the rates of return on environmental assets must be taken into account in trying to identify efficient and optimal paths of environmental resource use over time. The arising theory of the efficient and optimal use of natural and environmental resources over time is examined in Chapters 7 to 10, and is drawn on in Chapter 17. As discussed in Chapter 11, many pollution problems also have an intratemporal dimension, and it turns out that the analysis developed for thinking about the intertemporal problems of resource use can be used to analyse those problems.

Exhaustibility, substitutability and irreversibility

Natural resource stocks can be classified in various ways. A useful first cut is to distinguish between 'renewable' and 'non-renewable' resources. Renewable resources are biotic, plant and animal populations, and have the capacity to grow in size over time, through biological reproduction. Non-renewable resources are abiotic, stocks of minerals, and do not have that capacity to grow over time. The distinction is sometimes made between exhaustible, or depletable, and inexhaustible, or non-depletable, resources. This is not a useful distinction, and does not correspond to the renewable versus non-renewable distinction. Renewable resources are exhaustible if harvested for too long at a rate exceeding their regeneration capacities.

There is a useful distinction between stock and flow resources. Whereas stock resources, plant and animal populations and mineral deposits, have the characteristic that today's use has implications for tomorrow's availability, this is not the case with flow resources. Examples of flow resource are solar radiation, and the power of the wind, of tides and of flowing water.

Another property of natural resources that will be of interest is the extent to which they are substitutable for one another. Can, for example, solar power substitute for the fossil fuels on a large scale? As we shall see, the combustion of fossil fuels not only involves the depletion of non-renewable resources, but also is a source of some major environmental pollution problems, such as the so-called 'greenhouse effect' which entails the prospect of global climate change, to be discussed in Chapter 13.

A related matter of central importance is the degree to which environmental resources can be substituted for by other inputs, especially the man-made capital resulting from saving and investment. As we shall see, in Chapters 7 and 17 particularly, this is of particular significance when we address questions concerning long-run economy–environment interactions, and the problem of sustainability.

Man-made capital is sometimes referred to as reproducible capital, identifying an important difference between stocks of it and stocks of non-renewable resources. The latter are not reproducible, and their exploitation is irreversible in a way that the use of man-made capital is not. We shall discuss this further in the next chapter, and some arising implications in later chapters, especially 7 and 17. With renewable resource stocks, depletion is reversible to the extent that harvesting is at rates that allow regeneration. Some of the implications are discussed in Chapter 9. Some pollution problems may involve irreversible effects, and the extinction of a species of plant or animal is certainly irreversible.

Some assemblages of environmental resources are of interest for the amenity services, recreation and aesthetic enjoyment that they provide, as well as for their potential use as inputs to production. A wilderness area, for example, could be conserved as a national park or developed for mining. A decision to develop would be effectively irreversible, whereas a decision to conserve would be reversible. We show in Chapter 14 that under plausible conditions this asymmetry implies a stronger preference for non-development than would be the case where all decisions are reversible, and that this is strengthened when it is recognised that the future is not known with certainty.

Conclusions

There is not a single methodology used by all economists working on matters related to natural resources and the environment. Ecological economists have urged the need to work towards a more holistic discipline that would integrate natural scientific and economic paradigms. Some ecological economists argue further that the sustainability problem requires nothing less than a fundamental change in social values, as well as a scientific reorientation. While some movement has been made in the direction of interdisciplinary cooperation, most analysis is still some way from having achieved integration. At the other end of a spectrum of methodologies are economists who see no need to go beyond the application of neoclassical techniques to environmental problems, and stress the importance of constructing a more complete set of quasi-market incentives to induce efficient behaviour. Such economists would reject the idea that existing social values need to be questioned, and many have great faith in the ability of continuing technical progress to ameliorate problems arising with natural resources and the environment. Ecological economists tend to be more sceptical about the extent to which technical progress can overcome such problems.

However, there is a lot of common ground as between economists working in the area, and it is this that we mainly focus upon in this text. Nobody who has seriously studied the issues believes that the economy's relationship to the natural environment can be left entirely to market forces. Hardly anybody argues now that market-like incentives have no role to play in that relationship. In terms of policy, the arguments are about how much governments need to do, and the relative effectiveness of different kinds of policy instruments. Our aim in this book is to work through some economic analysis relevant to these kinds of questions, and to provide information on the resource and environmental problems that they arise from. We begin, in the next chapter, by discussing the general interdependence of the economic and environmental systems, and the concerns about sustainability that this has given rise to.

Discussion questions

1 Many economists accept that a 'Spaceship Earth' characterisation of the global economy is valid in the final analysis, but would dispute a claim that we are currently close to a point at which it is necessary to manage the economy according to strict principles of physical sustainability. On the contrary, they would argue that urgent problems of malnutrition and poverty dominate our current agenda, and the solution to these is more worthy of being our immediate objective. The objective of physically sustainable management must be attained eventually, but is not an immediate objective that should be pursued to the exclusion of all else. To what extent do you regard this as being a valid argument?

2 Do environmental resources have intrinsic values, independent of any use that human beings may have for them now or at any point in the future, and independent of any values that human beings would be willing to pay to preserve them in existence? If your answer is in the affirmative, how could one establish a figure for the magnitude of such an intrinsic value?

Problems

This problem is concerned with the distinction between private and social costs of production and the implications of external costs for the overall, social level of well-being. It should be solvable by anyone with prior knowledge of economics, but if you find it difficult, leave it for now and return to it after reading Chapter 6.

Suppose that a wood pulp mill is situated on a bank of the River Tay. The private marginal cost (MC) of producing wood pulp (in £ per ton) is given by the function

$$MC = 10 + 0.5Y$$

where Y is tons of wood pulp produced. In addition to this private marginal cost, an external cost is incurred. Each ton of wood pulp produces pollutant flows into the river which cause damage valued at £10. This is an external cost, as it is borne by the wider community but not by the polluting firm itself. The marginal benefit (MB) to society of each ton of produced pulp, in £, is given by

$$MB = 30 - 0.5Y$$

The following questions can be answered using carefully drawn diagrams or with algebra. Profit maximisation requires selection of an output level that equates marginal revenue and marginal cost. Furthermore, maximisation of social net benefits should be taken to imply equating marginal social benefits with marginal social costs.

1 Draw a diagram illustrating the marginal cost (MC), marginal benefit (MB), external marginal cost (EMC) and social marginal cost (SMC) functions.
2 Derive the profit-maximising output of wood pulp, assuming the seller can obtain marginal revenue equal to the marginal benefit to society derived from wood pulp.
3 Derive the pulp output which maximises social net benefits, defined as

Social net benefit
   = (gross) social benefit − social cost

4 Explain why the socially efficient output of wood pulp is lower than the private profit-maximising output level.
5 How large would external marginal cost have to be in order for it to be socially desirable that no wood pulp is produced?

Further reading

As all save one of the topics and issues discussed in this chapter will be dealt with more comprehensively in subsequent chapters, we shall not make any suggestions for further reading on them here. The one topic that we do not take further is the history of economics, on which the classic reference is Blaug (1985), *Economic Theory in Retrospect*.

CHAPTER 2

The origins of the sustainability problem

Certainly it is a problem to sustain many billions of people, a problem for each human to sustain himself and his/her own family. But the growth in numbers over the millennia from a few thousands or millions of humans living at low subsistence, to billions living well above subsistence, is a most positive assurance that the problem of sustenance has eased rather than grown more difficult with the years. The trend in population size by itself should suggest cheer rather than gloom.

Mark Perlman, in Simon and Kahn (1984), page 63

Introduction

We inhabit a world in which the human population has risen dramatically over the past century and will probably double during the next. The material demands being made by the average individual have been increasing rapidly, though many human beings now alive are desperately poor. Since the 1950s and 1960s economic growth has been generally seen as *the* solution to the problem of poverty. Without economic growth, poverty alleviation involves redistribution from the better-off to the poor, which encounters resistance from the better-off. In any case, there may be so many poor in relation to the size of the better-off group, that the redistributive solution to the problem of poverty is simply impossible – the cake is not big enough to provide for all, however thinly the slices are cut. Economic growth increases the size of the cake. With enough of it, it may be possible to give everybody at least a decent slice, without having to reduce the size of the larger slices.

However, the world's resource base is limited, and contains a complex, and inter-related, set of ecosystems that are currently exhibiting signs of fragility. It is increasingly questioned whether the global economic system can continue to grow without undermining the natural systems which are its ultimate foundation.

This set of issues we call 'the sustainability problem'. In this chapter we set out the basis for the belief that such a problem exists. In the next we shall examine some different ways of conceptualising and structuring the problem for analysis and policy prescription. For the moment we can say that the sustainability problem is: how to alleviate poverty in ways that do not affect the natural environment in such a way that future economic prospects suffer.

This chapter is organised as follows. We first provide a brief overview of the global situation in terms of the conditions of human life, and discuss the report which, in 1987, brought the sustainability problem to prominence. The second section then considers the interdependence of economic and natural systems, which is the basis for the concern that increasing economic activity could damage the environmental base that supports it. In the third section of the chapter we look at a controversial work from the 1970s that argued that the environment would put limits on economic growth. In the past few years an argument has emerged to the effect that far from damaging the environment, economic growth is, in the long run anyway, good for it. We examine this argument in the fourth section. As noted above, the origin of the sustainability problem involves increasing numbers of humans, as well as increasing per capita levels of income and consumption. In the fifth section we discuss population growth and the environment. The chapter ends with a section on biodiversity. Many regard biodiversity loss due to human activity as the most serious threat to sustainability.

Poverty and sustainable development

Many people live in conditions that do not meet reasonable standards. This is particularly true for people living in the poor nations of the world, but is by no means restricted to them. Even in the richest countries, income and wealth inequalities are such that many people live in conditions of material and social deprivation. For many years, it was thought that the eradication of poverty required well-designed development programmes that were largely independent of considerations relating to the natural environment. The goal of economic and political debate was to identify growth processes that could allow continually rising living standards. Economic development and 'nature conservation' were seen as quite distinct and separate problems. For some commentators, concern for the natural environment was a rather selfish form of self-indulgence on the part of the better-off.

Perspectives have changed significantly since the 1970s. While the pursuit of economic growth and development continues, it is recognised that the maintenance of growth has an important environmental dimension. During the 1970s, a concern for 'sustainability' began to appear on the international political agenda, most visibly in the proceedings of a series of international conferences. The common theme of these debates was the interrelationship between poverty, economic development and the state of the natural environment.

Perhaps the best known statement of the sustainability problem derives from the 1987 report of an institution established by the United Nations in 1983, the World Commission on Environment and Development (WCED). The report – *Our Common Future* (WCED, 1987) – set the agenda for much of the subsequent discussion of sustainability. We discuss this report and its impact at the end of this section after briefly describing the global state of human development in the late twentieth century.

The current state of human development

There are a number of very useful annual publications which report on various aspects of human development. Here we draw on those from the United Nations Development Programme (UNDP, 1995, 1997, 1998), the World Health Organization (WHO, 1995) and the World Resources Institute (WR, 1996, 1998).

Life expectancy

WHO estimates that between 1980 and 1993, overall life expectancy increased from 61 to 65 years. But this statistic masks big differences between countries, as can be seen in Table 2.1 (based on WHO, 1995).

The life expectancy gap between the least developed country (43 years) and the most developed country (78 years) is 35 years, a figure which WHO expects to grow further. Life expectancy is below 60 years in 45 developing countries that collectively contain 15% of the global population. Moreover the previous, seemingly uninterrupted, trend towards greater life expectancy has been broken in many countries, including the nations of the former Soviet Union, many central European transition economies and in many parts of sub-Saharan Africa. This last group has been affected by ravages of the AIDS virus; in 15 central African states life

Table 2.1 Life expectancy at birth in various regions.

Life expectancy at birth in	1980	1993
Developed regions	71.2	78.6
Less developed regions	62.4	65.3
Least developed regions	51.5	53.6

expectancy has been reduced by over 7 years to 49.6 years (and in the worst case, Zimbabwe, by 14.8 years).

Russia's dramatic falls in male and female life expectancy are possibly of a more short-term nature. Male life expectancy has fallen from 65.1 years in 1987 to 57.3 in 1996 (WR, 1996). Especially implicated are alcohol and cigarette consumption, operating in conjunction with very difficult living conditions and a major breakdown in preventive health care. Also culpable may be the cumulative effects of serious environmental contamination over many years in the Soviet Union, especially toxic wastes from chemical plants, pesticides from agriculture and nuclear radiation from various sources.

Health

A clear and concise summary of present health conditions is found in chapter 8 of *World Resources 1996–97* (WR, 1996):

> Broad indicators of human health show that significant progress has been made over the past few decades. Yet the conditions in many developing countries remain difficult – especially for the poorest groups. Furthermore, new outbreaks of infectious diseases pose potentially significant new medical challenges.

Large health discrepancies exist between countries and within countries. Poor urban dwellers in many developed countries have inadequate health facilities, and are beyond the reach of the most basic health and social services. The major cause of mortality world-wide is infectious and parasitic diseases (implicated in one-third of all deaths), followed by respiratory diseases (one-fifth of all deaths). But infectious diseases strike extremely unevenly, accounting for only 1% of deaths in developed countries but 41.5% in developing countries. Many individual causes of death are, in principle, easily preventable, such as diarrheal diseases and TB (which kills more than any other infectious disease, and is on the increase). Other big killers, including HIV and malaria, can be dramatically reduced where sufficient resources are

available to mount continuing public health schemes.

Of particular concern to WHO are problems of emerging and re-emerging infectious diseases. The Institute of Medicine identifies six contributory factors (Lederberg *et al.*, 1992):

(a) environmental change/habitat disturbance: for example, urbanisation, road building, irrigation, and logging all bring humans into new areas and displace microbes, which then seek new hosts, becoming evident in diseases such as new forms of malaria, and Rift Valley fever;

(b) human demographics and behaviour: particularly related to urbanisation, water projects, hygiene problems and urban poverty; TB and dengue virus exemplify this link;

(c) international travel and commerce;

(d) complications of modern medicine;

(e) microbial adaptation and change;

(f) breakdown of public health measures.

A salutary lesson is drawn by the World Resources Institute from this and similar analyses: any intervention that changes a local ecology is likely to bring with it a health cost; these costs should be factored into any investment appraisal of development projects.

Poverty and inequality

Measured in terms of GDP the world economy has grown fivefold between 1950 and 1995. Yet the industrialised economies accounted for US$22.5 trillion of the US$27.7 trillion global GDP in 1993 (WR, 1998). An important factor in the growth of global GDP since about 1980 has been the rapid growth of a number of developing economies, particularly in eastern and southern Asia. Countries such as Brazil, China, Malaysia and Mexico have attracted much foreign direct and indirect investment, reduced their dependence on agriculture, diversified their economies and participated in export-led growth. It remains to be seen whether this period of very rapid growth will continue after the Asian economic crisis of the late 1990s.

But this success has not been shared by all developing economies, and an increasing disparity is evident within this group of countries. About 100 countries have experienced stagnating or declining real per capita incomes, and 70 of these (containing one-fifth of the world's population) have average real incomes lower today than in 1980 (UNDP, 1996; World Bank, 1996). A simple dichotomy between developing and industrialised countries is now of little use for classifying regions of the world in terms of relative prosperity.

These trends in per capita real GDP are illustrated in Figure 2.1. Income disparities have widened despite the rapid growth in many developing countries. Some statistics reported in *World Resources 1998–99* (WR, 1998) graphically illustrate this gap: the poorest 20% of the world's population claims 1.1% of global income while the richest 20% claims 80% of global income. Between 1960 and 1994, the ratio of incomes in the most rich relative to the least rich country increased from 30 : 1 to 78 : 1. The latest report from the United Nations Development Programme (UNDP, 1998) contains similar data, and relates income inequalities to inequalities in consumption, and thus to demands upon the world's natural resources.

Given these income inequalities, it is not surprising that poverty still exists on a large scale. About one third of people in developing countries fall below the World Bank's poverty line (an income of less than US$1 per day). And while the percentage of people living in poverty has marginally fallen over the last decade, the absolute number of those involved has increased (UNDP, 1997).

The World Commission on Environment and Development

The 1987 report from the World Commission on Environment and Development, *Our Common Future* (WCED, 1987), is often referred to as 'the Brundtland report' after the name of its chair, Gro Harlem Brundtland, who had previously been both Minister for the Environment and Prime Minister of Norway. It advanced, with great effect, the concept of 'sustainable development', which is now on political agendas, at least at the level of rhetoric, around the world. The Brundtland report was, in political terms, an outstanding and influential piece of work.

It provides much information about what we have called here the sustainability problem, identifying a number of potential environmental constraints on future eco-

(per capita income in constant international dollars)

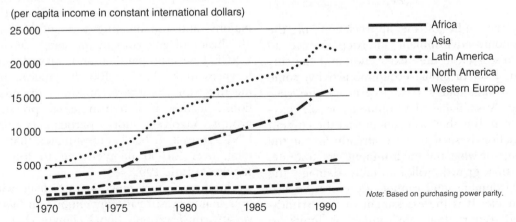

Africa
Asia
Latin America
North America
Western Europe

Note: Based on purchasing power parity.

Figure 2.1   Per capita income by region, 1970–91
Source: WR (1998), based on United Nations (1997), page 58.

nomic growth, and arguing that current trends cannot be continued far into the future. It does not, however, conclude that future economic growth is either infeasible or undesirable. Having defined sustainable development as development that 'seeks to meet the needs and aspirations of the present without compromising the ability to meet those of the future', it states that:

> Far from requiring the cessation of economic growth, it [sustainable development] recognises that the problems of poverty and underdevelopment cannot be solved unless we have a new era of growth in which developing countries play a large role and reap large benefits.

Nor does it require that those nations already developed cease to pursue economic growth:

> Growth must be revived in developing countries because that is where the links between economic growth, the alleviation of poverty, and environmental conditions operate most directly. Yet developing countries are part of an interdependent world economy; their prospects also depend on the levels and patterns of growth in industrialised nations. The medium term prospects for industrial countries are for growth of 3–4 per cent, the minimum that international financial institutions consider necessary if these countries are going to play a part in expanding the world economy. Such growth rates could be environmentally sustainable if industrialised nations can continue the recent shifts in the content of their growth towards less material- and energy-intensive activities and the improvement of their efficiency in using materials and energy.
>
> WCED (1987), pages 40 and 51

In the light of an appreciation of the economy–environment interdependence to be discussed in the next section and the current level of global economic activity, some environmentalists have expressed the view that 'sustainable development' is an oxymoron. It is their assessment that the current situation is such that we already are at the limits of what the environment can tolerate, so that growth will inevitably damage the environment, and cannot, therefore, be sustainable. It is the assessment of the Brundtland report that environmental limits to growth can be avoided given the adoption,

worldwide, of policies to affect the form that economic growth takes. To make growth sustainable, those policies would have to involve reducing, at the global level, the material content of economic activity, economising in the use of resources as the value of output increases, and substituting the services of man-made capital for environmental services. Much of resource and environmental economics is about the policy instruments for doing that, as we shall see in later chapters.

The 1992 Rio de Janeiro conference

WCED believed that an active follow-up to its report was imperative if the policy changes necessary for the attainment of sustainable development were to occur. It called for the transformation of its report into a UN Programme of Action on Sustainable Development, and recommended that:

> Within an appropriate period after the presentation of the report to the General Assembly, an international Conference could be convened to review progress made and promote follow-up arrangements that will be needed over time to set benchmarks and to maintain human progress within the guidelines of human needs and natural laws.

As a result, the United Nations Conference on Environment and Development, UNCED, took place in Rio de Janeiro in June 1992. The conference itself was preceded by over two years of preparatory international negotiations. Delegations were sent from 178 nations, and the meeting was attended by 107 heads of government (or state). During UNCED several parallel and related conferences took place in Rio de Janeiro; the meeting for 'non-governmental organisations', mainly pro-environmental pressure groups, involved more participants than UNCED itself. It has been estimated that, in total, over 20 000 people went to Rio de Janeiro in June 1992.

The preparatory negotiations dealt with four main areas: draft conventions on biodiversity conservation, global climate change, forest management, and the preparation of two documents for adoption at UNCED. The main outcomes were as follows. There was complete agreement on the non-binding adoption of the *Rio Declaration* and *Agenda 21*. The first of these comprises 27 statements of principle in regard to global sustainable development. The second is an 800-page document covering over 100 specific programmes for the attainment of global sustainable development: many of these programmes involve resource transfers from the industrial to the developing nations. UNCED also agreed on the creation of a new UN agency, a Commission for Sustainable Development, to oversee the implementation of *Agenda 21*. Agreement was also reached on the non-binding adoption of a set of principles for forest management. The industrial nations re-affirmed their previous, non-binding, commitments to a target for development aid of 0.7% of their GNP. It should be noted that it is still true that only a few of the industrial nations actually attain this target.

Two conventions were adopted, by some 150 nations in each case, which would be binding on signatories when ratified by them. These covered global climate change and biodiversity conservation: the latter was not signed by the USA at the Rio meeting, but the USA did sign in 1993 after a change of administration. Although binding, these conventions did not commit individual nations to much in the way of specific actions. The climate change convention and subsequent related developments are discussed in Chapter 13. Many environmental activists, as well as many concerned to promote economic development in poor nations, regarded the actual achievements at UNCED as disappointing, but it did confirm that sustainable development was, and would remain, firmly on the world political agenda. While specific commitments were not a major feature of the outcomes, there were agreements with the potential to lead to further developments. The creation of the Commission for Sustainable Development is clearly an important institutional innovation at the international level.

The convening of, and the outcomes at, UNCED suggest that the need to address the economic and environmental problems arising from economy–environment linkages is widely accepted. Equally, UNCED and subsequent events suggest that even when the existence of a problem is widely agreed by national governments, agreement on the nature of appropriate policy responses is limited. Further, there is clearly reluctance on the part of national governments to incur costs associated with policy responses, and agreed action is even more difficult to realise than agreement about what should be done. The difficulties involved in achieving international action on environmental problems are discussed in Chapter 13.

Economy–environment interdependence

Economic activity takes place within, and is part of, the system which is the earth and its atmosphere. This system we call 'the natural environment', or more briefly 'the environment'. This system itself has an environment, which is the rest of the universe. Figure 2.2 is a schematic representation of the two-way relationships between, the interdependence of, the economy and the environment.[1] The heavy black lined box represents the environment, which is a thermodynamically closed system, in that it exchanges energy but not matter with its environment. The environment receives inputs of solar radiation. Some of that radiation is absorbed and drives environmental processes. Some is reflected back into space. This is represented by the arrows crossing the heavy black line at the top of the figure. Matter does not cross the

[1] Figure 2.2 is taken from Common (1995), where economy environment interdependence is discussed at greater length than here. References to works which deal more fully, and rigorously, with the natural science matters briefly reviewed here are provided in the Further Reading section at the end of the chapter.

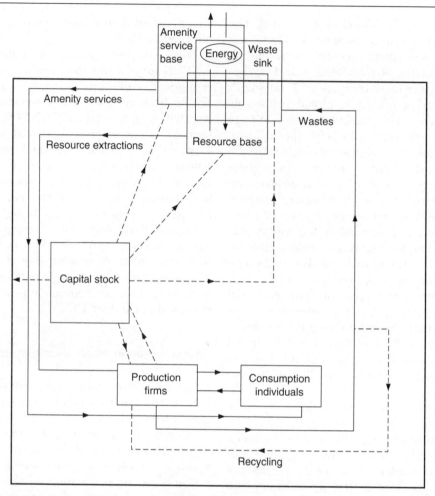

Figure 2.2 Economic activity in the natural environment.

heavy black line. The balance between energy absorption and reflection determines the way the global climate system functions. The energy in and out arrows are shown passing through three boxes, which represent three of the functions that the environment performs in relation to economic activity. The fourth function, represented by the heavy black lined box itself, is the provision of the life support services and those services which hold the whole functioning system together. Note that the three boxes intersect one with another and that the heavy black line passes through them. This is to indicate that the four functions interact with one another, as discussed below.

Figure 2.2 shows economic activity located within the environment and involving production and consumption, both of which draw upon environmental services, as shown by the solid lines inside the heavy lined box. Not all of production is consumed. Some of the output from production is added to the man-made, reproducible, capital stock, the services of which are used, together with labour services, in production. Figure 2.2 shows production using a third type of input, resources extracted from the environment. Production gives rise to wastes inserted into the environment. So does consumption. Consumption also uses directly a flow of amenity services from the environment to individuals without the intermediation of productive activity.

We now discuss these four environmental functions, and the interactions between them, in more detail.

The services that the environment provides

As noted in the previous chapter, natural resources used in production are of several types. One distinguishing characteristic is whether the resource exists as a stock or a flow. The difference lies in whether the level of current use affects future availability. A second standard distinction concerns the nature of the link between current use and future availability. Renewable resources are biotic populations – flora and fauna. Non-renewable resources are minerals, including the fossil fuels. In the former case, the stock existing at a point in time has the potential to grow by means of natural reproduction. If in any period use of the resource is less than natural growth, stock size grows. If use, or harvest, is always the same as natural growth, the resource can be used indefinitely. Such a harvest rate is often referred to as a 'sustainable yield'. Harvest rates in excess of sustainable yield imply declining stock size. For non-renewable resources there is no natural reproduction, except on geological time-scales. Consequently, more use now necessarily implies less future use.

Within the class of non-renewables the distinction between fossil fuels and the other minerals is important. First, the use of fossil fuels is pervasive in industrial economies, and could be said to be one of their essential characteristics. Second, fossil fuel combustion is an irreversible process in that there is no way in which the input fuel can be even partially recovered after combustion. In so far as coal, oil and gas are used to produce heat, rather than as inputs to chemical processes, they cannot be recycled. Minerals used as inputs to production can be recycled. This means that whereas in the case of minerals there exists the possibility of delaying, for a given use rate, the date of exhaustion of a given initial stock, in the case of fossil fuels there does not. Third, fossil fuel combustion is a major source of a number of waste emissions, especially into the atmosphere.

Many of the activities involved in production and consumption give rise to waste products, or residuals, to be discharged into the natural environment. Indeed, as we shall see when we discuss the materials balance principle, such insertions into the environment are the necessary corollary of the extraction of material resources from it. In economics, questions relating to the consequences of waste discharge into the environment are generally discussed under the heading of 'pollution'. To the extent, and only to the extent, that waste discharge gives rise to problems perceived by humans economists say that there is a pollution problem. Pollution problems can be conceptualised in two ways. One, which finds favour with economists, sees pollution as a stock of material resident in the natural environment. The other, which finds favour more with ecologists, sees pollution as a flow which affects the natural environment.

In the former case, pollution is treated in the same way as a stock resource, save that the stock has negative value. Residual flows into the environment add to the stock, natural decay processes subtract from it. We will look at pollution modelled this way in Chapter 11. The flow model treats the environment as having an 'assimilative capacity', defined in terms of a rate of residual flow. Pollution is then the result of a residual flow rate in excess of 'assimilative capacity'. There is no pollution if the residual flow rate is equal to, or less than, assimilative capacity. If the residual flow rate is persistently in excess of assimilative capacity, the latter declines over time, and may eventually go to zero.

In Figure 2.2 amenity services flow directly from the environment to individuals. The biosphere provides humans with recreational facilities and other sources of pleasure and stimulation. Swimming from an ocean beach does not require productive activity to transform an environmental resource into a source of human satisfaction, for example. Wilderness recreation is defined by the absence of other human activity. Some people like simply lying out of doors in sunshine. The role of the natural environment in regard to amenity services can be appreciated by imagining its absence, as would be the case for the occupants of a space vehicle. In many cases the flow to individuals of amenity services does not directly involve any consumptive material flow. Wilderness recreation, for example, is not primarily about exploiting resources in the wilderness area, though it may involve this in the use of wood for fires, the capture of game for food and so on. A day on the beach does not involve any consumption of the beach in the way that the use of oil involves its consumption. This is not to say that flows of amenity services never impact physically on the natural environment. Excessive use of a beach area can lead to changes in its character, as with the erosion of sand dunes following vegetation loss caused by human visitation.

The fourth environmental function, shown in Figure 2.2 as the heavy box, is difficult to represent in a simple and concise way. Over and above serving as resource base, waste sink and amenity base, the biosphere currently provides the basic life support functions for humans. While the range of environmental conditions that humans are biologically equipped to cope with is greater than for most other species, there are limits to the tolerable. We have, for example, quite specific requirements in terms of breathable air. The range of temperatures that we can exist in is wide in relation to conditions on earth, but narrow in relation to the range on other planets in the solar system. Humans have minimum requirements for water input. And so on. The environment functions now in such a manner that humans can exist in it. An example will illustrate what is involved.

Consider solar radiation. It is one element of the resource base, and for some people

sunbathing is an environmental amenity service. In fact, solar radiation as it arrives at the earth's atmosphere is harmful to humans. There it includes the ultraviolet wavelength UV-B, which causes skin cancer, adversely affects the immune system, and can cause eye cataracts. UV-B radiation affects other living things as well. Very small organisms are likely to be particularly affected, as UV-B can only penetrate a few layers of cells. This could be a serious problem for marine systems, where the base of the food chain are very small organisms living in the surface layers of the ocean, which UV-B reaches. UV-B radiation also affects photosynthesis in green plants adversely.

Solar radiation arriving at the surface of the earth has much less UV-B than it does arriving at the atmosphere. Ozone in the stratosphere absorbs UV-B, performing a life support function by filtering solar radiation. In the absence of stratospheric ozone, it is questionable whether human life could exist. Currently, stratospheric ozone is being depleted by the release into the atmosphere of chlorofluorocarbons (CFCs), compounds which exist only by virtue of human economic activity. They have been in use since the 1940s. Their ozone depleting properties were recognised in the 1980s, and, as discussed in Chapter 13, policy to reduce this form of pollution is now in place.

The interdependencies between economic activity and the environment are pervasive and complex. The complexity is increased by the existence of processes in the environment that mean that the four classes of environmental services each interact one with another. In Figure 2.2 this is indicated by having the three boxes intersect one with another, and jointly with the heavy black line representing the life support function. What is involved can be illustrated with the following example.

Consider a river estuary. It serves as resource base for the local economy in that a commercial fishery operates in it. It serves as waste sink in that urban sewage is discharged into it. It serves as the source of amenity services, being used for recreational purposes such as swimming and boating. It contributes to life support functions in so far as it is a breeding ground for marine species which are not commercially exploited, but which play a role in the operation of the marine ecosystem. At rates of sewage discharge equal to or below the assimilative capacity of the estuary, all four functions can coexist. If, however, the rate of sewage discharge exceeds assimilative capacity, not only does a pollution problem emerge, but the other estuarine functions are impaired. Pollution will interfere with the reproductive capacity of the commercially exploited fish stocks, and may lead to the closure of the fishery. This does not necessarily mean its biological extinction. The fishery may be closed on the grounds of the danger to public health. Pollution will reduce the capacity of the estuary to support recreational activity, and in some respects, such as swimming, may drive it to zero. Pollution will also impact on the non-commercial marine species, and may lead to their extinction with implications for marine ecosystem function.

An example at the global level of the interconnections between the environmental services arising from interacting environmental processes affected by economic activity is provided by the problem of global climate change, which is discussed in Chapter 13.

Substituting for environmental services

One feature of Figure 2.2 remains to be considered. We have so far discussed the solid lines. There are also some dashed lines. These represent possibilities of substitutions for environmental services.

Consider first recycling. This involves interception of the waste stream prior to it reaching the natural environment, and the return of some part of it to production. Recycling substitutes for environmental functions in two ways. First, it reduces the demands made upon the waste sink function. Second, it reduces the demands made upon the

resource base function, in so far as recycled materials are substituted for extractions from the environment.

Also shown in Figure 2.2 are four dashed lines from the box for capital running to the three boxes and the heavy black line representing environmental functions. These lines are to represent possibilities for substituting the services of capital for environmental services.

In relation to the waste sink function consider again, as an example, the discharge of sewage into a river estuary. Various levels of treatment of the sewage prior to its discharge into the river are possible. According to the level of treatment, the demand made upon the assimilative capacity of the estuary is reduced for a given level of sewage. Capital in the form of a sewage treatment plant substitutes for the natural environmental function of waste sink to an extent dependent on the level of treatment that the plant provides.

An example from the field of energy conservation illustrates the substitution of capital for resource base functions. For a given level of human comfort, the energy use of a house can be reduced by the installation of insulation and control systems. These add to that part of the total stock of capital equipment which is the house and all of its fittings, and thus to the total capital stock. Note, however, that the insulation and control systems are themselves material structures, the production of which involves extractions, including energy, from the environment. Similar fuel saving substitution possibilities exist in productive activities.

Consider next some examples in the context of amenity services. An individual who likes swimming can either do this in a river or lake, or from an ocean beach, or in a man-made swimming pool. The experiences involved are not identical, but they are close substitutes in some dimensions. Similarly, it is not now necessary to actually go into a natural environment to derive pleasure from seeing it. The capital equipment in the entertainment industry means that it is possible to see wild flora and fauna without leaving an urban environment. Apparently it is envisaged that computer technology will, via virtual reality devices, make it possible to experience many of the sensations involved in actually being in a natural environment without actually being in it.

It appears that it is in the context of the life support function that many scientists regard the substitution possibilities as most limited. However, from a technical point of view, it is not clear that this is the case. Artificial environments capable of supporting human life have already been created, and in the form of space vehicles and associated equipment have already enabled humans to live outside the biosphere, albeit for limited periods. It would apparently be possible, if expensive, to create conditions capable of sustaining human life on the moon, given some suitable energy source. However, the quantity of human life that could be sustained in the absence of natural life support functions would appear to be quite small. It is not that those functions are absolutely irreplaceable, but that they are irreplaceable on the scale that they operate. A second point concerns the quality of life. One might reasonably take the view that while human life on an otherwise biologically dead earth is feasible, it would not be in the least desirable.

The possibilities for substituting for environmental services have been discussed in terms of capital equipment. Capital is accumulated when output from current production is not used for current consumption. Current production is not solely of material structures, and capital does not only comprise equipment – machines, buildings, roads and so on. 'Human capital' is increased when current production is used to add to the stock of knowledge, and is what forms the basis for technical change. However, while the accumulation of human capital is clearly of great importance in regard to environmental problems, in order for technical change to impact on economic activity, it generally requires embodiment in new equipment. Knowledge that could reduce the demands made upon environmental functions does not actually do so until it is incorporated into equipment that substitutes for environmental functions.

Capital for environmental service substitution is not the only form of substitution that is relevant to economy–environment interconnections. In Figure 2.2 flows between the economy and the environment are shown as single lines. Of course, these single lines each represent what are in fact a whole range of different flows. With respect to each of the aggregate flows shown in Figure 2.2, substitutions as between components of the flow are possible and affect the demands made upon environmental services. The implications of any given substitution may extend beyond the environmental function directly affected. For example, a switch from fossil fuel use to hydroelectric power reduces fossil fuel depletion and waste generation in fossil fuel combustion (and also impacts on the amenity service flow in so far as a natural recreation area is flooded).

Some environmental science

We now briefly review some elements of the environmental sciences which relate to economy–environment interdependence and its implications.

The materials balance principle

The materials balance principle is the term that economists tend to use to refer to the law of conservation of matter, which states that matter can neither be created nor destroyed. An early exposition of the principle as it applies to economic activity is found in Kneese et al. (1970). As far as economics goes, the most fundamental implication of the materials balance principle is that economic activity essentially involves transforming matter extracted from the environment. Economic activity cannot, in a material sense, create anything. It does, of course, involve transforming material extracted from the environment so that it is more valuable to humans. But, another implication is that all of the material extracted from the environment must, eventually, be returned to it, albeit in a transformed state. The 'eventually' is necessary because some of the extracted material stays in the economy for a long time – in buildings, roads, machinery and so on.

Figure 2.3 shows the physical relationships implied by the materials balance principle. It abstracts from the lags in the circular flow of matter due to capital accumulation in the economy. It amplifies the picture of material extractions from and insertions into the environment provided in Figure 2.2. Primary inputs (ores, liquids and gases) are taken from the environment and converted into useful products (basic fuel, food and raw materials) by 'environmental' firms. These outputs become inputs into subsequent production processes (shown as a product flow to non-environmental firms) or to households directly. Households also receive final products from the non-environmental firms sector.

The materials balance principle states an identity between the mass of materials flow from the environment (flow A) and the mass of residual material discharge flows to the environment (flows $B + C + D$). So, in terms

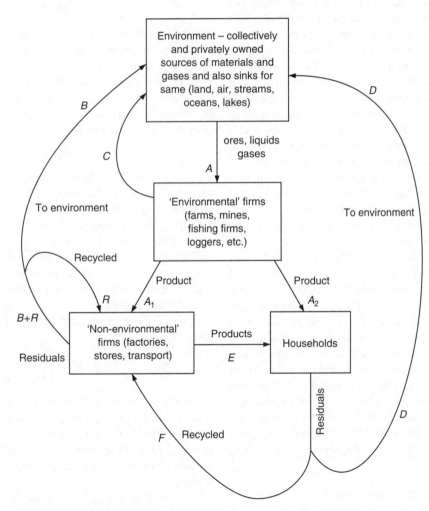

Figure 2.3 A materials balance model of economy–environment interactions.
Source: adapted from Herfindahl and Kneese (1974).

of mass, we have $A \equiv B + C + D$. In fact several identities are implied by Figure 2.3. Each of the four sectors shown by rectangular boxes receives an equal mass of inputs to the mass of its outputs. So we have the following four identities:

The environment: $A \equiv B + C + D$ as above
Environmental firms: $A \equiv A_1 + A_2 + C$
Non-environmental firms:
$\quad B + R + E \equiv R + A_1 + F$
Households: $A_2 + E \equiv D + F$

Several insights can be derived from this model. Firstly, in a materially-closed economy in which no net stock accumulation takes place (that is, physical assets do not change in magnitude) the mass of residuals into the environment $(B + C + D)$ must be equal to the mass of fuels, foods and raw materials extracted from the environment and oxygen taken from the atmosphere (flow A). Secondly, the treatment of residuals from economic activity does not reduce their mass although it alters their form. Nevertheless, while waste treatment does not 'get rid of' residuals, waste management can be useful by transforming residuals to a more benign form (or by changing their location).

Thirdly, the extent of recycling is important. To see how, look again at the identity $B + R + E \equiv R + A_1 + F$. For any fixed magnitude of final output, E, if the amount of recycling of household residuals, F, can be increased, then the quantity of inputs into final production, A_1, can be decreased. This in turn implies that less primary extraction of environmental resources, A, need take place. So the total amount of material throughput in the system (the magnitude A) can be decreased for any given level of production and consumption if the efficiency of materials utilisation is increased through recycling processes. We return to the question of recycling below.

Production function specification

In most of microeconomics, production is taken to involve inputs of capital and labour.

For the ith firm, the production function is written as

$$Q_i = f_i(L_i, K_i) \tag{2.1}$$

where Q represents output, L labour input and K capital input. According to the materials balance principle, this cannot be an adequate general representation of what production involves. If Q_i has some material embodiment, then there must be some material input to production – matter cannot be created.

If we let R represent some natural resource extracted from the environment, then the production function could be written as:

$$Q_i = f_i(L_i, K_i, R_i) \tag{2.2}$$

Production functions with these arguments are widely used in the resource economics literature. In contrast, the environmental economics literature tends to stress insertions into the environment – wastes arising in production and consumption wastes – and often uses a production function of the form

$$Q_i = f_i(L_i, K_i, M_i) \tag{2.3}$$

where M_i is the flow of waste arising from the ith firm's activity. Equation 2.3 may appear strange at first sight as it treats waste flows as an input into production. However, this is a reasonable way of proceeding given that reductions in wastes will mean reductions in output for given levels of the other inputs, as other inputs have to be diverted to the task of reducing wastes.

A more general version of Equation 2.3 is given by

$$Q_i = f_i\left(L_i, K_i, M_i, A\left[\sum_i M_i\right]\right) \tag{2.4}$$

in which A denotes the ambient concentration level of some pollutant, which depends on the total of waste emissions across all firms. Thus, Equation 2.4 recognises that ambient pollution can affect production possibilities.

However, as it stands Equation 2.4 conflicts with the materials balance principle. Now matter in the form of waste is being created by economic activity alone, which is not possible. A synthesis of resource and environmental economics production functions is desirable, which recognises that material inputs – in the form of environmental resources – enter the production function and material outputs – in the form of waste as well as output – emanate from production. This yields a production function such as

$$Q_i = f_i \left(L_i, K_i, R_i, M_i[R_i], A \left[\sum_i M_i \right] \right) \quad (2.5)$$

Where some modelling procedure requires the use of a production function, the use of a form such as Equation 2.5 has the attractive property of recognising that, in general, production must have a material base, and that waste emissions necessarily arise from that base. It is consistent, that is, with one of the fundamental laws of nature. This production function also includes possible feedback effects of wastes on production, arising through the ambient levels of pollutants. It is, however, relatively uncommon for such a fully specified production function to be used in either theoretical or empirical work in economics. In particular cases, this could be justified by argument that for the purpose at hand – examining the implications of resource depletion, say – nothing essential is lost by an incomplete specification, and the analysis is simplified and clarified. We shall implicitly use this argument ourselves at various points in the remainder of the book, and work with specialised versions of Equation 2.5. However, it is important to keep in mind that it is Equation 2.5 itself that is the correct specification of a production process that has a material output.

The second law of thermodynamics

Thermodynamics is the science of energy. Energy is the potential to do work. It is a characteristic of things, rather than a thing itself. Work is involved when matter is changed in structure, in physical or chemical nature, or in location. In thermodynamics it is necessary to be clear about the nature of the system under consideration. An 'open' system is one which exchanges energy and matter with its environment. An individual organism is an open system. A 'closed' system exchanges energy but not matter with its environment. We noted above that planet earth and its atmosphere are a closed system. An 'isolated' system exchanges neither energy nor matter with its environment. Apart from the entire universe, an isolated system is an ideal, an abstraction.

The first law of thermodynamics says that energy can neither be created nor destroyed. It can only be converted from one form to another. The second law of thermodynamics is also known as the 'entropy law'. It says that heat flows spontaneously from a hotter to a colder body, and that heat cannot be transformed into work with 100% efficiency. It follows that all conversions of energy from one form to another are less than 100% efficient. This appears to contradict the first law, but does not. The point is that not all of the energy of some store, such as a fossil fuel, is available for conversion. Energy stores vary in the proportion of their energy that is available for conversion. 'Entropy' is a measure of unavailable energy. All energy conversions increase the entropy of an isolated system. All energy conversions are irreversible, since the fact that the conversion is less than 100% efficient means that the work required to restore the original state is not available in the new state. Fossil fuel combustion is irreversible, and of itself implies an increase in the entropy of the system, which is the environment in which economic activity takes place. However, that environment is a closed, not an isolated, system, and is continually receiving energy inputs from its environment, in the form of solar radiation. This is what makes life possible.

Thermodynamics is difficult for non-specialists to understand. Even within physics it has a history involving controversy, and disagreements persist, as will be noted below. There exist some popular myths about thermodynamics and its implications. It is, for example, often said that entropy always increases. This is true only for an isolated system. Classical thermodynamics involved the study of equilibrium systems, but the systems directly relevant to economic activity are open and closed systems which are far from equilibrium. Such systems receive energy from their environment. As noted above, a living organism is an open system which is far from equilibrium. Some energy input is necessary for it to maintain its structure and not become disordered; in other words, dead.

The relevance of thermodynamics to the origins of the problem of sustainability is clear. The economist who did most to try to make his colleagues aware of the laws of thermodynamics and their implications, Nicholas Georgescu-Roegen (who started academic life as a physicist), described the second law as the 'taproot of economic scarcity' (Georgescu-Roegen, 1979). His point was, to put it graphically, that if energy conversion processes were 100% efficient, one lump of coal would last forever. Material transformations involve work, and thus require energy. Given a fixed rate of receipt of solar energy, there is an upper limit to the amount of work that can be done on the basis of it. For most of human history, human numbers and material consumption levels were subject to this constraint. The exploitation of fossil fuels removes this constraint. The fossil fuels are accumulated past solar energy receipts, initially transformed into living tissue, and stored by geological processes. Given this origin, there is necessarily a finite amount of the fossil fuels in existence. It follows that in the absence of an abundant substitute energy source with similar qualities to the fossil fuels, such as nuclear fusion, there would eventually be a reversion to the energetic situation of the pre-industrial phase of human history, which involved total reliance on solar radiation and other flow sources of energy. Of course, the technology deployed in such a situation would be different to that available in the pre-industrial phase. It is now possible,

for example, to use solar energy to generate electricity.

Recycling

The laws of thermodynamics are generally taken to mean that given enough available energy, all transformations of matter are possible, at least in principle. On the basis of that understanding it has generally been further understood that, at least in principle, complete material recycling is possible. On this basis, given the energy, there is no necessity that shortage of minerals constrain economic activity. Past extractions could be recovered by recycling. It is in this sense that the second law of thermodynamics is the ultimate source of scarcity. Given available energy, there need be no scarcity of minerals. This is what drives the interest in nuclear power, and especially nuclear fusion, which some claim offers the prospect of a clean and effectively infinite energy resource.

Nicholas Georgescu-Roegen, noted above as the economist who introduced the idea of the second law as the ultimate basis for economic scarcity, subsequently attacked the view just sketched as 'the energetic dogma', and insisted that 'matter matters' as well (Georgescu-Roegen, 1979). He argued that even given enough energy, the complete recycling of matter is, in principle, impossible. This has been dubbed 'the fourth law of thermodynamics' and its validity denied: 'complete recycling is physically possible if a sufficient amount of energy is available' (Biancardi et al., 1993). The basis for this denial is that the fourth law would be inconsistent with the second. This disagreement over what is a very basic scientific issue is interesting for two reasons. First, if qualified scientists can disagree over so fundamental a point, then it is clear that many issues relevant to sustainability involve uncertainty. Second, both sides to this dispute would agree that as a practical matter, complete recycling is impossible, however much energy is available. Thus, the statement above rebutting the fourth law is immediately followed by: 'The problem is that such expenditure of energy would involve a tremendous increase in the entropy of the environment, which would not be sustainable for the biosphere' (Biancardi *et al.*, 1993). Neither party to the dispute is suggesting that policy should be determined on the basis of an understanding that matter can actually be completely recycled.

Ecology

Two concepts of fundamental importance in ecology are stability and resilience. The ecologist Holling (1973, 1986) distinguishes between stability as a property attaching to the populations comprising an ecosystem, and resilience as a property of the ecosystem. Stability is the propensity of a population to return to some kind of equilibrium following a disturbance. Resilience is the propensity of an ecosystem to retain its functional and organisational structure following a disturbance. The fact that an ecosystem is resilient does not necessarily imply that all of its component populations are stable. It is possible for a disturbance to result in a population disappearing from an ecosystem, while the ecosystem as a whole continues to function in broadly the same way, so exhibiting resilience.

Common and Perrings (1992) put these matters in a slightly different way. Stability is a property that relates to the levels of the variables in the system. Cod populations in North Atlantic waters would be stable, for example, if their numbers returned to prior levels after a brief period of heavy fishing was brought to an end. Resilience relates to the sizes of the parameters of the relationships determining ecosystem structure and function in terms, say, of energy flows through the system. An ecosystem is resilient if those parameters tend to remain unchanged following shocks to the system, which will mean that it maintains its organisation in the face of shocks to it, without undergoing catastrophic, discontinuous, change.

Some economic activities appear to reduce resilience, so that the level of disturbance to which the ecosystem can be subjected without parametric change taking place is reduced. Expressed another way, the threshold levels of some system variable, beyond which major changes in a wider system take place, can be reduced as a consequence of economic behaviour. Safety margins become tightened, and the integrity and stability of the ecosystem is put into greater jeopardy. This aligns with the understanding, noted above, of pollution as that which occurs when a waste flow exceeds the assimilative capacity of the receiving system, and that which if it occurs itself reduces the system's assimilative capacity.

When such changes takes place, dose–response relationships may also exhibit very significant non-linearities and discontinuities. Pollution of a water system, for example, may have relatively small and proportional effects at low pollution levels, but at higher pollutant levels, responses may increase sharply and possibly jump discontinuously to much greater magnitudes. Such a dose–response relationship is illustrated in Figure 2.4.

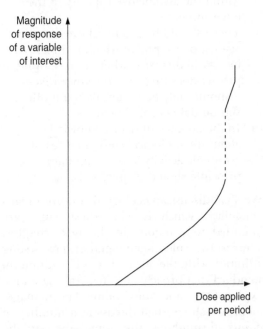

Figure 2.4 Non-linearities and discontinuities in dose-response relationships.

A matter that has become of great concern to ecologists, and others, in recent years, is loss of biological diversity (or biodiversity for short). Although natural phenomena cause changes in the composition and extent of biodiversity, it is human-caused losses that are of most concern. The extent of biodiversity appears to be falling at unprecedentedly high rates. This is understood to threaten the resilience of many ecosystems and, thereby, to have important long-term economic implications. Later in this chapter we consider more fully what biodiversity is, how it is measured, and how fast it is declining. In subsequent chapters we shall investigate the causes and consequences of biodiversity decline, and the policies available to arrest that decline.

Ecologists suggest several behavioural rules that should be followed to minimise the likelihood of ecosystem disruption:

(a) Harvesting of renewable resources should take place within natural and managed rates of regeneration.
(b) Emission of wastes should take place within the assimilative capacity of the environment.
(c) There should be a general presumption against development which reduces biological diversity; where a development project does threaten to reduce diversity, it should only be undertaken if it offers substantial net social benefits.
(d) In the absence of strong knowledge about the ecological consequences of economic activity, a precautionary principle should be pursued.

We shall discuss an ecological concept of sustainability, which is what these rules are intended to promote, in the next chapter. The last two rules taken together have strong affinities with the idea of a 'safe minimum standard' approach to natural resource exploitation and environmental management, which we shall discuss at a number of points throughout the remainder of the book.

Limits to growth?

An important event in the emergence in the last decades of the perception that there is a sustainability problem was the publication in 1972 of a book, *The Limits to Growth* (Meadows *et al.*, 1972), which was widely understood to claim that environmental limits would cause the collapse of the world economic system in the middle of the twenty-first century.

The book was roundly condemned by most economists, but influenced many people. It is arguable that it was a stimulus to the re-emergence of interest in natural resources on the part of economists in the early 1970s noted in Chapter 1. One economist argued, at around the same time, that the limits to growth were social rather than environmental.

Environmental limits

The Limits to Growth reported the results of a study in which a computer model of the world system, World3, was used to simulate its future. World3 represented the world economy as a single economy, and included interconnections between that economy and its environment. According to its creators, World3

> was built to investigate five major trends of global concern – accelerating industrialisation, rapid population growth, widespread malnutrition, depletion of non-renewable resources, and a deteriorating environment. These trends are all interconnected in many ways, and their development is measured in decades or centuries, rather than in months or years. With the model we are seeking to understand the causes of these trends, their interrelationships, and their implications as much as one hundred years in the future.
>
> Meadows *et al.* (1972), page 21

It incorporated:

(a) a limit to the amount of land available for agriculture;
(b) a limit to the amount of agricultural output producible per unit of land in use;

(c) a limit to the amounts of non-renewable resources available for extraction;

(d) a limit to the ability of the environment to assimilate wastes arising in production and consumption, which limit falls as the level of pollution increases.

The behaviour of the economic system was represented as a continuation of past trends in key variables, subject to those trends being influenced by the relationships between the variables represented in the model. These relationships were represented in terms of positive and negative feedback effects. Thus, for example, population growth is determined by birth and death rates, which are determined by fertility and mortality, which are in turn influenced by such variables as industrial output per capita, the extent of family planning and education – for fertility – and food availability per capita, industrial output per capita, pollution, and the availability of health care – for mortality. The behaviour over time in the model of each of these variables, depends in turn on that of others, and affects that of others.

On the basis of a number of simulations using World3, the conclusions reached by the modelling team were as follows:

> 1. If the present growth trends in world population, industrialisation, pollution, food production and resource depletion continue unchanged, the limits to growth on this planet will be reached sometime within the next 100 years. The most probable result will be a sudden and uncontrollable decline in both population and industrial capacity.
>
> 2. It is possible to alter these trends and to establish a condition of ecological and economic stability that is sustainable far into the future. The state of global equilibrium could be designed so that the basic material needs of each person on earth are satisfied and each person has an equal opportunity to realise his or her individual human potential.
>
> 3. If the world's people decide to strive for this second outcome rather than the first, the sooner they begin working to attain it, the greater will be their chances of success.
>
> Meadows *et al.* (1992)

What *The Limits to Growth* actually said was widely misrepresented. It was widely reported that it was an unconditional forecast of disaster sometime in the next century, consequent upon the world running out of non-renewable resources. In fact, as the quotation above indicates, what was involved was conditional upon the continuation of some existing trends. Further, this conditional prediction was not based upon running out of resources.

The first model run reported did show collapse as the consequence of resource depletion. Figure 2.5 is a reproduction of the figure in *The Limits to Growth* that reports the results for 'World Model Standard Run'. This run assumes no major changes in social, economic or physical relationships. Variables follow actual historical values until the year 1970. Thereafter, food, industrial output and population grow exponentially until the rapidly diminishing resource base causes a slowdown in industrial growth. System lags result in pollution and population continuing to grow for some time after industrial output has peaked. Population growth is finally halted by a rise in the mortality rate, as a result of reduced flows of food and medical services.

However, the next reported run involved the model modified by an increase in the resource availability limit such that depletion did not give rise to problems for the economic system. In this run, the proximate source of disaster was the level of pollution consequent upon the exploitation of the increased amount of resources available, following from the materials balance principle. A number of variant model runs were reported, each relaxing some constraint. The conclusions reached were based on consideration of all of the variant model runs. Successive runs of the model were used to ascertain those changes to the standard configuration that were necessary to get the model to a sustainable state, rather than to collapse mode.

It was widely reported that the World3 results said that there were limits to 'eco-

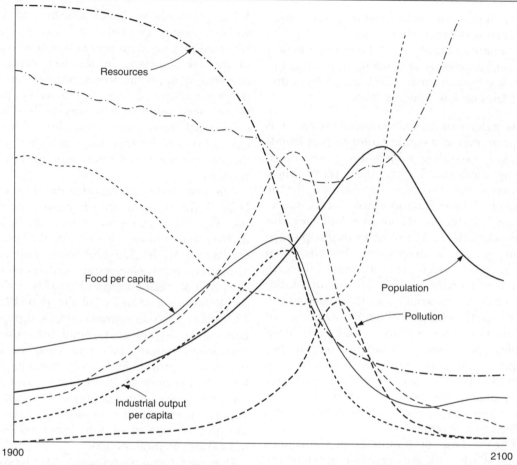

Figure 2.5 Base run projections of the 'limits to growth' model.
Source: Meadows *et al.* (1972), page 124.

nomic growth'. In fact, what it said, as the conclusions quoted above indicate, is that there were limits to the growth of material throughput for the world economic system. As economic growth is measured it includes the consumption of the output of the service sector, as well as the agricultural and industrial sectors.

A sequel to *The Limits to Growth*, written by the same team, and entitled *Beyond the Limits*, was published in 1992 to coincide with the UNCED conference held in Rio de Janeiro (Meadows *et al.*, 1992). To date, the publication of the sequel appears to have generated much less controversy than the original did. This might suggest some major change in analysis and conclusions as between original

and sequel. In fact there is very little substantive difference in the conclusions, and apart from updating of numerical values used, the model is stated to be modified in only minor ways from the original World3. The position on this as stated in the sequel is:

> As far as we can tell from the global data, from the World3 model, and from all we have learned in the past twenty years, the three conclusions we drew in *The Limits to Growth* are still valid, but they need to be strengthened.

Economists on environmental limits

The response by economists to *The Limits to Growth* was almost entirely hostile. Prominent among these responses were those by Page

(1973), Nordhaus (1972), Beckerman (1972, 1974), Cole *et al.* (1973) and Lecomber (1975). According to one eminent economist it was 'a brazen, impudent piece of nonsense that nobody could possibly take seriously' (Beckerman, 1972). Economists have had much less to say, and much less critical things to say, about the sequel *Beyond the Limits*. In a foreword to it, a Nobel laureate in economics, Jan Tinbergen, says of it: 'We can all learn something from this book, especially we economists'.

The main line of the criticism of the original by economists was that the feedback loops in World3 were poorly specified in that they failed to take account of behavioural adjustments operating through the price mechanism. In particular, it was argued that changing patterns of relative scarcity would alter the structure of prices, inducing behavioural changes in resource-use patterns. Given a well-functioning market mechanism, it was argued, limits to growth would not operate in the way reported by the modelling team. It was conceded by some of the economist critics that the force of this argument was weakened by the fact that for many environmental resources and services, markets did not exist, or functioned badly where they did. However, it was also argued that such 'market failure' could be corrected by the proper policy responses to emerging problems. This presumes that the sorts of substitutions for environmental services that we discussed above can be made, given properly functioning markets or policy-created surrogates for such, to the extent that will overcome limits that would otherwise exist. At the end of the day, a major, and largely unresolved, question in the debates about the existence of a sustainability problem is the existence and effectiveness of substitutes for environmental services.

Social limits to growth

Daly (1987) argues that there are two classes of limits to growth. First, there are the biophysical limits arising from the laws of thermodynamics and from the fragility of ecosystems. The second class relates to the desirability of growth, rather than its feasibility. Daly states four propositions about the desirability of growth:

(1) The desirability of growth financed by running down resources is limited by the cost imposed on future generations.
(2) The extinction or reduction in the number of sentient non-human species whose habitat disappears limits the desirability of growth financed by takeover.
(3) The self-cancelling effects on welfare limit the desirability of aggregate growth.
(4) The desirability of growth is limited by the corrosive effects on moral standards of the very attitudes that foster growth, such as glorification of self-interest and a scientific-technocratic world view.

The last two of these propositions concern what have been called 'social limits to growth'.

The argument for 'social limits to growth' was explicitly advanced in a book with that title (Hirsch, 1977), published five years after *The Limits to Growth*. Hirsch argued that the process of economic growth becomes increasingly unable to yield the satisfaction which individuals expect from it, once the general level of material affluence has satisfied the main biological needs for life-sustaining food, shelter and clothing. As the average level of consumption rises, an increasing portion of consumption takes on a social as well as an individual aspect, so that:

> the satisfaction that individuals derive from goods and services depends in increasing measure not only on their own consumption but on consumption by others as well.
>
> Hirsch (1977), page 2

The satisfaction a person gets from the use of a car, for example, depends on how many other people do the same. The greater the number of others who use cars, the greater is the amount of air pollution and the extent of congestion, and so the lower is the satisfaction one individual's car use will yield. However, Hirsch's main focus was on what he calls 'positional goods', the satisfaction from which depends upon the individual's consumption relative to that of others, rather than the absolute level of consumption. Consider, as an example, expenditure on education in an attempt to raise one's chances of securing sought-after jobs. The utility to a person of a given level of educational expenditure will decline as an increasing number of others also attain that level of education. Each person purchasing education seeks to gain individual advantage, but the simultaneous actions of others frustrate these objectives for each individual. As the average level of education rises, individuals will not receive the gains they expect from higher qualifications.

Once basic material needs are satisfied, further economic growth is associated with an increasing proportion of income being spent on such positional goods. As a consequence, growth is a much less socially desirable objective than economists have usually thought. It does not deliver the increased personal satisfactions that it is supposed to. Traditional utilitarian conceptions of social welfare (see Chapter 4) may be misleading in such circumstances, as utilities are interdependent. An external effect arises if the consumption of others affects the utility that an individual derives from his or her own consumption. The simple summation of individual consumption levels to yield a measure of social welfare is highly problematic.

Can economic growth improve the environment? The Environmental Kuznets Curve

The World Bank's *World Development Report 1992* (IBRD, 1992) was subtitled 'Development and the Environment'. It noted that, 'The view that greater economic activity inevitably hurts the environment is based on static assumptions about technology, tastes and environmental investments'. If we con-

sider, for example, the per capita emissions of some pollutant into the environment, e, and per capita income, y, then the view that is being referred to can be represented as

$$e = \alpha y \tag{2.6}$$

so that e increases linearly with y, as shown in Figure 2.6(a). This is the sort of relationship that critics of *The Limits to Growth* claimed were operative in World3. Suppose, alternatively, that the coefficient α is itself a linear function of y:

$$\alpha = \beta_0 - \beta_1 y \tag{2.7}$$

Then, substituting Equation 2.7 into Equation 2.6 gives the relationship between e and y as:

$$e = \beta_0 y - \beta_1 y^2 \tag{2.8}$$

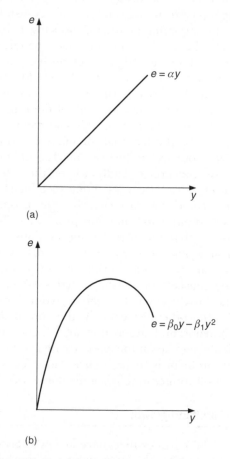

(a)

(b)

Figure 2.6 Environmental impact and income.
Source: Adapted from IBRD (1992).

For β_1 sufficiently small in relation to β_0, the e/y relationship takes the form of an inverted U, as shown in Figure 2.6(b). With this form of relationship, economic growth means higher emissions per capita until per capita income reaches the turning point, and thereafter actually reduces emissions per capita.

It has been hypothesised that a relationship like that shown in Figure 2.6(b) holds for many forms of environmental degradation. Such a relationship is sometimes called an 'Environmental Kuznets Curve' (EKC) after Kuznets (1955), who hypothesised an inverted U for the relationship between a measure of inequality in the distribution of income and the level of income. If the EKC hypothesis held generally, it could imply that instead of being a threat to the environment as argued in *The Limits to Growth*, economic growth is the means to environmental improvement. That is, as countries develop economically, moving from lower to higher levels of per capita income, overall levels of environmental degradation will eventually fall.

The argument for an EKC hypothesis has been succinctly put as follows:

> At low levels of development both the quantity and intensity of environmental degradation is limited to the impacts of subsistence economic activity on the resource base and to limited quantities of biodegradable wastes. As economic development accelerates with the intensification of agriculture and other resource extraction and the take off of industrialisation, the rates of resource depletion begin to exceed the rates of resource regeneration, and waste generation increases in quantity and toxicity. At higher levels of development, structural change towards information-intensive industries and services, coupled with increased environmental awareness, enforcement of environmental regulations, better technology and higher environmental expenditures, result in levelling off and gradual decline of environmental degradation.
>
> Panayotou (1993)

Clearly, the empirical status of the EKC hypothesis is a matter of great importance. If economic growth is actually and generally good for the environment, there is no need to curtail growth in the world economy in order to protect the global environment, and the prospects for sustainable development as envisaged by the Brundtland report are good. In recent years there have been a number of attempts to use econometric techniques to test the EKC hypothesis against the data. Some of the results arising are discussed below. According to one economist, the results support the conclusion that:

> there is clear evidence that, although economic growth usually leads to environmental degradation in the early stages of the process, in the end the best – and probably the only – way to attain a decent environment in most countries is to become rich.
>
> Beckerman (1992)

With respect to the global sustainability problem, two questions arise. First, are the data generally consistent with the EKC hypothesis? Second, if the EKC hypothesis holds, does the implication that growth is good for the global environment follow? We now consider each of these questions.

Evidence on the EKC hypothesis

Shafik and Bandyopadhyay (1992) estimated the coefficients of relationships between environmental degradation and per capita income for ten different environmental indicators as part of a background study for the *World Development Report 1992* (IBRD, 1992). The indicators are: lack of clean water, lack of urban sanitation, ambient levels of suspended particulate matter in urban areas, urban concentrations of sulphur dioxide, change in forest area between 1961 and 1986, the annual rate of deforestation between 1961 and 1986, dissolved oxygen in rivers, faecal coliforms in rivers, municipal waste per capita, and carbon dioxide emissions per capita. Some of their results, in terms of the relationship fitted to the raw data, are shown in Figure 2.7. Lack of clean water and lack of urban sanitation were

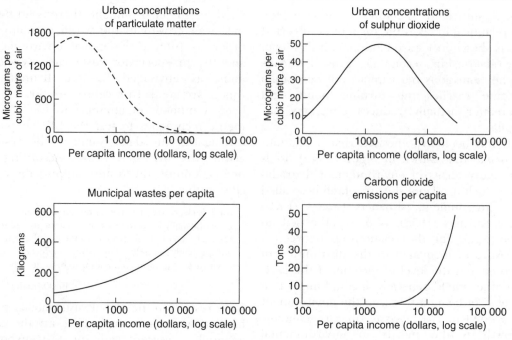

Figure 2.7   Some evidence on the EKC. Estimates are based on cross-country regression analysis of data from the 1980s.
Source: adapted from IBRD (1992).

found to decline uniformly with increasing income. Both measures of deforestation were found not to depend on income. River quality tends to worsen with increasing income. As shown in Figure 2.7, two of the air pollutants were found to conform to the EKC hypothesis. Note, however, that CO_2 emissions, a major contributor to the 'greenhouse gases' to be discussed in relation to global climate change in Chapter 13, do not fit the EKC hypothesis, rising unambiguously with income, as do municipal wastes. Shafik and Bandyopadhyay summarise the implications of their results by stating:

> It is possible to 'grow out of' some environmental problems, but there is nothing automatic about doing so. Action tends to be taken where there are generalised local costs and substantial private and social benefits.

Panayotou (1993) investigated the EKC hypothesis for sulfur dioxide (SO_2), nitrous oxide (NO_x), suspended particulate matter (SPM) and deforestation. The three pollu-

tants are measured in terms of emissions per capita on a national basis. Deforestation is measured as the mean annual rate of deforestation in the mid-1980s. All the fitted relationships are inverted Us, consistent with the EKC hypothesis. The result for SO_2 is shown in Figure 2.8, where the turning point is around $3000 per capita.

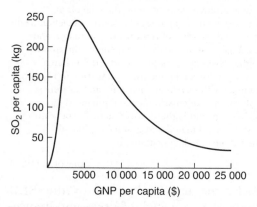

Figure 2.8   An EKC for SO_2.
Source: adapted from Panayotou (1993).

Implications of the EKC

Relationships such as that shown in Figure 2.8 might lead one to believe that, given likely future levels of income per capita, the global environmental impact concerned would decline in the medium-term future. In Figure 2.8 the turning point is near world mean income. In fact, because of the highly skewed distribution for per capita incomes, with many more countries – including some with very large populations – below rather than above the mean, this may not be what such a relationship implies.

This is explored by Stern et al. (1996), who also critically review the literature on the existence of meaningful EKC relationships. Stern et al. use the projections of world economic growth and world population growth published in the *World Development Report 1992* (IBRD, 1992), together with Panayotou's EKC estimates for deforestation and SO_2 emissions, to produce global projections of these variables for the period 1990–2025. These are important cases from a sustainable development perspective. SO_2 emissions are a factor in the acid rain problem: deforestation, especially in the tropics, is considered a major source of biodiversity loss. They projected population and economic growth for every country in the world with a population greater than 1 million in 1990. The aggregated projections give world population growing from 5265 million in 1990 to 8322 million in 2025, and mean world per capita income rising from $3957 in 1990 to $7127 in 2025. They then forecast deforestation and SO_2 emissions for each country individually using the coefficients estimated by Panayotou. These forecasts were aggregated to give global projections for forest cover and SO_2 emissions. Notwithstanding the EKC relationship shown in Figure 2.8, total global SO_2 emissions rise from 383 million tonnes in 1990 to 1181 million tonnes in 2025; emissions of SO_2 per capita rise from 73 kg to 142 kg from 1990 to 2025. Forest cover declines from 40.4 million km^2 in 1990 to a minimum of 37.2 million km^2 in 2016, and then increases to 37.6 million km^2 in 2025. Biodiversity loss on account of deforestation is an irreversible environmental impact, except on evolutionary time-scales, so that even in this case the implications of the fitted EKC are not reassuring.

Generally, the work of Stern et al. shows that the answer to the second question is that even if the data appear to confirm that the EKC fits the experience of individual countries, it does not follow that further growth is good for the global environment. Arrow et al. (1995) reach a similar position on the relevance of the EKC hypothesis for policy in relation to sustainability. They note that:

> The general proposition that economic growth is good for the environment has been justified by the claim that there exists an empirical relation between per capita income and some measures of environmental quality.

They then note that the EKC relationship has been 'shown to apply to a selected set of pollutants only', but that some economists 'have conjectured that the curve applies to environmental quality generally'. Arrow et al. conclude that 'Economic growth is not a panacea for environmental quality; indeed it is not even the main issue', and that 'policies that promote gross national product growth are not substitutes for environmental policy'.

In Box 2.1 we report some simulation results that indicate that even if an EKC relationship between income and environmental impact is generally applicable, given continuing exponential income growth, it is only in very special circumstances that there will not, in the long run, be a positive relationship between income and environmental impact.

Box 2.1 The Environmental Kuznets Curve and environmental impacts in the very long run

The Environmental Kuznets Curve (EKC) implies that the magnitude of environmental impacts of economic activity will fall as income rises above some threshold level, when both these variables are measured in per capita terms. Here we assume for the sake of argument that the EKC hypothesis is correct. Common (1995) examines the implications of the EKC hypothesis for the long-run relationship between environmental impact and income. To do this he examines two special cases of the EKC, shown in Figure 2.9. In case **a** environmental impacts per unit of income eventually fall to zero as the level of income rises. Case **b** is characterised by environmental impacts per unit income falling to some minimum level, k, at a high level of income, and thereafter remaining constant at that level as income continues to increase. Both of these cases embody the basic principle of the EKC, the only difference being whether environmental impacts per unit income fall to zero or just to some (low) minimum level.

Suppose that the world consists of two countries that we call 'developed' and 'developing', which are growing at the same constant rate of growth, g. However, the growth process began at an earlier date in the developed country and so at any point in time its per capita income level is higher than in the developing country. Common investigates what would happen in the long run if case **a**, the highly optimistic version of the EKC, is true. He demonstrates that the time path of environmental impacts one would observe would be similar to that shown in the upper part of Figure 2.10. Why should there be a dip in the central part of the curve? For some period of time, income levels in the two countries will be such that the developed country is on the downward sloping portion of its EKC while the developing country is still on the upward sloping part of its EKC. However,

as time passes and growth continues, both countries will be at income levels where the EKC curves have a negative slope; together with the assumption in case **a** that impacts per unit income fall to zero, this implies that the total level of impacts will itself converge to zero as time becomes increasingly large.

But now consider case **b**. No matter how large income becomes the ratio of environmental impacts to income can never fall below some fixed level, k. Of course k may be large or small, but this is not critical to the argument at this point; what matters is that k is some constant positive number. As time passes, and both countries reach high income levels, the average of the impacts to income ratio for the two countries must converge on that constant value, k. However, since we are assuming that each country is growing at a fixed rate, g, the total level of impacts (as opposed to impacts per unit income) must itself eventually be increasing over time at the rate g. This is shown in the lower part of Figure 2.10.

What is interesting about this story is that we obtain two paths over time of environmental impacts which are entirely different from one another in qualitative terms for very small differences in initial assumptions. In case **a**, k is in effect zero, whereas in case **b**, k is greater than zero. Even if environmental impacts

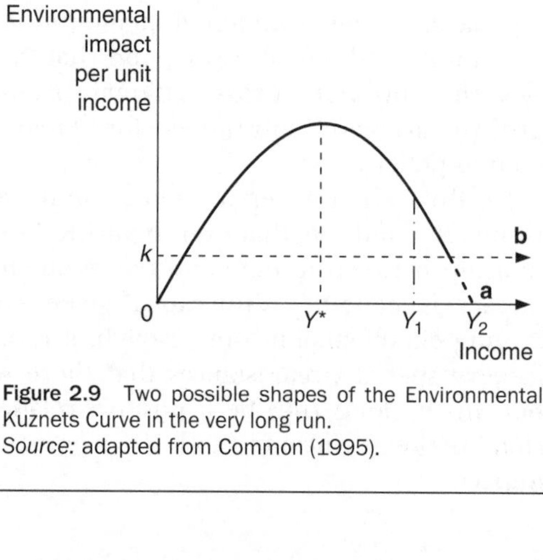

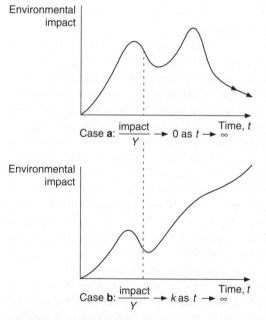

Figure 2.9 Two possible shapes of the Environmental Kuznets Curve in the very long run.
Source: adapted from Common (1995).

Figure 2.10 Two scenarios for the time profile of environmental impacts.
Source: adapted from Common (1995).

Box 2.1 continued

per unit of income eventually fell to a tiny level, the total level of impacts would eventually grow in line with income.

Which of these two possibilities – case **a** or case **b** – is the more plausible? Common argues that the laws of thermodynamics imply that k must be greater than zero. If so, the very long run relationship between total environmental impacts and the level of world income would be of the linear form shown (for per capita income) in Figure 2.6 The inference from the inverted U shape of the EKC that growth will reduce environmental damage in the very long run would be incorrect.

Population growth and the environment

Past, current and estimated future levels of human population are shown in Figure 2.11. It is estimated[2] that 5.7 billion people were living in 1995. The staggering increase in human population in the second half of the twentieth century can be gauged by the fact that in 1950 world population was less than half that size, at 2.5 billion. United Nations Population Division forecasts suggest that the world population will grow to about 8.3 billion by the year 2025, reaching 10.4 billion by 2100, before stabilising at just under 11 billion by around 2200. These forecasts are dependent on an assumption of 'average' levels of the fertility rate being maintained (slightly above two children per woman, the population replacement ratio).

However, inspection of Figure 2.12 shows that population outcomes are very sensitive to trends in the fertility rate. Under baseline assumptions about fertility rates, world population stabilises by 2200 at a level roughly twice its 1990 size. However, under high rates of fertility (an additional half child per woman compared with the 'average' case), no such plateau is reached, with population rising at an increasing rate to 30 billion and beyond.

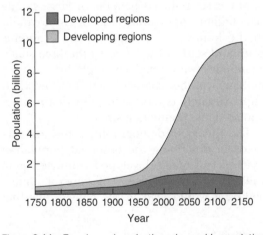

Figure 2.11 Trends and projections in world population growth, 1750–2150.
Source: Figure 8.1, *World Resources 96–97*. Based on United Nations Population Fund (UNFPA), 1995.

[2] Demographic statistics in this section are taken from various editions of the publication *World Resources* by the World Resources Institute. Editions used were those for 1994–95, 1996–97 and 1997–98. These statistics were derived, in turn, from the United Nations Population Division and the United Nations Population Fund (UNFPA). In addition, at the time of writing, unpublished population data from the United Nations Population Division 1998 report became available, and has been incorporated in the figures we have used.

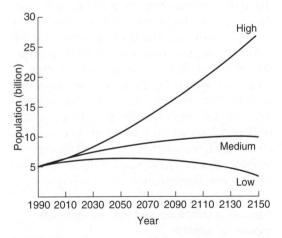

Figure 2.12 Long-range population projections using alternative fertility rate assumptions.
Source: derived from *World Resources 96–97*, based in turn on United Nations.

Whether this is plausible is a moot point; at levels such as this even simple Malthusian crisis processes would probably begin to operate. But under low fertility rate assumptions (one half child less per woman relative to the average case) an end to population growth is in sight: population would peak at just under 8 billion by 2050, and would fall rapidly thereafter. Policies aimed at reducing fertility rates can be designed and offer the prospect of eliminating overpopulation as a contribution to the sustainability problem.

In fact, the percentage rate of increase of global population is already well below its historical peak, having decreased in recent years in all regions of the world. Growth rates are currently less than 0.5% per year in developed countries and just over 2% in developing countries. Several countries now have falling populations (for example Germany, Austria, Denmark and Sweden), and many others are expected to move into this category in the near future. In many countries (including all industrialised countries and China), fertility rates are below the replacement rates that are required for a population size to be stationary in the long run. For these countries, population is destined to fall at some point in the future even though the momentum of population dynamics implies that population will continue to rise for some time to come. For example, although the Chinese birth rate fell below the replacement rate in 1992, population is committed to rise from 1.2 billion in 1995 to 2 billion by 2050, and subsequently increase further. However, if the fertility rate were to fall slightly, the population could peak at 1.5 billion in 2050, and then decline. Once again, we see that very small changes in fertility rates can have major effects upon the level to which population eventually grows.

Population dynamics and the economics of population control

A statistical relationship that is often remarked upon is the negative correlation between income level and population growth rate. Several attempts have been made to explain this observed relationship, the most well known of which is the theory of demographic transition (Todaro, 1989). The theory postulates four stages through which population dynamics progress, shown in Figure 2.13. In the first stage, populations are characterised by high birth-rates and high death-rates. In some cases, the death-rates reflect intentions to keep populations stable, and so include infanticide, infant neglect and senilicide (see Harris and Ross, 1987). In the second stage, rising real incomes result in improved nutrition and developments in public health, which lead to declines in death-rates and rapidly rising population levels. In the third stage of the demographic transition, economic forces lead to reduced fertility rates. These forces include increasing costs of childbearing and family care, reduced benefits of large family size, higher opportunity costs of employment in the home, and changes in the economic roles and status of women. In the final stage, economies with relatively high income per person will be characterised by low, and approximately equal, birth- and death-rates, and so stable population sizes.

The theory of demographic transition succeeds in describing the observed population dynamics of many developed countries quite well. If the theory were of general applicability, it would lead to the conclusions that

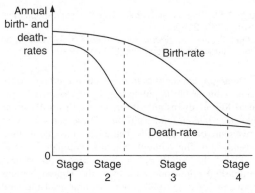

Figure 2.13 The theory of demographic transition.

rising population is a transient episode, and that programmes which increase rates of income growth in developing countries would lower the time profile of world population levels. But it remains unclear whether the theory does have general applicability. For many developing countries the second stage was reached not as a consequence of rising real income but rather as a consequence of knowledge and technological transfer. In particular, public health measures and disease control techniques were introduced at a very rapid rate. The adoption of such measures was compressed into a far shorter period of time than had occurred in the early industrialising countries, and mortality rates fell at unprecedented speed. During the nineteenth century, the higher-income countries typically experienced falls in birth-rates relatively soon after falls in mortality rates. However, while birth-rates are falling in most developing countries, these falls are lagging behind drops in the mortality levels, and challenging the relevance of the theory of demographic transition. Dasgupta (1992) argues that the accompanying population explosions created the potential for a vicious cycle of poverty, in which the resources required for economic development (and so for a movement to the third stage of the demographic transition) were crowded out by rapid population expansion.

Two important determinants of the rate at which a population changes over time are the number of children born to each female of reproductive age, and the life expectancy of each child. There have been dramatic increases in life expectancy throughout the world, attributed to improved medical and public health services. The number of children born into each household is primarily the outcome of a choice made by (potential) parents. Family size is choice variable; contraceptive and other family planning practices are the means by which these choices are effected. Microeconomic theory suggests that the marginal costs and the marginal benefits of children within the family (see Figure 2.14)

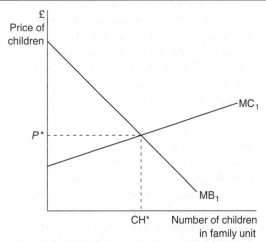

MC = The marginal cost to the family of a child
MC = The marginal benefit to the family of a child
    = (the demand curve for children)

Figure 2.14   The microeconomics of fertility.

determine family size. The marginal costs of children depend on the costs of childbearing, child rearing and education, including the opportunity costs of parental time in these activities. Marginal benefits of children to the family include the psychic benefits of children, the contribution of children to family income, and the extent to which old age security is enhanced by larger family size.

An important advantage of this line of analysis is that it offers the prospect of deriving guidelines for population policy: attempts to alter desired family size should operate by shifting the marginal cost of bearing and raising children, or the marginal benefits derived from children within the family. What measures might government take, or what intermediate goals might they pursue, to reduce the desired family size? Several suggest themselves:

- Increased levels of education, particularly education of women. This could affect fertility through three related routes. Firstly, education enhances the effectiveness of family planning programmes; families become more proficient at having the number of children that they choose. Secondly, greater participation in education increases the status of women; it is now widely agreed that where females have low status roles in the culture of a society, fertility rates are likely to be high. Thirdly, greater education decreases labour market gender discrimination, allows females to earn market incomes, and raises real wage rates in the labour market. These changes increase the opportunity cost of children, and may well also reduce the marginal benefits of children (for example, by salaried workers being able to provide for old age through pension schemes).

- Financial incentives can be used to influence desired family size. Financial penalties may be imposed upon families with large numbers of children. Alternatively, where the existing fiscal and welfare state provisions create financial compensation for families with children, those compensations could be reduced or restructured. There are many avenues through which such incentives can operate, including systems of tax allowances and child benefits, subsidised food, and the costs of access to health and educational facilities. There may well be serious conflicts with equity if financial incentives to small family size are pushed very far, but the experiences of China suggest that if government is determined, and can obtain sufficient political support, financial arrangements that increase the marginal cost of children or reduce the marginal benefits of children can be very powerful instruments.

- Provision of care for and financial support of the elderly, financed by taxation on younger groups in the population. If the perceived marginal benefits of children to parents in old age were to be reduced (by being substituted for in this case), the desired number of children per family would fall. As the tax instrument merely redistributes income, its effect on welfare can be neutral. But by reducing the private marginal benefits of children it can succeed (at little or no social cost) in reducing desired family size.

- The most powerful means of reducing desired family size is almost certainly economic development, including the replacement of subsistence agriculture by modern farming practices, giving farm workers the chance of earning labour market incomes. There may, of course, be significant cultural losses involved in such transition processes, and these should be weighed against any benefits that agricultural and economic development brings. Nevertheless, to the extent that subsistence and non-market farming dominates an economy's agricultural sector, there will be powerful incentives for large family size. Additional children are valuable assets to the family, ensuring that the perceived marginal benefits of children are relatively high. Furthermore, market incomes are not being lost, the marginal cost of child-rearing labour time is low. Important steps in the direction of creating markets for labour (and reducing desired family size) can be taken by defining property rights more clearly, giving communities greater control over the use of local resources, and creating financial incentives to manage and market resources in a sustainable way.

The impacts of population growth on the environment

Human population growth, in conjunction with pressures for higher standards of living, increases the demands for agricultural land, energy and water resources, and intensifies the problems of managing and disposing of waste products. These are associated with a number of serious environmental changes including forest depletion, declining soil fertility, loss of topsoil, desertification, loss of biodiversity, unsustainable rates of water usage, and groundwater and air pollution. While it would be wrong to attribute each of these processes exclusively or primarily to population growth, it is evident that the increasing pressure placed on environmental resources by a growing population will exacerbate these problems.

The linkages between population growth and the environment are complicated. Some of these linkages operate directly, others indirectly. The following appear to be particularly important:

- higher levels of population place greater demands on non-renewable material resources and greater strain on renewable resource stocks, including world food resources;
- higher levels of population tend to be associated with greater volumes of material and energy throughput, increasing the likelihood that carrying capacities of environmental sinks will be exceeded;
- higher levels of population will tend to increase ecological pressures generally and promote changes in agricultural practices in particular that will reduce biological diversity;
- high rates of population growth may contribute to low and possibly falling rates of real per capita income, which can exacerbate environmental pressures.

No consensus has emerged about the economic and environmental consequences of continued population increases despite a growing awareness of the linkages we have described. The major difficulty in arriving at reliable conclusions seems to be associated with uncertainties about the scope for behavioural adjustments in the face of changing prices or other indicators of changing relative scarcities.

Population, agriculture and the availability of food

Common sense suggests that continuing population increases will place increasing pressure on world agriculture and threaten the availability of adequate supplies of food. But the evidence does not give any strong support for this view. Johnson (1984), in summarising the principal features of the

world food system, noted that a family's access to food had become primarily dependent upon the family's income, and not on the availability of food *per se*. A food system had become established that was capable of making food available to almost every person in the world, a situation that had been impossible just a few years prior to 1980. This change had taken place in spite of the fact that global population had doubled in the previous 30 years. Johnson argued that hunger and malnutrition should be tackled by policy directed at reducing inequalities of income within and between countries, rather than by supply-side targeted measures.

Johnson's analysis suggested that real food price data show very little evidence of rising food scarcity. The real price of grains (the major source of calories for poor people) and the prices of many other food products, including rice, sugar cane, corn, poultry and eggs, had declined in the decades leading up to 1980. Livestock prices (beef cattle, hogs), however, exhibited slowly rising trends. Where food shortages had occurred, these were primarily attributable to government intervention in the markets for food or to other political factors (including wars and civil strife). In particular, trade restrictions and government interventions in some regional markets reduced food prices in 'uncontrolled' areas, reducing incentives to supply commercial food crops and to modernise and improve agricultural inputs.

Johnson's analysis was not, however, uniformly optimistic. He also noted that:

(1) Increasing affluence tends to change demand in the direction of meat and away from direct consumption of vegetables and grain. This imparts considerable physical inefficiency in food production, and causes prices to rise, reducing food access to lower-income families.
(2) There was limited availability of land to bring under cultivation. The scope for expanding the extensive margin of

agriculture had become quite restricted. However, the most cost-effective method of obtaining output increases has been through expanding the intensive margin of agriculture. Furthermore, large productivity increases remained to be exploited through land irrigation.

(3) Increasing the intensive margin was likely to become more difficult as a consequence of higher energy prices, leading to higher relative prices for inorganic fertilisers.

To what extent do Johnson's conclusions remain valid today? Studies by the Food and Agriculture Organization of the United Nations (FAO, 1994) and the World Bank (World Bank, 1993) concluded that production increases can accommodate effective demand for food over the period to 2020. In *World Resources 1996–97*, the World Resources Institute concludes that agricultural production in much of the developing world has been very successful in recent decades. Production is growing and will continue to do so in the next couple of decades. This has been true in all regions of the world with the exception of the dramatic (but probably only temporary) collapse in the countries of the former Soviet Union. Those developing countries that are most dependent on agriculture (with over one-third of the economically active engaged in agriculture, but with low levels of food per capita and low purchasing power on world markets) have seen agricultural output not merely growing but doing so increasingly quickly.

However, Africa (particularly sub-Saharan Africa) has not fully participated in these successes. African food production has more than doubled since 1961, but this output growth has been insufficient to keep pace with population. As a result per capita food production has fallen by 20% since 1970, and low real income prevents Africa from gaining access to food on world markets. To use Sen's phrase (Sen, 1981), many Africans have insufficient food entitlements to stave off the chronic malnutrition that prevails. Africa will regularly face serious food shortages during the next few decades unless income grows or food output rises at historically unprecedented rates.

There are other causes for concern about the current state of agriculture. First, the prices of agricultural commodities have been falling in real terms for the past 15 years, thereby squeezing monetary incomes and adding to problems of national debt even where output has been rising. This is a worrying trend on at least two counts:

(1) Large proportions of the population in many developing countries are seriously undernourished, because low incomes constrain their effective demand for food.

(2) Continuing indebtedness and low per capita incomes appear to be contributors to environmental degradation.

The second cause for concern is a slowing of the growth of agricultural production in many regions of the world. This seems to be partly associated with slowed yield growth rates. While crop yields have typically continued to increase, they have generally increased at much slower rates in the 1980s and 1990s than previously, particularly in developing countries. Some evidence on this is presented in Figure 2.15. Other contributory factors are increasing scarcities of water, limits to the biological productivities of fisheries and rangelands, soil erosion, fragility of ecosystems in tropical and subtropical countries, and the fact that the 'green revolution' has involved a series of technological leaps which cannot be repeated indefinitely. (See, for example, Brown and Kane, 1994; Carruthers, 1994; Pimental *et al.*, 1995). The prospect for increasing agricultural output is far higher in the temperate regions of Europe, the United States and Australasia than in much of the developing world, but that is of little help to food security for families in developing countries unless they are able to expand their export earning potential to purchase food requirements externally.

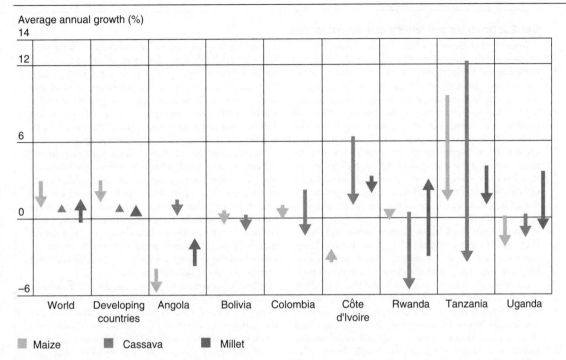

Average annual growth (%)

Figure 2.15 Change in crop yields in selected countries, 1970–1990. Arrows show change between 1970–80 and 1980–90 (note that millet is not a significant crop in Bolivia or Colombia).
Source: adapted from World Bank data.

A third cause for concern is the consequences of the growing use of pesticides, herbicides and inorganic fertilisers in agriculture. Pesticides, one foundation of the remarkable production hikes over the past few decades, continue to underpin many national development strategies in developing countries. Yet research suggests that the benefits of pesticides have been exaggerated and that they pose substantial dangers both to the environment and to human health. The situation in regard to pesticides is examined in the report *World Resources 1994–95* (WR, 1994). Similar worries apply to the consequences of inorganic fertilisers, the use of which is growing at 3.4% per year (FAO, 1994) in spite of evidence suggesting that fertiliser applications are of declining effectiveness (Brown and Kane, 1994). Finally, there are reasons to believe that agricultural intensification, in conjunction with long-term climate change, is contributing to the loss of soil fertility and increasing desertification, although these remain poorly understood phenomena. We examine soil fertility changes and desertification in Box 2.2.

However, future prospects also offer some grounds for optimism. One of these is the likely future stabilisation and then decline of global population levels that we noted above. Another derives from the application of new technology in agriculture, which we discuss in a little more detail in Box 2.3. Concerning biotechnology in particular, the World Resources Institute has written:

Agricultural biotechnology is an important source of hope for the future. Biotechnology offers numerous possibilities for agriculture. But these potential advances are decades away from realisation, carry some risk, and will not displace current agricultural practice altogether. Moreover, while the developing world is most in need of biotechnology's innovations, current research is concentrated on high-value crops grown in the industrialised world.

WR (1996)

Box 2.2 Declining soil fertility and desertification

A June 1994 conference of the United Nations Environment Programme (UNEP) examined the issues of declining soil fertility and desertification. Delegates to the conference were told that 900 million people were at risk from dependence on agriculture in dryland in the Americas, Africa and Asia, in which soil fertility was being lost at an alarming rate. The United Nations believes that loss of soil fertility is a greater threat to poor people than global warming or upper atmosphere ozone depletion. UNEP estimates that just under one-tenth of the earth's land surface is significantly degraded, and that an area equal to the size of Italy has been more or less permanently lost to agricultural use.

More recent work by the International Soil Reference and Information Centre suggests that the losses are somewhat lower, estimating that 9 million hectares are extremely degraded (more or less complete breakdown of all biotic functions) and that 1.2 billion hectares – about 10% of the earth's vegetative cover – are moderately degraded. There are several causes of soil fertility losses. In some cases, it is a consequence of the lack of organic inputs, combined with intensification of agriculture on already fragile lands. This process steadily depletes nutrients. Very often, these deficiencies cannot be compensated by use of inorganic fertilisers. A second cause is faulty agricultural practice – such as overgrazing, poor draining of irrigated land and too short fallow periods – which is thought to account for about 28% of degraded soils (including two-thirds of degraded land in North America).

Extreme soil fertility losses can be a precursor to desertification. It is now widely accepted that the predictions, made in the 1970s and 1980s, about the rapidly growing spread of desert areas, were severely overestimated. Satellite surveys show that deserts expand and contract in natural cycles, and that most of the changes noted in those earlier decades can be attributed to such cyclical behaviour.

However, large areas of land are subject to potential desertification as a result of economic activity. Desertification can be induced by chronic losses of soil fertility in association with some forms of agricultural practices introduced in attempts to mitigate those losses. In Africa, for example, peasant farmers in arid areas lack resources to maintain output as fertility falls, and tend to shift production to more marginal land. Soil fertility soon diminishes in these areas, and so agriculture follows a path of continuously shifting cultivation. However, environmental conditions are not conducive to restoring fertility in the vacated land areas. Wood clearing and burning for fuel, and overgrazing of savannah land by cattle, thins roots and leaves soils vulnerable to wind and water erosion. Irrigation has also had unintended effects; while often being seen as a way of raising yields, it has often been counterproductive, damaging soil through raising salt to upper soil surfaces.

Institutional factors play an important part in soil fertility losses. Land tenure is often very insecure, and environmental resources in arid regions are often effectively open access resources, destroying any incentives that farmers may have to conserve woodlands and soils. Finally, mention must be made of the effect that crippling poverty has on land degradation. Poverty denies peasant farmers access to credit and the resources necessary for sustainable and conservationist agricultural practices.

What policy initiatives offer hope for controlling or reducing the extent of these environmental and economic problems? Clearly, any changes that can offer the prospect of increasing the levels of real income of farmers in arid regions would be of substantial benefit, making possible the investments that are required for conservationist agricultural policy. The key step in avoiding severe cases of soil fertility losses is implementation of good agricultural practice. However, that may require substantial institutional reform. This would take the form of building local capacity for developing good practices and reforming the patterns of incentives affecting those who make a living from the land. It would be desirable to move towards more clearly defined property rights to land and other environmental resources, and to ensure more security in the tenure of land. Property rights need not necessarily be vested in individuals; common-property ownership rights can be effective in regulating the demands made on land, provided institutional mechanisms are established that prevent common-property resources degenerating into conditions of open-access. This implies establishing local incentives to manage resources, enabling communities to regulate access, and reducing restrictions on how resources can be used. For example, simple restrictions prohibiting tree felling are almost certainly counterproductive; they will be largely unenforceable, and will act as severe disincentives for future replanting by local communities.

Source: The June 1994 UNEP Conference on Soil Erosion and Desertification.

Box 2.3 Scientific advance, new crop varieties and biotechnology in agriculture

Agricultural research institutes have had astonishing success in cultivating new crop varieties with improved yield or lower susceptibility to disease characteristics. This has been particularly evident in the case of rice, where new hybrids have raised yields, lowered the cost of seed and increased the geographical area where rice can be profitably grown (CGIAR, 1994; Alexandratos, 1995).

However, the intensification in agricultural practice associated with the employment of new crop varieties has contributed to adverse environmental impacts (discussed elsewhere in this chapter). The tools of biotechnology offer the prospect of dramatic gains in future food production potential without the imposition of significant environmental stresses. The principal benefits which it is hoped will be derived from biotechnology applications are:

- insect and disease resistance
- greater stress tolerance
- improved fruit ripening characteristics
- improved nutritional content of plants
- development of crops with special 'target' qualities, such as plant-produced biodegradable plastic (as a substitute for plastics from petroleum).

The key technologies include:

- Genetic engineering: useful DNA material is identified in one organism and transferred into another unrelated organism. This technique can increase yields, promote pest resistance (and so avoid reliance on pesticides), alter harvesting characteristics of crops, and improve resistance of crops to environmental stresses such as drought or climate change. These techniques are at an advanced state in tomatoes, soybeans, cotton and rapeseed. Progress is also being made with cereal crops.
- Cell and tissue culture, by which plant cells or tissue are used to promote plant development in vitro. Commercial applications include clonal propagation, the mass production of genetic duplicates. These duplicates are guaranteed to be disease free, and can be planted in place of conventionally produced seeds, seedlings, cuttings or tubers. Crops that are currently cloned include potatoes, bananas, and oil palms.
- Production of monoclonal antibodies: allowing mass production of specific antibodies that can be used as diagnostic test materials for the presence of diseases, and in animal vaccines.

Limitations and costs of biotechnology

As in many areas of scientific advance, expectations tend to focus on the positive potentials of the technology and (at least initially) pay insufficient attention to limitations and potential costs. The limitations are twofold. First, while the technology itself has advanced rapidly, the pace of innovation – the commercial application of biotechnology – has been relatively slow. Few major applications are widely diffused so far, and large-scale effects will probably not be felt for two or three decades.

The second limitation is also an economic one. Biotechnology is research intensive, and its applications tend to be directed at where profit potential is greatest. Researchers and innovators tend to be very conscious of intellectual property rights, being unwilling to allow their findings to freely enter the public domain. Thus, applications have so far largely been applied to high value added crops in the industrialised world, and have not been devoted to crop development in poor countries where, despite the most pressing needs, the ability to pay is low.

Much of the genetic source material that is employed in biotechnology applications is obtained from biota taken from biologically diverse developing countries, where no mechanisms have yet been found to impose property rights on (and so gain income from) these materials. Once the technology has produced commercially profitable outputs, property rights over these products are fiercely defended. Yet the inability of the countries whose biodiversity is the source of the valuable genes to obtain financial rewards from it does not give them proper incentives to conserve that biodiversity. Here is an example of the failure (or in this case, absence) of market mechanisms to allocate and conserve resources in an efficient way.

The costs are harder to identify, but stem from the largely unknowable consequences of human directed genetic manipulation and consequent disturbances to ecosystem balances. Genetic engineering may alter the relative competitive advantages of species in very dramatic ways, reducing biodiversity, and upsetting ecosystem dynamics. These fears, in conjunction with ethical concerns about genetic engineering, have promoted a rather conservative regulatory regime in some countries.

Sources: WR (1994), chapter 6; WR (1996), box 10.1.

Biodiversity

Biological diversity, or biodiversity, is important in the provision of environmental services to economic activity in a number of ways. In regard to life support services, diverse ecological systems facilitate environmental functions, such as carbon cycling, soil fertility maintenance, climate and surface temperature regulation, and watershed flows. The diversity of flora and fauna in ecosystems contributes to the amenity services that we derive from the environment. In relation to inputs to production, those flora and fauna are the source of many useful products, particularly pharmaceuticals, foods and fibres; the genes that they contain also constitute the materials on which future developments in biotechnology will depend. In terms of agriculture, biodiversity is the basis for crop and livestock variability and the development of new varieties. But of the greatest long-term importance is the evolutionary potential afforded by biodiversity. Diverse gene pools represent a form of insurance against ecological collapse; the greater is the extent of diversity, the greater is the capacity for adaptation to stresses and benign evolutionary change in response to them.

Current development patterns are implicated in what are thought to be unprecedented rates of loss of biodiversity. Concern with this phenomenon culminated in the signing of the Convention on Biological Diversity, one of the international treaties adopted at the UNCED conference in Rio de Janeiro in 1992. The Convention calls for

- the conservation of biological diversity
- the sustained use of its components
- an equitable sharing of its benefits.

What is biodiversity and how is it measured?

A working definition of biodiversity can be taken from that Convention:

Biodiversity refers to the number, variety and variability of all living organisms in terrestrial, marine and other aquatic ecosystems and the ecological complexes of which they are parts.

It is evident from this definition that biodiversity is intended to capture two dimensions: firstly, the number of biological organisms and, secondly, their variability. There are three levels at which biodiversity can be considered:

(1) Population: genetic diversity within the populations that comprise a species is important as it affects evolutionary and adaptive potential of the species, and so we might measure biodiversity in terms of the number of populations.[3]
(2) Species: we might wish to measure biodiversity in terms of the numbers of distinct species in particular locations, the extent to which a species is endemic (unique to a specific location), or in terms of the diversity (rather than the number) of species.
(3) Ecosystems: in many ways, the diversity of ecosystems is the most important measure of biodiversity; unfortunately, there is no universally agreed criterion for either defining or measuring biodiversity at this level.

Biodiversity is best thought of as a multi-dimensional concept, which cannot be reduced to a single measure. As a matter of practice, however, biodiversity is usually considered in terms of species, and the number of distinct species is often used as a single indicator of biodiversity. There are problems with this measure. For example, within one population of any species there will be considerable genetic variation. Suppose a harvesting programme targets individuals within that population with a particular characteristic (such as

[3] For the purposes of this classification of levels, a species can be taken to be a set of individual organisms which have the capacity to reproduce, while a population is a set that actually do reproduce. A population is, that is, a reproductively isolated subset of a species.

large size). The target individuals are likely to possess genetic material favouring that characteristic, and so the harvesting programme reduces the diversity of the gene pool in the remaining population. Managed harvesting programmes, therefore, may result in loss of biodiversity even though the number of extant species shows no change.

What this tells us is that biodiversity is best measured by a variety of indicators rather than by any single statistic. Unfortunately, many of the qualities we wish to capture in such a variety of indicators are conceptually difficult to measure or very costly to collect on a systematic basis. As a result, a set of surrogate measures are often used in practice, such as the magnitude of undisturbed ecosystems.

The current extent of biodiversity

Given these observations, it is not surprising that we have very poor information about the current extent of biodiversity. Even if we restrict attention to one relatively straightforward indicator – the number of species that currently exist – we confront considerable uncertainty. This number is not known even to within an order of magnitude. Estimates that can be found in the literature range from 3–10 million (May, 1988) to 50–100 million (Wilson, 1992). A current best guess of the actual number of species is 12.5 mil-

lion (Groombridge, 1992).

Even the currently-known number of species is subject to some dispute, with a representative figure being 1.7 million species described to date (Groombridge, 1992). About 13 000 new species are being described each year. Table 2.2 details current knowledge about species numbers for a variety of important taxonomic classes.

Biodiversity loss

How fast is the stock of genetic resources being lost? Once again, we only have a partial picture of this, and only for one measure, the rate of species loss. Known extinctions to date are small in number (see Table 2.3), but the actual rate of extinction is much higher. For birds and mammals combined, the rate of extinction has been about 1% in the twentieth century. However, ecologists expect there to be a dramatic increase in this rate in the future, with a loss of half of all extant birds and mammals within 200–500 years (Wilson, 1992).

But species loss is slowest among the higher animals and birds. For all biological species, various predictions suggest an overall loss of between 1% and 10% of all species over the next 25 years, and between 2% and 25% of tropical forest species (UNEP, 1995). In the longer term it is thought that

Table 2.2 Numbers of described species and estimates of actual numbers for selected taxa (thousands).

Taxa	Species described	Estimated number of species: high	Estimated number of species: low	Working figure
Viruses	4	1000	50	400
Bacteria	4	3000	50	1000
Fungi	72	2700	200	1500
Protozoa and algae	80	1200	210	600
Plants	270	500	300	320
Nematodes[a]	25	1000	100	400
Insects	950	100 000	2000	8000
Molluscs	70	200	100	200
Chordates	[b]45	55	50	50

Source: adapted from Jeffries (1997), page 88, based in turn on Groombridge (1992) and Heywood (1995).
[a] Worms.
[b] Of the 45 000 chordates (vertebrate animals), there are about 4500 mammals, 9700 birds, 4000 amphibians and 6550 reptiles.

Table 2.3   Known extinctions up to 1995.

Group	Extinctions
Mammals	58
Birds	115
Molluscs	191
Other animals	120
Higher plants	517

Source: adapted from Groombridge (1992).

50% of all species will be lost over the next 70–700 years (Smith *et al.*, 1995; May, 1988). About 10–30% of species in well-studied groups are currently listed as being threatened with extinction. The rates of extinction we have described in this section are of an order one million times greater than the geological average. We shall discuss the causes of biodiversity loss in Chapter 9, and consider some of the policy options that might reduce this loss in Chapters 12 and 13.

Conclusions

Our objectives in this chapter have been to describe some aspects of the current state of human development, and of the fundamental material and biological conditions within which future development must take place. We have also examined some of the consequences that human activity currently has, and may have in the future, on the natural environment. While our discussion has not been comprehensive, it has demonstrated that the natural environment and the human economy are not independent systems. On the contrary, they are intimately related through a complex set of interactions. Economic activity affects the environment, which in turn affects the economy. Whatever 'sustainability' might mean, it is clear from our analysis here that a necessary condition for an economy to be sustainable is that its natural environment should be maintained so as to continue to deliver a diverse set of services.

In the next chapter, we shall present and discuss several alternative interpretations of the concept of sustainability, and the implications which follow from them. In so doing, we introduce some models of sustainability. These models are useful because they help us to think about what conditions are necessary for sustainable development, what behavioural constraints these conditions imply, and what other consequences might follow from adopting sustainability constraints on economic activity.

Discussion questions

1 Examine the effects of alternative patterns of land tenure and property rights on the likelihood of soil fertility losses and desertification.
2 How effective are measures designed to increase the use of contraception in reducing the rate of population growth?
3 How may the role and status of women affect the rate of population growth? What measures might be taken to change that role and status in directions that reduce the rate of population growth?
4 Does economic growth inevitably lead to environmental degradation?

Problems

1 Use the microeconomic theory of fertility to explain how increasing affluence may be associated with a reduction in the fertility rate.
2 Suppose that families paid substantial dowry at marriage. What effect would this have on desired family size?
3 What effect would one predict for desired family size if family members were to cease undertaking unpaid household labour and undertake instead marketed labour?

Further reading

Good sources of data on many of the issues considered in this chapter are found in IBRD (1992) and various editions of the UNEP Environmental Data Reports and World Resources. See, in particular, UNEP (1991), part 4, 'Population/settlements', WR (1992), chapter 6 'Population and human development' (which includes an analysis of the major causes of death in industrialised and developing countries), and WR (1996), chapter 8 'Population and human development'. Some of these data sources can now be obtained online via the internet. For example, the full text of the current issue of *World Resources* is available at no charge on the World Resources Institute Web site: (current address: http://www.wri.org). The United Nations Development Programme's *Human Development Report* is an authoritative attempt to give a complete account of the present and future human condition in terms of income and wealth, health, education, literacy and socio-economic opportunities.

McCormick (1989) provides a useful account of the modern history of environmental concerns and their impact on politics, and traces the evolution of the development versus the environment debate through the various international conferences which preceded the publication of the Brundtland report. That report is essential reading on sustainable development.

There is a vast range of books on the environmental sciences. Watt (1973), Peet (1992), Ramage (1983), Krebs (1972) and Bowler (1992) are likely to be useful to those without a strong background in the natural sciences. Common (1995), Dasgupta (1982), and Perrings (1987) consider economy environment interdependence and some of its implications from an economics perspective. D'Arge and Kogiku (1972) is an early contribution to the resource and environmental economics literature that contains a growth model which obeys the law of conservation of matter. Durning (1989) discusses the relationships between poverty, development and the environment.

Useful accounts of debates over limits to growth are to be found in Simon (1981), Simon and Kahn (1984) and Repetto (1985). The EKC hypothesis was the subject of a special issue of the journal *Environment and Development Economics* in October 1997 (volume 2, part 4), and also of the journal *Ecological Economics* in May 1998 (volume 25, no. 2).

Becker (1960) is the classic original source of the literature on the economics of population. Easterlin (1978) provides a comprehensive and non-mathematical survey of the economic theory of fertility, and his 1980 volume provides an excellent collection of readings.

Useful official data on food and agriculture issues are found in United Nations FAO, *The State of Food and Agriculture* (1979, 1981, 1985, 1989 and subsequent issues). Useful discussions are to be found in Alexandratos (1995), Browder (1988), Crosson and Brubaker (1982), Hall *et al.* (1989) and Johnson (1989). An excellent collection of articles on agriculture and development is found in Streeten (1987).

Wilson's classic work on biodiversity has recently been updated as *Biodiversity II*, edited by Reaka-Kudla *et al.* (1996). UNEP (1995) is the definitive reference work in this field, dealing primarily with definition and measurement of biodiversity loss, but also containing good chapters on economics and policy. See also Groombridge (1992) and Jeffries (1997) for excellent accounts of biodiversity from an ecological perspective. Measurement and estimation of biodiversity are examined in depth in Hawksworth (1995), and regular updated accounts are provided in the biennial publication *World Resources*.

CHAPTER 3

Concepts of sustainability

But we can be fairly certain that no new technology will abolish absolute scarcity because the laws of thermodynamics apply to all possible technologies. No one can be absolutely certain that we will not some day discover perpetual motion and how to create and destroy matter and energy. But the reasonable assumption for economists is that this is an unlikely prospect and that while technology will continue to pull rabbits out of hats, it will not pull an elephant out of a hat – much less an infinite series of ever-larger elephants!

Daly (1974), page 19

Introduction

The general notion of sustainability that we explore in this chapter concerns the potential for some acceptable state of human well-being to be maintained over an indefinite period of time. We shall present some more precise definitions shortly, but this one will suffice as a starting point. The principal purpose of this chapter is to show how economists think about sustainability. In particular, we explain how economists establish models that can be used to examine conditions required for sustainability, to assess whether patterns of economic activity are likely to satisfy sustainability objectives, and to provide a solid foundation for policy recommendations. We also consider the way in which ecologists think about sustainability.

There are two things we shall not be doing in this chapter. Firstly, we shall not be advocating any concrete 'sustainability programmes' that assert what should be done to attain sustainable outcomes. Secondly, we shall not discuss whether sustainability should or should not be a policy objective. We simply take it for granted that sustainability is an important issue that warrants examination using the tools of economic analysis. Having said this, it is useful to recognise from the outset that arguments in support of economic activity being organised on a sustainable basis are, in the final analysis, ethical arguments.

Sometimes this is transparently the case. Many writers deduce that sustainability follows from a moral obligation: the present generation has a moral obligation to those generations that will come after it. Such an obligation implies that we do not act in ways that jeopardise the chances of future generations having equal opportunities to those that are currently enjoyed. An alternative ethical basis for a commitment to sustainability comes from a notion introduced in the previous chapter, and expressed in the Brundtland report, that all individuals living now and in the future have a right to at least a decent minimum standard of life. Sustainable development, then, is a way of organising behaviour so that this objective is achieved. No doubt there are many other kinds of ethical argument that could be used to make a case for sustainability.

At times, arguments for sustainability seem to have a different basis. Suppose that ecological diversity is believed to be an important objective in its own right. Then economic activity which threatens to reduce biodiversity is intrinsically undesirable. We should organise our behaviour so as to avoid serious ecological disruption, to make economic activity be consistent with ecological diversity. Once again, there are different ways in which an ecological case for sustainability could be argued, possibly in terms of ecological stability or integrity rather than diversity. Nevertheless, any such argument remains fundamentally an ethical one. Asserting that an ecological objective *should* be pursued can only be done on the basis of an ethical principle.

Much the same can be said about economic arguments for sustainability. To make a purely economic case, one would need to take as given some goal and then show that either sustainable economic behaviour is necessary, or sufficient, for attaining that goal. But as we show later, there seems to be no good reason for claiming that efficient behaviour is sustainable, nor that sustainable behaviour is more efficient than non-sustainable behaviour. Efficiency arguments alone cannot be used in support of sustainability as a goal. Suppose, however, that you were able to show that sustainable behaviour (somehow defined) is a necessary condition for maximising intertemporal social welfare. Is this not a purely economic argument? Even if it were, the argument presupposes an ethical criterion (the social welfare function) as we explain in Chapter 4. We are led to the conclusion, therefore, that arguments for sustainability are intrinsically ethical in nature.

Our next task is to establish some definitions and meanings. Without getting clear what sustainability is, there is little chance that any useful analysis can be undertaken. It is to this task that we now turn.

Definitions and meanings of sustainability

There is no universally agreed definition of the concept of sustainability. On the contrary, in the literature, one finds a vast array of definitions, meanings and interpretations. In one recent paper, John Pezzey writes

> So I see little point in expanding the collection of fifty sustainability definitions which I made in 1989, to the five thousand definitions that one could readily find today ...
>
> Pezzey (1997), page 448

A more useful exercise than listing definitions (and engaging in the probably fruitless task of trying to distil a common essence from them) is to classify the major forms. This will help in understanding the relative merits of various approaches to sustainability, and in identifying the major issues which they address.

It turns out to be the case that several of these concepts view sustainability in terms of constraints on economic behaviour. These approaches to sustainability do not explicitly concern themselves with what society is or should be trying to achieve as an ultimate objective. But whatever that objective is, sustainability is defined in terms of a constraint on that goal or the process of achieving it.

In the cases where sustainability is seen as a constraint, it is also useful to distinguish between a number of distinct types of constraint. One useful classification has been proposed by Pezzey (1997), who distinguishes between 'sustainable' development, 'sustained' development and 'survivable' development. These are defined in Box 3.1, which you should now read.

As a prelude to our examination of sustainability concepts, we will use some hypothetical time paths of consumption to illustrate some of the notions of sustainability that will be considered shortly. These time paths are represented in Figure 3.1. The vertical axis measures the level of consumption at any point in time. The passage of time from the present $(t = 0)$ onwards corresponds to movement from left to right along the horizontal axis. Six alternative time paths of consumption are shown, labelled $C(1)$ to $C(6)$. In addition, the heavy horizontal line denoted $C \cdot MIN$ represents the level of consumption which is the minimum that society deems as being morally acceptable, and the dotted line, C^{SURV}, represents the minimum consumption level consistent with survival of the given population.

We suggest that you now try to rank the six alternative time paths. Put yourself in the position of a social planner aiming to do the best for society over many generations. Then how would you rank the alternatives? Keep a note of your choice for comparison with some rankings we discuss later.

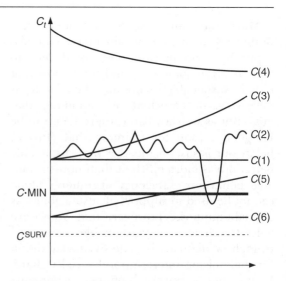

Box 3.1 Sustainable, sustained and survivable development

The following notation is used:

U_t = the utility level at time t
$\dot{U}_t$ = the rate of change of utility at time t
U_t^{MAX} = the maximum utility which can be held constant forever from time t onwards, given production opportunities available at time t
U^{SURV} = the minimum utility level consistent with survival of the given population

Development is **sustainable** if $U_t \leqslant U_t^{\text{MAX}}$ always
Development is **sustained** if $\dot{U}_t \geqslant 0$ always
Development is **survivable** if $U_t > U^{\text{SURV}}$ always

If utility is a function of consumption alone, then it is possible to replace the word 'utility' by 'consumption' in each of these criteria (and to change symbols from U to C commensurably) and thereby to define the three types of constraint in terms of consumption rather than utility. Doing this we obtain:

Development is **sustainable** if $C_t \leqslant C_t^{\text{MAX}}$ always
Development is **sustained** if $\dot{C}_t \geqslant 0$ always
Development is **survivable** if $C_t > C^{\text{SURV}}$ always

Note that the level of utility (or consumption) corresponding to survivability is taken to be constant over time (hence C^{SURV} carries no time subscript). But C_t^{MAX} does (and must) include a time subscript. The highest level of constant, sustainable consumption an economy can obtain from any point of time onwards does depend on which point in time we consider. For example, at the end of a prolonged and major world war, in which large stocks of resources have been consumed or irretrievably degraded, the maximum feasible level of sustainable consumption is likely to be smaller than it was before the war broke out.

Figure 3.1 Consumption paths over time.

concepts we will discuss are laid out in Table 3.1. Implicit in these concepts are a number of alternative ways of thinking about sustainability.

There are several points to note about this set of concepts from the outset. First, not all of them are purely economic conceptualisations. It is difficult, for example, to claim that satisfying ecosystem stability and resilience is an economic objective *per se*. Much the same could be said about the third and fourth concepts. Nevertheless, one (or more) of them might be, and has been argued to be, a necessary condition for a notion of sustainability couched in more standard economic

Concepts of sustainability

Having now seen some different forms that a sustainability constraint might take, we turn to looking at several concepts of 'sustainability' that are widely used and discussed. Unless explicitly stated otherwise, we use the term sustainability from now on in a general way, without trying to distinguish between sustainable and sustained development. (None of the concepts we discuss will correspond to survivable development.) The six

Table 3.1 Six concepts of sustainability.

(1) A sustainable state is one in which utility (or consumption) is non-declining through time.
(2) A sustainable state is one in which resources are managed so as to maintain production opportunities for the future.
(3) A sustainable state is one in which the natural capital stock is non-declining through time.
(4) A sustainable state is one in which resources are managed so as to maintain a sustainable yield of resource services.
(5) A sustainable state is one which satisfies minimum conditions of ecosystem stability and resilience through time.
(6) Sustainable development as capacity and consensus building.

terms, and it is for this reason that we include them.

Second, the concepts are not necessarily mutually exclusive. The first may imply the third, because if utility or consumption is not to decline, resources must be managed so that productive opportunities are maintained for subsequent generations. Similarly, it may be the case that the first requires the fifth because production and consumption cannot be maintained over time in the face of eco-system collapse.

Third, as we observed earlier, some of these concepts view sustainability as a constraint on economic behaviour. This is clearly the case for the first and third concepts, and is probably the right way of thinking about all except the last (which sees sustainability as being about capacity and consensus building).

Finally, none explicitly specifies the duration of time over which sustainability is to operate. Presumably one must have in mind very long horizons for the idea of sustainability to have substance. But this merely begs the question of what is meant by a long period of time. Some writers choose to think of indefinitely long (or infinite) time horizons: a state is sustainable if it is capable of being reproduced in perpetuity. Others conceive of millennia or the like; periods of time over which human populations are approximately genetically constant. However, it is not necessary to decide upon any particular span of time; we could define a sustainable state as one in which some relevant magnitude is bequeathed to the following period in at least as good a state as it is in the initial period. Provided no finite terminal time is set, this implies that one is thinking about unlimited time spans. Let us now discuss each of the conceptualisations of sustainability.

A sustainable state is one in which utility (consumption) is non-declining through time

We present this concept in two variants. In one case it is utility that is required to not decline through time. The second constrains consumption to be non-declining. These are equivalent in some (but not all) circumstances, and so it is convenient to treat them together for expositional purposes. One or other of these criteria has been the conventional way in which economists have defined and used the concept of sustainability in recent years. For example, John Pezzey has written that

> Sustainability is defined as ... non-declining utility of a representative member of society for millennia into the future.
>
> Pezzey (1992), page 323

This concept is one of the class in which sustainability is viewed as a constraint on economic behaviour, with the constraint being couched in terms of the profile of human well-being (utility or consumption) over time. Strictly speaking, it relates to *sustained* rather than sustainable development, using the terminology of Box 3.1.[1]

John Hartwick (1977, 1978) has been another advocate of this first concept of sustainability, although in contrast to Pezzey he chooses to interpret sustainability in terms of non-declining consumption. As we have noted, where utility depends only on consumption, non-declining utility and non-declining consumption are equivalent. Hartwick (1977, 1978) works with models where there is only one consumption good, and where, implicitly, it is the only argument in the utility function. Hartwick has sought to identify conditions under which non-declining consumption could be achieved. The conditions he derives centre around a particular savings rule, commonly known as Hartwick's rule. This states that if the rents (the surplus of revenues over marginal extraction costs) derived from non-renewable resource extraction are saved and then

---

[1] In his 1997 *Land Economics* paper, Pezzey states that he now regards 'sustainable' rather than 'sustained' development as the appropriate criterion of sustainability.

invested entirely in reproducible (physical) capital, then under certain conditions the levels of output and consumption will remain constant over time. We shall discuss and interpret this result in Chapter 17; see also Chapter 7.

A third influential advocate of this criterion of sustainability has been Robert Solow. In a seminal paper, Solow (1974a) begins from the premise that a sustainable state is one which satisfies some relevant criterion of intergenerational equity. Solow argues that a Rawlsian ethical framework (see Chapter 4, where we discuss this at length) is an appropriate one in which to develop principles of intertemporal distributive justice. Suppose that society were to make a decision as to how utility should be allocated over time. A Rawlsian ethic suggests that the allocation would confer equal utility on each generation of people. Solow asserts that a consistent application of this framework leads one to the conclusion that the undiscounted utility of per capita consumption should be constant over infinite time. Constant utility over time is, of course, a stricter criterion than non-declining utility, but the two are in the same spirit.

It is very difficult to deduce the conditions that would be necessary or sufficient for an economy to reach and sustain a constant level of undiscounted utility of per capita consumption. Analysis becomes much easier if the problem is converted to one in terms of consumption rather than utility. For reasons of simplicity, Solow (like Hartwick) uses a sustainability criterion in terms of consumption rather than utility.

The rule which constrains consumption to be non-declining over time is often known as the Hartwick–Solow sustainability criterion. Which of the consumption paths in Figure 3.1 satisfy it? Four of the paths – $C(1)$, $C(3)$, $C(5)$ and $C(6)$ – do so. Notice that because sustainability is here a constraint, it cannot be used to rank paths which satisfy the constraint. A consumption path either satisfies the criterion or it does not. However, under

many forms of social objective function,[2] path $C(3)$ would be preferred to $C(1)$, $C(5)$ and $C(6)$, because consumption is higher at each point in time on the former than any of the latter.

Note that using a sustainability rule does not necessarily lead to outcomes that all would regard as being sensible. Figure 3.1 is also helpful in understanding this point. Consider path $C(2)$. It is clearly not Solow–Hartwick sustainable, as consumption falls at several points in time, and falls by a particularly large amount near the end of the time interval shown. But if one were less strict in interpreting the non-declining requirement (possibly by allowing some limited 'averaging') then one might be tempted to regard $C(2)$ as sustainable because it does not exhibit a downward trend.

But a more serious objection to the Solow–Hartwick criterion is that it does not impose any requirements on how large the non-declining level of consumption should initially be. An economy can be sustainable even if living standards are abysmally low and remain so, provided they do not get any lower! This suggests that we might wish to build into the Hartwick–Solow criterion a threshold level of consumption that should always be achieved.

This was the purpose of Pezzey's concept of survivable development that we came across in Box 3.1. You will recall that the symbol C^{SURV} was used there to denote the minimum level of consumption consistent with reproducibility of a population of some given size. This level is indicated by the broken horizontal line in Figure 3.1.

But one might feel that this is an insufficiently ambitious criterion of 'sustainability'. In discussions of poverty, for example, it is now widely agreed that the poverty line is culturally rather than biologically determined, and is set at a level of access to resources considerably greater than what is

---

[2] We discuss various forms of social objective function in Chapter 4.

Table 3.2 Various sustainability criteria applied to the hypothetical consumption paths.

Consumption path	Criterion		
	Solow–Hartwick	Survivability	Minimum condition
$C(1)$	S	S	S
$C(2)$	NS	S	S
$C(3)$	S	S	S
$C(4)$	NS	S	S
$C(5)$	S	S	NS
$C(6)$	S	S	NS

Key: S = sustainable, NS = not sustainable

required merely to reproduce a population over time. In this spirit, we might argue that consumption should not fall below some minimum, decent, culturally-determined level over time. Let us assume that such a level can be defined, and label it as $C\cdot$MIN (shown by the heavy solid line in the diagram). We use the term 'minimum condition' to describe the requirement that consumption should never fall below $C\cdot$MIN. Which of the consumption time paths satisfy the survivability criterion and which the minimum condition? The answers are grouped together in Table 3.2 (along with those satisfying the Hartwick–Solow criterion).

All of the six consumption paths satisfy the survivable development criterion (although we have noted that this is a relatively undemanding requirement). Four of them – paths $C(1)$, $C(2)$, $C(3)$ and $C(4)$ – also satisfy the minimum condition.

Which paths satisfy all of the three criteria we have examined? Just two, $C(1)$ and $C(3)$. For reasons given earlier, one might well choose $C(3)$ over $C(1)$ on conventional maximisation of benefits grounds. But on that score, $C(4)$ would appear to be best, even though it fails the Hartwick–Solow sustainability criterion.

What conclusions may be drawn from all of this? The first point to note is that whether or not a path of consumption over time is sustainable can vary according to the criterion we use. Secondly, there may well be conflicts between choices made on sustainability criteria and choices made using conventional net benefit maximisation criteria. Sustainable outcomes may not be 'best' outcomes according to standard economic criteria, therefore. (This is something we examine further in Chapter 4.)

A sustainable state is one in which resources are managed so as to maintain production opportunities for the future

In some important later works, Solow proposes a concept of sustainability centred around maintaining production opportunities for future generations of people (Solow, 1986, 1991). He observes that a very common way of discussing distributional ethics is in terms of the so-called cake-eating problem. It is assumed that some fixed quantity of a non-renewable resource is available; how should the resource be distributed over time? Put another way, what is the appropriate way of dividing the cake intertemporally?

Solow (1986) regards as erroneous and unhelpful attempts to define sustainability in terms of the way in which non-renewable resources should be distributed, arguing that:

> [The cake-eating problem] is a damagingly narrow way to pose the question. We have no obligation to our successors to bequeath a share of this or that resource. Our obligation refers to generalised productive capacity or, even wider, to certain standards of consumption/living possibilities over time.

The cake-division problem is inappropriate because the present generation can have no firm knowledge of what future people's preferences will be, nor of what technologies will be available. Unless one knew these things, it would not be possible to arrive at any ethically defensible decision about how environmental resources should be distributed through time. Ultimately, claims Solow, what we owe our successors is the potential to do as well as we have done. Providing we bequeath them sufficient to do that, we will have done all that can be reasonably expected. It might make very good sense to bequeath a smaller non-renewable resource stock to future generations if that is compensated for by a more developed stock of scientific knowledge.

This opportunities-based view underpins the most well-known statement of sustainability, that due to the Brundtland report (WCED, 1987, page 43):

> Sustainable development is development that meets the needs of the present without compromising the ability of future generations to meet their own needs.

The idea that preservation of opportunities is what sustainability is about also seems to be what Talbot Page has in mind. Page appeals to John Locke's concept of just acquisition: the present generation does not have the right to deplete the opportunities afforded by the resource base since it does not 'own' it. Page proposes

> Preserving opportunities for future generations as a common sense minimal notion of intergenerational justice

Page (1977, page 202; 1982, page 205)

What does it mean to say that opportunities should be preserved for the future? Production potential at any point in time depends predominantly on the stock of productive assets available for use. This stock can be classified into human labour and all other productive resources. Now define the term capital in a very broad sense, to include any economically useful stock, other than raw labour power. In this broad sense capital consists of:

(a) Natural capital: any naturally provided stock, such as aquifers and water systems, fertile land, crude oil and gas, forests, fisheries and other stocks of biomass, genetic material, and the earth's atmosphere itself. This category is often called natural resources. It can be decomposed into renewable stock and non-renewable stock resources. Renewable flow resources, such as solar radiation and wind resources, are clearly flows, not capital stocks, but it is sensible to account for these as services of a component of natural capital. We do not include the human population stock in this category.

(b) Physical capital: plant, equipment, buildings and other infrastructure, accumulated by devoting part of current production to capital investment.

(c) Human capital: stocks of learned skills, embodied in particular individuals, which enhances the productive potential of those people.

(d) Intellectual capital: disembodied skills and knowledge. This comprises the stock of useful knowledge, which we might otherwise call the state of technology. These skills are disembodied in that they do not reside in particular individuals, but are part of the culture of a society. They reside in books and other cultural constructs, and are transmitted and developed through time by social learning processes.

If human-made capital is defined to be the sum of physical, human and intellectual capital, then the capital stock consists of two parts: natural and human-made capital. In terms of the production function notation that we introduced in Chapter 2, this way of classifying production inputs suggests that output Q is a function of labour L, natural capital, K_N and human-made capital K_H, so we could write the economy's production function[3] as

$$Q = Q(L, K_N, K_H)$$

Maintenance of the productive potential of the economy will be achieved if the levels of L, K_H and K_N change only in ways that allow output to be non-declining over time. (Note that we have defined technology as part of K_H so that our formulation does not allow the function itself to change with changing technology.)

If there were zero substitution possibilities between individual resource categories and each element were necessary for production, then maintenance of productive potential would imply that each element should be non-declining over time.[4] Most economists would argue that the different elements are substitutable to some degree. If so, then while it is necessary to bequeath some aggregate value of capital assets to ensure the maintenance of productive opportunities, there is no necessary reason why any particular element of the capital stock has to remain at a non-decreasing level. In particular, two kinds of substitution effect are particularly important. First, productive potential can in some circumstances be maintained in the face of falling availability of non-renewable resources if these can be substituted for by rising quantities of physical capital. Second, knowledge appears to be a good substitute for non-renewable resources, and so it may well be the case that falling

quantities of non-renewable resources could be more than compensated for by increasing human and intellectual capital.

What seems to be far more problematic, however, is the substitutability between human-made capital and those elements of natural capital other than non-renewable energy and mineral resources. This becomes clear when we turn our attention to some of the functions performed by natural resources. In particular, it is hard to envisage any resource effectively substituting for the ecosystem and climate maintenance functions of natural capital. We will discuss this matter further in the following subsection.

A sustainable state is one in which the natural capital stock is non-declining through time

The argument that policy should be directed towards maintaining a non-declining natural capital stock has found some support among economists, as can be seen from the following extracts (and from the discussion of the Atkinson and Pearce measure of sustainability in Box 3.2).

> Sustainable activity is … that level of economic activity which leaves the environmental quality level intact, with the policy objective corresponding to this notion being the maximisation of net benefits of economic development, subject to maintaining the services and quality of natural resources over time.
>
> Barbier and Markandya (1990), page 659

> The alternative approach [to sustainable development] is to focus on natural capital assets and suggest that they should not decline through time.
>
> Pearce *et al.* (1989), page 37

Clearly, and like the first two concepts of sustainability that we have examined, this concept sees sustainability in terms of a constraint. A non-declining natural capital stock would be a necessary condition for sustaining the economy's productive potential if natural capital is both essential to production and not substitutable by other productive resources. In the final analysis, the extent to which natural capital is substitutable by other

---

[3] But note that this is a very narrow way of specifying the production function, as we explained in Chapter 2.

[4] If resources cannot be substituted for one another, this means that more of one type cannot be used in place of less of another, with output remaining unchanged. So if we wished to at least maintain the existing level and pattern of output, each different element of the resource input mix would need to be maintained at non-declining levels. However, if we were prepared to accept changes in the output mix, it may be possible to maintain overall output by producing more of those goods using large shares of the growing resource and less of those goods using large shares of the depleting resource.

Box 3.2 Measuring sustainable development

Rather than try to measure total capital, and so look at the question of sustainable outcomes, it might be easier and less controversial to measure whether the conditions considered necessary for sustainable development are being achieved. Here we examine an attempt by Atkinson and Pearce to develop such a measure. They adopt a non-declining capital stock as the criterion for sustainability. The concept of capital here is a broad one, including physical and natural capital. In a world in which the population level is changing, we might wish to amend the rule to one in which the nation's stock of capital in per capita terms is non-declining. (This is a rather important choice, of course, and it may well be that ecological considerations require that we always place attention on the total stock sizes, not their per capita levels.)

Atkinson and Pearce propose two variants of the constant capital stock rule. Weak sustainability is achieved when the total capital stock – physical, human and natural – is non-declining through time. In this variant, development is sustainable even if some component (such as natural capital) is declining, provided the total capital stock is not falling. For this to be a meaningful criterion, it is necessary that different elements of the capital stock are substitutes for one another. An example of substitutability of this sort would be if the loss of a particular ecosystem is compensated for by an increase in the stock of human knowledge. By 'compensated for', one presumably means that the environmental and economic losses due to the former are more than outweighed by environmental and economic benefits from the latter, and that the overall system stability and resilience do not suffer in the process. Weak sustainability (and the strong sustainability variant discussed next) also requires that we can put relative values on different elements of capital, so that measures of depletion in some common metric can be obtained; this confronts the problems we have alluded to in the text.

The second variant – strong sustainability – affords environmental (or natural) capital a special place. Sustainable development is attained, in a strong sense, if the nation's stock of environmental capital is non-decreasing. Atkinson and Pearce point out that one may wish to modify this; some part of the capital stock is likely to be of particular importance, providing valuable and non-substitutable environmental services to the economic process. If we call this critical natural capital, then the modified version of strong sustainable development requires that development does not lead to a decline through time of a nation's stock of critical natural capital.

Table 3.3, reproduced from Atkinson and Pearce (1993), shows the results of a simple test for weak sustainability. The test statistic measures the nation's savings less the depreciation of man-made and natural capital, each expressed as a proportion of Gross Domestic Product (Y). The resulting number, Z, constitutes a measure of satisfaction of a necessary condition for sustainable development. If Z is positive, the condition is satisfied; if Z is negative, it is not. The authors obtained the value of this index for 22 economies. Of these, 8 failed the weak sustainability test, and another 3 just marginally passed it. Atkinson and Pearce concluded that 'even on a weak rule many countries are unlikely to pass a sustainability test'.

The authors urge caution in the degree of reliance that should be placed on the index. And they are correct to do so! As we shall see in Chapter 17, where we discuss the basis for this test further, the principal difficulty arises in arriving at valid measures of capital depreciation, particularly for natural capital. As explained in Chapter 17, the difficulty is enhanced by the following problem: as the test is one for sustainability, the relevant prices of capital needed for the calculation are not observed market prices, but the prices that would emerge if the economy were actually pursuing a sustainable path. But since we do not know whether it is (otherwise the test would not be needed) then it is not possible to know whether observed prices are relevant. Moreover, there seems no way in practice of calculating these prices from first principles. At best, therefore, the Atkinson and Pearce measure (and all others like it) can only give us approximate answers.

An alternative approach to defining conditions for sustainable development is to use ecological indicators. One might define an economy–environment system as being sustainable if it is resilient to a wide variety of shocks and stresses. Given this, a sustainable development indicator would be some indicator of resilience. This is likely, however, to be difficult to construct in practice. If resilience is a function of the degrees of complexity and diversity of an ecosystem, one might develop indirect measures of resilience (and hence of sustainability) using indicators of a system's complexity and/or diversity. Conway (1992) has developed and applied a variety of such indicators.

Source: Atkinson and Pearce (1993).

Table 3.3 Testing for sustainable development.

National economy	Test calculations[a]			
	S/Y	$-\delta M/Y$	$-\delta N/Y$	$= Z$
Sustainable economies				
Brazil	20	7	10	+3
Costa Rica	26	3	8	+15
Czechoslovakia	30	10	7	+13
Finland	28	15	2	+11
Germany (pre-unification)	26	12	4	+10
Hungary	26	10	5	+11
Japan	33	14	2	+17
Netherlands	25	10	1	+14
Poland	30	11	3	+10
USA	18	12	3	+3
Zimbabwe	24	10	5	+9
Marginally sustainable				
Mexico	24	12	12	0
Philippines	15	11	4	0
United Kingdom	18	12	6	0
Unsustainable				
Burkina Faso	2	1	10	−9
Ethiopia	3	1	9	−7
Indonesia	20	5	17	−2
Madagascar	8	1	16	−9
Malawi	8	7	4	−3
Mali	−4	4	6	−14
Nigeria	15	3	17	−5
Papua New Guinea	15	9	7	−1

[a] An economy is sustainable if it saves more than the depreciation on its man-made and natural capital, i.e. $Z \geqslant 0$
S = Gross Domestic Savings
Y = Gross Domestic Product
δM = Value of depreciation of man-made capital
δN = Value of depreciation of natural capital
Z = Sustainability Index

Source: Atkinson and Pearce (1993), page 3.

forms of productive input is an empirical matter, not one that can be decided by theoretical considerations alone.

A number of writers argue that substitutability is much lower than has been previously thought. Moreover, as the natural capital stock depletes, the degree of substitutability may fall too. Therefore, even if there were strong evidence that substitution possibilities have been high, this does not constitute grounds for asserting that they will remain so in the future. When we look at the various functions of the natural environment, it seems clear that some of these functions can be performed only by natural capital stocks, and so these functions are ones for which no substitutability is possible. Daly points out (see the summary in Box 3.3) that ultimately substitution implies the replacement of one form of low entropy matter-energy for another. But there is no substitute for low entropy itself, and low entropy is scarce and inevitably declining. Finally, as we argue in Chapter 15, economic progress and development may well lead societies to place increasing emphasis and value on the amenity services yielded by natural capital. Taken together, these arguments suggest that it would be wise to be pessimistic rather than optimistic about substitution possibilities between natural capital and other forms of resources.

A stronger version of this criterion retains the principle that the natural capital stock should be non-declining, but strengthens it by requiring that the non-declining rule also be applied to some subsets of natural capital. For example, a very strong version of the non-declining natural capital stock criterion is implied by UNESCO in its assertion that

> Every generation should leave water, air and soil resources as pure and unpolluted as when it came on earth. Each generation should leave undiminished all the species of animals it found on earth.

But such a criterion appears to be completely unfeasible. Almost every form of human activity will have some adverse impact on the environment. For example, human impacts will lead to the loss of some species no matter how cautious and environmentally-conscious is our behaviour. Advocates of the UNESCO position might respond by arguing that this criterion should not be taken too literally. It is not meant to imply that every single species, or that every particular narrowly defined category of natural capital, should suffer no loss in terms of quality or quantity. Rather, the requirement applies to wider classes. Thus, some moist tropical forests might be allowed to decline if that is compensated for by an extension of natural temperate forest cover. But this form of defence is unsatisfactory: once some kind of substitutability is permitted between subsets of natural capital, why not just accept that the relevant object of interest – the thing to be defended, if you like – is the total stock of natural capital.

Unfortunately, this does not necessarily avoid the problems inherent in any version of this concept. The reason is simple. Natural capital is not a homogeneous thing, but rather consists of many components, each of which is different from the others. How, then, does one define a single-valued measure of the natural capital stock? How do we add two lakes plus one forest into a single value for natural capital, for example? Anyone familiar with national income accounting will recog-

nise this difficulty. National income accounts do have a single-valued measure of the quantity of output. To obtain this, weights are employed. For example, 2 cars plus 3 televisions would correspond to an output of 26 if we agreed to give each car a weight of 10 and each television a weight of 2 in the summation. For output of goods, an obvious weight to use is relative prices, and this is what is done in the national accounts.

But there are no obvious weights to use for aggregating individual items of natural capital. Prices do not exist for many items of natural capital, and even where they do, there are many reasons why one would not be willing to accept them as correct reflections of 'true' values. If prices are to be used as weights, these prices will have to be imputed somehow or other. We will leave a discussion of how this might be done until Chapter 14 (on valuation of environmental goods and services) and Chapter 17 (on environmental accounting). However, to anticipate some conclusions we reach in those chapters, no fully satisfactory method yet exists for valuing environmental resources, and it may be that none could ever exist. This means that a criterion which says that the total stock of natural capital should not be allowed to fall comes up against the fundamental problem that there is no satisfactory method of measuring the total stock of natural capital.

A sustainable state is one in which resources are managed so as to maintain a sustainable yield of resource services

The concept of a sustainable yield is often used in biological models of renewable resource stocks, such as forests and fisheries. These models will be investigated in Chapters 9 and 10, and so we here make only a few general remarks. A sustained yield refers to a constant flow of services from a resource stock which is being maintained at a constant level through time. For example, a forest stand, when subjected to a suitable thinning and replanting regime, can deliver a constant flow of felled timber.

The maximum sustainable yield of a resource is the highest feasible flow of services that can be maintained over time from some environmental system. Some writers advocate that stocks should be managed to deliver maximum sustained yields, equating such yields with optimal practice. We show in Chapter 9 that a maximum sustainable yield may be, but is not necessarily, optimal on conventional economic criteria. Moreover, in some circumstances, it may not even be desirable to have a sustainable yield.

One possible interpretation of 'sustainable development' is in terms of sustainable yields from resource stocks looked at in some aggregate sense, although not necessarily maximum sustainable yields. But choosing to think in terms of aggregates poses the same kind of difficulties that we discussed earlier. What does 'maintaining a flow of resource services constant' mean when the flow is made up of heterogeneous elements? Does it mean that each different element must be kept constant, or rather that some weighted sum should be maintained? If the latter interpretation is chosen, how are the weights to be selected and should they be constant?

An alternative interpretation of this concept follows from the steady state models of Daly (see Box 3.3) and Boulding (see Box 1.1), which are derived from an application of the laws of thermodynamics. In Boulding's 'Spaceship Earth' economy, perpetual reproducibility of the economic/physical system (the spaceship) requires that a steady state be achieved in which the waste flows from production and consumption are equated with the system's recycling capacity. Reproducibility of the spaceship as a functioning system over time implies that waste flows cannot be ejected into outer space through the air lock, as that would lead to a gradual depletion of the material resource base upon which the spaceship is reliant. As the maximum recycling capacity of the system is determined by the (constant) flow of incoming energy that can be harnessed from extraterrestrial sources, so there must be in this steady state a maximum rate of sustainable materials usage in the economy. You should now read Box 3.3 to see how Daly envisages a steady state.

A sustainable state is one which satisfies minimum conditions of ecosystem stability and resilience through time

Two definitions illustrate the notion that sustainability is primarily about maintaining the integrity of the earth's ecosystems:

> A safe minimum standard of conservation is a matter of resources and economic policy. It is to be achieved by avoiding the critical zone – that is, the physical conditions, brought about by human action, which would make it uneconomical to halt and reverse depletion.
>
> S.V. Ciriacy-Wantrup (1968), page 253

> Sustainability is a relationship between human economic systems and larger dynamic, but normally slower-changing ecological systems in which 1) human life can continue indefinitely, 2) human individuals can flourish, and 3) human cultures can develop; but in which effects of human activities remain within bounds, so as not to destroy the diversity, complexity, and function of the ecological life support system.
>
> Costanza et al. (1991), page 8

Ecological science looks at its subject matter within a systems perspective. The whole system – the biosphere – consists of an interlocking set of ecological subsystems or ecosystems. Systems analysts are concerned with organisational characteristics and structure, and with the systems dynamics; the processes of evolution and change.

Ecologists look at sustainability from the point of view of the ecological system of which humans are just one part. Sustainability is assessed, loosely speaking, in terms of the extent to which the structure and properties of the prevailing ecosystem can be maintained. Human interests are not regarded as paramount; rather, they are

Box 3.3 Herman Daly: the steady state economy

In his article 'The economics of the steady state' (1974), Daly begins by defining his concept of a steady state economy:

> A steady-state economy is defined by constant stocks of physical wealth (artefacts) and a constant population, each maintained at some chosen, desirable level by a low rate of throughput – i.e., by low birth rates equal to low death rates and by low physical production rates equal to low physical depreciation rates, so that longevity of people and durability of physical stocks are high. The throughput flow, viewed as the cost of maintaining the stocks, begins with the extraction (depletion) of low entropy resources at the input end, and terminates with an equal quantity of high entropy waste (pollution) at the output end. The throughput is the inevitable cost of maintaining the stocks of people and artefacts and should be minimised subject to the maintenance of a chosen level of stocks.
>
> Daly (1974), page 15

The ultimate benefit of economic activity is the services (want satisfaction) yielded by the stocks of artefacts and people. Conventional indicators of economic performance measure the wrong thing: instead of measuring service flows, GDP and the like measure throughputs. But there is no longer any reason to believe that these two will be closely correlated, or have a stable relationship over time.

It is possible to make progress in the steady state through two types of efficiency improvement: either by maintaining a given stock level with less throughput, or by obtaining more services per unit of time from the same stock. Unfortunately, the fundamental laws of thermodynamics imply that these two forms of efficiency gain are likely to be unobtainable in the long term; we are condemned to efficiency losses not gains. The main reason for this arises from the fact that

> as better grade (lower entropy) sources of raw materials are used up, it will be necessary to process ever larger amounts of materials using ever more energy and capital equipment to get the same quantity of needed mineral.

Daly notes that a choice must be made about the level of stocks in the steady state. Selecting from the large number of feasible stock levels is a difficult choice problem, involving economic, ecological and ethical principles. We will never be able to identify an optimal stock level and so, as a matter of practice, should learn to be stable at or near to existing stock levels.

Ultimately there is no real choice over whether to seek a steady state. If the economic subsystem is not to eventually disrupt the functioning of the larger system of which it is a part, then at some point the economy will have to be run in a steady state. Daly does not claim that the steady state is infinitely sustainable. Indeed, his view is quite the opposite:

> Thus a steady state is simply a strategy for good stewardship, for maintaining our spaceship and permitting it to die of old age rather than from the cancer of growthmania.

The necessary ultimate demise of the system arises from the irresistible force of increasing entropy. Daly pours particular scorn upon those economists who see substitution as the salvation of perpetual growth. Conventional economists envisage a sequence of substitution effects; as one input becomes relatively scarce, it will be replaced by another that is less relatively scarce. The possibility of absolute scarcity is assumed away in this approach. But for Daly:

> Substitution is always of one form of low entropy matter-energy for another. There is no substitute for low entropy itself, and low entropy is scarce, both in its terrestrial source (finite stocks of concentrated fossil fuels and minerals) and in its solar source (a fixed rate of inflow of solar energy).

Technology does not offer the solution to perpetual economic growth that is often claimed. All technologies obey the logic of thermodynamics, and so we cannot appeal to any technology to wrench us from the grasp of the entropy principle. (See the epigraph at the start of this chapter.)

---

identified with the continuing existence and functioning of the biosphere in a form more or less similar to that which exists at present.

However, ecological views are often more human-centred than is admitted, as there is a presumption that the present system structure, including the important place in it occupied by humans, is preferred to others.

To confirm that this is so, consider the attitude an ecologist might take to the threat of global warming. If large-scale global warming were to occur, there is a reasonably high chance that major ecosystem change would occur. The biosphere would not cease to operate, of course – it would just operate in a different way. We guess that nearly all ecological scientists would take a stand against global warming, and most would do so on the grounds that human life is more threatened in a changed ecosystem than in the present one.

Let us now relate the ecological concepts of stability and resilience discussed in the previous chapter to the concept of sustainability. Common and Perrings (1992) define a system as being ecologically sustainable if it is resilient. By implication, therefore, any behaviour which reduces the system's resilience is potentially unsustainable. Unfortunately, while we are able to observe whether a system is resilient after a disturbance has taken place, the best we can do *ex ante* is to make an informed guess about whether a system would be resilient in the face of future shocks. Uncertainty pervades the behaviour of ecological systems, ensuring that we cannot know in advance whether some system is or is not resilient.

Suppose that it were accepted that ecological sustainability is a good objective (or that it should be imposed as a constraint on economic behaviour). Then economic affairs should be organised so as to keep to a reasonably low level the likelihood that disturbances alter the system's parameters to a point where the resilience of the whole ecosystem is threatened. One task of ecological and environmental economics is to identify what kinds of economic activity seem to be consistent with ecological sustainability, and what kinds do not.

For the reasons suggested above, it will never be possible to answer such questions with certainty. Prudent behaviour, based on informed judgement, may be the best we can do. Some authors have suggested that some indicators are useful as monitoring devices: they can be used to make inferences about potential changes in the degree of resilience of ecosystems in which we are interested. Schaeffer *et al.* (1988) propose a set of indicators, including:

- changes in the number of native species
- changes in standing crop biomass

- changes in mineral micronutrient stocks
- changes in the mechanisms of and capacity for damping oscillations

Suggestive as these and other indicators might be, none can ever be a completely reliable instrument in the sense that a satisfactory rating can be taken as a guarantee of resilience. They may, nonetheless, help us to avoid entering the 'critical zone' about which Ciriacy-Wantrup warns.

Sustainable development as capacity and consensus building

The final concept of 'sustainability' that we discuss focuses on processes rather than outcomes or constraints. It differs from the other concepts by viewing the issue primarily in terms of institutions and processes. A good example of this school of thought is to be found in a recent paper by de Graaf *et al.* (1996). In this paper, sustainable development is defined in two ways:

> ... a development of a socio-environmental system with a high potential for continuity because it is kept within economic, social, cultural, ecological and physical constraints.
> ... sustainable development [is] a development on which the people involved have reached consensus.

The first definition is described as 'formal but not operational', the second as 'procedural, but does not guarantee stability'. De Graaf *et al.* begin from the premise that one cannot separate environmental objectives – such as preventing catastrophic environmental problems – from other social and political objectives, such as the elimination of poverty. It is therefore very much within the spirit of the World Commission on Environment and Development. The authors consider, however, that conventional approaches to sustainable development are fundamentally flawed by information problems and by their failure to address issues of political will and feasibility. They classify conventional approaches as:

(1) Recognising that human societies are parts of ecosystems, determining the carrying capacity of those ecosystems, and then legislating to prevent human activity exceeding carrying capacities.

(2) Conceptualising environmental decline as external costs, evaluating these costs in monetary terms, and then using a price mechanism to internalise these costs.

The first strategy is not sufficient because its success is dependent on persuading citizens of the need to respect carrying capacities. It is flawed because carrying capacities are unknown (and probably unknowable), and are not simply technical data but depend on human choices. To quote de Graaf et al. on this:

> Summing up, it is difficult or impossible to prove that environmental limits exist and, if they do, what they are. It is perhaps even more difficult to convince people to respect those limits and to provide strategies for doing so. One could say that this strategy overestimates our knowledge of human carrying capacity and underestimates the importance of socio-economic factors.
>
> de Graaf et al. (1996), page 208

They argue that the second of the conventional approaches is also of limited usefulness for similar reasons, and ultimately because it 'overestimates the possibilities of pricing under difficult social circumstances' (page 209). In arriving at this claim, they argue that some values are unpriceable, giving as examples cultural development, nature conservation and landscape planning.

In proposing a new strategy, de Graaf et al. urge that we do not view the attainment of sustainability as simply a technical problem. Fundamental limits to our ability to know the consequences of human behaviour mean that it is futile to look for necessary or sufficient conditions for sustainability. De Graaf et al. take a different tack altogether, proposing consensus building through negotiations. It is our success in building a consensus about what should and should not be done that is their criterion of sustainability. The notion of

negotiation that they have in mind is very broad, referring to an institutional process of social choice that involves people as widely as possible, and involves a process of trade-offs in which all benefit from the avoidance of environmental disturbances. It is not yet clear, however, exactly what this negotiation process will consist of. According to de Graaf et al., research should be focused on the structure and management of these negotiations, and on the supply of relevant information about preventable problems and steerable development.

Steps towards attaining sustainable economic behaviour

What steps could be taken – by national and local government, by international organisations, and by firms and individuals – that would move us along a path towards sustainable behaviour? And what rules would need to be followed for a state to be sustainable over infinite time? There has been an explosion in the literature trying to answer questions of this sort in recent years. We do not attempt to summarise that huge and diverse literature, but instead select a small number of important themes, several of which will be taken further in later chapters.

Economic models of sustainability

Economic models are rarely designed to address the first question that we posed at the start of this section. Where economic models have been used to analyse sustainability issues, it is the second question that they typically address. That is, economists have constructed abstract models, which are then used to deduce rules that must be followed if the economy is to be sustainable according to some chosen criterion.

Herein lie both the strength and the weakness of much of the conventional economics contribution to sustainability. Analytical models can sharpen our insights, and force us to think about what is crucial in any problem. Beginning with a set of assumptions, we can often deduce very powerful conclusions. These conclusions can form the basis of behavioural rules. But these rules and conclusions are rarely of immediate practical relevance. The deductions from a model are highly dependent on the particular assumptions built into it. These assumptions are not usually based on concrete descriptions of conditions that actually prevail, but are idealised mental constructs. So it would be a serious misunderstanding of what economic models are all about if one were to regard their role as giving prescriptions for actual behaviour in particular circumstances.

It is precisely this inability of an economic model to generate detailed prescriptions for behaviour that many regard as its weakness. The person who seeks a detailed programme of actions for making Glasgow a sustainable city, for example, will find little direct help from an economic model (except possibly discovering that this is a meaningless goal). Our discussions may also have alerted you to another weakness of economic models that address sustainability issues. Both the economic sphere and, more fundamentally, the environmental systems in which the economy is located, and on which it depends, are subject to considerable uncertainty and unpredictability. Moreover, our discussions of the physical principles governing matter and energy might imply (as Daly claims in Box 3.3) that sustainability over infinite time is an impossibility. These two considerations suggest that it may simply be impossible to find any rules that guarantee sustainable behaviour. The best we can do is to avoid behaviour which has a high probability of causing future problems.

The Hartwick rule

One important example of this approach has been the analysis of the conditions required for economic behaviour to be sustainable,

associated with the names, particularly, of Hartwick and Solow. The sustainability criterion here, as we have seen, is that of non-declining consumption. The analysis proceeds by characterising the economy and the technological relationships governing production in a very simple way. The emphasis throughout this analysis is on the substitution possibilities between different productive inputs. It is possible to deduce a particular condition – the Hartwick rule – which, if satisfied, would in this simple economy be a sufficient condition for sustainability. The conclusion is that constant consumption through time is possible in an economy which is extracting and using a non-renewable resource if the Hartwick saving rule is followed (provided also that some feasibility conditions described in Chapter 7 are satisfied).

Let us explore the thinking here. Suppose that an economy has a fixed quantity of some non-renewable resource, and that recycling is impossible. Consuming this resource directly is the only source of human utility. What is the largest constant rate of consumption of this stock that is feasible over indefinite time? The answer must be zero, because of finiteness of the stock. But next suppose that the resource stock is not consumed directly for consumption, but is an input, together with physical capital, into the production process: the output of this production process can be either consumed or accumulated as capital. Let us now repose the question, but in a slightly different form: what is the largest constant rate of consumption in this economy that is feasible over indefinite time? The analysis of the model shows that under certain conditions, the answer is no longer zero; some positive amount of consumption can be maintained in perpetuity. What conditions are required to obtain this result?

The first condition concerns substitutability between the non-renewable resource and physical capital: these two inputs must be substitutable for one another in a particular way (to be defined precisely in Chapter 7).

Intuitively, the condition requires that as the non-renewable resource is depleted, and the physical capital stock is accumulated, the latter can substitute for the former in the production process in such a way that output does not diminish.

The second condition is the Hartwick rule and concerns the rate at which physical capital is accumulated. This rule requires that the rents (the surplus of revenues over production costs) derived from non-renewable resource extraction should be saved and then accumulated entirely in physical capital. A third condition is also required: the non-renewable resource should be extracted according to an efficient programme. We shall define and explain exactly what is meant by an efficient programme in Chapter 5; suffice it to say at the moment that the resource should not be extracted wastefully.

Lying behind this result is a very simple idea: while non-renewable resources are being depleted, the savings rule implies that a compensating increase in the stock of reproducible resources is taking place. In some sense, therefore, the Hartwick rule ensures that an aggregate measure of capital is being maintained at a constant level.

Unfortunately, very strong assumptions are required for the validity of this rule, including, as we have seen, the requirements that the resource is extracted efficiently over time and that sufficient substitutability exists between non-renewable resources and capital. Since not all of these conditions will be met in practice, one might argue that the practical usefulness of this rule is very limited. However, for the reasons we discussed earlier, this is not a fair way in which to appraise the value of this model. On the contrary, its value lies in disciplining us to think in terms of the important roles that substitutability and efficiency play.

What implications for actual practice follow from the Solow–Hartwick model? The first thing to note is that there is no guarantee that following the Hartwick rule will ensure that consumption will not decline over time, because the actual economy is not identical to the economy in Hartwick's model. However, there are very good grounds for believing that if the rule were adopted sustainable outcomes would be more likely than if the rule were not adopted. It does make sense to argue that as the non-renewable resource is depleted, the physical capital stock should be accumulated to compensate for the diminishing non-renewable resource base. If we do not do this, then future consumption is more likely to fall as the stock of productive assets declines.

How could the Hartwick rule be implemented? The required level of accumulation of physical capital would only be forthcoming in a market economy if all decision makers used a particular socially-optimal discount rate. As this will almost certainly not happen in any market economy, another mechanism would be required. To bring forth the optimal amount of savings over time, government could tax resource rents, and invest the proceeds in physical capital.

We now briefly discuss other ways that government might act to promote sustainable development.

The role of government

Information provision

The prospects for sustainable development will be enhanced if pollution flows are reduced, recycling is encouraged, and more attention is given to the regulation, management and disposal of waste. How can this be achieved? One school of thought argues that information is of central importance. Businesses sometimes seem able to increase profitability by behaving in environmentally friendly ways, and consumers sometimes appear to give preference to sellers with good environmental credentials. It is easy to find examples to support such claims. Consider the Dow Chemical Corporation: this organisation, by refining its method of synthesising agricultural chemicals at its Pittsburgh (California) plant, reduced its demand for a key reactant by 80%, eliminated 1000 tons of waste annually, and reduced costs by $8 million per year (Schmidheiny, 1992, page 268). Much has also been made of the power that the green consumer can have in altering producer behaviour (see Smart, 1992, for one example).

Proponents of the view that self-interest will stimulate environmentally friendly behaviour sometimes argue that the potential of this is limited only by the amount of relevant information that consumers and producers possess. On this view, environmental problems largely reflect ignorance; if that ignorance were to be overcome by improving the quality of information flows, much progress could be made towards sustainable economic behaviour.

An example of the role that can be played by information is given by the US Toxics Release Inventory (TRI). In 1986, the US government enacted legislation which required businesses to quantify their emissions of any of the 313 toxic substances covered by the TRI. The public exhibition of this information, no doubt linked with fears of possible future control, has served as a powerful incentive for firms to revise their production processes, and many large firms have voluntarily committed themselves to very demanding clean-up targets. Similar disclosure schemes are planned or are in operation in the European Union, Canada, Australia and India (Sarokin, 1992; WWF, 1993; *Business Week*, 1991).

While the provision of better information may assist environmental protection, there is no guarantee that it will do so. Private incentives are not necessarily consistent with environmentally friendly behaviour, and improved information flows will be of no help if private interests conflict with the public good. As we show in Chapter 6, externalities often drive a wedge between what is privately and socially efficient, and better information is not, in general, a solu-

tion to this problem. In the absence of the right incentives, the argument that better information will lead decision makers to behave in more socially responsive ways may be wishful thinking.

Education

A major vehicle for the dissemination of information is education. One often comes across arguments that government should educate its young citizens to be more aware of the impacts of human activities on the environment. Much the same kind of comments as we made about the role of information apply to this argument. There is, however, one important difference. Education is not only about the dissemination of information. It is also one of the ways in which cultural values are developed and transmitted. One may believe that education should teach people to behave in certain ways, but if so, it is sensible to be clear that the role that education is being expected to play is one of socialisation rather than the provision of information *per se*.

Before we leave this point, let us note that the consensus-building approach to sustainability that we discussed earlier does see information dissemination as having the decisive role in the attainment of sustainability. De Graaf *et al.* recognise that individuals do not have identical self-interests, and that the provision of information by itself will not produce consensus. That can only come through some ongoing negotiation process in which 'all parties can expect to gain something from a development that lowers the risk of future problems'.

Research

A strong case can be made that generous funding and promotion of pure and applied research by the public sector will assist in the pursuit of sustainability goals. There are two points to be made here. First, the products of research are often public goods, being nondepletable. As we demonstrate in Chapter 6, public goods will tend to be under-provided (or not provided at all) by profit-seeking organisations. So if one thinks that research is socially valuable, there are good grounds for the argument that it should be publicly funded.

The second point is that research is likely to be socially valuable, particularly where environmental preservation is concerned. It can, for example, generate new pollution abatement technologies, contribute to economically viable methods of harnessing renewable energy flow resources, lead to organic substitutes for materials such as plastics currently derived from crude oil, and produce crop varieties that can more easily tolerate environmental stresses.

Financial incentives and regulatory programmes

It is difficult to believe that purely self-interested behaviour will succeed in moving economies very far towards sustainability targets unless additional incentives are provided to steer that behaviour in an appropriate direction. Attempts to show that 'green' behaviour can be privately profitable tend to rely on evidence that is both anecdotal and selective. As we show repeatedly in later chapters, there are strong grounds for believing that, in the absence of policy interventions, financial incentives typically work in the opposite direction: environmentally responsible behaviour is costly, individuals have incentives to pass costs onto others and it is often in the interests of individual resource harvesters to maximise current rates of harvest rather than to manage the resource on a sustainable basis. The fishing industry throughout the world provides one clear example of the last-mentioned point.

This is not the place to discuss at length the instruments available to government in this regard. We shall leave that until later chapters, particularly Chapter 12. Suffice it to say that two broad approaches are available. First, governments may use direct controls over behaviour, requiring that things be done or prohibiting other things. Second, it may use financial incentives in the form of taxes and subsidies. These can achieve any desired target for corporate and consumer behaviour, although there may be considerable uncertainty about the magnitude of the required tax or subsidy change. Sometimes the threat of penalties is enough to modify business behaviour. An important tool that government has is the early announcement of targets and timetables for their implementation. If these are credible, businesses will often act proactively rather than reactively, as the costs of planned, gradual adjustments are lower than those of enforced, rapid change. One important case in point concerns the distinction between the reduction of waste or pollution at source, as compared with the more conventional 'end-of-pipe' treatment. Because of lower adjustment costs, there are important economic gains to be got from preannounced programmes, particularly when firms are in partnership with government in the programme design. Case Study 1 at the end of this chapter shows how the Dutch environmental policy planners hope to secure these gains from preannounced programmes.

Property rights and the legal system

As we explain in some depth in Chapters 6 to 10, when property rights over the use of and the income from natural resources are vested neither in small and clearly defined groups of individuals, nor in a system of common ownership with well-established rules and conventions about resource use, it is not likely that the resource will be sensibly managed. Conditions of open access to a resource will tend to result in environmental degradation, sometimes to a catastrophic degree.

The creation and maintenance of private property rights or well-managed common ownership can be a powerful instrument for achieving some environmental objectives, and will have an important part to play in any programme of sustainable development. A corollary of this is a need for the existence of a well-functioning legal system, in which grievances about infringement of property rights can be settled at relatively low costs in terms of time and money.

Environmental accounting

It does not seem sensible to pursue a sustainability objective unless measures (or indicators) exist which allow assessment of whether the objective is being realised. This will probably require the development of new indicators. Two approaches are available.

First, we might try to find some indicators which are related very closely to whatever criteria of sustainability has been chosen, as in the case considered in Box 3.2. Second, and more ambitiously, we might attempt to construct a set of national accounts which measure economic flows and stocks, environmental flows and stocks, and the linkages between the two. This is not the place to examine sustainability indicators nor integrated economic–environmental accounts in detail. That task will be left until Chapter 17. We focus here on the way in which the requirements at the level of the firm that a national environmental accounting strategy would imply could affect the behaviour of firms.

Presenting new information does not in itself alter the incentives facing decision makers, but by drawing attention to the consequences of activities, or by putting these in sharper relief, behavioural changes may be facilitated. For example, many firms appear to have very poor procedures for recording quantities of waste flows, where they originate, how much cost is associated with waste controls and to which activity these costs can be attributed. More generally, environmental impacts and the costs of environmental management within firms are not usually adequately represented in a cost-accounting framework. Similarly, when legislative or administrative controls impose costs of environmental control on firms, these costs are not usually attributed to particular production processes, but are treated as general environmental management expenses. This hides the true costs of particular products

and processes from managers, and undervalues the benefits to the firm of pollution control programmes. An implication is that firms should be encouraged to develop cost-accounting procedures so that pollution control costs and benefits can be evaluated at the level of individual products and processes within the firm. Not only will this create correct signals for resource allocation decisions within the firm, but it will create a recording framework that will enable the government to more easily and accurately compile national accounts that pay due attention to environmental impacts of economic activity. The final chapter of this book will examine such national accounting procedures.

The pursuit of sustainability can also be helped by encouraging firms to adopt what are sometimes called green design principles, which would build on better information. The objective of green design is to minimise the environmental impact of a product through its life cycle without compromising the product's performance or quality. Green design can be assisted by life cycle assessment, a process which attempts to measure the total environmental impact of a product from its conception through to any effects that result from its final disposal (in whole or in parts) to the environment. Government can encourage firms to adopt green design by extending the legal liability of firms to all damages over the life cycle of the products that they sell (see Chapter 12 for a discussion of this policy instrument).

Policy coordination at regional and local levels

While one would expect national (and possibly international) governmental organisations to have the principal responsibility for designing policies and administering programmes that are consistent with the goal of sustainability, there is also a role to be played by regional and local governments. These organisations have an important contribution to make for the following reason. Modern economies are complex, interrelated systems; the component parts are highly interconnected. While individual units can do much to reduce their environmental impacts, the existence of interconnectedness suggests there are substantial additional gains to be achieved by environmental planning at higher levels. A well-known example which illustrates this point is integrated systems of waste disposal, power generation and district heating. Establishing and implementing such schemes cannot easily be done at the level of individual units, as the decisions cut across institutional boundaries. A substantial literature on this approach – known as industrial ecology – has developed in recent years. It examines systems in terms of the extent to which flows of materials and energy are efficient and sustainable, and tries to identify 'closed loops' in which no net residual flows occur between the system and its environment. While no integrated process can ever be a perfect closed loop, with careful design it may be possible to approach such a target.

Project appraisal

Another role for government concerns project appraisal and approval. In many countries, projects which have environmental impacts can only be implemented with the approval of the relevant local or regional planning authority. Sustainability criteria could be given some weighting in this approval process, although doing so is problematic. The suggested general strategy would involve adding to the standard criteria for approval the requirement that a project have no environment impacts that might threaten sustainability.

There are two problems here. First, a strict adherence to the added criterion would probably close off most project proposals. Second, suppose that the decision maker chose, in the light of this, to insert the qualifier 'significant' into the additional condition so that only projects that had significant negative environmental effects were to be disqualified. The problem then is to decide in any particular case what 'significant' means.

Even if this problem could be solved, such a procedure would be of little help in achieving sustainability. A large number of projects could jointly produce catastrophic environmental effects even if the marginal impact of each is not significant. A variant on these conditions is that an environmentally damaging project may be accepted if it is associated with another that entails matching environmental benefits, an idea which is currently popular. Matching benefits refer to proposals whereby a package is proposed in which environmental losses arising from one activity are at least compensated for by environmental benefits from other elements of the package. This concept is related to the notion of sustainability as a non-declining natural capital stock, which was examined in the previous section.

Irreversibility

An issue related to project appraisal is that of irreversibility. If all resource-use decisions were reversible, then much of the force behind sustainability arguments would be lost. If we were to discover that present behaviour is unsustainable, then our decisions could be changed in whatever way and at whatever time was deemed appropriate. Reversibility implies that nothing would have been irretrievably lost.

But reversibility does not apply in all matters of environmental resource use. Many resource-use decisions cannot be reversed, particularly those that involve extraction of resources or development of undisturbed ecosystems. When irreversibility is combined with imperfect knowledge of the future then optimal decision rules can change significantly. In these circumstances, there are good reasons for keeping options open and behaving in a relatively cautious manner (with a presumption against development built into each choice). Clearly, this has important implications for project appraisal methods and rules, as we demonstrate in Chapter 15.

Conclusions

As we saw in our discussion of the Hartwick rule, one line of analysis taken within environmental economics has been to identify necessary or sufficient conditions for sustainability. If one is able to identify sufficient conditions, then by definition, sustainability will be realised if those conditions are satisfied. Unfortunately, this kind of reasoning is usually of little help in ascertaining whether existing economies have embarked on sustainable development courses. The main reason for this is that the conditions are typically pitched at high levels of abstraction and it is simply not possible to establish whether the 'real world' satisfies those conditions. For example, the standard presentation of the Hartwick rule establishes that constant consumption is possible if, among other things, natural resource rents from an economically efficient depletion programme are saved and invested in man-made capital, and if the economy's production function has the necessary substitution possibilities between natural and man-made capital. But each of these conditions is unobservable; we do not observe a single production function, we will be unable to know if resources are being extracted and used efficiently, and cannot observe the appropriate measure of rent that the Hartwick rule refers to.

A second line of reasoning has focused on the role of pricing. Some economists argue that, given a 'correct' set of prices, economic incentives will bring about outcomes in which pollution flows and environmental damage levels are socially efficient. Strong versions of this argument suggest that the correct set of prices would also bring about outcomes that are sustainable. Advocates of this view do not claim that the currently prevailing market prices are those that would bring about these outcomes. Rather, they suggest that prices could be made correct by an appropriate use of tax or subsidy instruments (or by other methods that we shall explore in Chapter 12). At this early stage in our studies, we cannot evaluate this claim. We will do so, however, in later chapters. However, two reasons should lead one to be sceptical about the claim that sustainable outcomes can be attained through markets in which agents respond to correct sets of prices.

The first concerns the part played in market processes by future generations. If there were some mechanism that enabled future generations to express preferences and enter into current market contracts, resource allocation decisions would at least have the potential to be sustainable. Unfortunately, no such mechanism exists or could ever exist. As yet unborn individuals cannot participate in current markets. However, it is decisions taken currently, whether through markets or otherwise, that will determine whether patterns of activity can be sustained over time. The fact that future generations cannot affect current resource allocation decisions should urge one to be cautious about the claim that a set of prices could be found that would be consistent with sustainable behaviour.

The second caution follows from the way in which market mechanisms take cognisance of ecological considerations. We suggested earlier that sustainability might require that human activity does not impair the resilience of the biosphere in its present form. Can prices be found that could ever guarantee that resilience is not lost? They probably can not. It is not possible to know *a priori* what kinds of behaviour will and will not threaten ecosystem resilience. But if that is unknowable, then there is no set of prices that can guarantee sustainable outcomes either.

None of this implies that human society cannot and will not behave in a sustainable way. But it does suggest that there are limits to the extent to which the price mechanism alone can bring about such an outcome. A belief that pricing mechanisms can lead to sustainability is at best an article of faith. If we believe that the current generation has an obligation to bequeath to the future a world in which conditions of life are at least as good as those currently enjoyed, then some form of risk averse, precautionary behaviour is probably warranted. It is sensible to presume that interference with ecosystems is potentially damaging, and that the consequences of such interference are highly uncertain (and unknowable). Hence, economic behaviour should be more cautious or 'conservative' than it would need to be otherwise. 'How much more cautious?' is a difficult question that we shall often return to in this book.

CASE STUDY 1:   Sustainable development: the case of the Netherlands

The Netherlands has been one of the first countries to unilaterally adopt a programme of environmental policies that seek to attain sustainable development. During the 40 years until 1985, the Dutch economy experienced a rapid rate of industrial development, transforming the Netherlands into one of the richest nations in the world in terms of per capita income. However, this growth success came at the expense of a deteriorating state of the country's environment. By the mid-1980s, the Netherlands had become one of the most heavily polluted of all industrial economies. This was partly a self-inflicted consequence of industrial development, with chemical manufacturing, oil refining and intensive agriculture in particular generating very large quantities of hazardous residuals. But this environmental pollution is also a consequence of geographical location, as can be seen from Figure 3.2.

First, the Netherlands is located in the centre of the heavily industrialised areas of northern Europe, leaving Dutch territories subject to transboundary airborne pollution from Britain, Germany and other European states. (See Chapter 13 for a discussion of transboundary pollution.) The most serious transboundary pollution problems are waterborne. The Netherlands includes the huge delta formed by three major river systems: the Rhine, Meuse and Scheldt. The Rhine basin acts as a receptacle for vast quantities of waste over an area of more than 185 000 square kilometres in five countries. As more than one-third of Dutch drinking water is drawn from the Rhine and Meuse rivers, their heavy pollution poses serious health risks to Netherlanders. The Dutch economy borders the North Sea, one of the most polluted

continued

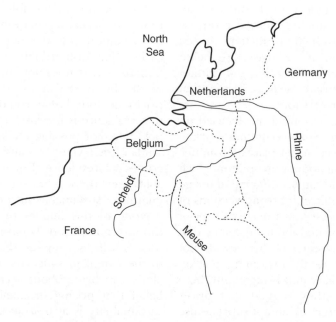

Figure 3.2   The Netherlands: the role of size and location.

CASE STUDY 1   continued

marine areas in the world, acting as it does as a final receptacle for river-borne pollutants from a variety of north European nations, and as a direct waste disposal facility from many sources.

The economic success of the Netherlands has, to a large extent, been dependent on the land reclamation and coastal defence systems that have been implemented since medieval times. More than 30% of the country's land area lies below sea level, with over 60% of the population living on reclaimed land. Land reclamation has enabled an intensive agricultural sector to flourish, but this activity is becoming increasingly vulnerable to periodic flood damage. The value of damages that can be caused in this way were vividly illustrated in the floods of January 1995.

The impetus for change

In the years since 1985, the Netherlands has made remarkable and unprecedented progress towards environmentally and economically sustainable behaviour. The main explanation for this was given in the preceding paragraphs: the Dutch economy had

become intolerably dirty. The fact of severe environmental degradation is not, in itself, sufficient to create a political force for drastic environmental policy initiatives; that required the existence of an environmentally conscious electorate in conjunction with a government composed of individuals willing to take the risks inherent in introducing costly control packages. The catalyst to change appears to have been the 1987 Brundtland Report. Whatever the particular circumstances were, 1987/88 saw a number of official and academic surveys of the state of the Dutch environment, prognoses for the future, and statements of the appropriate way forward. Queen Beatrix of the Netherlands expressed the Dutch mood in her 1988 Christmas message

The Earth is dying slowly, and the inconceivable – the end of life itself – is actually becoming conceivable.

continued

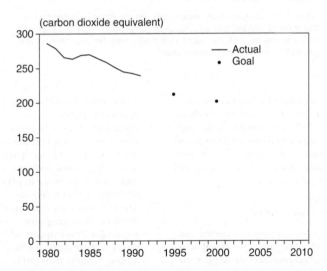

Figure 3.3 Greenhouse gas emissions index, the Netherlands, 1980–91.
Source: adapted from Albert Adriaanse, *Environmental Policy Performance Indicators* (Sdu Uitgeverij Koninginnegracht, The Hague, 1993), pp. 20 and 24.

Note: The Greenhouse Gas Emissions Index was calculated by estimating the emissions of carbon dioxide from fossil fuels, methane – mostly from agricultural activities – nitrogen oxides from combustion processes, and chlorofluorocarbons and halons. These were each weighted by their warming potential compared to carbon dioxide to estimate their carbon dioxide equivalent warming.

CASE STUDY 1:   continued

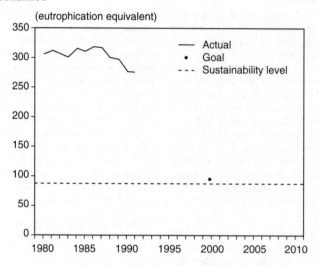

Figure 3.4 Eutrophication index, the Netherlands, 1980–91.
Source: adapted from Albert Adriaanse, *Environmental Policy Performance Indicators* (Sdu Uitgeverij Koninginnegracht, The Hague, 1993), pp. 39 and 44.

Note: The Eutrophication Index uses emissions of phosphorus (in the form of phosphate) and nitrogen (calculated from fertiliser and manure use as well as waste dumping), weighted by their natural proportion in the Dutch environment.

By 1990, the Dutch government had adopted a major environmental programme: the National Environmental Policy Plan (NEPP). It is a mark of the political success of the environmental control lobby in the Netherlands that environmental protection is now ranked equally with full employment and a balanced budget as pre-eminent policy targets.

NEPP – The main themes
Six principles form the basis of NEPP:

(1) Environmental problems are interconnected and cannot be tackled effectively on a piecemeal basis.
(2) Users of environmental resources should pay for any consequent environmental degradation, and cannot pass on costs to others (now, or in the future, in the Netherlands or elsewhere). The 'polluters pay' principle is to be interpreted strictly: wherever identifiable, individual polluters should pay any clean-up costs to which their behaviour contributes.
(3) The basis for environmental control is economic instruments, centred around the use of tax and subsidy to provide appropriate signals and incentives. Traditional 'command-and-control'

instruments should be replaced by these fiscal control measures.
(4) Environmental policy should be, as far as possible, based on self-regulation and social institutions, rather than being handed down from above. Negotiated covenants between government and business are to play a central role in attaining interim objectives.
(5) The principal long-run objective of the environmental control programme is the attainment of sustainable development, which is defined in terms of three particular targets: consumption of no more energy than can be harnessed from the sun, the treatment of all waste as raw material, and the promotion of high quality products – products that last, can be repaired, and are recyclable.
(6) Medium-term goals, consistent with the long-run objective of sustainable development, and the means of achieving these goals, are to be provided in a four-year environmental plan. The rolling plan is to be revised annually.

continued

CASE STUDY 1:   continued

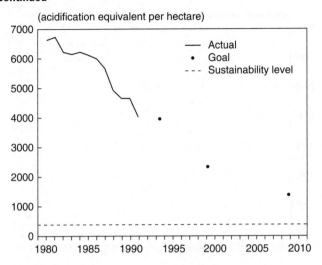

(acidification equivalent per hectare)

Figure 3.5 Acidification index, the Netherlands, 1980–91.
Source: adapted from Albert Adriaanse, *Environmental Policy Performance Indicators* (Sdu Uitgeverij Koninginnegracht, The Hague, 1993), pp. 33 and 36.

Note: The Acidification Index was calculated using the three main substances responsible for acid deposition in the Netherlands, sulphur dioxide, nitrogen oxides, and ammonia. The index is the number of acid equivalents deposited per hectare per year (from both domestic and foreign sources) and converts these substances to an acidification equivalent corresponding to 32 grams (g) of sulphur dioxide, 46 g of nitrogen dioxide, and 17 g of ammonia.

Some elements of the programme

NEPP instituted some demanding targets for emissions control. Very large proportionate reductions were called for in the use of energy, water and materials; most emissions are to be reduced to 10–20% of their 1990 levels within 20 years. CFCs were to be phased out entirely by 1998, and greenhouse gas emissions should be below their 1989 levels by the year 2000. Lower materials usage is to be achieved through recycling, and integrated life cycle management. The programme was expected to cost the Netherlands government authorities $46 billion over the period 1990–1994; to put this in a context which is readily interpretable, this is equivalent to a lump sum tax on each household of $20 per month over the same period. The major costs of the programme however – in accord with the polluter pays principle – are to be met by industry. Substantial progress has already been made in controlling a variety of pollutants, as is evident from Figures 3.3–3.6. Nevertheless, the figures also show that longer term targets

are much tighter than the levels of control achieved so far.

Target groups

Agriculture The Netherlands economy contains a highly efficient agricultural sector, with extremely high crop yields supported by inorganic fertiliser, herbicide and pesticide use. Agriculture contributes about 5% to the nation's GDP, but is very important to the Dutch balance of payments, representing about one quarter of her export value. Despite the low share of output for which it accounts, the agricultural sector's share of total pollution rose to 35% in 1992 (from 20% just ten years earlier). Agricultural pollution is a consequence of intensive use of fertilisers, herbicides and pesticides, and the failure of the economy to be able to process animal manure into benign forms in sufficient quantity. Contamination of water systems by residuals in untreated manure

continued

CASE STUDY 1:   continued

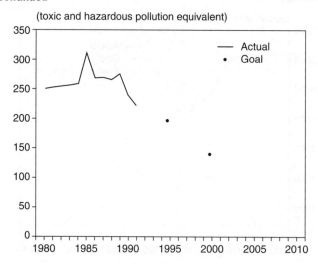

Figure 3.6 Toxic and hazardous pollution index, the Netherlands, 1980–91.
Source: adapted from Albert Adriaanse, *Environmental Policy Performance Indicators* (Sdu Uitgeverij Koninginnegracht, The Hague, 1993), pp. 47 and 53.

Note: The Toxic and Hazardous Pollution Index was calculated by using the emissions of the most hazardous substances in three main categories (pesticides, other wastes of high priority, and radioactive substances) weighted according to their toxicity and residence time in the environment.

causes eutrophication (the harmful loading of soil and water media with dissolved nutrient matter). This process harms animal and plant life, reduces the quality of water supplies, and generates feedback effects that reduce crop yields and, ultimately, cattle growth rates. NEPP contains provision for a substantial increase in manure processing capacity. With regard to pesticide use, the Dutch government estimates that of the 21 million kilograms of active pesticide ingredient applied annually, between 4 and 5 million kilograms enters air, groundwater and soil media as waste residuals. The Environment Plan provides for a 50% reduction in pesticide use by 2000.

Industry Industrial emissions are the principal form of pollution in the Netherlands, but the early stages of the environmental programme have already achieved much success in reducing industrial pollution flows (see Figure 3.5). However, cost-minimising behaviour implies that initial abatement efforts will be focused on the least expensive forms and areas of control; as the overall scale of abatement increases, the marginal cost of pollution reduction will rise, making further

control more expensive to the economy than has been the case hitheto.

Transportation Attempts to reduce pollution associated with transport are based upon a threefold approach. Fiscal measures are being implemented to provide economic incentives to reduce fuel demand; regulations will be used to control vehicle use in urban areas; and supply-side improvements, together with price incentives, are intended to increase the use of public rather than private transport.

Other elements of NEPP The NEPP places a strong emphasis on attempts to reduce acidification effects associated with energy production, and envisages that the incineration of waste products will play an important role in the provision of energy in the future. The construction sector is expected to modify its choice of methods and materials; more recycled materials are to be used, and design should incorporate the potential for recyclability. Less use is to be made of non-

continued

CASE STUDY 1:   continued

renewable and tropical region materials. Very demanding targets have been set to reduce the sector's environmental impact. In the consumption sector, separated waste collection systems are gradually being introduced, the composting of biological waste is to be increased, and pricing policy is designed to increase end-use energy efficiency. The retail trade sector is expected to provide sufficient information to enable consumers to make choices that are well-informed in terms of their environmental consequences.

Economic costs and political support

To date, NEPP appears to have won widespread support throughout the Netherlands. Business participation and involvement in designing programmes has been important not only in creating corporate support for NEPP, but also in minimising the costs of attaining the standards that have been achieved so far.

But the costs of abatement are large, and are expected to become substantially larger as the target constraints bite more strongly. Many of the elements in NEPP are being pursued unilaterally by the Netherlands, or are being taken to higher degrees of control than in other countries. Environmental control does impose real costs, although it also yields real benefits. However, these benefits will not typically be incorporated in the traded output of Dutch business. To the extent that control has this effect, the competitive position of Dutch goods and services in world markets will deteriorate. This is of course a problem that could be experienced by any single country or group of countries imposing unilateral or regional pollution control programmes. The Netherlands is a small open economy, very dependent on international trade, and with an export portfolio that includes large shares of goods that have adverse environmental impacts (such as agriculture and chemicals). The magnitude of this competitive disadvantage could, therefore, be quite large.

Source: WR (1994), chapter 14.

Discussion questions

1 Strong sustainability was defined as a process of development through time in which the nation's stock of environmental capital is non-decreasing. Is activity sustainable, however, even if the stocks of other forms of capital are falling through time?

2 To what extent are the ecologist's and the economist's concepts of sustainable behaviour mutually consistent?

3 Discuss the implications for accounting practices at the level of the firm if government seeks to pursue a programme of sustainable economic development.

Problems

1 Suppose Mr Field owns a plot of land which contains an oil well containing 1 million barrels of oil. A local extraction company has offered to extract this oil for Mr Field at $1 per barrel, the best deal he can obtain. The current market price of extracted oil is $3 a barrel, and is expected to stay at that level indefinitely. Now suppose that Mr Field decides to extract immediately and sell all the oil on his plot of land.

(a) How much economic profit (or rent) does Mr Field obtain?

(b) What is the effect on the GDP of the country in which Mr Field's plot is located?

(c) What will be the effect of the extraction decision on Mr Field's descendants?

(d) If Mr Field wished to arrange his affairs so that his descendants were at least as well off as he is, what actions might Mr Field take?

2 With computer economic modelling, Dow Chemical Corporation has been able to cut the need for a key reactant by 80%, eliminating 1000 metric tonnes of waste per year, and saving $8 million annually (WR, 1994, page 218).

(a) Has this change been economically efficient?

(b) Has this change contributed to more sustainable economic behaviour?

Further reading

Sustainability and sustainable development

There are many different interpretations of what sustainable development actually involves, and many different views on whether it can be achieved. Redclift (1992) examines a number of the dimensions within which the idea can be explored, as do Pezzey (1992, 1997), Barbier and Markandya (1990), Common and Perrings (1992), Common (1995) and Lele (1991). Farmer and Randall (1997) present an overlapping generations model in which sustainability issues are examined. Good general surveys are presented in Barbier (1989a), Klassen and Opschoor (1991) and Markandya and Richardson (1992). Beckerman (1994) debates whether the concept is a useful one. The argument that policy should be directed towards maintaining a non-declining natural capital stock is developed in Pearce and Turner (1990). The particular contributions of environmental economists to the debates are well represented by Pearce et al. (1989), Pearce (1991a), Common and Perrings (1992), Common (1995), Pezzey (1992) and Toman et al. (1993). More conventional economic contributions to the discussions, in the framework of a neoclassical growth model, are to be found in Solow (1974b, 1986) and Hartwick (1977, 1978). Cost–benefit analysis is often advocated as a device for achieving an efficient intertemporal allocation of resources. But its use may not be consistent with sustainable outcomes. Page (1997) compares two approaches to the problem of achieving the goals of sustainability and intergenerational efficiency. The long-term system implications of economic development and growth are discussed in Boulding (1966) and Daly (1974, 1977, 1987). An interesting assessment of the contribution of scientific understanding to the debate is to be found in Ludwig et al. (1993).

Ecological economics

Further discussion of ecological sustainability can be found in Common and Perrings (1992), on which our presentation relies heavily, Pearce (1987), Common (1995) and various articles in Costanza (1991). Conway (1985) discusses agriculture and ecology. A proposed system of environmental indicators for the UK is presented and discussed in RSPB (1994).

Environmental assessments and profiles

The basic references here are the biennial editions of *World Resources* and the United Nations Development Report. All of the recent issues of these two periodic publications contain a wealth of environmental data and case study analysis.

Accounting and pollution control at the firm level

Useful additional sources are *World Resources 1994-95*, especially chapter 12, Hirschborn (1991), EPA (1993), Schmidheiny (1992), Sarokin (1992), WWF (1993) and *Business Week* (1991). The role of the green consumer is examined in Smart (1992).

CHAPTER 4

Ethics and the environment

And God said, Let us make man in our image, after our likeness: and let them have dominion over the fish of the sea, and over the fowl of the air, and over the earth, and over every creeping thing that creepeth upon the earth.

Genesis 1: 24–8.

Introduction

Environmental economics is concerned with the allocation, distribution and use of environmental resources. To some extent, these matters can be analysed in a framework that does not require the adoption of any particular ethical viewpoint. We can focus our attention on answering questions of the form 'If X happens in a particular set of circumstances, what are the implications of X for Y?' Analyses of this form constitute what is sometimes described as positive economics.

However, limiting our scope to answering questions of this form is very restrictive. Many economists wish to address questions about what *should* be done in a particular set of circumstances. To do this it is necessary to make or use ethical judgements. Economists have usually employed some variety of utilitarianism whenever their work has gone beyond matters of positive economics. In particular, mainstream resource and environmental economics is infused with a predominantly utilitarian ethic.

Utilitarianism is not universally accepted, however. Other moral philosophies exist, with quite different implications for right or just behaviour. Part 1 of this chapter investigates a variety of ethical positions which have contributed to debate about environmental issues, and which continue to do so. However, our investigations will principally concern utilitarianism, particularly its limitations when being used as a framework in which the allocation of resources over many generations is being studied.

Part 2 of the chapter looks in detail at the discounting of future costs and benefits, a practice that has been the subject of much controversy. Within the economics profession, views differ widely as to when, how and why discounting should be undertaken and what criteria should be used in selecting a discount rate. Many non-economists regard the entire practice of discounting as being ethically indefensible.

In the third part of the chapter, the relationship between ethics and sustainable development is explored. Of central concern here is how sustainability goals can be incorporated into society's 'objective function': the ethical criterion that determines what policy makers try to maximise and how programmes or outcomes can be assessed. Some writers take the view that it is either not possible or not desirable to build a concern for sustainability directly into society's objectives. Instead, sustainability should be handled by imposing constraints on what actions or behaviour are permissible. Policy makers should them maximise the social objective function (whatever that may be) subject to these sustainability constraints.

PART 1
Ethical foundations for environmental economics[1]

Naturalist moral philosophies

A fundamental distinction can be drawn between two broad families of ethical sys-

---

[1] This section draws extensively upon the discussion in Kneese and Schulze (1985).

tems, humanist and naturalist moral philosophies. In humanist philosophies, rights and duties are accorded exclusively to human beings, either as individuals or as communities. While humans may be willing to treat other species tenderly or with respect, non-human things have no rights or responsibilities in themselves. A naturalist ethic denies this primacy or exclusivity to human beings. In this ethical framework, values do not derive from human beings, have no human psychological basis, nor reside in humans exclusively. Rather, rights can be defined only with respect to some natural system, including living and non-living components. A classic exposition of this ethic is to be found in Aldo Leopold's 'A Sand County Almanac' (1949), page 262:

> A thing is right when it tends to preserve the integrity, stability and beauty of the biotic community. It is wrong when it tends otherwise.

Peter Singer (1993) describes this position as a 'deep ecology' ethic. When a development is proposed, a deep ecologist might argue that the project would not be right if significant disturbances to ecosystems are likely to occur. Given that a large part of human behaviour does have significant ecological implications, strict adherence to a naturalist philosophy would prohibit much current and future human activity. The implications of a thoroughgoing adherence to such a moral philosophy seem to be quite profound, although much depends upon what constitutes a *significant* impact.

A weak form of naturalist ethic – roughly speaking, the notion that behaviour which has potentially large impacts on those parts of the biosphere that are deserving of safeguard because of their unusualness or scarcity should be prohibited – has had some impact on public policy in many countries. Examples include the designation of Sites of Special Scientific Interest and the consequent special provisions for management of these sites in the United Kingdom, the system of National Parks in the USA, and the designation of Internationally Important Sites by the World Wide Fund for Nature.

In the period since 1970, a number of important works have emerged which attempt to establish the nature of mankind's obligation to non-human beings. Much of this writing has made use of Kant's categorical imperative as the basis for ethical behaviour. An action is morally just only if it is performed out of a sense of duty and is based upon a valid ethical rule. Justice is not to be assessed in terms of the consequence of an action.

But what is a valid rule? According to Kant, a valid rule is a universal rule. Universality here means that such a rule can be applied consistently to every individual. He writes

> I ought never to act except in such a way that I can also will that my maxim [rule] should become a universal law.

This principle is Kant's categorical imperative. The basis of ethical behaviour is found in the creation of rules of conduct that each person believes should be universalised. For example, I might legitimately argue that the rule 'No person should steal another's property' is an ethical rule if I believe that everyone should be bound by that rule.

One categorical imperative suggested by Kant is the principle of respect for persons: no person should treat another exclusively as a means to his or her end. It is important to stress the qualifying adverb *exclusively*. In many circumstances we do treat people as means to an end; an employer, for example, regards members of his or her workforce as means of producing goods, to serve the end of achieving profits for the owner of the firm. This is not wrong in itself. What is imperative, and is wrong if it is not followed, is that all persons should be treated with the respect and moral dignity to which any person is entitled.

Kant was a philosopher in the humanist tradition. His categorical imperatives belong only to humans, and respect for 'persons' is similarly restricted. However, naturalists deny that such respect should be accorded only to humans. Richard Watson (1979) begins from this Kantian imperative of respect for persons, but amends it to the principle of respect for others. In discussing who is to count as 'others', Watson makes use of the principle of reciprocity, the capacity to knowingly act with regard to the welfare of others. He denies that only humans have the capacity for reciprocal behaviour, arguing that it is also evident in some other species of higher animal, including chimpanzees, dolphins and dogs. Such animals, Watson argues, should be attributed moral rights and obligations: at a minimum, these should include intrinsic rights to life and to relief from unnecessary suffering.

But many writers believe that human obligations extend to a far broader class of 'others'. The philosopher G. J. Warnock (1971) grappled with the concept of consideration, the circumstances that imply that something has a right for its interests to be taken into account in the conscious choices of others. Warnock concluded that all sentient beings – beings which have the capacity to experience pleasure or pain – deserve to be considered by any moral agent. So for Warnock, when you and I make economic decisions, we have a moral obligation to give some weight to the effects that our actions might have on any sentient being. This moral obligation is independent of any self-interest one may have.

Some other naturalist philosophers, while agreeing with the general premise that not only human interests matter, argue that the condition of sentience is too narrow. Our obligations to others extend beyond the class of other animals that can experience pain and pleasure. Kenneth Goodpaster (1978) concludes that all living beings have rights to be considered by any moral agent. W. Murray Hunt (1980) adopts an even stronger position. He concludes that 'being in existence', rather than being alive, confers a right to be considered by others. For Hunt, all

things that exist, living or dead, animate or inanimate, have intrinsic rights. This is, in effect, the deep ecology position of Leopold that we mentioned earlier.

Although our summary of naturalistic philosophies has been brief, it does demonstrate that the typical humanist philosophy adopted by most economists has not gone unchallenged. It seems to be the case that the moral foundations of some ecological and environmentalist arguments owe much to naturalistic ethics. This may account for why conventional economists and ecologists have found it difficult to agree on environmental issues.

Humanist moral philosophies

Two broad strands exist within the humanist tradition, the utilitarian and libertarian schools. Both see rights as residing exclusively within humans, but thereafter differ radically. We now briefly describe the libertarian ethical position, and follow that by a more extensive discussion of utilitarianism, the principal ethical basis of most economic analysis.

Libertarian moral philosophy

Libertarianism takes as its central axiom the fundamental inviolability of individual rights. There are no rights other than the rights of individuals, and economic and social behaviour is assessed in terms of whether or not it respects those rights. Actions that infringe individual rights cannot be justified by appealing to some supposed improvement in the level of social well-being. Libertarianism asserts the primacy of processes, procedures and mechanisms for ensuring that fundamental liberties and rights of individual human beings are respected and sustained. Rights are inherent in persons as individuals, and concepts such as community or social rights are not meaningful.

We will discuss the work of one influential libertarian philosopher, Robert Nozick

(1974). Nozick's intellectual foundations are in the philosophy of John Locke, and in particular his principle of just acquisition. Locke argued that acquisition is just when that which is acquired has not been previously owned and when an individual mixes his labour power with it. For Locke, this is the source of original and just property rights.

Nozick extends this argument. He asks when someone is entitled to hold (that is, own) something. His answer is a simple one:

> Whoever makes something, having bought or contracted for all other held resources used in the process (transferring some of his holdings for these co-operating factors), is entitled to it.

So any holding is a just holding if it was obtained by a contract between freely consenting individuals, provided that the seller was entitled to dispose of the object of the contract. (Not all people will be entitled to their holdings because they were obtained by theft or deception.) The key point in all of this is free action. Distributions are just if they are entirely the consequence of free choices, but not otherwise.

Libertarians are entirely opposed to concepts of justice based on consequences or outcomes. An outcome cannot in itself be morally good or bad. This kind of moral philosophy is likely to drastically limit the scope of what government may legitimately do. For example, redistributive policy (either between people, between countries or between generations) that requires taxation is coercive, and so unjust unless every affected person consents to it. Government action would be limited to maintaining the institutions required to support free contract and exchange. Those who believe in a limited role for government have adopted libertarianism most enthusiastically. However, it is by no means clear that a laisser-faire approach is necessarily implied, as can be seen when considering the following three questions that arise from the notion of just acquisition:

(1) What should government do about unjust holdings?

(2) How are open access or common property resources to be dealt with?
(3) How do external effects and public goods relate to the concept of just acquisition?

Utilitarianism

Utilitarianism originated in the writings of David Hume (1711–1776) and Jeremy Bentham (1748–1832), and found its most complete expression in the work of John Stuart Mill (1806–1873), particularly in his *Utilitarianism* (1863). There are two facets of utilitarianism. The first concerns how an individual derives pleasure or happiness. We shall have little to say about this aspect in this book, except when discussing the nature of individual valuation of non-traded and possibly intangible resources in Chapter 14. The second facet concerns the linkage between the individuals' utilities and social well-being. It is this facet to which our attention is mainly directed.

In terms of its ethical basis, utilitarianism is a consequentialist philosophy. The consequences or outcomes of an action determine the moral worth of the action. In this respect, it is fundamentally different from libertarianism. As we shall see, there are many possible variants of utilitarianism. One of these forms – classical utilitarianism – possesses three main components:

(1) an assertion that outcomes can be assessed only in terms of the extent to which they contribute to the social good;
(2) a criterion as to what constitutes individual good;
(3) the principle that individual good or well-being is comparable over persons and time.

The first component states that behaviour should be directed to producing the greatest amount of good for all persons in the aggregate. Utility was the term used by early utilitarian writers for the individual's pleasure or happiness. The social good (what we shall subsequently call well-being or welfare) is some aggregate of individual utilities. Subsequent utilitarian writers have adopted a broader view, arguing that things such as friendship, knowledge, courage and beauty have intrinsic worth, and so affect individual utilities and the social good.

One goal of the early utilitarians was to establish what utility consisted of, and which things conferred utility. Later writers have regarded this as a futile exercise. As individuals have different preferences, and these preferences are satisfied in different ways, it is not possible to develop a general description of what utility is, nor what things lead to it.

One thing that is agreed by all utilitarians is that the social well-being is some function of the utilities of all relevant persons. We shall examine shortly what form or forms this function might take. But whatever the answer to this, we can only obtain such an aggregate measure if individual utilities are comparable over persons (and over time if we wish to have an intertemporal measure of social well-being). This explains the need for the third component of utilitarianism that we identified earlier.

The majority of economists operate from the premise that the only relevant utilities are human utilities. But this is not the only possible position. We mentioned earlier a conclusion reached by the philosopher Peter Singer. In his book *Practical Ethics*, Singer adopts what he regards as being a utilitarian position, but he applies the concept in a rather different way. Utility is derived from gaining pleasure and avoiding pain. But since all sentient beings (by definition) can experience pleasure or pain, all can be regarded as capable of enjoying utility. Utility is a characteristic of sentience, not only of humanity. Singer concludes that the principle of judging actions on the basis of maximisation of utility is morally valid, but asserts that weight should be given to non-human as well as human utilities. Note, however, that even if one regarded human utilities as the sole component of the social good, this need not imply purely human-centred behaviour.

Human utility may depend upon the condition of other (animal or plant) lives, and if it does this will be incorporated in human utility functions.

Different writers use utilitarianism today in a variety of ways. According to Robert Solow (1974b), utilitarianism, in its broad sense, values social well-being as some function of the utilities of the individuals in a society. The particular form of this function assumed by classical utilitarians (and still widely used by economists) is additive: welfare is a weighted sum of the utilities of the individual members of the society. Solow describes utilitarianism using an additive form for welfare as narrow sense utilitarianism.

Utilitarianism and social well-being

We remarked earlier that classical economists regarded utility as being comparable over persons and over time. In fact, this is a premise of all forms of utilitarianism which assert the possibility of defining a measure of social well-being. In the absence of the ability to rank different sets of individual utilities (at one time or at different times), no function representing social well-being could be constructed.

It is now time to be more precise about how utilitarian measures of social well-being might be constructed. Let us first introduce some notation. Consider a hypothetical society consisting of two individuals, A and B, living at some particular point in time. One good (X) exists, the consumption of which is the only source of utility. Let U^A denote the total utility enjoyed by A, and U^B the total utility enjoyed by B, so we have

$$U^A = U^A(X^A)$$
$$U^B = U^B(X^B)$$
(4.1)

where X^A and X^B denote the quantities of the good consumed by A and B respectively. Solow's broad sense utilitarianism asserts that social welfare, W, is determined by a function of the form

$$W = W(U^A, U^B)$$
(4.2)

so that social welfare depends in some particular (but unspecified) way on the levels of utility enjoyed by each person in the relevant community. The social welfare function allows us to rank different configurations of individual utilities in terms of their social worth.

A narrow form utilitarian special case of the social welfare function (SWF) given by Equation 4.2 is obtained by making the SWF a weighted sum of individual utilities. The weights in such an aggregate measure reflect society's judgement of the relative worth of each person's utility. In the simplest case, weights are equal and social welfare is a simple sum of utilities of all individuals. For this special case we have

$$W = U^A + U^B \qquad (4.3)$$

Figure 4.1 illustrates one indifference curve, drawn in utility space, for such a welfare function. The social welfare indifference curve is a locus of combinations of individual utilities that yield a constant amount of social welfare, $\bar{W}$. The assumption that the welfare function is additive implies that the indifference curve, when drawn in utility space, is linear.

Distributional implications of utilitarianism

In general, utilitarianism does not carry any particular implication for the way output should be distributed between individuals in a society. However, if one is prepared to specify a particular form for the social welfare

function and also to specify the particular form of utility function for each individual, then matters change: one can then obtain specific distributional implications.

Let us see what implications follow in the special case we have just been discussing (a single good, two individuals with utility functions given by Equations 4.1 and the additive SWF specified in Equation 4.3). For simplicity, we also assume that there is a fixed total quantity of the good, denoted $\bar{X}$. In order to maximise welfare, X^A and X^B are chosen to maximise

$$W = U^A + U^B \qquad (4.4)$$

subject to the constraint that

$$X^A + X^B \leq \bar{X}$$

It is shown in Appendix 4.2 (using Lagrange's method of solving constrained optimisation problems that is outlined in Appendix 4.1) that the solution to this problem requires that

$$\frac{\mathrm{d}U^A}{\mathrm{d}X^A} = \frac{\mathrm{d}U^B}{\mathrm{d}X^B} \qquad (4.5)$$

This condition states that at a welfare maximum, the marginal utilities of consumption are the same for each individual. However, this still does not tell us how goods should be distributed. To find this, we need some information about the utility function of each individual. Consider the case where each person has the same utility function. That is

$$U^A = U^A(X^A) = U(X^A)$$
$$U^B = U^B(X^B) = U(X^B) \qquad (4.6)$$

It is then easy to see that in order for marginal utility to be equal for each person, the consumption level must be equal for each person. An additive welfare function, with equal weights on each person's utility, and identical utility functions for each person, implies that, at a social welfare maximum, individuals have equal consumption levels.

The solution to this problem is illustrated in Figure 4.2. Notice carefully that the diagram is now drawn in commodity space, not utility

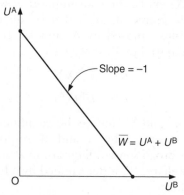

Figure 4.1 An indifference curve from a linear form of social welfare function.

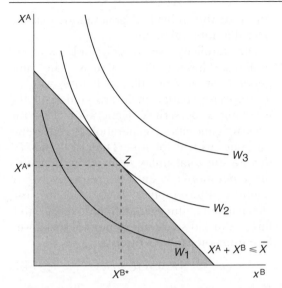

Figure 4.2 Maximisation of social welfare subject to a constraint on the total quantity of goods available.

space. Under the common assumption of diminishing marginal utility, the linear indifference curves in utility space in Figure 4.1 map into indifference curves that are convex from below in commodity space. The curves labelled W_1, W_2 and W_3 are social welfare indifference curves, with $W_1 < W_2 < W_3$. Remember that we assume that there is a fixed quantity of the good $\bar{X}$ available to be distributed between the two individuals. Max-

imum social welfare, W_2, is attained at the point Z where the consumption levels enjoyed by each person are X^{A*} and X^{B*}. The maximised level of social welfare will, of course, depend on the magnitude of $\bar{X}$. But irrespective of the level of maximised welfare, the two consumption levels will be equal.

In the example we have just looked at, the result that consumption levels will be the same for both individuals was a consequence of the particular assumptions that were made. But utilitarianism does not necessarily imply equal distributions of goods. An unequal distribution at a welfare maximum may occur under any of the following conditions:

(1) the weights attached to individual utilities are not equal;
(2) utility functions differ between individuals;
(3) the SWF is not of the additive form specified in Equation 4.3.

To illustrate the second condition, suppose that the utility functions of two persons, A and B, are as shown in Figure 4.3. Individual A enjoys a higher level of utility than individual B for any given level of consumption. It is evident that A and B have different utility functions. Because of that difference in the utility functions, the marginal utilities of the

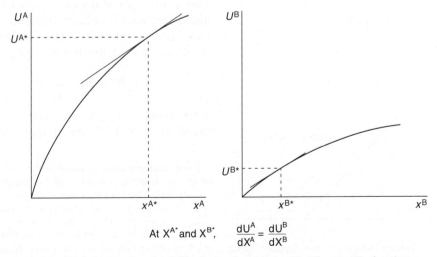

At X^{A*} and X^{B*}, $\quad \dfrac{dU^A}{dX^A} = \dfrac{dU^B}{dX^B}$

Figure 4.3 Maximisation of social welfare for two individuals with different utility functions.

two individuals can only be equal at different levels of consumption by A and B. It may help in interpreting the diagram to recall that the value of marginal utility at a particular level of consumption is indicated by the slope of the (total) utility function at that point.

Individuals and generations: the intertemporal social welfare function

Many of the issues with which we deal in this text involve choices that affect the time at which a given set of individuals enjoys consumption, or which affect different generations of people over time. It will be useful, therefore, to place our discussion of utilitarianism in an intertemporal framework. One way of doing this is to reinterpret 'individuals' and 'society'. We could think of an individual as one particular generation of people. Another individual is another generation of people. Society is then a sequence of generations living through some specified interval of time. With this change in interpretation, utilitarianism can address the relationship between the social welfare of a society of consecutive generations and the

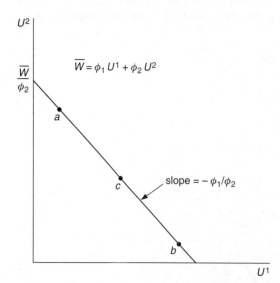

Figure 4.4   Intertemporal utilitarian social welfare function indifference curve.

utility of the individual generations existing over that interval of time.

For simplicity, we consider only two generations. This will allow us to use the same general form of notation as before, with an appropriate change in interpretation of the indexing superscripts. Generation 1 is the present generation; generation 2 represents the one which follows. Then U^1 and U^2 denote the total utility enjoyed by members of generations 1 and 2, respectively. W denotes intertemporal social welfare (or, alternatively, intergenerational social welfare). A broad sense intertemporal social welfare function can be written as[2]

$$W = W(U_1, U_2) \qquad (4.7)$$

Narrow sense utilitarianism, as illustrated in Figure 4.4, implies an additive form of welfare function

$$W = \phi_1 U_1 + \phi_2 U_2 \qquad (4.8)$$

so that W is a weighted average of the utilities of each generation, where ϕ_1 and ϕ_2 are the weights used in summing utility over generations to obtain a measure of social welfare. From where might such weights come? One answer is given by the common practice of 'time discounting' in which the weights can be interpreted as time discount factors. For example, setting $\phi_1 = 1$ and $\phi_2 = 1/(1 + \rho)$, where ρ is a social discount rate, we obtain a utilitarian social welfare function in which (one period ahead) future utility is discounted at the proportionate rate ρ. That is

$$W = U_1 + \frac{U_2}{1 + \rho} \qquad (4.9)$$

Time discounting, as we shall see in more detail in Part 2 of this chapter, implies (if

---

[2] Note that this form of social welfare is already quite restrictive. It assumes that we can meaningfully refer to an aggregate level of total utility for each generation, and that social welfare is a function of these aggregate quantities, but not of the distributions of well-being within generations (except in so far as this affects the relevant aggregate). We do not pursue this any further, but see Broome (1992) for further analysis.

$\rho > 0$) that future utility 'counts for less' than the same quantity of present utility in obtaining a measure of intertemporal welfare.

Rawls: a theory of justice

The work of John Rawls in *A Theory of Justice* (1971) has had a remarkable influence upon the consideration given by economists to ethical issues. Rawls's work appears to challenge utilitarianism, or more precisely classical utilitarianism. His objection to that ethic is grounded in the following assertion, that being indifferent to the distribution of satisfaction between individuals (and only being concerned with the sum of utilities), a distribution of resources produced by maximising utility could violate fundamental freedoms and rights that are inherently worthy of protection.

In common with many moral philosophers, Rawls seeks to establish the principles of a just society. Rawls adopts an approach that owes much to the ideas of Kant. Valid principles of justice are those which would be agreed by everyone if we could freely, rationally and impartially consider just arrangements. In order to ascertain the nature of these principles of justice, Rawls employs the device of imagining a hypothetical state of affairs (the 'original position') prior to any agreement about principles of justice, the organisation of social institutions, and the distribution of material rewards and endowments. In this original position, individuals exist behind a 'veil of ignorance'; each person has no knowledge of his or her inherited characteristics (such as intelligence, race and gender), nor of the position he or she would take in any agreed social structure. Additionally, individuals are assumed to be free of any attitudes that they would have acquired through having lived in particular sets of circumstances. The veil of ignorance device would, according to Rawls, guarantee impartiality and fairness in the discussions leading to the establishment of the social con-

tract. Rawls then seeks to establish the nature of the social contract that would be created by freely consenting individuals in the original position.

He reasons that, under these circumstances, people would unanimously agree on two fundamental principles of justice. These are:

> First: each person is to have an equal right to the most extensive basic liberty compatible with a similar liberty for others.

> Second: social and economic inequalities are to be arranged so that they are both (a) reasonably expected to be to everyone's advantage, and (b) attached to positions and offices and open to all ...[The Difference Principle]

It is the second principle that is of interest here. The Difference Principle asserts that inequalities are only justified if they enhance the position of everyone in society (if they lead to Pareto improvements).[3] The Difference Principle has been interpreted as a presumption in favour of equality of position; deviations from an equal position are unjust except in the special cases where all persons would benefit (or perhaps where the least advantaged benefit). Economists have tried to infer what a Rawlsian position would imply for the nature of a social welfare function (SWF).[4] Robert Solow, for example, argues that a Rawlsian SWF for a society of individuals at one point in time is of the so-called 'max–min' form, which for two individuals would be:

$$W = \min\{U^{A}, U^{B}\} \qquad (4.10)$$

Two SWF indifference curves from such a function are illustrated in Figure 4.5. As the utility level of the least advantaged person

---

[3] In other places, Rawls seems to advocate a rather different position, however, arguing that inequalities are justified in particular when they maximally enhance the position of the least advantaged person in society.

[4] However, notice that one could argue that such an attempt forces Rawls's theory into a utilitarian framework, something of which he would probably strongly disapprove.

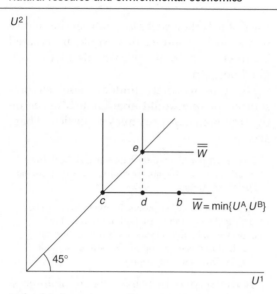

Figure 4.5 Intertemporal Rawlsian social welfare function indifference curve.

determines welfare, a Rawlsian SWF implies that raising the utility of the person with the lowest utility level can increase welfare. Compare the two points labelled b and c in Figure 4.5, which by virtue of lying on one indifference curve generate identical levels of social welfare. Starting from point b, reallocate utility between persons, by subtracting $\{b - d\}$ utility from person 1 and adding this to person 2. The point labelled e will have been attained on another indifference curve with a higher level of social welfare. It is clear that the only combinations of utility for which higher welfare levels are not possible through interpersonal transfers of utility are those which lie along the 45° ray from the origin. Along this locus, utility is allocated equally between individuals. So for any given total amount of utility, a Rawlsian social welfare function implies that, whenever utility levels differ between individuals, it is possible to increase social welfare by redistributing utility from individuals with higher utility to those with lower utility. An egalitarian distribution is implied by this logic.

However, the validity of this argument requires that the total level of utility will necessarily be independent of its distribution.

This is not necessarily true. There are some grounds for believing that total utility could be higher in an unequal position if incentive effects enhance productive efficiency. But note carefully that Rawls is not a utilitarian, and the fact that total utility might be higher in a situation in which utility is unequally distributed than one in which it is equally distributed does not of itself make the former a just distribution. Rawls's Difference Principle asserts that it is only just to have an unequal distribution if all persons benefit from that allocation.

But let us now turn our attention to the distribution of resources between generations; that is, intertemporal distributions. Rawls writes very little about this, and he does not reach any firm conclusion. Robert Solow suggests that a consistent extension of Rawls's logic implies that a two-period SWF would be of the form given in Equation 4.10, with A and B now denoting generations. By similar reasoning to that we used earlier, intertemporal social welfare maximisation implies that utility should be distributed equally between generations. Moreover, if utility functions were the same at all time periods, this would also imply equality of consumption levels over time.

Criticisms of utilitarianism

We have looked at several variants of the utilitarian ethic. However, utilitarianism has not been without its critics. One line of criticism comes from those who challenge the philosophical basis of utilitarianism itself. It is clear that an adherent to a naturalistic moral philosophy will be unable to accept the validity of an ethic which views rights and values as being inherent only in human beings. It should be noted, however, that it is possible to broaden the scope of utilitarianism so that the pleasure or happiness of non-human beings is accorded weight in a social welfare function. A libertarian moral philosophy also poses a fundamental challenge to utilitarianism. However, in this section attention is limited to criticisms of the kind of utilitarianism that is commonly used by economists.

One critique argues that the economist's concept of utility is defined too narrowly to be an adequate description of human economic behaviour. Utilitarians regard the objective of economic behaviour as being the maximisation of the enjoyment derived from the goods and services consumed in a given period of time. But there are grounds for believing that individuals are motivated by something broader than utility in this sense. For want of a better term, let us call this well-being. Whether this matters depends on the extent to which the distinction between utility and well-being is significant.

Sen (1987) regards it as being so. He sees well-being as a multidimensional quantity, depending not only on what goods and services are possessed or consumed, but also on various attributes that people possess as citizens. Of particular importance are the freedoms individuals possess. Democracy, free speech, tolerance and the other liberal freedoms are intrinsically valuable. This value is over and above the instrumental benefits that may arise from exercising these freedoms. So for Sen, social welfare is much broader than merely satisfaction derived from consumption.

But Sen's critique does not stop there. Well-being, even in this broad sense, is not the only thing that is valuable. All persons have a fundamental dualism, being concerned with their well-being but also pursuing objectives which are not exclusively self-interested. Individuals may seek to eliminate nuclear defence, promote the conservation of whales, or may wish poverty to be eliminated. For some people, much of their activity may be directed to pursuing such goals even though this does not affect their personal well-being. Once the scope of things regarded as being inherently valuable is extended in these two directions, the problems of quantification and comparability mentioned earlier become more complex. This does not in itself imply that utilitar-

ianism should be abandoned, but rather that its practice is far more problematic than many would usually admit.

The final criticism of utilitarianism that we consider is the problem of unjust consequences. In simple versions of utilitarianism, the goodness of an action is judged by its effect on aggregate welfare. But this poses great difficulties in cases where sacrifices by a few are demanded to improve the overall lot. The logic of utilitarianism might lead someone to advocate the killing of all persons over the age of 65 on the grounds that this would improve social welfare. To some extent, such 'problems' arise from the fact that classical utilitarianism is essentially a consequentialist philosophy, in which good is measured only by the outcome attained, and not by the means of achieving that outcome. If the nature of social welfare is defined in a broad way, taking adequate account of well-being and agency, the problems inherent in a philosophy in which unbridled self-interest is the only source of value can be avoided.

PART 2
Utilitarianism and discounting

> Two forms of discount rate:
> the utility discount rate and the
> consumption discount rate

We have seen that the ethical framework that underpins conventional economics is utilitarianism, and that a form of intertemporal social welfare function commonly used in economic analysis is:

$$W = \frac{1}{(1+\rho)^0} U_0 + \frac{1}{(1+\rho)^1} U_1$$
$$+ \ldots + \frac{1}{(1+\rho)^T} U_T \qquad (4.11)$$
$$= \sum_{t=0}^{t=T} \frac{1}{(1+\rho)^t} U_t$$

This is equivalent to Equation 4.9 but for the fact that welfare is being summed not over two periods but over $T + 1$ periods (i.e. period 0, the present period, through to period T).

In many problems we shall be investigating, an infinite time horizon will be used, in which case Equation 4.11 will be

$$W = \sum_{t=0}^{t=\infty} \frac{1}{(1+\rho)^t} U_t \qquad (4.12)$$

In later chapters it will be convenient to work with the continuous time version of Equation 4.12:

$$W = \int_{t=0}^{t=\infty} U_t e^{-\rho t} dt \qquad (4.13)$$

In this formulation, ρ is known as the utility discount rate. This is the rate at which the value of a small increment of utility falls as its date of receipt is delayed. Thus if one unit of utility received next period were regarded as less valuable by a proportion of 0.1 (i.e. 10%) than one unit of utility received this period, then $\rho = 0.1$.

The versions of the intertemporal SWF we have just described contain utility levels as arguments. However, it is conventional to suppose that utility is a function of consumption. Most writers specify that

$$U_t = U(C_t) \qquad (4.14)$$

so that utility at time t is determined only by consumption at that time. This is what Pezzey (1997) has recently labelled absolute materialism. However, as we shall see later, in the section on ethics and sustainable development, it is not the only possible formulation, nor is it necessarily the most appropriate one to use.

Given the assumption of absolute materialism, and working in discrete time with a finite time horizon, the intertemporal SWF can be written more explicitly as

$$W = \frac{1}{(1+\rho)^0} U(C_0) + \frac{1}{(1+\rho)^1} U(C_1)$$

$$+ \ldots + \frac{1}{(1+\rho)^T} U(C_T) \qquad (4.15)$$

$$= \sum_{t=0}^{t=T} \frac{1}{(1+\rho)^t} U(C_t)$$

As W is indirectly a function of C, it is possible to rewrite the welfare function directly in terms of consumption (as opposed to utility). The precise form taken by this function will depend upon $U(C)$, the relationship between consumption and utility. For some special cases of utility function, the welfare function can be written in the form:

$$W = \frac{1}{(1+r)^0} C_0 + \frac{1}{(1+r)^1} C_1$$

$$+ \ldots + \frac{1}{(1+r)^T} C_T \qquad (4.16)$$

In this case, r is a constant parameter that we shall call the consumption discount rate. This is the rate at which the value of a small increment of consumption changes as its date is delayed. However, in general it will not be the case that there is a single consumption discount rate as in Equation 4.16; instead that rate will change over time, as we show later in this section.

We have now seen that there is not one discount rate but two – a utility rate and a consumption rate. It is important to be careful about which rate is being referred to in discussions of discounting. Much confusion arises in the literature as a result of a failure to make this distinction when discussing 'the discount rate'.

The consequences of discounting

Let us examine the consequences of discounting. We deal with the discounting of utility, but similar arguments can be made about consumption discounting. Consider the relative contributions to welfare of utility at different points in time, using the welfare function given in Equation 4.11. Suppose that the level of utility in each generation is 100 units, and that the utility discount rate is 0.1 (or 10%) per period. Let T be 50. Now compare the contributions to welfare of these 100 units of utility today (period 0) and 50 periods later. The welfare contribution of 100 units of utility in period 0 is 100;

that is, $100/(1.1)^0 = 100$. The welfare contribution of 100 units of utility in period 50 is approximately 0.852 (i.e. $100/(1.1)^{50} = 0.852$), about 117 times smaller.

If policy is dictated by trying to maximise the value of W, a utility-discounted welfare function might be loosely described as discriminating against future generations, by giving their utility levels less weight in the maximisation exercise. It is this feature of discounting which leads many persons to regard any positive discount rate as ethically indefensible.

In subsequent chapters (especially Chapters 7 to 10) we shall be analysing the optimal use of resources over time, assuming that society's welfare function is of the discounted utilitarian form. It will be shown that the optimal path over time of consumption and resource use does depend critically upon the particular utility discount rate selected. Intuition suggests that higher utility discount rates will lead to patterns of resource use that are more rapacious, implying greater depletion in earlier years. This intuition is shown to be more or less correct. However, it is not valid to argue that consumption (or real income) will fall over time if high discount rates are used. We will demonstrate that rising consumption over time may be consistent with a positive utility discount rate.

The relationship between the utility and consumption discount rates

To deduce the relationship between the utility and consumption discount rates we work with the discounted utilitarian function in continuous time, continuing to assume that utility is a function only of current consumption. That is:

$$W = \int_{t=0}^{t=T} U(C_t)e^{-\rho t}dt$$

Furthermore, we make the conventional assumptions that, in the utility function $U = U(C)$, utility is an increasing function of consumption, but that it increases at a decreasing rate. That is, the first derivative of utility with respect to consumption is positive, but its second derivative is negative

$$\frac{dU}{dC} = U'(C) > 0, \; \frac{d^2U}{dC^2} = U''(C) < 0$$

A utility function that satisfies these assumptions is illustrated in Figure 4.6.

Now define the elasticity of marginal utility with respect to consumption, η, to be

$$\eta(C) = -\frac{C \cdot U''(C)}{U'(C)} > 0$$

We know that the consumption rate of discount, r, is the rate at which the value of a small increment of consumption changes as its date is delayed. It is shown in Appendix 4.3 that the consumption discount rate, r, can be expressed as

$$r = \rho + \eta \frac{\dot{C}}{C} \tag{4.17}$$

It is clear from this expression that the consumption rate of discount depends upon three things:

(1) the utility discount rate ρ

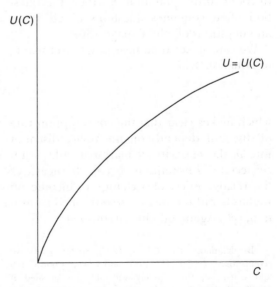

Figure 4.6 Conventional form of an individual's utility function.

(2) the elasticity of marginal utility with respect to consumption η

(3) the proportionate rate of growth of consumption, $\dot{C}/C$.

The consumption and utility discount rates will only be equal when $\eta\dot{C}/C$ is zero. This would occur if (i) $\dot{C}/C = 0$, implying that $\dot{C} = 0$, and so that consumption remains at a constant level over time, or (ii) $\eta = 0$. It can be shown that $\eta = 0$ only if utility is a linear function of consumption.[5] Notice also, from Equation 4.17, that even if the utility discount rate ρ is greater than zero, it is possible that the consumption discount rate r will be negative. This would occur if the level of consumption is falling at a sufficiently high rate.

What numerical values should be selected for the utility and consumption discount rates?

Discussions about which value to set for the discount rate are often confusing because, as Arrow et al. (1996) point out, 'three separate issues are being addressed: how to discount the *welfare* or *utility* of future generations, how to discount future dollars, and how to discount future pollution. Further, the question often combines questions of efficiency and questions of ethics' (page 130).

We can make some headway by returning to Equation 4.17

$$r = \rho + \eta\frac{\dot{C}}{C}$$

which makes clear that the consumption rate of discount depends on the utility discount rate ρ, the elasticity of marginal utility with respect to consumption η (which measures the relative effect of a change in income on welfare), and the rate of growth of consumption, $\dot{C}/C$. Again, quoting Arrow et al.:

This equation sets out explicitly the two reasons for discounting future consumption: either (1) one cares less about tomorrow's consumer than today's, or about one's own welfare tomorrow than today's (reflected in the first term, ρ); or else (2) one believes tomorrow's consumer will be better off than today's (reflected in the second term).

The utility discount rate

The utility discount rate is sometimes described as the pure rate of time preference. If the time preference rate is positive, this implies some form of impatience; utility is preferred sooner rather than later. While it may be true that individuals exhibit such impatience, it is not necessarily the case that society as a whole either does or should exhibit such impatience. Indeed, many people argue that in comparing utilities over successive generations, the only ethically defensible position is that utilities attaching to each generation should be treated equally, implying a zero rate of utility discounting.

One argument used to justify a positive utility discount rate is that there is, for every point in time in the future, a positive probability that the human species will become extinct. Presumably this probability is very small, but one would expect it to increase as the length of time into the future exists. One may take the view that future generations should be given less weight than the present, given that we cannot be certain of the existence of any future generation.

It seems reasonable to say that those who have attempted to derive values for ρ from first principles, and who are concerned with matters of intergenerational choice, have generally concluded that the value should be zero, or at most only slightly above it (no higher than 1% or 2%).

The consumption discount rate

Even if one were to accept that ρ should be (or actually is) zero, this does not imply that the consumption discount rate will necessarily be zero, as the term $\eta\dot{C}/C$ may be non-

---

[5] By definition, $\eta = -C\,U''(C)/U'(C)$. So for $\eta = 0$, we require that $-C\,U''(C)/U'(C) = 0$. As by assumption $C > 0$ and $U'(C) > 0$, this equality will only be satisfied if $U''(C) = 0$. The second derivative of the utility function will only be zero everywhere if the utility function is linear.

zero. Under the plausible assumptions we have made about the form of the utility function, η will be a positive number. It is generally thought (see Arrow *et al.*, page 132) that this value lies in the range 1 to 2.

The relative sizes of t and p will then depend on the sign of the consumption growth rate, $\dot{C}/C$. If consumption is growing over time $\dot{C}/C > 0$ and so the consumption discount rate would exceed the utility discount rate. To many people, this is an intuitively reasonable conclusion. If an economy is experiencing a growth in income and consumption through time, then an additional unit of consumption will be worth less to a typical person in the future than to such a person now, as the former will be more affluent. Suppose that an individual receives less additional (marginal) utility from further units of the good as his or her total consumption level increases, then additional units of consumption are worth less to an individual the higher the initial level of consumption. Arguments that the expectation of continuing technical progress justifies discounting can be regarded as a variation on this theme. Technical progress leads, other things being equal, to consumption possibilities being increased over time. Note that the arguments based on consumption growth and technical progress are related to the consumption (but not the utility) discount rate.

This shows the central problem in selecting discount rates: we need to make an assumption about appropriate future values of the growth rate of consumption (g, let us say). But the range of plausible estimates is immense, covering at least the interval 1% to 5% for the world as a whole, and up to as much as 10% for growth in particular places.

Where does this leave us? With $\rho = 0$ and $\eta = 1.5$ and $g = 1.6$, for example (as suggested by Cline, 1992), we obtain $r = 2.4\%$. But with $\rho = 0$ and $\eta = 1.0$ and $g = 1$, reflecting slower long-term trend growth, $r = 1\%$.

Market interest rates and the consumption rate of interest

Some economists are unhappy with the approach of trying to deduce discount rates from first principles, arguing instead that the consumption discount rate should be based on observed or revealed behaviour.

We demonstrate in the next chapter that, under certain conditions, the market rate of interest will be equal to the consumption discount rate. The result we shall demonstrate there is that

$$i = r = \delta \qquad (4.18)$$

where i denotes the market interest rate on risk-free lending and borrowing, δ denotes the rate of return on capital, and r is the consumption discount rate. As i (and possibly δ) is an observable quantity, Equation 4.18 provides us with a criterion for selecting r, should we need it. Notice also that Equation 4.18 states that $r = \delta$. This provides the rationale for an alternative criterion: the discount rate should be equal to the marginal product of capital.

This approach typically yields substantially higher rates than the previous method, usually in the neighbourhood of 5–7%. However, there is great variation in the rates obtained in this way, with some observed real rates of return as high as 20%. It is also by no means clear that the preferences underlying these rates are the ones that are relevant for the discount rate choices that confront the environmental economist.

Divergences between the social and private rates of time preference

The argument that the market rate of interest serves as an observable benchmark for the consumption discount rate is an attractive one. But its validity depends on the existence of a set of conditions that are unlikely to be met in practice. These amount to the requirement that no forms of market

---

Box 4.1 Discount rate choices in practice

As our analysis has shown, there is no unequivocally correct single rate of discount. Indeed, Heal (1981) argues that 'The discount rate is not something we measure; it is something we choose', and Page (1977) writes 'After a lot of time trying to discover an unassailable definition of the social rate of discount, economists are beginning to decide that a totally satisfactory definition does not exist'.

In practice, what is usually wanted is a number for the consumption discount rate, so as to compare flows of consumption or income (rather than utility) over time. When pressed for a particular number, economists have conventionally advocated setting the social (consumption) discount rate at the level of long-term interest rates on government bonds, plus a risk premium where appropriate. This would suggest values in the neighbourhood of 5% per annum. What values have been used 'officially' for social discount rates in the USA and the UK?

In 1969, a United States Congressional hearing found that agencies were using discount rates from zero to 20%, with no clear logic dictating the level in any particular instance. Very often, rates are set reflecting political pressures and goals. For example, in the years of the Nixon administration, the federal government chose to use rates near the top of the then prevailing 3–12% band in order to reduce the level of public expenditure. From time to time, single target rates have been set by the federal authorities. In 1970, the Office of Management and Budget required all federal agencies to use a 10% discount rate, although some project areas were treated differently. In particular, discount rates for water resource projects were set annually by the US Treasury Department, and have typically been around 2.5%. In 1986, the US Congressional Budget Office required the general use of a 2% discount rate, roughly equal to the real cost of borrowing on world markets. A detailed analysis of US discounting practices can be found in the March 1990 Special Issue of the *Journal of Environmental Economics and Management* (Vol 18, No 2, Part 2).

Little more consistency seems to characterise choices of social discount rates in the UK. Some recent choices have been:

- 1988: UK Treasury 'Test' Discount Rate of 5%
- 1990: UK Treasury: 6% rate on most public sector investments, but 8% for public transport
- 1994: UK Treasury 'Target' Discount Rate for public sector investment, 8%. Forestry projects to be discounted at 6% if non-market benefits included

One particularly awkward matter has been the use of different discount rates where project areas are deemed to carry positive external benefits. In the USA, this has been true for water resource project appraisal, while in the UK, forestry projects have often been discounted at unusually low rates. This practice is not desirable and the appropriate way of proceeding is to measure externalities in a project appraisal, rather than to assume they exist and set *ex ante* an adjusted discount rate to reflect this assumption.

---

failure exist[6] in the economy. The rates of time preference or rates of return on capital observed in actual markets may, however, be inappropriate guides to their unobservable 'social' counterparts.

Marglin (1963) compares individual and social time preference. He argues that society as a whole would choose to save more collectively than the sum of individuals' private savings decisions. This follows from the fact that the investment of saved funds provides external consumption benefits in the future. No individual expects to be able to appropriate more than a tiny proportion of these

external benefits, and so private savings decisions will tend to ignore these external returns. An example of this might be investment in water resource projects: if such investments improve public health, the project will certainly have positive external effects in the future. The government, acting as a collective agent, can compare total returns with total sacrifices of present consumption. In evaluating projects with substantial external future consumption benefits, therefore, a lower discount rate should be adopted than that used in private markets. The essence of this argument is that the social rate of time preference is the relevant magnitude to use when trying to determine a social discount rate. Market failure makes it

---

[6] The concept of market failure is explained at length in Chapter 6.

unlikely that social and market (private) rates of time preference will coincide.

A similar argument revolves around the distinction that Sen draws between the roles of individuals as citizens and as consumers. As citizens, individuals may prefer to discount future costs and benefits at a lower rate than they do as consumers. However, even if this were true, the question arises of whether it would be legitimate for government or some other environmental planner to impose what it regards as people's citizen-preferences on their behalf.

Pigou (1920) argued that individuals might underestimate the pleasure that future consumption would in fact give them. Individuals who are myopic in this way, underestimating the utility of future consumption, are suffering from 'defective telescopic faculty'. One might then argue that the discount rates that should be used in intertemporal comparisons are lower than those that myopic individual behaviour implies. Once again, this raises the very difficult question of the extent to which government should act against the expressed opinions of individuals.

The principles and practice of discounting are very controversial, with many fundamental and largely unresolved theoretical controversies. In addition, many practical problems exist that are difficult to resolve satisfactorily. For example, taxes and transaction costs drive a wedge between market rates of return and time preference rates; in practice, the market rate of return exceeds the time preference rate, destroying the equality given in Equation 4.18. Unfortunately, all of this leaves us in a rather unsatisfactory situation: the choice of discount rate does matter, but we have no easy way of knowing what that rate should be.

PART 3
Ethics and sustainable development

We argued in Chapter 3 that sustainability and sustainable development are fundamen-

tally ethical in nature. A belief that development should be sustainable asserts that those people currently living have moral obligations to future generations. We also argued in the first two parts of this chapter that the ethical dimension of utilitarianism is reflected in the forms of social welfare function (SWF) typically adopted in economic analysis.

However, these ethics may not be compatible. It is possible that the consequences of maximising a conventional utilitarian SWF may be incompatible with sustainability. We will demonstrate later that this is indeed so. To anticipate the conclusions we shall reach, only under special circumstances will maximising a conventional utilitarian SWF be consistent with sustainability. In general, there is no reason to believe that conventional optimality criteria will yield sustainable outcomes.

How do those economists who believe that sustainability matters propose that concern for the well-being of future generations be incorporated into economic analysis? Three approaches can be identified.

(1) Adoption of an intertemporal social welfare function, the maximisation of which leads to a sustainable outcome.
(2) Imposition of one or more constraints that ensure that a (constrained) maximum of the intertemporal social welfare function will yield a sustainable outcome.
(3) Selection of an appropriate discount rate that will guarantee a sustainable outcome.

Let us now examine each of these approaches.

(1) Specification of a social welfare function that incorporates sustainability.
The steps here are simple in principle. First, a criterion of sustainability is chosen. Second, a SWF is specified which has the following property: any optimal solution to a problem involving that SWF satisfies that sustainability criterion (provided that sustainability is feasible).

One example is the approach taken by Solow (1974b) that we examined earlier. Solow equates sustainability with intergenerational equity. In particular, he advocated using a Rawlsian ethical framework, and suggested that this led to a SWF of the form

$$W = \min\{U_1, U_2\}$$

Maximisation of this welfare function would entail each generation of people having equal utility, and so being sustainable according to his criterion.

Unfortunately, there are some problems with this approach, not least of which is that we may not all agree on what is the relevant criterion of sustainability. Solow's criterion, for example, has been widely criticised. Second, this kind of approach imposes sustainability as an absolute, binding constraint. It may be more appropriate to specify a SWF in which sustainability matters but not to the exclusion of all else. In other words, it is not given a weighting of infinity in society's objective function.

Pezzey (1997) suggests a way of making sustainability matter but not absolutely so. He proposes replacing a social welfare function built upon the premise of absolute materialism such as

$$W = \sum_{t=0}^{t=\infty} \frac{1}{(1+\rho)^t} U(C_t)$$

with one based upon relative materialism[7]

$$W = \sum_{t=0}^{t=\infty} \frac{1}{(1+\rho)^t} U(\{C_t\})_t$$

What is the difference between these two expressions? Both state that social welfare is a discounted sum of utilities in each period (or each generation). They differ in terms of what each generation's utility depends upon. In the first case,

the utility of generation t depends only on consumption by that generation. The second case allows the utility of generation t to depend on the consumption levels of all generations (the term $\{C_t\}$ denotes the whole time path of consumption, that is C_t for $t = 0$ to $t = \infty$). This allows concern for the future, a commitment to improvement over time, and various other forms of 'socially responsible' attitudes to enter the welfare function. The precise way in which these concerns enter the SWF depends on the particular functional forms chosen. Pezzey suggests that this is an important area for further research.

(2) Adoption of constraints that ensure a sustainable outcome. What might these constraints be? Our discussion of sustainability in Chapter 3 suggests a number of possibilities. These include not allowing the size of the natural capital stock to fall (that is, imposing what Pearce *et al.* (1989) call a 'strong sustainability' constraint), or disallowing developments that have a high likelihood of leading to ecological disruption (although this will not itself guarantee the attainment of sustainability).

There are three principal difficulties in this approach. First (as we discussed earlier), imposing an absolute sustainability constraint may be too strong. Second, it may be difficult to establish what kind of constraints would in fact be consistent with sustainability. Indeed, in the presence of uncertainty, there can be no guarantee of sustainability whatever we do. Finally, the approach leaves the original SWF unchanged. To many writers, our principal concern should lie with the appropriate form of SWF – reflecting the mechanisms by which social choices are made and through which cultural values of what is 'socially good' are constructed – not with constraints we may choose to impose on behaviour.

---

[7] In fact Pezzey also suggests using a different form of discounting. But that is not an issue we wish to discuss here.

(3) The use of a 'sustainability' discount rate. A central issue in the theory of project appraisal has been what value to select for the discount rate to use in weighting future costs or benefits that are likely to accrue over very long time scales. We shall have something more to say about this issue in Chapters 6 and 15, but mention it here because it is sometimes argued that discount rates should be lower than 'normal' (and possibly zero) when long spans of time are involved.

The rationale for this is not clear. One line of argument seems to be that there is a fundamental difference between the way we should handle the passage of time when attention is being paid to a given set of individuals and when successive generations are affected. The usual practice in conventional environmental economics analysis is to use positive consumption discount rates, even when very long time periods are being considered, and to deny that there is any difference between discounting consumption flows over one individual's lifetime and over successive generations. But many economists are uneasy about using this equivalence.

However, it is difficult to find a convincing criterion for making choices about discount rates when long-term intergenerational comparisons are being made. A number of writers argue that a discount rate based on the time preferences of currently living people is inappropriate as a long-term social discount rate. While currently living people might give proper attention to the needs of future persons, this is rather unlikely. Individuals with finite life expectancies are likely to behave differently from a planner presiding over a society that is expected to remain in existence for perpetuity. It is this distinction that lies at the heart of two of the most famous statements regarding discounting. Frank Ramsey (1928)

pronounced discounting to be 'ethically indefensible and arises merely from the weakness of the imagination'. Roy Harrod (1948) remarked that discounting is 'a polite expression for rapacity and the conquest of reason by passion'.

Many writers argue that the only ethically defensible consumption discount rate for projects having effects spread over several generations is zero. Without wishing to deny that zero may be a valid rate for some purposes, our arguments should have made it clear that non-zero rates may also be ethically defensible. If consumption is growing rapidly over time, there are grounds for using a positive consumption discount rate even if the utility discount rate is zero. On the other hand, if consumption is falling over time, a negative consumption discount rate could be defended. It is also important to ask which rate – the utility or consumption rate of discount – is being referred to whenever a writer is proposing a zero rate of discount.

Discounting: efficiency, equity and sustainability

Any attempt to deduce from ethical criteria what the discount rate should be in order to ensure that some specified objective is achieved is ill conceived. Questions relating to the equitable distribution of wealth between generations are not amenable to being translated into selection of an appropriate discount rate. If, for example, one believes that future generations have certain intrinsic rights, there is almost certainly no way in which those rights could be safeguarded merely by the choice of some particular discount rate. Similar arguments can and have been made about sustainability. It is not possible to define *a priori* a discount rate that will ensure that a sustainability goal is attained.

Discounting is essentially to do with allocative efficiency, specifically the efficient allocation of resources over time. This theme will be explored fully in the two following chapters. If society also wishes to pursue another objective – an ethical one, such as sustainability, for example – another instrument is necessary for that purpose. What might that instrument be? We have already seen one answer to this. We can define a social welfare function that incorporates the objective, or establish absolute constraints on behaviour to rule out efficient outcomes that would not satisfy that objective.

Discussion questions

1 We argued in the text that Rawls's Difference Principle asserts that it is only just to have an unequal distribution of wealth if all persons benefit from that allocation, relative to the situation of an equal distribution. But we also argued that the total level of utility attainable might depend on the distribution of wealth, as utility could be higher in an unequal position if incentive effects enhance productive efficiency. Discuss the implications of these comments for a morally just distribution of resources within and between countries.

2 In discussing the work of Robert Nozick, it was argued that libertarian ethics have been adopted most enthusiastically by those who believe in a limited role for government. But we also noted that it is by no means clear that a laisser-faire approach is necessarily implied. Three difficult issues arise in connection with the principle of just acquisition:

(a) What should government do about unjust holdings?

(b) How are open access or common property resources to be dealt with?

(c) How do external effects and public goods relate to the concept of just acquisition?

Sketch out reasoned answers to these three questions.

3 If society deemed it to be correct that some animals or plants have intrinsic rights (such as rights to be left undisturbed or rights to be reasonably protected), then such rights can be protected by imposing them as constraints on what is legitimate human behaviour. Do humans appear to regard whales as having intrinsic rights, and if so, what rights are these? In what ways, if at all, do humans defend these rights by imposing constraints on human behaviour?

4   A river tumbles through forested ravines and rocky gorges towards the sea. The state hydro-electricity commission sees the falling water as untapped energy. Building a dam across one of the gorges would provide three years of employment for a thousand people, and provide longer-term employment for twenty or thirty. The dam would store enough water to ensure that the state could economically meet its energy needs for the next decade. This would encourage the establishment of energy-intensive industry thus further contributing to employment and economic growth.

The rough terrain of the river valley makes it accessible only to the reasonably fit, but it is nevertheless a favoured spot for bush-walking. The river itself attracts the more daring whitewater rafters. Deep in the sheltered valleys are stands of rare Huon Pine, many of the trees being over a thousand years old. The valleys and gorges are home to many birds and animals, including an endangered species of marsupial mouse that has seldom been found outside the valley. There may be other rare plants and animals as well, but no one knows, for scientists are yet to investigate the region fully.

Singer (1993), page 264

Peter Singer's discussion of ethics and the environment begins with this scenario. His description is loosely based on a proposed dam on the Franklin River in southwest Tasmania. Singer notes that this is an example of a situation in which we must choose between very different sets of values. Please answer the following question, as put by Singer:

Should the dam be built?

Problems

1 Suppose that one believed that each generation should have the same level of well-being as every other one. Demonstrate that we could not ensure the attainment of this merely by the choice of a particular discount rate, zero or otherwise.
2 Prove that, under the assumption of diminishing marginal utility, the linear indifference curves in utility space in Figure 4.1 map into indifference curves that are convex from below in commodity space, as illustrated in Figure 4.2.
3 Demonstrate that an unequal distribution of goods at a welfare maximum may occur when the weights attached to individual utilities are not equal, and/or when individuals have different utility functions.

Further reading

Ethics

A good introduction to ethics, including environmental applications, may be found in Singer (1993). Beauchamp and Bowie (1988) give a good presentation, especially in chapters 1 and 9; the book contains an interesting analysis of the business implications of ethical principles. Other useful sources include Sen (1987) and Kneese and Schulze (1985). Interesting applications and discussions of ethical issues are to be found in the journal *Environmental Values*.

Discounting

Excellent extensive presentations are found in Hanley and Spash (1993, chapter 8) and in Layard and Glaister (1994), particularly in the introduction, chapter 3 (by Stiglitz), chapter 4 (by Arrow and Lind), and chapter 11 (by Dasgupta, on discounting and the environment). Lind (1982) investigates discounting and risk in energy policy, and Harberger (1971), Common (1995), Heal (1981), Marglin (1963) and Broome (1992) provide

stimulating analyses of discounting. Mikesell (1977) looks in detail at the practical choice of discount rates, and the implications of that choice. The issue of how sustainability might be built into a social welfare function, or what constraints might be set, is examined by Pezzey (1997).

Appendix 4.1 The Lagrange multiplier method of solving constrained optimisation problems

In this appendix, we state one method for solving maximisation problems with equality constraints. Suppose that we have the following problem in which a function of three variables is to be maximised subject to two constraints:

$$\max f(x_1, x_2, x_3)$$

subject to

$$g(x_1, x_2, x_3) = 0$$
$$h(x_1, x_2, x_3) = 0$$

To obtain a solution to this problem, we begin by writing the Lagrangian (L) for the problem. The Lagrangian consists of two components. The first of these is the function to be maximised. The second contains the constraint functions (but without being set equal to zero), with each constraint being preceded by a separate Lagrange multiplier variable. The Lagrangian is the sum of all these terms.

So in this case the Lagrangian, L, is

$$L(x_1, x_2, x_3, \lambda_1, \lambda_2) = f(x_1, x_2, x_3)$$
$$+ \lambda_1 g(x_1, x_2, x_3) + \lambda_2 h(x_1, x_2, x_3)$$

in which λ_1 and λ_2 are two Lagrange multipliers (one for each constraint) and the term $L(x_1, x_2, x_3, \lambda_1, \lambda_2)$ signifies that we are now to regard the Lagrangian as a function of the original choice variables of the problem and of the two Lagrange multiplier variables.

We now proceed by using the standard method of unconstrained optimisation to find a maximum of the Lagrangian with respect to x_1, x_2, x_3, λ_1 and λ_2.

The necessary first-order conditions for a maximum are

$$\frac{\partial L}{\partial x_1} = f_1 + \lambda_1 g_1 + \lambda_2 h_1 = 0$$

$$\frac{\partial L}{\partial x_2} = f_2 + \lambda_1 g_2 + \lambda_2 h_2 = 0$$

$$\frac{\partial L}{\partial x_3} = f_3 + \lambda_1 g_3 + \lambda_2 h_3 = 0$$

$$\frac{\partial L}{\partial \lambda_1} = g(x_1, x_2, x_3) = 0$$

$$\frac{\partial L}{\partial \lambda_2} = h(x_1, x_2, x_3) = 0$$

where

$$f_i = \frac{\partial f}{\partial x_i}, g_i = \frac{\partial g}{\partial x_i}, h_i = \frac{\partial h}{\partial x_i} \text{ for } i = 1, 2, 3$$

These are solved simultaneously to obtain solution values for the choice variables.

The second-order conditions for a maximum require that the following determinant be positive:

$$\begin{vmatrix} L_{11} & L_{12} & L_{13} & g_1 & h_1 \\ L_{21} & L_{22} & L_{23} & g_2 & h_2 \\ L_{31} & L_{32} & L_{33} & g_3 & h_3 \\ g_1 & g_2 & g_3 & 0 & 0 \\ h_1 & h_2 & h_3 & 0 & 0 \end{vmatrix} > 0$$

where

$$L_{ij} = \frac{\partial^2 L}{\partial x_i \, \partial x_j}$$

For a constrained maximum, a sufficient second-order condition can be stated in terms of the signs of the bordered principal minors of the Hessian matrix. Details of this condition are beyond the scope of this appendix, but can be found on page 386 of Chiang (1984).

The Lagrange multiplier method is widely used in economic analysis generally, and in resource and environmental economics particularly. This is because the Lagrange multipliers have a very useful interpretation in analysis. They are 'shadow prices' on the constraints. In the case of a constrained maximisation problem as considered above, this means that the value of a Lagrange multiplier tells us what the effect on the maximised value of the objective function would be for a small – strictly an infinitesimal (or vanishingly small) – relaxation of the corresponding constraint. The same interpretation arises in constrained minimisation problems. Clearly, this is very useful information. We now illustrate this interpretation using a simple example from an environmental economics context. We consider the problem of the least-cost allocation across sources of a reduction in total emissions, which will be discussed at length in Chapter 12.

Suppose that there are two firms, 1 and 2, where production gives rise to emissions M_1 and M_2. In the absence of any regulation of their activities, the firms' profit maximising emissions levels are 1000 and 7500 tonnes, respectively. The firms can cut back, or abate, emissions, but in so doing reduces profits and is costly. Further, abatement costs as a function of the level of abatement vary as between the two firms. The abatement cost functions are

$$C_1 = 10A_1 + 0.01A_1^2 = 10(1000 - M_1) \\ + 0.01(1000 - M_1)^2 \quad (4.19\text{a})$$

$$C_2 = 5A_2 + 0.001A_2^2 = 5(7500 - M_2) \\ + 0.001(7500 - M_2)^2 \quad (4.19\text{b})$$

where A_1 and A_2 are the levels of abatement, the amount by which emissions in some regulated situation are less than they would be in the absence of regulation.

The regulatory authority's problem is to determine how a reduction in total emissions from $8500 \, (= 1000 + 7500)$ to 750 tonnes should be allocated as between the two firms. Its criterion is the minimisation of the total cost of abatement. The problem is, that is, to find the levels of A_1 and A_2, or equivalently of M_1 and M_2, which minimise C_1 plus C_2 given that M_1 plus M_2 is to equal 750. Formally, using M_1 and M_2 as the control or choice variables, the problem is

$$\min C_1 + C_2$$

subject to

$$M_1 + M_2 = 750$$

Substituting for C_1 and C_2 from Equations 4.19a and 4.19b, and writing the Lagrangian, we have

$$L = 113\,750 - 30M_1 - 20M_2 + 0.01M_1^2 \quad (4.20)$$
$$+ 0.001M_2^2 + \lambda[750 - M_1 - M_2]$$

where the necessary conditions are

$$\partial L/\partial M_1 = -30 + 0.02M_1 - \lambda = 0 \quad (4.21a)$$

$$\partial L/\partial M_2 = -20 + 0.002M_2 - \lambda = 0 \quad (4.21b)$$

$$\partial L/\partial \lambda = 750 - M_1 - M_2 = 0 \quad (4.21c)$$

Eliminating λ from Equations 4.21a and 4.21b gives

$$-30 + 0.02M_1 = -20 + 0.002M_2 \quad (4.22)$$

and solving Equation 4.21c for M_1 gives

$$M_1 = 750 - M2 \quad (4.23)$$

so that substituting Equation 4.23 into Equation 4.22 and solving leads to M_2 equal to 227.2727, and then using Equation 4.23 leads to M_1 equal to 522.7272. The corresponding abatement levels are A_1 equal to 477.2728 and A_2 equal to 7272.7273. Note that firm 2, where abatement costs are much lower than in firm 1, does proportionately more abatement.

Now, in order to get the allocation of abatement across the firms we eliminated λ from Equations 4.21a and 4.21b. Now that we know M_1 and M_2 we can use one of these equations to calculate the value of λ as -19.5455. This is the shadow price of pollution, in the units of the objective function, which are here £s, when it is constrained to be a total emissions level of 750 tonnes. This shadow price gives what the impact on the minimised total cost of abatement would be for a small relaxation of the constraint that is the target regulated level of total emissions. To see this, we can compare the minimised total cost for 750 tonnes and 751 tonnes. To get the former, simply substitute $M_1 = 522.7272$ and $M_2 = 227.2727$ into

$$C = 113\,750 - 30M_1 - 20M_2 + 0.01M_1^2$$
$$+ 0.001M_2^2 \quad (4.24)$$

to get 96 306.819. To get the latter, replace 750 by 751 in Equation 4.21c, and then solve Equations 4.21a, 4.21b and 4.21c as before to get $M_1 = 522.8181$ and $M_2 = 228.1818$, which on substitution into Equation 4.24 for C gives the total cost of abatement to 751 tonnes as 96 287.272. The difference between 96 287.272 and 96 306.819 is -19.547, to be compared with the value for λ calculated above as -19.5455. The two results do not agree exactly because strictly the value for λ is for an infinitesimally small relaxation of the constraint, whereas we actually relaxed it by one tonne.

Note that the shadow price is £s per tonne, so that the Lagrangian multiplier is in the same units as the objective function, £s.

It is not always necessary to use the method of Lagrange multipliers to solve constrained optimisation problems. Sometimes the problem can be solved by substituting the constraint(s) into the objective function. This is the case in our example here. We want to find the values for M_1 and M_2 which minimise C as given by Equation 4.24, given that $M_1 + M_2 = 750$. That means that $M_1 = 750 - M_2$, and if we use this to eliminate M_1 from Equation 4.24, after collecting terms we get

$$C = 96\,875 - 5M_2 + 0.011M_2^2 \quad (4.25)$$

where the necessary condition for a minimum is

$$\partial C/\partial M_2 = -5 + 0.022M_2 = 0$$

which solves for $M_2 = 227.2727$, and from $M_1 = 750 - M_2$ we then get M_1 as 522.7273.

Even where solution by the substitution method is possible, using the method of Lagrange multipliers is generally preferable in that it provides extra information on shadow prices, with the interpretation set out above. In fact, these shadow prices often are useful in a further way, in that they have a natural interpretation as the prices that could be used to actually achieve a solution to the problem under consideration. Again, this can be illustrated with the emissions control example. If the regulatory authority had the information on the abatement cost functions for the two firms, it could do the calculations as above to find that for the least cost attainment of a reduction to 750 tonnes firm 1 should be emitting 522.7272 tonnes and firm 2227.2727 tonnes. It could then simply instruct the two firms that these were their permissible levels of emissions.

Given that it can also calculate the shadow price of pollution at its desired level, it can achieve the same outcome by imposing on each firm a tax per unit emission at a rate which is the shadow price. A cost minimising firm facing a tax on emissions will abate to the point where its marginal abatement cost is equal to the tax rate. With t for the tax rate, and M^* for the emissions level in the absence of any regulation or taxation, total costs are

$$C(A) + tM = C(A) + t(M^* - A)$$

so that total cost minimisation implies

$$\text{or} \quad \begin{aligned} dC/dA - t &= 0 \\ dC/dA &= t \end{aligned} \quad (4.26)$$

For firm 1, the abatement cost function written with A_1 as argument is

$$C_1 = 10A_1 + 0.01A_1^2 \quad (4.27)$$

so that marginal abatement costs are given by

$$dC_1/dA_1 = 10 + 0.02A_1 \quad (4.28)$$

Using the general condition which is Equation 4.26 with Equation 4.28, we get

$$10 + 0.02A_1 = t$$

and substituting for t equal to the shadow price of pollution, 19.5455, and solving yields A_1 equal to 477.275, which is, rounding errors apart, the result that we got when considering what level of emissions the authority should regulate for in firm 1. Proceeding in

the same way for firm 2, it will be found that it will do as required for the least cost allocation of total abatement if it faces a tax of £19.5455 per tonne of emissions.

When we return to the analysis of instruments for pollution control in Chapter 12 we shall see that the regulatory authority could reduce emissions to 750 by issuing tradable permits in that amount. Given the foregoing, it should be intuitive that the equilibrium price of those permits would be £19.5455.

Appendix 4.2 Social welfare maximisation

The problem is defined as follows. Choose X^A and X^B to maximise

$$W = U^A(X^A) + U^B(X^B)$$

subject to the constraint

$$X^A + X^B \leq \bar{X}$$

The Lagrangian for this problem is

$$L = U^A + U^B + \lambda(\bar{X} - X^A - X^B)$$

The first order conditions include

$$\frac{\partial L}{\partial X^A} = \frac{dU^A}{dX^A} - \lambda = 0$$

$$\frac{\partial L}{\partial X^B} = \frac{dU^B}{dX^B} - \lambda = 0$$

which together imply that

$$\frac{dU^A}{dX^A} = \frac{dU^B}{dX^B}$$

as given in the text. Maximisation of welfare requires that the good be distributed so that marginal utilities are equal for each individual. If $U^A(X^A) = U^B(X^B) = U(X)$ (that is, both individuals have an identical utility function) then this maximisation condition gives

$$\frac{dU}{dX^A} = \frac{dU}{dX^B}$$

This equality can only hold when $X^A = X^B$.

Appendix 4.3 The relationship between the utility and consumption discount rates

The welfare function is

$$W = \int_{t=0}^{t=T} U(C_t)e^{-\rho t}\, dt$$

and the utility function

$$U = U(C)$$

satisfies the restrictions

$$\frac{dU}{dC} = U'(C) > 0, \; \frac{d^2U}{dC^2} = U''(C) < 0$$

The elasticity of marginal utility with respect to consumption, η, is

$$\eta(C) = -\frac{C \bullet U''(C)}{U'(C)}$$

and so η is positive under the assumptions made about the utility function.

We have defined the consumption rate of discount, r, to be the rate at which the value of a small increment of consumption changes as its date is delayed. The value of an incremental unit of consumption at date t is given by the marginal utility of consumption at that date, which is

$$\frac{d}{dC_t}\left[U(C_t)\,e^{-\rho t}\right] = U'(C_t)e^{-\rho t}$$

The proportionate rate of change of this value with respect to time is

$$\frac{\dfrac{d}{dt}\left[U'(C_t)e^{-\rho t}\right]}{U'(C_t)e^{-\rho t}}$$

Differentiating the numerator with respect to time we obtain

$$\frac{U''(C_t)\dfrac{dC}{dt}e^{-\rho t} - \rho U'(C_t)e^{-\rho t}}{U'(C_t)e^{-\rho t}}$$

Letting $\dot{C} = dC/dt$, this simplifies to

$$\frac{U''(C_t)}{U'(C_t)}\dot{C} - \rho$$

Now, as we have defined the consumption rate of discount, r, to be the negative of this magnitude, we obtain

$$r = \rho - \frac{U''(C_t)}{U'(C_t)}\dot{C}$$

Finally, to obtain an expression for r in its most useful form, note that using the definition of η we obtain

$$r = \rho + \eta\frac{\dot{C}}{C}$$

CHAPTER 5

Welfare economics: efficiency and optimality

Welfare economics is the branch of economic theory which has investigated the nature of the policy recommendations that the economist is entitled to make.

Baumol (1977) page 496

Introduction

The concepts of efficiency and optimality will play a central role throughout the rest of this book. The purpose of this chapter is to explain what these terms mean, and so to provide a foundation for what follows. If you have previously studied a course in welfare economics, you should be able to read through the material of this chapter rather quickly. If not, the chapter will fill in that gap.

There are three parts to this chapter. The first states and explains the conditions required for resource use to be (i) efficient and (ii) optimal. These conditions are derived without regard to any particular institutional setting. In the second part of the chapter, we consider how efficient and optimal resource use might be brought about in the context of a market economy. The third part of the chapter uses a simpler partial equilibrium framework to examine economic efficiency. It develops the ideas of marginal analysis and consumers' and producers' surpluses that are used throughout the text, and which underpin much applied work in environmental economics.

PART 1
Efficiency and resource allocation

Environmental economics places considerable importance on economic efficiency (or just efficiency, for short) in resource allocation. The criterion of economic efficiency, as

you will see in Chapters 11, 12 and 13, dominates discussions about pollution targets and the choice of alternative instruments for achieving pollution targets. It also plays a central role in the analysis of non-renewable resource depletion and renewable resource harvesting (see Chapters 7 to 10).

However, the concept of efficiency is often poorly understood, and it is common for efficiency and optimality to be confused. In order to understand these ideas, it will be useful to devote a little attention to resource scarcity and its implications.

Environmental resources: scarcity and choice

Environmental resources are available in limited quantities. This is evidently true for non-renewable stock resources, such as mineral deposits and fossil fuels. And while the situation is not identical for renewable resources, it remains true that there are limits to the quantities that can be harvested in any period of time. Furthermore, if harvesting is persistently above sustainable levels, the possibility of the stock irreversibly collapsing to zero arises.

Environmental resources provide a set of useful services, yet they are available in limited quantities. They are, therefore, scarce. Scarcity requires that two sets of choices be made about how the resources are allocated among competing uses. First, at any point in time there are many uses to which resources could be put and many different ways in which they could be distributed over individuals and between nations. Second, choices relate to the patterns of use over time – the intertemporal allocation of resources. Any 'sensible' allocation will involve resources being used efficiently. But what precisely does this mean?

Economic efficiency

At any point in time, an economy will have access to particular quantities of a set of productive resources. Individuals have preferences about the various goods that it is feasible to produce. An allocation of resources describes what goods are produced, which combinations of inputs are used in producing those goods, and how the outputs are distributed between persons. A static allocation of resources refers to the allocation at some single point in time. Resource allocation over time is known as the intertemporal allocation of resources.

Static economic efficiency

We consider an economy in which particular individuals own all resources. Ownership of resources implies rights about how they are used and who is entitled to income from their use. The prevailing pattern of ownership can be called the initial distribution of property rights, or initial distribution for short. For some particular initial distribution, an allocation of resources is said to be efficient if it is not possible to make one or more persons better off without making at least one other person worse off. Conversely, an allocation is inefficient if it is possible to improve someone's position without worsening the position of anyone else. A gain by one or more persons without anyone else suffering is known as a Pareto improvement.

What conditions would have to be satisfied in order that an allocation of resources is efficient? To answer this question, we strip the problem down to its barest essentials. Our economy consists of two persons (A and B);

two goods (X and Y) are produced; and production of each good uses two inputs (K and L) each of which is available in a fixed quantity. We make two assumptions that will be explained later in this chapter. Firstly, no externalities exist in either consumption or production; roughly speaking, this means that consumption or production activities by any person do not have uncompensated effects upon others. Secondly, X and Y are private (not public) goods.

Let U denote an individual's total utility, which depends only on the quantity that he or she consumes. Then we can write the utility functions for A and B in the form shown in Equations 5.1.

$$U^A = U^A(X^A, Y^A)$$
$$U^B = U^B(X^B, Y^B) \qquad (5.1)$$

The total utility enjoyed by individual A (U^A) depends upon the quantities he or she consumes of the two goods, X^A and Y^A. An equivalent statement can be made about B's utility.

Next, we suppose that the quantity produced of good X depends only on the quantities of the two inputs K and L used in producing X, and the quantity produced of good Y depends only on the quantities of the two inputs K and L used in producing Y. Thus, we can write the two production functions in the form shown in Equations 5.2.

$$X = X(K^X, L^X)$$
$$Y = Y(K^Y, L^Y) \qquad (5.2)$$

Finally, we establish some additional notation. The marginal utility that A derives from the consumption of good X is denoted U_X^A; that is, $U_X^A = \partial U^A / \partial X^A$. The marginal product of the input L in the production of good Y is denoted as MP_L^Y; that is, $MP_L^Y = \partial Y / \partial L^Y$. Equivalent notation applies for the other three marginal utilities and the other three marginal products. We are now in a position to state and explain three conditions that must be satisfied if resources are to be allocated efficiently at any point in time.

Efficiency in consumption

Consumption efficiency requires that the ratios of the marginal utilities of goods X and Y are the same for each consumer. That is

$$\frac{U_X^A}{U_Y^A} = \frac{U_X^B}{U_Y^B} \qquad (5.3)$$

If this condition is not met, then the two consumers can exchange commodities at the margin in such a way that both gain. For example, suppose that the ratios of marginal utilities were as follows

$$\left(\frac{6}{3}\right)^A \neq \left(\frac{2}{4}\right)^B$$

A values X twice as highly as Y at the margin, whereas B values X at only half the value of Y. Clearly, if A exchanged one unit of Y for one unit of X from B, both would gain; each would be giving up something judged to be half as valuable as the thing gained. A Pareto improvement is possible, and so the initial position could not have been efficient. The only situation in which a mutually beneficial gain would not be possible is that in which the ratios of marginal utilities are equal.

Efficiency in production

Turning now to the production side of the economy, recall that we are considering an economy with two inputs, L and K, which can be used (via the production functions of Equations 5.2) to produce the goods X and Y. Efficiency in production requires that the ratio of the marginal product of each input be identical in the production of both goods. That is

$$\frac{MP_L^X}{MP_K^X} = \frac{MP_L^Y}{MP_K^Y} \qquad (5.4)$$

If this condition is not satisfied, the allocation must be inefficient as it would be possible for producers to exchange some K for some L so that the total production of both goods could be increased from the same total volume of inputs.

Product-mix efficiency

The final condition necessary for economic efficiency is product-mix efficiency. This requires that

$$\frac{U_X}{U_Y} = \frac{MP_K^Y}{MP_K^X} \qquad (5.5)$$

How can this condition be interpreted? The term on the left-hand side is the ratio of the marginal utilities of goods X and Y. We have omitted specifying to which person this refers as, from Equation 5.3, the ratio will be the same for both individuals if an allocation is efficient. It can be interpreted as the relative marginal valuation put on the two goods by all consumers; it gives the terms at which consumers are willing to trade Y for X at the margin. The term on the right-hand side of Equation 5.5 is the ratio of the marginal products of capital in the production of the two goods, Y and X. It indicates the rate at which units of Y are sacrificed for units of X, in using a unit of capital.

Hence, the product-mix efficiency condition requires that the rate at which consumers value one good in terms of another is equal to the opportunity cost of one good in terms of the other in production. If this condition were not satisfied, inputs could be reallocated into making an alternative configuration of outputs in such a way that each consumer could achieve higher total utility, and so a Pareto improvement would be possible.

We could have written the right-hand side of Equation 5.5 in terms of the marginal products of labour without changing the nature of this condition. To see this, note that Equation 5.4 can be rearranged to:

$$\frac{MP_L^Y}{MP_L^X} = \frac{MP_K^Y}{MP_K^X}$$

So provided productive efficiency (Equation 5.4) is satisfied, it does not matter whether we have the relative marginal products of capital or labour (or both) on the right-hand side of Equation 5.5.

An economy attains a fully efficient static allocation of resources if the conditions given by Equations 5.3, 5.4 and 5.5 are satisfied simultaneously. Moreover, it does not matter that we have been dealing with an economy with just two persons and two goods. The results readily generalise to economies with many inputs, many goods and many individuals. The only difference will be that the three efficiency conditions will have to hold for each possible pairwise comparison that one could make, and so would be far more tedious to write out.

An efficient allocation of resources is not unique

In general, there will be many efficient allocations of resources. To understand this result, recall that we have been discussing an economy with one particular initial distribution of property rights. With knowledge of that initial distribution and of all the relevant utility and production functions, it would be possible to work out the efficient allocation of resources in this case. The solution would tell us what quantities of goods are produced, how the inputs are allocated between different products, and what quantities of goods each individual would receive.

What happens if everything remains the same except that the initial distribution of property rights is different? Repeating the above exercise, one would find that a different efficient allocation would result. Different quantities of goods would be produced, inputs would be allocated in another way, and the quantities of goods that

---

Box 5.1 Productive inefficiency in ocean fisheries

The total world marine fish catch has increased steadily since the 1950s, rising by 32% between the periods 1976–1978 and 1986–1988 (UNEP, 1991). However, the early 1990s witnessed downturns in global harvests, although it is not yet clear whether this is indicative of longer-term trends. The steady increase in total catch until 1989, however, masked significant changes in the composition of that catch; as larger, higher-valued stocks became depleted, effort was redirected to smaller-sized and lower-valued species. This does sometimes allow depleted stocks to recover, as happened with North Atlantic herring, which recovered in the mid-1980s after being overfished in the late 1970s. However, many fishery scientists believe that these cycles of recovery have been modified, and that species dominance has shifted permanently towards smaller species.

So rising catch levels have put great pressure on some fisheries, particularly those in coastal areas, but also including some pelagic fisheries. Among the species whose catch has declined over the period 1976–1988 are Atlantic cod and herring, haddock, South African pilchard and Peruvian anchovy. Falls in catches of these species have been compensated for by much increased harvests of other species, including Japanese pilchard in the north-west Pacific, but it is widely agreed that the prospects of the total catch rising in the future are now very remote (WR, 1992).

Where do inefficiencies enter into this picture? We can answer this question in two ways. Firstly, a strong argument can be made to the effect that the total

amount of resources devoted to marine fishing is excessive, probably massively so. We shall defer giving evidence to support this claim until Chapter 9 (on renewable resources), but you will see there that a smaller total fishing fleet would be able to catch at least as many fish as the present fleet does; furthermore, if fishing effort were temporarily reduced so that stocks were allowed to recover, a greater steady-state harvest would be possible, even with a far smaller world fleet of fishing vessels. There is clearly an intertemporal inefficiency here.

A second insight into inefficiency in marine fishing can be gained by recognising that two important forms of negative external effect operate in marine fisheries, both largely attributable to the fact that marine fisheries are predominantly open-access resources. One type is a so-called crowding externality, arising from the fact that each boat's harvesting effort increases the fishing costs that others must bear. The second type may be called an intertemporal externality: as fisheries are often subject to very weak (or even zero) access restrictions, no individual fisherman has an incentive to conserve stocks for the future, even if all would benefit if the decision were taken jointly.

As the concepts of externalities and open access will be explained and analysed in the second part of this chapter, and applied to fisheries in Chapter 9, we shall not explain these ideas any further now. Suffice it to say that production in market economies will, in general, be inefficient in the presence of external effects.

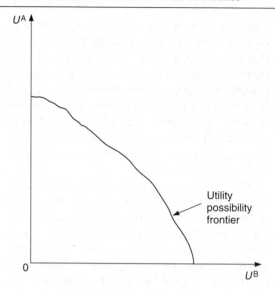

Figure 5.1 The utility possibility frontier.

each person receives would change. For each possible initial distribution of property rights there will be a corresponding efficient allocation of resources.

This idea can be represented using the concept of the utility possibility frontier, illustrated in Figure 5.1. The shape of the utility possibility frontier depends on the particular forms of the utility and production functions, so the way in which it is represented in Figure 5.1 is merely one possibility. However, one would expect the frontier to be generally bowed outwards in the manner shown. Each point on the frontier is an efficient allocation of resources, satisfying the three necessary conditions. Each point on the frontier also describes a particular pair of utility levels enjoyed by the two individuals. If an economy were to allocate resources efficiently, the position it takes on this frontier would depend upon the initial distribution of property rights to the productive resources.

Is it possible, using this information, to say which of the points on the frontier is best from the point of view of society? It is not possible, for the simple reason that the criterion of economic efficiency does not provide any basis for making interpersonal comparisons. Put another way, efficiency does not give us a criterion for judging which allocation is best from a social point of view.

The social welfare function and optimality

However, there is a way forward. Our discussions in the previous chapter show how a social welfare function (SWF) can be used to rank alternative allocations. For the economy we are examining here, a SWF will be of the general form:

$$W = W(U^A, U^B) \qquad (5.6)$$

The only assumptions we make at this point regarding the SWF are that one exists (and can be identified, somehow or other) and that welfare is non-decreasing in U^A and U^B. That is, for any given level of U^A, welfare cannot decrease if U^B were to rise and vice versa.

Armed with the tool of a social welfare function, we can conclude that resources are allocated in a socially optimal way at the point on the utility possibility frontier associated with the highest level of social welfare. This is a standard problem of constrained optimisation, and is illustrated in Figure 5.2. W_1, W_2 and W_3 are social welfare indifference curves. Each one represents combinations of individual utilities that yield a constant level of social welfare. The social welfare maximum is

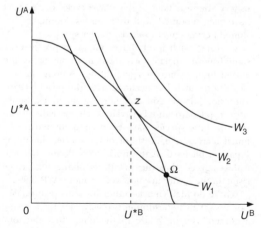

Figure 5.2 Maximised social welfare.

attained at point z, where social welfare is W_2 and the utility levels enjoyed by each person are U^{*A} and U^{*B} respectively.

Not surprisingly, it is a necessary condition for a welfare maximum that resources are allocated efficiently. Since 'more is better', society cannot be in the best position possible if resources are not efficiently used. As a result, conditions 5.3, 5.4 and 5.5 will be satisfied simultaneously at the welfare optimum. However, maximised welfare implies an additional necessary condition:

$$\frac{U_X^B}{U_X^A} = \frac{W_{U^A}}{W_{U^B}} \qquad (5.7)$$

where $U_X^B = \partial U^B/\partial X$, $U_X^A = \partial U^A/\partial X$, $W_{U^A} = \partial W/\partial U^A$ and $W_{U^B} = \partial W/\partial U^B$. The left-hand side of this equality is the slope of the utility possibility frontier (which could have been written in terms of good Y rather than good X). The right-hand side is the slope of the social welfare indifference curve. At a social welfare maximum, these slopes must be equal. This condition implies that it is not possible to increase social welfare by transferring goods between persons.

An example may help in understanding this conclusion. Consider the point labelled Ω in Figure 5.2. Imagine that goods were exchanged between the two individuals in such a way that B's utility falls and A's utility rises. The economy would move upwards and to the left along the utility possibility frontier (UPF). But in so doing, the economy can move onto a higher social welfare indifference, and so social welfare would rise. The only circumstance where this is not possible is where the slope of the SWF is identical to that of the UPF. Then, small movements along the UPF would be equivalent to movements along a SWF indifference curve, and not movements between indifference curves. We can also think about this numerically. At the point Ω, the slope of the social welfare function is lower than the slope of the utility possibility frontier in absolute terms. Suppose that the slope of SWF is $-1/1$, and the slope of the UPF is $-2/1$. The latter ratio

implies that if B gave up sufficient goods for his or her utility to fall by 1, A's utility would rise by 2. However, the slope of the SWF tells us that if A's utility fell by 1, it would only be necessary for B's utility to rise by 1 if social welfare is to remain constant. As B's utility would in fact rise by 2, this would imply an increase in welfare.

Intertemporal economic efficiency

As much of the content of environmental economics concerns decision making over time, we next extend the analysis to take account of this time dimension. Decisions taken today have implications for the consumption and production possibilities available in the future. When making decisions about the current use of resources, provided that we think the future matters, it will not be desirable to do so without reference to the subsequent consequences of our actions.

It was argued earlier, in considering the static allocation of resources, that a minimum condition one might require of an allocation of resources is that it be efficient. It seems sensible to apply this idea to intertemporal choices as well. To derive a criterion for intertemporal efficiency, a simplification is adopted. We define an aggregate of all living people and suppose that it is possible to define the utility of this aggregate for any period of time. Given this, an allocation of resources over time is intertemporally efficient if, for some given level of utility at the present time, utility at all future points in time is as high as is economically feasible. In other words, future utility can only be increased at the expense of current utility.

Before we work out some of the implications of this general criterion of intertemporal efficiency, some clarification is needed about our use of the words 'current' and 'future'. At least three interpretations can be offered. The first – and in some ways the most natural – is to think of the simple passage of time as it relates to a particular set of people. Current utility is how much satisfaction individuals now obtain; future utility is how much satisfaction those same individuals at some future instant of time obtain.

This presents a problem if we wish to consider indefinitely long passages of time, as it supposes the existence of infinitely long-lived individuals. A second alternative is to conceive of sets of overlapping generations. Members of any generation have finite lives, and so generations are born and die. Overlapping implies that the next generation is born before the current one dies. There are, of course, many ways in which we could specify the manner of this overlapping.

This second interpretation is attractive but presents modelling difficulties that are beyond the scope of this book. So we shall often make use of a third, simpler interpretation. We stick with the idea of generations, but these are not overlapping. Each individual is a member of a particular generation. Generation 0 is the set of people living today. At some point of time, Generation 0 is replaced by Generation 1, and so on. We envisage a sequence of generations, each new one replacing the previous one. We could then think about current utility as referring to the utility enjoyed through the span of Generation 0 and the future utility as referring to utilities enjoyed by members of later generations.

Let us now derive some specific conditions that must be satisfied if resources are to be allocated efficiently over time. We focus on two such conditions, which arise from the fact that assets may be productive over time. This is certainly true for some biological resources (such as forests and fisheries) which have the property of natural growth. It is also considered to be an inherent property of many forms of capital. Thus, if I defer some consumption today, and allow capital to be accumulated instead, my consumption tomorrow may well have increased by a larger quantity than the magnitude of the initial sacrifice. Let δ denote a real rate of return on a single homogeneous asset, and suppose there are M different sectors of the economy in which the asset can be used as a productive input. Call δ_i the return on this asset in the ith sector (where $i = 1, 2, \ldots, M$).

The first intertemporal efficiency condition

The real rate of return on assets is equalised across all sectors and between all assets at any point in time. That is, $\delta_i = \delta$ for all i, $i = 1, \ldots, M$.

Why is this condition required for intertemporal efficiency? If these rates of return differed, it would be possible to reallocate some resources from low productivity into higher productivity sectors, so that total returns would be increased. But if total returns could be increased in this way, current utility could be higher without there being any reduction in future utility, and so the general condition for intertemporal efficiency fails. The only circumstance where such a Pareto improvement would not be possible is that in which the rate of return on assets is equalised throughout the economy. However we interpret the phrases current and future utility, it should be clear that this condition must be satisfied if intertemporal efficiency is to be satisfied.

The second intertemporal efficiency condition

Suppose that the marginal social worth of present consumption relative to that of consumption next period is judged to be in the ratio $(1 + r)/1$. That is, one unit of the consumption good in the current period is perceived as having the same effect on overall well-being as $(1 + r)$ units of the good next period. Expressed differently, an additional unit of consumption in the present period is valued $(1 + r)$ times more highly than the same quantity of consumption next period. Clearly, r is the consumption discount rate that we referred to previously. As before, denote the real rate of return that is attained by deferring a marginal unit of consumption by one period and investing those resources by δ. In other words, if one unit of consumption is foregone today, this can be transformed into $(1 + \delta)$ units of consumption in the following period.

A second necessary condition for the efficient intertemporal allocation of resources is that the real rate of return on investment (δ) is equal to the consumption discount rate (r).

This condition is illustrated in Figure 5.3. The consumption indifference curve is a locus of all combinations of consumption in the current period (C_0) and consumption in the next period (C_1) that confer a constant amount of utility. At any point, the slope of this indifference curve is given by $-(1 + r)$. Note that r is not a constant number; as one moves along any given indifference curve, its slope changes and so r changes. The production possibility frontier shows the combinations of consumption goods that can be produced in each period; its slope at any point is given by $-(1 + \delta)$. Like r, δ is not a constant number; as one moves along any given production possibility frontier, its slope changes and so δ changes. An explanation of these expressions for the slopes of the curves is given in Appendix 5.2.

An efficient intertemporal consumption allocation is shown by the point Θ at which the slopes of the intertemporal production possibility frontier and the consumption indifference curve are equalised, and the highest possible consumption indifference curve is attained. At any such point, $r = \delta$.

If this condition were not satisfied, then it would be possible to attain a higher level of two-period utility by moving along the production possibility curve. For example, suppose the economy was currently at the point labelled ϕ in Figure 5.3. An indifference curve going through that point would yield lower two-period utility than the one illustrated in the diagram that passes through the point Θ. By reducing present consumption to C_0^*, consumption could be increased in the next period to C_1^*. At the combination $\{C_0^*, C_1^*\}$ utility is as high as it can be, given the available intertemporal production opportunities.

The intertemporal social welfare function and an intertemporally optimal resource allocation

An allocation of resources over time is efficient if, for any given level of utility today, future utilities are at their maximum feasible levels. However, just as in the static case, there is no unique intertemporally efficient allocation. On the contrary, there will be an infinite quantity of them. This is illustrated in Figure 5.4.

Figure 5.4 collapses all generations into two; generation 1 is the present one; 2 represents all future generations. U^{G1} and U^{G2} denote the total utility enjoyed by members of each generation. The intertemporal utility possibility frontier shows all feasible combinations of total utilities. Each point on the frontier corresponds to a particular allocation of rights to use resources between generations. Since there are many different possible ways in which these rights of resource use could be distributed, there are many possible efficient paths of resource usage over time. An example might help you to understand this

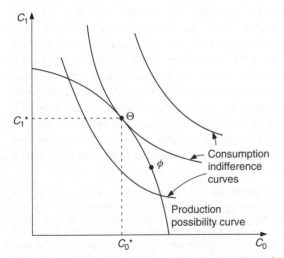

Figure 5.3 An intertemporally efficient allocation of resources.

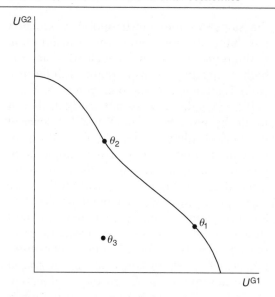

Figure 5.4 The intertemporal utility possibility frontier.

statement. Suppose that there are no constraints on how much or in what way resources are used by the present generation. The point θ_1 denotes a feasible combination of current and future utilities; let us assume that in the absence of any constraints this is the allocation chosen by the current generation. Now suppose that government restricts the quantity of resources that the current generation is allowed to use with the effect that the maximum attainable current utility falls to the level shown at the point θ_2. The increased resource stock bequeathed to the next generation allows it to obtain greater utility than in the first case. Both θ_1 and θ_2 are intertemporally efficient: present utility cannot be increased without future utility falling. However, a point such as θ_3 is inefficient, as no such trade-off is necessary.

It is important to be clear about the interpretation of the rights of resource use, as this is not a common way of thinking about resource use. In some sense, our generation has at its disposal all the resources known to exist. But having the ability to use resources in any way it chooses is not the same thing as having the right to do so. It is not our intention to suggest how these rights should be

distributed, only to make it clear that there are different ways in which such rights could be distributed, and so there are many different possible efficient allocations of resources. Of course, even if agreement could be reached on how rights of this kind should be distributed, it is not clear how such an agreement could be implemented.

Once again, if we are to make any claim about which of these efficient paths is best, in the sense of maximising intertemporal social welfare, we shall need a social welfare function – more precisely, what we require is an intertemporal social welfare function. Let W denote social welfare, this time interpreted in an intertemporal sense. An intertemporal social welfare function (for two generations) can be written in the general form:[1]

$$W = W(U^{G1}, U^{G2}) \qquad (5.8)$$

As we discussed earlier, it is common in economic analysis to use the classical utilitarian form:

$$W = \Phi_1 U^{G1} + \Phi_2 U^{G2} \qquad (5.9)$$

so that W is a weighted average of the utilities of each generation, where Φ_1 and Φ_2 are the weights used in summing utility over generations to obtain a measure of social welfare. If Φ_1 is set equal to unity and Φ_2 to $1/(1 + \rho)$, then we obtain the standard discounted utilitarian SWF in which future utility is discounted at the utility discount rate ρ. Not surprisingly, if we employ a discounted utilitarian social welfare function, the optimal rates of use of resources over time will depend upon the particular discount rate selected. This will be verified as you read our discussions of the extraction and harvesting of environmental resources in Chapters 7 to 10.

---

[1] Note that this form of social welfare function is already quite restrictive, as it assumes that we can meaningfully refer to an aggregate level of total utility for each generation. Social welfare is a function of these aggregate quantities, but not of the distributions of well-being within generations (except in so far as this affects the relevant aggregate). Despite these limitations, we shall work with this form in most of this text.

PART 2
Achieving an efficient allocation in a market economy

Static and intertemporal allocations and market economies

A variety of institutional arrangements might be employed to allocate resources, such as dictatorship, central planning and free markets. Any of these can, but will not necessarily, achieve an efficient allocation of resources. We are particularly interested in the consequences of free market resource allocation decisions. Welfare economics theory points to a set of circumstances such that, if they prevailed, markets would sustain an efficient allocation of resources. For an efficient static allocation, these 'institutional arrangements', as we shall call them from now on, include the following:

(a) Markets exist for all goods and services exchanged.
(b) All markets are perfectly competitive.
(c) All transactors have perfect information.
(d) Property rights are fully assigned.
(e) No externalities exist.
(f) All goods and services are private goods. That is, no public goods exist, nor are any resources common property resources.
(g) Long run average costs are non-decreasing.[2]

An efficient static and intertemporal allocation would be sustained if these seven institutional circumstances generalised to refer to all points in time now and in the future, were satisfied. Thus, for example, we would need to interpret condition (a) as referring to markets for all goods and services being exchanged currently (i.e. spot markets) and at all points of future time (forward markets).

[2] This is required for the existence of a competitive equilibrium. If production were characterised by economies of scale, then natural monopolies would exist, and a competitive equilibrium could not be sustained.

Static efficiency in a market economy

We now explain why a market allocation of resources would be an efficient allocation if the institutional arrangements listed above were to exist. Assume that all firms are profit maximisers and all individuals maximise utility. A result from microeconomic theory (a proof of which is given in Appendix 5.1) is that utility maximisation subject to a budget constraint requires that the ratio of marginal utilities is equal to the ratio of prices. That is, for any two goods X and Y, and for an individual indexed by i:

$$\left(\frac{U_X}{U_Y}\right)^i = \left(\frac{P_X}{P_Y}\right)^i \qquad (5.10)$$

In competitive markets, all consumers face identical prices for each good, so the right-hand side of Equation 5.10 is identical for all consumers. Given this, Equation 5.10 implies that the left-hand side will be identical across persons. This ensures satisfaction of the consumption efficiency condition, Equation 5.3.

Profit maximisation requires that the ratio of marginal products of the productive inputs is equal to the ratio of the input prices. That is, for any firm producing the good j and using the inputs L and K we have

$$\left(\frac{MP_L}{MP_K}\right)^j = \left(\frac{P_L}{P_K}\right)^j \qquad (5.11)$$

where P_L and P_K are the unit input prices of L and K. Because all producers face identical input prices in competitive markets, this ensures satisfaction of the production efficiency condition 5.4, as the left-hand side of Equation 5.11 must then be equalised over products, and by implication over all firms.

Furthermore, profit maximisation in the production of any good j implies that

$$P_j = MC_j = \frac{P_K}{MP_K} = \frac{P_L}{MP_L} \qquad (5.12)$$

where P_j denotes the output price of good j and MC_j is marginal cost. This ensures the satisfaction of the product-mix efficiency condition 5.5. You should try to convince yourself of why it is that Equation 5.12 does satisfy the product-mix efficiency condition; a proof is given in Appendix 5.1 if you need some help. The intuition behind Equation 5.12 is not easy to obtain. But note that the first equality states that (in profit maximising competitive equilibrium) price is equal to marginal cost. This result will probably be one with which you are familiar. It is quite difficult, though, to understand the two other equalities in Equation 5.12 at an intuitive level, except by noting that the last two terms on the right-hand side of the equation are both interpretable as long-run marginal cost. As it is not very satisfactory to take results on trust, the authors strongly recommend that you read through the derivations given in Appendix 5.1.

Intertemporal allocation and efficiency in a market economy

The circumstances we have just described thus sustain an efficient static allocation of resources. What will ensure an intertemporally efficient allocation? Before we explore this question, recall that an intertemporally efficient allocation requires that:

(i) $\delta_i = \delta$ for all $i = 1, \ldots, M$

so the return on each asset in each sector of the economy is equalised, and

(ii) $\delta = r$

so the rate of return on investment is equal to the consumption discount rate.

In looking at behaviour in market economies, we have assumed that the goal of firms is to maximise profits, and the goal of consumers is to maximise utility. The intertemporal generalisations of these assumptions are that firms maximise the present value of profit flows over time, and that consumers maximise the present value of utility flows over time.

It is easy to understand how the first of these conditions will be satisfied in a multi-

sector, competitive market economy. Perfectly mobile capital will be invested in the sector yielding the highest rate of return; this will have the effect of equalising the equilibrium real rates of return across all sectors in the economy. Another explanation goes as follows: maximisation of present value by competitive firms implies that they invest to the point where the rate of return on a marginal project equals the market rate of interest, i. But in an economy in which all markets are perfect, firms face a single interest rate. Thus, since i is at each point in time a constant number, marginal rates of return across sectors will be equalised.

The second condition is satisfied through the mechanism of the market for loanable funds. Those individuals deferring consumption supply loanable funds to the market; individuals or firms undertaking investment projects demand loanable funds from the market. The rate of interest, i, serves as a price which adjusts until equilibrium is achieved in the market, at which demand and supply of loanable funds are equal. This interest rate will be equal to the consumption discount rate, as individual lenders will adjust the quantities of funds lent until the return they receive on the market (i) is equal to their marginal consumption discount rate (r). A similar mechanism operates on the demand side of the market. In equilibrium, the market interest rate will be equal to the real rate of return on capital, as individual borrowers will adjust the quantities of funds invested until the interest rate paid on borrowed funds (i) is equal to their marginal rate of return on investment projects (δ).

Therefore, we obtain the result that in equilibrium

$$\delta = i = r \qquad (5.13)$$

and so the efficiency condition $\delta = r$ is satisfied. A more complete account of the mechanisms by which Equation 5.13 is obtained is given in Appendix 5.2. Of course, as is well known, the equalities in that equation are only obtained under special conditions, amounting to all the standard assumptions of perfectly competitive markets. However, since at this stage in our discussions we are assuming that all markets are competitive, there is no difficulty here.

The welfare-optimal allocation and a market economy

Our earlier analysis has identified the nature of a welfare maximising allocation of resources. Unfortunately, no 'automatic' (that is, market based) tendency exists in a market economy for such a welfare maximum to be reached. Perfect competition plus the other circumstances listed above would lead to an efficient allocation, but does not lead to the attainment of a welfare maximum. The only exception to this would be where some chance outcome happened to allocate property rights in the unique configuration that would correspond to optimal welfare. Of course, government can pursue redistributive policy, which might move the economy to such a position. But that is not a process which is in any way intrinsic to the notion of a market economy itself.

In later chapters of this text, we shall often investigate the use by government of a variety of policy instruments. Our discussion of efficiency and welfare should alert us to some problems we might encounter in assessing policy measures. Ideally, all statements about the desirability of changes in resource allocation should be made in terms of their effects upon social welfare. For a variety of reasons, however, it is often not possible to obtain good estimates of the welfare implications of some projects. In these circumstances, the projects are sometimes advocated on the grounds of efficiency gains. But it is easy to see that efficiency improvements are not unambiguously desirable. An efficiency improvement might result in a lower value of social welfare. This possibility is illustrated in Figure 5.5 by the

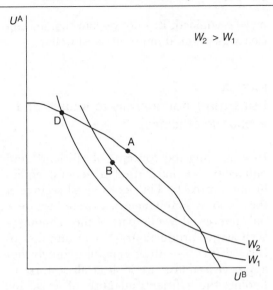

Figure 5.5 Efficient and inefficient static allocations.

efficiency improvement attained by moving from point B to point D. Such a move would result in a welfare loss (as $W_1 < W_2$), even though there is an efficiency gain. Having made this point, it should also be said that whenever there is an inefficient allocation, there is always some other allocation which is both efficient and superior in welfare terms. For example, the move from B to A is both an efficiency gain and a welfare improvement. The reason why the move from B to A is certainly welfare beneficial is that it is a Pareto improvement. On the other hand, going from B to D was an efficiency gain in the sense that an inefficient allocation is replaced by an efficient one; but the change is not a Pareto improvement.

The very simple observation that efficiency gains are not necessarily welfare gains, or in other words are not necessarily socially beneficial, is often ignored. Sometimes, claims are made (explicitly or implicitly) that the eradication of a market failure is intrinsically desirable. It is clear that if desirability is defined in terms of effects upon social welfare, an efficiency gain may or may not be beneficial. While it is perfectly reasonable to discuss the means by which efficiency gains may be attained, it is not certain that an efficiency gain would improve social welfare.[3]

PART 3
Using marginal analysis to understand economic efficiency

In examining the concepts of efficiency and optimality, we have used a general equilibrium approach. This looks at all sectors of the economy simultaneously. Even if we were only interested in one part of the economy – such as the production and consumption of cola drinks – the general equilibrium approach requires we look at all sectors. In finding the efficient quantity of cola, for example, the solution we get from this kind of exercise would give us the efficient quantities of all goods, not just cola.

There are several very attractive properties of proceeding in this way. Perhaps the most important of these is the theoretical rigour it imposes. In developing economic theory, it is often best to use general equilibrium analysis. Much (although by no means all) of the huge body of theory that makes up resource and environmental economics analysis has such a general approach at its foundation.

But there are penalties to pay for this rigour. Doing practical work in this way can be expensive and time consuming. And in some cases data limitations make it impossible. The exercise may not be quite as daunting as it sounds, however. We could define categories in such a way that there are just two goods in the economy: cola and a

composite good that is everything except cola. Indeed, this kind of 'trick' is commonly used in economic analysis. But even with this type of simplification, a general equilibrium approach is likely to be difficult and costly, and may be out of all proportion to the demands of some problem for which we seek an approximate solution.

Given the cost and difficulty of using this approach for many practical purposes, many applications use a different framework that is much easier to operationalise. This involves looking at only the part of the economy of direct relevance to the problem being studied. Let us return to the cola example, in which our interest lies in trying to estimate the efficient amount of cola to be produced. The partial approach examines the production and consumption of cola, ignoring the rest of the economy. It begins by identifying the benefits and costs to society of using resources to make cola. Then, defining *net* benefit as total benefit minus total cost, an efficient output level of cola would be one that maximises net benefit.

Let X be the level of cola produced and consumed (we assume these are equal). Figure 5.6(a) shows the total benefits of cola (labelled B) and the total costs of cola (labelled C) for various possible levels of cola production. The reason we have labelled the curves $B(X)$ and $C(X)$, not just B and C, is to make it clear that benefits and costs each depend on (or, more precisely, are functions of) X. In principle, any common unit could be used to measure these costs and benefits; in practice, they are measured in money units.

The shapes and relative positions of the curves we have drawn for B and C are, of course, just stylised representations of what we expect them to look like. A researcher trying to answer the question we posed above would have to estimate the shapes and positions of these functions from whatever evidence is available, and they may differ considerably from those drawn in the diagram. However, the reasoning that follows is

---

[3] In this discussion, we have ignored the possibility of compensation. Thus, imagine some resource reallocation benefited one person but was damaging to another. If, in absolute terms, the size of the gain is greater than the size of the loss, the two parties may be able to negotiate a compensating transfer so that, after compensation is paid, both parties benefit. If the resource reallocation takes place, we can say that there is a potential Pareto improvement (also known as a Kaldor improvement). If the resource reallocation and compensation take place, an actual Pareto improvement will have occurred.

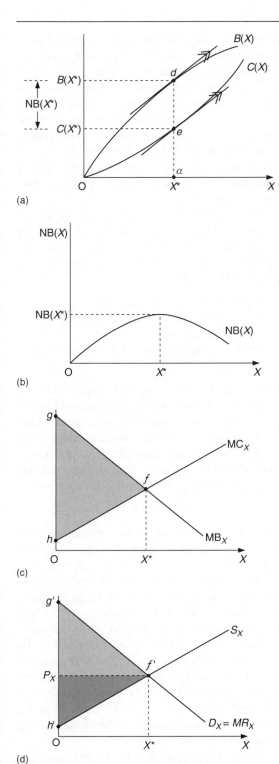

(a)

(b)

(c)

(d)

Figure 5.6 A partial equilibrium interpretation of economic efficiency.

essentially valid whatever the actual shapes of the functions.

Given that we call an outcome that maximises net benefits efficient, it is clear from Figure 5.6(a) that X^* is the efficient level of cola production. Net benefits (indicated by the distance de) are at their maximum at that level of output. This is also shown in Figure 5.6(b), which plots the *net* benefits for various levels of X. Observe the following points:

- At the efficient output level X^* the total benefit and total cost curves are parallel to one another (Figure 5.6(a)).
- The net benefit function is horizontal at the efficient output level (Figure 5.6(b))

The distance de, or equivalently the magnitude $NB(X)$, can be interpreted in efficiency terms. It is a measure, in money units, of the efficiency gain that would come about from producing X^* cola compared with a situation in which no cola was made.

These ideas are often expressed in a different, but exactly equivalent way, using marginal rather than total functions. As much of the environmental economics literature uses this way of presenting ideas (and we shall do so also in several parts of this book), let us see how it is done. For notational simplicity, we use MC_X to denote the marginal cost of X, dC/dX; similarly, MB_X denotes the marginal benefit of X, dB/dX. Figure 5.6(a), shows the marginal functions which correspond to the total functions in Figure 5.6(c). We drew the curves for $B(X)$ and $C(X)$ in Figure 5.6(a) so that the corresponding marginal functions are straight lines. This is convenient and simplifies the exposition of the subsequent analysis. But, the conclusions do not depend on the marginal functions being straight lines. The results to be stated hold so long as marginal benefits are positive and declining with X and marginal costs are positive and increasing with X – as they are in Figure 5.6(c).

By definition, the net benefit for any given level of X is given by $NB(X) = B(X) - C(X)$. Net benefit maximisation requires that X is chosen so as to equate the marginal benefit of

X and the marginal cost of X. This result follows from some elementary calculus. A necessary condition for net benefit maximisation is that the first derivative of net benefits with respect to the level of X be zero. That is

$$\frac{\mathrm{dNB}(X)}{\mathrm{d}X} = \frac{\mathrm{d}B(X)}{\mathrm{d}X} - \frac{\mathrm{d}C(X)}{\mathrm{d}X} = 0$$

which implies that

$$\frac{\mathrm{d}B(X)}{\mathrm{d}X} = \frac{\mathrm{d}C(X)}{\mathrm{d}X}$$

or the marginal cost of X must equal its marginal benefit. Not surprisingly, this occurs at the level X^*; at this output level $\mathrm{dNB}/\mathrm{d}X$ has a value of zero, so the slope of the net benefit function is horizontal there. This is something we remarked on earlier (and is shown in Figure 5.6(b)).

Can we obtain a measure of maximised net benefits from Figure 5.6(c) that corresponds to the distance de in Figure 5.6(a)? Such a measure is available; it is the area of the triangle gfh. The area beneath a marginal function over some range gives the value of the change in the total function for a move over that range. So the area beneath MB_X over the range $X = 0$ to $X = X^*$ gives us the total benefits of X^* cola (i.e. B^*), which is equal to the distance αd in Figure 5.6(a). Similarly, the area beneath MC_X over the range $X = 0$ to $X = X^*$ gives us the total cost of X^* (i.e. C^*), which is the same as the distance αe in Figure 5.6(a). By subtraction we find that the area gfh in Figure 5.6(c) is identical to the distance de in Figure 5.6(a).

Finally, we want to offer one other interpretation of efficiency that is also widely used in practice by environmental economists. To do so, some institutional data is introduced into the story. Specifically, we assume that all the institutional conditions listed at the start of Part 2 of this chapter are satisfied. Then all those who wish to drink cola will obtain it from the market, and pay the going market price. The market demand curve for cola will be identical to the MB_X curve, as that describes consumers' *willingness to pay* for

additional units of the good – and that is exactly what we mean by a demand curve.

Under our assumptions, cola is produced by a large number of price-taking firms in a competitive market. The market supply curve – let us call this S_X – is identical to the curve MC_X in Figure 5.6(c). (This result comes from the standard theory of perfect competition.) It shows the cost of producing additional (or marginal) cans of cola at various output levels.

The market demand and supply curves are drawn in Figure 5.6(d). When all mutually beneficial transactions have taken price, the equilibrium market price of the good will be P^*, equal to both

- consumers' subjective valuations of additional units of the good (expressed in money terms); and
- the costs of producing an additional unit of the good.

Put another way, all consumers face a common market price P_X, and each will adjust their consumption until his or her marginal utility (in money units) is equal to that price. Each firm faces that same fixed market price, and adjusts its output so that its marginal cost of production equals that price. So we have

$$P = \mathrm{MC} = \mathrm{MB}$$

a result obtained earlier (see Equations 5.10 and 5.12) and derived formally in Appendix 5.1.

The area beneath the demand curve between zero and X^* units of the good shows the total consumers' willingness to pay (WTP) for X^* cans of cola per period. (You can think of this area as adding up or 'integrating' the WTP for each successive unit up to the total of X^* units.) Now consider the area beneath the supply curve over the same range. This shows the total cost of producing X^* units. It is the sum of the incremental costs of producing each successive unit up to X^*.

Value is being added in the economy by producing cola to this level, as consumers' WTP (the total benefits) is greater than the

Box 5.2 Saturday effects in tanker oil spills

In a paper in the *Journal of Environmental Economics and Management* (1992), Eban Goodstein examines what he calls 'Saturday effects' in tanker oil spills. He writes that

> certain types of spills happen much more frequently on this day than one would expect if the spills were uniformly distributed. The phenomenon is restricted to Europe and North America, and is associated with 'vessel guidance' accidents – groundings, collisions, and rammings. Eliminating the Saturday effect would reduce tanker oil spills by around 163,000 gallons per year.

(Goodstein, 1992, page 276)

The paper is an interesting use of marginal cost and marginal benefit functions to derive an efficient policy response to an environmental 'problem'. We will examine this kind of issue at greater length in Chapters 11 and 12, but the intuition of what is going on here should be fairly clear. Goodstein's main objective is to calculate the level of per-gallon tax on Saturday harbour operations that would bring about an efficient reduction of this Saturday effect. As you will see, Goodstein uses a mixture of empirical data and logical reasoning – the two principal information sources employed by economists – to obtain his answer.

Goodstein begins with two conjectures about the cause of the Saturday effect:

- spills are more frequent on Saturdays because there is more harbour traffic on those days
- spills are associated with alcohol abuse by seamen at weekends

His assessment of the evidence leads Goodstein to reject these explanations. There is more traffic in harbours at weekends, but not enough to generate the observed effect. Alcohol abuse is also rejected as a plausible explanation; heavy drinking, if it occurs, is likely on both Friday and Saturday nights, so we would expect a Sunday effect too if this were the cause. But that effect is not present. Indeed, Goodstein is unable to come up with any convincing explanation of the phenomenon.

Fortunately, Goodstein's task does not require that he be able to explain the Saturday effect. He proceeds in the following way. First, Goodstein's assessment of the problem and the feasible policy options leads him to conclude that a charge imposed on each gallon of oil landed on Saturdays is the best instrument. Next, he sets out to calculate the efficient level of such a charge. To do this, Goodstein reasons that the marginal benefits and marginal costs of reducing Saturday shipments are as shown in Figure 5.7. Note that the *marginal cost* of reducing Saturday shipments increases as the reduction becomes larger (going from right to left in the diagram). The rising

marginal cost schedule reflects the fact that scheduling flexibility is lost at an increasing rate as firms concentrate ship movements onto the rest of the week. In contrast, Goodstein assumes that the *marginal benefit* of reduction is constant, because of what he calls the 'lumpy nature of oil spills from vessel accidents'. By assumption, each gallon of oil spilled causes the same damage as any other gallon spilled.

The efficient tax rate will be at the intersection of the marginal cost and marginal benefit functions. In general, this intersection can only be identified with knowledge of the position of both functions. But the constancy of the marginal benefit curve greatly simplifies Goodstein's task. Because marginal benefits are assumed to be constant, all that is necessary is to estimate that (constant) value. Goodstein avoids the tricky problem of estimating the position of the marginal cost curve because, whatever it is, the marginal benefit (and so the efficient tax) will be the same.

Goodstein obtains a measure of the marginal benefit of reducing a gallon of oil shipped in or out of a US harbour on a Saturday in the following way. First, we introduce some notation he uses:

d = the marginal benefit of reducing each gallon spilled
b = the marginal benefit of reducing Saturday shipments by one gallon
p_s = the enhanced probability of a spill due to the Saturday effect

The marginal benefit of reducing Saturday shipments by one gallon, b, is the damage caused by that gallon actually being spilled multiplied by the probability that it will be spilled because of the Saturday effect. That is

$$b = p_s d$$

Goodstein calculates the probability p_s by dividing the total excess spillage due to the Saturday effect (163 000 gallons per year) by the total volume of oil shipments on Saturdays (22.4 billion gallons per year). This gives the value $p_s = 0.000\,007$. His estimate of d, the marginal benefit of reducing each gallon spilled, is based on previous research by Cohen (1986). Cohen obtained a 'conservative' estimate of the average value of damages as $4.05 per gallon. (All money values are in 1990 US dollars.) But the marginal benefit of not spilling one gallon of oil consists of three components: the averted damage, the value of the oil itself that would have been lost, and the avoided clean-up costs that would have had to be paid. So to the marginal damage figure must be added the value of the oil itself ($0.48 per gallon) and the cost of clean-up that the tanker operator must

Box 5.2 continued

pay in the event of a spill (on average, $1.07 per gallon). Combining these three figures gives a value for d of $5.60. Goodstein interprets this number as a very conservative, lower bound estimate of the true value of d. Some support for this view is evident from the fact that the damages paid by Shell for a spill in San Francisco Bay were over $27 per gallon, and by Exxon for the Valdez spill over $100 per gallon.

Multiplying the estimates of p_s and d (that is, $5.60 times 0.000 007) we obtain a value of $0.000 039 for the marginal benefit of reducing Saturday shipments by one gallon. For a fully laden average-sized tanker of 20 million gallons, the tax amounts to about $780 for each harbour entry. This is Goodstein's estimate of the efficient tax rate.

It is important to note that the efficient tax will not completely eliminate the Saturday effect. There are costs as well as benefits of reducing ship operations on Saturday. Only if there were no costs would it be efficient to completely eliminate the Saturday effect (by having no tanker traffic on that day).

The charge of $0.000 039 per gallon taken into or out of port on a Saturday will reduce Saturday shipments, but to a level which Goodstein's analysis cannot calculate. If the position of the marginal cost curve were known, the reduction in Saturday shipments would be calculable, but what Goodstein actually 'knows' is only the marginal benefit curve.

However, with an additional assumption (which Goodstein does not make) the size of the efficiency gain that the charge would bring about can be estimated. What we are trying to do is to measure the area of the shaded triangle ($\beta\gamma\delta$) in Figure 5.7. We know the vertical height of this triangle: it is $0.000 039, the efficient charge per gallon. What is the base-width of the triangle? Goodstein estimated that 22.4 billion gallons of oil per year were shipped on Saturdays. Let us assume that the tax reduces this by 50%, or 11.2 billion gallons. So the point δ corresponds to 22.4 and α to 22.4 minus 11.2, so the distance we are looking for is 11.2 billion.

The efficiency gain is half the area of the rectangle

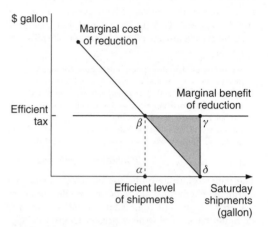

Figure 5.7 Assumed marginal costs and benefits of reducing Saturday shipments.

$\alpha\beta\gamma\delta$, or equivalently the area of the triangle $\beta\gamma\delta$; that is (11.2 billion × $0.000 039)/2 = $218 400. Looked at another way, society gains from avoided spills a total benefit equal to the area of the rectangle $\alpha\beta\gamma\delta$; however, the costs to society are only half of this, the triangle $\beta\alpha\delta$. That is why the value of net benefits is equal to the shaded area in Figure 5.7.

Can we describe this gain as a consumer or producer surplus? Given the context being considered here, it is quite difficult to do so. However, suppose that oil firms would be successfully sued for the full value of all the damages they caused. Then, as they would also incur any oil losses and clean-up costs, we can interpret the area of the rectangle $\alpha\beta\gamma\delta$ as the net cash flows gained by reducing spills. But as they only have to incur costs of $\beta\alpha\delta$ to achieve those cash flows, the difference between the two is producers' surplus. All the efficiency gain in this case is producers' surplus; the absence of consumers' surplus comes from the fact that the 'demand curve' (the marginal benefits curve) is in this case horizontal.

Source: Goodstein (1992)

value of the resources used (the total costs). But who actually gets this added value, consumers or producers or both? The answer is that the total added value is shared between the two. Consumers obtain a portion given by the area $P_X f'g'$ (known as consumers' surplus). Producers obtain a portion given by the area $P_X f'h'$ (known as producers' surplus). To see why this is so, reason as follows.

Consumers pay a fixed, market price for each unit. But for all except the last unit (the X*th one) the maximum amount of money they would pay is larger than the market price. Consumers are obtaining a total level of utility the money value of which they rate as being greater than their total expenditure. This difference is consumers' surplus, the portion of added value obtained by consumers.

Similarly, producers receive revenue in excess of the total cost that they incur in producing the cola; this difference is producers' surplus.

We conclude the chapter with a simple application of the partial equilibrium approach to measuring efficiency gains in Box 5.2.

Conclusions

In this chapter, we have defined and explained the terms efficiency and optimality. Efficiency was shown to have two dimensions: static and intertemporal. We also demonstrated that a perfectly functioning 'ideal' market economy would bring about an efficient outcome, but not necessarily an optimal one.

However, it is clear that economies in practice do not satisfy the conditions of an ideal competitive economy that we described above. Markets are often not perfectly competitive, information is not perfect, and consumption and production behaviour does generate uncompensated external effects upon others. These (and other) 'failures' will result in inefficient allocations of resources.

In the next chapter, we examine these inefficiencies, and their various causes, at some length. In doing so, we will bring the discussion back once again to a framework in which natural and environmental resources are given a central focus.

Discussion questions

1 To what extent do you believe that an economic criterion of efficiency is compatible with
   (a) an economic definition of sustainability?
   (b) an ecological definition of sustainability?
2 'If the market puts a lower value on trees as preserved resources than as sources of timber for construction, then those trees should be felled for timber.' Discuss.

Problems

1 Demonstrate that Equations 5.1 and 5.2 embody an assumption that there are no externalities in either consumption or production. Suppose that B's consumption of Y had a positive effect upon A's utility, and that the use of K by firm X adversely affects the output of firm Y. Show how the utility and production functions would need to be amended to take account of these effects.
2 The product-mix efficiency condition requires that there be an equality of the rate at which consumers value one good in terms of another with the opportunity costs of one good in terms of the other. Demonstrate that if this condition were not satisfied, inputs could be reallocated in such a way that a higher total utility could be achieved by each consumer for any given initial level of inputs.

Further reading

For a thorough general coverage of welfare economics principles, see Bator (1957), Baumol (1977), Just *et al.* (1982), Kreps (1990), Varian (1987) or Layard and Walters (1978), chapter 1. Applications of these principles to environmental economics are to be found in Baumol and Oates (1988), Hanley and Spash (1993), Common (1996), Dasgupta (1990), Johannson (1987), McInerney (1976) and Fisher (1981). An authoritative, but quite difficult, exposition is to be found in Mäler (1985).

Appendix 5.1 Economic efficiency in competitive markets

Utility maximisation in competitive markets

Consider an individual consumer, with a fixed money income M and gaining utility from the consumption of two goods, X and Y. The prices of these goods are determined in competitive markets, at the levels P_X and P_Y. Suppose this individual's utility function is given by

$$U = U(X, Y)$$

We can express the problem of maximising utility subject to a budget constraint mathematically as

$$\text{Max } U = U(X, Y)$$

subject to

$$M = P_X X + P_Y Y$$

Solving this problem by the method of Lagrange, we obtain

$$L = U(X, Y) + \lambda_1 (M - P_X X - P_Y Y)$$

The first-order conditions for a maximum require that

$$\frac{\partial L}{\partial X} = U_X - \lambda_1 P_X = 0$$

and

$$\frac{\partial L}{\partial Y} = U_Y - \lambda_1 P_Y = 0$$

in which $U_X = \partial U/\partial X$ and $U_Y = \partial U/\partial Y$, the marginal utilities of goods X and Y.

From these two equations we can deduce that

$$U_X = \lambda_1 P_X$$
$$U_Y = \lambda_1 P_Y$$

and so

$$\lambda_1 = \frac{U_x}{P_X} = \frac{U_Y}{P_Y}$$

Rearranging this expression, and noting that this is true for each consumer, indexed by i, we obtain

$$\left(\frac{U_X}{U_Y} \right)^i = \left(\frac{P_X}{P_Y} \right)^i$$

as given by Equation 5.10 in the main text.

Cost minimisation and profit maximisation in competitive markets

Suppose that a firm wishes to minimise its cost of production subject to satisfying an output constraint. (We will consider where this output constraint might come from shortly.) Let L and K be two inputs with prices P_L and P_K fixed in competitive input markets. Denote the required output level by $\bar{Q}$, and total costs by C. The cost minimisation problem is

$$\text{Min } C = P_L L + P_K K$$

subject to

$$\bar{Q} = Q(K, L)$$

Solving this problem by the method of Lagrange, we obtain

$$Y = P_L L + P_K K + \lambda_2 (\bar{Q} - Q(K, L))$$

The first-order conditions for a minimum require that

$$\frac{\partial Y}{\partial L} = P_L - \lambda_2 Q_L = 0$$

and

$$\frac{\partial Y}{\partial K} = P_K - \lambda_2 Q_K = 0$$

where $Q_K = \partial Q/\partial K$ and $Q_L = \partial Q/\partial L$, the marginal products of capital and labour.

From these two equations we can deduce that

$$\lambda_2 Q_L = P_L$$
$$\lambda_2 Q_K = P_K$$

and so

$$\lambda_2 = \frac{P_L}{Q_L} = \frac{P_K}{Q_K} \tag{5.14}$$

Given that we use the notation MP_K for Q_K in the main text, we can rewrite this expression in the form

$$\left(\frac{P_K}{\text{MP}_K} \right) = \left(\frac{P_L}{\text{MP}_L} \right) \tag{5.15}$$

as given by the last equality in Equation 5.12 in the main text.

Next we wish to demonstrate that in competitive markets, for any good, $\text{MC} = P_K/\text{MP}_K = P_L/\text{MP}_L$.

Denote L^* and K^* as the cost minimising levels of L and K. By definition

$$C = P_L L^* + P_K K^* \tag{5.16}$$

Marginal cost is obtained by differentiating this expression for cost with respect to output:

$$MC = \frac{dC}{dQ} = \left[P_L \frac{\partial L^*}{\partial Q} + P_K \frac{\partial K^*}{\partial Q} \right]$$

The term in square brackets is equal to the value of the Lagrange multiplier, λ_2. To see that this is so, take the expression for the output constraint at the cost-minimising levels of the inputs:

$$Q(K^*, L^*) = \bar{Q}$$

By differentiation with respect to $\bar{Q}$, we obtain

$$Q_K \cdot \frac{\partial K^*}{\partial \bar{Q}} + Q_L \cdot \frac{\partial L^*}{\partial \bar{Q}} = 1 \qquad (5.17)$$

Substituting from Equation 5.14 into Equation 5.17, we obtain

$$\frac{-P_K}{\lambda_2} \cdot \frac{\partial K^*}{\partial \bar{Q}} + \frac{P_L}{\lambda_2} \cdot \frac{\partial L^*}{\partial \bar{Q}} = 1$$

and then, after multiplication by $-\lambda_2$

$$MC = P_K \cdot \frac{\partial K^*}{\partial \bar{Q}} + P_L \cdot \frac{\partial L^*}{\partial \bar{Q}} = \lambda_2$$

So we have established that λ_2 is the marginal cost, MC. But from Equation 5.15 we also know that

$$\lambda_2 = \frac{P_L}{Q_L} = \frac{P_K}{Q_K} = \frac{P_L}{MP_L} = \frac{P_K}{MP_K}$$

This establishes the result we wish to prove, namely that $MC = P_K/MP_K = P_L/MP_L$.

Finally, we also wish to demonstrate that price equals marginal cost in long run competitive equilibrium. To do this, first note from Equation 5.16, together with the fact that L^* and K^* are functions of P_L, P_K and $\bar{Q}$, that

$$C = C(P_L, P_K, \bar{Q})$$

From the definition of profit we have

$$\Pi(\bar{Q}) = P\bar{Q} - C(P_L, P_K, \bar{Q})$$

The first-order condition for profit maximisation is that

$$\frac{d\Pi(\bar{Q})}{d\bar{Q}} = P - \frac{dC}{d\bar{Q}} = 0$$

which implies that $P = dC/dQ$, and hence at a profit maximum, output price equals marginal cost.

We have now established the result that

$$P = MC = \left(\frac{P_K}{MP_K} \right) = \left(\frac{P_L}{MP_L} \right) \qquad (5.18)$$

So for any two goods, X and Y, say, we have

$$P_X = MC_X = \left(\frac{P_K}{MP_K} \right)^X = \left(\frac{P_L}{MP_L} \right)^X \qquad (5.19)$$

and

$$P_Y = MC_Y = \left(\frac{P_K}{MP_K} \right)^Y = \left(\frac{P_L}{MP_L} \right)^Y \qquad (5.20)$$

and dividing Equation 5.19 by Equation 5.20 we obtain

$$\frac{P_X = \left(\frac{P_K}{MP_K} \right)^X}{P_Y = \left(\frac{P_K}{MP_K} \right)^Y}$$

which implies

$$\frac{P_X}{P_Y} = \frac{\left(\frac{P_K}{MP_K} \right)^X}{\left(\frac{P_K}{MP_K} \right)^Y}$$

But since all firms face the same price of capital, $P_K^X = P_K^Y$, and so this expression reduces to

$$\frac{P_X}{P_Y} = \frac{MP_K^Y}{MP_K^X}$$

Finally, using the result obtained earlier that in a competitive equilibrium

$$\frac{U_X}{U_Y} = \frac{P_X}{P_Y}$$

we obtain the product-mix efficiency condition

$$\frac{U_X}{U_Y} = \frac{P_X}{P_Y} = \frac{MP_K^Y}{MP_K^X}$$

By replacing K by L in this argument, the proof would be in terms of labour rather than capital, as here.

Appendix 5.2 The market for loanable funds

Assume that there exists a perfect capital market in which lending and borrowing can take place at a fixed rate of interest, i. Consider two successive periods of time, denoted 0 and 1 respectively. It will be convenient to consider one individual with a given level of income in each period. This person has two related sets of choices to make: firstly, a consumption choice – the amount to be consumed in each period – and secondly, an investment choice – which of the available investment projects should be taken up. The amounts produced and consumed in the two periods will depend upon the consumption and investment choices that are made.

Maximisation of the present value of utility

Given the interest rate i, an individual can exchange £1 income (and so consumption) today for £$1(1+i)$ in the next period, as illustrated in Figure 5.8. He or she can save £1 in period 0, earn interest on the saving at a rate i, and consume an additional quantity of £$1(1+i)$ in period 1.

The individual's preferences between present and future consumption are reflected in his or her intertemporal utility function

$$U = U(C_0, C_1)$$

Setting utility at some fixed level $\bar{U}$, an indifference curve can be constructed consisting of a locus of combinations of C_0 and C_1 yielding that level of utility. This is shown in Figure 5.9. If we denote by r the person's consumption discount rate, then the absolute value of the slope of an intertemporal indifference curve is given by $(1+r)$. A necessary condition for the consumer to have achieved an efficient allocation of consumption over time is that the rate at which present consumption can be exchanged for future consumption (that is, the slope of the intertemporal budget line in Figure 5.8) is equal to the marginal worth of present consumption relative to future consumption

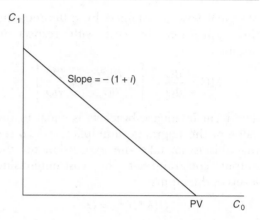

Figure 5.8 The market rate of exchange of present for future income.

(that is, the slope of an intertemporal utility indifference curve in Figure 5.9). One illustration of an efficient intertemporal consumption allocation is shown by the point Ω in Figure 5.10.

Maximisation of the present value of profits: intertemporal production possibilities

Assume a set of investment projects exists. For each project, an investment reduces present consumption by ΔC_0 and increases the next period's consumption by an amount ΔC_1. Let the rate of return on a project be denoted by δ, defined as

$$\frac{\Delta C_1}{-\Delta C_0} = 1 + \delta \text{ or } \frac{\Delta C_1 - \Delta C_0}{-\Delta C_0} = \delta$$

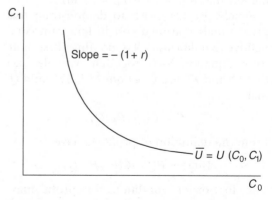

Figure 5.9 An intertemporal indifference curve.

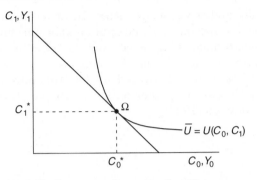

Figure 5.10 Intertemporal consumers' equilibrium.

Arranging all available projects in order of rate of return, we can represent available intertemporal production possibilities by means of the intertemporal production frontier shown in Figure 5.11. (In this diagram, we arbitrarily take the co-ordinates $\{C_0', C_1'\}$ to represent the consumption set if no investments are undertaken.)

As before, assume that unlimited borrowing and lending opportunities are available at the rate i. The rational individual (firm) will undertake all investment projects which have a positive net present value. That is, projects will be selected for which

$$PV = \Delta C_0 + \frac{\Delta C_1}{1+i} > 0$$

This implies that all projects should be done for which $\delta > i$, and in turn implies that at an

efficient allocation $\delta = i$ as indicated in Figure 5.12 at the point ϕ. Maximisation of present value by competitive firms implies that firms invest to the point where the rate of return on a marginal project, δ, equals the market rate of interest, i. An efficient production choice, therefore, requires that the rate at which future and present consumption can be exchanged (given by the slope of the intertemporal production frontier) is equal to the rate at which these can be exchanged in the market (determined by the prevailing rate of interest).

Intertemporal production and consumption efficiency

Finally, bringing together the two sides of our argument, we observe that simultaneous satisfaction of the conditions for efficiency in production and consumption requires that $(1 + r) = (1 + \delta)$, as illustrated in Figure 5.12. We assumed at the outset that all agents face a single given rate of interest. How is such a rate determined? To answer this, we need to look at the borrowing and lending decisions implicit in Figure 5.12. Note first that this individual borrows the amount $C_0^* - Y_0^*$ in period 0, and repays (lends) the amount $Y_1^* - C_1^*$ in period 1. The market rate of

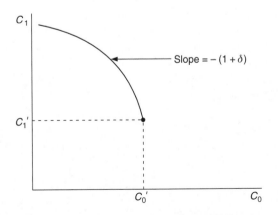

Figure 5.11 The intertemporal production possibility curve.

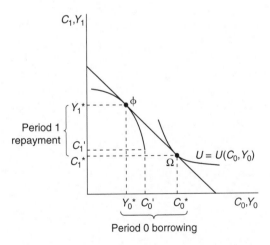

Figure 5.12 Intertemporal consumption–production equilibrium.

interest will be determined by the borrowing and lending decisions of all individuals in the economy. The equilibrium rate of interest (shown in all diagrams) is that for which aggregate lending equals aggregate borrowing at any point in time. Note that the individual we have investigated here is a net borrower initi-ally and a net lender later. In an economy where the interest rate is in equilibrium, this borrowing/lending stance must be offset by an opposite stance by all other persons.

The material covered in this Appendix is dealt with at greater length in chapter 6 of Commen (1996).

Market failure and public policy

[The contract between generations] is a partnership in all science; a partnership in all art; a partnership in every virtue, and in all perfection. As the ends of such a partnership cannot be obtained in many generations, it becomes a partnership not only between those living, but between those who are living, those who are dead, and those who are to be born.

Edmund Burke, *Reflections on the Revolution in France*

Introduction

In Chapter 5 we introduced and explained the concepts of efficiency and optimality as they relate to the allocation of resources at a point in time, and over time. We noted that, under certain conditions, a system of markets would realise efficiency in allocation. Where those conditions are not satisfied, 'market failure' is said to exist. Nobody believes that those conditions are satisfied in any actual economy. Economists think about public policy mainly, but not entirely, in terms of correcting market failure so as to realise efficiency in allocation. Economists also consider public policy in relation to optimality, when analysing measures intended to redistribute income and wealth so as to promote some concept of fairness or justice.

In Part 1 of this chapter we discuss, in a general way, the sources of market failure, concentrating on those that are of particular relevance to public policy in relation to environmental resources. In subsequent chapters we apply these ideas to particular issues, and explore the policy implications arising. In Part 2 we take a first look at cost–benefit analysis. This is a widely used technique for the social appraisal of investment projects. If there were no market failure, project appraisal could, at least as far as efficiency goes, be left to private agents using market prices. But where there is market failure, as there generally is in relation to projects with environmental impacts, the selection of projects in a manner consistent with efficiency requires appraisal by a public agency in a way that corrects for that failure. We shall explicitly discuss cost–benefit analysis in the environmental context in Chapters 14 and 15, though the ideas involved crop up at a number of points in subsequent chapters.

PART 1
Market failure

In the previous chapter, we laid out the conditions required for the allocation of resources within an economy to be efficient, in both static and intertemporal senses. As we shall make use of these conditions on a number of occasions in the rest of this chapter, it will be convenient to group and present them in a concise form. This is done in Box 6.1. A set of institutional arrangements was then described which would be sufficient to ensure that resource allocation through market processes is efficient. They are restated for convenience in Box 6.2.

The main arguments we shall be making in the first part of this chapter are as follows.

(1) Unregulated private market behaviour can, in principle, lead to efficient outcomes. However, in practice, some of the institutional arrangements required for market economies to allocate resources efficiently are not satisfied.

(2) The special characteristics of environmental resources play an important part in preventing the necessary institutional arrangements from existing or being likely to exist in any economy.

Box 6.1 Efficiency conditions in a competitive market

Static efficiency conditions

Efficiency in consumption:

$$\left(\frac{U_X}{U_Y}\right)^A = \left(\frac{U_X}{U_Y}\right)^B = \left(\frac{P_X}{P_Y}\right)$$

Efficiency in production:

$$\left(\frac{MP_L}{MP_K}\right)^X = \left(\frac{MP_L}{MP_K}\right)^Y = \left(\frac{P_L}{P_K}\right)$$

Product-mix efficiency

$$\left(\frac{U_X}{U_Y}\right) = \left(\frac{MP_K^Y}{MP_K^X}\right) = \left(\frac{MP_L^Y}{MP_L^X}\right) \Leftrightarrow P_X = MC_X$$

$$= \left(\frac{P_K}{MP_K}\right)^X = \left(\frac{P_L}{MP_L}\right)^X$$

Intertemporal efficiency conditions

$$r_i = r, i = 1, \ldots, M$$
$$\delta = r$$

Box 6.2 The institutional arrangements required for an efficient allocation of resources

(1) Markets exist for all goods and services exchanged.
(2) All markets are perfectly competitive.
(3) No externalities exist.
(4) All goods and services are private goods. There are no public goods.
(5) Property rights are fully assigned.
(6) All transactors have perfect information.
(7) All firms are profit maximisers and all individuals utility maximisers.
(8) Long-run average costs are non-decreasing.
(9) Transactions costs are zero.
(10) All relevant functions satisfy convexity conditions.

---

(3) If these two assertions are correct, market economies will not allocate resources efficiently; that is, the economy will be characterised by market failure.

(4) Even though markets by themselves may fail to allocate resources efficiently, public sector intervention offers the prospect of establishing alternative institutional arrangements that will, by altering behaviour, lead to efficient patterns of resource allocation.

Our objectives in this part of Chapter 6 are to explain and justify each of these assertions. We shall pay particular attention to points 2 and 4. Identification of the reasons why markets fail is an important step in designing appropriate environmental policy programmes. We present one example of an environmentally relevant market failure in Box 6.3.

Environmental resources and the existence of markets

Markets cannot allocate resources efficiently where markets do not exist. Many environmental resources are not transacted at all through market processes, or the markets in which they are exchanged are incomplete in some way. Examples of environmental resources that are not traded through markets include the earth's atmosphere, a large proportion of its water resources, and many wilderness areas. In the absence of regulation, pollution is also not subject to market exchange.

Some environmental resources are traded through markets. Most mineral deposits are privately owned, and when extracted are marketed commodities. But here markets are usually incomplete. Current (or spot) markets exist for such resources, but it is unusual for futures markets to exist for most commodities. There is no resource, good or service for which a complete set of future markets (for all points in time) exists.

It is possible to envisage alternative forms of organisation to that of the market which can bring about resource allocation efficiency. However, such substitutes do not exist in practice. The pervasive presence of public goods and externalities implies failure of the static efficiency conditions, and the

Evidence now suggests that the accumulation of tropospheric ozone in urban areas poses serious threats to human health, and also leads to agricultural crop damage in surrounding areas.[1] A major source of tropospheric ozone is road vehicle exhaust emissions. Because vehicle emissions have real effects on well-being through our utility and production functions, these emissions can be termed 'goods' (although it may be preferable to label them as 'bads' as the effects on utility are adverse). However, unlike goods that are exchanged through markets, no charge is made for such emissions in the absence of government intervention. In this example, conditions 1 and 5 of Box 6.2 are not being met, and the analysis below will demonstrate that resources are not being allocated efficiently. An efficient allocation would require lower exhaust emissions, implying lower traffic volumes, change in fuel type used, increased engine efficiency or enhanced exhaust control. We show in Chapter 12 how such objectives might be achieved, but it should be clear at this stage that one method would be through the use of taxes on emissions that cause ozone accumulation. Thus, an efficient emissions tax would impose a tax rate on each unit of emission equal to the value of the damages caused by that unit of emission.

In arriving at this conclusion, we did not explicitly consider the time dimension of pollution. But note that if ozone accumulates over time, and damage is dependent on the stock of ozone rather than the flow of emissions in any particular period, then we need to consider the accumulation of the pollutant over time. As Chapter 11 shows, where emission flows lead to accumulating stocks of pollutants, it may be efficient to impose a tax rate that rises over time.

[1] Note that the accumulation of ozone in lower layers of the atmosphere, causing lung-related health problems, among other things, is completely distinct from the destruction of the ozone layer in the earth's upper atmosphere (the stratosphere). The latter phenomenon – often known as 'holes in the ozone layer' – causes different problems, and is explained in Chapter 13.

The failure of markets to exist for many environmental resources is often a reflection of the fact that the resources in question are public goods. We shall examine the implications for resource use of public goods and the related issue of common property resources in the present chapter. Implications for the environment and environmental policy of public goods, common property resources and externalities will also be examined in several of the chapters that follow.

Environmental resources and markets

Where markets for environmental resources do exist they are not always competitive. It is well known from standard results in microeconomics that monopolistic and imperfectly competitive market structures can result in efficiency losses. We investigate these losses in the context of the extraction of exhaustible resources in Chapters 7 and 8, and so do not discuss the matter any further at this point.

Externalities

An external effect, or externality for short, is said to occur when the production or consumption decisions of one agent affect the utility or production possibilities of another agent in an unintended way, and when no compensation is made by the producer of the external effect to the affected party. In our analysis of efficient resource allocation in the previous chapter, we excluded the existence of externalities by the assumptions that were made about the utility and production functions. To confirm this, look again at the way we formulated these functions in Equations 5.1 and 5.2. An individual's utility depends only on the quantity of each good he or she consumes. Similarly, the quantity of each good produced depends only on the quantities of the two inputs that the producer employs.

risks and uncertainties introduced whenever markets are incomplete suggest that it is very unlikely that resource allocation over time will be efficient.

But in practice consumption and production behaviour by some agents does affect, in uncompensated ways, the utility gained by other consumers and the output produced by other producers. Economic behaviour does involve external effects. In Chapter 2, we discussed the materials balance approach to economic analysis. The seminal work in this field by Ayres and Kneese (1969) demonstrates that external effects, far from being rare in occurrence and limited in importance, are endemic in modern economies. Negative externalities are inevitable and pervasive in industrial economies, and are intrinsically associated with the use of environmental resources. Ayres and Kneese argued that it is not possible for these externalities to be 'internalised' through unregulated market behaviour, and so, in the absence of government intervention, inefficient outcomes are inevitable. Our objective here is to explain the basis of these claims, and to show how externalities result in resource misallocation.

Classification of externalities

A simple classification of the forms that external effects may take is given in Table 6.1. The effect may be the consequence of either consumption or production behaviour, and may be beneficial or adverse. This twofold classification leads to four types of externality. Vaccination against an infectious disease exemplifies the case of a beneficial consumption externality. Suppose a woman chooses to

Table 6.1 Example of a simple classification of externalities.

Effect on others	Consumption	Production
Beneficial	Vaccination against an infectious disease	Pollination of blossom arising from proximity to apiary
Adverse	Noise pollution from radio playing in park	Chemical factory spillage of contaminated water into water systems

vaccinate herself against the risk of contracting measles. This is a consumption decision taken presuming that the net benefits she derives will be positive. But her action has effects upon others; her reduced probability of contracting measles will reduce the probability of others contracting the disease. The effect is external in the sense that the effect on others did not influence her choice, and nor will she receive any compensation from others (through a market or otherwise). Put another way, the total benefits of a vaccination decision are greater than the effects derived directly by the individual who is vaccinated. We shall demonstrate later in this section that, relative to economically efficient levels, a market economy will tend to consume too small a quantity of goods that have beneficial external effects. Conversely, a market economy will tend to consume excessive quantities of goods that have adverse external effects.

The example we have just illustrated constitutes one in which the externality is a 'public good'. Public goods externalities include most types of air and water pollution. It is also possible for externalities to take the form of private goods. This suggests a third dimension in terms of which externalities may be classified: they can be public or private, depending upon whether the external effect is a public good or bad, or a private good or bad. The concepts of public and private goods will be defined in the next section. However, it is worth noting at this point that most environmentally relevant externalities are public. As we shall see, the public goods nature of many environmentally relevant externalities poses particular difficulties in designing and administering measures that seek to reduce the problems associated with market failure.

Externalities and economic efficiency

Do the efficiency conditions in Box 6.1 remain valid in an economy in which externalities do exist? Not surprisingly, they do not, or more precisely, they are only valid if we interpret them in a particular way.[2] So how does the presence of externalities change the required efficiency conditions? Let us consider first the production efficiency condition that we have written as

$$\frac{MP_L^X}{MP_K^X} = \frac{MP_L^Y}{MP_K^Y} \qquad (6.1)$$

In order for this to remain valid as a condition of productive efficiency, it is necessary to interpret the four marginal products in net terms, or if you prefer, as social marginal products. Let us define some new notation: PMP_L is the private marginal product of labour, EMP_L is the external marginal product of labour and SMP_L is the social marginal product of labour. An equivalent notation applies to capital. These three measures of marginal product are related as follows:

$$PMP_L + EMP_L = SMP_L$$

The idea here is a simple one: when a firm chooses to employ an additional unit of labour, the marginal product of labour to that firm is PMP_L. If this employment of labour has an external effect on others, we denote that external effect as EMP_L. The total, net, or social marginal product is the sum of these two. The productive efficiency condition for an economy in which external effects occur can then be written as either

$$\frac{SMP_L^X}{SMP_K^X} = \frac{SMP_L^Y}{SMP_K^Y} \qquad (6.2)$$

or

$$\frac{PMP_L^X + EMP_L^X}{PMP_K^X + EMP_K^X} = \frac{PMP_L^Y + EMP_L^Y}{PMP_K^Y + EMP_K^Y} \qquad (6.3)$$

We can now see why private profit maximising behaviour will fail to allocate resources efficiently in the presence of externalities. Left to act in their individual self-interests, firms will only take account of private marginal pro-

ducts. So profit maximisation will result in the ratio of private marginal products being equalised between goods. The analysis in Chapter 5, in the section on achieving an efficient allocation in a market economy, demonstrated that these would be equal to the ratio of input prices (see Equation 5.11). That is

$$\frac{PMP_L^X}{PMP_K^X} = \frac{PMP_L^Y}{PMP_K^Y} = \frac{P_L}{P_K} \qquad (6.4)$$

Clearly, except in the unlikely event that external effects are exactly offsetting in arithmetic terms, the equalisation of private marginal product ratios will yield a different allocation of resources from that which derives from the equalisation of social marginal product ratios. As the latter is required for efficiency, private market behaviour will be inefficient in the presence of externalities.

We can also think about inefficiency in the following way. If firms act uncooperatively (that is, maximising profits independently of one another) the outcome is less good compared with that where they act cooperatively (maximising combined profits). Suppose that one firm produces X and another produces Y. For simplicity, imagine that X is produced using one purchased input K, while Y is produced using another purchased input L. Each producer also makes use of the atmosphere as a productive input, but no charge is made for the use of this resource. In addition, we assume that the production of Y generates atmospheric pollution. This pollution generates a negative externality, adversely affecting the production of X, but not affecting the production of Y. We denote the quantity of this pollutant emission by M, and assume that its magnitude is an increasing function of the amount of L used in producing Y. Thus we can write the two production functions as

$$\begin{aligned} X &= X(K, M) \\ Y &= Y(L) \end{aligned} \qquad (6.5)$$

where $M = M(L)$

Assume that $\partial X/\partial K > 0$, $\partial X/\partial M < 0$, and $dY/dL > 0$. The production of Y only involves

---

[2] There is a general point here. None of the efficiency conditions listed in Box 6.1 remains true (without a suitable reinterpretation) whenever one or more of the institutional arrangements in Box 6.2 fails to hold.

inputs chosen by its own producer; however, the production of X is partly determined by inputs chosen by its own producer and partly by input choices of the other producer. In a competitive market economy, each firm maximises profits independently. What is the outcome of this process? The profit functions for the two firms can be written as

$$\Pi_X = P_X X - P_K K$$
$$= P_X X(K, M) - P_K K \qquad (6.6)$$
$$\Pi_Y = P_Y Y - P_L L = P_Y Y(L) - P_L L$$

Profit maximisation by each firm separately implies that K is chosen to maximise the profits in producing X, while, independently, L is chosen to maximise the profits in producing Y. It is necessary for profit maximisation that the input choices of the two firms satisfy the first-order conditions:

$$\frac{\partial \Pi_X}{\partial K} = P_X X_K - P_K = 0$$
$$\frac{\partial \Pi_Y}{\partial L} = P_Y Y_L - P_L = 0 \qquad (6.7)$$

where $X_K = \partial X/\partial K$ and $Y_L = \partial Y/\partial L$. Rearranging Equations 6.7 we obtain the profit maximising conditions

$$P_X X_K = P_K$$
$$P_Y Y_L = P_L \qquad (6.8)$$

The left-hand side of each of the Equations 6.8 is the value of the marginal product of the input. The right-hand side is a marginal cost. Equations 6.8, therefore, imply that the quantity employed of each input is chosen so that the value of its marginal product is equal to its marginal cost.

Note also that we can derive an alternative interpretation of these profit maximising conditions. Rearranging Equations 6.8 we can obtain

$$P_X = \frac{P_K}{X_K}$$
$$P_Y = \frac{P_L}{Y_L} \qquad (6.9)$$

Equations 6.9 state that in profit maximising equilibrium, the output price for each good equals its *private* marginal cost of production. We make use of this alternative interpretation later.

Return now to Equations 6.8. These describe the input demands that will exist in a competitive market economy where no price is charged for the pollution externality associated with the output of firm Y. However, this outcome is not one in which resources are allocated efficiently. Recall that an efficient allocation implies that no unexploited net benefits exist. But there are unexploited net benefits in this case, because individual competitive behaviour does not maximise overall or combined profits. To see this, consider how profits would change if there were to be a small increase in the use of the input L. The second of Equations 6.8 shows that there would be no change in profits in producing good Y, because the incremental cost of labour (P_L) would be just balanced by the value of the marginal product of the additional unit of labour ($P_Y Y_L$). But the profits of firm X are reduced; the increased use of L raises the quantity of harmful emissions M. Given that $\partial X/\partial M < 0$, this reduces the output of X, and lowers the profits of its producer. A corollary of this is that joint profits would be increased if a smaller quantity of labour were to be employed. Clearly the competitive equilibrium is not efficient; it leads to an excessive use of L, reducing combined profits below their maximum level, and leaving unexploited Pareto improvements.

Maximisation of joint profits

Let us now look more closely at the efficient solution, which maximises joint or combined profits. Combined profits, Π_{X+Y}, are given by

$$\Pi_{X+Y} = P_X X(K, M) + P_Y Y(L)$$
$$- P_K K - P_L L \qquad (6.10)$$

The necessary conditions for a maximum of this combined profit function are obtained by differentiation of the joint profit function with respect to K and L:

$$\frac{\partial \Pi_{X+Y}}{\partial K} = P_X X_K - P_K = 0 \qquad (6.11)$$

$$\frac{\partial \Pi_{X+Y}}{\partial L} = P_X \cdot \frac{\partial X}{\partial M} \cdot \frac{dM}{dL}$$
$$+ P_Y Y_L - P_L = 0 \quad (6.12)$$

Rearranging Equation 6.12 we obtain

$$P_X \cdot \frac{\partial X}{\partial M} \cdot \frac{dM}{dL} + P_Y Y_L = P_L \qquad (6.13)$$

The first term on the left-hand side of Equation 6.13 is the value of the marginal damage done to X by the pollution produced by Y. The marginal damage in physical units is given by $\partial X/\partial M$ multiplied by dM/dL, what we called earlier the external marginal product of labour. The *value* of marginal damage is found by multiplying this expression by P_X. The second term on the left-hand side is the value of the marginal product of L in the production of good Y. Combining the two components on the left-hand side gives the value of the marginal product of L, net of the value of the marginal damage done by L in the production of X. Equation 6.13 states that the value of the net marginal product of L should be equal to the marginal cost of L, P_L. Finally, another interpretation can be gleaned from inspection of Equation 6.13. Productive efficiency in the presence of externalities requires that the input L should be used to the point where the net value of its marginal contribution in the production of good Y $(P_Y Y_L - P_L)$ is just equal to the value of the marginal damage in the production of X, as shown in Figure 6.1.

Let us recap the argument. Profit-maximising behaviour in a market economy would result in the satisfaction of the second of Equations 6.7, in which $P_Y Y_L = P_L$. However, in the presence of an external effect, this is not economically efficient, as an unexploited Pareto gain exists. The efficient solution is given by Equation 6.13, which requires that the sum of $P_Y Y_L$ (the value of

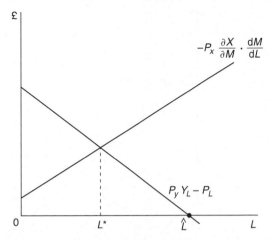

Figure 6.1 The efficient choice of an input in the presence of a production external effect.

the output of Y obtained by using an additional unit of labour) and the value of the associated external damage to the production of X is equal to the incremental cost of a unit of labour, P_L. Notice that the first term on the left-hand side of Equation 6.13 represents this adverse external effect, that we earlier called EMP$_L$. As P_L is a given constant to every firm, it must be equal in the two equations. Also, the first term in Equation 6.13 is negative. Therefore the product $P_Y Y_L$ must be higher in Equation 6.13 than in the second of Equations 6.7. This in turn implies that Y_L must be higher, implying a lower use of the input L. An illustration of this result is given in Figure 6.1. The efficient labour choice, L^*, is lower than that implied by private profit maximisation, $\hat{L}$.

Representing in a slightly different way the information contained in Figure 6.1 can help comprehension of this argument. This is done in Figure 6.2. The diagram on the left portrays the competitive (inefficient) solution, in which the quantity $\hat{L}$ is chosen so that $P_Y Y_L = P_L$. Put differently, if we denote marginal private net benefit by MB, and define this to be MB $= P_Y Y_L - P_L$, then private producers operate so as to employ an input up to the point where MB equals zero. The right-hand side of Figure 6.2 illustrates the

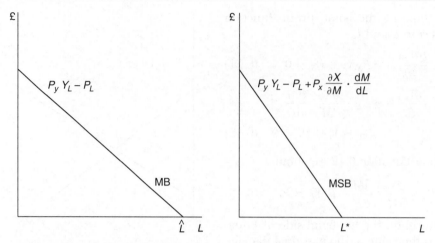

Figure 6.2 The marginal private benefit and the marginal social benefit from the use of labour in the presence of an adverse external effect.

combined efficient solution. Defining the marginal net social benefit (MSB) as

$$P_X \cdot \frac{\partial X}{\partial M} \cdot \frac{dM}{dL} + P_Y Y_L - P_L \quad (6.14)$$

we see (from Equation 6.12) that efficiency requires that L^* be chosen so that MSB = 0. Finally, Figure 6.3 combines the two sets of information from Figure 6.2, and allows us to compare L^* with $\hat{L}$. Another item of information can be obtained from Figure 6.3. The distance ab represents the magnitude of the value of the adverse external effect at the socially optimal labour input level, L^*. This magnitude is a shadow price, and we show in Chapter 11 that this shadow price determines the magnitude of an optimal emission tax.

An alternative interpretation of production externalities

Previously, in Equations 6.9, we derived an alternative formulation of the profit-maximising condition in competitive equilibrium, which for good Y was:

$$P_Y = \frac{P_L}{Y_L}$$

so that the output price of Y equals the private marginal cost of production of good Y.

However, we saw above that an efficient allocation requires that

$$P_X \cdot \frac{\partial X}{\partial M} \cdot \frac{dM}{dL} + P_Y Y_L = P_L$$

Rearranging this expression yields

$$P_Y = \frac{P_L}{Y_L} - \frac{P_X \cdot \frac{\partial X}{\partial M} \cdot \frac{dM}{dL}}{Y_L} \quad (6.15)$$

so that the socially efficient price of Y equals the private marginal cost of producing good $Y (P_L/Y_L)$ minus the marginal external cost of

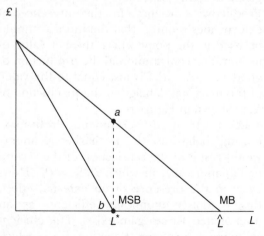

Figure 6.3 An adverse externality, driving a wedge between private and social costs.

Y, which is the second term on the right-hand side. This term is negative by virtue of $\partial X/\partial M < 0$, so that $P_Y > P_L/Y_L$. A comparison of the private but inefficient allocation of good Y with the socially efficient allocation is shown graphically in Figure 6.4, in terms of a familiar supply and demand curve representation.

Private profit maximisation in competitive markets leads to an output level $\hat{Y}$, at which private marginal cost is equal to private marginal revenue. The competitive market price of Y is P_Y, which takes no account of the external effect that Y has on X. The socially efficient output level is Y^*, which equates the marginal benefit derived from good Y with the social marginal cost of Y. This social cost exceeds the private cost by its inclusion of the external effect.

The distance cd represents a shadow price, which can be interpreted as an efficient externality tax on units of output of Y. The socially efficient price, P_{Y^*}, is greater than the competitive market price, P_Y, because of the presence of the adverse external effect. We discuss the concept of pollution taxes, designed to 'internalise' externalities, at length in Chapter 11. At this stage in our dis-

cussions we just note the pervasiveness of negative external effects in matters relating to the natural environment. Perhaps the most important example relates to negative external effects from the consumption of fossil fuels, discussed extensively throughout the text. There are several other examples of the external effects of economic activities that we shall investigate in subsequent chapters. These include overuse of wilderness areas, the loss of biodiversity as economic activity interferes with habitats, the build-up of inorganic pollutants associated with intensive agricultural practices, road congestion and the increasing real economic costs of waste disposal.

Our discussion of externalities has concentrated upon negative externalities arising from production. Clearly, the analysis carries over straightforwardly to beneficial externalities in production, with appropriate changes in sign on the external effects in the appropriate expressions. When it comes to externalities in consumption, whether they are adverse or beneficial, the method of analysis and the results obtained are similar in form. The consumption efficiency condition must be reinterpreted to require equality between the ratios of social marginal utilities. This will not be obtained, however, in an unregulated market economy; individual consumers will equate the ratios of their private marginal utilities to the ratios of goods prices. Whenever consumption externalities are present, this will lead to inefficient outcomes. Mention should also be made of 'mixed cases', where production externalities damage individuals as consumers, and vice versa. We will not go through the analyses for these cases, but you should be able to appreciate that these cases will also, in general, lead to market failure.

How can inefficiencies associated with externalities be eliminated? We will not attempt to answer this important question at this point, as it is the major theme of Chapter 11. It will be shown there that, under certain special circumstances, bargaining between producers and consumers of externalities can

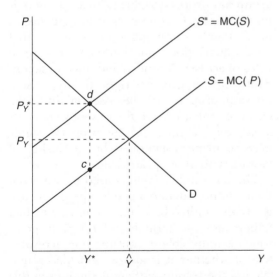

Figure 6.4 The private profit-maximising output and the socially efficient output of a good that creates an adverse external effect.

lead to efficient outcomes. Bargaining solutions are, however, very unlikely for most externalities that relate to the use of environmental resources. Our analysis has pointed to one measure that could bring about efficient outcomes: the use of pollution taxes. This policy instrument is examined in Chapter 12.

Public goods

Many environmental resources have the characteristics of public goods. The probability of markets existing to provide or conserve public goods is extremely low, even where their existence would yield positive net benefits. As a result, public goods will tend, in a pure market economy, to be provided in quantities that are too low from the point of view of social efficiency. Furthermore, even in the unlikely event that a private market did develop, the outcome would not be efficient. Once again, one is led to the conclusion that efficiency gains may be possible from government intervention.

Consider a good, service or resource with the following properties. Firstly, when one person consumes a unit of the good, that unit is not available for another person to consume. An ice cream exhibits this property; when a particular unit is consumed no one else can eat it. This property is variously called divisibility, rivalness, or depletability. We will henceforth use the first of these terms, and describe such a good as being a divisible good. Notice that divisibility implies that the marginal cost of providing the good will be positive.

Secondly, a good may have the property that its owner could prevent access to it (and so consumption of it) by other people. The owner of a gold mine, for example, could normally prevent access to and consumption of the gold if he or she chose to do so. A good possessing this property is said to be an excludable good.

A private good is divisible and excludable. However, not all goods and resources are both divisible and excludable. In particular, many environmental resources do not exhibit one or both of these characteristics. Consider an example. Wilderness areas are not divisible, provided the use rates to which they are subjected are not excessive. If one person visits a wilderness area and consumes its services – recreation, wildlife experiences and solitude, for example – that does not prevent others consuming those services as well. There is no rivalry between the consumption of different individuals, provided that the overall rate of usage is not beyond a threshold level at which congestion occurs (and so one person's visit does not detract from others' enjoyment). In this sense, we could describe the services provided by wilderness areas as indivisible. What does this imply about the marginal cost of providing an extra unit of the service to another user? Clearly this cost is zero because an additional user's consumption of the resource does not require that the resource stock be increased. This insight has important implications that we explore below.

Secondly, for many goods, it is not possible to exclude persons from consuming the good. There are really two issues here. The first concerns property rights; if no person or group has property rights to an asset, there is no legal basis for one person to deny access to another (assuming for the moment that government does not intervene to create rules of access). Secondly, and quite independently of what property rights (if any) exist, a physical property of the asset might make exclusion infeasible. In the case of wilderness areas, for example, private property rights may be firmly established but exclusion of visitors is often not practicable.

The term public good is used in two ways. Some authors define a good to be public if it is both indivisible and non-excludable. Others use the term to refer to any good which is indivisible in consumption, irrespective of whether it is also excludable or not. We use the second of these definitions in this text, and so take a public good to be indivisible in consumption.

Box 6.4 Examples of public goods

The classic textbook examples of public goods are lighthouses and national defence systems. These both possess the properties of being non-excludable and indivisible. If you or I choose not to pay for defence or lighthouse services, we cannot be excluded from the benefits of the service, once it is provided to anyone. Moreover, our consumption of the service does not diminish the amount available to others. Bridges also share the property of being indivisible (provided they are not used beyond a point at which congestion effects begin), although they are not typically non-excludable.

Many environmental resources are public goods, as can be seen from the following examples. You should check, in each case, that the key criterion of indivisibility is satisfied. The benefits from biological diversity, the services of wilderness resources, the climate regulation mechanisms of the earth's atmosphere, and the waste disposal and reprocessing services of environmental sinks all constitute public goods, provided the use made of them is not excessive. Indeed,

much public policy towards such environmental resources can be interpreted in terms of regulations or incentives designed to prevent use breaking through such threshold levels.

Some naturally renewing resource systems also share public goods properties. Examples include water resource systems and the composition of the earth's atmosphere. Although in these cases consumption by one person does potentially reduce the amount of the resource available to others (so the resource could be 'scarce' in an economic sense), this will not be relevant in practice as long as consumption rates are low relative to the system's regenerative capacity.

Finally, note that many public health measures, including inoculation and vaccination against infectious diseases, have public goods characteristics, by reducing the probability of any person (whether or not he or she is inoculated or vaccinated) contracting the disease. Similarly, educational and research expenditures are, to some extent, public goods.

As you will see, it is probably the case that most indivisible (public) goods are also non-excludable. Moreover, it is this latter aspect which is of most relevance to the place of public goods in market economies; if an owner were unable to exclude another person from consuming a good, it is difficult to see how the owner could sell the good at any positive price. But if prices cannot be charged for a good, it is difficult to imagine how a market could exist for that good. We are drawn to the conclusion that non-excludable public goods are unlikely to be provided in pure market economies.

Separating the issue of excludability from the defining characteristic of public goods (i.e. indivisibility) also allows us to define another class of goods for which private property rights have not been established. These are the common-property and open access goods and resources, analysed extensively in Chapters 9 and 10. Examples of these include some aquifers, fisheries, forests, the earth's atmospheric resources and wilderness areas.

Public goods and economic efficiency

We begin by recalling the static efficiency conditions for an economy in which all of the institutional arrangements of Box 6.2 are satisfied. For convenience, the production, consumption and product-mix efficiency conditions are restated in the upper part of Table 6.2. Remember that these conditions apply to the case where no public goods exist (and so X and Y are private goods).

How do we interpret these conditions? Note that $(U_X/U_Y)^A$ is the number of units of

Table 6.2 Private and public goods: consumption efficiency.

Efficiency conditions for two private goods, X and Y:

$$\left(\frac{U_X}{U_Y}\right)^A = \left(\frac{U_X}{U_Y}\right)^B = \frac{MP_K^Y}{MP_K^X} = \frac{MP_L^Y}{MP_L^X} \left[=\frac{P_X}{P_Y}\right]$$

Efficiency conditions for a private good (Y) and a public good (X)

$$\left(\frac{U_X}{U_Y}\right)^A + \left(\frac{U_X}{U_Y}\right)^B = \frac{MP_K^Y}{MP_K^X} = \frac{MP_L^Y}{MP_L^X} \left[=\frac{P_X}{P_Y}\right]$$

good Y that A is willing to pay for an additional unit of X. As the consumption of X is divisible, and so only one person can consume it, the social willingness to pay (WTP) for one unit of X is equal to one consumer's WTP. Given fixed market prices, P_X and P_Y, this measure of WTP will be identical over all consumers. The expressions involving marginal products refer to the reduction in production of Y that would result from transferring resources into the production of an extra unit of X. In other words, it is the opportunity cost of X in terms of Y. Efficiency requires that the individual WTP for X in units of Y is equal to the opportunity cost of X in units of Y.

Now consider the case where good Y is private and X is a public good. In this case, the relevant efficiency conditions are given in the lower part of Table 6.2. As the consumption of X is non-divisible, the social willingness to pay for one unit of X is the sum over all consumers of each person's WTP, rather than being equal to one person's WTP. The interpretation of the terms involving marginal products remains exactly as before. Thus efficiency in the allocation of resources requires that the sum of all individuals' WTP is equal to the opportunity cost of X in terms of Y. In a competitive market economy the opportunity cost of X in terms of Y is equal to the ratio of output prices, P_X/P_Y. We can re-express this result as follows. For one public and one private good, economic efficiency requires that

$$\sum \left(\frac{U_X}{U_Y} \right) = \frac{P_X}{P_Y} \qquad (6.16)$$

Another interpretation of these efficiency conditions is sometimes given. Recall that we obtained, for two private goods

$$\frac{U_X}{U_Y} = \frac{P_X}{P_Y}$$

and for one private good (Y) and one public good (X)

$$\sum \left(\frac{U_X}{U_Y} \right) = \frac{P_X}{P_Y}$$

Now choose units in such a way that $P_Y = 1$. Given this, we can now write the two efficiency conditions as

$$\frac{U_X}{U_Y} = P_X \qquad (6.17)$$

for two private goods, and

$$\sum \left(\frac{U_X}{U_Y} \right) = P_X \qquad (6.18)$$

for one private good (Y) and one public good (X). We may interpret Equation 6.17 as stating that for any two private goods, consumption efficiency requires that purchases be arranged so that the willingness to pay for X (in units of Y) is equal to the price of X (in units of Y). On the other hand, for the case of X being a public good, Equation 6.18 states that purchases should be arranged so that the sum of the willingness to pay for X (in units of Y) over all consumers of the good X is equal to the price of X (in units of Y).

What is the efficient level of provision of a public good?

Two questions are relevant here:

(1) Should a particular public good be provided at all if it does not already exist? If it should be, to what extent should it be provided?
(2) Once available, how much use should be made of the public good?

The first question is essentially one that should be answered by means of a cost–benefit analysis (CBA) project appraisal. The project should be undertaken if its social expected net present value exceeds zero. (See Part 2 of this chapter and Chapter 15 for an analysis of CBA.) As far as the second question is concerned, additional use is socially beneficial (and so should be encouraged) whenever a potential user can derive any positive marginal benefit from the good, provided the marginal cost of that provision is zero. This latter condition

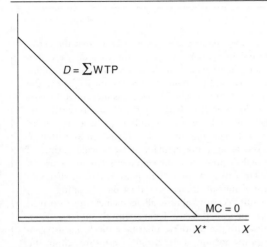

$D = \sum WTP$

$MC = 0$

X^* X

Figure 6.5 The socially efficient level of provision of a public good.

will be satisfied, by definition, for a pure public good. However, in circumstances where congestion exists or rivalry between users arises, as for example where the presence of visitors to a wildlife area detracts from other visitors' enjoyment, the good in question ceases to be a pure public good. Then limitation on use, possibly through the introduction of user charges, becomes efficient. Wherever a good is private, its use should be such that individual marginal costs and benefits from use are balanced. The efficient use rate of an existing pure public good is illustrated in Figure 6.5.

Property rights, common property resources and environmental resources

The extent to which an economy is able to reach an efficient allocation of resources will depend upon the nature of the property rights that prevail. Hartwick and Olewiler (1986) define a property right as 'A bundle of characteristics that convey certain powers to the owner of the right'.

These characteristics concern conditions of appropriability of returns, the ability to divide or transfer the right, the degree of exclusiveness of the right, and the duration and enforceability of the right. Where a right is exclusive to one person or corporation, a private property right is said to exist. In these circumstances, markets will tend to exist and efficient allocations of resources will be possible without government intervention. For several classes of environmental resources, well-defined property rights do not exist. Outcomes cannot be socially optimal in these circumstances.

Where property rights are non-exclusive, there are common property or open access rights. The title 'common property resources' is used whenever some customary procedures or conventions govern use of the resource in question. This is not implied by the phrase 'open access resources'. In the presence of open access, markets cannot by themselves allocate resources efficiently. It is possible, though unlikely, that resources will be allocated efficiently where common property rights prevail.

Many environmental resources are not privately owned, being characterised by either common property regimes or open access in which ownership is either ill defined or non-existent. In these circumstances, there are several sources of inefficiency in the use of the resource. Not surprisingly, the major problem arises from the fact that stewardship of the asset is likely to be poor where users cannot expect to receive the fruits of investment in the resource.

A rapacious attitude often characterises behaviour in the absence of regulatory control. However, since common property resource issues are intimately bound up with the use of resources over time, and because they are characteristic of many renewable resources, these conclusions will not be justified here. They will become evident as you study the economics of renewable resource harvesting in Chapters 9 and 10. Indeed, we shall demonstrate at several places in this book that many environmental assets have the characteristics of public goods, either wholly or partially, and that this can go a long way towards explaining the misuse of these resources.

Box 6.5 Property rights and biodiversity

Among the many sources of value that humans derive from biological diversity is the contribution it makes to the pharmaceutical industry. This is examined in a volume which brings together a collection of papers on the theme of property rights and biological diversity (Swanson, 1995a). In this box we summarise some of the central issues raised there.

Swanson begins by noting that the biological characteristics of plants (and, to a lesser extent, animals) can be classified into primary and secondary forms. Primary characteristics concern the efficiency with which an organism directly draws upon its environment. For example, plant growth – and the survivability of a population of that plant over time – depends upon its rate of photosynthesis, by which solar energy is converted into the biological material of the plant itself. The success of a species depends on such primary characteristics; indeed, the ecological dominance of humans can be described largely in terms of the massive increases in primary productivity attained through modern agriculture.

But another set of characteristics – secondary characteristics – are also of great importance in the survivability of an organism within its environment. To survive in a particular ecological complex, an organism must be compatible with other living components of its environment. The secondary metabolites which plants develop are crucial in this respect. Some plants develop attractors (such as fruits and aromas) which increase the spread of their reproductive materials. Acorns, for example, are transported and eaten by small animals, thereby encouraging the spread of oak woodlands. Other plants develop repellents in the form of (unattractive) aromas or toxins, which give defence against predatory organisms.

A diverse ecosystem will be characterised by a large variety of biological organisms in which evolutionary processes generate a rich mix of these secondary metabolites. Many of these will be highly context-specific. That is, even within one fairly narrow class of plants, there can be a large variety of these secondary metabolites that function to give relative fitness in a particular location. These secondary characteristics are helpful to plants and animals not only in aiding current survival but also in terms of long-term evolutionary sustainability. The presence of a diverse collection of secondary metabolites provides resources to help organisms survive environmental disruptions.

But these secondary characteristics are also of immense value to humans, and have been for much of recorded history. Let us look at a few examples discussed by Swanson. Lemons have been used to avoid scurvy in humans for hundreds of years, without any knowledge about how this beneficial effect was taking place. We now know that the active ingredient is vitamin C, one of the secondary metabolites of citrus fruits. Similarly, the bark of the willow tree was used for pain relief for centuries before the active substance (salicylic acid) was identified; its current form is the drug aspirin. More recently, the plant sweetclover was found to be causing severe internal bleeding in cattle. Trials showed that it served as an anti-coagulant across a wide variety of animals. Subsequent developments led to its use in warfarin (the major rodent poison) and in drugs to treat victims of strokes (to reduce blood clotting).

Until recently, almost all medicines were derived more-or-less directly from natural sources. Even today, in the modern pharmaceuticals industry, a large proportion of the drugs in use throughout the world are derived from natural sources. Much work within the pharmaceuticals industry is concerned with identifying medicinal uses of secondary metabolites within plant, animal and microbial communities. The first step in this process is to develop chemicals from these organisms that have demonstrable biological effects within humans. Possible uses of the chemicals can then be found. What is interesting is that even today, the drugs developed in this way (such as those used in general anaesthesia) are often used without good understanding of their mechanism.

Two things are virtually certain. First, a large number of substances are being, or have been, used in specific cultural contexts without their usefulness having become generally known. Secondly, we have only begun to scratch the surface of the range of possible uses that the biosphere permits. Our collective knowledge encompasses only a small part of what there is to know.

All of this suggests that the conservation of biological diversity is of enormous value. This was recognised in the 1992 Rio Convention on Biological Diversity, which states that biological diversity must be conserved and cultural/institutional diversity respected. Yet the institutional arrangements we have in place are poorly designed to conserve that diversity.

Swanson focuses on the role that property rights plays. The nub of the problem is that the system of property rights which has been built up over the past 100 years rewards the creators of information in very different ways. Consider a drug company that extracts biological specimens from various parts of the world and screens these for potential beneficial effects. Intellectual property rights will be awarded to the first individual or organisation that can demonstrate a novel use of information in a product or process. There is nothing wrong with this, of course. A system which rewards people who create

Box 6.5 continued

useful information by granting them exclusive rights to market products that incorporate that information is of immense value. Intellectual property rights, in the form of patents and the like, give market value to information, and create incentives to search for and exploit more information.

However, Swanson points out that not all forms of information have such market value. In particular, the existence of biologically diverse ecosystems creates a reservoir of potentially useful information, but no system of property rights exists which rewards those who build up or sustain biodiversity. He writes:

Internationally-recognised property rights systems must be flexible enough to recognise and reward the contributions to the pharmaceutical industry of each people, irrespective of the nature of the source of that contribution. In particular, if one society generates information useful in the pharmaceutical industry by means of investing in natural capital (non-conversion of forests etc.) whereas another generates such information by investing in human capital (laboratory-based research and school-based training) each is equally entitled to an institution that recognises that contribution.

What is needed, therefore, is a property rights system that brings the value of biodiversity back into human decision making. So-called 'intellectual' property

rights should be generalised to include not only intellectual but natural sources of information. Put another way, it is *information* property rights rather than just *intellectual* property rights that should be protected and rewarded. An ideal system would reward any investment that generates information, including that which is produced naturally.

It is ironic that the 'success' of modern scientific systems of medicine may be contributing to a loss of potentially useful information. Swanson points to the fact that knowledge which is used with demonstrable success in particular cultural contexts often fails to be widely recognised and rewarded. The difficulty has to do with the fact that this knowledge is not codified in ways that satisfy conventional scientific standards. Publication in academic and professional journals, for example, tends to require analysis in a standard form of each link in the chain running from chemical input to accomplished objective. Unconventional or alternative forms of medicine that cannot fit this pattern struggle to survive, even when they have demonstrable value and where no orthodox substitute exists (such as in the treatment of eczema). Reading the collection of papers in full will show you what Swanson and his co-authors recommend to rectify these shortcomings.

Source: Swanson (1995a)

Imperfect information, risk and uncertainty, and irreversibility

The attainment of efficient outcomes through unregulated market behaviour presupposes that all transactors of goods and services are perfectly informed about both direct and external effects. To continue our earlier example, those affected by ozone pollution should know its origin and the damage it causes. This is certainly not true for all persons affected by ozone, and this is likely to be so for many (or even most) forms of pollution externality. In some cases, poor information reflects fundamental scientific uncertainty (for example concerning the greenhouse effect). In other cases, poor information simply reflects the limits to what individuals will know in a complex world. Where ignorance is

particularly acute, and the potential costs of such ignorance are large, government intervention may, again, offer substantial efficiency gains. However, as we show in the next section, there is no guarantee that government intervention will actually achieve these potential net benefits.

Imperfect information and uncertainty become particularly important to our analyses in circumstances where actions have irreversible consequences. It does appear to be the case that many of the consequences of decisions about environmental resource use are irreversible. For example, it is arguable that once developed, a natural wilderness area cannot be returned to its natural state. We shall demonstrate in Chapter 15 how the conjunction of imperfect information and irreversibility is a cause of market failure.

Government policy, government failure and market failure

Government intervention offers the possibility of realising substantial efficiency gains, by eliminating or mitigating situations of market failure. Firstly, many environmental resources are not subject to well-defined and clearly established property rights. Efficiency gains may be obtained if government can create and maintain appropriate institutional arrangements for establishing and supporting property rights. Even where property rights exist, it may be very costly to enforce them. Where this is so, it may be beneficial to develop the legal and judicial structures so that redress for damages arising from external effects can be quickly and cheaply obtained. It would be desirable on efficiency grounds if arrangements could be put in place whereby generators of beneficial public goods and externalities received appropriate compensation for the benefits their activities generate but which are not reflected in market transactions. It is not easy, though, to devise ways of doing this.

Markets themselves may be undeveloped for a variety of legal, cultural and institutional reasons. This will tend to result in a proliferation of externalities unless cultural norms support bargaining structures that serve in place of market exchange.

Government intervention might consist of the use of regulatory instruments. These are often classified into two groups. So-called command-and-control instruments take the form of rules and regulations prohibiting, limiting or requiring certain forms of behaviour. Fiscal instruments – tax and subsidy systems, and marketable permits – are designed to create appropriate patterns of incentives for private behaviour. We explore these instruments in depth in Chapter 12. The use of fiscal incentive schemes is likely to be particularly appropriate where markets already exist, but fail, for one reason or another, to achieve efficient outcomes. However, for some goods – public goods – market

economies may simply fail to provide them, even though supply at some positive level would be socially desirable. The provision of public goods and services is one area where intervention offers the prospect of very large social benefits.

Governmental intervention may also take the form of providing information, or funding research activity that can reduce uncertainty and increase the stock of knowledge. Given that much research activity has the characteristics of a public good, there is a strong case for its provision or financing by the public sector.

The arguments we have used so far in this section have all pointed to the possibility of efficiency gains arising from public sector intervention in the economy. But intervention will not necessarily realise such gains. Firstly, the removal of the cause of market failure in one sector of the economy does not necessarily result in a more efficient allocation of resources if other sectors of the economy are characterised by market failure. This is one example of what is known as second-best theory, a brief analysis of which is undertaken in the context of establishing targets for pollution control in Chapter 11.

A second consideration is that government intervention may itself induce economic inefficiency. Poorly-designed tax and subsidy schemes, for example, may distort the allocation of resources in unintended ways. Any such distortions need to be offset against the intended efficiency gains when the worth of intervention is being assessed.

Intervention in the economy to secure particular policy targets often involves the establishment of regulatory organisational structures. This opens up the possibility of a third type of 'government failure' that is sometimes described as institutional capture.

In some cases, the chosen policy instruments may just fail to achieve desired outcomes. This is particularly likely in the case of instruments that take the form of quantity controls or direct regulation. One example of this is the attempt by the Greek government to reduce car usage in Athens. Regulations prohibiting entry into the city by cars with particular letters on their licence plates on particular days has served to promote the purchase of additional cars by households wishing to maintain freedom of mobility in the city. Similarly, the use of quantity controls in fisheries policy (such as determining minimum mesh sizes for nets, maximum number of days of permitted fishing, required days in port for vessels, and so on) have met with very little success. Fishermen have responded to the regulations by making behavioural adjustments to minimise their impact. The limited success of quantitative controls in fishing is explored at length in Chapter 9.

Finally, one should always remember that efficiency improvements are not unambiguously desirable, as they may (in the absence of redistributive and reallocative steps) reduce social welfare. It is possible in principle to use fiscal adjustments to transfer resources so as to achieve any distributions that might be regarded as fair. Put another way, it is possible to design policy packages that are distributionally neutral. However, this will often not be done in practice.

PART 2
Cost–benefit analysis

Principles of cost–benefit analysis

Cost–benefit analysis (CBA) is a widely practised technique of project appraisal. It is used in circumstances where it is felt that important components of either the real costs or the real benefits of a project would not be adequately represented by market prices, or would not be traded through markets at all (and so do not have market prices). In these circumstances, markets are failing to value all relevant flows correctly, and so a non-market evaluation procedure is required to assess the net worth of the project. Suppose that a project has been put forward, and that the gov-

ernment wishes to estimate the impact that this project would have on social welfare if it were to be undertaken. We begin by noting that any non-trivial project would tend to affect many individuals, and have impacts over many periods of time.

The key principle that underpins CBA is very simple. The impact of the project on each affected person at each point in time is identified. The value to each person of any gain or loss is then estimated. In principle, these valuations should be based on the preferences of the affected individuals, and ideally should reflect each person's willingness to pay for an improvement or compensation willingly accepted for a loss. The methods by which such valuations might be made are not described here, but are presented and discussed in Chapters 14 and 15. Having arrived at the values of the impacts of the project to each affected person, some procedure is then used to obtain an aggregate or social measure of the impacts of the project. The project is approved if its aggregate net value is positive.

For simplicity, imagine that three individuals (A, B and C) are affected in each of four consecutive intervals of time, labelled 0, 1, 2 and 3, where we take period 0 to be the present period. Table 6.3 presents the impacts on each person's utility at each time. Thus $\Delta U_{B,2}$ denotes the change in utility (post-project utility minus pre-project utility) experienced by individual B during time period 2.

However, utilities are unobservable, and not all economists believe that utilities are

Table 6.3 Changes in utility (ΔU) for individuals A, B and C over four consecutive time periods.

Individual	Time period				
	0	1	2	3	Overall
A	$\Delta U_{A,0}$	$\Delta U_{A,1}$	$\Delta U_{A,2}$	$\Delta U_{A,3}$	ΔU_A
B	$\Delta U_{B,0}$	$\Delta U_{B,1}$	$\Delta U_{B,2}$	$\Delta U_{B,3}$	ΔU_B
C	$\Delta U_{C,0}$	$\Delta U_{C,1}$	$\Delta U_{C,2}$	$\Delta U_{C,3}$	ΔU_C
Society	ΔU_0	ΔU_1	ΔU_2	ΔU_3	

Table 6.4 Net benefit (NB) of project for individuals A, B and C over four consecutive time periods.

Individual	Time period				
	0	1	2	3	Overall
A	$NB_{A,0}$	$NB_{A,1}$	$NB_{A,2}$	$NB_{A,3}$	NB_A
B	$NB_{B,0}$	$NB_{B,1}$	$NB_{B,2}$	$NB_{B,3}$	NB_B
C	$NB_{C,0}$	$NB_{C,1}$	$NB_{C,2}$	$NB_{C,3}$	NB_C
Society	NB_0	NB_1	NB_2	NB_3	

comparable across people. As a result, the usual practice in CBA is to assess changes in terms of observable consumption (or output) gains and losses. Then defining net benefit (NB) as the gross benefit from the project less the costs associated with the project, both being measured in units of consumption, we can re-express the impacts of the project as in Table 6.4.

The net value of the project is defined as

$$NV = NB_0 + NB_1 + NB_2 + NB_3$$

which is the sum of what are labelled in Table 6.4 the net benefits to society in each of the four time periods. Note that in this measure of net value, the gains or losses of each individual are weighted equally in arriving at the social net benefit for each time period, irrespective of characteristics or circumstances of the individuals concerned. Thus , for example, NB_0 is the simple sum of $NB_{A,0}$, $NB_{B,0}$ and $NB_{C,0}$.

More generally, for T time periods $(T > 0)$, the net value of a project is given by

$$NV = NB_0 + NB_1 + NB_2 + \ldots + NB_T$$

The net present value (NPV) of a project is then defined as

$$NPV = NB_0 + \frac{NB_1}{(1 + r_1)} + \frac{NB_2}{(1 + r_1) \cdot (1 + r_2)}$$
$$+ \ldots + \frac{NB_T}{(1 + r_1) \cdot (1 + r_2) \cdot \ldots \cdot (1 + r_T)}$$

Because we are here summing consumption (or consumption equivalents) over a sequence of periods, if a discount rate is deemed to be relevant the appropriate rate should be the consumption rate of discount. There is no reason why the consumption discount rate need be equal between periods, and so we have written the expression for NPV in a way that allows for varying consumption discount rates. However, if that rate were constant, so that $r_t = r$, for $t = 1, \ldots T$, as it is commonly assumed to be when CBA is undertaken in practice, then we can express the NPV of a project as

$$NPV = \sum_{t=0}^{t=T} \frac{NB_t}{(1 + r)^t}$$

As we mentioned earlier, the CBA decision rule is of the form:

Do the project if NPV > 0, otherwise do not do the project.

Why is this a sensible rule? Suppose for the moment that r denotes the marginal rate of return (in units of consumption) on the best available alternative project in the economy. If scarce resources were not used in the project they could be invested elsewhere at a rate of return r per period. The NPV of a project will only exceed zero if its marginal rate of return exceeds r. Therefore scarce funds will only be allocated to the project if its rate of return is at least as good as the best alternative returns available. But this is precisely what efficient investment appraisal requires – allocating scarce funds to their highest valued use. It is clear from this that CBA is a technique whose object is to ensure the attainment of economic efficiency in the allocation of resources.

Could this decision rule have any ethical justification as well? It turns out to be the case that we are able to claim that a positive net present value is equivalent to an increase in social welfare if some additional assumptions are satisfied. One condition required is that the marginal utility of consumption is equal for each individual. This ensures that if the sum of individual consumption (or consumption equivalent) changes is positive in any period, the sum of utility changes must also be positive in that period. Then, provided we are willing to accept the ethic underlying utilitarianism, it is valid to argue that the social welfare in that period has risen.

This is not enough by itself, though. The NPV criterion asserts that if the sum of the discounted welfare changes for each period is positive, then intertemporal social welfare has increased. This requires that we also accept that the intertemporal SWF has a utilitarian form, and that the discount rate chosen is a fair one. There are clearly a large number of assumptions here that underpin any attempt to give the cost–benefit analysis technique of appraisal ethical support.

As we shall see in the following chapter, another way of thinking about these assumptions is that they amount to a claim that the existing distribution of wealth, at each point in time, is an optimal one. In this situation, the distribution of the gains and losses between individuals does not affect the magnitude of the welfare gains arising from a project, provided the gains and losses are relatively small.

Do any additional complications arise when we undertake CBA for projects whose impacts are spread over several generations? Many writers would certainly answer in the affirmative. The technique was developed to

---

Box 6.6 Cost–benefit analysis in practice

The history of CBA is an interesting case study of the way in which a technique has been developed and refined gradually in response to the need to address practical problems. The original theoretical basis for CBA arose from the need in the USA to evaluate flood control and irrigation projects. The original applications made little or no attempt to analyse the welfare implications of the projects, requiring only that the aggregate total of benefits exceeded the aggregate costs, irrespective of distribution (see Maass *et al.*, 1962; Ecstein, 1958). After 1960, the types of project to which CBA was directed and the number of applications grew enormously. CBA has become a commonly used appraisal tool in developed countries, and is used routinely for some classes of project appraisal in developing countries where official assistance is sought from the World Bank, the United Nations, or other international agencies.

Most applications have tended to ignore certain problems associated with the technique. One of these – arriving at simple aggregate totals, without any clear theoretical justification for so doing – has already been mentioned. We have seen that distributional questions can be ignored under particular conditions. But it seems most unlikely that these would be satisfied in practice. A second set of difficulties concerns measurement issues, which we shall ignore in the present discussion but will cover in depth in Chapter 14. Finally, as many projects imply costs and benefits which are spread out through very long periods of time, often affecting generations long into the future, the question of the appropriate way in which to discount future net values has been an issue of continuing interest.

In the past 20 years, CBA has routinely been applied to the evaluation of schemes having significant environmental implications. There are a number of additional difficulties posed by this. First, there are several issues related to scale. In some cases, the projects have impacts that are considerably greater than 'marginal' impacts. Given that most applications of CBA either ignore the conditions required for valid aggregation, or simply assume that these are satisfied, this is particularly problematic. Consider, for example, the assumption of constancy of the marginal utility of income; this seems to be an untenable assumption when significant impacts change the real income of individuals by greater than marginal magnitudes.

Secondly, many projects affecting the environment in non-trivial ways imply actual physical harm or threats to life, rather than just small changes in the risk of certain types of ill health. There are profound problems in evaluating impacts of this form. Thirdly, projects may have very small impacts, but on very many individuals, over very long periods. In these cases, individuals may be unaware of the relevant impacts, or have great difficulty in identifying their magnitudes. Attempting to infer values through human behaviour that is assumed to reveal preferences may be a very poor basis for valuation in these cases. In circumstances where future impacts are likely to be significant, the analyst also faces the difficult task of deciding how the preferences of people not yet born are to be measured and incorporated. Finally, many of the costs and benefits of projects with environmental impacts possess the characteristics of public goods. There are additional valuation difficulties here that we shall discuss in Chapter 14.

Box 6.7 A CBA of temperate zone forestry

What are the benefits and costs of afforestation programmes in temperate zones such as the UK? David Pearce argues that afforestation programmes are multiple-output activities. The outputs he identifies are listed below.

T Timber values
R Recreational amenities
D Biological diversity
L Landscape values
W Water-related effects: watershed protection, affecting soil erosion and water run-off, fixation of airborne pollutants, typically increasing pollutant concentrations locally but reducing them elsewhere
M Microclimate effects
G Carbon stores
S Economic security
I Community integration

Each of these outputs can be beneficial, relative to alternative uses of the land. However, in some cases the benefits may be negative. For example, if single-species spruce afforestation displaces the provision of wilderness areas, biological diversity is likely to diminish. On the other hand, the creation of urban forests in areas of industrial dereliction would, in most cases, increase diversity.

What are the costs of afforestation? These costs comprise land acquisition, planting, maintenance, thinning and felling. Denoting the total benefits by B and the total costs by C, and using subscripts f and a to denote afforestation and the best alternative use, respectively, then ignoring time for a moment, Pearce argues that afforestation is economically justified if

$$B_f - C_f > B_a - C_a$$

although there are grounds for disagreeing with this particular formulation.[3]

Pearce then notes that only one of the joint products – the produced timber – is actually traded through market exchanges. All other products are beneficial (or sometimes adverse) external effects, not captured in market valuations. On the other hand, the costs of afforestation are internalised in market transactions. The consequence of this is that afforestation programmes in temperate regions such as the UK are rarely commercially profitable. By way of example, Pearce quotes results from an earlier study. He introduces time into his analysis, discounts consumption-equivalent benefits and costs at a discount rate of 6%, and then estimates the net present value of various types of forestry plantations (on various types of land) under a variety of assumptions about the costs of land.

Pearce investigates eight types of forestry scheme. For each scheme, the commercial[4] NPV is calculated under high and low (and sometimes zero) assumed costs of land. Of the 17 cases this generates, all but one result in negative NPVs. The sole exception is mixed fir/spruce and broadleaf plantations in lowlands, assuming the true value of land is zero (that is, the land has no alternative use)!

Having evaluated the commercial returns to afforestation, Pearce then investigates each of the non-marketed benefits, and gives estimates of the net benefits for each of the outputs R, D, L, W, G, S and I. For two of these (R and G) the benefits are quantified in money terms; for others (D, W, S and I) Pearce identifies and describes the benefits but does not attempt any monetary quantification. Unquantified benefits will have to be judgementally taken into account when project decisions are made.

Recreational benefits for various forms of afforestation are taken from Benson and Willis (1991). The gross values for recreational benefits in the UK range from £3 per hectare on low amenity woodlands in the uplands to £424 per hectare on very high amenity lowland woodlands (in 1989 prices). Pearce suggests these values are likely to grow in real terms by at least 1% per annum. Wildlife conservation and biodiversity benefits (W) and landscape amenity values (L) are two outputs that Pearce does not quantify and monetise. He argues that these benefits will vary widely depending upon woodland form and location, but that they are likely to be positive in the UK, where land for afforestation tends to be drawn from low wildlife-value agricultural land. However, if afforestation takes the form of non-native conifer species, and is at the expense of previously semi-natural land use,

---

[3] The problem with this expression is actually twofold. In a CBA, the benefits and costs of a project should be valued in opportunity cost terms – that is, they are valued in terms of the best alternative. This suggests that, if B and C are measured correctly, there is no need to make any comparison of the type Pearce does. Using a CBA criterion, afforestation should be done if $B_f > C_f$. Indeed, the logic of this approach suggests that if $B_f > C_f$ (and so afforestation is actually best), then $B_a < C_a$, as the cost of the alternative is the lost net benefits of afforestation.

[4] This is not a true calculation of the commercial NPV: in that case, the actual market price would enter the cost calculations. Pearce assumes the true (economic) cost of land is at most 80% of its market value, and at worst is of zero economic cost.

Box 6.7 continued

these effects on both landscape amenities and biological diversity could be strongly negative. The picture is thus a very mixed one, with the magnitude (and direction) of the effects varying greatly from one case to another.

Water-related ecological outputs (W) discussed by Pearce include the effects of afforestation on water supply, water quality, the deposition of air pollution, soil erosion, and the impacts of fertiliser and pesticide use and harvesting practices. Qualitative estimates only are presented for these impacts.

Greenhouse warming related effects (discussed in Chapter 13 of this book) are quantified in monetary terms by Pearce. His estimates of the present value of benefits from carbon fixing, in pounds per hectare at a 6% discount rate, range from £142 on upland semi-natural pinelands to £254 on lowland mixed woodlands.

Pearce's conclusions

In terms of the commercial costs and benefits, together with the two benefit categories that he was able to quantify (recreation and carbon-fixing), Pearce concludes that only four of the eight general classes of woodlands he investigates have a clear justification for increased afforestation at a discount rate of 6%. His summary conclusions are presented in Table 6.5

Table 6.5 The values of alternative classes of woodlands.

Forest type	Assumptions giving positive NPV at $r = 6\%$
FT5 Community forests	Very high recreational values
FT4 Spruce in uplands	Moderate recreational values and land values at $0.5 \times$ market price
FT8 Fir, spruce, broadleaves in lowlands	High recreational values and land values at $0.8 \times$ market price
FT7 Pine in lowlands	Moderate recreational values and land values at $0.5 \times$ market price

As explained above, these conclusions are drawn without looking at non-monetised benefits (or costs). In those cases where the NPV of an afforestation project is negative, however, the decision maker may regard the project as socially desirable if he or she forms a judgement that the non-monetised benefits are sufficiently large to offset the negative (monetised) NPV.

Source: adapted from Pearce (1994).

deal with project evaluation in which costs and benefits, while being spread out over time, were not thought to be distributed over very long periods of time into the future, having significant effects (adverse or beneficial) on future generations. It is by no means clear whether the technique can be applied in the simple manner we have just indicated, where significant intergenerational impacts take place.

One matter that remains unresolved is what criterion should be used in selecting the discount rate for projects with long-lasting impacts that impinge upon more than one generation. It is often argued that a lower discount rate should be used in these circumstances than in conventional, shorter-term project appraisal. Some writers take the view that the rate of discount to be used in

appraising projects that have long-term environmental impacts should be zero.

It is not always clear what the basis of these arguments is. One line of reasoning seems to be that a low (or zero) discount rate is consistent with environmentally friendly economic behaviour. Page (1977), for example, argues that a zero discount rate would prevent environmental damage from implicitly being ignored. However, it can easily be demonstrated that the selection of a low or zero discount rate does not necessarily reduce the rate of environmental degradation, nor does it necessarily create a bias towards accepting sustainable projects.

A second basis is the claim that a zero discount rate is the only one that is ethically defensible. But this view is very difficult to support. First, it is not always clear which discount rate it is that should be set to zero – the consumption or the utility discount rate. If it is consumption rates that are being referred to, then the assertion that the discount rate should be zero is at odds with many plausible ethical stances. If real income were expected to fall, it may be appropriate to have a negative consumption rate of discount, as consumption in the future will be worth more than consumption today. What if consumption were expected to rise over time – should one really argue that one unit of future consumption is of the same value as one unit of present consumption? It does not seem that any single discount rate can ever be right for all circumstances. Finally, it should be remembered that the technique of CBA is essentially a vehicle for achieving efficiency in resource allocation. If one accepts this view, then optimality goals will have to be pursued in some other way.

Discussion questions

1 How is the level of provision of national defence services, a public good, actually determined? Consider a practical method for determining the level of provision that would satisfy an economist.
2 Economists see pollution problems as examples of the class of adverse externality phenomena. An adverse externality is said to occur when the decisions of one agent harm another in an unintended way, and when no compensation occurs. Does this mean that if a pollution source, such as a power station, compensates those affected by its emissions, then there is no pollution problem?
3 While some economists argue for the creation of private property rights to protect the environment, many of those concerned for the environment find this approach abhorrent. What are the essential issues in this dispute?

Problems

1 Consider the two social welfare functions

$$W_U = U_1 + U_2 \text{ (Utilitarian)}$$
$$W_R = \min\{U_1 + U_2\} \text{ (Rawlsian)}$$

where $U_i = \ln(X_i)$ is the utility enjoyed by the ith generation from the consumption X_i, $i = 1, 2$. Consider two projects:

Project A: Generation 1 reduces consumption by 10 units. The investment yields 20 additional units of consumption for Generation 2.
Project B: Generation 1 reduces consumption by 15 units. The investment yields 15 additional units of consumption for Generation 2.

Let the pre-project level of consumption in Generation 1 be 100 units. Now consider three scenarios:

Scenario	Pre-project level of X_2
(i) No technology change	100
(ii) Technology improvement	120
(iii) Technology worsening (or loss of inputs)	80

Use a tick ($\checkmark$)to denote *Do project* or a cross ($\times$) to denote *Do not do project* in each cell of the following table to show whether the project (A or B) should be undertaken under each of the three scenarios, for the two cases of a utilitarian SWF (U) and a Rawlsian SWF (R).

		Scenario					
		(i)		(ii)		(iii)	
		U	R	U	R	U	R
Project	A						
	B						

2 The Safe Water Drinking Act required the United States Environmental Protection Agency to establish action standards for lead in drinking water. The EPA evaluated three options (labelled A, B and C in the

table) using cost–benefit techniques. A selection of the results of this analysis is presented in the following table.

	Option		
	A	B	C
Total benefits	$68 957	$63 757	$24 325
Total costs	$6272	$4156	$3655
Benefit to cost ratio	11.0	15.3	6.7
Marginal benefit (MB)	$5192	$39 440	$24 325
Marginal cost (MC)	$2117	$500	$3665
MB to MC ratio	2.5	78.8	6.67

Monetary values in the table are 1988 $ million, based on a 20-year life, discounted to present value at 3%. Option A involves the strictest standard, Option C the least strict, with B intermediate. The marginal cost and benefit figures refer to incremental costs/benefits incurred in moving from no control to Option C, from Option C to Option B, and from Option B to A respectively. The US Environmental Protection Agency selected Option B. Is Option B the economically efficient choice?

Source: based on EPA (1991). The EPA decision is discussed at length in Goodstein (1995), pages 133–140.

Further reading

Market failure, externalities and public goods

Good discussions of the theory of market failure can be found in Bator (1957) and Varian (1987). Market failure as it concerns environmental economics is rigorously discussed in Baumol and Oates (1988) and Mäler (1985). Classic articles on environmental externalities include Ayres and Kneese (1969) and D'Arge and Kogiku (1972). Discussions concerning welfare economics and the environment may also be found in Common (1996), Dasgupta (1990), Johannson (1987) and Fisher (1981). Swanson (1995a) examines the impacts of property rights.

CBA

The texts by Hanley and Spash (1993) and by Layard and Glaister (1994) are excellent surveys of the theory and practice of cost–benefit analysis. Good accounts are also to be found in the general microeconomic texts by Layard and Walters (1978) and Varian (1987). See also Chapter 15 of this text for a discussion of CBA under conditions of risk, uncertainty and irreversibility (and another set of suggestions for further reading).

CHAPTER 7

The efficient and optimal use of environmental resources

The Golden Rule is that there are no golden rules.

George Bernard Shaw, *Maxims for Revolutionists*

Introduction

In this chapter, we construct a framework to analyse the use of environmental resources over time. This will provide the basis for our investigations of non-renewable resource depletion and the harvesting of renewable resources that follow in Chapters 8, 9 and 10. It will also underpin our examination of choices about 'optimal' pollution levels in Chapter 11. Our objectives in the present chapter are:

- To develop a simple economic model, built around a production function in which environmental resources are inputs into the production process.
- To identify the conditions that must be satisfied by an economically efficient pattern of natural resource use over time.
- To establish the characteristics of a socially optimal pattern of resource use over time in the special case of a utilitarian social welfare function.

We shall be constructing a simple, stylised model of the economy in order to address questions about the use of resources. Although the economics of our model are straightforward, the mathematics required to analyse the model are quite advanced in places. To keep technical difficulties to a minimum, the main body of text avoids the use of mathematical derivations. It shows the logic behind, and the economic interpretations of, important results. Derivations of results are presented separately in appendices at the end of the chapter. It is not vital to read these appendices to follow the arguments in the chapter, but we strongly recommend that you do read them. The derivations use relatively straightforward techniques, which are explained thoroughly. Appendix 7.1 is of particular importance as it takes the reader through a key mathematical technique used in the book – dynamic optimisation using the Maximum Principle. You are also urged to read Appendices 7.2 and 7.3 to see how we have obtained the results discussed in the text.

PART 1
A simple optimal resource depletion model

The economy and its production function

Let us begin by specifying the model we shall be using in this chapter. The economy produces a single good, Q, which can be either consumed or invested. Consumption increases current well-being, while investment increases the capital stock, permitting greater consumption in the future. Output is generated through a production function, which contains a single 'composite' non-renewable resource, R, as an input to production. Beginning in this way, with just one type of environmental resource, abstracts from any substitution effects that might take place between different kinds of environmental resource. In Chapter 8, we shall see how our conclusions alter when more than one type of natural resource enters the production function.

In addition to the non-renewable resource, a second input – manufactured capital, K –

enters the production function, which is written as

$$Q = Q(K, R) \qquad (7.1)$$

This states that output has some functional relationship to the quantities of the two inputs which are used, but it does not tell us anything about the particular form of this relationship.[1] There are many such forms that the production function might actually take. One type of production technology is the Cobb–Douglas (CD) form, consisting of the class of functions

$$Q = AK^{\alpha}R^{\beta} \qquad (7.2)$$

where A, α, and $\beta > 0$. An alternative form, widely used in empirical analysis, is the constant elasticity of substitution (CES) type, which comprises the family of functional forms

$$Q = A(\alpha K^{-\theta} + \beta R^{-\theta})^{-\varepsilon/\theta} \qquad (7.3)$$

where A, ε, α, $\beta > 0$, $(\alpha + \beta) = 1$, and $-1 < \theta \neq 0$.[2]

The CD and CES forms of production function do not exhaust all possibilities. Many others exist, and we mention CD and CES only because they are commonly used in economic analysis. We shall not be making any assumption as to which type of production function best represents the production technology of an economy, but rather work with a general form that might be CD, might

be CES, or might be some other. Which functional form is the 'correct' one is an empirical question, and cannot be answered by theoretical argument alone.

Is the environmental resource essential?

Not surprisingly, it turns out to be the case that the characteristics of an optimal resource depletion path through time will be influenced by whether the environmental resource is 'essential' in some sense. At a general level, claiming that a resource is essential could mean several things. Firstly, a resource might be essential as a waste disposal and reprocessing agent. Given the ubiquitous nature of waste and the magnitude of the damages that waste can cause, resources do appear to be necessary as waste processing agents. A resource might also be essential for human psychic satisfaction. Many humans appear to need peace, quiet, solitude and the aesthetic enjoyment derived from observing or being in natural environments. Thirdly, some resource might be ecologically essential in the sense that some or all of a relevant ecosystem cannot survive in its absence.

In this chapter, we are concerned with a more specific fourth meaning: whether a resource is essential as a direct input to production. Some resources are undoubtedly essential for specific products – for example, crude oil is an essential raw material for the production of petrol, kerosene and paraffin. But we wish to look at resources at a high degree of aggregation, dealing with general classes such as non-renewable and renewable resources. A productive input is defined to be essential if output is zero whenever the quantity of that input is zero, irrespective of the amounts of other inputs used. That is, R is essential if

$$Q = Q(K, R = 0) = 0 \qquad \text{for any value of } K$$

In the case of the CD production function, R is essential (as too is K). To verify this, note that setting any input to zero in Equation 7.2

---

[1] Each output level Q satisfying the production function is the maximum attainable output for given quantities of the inputs, and implies that inputs are used in a technically efficient way. Throughout this text, we assume that technical efficiency is satisfied. You may also have noticed that the production function does not contain labour as a productive input. We have omitted labour to keep the algebra as simple as possible. It would be easy to generalise the model we develop in this chapter to include three (or more) inputs, but this would add little to the explanatory power of the model. Alternatively, you could choose to interpret K and R as being in per capita units, so that labour does implicitly enter as a productive input.

[2] It can be shown that the CD function is a special case of the CES functional form as θ goes to zero in the limit.

results in $Q = 0$. Matters are not so straightforward with the CES function. We state (but without giving a proof) that if $\theta < 0$, then none of the inputs is essential, and if $\theta > 0$ then all inputs are essential.

What is the relevance of this to our study of resource use over time? If we wish to answer questions about the long-run properties of economic systems, the essentialness of non-renewable resources will matter. Since, by definition, non-renewable resources exist in finite quantities it is not possible to use constant and positive amounts of them over infinite horizons. However, if a resource is essential, then we know that production can only be undertaken if some positive amount of the input is used. This seems to suggest that production and consumption cannot be sustained indefinitely if a non-renewable resource is a necessary input to production.

However, if the rate at which the resource is used were to decline asymptotically to zero, and so never actually become zero in finite time, then production could be sustained indefinitely even if the resource were essential. Whether output could rise, or at least stay constant over time, or whether it would have to decline towards zero will depend upon the extent to which other resources can be substituted for non-renewable resources and upon the behaviour of output as this substitution takes place.

What is the elasticity of substitution between *K* and *R*?

The extent of substitution possibilities is likely to have an important bearing on the feasibility of continuing economic growth over the very long run, given the constraints which are imposed by the natural environment. Let us examine substitution between the non-renewable resource and capital. The elasticity of substitution, σ, between capital and the non-renewable environmental resource (from now on just called the resource) is defined as the proportionate change in the ratio of

capital to the resource in response to a proportionate change in the ratio of the marginal products of capital and the resource (see Chiang, 1984). That is

$$\sigma = \frac{d(K/R)}{K/R} \bigg/ \frac{d(Q_K/Q_R)}{Q_K/Q_R} \qquad (7.4)$$

where the partial derivative $Q_R = \partial Q/\partial R$ denotes the marginal product of the resource and $Q_K = \partial Q/\partial K$ denotes the marginal product of capital.[3] The elasticity of substitution lies between zero and infinity. Substitution possibilities can be represented diagrammatically. Figure 7.1 shows what are known as production function isoquants. For a given production function, an isoquant is the locus of all combinations of inputs which, when used efficiently, yield a constant level of output. The three isoquants shown in Figure 7.1 each correspond to the level of output, $\overline{Q}$, but derive from different production functions. The differing substitution possibilities are reflected in the curvatures of the isoquants.

In the case where no input substitution is possible (that is, $\sigma = 0$), inputs must be combined in fixed proportions and the isoquants will be L-shaped. Production functions of this type, admitting no substitution possibilities, are sometimes known as Leontief functions. They are commonly used in input–output models of the economy. At the other extreme, if substitution is perfect ($\sigma = \infty$), isoquants will be straight lines. In general, one would expect production functions to

---

[3] It can also be shown (see Chiang, 1984, for example) that if resources are allocated efficiently in a competeitive market economy, the elasticity of substitution between capital and an exhaustible resource is equal to

$$\sigma = \frac{d(K/R)}{K/R} \bigg/ \frac{d(P_R/P_K)}{P_R/P_K}$$

where P_R and P_K denote the unit prices of the exhaustible resource and capital, respectively. That is, the elasticity of substitution measures the proportionate change in the ratio of capital to exhaustible resource used in response to a change in the relative price of the resource to capital.

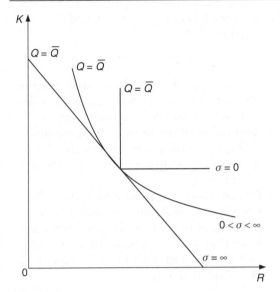

Figure 7.1 Substitution possibilities and the shapes of production function isoquants.

exhibit an elasticity of substitution somewhere between those two extremes (although not all production functions will have a constant σ for all input combinations). In these cases, isoquants will often be convex to the origin, exhibiting a greater degree of curvature the lower the elasticity of substitution, σ. Some evidence on empirically-observed values of the elasticity of substitution between different production inputs is presented later in Box 7.1.

For a CES production function, we can also relate the elasticity of substitution to the concept of essentialness. It can be shown (see, for example, Chiang (1984), page 428) that

$$\sigma = \frac{1}{1 + \theta}$$

We argued in the previous section that no input is essential where $\theta < 0$, and all inputs are essential where $\theta > 0$. Given the relationship between σ and θ, it can be seen that no input is essential where $\sigma > 1$, and all inputs are essential where $\sigma < 1$. Where $\sigma = 1$ (that is, $\theta = 0$), the CES production function collapses to the CD form, where all inputs are essential.

Resource substitutability and the consequences of increasing resource scarcity

As production continues throughout time, stocks of non-renewable resources must decline. One would expect that continuing depletion of the resource stock would be associated with a tendency for the non-renewable resource price to rise relative to the price of capital. We will show later that this intuition is correct.

Productive efficiency implies, that as the relative price of the non-renewable resource rises, the ratio of the resource to capital employed will fall, thereby raising the marginal product of the resource and reducing the marginal product of capital. However, the magnitude of this substitution effect will depend upon the value of the elasticity of substitution. Where the elasticity of substitution is high, only small changes in relative input prices will be necessary to induce a large proportionate change in the quantities of inputs used. 'Resource scarcity' will be of little consequence as the economy is able to replace the scarce resource by the reproducible substitute. Put another way, the constraints imposed by the finiteness of the non-renewable resource stock will bite rather weakly in such a case.

On the other hand, very low substitution possibilities mean that as resource depletion pushes up the relative price of the resource, the magnitude of the induced substitution effect will be very small. 'Resource scarcity' will have much more serious adverse effects, as the scope for replacement of the scarce resource by the reproducible substitute is much more limited. Where the elasticity of substitution is zero, then no scope exists for such replacement.

The feasibility of sustainable development

In Chapter 3, we considered what sustainability might mean, how economists have attempted to incorporate a concern with sustainability into their work, and (albeit rather briefly) why we might wish to incorporate sustainability into the set of objectives that society pursues. What we did not discuss there was whether sustainable development is actually possible.

To address this question, two things are necessary. First, we require a criterion of sustainability; unless we know what sustainability is, it is not possible to judge whether it is feasible. Second, we need to describe the material transformation conditions available to society, now and in the future. These conditions – the economy's production possibilities – determine what can be obtained from the endowments of natural and human-made capital over the relevant time horizon.

To make some headway in addressing this question, let us adopt a conventional criterion of sustainability, that of non-declining per capita consumption maintained over indefinite time (see Chapter 3). Turning attention to the transformation conditions, it is clear that a large number of factors enter the picture. What is happening to the size of the human population? What kinds of resources are available and in what quantities, and what properties do they possess? What will happen to the state of technology in the future? How will ecosystems be affected by the continuing waste loads being placed upon the environment, and how will ecosystem changes feed back upon productive potential? To make progress, economists typically simplify and narrow down the scope of the problem, and represent the transformation possibilities by making an assumption about the form of an economy's production function. A series of results have become established for several special cases, deriving mainly from papers by Dasgupta and Heal (1974), Solow (1974a) and Stiglitz (1974). For the CD and CES functions we have the following.

- Case A: Output is produced under fully competitive conditions through a CD production function with constant returns to scale and two inputs, a non-renewable resource, R, and manufactured capital, K,

as in the following special case of Equation 7.2.

$$Q = K^{\alpha} R^{\beta} \quad \text{with } (\alpha + \beta) = 1$$

Then, in the absence of technical progress and with constant population, it is feasible to have constant consumption across generations if the share of total output going to capital is greater than the share going to the natural resource (that is, if $\alpha > \beta$).

- Case B: Output is produced under fully competitive conditions through a CES production function with constant returns to scale and two inputs, a non-renewable resource, R, and manufactured capital, K, as in Equation 7.3:

$$Q = A(\alpha K^{-\theta} + \beta R^{-\theta})^{-1/\theta} \quad \text{with } (\alpha + \beta) = 1$$

Then, in the absence of technical progress and with constant population, it is feasible to have constant consumption across generations if the elasticity of substitution $\sigma = 1/(1 + \theta)$ is greater than or equal to one.

- Case C: Output is produced under conditions in which a backstop technology is permanently available. In this case, the natural resource is not essential. Sustainability is feasible, although there may be limits to the size of the constant consumption level that can be obtained.

It is relatively easy to gain some intuitive understanding of these results. For the CD case, although the resource is always essential in the sense we described above, if $\alpha > \beta$ then capital is sufficiently substitutable for the resource so that output can be maintained by increasing capital as the resource input diminishes. However, it should be noted that there is an upper bound on the amount of output that can be indefinitely sustained in this case; whether that level is high enough to satisfy 'survivability' (see Chapter 3) is another matter.

For the CES case, if $\sigma > 1$, then the resource is not essential. Output can be produced even in the absence of the environmental resource. The fact that the environmental resource is finite does not, therefore, prevent indefinite production (and consumption) of a constant, positive output. Where $\sigma = 1$, the CES production function collapses to the special case of CD, and so Case A applies. Where a backstop exists (such as a renewable energy source like wind or solar power, or perhaps nuclear fusion-based power) then it is always possible to switch to that source if the limited resource becomes depleted. We explore this process further in the next chapter.

The results we have just described assumed that the rate of technical progress and the rate of population growth were both zero. Not surprisingly, results change if one (or both) of these rates is non-zero. The presence of permanent technical progress increases the range of circumstances in which indefinitely long-lived constant per capita consumption is feasible whereas constant population growth has the opposite effect. However, there are circumstances in which constant per capita consumption can be maintained even where population is growing provided the rate of technical progress is sufficiently large and the share of output going to the resource is sufficiently low. Details of this result are given in Stiglitz (1974). Similarly, for a CES production function, sustained consumption is possible even where $\sigma < 1$ provided that technology growth is sufficiently high relative to population growth.

The general conclusion from this analysis is that sustainability requires either a relatively high degree of substitutability between capital and the resource, or a sufficiently large continuing rate of technical progress or the presence of a permanent backstop technology. Whether such conditions will prevail is a moot point.

Sustainability and the Hartwick rule

In our discussion of sustainability in Chapter 3, mention was made of the so-called Hartwick savings rule. Interpreting sustainability in terms of non-declining consumption through time, John Hartwick (1977, 1978) sought to identify conditions under which such a target would be achievable. Hartwick identified two sets of conditions which were sufficient to achieve constant (or more accurately, non-declining) consumption through time:

- A particular savings rule, known as the Hartwick rule, which states that the rents derived from an efficient extraction programme for the non-renewable resource are invested entirely in reproducible (that is, physical and human) capital.
- Conditions pertaining to the economy's production technology. These conditions are essentially those we described in the previous section, which we shall not repeat here.

We shall discuss the implications of the Hartwick rule further in Chapter 17. What is important to recognise at this point is that following the Hartwick rule alone is not sufficient to guarantee sustainability. The rents which are saved must be those that are generated from an efficient resource extraction programme in a competitive economy (see Chapter 6 for futher details on this). Even if the Hartwick rule is pursued subject to this qualification, it may still be the case that sustainability is not feasible. As we noted in the previous section, feasibility depends very much upon the extent of substitution possibilities open to an economy. Let us now explore this a little further.

How large are resource substitution possibilities?

Clearly, the magnitude of the elasticity of substitution between non-renewable resources and other inputs is a matter of considerable importance. But how large it is cannot be deduced by *a priori* theoretical reasoning; this magnitude has to be inferred empirically.

Whereas many economists believe that evidence points to reasonably high substitution possibilities (although there is by no means a consensus on this), environmental scientists and ecologists stress the limited substitution possibilities between resources and reproducible capital. Indeed some ecologists have argued that, in the long-term, these substitution possibilities are zero.

These disagreements reflect, in large part, differences in conceptions about the scope of services that environmental resources provide. For example, whereas it appears to be quite easy to economise on the use of fossil energy inputs in many production processes, reproducible capital cannot substitute for environmental capital in the provision of the amenities offered by wilderness areas, or in the regulation of the earth's climate. The reprocessing of harmful wastes is less clear cut; certainly reproducible capital and labour can substitute for the waste disposal functions of the environment to some extent (perhaps through increased use of recycling processes) but there appear to be limits to how far this substitution can proceed.

Finally, it is clear that even if we were to establish that substitutability had been high in the past, this does not imply that it will continue to be so in the future. It may be that as development pushes the economy to points where environmental constraints begin to bite, substitution possibilities reduce significantly. Recent literature from environmental science seems to suggest this possibility. On the other hand, a more optimistic view is suggested by the effect of technological progress, which appears in many cases to have contributed towards enhanced opportunities for substitution. You should now read the material on resource substitutability presented in Box 7.1.

Up to this point in our presentation, natural resources have been treated in a very special way. We have assumed that there is a single, non-renewable resource, R, of fixed, known size, and (implicitly) of uniform quality. Substitution possibilities have been limited to those between this resource and other, non-environmental, resources.

In practice, there are a large number of different natural resources, with substitution possibilities among members of this set. Of equal importance is the non-uniform quality of resource stocks. Resource stocks do not usually exist in a fixed amount of uniform quality, but rather in deposits of varying grade and quality. As high-grade reserves become exhausted, extraction will turn to lower-grade deposits, provided the resource price is sufficiently high to cover the higher extraction costs of the lower-grade mineral. Furthermore, while there will be some upper limit to the physical occurrence of the resource in the earth's crust, the location and extent of these deposits will not be known with certainty. As known reserves become depleted, exploration can, therefore, increase the size of available reserves. Finally, renewable resources can act as backstops for non-renewable, non-renewables; wind or wave power are substitutes for fossil fuels, and wood products are substitutes for metals for some construction purposes, for example.

Partha Dasgupta (1993) examines these various substitution possibilities. He argues that they can be classified into nine innovative mechanisms:

(1) An innovation allowing a given resource to be used for a given purpose. An example is the use of coal in refining pig-iron.
(2) The development of new materials, such as synthetic fibres.
(3) Technological developments which increase the productivity of extraction processes. For example, the use of large-scale earthmoving equipment facilitating economically viable strip-mining of low-grade mineral deposits.
(4) Scientific and technical discovery which makes exploration activities cheaper. Examples include developments in aerial photography and seismology.
(5) Technological developments that increase efficiency in the use of resources.

Box 7.1 Resource substitutability: one item of evidence

A huge amount of empirical research has been devoted to attempts to measure the elasticity of substitution between particular pairs of inputs. Results of these exercises are often difficult to apply to general models of the type we use in this chapter, because the estimates tend to be specific to the particular contexts being studied, and because many studies work at a much more disaggregated level than is done here. We restrict comments to just one estimate, which has been used in a much-respected model of energy–environment interactions in the United States economy.

Alan Manne, in developing the ETA Macro model, considers a production function in which gross output (Q) depends upon four inputs, K, L, E and N (respectively capital, labour, electric and non-electric energy). Manne's production function incorporates the following assumptions:

(a)   There are constant returns to scale in terms of all four inputs;
(b)   There is a unit elasticity of substitution between capital and labour;
(c)   There is a unit elasticity of substitution between electric and non-electric energy;
(d)   There is a constant elasticity of substitution between the two pairs of inputs, capital and labour on the one hand and electric and non-electric energy on the other. Denoting this constant elasticity of substitution by the symbol σ, the production function used in the ETA Macro model that embraces these assumptions is

$$Q = [a(K^\alpha L^{1-\alpha})^{-\theta} + b(E^\beta N^{1-\beta})^{-\theta}]^{-1/\theta}$$

where, as noted in the text,

$$\sigma = \frac{1}{1+\theta}$$

Manne selects the value 0.25, a relatively low figure, for the elasticity of substitution σ between the pair of energy inputs and the other input pair. How is this figure arrived at? First, Manne argues that the elasticity of substitution is approximately equal to the absolute value of the price elasticity of demand for primary energy (see Hogan and Manne, 1979). Then, Manne collects time series data on the prices of primary energy, incomes and quantities of primary energy consumed. This permits a statistically-derived estimate of the long-run price elasticity of demand for primary energy to be obtained, thereby giving an approximation to the elasticity of substitution between energy and other production inputs.

Manne's elasticity estimate of 0.25 falls near to the median of recent econometric estimates of this elasticity of substitution.

Being positive, this figure suggests that energy demand will rise relative to other input demand if the relative price of other inputs to energy rises, and so the composite energy resource is a substitute for other productive inputs (a negative sign would imply the pair were complements). However, as the absolute value of the elasticity is much less than one, the degree of substitutability is very low, implying that relative input demands will not change greatly as relative input prices change.

Source: Manne (1979)

Dasgupta illustrates this for the case of electricity generation; between 1900 and the 1970s, the weight of coal required to produce one kilowatt-hour of electricity fell from 7 lb to less than 1 lb.

(6)   Development of techniques which enable one to exploit low-grade but abundantly available deposits. For example, the use of froth-flotation, allowing low-grade sulphide ores to be concentrated in an economical manner.

(7)   Constant developments in recycling techniques which lower costs and so raise effective resource stocks.

(8)   Substitution of low-grade resource reserves for vanishing high-grade deposits.

(9)   Substitution of fixed manufacturing capital for vanishing resources.

In his assessment of substitution possibilities, Dasgupta argues that only the last of these nine mechanisms is of limited scope, the substitution of manufacturing capital for natural resources:

Such possibilities are limited. Beyond a point fixed capital in production is complementary to resources, most especially energy resources. Asymptotically, the elasticity of substitution is less than one.

There is a constant tension between forces which raise extraction and refining costs – the depletion of high-grade deposits – and those which lower such costs – discoveries of newer technological processes and materials. What implications does this carry for resource scarcity? Dasgupta argues that as the existing resource base is depleted, profit opportunities arise from expanding that resource base; the expansion is achieved by one or more of the nine mechanisms just described. Finally, in a survey of the current stocks of mineral resources, Dasgupta notes that after taking account of these substitution mechanisms, and assuming unchanged resource stock to demand ratios:

> the only cause for worry are the phosphates (a mere 1300 years of supply), fossil fuels (some 2500 years), and manganese (about 130 000 years). The rest are available for more than a million years, which is pretty much like being inexhaustible.

However, adjusting for population and income growth,

> the supply of hydrocarbons ... will only last a few hundred years ... So then, this is the fly in the ointment, the bottleneck, the binding constraint ...

> Dasgupta (1993), page 1126

Dasgupta's optimism is not yet finished. He conjectures that profit potentials will induce technological advances (perhaps based on nuclear energy, perhaps on renewables) that will overcome this binding constraint. Not all commentators share this sanguine view as we have seen previously, and we shall have more to say about resource scarcity in the next chapter. In the meantime, we return to our simple model of the economy, in which the heterogeneity of resources is abstracted from, and in which we conceive of there being one single, uniform, resource stock.

The social welfare function and an optimal allocation of environmental resources

The previous two chapters have established the meaning of the concepts of efficiency and optimality for the allocation of productive resources in general. We shall now apply these concepts to the particular case of natural resources. Our objective is to establish what conditions must be satisfied for natural resource allocation to be optimal, in the sense that the allocation maximises a social welfare function. The presentation in this chapter focuses upon non-renewable resources, although we also indicate how the ideas can be applied to renewable resources.

The first thing we require is a social welfare function. You already know that a general way of writing the social welfare function (SWF) is:

$$W = W(U_0, U_1, U_2, \ldots, U_T) \qquad (7.5)$$

where U_t, $t = 0, \ldots, T$, is the aggregate utility in period t.[4] We now assume that the SWF is utilitarian in form. A utilitarian SWF defines social welfare as a weighted sum of the utilities of the relevant individuals. As we are concerned here with intertemporal welfare, we can interpret an 'individual' to mean an aggregate of persons living at a certain point in time, and so refer to the utility in period 0, in period 1, and so on. Then a utilitarian intertemporal SWF will be of the form

$$W = \alpha_0 U_0 + \alpha_1 U_1 + \alpha_2 U_2 + \ldots + \alpha_T U_T \qquad (7.6)$$

Now let us assume that utility in each period is a concave function only of the level of consumption in that period, so that $U_t = U(C_t)$ for all t, with $U_C > 0$ and $U_{CC} < 0$. Notice that the utility function itself is not dependent upon time, so that the relationship between consumption and utility is the same in all periods. By interpreting the weights in

---

[4] Writing the SWF in this form assumes that it is meaningful to refer to an aggregate level of utility for all individuals in each period. Then social welfare is a function of these aggregates, but not of the distribution of utilities between individuals within each time period. That is a very strong assumption, and by no means the only one we might wish to make. We might justify this by assuming that, for each time period, utility is distributed in an optimal way between individuals.

Equation 7.6 as discount factors, related to a social utility discount rate ρ that we take to be fixed over time, the social welfare function can be rewritten as

$$W = U_0 + \frac{U_1}{1+\rho} + \frac{U_2}{(1+\rho)^2} + \ldots + \frac{U_T}{(1+\rho)^T}$$
(7.7)

For reasons of mathematical convenience, we switch from discrete time to continuous time notation, and assume that the relevant time horizon is infinite. This leads to the following special case of the utilitarian SWF:

$$W = \int_{t=0}^{t=\infty} U(C_t) e^{-\rho t}\, dt$$
(7.8)

There are two constraints that must be satisfied by any optimal solution. First, all of the resource stock is to be extracted and used by the end of the time horizon (as after this, any remaining stock has no effect on social well-being). Given this, together with the fact that we are considering a resource for which there is a fixed and finite initial stock, the total use of the resource over time is constrained to be equal to the fixed initial stock. Denoting the initial stock (at $t = 0$) as S_0 and the rate of extraction and use of the resource at time t as R_t, we can write this constraint as

$$S_t = S_0 - \int_{\tau=0}^{\tau=t} R_\tau\, d\tau$$
(7.9)

Notice that in Equation 7.9, as we are integrating over a time interval from period 0 to any later point in time t, it is necessary to use another symbol (here τ, the Greek letter tau) to denote any point in time in the range over which the function is being integrated. Equation 7.9 states that the stock remaining at time t (S_t) is equal to the magnitude of the initial stock (S_0) less the amount of the resource extracted over the time interval from zero to t (given by the integral term on the right-hand side of the equation). An equivalent way of writing this resource stock constraint is obtained by dif-

ferentiating Equation 7.9 with respect to time, giving

$$\dot{S}_t = -R_t$$
(7.10)

where the dot over a variable indicates a time derivative, so that $\dot{S}_t = dS/dt$. Equation 7.10 has a straightforward interpretation: the rate of depletion of the stock, $-\dot{S}_t$, is equal to the rate of resource stock extraction, R_t.

A second constraint on welfare optimisation derives from the accounting identity relating consumption, output and the change in the economy's stock of capital. Output is shared between consumption goods and capital goods, and so that part of the economy's output which is not consumed results in a capital stock change. Writing this identity in continuous time form we have[5]

$$\dot{K}_t = Q_t - C_t$$
(7.11)

It is now necessary to specify how output, Q, is determined. Output is produced through a production function involving two inputs, capital and a non-renewable resource:

$$Q_t = Q(K_t, R_t)$$
(7.12)

Substituting for Q_t in Equation 7.11 from the production function 7.12, the accounting identity can be written as

$$\dot{K}_t = Q(K_t, R_t) - C_t$$
(7.13)

We are now ready to find the solution for the socially optimal intertemporal allocation of the non-renewable resource. To do so, we need to solve a constrained optimisation problem. The objective is to maximise the economy's social welfare function subject to the non-renewable resource stock-flow constraint and the national income identity. Writing this mathematically, therefore, we have the following problem:

---

[5] Notice that by integration of Equation 7.11 we obtain

$$K_t = K_0 + \int_{\tau=0}^{\tau=t} (Q_\tau - C_\tau)\, dt$$

in which K_0 is the initial capital stock (at time zero). This expression is equivalent in form to Equation 7.9 in the text.

Select values for the choice variables C_t and R_t for $t = 0, \ldots, \infty$ so as to maximise

$$W = \int_{t=0}^{t=\infty} U(C_t)e^{-\rho t}dt$$

subject to the constraints

$$\dot{S}_t = -R_t$$

and

$$\dot{K}_t = Q(K_t, R_t) - C_t$$

The full solution to this constrained optimisation problem, and its derivation, are presented in Appendix 7.2. This solution is obtained using the Maximum Principle of optimal control. That technique is explained carefully in Appendix 7.1. We recommend that you now read Appendix 7.1. Having done that, then read Appendix 7.2, where we show how the Maximum Principle is used to solve the problem we have just posed in the text. If you find this material disconcerting, do not worry. The text of this chapter has been written so that it can be followed without having to read the appendices. In the following sections, we outline the nature of the solution, and provide economic interpretations of the results.

The nature of the solution

There are four equations which characterise the optimal solution:

$$U_{Ct} = \omega_t \tag{7.14a}$$
$$P_t = \omega_t Q_{Rt} \tag{7.14b}$$
$$\dot{P}_t = \rho P_t \tag{7.14c}$$
$$\dot{\omega}_t = \rho\omega_t - Q_{Kt}\omega_t \tag{7.14d}$$

Before we discuss the economic interpretations of these equations, it is necessary to explain several things about the notation we have used and the nature of the solution:

- The terms $Q_{Kt} = \partial Q/\partial K$ at t and $Q_R = \partial Q/\partial R$ at t are the partial derivatives of

output with respect to capital and the exhaustible resource. In economic terms, they are the marginal products of capital and the resource, respectively. These marginal products may vary over time in the optimal solution, which is why time subscripts are attached to them.

- The terms P_t and ω_t are the shadow prices of the two productive inputs, the natural resource and capital. These two variables carry time subscripts because the shadow prices will vary over time. The solution values of P_t and ω_t, for $t = 0, 1, \ldots, \infty$, define optimal time paths for the prices of the natural resource and capital.[6]
- The quantity being maximised in Equation 7.8 is a sum of (discounted) units of utility. Hence the shadow prices are measured in utility, not consumption, units. The prices with which you are most likely to be familiar are money prices, so this may cause a little consternation. You should now turn to Box 7.2 where an explanation of prices in utils is given.

Now we are in a position to interpret the four conditions 7.14a–d. First recall from our discussions in Chapter 5 that for any resource to be allocated efficiently, two kinds of conditions must be satisfied: static and dynamic efficiency. The first two of these conditions – 7.14a and 7.14b – are the static efficiency conditions that arise in this problem; the latter two are the dynamic efficiency conditions which must be satisfied. These are examined in a moment. The first two conditions – 7.14a and 7.14b – also implicitly define an optimal solution to this problem. We shall explain what this means shortly.

[6] A shadow price is a price that emerges as a solution to an optimisation problem; put another way, it is an implicit or 'planning' price that a good (or in this case, a productive input) will take if resources are allocated optimally over time. If an economic planner were using the price mechanism to allocate resources over time, then $\{P_t\}$ and $\{\omega_t\}$, $t = 0, 1, \ldots, \infty$, would be the prices he or she should establish in order to achieve an efficient and optimal resource allocation.

Box 7.2 Prices in units of utility: what does this mean?

The notion of prices being measured in units of utility appears at first sight a little strange. After all, we are used to thinking of prices in units of money: a Cadillac costs $40 000, a Mars bar 30 pence, and so on. Money is a claim over goods and services: the more money someone has, the more goods he or she can consume. So it is evident that we could just as well describe prices in terms of consumption units as in terms of money units. For example, if the price of a pair of Levi 501 jeans were $40, and we agree to use that brand of jeans as our 'standard commodity', then a Cadillac will have a consumption units price of 1000.

We could be even more direct about this. Money can itself be thought of as a good and, by convention, one unit of this money good has a price of one unit. The money good serves as a numeraire in terms of which the relative prices of all other goods are expressed. So one pair of Levis has a consumption units price of 40, or a money price of $40.

What is the conclusion of all this? Essentially, it is that prices can be thought of equally well in terms of consumption units or money units. They are alternative but equivalent ways of measuring some quantity. Throughout this book, the terms 'benefits' and 'costs' are usually measured in units of money or its consumption equivalent.

But we sometimes refer to prices in utils – units of utility – rather than in money/consumption units. It is here that matters may be a little baffling. But this turns out to be a very simple notion. Economists make extensive use of the utility function:

$$U = U(C)$$

where U is units of utility and C is units of consumption. Now suppose that the utility function were of the simple linear form $U = kC$ where k is some constant, positive number. Then units of utility are simply a multiple of units of consumption. So if $k = 2$, three units of consumption are equivalent to six units of utility, and so on.

But the utility function may be non-linear. Indeed, it is often assumed that utility rises with consumption but at a decreasing rate. One form of utility function that satisfies this assumption is the common logarithmic form $U = \log(C)$, sketched in Figure 7.2. The graph shows the amounts of utility (in units of utility) that correspond to various levels of consumption units.

It is equally valid to refer to prices in utility units as in any other units. From Figure 7.2 it is clear that a utility price of 2 corresponds to a consumption price of 100; and a consumption price of 1000 corresponds to a utility price of 3. What is the consumption units price equivalent to a price of 2.5 units of utility? (Use your calculator to find the answer, or read it off approximately from the diagram.)

Which units prices are measured in will depend on how the problem has been set up. In the chapters on resource depletion, what is being maximised is social

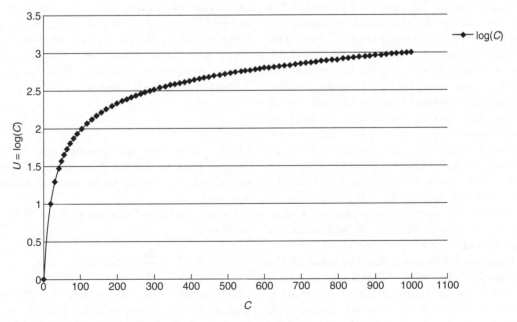

Figure 7.2 The logarithmic utility function.

Box 7.2 continued

welfare; given that the SWF is specified as a sum of utilities (of different people or different generations), it seems natural to denominate it in utility units as well, although our discussion makes it clear that we could convert units from utility into money/consumption terms if we wished to do so.

In other parts of the book, what is being maximised is net benefit. That measure is typically constructed in consumption (or money income) units, and so it is natural to use money prices when dealing with problems set up in this way.

In conclusion, it is up to us to choose which units are most convenient. And provided we know what the utility function is (or are willing to make an assumption about what it is) then we can always move from one to the other as the occasion demands.

The static and dynamic efficiency conditions

You will recall from our discussions in Chapter 5 that the efficient allocation of any resource consists of two aspects.

The static efficiency conditions

For any resource (or asset, if you like), static efficiency requires that, in each use to which it is put, the marginal value of the services from a resource should be equal to the marginal value of that resource stock. This ensures that the marginal net benefit (or marginal value) to society of the resource should be the same in all its possible uses.

Inspection of Equations 7.14a and 7.14b shows that this is what these equations do imply. Look first at Equation 7.14a. This states that, in each period, the marginal utility of consumption $U_{C,t}$ must be equal to the shadow price of capital ω_t (remembering that prices are measured in units of utility here). A marginal unit of output can be used for consumption now (yielding $U_{C,t}$ units of utility) or added to the capital stock (yielding an amount of capital value ω_t in utility units). An efficient outcome will be one in which the marginal net benefit of using one unit of output for consumption is equal to its marginal net benefit when it is added to the capital stock.

Equation 7.14b states that the value of the marginal product of the natural resource must be equal to the marginal value (or shadow price) of the natural resource stock. This shadow price is, of course, P_t. The value of the marginal product of the resource is the mar-

ginal product in units of output (i.e. $Q_{R,t}$) multiplied by the value of one unit of output, ω_t. But we have defined ω_t as the price of a unit of capital; so why is this the value of one unit of output? The reason is simple. In this economy, units of output and units of capital are in effect identical (along an optimal path). Any output that is not consumed is added to capital. So we can call ω_t either the value of a marginal unit of capital or the value of a marginal unit of output.

The dynamic efficiency conditions

As discussed in Chapter 5, dynamic efficiency requires that each asset or resource earns the same rate of return, and that this rate of return is the same at all points in time, being equal to the social rate of discount. Equations 7.14c and 7.14d ensure that dynamic efficiency is satisfied. Consider first Equation 7.14c. Dividing each side by P we obtain

$$\frac{\dot{P}_t}{P_t} = \rho$$

which states that the growth rate of the shadow price of the resource (that is, its own rate of return) should equal the social utility discount rate.

Finally, dividing both sides of 7.14d by ω, we obtain

$$\frac{\dot{\omega}_t}{\omega_t} + Q_{Kt} = \rho$$

which states that the return to physical capital (its price appreciation plus its marginal productivity) must equal the social discount rate.

Hotelling's rule: two interpretations

Equation 7.14c is known as Hotelling's rule for the extraction of non-renewable resources. It is often expressed in the form

$$\frac{\dot{P}_t}{P_t} = \rho \qquad (7.15)$$

The Hotelling rule is an intertemporal efficiency condition which must be satisfied by any efficient process of resource extraction. In one form or another, we shall return to the Hotelling rule during this and the following three chapters.

One interpretation of this condition was offered above. A second can be given in the following way. First rewrite Equation 7.15 in the form used earlier, that is

$$\dot{P}_t = \rho P_t \qquad (7.16)$$

By integration of Equation 7.16 we obtain

$$P_t = P_0 e^{\rho t} \qquad (7.17)$$

P_t is the undiscounted price of the environmental resource. The discounted price is obtained by discounting P_t at the social utility discount rate ρ. Denoting the discounted resource price by P^*, we have

$$P_t^* = P_t e^{-\rho t} = P_0 \qquad (7.18)$$

Equation 7.18 states that the discounted price of the resource is constant along an efficient resource extraction path. In other words, Hotelling's rule states that the discounted value of the resource should be the same at all dates. But this is merely a special case of a general asset-efficiency condition; the discounted (or present value) price of any efficiently managed asset will remain constant over time. This way of interpreting Hotelling's rule shows that there is nothing special about natural resources *per se* when it comes to thinking about efficiency. A natural resource is an asset. All efficiently managed assets will satisfy the condition that their discounted prices should be equal at all points in time. If we had wished to do so, the Hotelling rule could have been

obtained directly from this general condition.

Before we move on, note the effect of changes in the social discount rate on the optimal path of resource price. The higher is ρ, the faster should be the rate of growth of the resource price. This result is eminently reasonable given the two interpretations we have offered of the Hotelling rule. Its implications will be explored in the following chapter.

The growth rate of consumption

We show in Appendix 7.2 that Equations 7.14a and 7.14d can be combined to give:

$$\frac{\dot{C}}{C} = \frac{Q_K - \rho}{\eta}$$

The term η, the elasticity of marginal utility with respect to consumption, is necessarily positive under the assumptions we have made about the utility function. It therefore follows that:

$$\frac{\dot{C}}{C} > 0 \Leftrightarrow Q_K > \rho$$

$$\frac{\dot{C}}{C} = 0 \Leftrightarrow Q_K = \rho$$

$$\frac{\dot{C}}{C} < 0 \Leftrightarrow Q_K < \rho$$

Therefore, consumption is growing over time along an optimal path if the marginal product of capital Q_K exceeds the social discount rate, consumption is constant if $Q_K = \rho$, and consumption growth is negative if the marginal product of capital Q_K is less than the social discount rate.

Optimality in resource extraction

The astute reader will have noticed that we have described the Hotelling rule (and the other conditions described above) as an efficiency condition. But a rule that requires the growth rate of the price of a resource to be equal to the social discount rate does not give rise to a unique price path. This should be evident by inspection of Figure 7.3, in which two different initial prices, say 1 util and 2 utils, grow over time at the same discount rate, say 5%. If ρ were equal to 5%, each of these paths – and indeed an infinite quantity of other such price paths – satisfies Hotelling's rule, and so they are all efficient paths. But only one of these price paths can be optimal, and so the Hotelling rule is a necessary but not a sufficient condition for optimality.

How do we find out which of all the possible efficient price paths is the optimal one? An optimal solution requires that all of the conditions listed in Equations 7.14a–d, together with initial conditions relating to the stocks of capital and resources and terminal conditions (how much stocks, if any, should be left at the terminal time), are satisfied simultaneously. So Hotelling's rule – one of these conditions – is a necessary but not sufficient condition for an optimal allocation of environmental resources over time.

Let us think a little more about the initial and final conditions for the resource that must be satisfied. There will be some initial resource stock; similarly, we know that the resource stock must converge to zero as

elapsed time passes and the economy approaches the end of its planning horizon. If the initial price were 'too low', then this would lead to 'too large' amounts of resource use in each period, and all the resource stock would become depleted in finite time (that is, before the end of the planning horizon). Conversely, if the initial price were 'too high', then this would lead to 'too small' amounts of resource use in each period, and some of the resource stock would (wastefully) remain undepleted at the end of the planning horizon. This suggests that there is one optimal initial price that would bring about a path of demands that is consistent with the resource stock just becoming fully depleted at the end of the planning period.

In conclusion, we can say that while Equations 7.14a–d are each efficiency conditions, taken jointly as a set (together with initial values for K and S) they implicitly define an optimal solution to the optimisation problem, by yielding unique time paths for K_t and R_t and their associated prices that maximise the social welfare function.

PART 2
Extending the model to incorporate extraction costs and renewable resources

In our analysis of the depletion of resources up to this point, we have ignored extraction costs. Usually the extraction of an environmental resource will be costly. So it is desirable to generalise our analysis to allow for the presence of these costs.

It seems likely that total extraction costs will rise as more of the material is extracted. So denoting total extraction costs as G and the amount of the resource being extracted as R, we would expect that G will be a function of R. A second influence may also affect extraction costs. In many circumstances, costs will depend on the size of the remaining stock of the resource, typically rising as the stock becomes more depleted. Letting S_t denote the size of the resource stock at time t

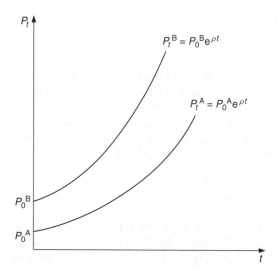

Figure 7.3 Two price paths, each satisfying Hotelling's rule.

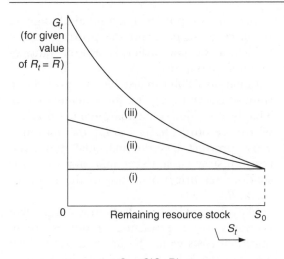

$$G_t = G(S_t, R_t)$$

Case (i) $G_t = G_1(R_t) \rightarrow \delta G_t/\delta S_t = 0$

Case (ii) $G_t = G_2(S_t, R_t)$

$$= \beta_1 R_t + \beta_2 S_t \quad (\beta_1 > 0, \beta_2 < 0)$$

$$\rightarrow = \delta G_t/\delta S_t = \beta_2 < 0$$

Case (iii) $G_t = G_3(S_t, R_t)$

$$= \beta_1 R_t + \beta_2 S_t^{1/2}$$

$$\rightarrow = \delta G_t/\delta S_t = \tfrac{1}{2}\beta_2 S_t^{-1/2} < 0$$

Figure 7.4 Three possible examples of the relationship between extraction costs and remaining stock for a fixed level of resource extraction, R.

(the amount remaining after all previous extraction) we can write extraction costs as

$$G_t = G(R_t, S_t) \tag{7.19}$$

To help understand what the presence of the stock term in Equation 7.19 implies about extraction costs look at Figure 7.4. This shows three possible relationships between total extraction costs and the remaining resource stock size for a constant level of resource extraction. The relationship denoted (i) corresponds to the case where the total extraction cost is independent of the stock size. In this case, the extraction cost function collapses to the simpler form $G_t = G_1(R_t)$, in which extraction costs depend only on the quantity extracted per period of time. In case (ii), the costs of extracting a given quantity of the

resource increase linearly as the stock becomes increasingly depleted. $G_S = \partial G/\partial S$ is then a constant negative number. Finally, case (iii) shows the costs of extracting a given quantity of the resource increasing at an increasing rate as S falls towards zero; G_S is negative but not constant, becoming larger in absolute value as the resource stock size falls. This third case is the most likely one for typical non-renewable resources. Consider, for example, the cost of extracting oil. As the available stock more closely approaches zero, capital equipment is directed to exploiting smaller fields, often located in geographically difficult land or marine areas. The quality of resource stocks may also fall in this process, with the best fields having been exploited first. These and other similar reasons imply that the cost of extracting an additional barrel of oil will tend to rise as the remaining stock gets closer to exhaustion.

The optimal solution to the resource depletion model incorporating extraction costs

The problem we now wish to solve can be expressed as follows:

Select values for the choice variables C_t and R_t for $t = 0, \ldots, \infty$ so as to maximise

$$W = \int_{t=0}^{t=\infty} U(C_t)e^{-\rho t}\,dt$$

subject to the constraints

$$\dot{S}_t = -R_t$$

and

$$\dot{K}_t = Q(K_t, R_t) - C_t - G(R_t, S_t)$$

Comparing this with the description of the optimisation problem for the simple model, you can see that there is one difference. The differential equation for $\dot{K}$ now includes extraction costs as an additional term. Output produced through the production function $Q(K, R)$ should now be thought of as gross output. Extraction costs make a claim on this gross output, and net-of-extraction cost output is gross output minus extraction costs (that is, $Q - G$).

The solution to this problem is once again obtained using the Maximum Principle of optimal control. If you wish to go through the derivations, you should follow the steps in Appendix 7.2, but this time ensuring that you take account of the extraction cost term which will now appear in the differential equation for $\dot{K}$, and therefore also in the Hamiltonian.

From this point onwards, we shall omit time subscripts for simplicity of notation unless their use is necessary in a particular context. The necessary conditions for a social welfare optimum now become:

$$U_C = \omega \qquad (7.20a)$$

$$P = \omega Q_R - \omega G_R \qquad (7.20b)$$

$$\dot{P} = \rho P + \omega G_S \qquad (7.20c)$$

$$\dot{\omega} = \rho \omega - Q_K \omega \qquad (7.20d)$$

Note that two of these four equations – 7.20a and 7.20d – are identical to their counterparts in the solution to the simple model we obtained earlier, and the interpretations of them offered then need not be repeated. However, the equations for the resource net price and for the rate of change of net price differ. Some additional comment is warranted on these two equations.

First, it is now necessary to distinguish between two kinds of price: gross price and net price. The gross price is the price at which the extracted resource sells. The net price is the price of the resource *in situ*, also referred to as 'royalty' or 'rent'. These two measures of the resource price are related as follows:

Net price = Gross price – Marginal cost

Equation 7.20b can be seen in this light:

$$P_t \quad = \quad \omega_t Q_R \quad - \quad \omega_t G_R$$
Net price = Gross price – Marginal cost

The term $\omega_t G_R$ is the value of the marginal extraction cost, being the product of the

impact on output of a marginal change in resource extraction and the price of capital (which, as we saw earlier, is also the value of one unit of output).

Equation 7.20b can also be interpreted in a similar way to that given for Equation 7.14b. That is, the value of the marginal net product of the resource ($\omega Q_R - \omega G_R$, the marginal gross product less the marginal extraction cost) must be equal to the marginal value (or shadow net price) of a unit of the resource stock, P.

If profit maximising firms in a competitive economy were extracting resources, these marginal costs would be internal to the firm and the market price would be identical to the gross price. Note that the level of the net (and the gross) price is only affected by the effect of the extraction rate, R, on costs. The stock effect does not enter Equation 7.20b.

The stock effect on costs does, however, enter Equation 7.20c for the rate of change of the net price of the resource. This expression is the Hotelling rule, but now generalised to take account of extraction costs. The modified Hotelling rule (Equation 20.c) is:

$$\dot{P} = \rho P + G_S \omega$$

Given that $G_S = \partial G / \partial S$ is negative (resource extraction is more costly the smaller is the remaining stock), efficient extraction over time implies that the rate of increase of the resource net price should be lower where extraction costs depend upon the resource stock size.

A little reflection shows that this is eminently reasonable. Once again, we work with an interpretation given earlier. Dividing Equation 7.20c by the resource net price we obtain

$$\rho = \frac{\dot{P}}{P} - \frac{G_S \omega}{P}$$

which says that, along an efficient price path, the social rate of discount should equal the rate of return from holding the resource (which is given by its rate of price appreciation, plus the value of the extraction cost increase that is avoided by not extracting an additional unit of the stock, $-[(G_S\omega)/P]$.)

There is yet another possible interpretation of Equation 7.20c. To obtain this, first rearrange the equation to the form:

$$\rho P = \dot{P} - G_S\omega \qquad (7.20^*)$$

The left-hand side of 7.20* is the marginal cost of not extracting an additional unit of the resource; the right-hand side is the marginal benefit from not extracting an additional unit of the resource. At an efficient (and at an optimal) rate of resource use, the marginal costs and benefits of resource use are balanced at each point in time. How is this interpretation obtained? Look first at the left-hand side. P, the net price of the resource, is the value that would be obtained by the resource owner were he or she to extract and sell the resource in the current period. With ρ being the social utility discount rate, ρP is the utility return foregone by not currently extracting one unit of the resource, but deferring that extraction for one period. This is sometimes known as the holding cost of the resource stock. The right-hand side contains two components. $\dot{P}$ is the price appreciation of one unit of the unextracted resource; the second component, $-G_S\omega$, is a return in the form of a postponement of a cost increase that would have occurred if the additional unit of the resource had been extracted.

Finally, note that whereas the static efficiency condition 7.20b is only affected by the current extraction rate, R, the dynamic efficiency condition (Hotelling's rule, 7.20c) is only affected by the stock effect on costs.

In conclusion, the presence of costs related to the level of resource extraction raises the gross price of the resource above its net price (or royalty) but has no effect on the growth rate of the resource net price. In contrast, a resource stock size effect on extraction costs will slow down the rate of growth of the resource net price. In most circumstances, this implies that the resource net price has to be higher initially (but lower ultimately) than it would have been in the absence of this stock effect. As a result of higher initial prices, the rate of extraction will be slowed down in the early part of the time horizon, and a greater quantity of the resource stock will be conserved (to be extracted later).

Generalisation to renewable resources

We reserve a full analysis of the allocation of renewable resources until Chapter 9, but it will be useful at this point to suggest the way in which the analysis can be undertaken. To do so, first note that in this chapter so far, S has represented a fixed and finite stock of a non-renewable resource. The total use of the resource over time was constrained to be equal to the fixed initial stock. This relationship arises because the natural growth of non-renewable resources is zero except over geological periods of time. Thus we wrote

$$S_t = S_0 - \int_{\tau=0}^{\tau=t} R_\tau \, d\tau \Rightarrow \dot{S}_t = -R_t$$

However, the natural growth of renewable resources is, in general, non-zero. A simple way of modelling this growth is to assume that the amount of growth of the resource, Ω_t, is some function of the current stock level, so that $\Omega_t = \Omega(S_t)$. Given this we can write the relationship between the change in the resource stock and the rate of extraction (or harvesting) of the resource as

$$\dot{S}_t = \Omega(S_t) - R_t \qquad (7.21)$$

Not surprisingly, the efficiency conditions required by an optimal allocation of resources, are now different from the case of exhaustible resources. However, a modified version of the Hotelling rule for rate of change of the net price of the resource still applies, given by

$$\dot{P} = \rho P - P\Omega_S \qquad (7.22)$$

where $\Omega_S = d\Omega/dS$, and in which we have assumed, for simplicity, that harvesting does not incur costs, nor that any environmental damage results from the harvesting and use of the resource. Inspection of the modified Hotelling rule for renewable resources (Equation 7.22) demonstrates that the rate at which the net price should change over time depends upon Ω_S, the rate of change of resource growth with respect to changes in the stock of the resource. We will not attempt to interpret Equation 7.22 here as that is best left until we examine renewable resources in detail in Chapter 9. However, it is worth saying a few words about steady-state resource harvesting.

A steady-state harvesting of a renewable resource exists when all stocks and flows are constant over time. In particular, a steady-state harvest will be one in which the harvest level is fixed over time and is equal to the natural amount of growth of the resource stock. Additions to and subtractions from the resource stock are thus equal, and the stock remains at a constant level over time. Now if the demand for the resource is constant over time, the resource net price will remain constant in a steady state, as the quantity harvested each period is constant. Therefore, in a steady state, $\dot{P} = \partial P/\partial t = 0$. So in a steady state, the Hotelling rule simplifies to

$$\rho P = P\Omega_S \qquad (7.23)$$

and so

$$\rho = \Omega_S \qquad (7.24)$$

It is common to assume that the relationship between the resource stock size, S, and the growth of the resource, Ω, is as indicated in Figure 7.5. This relationship is explained more fully in Chapter 9. As the stock size increases from zero, the amount of growth of the resource rises, reaches a maximum, known as the maximum sustainable yield (MSY) and then falls. Note that $\Omega_S = d\Omega/dS$ is the slope at any point of the growth-stock function in Figure 7.5.

We can deduce that if the social utility discount rate ρ were equal to zero, then the efficiency condition of Equation 7.24 could only be satisfied if the steady-state stock level is $\hat{S}$, and the harvest is the MSY harvest level. On the other hand, if the social discount rate was positive (as will usually be the case), then the efficiency condition requires that the steady-

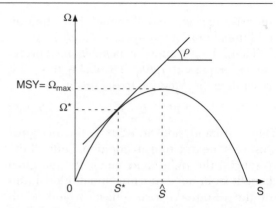

Figure 7.5 The relationship between the resource stock size, S, and the growth of the resource stock, Ω.

state stock level be less than $\hat{S}$. At the stock level S^*, for example, Ω_S is positive, and would be an efficient stock level, yielding a sustainable yield of Ω^*, if the discount rate were equal to this value of Ω_S. Full details of the derivation of this and other results relating to the Hotelling rule are given in Appendix 7.3.

Complications

The model with which we began in this chapter was one in which there was a single, known, finite stock of a non-renewable resource. Furthermore, the whole stock was assumed to have been homogeneous in quality. In practice, of course, both of these assumptions are often false. Rather than there existing a single stock resource, there are many different classes or varieties of non-renewable resource, some of which may be relatively close substitutes for others (such as oil and natural gas, and iron and aluminium).

While it may be correct to assume that there exists a given finite stock of each of these resource stocks in a physical sense, the following situations are likely:

(a) The total stock is not known with certainty.

(b) New discoveries increase the known stock of the resource.

(c) A distinction needs to be drawn between the physical quantity of the stock and the economically viable stock size.

(d) Research and development, and technical progress, take place, which can change extraction costs, the size of the known resource stock, the magnitude of economically viable resource deposits, and estimates of the damages arising from environmental resource use.

Furthermore, even when we focus on a particular kind of non-renewable resource, the stock is likely to be heterogeneous. Different parts of the total stock are likely to be uneven in quality, or to be located in such a way that extraction costs differ for different portions of the stock.

By treating all non-renewable resources as one composite good, our analysis in this chapter had no need to consider substitutes for the resource in question (except, of course, substitutes in the form of capital and labour). But once our analysis enters the more complex world in which there are a variety of different non-renewable resources which are substitutable for one another to some degree, analysis inevitably becomes more complicated. One particular issue of great potential importance is the presence of backstop technologies (see Chapter 8). Suppose that we are currently using some non-renewable resource for a particular purpose – perhaps for energy production. It may well be the case that another resource exists that can substitute entirely for the resource we are considering, but may not be used at present because its cost is relatively high. Such a resource is known as a backstop technology. For example, renewable power sources such as wind energy are backstop alternatives to fossil-fuel based energy.

The existence of a backstop technology will set an upper limit on the level to which the price of a resource can go. If the cost of the 'original' resource were to exceed the backstop cost, users would switch to the backstop. So even though renewable power is probably not currently economically viable, at least not on a large scale, it would become so at some fossil fuel cost, and so the existence of a backstop will lead to a price ceiling for the original resource.

Each of the issues we have raised in this section, and which we have collectively called 'complications', need to be taken account of in any comprehensive account of resource use. We shall do so in the next three chapters.

A numerical application: oil extraction and global optimal consumption

In this section we present a simple, hypothetical numerical application of the theory developed above. You may find the mathematics of the solution given in Box 7.3 a little tedious; if you wish to avoid the maths, just skip the box and proceed to Table 7.1 and Figures 7.6–7.8 at the end of the section where the results are laid out. (The derivation actually uses the technique of dynamic optimisation explained in Appendix 7.1, but applied in this case to a discrete time model.)

Suppose that the welfare function to be maximised is

$$W = \sum_{t=0}^{t=T-1} \frac{U(C_t)}{(1+\rho)^t}$$

where C_t is the global consumption of goods and services at time t; U is the utility function, with $U(C_t) = \log C_t$; ρ is the utility discount rate; and T is the terminal point of the optimisation period.

The relevant constraints are

$S_{t+1} = S_t - R_t$

$K_{t+1} = K_t + Q(K_t, R_t) - C_t$

$S_T = K_T = 0$

S_0 and K_0 are given

S_t denotes the stock of oil; R_t is the rate of oil extraction; K_t is the capital stock; and $Q(K_t, R_t) = A K_t^{0.9} R_t^{0.1}$ is a Cobb–Douglas production function, with A being a fixed 'efficiency' parameter. In this application, we assume that oil extraction costs are zero, and that there is no depreciation of the capital stock. Note that we assume that there are fixed initial stocks of the state variables (the oil stock and the capital stock), and that we specify that the state variables are equal to zero at the end of the optimisation period.

We also assume that a backstop technology exists that will replace oil as a productive input at the end (terminal point) of the optimisation period, $t = T$. This explains why we set $S_T = 0$, as there is no point having any stocks of oil remaining once the backstop technology has replaced oil in production. We assume that the capital stock, K_t, associated with the oil input will be useless for the backstop technology, and therefore will be consumed completely by the end of the optimisation period so $K_T = 0$.

Implicitly in this simulation, we assume that a new capital stock, appropriate for the backstop technology, will be accumulated out of the resources available for consumption. So C_t in this model should be interpreted as consumption plus new additions to the (backstop)

capital stock. The question of how much should be saved to accumulate this new capital stock is beyond the scope of our simple model.

As the notation will have made clear, this is a discrete time model. We choose each period to be 10 years, and consider a 10-period ($t = 0, 1, \ldots, 9$) time horizon of 100 years beginning in 1990 ($t = 0$). The following data are used in the simulation:

Estimated world oil reserve = 11.5 (units of 100 billion barrels)
World capital stock = 4.913 (units of 10 trillion $US)
Efficiency parameter $A = 3.968$
Utility discount rate = 5%

The value of the efficiency parameter is estimated under the assumption that world aggregate output over the 1980s was $US 179.3 trillion, and aggregate oil extraction was 212.7 billion barrels.

We cannot obtain an analytical solution for this problem. But it is possible to solve the problem numerically on a computer. Table 7.1

Table 7.1   Numerical solution to the oil extraction and optimal consumption problem.

Welfare (p.v.) = 46.67668

time	Ct	Q(Kt, Rt)	Kt	Rt	St	q(t + 1)	P(t + 1)	$\partial Q/\partial K(t)$
1990s	3.7342	18.0518	4.9130	2.2770	11.5000	0.2678	0.2123	3.3069
2000s	13.6819	60.8347	19.2306	1.9947	9.2230	0.0731	0.2229	2.8471
2010s	45.3301	182.8353	66.3834	1.7232	7.2283	0.0221	0.2341	2.4788
2020s	137.2777	493.8224	203.8886	1.4637	5.5051	0.0073	0.2458	2.1798
2030s	383.6060	1204.3708	560.4334	1.2167	4.0413	0.0026	0.2581	1.9341
2040s	997.3350	2654.7992	1381.1982	0.9824	2.8247	0.0010	0.2710	1.7299
2050s	2430.1080	5261.7198	3038.6624	0.7611	1.8423	0.0004	0.2845	1.5584
2060s	5584.8970	9217.1125	5870.2742	0.5525	1.0812	0.0002	0.2987	1.4131
2070s	12174.5621	13608.6578	9502.4897	0.3564	0.5287	0.0001	0.3137	1.2889
2080s	25298.4825	14361.8971	10936.5854	0.1724	0.1724	0.0000	0.3293	1.1819
2090s			0.0	0.0000	0.0000	0.0000	0.3548	

| | | ×10 trillion US$ | | | ×100 billion barrels | | | |

% Growth rates:

2000	266.3899	237.0006	291.4222	−12.4012	−19.8004	−74.0064	5.0000	
2010	231.3150	200.5443	245.1973	−13.6071	−21.6271	−71.2545	5.0000	
2020	202.8399	170.0914	207.1378	−15.0607	−23.8402	−68.5517	5.0000	
2030	179.4380	143.8874	174.8723	−16.8783	−26.5885	−65.9180	5.0000	
2040	159.9894	120.4304	146.4518	−19.2530	−30.1053	−63.3685	5.0000	
2050	143.6602	98.1965	120.0019	−22.5320	−34.7797	−60.9136	5.0000	
2060	129.8209	75.1730	93.1861	−27.4081	−41.3110	−58.5599	5.0000	
2070	117.9908	47.6456	61.8747	−35.4951	−51.0972	−56.3110	5.0000	
2080	107.7979	5.5350	15.0918	−51.3311	−67.3996	−54.1679	5.0000	

Box 7.3 Solution of the dynamic optimisation problem using the maximum principle

The current value of the Hamiltonian is

$$H_t = U(C_t) + P_{t+1}(-R_t) + q_{t+1}(Q(K_t, R_t) - C_t)$$
$$(t = 0, 1, \ldots, T-1)$$

where P_t is the shadow price of oil (at time t), and q_t is the shadow price of capital. The four necessary conditions for an optimum are:

1. $P_{t+1} - P_t = \rho P_t - \dfrac{\partial H_t}{\partial S_t} = \rho P_t$

   which implies Hotelling's efficiency rule

   $P_{t+1} = (1 + \rho)P_t \qquad (t = 1, \ldots, T)$

2. $q_{t+1} - q_t = \rho q_t - \dfrac{\partial H_t}{\partial K_t} = \rho q_t - q_{t+1}Q_{K_t}$

   which implies

   $q_{t+1} = \dfrac{1 + \rho}{1 + F_{K_t}}(t = 1, \ldots, T)$

   where

   $Q_{K_t} = Q_{K_t}(K_t, R_t) = \dfrac{\partial Q(K_t, R_t)}{\partial K_t}$

3. $\partial H_t / \partial R_t = 0 = -P_{t+1} + q_{t+1}Q_{R_t}$
   $(t = 0, 1, \ldots, T-1)$

   where

   $Q_{R_t} = Q_{R_t}(K_t, R_t) = \dfrac{\partial Q(K_t, R_t)}{\partial R_t}$

4. $\dfrac{\partial H_t}{\partial C_t} = 0 = U'(C_t) - q_{t+1} \qquad (t = 0, 1, \ldots, T-1)$

   where

   $U'(C_t) = \dfrac{dU(C_t)}{dC_t}$

Since we know $S_t = K_t = 0$, there are $6T$ unknowns in this problem as given below. The unknowns are:

Number	Unknowns
$T + 1$	$\{P_t\}_1^{T+1}$
$T + 1$	$\{q_t\}_1^{T+1}$
$T - 1$	$\{K_t\}_1^{T-1}$
$T - 1$	$\{S_t\}_1^{T-1}$
T	$\{C_t\}_0^{T-1}$
T	$\{R_t\}_0^{T-1}$
$= 6T$	

We have $6T$ equations to solve for these $6T$ unknowns. The equations are:

$U'(C_t) = q_{t+1} \qquad (t = 0, 1, \ldots, T-1)$
                                      [T equations]

$P_{t+1} = q_{t+1}F_{R_t} \qquad (t = 0, 1, \ldots, T-1)$
                                      [T equations]

$S_{t+1} = S_t - R_t \qquad (t = 0, 1, \ldots, T-1)$
                                      [T equations]

$P_{t+1} = (1 + \rho)P_t \qquad (t = 1, \ldots, T)$
                                      [T equations]

$q_{t+1} = \dfrac{1 + \rho}{1 + F_{K_t}}q_t \qquad (t = 1, \ldots, T)$
                                      [T equations]

$K_{t+1} = K_t + F(K_t, R_t) - C_t \quad (t = 0, 1, \ldots, T-1)$
                                      [T equations]

---

and Figures 7.6–7.8 show the numerical solution. Figure 7.6 shows that consumption rises exponentially through the whole of the optimisation period (the figure only shows the first part of that period, from 1990 up to 2080); output (Q_t) also rises continuously, but its growth rate slows down towards the end of the period shown in the figure; this arises because at the terminal point (not shown in these figures), the capital stock has to fall to zero for the reason indicated above.

In Figure 7.7 we observe the oil shadow price growing over time at the rate ρ, and so satisfying Hotelling's rule; the shadow price of capital falls continuously through time. In Figure 7.8, we see that the oil stock falls gradually from its initial level towards zero; note that as the shadow price of oil rises over time, so the rate of extraction falls towards zero. Not surprisingly, the optimal solution will require that the rate of extraction goes to zero at exactly the same point in time, t_f, that the stock is completely exhausted. Finally, note that within 100 years, the oil stock has fallen to a level not significantly different from zero; it is optimal to deplete the stock of oil fairly rapidly in this model.

What happens after the year 2090? You should now try to deduce the answer to this question.

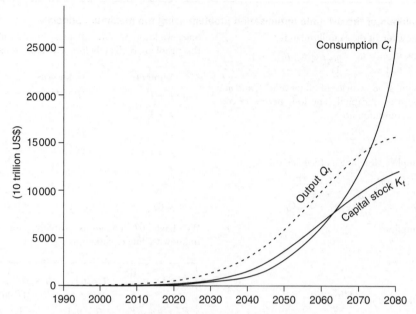

Figure 7.6 Numerical application: optimal time paths of output, consumption and capital stock.

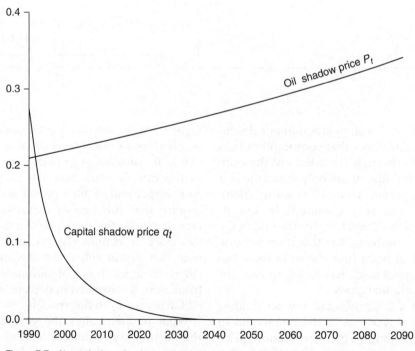

Figure 7.7 Numerical application: optimal time paths of the oil and capital shadow prices.

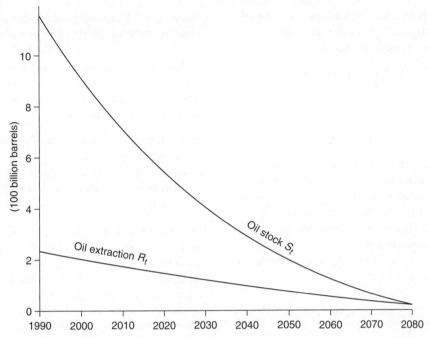

Figure 7.8 Numerical application: optimal time paths of oil extraction and the remaining oil stock.

Discussion questions

1 Are non-renewable resources becoming more or less substitutable by other productive inputs with the passage of time? What are the possible implications for efficient resource use of the elasticity of substitution between non-renewable resources and other inputs becoming
   (a) higher, and
   (b) lower
   with the passage of time?
2 Discuss the possible effects of technical progress on resource substitutability.
3 Recycling of non-renewable resources can relax the constraints imposed by finiteness of non-renewable resources. What determines the efficient amount of recycling for any particular economy?

Problems

1 Using the relationship

$$r = \rho + \eta \frac{\dot{C}}{C}$$

   demonstrate that if the utility function is of the special form $U(C) = C$, the consumption rate of discount (r) and the utility rate of discount are identical.
2 Using Equation 7.15 in the text (that is, the Hotelling efficiency condition), demonstrate the consequences for the efficient extraction of a non-renewable resource of an increase in the social discount rate, ρ.
3 The simplest model of optimal resource depletion is the so-called 'cake-eating' problem in which welfare is a discounted integral of utility, utility is a function of

consumption, and consumption is equal to the amount of the (non-renewable) resource extracted. That is:

$$W = \int_{t=0}^{t=\infty} U(C_t)e^{-\rho t}\, dt$$

$$C_t = R_t$$

and

$$\dot{S}_t = -R_t$$

(a) Obtain the Hamiltonian, and the necessary first-order conditions for a welfare maximum.
(b) Interpret the first order conditions.
(c) What happens to consumption along the optimal path?
(d) What is the effect of an increase in the discount rate?

Further reading

The mathematics underlying our analyses is presented simply and clearly in Chiang (1992). Kamien and Schwartz (1991) is also an excellent reference for optimal control theory. Excellent advanced level presentations of the theory of efficient and optimal resource depletion can be found in Baumol and Oates (1988), Dasgupta and Heal (1979), and Heal (1981). Kolstad and Krautkraemer (1993) is particularly insightful and relatively straightforward. Dasgupta and Heal (1974) is also a comprehensive study, and is contained along with several other useful (but difficult) papers in the May 1974 special issue of the *Review of Economic Studies*.

Less difficult presentations are given in Hartwick and Olewiler (1998), Anderson (1985, 1991), and the Fisher and Peterson survey article in the March 1976 edition of the *Journal of Economic Literature*. For an application of this theory to the Greenhouse Effect, see Barbier (1989b) or Nordhaus (1982, 1991a). Barbier (1989a) provides a critique of the conventional theory of resource depletion, and other critical discussions are found in Common (1995) and Common and Perrings (1992).

Appendix 7.1 The optimal control problem and its solution using the maximum principle

Optimal control theory, using the Maximum Principle, is a technique for solving constrained dynamic optimisation problems. In this appendix we aim to:

(a) explain what is meant by a constrained dynamic optimisation problem
(b) show one technique – the Maximum Principle – by which such a problem can be solved.

We will not give any proofs of the conditions used in the Maximum Principle. Our emphasis is on explaining the technique and showing how to use it. For the reader who wishes to go through these proofs, some recommendations for further reading are given above. After you have finished reading this appendix, it will be useful to go through Appendices 7.2 and 7.3. Appendix 7.2 shows how the maximum principle is used to derive the optimal solution to the simple non-renewable resource depletion problem discussed in Part 1 of this chapter. Appendix 7.3 considers the optimal allocation of a renewable or non-renewable resource in the case where extraction of the resource involves costs, the model discussed in Part 2 of this chapter.

Let us begin by laying out the various elements of a constrained dynamic optimisation problem. In doing this, you will find it useful to refer to Tables 7.2 and 7.3, where we have summarised the key elements of the optimal control problem and its solution.

(1) The function to be maximised is known as the objective function, denoted $J(u)$. This takes the form of an integral over a time period from an initial time t_0 to the terminal time t_T. Two points should be borne in mind about the terminal point in time, t_T:

- In some optimisation problems t_T is fixed; in others it is free (and so becomes an endogenous variable, the value of which is solved for as part of the optimisation exercise).

Table 7.2 The optimal control problem and its solution

Objective function	$J(u) = \max \int_{t_0}^{t_T} L(x,u,t)\mathrm{d}t$			
System	$\dot{x} = f(x,u,t), \quad x(t_0) = x_0$			
Terminal state	$x(t_T) = x_T$		$x(t_T)$ free	
Terminal point	t_T fixed	t_T free	t_T fixed	t_T free
Hamiltonian	$H = H(x,u,t,\lambda)$ $= L(x,u,t) + \lambda'f(x,u,t)$			
Equations of motion	$\dot{x} = f(x,u,t), \quad \dot{\lambda} = -\dfrac{\partial H}{\partial x}$			
Max H	$\dfrac{\partial H}{\partial u} = 0$			
Transversality condition	$x(t_T) = x_T$		$\lambda^*(t_T) = 0$	
		$H(t_T) = 0$		$H(t_T) = 0$

$x(t)$ is the vector of state variables
$u(t)$ is the vector of control variables
$J(u)$ is the objective function to be maximised
$\lambda(t)$ is the vector of co-state variables
t_0 is the initial point in time
t_T is the terminal point in time
H is the Hamiltonian function

Table 7.3 The optimal control problem with a discounting factor and its solution.[a]

Objective function	$J(u) = \max \int_{t_0}^{t_T} L(x,u,t)\mathrm{e}^{-\rho t}\mathrm{d}t$			
System	$\dot{x} = f(x,u,t), \quad x(t_0) = x_0$			
Terminal state	$x(t_T) = x_T$		$x(t_T)$ free	
Terminal point	t_T fixed	t_T free	t_T fixed	t_T free
Hamiltonian[b]	$H = H(x,u,t,\lambda)$ $= L(x,u,t) + \lambda'f(x,u,t)$			
Equations of motion	$\dot{x} = f(x,u,t), \quad \dot{\lambda} = \rho\lambda - \dfrac{\partial H}{\partial x}$			
Max H	$\dfrac{\partial H}{\partial u} = 0$			
Transversality condition	$x(t_T) = x_T$		$\lambda^*(t_T) = 0$	
		$H(t_T) = 0$		$H(t_T) = 0$

[a] ρ is the discount rate
[b] This version of the Hamiltonian function is known as the current-value Hamiltonian (see Chiang [1992], page 210). It is called current-value as the Hamiltonian does not contain the term $\mathrm{e}^{-\rho t}$ which would have the effect of putting the Hamiltonian in present-value terms.

- In some optimisation problems the terminal point is a finite quantity (it is a finite number of time periods later than the initial time); in others, the terminal point is infinite ($t_T = \infty$). When a problem has an infinite terminal point in time, t_T should be regarded as free.

(2) The objective function will, in general, contain as its arguments three types of variable:

- $x(t)$, a vector of n state variables at time t
- $u(t)$, a vector of m control (or instrument) variables at time t
- t, time itself

Although the objective function may contain each of these three types of variable, it is not necessary that all will be present in the objective function (as you will see from the examples worked through in Appendices 7.2 and 7.3).

(3) The solution to a dynamic optimal control problem will contain, among other things, the values of the state and control variables at each point in time over the period from t_0 to t_T. It is this that makes the exercise a dynamic optimisation exercise.

(4) Underlying the optimal control problem will be some economic, biological or physical system (which we shall call simply the economic system), describing the initial values of a set of state variables of interest, and how they evolve over time. The evolution of the state variables over time will, in general, be described by a set of differential equations (known as state equations) of the form:

$$\dot{x} = f(x,u,t)$$

where $\dot{x} = \mathrm{d}x/\mathrm{d}t$ is the time derivative of x (the rate of change of x with respect to time). Note that as x is a vector of n state variables, there will in general be n state equations. Any solution to the optimal control problem must satisfy these state equations. This is one reason why we use the phrase 'constrained' dynamic optimisation problems.

(5) A second way in which constraints may enter the problem is through the terminal conditions of the problem. There are two aspects

here: one concerns the value of the state variables at the terminal point in time, the other concerns the terminal point in time itself.

- Firstly, in some problems the values that the state variables take at the terminal point in time are fixed; in others these values are free (and so are endogenously determined in the optimisation exercise).
- Secondly, either the particular problem that we are dealing with will fix the terminal point in time, or that point will be free (and so, again, be determined endogenously in the optimisation exercise).

(6) The optimisation exercise must satisfy a so-called transversality condition. The particular transversality condition that must be satisfied in any particular problem will depend upon which of the four possibilities outlined in (5) applies. (Four possibilities exist because for each of the two possibilities for the terminal values of the state variables there are two possibilities for the terminal point in time.) It follows from this that when we read Tables 7.2 and 7.3, then (ignoring the column of labels) there are four columns referring to these four possibilities. Where cells are merged and so cover more than one column, the condition shown refers to all the possibilities it covers. We shall come back to the transversality conditions in a moment.

(7) The control variables are those instruments whose value can be chosen by the decision maker in order to steer the evolution of the state variables over time in a desired manner.

(8) In addition to the three kinds of variables we have discussed so far – time, state and control variables – a fourth type of variable enters optimal control problems. This is the vector of co-state variables, λ. Co-state variables are similar to the Lagrange multiplier variables one finds in static constrained optimisation exercises. But in the present context, where we are dealing with a dynamic optimisation problem over some sequence of time periods, the value taken by each co-state variable will in general vary over

time, and so it is appropriate to denote $\lambda(t)$ as the vector of co-state variables at time t.

(9) The analogy of co-state variables with Lagrange multipliers carries over to their economic interpretation: the co-state variables can be interpreted as shadow prices, which denote the decision maker's marginal valuation of the state variable at each point in time (along the optimal time path of the state and control variables).

(10) Finally, let us return to the transversality condition. Looking at the final rows in Tables 7.2 and 7.3 you will see four possible configurations of transversality condition. All relate to something that must be satisfied by the solution at the terminal point in time. Where the terminal value of the state variables is fixed, this will always be reflected in the transversality condition. On the other hand, where the terminal value of the state variables is free, the transversality condition will always require that the shadow price of the state variables is zero. Intuitively, this means that if we do not put any constraints on how large the stocks of the state variables must be at the terminal point in time, then they must have a zero value at that time. For if they had any positive value, it would have been optimal to deplete them further prior to the end of the planning horizon. Note also that whenever the terminal point in time is free (whether or not the state variables are fixed at the terminal point), an additional part of the transversality condition requires that the Hamiltonian have a zero value at the endogenously determined terminal point in time. If it did not, then the terminal point could not have been an optimal one!

The general case referred to in Tables 7.2 and 7.3, and special cases

In the description we have given above of the optimal control problem, we have been considering a general case. For example, we allow there to be n state variables and m control variables. In some special cases, m and n may each be one, so there is only one state and one control variable. Also, we have written the state equation for the economic system of interest as being a function of three types of variables: time, state and control. In many particular problems, not all three types of variables will be present as arguments in the state equation. For example, in many problems, time does not enter explicitly in the state equation. A similar comment applies to the objective function: while in general it is a function of three types of variables, not all three will enter in some problems.

Limitations to the optimal control technique outlined in this appendix

The statement of the optimal control problem and its solution given in this appendix is not as general as it might be. For example, the solution may involve corner solutions (rather than the interior solutions that we are assuming here). Secondly, the terminal condition might require that the state variables are greater than some particular quantity (but are otherwise unconstrained). Similar constraints might also apply to one or more of the control variables. As none of these (or other) complications arise in the examples discussed in this book, we do not go through them here. Details can be found in Chiang (1992).

The presence of a discount factor in the objective function

For some dynamic optimisation problems, the objective function to be maximised, $J(u)$, will be an integral over time of some function of time, state variables and control variables. That is:

$$J(u) = \int_{t_0}^{t_T} L(x, u, t) \, dt$$

However, in many dynamic optimisation problems that are of interest to economists, the objective function will be a discounted (or present-value) integral of the form:

$$J(u) = \int_{t_0}^{t_T} L(x, u, t) \, e^{-\rho t} \, dt$$

For example, Equation 7.8 in the text of this chapter is of this form. There, L is actually a utility function $U(\cdot)$ (which is a function of only one control variable, C). Indeed, throughout this book, the objective functions with which we deal are almost always discounted or present value integral functions.

The solution of the optimal control problem

The nature of the solution to the optimal control problem will differ depending on whether or not the objective function contains a discounting factor. Table 7.2 states formally the optimal control problem and its solution using general notation, for the case where the objective function does not include a discount factor. Table 7.3 presents the same information for the case where the objective function is a discounted (or present value) integral. Some (brief) explanation and discussion of how the conditions listed in Tables 7.2 and 7.3 may be used to obtain the required solution is provided with tables. However, we strongly urge you to read through Appendices 7.2 and 7.3 carefully, so that you can get a feel for how the general results we have described here can be used in practice (and how we have used them in this chapter).

Interpreting the two tables

It will help to focus on one case: we will look at an optimal control problem with a discounting factor, an infinite time horizon (so that t_T is deemed to be free), and no restriction being placed on the values of the state variable in the terminal time period (so that $x(t_T)$ is free. The relevant statement of the optimal control problem and its solution is, therefore, that given in the final column to the right in Table 7.3.

We can express the problem as

$$J(u) = \max \int_{t_0}^{t_T} L(x, u, t) \, e^{-\rho t} \, dt$$

subject to

$$\dot{x} = f(x, u, t) \text{ and } x(t_0) = x_0$$

$$(x_0 \text{ given}), x(t_T)\text{free}$$

To obtain the solution we first construct the Hamiltonian:

$$H = L(x, u, t) + \lambda' f(x, u, t)$$

The Hamiltonian consists of two components:

- The first $L(x, u, t)$ is the function which, after being multiplied by the discounting factor and then being integrated over the relevant time horizon, enters the objective function. Note carefully by examining Table 7.3 that in the Hamiltonian the L function itself enters, not its integral. Furthermore, although the discounting factor enters the objective function, it does not enter in the Hamiltonian.
- The second component that enters the Hamiltonian is the right-hand side of the state variable equation of motion, $f(x, u, t)$, after having been premultiplied by the co-state variable vector. Remember that in the general case there are n state variables, and so n co-state variables, one for each state equation. In order for this multiplication to be conformable, it is actually the transpose of the co-state vector λ that premultiplies the vector of functions from the state equations. The 'prime' symbol (') adjacent to the co-state variable vector denotes the transpose of the vector.

Our next task is to find the values of the control variables u which maximise the Hamiltonian at each point in time; it is this which gives this approach its name of 'the maximum principle'. Now this can be a difficult task in some circumstances. However, in the conditions given in Tables 7.2 and 7.3, it is assumed that the Hamiltonian function H is non-linear and differentiable in the control variables u. In this case, the problem will have an interior solution, which can be found by differentiating H with respect to u and setting the derivatives equal to zero.

Hence one of the necessary conditions for the solution will be

$$\frac{\partial H}{\partial u} = 0 \qquad \text{(a set of } m \text{ equations, one for each of the } m \text{ control variables)}$$

Bringing together all the necessary conditions for the complete solution of the optimisation problem we have:

The maximum principle conditions:

$$\frac{\partial H}{\partial u} = 0 \qquad \text{(a set of } m \text{ equations, one for each set of the } m \text{ control variables)}$$

Those given in the row labelled 'Equations of motion' in Table 7.3, that is

$$\dot{x} = f(x, u, t) \qquad \text{(a set of } n \text{ equations)}$$

$$\dot{\lambda} = \rho\lambda - \frac{\partial H}{\partial x} \qquad \text{(a set of } n \text{ equations)}$$

The initial condition $x(t_0) = x_0$

The transversality condition $H(t_T) = 0$

Solving these necessary conditions simultaneously, we can obtain the optimal time path for each of the m control variables over the (infinite) time horizon. Corresponding to this time path of the control variables are the optimised time paths of the n state variables and their associated shadow prices (values of the co-state variables) along the optimal path. It should be clear that obtaining this complete solution could be a daunting task in problems with many control and state variables. However, where the number of variables is small and the relevant functions are easy to handle, the solution can often be obtained quite simply. We demonstrate this assertion in the following two appendices.

One final point warrants mention. Tables 7.2 and 7.3 give necessary but not sufficient conditions for a maximum. In principle, to confirm that our solution is indeed a maximum, second-order conditions should be checked as well. However, in most problems of interest to economists (and in all problems investigated in this book), assumptions are made which guarantee that second-order conditions for a maximum will be satisfied, thereby obviating the need for checking second-order conditions.

Let us try to provide some intuitive content to the foregoing by considering a problem where there is just one state variable, x, and one control variable, u, where t does not enter either the objective function or the equation describing the system, and where $t_0 = 0$ and we have an infinite terminal point ($t_T = \infty$). Then the problem is to maximise

$$\int_0^\infty L(x_t, u_t)e^{-\rho t}\,\mathrm{d}t$$

subject to

$$\dot{x} = f(x_t, u_t) \quad \text{and} \quad x(t_0) = x_0$$

for which the current value Hamiltonian is

$$H_t = L(x_t, u_t) + \lambda_t f(x_t, u_t) = L(x_t, u_t) + \lambda_t \dot{x}_t$$

In the original problem, we are looking to maximise the integral of the discounted value of $L(x_t, u_t)$. The first term in the Hamiltonian is just $L(x_t, u_t)$, the instantaneous value of that we seek the maximum of. Recalling that co-state variables are like Lagrangian multipliers and that those are shadow prices (see Appendix 4.1), the second term in the Hamiltonian is the increase in the state variable, some stock, valued by the appropriate shadow price. So, H_t can be regarded as the value of interest at t plus the increase in the value of the stock at t. In that case, the maximum principle condition

$$\partial H_t/\partial u_t = 0$$

makes a good deal of sense. It says, at every point in time, set the control variable so that it maximises H_t, which is value plus an increase in value. It is intuitive that such maximisation at every point in time is required for maximisation of the integral.

The equation of motion condition

$$\dot{x} = f(x_t, u_t)$$

ensures that the optimal path is one that is feasible for the system. Aside from tranversality, the remaining condition is

$$\dot{\lambda} = \rho\lambda_t - \partial H_t/\partial x_t$$

which governs how the shadow, or imputed, price of the state variable must evolve over time.

This condition can be given some intuitive content by considering a model which is, mathematically, further specialised, and which has some economic content. Consider the simplest possible optimal growth model in which the only argument in the production function is capital. Then, the optimal paths for consumption and capital accumulation are given by maximising

$$\int_0^\infty U(C_t)e^{-\rho t}\,\mathrm{d}t$$

subject to

$$\dot{K} = Q(K_t) - C_t$$

giving the Hamiltonian

$$H_t = U(C_t) + \lambda_t(Q(K_t) - C_t) = U(C_t) - \lambda_t \dot{K}$$

Here the Hamiltonian is current utility plus the increase in the capital stock valued using the shadow price of capital. In Appendices 17.1 and 17.2 we shall explore this kind of Hamiltonian in relation to the question of the proper measurement of national income.

The maximum principle condition here is

$$\partial H_t/\partial C_t = \partial U_t/\partial C_t - \lambda_t = 0$$

which gives the shadow price of capital as equal to the marginal utility of consumption. Given that a marginal addition to the capital stock is at the cost of a marginal reduction in consumption, this makes sense. Here the condition governing the behaviour of the shadow price over time is

$$\dot{\lambda} = \rho\lambda_t - \partial H_t/\partial K_t = \rho\lambda_t - \lambda_t\partial Q_t/\partial K_t$$

where $\partial Q_t/\partial K_t$ is the marginal product of capital. This condition can be written with the proportionate rate of change of the shadow price on the left-hand side, as

$$\dot{\lambda}/\lambda_t = \rho - \partial Q_t/\partial K_t$$
$$= \rho - \partial Q_t/\partial K_t$$

where the right-hand side is the difference between the discount rate and the marginal product of capital. The first term on the right-hand side reflects impatience for future consumption and the second term the pay-off to delayed consumption. According to this expression for the proportional rate of change of the shadow price of capital:

(a) λ is increasing when 'impatience' is greater than 'pay-off'
(b) λ is constant when 'impatience' is equal to 'pay-off'
(c) λ is decreasing when 'impatience' is less than 'pay-off'

This makes sense, given that:

(a) when 'impatience' is greater than 'pay-off', the economy will be running down K
(b) when 'impatience' and 'pay-off' are equal, K will be constant
(c) when 'impatience' is less than 'pay-off', the economy will be accumulating K.

These remarks should be compared with the results in Table 7.1, where it will be seen that the calculated shadow price of capital decreases over time, while the shadow price of oil, which is becoming scarcer, increases over time.

Appendix 7.2 The optimal solution to the simple exhaustible resource depletion problem

In this appendix, we derive the optimal solution to the simple exhaustible resource depletion problem discussed in Part 1 of this chapter. In doing this, we will make extensive reference to the solution method outlined in Appendix 7.1.

The objective function to be maximised is:

$$W = \int_{t=0}^{t=\infty} U(C_t)e^{-\rho t}dt$$

Comparing this with the form and notation used for an objective function in Tables 7.2 and 7.3 it is evident that:

- we are here using W (rather than J) to label the objective function
- the initial time period (t_0) is here written as $t = 0$
- the terminal time (t_T) is infinity: therefore we describe the terminal point as free
- there is a discounting factor present in the objective function: Table 7.3 is therefore appropriate
- the integral function which in general takes the form $L(x, u, t)$ (ignoring the discounting term) here has the form $U(C_t)$. It is a function of one variable only, consumption, which is a control variable (u). Note that we have written this variable as C_t rather than C to make it explicit that the value of the control variable changes over time. No state variable enters the objective function in this problem, nor does time, t, enter the integral function directly (it enters only through the discounting factor).

Be careful not to confuse U and u. The term U in Appendix 7.2 denotes utility; it is what is being maximised in the objective function; u in Tables 7.2 and 7.3 is the notation used for control variables.

There are two state variables (the x variables in Table 7.3) in this problem: S_t and K_t, the resource stock at time t and the capital stock at time t, respectively. Corresponding to these two state variables are two state equations of motion (the equations $\dot{x} = f(x, u, t)$ in Table 7.3). These are

$$\dot{S} = -R_t$$

and

$$\dot{K}_t = Q_t - C_t$$

There are two control variables in this problem: C_t and R_t (the rate of resource extraction). These are the two variables whose values are chosen by the decision maker to form a time path that will maximise the objective function. Note that in neither of the state equations of motion does a state variable (x) or time (t) appear as an argument of the function.

The economic system consists of:

- the two state equations
- initial values for the state variables: the initial resource stock (S_0, see Equation 7.9) and the initial capital stock (K_0, see footnote 5 in the main text).
- a production function, linking output Q (which is neither a state nor a control variable) to the capital stock and rate of resource extraction at each point in time:

$$Q_t = Q(K_t, R_t)$$

One final thing remains to be specified: the terminal state conditions. We do not state these explicitly in the text. However, by implication, the problem is one in which both the capital stock and the resource stock become zero at the end of the (infinite) planning horizon, so we have $K_{t=\infty} = 0$ and $S_{t=\infty} = 0$ (i.e. $x(t_T) = x_T = 0$, in the notation of Table 7.3). As a result of $x(t_T) = 0$ and t_T free (with an infinite horizon), it is the penultimate column of Table 7.3 which is relevant for obtaining the solution to this problem.

The current-value Hamiltonian for this problem is

$$H_t = U(C_t) + P_t(-R_t) + \omega_t(Q_t - C_t)$$

in which P_t and ω_t are the co-state variables (shadow prices) associated with the resource stock and the capital stock at time t respectively. After substituting for Q_t from the production function, the Hamiltonian is

$$H_t = U(C_t) + P_t(-R_t) + \omega_t(Q\{K_t, R_t\} - C_t)$$

The necessary conditions for a maximum include:

$$\frac{\partial H_t}{\partial C_t} = U_{Ct} - \omega_t = 0 \qquad (7.25a)$$

$$\frac{\partial H_t}{\partial R_t} = -P_t + \omega_t Q_{Rt} = 0 \qquad (7.25b)$$

$$\dot{P}_t = -\frac{\partial H_t}{\partial S_t} + \rho P_t \Leftrightarrow \dot{P}_t = \rho P_t \quad (7.25c)$$

$$\dot{\omega}_t = -\frac{\partial H_t}{\partial K_t} + \rho \omega_t \Leftrightarrow \dot{\omega}_t = \rho \omega_t - Q_{Kt}\omega_t$$
$$(7.25d)$$

The pair of equations 7.25a and 7.25b correspond to the 'Max H' condition $\partial H / \partial u = 0$ in Table 7.3, for the two control (u) variables R and C. The second pair, 7.25c and 7.25d, are the equations of motion for the two co-state variables $[\dot{\lambda} = \rho\lambda - (\partial H / \partial x)]$ that are associated with the two state variables S and K. Note that in 7.25c the term $-\partial H / \partial S = 0$ as S does not enter the Hamiltonian function. The four equations 7.14a to 7.14d given in the main text of this chapter are identical to Equations 7.25a to 7.25d above.

Obtaining an expression for the growth rate of consumption

An expression for the growth rate of consumption along the optimal time path can be obtained by combining Equations 7.25a and 7.25d as follows (dropping the time subscripts for simplicity).

First, differentiate Equation 7.25a with respect to time, yielding:

$$\dot{\omega} = U''(C)\dot{C} \qquad (7.26)$$

Next, combine Equations 7.26 and 7.25d to obtain:

$$U''(C)\dot{C} = (\rho\omega - Q_K^\omega)$$

Hence

$$\dot{C}U''(C) = \omega(\rho - Q_K)$$

But since from Equation 7.25a we know that $U'(C_t) = \omega_t$ the previous equation can be re-expressed as

$$\dot{C}U''(C) = U'(C)(\rho - Q_K\omega)$$

Therefore

$$\frac{\dot{C}U''(C)}{C} = \frac{U'(C)(\rho - Q_K)}{C}$$

and so

$$\frac{\dot{C}}{C} = \frac{1}{\left[\dfrac{U''(C)C}{U'(C)}\right]}(\rho - Q_K) \qquad (7.27)$$

Now by definition the elasticity of marginal utility with respect to consumption, η, is

$$\eta = -\frac{\partial MU/MU}{\partial C/C}$$

Noting that $MU = U'(C)$, then the expression for η can be rearranged to give

$$\eta = -\frac{U''(C)C}{U'(C)}$$

Then 7.27 can be rewritten as

$$\frac{\dot{C}}{C} = -\frac{1}{\eta}(\rho - Q_K) = \frac{Q_K - \rho}{\eta}$$

which is the expression we gave for the growth rate of consumption in the text.

Appendix 7.3 Optimal and efficient extraction or harvesting of a renewable or non-renewable resource in the presence of resource extraction costs

In this appendix, we derive the optimal solution to the resource depletion problem discussed in Part 2 of this chapter. We allow for the resource to be either renewable or non-renewable, and its extraction or harvesting to be costly. Once again, we use the solution method outlined in Appendix 7.1.

So utility is a function of the level of consumption:

$$U_t = U(C_t)$$

The objective function to be maximised is:

$$W = \int_{t=0}^{t=\infty} U(C_t)e^{-\rho t}dt$$

There are two state variables in this problem: S_t, the resource stock at time t and K_t, the capital stock at time t. Associated with each state variable is a shadow price, P (for the resource stock) and ω (for the capital stock).

The two state equations of motion are

$$\dot{S}_t = \Omega(S_t) - R_t \qquad (7.28)$$

$$\dot{K}_t = Q(K_t, R_t) - C_t - G(R_t, S_t) \qquad (7.29)$$

There are several things to note about these equations of motion:

- If the natural resource being used is a non-renewable resource, $\Omega(S) = 0$ and so Equation 7.28 collapses to the special case $\dot{S}_t = -R_t$.
- Equation 7.29 incorporates resource extraction costs, which are modelled as reducing the amount of output available for either consumption or addition to the stock of capital.
- Equation 7.29 incorporates a production function of the same form as in Appendix 7.2.

There are two control variables in this problem: C_t (consumption) and R_t (the rate of resource extraction). Initial and terminal state conditions are identical to those in Appendix 7.2. The current-value Hamiltonian is

$$H = U(C_t) + P_t(\Omega(S_t) - R_t)$$
$$+ \omega_t(Q\{K_t, R_t\} - C_t - G(R_t, S_t))$$

Ignoring time subscripts, the necessary conditions for a maximum are:

$$\frac{\partial H}{\partial C} = U_C - \omega = 0 \qquad (7.30a)$$

$$\frac{\partial H}{\partial R} = -P + \omega Q_R - \omega G_R = 0 \qquad (7.30b)$$

$$\dot{P} = -\frac{\partial H}{\partial S} + \rho P \Leftrightarrow \dot{P} = \rho P - P\Omega_S + \omega G_S \qquad (7.30c)$$

$$\dot{\omega} = -\frac{\partial H}{\partial K} + \rho\omega \Leftrightarrow \dot{\omega} = \rho\omega - \omega Q_K \qquad (7.30d)$$

Special cases of these conditions

Let us consider the simplifications which take place in the Hotelling efficiency condition for the shadow price of the resource (Equation

7.30c) when some special cases are considered.

(a) Non-renewable resources. For non-renewables, as noted above, $\Omega(S) = 0$. The Hamiltonian does not, therefore, contain the term Ω_S. This implies that condition 7.30c simplifies to

$$\dot{P} = \rho P + \omega G_S$$

which is identical to the Hotelling rule given in the text for optimal depletion of a non-renewable resource that incurs extraction costs (Equation 7.20c).

(b) Extraction costs do not depend on the size of the resource stock. Next suppose that we are considering a non-renewable resource for which extraction costs are zero or, more generally, are positive but do not depend on the size of the remaining resource stock. In this case, we have either $G = 0$ or $G = G(R)$. In both cases, $G_S = 0$. Therefore, the final term in Equation 7.30c is zero and so (for non-renewable resources) the Hotelling rule collapses to Equation 7.14c, the one we used in Part 1 of the chapter. That is

$$\dot{P} = \rho P$$

CHAPTER 8

The theory of optimal resource extraction: non-renewable resources

Behold, I have played the fool, and have erred exceedingly.

1 Samuel 26: 21

Introduction

Non-renewable resources include fossil fuel energy supplies – oil, gas and coal – and non-energy minerals – copper and nickel, for example. These resources are formed by geological processes that usually take millions of years, so that they can be viewed as existing in the form of fixed stocks of reserves which, once extracted, cannot be renewed. The resource will be depleted as long as the use rate is positive. One question is of central importance: what is the optimal extraction path over time for any particular non-renewable resource stock?

We have answered this question to some extent in Chapter 7. However, in that earlier analysis, we solved the optimal extraction problem for one particular, very simple, case in which it was assumed that there was only one homogeneous non-renewable resource. No differences existed between different parts of the stock according to location, all of which was of uniform quality. By assuming a single homogeneous stock, we ruled out the possibility that alternative substitute non-renewable resources exist for the one under consideration. The only substitution possibilities we explicitly modelled in Chapter 7 were between the non-renewable resource and other production inputs (labour and capital).

But in practice, non-renewable resources comprise a set of different forms of resource. They vary in terms of chemical and physical type (oil, gas, uranium, coal, and the various categories of each of these) and in terms of costs of extraction as a result of differences in location, accessibility, quality and so on. In this chapter, we wish to analyse the optimal extraction of one component of this set of non-renewable resources, where possibilities exist for substituting other components if the price of the resource rises to such an extent that it makes alternatives economically more attractive. Consider, for example, the case of a country that has been exploiting its coal reserves, but in which coal extraction costs rise as lower quality seams are mined. Meanwhile, gas costs fall as a result of the application of superior extraction technology. One would expect a point to be reached where electricity producers will substitute gas for coal in power generation. It is this kind of process that we wish to be able to model in this chapter.

Although the analysis that follows will employ a different framework from that used in Chapter 7, one very important result carries over to the present case. If a resource is to be optimally extracted, the Hotelling rule continues to be a necessary condition for this. As we showed in Chapter 7, the Hotelling rule is an efficiency condition that must be satisfied by *any* optimal extraction programme.

Having discussed the socially optimal extraction path for a non-renewable resource stock, we then consider how a resource is likely to be depleted in a market economy. The discussions of Chapter 6 suggest that the extraction path in competitive market economies will, under certain circumstances, be socially optimal. We demonstrate that this intuition is indeed correct. However, the competitive market is not the only market form that can exist. We shall also study the influence of one other market form, pure monopoly, upon the depletion path of a non-renewable resource.

Our model is necessarily very simple, and abstracts considerably from reality so that we can identify and examine basic concepts. The assumptions are gradually relaxed so that we can deal with increasingly complex but more realistic situations. For convenience of presentation of the arguments, it is better to begin with a model in which only two periods of time are considered. Even from such a simple starting point, very powerful results can be obtained, which can be generalised to analyses involving many periods. If you have a clear understanding of Hotelling's rule from Chapter 7, you might wish to skip the two-period model in the next section; we have chosen to include it to lead the reader gently into the more powerful analyses that follow.

Having analysed optimal depletion in a two-period model, we then consider a more general model in which depletion takes place over T periods, where T may be a very large number. You will notice that in our worked examples in this chapter, the demand curve we use has a maximum price: a price at which demand would be choked off to zero. Clearly, this implies either that the resource is not essential (in the sense used in Chapter 7), or that substitutes exist for the resource which become economically more attractive at that price. It is the latter interpretation we shall have in mind in this chapter. We shall have more to say on this at the appropriate place below.

There are limits to what we try to cover here. In this chapter, we do not take any account of adverse external effects arising from the extraction or consumption of the resource. It is known, however, that the production and consumption of non-renewable fossil energy fuels are the primary cause of many of the world's most serious environmental problems. In particular, the combustion of these fuels accounts for between 55% and 88% of carbon dioxide emissions, 90% of sulphur dioxide, and 85% of nitrogen oxide emissions (IEA, 1990). In addition, fossil fuel use accounts for significant proportions of trace metal emissions.

We will show later (in Chapter 11) that the optimal extraction path will be different if adverse externalities are present, causing environmental damage. In this chapter, however, we ignore environmental impacts, assuming that they do not exist. Any results we obtain regarding socially optimal extraction paths are conditional upon this assumption, of course, and we will return to this matter in Chapter 11.

Finally, a word about presentation. A lot of mathematics is required to derive our results. The maths is not particularly difficult, but it can be tedious to go through. For this reason, we have tended to stress results and discuss them intuitively in the main text, while derivations (where they are lengthy) are placed in appendices. You may find it helpful to omit these on a first reading, and return to read them during a more careful second reading. The maths is presented fully and simply so you should have little difficulty in understanding the analysis. However, if you cannot cope with the appendices for any reason, do not worry; the arguments in the chapter do not require that they be read.

Our concern in this chapter is with the class of so-called non-renewable resources. For much of our discussion, we shall assume that there exists a known, finite stock of each kind of non-renewable resource. But as we show in later sections, this assumption is not always appropriate; new discoveries are made, increasing the magnitude of known stocks, and technological change alters the proportion of mineral resources that are economically recoverable. Box 8.1 discusses the extent to which it is reasonable to claim that there are fixed and finite quantities of non-renewable resources.

Box 8.1 Are non-renewable resources fixed and finite?

Are non-renewable resources really available in fixed and finite supply? This class of resources includes metals, oil, gases and other mineral deposits. Over sufficiently long timescales, they are renewable, but the rate of regeneration is so slow in timescales relevant to humans that it is sensible to label such resources non-renewable. It also seems reasonable to claim that they exist in finite quantities – albeit very large quantities in some cases. But what is of most interest is whether the amounts are 'fixed' in some sense.

Table 8.1 presents some relevant information. The final column – 'Base resource' – indicates the mass of each resource that is thought to exist in the earth's crust. Most of this resource base consists of the mineral in very dispersed form, or at great depths below the surface. Base resource figures such as these are the broadest sense in which one might use the term 'resource stocks', and these quantities are, to all intents and purposes, fixed and finite. In each case, the measure is purely physical, having little or no relationship to economic measures of stocks. Notice that each of these quantities is extremely large relative to any other of the indicated stock measures.

The column labelled 'Resource potential' is of more relevance to our discussions, comprising estimates of the upper limits on resource extraction possibilities given current and expected technologies. Whereas the resource base is a pure physical measure, the resource potential is a measure incorporating physical and technological information. But this illustrates the difficulty of classifying and measuring resources; as time passes, technology will almost certainly change, in ways that cannot be predicted today. As a result, estimates of the resource potential will change (usually rising), even where resource base figures are constant. Some writers are so confident of the prospects of future technological improvement as to assert that we shall never run out of any resource.

An economist is interested not in what is technically feasible but in what would become available under certain conditions. In other words, he or she is interested in resource supplies, or potential supplies. These will be shaped by physical and technological factors, but will also depend upon resource market prices and the costs of extraction. Prices and costs, introducing feedback into the relationships, will themselves influence exploration and research effort. Data in the column labelled 'World reserve base' consist of estimates of the upper bounds of resource stocks (including reserves that have not yet been discovered) that are economically recoverable under 'reasonable expectations' of future price, cost and technology possibilities. Those labelled 'Reserves' consist of quantities that are economically recoverable under present configurations of costs and prices.

In conclusion, while it might be reasonable to maintain as a working assumption the notion of fixed mineral resource stocks, in the longer term stocks are not fixed, and will vary with changing economic and technological circumstances.

Table 8.1 Production, consumption and reserves of some important mineral resources: 1991 (figures in millions of metric tons).

	Production	Reserves		World reserve base		Consumption	Resource potential	Base resource (crustal mass)
		Quantity	Reserve life (years)	Reserve base	Base life (years)			
Aluminium	112.22	23 000	222	28 000	270	19.460	3 519 000	1 990 000 000 000
Iron ore	929.754	150 000	161	230 000	247	959.6	2 035 000	1 392 000 000 000
Potassium	na	20 000	800	na	>800	25	na	408 000 000 000
Manganese	25	800	32	5000	200	22	42 000	31 200 000 000
Phosphorus	na	110	na	na	270	na	51 000	28 800 000 000
Fluorine	na	2.5	na	na	12	na	20 000	10 800 000 000
Sulphur	56.87	na	na	na	na	57.5	na	9 600 000 000
Chromium	13	419	32	1950	150	13	3260	2 600 000 000
Zinc	7.137	140	20	330	46	6.993	3400	2 250 000 000
Nickel	0.922	47	51	111	119	0.882	2590	2 130 000 000
Copper	9.29	310	33	590	64	10.174	2120	1 510 000 000
Lead	3.424	63	18	130	38	5.342	550	290 000 000
Tin	0.179	8	45	10	56	0.218	68	40 000 000
Tungsten	0.0413	3.5	80	>3.5	>80	0.044	51	26 400 000
Mercury	0.003	0.130	43	0.240	80	0.005	3.4	2 100 000
Silver	0.014	0.28	20	na	na	0.02	2.8	1 800 000
Platinum	0.0003	0.37	124	na	na	0.00029	1.2	1 100 000

na denotes figure not available.
Source: Figures compiled from a variety of sources.

A non-renewable resource two-period model

Consider a planning horizon that consists of two periods, period 0 and period 1. There is a fixed stock of known size of one type of a non-renewable resource. The initial stock of the resource (at the start of period 0) is denoted $\bar{S}$.

Let R_t be the quantity extracted in period t and assume that a demand[1] exists for this resource at each time, given by

$$P_t = a - bR_t$$

where P_t is the price in period t, with a and b being positive constant numbers. So, the demand functions for the two periods will be:

$$P_0 = a - bR_0$$
$$P_1 = a - bR_1$$

These demands are illustrated in Figure 8.1.

Before we go any further, note a point made in the introduction. A linear (and negatively sloped) demand function such as this one has the property that demand goes to zero at some price, in this case the price a. Hence, either this resource is non-essential or it possesses a substitute which at the price a becomes economically more attractive. This is not the only assumption one could make, and so you should bear in mind that the particular results we derive will, to some extent at least, be conditional upon the assumption that the demand curve is of this particular form.

The shaded area in Figure 8.1 (algebraically, the integral of P over the interval $R = 0$ to $R = R_t$) shows the total benefit consumers obtain from consuming the quantity R_t in

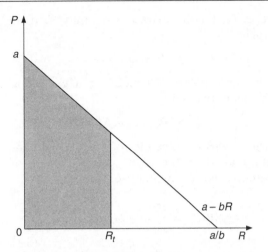

Figure 8.1 The exhaustible resource demand function for the two-period model.

period t.[2] From a social point of view, this area represents the gross social benefit, B, derived from the extraction and consumption of quantity R_t of the resource. We can express this quantity as

$$B(R_t) = \int_0^{R_t} (a - bR)\mathrm{d}R$$

$$= aR_t - \frac{b}{2}R_t^2$$

where the notation $B(R_t)$ is used to make explicit the fact that the gross benefit (B) is dependent on the quantity of the resource extracted and consumed (R).

However, the total gross benefit obtained by consumers is not identical to the net social benefit of the resource, as resource extraction involves costs to society. Let us define c to be the constant marginal cost of extracting the resource ($c \geqslant 0$).[3] Then total extraction

---

[1] Strictly speaking, this is an inverse demand function.

[2] One way of convincing yourself that this statement is correct is as follows. We can regard a demand curve as providing information about the marginal willingness to pay (or marginal benefit) for successive units of the good in question. The area under a demand curve up to some given quantity is thus the sum of a set of marginal benefits, and is equal to the total benefit derived from consuming that quantity. This was explained in Part 3 of Chapter 5.

[3] Constancy of marginal costs of extraction is a very strong assumption. In the previous chapter, we investigated a more general case in which marginal extraction costs are not necessarily constant. We do not consider this any further here, as little of importance would be gained, while it would complicate the derivations considerably. Later in this chapter, however, we do analyse the consequences for extraction of a once-and-for-all rise in extraction costs.

costs, C_t, for the extracted quantity R_t units will be

$$C_t = cR_t$$

The total net social benefit from extracting the quantity R_t is[4]

$$\text{NSB}_t = B_t - C_t$$

where NSB denotes the total net social benefit and B is the gross social benefit of resource extraction and use. Hence

$$
\begin{aligned}
\text{NSB}(R_t) &= \int_0^{R_t} (a - bR)\,\mathrm{d}R - cR_t \\
&= aR_t - \frac{b}{2}R_t^2 - cR_t
\end{aligned}
\tag{8.1}
$$

A socially optimal extraction policy

Our objective in this subsection is to identify an extraction programme that is socially optimal – in other words, a programme that maximises social welfare. This will serve as a yardstick in terms of which any particular extraction programme can be assessed. Later in the chapter, we try to find out what kind of depletion programme would be undertaken in a market economy, and can then discuss whether this would be socially optimal using the criterion we develop here. In order to find the socially optimal extraction programme, two things are required. The first is a social welfare function that embodies society's objectives; the second is a statement of the technical possibilities and constraints available at any point in time. Let us deal first with the social welfare function, relating this as far as possible to our discussion of social welfare functions in Chapters 4 and 5.

As in Chapter 4, the social welfare function that we shall use is discounted utilitarian in

form. So the general two-period social welfare function

$$W = W(U_0, U_1)$$

takes the particular form

$$W = U_0 + \frac{U_1}{1 + \rho}$$

where ρ is the social utility discount rate, reflecting society's time preference. Now let us regard the utility in each period as being equal to the net social benefit in each period.[5] Given this, the social welfare function may be written as

$$W = \text{NSB}_0 + \frac{\text{NSB}_1}{1 + \rho}$$

What are the relevant technical constraints? There is only one in this case. Society has available a fixed initial stock of the non-renewable resource, $\bar{S}$. Since we are adopting a two-period model, we assume that society wishes to have none of this resource stock left at the end of the second period. Then the quantities extracted in the two periods, R_0 and R_1, must satisfy the constraint:[6]

$$R_0 + R_1 = \bar{S}$$

We are now in a position to state precisely the optimisation problem that we wish to

---

[4] Strictly speaking, social benefits derive from consumption (use) of the resource, not extraction *per se*. However, we assume throughout this chapter that all resource stocks extracted in a period are consumed in that period, and so this distinction becomes irrelevant.

[5] In order to make such an interpretation valid, we shall assume that the demand function is 'quasilinear' (see Varian, 1987). Suppose there are two goods, X, the good whose demand we are interested in, and Y, money to be spent on all other goods. Quasilinearity requires that the utility function for good X is of the form

$$U = V(X) + Y$$

This implies that income effects are absent in the sense that changes in income do not affect the demand for good X. In this case, we can legitimately interpret the area under the demand curve for good X as a measure of utility.

[6] We could easily change the problem so that a determined quantity $S^*(S^* \geqslant 0)$ be left at the end of period 1 by rewriting the constraint as

$$R_0 + R_1 + S^* = \bar{S}.$$

This would not, in any important sense, alter the essence of the conclusion we shall reach.

solve. The problem is to choose R_0 and R_1 in such a way as to maximise social welfare, subject to the constraint that total extraction of the resources over the two periods equals $\bar{S}$ exactly. Mathematically, we write the objective as

$$\max_{R_0, R_1} W = \mathrm{NSB}_0 + \frac{\mathrm{NSB}_1}{1 + \rho}$$

subject to

$$R_0 + R_1 = \bar{S}$$

There are several ways of obtaining solutions to constrained optimisation problems of this form. We use the Lagrange multiplier method, a technique that was explained in Appendix 4.1. The first step is to form the Lagrangian function, L

$$L = W - \lambda(\bar{S} - R_0 - R_1)$$

$$= (\mathrm{NSB}_0) + \left(\frac{\mathrm{NSB}_1}{1 + \rho}\right) - \lambda(\bar{S} - R_0 - R_1)$$

$$= \left(aR_0 - \frac{b}{2}R_0^2 - cR_0\right) \qquad (8.2)$$

$$+ \left(\frac{aR_1 - \dfrac{b}{2}R_1^2 - cR_1}{1 + \rho}\right)$$

$$- \lambda(\bar{S} - R_0 - R_1)$$

in which λ is a 'Lagrange multiplier'. Remembering that R_0 and R_1 are choice variables – variables whose value we must select in order to optimise welfare – the necessary conditions for maximising this expression include:

$$\frac{\partial L}{\partial R_0} = a - bR_0 - c + \lambda = 0 \qquad (8.3)$$

$$\frac{\partial L}{\partial R_1} = \frac{a - bR_1 - c}{1 + \rho} + \lambda = 0 \qquad (8.4)$$

Since the right-hand side terms of Equations 8.3 and 8.4 are both equal to zero, this implies that

$$a - bR_0 - c + \lambda = \frac{a - bR_1 - c}{1 + \rho} + \lambda$$

and so

$$a - bR_0 - c = \frac{a - bR_1 - c}{1 + \rho}$$

Using the demand function $P_t = a - bR_t$, the last equation can be written as

$$P_0 - c = \frac{P_1 - c}{1 + \rho}$$

where P_0 and P_1 are gross prices and $P_0 - c$ and $P_1 - c$ are net prices. A resource's net price is also known as the resource rent or resource royalty. Rearranging this expression, we obtain

$$\rho = \frac{(P_1 - c) - (P_0 - c)}{P_0 - c}$$

If we change the notation used for time periods so that $P_0 = P_{t-1}$, $P_1 = P_t$ and $c = c_t = c_{t-1}$, we then obtain

$$\rho = \frac{(P_t - c_t) - (P_{t-1} - c_{t-1})}{P_{t-1} - c_{t-1}} \qquad (8.5)$$

which is equivalent to a result we obtained previously in Chapter 7, Equation 7.15, commonly known as Hotelling's rule. Note that in Equation 8.5 P is a gross price whereas in Equation 7.15 P refers to a net price, resource rent or royalty. However, since $P - c$ in Equation 8.5 is the resource net price or royalty, these two equations are identical (except for the fact that one is in discrete time notation and the other in continuous time notation).

What does this result tell us? The left-hand side of Equation 8.5, ρ, is the social utility discount rate, which embodies some view about how future utility should be valued in terms of present utility. The right-hand side is the proportionate rate of growth of the resource's net price. So if, for example, society chooses a discount rate of 0.1 (or 10%), Hotelling's rule states that an efficient extraction programme requires the net price of the resource to grow at a proportionate rate of 0.1 (or 10%) over time.

Now we know how much higher the net price should be in period 1 compared with period 0, if welfare is to be maximised; but what should be the level of the net price in period 0? This is easily answered. Recall that the economy has some fixed stock of the resource that is to be entirely extracted and consumed in the two periods. Also, we have assumed that the demand function for the resource is known. An optimal extraction programme requires two gross prices, P_0 and P_1 such that the following conditions are satisfied:

$$P_0 = a - bR_0$$
$$P_1 = a - bR_1$$
$$R_0 + R_1 = \bar{S}$$
$$P_1 - c = (1 + \rho)(P_0 - c)$$

This will uniquely define the two prices that are required for welfare maximisation: there are four equations in four unknowns, P_0, P_1, R_0 and R_1.

A non-renewable resource multi-period model

Having investigated resource depletion in the simple two-period model, let us now generalise our analysis to that of many periods. It will be convenient also to change from a discrete time framework (in which we have a number of successive intervals of time, denoted period 0, period 1, etc.) to a continuous time framework, in which we can refer to rates of extraction and use at particular points in time over some continuous time horizon.[7]

To keep the maths as simple as possible, we will push extraction costs somewhat into the background. To do this, we now define P to be the net price of the non-renewable resource, that is the price after deduction of the cost of extraction. Let $P(R)$ denote the

demand function for the resource, indicating that the resource net price is a function of the quantity extracted R.

The social utility at some point in time from consuming a quantity of the resource, R, which is equivalent to the net social benefit discussed in the previous section for the two-period case, may be defined as follows

$$U(R) = \int_0^R P(R) \, dR \qquad (8.6a)$$

which is illustrated by the shaded area in Figure 8.2. You will notice that the demand curve used in Figure 8.2 is non-linear. We shall have more to say about this particular form of the demand function shortly.

By differentiating total utility with respect to R, the rate of resource extraction and use, we obtain

$$\frac{\partial U}{\partial R} = P(R) \qquad (8.6b)$$

which states that the marginal social utility of resource use equals the net price of the resource.

Assume, as we did for the two-period model, that the intertemporal social welfare function is of the utilitarian form, in which future social utility is discounted at the social utility discount rate ρ. Then the value of

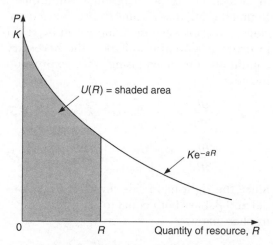

Figure 8.2 A resource demand curve, and the total utility from consuming a particular quantity of the resource.

---

[7] The material in this section, in particular the worked example investigated later, owes much to Heijman (1990).

social welfare over an interval of time from period 0 to period T can be expressed as[8]

$$W = \int_0^T U(R_t)e^{-\rho t}dt$$

Our problem is to make social welfare-maximising choices of

(a) R_t, for $t = 0$ to $t = T$ (that is, we wish to choose a quantity of resource to be extracted in each period), and
(b) the optimal value for T (the point in time at which further depletion of the resource stock ceases),

subject to the constraint that

$$\int_0^T R_t\,dt = \bar{S}$$

where $\bar{S}$ is the total initial stock of the non-renewable resource. That is, the total extraction of the resource is equal to the size of the initial resource stock. Note that in this problem, the time horizon to exhaustion is being treated as an endogenous variable chosen by the decision-maker, and not as a fixed, exogenous number.

We define the remaining stock of the natural resource at time t, S_t, as

$$S_t = \bar{S} - \int_0^t R_t\,dt$$

then by differentiation with respect to time, we obtain

$$\dot{S}_t = -R_t$$

---

[8] It may be helpful to relate this form of social welfare function to the discrete time versions we have been using previously. We have stated that a T-period, discrete time, discounted welfare function can be written as

$$W = U_0 + \frac{U_1}{1+\rho} + \frac{U_2}{(1+\rho)^2} + \dots + \frac{U_T}{(1+\rho)^T}$$

We could write this equivalently as

$$W = \sum_{t=0}^{t=T} \frac{U_t}{(1+\rho)^t}$$

A continuous time analogue of this welfare function is then

$$W = \int_{t=0}^{t=T} U_t e^{-\rho t}dt$$

where $\dot{S} = dS/dt$, the rate of change of the remaining resource stock with respect to time.

So the dynamic optimisation problem involves the choice of a path of resource extraction R_t over the interval $t = 0$ to $t = T$ that satisfies the resource stock constraint and which maximises social welfare, W. Mathematically, we have:

$$\max W = \int_0^T U(R_t)e^{-\rho t}\,dt$$

subject to $\dot{S}_t = R_t$

This problem is very similar to (although rather easier than) one we solved in Chapter 7, Appendix 7.2. It would be a useful exercise at this point for you to use that optimisation technique (explained in Appendix 7.1) to derive the solution to this problem. Your derivation can be checked against the answer given in Appendix 8.1.

Even without using formal optimisation techniques, intuition suggests one condition that must be satisfied if W is to be maximised. This is, R_t must be chosen so that the *discounted* marginal utility is equal at each point in time, that is

$$\frac{\partial U}{\partial R}e^{-\rho t} = \text{constant}$$

To understand this, let us use the method of contradiction. If the discounted marginal utilities from resource extraction were not equal in every period, then total welfare W could be increased by shifting some extraction from a period with a relatively low discounted marginal utility to a period with a relatively high discounted marginal utility. Rearranging the path of extraction in this way would raise welfare. It must, therefore, be the case that welfare can only be maximised when discounted marginal utilities are equal.

Given this result, how do we proceed? First note Equation 8.6b again:

$$\frac{\partial U_t}{\partial R_t} = P_t$$

So, the requirement that the discounted marginal utility be constant is equivalent to the requirement that the discounted net price is constant as well, a result noted previously in Chapter 7. That is

$$\frac{\partial U_t}{\partial R_t}\, e^{-\rho t} = P_t\, e^{-\rho t} = \text{constant} = P_0$$

Rearranging this condition, we obtain

$$P_t = P_0\, e^{\rho t} \qquad (8.7a)$$

By differentiation[9] this can be rewritten as

$$\frac{\dot{P}_t}{P_t} = \rho \qquad (8.7b)$$

This is, once again, the Hotelling efficiency rule. It now appears in a different guise, because of our switch to a continuous time framework. The rule states that the net price or royalty P_t of a non-renewable resource should rise at a rate equal to the social utility discount rate, ρ, if the social value of the resource is to be maximised.

We now know the rate at which the resource net price or royalty must rise. However, this does not fully characterise the solution to our optimising problem. There are several other things we need to know too. Firstly, we need to know the optimal initial value of the resource net price. Secondly, we need to know over how long a period of time the resource should be extracted – in other words, what is the optimal value of T? Thirdly, what is the optimal rate of resource extraction at each point in time? Finally, what

Table 8.2   The required optimality conditions.

	Initial ($t = 0$)	Interim ($t = t$)	Final ($t = T$)
Royalty, P	$P_0 = ?$	$P_t = ?$	$P_T = ?$
Extraction, R	$R_0 = ?$	$R_t = ?$	$R_T = ?$
Depletion time			$T = ?$

should be the values of P and R at the end of the extraction horizon? Table 8.2 summarises the information that is required for a full solution.

It is not possible to obtain answers to these questions without one additional piece of information: the particular form of the resource demand function. So let us suppose that the resource demand function is

$$P(R) = Ke^{-aR} \qquad (8.8)$$

which is illustrated in Figure 8.2.[10] Unlike the demand function used in the two-period analysis, this function exhibits a non-linear relationship between P and R, and is probably more representative of the form that resource demands are likely to take than the linear function used in the section on the two-period model. However, it is similar to the previous demand function in so far as it exhibits zero demand at some finite price level.

To see this, just note that $P(R = 0) = K$. K is the so-called *choke price* for this resource, meaning that the demand for the resource is driven to zero or is 'choked off' at this price. At the choke price people using the services of this resource would switch demand to some alternative, substitute, non-renewable

[9] Differentiation of Equation 8.7a with respect to time gives

$$\frac{\mathrm{d}P_t}{\mathrm{d}t} = P_0 \rho e^{\rho t}$$

By substitution of Equation 8.7a into this expression, we obtain

$$\frac{\mathrm{d}P_t}{\mathrm{d}t} = \dot{P}_t = \rho P_t$$

and dividing through by P_t we obtain

$$\frac{\dot{P}_t}{P_t} = \rho$$

as required.

[10] For the demand function given in Equation 8.8, we can obtain the particular form of the social welfare function as follows. The social utility function corresponding to Equation 8.6a will be:

$$U(R) = \int_0^R P(R)\mathrm{d}R = \int_0^R Ke^{-aR}\mathrm{d}R = \frac{K}{a}(1 - e^{-aR})$$

The social welfare function, therefore, is

$$W = \int_0^T U(R_t)e^{-\rho t}\mathrm{d}t = \int_0^T \frac{K}{a}(1 - e^{-aR_t})e^{-\rho t}\mathrm{d}t$$

Table 8.3 Optimality conditions: multi-period model

	Initial ($t = 0$)	Interim ($t = t$)	Final ($t = T$)
Royalty, P	$P_0 = K \exp\left(\sqrt{2\rho \bar{S} a}\right)$	$P_t = K e^{\rho(t - T)}$	$P_T = K$
Extraction, R	$R_0 = \sqrt{\dfrac{2\rho \bar{S}}{a}}$	$R_t = \dfrac{\rho}{a}(T - t)$	$R_T = 0$
Depletion time			$T = \sqrt{\dfrac{2 \bar{S} a}{\rho}}$

Note: Here, and in Table 8.4 and the appendices, it is in some cases convenient to use $\alpha \exp \beta$ in place of αe^{β}. The two expressions mean the same thing.

resource, or to an alternative final product not using that resource as an input.

Let us recap the argument so far. Given

- a particular resource demand function,
- Hotelling's efficiency condition,
- an initial value for the resource stock, and
- a final value for the resource stock,

it is possible to obtain optimal expressions for all the variables listed in Table 8.2. We now have all this information. A particular demand curve has just been assumed, we have derived the Hotelling condition, and we know the initial stock. What about the final stock level? This is straightforward. An optimal solution must have the property that the stock goes to zero at exactly the same point in time that demand and extraction go to zero.[11] If that were not the case, some resource will have been needlessly wasted. So we know that the solution must include $S_T = 0$ and $R_T = 0$, with resource stocks being positive, and positive extraction taking place over all time up to T.

Before we proceed to obtain all the details of the solution, one important matter must be made clear. As the solution we obtain requires information about the demand function of the natural resource, the solution will vary depending upon the demand function chosen. It is important to realise that the expressions derived below are conditional upon the particular demand function chosen,

and will not be valid in all circumstances. In particular, our model in this chapter assumes that the resource has a choke price, implying that a substitute for the resource becomes economically more attractive at that price.

As the mathematics required to obtain the full solution are rather tedious (but not particularly difficult), the derivations are presented in Appendix 8.1. You are strongly recommended to read this now, but if you prefer to omit these derivations, the results are presented in Table 8.3. You can see from Table 8.3 that all the expressions for the initial, interim and final resource royalty (or net prices) and rate of resource extraction are functions of the parameters of the model (K, ρ, and a) and T, the optimal depletion time. As the final expression indicates, T is itself a function of those parameters.

Given the functional forms we have been using in this section, if the values of the parameters K, ρ, and a were known, it would be possible to solve the model to obtain numerical values for all the variables of interest over the whole period for which the resource will be extracted.

Figure 8.3 portrays in a diagrammatic form the solution to our optimal depletion model. The diagram shows the optimal resource extraction and net price paths over time corresponding to social welfare maximisation. As we show subsequently, it also represents the profit-maximising extraction and price paths in perfectly competitive markets.

In the upper right quadrant, the net price is shown rising exponentially at the social uti-

[11] In terms of optimisation theory, this constitutes a so-called terminal condition for the problem.

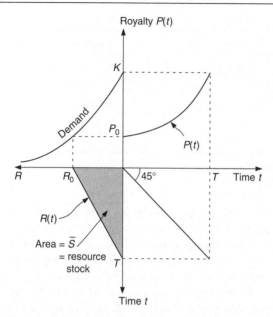

Figure 8.3 Graphical representation of solutions to the optimal resource depletion model.

lity discount rate, ρ, thereby satisfying the Hotelling rule. The upper left quadrant shows the resource demand curve with a choke price K. The lower left quadrant gives the optimal extraction path of the non-renewable resource, which is, in this case, a declining linear function of time.

The net price is initially at P_0, and then grows until it reaches the choke price K at time T. At this point, demand for the resource goes to zero, and the accumulated extraction of the resource (the shaded area beneath the extraction path) is exactly equal to the total initial resource stock, $\bar{S}$. The lower right quadrant maps the time axes by a 45° line. A worked numerical example illustrating optimal extraction is presented in Appendix 8.3.

Non-renewable resource extraction in perfectly competitive markets

Until this point, we have said nothing about the kind of market structure in which decisions are made. Put another way, it is as if we have been imagining that a rational social planner were asked to make decisions that

maximise social welfare, given the constraints facing the economy. All of the optimality conditions listed in Table 8.3, plus the Hotelling efficiency condition, are the outcome of the social planner's calculations.

How will matters turn out if decisions are not taken by a rational and perfectly informed social planner, but are instead the outcome of profit-maximising decisions in a perfectly competitive market economy? A remarkable result we demonstrate in this section is that, ceteris paribus, the outcomes will be identical. We will show that Hotelling's rule and the optimality conditions of Table 8.3 are also obtained under a perfect competition assumption.

Suppose there are m competitive firms in the market. Use the subscript j to denote any one of these m firms. Assume, for simplicity, that all firms have equal and constant marginal costs of extracting the resource. Now as all firms in a competitive market face the same fixed selling price at any point in time, the market royalty will be identical over firms. Given the market royalty P_t, each firm chooses an amount to extract and sell, $R_{j,t}$, to maximise its profits. Mathematically

$$\max \int_0^T \Pi_{j,t}\,e^{-it}\,dt$$

subject to

$$\int_0^T \left(\sum_{j=1}^m R_{j,t}\right) dt = \bar{S}$$

where $\Pi_j = P \cdot R_j$ is firm j's profit and i is the market interest rate.

Note that the stock constraint operates on all firms collectively; in other words, the industry as a whole cannot extract more than the fixed initial stock over the whole time horizon. The profit-maximising extraction rate is obtained when each firm selects an extraction $R_{j,t}$ so that its discounted marginal profit will be the same at any point in time t, i.e.

$$M\Pi_{j,t}\,e^{-it} = \frac{\partial \Pi_{j,t}}{\partial R_{j,t}}\,e^{-it} = \frac{\partial PR_{j,t}}{\partial R_{j,t}}\,e^{-it}$$

$$= P_t\,e^{-it} = \text{constant}$$

where $M\Pi_j$ is firm j's marginal profit function. If discounted marginal profits were *not* the same over time, total profits could be increased by switching extraction between time periods so that more was extracted when discounted profits were high and less when they were low.

The result that the discounted marginal profit is the same at any point in time implies that

$$P_t \mathrm{e}^{-it} = P_0 \text{ or } P_t = P_0\, \mathrm{e}^{it}$$

Not surprisingly, Hotelling's efficiency rule continues to be a required condition for profit maximisation, so that the market net price of the resource must grow over time at the rate i. The interest rate in this profit maximisation condition is the market rate of interest. Our analysis in Chapter 5 showed that, in perfectly competitive capital markets, the market interest rate will be equal to r, the consumption rate of interest, and also to δ, the rate of return on capital.

We appear now to have two different efficiency conditions,

$$\frac{\dot{P}}{P} = \rho \quad \text{and} \quad \frac{\dot{P}}{P} = i$$

the former emerging from maximising social welfare, the latter from private profit maximisation. But these are in fact identical conditions under the assumptions we have made in this chapter; by assuming that we can interpret areas under demand curves (that is, gross benefits) as quantities of utility, we in effect impose the condition that $\rho = r$. Given this result, it is not difficult to show, by cranking through the appropriate maths in a similar manner to that done in Appendix 8.1, that all the results of Table 8.3 would once again be produced under perfect competition, provided the private market interest rate equals the social consumption discount rate. We leave this as an exercise for the reader.

Finally, note that the appearance of a positive net price or royalty, $P_t > 0$, for non-renewable resources reflects the fixed stock assumption. If the resource existed in unlimited quantities (that is, the resource were not scarce) net prices would be zero in perfect competition, as the price of the product will equal the marginal cost (c), a result which you may recall from standard theory of long-run equilibrium in competitive markets. In other words, scarcity rent would be zero as there would be no scarcity!

Resource extraction in a monopolistic market

It is usual to assume that the objective of a monopoly is to maximise its discounted profit over time. Thus, it selects the net price P_t (or royalty) and chooses the output R_t so as to obtain

$$\max \int_0^T \Pi_t \mathrm{e}^{-it}\mathrm{d}t$$

subject to

$$\int_0^T R_t \mathrm{d}t = \bar{S}$$

where $\Pi_t = P(R_t) \cdot R_t$.

For the same reason as in the case of perfect competition, the profit-maximising solution is obtained by allocating the output R_t such that the discounted marginal profit will be the same at any time, so we have

$$M\Pi_t\, \mathrm{e}^{-it} = \frac{\partial \Pi_t}{\partial R_t} e^{-it} = \text{constant} = M\Pi_0$$

that is,

$$M\Pi_t = M\Pi_0 \mathrm{e}^{it} \qquad (8.9)$$

Looking carefully at Equation 8.9, and comparing this with the equation for marginal profits in the previous section, it is clear why the profit-maximising solutions in monopolistic and competitive markets will differ. Under perfect competition, the market price is exogenous to (fixed for) each firm. Thus we are able to obtain the result that in competitive markets, marginal cost equals price. However, in a monopolistic market, price is

Table 8.4 The comparison table: perfect competition vs monopoly.

	Perfect competition	Monopoly
Objective	$\max \int_0^T P_t R_{jt} \exp(-it) dt$	$\max \int_0^T P_t R_t \exp(-it) dt$
Constraint	$\int_0^T \left(\sum_j R_{jt} \right) dt = \bar{S}$	$\int_0^T R_t dt = \bar{S}$
Demand curve	$P_t = K \exp(-aR_t)$	$P_1 = K \exp(-aR_t)$
Optional solution		
Exhaustion time	$T = \sqrt{2\bar{S}a/i}$	$T = \sqrt{2\bar{S}ah/i}$
Initial royalty	$P_0 = K \exp(-\sqrt{2i\bar{S}a})$	$P_0 = K \exp(-\sqrt{2i\bar{S}a/h})$
Royalty path	$P_t = P_0 \exp(it)$	$P_t = P_0 \exp(it/h)$
Extraction path	$R_t = \dfrac{i}{a}(T - t)$	$R_t = \dfrac{i}{ha}(T - t)$
	(where $R_t = \sum_j R_{jt}$)	$R_0 = \sqrt{2i\bar{S}/ha}$
	$R_0 = \sqrt{2i\bar{S}/a}$	

not fixed, but will depend upon the firm's output choice. Marginal revenue will be less than price in this case.

The necessary condition for profit maximisation in a monopolistic market states that the marginal profit (and not the net price or royalty) should increase at the rate of interest i in order to maximise the discounted profits over time. The solution to the monopolist optimising problem is derived in Appendix 8.2. If you wish to omit this, you will find the results in Table 8.4.

A comparison of competitive and monopolistic extraction programmes

Table 8.4 summarises the results concerning optimal resource extraction in perfectly competitive and monopolistic markets. The analytical results presented are derived in Appendices 8.1 and 8.2. For convenience, we list below the notation used in Table 8.4.

P_t is the net price (royalty) of non-renewable resource with fixed stock $\bar{S}$

R_t is the total extraction of the resource at time t

R_{jt} is the extraction of individual firm j at time t

i is the interest rate

T is the exhaustion time of the natural resource

K, h and a are fixed parameters

Two key results emerge from Tables 8.3 and 8.4. Firstly, under certain conditions, there is equivalence between the perfect competition market outcome and the social welfare optimum. If all markets are perfectly competitive, and the market interest rate is equal to the social consumption discount rate, the profit-maximising resource depletion programme will be identical to the one that is socially optimal.

Secondly, there is non-equivalence of perfect competition and monopoly markets: profit-maximising extraction programmes will be different in perfectly competitive and monopolistic resource markets. Given the result stated in the previous paragraph, this implies that monopoly must be sub-optimal in a social welfare-maximising sense.

For the functional forms we have used in this section, a monopolistic firm will take $\sqrt{h}$ times longer to fully deplete the non-renew-

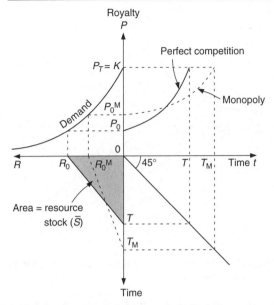

Figure 8.4 A comparison of resource depletion in competitive and monopolistic markets.

able resource than a perfectly competitive market in our model. As Figure 8.4 demonstrates, the initial net price will be higher in monopolistic markets, and the rate of price increase will be slower. Extraction of the resource will be slower at first in monopolistic markets, but faster towards the end of the depletion horizon. Monopoly, in this case at least, turns out to be an ally of the conservationist, in so far as the time until complete exhaustion is deferred further into the future.[12] As the comparison in Figure 8.4 illustrates, a monopolist will restrict output and raise prices initially, relative to the case of perfect competition. The rate of price increase, however, will be slower than under perfect competition. Eventually, an effect of monopolistic markets is to increase the time horizon over which the resource is extracted.

---

[12] Note that this conclusion is not *necessarily* the case. The longer depletion period we have found is a consequence of the particular assumptions we have made. Although in most cases one would expect this to be true, it is possible to make a set of assumptions such that a monopolist would extract the stock in a shorter period of time.

Extensions of the multi-period model of non-renewable resource depletion

To this point, we have made a number of simplifying assumptions in developing and analysing our model of resource depletion. In particular, we have assumed that

- the utility discount rate and the market interest rate are constant over time;
- there is a fixed stock, of known size, of the non-renewable natural resource;
- the demand curve is identical at each point in time;
- no taxation or subsidy is applied to the extraction or use of the resource;
- marginal extraction costs are constant;
- there is a fixed 'choke price' (hence implying the existence of a backstop technology);
- no technological change occurs;
- no externalities are generated in the extraction or use of the resource.

We shall now undertake some comparative dynamic analysis. This consists of finding how the optimal paths of the variables of interest change over time in response to changes in the levels of one or more of the parameters in the model, or of finding how the optimal paths alter as our assumptions are changed. We adopt the device of investigating changes to one parameter, holding all others unchanged, comparing the new optimal paths with those derived above for our simple multi-period model. (We shall only discuss these generalisations for the case of perfect competition; analysis of the monopoly case is left to the reader as an exercise.)

An increase in the interest rate

Let us make clear the problem we wish to answer here. Suppose that the interest rate we had assumed in drawing Figure 8.3 was 6% per year. Now suppose that the interest rate was not 6% but rather 10%; how would Figure 8.3 have been different if the interest

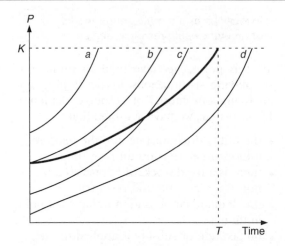

Figure 8.5 The effect of an increase in the interest rate on the optimal price of the exhaustible resource.

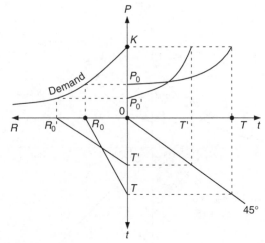

Figure 8.6 An increase in interest rates in a perfectly competitive market.

rate had been higher in this way? This is the kind of question we are trying to answer in doing comparative dynamics.

Since the royalty must grow at the market interest rate, an increase in i will raise the growth rate of the resource royalty, P_t. The initial price will be lower than in the base case, but the price grows more quickly, and the final price (the choke price) is reached earlier. This result follows from the fact that the change in interest rate does not alter the quantity that is to be extracted; the same total stock is extracted in each case. But this means that if the initial price is lower (and so the quantity extracted is higher), then the final price must be higher (and so the quantity extracted is lower). The resource price path will change position as shown in Figure 8.5 by the switch from the original

path to the path labelled c.[13] The initial royalty has to be lowered to increase the demand so that within a shorter time horizon, the stock of resource is depleted completely. The implications for all the variables of interest are summarised in Figure 8.6. This shows that a higher discount rate will tend to mean more rapid exhaustion of the non-renewable resource.

An increase in the size of the known resource stock

In practice, estimates of the size of reserves of non-renewable resources such as coal and oil are under constant revision. Proven reserves are those unextracted stocks known to exist and be recoverable at current prices and costs.

---

[13] If the rate of price increase is higher than in the initial case, this does not of itself tie down the exact position of the new price path. In Figure 8.5, each of the price paths a, b, c and d shows a higher rate of price increases than the original path. However, only path c can be optimal.

To see this, note that paths a and b have a higher price than the original path at all times (except $t = 0$ for b). Therefore, on paths a and b, not all of the resource would be extracted before the choke price, K, is reached. These two paths cannot, therefore, be optimal ones. Case d is not feasible; it implies a lower price at all times than in the original case, and a longer time until the choke price is reached. But this implies, in turn, that a greater quantity is extracted over time than on the original path, which is not feasible.

Only a path such as c is optimal. The price is initially lower (implying more extraction early on than under the original path) but after a certain point in time, the price becomes higher and remains so (and therefore less is extracted later). If the new price path intersects the original in this manner, the optimal time to exhaustion (the time in which the resource price reaches K, the choke price) must be shorter.

Probable reserves relate to stocks that are known, with near certainty, to exist but which have not yet been fully explored or researched. They represent the best guess of additional amounts that could be recovered at current price and cost levels. Possible reserves refer to stocks in geological structures near to proven fields. As prices rise, what were previously uneconomic stocks become economically recoverable.

Consider the case of a single new discovery of a fossil fuel stock. Other things being unchanged, if the royalty path were such that its initial level remained unchanged at P_0, then given the fact that the rate of royalty increase is unchanged, some proportion of the reserve would remain unutilised by the time the choke price, K, is reached. This is clearly neither efficient nor optimal. It follows that the initial royalty must be lower and the time to exhaustion is extended. At the time the choke price is reached, T', the new enlarged resource stock will have just reached complete exhaustion, as shown in Figure 8.7.

Now suppose that there is a sequence of new discoveries taking place over time, so that the size of known reserves increases in a

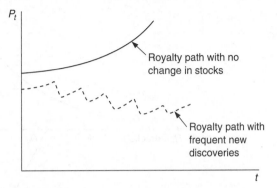

Figure 8.8 The effect of frequent new discoveries on the resource net price or royalty.

series of discrete steps. Generalising the previous argument, we would expect the behaviour of the net price or royalty over time to follow a path similar to that illustrated in Figure 8.8. This hypothetical price path is one that is consistent with the actual behaviour of oil prices.

Changing demand

Suppose that there is an increase in demand for the resource, possibly as a result of population growth or rising real incomes. The demand curve thus shifts outwards. Given this change, the old royalty or net price path would result in higher extraction levels, which will exhaust the resource before the net price has reached K, the choke price. Hence the net price must increase to dampen down quantities demanded; as Figure 8.9 shows, the time until the resource stock is fully exhausted will also be shortened.

A fall in the price of backstop technology

In the model developed in this chapter, we have assumed there is a choke price K. If the net price were to rise above K, the economy will cease consumption of the non-renewable resource and switch to an alternative source – the backstop source. Suppose that technological progress occurs, increasing the efficiency of a backstop technology. This will tend to

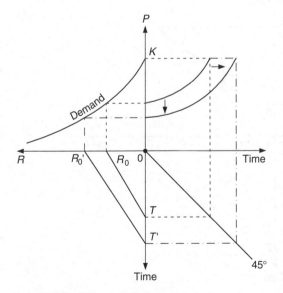

Figure 8.7 An increase in the resource stock.

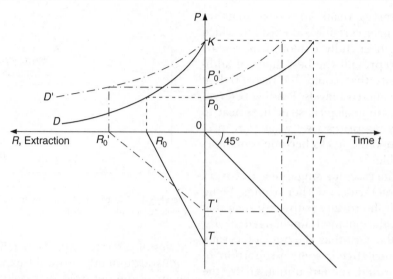

Figure 8.9   The effect of an increase in demand for the resource.

reduce the price of the backstop source, P_B. If P_B falls, P_0 will be too high to be optimal since the net price would reach the new backstop price, P_B, before T, leaving some of the economically useful resource unexploited. So the initial price of the non-renewable resource, P_0, must fall to encourage an increase in demand so that a shorter time horizon is required until complete exhaustion of the non-renewable resource reserve. This process is illustrated in Figure 8.10. Note that when the resource price reaches the new, reduced backstop price, demand for the non-renewable resource discontinuously falls to zero.

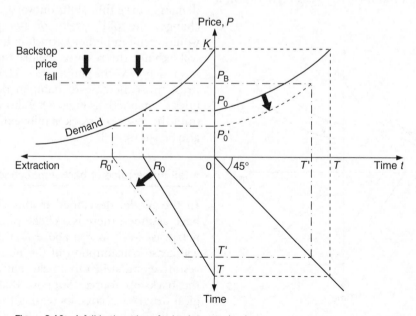

Figure 8.10   A fall in the price of a backstop technology.

A change in resource extraction costs

Let us begin by considering the case of an increase in extraction costs, possibly because labour charges rise in the extraction industry. To analyse the effects of an increase in extraction costs, it is important to distinguish carefully between the net price and the gross price of the resource. Let us define:

$$p_t = P_t - c$$

where p_t is the resource royalty (or net price), P_t is the gross price of the non-renewable resource, and c is the marginal extraction cost, assumed to be constant. Hotelling's rule, you recall, requires that the resource *net price* grows at a constant rate, equal to the discount rate (that we take here to be constant at the rate i). Therefore, efficient extraction requires that

$$p_t = p_0 e^{it}$$

Now suppose that the cost of extraction, while still constant, now becomes somewhat higher than was previously the case. We suppose that this change takes place at the initial time period, period 0. Consider first what would happen if the gross price remained unchanged at its initial level. The increase in unit extraction costs would then result in the net price being lower than its initial level. However, with no change having occurred in the interest rate, the net price must *grow* at the same rate as before. It therefore follows that the net price p_t would be lower at all points in time. The gross price will be lower at all points in time, except in the original period. This is illustrated in Figure 8.11. Note carefully that the reason why the gross price will be lower is the changed profile of the net price curve; the net price grows at the same rate as before, but from a lower starting value.

But if the gross or market price is lower at all points in time except period 0, more extraction would take place in every period. This would cause the reserve to become completely exhausted before the choke price (K) is reached. This cannot be optimal, as any

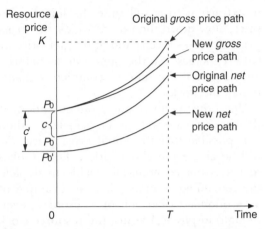

Figure 8.11 An increase in extraction costs: effects on gross and net prices.

optimal extraction path must ensure that demand goes to zero at the same point in time as the remaining resource stock goes to zero. Therefore, optimal extraction requires that the initial market price, P_0 must be greater than its initial level, causing less of the reserve to be extracted at each point in time, and the time to exhaustion to be lengthened. This is the final outcome that we illustrate in Figure 8.12. In conclusion, a rise

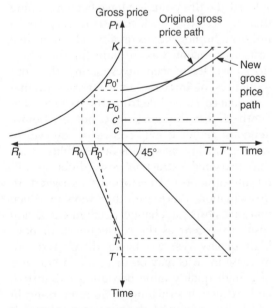

Figure 8.12 A rise in extraction costs.

in extraction costs will raise the initial gross price, slow down the rate at which the gross price increases (even though the net price or royalty increases at the same rate as before), and lengthen the time to complete exhaustion of the stock.

One other point requires our attention. If the cost increase were to be very large, then it is possible that the initial gross price, P_0, will be above the choke price. This implies that it is not economically viable to deplete the remaining reserve – it is an example of an economic exhaustion of a resource, even though, in physical terms, the resource stock has not become completely exhausted.

Let us now briefly consider the effects of a fall in extraction costs. This may be the consequence of technological progress decreasing the costs of extracting the resource from its reserves. By following similar reasoning to that we used above, it can be deduced that a fall in extraction costs will lower the initial gross price, increase the rate at which the gross price increases (even though the net price or royalty increases at the same rate as before), and shorten the time to complete exhaustion of the stock.

One remaining point needs to be considered. To this point, we have been assuming that the resource stock consists of reserves of uniform, homogeneous quality. The marginal cost of extraction was constant for the whole stock. We have been investigating the consequences of increases or decreases in that marginal cost schedule from one fixed level to another. But the stock may not be homogeneous; rather it may consist of reserves of varying quality or varying accessibility, such that marginal extraction costs differ as different segments of the stock are extracted. In this situation, there are other ways in which marginal costs can change. A fall in extraction costs may occur as the consequence of new, high quality reserves being discovered. An increase in costs may occur as a consequence of a high quality mine becoming exhausted, and extraction switching to another mine in which the quality of the resource reserve is

somewhat lower. We do not formally analyse these cases in this text. The interested reader can find a good treatment in Hartwick and Olewiler (1986). An important dimension that is introduced into the analysis by generalising the model in this way is that we must give up the assumption that there is a known, fixed quantity of the resource. Instead, the amount of the resource 'economically' available will be a variable, the value of which depends upon resource demand and extraction cost schedules. This also implies that we could analyse a reduction in extraction costs as if it were a form of technological progress; this can increase the stock of the reserve that can be extracted in an economically viable manner.

The introduction of taxation/subsidies

A royalty tax or subsidy

A royalty tax or subsidy will have no effect on a resource owner's extraction decision in the case of a reserve that is currently being extracted. The tax or subsidy will alter the present value of the resource being extracted, but there can be no change in the rate of extraction over time that can offset that decline or increase in present value. The government will simply collect some of the mineral rent (or pay some subsidies), and resource extraction and production will proceed in the same manner as before the tax/subsidy was introduced.

This result follows from the Hotelling rule of efficient resource depletion. To see this, define α to be a royalty tax rate (which could be negative, that is, a subsidy), and denote the royalty or net price at time t by p_t. Then the post-tax royalty becomes $(1 - \alpha)p_t$. But Hotelling's rule implies that the post-tax royalty must rise at the discount rate, i, if the resource is to be exploited efficiently. That is:

$$(1 - \alpha)p_t = (1 - \alpha)p_0 e^{it}$$

or

$$p_t = p_0 e^{it}$$

Hotelling's rule continues to operate unchanged in the presence of a royalty tax, and no change occurs to the optimal depletion path. This is also true for a royalty subsidy scheme. In this case, denoting the royalty subsidy rate by β, we have the efficiency condition

$$(1 + \beta)p_t = (1 + \beta)p_o e^{it} \Rightarrow p_t = p_o e^{it}$$

We can conclude that a royalty tax or subsidy is neutral in its effect on the optimal extraction path. However, a tax may discourage (or a subsidy encourage) the exploration effort for new mineral deposits by reducing (increasing) the expected payoff from discovering the new deposits.

Revenue tax/subsidy

The previous subsection analysed the effect of a tax or subsidy on resource royalties. We now turn our attention to the impact of a revenue tax (or subsidy). In the absence of a revenue tax, the Hotelling efficiency condition is, in terms of net prices and gross prices:

$$p_t = p_o e^{it}$$
$$\Rightarrow (P_t - c) = (P_o - c)e^{it}$$

Under a revenue tax scheme, with a tax of α per unit of the resource sold, the post-tax royalty or net price is

$$p_t = (1 - \alpha)P_t - c$$

So Hotelling's rule becomes:

$$[(1 - \alpha)P_t - c] = [(1 - \alpha)P_o - c]e^{it} \quad (0 < \alpha < 1)$$
$$\Rightarrow \left(P_t - \frac{c}{1 - \alpha}\right) = \left(P_o - \frac{c}{1 - \alpha}\right)e^{it}$$

Since $c/(1 - \alpha) > c$, an imposition of a revenue tax is equivalent to an increase in the resource extraction cost. Similarly, for a revenue subsidy scheme, we have

$$\left(P_t - \frac{c}{1 + \beta}\right) = \left(P_o - \frac{c}{1 + \beta}\right)e^{it} \quad (0 < \beta < 1)$$

A revenue subsidy is equivalent to a decrease in extraction cost. We have already discussed the effects of a change in extraction costs, and you may recall the results we obtained: a decrease in extraction costs will lower the initial gross price, increase the rate at which the gross price increases (even though the net price or royalty increases at the same rate as before) and shorten the time to complete exhaustion of the stock.

The resource depletion model: some extensions and further issues

Discount rate

We showed above that resource extraction under a system of perfectly competitive markets might produce the socially optimal outcome. But this equivalence rests upon several assumptions, one of which is that firms choose a private discount rate identical to the social discount rate that would be used by a rational planner. If private and social discount rates differ, however, then market extraction paths may be biased toward excessive use or conservation relative to what is socially optimal.

Forward markets and expectations

The Hotelling model is an abstract analytical tool; its operation in actual market economies is, as we have seen, dependent upon the existence of a set of particular institutional circumstances. In many real situations, these institutional arrangements do not exist, and so the rule lies at a considerable distance from the operation of actual market mechanisms. In addition to the discount rate equivalence mentioned in the previous section, two very strict assumptions are required to ensure a social optimal extraction in the case of perfect competition, Firstly, the resource must be owned by the competitive agents. Secondly, each agent must know at each point in time all current and future prices.

One might just assume that agents have perfect foresight, but this hardly seems tenable for the case we are investigating. In the absence of perfect foresight, knowledge of these prices requires the existence of both spot markets and a complete set of forward markets for the resource in question. But no resource does possess a complete set of forward markets, and in these circumstances there is no guarantee that agents can or will make rational supply decisions.

Optimal extraction under uncertainty

Uncertainty is prevalent in decision making regarding non-renewable resource extraction and use. There is uncertainty, for example, about stock sizes, extraction costs, how successful research and development will be in the discovery of substitutes for non-renewable resources (thereby affecting the cost and expected date of arrival of a backstop technology), pay-offs from exploration for new stock, and the action of rivals. It is very important to study how the presence of uncertainty affects appropriate courses of action. For example, what do optimal extraction programmes look like when there is uncertainty, and how do they compare with programmes developed under conditions of certainty?

Let us assume an owner of a natural resource (such as a mine) wishes to maximise the net present value of utility over two periods:[14]

$$\max U_o + \frac{U_1}{1 + \rho}$$

If there is a probability (π) of a disaster (for example, the market might be lost) associated with the second period of the extraction programme, then the owner will try to maximise the expected net present value of the utility (if he or she is risk-neutral):

[14] This argument follows very closely a presentation in Fisher (1981).

$$\max U_o + \pi \cdot 0 + (1 - \pi)\frac{U_1}{1 + \rho}$$

$$= \max U_o + (1 - \pi)\frac{U_1}{1 + \rho}$$

$$\Rightarrow \max U_o + \frac{U_1}{1 + \rho^*}$$

where

$$\frac{1}{1 + \rho^*} = \frac{1 - \pi}{1 + \rho}$$

To solve for ρ^*

$$(1 + \rho^*)(1 - \pi) = 1 + \rho$$

$$\Rightarrow \quad \rho^* - \rho = \pi(1 + \rho^*) > 0 \quad (\text{if } 1 \geqslant \pi > 0)$$

$$\Rightarrow \quad \rho^* > \rho$$

Therefore, in this example, the existence of risk is equivalent to an increase in the discount rate for the owner, which implies, as we have shown before, that the price of the resource must rise more rapidly and the depletion is accelerated.

Do resource prices actually follow the Hotelling rule?

The Hotelling rule is an economic theory. It is a statement of how resource prices should behave under a specified (and very restrictive) set of conditions. Economic theory begins with a set of axioms (which are regarded as not needing verification) and/or a set of assumptions (which are treated as being provisionally correct). These axioms or assumptions typically include goals or objectives of the relevant actors and various rules of how those actors behave. Then logical reasoning is used to deduce outcomes that should follow, given those assumptions.

But a theory is not necessarily correct. Among the reasons why it may be wrong are inappropriateness of one or more of its assumptions, and flawed deduction. A theory may also fail to 'fit the facts' because it refers to an idealised model of reality that does not take into account some elements of real world-complexity. However, failing to fit the facts does not make the theory *false*; the theory only applies to the idealised world for which it was constructed.

But it would be interesting to know whether the Hotelling principle is sufficiently powerful to fit the facts of the real world. Indeed, many economists take the view that a theory is useless unless it has predictive power: we should be able to use the theory to make predictions that have a better chance of being correct than chance alone would imply. A theory is unlikely to have predictive power if it cannot describe or explain current and previous behaviour. Of course, even if it could do that, this does not necessarily mean it will have good *ex ante* predictive power.

In an attempt to validate the Hotelling rule (and other associated parts of resource depletion theory), much research effort has been directed to empirical testing of that theory. What conclusions have emerged from this exercise? Unfortunately, no consensus of opinion has come from empirical analysis. As Berck (1995) writes in one recent survey of results, 'the results from such testing are mixed'.

A simple version of the Hotelling rule for some marketed non-renewable resource was given by Equation 8.7b; namely

$$\frac{\dot{P}_t}{P_t} = \rho$$

In this version, all prices are denominated in units of utility, and ρ is a utility discount rate. These magnitudes are, of course, unobservable, so Equation 8.7b is not directly testable. But we can rewrite the Hotelling rule in terms of money-income (or consumption) units that can be measured:

$$\frac{\dot{p}_t^*}{p_t^*} = \delta \qquad (8.10)$$

Here, p^* denotes a price in money units, and δ is a consumption discount rate. Empirical testing normally uses discrete time series data, and so the discrete-time version of Hotelling's rule is employed:

$$\frac{\Delta p_t^*}{p_t^*} = \delta \qquad (8.11)$$

or, expressed in an alternative way,

$$p_{t+1}^* = p_t^*(1 + \delta) \qquad (8.12)$$

Notice right away that Equations 8.11 and 8.12 are assuming that there is a constant discount rate over time. If this is not correct (and there is no reason why it has to be) then δ should enter those two equations with a time subscript, and the Hotelling principle no longer implies that a resource price will rise at a fixed rate. But this is a complication we ignore in the rest of this section.

One way of testing Hotelling's rule seems to be clear: collect time-series data on the price of a resource, and see if the proportionate growth rate of the price is equal to δ. This was one thing that Barnett and Morse (1963) did in a famous study. They found that resource prices – including iron, copper, silver and timber – fell over time, a most disconcerting result for proponents of the standard theory. Subsequent researchers, looking at different resources or different time periods, have come up with a bewildering variety of results. There is no clear picture of whether resource prices typically rise or fall over time. We can no more be confident that the theory is true than that it is not true, a most unsatisfactory state of affairs.

But we now know that the problem is far more difficult than this to settle, and that a direct examination of resource prices is not a reasonable way to proceed. Note first that the variable p^* in Hotelling's rule is the *net* price (or rent, or royalty) of the resource, not its *market* price. Roughly speaking, these are related as follows

$$P^* = p^* + mc \qquad (8.13)$$

where P^* is the gross (or market) price of the extracted resource, p^* is the net price of the resource *in situ* (i.e. unextracted), and mc is the marginal extraction cost. It is clear from Equation 8.13 that if the marginal cost of extraction is falling, P^* might be falling even though p^* is rising. We noted this earlier in examining the effect of a fall in extraction costs. So evidence of falling market prices cannot, in itself, be regarded as invalidating the Hotelling principle.

This suggests that the right data to use is the resource net price. But that is an unobservable variable, for which data does not therefore exist. And this is not the only unobservable variable: δ is also unobserved, as we shall see shortly. In the absence of data on net price, one might try to construct a proxy for it. The obvious way to proceed is to subtract marginal costs from the gross, market price to arrive at net price. This is also not as easy as it seems; costs are observable, but the costs recorded are usually averages, not marginals. We shall not discuss how this (rather serious) difficulty has been dealt with. However, many studies have pursued this approach. Slade (1982) was one of the earliest studies of this type; she concluded that some resources have U-shaped quadratic price paths, having fallen in the past but latterly rising. Other studies of this type are Stollery (1983), which generally supported the Hotelling hypothesis, and Halvorsen and Smith (1991), which was unable to support it.

Any attempt to construct a proxy measure for net price comes up against an additional problem. The measure that is obtained is a proxy, and it will contain estimation errors. If this variable is simply treated as if it were the unobserved net price itself, a statistical problem – known to econometricians as an errors-in-variables problem – will occur, and estimates of parameters will in general be biased (and so misleading) no matter how large is the sample of data available to the researcher. This casts doubt on all studies using proxies for the net price which have not taken account of this difficulty. Appropriate statistical techniques in the presence of errors-in-variables are discussed in most intermediate econometrics texts, such as Greene (1993). Harvey (1989) is a classic text on the Kalman filter, which is one way of resolving this problem.

Other approaches have also been used to test the Hotelling rule, and we shall mention only two of them very briefly. Fuller details can be found in the survey paper by Berck (1995). Miller and Upton (1985) use the valuation principle. This states that the stock market value of a property with unextracted resources is equal to the present value of its resource extraction plan; if the Hotelling rule is valid this will be constant over time, and so the property's stock market value will be constant. Evidence from this approach gives reasonably strong support for the Hotelling principle. Farrow (1985) adopts an approach that interprets the Hotelling rule as an asset-efficiency condition, and tests for efficiency in resource prices, in much the same way that finance theorists conduct tests of market efficiency. These tests generally reject efficiency, and by implication are taken to not support the Hotelling rule. However, it has to be said that evidence in favour of efficient asset markets is rarely found, but that does not stop economists assuming (for much of the time) that asset markets are efficient.

Let us now return to a comment we made earlier. The right-hand side of the Hotelling rule equation consists of the consumption discount rate δ. But this is also a theoretical construct, not directly observable. What we do observe are market rates of interest, which will include components reflecting transaction costs, various degrees of risk premia, and other market imperfections. Even if we could filter these out, the market rate of interest measures realised or *ex post* returns; but the Hotelling theory is based around an *ex ante* measure of the discount rate, reflecting expectations about the future. This raises a whole host of problems concerning how expectations might be proxied that are beyond the scope of this text.

Finally, even if we did find convincing evidence that the net price of a resource does not rise at the rate δ (or even that it falls), should we regard this as evidence that invalidates the Hotelling rule? The answer is that we should not draw this conclusion. There are several circumstances where resource prices may fall over time even where a Hotelling rule is being followed. For example, in Figure 8.8 we showed that a sequence of new mineral discoveries could lead to a downward sloping path of the resource's net price. Pindyck (1978) first demonstrated this in a seminal paper. If resource extraction takes place in non-competitive markets, the net price will also rise less quickly than the discount rate (see Figure 8.4). And in the presence of technical progress continually reducing extraction costs, the market price may well fall over time, thereby apparently contradicting a simple Hotelling rule.

The history of attempts to test the Hotelling principle is an excellent example of the problems faced by economists in all branches of that discipline. Many of the variables used in our theories are unobservable or latent variables. Shadow prices are one class of such latent variables. The best we can do is to find proxy variables for them. But if the theory does not work, is that because the theory is poor or because our proxy was not good? More generally, a theory pertains to a particular model. So unless it contains a logical error, a theory can never be wrong. What can be, and often is, incorrect, is a presumption that a theory that is correct in the context of one particular model will generate conclusions that are valid in a wide variety of 'real' situations.

Natural resource scarcity

Concern with the supposed increasing scarcity of natural resources, and the possibility of running out of strategically important raw materials or energy sources, is by no means new. Worries about resource scarcity can be traced back to at least medieval times in Britain, and have surfaced periodically ever since. The scarcity of land was central to the theories of Malthus and the other classical economists. In the twentieth century, fears about timber shortages in several countries

led to the establishment of national forestry authorities, charged with rebuilding timber stocks. As we have seen earlier, pessimistic views about impending resource scarcity have been most forcibly expressed in the 'limits to growth' literature; during the 1970s, the so-called oil crises further focused attention on mineral scarcities.

What do we mean by resource scarcity? One use of the term – what might be called absolute scarcity – holds that all resources are scarce, as the availability of resources is fixed and finite at any point in time, while the wants which resource use can satisfy are not limited. Where a market exists for a resource, the existence of any positive net price is viewed as evidence of absolute scarcity; where markets do not exist, the existence of a positive shadow price – the implicit net price that would be necessary if the resource were to be used efficiently – similarly is an indicator of absolute scarcity for that resource.

But this is not the usual meaning of the term in general discussions about natural resource scarcity. In these cases, scarcity tends to be used to indicate that the natural resource is becoming harder to obtain, and requires more of other resources to obtain it. The relevant costs to include in measures of scarcity are both private and external costs; it is important to recognise that if private extraction costs are not rising over time, social costs may rise if negative externalities such as environmental degradation or depletion of common property resources are increasing as a consequence of extraction of the natural resource. Thus, a rising opportunity cost of obtaining the resource is an indicator of scarcity – let us call this use of the term *relative scarcity*. In the rest of this section, our comments shall be restricted to this second form.

Before we take this matter any further, it is necessary to say something about the degree of aggregation used in examining resource scarcity. To keep things as simple as possible, first consider only non-renewable natural resources. There is not one single resource but a large number, each distinct from the others in some physical sense. However, physically distinct resources may be economically similar, through being substitutes for one another. Non-renewable resources are best viewed, then, as a structure of assets, components of which are substitutable to varying degrees. In Chapter 7, when we discussed the efficient extraction of a single non-renewable resource, what we had in mind was some aggregate set of resources in this particular sense. Moreover, when the class of resources is extended to incorporate renewable resources, so the structure is enlarged, as are the substitution possibilities.

Except for resources for which no substitution possibilities exist – if indeed such resources exist – it is of limited usefulness to enquire whether any individual resource is scarce or not. If one particular resource, such as crude oil, were to become excessively costly to obtain for any reason, one would expect resource use to substitute to another resource, such as natural gas or coal. A well-functioning price mechanism should ensure that this occurs. Because of this, it is more useful to consider whether natural resources in general are becoming scarcer – is there any evidence of increasing generalised resource scarcity?

What indicators might one use to assess the degree of scarcity of particular natural resources, and natural resources in general? There are several candidates for this task, including physical indicators (such as reserve quantities or reserve-to-consumption ratios), marginal resource extraction cost, marginal exploration and discovery costs, market prices, and resource rents. We shall now briefly examine each of these. In doing so, you will see that the question of whether resources are becoming scarce is closely related to the question of whether the Hotelling rule is empirically validated.

Physical indicators

A variety of physical indicators have been used as proxies for scarcity, including various measures of reserve quantities, and reserve-to-consumption ratios. Several such measures were discussed earlier in this chapter and appropriate statistics listed (see Box 8.1 and Table 8.1). Inferences drawn about impending resource scarcity in the 'limits to growth' literature were drawn on the basis of such physical indicators. Unfortunately, they are severely limited in their usefulness as proxy measures of scarcity for the reasons discussed in Box 8.1. Most importantly, most natural resources are not homogeneous in quality, and the location and quantities available are not known with certainty; extra amounts of the resource can be obtained as additional exploration, discovery and extraction effort is applied. A rising resource net price will, in general, stimulate such effort. It is the absence of this information in physical data that limits its usefulness.

Real, marginal resource extraction cost

We argued earlier that scarcity is concerned with the real opportunity cost of acquiring additional quantities of the resource. This suggests that the marginal extraction cost of obtaining the resource from existing reserves would be an appropriate indicator of scarcity. The classic study by Barnett and Morse (1963) used an index of real unit costs, c, defined as

$$c = \frac{(\alpha L + \beta K)}{Q}$$

where L is labour, K is capital and Q is output of the extractive industry, and α and β are weights to aggregate inputs. Rising resource scarcity is proxied by rising real unit costs. Note that ideally marginal costs should be used, although this is rarely possible in practice because of data limitations. An important advantage of an extraction costs indicator is that it incorporates technological change. If technological progress relaxes resource constraints by making a given quantity of resources more productive, then this reduction in scarcity will be reflected in a tendency for costs to fall. However, the measure does have problems. Firstly, the measurement of capital is always difficult, largely because of the aggregation that is required to obtain a single measure of the capital stock. Similarly, there are difficulties in obtaining valid aggregates of all inputs used. Secondly, the indicator is backward looking, whereas an ideal indicator should serve as a signal for future potential scarcity. Finally, it may well be the case that quantities and/or qualities of the resource are declining seriously, while technical progress that is sufficiently rapid results in price falling. In extreme cases, sudden exhaustion may occur after a period of prolonged price falls. Ultimately, no clear inference about scarcity can be drawn from extraction cost data alone.

Barnett and Morse (1963) and Barnett (1979) found no evidence in US data of increasing scarcity, except for forestry. As we mentioned previously, they concluded that agricultural and mineral products, over the period 1870 to 1970, were becoming more abundant rather than more scarce, and explained this in terms of the substitution of more plentiful lower-grade deposits as higher grades were depleted, the discovery of new deposits, and technical change in exploration, extraction and processing. References for other, subsequent studies are given at the end of the chapter.

Marginal exploration and discovery costs

An alternative measure of resource scarcity is the opportunity cost of acquiring additional quantities of the resource by locating as yet unknown reserves. Higher discovery costs are interpreted as indicators of increased resource scarcity. This measure is not often used, largely because it is difficult to obtain long runs of reliable data. Moreover, the same kinds of limitations possessed by extraction cost data apply in this case too.

Real market price indicators and net price indicators

The most commonly used scarcity indicator is time-series data on real (that is, inflation-adjusted) market prices. It is here that the affinity between tests of scarcity and tests of the Hotelling principle is most apparent. Market price data are readily available, easy to use and, like all asset prices, are forward-looking, to some extent at least. Use of price data is beset by three main problems. Firstly, prices are often distorted as a consequence of taxes, subsidies, exchange controls and other governmental interventions; reliable measures need to be corrected for such distortions. Secondly, the real price index tends to be very sensitive to the choice of deflator. Should nominal prices be deflated by a retail or wholesale price index (and for which basket of goods), by the GDP deflator, or by some input price index such as manufacturing wages? There is no unambiguously correct answer to this question, which is unfortunate as very different conclusions can be arrived at about resource scarcity with different choices of deflator. Some evidence on this is given in the chapter on resource scarcity in Hartwick and Olewiler (1986); these authors cite an analysis by Brown and Field (1978) which compares two studies of resource prices using alternative deflators. For eleven commodities, Nordhaus (1973) used capital goods prices as a deflator and concluded that all eleven minerals were becoming less scarce. However, Jorgensen and Griliches (1967) used a manufacturing wages deflator and concluded that three of the minerals – coal, lead and zinc – were becoming scarcer over the same period.

The third major problem with resource price data is one we came across earlier. Market prices do not in general measure the right thing; an ideal price measure would reflect the net price of the resource. Hotelling's rule shows that it is this that rises through time as the resource becomes progressively scarcer. But we have seen that net resource prices are not directly observed variables, and so it is rather difficult to use them as a basis for empirical analysis.

Despite the limitations of market price data, the early studies show a broad agree-

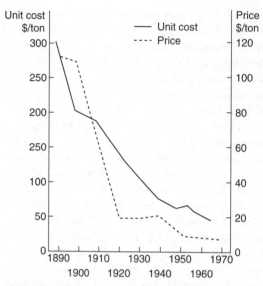

Figure 8.13 Price and unit costs for all metals, 1890–1970.
Source: Brown and Field (1979). Copyright, Resources for the Future, Inc.

ment between this measure and the others discussed in this section. One illustration is given in Figure 8.13, taken from Brown and Field (1979), that suggests that, for an aggregate index of all metals, scarcity was decreasing over the period 1890 to 1970. More recent studies present a much less clear picture however, as we noted above.

Can any general conclusions about resource scarcity be obtained from the literature? The majority of economic analyses conducted up to the early 1980s concluded that few, if any, non-renewable natural resources were becoming more scarce. In the last 20 years, concern about increasing scarcity of non-renewable resources has increased, and an increasing proportion of studies seems to lend support to an increasing scarcity hypothesis.

Paradoxically, these studies also suggested it was in the area of *renewable* resources that problems of increasing scarcity were to be found, particularly in cases of open access. The reasons why scarcity may be particularly serious for some renewable resources will be examined in the following chapter.

Discussion questions

1 Discuss the merits of a proposal that the government should impose a tax or subsidy where a non-renewable resource is supplied monopolistically in order to increase the social net benefit.

2 'An examination of natural resource matters ought to recognise technical/scientific, economic, and socio-political considerations.' Explain.

3 'The exploitation of resources is not necessarily destructive ... need not imply the impoverishment of posterity ... It is the diversion of national income from its usual channels to an increased preservation of natural wealth that will harm posterity' (Anthony Scott). Explain and discuss.

4 The notion of sustainability is used differently in economics than in the natural sciences. Explain the meaning of sustainability in these two frameworks, and discuss the attempts that have been made by economists to make the concept operational.

Problems

1 The version of Hotelling's rule given in Equation 8.5 requires the net price to grow proportionately at the rate ρ. Under what circumstances would this imply that the gross price also should grow at the rate ρ?

2 In Equation 8.5, if $\rho = 0$, what are the implications for
   (a) P_0 and P_1?
   (b) R_0 and R_1?
   (Problems 3, 4 and 5 are based on Table 8.4.)

3 Explain, with diagrams, why a monopolistic non-renewable resource market is biased towards conservation and therefore will increase the 'life' of the resource.

4 In the case of perfect competition, if the private discount rate is higher than the

correct social discount rate, explain, with diagrams, why the market will exhaust the resource too quickly.
5 Discuss, with diagrams, the consequences of the discovery of North Sea oil for
   (a) the price and output levels for the oil market;
   (b) the date of exhaustion of oil reserves.

What will be the probable path over time of oil prices if there are frequent discoveries of oil?

Further reading

The references for further reading given at the end of Chapter 7 are all relevant for further reading on the material covered in this chapter. In particular, very good (but rather advanced level) presentations of the theory of efficient and optimal resource depletion can be found in Baumol and Oates (1988), Dasgupta and Heal (1979), Heal (1981) and the collection of papers in the May 1974 special issue on resource depletion of the *Review of Economic Studies*. As stated previously, less difficult presentations are given in Hartwick and Olewiler (1986), Anderson (1991) and Fisher (1981). Pindyck (1978) is the classic reference on resource exploration.

Good general discussions of resource scarcity can be found in Hartwick and Olewiler (1986, chapter 6), which provides an extensive discussion of the evidence, Barbier (1989a), Fisher (1979, 1981) and Harris (1993). Important works in the field of resource scarcity include Barnett (1979), Barnett and Morse (1963), Brown and Field (1979), Deverajan and Fisher (1980, 1982), Hall and Hall (1984), Jorgensen and Griliches (1967), Leontief *et al.* (1977), Nordhaus (1973), Norgaard (1975), Slade (1982), Smith (ed.) (1979) and Smith and Krutilla (1979). Examinations of the extent to which the Hotelling rule are satisfied in practice are extensively referenced in the text, but the best place to go next is probably Berck (1995).

An excellent discussion on natural resource substitutability can be found in Dasgupta (1993). Adelman (1990, 1995) covers the economics of oil depletion. Prell (1996) deals with backstop technology.

Appendix 8.1   Solution of the multi-period resource depletion model

In this appendix, we derive the optimal solution to the multi-period non-renewable resource depletion problem discussed in this chapter. The technique we shall use – the Maximum Principle – is explained in Appendix 7.1.

We wish to maximise

$$W = \int_{t=0}^{t=T} U(R_t)e^{-\rho t}dt$$

subject to

$$\dot{S} = -R_t$$

The current-valued Hamiltonian for this problem is

$$H = U(R_t) + P_t(-R_t)$$

The necessary conditions for maximum social welfare are

$$\dot{P}_t = \rho P_t \tag{8.14}$$

$$\frac{\partial H}{\partial R} = -P_t + \frac{dU}{dR} = 0 \tag{8.15}$$

Rearranging Equation 8.15 we obtain

$$P_t = \frac{dU}{dR}$$

so that the resource shadow price (P_t) is equal to the marginal utility of the non-renewable resource, an equality used in the main text. Equation 8.14 is, of course, the Hotelling efficiency condition, given as Equation 8.7b in the chapter.

As we noted in the chapter, an optimal solution must have the property that the stock goes to zero at exactly the point that demand goes to zero. In order for demand to be zero at time T (which we determine in a moment) the net price must reach the choke price at time T. That is

$$P_T = K$$

This, together with Equation 8.7a in the main text, implies

$$K = P_0 e^{\rho T} \qquad (8.16)$$

To solve for $R(t)$, it can be seen from Equations 8.7a and 8.8 that

$$P_0 e^{\rho t} = K e^{-aR}$$

Substituting for K from Equation 8.16 we obtain

$$P_0 e^{\rho t} = P_0 e^{-(aR - \rho T)}$$

$$\Rightarrow \quad \rho t = -aR + \rho T \qquad (8.17)$$

$$\Rightarrow \quad R(t) = \frac{\rho}{a}(T - t)$$

This gives an expression for the rate at which the resource should be extracted along the optimal path. To find the optimal time period, T, over which extraction should take place, we need to recall that the fixed stock constraint is:

$$\int_0^T R(t)\,\mathrm{d}t = \bar{S}$$

and so by substitution for $R(t)$ from Equation 8.17 we obtain

$$\int_0^T \left[\frac{\rho}{a}(T - t) \right] \mathrm{d}t = \bar{S}$$

Therefore

$$\frac{\rho}{a} \left[Tt - \frac{t^2}{2} \right]_0^T = \bar{S}$$

$$\frac{1}{2}\frac{\rho}{a} \cdot T^2 = \bar{S}$$

or

$$T = \sqrt{\frac{2\bar{S}a}{\rho}}$$

Next we solve, using Equation 8.16, for the initial royalty level, P_0:

$$P_0 = K e^{-\rho T} = K e^{-\sqrt{2\rho \bar{S} a}}$$

To obtain an expression for the resource royalty at time t, we substitute Equation 8.7a into the expression just derived for the initial royalty level to obtain the required condition:

$$P_t = K e^{\rho(t - T)}$$

The optimal initial extraction level is, from Equation 8.17,

$$R_0 = \frac{\rho}{a}(T - 0) = \frac{\rho T}{a} = \sqrt{\frac{2\rho \bar{S}}{a}}$$

Appendix 8.2   The monopolist's profit-maximising extraction programme

To solve for the monopolist's profit-maximising extraction programme, we need to do some additional calculation. First let us derive an expression for the firm's marginal profit function, $M\Pi$:

$$M\Pi_t = \frac{\partial \Pi_t}{\partial R_t} = \frac{\partial (P(R)R_t)}{\partial R_t}$$

$$= \frac{\partial P_t}{\partial R_t} R_t + P(R) \qquad (8.18)$$

Now, substituting for $P(R)$ from the resource demand function (Equation 8.8) we can express this equation as

$$M\Pi_t = -aR_t K e^{-aR_t} + K e^{-aR_t}$$

$$= K(-aR_t + 1)e^{-aR_t} \approx K e^{-ahR_t} \qquad (8.19)$$

where $h = 2.5$

Notice the approximation here: why do we do this? Because if this is not done, it will not be possible to obtain an analytical solution, given the double appearance of R_t.

But since resource extraction at the end of the planning horizon must be zero ($R_T = 0$) we have

$$M\Pi_T = K e^{-ahR(T)} = K \qquad (8.20)$$

To obtain $M\Pi_0$, using Equation 8.9 we obtain

$$M\Pi_0 = M\Pi_T e^{-iT} = K e^{-iT} \qquad (8.21)$$

To obtain an expression for $M\Pi_t$, using Equations 8.9 and 8.21, we have

$$M\Pi_t = M\Pi_0 e^{it} = K e^{i(t - T)} \qquad (8.22)$$

Now we may obtain a solution equation for R_t, using Equations 8.19 and 8.22:

$$Ke^{-ahR_t} = Ke^{i(t-T)}$$
$$\Rightarrow i(t-T) = -ahR_t$$

$$\Rightarrow R_t = \frac{i}{ha}(T-t) \qquad (8.23)$$

In order to obtain the optimal depletion time period T we use the fixed stock constraint together with Equation 8.23, the result we have just obtained:

$$\int_0^T R_t dt = \bar{S}$$

$$\Rightarrow \int_0^T \frac{i}{ha}(T-t)dt = \bar{S}$$

$$\Rightarrow \frac{i}{ha}\left[Tt - \frac{t^2}{2}\right]_0^T = \bar{S}$$

$$\frac{1}{2} \cdot \frac{i}{ha}T^2 = \bar{S}$$

$$\therefore \quad T = \sqrt{\frac{2\bar{S}ha}{i}}$$

To solve the initial extraction R_0, from Equation 8.22:

$$R_0 = \frac{i}{ha}(T-0) = \frac{iT}{ha} = \sqrt{\frac{2i\bar{S}}{ha}}$$

Finally, to solve the initial net price P_0, from Equation 8.8, (the demand curve)

$$P_0 = Ke^{-aR_0} = K\exp\left(-\sqrt{\frac{2i\bar{S}a}{h}}\right)$$

Let us take 1990 as the 'initial year' of the study. In 1990, the oil price was $P_0 = \$20$ per barrel, and oil output was $R_0 = 21.7$ billion barrels. From our demand function (Equation 8.8)

$$P_0 = Ke^{-aR_0} = K\exp(-aR_0)$$

we obtain

$$R_0 = \frac{\ln K}{a} - \frac{1}{a} \cdot \ln P_0$$

The price elasticity of the initial year is, therefore:

$$\varepsilon_0 = \frac{dR_0}{dP_0} \cdot \frac{P_0}{R_0} = \left[-\frac{1}{aP_0}\right] \cdot \frac{P_0}{R_0} = -\frac{1}{aR_0}$$

Assume that $\varepsilon = 0.5$, then we can estimate a:

$$a = -\frac{1}{\varepsilon R_0} = \frac{1}{0.5 \times 21.7} \approx 0.1$$

We can also estimate the parameter K, as follows:

$$K = P_0 \exp(aR_0) = 20\exp(0.1 \times 21.7) \approx 175$$

The global oil reserve stock is $S = 1150$ billion barrels. The optimal oil extraction programme under the assumptions of a discount rate $\rho = 3\%$ and perfect competition are given by the following. The optimal exhaustion time is:

$$T^* = \sqrt{\frac{2Sa}{\rho}} = \sqrt{\frac{2 \times 1150 \times 0.1}{0.03}} = 87.5 \text{ years}$$

The optimal initial oil output is:

$$R_0^* = \sqrt{\frac{2\rho S}{a}} = \sqrt{\frac{2 \times 0.03 \times 1150}{0.1}}$$
$$= 26.26 \text{ billion barrels}$$

The corresponding optimal initial oil price is:

$$P_0^* = K\exp(-aR_0^*) = 175\exp(-0.1 \times 26.26)$$
$$= \$12.7/\text{barrel}$$

The optimal oil output is obviously higher than the actual output in 1990, and the optimal price is lower than the actual one. So there is apparent evidence of distortion (inefficiency) in the world oil market.

CHAPTER 9

The theory of optimal resource extraction: renewable resources

It will appear, I hope, that most of the problems associated with the words 'conservation' or 'depletion' or 'overexploitation' in the fishery are, in reality, manifestations of the fact that the natural resources of the sea yield no economic rent. Fishery resources are unusual in the fact of their common-property nature; but they are not unique, and similar problems are encountered in other cases of common-property resource industries, such as petroleum production, hunting and trapping, etc.

Gordon (1954)

Introduction

Environmental resources are described as renewable when they have a capacity for reproduction and growth. The class of renewable resources is both wide and diverse. One type consists of populations of living organisms, such as fish, cattle and forests, which have a natural capacity for growth. A second variety includes inanimate systems (such as water and atmospheric systems), which are reproduced through time by physical or chemical processes. While these do not possess biological growth capacity, water and atmospheric stocks do have some ability to assimilate and cleanse themselves of pollution inputs (thereby maintaining their quality) and, at least in the case of water resources, can self-replenish as stocks are run down (thereby maintaining their quantity).

It is also conventional to classify arable and grazing lands as renewable resources. In these cases, reproduction and growth take place by a combination of biological processes (such as the recycling of organic nutrients) and physical processes (irrigation, exposure to wind etc.). Fertility levels can naturally regenerate so long as the demands made on the soil are not excessive. We may also consider more broadly-defined environmental systems (such as wilderness areas or tropical moist forests) as being sets of interrelated renewable resources.

The categories we have just described are sometimes called renewable stock resources. A broad criterion of renewable resources would also include renewable flow resources, such as solar, wave, wind and geothermal energy. These share with biological stock resources the property that harnessing some units of the flow does not necessarily mean that the total magnitude of the flow at the next instant in time will be smaller. Indeed, energy flow resources are non-depletable: the total size of the available flow is unaffected by the amount of the flow that is harnessed at any point in time.

Given this diversity of forms, one may be tempted to treat each type separately. Indeed, many texts do just that, having separate chapters on fisheries, forests and so on. Our approach in this chapter is to analyse the economics of renewable resources at a general level, developing a framework that can be applied to all forms of renewable stock resources. Despite this goal of generality, it will be convenient to illustrate the analysis by considering one particular case in some detail. The example of fisheries will be used for this purpose.

Although our framework can be used to analyse harvesting and depletion processes for most forms of renewable stock resources, important differences do exist between fisheries, forests, wilderness areas, water systems and other kinds of renewable stock resources. Because of the great importance of forest resources, we shall in the next chapter devote some time to a particular investigation of forestry. Doing this will allow us to identify how our general framework needs to be modified when we choose to deal more comprehensively with particular cases of the general class of renewable resources.

It will also allow us to develop a crucial ancillary theme. Very often, environmental resources provide multiple services. Forests and other woodland areas serve not only as sources of timber but also offer recreational facilities, sustain diverse stocks of genetic material, and provide a wide-range of environmental support services (such as water retention and flood control, pollution scrubbing and climate regulation). It will not be surprising that sensible policy concerning resource use should take into account these multiple functions of environmental resources.

As with non-renewable resources, it is important to distinguish between stocks and flows of the renewable resource. The stock is a measure of the quantity of the resource existing at a point in time, measured either as the aggregate mass of the biological material (the biomass) in question (such as the total weight of fish of particular age classes or the cubic metres of standing timber), or in terms of population numbers. The flow is the change in the stock over an interval of time, where the change results either from biological factors, such as the entry of new fish into the population through birth (called recruitment), or from the exit from the population due to natural death, or from economic factors such as harvesting of the species in question.

One similarity between renewable and non-renewable resources is that both are capable of being fully exhausted (that is, the stock is driven to zero) if too much harvesting or extraction activity is carried out over some time period. In the case of non-renewable resources, exhaustibility is a con-

sequence of the finiteness of the stock. For renewable resources, although the stock can grow, it can also be driven to zero if conditions interfere with the reproductive capability of the renewable resource, or if rates of harvesting continually exceed natural growth.

As the analysis in this chapter will make clear, private property rights do not exist for many forms of renewable resource. In the absence of government regulation or some other form of collective control over harvesting behaviour, the resource stocks are subject to open access. Open-access resources tend to be overexploited, and the likelihood of the resource being harvested to the point of exhaustion is higher than in situations where private property rights are established and access to harvesting can be restricted.

We begin our analysis by examining how an open access, renewable resource stock tends to be harvested. We then identify a privately optimal (that is, profit-maximising) harvesting programme for a renewable resource, and compare this with the behaviour expected under conditions of open access. In doing this, a matter of particular importance will be the relationship between harvesting behaviour and the discount rate used by potential or actual harvesters. Open-access harvesting is then revisited and socially optimal harvesting programmes discussed.

Under certain conditions, a perfectly competitive industry in which private property rights to the resource stocks are established and enforceable will follow a harvesting programme which is socially optimal. This is not the case if the resource is in monopolistic ownership, discussed in a section to itself. We then examine a set of policy instruments that could be introduced, in conditions of open access, in an attempt to move harvesting behaviour closer to a socially optimal programme. The following chapter presents an outline of the economics of forestry.

Biological growth processes for renewable resources

In order to investigate the economics of a renewable resource, the first thing we need to do is to describe the pattern of biological (or other) growth of the resource in the absence of human predation. Immediately we confront the problem of diversity of resources. It seems likely that trees, fish and cattle, for example, will have very different natural growth processes.

We begin by considering the growth function for a population of some species of fish. In later parts of the chapter, the question of whether this function adequately describes the growth of other renewable resources will be addressed. Let us suppose that in the absence of any environmental constraints the fish population has an intrinsic growth rate, denoted χ. The intrinsic growth rate χ may be thought of as the difference between the population's birth-rate and its mortality rate. If the population stock is S and it grows at a fixed rate χ the rate of change of the population over time is given by

$$\frac{dS}{dt} = \dot{S} = \chi S \qquad (9.1)$$

By integrating this equation, we obtain an expression for the stock level at any point in time:

$$S_t = S_0 e^{\chi t}$$

In other words, for a positive value of χ, the population grows exponentially over time and without bounds. Now this is clearly implausible over anything except a very brief period of time. The reason why it is not plausible is that a population of fish will exist in a particular environmental milieu, with a finite carrying capacity, which sets bounds on the population's growth possibilities.

A simple way of representing this effect is by making the growth rate depend on the stock size rather than being constant. So we may then write the growth function as

$$\dot{S} = \chi(S)S$$

where $\chi(S)$ shows the dependence of the growth rate on the stock size. If this function has the property that the growth rate declines as the stock size rises then the function is said to have the property of compensation.

Now let us suppose that there is a finite upper bound on the size the population can grow to. We will denote this as S_{MAX}. A commonly used functional form for $\chi(S)$ is the logistic function:

$$\chi(S) = g\left(1 - \frac{S}{S_{MAX}}\right)$$

in which $g > 0$ is a constant parameter. Where the logistic function determines the intrinsic (or natural) growth rate of the population, we may therefore write the biological growth function as

$$\dot{S} = \frac{dS}{dt} = g\left(1 - \frac{S}{S_{MAX}}\right)S \qquad (9.2)$$

It is important to be clear that $\dot{S}$ (or dS/dt which is the same thing) describes the amount of biological growth over some interval of time, and is not the same thing as the 'intrinsic' or unconstrained rate of growth (which is g in the logistic function). As we want to use the symbols $\dot{S}$ and dS/dt in a slightly different way later, we shall use an alternative symbol in place of them now. This will be G, or $G(S)$ to make it clear that G depends on S (as you can see from Equation 9.2). With this change in notation we write the logistic biological growth function as

$$G(S) = g\left(1 - \frac{S}{S_{MAX}}\right)S \qquad (9.3)$$

The logistic form appears to approximate very well to the natural growth processes of many fish, animal and bird populations (and indeed to some physical systems such as the quantity of fresh water in an underground reservoir). Some additional information on the logistic growth model, and an alternative form of logistic growth, is given in Box 9.1. You should now read the contents of that box. Problem 1 at the end of the chapter also explores the logistic model a little further.

Box 9.1 The logistic form of the biological growth function

Logistic growth is one example of the general class of growth processes where the growth rate of a population depends on the population size. This class is known as density-dependent growth. The logistic growth model was first applied to fisheries by Schaeffer (1957). The equation for logistic growth of one species or type of renewable resource at a particular location was given by Equation 9.3.

Logistic growth is illustrated in Figure 9.1(a), which represents the relationship between the stock size and the associated magnitude of biological growth. There are three properties which should be noted by inspection of that diagram.

(a) S_{MAX} is the maximum stock size that can be supported in the environmental milieu. This arises from the fact that the environmental system in which the population is resident is assumed to have a maximum carrying capacity for that particular population. Of course it is possible that this carrying capacity might change for some reason (such as a change in ocean temperatures or stocks of nutrients). But unless environmental characteristics do become more favourable, S_{MAX} is the maximum size to which the population biomass can grow.

(b) By multiplication through of the terms on the right-hand side of Equation 9.3, it is clear that the amount of growth, G, is a quadratic function of the resource stock size, S. For this standard version of the logistic function, the maximum amount of growth (S_{MSY}) will occur when the stock size is equal to half of S_{MAX}.

(c) The amount of biological growth G is zero at exactly the point where the stock size is zero.

This last property may appear at first sight to be obviously true, but it turns out to be seriously in error in many cases. That property implies that for any population size greater than zero natural growth will lead to a population increase if the system is left undisturbed. In other words, the population does not possess any positive lower threshold level.

However, suppose there is some positive population threshold level, S_{MIN}, such that the population would inevitably and permanently decline to zero if the actual population were ever to fall below that threshold. (Moreover, if the 'population' in question were the entire population of a particular species, then the species itself would become extinct.)

A simple generalisation of the logistic growth function that has this property is:

$$G(S) = g(S - S_{MIN})\left(1 - \frac{S}{S_{MAX}}\right) \qquad (9.4)$$

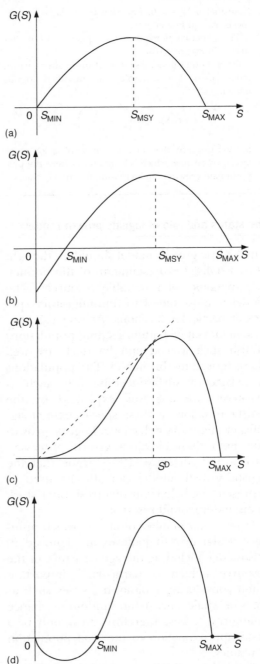

Figure 9.1 (a) Simple logistic growth. (b) Logistic growth with a minimum population threshold. (c) Logistic growth with depensation. (d) Logistic growth with critical depensation.

The status and role of logistic growth models

The logistic growth model should be thought of as a stylised representation of the population dynamics of renewable resources. The model is most suited to non-migratory species at particular locations. Among fish species, demersal or bottom-feeding populations of fish such as cod and haddock are well characterised by this model. The populations of pelagic or surface-feeding fish, such as mackerel, are less well explained by the logistic function, as these species exhibit significant migratory behaviour. Logistic growth does not only fit biological growth processes. Brown and McGuire (1967) argue that the logistic growth model can also be used to represent the behaviour of a freshwater stock in an underground reservoir.

However, a number of factors which influence actual growth patterns are ignored in this model, including the age structure of the resource (which is particularly important when considering long-lived species such as trees or whale stocks) and random or chance influences. At best, therefore, it can only be a good approximation to the true population dynamics.

But judging the logistic model on whether it is the best available at representing renewable resources is probably the wrong way of thinking about what is being done here. One would not expect to find that specialised bio-

logical or ecological modellers would use logistic growth functions. They will use more complex growth models designed specifically for particular species in particular contexts. But our needs differ from those of ecological modellers. We are willing to trade-off some realism to gain simple, tractable models that satisfy the requirement of being reasonably good approximations. It is for this reason that most economic analysis makes use of some version of the logistic growth function.

Steady-state harvests

Consider a period of time in which the amount of the stock being harvested is equal to the amount of net natural growth of the resource. Now imagine that the magnitudes of harvests (H) and net natural growth (G) remain constant and equal over a sequence of consecutive periods. We call this *steady-state* harvesting.

If we now redefine $\dot{S}$ as the actual rate of change of the renewable resource stock, that is

$$\dot{S} = G - H$$

then it follows that in steady-state harvesting, because $G = H$, $\dot{S} = 0$ and so the resource stock size remains constant over time. What kinds of steady states are available? To answer this, look at Figure 9.2. First note that

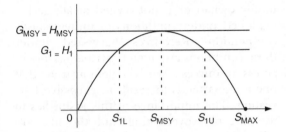

Figure 9.2   Steady-state harvests.

there is one particular stock size at which the quantity of net natural growth is at a maximum (the level labelled G_{MSY}). Clearly a steady state is feasible if the harvest is set at a constant rate of H_{MSY}. In this way, we obtain a maximum sustainable yield (MSY) steady state. A resource management programme could be devised which takes this MSY in perpetuity provided that the stock size is maintained at level S_{MSY}. Many people believe it to be self-evident that a fishery, forest or other renewable resource should be managed so as to produce its maximum sustainable yield. We shall see later in this chapter whether this suggestion finds any support in economic theory.

It is clear from Figure 9.2 that any steady-state harvest level between zero and H_{MSY} is feasible. For example, the level H_1 can be had as a steady-state harvest if the stock size is maintained at either S_{1L} or S_{1U}. Which of these two stock sizes would be more appropriate for attaining a harvest level of H_1 is a matter we shall investigate later.

Static analysis of the harvesting of a renewable resource

Our first economic model of renewable resource harvesting is a static model. We investigate resource growth and harvesting in a single period of time. We can justify this in one of two ways. Either the future is deemed to be irrelevant for the purposes of making decisions in this period, or each period has the same characteristics as any other, so any results we obtain for one period

will be true for all others too. Proceeding in this way means that there is no need to introduce time into our model. There are several important limitations, however, in doing static analysis. These become important when neither of the justifications we mentioned above is valid. However, for the moment we shall ignore these limitations. We will examine them carefully at the end of our discussions of static resource harvesting models.

What determines H, the size of the harvest, in any given period? First, the harvest will depend upon the amount of 'effort' devoted to harvesting. In the case of marine fishing for example, harvesting effort describes the number of boats deployed and their efficiency, the number of days when fishing is undertaken and so on. Let us assume, for simplicity, that all the different dimensions of harvesting activity can be aggregated into one magnitude called effort, E. Second, it is probable that the harvest will depend upon the size of the resource stock; the larger the stock, the greater the harvest for any given level of effort, other things being equal. The size of harvest will also depend upon other factors, including random influences, but we abstract from these in our analysis, and take harvest to depend upon the effort applied and the stock size. That is

$$H = H(E, S) \qquad (9.5)$$

This relationship can take a variety of particular forms. One very simple form appears to be a good approximation to actual relationships (see Munro, 1981, 1982), and is given by

$$H = eES \qquad (9.6)$$

where e is a constant number, often called the catch coefficient. Dividing each side by E, we have

$$\frac{H}{E} = eS$$

which says that the quantity harvested per unit effort is equal to some multiple (e) of the stock size.

We have already defined the renewable stock growth function taking into account human predation as the biological growth function less the quantity harvested. That is

$$\dot{S} = G(S) - H \qquad (9.7)$$

The costs and benefits of harvesting the renewable resource can now be described. Assume, for simplicity, that the costs of harvesting the resource are a linear function of effort,

$$C = wE$$

where C is the total cost of harvesting, and w is the cost per unit of harvesting effort, taken to be a constant. Let B denote the total gross benefit from harvesting a given quantity of the renewable resource. In general, the gross benefit will depend upon the quantity harvested, so we have

$$B = B(H)$$

As we wish to begin our analysis by looking at the commercially chosen levels of renewable resource harvesting, the appropriate measure of gross benefits is the total revenue that accrues to firms. Denoting the revenue obtained from the harvest as V, by definition

$$V = PH$$

where P is the gross (market) price of the harvested resource. At this point, it is necessary to make an assumption about the determination of this gross price. We will continue to assume, as was done for non-renewable resources in Chapter 8, that a market demand function exists for the renewable resource in which the resource gross price is negatively related to the quantity harvested. That is

$$P = P(H) \qquad \frac{dP}{dH} < 0$$

Harvesting a renewable resource under open-access conditions

What are the consequences of harvesting a renewable resource under conditions in which the resource in question is either com-monly owned or is not owned at all, and is exploited under conditions of individualistic competition? Resources harvested under these conditions are often described as 'open-access resources'. We will demonstrate that open access tends to result in excessive harvesting. The importance of this result lies in the fact that overfishing and the like are often the consequence of particular institutional arrangements, not the result of ecological problems as such.

Our objective is to identify an open-access outcome in which decision makers have no incentive to their behaviour (that is, the outcome is an equilibrium). In equilibrium

$$C = V$$

The fundamental property of an open-access equilibrium is that it is characterised by all firms (meaning here resource harvesters) earning zero economic rent. Equivalently, we could say that open-access equilibria are characterised by zero royalties, or that the *net* price is zero. Economic rent is the difference between the total revenue from the sale of harvested resources (V) and the total cost (C) incurred in resource harvesting. The zero rent condition applies to each harvester and to the industry as a whole.

Why does this occur? For an open-access resource, there is no method of excluding incomers into the industry, nor is there any way in which existing firms can be prevented from changing their level of harvesting effort. If we assume that markets in the rest of the economy are perfectly competitive and so economic profit is zero in long-run equilibrium in each market, then the existence of positive rent in fishing will attract new firms into the industry, or cause existing firms to increase their fishing effort, in an attempt to appropriate part of these rents. An open-access equilibrium is only possible when rents have been driven down to zero, so that there is no longer an incentive for entry into or exit from the industry, nor for the fishing effort on the part of existing fishermen to change.

The essence of the argument here is that the resource is subject to free or open access. This is equivalent to saying that property rights do not exist in the resource, or, more precisely, that *enforceable* property rights are not in existence. If they were, then the holder of the property rights could extract compensation from the harvesters and, as we shall see later, a very different outcome would emerge.

An alternative perspective on open-access resources comes from considering the incentives that face individual harvesters. Let us consider incentives in the case of a commercial fishery in which there are no access restrictions and no entry charges to fishermen. Firms will exploit the fishery as long as profit opportunities are available. Each fishing vessel has an incentive to maximise its catch. Although reducing the total catch today may be in the collective interest (by allowing fish stocks to recover and grow, for example), it is not rational for any individual fisherman to restrict his fishing effort; there is no guarantee that he will receive any of the rewards that this may generate in terms of higher catches later. Indeed, for some fisheries, there is no certainty that the stock will even be available tomorrow. In such circumstances, each firm will exploit the fishery today to its maximum potential, subject only to the constraint that its revenues must at least cover its costs.

Our task now is to find out what the stock level and harvest rate will be in an open-access equilibrium. To do this, recall the assumptions we have made about the costs and revenues associated with resource harvesting. The total cost function is taken to be

$$C = wE \qquad (9.8)$$

and we choose Equation 9.6, the special form of the relationship between the harvest rate, effort and stock size proposed by Munro (1981, 1982)

$$H = eES$$

Substituting Equation 9.6 into Equation 9.8 we obtain

$$C = w\left(\frac{H}{eS}\right) \qquad (9.9)$$

so that total fishing costs are a function of the harvesting rate and stock level. Note carefully that we are here regarding the cost per unit effort (w) and the catchability coefficient (e) as constant parameters. In many circumstances, these will be untenable assumptions.

Now suppose that the simple logistic function describes the biological growth process of the species (see Equation 9.3). That is

$$G(S) = gS\left(1 - \frac{S}{S_{MAX}}\right)$$

But as we are considering only equilibrium states, it must be the case that $H = G(S)$, and so we can substitute for H in Equation 9.9 to obtain

$$C = \frac{w}{eS}gS\left(1 - \frac{S}{S_{MAX}}\right) = \frac{wg}{e}\left(1 - \frac{S}{S_{MAX}}\right) \qquad (9.10)$$

Equation 9.10 shows the total cost of harvesting the sustainable yields associated with different resource stock levels. It is clear from inspection of Equation 9.10 that C, the total cost, is a linear function of the resource stock, S. Moreover, when $S = S_{MAX}$, $C = 0$. As S falls below S_{MAX}, C will rise, becoming wg/e when $S = 0$. This cost–stock relationship is illustrated in Figure 9.3 by the negatively sloped straight line.

We next turn our attention to the income side. From the definition of total revenue, V, we have

$$V = HP(H) \qquad (9.11)$$

However, our particular interest is in the relationship between V and S (rather than V and H), in order to derive the equilibrium resource *stock* level under open access. We have already made an assumption about the relationship between S and H; that was illustrated in Figure 9.2. But we need the S–V relationship, which requires in turn that we know the relationship between H and V. This latter relationship depends on the form taken by the resource demand function. So it is not possible to give any general result here.

However, under one plausible, and quite likely, form of demand equation, it turns out to be the case that the revenue–stock relationship has an inverted U-shaped form, with the revenue-maximising stock level being identical to the harvest-maximising stock level. That is, revenue is maximised at the MSY stock level, as shown in Figure 9.3. We show this result in Appendix 9.1.

We now know:

- how industry revenue is related to the resource stock
- how industry cost is related to the resource stock
- what an open-access equilibrium will be characterised by.

Putting together all these pieces, a unique open-access equilibrium will occur at a stock level where total cost equals total revenue. Such an equilibrium is shown by point A in Figure 9.3, corresponding to the stock level S_{OA}. At this point, a double bio-economic equilibrium is attained:

(1) economic equilibrium: the industry is in an open-access zero rent equilibrium, as $V = C$.

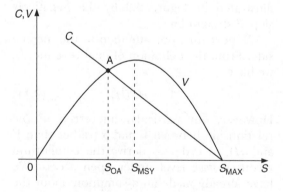

C = Total harvesting costs ($C = wE$)

V = Total harvest revenue ($V = H.P(H)$)

S_{OA} = Open access steady state equilibrium

Figure 9.3 A static model of fish harvesting.

(2) biological equilibrium: the resource stock is constant through time, as $G(S) = H$.

The nature of such a bio-economic equilibrium is explored a little further in Problem 2 at the end of this chapter.

Under the assumptions we have made, the open-access equilibrium is unique, and is also stable. If the resource stock were to fall below S_{OA}, the cost of harvesting the sustainable yield associated with that lower stock would exceed the revenue obtained from that sustainable yield and so harvesting profits would become negative. This would lead to reduced harvesting activity. The amount being harvested would be lower than the sustainable yield at that stock level, and so stocks would recover towards S_{OA}. By a similar argument, a rise in stocks above S_{OA} would result in positive industry profits, greater harvesting activity, and an adjustment process leading, once again, to the open access equilibrium at point A.

Further analysis of open-access equilibria

In our illustration of an open-access equilibrium, the stock S_{OA} is less than the stock size at which the sustainable yield is maximised. However, such an outcome is not inevitable. The level of S_{OA} will depend on several factors, including the cost of a unit of harvesting effort, w, and the form and parameters of the demand function (which will influence the steady-state price). Consider, for example, the consequence of an increase in w. The cost function will rotate clockwise about a fixed point at $S = S_{MAX}$. In so doing, the open-access equilibrium would correspond to an increasingly large steady-state stock. Clearly, for a sufficiently large w, the intersection of C and V will occur at a point where the revenue curve has a negative slope, and so the open-access stock level will exceed S_{MSY}, as shown in Figure 9.4. Consider two particular cases. If the cost function intersected the revenue function at its maximum point, the open-access equilibrium stock level would be

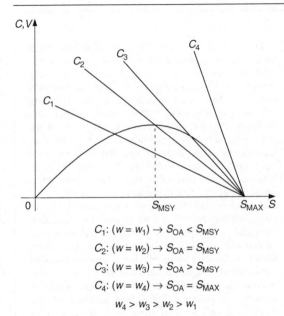

C_1: $(w = w_1) \to S_{OA} < S_{MSY}$

C_2: $(w = w_2) \to S_{OA} = S_{MSY}$

C_3: $(w = w_3) \to S_{OA} > S_{MSY}$

C_4: $(w = w_4) \to S_{OA} = S_{MAX}$

$w_4 > w_3 > w_2 > w_1$

Figure 9.4 Open-access equilibria with alternative cost functions.

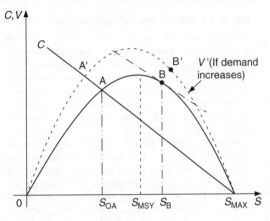

C = Total cost ($=w(H/eS)$)

V = Total revenue ($=P(H) \cdot H$)

A = Open access equilibrium

A' = New open access equilibrium if demand increases

Figure 9.5 The effects of an increase in demand in open access.

the one generating the maximum sustainable yield. Clearly, open access is not necessarily anti-conservationist. The second case of interest arises when harvesting costs are so high (relative to fishing revenues) that no level of fishing is commercially viable. In this case, stocks would rise to S_{MAX}.

If demand increases in such a way that the resource price becomes higher at any harvested quantity, the revenue function will have a higher maximum value (see Appendix 9.1). In this case, the equilibrium open-access resource stock level will be lower than it was prior to the demand increase. This is illustrated in Figure 9.5 by the shift of the revenue function from V to V', and the associated change in the open-access equilibrium from A to A', at a lower stock level.

In our analysis to date, we have presumed that environmental conditions remain unchanged over time. However, in practice these conditions do change, and sometimes very rapidly. When open access to a resource is accompanied by worsening environmental conditions, and when these changes are either rapid or unforeseen or both, har-

vesting outcomes can be catastrophic. The recent history of the Peruvian anchovy fishery in Box 9.2 illustrates such an outcome. Another facet of open access is shown in Box 9.2. Overfishing does not usually happen because of ignorance; it tends to result from the forces of competition in conditions where access is poorly regulated. The New England fisheries demonstrates that self-regulation on the part of fishermen may do little to overcome the consequences of open access.

Static equilibrium when the resource is held under private property

The main characteristic of an open-access equilibrium is zero long-run rent or profit. Price equals average cost, including a normal return on capital. The zero rent condition is a consequence of non-excludability – under open-access arrangements, no institutional barriers exist to exclude those seeking to harvest the resource. The process of unrestricted individualistic competition drives rents to zero.

But if the fishery were organised into private ownership, and owners could enforce

---

Box 9.2 A story of two fish populations

One species of fish – the Peruvian anchovy – and one group of commercial fish – New England groundfish – present case studies of the mismanagement and economic inefficiency which often characterise the world's commercial fisheries. In this box, we summarise reviews of the recent historical experiences of these two fisheries; the reviews are to be found in WR (1994), chapter 10.

Peruvian anchovy are to be found in the Humboldt upswelling off the west coast of South America. Upswellings of cold, nutrient-rich water create conditions for rich commercial fish catches. During the 1960s and 1970s, this fishery provided nearly 20% of the world's fish landings. Until 1950, Peruvian anchovy were harvested on a small scale, predominantly for local human consumption, but in the following two decades the fishery increased in scale dramatically as the market for fishmeal grew. The maximum sustainable yield (MSY) was estimated as 9.5 million tonnes per year, but that figure was being exceeded by 1970, with harvests beyond 12 million tonnes. In 1972, the catch plummeted. This fall was partially accounted for by a cyclical natural phenomenon, the arrival of the El Niño current. However, it is now recognised that the primary cause of the fishery collapse (with the catch down to just over 1 million tonnes in the 1980s) was the conjunction of overharvesting with the natural change associated with El Niño. Harvesting at rates above the MSY can lead to dramatic stock collapses that can persist for decades, and may be irreversible (although, in this case, anchovy populations do now show signs of recovery).

The seas off the New England coast have been among the most productive, the most intensively studied and the most heavily overfished in the world since 1960. The most important species in commercial terms have been floor-living species including Atlantic cod, haddock, redfish, hake, pollock and flounder. Populations of each are now near record low levels. Although overfishing is not the only contributory factor, it has almost certainly been the principal cause of stock collapses. The New England fisheries are not unusual in this; what is most interesting about this case is the way in which regulatory schemes have failed to achieve their stated goals. In effect, self-regulation has been practised in these fisheries and, not surprisingly perhaps, regulations have turned out to avoid burdening current harvesters. This is a classic example of what is sometimes called 'institutional capture'; institutions which were intended to regulate the behaviour of firms within an industry, to conform with some yardstick of 'the common good', have in effect been taken over by those who were intended to be regulated, who then design administrative arrangements in their own interest. The regulations have, in the final analysis, been abysmal failures when measured against the criterion of reducing the effective quantity of fishing effort applied to the New England ground fisheries.

Long-term solutions to overfishing will require strict quantity controls over fishing effort, either by direct controls over the effort or techniques of individual boats, or through systems of transferable, marketable quotas. We investigate some of these instruments later in this chapter and in Chapter 12.

---

exclusion (or could charge a rent for entry), then the open-access equilibrium would not optimise the profits of the resource owners. It is easy to see why this is by looking again at Figure 9.5 (but focusing only on the revenue curve prior to the demand increase). Compare the open-access equilibrium (point A) with another equilibrium, indicated by point B. Whereas profits are zero at point A, they are positive at point B. Therefore, an open-access equilibrium cannot be a profit maximising equilibrium.

We might continue our reasoning as follows. Point B is not only superior to A in that it generates positive rent, it is also the point at which the steady-state profit level (the difference between V and C) is maximised. This is clear by thinking of the relevant marginal conditions. At any point, the function labelled C shows the total cost of harvesting the sustainable yield associated with that resource stock level. The slope of this curve is, therefore, the marginal cost. The V curve shows the total revenue associated with the sustainable harvest at a given stock level, and so its slope indicates marginal revenue. A stock level which maximises profit is one which equates the stock marginal cost and marginal revenue. This is uniquely given by the stock level S_B in Figure 9.5. Under the assumptions we have made, the equilibrium for resource extraction under conditions of private ownership, in which excludability is possible, will lead to a higher resource stock level than that which prevails under open access.

Unfortunately, there is an important deficiency in this argument, and it turns out to be the case that the conclusion we have just reached is only valid in the special circumstance that the private discount rate is zero. It is to this deficiency that we now turn our attention.

Steady-state harvesting when the resource is held under private property

To give a more complete explanation of renewable resource harvesting, and to explain the source of the deficiency in the previous argument, it is necessary to analyse the dynamics of resource harvesting and to bring time explicitly into our analysis. We first establish what the objective of a resource owner is.

Economic theory assumes that the owner acts so as to maximise the present value of the stream of profits over what he or she regards as the relevant time horizon. In other words, the owner maximises the wealth of the firm. Suppose that the owner could invest his or her capital elsewhere in the economy at the rate of return i. The fishery resource owner will only keep his or her capital in the fishery provided it too produces a return at least equal to i.

The reader is likely to be familiar with the formula for the present value of a series of discrete returns, each of which is Z_t, over $T + 1$ periods, which is given by

$$PV = \sum_{t=0}^{t=T} \frac{Z_t}{(1+i)^t}$$

where the discount rate i is the opportunity cost of the firm's capital (the highest rate of return it can obtain elsewhere in the economy). The continuous time analogue of this expression is

$$PV = \int_{t=0}^{t=T} Z_t \, e^{-it} \, dt$$

We assume that total harvesting costs, C, depend positively on the amount harvested, H, and negatively on the size of the resource stock, S. That is

$$C_t = C(H_t, S_t) \qquad C_H > 0, C_S < 0$$

How is the present value of profits maximised? The key to understanding profit-maximising behaviour when access to the resource can be regulated lies in capital theory. A renewable resource is a capital asset. To fix ideas, think about a fishery with a single owner who can control access to the resource and appropriate all returns from it. We wish to consider the owner's decision about whether to marginally change the amount of fish harvesting currently being undertaken.

Choosing not to harvest some fish is equivalent to a capital investment. The uncaught fish will be there next period; moreover, biological growth will mean that there is an additional increment to the stock next period (over and above the quantity of fish left unharvested). This amounts to saying that the asset – in this case the fishery – is productive.

A decision about whether to defer some harvesting until the next period is made by comparing the marginal costs and benefits of adding additional units to the resource stock. By choosing not to harvest an incremental unit, the fisher incurs an opportunity cost in holding a stock of unharvested fish. Holding these units sacrifices an available return. Sale of the harvested fish would have led to revenue which can be invested at the prevailing rate of return on capital, i. So the marginal cost is the foregone current return, the value of which is the net price of the resource, p. Note that $p = P - c$, where P is the gross (or market) price of the resource and $c = \partial C / \partial H$ is the marginal cost of one unit of the harvested resource. However, since we are considering a decision to defer this revenue by one period, the present value of this sacrificed return is ip.

The owner compares this cost with the benefits obtained by the resource investment. There are three categories of benefit:

(1) The unit of stock may appreciate in value by the amount dp/dt.
(2) As a consequence of an additional unit of stock being added, *total* harvesting costs will be reduced by the quantity $\partial C/\partial S$ (note that $\partial C/\partial S < 0$).
(3) The additional unit of stock will grow by the amount dG/dS. The value of this additional growth is the amount of growth valued at the net price of the resource, that is dG/dS multiplied by p.

A present value-maximising owner will add units of resource to the stock provided the marginal cost of doing so is less than the marginal benefit. That is (omitting time subscripts for simplicity):

$$ip < \frac{dp}{dt} - \frac{\partial C}{\partial S} + \frac{dG}{dS}p \qquad (9.12a)$$

This states that a unit will be added to stock provided its holding cost is less than the sum of its price appreciation, harvesting cost reduction and value-of-growth benefits. Conversely, a present value-maximising owner will harvest additional units of the stock if marginal costs exceed marginal benefits:

$$ip > \frac{dp}{dt} - \frac{\partial C}{\partial S} + \frac{dG}{dS}p \qquad (9.12b)$$

These imply the asset equilibrium condition:

$$ip = \frac{dp}{dt} - \frac{\partial C}{\partial S} + \frac{dG}{dS}p \qquad (9.13)$$

A formal derivation of this condition using the Maximum Principle is provided in Appendix 9.2 (except there we use the consumption discount rate r instead of the private discount rate i). Whether or not you read that appendix, what is important to understand is the interpretation of the asset equilibrium condition, Equation 9.13. When this is satisfied, the rate of return the resource owner obtains from the fishery is equal to i, the rate of return that could be obtained by investment elsewhere in the economy. This is one of the efficiency conditions we identified in Chapter 5. To confirm

that this equality exists, divide both sides of Equation 9.13 by the net price p to give

$$i = \frac{\left(\frac{dp}{dt}\right)}{p} - \frac{\left(\frac{\partial C}{\partial S}\right)}{p} + \frac{dG}{dS} \qquad (9.14)$$

This reformulation of Equation 9.13 shows that it is Hotelling's rule of efficient resource use, albeit in a modified form. (It is instructive to compare this version of Hotelling's rule with other versions that we have derived previously. See, for example, the reformulation of Equation 7.20c in Chapter 7.) The left-hand side of Equation 9.14 is the rate of return that can be obtained by investing in assets elsewhere in the economy. The right-hand side is the rate of return that is obtained from the renewable resource. This is made up of three elements:

(a) the proportionate growth in net price
(b) the proportionate reduction in harvesting costs that arises from a marginal increase in the resource stock
(c) the natural rate of growth in the stock from a marginal change in the stock size.

Private profit-maximising outcomes when harvest costs do not depend on the stock size

We are now in a position to make some deductions about the nature of the stock level that will be associated with a privately optimal outcome. To compare our present results with those we obtained in the previous two sections, we focus on steady-state situations only. In a steady-state equilibrium, the net price does not change over time. Therefore Equation 9.14 simplifies to

$$i = -\frac{\left(\frac{\partial C}{\partial S}\right)}{p} + \frac{dG}{dS} \qquad (9.15)$$

Where total harvesting costs do not depend on the stock size $\partial C/\partial S = 0$ and so Equation 9.15 simplifies further to

$$i = \frac{dG}{dS} \qquad (9.16)$$

This is an interesting result. It tells us that a private profit-maximising steady-state equilibrium, where access can be controlled and costs do not depend upon the stock size, will be one in which the resource stock is maintained at a level where the rate of biological growth (dG/dS) equals the market rate of return on investment (i) – exactly what standard capital theory suggests should happen. This is illustrated in Figure 9.6. At the present value-maximising resource stock size (which we denote by S_{PV}), $i = $ dG/dS. It is clear from this diagram that as the interest rate rises, the profit-maximising stock size will fall. Furthermore, it is also clear from inspection of Figure 9.6 that if $i > 0$ and $\partial C/\partial S = 0$, then S_{PV} is less than the maximum sustainable yield stock, S_{MSY}. With positive discounting and no stock-effect on costs, the stock is drawn down below the maximum sustainable yield as future losses in income from higher harvests are discounted and there is no penalty from harvest cost increases.

A further deduction can be made from Equation 9.16. If

(1) harvesting costs do not depend on the stock size (which is you will recall an assumption we used in simplifying Equation 9.15 to Equation 9.16) and
(2) decision makers used a zero discount rate, so that $i = 0$

then the stock rate of growth (dG/dS) should be zero, and so the present-value maximising steady-state stock level, S_{PV}, would be the one which leads to the maximum sustainable yield, S_{MSY}. It makes sense to pick the stock level that gives the highest yield in perpetuity if costs are unaffected by stock size and the discount rate is zero. This result is of little practical relevance in commercial fishing as it is not conceivable that owners would select a zero discount rate.

Private profit maximising outcomes when harvest costs depend on the stock size

The two results we have just derived assumed that costs are not dependent on the stock size. But it is likely to be the case in practice that the total costs of harvesting a given quantity will rise as the stock size falls. When we allow for this dependency, it is not legitimate to make the simplification used in obtaining Equation 9.16. On the contrary, the relevant present-value maximising condition is Equation 9.15. Not surprisingly, the results will then be somewhat different.

The key result we find is that when costs depend negatively on the stock size, the present value-maximising stock will be higher than it would be otherwise. The discount rate i must be equated not with dG/dS but with (dG/dS − {$\partial C/\partial S$}/p). Given that {$\partial C/\partial S$}/p is a negative quantity, this implies that dG/dS must be lower for any given value of R, and so the equilibrium stock size must be greater than where there is no stock effect on costs. The intuition behind this is that benefits can be gained by allowing the stock size to rise (which causes harvesting costs to fall). We illustrate this in Figure 9.7, which compares the present value optimal stock levels with and without the dependence of costs on the stock size, S^*_{PV} and S_{PV}.

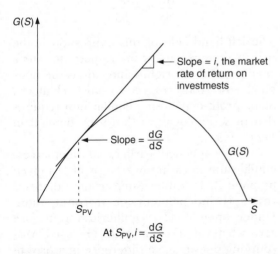

Figure 9.6 The relationship between the interest rate and the present value maximising stock size in steady-state equilibrium.

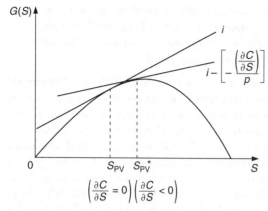

$$\left(\frac{\partial C}{\partial S} = 0\right)\left(\frac{\partial C}{\partial S} < 0\right)$$

Notes to Figure 9.7

No dependence of C on S	Dependence of C on S
$i = \dfrac{\partial G}{\partial S}$	$i = \dfrac{-\left(\dfrac{\partial C}{\partial S}\right)}{p} + \dfrac{\partial G}{\partial S}$
	$\dfrac{\partial C}{\partial S} < 0$
$\therefore i = \dfrac{\partial G}{\partial S}$	$\therefore i > \dfrac{\partial G}{\partial S}$
is required in equilibrium	is required in equilibrium

As i is a constant, this implies

$$\left.\frac{\partial G}{\partial S}\right|_{\substack{\text{no dependence of}\\ \text{costs on stock case}}} > \left.\frac{\partial G}{\partial S}\right|_{\substack{\text{dependence of}\\ \text{costs on stock case}}}$$

$$\downarrow \qquad\qquad\qquad \downarrow$$

$$S_{PV} \qquad < \qquad S^*_{PV}$$

Figure 9.7 Present value maximising fish stocks with and without the dependence of costs on stock size.

The static and dynamic steady-state analyses compared

We appear to have two fundamentally different sets of results in this chapter: those from the static model, and those from the dynamic (steady-state) model. However, it turns out to be the case that these sets of results are not inconsistent with each other. The static results can be thought of as a special case of the dynamic results.

It was stated earlier that there is a limitation in static analysis. This comes from the fact that static analysis looks at one period only. It abstracts from the passage of time. But the passage of time does matter when people have time preference and/or when assets are productive. In either case, the discount rate will not be zero.

Static analysis can be thought of as being applicable when discount rates are zero. It is in this sense that static analysis is a special case of the steady-state dynamic analysis. We can show that the steady-state dynamic results developed in this section collapse to the static results shown in Figure 9.2 when the discount rate is zero.

Let us see how this happens. First we return to the dynamic asset-equilibrium condition given by Equation 9.13:

$$ip = \frac{dp}{dt} - \frac{\partial C}{\partial S} + \frac{dG}{dS}p$$

A static model abstracts from the passage of time (it is as if we are in a steady-state in which all variables are unchanging with respect to time) so $dp/dt = 0$. So the asset-equilibrium condition collapses to

$$ip = -\frac{\partial C}{\partial S} + \frac{dG}{dS}p$$

When $i = 0$, this in turn collapses to

$$\frac{dG}{dS}p = \frac{\partial C}{\partial S}$$

The left-hand side of this expression is the marginal revenue (with respect to stock changes) and the right-hand side is the marginal cost (with respect to stock changes). Static profit-maximising equilibrium requires that these be equal, as shown by point B in Figure 9.5.

As we explained earlier, an open-access equilibrium must imply zero profit, as given by point A. It is interesting to note that this result is independent of discount rates. Under open access, equilibrium rents are zero whatever discount rates are used. Discounting does make a difference in a private property equilibrium in which rents can exist. Where positive discount rates are used, the static model will, therefore, give misleading results.

Socially optimal resource harvesting

How do the commercial privately optimal outcomes identified so far compare with the socially optimal harvesting programme? To derive the socially optimal programme, we maximise a social net benefits function over an infinite time horizon. Net benefits are discounted at a social consumption discount rate r. If you wish to see how this solution is obtained, please read Appendix 9.2.

The main result obtained from this exercise is that the socially optimal harvesting programme is identical to a privately optimal programme, provided that $i = r$ (that is, there is no difference between the private and social discount rates). This result is subject to three qualifications, however:

(1) the private outcome is one in which there is a competitive industry;
(2) individual owners of the resource have enforceable property rights, so that they are able to control access to the resource which they own and appropriate all returns from the resource;
(3) no externalities are associated with the harvesting or use of the renewable resource.

We shall discuss the qualification relating to the industry being competitive in the next section. The property rights qualification should be evident from our previous discussions of the consequences of open access. As far as externalities are concerned, while the absence of externalities is plausible for some renewable resources, it is not for others. Fishing activities do not generate significant external effects, for example (except by one fisherman on another, as we see shortly), but forestry harvesting often does result in important externalities. We shall discuss why these exist in the next chapter.

Harvesting by a monopolist owner

It is important to be clear in what sense we are referring to monopoly in this section. Firstly, we are restricting attention to a renewable resource for which enforceable property rights exist and so access can be controlled by the owners. If an individual harvester makes positive profits, or if this is achieved by the industry as a whole, these controls over access prevent the rents being dissipated by new entry. In this sense, any private property resource could be said to have monopolistic characteristics, in so far as an important component of a monopolistic market is the ability of an established producer to prevent the entry of rivals into the market.

But this is not the meaning that we wish to ascribe to a 'monopolistic market' in this section. Rather, a resource market is monopolistic if there is one single harvester or a small number of harvesters that dominate the industry and are price setters. As is well known from standard microeconomic theory, marginal revenue will exceed marginal cost at a monopolistic market equilibrium. A competitive market, on the other hand, has a large number of producers, each of which is a price taker with no individual control over market price. In the fishing case, a competitive industry in which access is restricted is a form of cartel, in which the co-operation among the members of the cartel is restricted to one thing: action to restrict access to the fishery by non-members of the cartel. In competitive market equilibrium, marginal revenue will equal marginal cost, as is the case for a competitive (but limited access) fishing industry.

As shown in Appendix 9.2, if a renewable resource were harvested under monopolistic market conditions rather than competitive conditions, then an economically inefficient harvesting level may result. A monopoly owner would tend to harvest less each period, and sell the resource at a higher market price, than is socially optimal. If we define a 'conservationist' as someone who regards high stock sizes as intrinsically desirable (and perhaps as someone who does not accord economic efficiency arguments much weight), then he or she may regard monopoly as more desirable than competition in renewable resource markets, however.

The dynamics of renewable resource harvesting

Although we have made use of 'dynamic analysis' to investigate resource harvesting decisions, our focus has been exclusively on steady states. A complete dynamic analysis, however, would involve far more than we have done in this chapter. It might include, for example:

- specifying initial and terminal conditions
- finding time paths for variables of interest over the relevant time horizon
- establishing whether these time paths will converge eventually to a steady state
- investigating how variables respond to shocks or disturbances to the system being studied.

Answering these kinds of questions can be very difficult, and is beyond the scope of this book. This is unfortunate, though, as many resource 'problems' can only be investigated properly in a dynamic framework. For example, to understand how sudden collapses of fish populations can take place as environmental conditions change in unpredictable ways requires that we know something about the adjustment processes that take place when disturbances knock systems out of equilibrium.

The reason why we draw your attention to this matter is so that the limitations of static and steady-state analysis are understood. These techniques are useful starting points for analysing resource economics, but they are far from complete. We explore these matters a little further in the next section. The further readings at the end of the chapter will suggest where you might go next to take your studies further.

Resource harvesting, stock collapses and the extinction of target species

Human activity has adverse effects on biological resources in a variety of ways. It is useful to distinguish two general classes of effects. One operates on particular species (or local populations of species) that are the direct targets of, predominantly commercial, harvesting activity. In this category we shall also include effects on related species or populations that are strongly dependent on or interrelated with the targets. The second class concerns more widely diffused, indirect impacts on systems of biological resources, induced in the main by disruptions of ecosystems. Much of this generalised impact on biological resources is brought together under the rubric of decline of biological diversity. In this section, we consider the first of these two classes of impact. The next section will investigate the causes of biodiversity decline.

In our discussions of resource harvesting, we have noted that when harvest rates are persistently above natural population growth rates, stock levels of the targeted populations will trend downwards. Where a population has some minimum threshold size, a fall in the stock below that level can cause the population in question (and possibly a species itself) to disappear. It is also important to note that non-targeted species may be casualties in this process too. Many forms of resource harvesting, particularly marine fishing, directly or indirectly reduce stocks of other plants or animals that happen to be in the neighbourhood, or which have some biologically complementary relationship with the target resource.

Elementary theories of commercial resource harvesting tend to ignore these possibilities, as we did in much of the exposition given to this point in this chapter. Steady-state fishing involves a balance between regeneration and harvesting rates, and so precludes population collapses. And most dynamic models of commercial resource harvesting suggest that species extinction, while being possible in principle, is likely only under very special circumstances.

But even a casual inspection of the evidence suggests that much resource harvesting does not conform to the theoretical models we have outlined, nor does it have the consequences that those models predict. Reading the sections on the state of renewable resources in general, or fishing or forestry in particular, in recent issues of *World Resources* makes it clear that we are experiencing extensive losses of many renewable resource population stocks, and unprecedented rates of species extinction. Some examples of these phenomena, looking particularly at cases where harvesting rates of target animal populations have been high relative to natural rates of regeneration, are presented in Box 9.3.

There are many reasons why human behaviour may cause population levels of some renewable resources to fall dramatically or, in extreme cases, cause species extinction. These include:

- The existence of open access harvesting regimes in which incentives to conserve stocks for the future are very weak.
- A privately optimal harvesting programme (where access to the resource is controlled) may be one in which it is 'optimal' to harvest a resource to extinction. Clark (1990) demonstrates, however, that this is highly improbable.
- Ignorance of or uncertainty about current and/or future conditions results in unintended collapse or extinction of the population.
- Shocks or disturbances to the system push populations below minimum threshold population survival levels.

It is sometimes thought that the existence of open access to a resource stock inevitably leads to the collapse or even extinction of the population where the species in question is commercially valuable. But this is not correct. The extinction of renewable resource stocks is a possibility in conditions of open access, but open access does not necessarily result in extinction of species. Our earlier discussion of resource harvesting under conditions of open access showed that there is not an inevitable conflict between a resource being harvested under open-access conditions and the conservation of the stock or species. Equilibria in which both harvests and stocks are positive amounts over indefinite periods of time are possible and likely. Open access does not necessarily result in renewable resource stock exhaustion.

In some circumstances, open access conditions do lead to the stock levels being driven to zero. But this is not only true under open access – even with private property rights established and enforceable, it can be commercially optimal to harvest a resource stock to extinction. Some of the results which emerge from the literature about species extinction can be easily summarised. Species extinction is more likely, irrespective of whether the resource is harvested under conditions of open access or private property:

- the higher is the market (gross) resource price of the resource,
- the lower is the cost of harvesting a given quantity of the resource,
- the more that market price rises as the catch costs rise or as harvest quantities fall,
- the lower the natural growth rate of the stock, and the lower the extent to which marginal extraction costs rise as the stock size diminishes.
- the higher is the discount rate.

Thus, even under private property conditions, it may be the case that optimal harvesting programmes drive a fish stock to zero if the prey are simple to catch as the stock diminishes towards its critical minimum threshold level and if it is very valuable. In this case, the optimal harvest level could exceed biological growth rates at all levels of stock.

Box 9.3 Some population collapses of biological resources arising from human predation

The number of species which are known to have been driven to extinction as a result of targeted human action is relatively small. A much larger number have a high probability of becoming extinct in the medium- to long-term future. Several examples are well known. While blue whales (and several other whale species) and African elephants are not extinct, there have been fears that they could easily become so. These fears are justified not only because present numbers are small, but also because several of the conditions favouring extinction (and listed earlier) seem to be present in these cases.

Populations of large mammals are particularly vulnerable. Unlike most fish species, the biotic growth potential of large mammals is sufficiently low to mean that heavy harvesting can drive the stock to zero. A well-known example is the American plains buffalo, which has survived only through a combination of good fortune and careful nurturing of small numbers of the animals in some safe havens. Indeed, hunting and trapping have left many land creatures perilously close to or beyond the point of extinction.

African elephants have long been regarded as common property resources. In recent decades, elephant stocks have fared quite differently from place to place, depending on how governments and local communities have managed stocks, arranged economic incentives and controlled access. Several southern African states (such as Zimbabwe, Botswana and South Africa) manage the stocks as capital assets, strictly limiting access and allowing limited high-income-generating hunting. The most successful conservation programmes seem to have taken place where local people have had strong financial incentives for participating in these programmes, and so support strong anti-poaching measures. Kenya has experienced serious falls in its elephant population, not having established strong economic incentives for local people to participate in elephant protection.

Two large Asian countries – China and India – are threatened with substantial losses of species in the near future. Threatened species in China include a number of large mammals, including the giant panda, tiger, snow leopard, white-lip deer and golden monkey (see WR, 1994, page 79). The main influences appear to be general habitat change arising from population growth and the associated pressures for increasing food output. Other contributory factors are hunting, and collection of specimens for taxidermy and for preparation of medicines (particularly in the case of plants). Similarly, many large mammal populations are threatened in India, including the tiger, elephant and some apes.

Both China and India have recognised these threats for at least two decades, have instituted systems of protected areas, and have plans to increase the protected land area by large quantities over the next two decades. These schemes show many interesting qualities; for example, Chinese plans include attempts to create corridors, providing natural links between nature reserves within the country and to reserves outside China.[1] However, the limited success to date of these protected areas in attaining conservation objectives demonstrates the importance of providing appropriate economic incentives to local populations. In India, for example, local tribespeople displaced from land devoted to tiger reserves have no incentive to conserve the animal, and their poaching has added to the pressures on tiger numbers (WR, 1994, page 99). As we remarked earlier, the designation of protected status is of little use in itself unless there are concomitant changes in human behaviour; these can only be expected if local people are granted secure land tenure, property rights are firmly established, and the enforcement of those rights is supported by the state.

This brings us back to the question of open access. Blue whale stocks have suffered from open access, together with very slow rates of natural growth. Efforts by the International Whaling Commission to conserve blue whale stocks have been largely ineffective. The passenger pigeon, which effectively became extinct through hunting in the late-nineteenth century, also shows the dangers of extinction associated with open access.

While hunting or harvesting has been a major cause of extinction (or threats to extinction) of many large animal species, there are strong grounds for believing that most cases of species extinction do not result directly from excessive harvesting of the resource. Indeed, very often, species becoming extinct were never harvested at all. Most species extinction results from habitat change. Habitats do evolve naturally, of course, and so extinction is not only the result of human activity. But economic activity imposes very rapid and substantial changes to environmental systems, and it is this that is the cause of most species loss.

[1] Similar proposals to construct corridors have been mooted for the former socialist countries of Central and Eastern Europe. Previous no-go areas along national boundaries offer the prospects of providing, at little real cost, very ecologically diverse nature reserves connected to one another by ecological corridors following the national boundaries.

Box 9.3 continued

The important point that emerges from this is the potential for irreversible effects of resource use. This characteristic of irreversibility suggests that there may be benefits from cautious or conservative use of resources, especially when there is uncertainty about the role and functions of species that might be lost by development. We investigate this issue further in Chapter 15.

Extinction is also more likely, other things being equal, where the critical minimum threshold population size is relatively large. In this case, a greater proportion of possible harvesting programmes will lead to harvest rates that cannot be maintained over time. The existence of uncertainty also plays a very important role. Uncertainty may relate to the size of the minimum threshold population, to the actual stock size, or to the current and forecast harvesting rates. If errors are made in estimating any of these magnitudes, then it is clear that the likelihood of stock extinction is increased.

Another influence is the role of chance or random factors. Our presentation has assumed that all functions are deterministic – for given values of explanatory variables, there is a unique value of the explained variable. But many biological and economic processes are stochastic, with chance factors playing a role in shaping outcomes. In these circumstances, there will be a distribution of possible outcomes rather than one single outcome for given values of explanatory variables. We discuss some consequences of risk and uncertainty in Chapter 15.

Having said all this, it still remains true that any given resource stock is more likely to be harvested to exhaustion, or a species driven to extinction, when it is harvested under conditions of open access than under a system in which property rights have been established and are enforceable. Why is this? The main reason is that in these circumstances there is no collectively rational management of harvesting taking place. Even where what should be done is evident, an institutional mechanism to bring this about is missing. So harvest rates are typically higher under conditions of open access; other things being equal, the greater are harvesting rates, the higher is the likelihood of extinction.

Another way of thinking about this is in terms of economic efficiency. Open-access harvesting programmes are inefficient because the resource harvesters are unable to appropriate the benefits of investment in the resource. If a single fisher were to defer the harvesting of some fish until a later period, all fishers would benefit from this activity. It would be in the interests of all if a bargain were made to reduce fishing effort by the industry. However, the conditions under which such a bargain could be made and not reneged upon are very unlikely to exist. Each potential bargainer has an incentive to free ride once a bargain has been struck, by increasing his or her harvest while others reduce theirs. Moreover, even if all existing parties were to agree among themselves, the open-access conditions imply that others could enter the market as soon as rents became positive. Open-access resources thus have one of the properties of a public good – non-excludability – and this alone is sufficient to make it likely that markets will fail to reach efficient outcomes.

An important externality also arises in open-access situations; this is often known as a crowding diseconomy. Under conditions of open access, there will be a tendency for the industry to consist of more harvesters and harvesting capital than is economically efficient. In the case of a fishery, for example, each boat's catch imposes an external cost on every other boat; by taking fish from the water, the costs of harvesting a given quantity of fish become higher for all other boats, provided fishing costs are related to stock size. In effect, each fisherman imposes an external cost on all others. This externality drives the average costs of fishing for the fleet as a whole above the marginal costs of an individual fisher.

There is no way that such external effects can be avoided, in the case of fishing at least. The crowding diseconomy is a technical effect that will operate whenever more than one vessel harvests from a particular fish population. However, if the fishery were in private property ownership and access were regulated, it would be feasible for the size of the fishing fleet to be chosen at an optimal size. The optimal size of fleet would balance the additional benefits of extra boats against the additional external costs of extra boats – what we have called crowding diseconomies. The negative effects become internalised in this way, leading to efficient outcomes. There is ample evidence that fishing effort is massively excessive and inefficient in many open access fisheries throughout the world. We give some evidence on this later, in Box 9.6.

What is causing the loss of biological diversity?

As Fisher (1981, page 75) argues, much of the concern about resource exhaustion appears to involve renewable resource use and the endangerment of species. He quotes one early assessment by a biologist:

> The worst thing that can happen – will happen [in the 1980s] – is not energy depletion, economic collapse, limited nuclear war, or conquest by a totalitarian government. As terrible as these catastrophes would be, they can be repaired within a few generations. The one ongoing process in the 1980s that will take millions of years to correct is the loss of genetic and species diversity by the destruction of natural habitats. This is the folly our descendants are least likely to forgive us.

> Wilson (1980)

This prognosis is supported by the following assessment that introduces the discussion of diversity found in Chapter 8 of the 1994–95 edition of *World Resources*:

> By some accounts, the world is on the verge of an episode of major species extinction, rivalling five other documented periods over the past half billion years during which a significant portion of global flora and fauna were wiped out. Unlike previous die-offs, for which climatic, geologic and other natural phenomena were to blame, the current episode is driven by anthropogenic factors: the rapid conversion and degradation of habitat for human use; the accidental and deliberate introduction of exotic species; overharvesting animals, fish and plants; pollution; human-caused climate change; industrial agriculture and forestry; and other activities that destroy or impair natural ecosystems and the species within them.

> WR (1994), page 147

It is common to have in mind land-based organisms when discussing loss of biodiversity. However, there is evidence that freshwater lakes, streams and rivers may be the most threatened terrestrial ecosystem. Furthermore, marine waters, which contain over 90% of the world's living biomass, may also be experiencing substantial loss of biodiversity (see WR (1994), pages 184 and 192).

A general assessment of the nature and extent of biodiversity decline was given in Chapter 2, so there is no need to dwell on this evidence any further here. Rather, we turn our attention to the causes of biodiversity decline. It has already been shown that a part of this phenomenon is due to the hunting or harvesting of particular species for recreational or commercial purposes. But this explains only a small part of the total picture.

Far more important are losses associated with general economic activity. The drainage of wetlands for agriculture, dam construction and the flooding of valleys for power generation, the use of pesticides, the development of wilderness areas, and toxic contamination of soils have all been associated with unintended species collapses or extinction. In fact, almost all forms of human activity pose this threat. Incidental and unintended impacts are the most important causes of species extinction, dwarfing in significance species loss arising from excessive harvesting.

The causes of biodiversity decline are, therefore, many and diffuse. It is useful to draw a distinction between proximate and underlying or fundamental causes. Proximate causes refer to the mechanisms that trigger the loss of biological diversity; the immediate neighbours, if you like, in the chains of cause and effect links. Fundamental causes are those conditions – cultural, economic, and institutional – which generate and sustain the proximate causes. This distinction is important for policy purposes. Attempts to reduce the loss of biodiversity must take account of the fundamental causes. Efforts concentrated on proximate causes may be doomed to failure if the pressures emanating from underlying conditions are not redirected.

Proximate

Even in the absence of human pressures, there are several natural mechanisms that can result in biodiversity loss or species extinction. These include environmental and demographic stochasticity (random variability), genetic failure and natural catastrophes. Details of the ways in which these mechanisms operate can be found in Jeffries (1997).

But our interest lies in human induced processes. Each of the following processes can induce biodiversity decline:

- land conversion away from high diversity supporting uses
- exploitation of wild species
- introduction of exotic species into new environments
- homogenisation of agricultural practices
- air, water and ground pollution
- climate change.

Some examples of each of these are given in Box 9.4.

Fundamental

While there is little disagreement about the proximate causes of biodiversity decline, there is less consensus about the underlying causes. The explanations given are not mutually inconsistent with each other, however. Rather, they differ in terms of how the problem is conceptualised, and what are perceived as most 'fundamental'. A very useful classification of suggested underlying causes of biodiversity loss was given by Swanson (1995b). He identifies four classes of explanation

(1) *The expansion of human society*. This explanation is essentially one of scale and dominance. Human population growth and changes in its geographical distribution have dramatically increased pressures on the environment. These pressures have intensified as per capita production and consumption have risen with economic development.

Economic and ecological systems are linked. As the scale of the economic system grows relative to that of the natural environment, the dynamics of both systems are affected. In particular, the dynamics become more discontinuous. Threshold effects start to come into play as assimilative and carrying capacities are exceeded (see Perrings, 1995). In this view, biodiversity and the resilience of ecological and economic systems interact in a reciprocal causal relationship: biodiversity is a contributor to ecological and economic resilience (and so provides insurance against the loss of ecological services). But at the same time, a loss of ecological resilience tends to reduce the extent of biodiversity.

This perspective gives the greatest cause for concern. It sees human interests as being fundamentally in competition or conflict with the interests of other species. Policies designed to save biodiversity require the general processes of human expansion be stopped.

(2) *Poverty and underdevelopment*. A second candidate for the underlying cause of biodiversity loss is poverty and underdevelopment. There are various mechanisms through which this may act including deforestation and the loss of

Box 9.4 Some examples of biodiversity decline

Land conversion away from high diversity supporting uses

Possibly the most well known (and well-researched) example of land use change leading to biodiversity decline is the clearing of rainforests. These ecosystems are the most diverse terrestrial systems; forest conversion breaks up continuous woodland areas into parcels which are unable to support the diversity of species that they held in their natural states. We will look at one example of this.

In 1973, a new species of frog – the gastric brooding frog, named because the female nurtures her young in her stomach – was discovered in the Conondale range of Queensland, Australia. Initial studies suggested that its biological materials were potentially of immense medicinal benefit. However, the frogs' habitat was suffering from severe logging pressures, and fears were expressed that habitat conversion would lead to a loss of the species. The gastric brooding frog became the symbol of an intense local and international conservation campaign, organised under the slogan 'Don't log the frog'. All was to no avail. The last wild gastric brooding frogs were seen in 1979, and the species is now thought to be extinct.

Exploitation of wild species

This topic has been discussed earlier in Box 9.3, in which several examples were given, including the passenger pigeon and the near extinction of the American buffalo.

Introduction of exotic species into new environments

The last known member of the *Partula turgida* population, a snail species endemic to French Polynesia, died in London Zoo in 1996 (Jeffries, 1997). This species, along with many other Polynesian island snails, was driven to extinction by the introduction of a predatory snail, *Englaninia rosea*. The latter species had, in turn, been introduced as a device to control the population of giant African land snails. These had been imported for human consumption. Escape of African land snails was followed by an explosion in their numbers, with the species becoming a serious pest through crop damage.

Homogenisation of agricultural practices

One component of the so-called green revolution in agriculture has been the selection and development of crop cultivars with high yield characteristics (see the previous discussions on this in Chapter 2). Using some terminology that we introduced in Box 6.5, these crop development processes involve selection of genetic varieties with high primary productivity potential – that is, they grow quickly and deliver high crop yields. Secondary characteristics of plants are of little or no commercial relevance, and are correspondingly selected out of the commercial varieties. But this process leads to crops which are critically dependent upon the maintenance of unchanging environmental conditions. When those change – due to climate change, entry of new diseases or predators, or when soil conditions change, for example – the selected species is vulnerable to collapsing primary productivity or worse. The Irish potato famine of the nineteenth century illustrates the possible consequences of dependence on one genetic variety that is particularly vulnerable to disease.

But more importantly in the long-term, selection processes of this kind promote genetic uniformity; even where species do not become extinct, the extent of genetic diversity can fall significantly. This loss is enhanced by spillover effects on surrounding ecosystems. Monocultural agriculture – be it timber plantations, cereal crops or whatever – tends to be associated with changes in the pattern of land use which cause the loss of habitats for other plant and animal communities.

Air, water and ground pollution

Pollution has very pervasive effects on biological diversity. European forests and water systems have been badly damaged by acid precipitation (see Chapter 13), and the use of pesticides and herbicides in agriculture has serious ecological effects (discussed in Chapter 2), including the loss of several bird species due to DDT impacts. It has been conjectured that the large falls that have been observed in male fertility in many parts of the world are the result of long-term accumulations of pollutants in various environmental media. As yet, it is too early to say whether this speculation is well founded (and whether the human race is near its end as a result!).

Climate change

We know that major episodes of rapid climate change in the past have been associated with catastrophic episodes of biodiversity loss. For example, at the end of the Palaeozoic period (about 250 million years in the past), over 95% of species were lost in the Permian extinction. This is thought to have been caused by major climate change associated with continental plate movements forming the supercontinent, Gondwanaland.

What is not yet clear is whether the current human-caused climate change due to the so-called greenhouse effect (to be investigated in Chapter 13) will have an effect anywhere near so large in magnitude. Much will depend on the pace of climate

---

Box 9.4 continued

change, rather than the level of eventual climate change. If the change is sufficiently slow, natural adaptation and evolutionary processes may be sufficient to avoid a great loss of biodiversity, even though its composition may change. The high degree of homogenisation of land use today, though, suggests that these natural mechanisms may not work very successfully.

---

soil fertility by an inappropriately managed expansion of extensive margin of agriculture. Essentially, this kind of explanation is one which stresses some form of vicious cycle of poverty. Poverty is associated with extensive, wasteful and short-term use of resources. This has three consequences: first, economic activity is very damaging to the environment, with little or no attention being paid to these impacts; second, environmental damages generates negative feedback on future production possibilities; and third, little value is added by these activities, and so financial resources to break out of underdevelopment are not forthcoming. The initial position of poverty is thereby reproduced over time. Chapter 2 examined several of the links between environmental degradation and poverty. It is the general environmental degradation we discussed there that gives rise to the proximate causes of biodiversity loss.

In one important respect, this explanation is somewhat misleading. There is a reasonable degree of positive correlation between poverty and environmental richness. The more diverse a region is currently, the greater will be the absolute amount of biodiversity loss from any given set of impacts. Most of the industrialised countries are located in northern regions where biodiversity has naturally been lower. Moreover, these countries have already lost many of their large reserves of genetic material, through forest and wilderness conversion.

Having said this, if this explanation does have validity, it does give cause for optimism. Poverty and underdevelopment can be overcome, and major strides in this direction have been taken in recent decades. Matters are far more difficult to deal with where the problem is associated with high levels of economic activity, as in the previous explanation.

(3) *Human choices about the pattern of development*. Biodiversity loss may be viewed as a result of our development choices. In his summary of this perspective Swanson writes:

> human society has a choice in regard to the amount of diversity that will be retained along its development path, and ... this choice has thus far been made in a haphazard fashion, resulting in unmanaged diversity depletion
>
> Swanson (1995b), page 2

Swanson uses the notion of society's asset portfolio. Existing plans have a bias towards a low weight being attached to biological assets in that portfolio. We have freely chosen, for whatever reason, a narrowly constructed portfolio. It is perfectly conceivable for us to select a more diverse portfolio 'either through the more intensive use of a smaller area of land or by the more extensive use of a wider range of species'. Swanson (1995b), page 1.

Stressing the role of free choice may be important in putting responsibility firmly on human shoulders, but one cannot avoid feeling that this perspective is a good description of what has happened but does not constitute a satisfactory explanation (much in the same way that to say that peoples' free choices explain population growth).

(4) *Inappropriate policies and policy failure.* It is relatively easy to make a good case for the proposition that consistently poor policy choices, or failures to properly think through the consequences of choices, are causes of biodiversity decline. Examples can easily be cited: development programmes introduced in response to poverty or perceived need to develop quickly; agricultural support programmes; the ineffective use of extensive margins – these are just a few.

The kinds of misguided policy are too numerous to list. But underlying most cases of policy failure seem to be two factors: the presence of formidable amounts of ignorance and uncertainty; and the lack of policy integration – different arms of government pursue what are perceived as independent objectives without coordination, when in reality the objectives are interconnected (and so their pursuit warrants integration).

Anyone trained as an economist is likely, however, to feel that an important element is lacking in this story, plausible as it is in other respects. The explanation does not address the patterns of incentives facing individuals or organisations. Perhaps decision makers are not failing at all in terms of their own objectives. This suggests that we should look at the institutional framework within which choices are made and incentive structures are determined.

(5) *Institutional failure.* Swanson characterises this explanation as 'failure to create institutions that internalise the values of biodiversity within the decision-making of states and individuals making conversion decisions. (Swanson, 1995b).

This brings us back to the ideas of 'market failure' that we discussed at length in Chapter 6. You will recall from that discussion that resources may be inefficiently allocated (in this case, biodiversity being insufficiently conserved) for a variety of institutional reasons. One of these which is directly relevant to biodiversity was discussed in Box 6.5. This concerns the bias in information property rights towards information deriving from human capital and against information retained in conserved natural capital. Here we have a situation where no institutional framework exists that rewards diversity for its information content.

Many other instances of market failure could be cited, and their linkages to biodiversity decline traced out. We will leave this to your further reading. However, the institutional failure explanation does imply in a fairly clear way some directions that might be taken in constructing instruments to stem the loss of biodiversity. We will leave this matter until Chapter 12, in which the relative advantages of environmental policy instruments is our chief concern.

Renewable resources policy

What goals might one reasonably expect governmental policy towards the use of renewable resources to adopt? Firstly, there are efficiency goals; when the use of resources is economically inefficient, there are potential welfare benefits to the community from policy which leads to efficiency gains. This suggests that policy may be directed towards removing externalities, improving information, developing property rights, removing monopolist industrial structures, and using direct controls or fiscal incentives to alter rates of harvesting whenever there is reason to believe that harvesting programmes are inefficient. Chapter 11 examines economic policy towards the environment and the instruments it has available to attain policy targets, so we shall defer a full consideration of how these objectives might be attained until then. However, some comment is warranted at this stage.

A key issue in renewable resource exploitation, as you have seen, is the adverse consequences of open access to many resources. This is a particularly significant problem in the case of ocean fisheries, but also applies to water and land resources, primary forests, and many other environmental systems. The simplest way of dealing with this may be to define and allocate property rights to the resource. Many nations have done something similar to this by extending their limits of national jurisdiction to 200 miles over their coastal waters. However, in order for this approach to yield efficient outcomes, two conditions must be satisfied. First, the access restriction must be enforceable. Second, the individual boats and their crews should harvest the resource in a collectively efficient manner. This latter condition is not likely to be satisfied purely as a consequence of extended national jurisdiction.

Secondly, given that uncertainty is so great in matters relating to natural resources, the government's role in the provision of information is likely to be crucial. In the case of commercial fisheries, for example, individual fishermen will not be in a position to know, in quantitative terms, how previous and current behaviour has affected and is likely to affect the population levels of relevant species. The consequences of cyclical natural phenomenon, such as the El Niño current mentioned in Box 9.2, will similarly be largely unpredictable by individual agents. Obtaining this kind of information requires a significant monitoring and research effort which is unlikely to be undertaken by the industry itself. Even if it were obtained privately, the dissemination of such information would probably be suboptimal, as those who devote resources to collecting the information may well seek to limit its availability to others.

Efficiency gains, in the form of improved intertemporal resource extraction programmes, may also be obtained if government assists in the establishment of forward or futures markets. As we saw in Chapter 5, efficient outcomes are not possible in general unless all relevant markets exist. The absence of forward markets for most non-renewable and renewable resources suggests that it is most unlikely that extraction and harvesting programmes will be intertemporally efficient.

As far as the use of fiscal incentives is concerned, one way in which the fishing industry might be led into efficient resource harvesting is through the use of a tax levied at a fixed rate per unit of the resource landed. How should the level of such a tax be set? Look at Equation 9.22 in Appendix 9.2: this states that in an optimal harvesting regime, the market price (P) should equal the net price or royalty (p) plus the marginal cost of harvesting the resource. On the other hand, under open access, the zero rent result means that market price equals the average cost of harvesting. To bring about an optimal outcome, a two-part tax is therefore required. The first component of the tax rate is equal to the net price or royalty, p; the second component is the difference between marginal and average extraction costs. If a tax is levied at a rate equal to the sum of these two components, harvesting will take place at the optimal level. The royalty component corrects for the fact that fishermen in open access take no account of the future benefits to be obtained by refraining from harvesting. The second component internalises the crowding externalities referred to earlier.

Tax systems of this kind are very uncommon; an alternative to a tax regime is a system of transferable or marketable catch permits to harvest the resource. Let us call these catch permits 'individual transferable quotas' (ITQ). The ITQ system operates in the following way. Scientists assess fish stock levels, and determine maximum total allowable catches (TAC) for controlled species. The TAC is then divided among fishers. Each fisher can catch fish up to the amount of the quota it holds, or the quotas can be sold to other fishers. No entitlement exists to harvest fish in the absence of holding ITQs. In principle, the ITQ system can ensure that a given target quantity of fish can be harvested in a cost-efficient manner. To see how this operates, consider the following hypothetical example.

Suppose that a fishing industry consists of two groups of fishers – low cost ($2 per tonne) and high cost ($4 per tonne) – and assume that a tonne of fish can be sold for $10. Each group has historically caught and sold 100 tonnes of fish each period. Now consider what will happen if the government imposes a TAC of 100 tonnes.

In the first case, suppose that a non-transferable quota of 50 tonnes is imposed on each fisher. The total catch will be 100 tonnes, at a total cost of $300 (that is, $50 \times 4 + 50 \times 2$). Next, suppose that a transferable quota of 50 tonnes is allocated to each fisher; what will happen in this case? Given that the low-cost fishers make a profit (net price) of $8 per tonne, while high-cost fishers make a profit (net price) of $6 per tonne, a mutually advantageous trade opportunity arises. Suppose, for example, that an ITQ price is $7. High-cost producers will sell quotas at this price, obtaining a higher value per sold quota ($7) than the profit foregone on fish they could otherwise catch ($6). Low-cost producers will purchase ITQs at $7, as this is lower than the marginal profit ($8) they can make from the additional catch that is permitted by possession of an ITQ. A Pareto gain takes place, relative to the case where the quotas are non-transferable. This gain is a gain for the economy as a whole as can be seen by noting the total costs after ITQ trading. In this case, all 50 ITQs will be transferred, and so 100 tonnes will be harvested by the low-cost fishers, at a total cost of $200.

Although this example is unrealistically simple, the underlying principle is correct and applies to all marketable permit or quota systems. Transferability ensures that a market will develop in the quotas. In this market, high-cost producers will sell entitle-ments to harvest, and low-cost producers will purchase rights to harvest. The market price will be set at some level intermediate between the net prices or profits of the different producers. (We will demonstrate in Chapter 12 that this efficiency property is also shared by a tax system; indeed, a tax rate of $7 per tonne of harvested fish would bring about an identical outcome to that described above. Why is this so?) The transferable quota system has been used successfully in several fisheries, including some in Canada and New Zealand, and is examined in Box 9.5.

However, most regulatory policy has not used a tax/subsidy or marketable catch quota instrument. A common approach is to impose technical restrictions on the capital equipment used by fishermen – for example, restrictions on fishing gear, mesh or net size, boat size and so on. Such controls deliberately impose economic inefficiency on the industry, in an effort to reduce harvest sizes, and so cannot be cost-efficient methods of attaining harvest reduction targets. An alternative approach is to restrict the amount of fishing effort taking place by limitations on the times at which fishing may take place. Like the previous instrument, such restrictions fail to tackle at its root the excess fishing capacity that tends to be a consequence of open access.

The restrictions we have just discussed all attempt to reduce fishing effort, or to reduce the catch coefficient (the catch rate per unit effort). However, they cannot be cost-effective relative to a scheme which reduces the fishing industry capital stock to an optimal level. Governments might try to attain this by incentives for firms to leave the industry, but this will be useless if the reduced effort that results is just matched by increased effort from other firms, as seems very likely.

Another approach that is often used is to impose controls in the form of quantity restrictions on catches. This is the centrepiece of fishing regulation in the European Community, for example, in the Total Allowable Catch system. This often has the per-

Box 9.5 The Individual Transferable Quota system in New Zealand fisheries

New Zealand introduced in 1986 an individual transferable quota (ITQ) system for its major fisheries. The ITQ management system operates in the way we described earlier. Government scientists annually assess fish stock levels, and determine maximum total allowable catches (TACs) for controlled species. New Zealand legislation requires that the TAC levels are consistent with the stock levels that can deliver maximum sustainable yields (although that is not the only way in which TAC levels could be set). The TAC is then divided among fishers, with the shares being allocated on the basis of individual catches in recent years. Each fisher can catch fish up to the amount of the quota it holds, or the quotas can be sold or otherwise traded.

The ITQ system has a number of desirable properties. First, fishermen know at the start of each season the quantity of fish they are entitled to catch; this allows effort to be directed in a cost-minimising efficient manner, avoiding the mad dash for catches that characterises free-access fishery. Secondly, as a market exists in ITQs, resources should be allocated in such a way that firms with low harvesting costs undertake fishing. The reasoning behind this assertion is explained in the main text.

The ITQ system operates in conjunction with strictly enforced exclusion from the fishery of those not in possession of quotas. This access restriction generates appropriate dynamic incentives to conserve fish stocks for the future whenever the net returns of such 'investments' are sufficiently high.

The evidence of the ITQ system in operation suggests that, in comparison with alternative management regimes that might have been implemented, it has been successful both as a conservation tool and in terms of reducing the size of the uneconomically large fleets. The ITQ system has not eliminated all problems, however. The fishing industry creates continuous pressure to push TAC levels upwards, and great uncertainty remains as to the levels at which the TAC can be set without jeopardising population numbers. The ITQ system has failed to find a clear solution to the problems of bycatch – the netting of unwanted, untargeted species – and high-grading – the discarding of less valuable species or smaller-sized fish, in order to maximise the value of quotas set in terms of fish quantities.

The ITQ system now operates, to varying extents, in the fisheries of Australia, Canada, Iceland and the United States.

Source: WR (1994), chapter 10

verse effect of increasing fishing effort; individual firms buy larger boats, or more boats, or install more sophisticated harvesting technology in order to win a larger share of the fixed quota for themselves. This results in shorter fishing seasons (often imposed by regulation), and the larger capital stock either lying idle for even longer periods, or turning to exploit other fisheries, thereby imposing stock depletion problems elsewhere. For example, the season for eastern Pacific yellowfin tuna fell from 9 months prior to catch quotas being introduced to just three months after a quota restriction was imposed. Gordon (1954) provides an interesting account of the use of quota restrictions in the Pacific halibut fishery. During the 1930s, Canada and the USA agreed to fixed-catch limits. For many years, the scheme was hailed as an outstanding success, with catch per unit effort quantities rising over two decades, one of the few quota schemes to have achieved this goal. However, Gordon shows that the improvements were not the result of quotas, but of a natural cyclical improvement in Pacific halibut stocks; catches rose rather than fell during the period when quotas were introduced, yet the total catch taken was only a small fraction of the estimated population reduction prior to regulation. Furthermore, the efficiency loss of the regulations was enormous, with the fishing season before quotas were met falling from six months in 1933 to between one and two months in 1952. Despite their widespread use, these quantitative restrictions on either effort or catch have very little justification in either economic or biological terms.

You may wonder at this point why aggregate catch quotas have inefficient (or even counterproductive) outcomes, whereas we argued earlier that marketable or transferable quota regimes lead to efficient outcomes. The difference arises precisely because of marketability. Where quotas are marketable, an economic incentive exists to reduce fishing – such an incentive does not exist in non-transferable, non-marketable quota regimes. We shall explore the implications of this in depth in Chapter 12.

Finally, it is important to note that many writers (particularly non-economists) would argue that correcting market failure and eliminating efficiency losses is not sufficient as an objective for government. They would argue that policy should be directed to prevention of species extinction or the loss of biological diversity whenever that is reasonably practical. This introduces the principle that policy should satisfy a criterion of a safe minimum standard of conservation.

Our discussion of the 'best' level of renewable resource harvesting and policy has placed emphasis very heavily upon the criterion of economic efficiency. However, if harvesting rates pose threats to the survival or sustainability of some renewable resource (such as North Atlantic fisheries or primary forests) or jeopardise an environmental system itself (such as a wildlife reserve containing extensive biodiversity) then the criterion of efficiency may not be appropriate by itself. We have seen that the pursuit of an efficiency criterion is not sufficient to guarantee the survival of a renewable resource stock or an environmental system in perpetuity, particularly when resource prices are high, harvesting costs are low, discount rates are high, and uncertainty pervades the relevant functions.

When a renewable resource or environmental system is of high intrinsic value, so that we would be strongly averse to outcomes that involve the resource being driven to extinction or being unable to yield valuable

---

Box 9.6 Overcapacity in fishing fleets

Our discussions of open-access resources implied that rents will be driven down to zero in an open-access equilibrium. Recent UNFAO calculations suggest that the global fishing fleet did not even succeed in attaining zero rent. In 1989, the fleet was operating at a loss of $22 million; the loss including capital costs was $54 million. Summary statistics, taken from WR (1994), are presented in Table 9.1.

The industry is able to survive on such a loss-making basis partly as a result of government subsidies. For example, some governments pay entry fees for their nation's boats to enter foreign fisheries, while allowing domestic boats free access to their own territorial waters. The losses referred to above also reflect chronic overcapitalisation in the fishing industry; far more fishing capacity is actually available and used than is necessary to catch at current levels. As a result of this, the industry is, overall, massively inefficient.

To some extent overcapacity is a result of government and commercial responses to fluctuations in fish populations. As stocks rise, perhaps as a result of unusually beneficial environmental conditions, the industry installs new capital, often with government support. Subsequently, as stocks fall, either because of natural changes in environments or because of excessive harvesting, the industry is left heavily overcapitalised. Normal market mechanisms, driving firms out of loss-making industries, commonly work slowly or not at all, as government protective subsidies are introduced to maintain employment in areas where fishing activity is heavily concentrated.

Huppert (1990) presents some evidence on overcapitalisation in a fishery in the Bering Sea and Aleutian Islands. The efficient number of mother ships – those required to process the catches of fish from the fishing vessels – was estimated to be nine for the whole fishery. In fact, the number of mother ships was 140. A financial measure of this inefficiency is given by Huppert's calculation of $124 million per annum in lost benefits to the fishery.

Table 9.1 Operating costs and revenues for the global fishing fleet, 1989

Annual operating costs	Amount (millions of US$)
Routine maintenance	30 207
Insurance	7 193
Supplies and gear	18 506
Fuel	13 685
Labour	22 587
Total annual operating costs	92 178
Gross revenue from 1989 catch	69 704
1989 deficit (excluding debt servicing)	22 474

Source: adapted from FAO (1992), pages 20 and 58. Printed in WR (1994), page 183.

environmental services, constraints on harvesting behaviour may be deemed appropriate. The notion of a Safe Minimum Standard of conservation (SMS) has been advocated as a response to this set of circumstances, and we shall now examine this principle, and see how it can be applied to renewable resource policy.

A strict version of SMS would involve imposing constraints on resource harvesting and use so that all risks to the survival of a renewable resource are eliminated. This is unlikely to be of much relevance, however. Virtually all human behaviour entails some risks to species survival, and so strict SMS would appear to prohibit virtually all economic activity. In order to obtain a useful version of SMS, it would appear to be necessary to impose weaker constraints, so that the adoption of an SMS approach will entail that, under *reasonable* allowances for uncertainty, threats to survival of *valuable* resource systems are eliminated, provided that this does not entail *excessive cost*.

For decisions to be made that are consistent with such a weaker SMS criterion, judgements will be necessary about each of the italicised words or phrases in the previous sentence. Decisions will be required as to what constitutes 'reasonable uncertainty' and 'excessive cost', and which resources are deemed 'sufficiently valuable' for application of the SMS criterion. The idea of an SMS is examined further in Chapter 15.

Discussion questions

1 Would the extension of territorial limits for fishing beyond 200 miles from coastlines offer the prospect of significant improvements in the efficiency of commercial fishing?
2 Discuss the implications for the harvest rate and possible exhaustion of a renewable resource under circumstances where access to the resource is open, and property rights are not well defined.

3 To what extent do environmental 'problems' arise from the absence (or unclearly defined assignation) of property rights?

Problems

1 The simple logistic growth model given as Equation 9.3 in the text

$$G(S) = g\left(1 - \frac{S}{S_{MAX}}\right)S$$

gives the amount of biological growth, G, as a function of the resource stock size, S. This equation can be easily solved for $S = S(t)$, that is the resource stock as a function of time, t. The solution may be written in the form

$$S(t) = \frac{S_{MAX}}{1 + ke^{-gt}}$$

where $k = (S_{MAX} - S_0)/S_0$ and S_0 is the initial stock size (see Clark (1990), page 11 for details of the solution). Sketch the relationship between $S(t)$ and t for:
(a) $S_0 > S_{MAX}$
(b) $S_0 < S_{MAX}$

2 A simple model of bioeconomic (that is, biological and economic) equilibrium in an open-access fishery in which resource growth is logistic is given by

$$G(S) = g\left(1 - \frac{S}{S_{MAX}}\right)S - eES$$

and

$$V - C = PeES - wE = 0$$

with all variables and parameters defined as in the section entitled 'Static analysis of the harvesting of a renewable resource'.
(a) Demonstrate that the equilibrium fishing effort and equilibrium stock can be written as

$$E = \frac{g}{e}\left(1 - \frac{w}{PeS_{MAX}}\right) \text{ and } S = \frac{w}{Pe}$$

(b) Using these expressions, show what happens to fishing effort and the stock size as the 'cost-price ratio' w/P changes. In particular, what happens to effort as this ratio becomes very large? Explain your results intuitively.

Further reading

Excellent reviews of the state of various renewable resources in the world economy, and experiences with various management regimes are contained in the biannual editions of *World Resources*. See, in particular, the sections in *World Resources 1994–95* on biodiversity (chapter 8) and marine fishing (chapter 10). Various editions of the *United Nations Environment Programme, Environmental Data Report* also provide good empirical accounts.

Clark (1990), Conrad and Clark (1987) and Dasgupta (1982) provide graduate-level accounts, in quite mathematical form, of the theory of renewable resource depletion, as do Wilen (1985), Conrad (1995) and Rettig (1995). Good undergraduate accounts are to be found in Fisher (1981, chapter 3), the survey paper by Peterson and Fisher (1977), Hartwick and Olewiler (1986) and Tietenberg (1992). A lobster fishery is examined by Henderson and Tugwell (1979), and Huppert (1990) studies Alaskan groundfish.

Gordon (1954) is a classic paper developing the idea of open access resources. Munro (1981, 1982) provides rigorous accounts of the theory of resource harvesting. F.J. Anderson (1991, chapter 7) gives a very thorough and readable analysis of policy instruments that seek to attain efficient harvesting of fish stocks, using evidence from Canadian experience. That book also provides a good account of models of fluctuating fish populations, an issue of immense practical importance. More advanced discussions of fisheries management can be found in L.G. Anderson (1977, 1981, 1995), the last of which examines the ITQ system.

Species extinction and biodiversity decline

A relatively simple, non-technical account of species loss arising from harvesting and human predation is given in Conrad (1995). For a more rigorous and complete account, see Clark (1990). Barbier *et al.* (1990b) examine elephants and the ivory trade from an economics perspective. Several references to the meaning, measurement, and statistics/estimates regarding biodiversity decline were given at the end of Chapter 2. In addition to those, important ecological accounts of the issue are Lovelock (1989, developing the Gaia principle), Ehrenfeld (1988) and Ehrlich and Ehrlich (1981, 1992). The classic book in this field is Wilson (1988). More recent evidence is found in Groombridge (1992), Hawksworth (1995), Jeffries (1997) and UNEP (1995).

Krebs (1972, 1985) contain good expositions of ecology. Perrings (1995), Jansson *et al.* (1994) and Perrings *et al.* (1995) examine biodiversity loss from an integrated ecology–economy perspective. Several other ecological accounts, together with more conventional economic analyses of the causes, are found in Swanson (1995a,b) and OECD (1996). Repetto and Gillis (1988) examine biodiversity in connection with forest resource use. The economics of biodiversity is covered at an introductory level in Pearce and Moran (1994), McNeely (1988) and Barbier *et al.* (1994). Other economics-oriented discussions are Simon and Wildavsky (1993). There is also a journal devoted to this topic, *Biodiversity and Conservation*. Articles concerning biodiversity are regularly published in the journal *Ecological Economics*. Policy options for conserving biodiversity are covered in OECD (1996). Common and Norton (1992) study conservation in Australia.

A large literature now exists examining the economics of wilderness conservation, including Porter (1982), Krutilla (1967) and Krutilla and Fisher (1975).

Excellent accounts of the notion of a Safe

Minimum Standard of conservation are to be found in Randall and Farmer (1995) and Bishop (1978). Other good references in this area include Ciriacy-Wantrup (1968), Norgaard (1984, 1988), Ehrenfeld (1988) and Common (1995).

Water may, of course, be regarded as a renewable resource. Good discussions of the valuation of water quality improvements are found in Desvousges et al. (1987) and Mitchell and Carson (1984) (which both emphasise valuation issues), Ecstein (1958) and Maass et al. (1962), both of which focus on CBA. Water quality management is considered by Johnson and Brown (1976), Kneese (1984) and Kneese and Bower (1968).

Appendix 9.1 The revenue from resource harvesting

The relationship between total revenue from resource harvesting, V, and the resource stock size, S, depends on the form taken by the resource demand function. Under plausible and likely conditions, we can show that the relationship will be of the form shown in Figure 9.3, with the revenue to the industry being at a maximum at S_{MSY}.

Assume that the resource growth function is given by

$$G(S) = gS\left(1 - \frac{S}{S_{MAX}}\right) \qquad (g > 0) \quad (9.17)$$

and the demand for the renewable resource has a constant price elasticity ε_d:

$$P = aG(S)^{1/\varepsilon_d} \qquad \text{where } a > 0 \quad (9.18)$$

The revenue function is

$$V(S) = PG(S) \tag{9.19}$$

By substituting Equation 9.18 into 9.19 we have

$$V(S) = PG(S) = aG(S)^{1+\frac{1}{\varepsilon_d}}$$

Hence

$$\frac{dV(S)}{dS} = \left(1 + \frac{1}{\varepsilon_d}\right)aG(S)^{\frac{1}{\varepsilon_d}}\frac{dG(S)}{dS}$$

$$= agG(S)\frac{1}{\varepsilon_d}\left(1 - \frac{2S}{S_{MAX}}\right)\left(1 + \frac{1}{\varepsilon_d}\right)$$

If $\varepsilon_d < -1$, then

$$\frac{dV(S)}{dS} > 0 \text{ for } 2S < S_{MAX}$$

and

$$\frac{dV(S)}{dS} < 0 \text{ for } 2S > S_{MAX}$$

So when $S = S_{MAX}/2$, revenue $V(S)$ reaches its maximum. It can also be shown (although we do not do so here) that, in these circumstances, if the parameters of the demand function shift so that demand increases and the resource price becomes higher at any harvested quantity, the revenue function shown in Figure 9.2 will have a higher maximum value. Note that the results we have obtained here depend upon the assumptions we made about functional forms of demand and growth functions. They will not necessarily be true in other cases.

Appendix 9.2 The dynamics of renewable resource harvesting

A socially optimal harvesting programme

Let r be the social consumption discount rate. The objective is to maximise discounted social net benefits over an infinite horizon, subject to a resource growth constraint. We may state the problem as

$$\text{Max} \int_0^\infty \{B(H_t) - C(H_t, S_t)\}\, e^{-rt}\, dt$$

subject to

$$\frac{dS}{dt} = G(S_t) - H_t$$

Let the Hamiltonian be labelled as L. The current-value Hamiltonian for this problem is

$$L_t = B(H_t) - C(H_t, S_t) + p_t(G(S_t) - H_t)$$

where p is a Lagrange multiplier, interpretable as the shadow net price of one unit of the stock of the renewable resource.

The necessary conditions for a maximum are

$$\frac{\partial L_t}{\partial H_t} = 0 = \frac{dB}{dH_t} - \frac{\partial C}{\partial H_t} - p_t \qquad (9.20)$$

$$\frac{dp_t}{dt} = rp_t - p_t\frac{dG}{dS_t} + \frac{\partial C}{\partial S_t} \qquad (9.21)$$

and the resource net growth equation

$$\frac{dS}{dt} = G(S_t) - H_t$$

Equation 9.20 defines the relationship between the resource net price, gross price and marginal cost. We assume that there is an inverse demand function for the resource given by $P_t = P(H_t)$, where P denotes the gross price of the resource. (Be careful with the notation here; P denotes the resource gross price, p the resource net price.) The demand function implies that $dB/dH_t = P_t$, and so Equation 9.20 can be rewritten as

$$p_t = P_t - \frac{\partial C}{\partial H_t} \qquad (9.22)$$

which states that the net price is equal to the gross price minus the marginal cost of a unit of resource harvested.

Equation 9.21 is the Hotelling efficient harvesting condition for a renewable resource in which costs depend upon the stock level. It is also sometimes called the asset-equilibrium condition. Equation 9.14 in the main text is identical to Equation 9.21 with the exception that the former uses i, the market rate of interest, as the discount rate, whilst the latter uses r, the social (consumption) discount rate. An interpretation of this Hotelling efficiency

rule is given in the discussion surrounding Equation 9.14.

Initial and terminal conditions

This problem has a single initial condition, namely that there exists a fixed, positive initial stock level, S_0. Let $\{H_T, S_T\}$ denote the terminal, steady-state values of the harvest rate and resource stock, such that

$$\frac{dH}{dt} = 0 \text{ and } \frac{dS}{dt} = 0$$

When $S_t < S_T$, H_t should be set at a level such that $H_t < G(S_t)$, so that S_t grows over time and gradually converges to its steady-state value, S_T. Then, as dH/dt gradually converges to zero, the process converges to the terminal steady-state equation

$$rp = p\frac{dG}{dS} - \frac{\partial C}{\partial S}$$

which is identical to Equation 9.15 in the text, with i replaced by r and the equation then multiplied through by r.

Private present value-maximising harvesting in a competitive market with enforceable property rights

Let i be the appropriate private discount rate. In this case, the problem is defined as

$$\text{Max} \int_0^\infty \{V(H)_t - C(H_t, S_t)\}e^{-it} \, dt$$

subject to

$$\frac{dS}{dt} = G(S_t) - H_t$$

The current-valued Hamiltonian for this problem is

$$L_t = V(H_t) - C(H_t, S_t) + p_t(G(S_t) - H_t)$$

The necessary conditions for a maximum are the same as in the previous case (with i replacing r) except for Equation 9.20 which is now

$$\frac{\partial L_t}{\partial H_t} = 0 = \frac{dV}{dH_t} - \frac{\partial C}{\partial H_t} - p_t \qquad (9.23)$$

Now $V = PH$. In a competitive market, each firm is a price-taker and so we have $dV/dH = P$ in equilibrium. Given this, the profit-maximising conditions for a perfectly competitive industry in which the resource is privately owned and excludable will be identical to that for the social optimum, provided the social discount rate, r, equals the private discount rate, i.

Private present value-maximising harvesting in a monopolistic market with enforceable property rights

For a monopolistic industry, $V = P(H)H$ and so

$$\frac{dV}{dH} = \frac{d}{dH}(P(H)H) = \frac{dP}{dH}H + P(H)$$

and so $dV/dH < P$, as $dP/dH < 0$. Hence the monopolistic profit-maximising solution is different from the socially optimal solution. To see precisely how it is different, look at Equations 9.20 and 9.23 under the two alternative market structures.

Monopoly:

$$P(H) = \frac{\partial C}{\partial H} + p_T - \frac{dP}{dH}H$$

Competition:

$$P(H) = \frac{\partial C}{\partial H} + p_T$$

Now as dP/dH is negative, this implies that the market price is higher in monopolistic than in competitive markets, and so less is harvested and sold. One would expect the stock size to be larger in monopolistic than in competitive markets.

Appendix 9.3 The condition for maximising the net present value of a renewable resource

As we are considering steady-states only, the stock level S and the harvest rate H are each constant. So, provided the demand function does not change over time, dp/dt is zero in a steady state. Imposing this on the Hotelling rule, Equation 9.13, we obtain

$$ip = -\frac{\partial C}{\partial S} + \frac{dG}{dS}p \qquad (9.24)$$

Now if $i = 0$, then from Equation 9.24 we would have

$$\frac{\partial C}{\partial S} = \frac{dG}{dS}p \qquad (9.25)$$

But as $p = P - c$ (where $c = \partial C/\partial H$) then

$$\frac{\partial C}{\partial S} = \frac{dG}{dS}(P - c)$$

$$\frac{\partial C}{\partial S} = \frac{dG}{dS}P - \frac{dG}{dS}c$$

or

$$\frac{\partial G}{\partial S}P = \frac{dG}{dS}c + \frac{\partial C}{\partial S}$$

This is the condition for maximising the net present value of the renewable resource. The left-hand side can be interpreted as the steady-state marginal revenue of harvesting, the right-hand side the steady-state marginal cost of harvesting, taking account of the dependence of costs on effort, the cost per unit effort and the dependence of cost on the size of the resource stock.

CHAPTER 10

Forest resources

This was the most unkindest cut of all.

William Shakespeare, *Julius Caesar* III.ii. (188)

Introduction

This chapter is concerned with forests and other wooded land. As Table 10.1 shows, in 1990 these covered over 5.1 billion hectares, about 40% of the earth's land surface. The total of 5.1 billion hectares consists of 3.4 billion hectares of forest (land with a high density of tree coverage) and 1.7 billion hectares of other wooded land (that is, open woodland, scrubland and brushland, and land under shifting cultivation).

Our focus is directed on the larger share consisting of forestland (defined by the United Nations Food and Agriculture Organization as land with a minimum tree cover of 20% in developed countries and 10% in developing countries). Forestland can be divided into two categories: natural forests and plantation forests. While the former is typically not managed at all (and where it is managed, is not done so primarily for timber production), plantations are commercially operated resources, managed predominantly for timber revenues.

The analysis of plantation forestry is well developed, and it has been the object of an important sub-discipline within economics for well over a century. A forest is a renewable resource, and the techniques we outlined in the previous chapter carry over fairly easily to the analysis of plantation forestry. The first part of this chapter shows how this is done, and draws your attention to some of the particular characteristics of forest resources that differentiate its study from fisheries, the principal focus of Chapter 9.

However, readers may think it rather strange that so much attention has been given to plantation forestry given the relatively small proportion that such forests form of total forested area. As Table 10.1 shows, the ratio of planted to natural forests is not known for all regions and countries, but it is typically small. For example, plantations constitute less than 1% of Africa's forest cover, and an even smaller proportion of the forest area of tropical South America. Proportions as small as this are not universally true, of course, particularly when one looks at individual countries (not shown here, but available in each issue of *World Resources*). India, for example, has 20% of forestland in plantations. In those parts of the world that industrialised earliest and most extensively, natural forest loss has been far greater and plantation forestry is proportionately far more important. Unfortunately, the *World Resources* data in Table 10.1 does not provide the information needed to find this ratio for Europe and North America, but one would expect that in many countries in these regions plantation forests form large proportions of total forest area.

As time goes by, plantation forestry will inevitably become of greater significance. Natural forests are similar in one fundamental way to non-renewable resources: under present conditions, they exist in more-or-less fixed quantities and once 'mined' are irreversibly lost as natural forests. Although trees may subsequently grow in areas once occupied by natural forest, the essence of what constitutes a natural forest cannot be replaced (except over extremely long spans of time). Plantation forestry will tend to increase through time as previously natural forestland is converted and land use changes. Nevertheless, there is no guarantee that forested land will simply change the form of its wood cover with no loss of total forested

Table 10.1 Global forest resources.

| | Forest and other wooded land | Total forest | Forest area | | | | Annual logging of closed broadleaf forest | | |
| | | | Natural forest | | Plantations | | | | |
	1990 Extent (000 ha)	1990 Extent (000 ha)	1990 Extent (000 ha)	Change 1981–90 (%)	1990 Extent (000 ha)	Change 1981–90 (%)	1990 Extent (000 ha)	Closed Forests (%)	Primary forest (%)
World	5 120 227	3 442 369	na	na	na	na	na	na	na
Africa	1 136 676	545 085	540 669	−0.73	4416	5.55	na	na	na
North Africa	11 137	6905	5655	−1.11	1250	6.82	na	na	na
West Sahelian Africa	105 956	40 941	40 766	−0.68	175	49.95	6	0.2	78
East Sahelian Africa	161 048	65 983	65 450	−0.83	533	7.03	4	0.1	65
West Africa	149 764	55 919	55 607	−0.96	312	4.72	312	2.0	47
Central Africa	296 704	204 238	204 113	−0.53	125	16.12	571	0.4	90
Tropical Southern Africa	346 896	146 609	145 869	−0.84	740	8.14	9	0.1	38
Temperate Southern Africa	41 172	8361	7317	−0.79	1044	1.82	na	na	na
Insular Africa	23 457	16 127	15 892	−0.78	235	1.69	20	0.3	31
Asia	657 361	489 466	na	na	na	na	na	na	na
Temperate and Middle East Asia	252 339	192 386	na	na	33 566	5.80	na	na	na
South Asia	100 164	77 762	63 931	−0.79	13 831	29.84	62	0.2	17
Continental South and East Asia	123 400	77 484	75 239	−1.49	2245	7.77	304	0.5	76
Insular Soth East Asia	181 458	141 834	135 425	−1.25	6409	11.12	1721	1.5	85
The Americas	2 009 006	1 424 206	959 704	−0.74	7765	7.09	na	na	na
Temperate North America	749 289	456 737	na	na	na	na	na	na	na
Central America and Mexico	158 034	68 289	68 097	−1.40	192	16.13	90	0.4	65
Caribbean Subregion	50 989	47 447	47 138	−0.25	309	11.31	42	0.1	73
Nontropical South America	68 453	43 283	41 564	−0.62	1719	5.51	na	na	na
Tropica South America	982 242	808 450	802 905	−0.71	5545	7.24	2445	0.4	90
Europe	174 340	140 197	na	na	na	na	na	na	na
USSR (former)	941 530	754 958	na	na	na	na	na	na	na
Oceania	200 971	88 524	na	na	na	na	na	na	na

area. During the 1990s, for example, only one-fifth of lost natural forestland was taken up in plantation growth. It is worth noting that China has been unusual in this respect. Its tree-planting programme of the 1980s was so massive in scale that afforestation exceeded deforestation in the whole of the Asia and Pacific region.

The reason why we have written at some length on this matter is that natural forests and plantation forests are very different kinds of resources in terms of the services that they provide. Natural forests are biologically more diverse and perform a much broader range of ecological, amenity and recreational and other economic services. We devote the latter part of this chapter, therefore, to looking at deforestation of natural forestland, an issue that has become the subject of extensive study within environmental economics in recent decades.

Characteristics of forest resources

Let us begin by summarising some of the key characteristics of forest resources, noting some of the similarities and differences between forest and fish resources.

(1) While fisheries typically provide a single service, forests are multi-functional, providing a wide variety of goods and services, including raw materials and fuels, habitats for wildlife, watershed maintenance, regulation of atmospheric quality, recreational facilities and other amenities. Because of the wide variety of functions that forests perform, timber managed for any single purpose generates a large number of important external effects. We would expect that the management of woodland resources is often economically inefficient because of the presence of these external effects.

(2) Woodlands are capital assets that are intrinsically productive. In this, they are no different from fisheries, and so the techniques we developed earlier for analysing efficient and optimal exploitation should also be applicable (albeit with amendments) to the case of forest resources.

(3) Trees typically exhibit very long lags between the date at which they are planted and the date at which they attain biological maturity. A tree may take more than one century to reach its maximum size. The length of time between planting and harvesting is usually at least 25 years, and can be as large as 100 years. This is considerably longer than for most species of fish, but not greatly different from some large animals.

(4) Unlike fisheries, tree harvesting does not involve a regular cut of the incremental growth. Forests, or parts of forests, are usually felled in their entirety. It is possible, however, to practice a form of forestry in which individual trees are selectively cut. Indeed, this practice is becoming increasingly common, particularly where public pressure to manage forests in a multiple-use way is strong. This form of felling is similar to the 'ideal' form of commercial fishing in which adult fish are taken, leaving smaller, immature fish unharvested for a later catch.

(5) Plantation forestry is intrinsically more controllable than commercial marine fishing. Tree populations do not migrate spatially, and population growth dynamics are simpler, with less interdependence among species and less dependence on relatively subtle changes in environmental conditions.

(6) Trees occupy potentially valuable land. The land taken up in forestry often has an opportunity cost. This distinguishes woodlands from both ocean fisheries (where the ocean space inhabited by fish stocks usually has no value other than as a source of fish) and mineral deposits (where the space occupied by deposits has little or no economic value).

(7) The growth in volume or mass of a single stand of timber, planted at one point in time, resembles that illustrated for fish populations in the previous chapter.

To illustrate the assertion made in point (7), we make use of some data reported in Clawson (1977). This refers to the volume of timber in a stand of US northwest Pacific region Douglas firs. Let S denote the volume, in cubic feet, of standing timber and t the age in years of the stand since planting. (For simplicity, we shall use a year to denote a unit of time.) The age–volume relationship estimated by Clawson for a typical single stand is

$$S = 40t + 3.1t^2 - 0.016t^3$$

Figure 10.1(a) plots the volume of timber over a period of up to 145 years after planting. The volume data is also listed in the second column in Table 10.2. It is evident from the diagram that an early phase of slow growth in volume is followed by a period of rapid volume growth, after which a third phase of slow growth takes place as the stand moves towards maturity. Eventually, growth ceases altogether (and in this case even becomes negative). The stand becomes mature (reaches maximum volume) at approximately 135 years.

How does the amount of growth (that is, $G(S)$ in the notation we used in Chapter 9) from one year to the next vary with the volume of timber, S? The amount of growth is listed in the third column of Table 10.2, and the growth–volume relationship is plotted in Figure 10.1(b). Although the biological growth function is not logistic in this case, it is very similar in form to simple logistic growth, being a quadratic function (with an inverted U-shaped profile).

Inspection of Figure 10.1(b) or Table 10.2 shows that the biological growth function for one stand reaches a peak increment of 240 cubic feet 65 years after planting at a total standing timber volume of approximately 11 300 cubic feet. When discussing a fishery, we labelled an increment such as this (the

one where the growth function is maximised) the maximum sustainable yield. But for a single forest stand of trees all planted at one point in time, the concept of a maximum sustainable yield (MSY) of timber is not meaningful. While we can imagine (perhaps a little simplistically) that fishing involves catching the old, large fish while younger fish are left to grow to maturity, this does not apply in the single-aged forest stand we are now considering. However, when we have more than one stand, or a stand of trees of different ages, it is meaningful to talk about sustainable yields. But this is something we shall discuss later.

Commercial plantation forestry

There is a huge literature dealing with optimal timber extraction. We attempt to do no more than present a flavour of some basic results, and refer the reader to specialist sources of further reading at the end of the chapter. An economist derives the criterion for an efficient forest management and felling programme by trying to answer the following question:

What harvest programme is required in order that the present value of the profits from the stand of timber is maximised?

The particular aspect of this question that has most preoccupied forestry economists is the appropriate time after planting at which the forest should be felled. As always in economic analysis, the answer one gets to any question depends on what model is being used. We begin with one of the most simple forest models, the single rotation model. Despite its lack of realism, this model offers useful insights into the economics of timber harvesting.

A single rotation forest model

Suppose there is a stand of timber of uniform type and age. All trees in the stand were

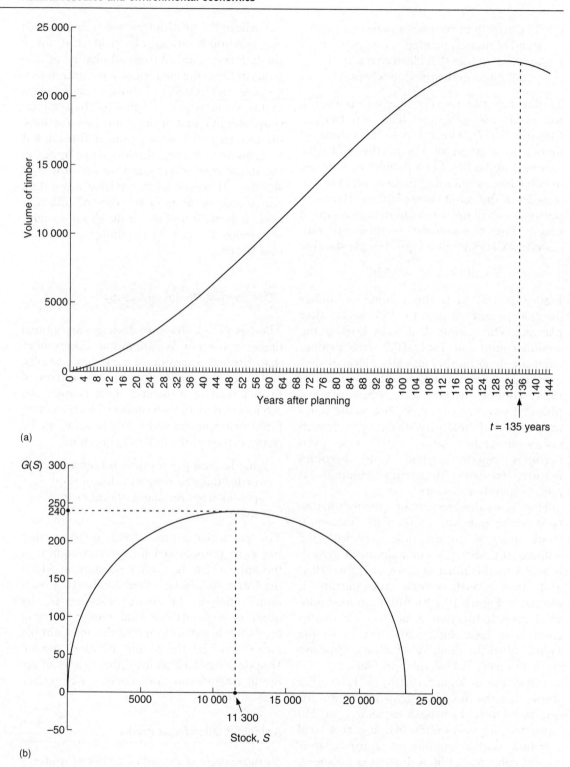

Figure 10.1 (a) The volume of timber in a single stand over time. (b) Biological growth of a single stand of timber.

Table 10.2 Present values of revenue, costs and net benefits undiscounted and discounted at 3%.

Age of stand, t years	Volume of timber, S (cu. ft.)	Annual growth, $S_t - S_{t-1}$	Interest rate $i = 0.00$			Interest rate $i = 0.03$		
			Revenue, R1	Cost, C1	Net benefit, NB1	Revenue, R2	Cost, C2	Net benefit, NB2
1	43.1	43.1	430.8	5 086.2	−4 655.3	418.1	5083.6	−4665.5
5	275.5	66.9	2 755.0	5 551.0	−2 796.0	2 371.3	5474.3	−3103.0
10	694.0	94.6	6 940.0	6 388.0	552.0	5 141.3	6028.3	−887.0
15	1 243.5	119.8	12 435.0	7 487.0	4 948.0	7 928.9	6585.8	1343.1
20	1 912.0	142.6	19 120.0	8 824.0	10 296.0	10 493.3	7098.7	3394.6
24	2 524.4	159.2	25 244.2	10 048.8	15 195.3	12 287.6	7457.5	4830.1
25	2 687.5	163.1	26 875.0	10 375.0	16 500.0	12 694.8	7539.0	5155.9
27	3 025.0	170.6	30 249.7	11 050.0	19 199.8	13 456.8	7691.4	5765.5
30	3 558.0	181.1	35 580.0	12 116.0	23 464.0	14 465.8	7893.2	6572.6
32	3 930.1	187.7	39 301.1	12 860.2	26 441.0	15 048.1	8009.6	7038.5
35	4 511.5	196.8	45 115.0	14 023.0	31 092.0	15 787.4	8157.5	7630.0
39	5 326.0	207.5	53 260.0	15 652.0	37 608.0	16 530.1	8306.0	8224.1
40	5 536.0	210.0	55 360	16 072.0	39 288.0	16 674.1	8334.8	8339.3
50	7 750.0	229.3	77 500.0	20 500.0	57 000.0	17 292.6	8458.5	8834.1
60	101 04.0	239.0	101 040.0	25 208.0	75 832.0	16 701.8	8340.4	8361.4
65	113 03.5	240.2	113 035.0	27 607.0	85 428.0	16 082.0	8216.4	7865.6
70	125 02.0	239.0	125 020.0	30 004.0	95 016.0	15 309.5	8061.9	7247.6
80	148 48.0	229.5	148 480.0	34 996.0	113 784.0	13 469.8	7694.0	5775.8
90	170 46.0	210.4	170 460.0	39 092.0	131 368.0	11 455.9	7291.2	4164.7
100	190 00.0	181.7	190 000.0	43 000.0	147 000.0	9 459.5	6891.9	2567.6
110	206 14.0	143.4	206 140.0	46 228.0	159 912.0	7 603.1	6520.7	1082.5
120	217 92.0	95.4	217 920.0	48 584.0	169 336.0	5 954.4	6190.9	−236.5
130	224 38.0	37.9	224 380.0	49 876.0	174 504.0	4 541.9	5908.4	−1366.5
135	225 31.5	5.6	225 315.0	50 063.0	175 252.0	3 925.5	5785.1	−1859.6
140	224 56.0	−29.2	224 560.0	49 912.0	174 648.0	3 367.4	5673.5	−2305.1
145	221 99.5	−66.4	221 995.0	49 399.0	172 596.0	2 865.2	5573.1	−2707.8

planted at the same time, and are to be cut at one point in time. Once felled, the forest will not be replanted. So only one cycle or rotation – plant, grow, cut – is envisaged. For simplicity, we also assume that

- the land has no alternative uses so its opportunity cost is zero;
- planting costs (k), marginal harvesting costs (c) and the gross price of felled timber (P) are constant over time;
- the forest generates value only through the timber it produces, and its existence (or felling) has no external effects.

Looked at from the point of view of the forest owner (which, for simplicity we take to be the same as the landowner), what is the optimum time at which to fell the trees? The answer is obtained by choosing the age at which the present value of profits from the stand of timber is maximised. Profits from felling the stand at a particular age of trees are given by the value of felled timber less the planting and harvesting costs. Notice that because we are assuming the land has no other uses, the cost of the land is zero and so does not enter this calculation. If the forest is clear-cut at age T, then the present value of profits is

$$(P - c)S_T e^{-iT} - k = pS_T e^{-iT} - k \quad (10.1)$$

where S_T denotes the volume of timber available for harvest at time T, p is the net price of the harvested timber, and i is the private consumption discount rate (which we suppose is equal to the opportunity cost of capital to the forestry firm).

The present-value of profits is maximised at that value of T which gives the highest value for $pS_T e^{-iT} - k$. To maximise this quantity, we differentiate Equation 10.1 with respect to T, using the product rule, set the derivative equal to zero and solve for T:

$$\frac{d}{dT}((pS_T)\,e^{-iT} - k) = \frac{d}{dT}((pS_T)\,e^{-iT})$$

Differentiating, we obtain

$$pe^{-iT}\frac{dS}{dT} + pS_T\frac{de^{-iT}}{dT} = 0$$

which implies that

$$pe^{-iT}\frac{dS}{dT} - ipS_T\,e^{-iT} = 0$$

and so

$$p\frac{dS}{dT} = ipS_T$$

or

$$i = \frac{\dfrac{dS}{dT}}{S_T} \qquad (10.2)$$

Equation 10.2 states that the present value of profits is maximised when the growth rate of the resource stock is equal to the private discount rate. Note that with the timber price and harvesting cost constant, this can also be expressed as an equality between the rate of growth of the (undiscounted) value of profits and the discount rate.

We can calculate the optimal, present-value maximising age of the stand for the illustrative data in Table 10.2. In these calculations, we assume that the market price per cubic foot of felled timber is £10, planting costs are £5000, incurred immediately the stand is established, and harvesting costs are £2 per cubic foot, incurred at whatever time the forest is felled. The columns labelled R1 and C1 list the present values of revenues and costs and profits for a discount rate of zero. Note that when $i = 0$, present values are identical to undiscounted values. The present value of profits is listed in the table under the title NB1, and its level over time is shown in Figure 10.2. Net benefits are maximised at 135 years, the point at which the biological growth of the stand (dS/dt) becomes zero. With no discounting and fixed timber prices, the profile of net value growth

of the timber is identical to the profile of net volume growth of the timber, as can be seen by comparing Figure 10.1(b) and 10.2.

It is also useful to look at this problem in another way. The interest rate to a forest owner is the opportunity cost of the capital tied up in the growing timber stand. As we are here supposing that the interest rate is zero, that opportunity cost is zero. It will, therefore, be in the interests of the owner to not harvest the stand as long as the volume (and value) growth is positive, which it is up to an age of 135 years.

Now consider the case where the discount rate is 3%. The columns labelled R2, C2 and NB2 in Table 10.2 refer to the present values of revenues, costs and profits when the interest rate is 3%. The present value of profits at a discount rate of 3% is also plotted in Figure 10.2, under the legend NB2. With a 3% discount rate, the present-value of the forest is maximised at a stand age of 50 years. Expressed another way, the growth of undiscounted profits falls to 3% at year 50, and is less than 3% thereafter. This is shown in Figure 10.3. If the interest rate is 3%, a wealth-maximising owner should harvest the timber when the stand is of age 50 years – up to that point, the return from the forest is above the interest rate, and beyond that point the return to the forest is less than the interest rate. Before leaving this example, note the huge effect that discounting can have. A rise in the discount rate from zero to 3% not only dramatically lowers the profitability of the forest but also significantly changes the shape of the present-value profile, reducing the age at which the forest should be felled (in our illustrative example) from 135 to 50 years.

The single rotation model we have used shows that the optimal time for felling will depend upon the discount rate used. As the discount rate rises, it is clear from Figure 10.3 that the age at which the stand is felled will have to be shortened in order to bring about equality between the rate of change of undiscounted net benefits and the discount

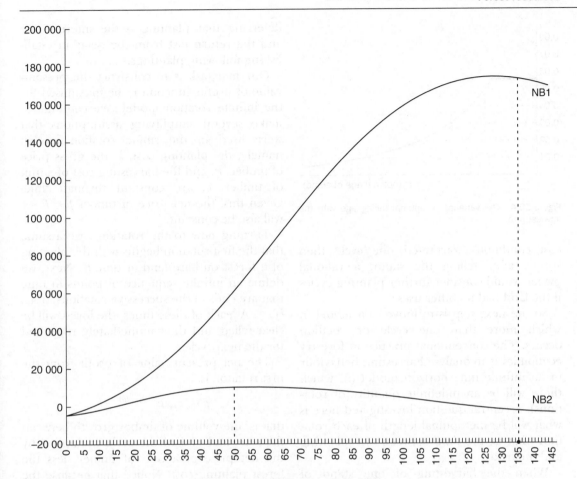

Figure 10.2   Present values of net benefits at $i = 0.00$ (NB1) and $i = 0.03$ (NB2).

rate. This sensitivity of the optimal felling age to the level of the interest rate can be large. In Figure 10.4, we illustrate how the optimal felling age varies with the interest rate. The

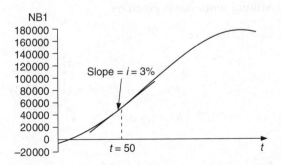

Figure 10.3   The optimal felling time is when the growth rate of undiscounted net benefits equals the interest rate.

relationship that is shown is valid only for the growth model used here, and the various assumptions we made about parameter values, prices and costs. However, it does indicate that under plausible circumstances, small changes in interest rates can dramatically alter privately optimal harvesting programmes.

Infinite rotation forestry models

The forestry model we investigated in the previous section is unsatisfactory in a number of ways. In particular, it is hard to see how it would be meaningful to have only a single rotation under the assumption that there is no alternative use of the land. If price and

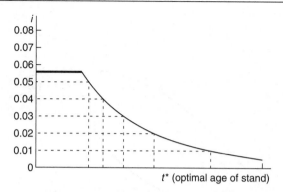

Figure 10.4 The variation of optimal felling age with the interest rate.

cost conditions warranted one cycle then surely, after felling the stand, a rational owner would consider further planting cycles if the land had no other uses?

So the next step is to move to a model in which more than one cycle or rotation occurs. The conventional practice in forestry economics is to analyse harvesting behaviour in an infinite time horizon model (in which there will be an indefinite quantity of rotations). A central question investigated here is what will be the optimal length of each rotation (that is, the time between one planting and the next).

When the harvesting of one stand of timber is to be followed by the establishment of another, an additional element enters into the calculations. In choosing an optimal rotation period, a decision to defer harvesting incurs an additional cost over that in the previous model. We have already taken account of the fact that a delay in harvesting has an opportunity cost in the form of interest that is foregone on the (delayed) revenues from harvesting. But a second kind of opportunity cost now enters into the calculus. This arises from the delay in establishing the next and all subsequent planting cycles. Timber that would have been growing in subsequent cycles will have later starts. So an optimal harvesting and replanting programme must equate the benefits of deferring harvesting – the rate of growth of the undiscounted net benefit of the timber stand – with the costs of

deferring that planting – the interest rate and the return lost from the delay in establishing following plantings.

Our first task is to construct the present-value of profits function to be maximised for the infinite rotation model. We continue to make several simplifying assumptions that were used in the single rotation model: namely, the planting cost, k, the gross price of timber, P, and the harvesting cost of a unit of timber, c, are constant through time. Given this, the net price of timber $p = P - c$ will also be constant.

Turning now to the rotations, we assume that the first rotation begins with the planting of a forest on bare land at time t_0. Next, we define an infinite sequence of points in time that are ends of the successive rotations, $t_1, t_2, t_3 \ldots$. At each of these times, the forest will be clear-felled and then immediately replanted for the next cycle.

The net present value of profit from the first rotation is

$$pS_{(t_1 - t_0)} \, e^{-i(t_1 - t_0)} - k$$

that is, the volume of timber growth between the start and end of the cycle multiplied by the net price of a unit of timber, less the forest planting cost. Notice that because the planting cost is incurred at the start of the rotation, no discounting is required to bring it into present value terms. But as the timber is felled at the end of the rotation (t_1), the timber revenue has to be discounted back to its present (t_0) value equivalent.

The net present value of profits over this infinite sequence is given by

$$\Pi = \left[pS_{(t_1 - t_0)} \, e^{-i(t_1 - t_0)} - k \right]$$
$$+ e^{-i(t_1 - t_0)} \left[pS_{(t_2 - t_1)} \, e^{-i(t_2 - t_1)} - k \right]$$
$$+ e^{-i(t_2 - t_0)} \left[pS_{(t_3 - t_2)} \, e^{-i(t_3 - t_2)} - k \right] \quad (10.3)$$
$$+ e^{-i(t_3 - t_0)} \left[pS_{(t_4 - t_3)} \, e^{-i(t_4 - t_3)} - k \right]$$
$$+ \ldots$$

Reading this, we can see that the present value of profits from the infinite sequence of rotations is equal to the sum of the present values of the profit from each of the individual rotations.

Provided conditions remain constant through time, the optimal length of any rotation will be the same as the optimal length of any other. Call the interval of time in this optimal rotation T. Then we can rewrite the present value function as

$$\Pi = \left[pS_T\,e^{-iT} - k\right]$$
$$+\,e^{-iT}\left[pS_T\,e^{-iT} - k\right]$$
$$+\,e^{-i2T}\left[pS_T\,e^{-iT} - k\right] \qquad (10.4)$$
$$+\,e^{-i3T}\left[pS_T\,e^{-iT} - k\right]$$
$$+\,\dots$$

Next, factorise out the term e^{-iT} from the second term on the right-hand side of Equation 10.4 onwards to give

$$\Pi = \left[pS_T\,e^{-iT} - k\right] + e^{-iT}$$
$$\left\{\left[pS_T\,e^{-iT} - k\right] + e^{-iT}\left[pS_T\,e^{iT} - k\right]\right.$$
$$\left. + e^{-i2T}\left[pS_T\,e^{-iT} - k\right] + \dots\right\} \qquad (10.5)$$

Now look at the term in curly braces on the right-hand side of Equation 10.5. This is identical to Π in Equation 10.4. Therefore, we can rewrite Equation 10.5 as

$$\Pi = \left[pS_T\,e^{-iT} - k\right] + e^{-iT}\Pi \qquad (10.6)$$

which, on solving for Π gives

$$\Pi = \frac{pS_T\,e^{-iT} - k}{1 - e^{-iT}} \qquad (10.7)$$

Equation 10.7 gives the present value of profits for any rotation length, T, given values of p, k, i and the timber growth function S_t. The wealth-maximising forest owner selects that value of T which maximises the present value of profits. For the illustrative data in Table 10.2, we have used a spreadsheet programme to calculate the present-value-maximising rotation intervals for different values of the discount rate. (The present values were obtained by substituting the assumed values of p, k and i into Equation 10.7, and using the spreadsheet to calculate

Table 10.3 Optimal rotation intervals for various discount rates.

i	T	(Single rotation harvest age)
0	135	(135)
1	70	
2	50	
3	39	(50)
4	32	
5	27	
6	24	

the value of Π for each possible rotation length, using Clawson's timber growth equation.) The results of this exercise are presented in Table 10.3. Discount rates above 6% result in negative present values at any rotation, and so are not tabulated. Note that when the discount rate is zero, the optimal rotation interval (135 years) is unchanged from the age at which a forest would be felled in a single rotation model. But for a 3% discount rate, the optimal rotation interval in an infinite sequence of rotations is 39 years, substantially less than the 50 year harvest age in a single rotation. We will explain why this is so shortly.

It is also useful to think about the optimal rotation interval in another way. Let us proceed as was done in the section on single rotation forestry. The first derivative of Π with respect to T is obtained, this derivative is set equal to zero, and the resulting equation is solved for the optimal value of T, the rotation length. After some rearrangement, this yields the efficiency condition

$$p\frac{dS}{dT} = ipS_T + i\Pi \qquad (10.8)$$

Equation 10.8 is known as the Faustmann rule. It implicitly determines the optimal rotation length for an infinite rotation model in which prices and costs are constant. Given knowledge of the function $S = S(t)$, and values of p, i and k, one could deduce which value of T satisfies Equation 10.8 (assuming the solution is unique which it usually will be). The term Π in Equation 10.8 is the site value of the land – the value of the bare land on which the forest is located. This site value is equal to the maximised present value of an endless number of stands of timber that could be grown on that land.

How can we interpret Equation 10.8? The left-hand side is the value of the marginal product of timber left growing for an additional period. The right-hand side is the value of the marginal opportunity cost of this choice, which consists of the interest foregone on the capital tied up in the growing timber and the interest foregone on the site value of the land.

Equation 10.8 is in fact a Hotelling dynamic efficiency condition for the harvesting of timber. This is seen more clearly by rewriting the equation in the form:

$$\frac{p\left(\frac{dS}{dT}\right)}{pS_T} = i + \frac{i\Pi}{pS_T} \qquad (10.9)$$

Equation 10.9 states that, with an optimal rotation interval, the proportionate rate of return on the growing timber (the term on the left-hand side) is equal to the interest rate that could be earned on the capital tied up in the growing timber (given by the first term on the right-hand side) plus the interest that could be earned on the capital tied up in the site value of the land ($i\Pi$) expressed as a proportion of the value of the growing timber (pS_T).

How does a positive site value affect the length of a rotation?

To see the effect of land site values on the optimal rotation interval, compare Equation 10.9 (the Hotelling rule taking into consideration positive site values) with Equation 10.10, which is the Hotelling rule when site values are zero (and is obtained by setting $\Pi = 0$ in Equation 10.9):

$$\frac{p\frac{dS}{dT}}{pS_T} = i \qquad (10.10)$$

In this case, an optimal rotation interval is one in which the rate of growth of the value

of the growing timber is equal to the interest rate on capital alone.

But it is clear from inspection of Equation 10.9 that for any given value of i, a positive site value will mean that $(dS/dt)/S$ will have to be larger than when the site value is zero, if the equality is to be satisfied. This requires a shorter rotation length, in order that the rate of timber growth is larger at the time of felling. Intuitively, the opportunity cost of the land on which the timber is growing requires a compensating increase in the return being earned by the growing timber. With fixed timber prices, this return can only be achieved by harvesting at a point in time at which its biological growth is higher, which in turn then requires that trees be felled at a younger age. Moreover, the larger is the site value, the shorter will be the optimal rotation.

It is this which explains why the optimal rotation interval for a 3% discount rate shown in Table 10.3 is shorter than the length of an optimal single rotation. In an infinite rotation model, land is valuable (because the timber that can be grown on it in the future can yield profits), and the final term in Equation 10.9 comes into play. In the special case when $i = 0$, however, the interest on this land value is zero, so it plays no role.

It is worth noting that the basis of valuing bare land in the Faustmann rule – the present value of profits from an infinite sequence of optimal timber rotations – is not the only basis on which one might choose to arrive at land values. Another method would be to value the land at its true opportunity cost basis; that is, the value of the land in its most valuable use other than forestry. In many ways, this is a more satisfactory basis for valuation.

This approach can give some insights into forestry location. In remote areas with few alternative land uses, low land prices may permit commercial forest growth even at high altitude where the intrinsic rate of growth of trees is low. In urban areas, by contrast, the high demand for land is likely to make site costs high. Timber production is only profitable if the rate of growth is sufficiently high to offset interest costs on tied-up land capital costs. There may be no species of tree that has a fast enough growth potential to cover such costs. In the same way, timber production may be squeezed out by agriculture where timber growth is slow relative to crop potential (especially where timber prices are low).

All of this suggests that one is not likely to find commercial plantations of slow growing hardwood near urban centres unless there are some additional values that should be brought into the calculus. It is to this matter that we now turn.

Multiple use forestry

In addition to the timber values that we have been discussing so far, forests are capable of producing a wide variety of non-timber benefits. These include soil and water control, habitat support for a biologically diverse system of animal and plant populations, recreational and aesthetic amenities, wilderness existence values, and climate control. Where forests do provide one or more of these benefits to a significant extent, they are called multiple-use forests. One would expect that the choices of how a forest should be managed and how frequently it should be felled (if at all) should take account of the multiplicity of forest uses.

For the moment we will assume that bare land is privately owned, and that the owner can appropriate the value generated by all the benefits of the forest: both timber and non-timber benefits. Our first task is to work out how the inclusion of these additional benefits into the calculations alters the optimal rotation age of a forest.

Once again we imagine beginning at time zero with some bare land. Let NT_t denote the undiscounted value of the flow of non-timber benefits t years after the forest is established. The present value of these non-

timber value flows over the whole of the first rotation of duration T is

$$\int_{t=0}^{t=T} NT_t \, e^{-it} dt$$

Now for simplicity denote this integral as N_T, so that we regard the present value of the stream of non-timber values (N) during one rotation as being a function of the rotation interval (T).

Adding the present value of the non-timber benefits to the present value of timber benefits, the present value of all forest benefits for the first rotation is

$$PV_1 = (pS_T - k) e^{-iT} - k + N_T$$

For an infinite succession of rotations of equal duration, the present-value of the whole sequence is given

$$\begin{aligned}
\Pi^* = & \left[pS_T \, e^{-iT} - k + N_T \right] \\
& + e^{-iT} \left[pS_T \, e^{-iT} - k + N_T \right] \\
& + e^{-i2T} \left[pS_T \, e^{-iT} - k + N_T \right] \quad (10.11) \\
& + e^{-i3T} \left[pS_T \, e^{-iT} - k + N_T \right] \\
& + \cdots
\end{aligned}$$

which is just a generalisation of Equation 10.4 including non-timber benefits. Alternatively, we could interpret Equation 10.11 as saying that the present value of all benefits from the rotation (Π^*) is equal to the sum of the present value of timber-only benefits from the rotation (Π) and the present value of non-timber-only benefits from the infinite sequence of rotations.

A forest owner who wishes to maximise the net present value of timber and non-timber benefits will choose a rotation length which maximises this expression. Without going through the derivation (which follows the same steps as before), wealth maximisation requires that the following first-order condition is satisfied

$$p \frac{dS}{dT^*} + N_{T^*} = ipS_{T^*} + i\Pi^* \quad (10.12)$$

in which asterisks have been included to emphasise the point that the optimal rotation interval when all benefits are considered (T^*) will in general differ from the interval which is optimal when only timber benefits are included in the function being maximised (T). For the same reason, the optimised present value (and so the land site value) will in general be different from their earlier counterparts, and we will denote these as Π^*.

What effect does the inclusion of non-timber uses of forests have on the optimal rotation length? Inspection of Equation 10.12 shows that non-timber benefits affect the optimal rotation in two ways:

- the present-value of the flows of non-timber benefits over any one rotation (N_T^*) enter Equation 10.12 directly; other things being equal, a positive value for N_T^* implies a reduced value of dS/dT, which means that the rotation interval is lengthened;
- positive non-timber benefits increase the value of land (from Π to Π^*) and so increase the opportunity cost of maintaining timber on the land; this will tend to reduce the rotation interval.

Which of these two opposing effects dominates depends on the nature of the functions $S(t)$ and $N(t)$. It is often assumed that N increases with the age of the forest; while this may happen, it need not always be the case. Studies by Calish et al. (1978) and Bowes and Krutilla (1989) suggest that some kinds of non-timber values rise strongly with forest age (for example, the aesthetic benefits of forests), others decline (including water values) and yet others have no simple relationship with forest age. There is also reason to believe that total forest benefits are maximised when forests are heterogeneous (with individual forests being specialised for specific purposes) rather than being managed in a uniform way (see Swallow and Wear, 1993; Vincent and Blinkley, 1993). All that can be said in general is that it is most unlikely that total non-timber benefits will be independent of the age of forests, and so the inclusion of these benefits into rotation calculations will

make some difference.

Some of the results which follow from analysis of Equation 10.12 are:

- Inclusion of non-timber values could shorten, lengthen or leave unchanged the optimal rotation length.
- If the flow of non-timber benefits is constant over the forest cycle, the optimal rotation interval is unaffected. It is variation over the cycle in N that causes the rotation ages to diverge.
- If non-timber values increase rapidly with age of the forest, particularly at higher ages, then the optimal rotation interval will tend to lengthen.
- In extreme cases the magnitude and timing of non-timber benefits could result in no felling being justified. Where this occurs, we have an example of what is called 'dominant-use' forestry. It suggests that the woodland in question should be put aside from any further commercial forest use, perhaps being maintained as a national park or the like.
- One would expect that the optimal rotation interval will lie somewhere between that which comes from considering timber benefits alone and that which considers non-timber benefits alone.

There is no guarantee that the objective function is convex; where it is not, multiple equilibria are possible and so the first-order condition presented above will not be sufficient to determine which is the best of the multiple equilibria.

Socially and privately optimal multiple use plantation forestry

Our discussions of multiple-use forestry have assumed that the forest owner either directly receives all the forest benefits or is able to appropriate the values of these benefits (presumably through market prices). In that case, what is privately optimal will also be what is socially optimal (provided, of course, that there is no divergence between social and private consumption discount rates).

But it is most implausible that forest owners can appropriate all forest benefits. Many of these are public goods; even if exclusion could be enforced and markets brought into existence, market prices would undervalue the marginal social benefits of those public goods. In many circumstances, exclusion will not be possible and open-access conditions will prevail.

Where there is a divergence between private and social benefits, the analysis of multiple-use forestry we have just been through is best viewed as providing information about the socially optimal rotation length. In the absence of efficient bargaining (see Chapter 12), to achieve such outcomes would involve public intervention. This might consist of public ownership and management, regulation of private behaviour, or the use of fiscal incentives to bring social and private objectives into line. The fact that forestland often satisfies multiple uses suggests that there are likely to be efficiency gains available where government integrates environmental policy objectives with forestry objectives.

Natural forests and deforestation

A vivid picture of the pattern and extent of deforestation can be found in FAO (1995). The statistics given below have been taken from that report, and from the survey of forestry contained in WR (1996), chapter 9. The extent of human impact on the natural environment can be gauged by noting that by 1990 almost 40% of the earth's land area had been converted to cropland and permanent pasture. Most of this has been at the expense of forest and grassland.

Until the second half of the twentieth century, deforestation largely affected temperate regions. In several of these, the conversion of temperate forests has been effectively completed. North Africa and the Middle East now have less than 1% of land area covered

by natural forest. It is estimated that only 40% of Europe's original forestland remains, and most of what currently exists is managed, secondary forest or plantations. The two remaining huge tracts of primary temperate forest – in Canada and Russia – are now being actively harvested, although rates of conversion are relatively slow. Russia's boreal (coniferous) forests are now more endangered by degradation of quality than by quantitative change, and the same is true for all forms of temperate woodland throughout Europe, which appear to be experiencing severe pollution damage, with about one quarter of trees suffering moderate to severe defoliation. The picture is not entirely bleak, however. China has recently undertaken a huge reforestation programme, and the total Russian forest area is currently increasing. And in developed countries, management practices in secondary and plantation forests are becoming more environmentally benign, partly as a result of changing public opinion and political pressure.

Not surprisingly, the extent of deforestation tends to be highest in those parts of the world which have the greatest forest coverage. With the exceptions of temperate forests in China, Russia and Canada, it is tropical forests that are the most extensive. And it is tropical deforestation that is now perceived as the most acute problem facing forest resources. In the 30 years from 1960 to 1990 one-fifth of all natural tropical forest cover was lost, and the rate of deforestation has been increasing steadily during that period. Box 10.1 contains a summary of the consequences of tropical deforestation and a discussion of its various causes.

We remarked earlier that natural (or primary) forests warrant a very different form of treatment from that used in investigating plantation forestry. We are essentially dealing here with something akin to the mining of a resource. These forests represent massive and valuable assets, with a corresponding huge income potential. While it is conceivable that a forest owner might choose

Box 10.1 Tropical deforestation

Tropical deforestation has many adverse consequences. As far as the countries in which the forests are concerned, valuable timber assets are irretrievably lost, and the loss of tree cover (particularly when it is followed by intensive agriculture or farming) can precipitate severe losses of soil fertility. Indigenous people may lose their homelands (and their distinctive cultures), water systems may be disrupted, resulting in increased likelihood of extreme hydrological conditions (more droughts and more floods, for example), and local climates may be subtly altered. Perhaps most pernicious are the losses in potential future incomes which deforestation may lead to. Tropical forests are immense stores of biological diversity and genetic material, and quasi-option values (see Chapter 15) are forfeited as this diversity is reduced. With the loss of animal and plant species and the *gestalt* of a primary tropical forest will go recreational amenities and future tourism potential.

All of this is reinforcing a point made earlier: tropical forests are multiple-service resources par excellence. Many of these forest services benefit the world as a whole of course, rather than just local inhabitants. Of particular importance here are the losses of stores of diverse genetic material, the climate control mechanisms that are part of tropical forest systems, and the emission of greenhouse gases when forests are cleared (see Chapter 13 for further details).

Given these adverse consequences, why are tropical forests being lost? There appears to be no single, predominant cause. To some extent, tropical deforestation is a result of the absence of clearly defined and enforceable property rights. The lack of access restrictions must at least partially explain the fact that less than 0.1% of tropical logging is currently being done on a sustainable yield basis (WR, 1996).

Many commentators give a large role to population pressure, especially when significant numbers of people in burgeoning populations have no land entitlement or are living close to the margin of poverty. It is not difficult to understand why governments, in these circumstances and faced with mounting debt and growing problems in funding public expenditure, will tend to regard tropical forests as capital assets that can be quickly turned into revenues. Moreover, cleared forestland can also provide large additional sources of land for agriculture and ranching, each of which may offer far greater financial returns than are obtainable from natural forests.

This suggests that the conversion of forestland to other uses (principally agriculture) may well be optimal from the point of view of those who make land-use choices in tropical countries. Of course, it may be the case that the incentive structures are perverse, as a result of widespread market failure. But this does not detract from the fact that tropical deforestation is not simply the result of ignorance, short-sightedness, or commercial pressure from organised business (although any of these may have some bearing on the matter). It is the result of the patterns of incentives that exist. This way of thinking is important because it suggests ways of changing behaviour, based on altering those incentive structures.

Several writers have developed models of tropical forest conversion arising from optimising, rational behaviour. Hartwick (1992) suggests that the use of any single piece of land will be determined by the relative magnitudes of B^F, the net benefits of the land in forestry (which includes both timber and non-timber values) and B^A, the net benefits of the land in agriculture. At the level of the whole economy, there will be many individual natural forest stands, and we can envisage deforestation as a gradual process by which an increasing proportion of these stands is converted to agriculture over time. The socially efficient rate of conversion at any point in time is that at which these benefits are equalised at the margin. That is

$$MB^F = MB^A$$

One might expect MB^F to rise as the remaining area of tropical forest becomes ever smaller. This would tend to slow down forest conversion. However, this effect may be offset by a rise in MB^A which could arise because of population increases or higher incomes. It is not inconceivable that the outcome of this process would be one in which all forestland is converted. That likelihood is increased if MB^F only includes timber benefits, and excludes the non-timber, or environmental, benefits. For the reasons we gave in the text, there are good reasons to believe that the non-timber benefits will be excluded from the optimising exercise.

Barbier and Burgess (1997) develop Hartwick's ideas a little further. Their optimising model allows the authors to construct a demand and supply function for forestland to be converted to agriculture. At any point in time, the supply and demand for forestland conversion, taking account of both timber and non-timber benefits, can be represented by the functions labelled S_t^* and D_t^* in Figure 10.5. The price shown on the vertical axis is the opportunity cost of land converted to agriculture: that is, foregone timber and non-timber benefits. The demand function is of the form:

$$D = D(P, Y, POP, Q)$$

where Y is income, POP is the level of population and Q is an index of agricultural yields. Barbier and Burgess expect that dD/dPOP is positive, and so population increases will shift the demand curve rightwards, so increasing deforestation.

Box 10.1 continued

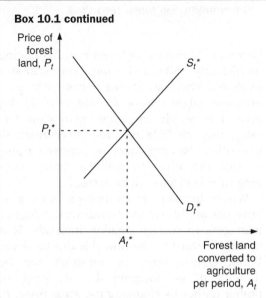

Figure 10.5 The optimal rate of conversion of forested land at time t.

If, however, forest owners are unable to appropriate non-timber benefits, the supply curve will shift to the right relative to that shown in the diagram (which supposes that both timber and non-timber benefits are appropriable by forest owners). Clearly this would also increase the rate of deforestation (by depressing the price of forestland).

We mentioned in the text that the non-timber benefits of tropical forests are received by people throughout the world, not just in the forest vicinities. The benefits are global environmental goods. An interesting attempt to estimate the size of these benefits has recently been made. Kramer and Mercer (1997) used a contingent valuation approach (discussed later in Chapter 14) to estimate the size of the one-off monetary payment that US residents would be willing to pay to conserve 5% of tropical forests. Kramer and Mercer's survey responses gave an average value per household of between $21 and $31. Aggregated over the US population, this is equivalent to a total single payment of between $1.9 billion and $2.8 billion.

to extract the sustainable income that these assets can deliver, that is clearly not the only possibility. In many parts of the world, as we noted earlier, these assets have been converted into income a long time ago. In others, the assets have been left almost entirely unexploited until the period after the Second World War. What appears to be happening now is that remaining forest assets are being converted into current income at rates far exceeding sustainable levels.

Where a natural forest is held under private property, and the owner can exclude others from using (or extracting) the forest resources, the management of the resource can be analysed using a similar approach to that covered in Chapter 8 (on non-renewable resources). Without going into details, the basic point is that the owner will devise an extraction programme that maximises the present value of the forest. Whether this results in the forest being felled or maintained in its natural form depends on the composition of the benefits or services the forest yields, and from which of these services the owner can appropriate profits. This explanation is developed further in Box 10.1.

Where private ownership exists, the value of the forest as a source of timber is likely to predominate in the owner's management plans even where the forest provides a multiplicity of socially valuable services. This is because the market mechanism does not provide an incentive structure which reflects the relative benefits of the various uses of the forest. Timber revenues are easily appropriated, but most of the other social benefits of forestry are external to the owner. The signals given to owners by the relative returns to the various forest services lead to a socially inefficient allocation of resources, as we explained in Chapter 6 in discussing the consequences of externalities and public goods.

These mechanisms go a long way to explaining why the rate of conversion of natural forests is so high, and why forestland is often inefficiently converted to other land uses, and why the incentives to replant after clearing are sometimes too low to generate reforestation.

These arguments have been premised on the assumption that forestland is privately owned and its use correspondingly controlled. But this analysis is of little relevance in circumstances where forests are not privately owned or where access cannot be controlled. There are two main issues here: the first is the consequence of open-access conditions, and the second is the temptation to 'mine' forests for quick returns.

Many areas of natural forest are *de facto* open-access resources. There is no need to repeat the analysis in Chapter 9 of the consequences of open access for renewable resource exploitation. However, in some ways, the consequences will be more serious in this instance. We argued that open-access fisheries have a built-in defence against stocks being driven to zero; as fish numbers decline to low levels, marginal harvesting costs rise sharply. It usually becomes uneconomic to harvest fish to the point where stock levels have reached critical minimum levels. This does not apply in the case of woodland, however. Trees are not mobile and harvesting costs tend to be affected very little by the stock size. So as long as timber values are high (or the return from other uses of the land is sufficiently attractive), there is no in-built mechanism stopping stock declines to zero. Open access also implies that few individuals are willing to incur the large capital costs in restocking felled timber, particularly when returns are so far into the future.

The second issue we raised above was the temptation of governments and individuals granted tenure of land to convert natural timber assets into current income, or to switch land from forestry to another use which offers quicker and more easily appropriated returns. There is, of course, nothing new about this. It has been happening throughout history, and goes a long way to explaining the loss of natural forest cover in Europe, North Africa and the Middle East. The process is now most acute in tropical forests, as we show in Box 10.1.

Government and forest resources

Given the likelihood of forest resources being inefficiently allocated and unsustainably exploited, there are strong reasons why government might choose to intervene in this area. For purely single-use plantation forestry, there is little role for government to play other than guaranteeing property rights so that incentives to manage timber over long time horizons are protected.

Where forestry serves multiple uses, government might use fiscal measures to induce managers to change rotation intervals. It is straightforward to see how this can be done. Well-designed taxes or subsidies can be thought of as changing the net price of timber (either by changing the gross price, P, or the marginal harvest cost, c). We will leave you to deduce what kind of taxes and subsidies would have this effect. In principle, any desired rotation length can be obtained by an appropriate manipulation of the after-tax net price.

Where non-timber values are large and their incidence is greatest in mature forests, no felling may be justified. Government might seek such an outcome through fiscal incentives, but is more likely to do so through public ownership. The most important role for government, though, concerns its policy towards natural forestland. It is by no means clear that public ownership *per se* has any real advantages over private ownership in this case. What matters here is how the assets are managed, and what incentive structures exist.

Finally, we need to give some attention to international issues here. Many of the non-timber values of forest resources are derived by people living not only outside the forest area but also in other countries. Many of the externalities associated with tropical deforestation, for example, cross national boundaries. This implies limits to how much individual national governments can do to promote efficient or sustainable forest use.

Internationally concerted action is a prerequisite of efficient or sustainable outcomes. We discuss these issues – including internationally organised tax or subsidy instruments, debt for nature swap arrangements and international conservation funds – in Chapter 13.

Conclusions

If all markets exist, all the conditions described in Chapter 5 for efficient allocation of resources are satisfied throughout the economy, and if the interest rate used by private foresters is identical to the social consumption discount rate, privately optimal choices in forestry will be socially efficient, and, given appropriate distributions of initial endowments of property rights, could be socially optimal too. Unfortunately these conditions are not likely to be satisfied. Apart from the fact that the 'rest of the economy' is unlikely to satisfy all the necessary efficiency conditions, there are particular aspects of forestry that imply a high likelihood of private decisions not being socially efficient. What are these aspects?

Where forests are privately owned, externalities tend to drive a wedge between privately and socially efficient incentive structures whenever forests serve multiple uses. Forests are multi-functional, providing a wide variety of economic and other benefits. Private foresters are unlikely to incorporate all these benefits into their private net benefit calculations, as they often have very weak or no financial incentives to do so. Non-timber benefits may be very substantial. Where plantation forests are being managed, the presence of these benefits is likely to cause the length of socially optimal rotations to diverge from what is privately optimal. In the case of natural forests, it will also be difficult for whoever has responsibility for land-use decisions to extract appropriate monetary values for these non-timber benefits, particularly when the benefits are received by citizens of other countries. These problems are particularly acute in the case of tropical forests and other open access woodlands.

Governments might attempt to internalise externalities by fiscal measures or by the regulation of land use. Alternatively, public ownership of forestland may be used as a vehicle for promoting socially efficient forest management. The record of public ownership does not, however, give much cause for confidence that forest policy will be pursued prudently.

Discussion questions

1 Is it reasonable for individuals living in Western Europe today to advise others to conserve tropical forests given that the countries in which they live effectively completed the felling of their natural forests centuries ago?

2 Discuss the implications for the harvest rate and possible exhaustion of a renewable resource under circumstances where access to the resource is open, and property rights are not well defined.

3 Discuss the contention that it is more appropriate to regard natural forests as non-renewable than as renewable resources.

4 In what circumstances, and on what criterion, can the conversion of tropical forestry into agricultural land be justified?

5 How will the optimal rotation interval be affected by extensive tree damage arising from atmospheric pollution?

Problems

1 Using a spreadsheet programme, calculate the volume of timber each year after planting for a period of up to 200 years for a single unfelled stand of timber for which the age-volume relationship is given by $S = 50t + 2t^2 - 0.02t^3$ (where S and t are defined as in the text of this chapter).

Also calculate:

(a) The year after planting at which the amount of biological growth, $G(S)$, is maximised.

(b) The present-value-maximising age for clear felling (assuming the stand is not to be replanted) for the costs and prices used in Table 10.2 and a discount rate of 5%.

2 Demonstrate that a tax imposed on each unit of timber felled will increase the optimal period of any rotation (that is, the age of trees at harvesting) in an infinite rotation model of forestry. What effect would there be on the optimal rotation length if the expected demand for timber were to rise?

3 How would the optimal rotation interval be changed as a result of

(a) an increase in planting costs;

(b) an increase in harvesting costs;

(c) an increase in the gross price of timber;

(d) an increase in the discount rate;

(e) an increase in the productivity of agricultural land?

Further reading

Excellent reviews of the state of forest resources in the world economy, and experiences with various management regimes, are contained in the biannual editions of *World Resources*. See, in particular, the sections in WR (1994) and WR (1996). This source also contains an excellent survey concerning trends in biodiversity. Various editions of the *United Nations Environment Programme, Environmental Data Report* also provide good empirical accounts. Extensive references on biodiversity were given in Chapter 9.

A more extensive account of forestry economics (at about the same level as this text), examining the effects of various tax and subsidy schemes, is to be found in Hartwick and Olewiler (1998), chapter 10. Other excellent surveys of the economics of forestry can be found in Anderson (1991), Pearse (1990), Berck (1979) and Johansson and Löfgren (1985). Montgomery and Adams (1995) contains a good account of optimal management, but at a relatively advanced level.

Bowes and Krutilla (1985, 1989) are standard references for multiple-use forestry. Hartman (1976) is an early work in the area, which is also examined in Calish *et al.* (1978), Swallow *et al.* (1990), Swallow and Wear (1993), Pearce (1994) and Vincent and Blinkley (1993).

The value of forests for recreation is analysed by Clawson and Knetsch (1966), Benson and Willis (1991) and Cobbing and Slee (1993), although you should note that these references are primarily concerned with the techniques of valuation of non-marketed goods that we discuss in Chapter 14. Browder (1988) examines the conversion of forestland in Latin America. The state of tropical and other natural forest resources, with an emphasis on sustainability and policy, is discussed in Sandler (1993), Barbier and Burgess (1997), Vincent (1992) and Repetto and Gillis (1988). For the effects of acid rain on forests, see CEC (1983) and Office of Technology Assessment (1984).

CHAPTER 11

Pollution control: targets

The use of coal was prohibited in London in 1273, and at least one person was put to death for this offence around 1300. Why did it take economists so long to recognise and analyse the problem?

Fisher (1981), page 164

Introduction

Pigou (1920) appears to have been the first writer to present a systematic economic analysis of pollution. This arose from his development of the concept of externalities. Despite Pigou's original work, little further attention was given either to externalities or to the economics of pollution prior to 1950. During the 1950s, the theory of externalities was extended and developed, and in the 1960s economists began to turn their attention to pollution using the concept of externalities as an organising analytical principle.

At the same time, other economists began to use the material balance principle as a vehicle for investigating pollution problems. While this approach did not ignore externalities, it had a somewhat different purpose. Most of the externalities-based models of pollution adopted a partial perspective, building a framework for thinking about particular pollution problems in isolation from the rest of the economy. In contrast, materials balance models of pollution have usually taken a more system-wide or macro viewpoint.

Both approaches are valuable. One advantage of the materials-balance approach lies in its insistence that pollution problems have a material – not merely an institutional – basis. This approach forces us to think carefully about flow interactions between the economy and the environment. Production and consumption activities draw upon materials and energy from the environment. Residuals from economic processes are returned to various environmental receptors (air, soils, biota and water systems). Of course, there may be significant delays in the timing of residual flows from and to the environment. So in a growing economy, a significant part of the materials taken from the environment may be assembled in long-lasted structures, such as roads, buildings and machines. Thus flows back to the natural environment may be substantially less than extraction from it over some interval of time. However, in the long run the materials balance principle points to an equality between outflows and inflows, and if we defined the environment broadly (to include human-made structures as well as the natural environment) the equality would hold perfectly at all times.

While the masses of flows to and from the environment are identical, the return flows are in different physical forms and to different places from those of the original, extracted materials. To envisage this, think about the material and energy flows associated with the extraction and transportation of oil, its refining and burning for energy generation, and the subsequent transportation and chemical changes of the residuals in this process. Box 11.1 outlines the stages, and some characteristics of, this fuel cycle as described by researchers in the ExternE project, commissioned by the European Union.

Residual flows impose loads upon environmental systems. These loads can result in impacts which are harmful (judged from a human perspective). The extent to which these waste loads cause subsequent damage depends upon several things, including:

- the assimilative (or absorptive) capacity of the receptor environmental media
- the existing loads on the receptor environmental media
- the location of the environmental receptor

Box 11.1 The oil-to-electricity fuel cycle

Figure 11.1 describes the process steps of the oil-to-electricity fuel cycle. At each of these steps, some material transformation occurs, with potential for environmental, health and other damage.

The task given to the ExternE research team was, among other things, to estimate the external effects of power generation in Europe. A standard methodology framework – called the Impact Pathway Methodology – was devised for this task. The stages of the impact pathway are shown on the left-hand side of Figure 11.2. Each form of pollutant emission associated with each fuel cycle was investigated in this standard framework. One example of this, for one pollutant and one kind of impact of that pollutant, is shown on the right-hand side of Figure 11.2; coal use results in sulphur dioxide emissions, which contribute to the acidification of air, ground and water systems.

An indication of the pervasiveness of impacts and forms of damage is shown in Table 11.1, which lists

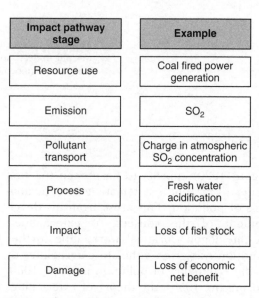

Figure 11.2 The impact pathways methodology and one example.
Source: adapted from ExternE (1995), figure 1, page iii.

the major categories of damages arising from the oil-to-electricity fuel cycle. In fact, ExternE identified 82 sub-categories of the items listed in Table 11.1. It attempted to measure each of these 82 impacts for typical oil-fired power stations in Europe, and place a monetary value on each sub-category.

Table 11.1 Major categories of damage arising from the oil-to-electricity fuel cycle.

Damage category
Oil spills on marine ecosystems
Public health:
Acute mortality
Acute morbidity
Ozone
Chronic morbidity
Occupational health
Agriculture
Forests
Materials
Noise
Global warming

Source: adapted from ExternE (1995).

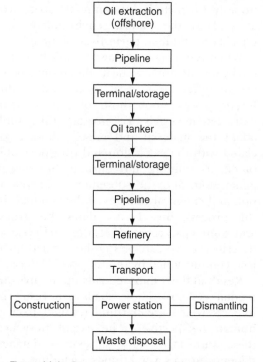

Figure 11.1 Process steps of the oil-to-electricity fuel cycle.
Source: ExternE (1995), figure 3.1, page 30.

media, and so the number of people living there and the characteristics of the affected ecosystems

• tastes and preferences of affected people.

Figure 11.3 illustrates some of these ideas and points forward to some additional matters that we shall investigate in this chapter. Some proportion of the emission flows from economic activity is quickly absorbed and transformed by environmental media into harmless forms. The assimilative capacity of the environment will in many circumstances be sufficient to absorb and transform into harmless forms some amount of wastes. However, carrying capacities will often be insufficient to deal with all wastes in this way, and in extreme cases carrying capacities will become zero when burdens become excessive. Furthermore, physical and chemical processes take time to operate. Some greenhouse gases, for example, require decades to be fully absorbed in water systems or chemically changed into non-warming substances.

This implies that some proportion of wastes will, in any time interval, remain unabsorbed or untransformed. These may cause damage at the time of their emission, and may also, by accumulating as pollutant stocks, cause additional future damage. Stocks of pollutants will usually decay into harmless forms but the rate of decay is often very slow. The half-lives of some greenhouse gases are close to a century and for some forms of radioactive material thousands of years. In some cases (infinitely persistent pollutants, such as the heavy metals) the rate of decay is approximately zero.

You will have noticed that we are not drawing a distinction in usage between the words pollution and residuals. Some writers believe we should do so, reserving the word 'pollution' for that subset of waste/emission flows which has harmful impacts on human well-being. Despite its attractions, this distinction does not in fact get used in the environmental economics literature, and so we shall use the terms residuals, pollution flows and emissions interchangeably. It is not correct, however, to regard emissions and pollution stocks as being synonymous. As you will see later in this chapter, there is a fundamental difference between pollution flows and stocks.

Until recently, the conventional way in which pollution has been modelled in economics has been in isolation from the material basis we have just outlined. While it is recognised that pollution has a basis in the residual flows arising from production and consumption activity, little or no attempt is made to link those residual flows back to resource extraction, harvesting and use. This approach has the important benefit of being simple, and it is the one we shall begin with

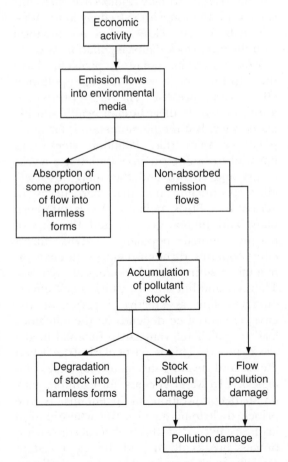

Figure 11.3 Economic activity, residual flows and environmental damage.

in this chapter. However, this simplicity does not come without a cost. In some circumstances we wish to look at the 'big picture', and to see whether pollution targets can be obtained from the kind of resource depletion models we investigated earlier in Chapter 7. Later in this chapter, some further analysis of that kind is undertaken.

Pollution flows, pollution stocks and pollution damage

Before we begin to develop some economic models of pollution, it will be useful to classify pollution in terms of the way in which it is associated with damage. This has important implications for the way in which pollution control targets are set and for the way in which pollution is most appropriately controlled. The distinction we wish to draw here concerns whether damage arises from the flow of the pollutant (that is, the rate of emissions), from the stock (or concentration rate) of pollution in the relevant environmental medium, or from both. We define the following three classes of pollution: flow-damage pollution, stock-damage pollution and mixed stock-flow pollution.

Flow-damage pollution occurs when damage results only from the flow of residuals; that is, the rate at which they are being discharged into the environmental system. By definition, for pure cases of flow-damage pollution, the damage will instantaneously drop to zero if the emissions flow becomes zero. This can only be exactly true when the pollutant exists in an energy form such as noise or light so that when the energy emission is terminated no residuals remain in existence. However, this characterisation of damages may be approximately true in a wider variety of cases, particularly when the residuals have very short life spans before being transformed into benign forms.

Stock-damage pollution describes the case in which damages depend only on the stock of the pollutant in the relevant environmental system at any point in time. For a stock of the pollutant to accumulate, it is necessary that the residuals have a positive life span and that emissions are being produced at a rate which exceeds the assimilative capacity of the environment. An extreme case is that in which the assimilative capacity is zero, as seems to be the case for some synthetic chemicals and a number of heavy metals. Metals such as mercury or lead accumulate in soils, aquifers and biological stocks, and subsequently in the human body, causing major damage to human health. Persistent synthetic chemicals, such as PCBs (polychlorinated biphenyls), DDT and dioxins, have similar cycles and effects. Rubbish which cannot biodegrade is another case. Strongly radioactive elements such as plutonium with extremely long radiation half-lives are close to but not identical with the pure stock-damage pollution case.

Most important pollution problems have the attribute of a stock-damage pollution effect being present. The most prominent are those which affect human health and life expectancy. But the phenomenon is far more pervasive than this. Pollution stocks are harmful to built structures (buildings, works of art and so on) and they may adversely affect production potential, particularly in agriculture. Stock pollution levels influence plant and timber growth, and the size of marine animal populations. Less direct effects operate through damages to environmental resources and ecological systems. There is another way in which stock effects operate. The assimilative capacity of the environment often depends on the emissions load to which relevant environmental media are exposed. This is particularly true when the natural cleaning mechanism operates biologically. In water systems, for example, bacterial decomposition of pollutants is the principal cleaning agency. But where critical loads are exceeded, this biological conversion process breaks down, and the water system can effectively become dead. Its assimilative capacity has fallen to zero.

Stock-flow pollution occurs where pollution damage arises from both flow and stock effects. Waste emissions into water systems are sometimes modelled as mixed stock-flow pollutants. So too are damages arising from the emissions of compounds of carbon, sulphur and nitrogen. It is rather difficult to find a clear example of a pollution type which fits this description perfectly; most pollutants seem to be either flow-damage or stock-damage cases, but not mixed. One example that may fit this description is river pollution by chemical effluents; damage is related to the stock level of biological oxygen demand, but also possibly by the rate of throughput of effluents at particular locations in the river. However, even in this case, it may be preferable to view the problem as one of a pure stock pollutant, in which the stock level is spatially varying within the river system.

Using M to denote the pollution flow, A to denote the pollution stock and D to denote pollution damage, we therefore have three variants of damage function:

Flow-damage pollution: $D = D(M)$ (11.1a)

Stock-damage pollution: $D = D(A)$ (11.1b)

Stock-flow pollution: $D = D(M, A)$ (11.1c)

Optimal pollution and efficient pollution

We now begin our analysis of pollution targets. Given that pollution is harmful, the reader may wonder how any non-zero level of pollution can constitute a sensible target. But a little reflection should suggest that pollution is also beneficial. More precisely, producing goods and services that we do find useful may not be possible without generating some pollution; or goods might only be producible in non-polluting ways at large additional expense. Decisions about the appropriate level of pollution involve the evaluation of trade-offs. Indeed, if we think

about pollution as an externality arising from production or consumption activities, this trade-off becomes particularly clear; it is well-known that the socially efficient level of an externality is not, in general, zero, as the marginal costs of reducing the external effect will, beyond a certain point, exceed the marginal benefits of that reduction.

It will be convenient to divide our discussions of optimal pollution into three parts. In the first we use a simple static modelling framework based around the theory of externalities to analyse a flow-damage pollutant. This will allow us to understand the key principles involved in dealing with the trade-offs just described. In the second part, we use a steady-state model to investigate the optimal level of stock-damage pollution. The third approach employs the dynamic modelling framework that was introduced in Chapter 7. This will generate considerable additional insights into the economics of pollution.

Suppose we wished to find out what is the socially *optimal* level of pollution. How would we go about doing this? You know from our previous discussions (see in particular Chapter 4) that a solution to any problem will be socially optimal only if it maximises the relevant social welfare function, subject to whatever constraints operate. The solution to such an exercise will give (among other things) the optimal level of pollution that we seek.

For much of this chapter we will continue to have a social objective in mind, although it will not be a fully-fledged social welfare function. The objective is to maximise the net benefits from pollution, where net benefits are defined as the advantages society gets from pollution minus the costs (or damages) it bears from pollution. A question that then arises is whether we can legitimately call a solution that maximises net benefits an optimal solution.

It is difficult to give a definite answer to that question. The best way of dealing with this question is as follows. If we are looking at pollution in a model that describes the economy as a whole and if the objective of maximising the net benefits of pollution is entirely consistent with maximising society's social welfare function, then it is legitimate to call the solution an optimal one.

However, we should be cautious about using the term optimal. Very often, economists look at pollution problems in isolation from other parts of the economy, and without making any assumptions about whether or not the current pattern of resource allocation or the current distribution of wealth is anywhere near what could be called optimal. Moreover, we often wish to investigate particular pollution problems in isolation from everything else, such as air pollution in Los Angeles, water pollution in the Rhine or nitrate pollution of agricultural land. In such circumstances, there can be no guarantee that the pollution level that arises from maximising social net benefits does correspond to a full social welfare optimum. It is preferable to describe the net benefit maximising level of pollution as 'economically efficient' (or just efficient, for short) rather than optimal.

A justification for this terminology is that if the net benefits of pollution were not maximised, it would be possible to change the pollution level and, after redistributing wealth, make some people better off with none worse off. The initial allocation could not have been efficient. Only at a pollution level which maximises social net benefits is this not possible, and so it is economically efficient.

If you think carefully about what we have said here, it should also be apparent that a pollution control programme which moves the economy from an 'inefficient' to an 'efficient' level of pollution does not necessarily improve economic welfare. This suggests that one should be wary of supposing that efficient pollution control programmes are necessarily good things to have. They certainly can be in some circumstances, but they will not always be so.

Bearing in mind all of this, we shall adopt the following convention. The term 'efficient' will be used to describe the net benefit maximising level of pollution. Only in the part of the chapter where a social welfare function is being maximised (by an appropriate use of resources) will we use the term optimal. In that case, we can also describe the outcome as efficient because, as we saw in Chapter 5, an optimal outcome must also be efficient.

A simple static model of efficient flow-damage pollution

Our first model views pollution as a negative externality arising from production activities. It uses a static framework to identify the efficient level of a flow-damage pollutant. Static analysis investigates equilibrium states in one single period of time. We take various parameters and levels of exogenous variables as given and analyse the properties of an equilibrium that will emerge in this context. The advantages of a static modelling derive from its simplicity. Powerful insights can be obtained at relatively little cost in terms of modelling effort. This makes it an attractive starting point. The model is also 'partial' in the sense that it examines one activity or one sector in the economy in isolation from any links that may exist between that sector and the rest of the economy. In a later part of this chapter, an alternative model of pollution will adopt a system-wide (general) perspective.

Additional assumptions we shall be making, again for reasons of simplicity, are that emissions have no affect outside the economy being studied and that damage is independent of the time or source of the emissions. We shall look at some of these complications later.

How can we identify the statically efficient level of pollution? Pollution flows are intrinsically undesirable, yet they are largely unavoidable if we wish to produce valuable goods and services. This generates the trade-off referred to earlier: economic activity produces desirable and undesirable outputs. An efficient output level maximises net benefits, the difference between the values of the components generating positive utility and those yielding negative utility.

The costs and benefits of pollution

With flow-damage pollution, damage – the externality arising from the economic activity in question – is dependent only on the magnitude of the emissions flow:

$$D = D(M) \qquad (11.2)$$

where D is the value of damage and M is the flow of emissions. Gross benefits (B) from pollution are given by[1]

$$B = B(M) \qquad (11.3)$$

The net social benefit of pollution

We define the net benefits to society (NB) from a given level of pollution as

$$\text{NB} = B(M) - D(M) \qquad (11.4)$$

It will be convenient to work with the marginal damage and marginal benefits functions, rather than their total counterparts. Thus dB/

[1] Remember that the relevant measure of the benefits of pollution is the benefit that is derived from the output of goods and services with which the pollution is associated, net of the private costs of producing those goods. It will not be an easy matter to identify a particular, numerically specified, form of this latter relationship. There are few difficulties, at least in principle, in estimating consumer benefits associated with various levels of output. Then, if there were a unique output–emissions relationship, it would be a simple matter to map output levels into their associated emission levels. But there are several reasons why we would not expect there to be a unique emissions–output relationship. One reason is that environmental policy measures (such as pollution taxes) alter firms' behaviour, thereby possibly shifting the emissions–output relationship. If benefits have a constant relationship to output, but output does not have a fixed-proportion relationship to emissions, then the mapping of emissions into benefits clearly becomes difficult. However, while not denying the importance of this difficulty, we put it to one side for now and simply assume that there is one relationship of the form specified in Equation 11.3. There is another difficulty to consider as well. The benefit being measured here is net of private costs of producing output. This may change too. Note that if the problem is transformed into one comparing the marginal benefits and marginal costs of pollution abatement (rather than emissions) these problems largely become irrelevant. We will look at things from this perspective a little later.

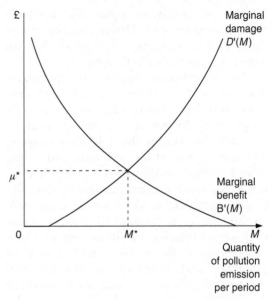

Figure 11.4   The efficient level of flow pollution.

dM is the marginal benefit of pollution and dD/dM is the marginal damage of pollution.[2] Economists often assume that the marginal damage and marginal benefit of pollution functions have the general forms shown in Figure 11.4. The marginal damage arising from a pollutant is expected to rise with the size of the pollution flow, whereas the marginal benefit of pollution is expected to fall as pollution flows increase.

To maximise the net benefits of economic activity, we require that the pollution flow, M, be chosen so that

$$\frac{d\text{NB}(M)}{dM} = \frac{dB(M)}{dM} - \frac{dD(M)}{dM} = 0 \quad (11.5a)$$

or equivalently that

$$\frac{dB(M)}{dM} = \frac{dD(M)}{dM} \qquad (11.5b)$$

which states that the net benefits of pollution can be maximised only where the marginal

[2] If benefits and damages depended not only on emissions but also on other variables, it would be appropriate to use partial derivative notation, such as $\partial B/\partial M$. However, for simplicity, we shall use ordinary derivative notation (such as dB/dM), thereby implicitly assuming that these are single variable functions.

benefits of pollution equal the marginal damage of pollution.[3] This is a special case of the familiar efficiency condition for an externality, as shown in Chapter 6.

The equilibrium 'price' of pollution, denoted as μ^* in Figure 11.4, is a shadow price and has a particular significance in terms of an efficient rate of emissions tax, as we shall discover in the following chapter. There is no market for pollution, and so this price is not an existing market price. Rather, it is a hypothetical price, implied by the solution to a problem in which we are interested. In this case, μ^* is the implied price (in whatever metric benefits are measured) of a unit of pollution at the socially efficient level of pollution, and is equal to the marginal damage of pollution at that level. In other terminology, we could describe μ^* as the shadow price of the pollution externality. If a market were, somehow or other, to exist for the pollutant itself (thereby internalising the externality) so that firms had to purchase rights to emit units of the pollutant, μ^* would be the efficient market price.

The efficient level of pollution is M^*. If pollution is less than M^* the marginal benefits of pollution are greater than the marginal damage from pollution, so higher pollution will yield additional net benefits. Conversely, if pollution is greater than M^*, the marginal benefits of pollution are less than the marginal damage from pollution, so less pollution will yield more net benefits.

Another interpretation of this efficiency result is obtained by inspection of Figure 11.5. The efficient level of pollution is

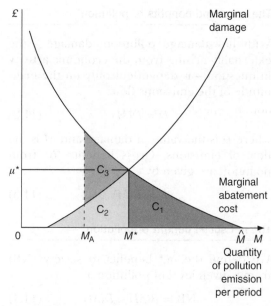

Figure 11.5 The economically efficient level of pollution minimises the sum of abatement and damage costs.

the one that minimises the sum of total abatement costs plus total damage costs. Notice that in the diagram, we have relabelled the curve previously called marginal benefit as marginal abatement cost. The logic here is straightforward: reducing emissions incurs abatement costs. We are supposing that these costs are equal to the marginal benefits that will be lost if emissions fall (and so either output has to be reduced or expenditure has to be made on emissions abatement technology or both).

To confirm this cost-minimising result, note that at the efficient pollution level, the sum of total damage costs (the area C_2) and total abatement costs (the area C_1) is $C_2 + C_1$. Any other level of pollution yields higher total costs. If, for example, too little pollution is produced (or too much abatement is undertaken) with a pollution flow restricted to M_A, it can be deduced that total costs rise to $C_1 + C_2 + C_3$, so C_3 is the welfare loss arising from the excessive abatement. If you cannot see how this conclusion is reached, look now at Problem 2 at the end of this chapter. You should also convince yourself

[3] A proof of this proposition follows. $NB(M) = B(M) - D(M)$. Maximisation of net benefits requires that the following first-order condition is satisfied: $dNB/dM = dB/dM - dD/dM = 0$. Rearranging this we obtain $dB/dM = dD/dM$, the condition given in the text. A sufficient second-order condition for this extremum to be a maximum is that $d^2NB/dM^2 = d^2B/dM^2 - d^2D/dM^2 < 0$. That is satisfied given the slopes of the marginal benefit and marginal damage functions assumed in the text and shown in Figure 11.4. The marginal equality given in the text assumes that the solution is an 'interior solution' (see Chiang, 1984).

that too much pollution (too little abatement) results in higher costs than $C_1 + C_2$.

It can also be deduced from Figures 11.4 and 11.5 that the efficient level of pollution will not, in general, be zero. (By implication, the efficient level of pollution abatement will not, in general, correspond to complete elimination of pollution.) Problem 1 examines this matter.

Steady-state analysis of stock-damage pollution

Our attention now turns from flow-damage to stock-damage pollution. We have defined stock-damage pollution to be the case in which damages are determined by the stock size or concentration rate of the pollutant in an environmental medium. For example, we might be thinking about urban air particulate pollution, in which case what is sometimes called the ambient pollution level would be measured in terms of the proportion of particles, in parts per billion, in the relevant air shed. So for a stock-damage pollutant:

$$D = D(A) \qquad (11.6)$$

Once again, we assume that gross benefits B are a function of the flow level of pollution M:

$$B = B(M) \qquad (11.7)$$

Stock pollutants have the property of persistence, and so the pollution flows accumulate over time. The analysis of the efficient level of a stock pollutant is more complex than was the case for a flow pollutant. Where a flow pollutant is concerned, the fact that damages in any period relate only to the emission level in that period means that time periods may be treated as independent of one another. The researcher can, in principle, establish the efficient level of flow emission in 1995 without reference to any other year. Furthermore, ceteris paribus, the solution for any one period is also the solution for every other period. And it is this that justified the

use of a static model in looking at flow-damage pollution.

However, the essential nature of a stock pollutant leads to a breakdown of this independence between time periods. Stock pollutants persist through time, and so current emissions add to the current and future stock levels, causing damage which will persist through time, even if the emission were to be stopped immediately. In extreme cases where the pollutant is perfectly persistent, the stock of the pollutant will be the sum of all previous emission flows, and the damages that arise will last indefinitely. This is approximately true for some synthetic chemicals, such as heavy metal residuals, and toxins such as DDT and dioxin. More generally, the pollutant stock will gradually decay over time, being converted into relatively harmless elements or compounds. Greenhouse gases, for example, are not perfectly persistent, but do nevertheless have very slow rates of decay (see Chapter 13 for further details).

In determining the efficient level of stock-damage pollution, therefore, we must take into account the fact that the pollutant may accumulate over time. Even if the flow of pollution emissions were constant, the damage associated with that flow might rise. A complete description of efficient pollution must define a path of pollution flows through time, rather than the flow in just one time period.

However, we can avoid the complexities of a complete description by analysing the efficient pollution level in a steady-state situation. A steady-state requires an unchanging pollutant stock and an unchanging pollution flow. How can this be true for a pollutant that accumulates over time? The pollution stock can only be constant if outflows from and inflows to the stock are balanced – that is, when the amount which decays each period is equal to the pollution flow each period.

Assume that the rate of change of the pollutant stock over time is governed by the differential equation

$$\dot{A}_t = M_t - \alpha A_t \qquad (11.8)$$

where a dot over a variable indicates its derivative with respect to time, so $\dot{A}_t = dA/dt$. How can we interpret this equation? To answer this, let us think about the example of the ambient level of sulphur dioxide in the atmosphere. One source of sulphur dioxide (SO_2) is the emissions that arise from the combustion of coal. So current emissions, M_t, add to SO_2 concentrations, causing the ambient level to rise. However, a natural offsetting factor is at work too. Some of the existing SO_2 stock will be transformed into harmless substances by physical or chemical processes, or will be moved to places where it has no damaging effect. In other words, part of the pollution stock decays. Stock decay is captured by the term αA_t.

It is important to be aware that in writing Equation 11.8 a major simplification has been used. By setting the parameter α to be a constant, we impose the restriction that a constant proportion of the pollution stock decays over any given interval of time. Moreover, interpreting α as a proportion implies that it must lie in the interval zero to one. A perfectly persistent pollutant – one for which no decay takes place – corresponds to $\alpha = 0$. What we shall call an imperfectly persistent pollutant occurs where $0 < \alpha < 1$. The case where $\alpha = 1$ implies instantaneous decay, and so the pollutant is not, properly speaking, a stock pollutant at all.

The simplification in all this, of course, is that our specification of Equation 11.8 means that we exclude the possibility that the decay rate (or assimilation rate as it is often called) can change over time as the level of A or M changes. Clearly this is unrealistic. However it helps our exposition to make this simplification. We will return to this matter later in the chapter.

In a steady state the rate of change of the ambient pollution stock is zero and so we have

$$0 = M - \alpha A \Rightarrow A = \frac{M}{\alpha} \qquad (11.9)$$

In the steady state, emissions are constant over time at the level M. The contribution

these make to increasing the stock will be exactly offset by the stock decay each period, αA. Two points should be noted from this steady state equation for M:

- for any given level of pollution emissions M, the smaller is the value of α the larger will be the ambient pollution level A;
- if $\alpha = 0$ (that is, the decay rate is zero and so the pollutant is infinitely persistent) the ambient level will increase without bounds through time as long as M is positive. The pollutant stock at any point in time will be equal to the cumulative total of all current and previous emissions.

We now define the objective function for this problem. The objective is to choose M so as to maximise

$$\int_{t=0}^{t=\infty} (B(M_t) - D(A_t))e^{-rt}dt$$

Because we are restricting the solution here to be a steady-state, the maximising value of M must be the same in every period. So for any one period, net benefit (NB) is the gross benefit of the pollution B less the damage D arising from the ambient pollution level. Thus we have

$$NB = B(M) - D(A) \qquad (11.10)$$

The right-hand side is a function of two variables. However, we know that in steady state $A = M/\alpha$, so we can write

$$NB(M) = B(M) - D(M/\alpha) \qquad (11.11)$$

The derivation of the solution to this problem is presented in Appendix 11.1. Here, we just state the solution, interpret it intuitively, and discuss some of its characteristics. The necessary conditions for a maximum include:

$$\frac{dB_t}{dM_t} = -\mu_t \qquad (11.12)$$

$$-r\mu_t = -\frac{d\mu_t}{dt} + \frac{dD_t}{dA_t} + \alpha\mu_t \qquad (11.13)$$

In a steady state, all variables are constant through time so these two equations become:

$$\frac{dB}{dM} = -\mu \qquad (11.14)$$

$$-r\mu = \frac{dD}{dA} + \alpha\mu \qquad (11.15)$$

Equation 11.15 can also be written as

$$-\mu = \frac{\dfrac{dD}{dA}}{r + \alpha} \qquad (11.16)$$

The first thing to ask about these two equations is what μ denotes. It is a price, the price of one unit of pollutant emissions. But it is a special kind of price: a shadow price. A shadow price derives from the solution to an optimising exercise. So μ is the equilibrium price (or if you prefer, the marginal social value) of a unit of emissions at a social net benefits maximum. As pollution is a bad, not a good, the shadow price, μ, will be negative (and so $-\mu$ will be positive).

The conditions 11.14 and 11.16 say that two things have to be equal to $-\mu$ at a net benefit maximum. Therefore those two things must be equal to one another. Combining Equations 11.14 and 11.16 we obtain:

$$\frac{dB}{dM} = \frac{\dfrac{dD}{dA}}{r + \alpha} \qquad (11.17)$$

Equation 11.17 is one example of a familiar marginal condition for efficiency: in this case, an efficient solution requires that the present value of net benefit of a marginal unit of pollution equals the present value of the loss in future net benefit that arises from the marginal unit of pollution. However, it is quite tricky to get this interpretation from Equation 11.17, so we shall take you through it in steps.

The term on the left-hand side of Equation 11.17 is the increase in *current* net benefit that arises when the rate of emissions is allowed to rise by one unit. This marginal benefit takes place in the current period only. In contrast, the right-hand side of

Equation 11.17 is the present value of the loss in future net benefit that arises when the output of the pollutant is allowed to rise by one unit. Note that dD/dA itself lasts forever; it is a form of perpetual annuity (although an annuity with a negative effect on utility). To obtain the present value of an annuity, we divide its annual flow, dD/dA, by the relevant discount rate, which in this case is r. The reason why we *also* divide the annuity by α is because of the ongoing decay process of the pollutant. If the pollutant stock were allowed to rise, then the amount of decay in steady state will also rise by a proportion α of that increment in the stock size. This reduces the magnitude of the damage. Note that α acts in an equivalent way to the discount rate. The greater is the rate of decay, the larger is the 'effective' discount rate applied to the annuity and so the smaller is its present value.

For the purpose of looking at some special cases of Equation 11.17, it will be convenient to rearrange that expression as follows:

$$\frac{dD}{dA} = \frac{dB}{dM} \cdot \alpha + \frac{dB}{dM} \cdot r$$

$$\frac{dD}{dA}\frac{1}{\alpha} = \frac{dB}{dM} + \frac{dB}{dM}\frac{r}{\alpha} \qquad (11.18')$$

Now, given that in steady-state Equation 11.9 holds, then using that equation and the chain-rule of differentiation we can write

$$\frac{dD}{dM} = \frac{1}{\alpha}\frac{dD}{dA}$$

This allows us to write Equation 11.18' as

$$\frac{dD}{dM} = \frac{dB}{dM} + \frac{dB}{dM}\frac{r}{\alpha}$$

or

$$\frac{dD}{dM} = \frac{dB}{dM}\left(1 + \frac{r}{\alpha}\right) \qquad (11.18)$$

Four special cases of Equation 11.18 can be obtained, depending on whether $r = 0$ or $r > 0$, and on whether $\alpha = 0$ or $\alpha > 0$. We portray these combinations in Table 11.2.

Let us now examine these four cases.

Table 11.2   Special cases of Equation 11.18.

	Imperfectly persistent pollutant $\alpha > 0$	Perfectly persistent pollutant $\alpha = 0$
$r > 0$	C	B
$r = 0$	A	D

Case A: $r = 0$, $\alpha > 0$

Given that $\alpha > 0$, the pollutant is imperfectly persistent and eventually decays to a harmless form. With $r = 0$, no discounting of costs and benefits is being undertaken. Equation 11.18 collapses to:[4]

$$\frac{\mathrm{d}D}{\mathrm{d}M} = \frac{\mathrm{d}B}{\mathrm{d}M} \qquad (11.19)$$

Equation 11.19 has a straightforward interpretation. An efficient steady-state rate of emissions for a stock pollutant requires that the contribution to benefits from a marginal unit of pollution flow be equal to the contribution to damage from a marginal unit of pollution flow. Remembering that $\mathrm{d}D/\mathrm{d}M = (\mathrm{d}D/\mathrm{d}A)\cdot(1/\alpha)$, we can also write this expression as

$$\frac{\mathrm{d}D}{\mathrm{d}A}\frac{1}{\alpha} = \frac{\mathrm{d}B}{\mathrm{d}M} \qquad (11.20)$$

which says that the contribution to damage of a marginal unit of emissions flow should be set equal to the damage caused by an additional unit of ambient pollutant stock divided by α. The steady-state equilibrium for an imperfectly persistent stock pollutant with no discounting is shown in Figure 11.6. Net benefits are maximised at the steady-state pollution flow M^*. In the steady state, A will have reached a level at which $\alpha A^* = M^*$, and both the pollution stock and emissions track

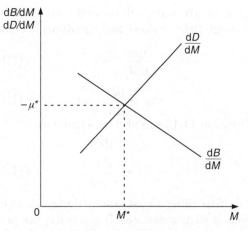

Figure 11.6   Efficient steady-state emission level for a stock pollutant ($r = 0$ and $\alpha > 0$).

along through time at constant levels. You may find it useful to look at Box 11.2 at this point; this goes through a simple numerical example in order to illustrate the nature of the equilibrium.

Case C: $r > 0$, $\alpha > 0$

Equation 11.18 remains unchanged here.

$$\frac{\mathrm{d}D}{\mathrm{d}M} = \frac{\mathrm{d}B}{\mathrm{d}M}\left(1 + \frac{r}{\alpha}\right)$$

The marginal equality we noted in Case A remains true but in an amended form (to reflect the presence of discounting at a positive rate). We show this amended equality condition diagrammatically in Figure 11.8, using M^{**} to denote the equilibrium in this case (and including the Case A equilibrium, denoted M^* for comparison). Note that as r increases above zero, the marginal benefits function rotates clockwise about the point $\widehat{M}$. Discounting, therefore, increases the steady-state level of emissions. Intuitively, the reason it does so is because a larger value of r reduces the present value of the future damages that are associated with the pollutant stock. In effect, higher weighting is given to present benefits relative to future costs the larger is r. However, notice that the shadow price of one unit of the pollutant emissions becomes larger as r increases.

---

[4] We can arrive at this result another way. Recall that $\mathrm{NB}(M) = B(M) - D(A)$. Maximisation of net benefits requires that the following first-order condition is satisfied: $\mathrm{dNB}/\mathrm{d}M = \mathrm{d}B/\mathrm{d}M - \mathrm{d}D/\mathrm{d}M = 0$. Differentiating (using the chain rule in the damage function) and then rearranging we obtain $\mathrm{d}B/\mathrm{d}M = (1/\alpha)(\mathrm{d}D/\mathrm{d}A) = \mathrm{d}D/\mathrm{d}M$.

Box 11.2 Steady-state efficient solution for a stock pollutant: a numerical example.

Let: $\alpha = 0.5$, $D = A^2$, $B = 24M - 2M^2$

What are M^* and A^*?

$B = 24M - 2M^2 \Rightarrow dB/dM = 24 - 4M$

$D = A^2 = (M/\alpha)^2 = (1/0.5)^2 M^2 = 4M^2$
$\qquad \Rightarrow dD/dM = 8M$

Now setting $dB/dM = dD/dM$ we obtain:

$24 - 4M = 8M \Rightarrow M^* = 2$

Therefore $A = (M/\alpha) \Rightarrow A^* = 4$

This result is illustrated in Figure 11.7.

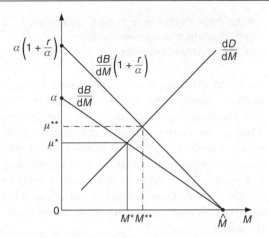

Figure 11.8 Efficient steady-state pollution flow for a stock pollutant (for $r > 0$, $\alpha > 0$).

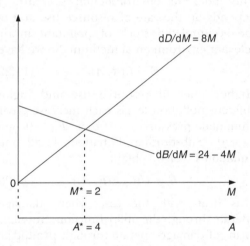

Figure 11.7 The steady-state solution for the illustrative example.

Cases B ($r > 0$, $\alpha = 0$) and D ($r = 0$, $\alpha = 0$)

Given that $\alpha = 0$, case B and D are each one in which the pollutant is perfectly persistent – the pollutant does not decay to a harmless form. One might guess that something unusual is happening here by noting that Equation 11.18 is undefined when $\alpha = 0$; division by zero is not a legitimate mathematical

operation. The intuition that lies behind this is straightforward. No positive and finite steady-state level of emissions can be efficient. The only possible steady-state level of emissions is zero. If emissions were positive, the stock will increase without bound, and so stock-pollution damage will rise to infinity. The steady-state equilibrium solution for any value of r when $\alpha = 0$, therefore, gives zero pollution. The pollution stock level in that steady-state will be whatever level A had risen to by the time the steady-state was first achieved, say time T. Pollution damage continues indefinitely, but no additional damage is being caused in any period.

This is a very strong result – any activity generating perfectly persistent pollutants that lead to any positive level of damage cannot be carried on indefinitely. At some finite time in the future, a technology switch is required so that the pollutant is not emitted. If that is not possible, the activity itself must cease. Note that even though a perfectly persistent pollutant has a zero natural decay rate, policy makers may be able to find some technique by which the pollutant may be artificially reduced. This is known as clean-up expenditure. We examine this possibility in the following section.

A dynamic model of pollution associated with depletion of non-renewable environmental resources

So far in this chapter, we have been using a partial equilibrium mode of analysis for investigating specific pollution problems. That is, we take a part of the economy in which a pollution problem arises and investigate that separately from what is happening elsewhere. A cost–benefit approach is used to decide what is the best level of pollution. This approach is appropriate for addressing questions like:

What is the best level of sulphur dioxide pollution in the United Kingdom?
How much effort should be devoted to water pollution abatement in the Great Lakes region of the United States?

The decision variable being focused upon in this framework has been the rate of emission of the pollutant in question. Pollution flows have costs and benefits. The criterion for choice of the best emission flow is maximisation of net benefits, the difference between the benefits and costs of emission flows. But we also wish to devote some attention to analysing pollution in a more general, system-wide perspective, and to relate this analysis to our earlier study of resource depletion in Chapters 7 to 10. This suggests that pollution can be seen as arising from the extraction and consumption of natural resources.

In this section we use the Maximum Principle to determine the characteristics of an optimal path for a mixed stock-flow pollutant. The stock-damage and flow-damage pollution results are obtainable as special cases of our general result. Our model will be a direct extension of that developed in Chapter 7. We retain the assumption that extraction costs are present, but simplify by having those costs dependent on the rate of resource extraction but not on the size of the remaining stock. We will restrict attention only to pollution arising from the use of non-renewable resources.

There are various ways in which pollution damages can be incorporated into a resource depletion model. Two of these are commonly used in environmental economics:

- damages operate through the utility function
- damages operate through the production function.

In order to handle these kinds of effects in a fairly general way, we use the symbol E to denote an index of environmental pressures. These environmental pressures have a negative effect upon utility. To capture these effects, we write the utility function as

$$U = U(C, E) \qquad (11.21)$$

in which, by assumption, $U_C > 0$ and $U_E < 0$. The index of environmental pressures E depends on the rate of resource use and on the accumulated stock of pollutant in the relevant environmental medium. So we have

$$E = E(R, A) \qquad (11.22)$$

Higher rates of resource use and higher ambient pollution levels each increase environmental pressures, so that $E_R > 0$ and $E_A > 0$. Substituting Equation 11.22 into Equation 11.21 we obtain

$$U = U(C, E(R, A)) \qquad (11.23)$$

This deals with the case where damages operate through the utility function. But many forms of damage operate through production functions. For example, greenhouse gas-induced climate change might reduce crop yields, or tree growth may be damaged by sulphur dioxide emissions. A production function that incorporates damages of this kind is

$$Q = Q(R, K, E(R, A)) \qquad (11.24)$$

where the index of environmental pressures E is as explained above.

The utility and production functions both contain the variable A, the ambient level of pollution. The way in which A changes over time is modelled in the same way as in previous parts of this chapter. That is:

$$\dot{A} = M(R) - \alpha A \qquad (11.25)$$

which assumes, as before, that a constant proportion α of the ambient pollutant stock decays at each point in time. Note that Equation 11.25 specifies that emissions depend upon the amount of resource use, R. By integration of Equation 11.25 we obtain

$$A_t = \int_0^t (M(R_\tau) - \alpha A_\tau)\, d\tau$$

so for a pollutant which is not infinitely long-lived ($\alpha > 0$) the pollution stock at time t will be the sum of all previous pollution emissions less the sum of all previous pollution decay, whilst for a perfectly persistent pollutant ($\alpha = 0$) A grows without bounds as long as M is positive.

Defensive or clean-up expenditure

We now introduce an additional control variable (or instrument), which is expenditure on cleaning-up pollution. In the model clean-up activity operates as additional to natural decay of the pollution stock. For example, rivers may be treated to reduce biological oxygen demand, air may be filtered to remove particles, and so on. We shall measure the level of such activity by expenditure on it, for which we use the symbol V. We shall refer to V as 'defensive expenditure'. This is a term which is widely used in the literature, where it sometimes refers to expenditure on coping with, or ameliorating the effects of, an existing level of pollution. Thus, for example, in some contexts the term would be used to cover expenditure by individuals on personal air filters, 'gas masks', for wear while walking the streets of a city with an air pollution problem. As we use the term here, it would in that context refer to expenditure on an activity intended to reduce the level of air pollution in the city.

The consequences of defensive expenditure for the pollutant stock is described by the equation:

$$F = F(V) \qquad (11.26)$$

in which $F_V > 0$. The term F, therefore, describes the reduction in the pollution stock brought about by some level of defensive expenditure V. Incorporating this in the differential equation for the pollutant stock we obtain

$$\dot{A} = M(R) - \alpha A - F(V) \qquad (11.27)$$

which says that the pollution stock is increased by emissions arising from resource use and is decreased by natural decay and by defensive expenditure.

This completes our statement of the scenario being studied. We can now state the dynamic optimisation problem formally as:

Select values for the control variables C_t, R_t and V_t for $t = 0, \ldots, \infty$ so as to maximise

$$W = \int_{t=0}^{t=\infty} U(C_t, E(R_t, A_t)) e^{-\rho t}\, dt$$

subject to the constraints

$$\dot{S} = -R_t$$

$$\dot{A}_t = M(R_t) - \alpha A_t - F(V)$$

$$\dot{K}_t = Q(K_t, R_t, E(R_t, A_t)) - C_t - G(R_t) - V_t$$

Note that because we are maximising a utility-based social welfare function,

(1) the discount rate being used here is a utility discount rate (unlike the consumption rate used previously in the chapter)
(2) prices are in utility (not consumption) units.

There are three state variables in this problem: S_t, the resource stock at time t; A_t, the level of ambient pollution stock at time t; and K_t, the capital stock at time t. Associated with each state variable is a shadow price, P (for the resource stock), ω (for the capital stock) and λ (for the ambient pollution stock). Note that the shadow price of the ambient pollution stock, λ, corresponds to the shadow price μ used earlier in the chapter, except that the former price is denominated in units of utility whereas the latter price is in units of consumption.

You can see that Equation 11.24 incorporates a production function of the form $Q = Q(K_t, R_t, E(R_t, A_t))$ in which we assume that $Q_E < 0$ (and also, as before, $E_R > 0$ and $E_A > 0$). The rate of extraction of environmental resources thus has a direct and an indirect effect upon production. The direct effect is that using more resources increases Q. The indirect effect is that using more resources increases environmental pressures, and so reduces production. The overall effect of R on Q is, therefore, ambiguous and cannot be determined *a priori*.

The optimal solution to the model

The current-valued Hamiltonian is

$$H = U(C_t, E(R_t, A_t)) + P_t(-R_t)$$
$$+ \omega_t(Q[K_t, R_t, E(R_t, A_t)] - C_t - G(R_t) - V_t)$$
$$+ \lambda_t(M(R_t) - \alpha A_t - F(V_t))$$

Ignoring time subscripts, the necessary conditions for a social welfare maximum are:[5]

$$\frac{\partial H}{\partial C} = U_c - \omega = 0$$

$$\frac{\partial H}{\partial R} = U_E E_R - P + \omega Q_R + \omega Q_E E_R$$
$$- \omega G_R + \lambda M_R = 0$$

$$\frac{\partial H}{\partial V} = -\omega - \lambda F_V = 0$$

$$\dot{P} = -\frac{\partial H}{\partial S} + \rho P \Leftrightarrow \dot{P} = \rho P$$

$$\dot{\omega} = -\frac{\partial H}{\partial K} + \rho \omega \Leftrightarrow \dot{\omega} = \rho \omega - Q_K \omega$$

$$\dot{\lambda} = -\frac{\partial H}{\partial A} + \rho \lambda \Leftrightarrow \dot{\lambda} = \rho \lambda + \alpha - U_E E_A - \omega Q_E E_A$$

These can be rewritten as:

$$U_C = \omega \qquad (11.28a)$$

[5] We will leave you to verify that these first-order conditions are correct, using the method of the Maximum Principle explained in Appendix 7.1.

$$P = U_E E_R + \omega Q_R + \omega Q_E E_R - \omega G_R + \lambda M_R$$
$$\qquad (11.28b)$$

$$\omega = -\lambda F_V \qquad (11.28c)$$

$$\dot{P} = \rho P \qquad (11.28d)$$

$$\dot{\omega} = \rho \omega - Q_K \omega \qquad (11.28e)$$

$$\dot{\lambda} = \rho \lambda + \alpha \lambda - U_E E_A - \omega Q_E E_A \qquad (11.28f)$$

Interpreting the solution

Three of these first-order conditions for an optimal solution – Equations 11.28a, 11.28d and 11.28e – have interpretations essentially the same as those we offered in Chapter 7. No further discussion of them is warranted here, except to note that Equation 11.28d is a Hotelling dynamic efficiency condition for the resource net price, which can be written as:

$$\frac{\dot{P}}{P} = \rho$$

Provided that the utility discount rate is positive, this implies that the net price of the resource must always grow at a positive rate. Note that the ambient pollution level does not affect the growth rate of the net resource price.

Three conditions appear in a form we have not seen before, Equations 11.28b, 11.28c and 11.28f. The last of these is a dynamic efficiency condition which describes how the shadow price of pollution, λ, must move along its optimal path. As this condition is not central to our analysis, and because obtaining an intuitive understanding of it is difficult, we shall consider it no further. However, some important interpretations can be drawn from Equations 11.28b and 11.28c. We now turn to these.

The static efficiency condition for the resource net price

Equation 11.28b gives the shadow net price of the environmental resource. It shows that the net price of the environmental resource equals the value of the marginal net product of the environmental resource (that is, ωQ_R, the value of the marginal product less ωG_R, the value of the extraction costs) minus three kinds of damage cost:

- $U_E E_R$, the loss of utility arising from the impact of a marginal unit of resource use on environmental pressures;
- $\omega Q_E E_R$, the loss of production arising from the impact of a marginal unit of resource use on environmental pressures;
- λM_R the value of the damage arising indirectly from resource extraction and use. This corresponds to what we have called previously stock-damage pollution damage. This 'indirect' damage cost arises because a marginal increase in resource extraction and use results in pollution emissions and then an increase in the ambient pollution level, A. To convert this into value terms, we need to multiply this by a price per unit of ambient pollution.

Note that we have stated that these three forms of damage cost must be *subtracted* from the marginal net product of the environmental resource, even though they are each preceded by an addition symbol in Equation 11.28b. This can be verified by noting that U_E and Q_E are each negative, as is the shadow price λ_t, given that ambient pollution is a 'bad' rather than a 'good' and so will have a negative price.

In a competitive market economy, none of these pollution damage costs will be internalised – they are not paid by whoever it is that generates them. This has implications for efficient and optimal pollution policy. A pollution control agency could set a tax rate per unit of resource extracted equal to the value of marginal pollution damages, $U_E E_R, + \omega Q_E E_R + \lambda M_R$.

The nature of the required tax is shown more clearly in Figure 11.9. To interpret this diagram, it will be convenient to rearrange Equation 11.28b to:

$$\omega Q_R = P + \omega G_R - U_E E_R - \omega Q_E E_R - \lambda M_R$$

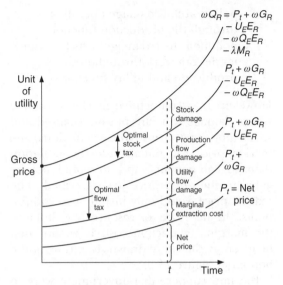

Figure 11.9 Optimal pollution taxes.

We can read this as saying that:

> Gross price = net price + extraction cost + value of flow damage operating on utility + value of flow damage operating on production + value of stock damage

Figure 11.9 can be interpreted in the following way. In a perfectly functioning market economy with no market failure, in which all costs and benefits are fully and correctly incorporated in market prices, the gross (or market) price of the resource would follow a path through time indicated by the uppermost curve in the diagram (and denoted by ωQ_R). We can distinguish several different cost components of this *socially optimal* gross price:

(a) the net price of the resource (the rent that must be paid to the resource owner to persuade him or her to extract the resource);

(b) the marginal cost of extracting the resource;

(c) the marginal pollution damage cost. This consists of three different types of damage:
   - pollution flow damage operating through the utility function;

- pollution flow damage operating through the production function;
- pollution stock damage (which in our model can work through both production and utility functions).

However, in a competitive market economy where damage costs are not internalised and so do not enter firms' cost calculations, the market price will not include the pollution damage components, and so would not be equal to the gross price just described. The market price would only include two components: the net price (or resource royalty) and the marginal extraction cost. It would then be given by the curve drawn second from the bottom in Figure 11.9.

But now suppose that government were to introduce a socially optimal tax in order to bring market prices into line with the socially optimal gross price. It is now easy to see what such a tax would consist of. The tax should be set at a rate equal in value (per unit of resource) to the sum of the three forms of damage cost, thereby internalising the damages arising from resource use. We could regard this tax as a single pollution tax, or we might think of it as a three-part tax (one on

utility flow damages, one on production flow damages and one on stock damages). The three-part tax has the advantage that it shows clearly what the government has to calculate in order to arrive at a socially optimal tax rate.

Figure 11.10 shows this interpretation of the optimal tax rate in terms of a 'wedge' between the private and the social marginal cost. As you can see from the notes that accompany the diagram, the private marginal cost is given by $P + \omega G_R$. The optimal tax is set equal to the marginal value of the three damage costs. When imposed on firms, the wedge between private and social marginal costs is closed. Be careful to note, however, that Figure 11.10 can only be true at one point in time. We know that all the components of costs change over time, and so the functions shown in the diagram will be shifting as well.

Efficiency in defensive expenditure

The necessary conditions for a solution of our pollution problem include one equation, Equation 11.28c, that concerns defensive expenditure

$$\omega = -\lambda F_V \qquad (11.28c)$$

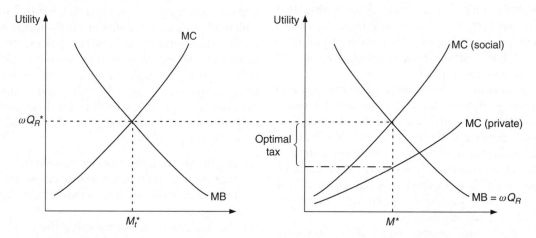

Notes: MC = MC (social) = $P + \omega G_R - U_E.E_R - \omega Q_E.E_R - \lambda M_R$
MC (private)   = $P + \omega G_R$
Optimal tax   = $-U_E.E_R - \omega Q_E.E_R - \lambda M_R$
MB   = ωQ_R

Figure 11.10 Optimal taxes and the wedge between private and social costs.

To understand this condition, let us recall the meanings of its terms. First, the variable ω is the shadow price of capital; it is the amount of utility lost when one unit of output is diverted from consumption (or investment in capital) to be used for defensive expenditure. Be careful to note that these values are being measured at the optimal solution. That is, it is the amount of utility lost when output is diverted to pollution clean-up when consumption and clean-up are already at their socially optimal levels.[6] You can imagine that finding out what these values are going to be is a very difficult task indeed; this is a matter we shall return to shortly.

Second, λ is the optimal value of one unit of ambient pollution; remember that this is a negative quantity, as pollution is harmful. Third, F_V is the amount of pollution stock clean-up from an additional unit of defensive expenditure.

Putting these pieces together, we can deduce the meaning of Equation 11.28c. The right-hand side, $-\lambda F_V$, is the utility value gained from pollution clean-up when one unit of output is used for defensive expenditure. This must be set equal to the value of utility lost by reducing consumption (or investment) by one unit. Put another way, the optimal amount of pollution clean-up expenditure will be the level at which the marginal costs and the marginal benefits of clean-up are equal.

Some complications and extensions

Variable decay

Throughout this chapter, we have assumed that the proportionate rate of natural decay

of the pollution stock, α, is constant. So although a larger amount of decay will take place the greater is the size of the pollution stock, the proportion that naturally decays is unaffected by the pollution stock size (or by anything else). This assumption is very commonly employed in environmental economics analysis.

While this is certainly one possibility it is by no means the only one. There are likely to be circumstances in which the rate of decay changes over time, perhaps because that rate depends on the size of the pollution stock. Of particular importance are the existence of threshold effects and irreversibilities. For example, it may be that at some threshold level of biological oxygen demand (BOD) on a river, the decay rate collapses to zero. An irreversibility exists if the decay rate of the pollutant in the relevant environmental medium remains below its previous levels even when the pollutant stock falls below the threshold level. An irreversibility implies some hysteresis in the environmental system: the history of pollutant flows matters, and reversing pollution pressures does not bring one back to the status quo *ex ante*.

Another way of thinking about this issue is in terms of carrying capacities (or assimilative capacities, as they are sometimes called) of environmental media. In the case of water pollution, for example, we can think of a water system as having some pollution assimilative capacity. This enables the system to carry and to continuously transform some proportion of these pollutants into harmless forms through physical or biological process. Our model has in effect assumed unlimited carrying capacities: no matter how large the load on the system, more can always be carried and transformed at a constant proportionate rate.

Whether this assumption is plausible is, in the last resort, an empirical question. However, there are good reasons to believe that it is not plausible for many types of pollution. The reason we made that assumption was not because we believe it to be true but to

---

[6] The reason why we can use the value lost by dividing expenditure from either consumption *or* investment follows from this point: at the social optimum, the value of an incremental unit of consumption will be identical to the value of an incremental unit of investment. They will not be equal away from such an optimum.

simplify our analysis. It follows from this, of course, that where that assumption is false, the results obtained from the modelling exercise will not be valid. It is beyond the scope of this text to study models with variable decay rates. The suggestions for further reading point you to some literature that explores outcomes in models with variable pollution decay rates.

The spatial dimension

Our discussions in this chapter have ignored the spatial dimension of pollution. In effect, we have been thinking of uniformly mixing pollutants, in which there is no variation over space in ambient pollution levels. The source of the pollutant is irrelevant where physical processes mix the pollutant into a uniform spatial distribution.

But matters are more complicated for non-uniformly mixing pollutants. There, location of the polluting source does matter: X units of emissions from one place may do much more damage than X units from another place. For pollutants that do not mix perfectly, we need a pollution model which 'maps' pollution flows from various pollution sources to ambient pollution levels at various receptor points. Optimal emissions targets require that this spatial dimension be taken into consideration. So it may be necessary to have different rates of tax on emissions depending on where (and possibly when) they are emitted. We will consider this matter, but it will be convenient to do so at the same time as we investigate the instruments that can be used for achieving pollution targets. So we will defer a consideration of non-uniformly mixing pollution until the following chapter.

Convexity and non-convexity in damage and abatement cost functions

In the conventional exposition of the theory of optimal pollution, an assumption is made about the form of the total damage cost and total abatement cost functions. These functions are each assumed to be strictly convex. We will first define the concept of a strictly convex function, and then show how the analysis in this chapter incorporates that assumption. Having done this, we explain why these functions may not be convex in practice.

When one or both of the total damage or total abatement cost functions are non-convex, the marginal analysis of optimal pollution can be misleading. At the least, the investigator must check to see whether equalising marginal damages and marginal abatement costs does, in fact, correspond to an optimal level of pollution (or pollution abatement). The last part of this section explains this point carefully.

Consider a function, $f(x)$, of a single variable x. The function is strictly convex if its graph, when viewed from the horizontal axis, has a smooth and continuous U shape, so that its graph is of the form indicated in Figure 11.11.

More precisely, a strictly convex function requires that if we choose any two distinct points on the function (such as **a** and **b**), the line segment connecting those two points lies everywhere above the function $f(x)$, except at the points **a** and **b** themselves. A function is

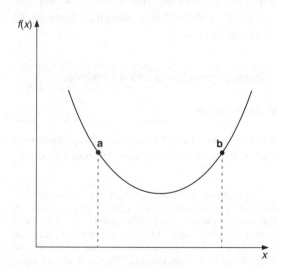

Figure 11.11 A strictly convex function.

convex (as opposed to strictly convex) if the line segment lies everywhere above or on the function $f(x)$, but not below it.

Conventional environmental economics theory assumes that the total damage costs function

$$D = D(M)$$

and the total abatement costs function

$$C = C(Z)$$

are strictly convex functions (where M is the level of pollution and Z is the amount of pollution abatement, equal to $\widehat{M} - M$, where $\widehat{M}$ is the uncontrolled level of pollution and M is the actual level of pollution). In graphical terms, this implies that the functions have the shapes shown in Figure 11.12(a) and (b).

However, as $Z = \widehat{M} - M$, the abatement function can be redrawn in terms of pollution as illustrated in Figure 11.12(c). The functions drawn in Figure 11.12(a) and (b) are for total functions – we have used marginal functions in the analysis in this chapter. So what do the marginal damage cost and marginal abatement cost functions look like

when the total functions are convex? They will be of the form indicated in Figure 11.12(d)–(f). Let us look at this relationship in more detail for the total and marginal damage functions. In order for the quantity of total damages to rise at an increasing rate (as in Figure 11.12(a)) the marginal damage function (in Figure 11.12(d)) must be continuously increasing. The marginal damage function will not necessarily have the same shape as that shown in the diagram, but it must be continuously rising.

Gathering the threads of our argument together, the conventional convexity assumptions imply that, as functions of pollution, marginal damages are continuously increasing and marginal costs of abatement are continuously decreasing, as shown in Figure 11.13. If you compare this diagram with Figure 11.4 that we used in our analysis of the optimal level of pollution (or pollution abatement), you will see that they are essentially identical. We have been assuming convexity in drawing the functions used in this chapter (and, indeed, throughout the book as a whole).

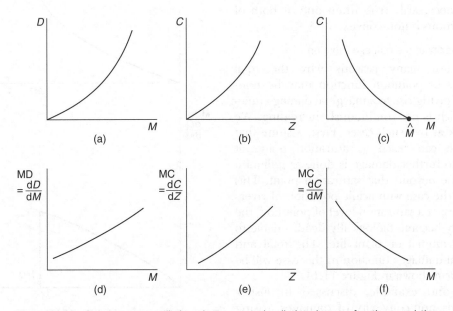

Figure 11.12 Strictly convex pollution abatement and pollution damage functions, and the counterpart marginal functions.

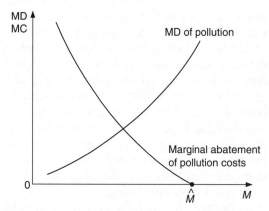

Figure 11.13 The unique efficient level of pollution when damage and abatement cost functions are convex.

Convexity and efficiency

If total cost and total damage functions are convex, it is clear from Figure 11.13 that there can be only one level of pollution at which the marginal costs of pollution abatement are equal to the marginal damage of pollution. This implies that marginal analysis is sufficient for identifying the optimal level of pollution – that level occurs at the unique pollution level at which those two marginal quantities are equalised. As you will see shortly, this is no longer necessarily true when one or both of the functions is non-convex.

Non-convexity of the damage function

There are many reasons why the total damages of pollution function may be non-convex, giving rise to a marginal damage function which is not continuously increasing. We will look at two such cases. First, assume that pollution can reach a saturation point, at which no further damage is done as pollution levels rise beyond that saturation point. This may be the case with acidic pollution of rivers and lakes; at a saturation level of pollution, the lake may become biologically dead, unable to support animal or plant life. The total and marginal damages function in this case will be of the form shown in Figure 11.14.

A second example, discussed in Fisher (1981), is non-convexity of damages arising from aversive behaviour by an individual.

Suppose a factory emits particulate emissions that create external damages for an individual living in the neighbourhood of the factory. The marginal damage initially rises with the amount of the pollution. However, at some critical level of pollution flow, the affected individual can no longer tolerate living in the neighbourhood of the factory, and moves to live somewhere else where the damage to him or her becomes zero. As far as this particular individual is concerned, his or her marginal damage function is also of the form shown in Figure 11.14. However, if there are many individuals living in the neighbourhood, with varying tolerance levels, many of whom are prepared to move at some level of pollution, the aggregate marginal pollution damage function will be the sum of a set of individual functions, each of which has the same general form but with

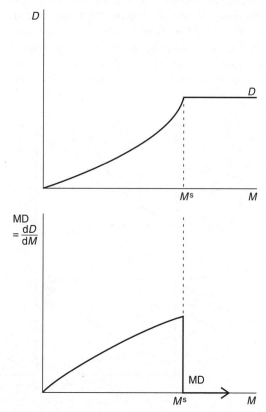

Figure 11.14 A non-convex damage function arising from pollution reaching a saturation point.

differing pollution tolerance levels M^S. The aggregate function will be of the form shown in Figure 11.15, a 'smoothed' version of an individual counterpart. Clearly, the two damage functions are non-convex.

Implications of non-convexity

Suppose the marginal damage function is of the form shown in Figure 11.16, and that the abatement cost function is of a conventional shape. Marginal costs and benefits are equalised here at three pollution levels. To ascertain which is the best (that is, the optimal) level of pollution, it is necessary to inspect the level of total net benefits at these three points, and at all other levels of pollution. The two points labelled A and B are 'local optima', as they satisfy the second-order conditions for a local maximum of net benefits, as shown in the lower half of Figure 11.16. In

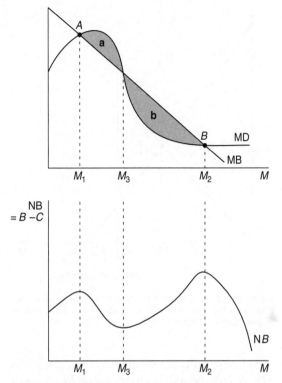

Figure 11.16 The case of a convex abatement cost function and a non-convex damage function.

this case M_2 is a 'global' net benefits maximising pollution level. Note that in moving from M_1 to M_2, net benefits at first fall (by the area labelled **a**) and then rise (by the area labelled **b**).

A more serious consequence of non-convexity for policy making may be its implications for cost–benefit analysis-based calculations of small projects. Consider Figure 11.17. The damage function in this diagram is a little unusual, but an example that would generate such a function is given in Goodstein (1995). Nitrogen oxides (NO_x), in combination with some volatile organic compounds and sunlight, can produce damaging lower atmosphere ozone smog. Initially, the damage rises at an increasing rate with NO_x emissions. However, high levels of NO_x act as ozone inhibitors, and so beyond M_2 higher levels of NO_x reduce ozone damage; hence the negative part of the marginal damage function.

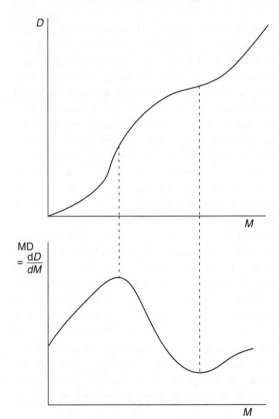

Figure 11.15 A non-convex damage function arising from behavioural adjustments of individuals.

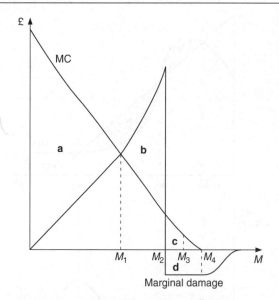

Figure 11.17 A non-convex damage function arising from pollutants harmful at low concentrations but beneficial at higher concentrations.

Suppose an economy was at a point such as M_3. A cost–benefit analysis of small changes in NO_x emissions would suggest that the pollutant flow should be increased, as this will both reduce abatement expenditures and result in lower total damage. But this would be a misleading conclusion. Inspection of the areas **a**, **b**, **c** and **d** shows that the economically optimal pollution level (over the whole range of possible pollution levels) is in fact M_1. The cost–benefit analysis prescription would lead the economy further away from the optimal allocation of resources.

There are many other reasons why damage functions may be non-convex. Furthermore, it is possible (although less likely) that abatement costs exhibit non-convexities too. Space prevents us continuing the analysis any further. An excellent survey of the non-convexity issue can be found in Burrows (1995).

Difficulties in identifying optimal pollution

Most of this chapter has been concerned with efficient or optimal pollution targets. But

many would argue that the analyses we have been through are of theoretical interest only and have little practical significance. What is the basis for such a claim?

The main point here is that it may be impossible to identify in practice efficient or optimal targets. To see why, consider what policy makers must know in order to set an optimal target.[7] They must know the functional forms, and parameter values of, all the relevant functions for the pollution problem being considered. In particular, exact knowledge of the benefits and costs of pollution (or pollution abatement) is required. Moreover, it is not sufficient to know the values of such things as marginal costs and marginal benefits of pollution abatement at the current position; these have to be known across the whole range of abatement possibilities in order for an optimum to be found.

But this puts us in a rather awkward logical trap: empirical data may be obtainable on costs and benefits of pollution abatement, but that data will reflect the position we are in now. But without knowing values of costs and benefits over the whole range of possible abatement levels, we do not know whether the current position is optimal, and whether available data is valid for our problem. This is something of an oversimplification, but it does serve to indicate the nature of the difficulty faced by anyone trying to identify optimal targets. Essentially the problem is one of insufficient information.

Another difficulty faced by the environmental protection agency relates to valuation of environmental services. The cost and benefit functions that enter into optimisation exercises are denominated in monetary, not physical, terms. It is not sufficient to know how much biological damage a pollutant does; we need a monetary value for that damage. But, as we show in Chapter 14, valuation of environmental services is beset by a host of theore-

---

[7] In the rest of this section we shall talk about optimal targets but much the same applies to efficient targets.

tical and practical problems, and there is no consensus about the validity of current valuation techniques. While there are now many good indications of the costs involved in abating pollution (see the suggestions for further reading) valuation problems have particularly plagued efforts to get reliable estimates of the benefits of environmental improvements.

One may, of course, counter by saying that even if we do not 'know' the relevant functions, it may be possible to make good estimates of them and construct policy targets on that basis. But note that this does not really avoid the logical problem just described: knowledge (or estimates) of appropriate prices and costs may only be obtainable when the economy is already at an optimum. Furthermore, information and uncertainty do not simply mean that decisions should be taken in the same way (but have less 'accuracy') as under conditions of full information. As we show in Chapter 15, there can be profound implications for appropriate decision making under conditions of risk or uncertainty.

If this were not enough, there are also formidable computational problems involved. Even if one did have sufficient information, computing optimal targets may be very difficult for the kinds of problems we have considered above. And finally, there are nasty 'second-best' considerations to contend with. If the economy suffers from other forms of market failure too, then the 'first best' outcomes we investigated earlier are not optimal.

Arbitrary environmental standards and precautionary approaches

If it is not possible to set optimal or efficient targets, then some other criterion must be used. Several possibilities exist. For example, targets may be chosen on the basis of health or safety considerations. An alternative approach is one based on what is technically feasible, usually subject to some 'reasonable

cost' qualification. We discuss instruments such as this that implicitly set technology- or health-based targets in the next chapter. Table 11.3 lists some existing environmental standards and the criterion used in their selection.

All of these approaches could be called 'arbitrary standards'. While some more-or-less well defined criterion is being employed in setting the target or standard, they are arbitrary in the sense that the standard is not explicitly chosen on the basis of any comparison of the magnitudes of costs and benefits.

Another influence which shapes standard setting is political feasibility. This has been particularly important in the area of international environmental agreements over such things as ozone depletion, acid rain and the greenhouse effect (see Chapter 13). Lying behind this appears to be a presumption that current levels of pollution control are too little (relative to some unknown 'optimal' level), and that any additional control must be moving in the right direction. This may well be right in most cases but it is, in the last resort, nothing more than a presumption which may or may not be correct.

We conclude with a brief mention of a precautionary approach to target setting. In our discussions of the 'best' level of pollution, emphasis was placed almost exclusively upon the single criterion of economic efficiency. However, if pollution levels pose threats to the survival or sustainability of some renewable resource (such as European marine fisheries or tropical forests) or jeopardise an environmental system itself (such as a wilderness area characterised by extensive biodiversity) then the criterion of efficiency may be regarded as inappropriate. Our analysis in Chapter 9 demonstrated that the efficiency criterion is not sufficient to guarantee the survival of a renewable resource stock or environmental system in perpetuity. This conclusion is strengthened by the presence of uncertainty.

In Chapter 15, we discuss the notion of a Safe Minimum Standard (SMS) and explain

Table 11.3 Environmental targets

Pollutant	Target	Relevant criterion
United Kingdom		
Grains emitted in cement production	0.1–0.2 grains per cubic foot	Best practicable means
Sewage concentration	Max. 30 mg/litre suspended solids. Max BOD 20 mg/litre	1976 National Water Council: Precautionary principle, perceived health risks
Cadmium/lead	Discharges into North Sea to fall by 70% between 1985 and 1995	Health criterion
PCBs	Phase out by 1999	Strict precautionary principle – health risks
Waste recycling	50% domestic waste to be recycled	Political target?
United states		
Particulates	Ambient air concentration of TSP to not exceed 50 $\mu g/m^3$ average annual or 150 $\mu g/m^3$ average 24 hours	Health risks
Sulphur dioxide	Ambient air concentration of SO$_2$ to not exceed 80 $\mu g/m^3$ average annual or 365 $\mu g/m^3$ average 24 hours	Health risks/ significant respiratory problems
Lead	Concentration to not exceed 1.5 $\mu g/m^3$ maximum in any quarter	
International		
CFCs	CFC production to fall to 80% and 50% of 1986 levels by 1994 and 1999 respectively	Political feasibility, with final targets set in terms of critical load

Notes: BOD, Biochemical oxygen demand; TSP, total suspended particulate matter. The concepts of 'best practicable means', and 'critical load' are explained in the next chapter. The concept of the precautionary principle is explained in Chapter 15.

why this criterion is sometimes proposed as a means of formulating policy concerning pollution control. The SMS criterion may be appropriate where there are grounds for believing that an efficiency criterion may be insufficient to ensure sustainability of valuable or potentially valuable resources. When applied to pollution policy, the adoption of an SMS approach entails that threats to survival of valuable resource systems from pollution flows are eliminated. This is a strict interpretation of SMS. As discussed in Chapter 15, a modified SMS would eliminate the pollution flow, provided that so doing does not entail 'excessive cost'. It remains, of course, to determine what is an 'excessive cost'. One may view the SMS criterion in terms of constraints – pollution policy should in general be determined using an efficiency criterion, but subject to the overriding constraint that an SMS is satisfied. This formulation of pollution policy recognises the importance of economic efficiency but accords it a lower priority than conservation when the two conflict, provided that the opportunity costs of conservation are not excessive.

This compromise between efficiency and conservation criteria implies that 'correct' levels of pollution cannot be worked out analytically. Instead, judgements will need to be made about what is reasonable uncertainty, what constitutes excessive costs, and which resources are deemed sufficiently valuable for application of the SMS criterion.

would not be received by firms (although they would by society). Hence, in considering pollution abatement, the control level that maximises net benefits to firms is different from the level which maximises social net benefits.

We have shown how, in principle at least, a policy maker might try to identify an efficient or optimal level of pollution. In practice this is a very difficult undertaking, and may well be impossible in many circumstances. Targets, or environmental standards if you like, are often chosen in practice on the basis of some criterion other than economic efficiency. In the next chapter we investigate which instruments are available to an environmental protection agency for attaining some pollution target (however that target may have been determined).

Discussion questions

1 'Only the highest standards of environmental purity will do'. Discuss.
2 'A clean environment is a public good whose benefits cannot be privately appropriated. Therefore private industry which is run for private gain will always be the enemy of a clean environment'. Examine this proposition.
3 Discuss the relevance and application of the concept of externalities in environmental economics.

Conclusions

We do not expect pure market economies to deliver optimal or efficient outcomes in terms of pollution. Pollution tends to be an externality to the market process and as a result is not adequately reflected in private market decisions. Put another way, while the costs of controlling or abating pollution would be met by firms, the benefits of abatement

Problems

1 Under which circumstances will the economically optimal level of pollution be zero? Under which circumstances will it be optimal to undertake zero pollution abatement?
2 We have seen that the efficient level of pollution is the one that minimises the sum of total abatement costs plus total damage

costs. Refer now to Figure 11.5. Show that if pollution abatement takes place to the extent $\hat{M} - M_A$ the sum of total damage costs and total abatement costs is $C_1 + C_2 + C_3$. Prove that 'too little' abatement (relative to the optimal quantity) results in higher costs than $C_1 + C_2$.

3 Explain the concept of the 'economically optimal level of pollution'. What information is required in order to identify such an optimal quantity? Discuss the relative merits of alternative policy instruments that could be used to attain particular pollution targets.

4 Using Equation 11.18, deduce the effect of an increase in α for a given value of r, all other things being equal, on:
   (a) M^*
   (b) A^*

Further reading

Excellent and extensive presentations of the economics of pollution are to be found in F.J. Anderson (1985), Hartwick and Olewiler (1998) and Fisher (1981, chapters 5 and 6). Tietenberg (1992) gives little attention to the economic analysis of pollution in general, but gives a very extensive, descriptive coverage of specific types of pollution. Baumol and Oates (1988) is a classic source in this area, although the analysis is formal and quite difficult. Other useful treatments which complement the discussion in this chapter are Dasgupta (1982, chapter 8), and two survey articles by Fisher and Peterson (1976) and Cropper and Oates (1992). Smith (1972) gives a very interesting mathematical presentation of the theory. Several excellent articles can be found in the edited volume by Bromley (1995).

The original references for stock pollution are Plourde (1972) and Forster (1975). Conrad and Olson (1992) apply this body of theory to one case, Aldicarb on Long Island. One of the first studies about the difficulties in designing optimal taxes (and still an excellent read) is Rose-Ackerman (1973). Stebbing (1992) discusses the notion of a precautionary principle applied to pollution policy. Pezzey (1996) surveys the economic literature on assimilative capacity, and an application can be found in Tahvonen (1995). Forster (1975) analyses a model of stock pollution in which the decay rate is variable.

Some journals provide regular applications of the economic theory of pollution. Of particular interest are the *Journal of Environmental Economics and Management*, *Ambio*, *Environmental and Resource Economics*, *Land Economics*, *Ecological Modelling*, *Marine Pollution Bulletin*, *Ecological Economics* and *Natural Resources Journal*.

Appendix 11.1 Dynamic optimisation with stock-damage pollutants

The objective is to choose a sequence of pollutant emission flows, M_t, $t = 0$ to $t = \infty$, to maximise

$$\int_{t=0}^{t=\infty} (B(M_t) - D(A_t))e^{-rt}dt \quad (11.29)$$

subject to the constraint

$$\frac{dA_t}{dt} = M_t - \alpha A_t \quad (11.30)$$

The current-valued Hamiltonian for this problem is

$$H_t = B(M_t) - D(A_t) + \mu(M_t - \alpha A_t) \quad (11.31)$$

The necessary conditions for a maximum include (dropping time subscripts for brevity of notation):

$$\frac{\partial H}{\partial M} = 0 \Rightarrow \frac{dB}{dM} + \mu = 0 \quad (11.32)$$

$$\frac{d\mu}{dt} = r\mu - \frac{\partial H}{\partial A} = r\mu + \frac{dD}{dA} + \alpha\mu \quad (11.33)$$

The steady state

The two necessary conditions for an optimal outcome can be rewritten as

$$\frac{dB}{dM} = -\mu \qquad (11.34)$$

$$\frac{d\mu}{dt} = \frac{dD}{dA} + (\alpha + r)\mu \qquad (11.35)$$

In a steady state, all variables are constant over time and so $d\mu/dt$ is zero. Equation 11.34 remains unchanged but Equation 11.35 collapses to

$$\frac{dD}{dA} = -(\alpha + r)\mu \qquad (11.36)$$

Also, in a steady state the pollution stock differential equation

$$\frac{dA_t}{dt} = M_t - \alpha A_t$$

collapses to

$$M = \alpha A \qquad (11.37)$$

Substituting 11.34 into 11.36 we obtain

$$\frac{dD}{dA} = (\alpha + r)\frac{dB}{dM} \qquad (11.38)$$

Note that if $r = 0$, then 11.38 can be rewritten as

$$\frac{dD}{dA}\frac{1}{\alpha} = \frac{dB}{dM} \qquad (11.39)$$

which is identical to Equation 11.12 in the main text.

However, where $r > 0$, 11.38 gives (after some rearrangement):

$$\frac{dD}{dA}\frac{1}{\alpha} = \frac{dB}{dM}\left(1 + \frac{r}{\alpha}\right)$$

or

$$\frac{dD}{dM} = \frac{dB}{dM}\left(1 + \frac{r}{\alpha}\right) \qquad (11.40)$$

Imperfectly persistent pollutants

With pollutants that are imperfectly persistent, $\alpha > 0$. A steady state will be characterised by positive emissions

$$M = \alpha A = k$$

where $k > 0$. The decay rate is positive for imperfectly persistent pollutants. The steady state will be characterised by a constant stock and positive emissions of the pollutant. From Equation 11.36, we have that in a steady state the pollutant price will be

$$\mu = -\frac{dD/dA}{r + \alpha}$$

Perfectly persistent pollutants

Given that, by definition, α is zero for perfectly persistent pollutants, no pollution stock decay can occur. A steady state in which the pollution stock is constant over time therefore requires zero emissions. That is

$$M = \alpha A = 0$$

Also, from Equation 11.36 we obtain

$$\mu = -\frac{dD/dA}{r}$$

Dynamics

To obtain the dynamics of the control variable, M_t, we take the time derivative of Equation 11.32:

$$\frac{d\mu}{dt} = -\left(\frac{d^2B}{dM^2}\right)\frac{dM}{dt} \qquad (11.41)$$

Substituting Equation 11.41 into Equation 11.33 we have:

$$(r + \alpha)\mu + \frac{dD}{dA} = -\left(\frac{d^2B}{dM^2}\right)\frac{dM}{dt} \qquad (11.42)$$

Substituting Equation 11.32 into Equation 11.42 we have

$$\frac{dM}{dt} = \frac{(r + \alpha)\left(\frac{dB}{dM}\right) - \frac{dD}{dA}}{\frac{d^2B}{dM^2}} \qquad (11.43)$$

We can then solve into Equation 11.43 together with into Equation 11.30 to obtain the efficient time paths of $\{M_t, A_t\}$.

The terminal conditions for pollution emissions are $M_T = \alpha A_T$ from Equation 11.30 and

$$(r + \alpha)\frac{\mathrm{d}B(M_T)}{\mathrm{d}M_T} - \frac{\mathrm{d}D(A_T)}{\mathrm{d}A_T} = 0$$

from Equation 11.38.

Subject to some qualifications that are not discussed here, we have the following. If the initial pollution stock $A_0 < A_T$, then the pollution flows are positive and moving towards the steady-state terminal condition. If $A_0 > A_T$, then the pollution flows are kept to $M_T < \alpha A_T$ so that $\mathrm{d}A/\mathrm{d}t < 0$, and the pollution stock will decline to A_T. If $A_0 = A_T$, then we can set $M_t = M_T = \alpha A_T$ so that $\mathrm{d}A/\mathrm{d}t = 0$, and the pollution stock remains at the steady-state level.

CHAPTER 12

Pollution control: instruments

Economists can only repeat, without quite understanding, what geologists, ecologists, public health experts, and others say about physical and physiological facts. Their craft is to perceive how economies and people in general will respond to those facts.

Dorfman (1985), page 67

Introduction

The previous chapter dealt with how pollution targets might be set. In this chapter we shall assume that some overall pollution target has already been determined, and turn our attention to how government might attain that target through the use of one or more pollution control instruments. In the next section of this chapter, we describe a set of attributes that one might wish good pollution control instruments to possess. Having done this, we then classify the available pollution control instruments, describe the way in which each instrument is intended to operate, and assess their relative strengths. In doing this, emphasis will be placed (although not exclusively so) on the criterion of cost-effectiveness.

In the previous chapter we viewed pollution within the framework of the economic theory of externalities. It follows from such a perspective that, if an externality can be internalised, market behaviour could (under the conditions discussed in Chapter 5) lead to an efficient outcome. We show in this chapter that some policy instruments, including emissions taxes and pollution abatement subsidies, have this property and so can be used to obtain an efficient allocation of resources where unregulated markets would fail to do so.

Our initial discussions of pollution control instruments will be set in the context of a uniformly mixing pollutant, to be defined shortly. Some discussion of how instruments will need to be modified for controlling pollutants that do not mix uniformly, and so

have spatially-specific effects, is presented later. We then discuss mobile-source (principally traffic) pollution, and conclude with a brief look at instruments for conserving biological diversity.

Criteria for choice of pollution control instruments

Policy makers have multiple objectives and so there are likely to be many properties that a 'good' instrument would ideally possess. We list several of these properties in Table 12.1. At this point, we shall not say very much about these criteria. Table 12.1 is intended as a checklist of instrument properties to be examined at various points in the chapter.

The importance attached to each of these criteria by the pollution control authority, by the policy maker, and perhaps by the general public will influence the choice of instrument for any desired control programme. It is likely that the weights attached to these properties (and so the selection of instrument) will vary over different types of pollution. For example, where a dangerous and persistent toxin is concerned, certainty or dependability of control is of great importance and will dominate instrument choice. But in general, no single instrument is best for all types of pollution in all circumstances. One criterion of instrument choice – cost-efficiency – is so important in economic analysis that it warrants special attention. So let us now investigate what cost efficiency means.

Table 12.1   Criteria for selection of pollution control instruments.

Criterion	Brief description
Cost-effectiveness	Does the instrument attain the target at least cost?
Dependability	To what extent can the instrument be relied upon to achieve the target?
Information requirements	How much information does the instrument require that the control authority possess, and what are the costs of acquiring it?
Enforceability	How much monitoring is required for the instrument to be effective, and can compliance be enforced?
Long-run effects	Does the influence of the instrument strengthen, weaken or remain constant over time?
Dynamic efficiency	Does the instrument create continual incentives to improve products or production processes in pollution-reducing ways?
Flexibility	Is the instrument capable of being adapted quickly and cheaply as new information arises, as conditions change or as targets are altered?
Equity	What implications does the use of an instrument have for the distribution of income or wealth?
Costs of use under uncertainty	How large are the efficiency losses when the instrument is used with incorrect information?

Cost efficiency and cost-effective pollution abatement instruments

Our objective in this section is to define and examine the concept of cost efficiency. A pollution abatement instrument is cost effective if it attains a target at minimum cost. The so-called least-cost theorem of pollution control states that a necessary condition for abatement at least total cost is that the marginal cost of abatement is equalised over all abaters. This theorem is derived algebraically in the first part of Appendix 12.1. You will find it useful to read that now.

The intuition behind this result is easily obtained. Consider the case where marginal abatement costs are not equalised. For example suppose that at present abatement levels two firms, A and B, have marginal abatement costs of 60 and 100 respectively. Clearly if B did one unit less abatement and A did one more (so that total abatement is unchanged) there would be a total cost reduction of 40. Cost savings will accrue for further switches in abatement effort from B to A as long as it is more expensive for B to abate pollution at the margin than it is for A.

Let us examine these ideas a little further. Suppose government wishes to reduce the emission of a particular pollutant from the current (uncontrolled) level $\hat{M}$ (say, 90 units per period) to a target level M^* (say, 50 units). This implies that the abatement target is 40 units of pollutant per period. Emissions arise from the activities of two firms, A and B. Firm A currently emits 40 units and B 50 units.

The following notation is used. The subscript i indexes one firm (so here $i = $ A or B). M_i is the actual level of the ith firm's emissions, which will depend on what regime is in place. Two particular levels are of special interest. $\hat{M}_i$ is the level of emissions by firm i in the absence of any controls set by government and in the absence of any pollution charges. M_i^* is an emission ceiling (upper limit) set for the firm by the environmental protection agency (EPA). The quantity of pollution abatement by the ith firm is denoted by Z_i, and is given by $Z_i = \hat{M}_i - M_i^*$ so that we assume that whenever an emissions regulation is in operation the amount of emissions the firm actually produces is that set by the EPA. C_i is the total abatement cost of the ith firm.

The total abatement cost functions of the two firms are $C_A = 100 + 1.5Z_A^2$ and $C_B = 100 + 2.5Z_B^2$. Therefore, the marginal abatement cost functions are $MC_A = 3Z_A$ and $MC_B = 5Z_B$. These are sketched in Figure

12.1. Firm A has a lower marginal abatement cost schedule. Does this imply it should undertake all 40 units of abatement? If we wish to achieve the target at minimum cost, the answer is no. This objective requires that marginal abatement costs be equalised. Figure 12.1 shows the situation where firm A undertakes 25 units of abatement and firm B undertakes 15 units. Inserting these values into the two abatement cost functions, we see that both firms have marginal abatement costs of 75. As marginal abatement costs are equal and the total abatement target of 40 units is exactly satisfied, this corresponds to a least-cost solution to the problem.

Minimised total abatement costs can be read from the diagram. The solidly shaded area denoted β shows B's total abatement costs, while the hatched area denoted α represents A's total abatement costs. Any other combination of abatement efforts, adding up to 40 units in total, can only be attained at a higher cost than $\alpha + \beta$. For example, it can be seen by inspection of Figure 12.1 that if each firm undertook 20 units of abatement, marginal abatement costs would be 60 for firm A and 100 for firm B (the numbers we used earlier). Using geometry, you should be able to convince yourself that this would lead to higher total abatement costs. Alternatively, using the total abatement cost functions given earlier, you can confirm that total abatement costs are 1700 at the least-cost solution, and 1800 in the case where each firm does 20 units of abatement.

Some conclusions emerge from our discussions so far:

- An instrument that attains a pollution target at least cost is known as a cost-effective instrument.
- A least-cost control regime implies that the marginal cost of abatement is equalised over all firms undertaking pollution control.
- A least-cost solution will in general not involve equal abatement effort by all polluters.
- Where abatement costs differ, cost efficiency implies that relatively low-cost abaters will undertake most of the total abatement effort, but not all of it.

We shall demonstrate later that some pollution control instruments will tend to bring about cost-efficient abatement but others are unlikely to do so. We will also demonstrate that some instruments can only be cost effective where the EPA knows the marginal abatement costs of all polluters. Others do not require that the agency know this information.

Instruments for achieving pollution abatement targets

In this section, we describe and explain the instruments available for pollution control.

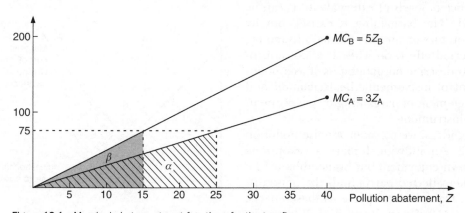

Figure 12.1 Marginal abatement cost functions for the two firms.

Table 12.2   Classification of pollution control instruments.

Institutional approaches to facilitate internalisation of externalities

Enabling bargaining
Legal redress
Education/awareness/social responsibility
Creation of property rights

Command and control instruments

Inputs/technique	Minimum technology requirements, BAT, BATNEEC
Outputs	
Intended output	Quotas
Pollutant	Emission, permits, licenses, quotas
Location	
Of source	Zoning, planning controls, relocation
Of individual	Relocation away from toxic areas
Timing	Noise regulations
Prohibition of activity	

Economic incentive (market-based) instruments

'Pollution' taxes	On inputs
	On emissions
Pollution abatement subsidies	
Marketable (transferable) emissions permits	

For convenience, these are listed in Table 12.2. Our emphasis here is on the method of operation of each instrument and whether the instrument is cost efficient. A more complete examination of the relative advantages of the instruments is left until later in the chapter.

Institutional approaches which facilitate internalisation of externalities

Bargaining solutions

Bargaining is one method by which economically efficient levels of external effects can be achieved. The bargaining is carried out by the generators of, and the parties affected by, the external effect. So while it is not appropriate to describe bargaining itself as a pollution control instrument, the facilitation and encouragement of bargaining by government is as an instrument.

To fix ideas, we consider a noise pollution example. An individual plays a saxophone for his own enjoyment but his neighbour (the only other affected party) finds the noise disturbing. Figure 12.2 represents these effects, the curve MB denoting the marginal benefits

to the musician, and MC denoting the marginal cost of the noise to his neighbour. The horizontal axis is measured in units of noise, M.

If the musician behaved without regard for others, and were not subject to any external control, he would maximise his private benefit at the output M_3, where all his additional benefits from sax playing have been exhausted. But this would not be an efficient outcome. That is found at the output M_2, and can be achieved by bargaining. Starting from the

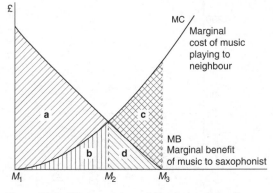

Figure 12.2   The bargaining solution to an externality.

noise level M_3 a mutually beneficial bargain (a Pareto improvement) is possible. If the musician reduced his noise output to M_2 the gain to the neighbour would be shown by the area **c + d**. The loss to the musician is represented by the area **d**. Then if the neighbour compensated the musician by some payment greater than **d** but less than **c + d** both individuals would be in a better position than they were initially. Moreover, since this bargain yields the largest possible aggregate gain, an efficient outcome would have been achieved. Potentially inefficient outcomes can be avoided, therefore, if the affected parties can bargain with one another.

Does the manner in which property rights are distributed matter? Continuing our example, let us focus on two of the ways in which they might be distributed. Individuals may have unlimited rights to make noise. Alternatively, individuals may be granted the right to noise-free environments. In a classic article Ronald Coase (1960) argued that where the costs of bargaining are negligible efficient outcomes will be achieved through bargaining between affected parties. Moreover, he claimed that the same efficient outcome would be attained irrespective of the way in which property rights are distributed. The distribution of property rights does matter, but only in determining the division of the net gains which arise from the bargain. They do not matter in terms of the way in which resources are eventually allocated. This second result is commonly known as the Coase Theorem.

To see the basis for the Coase Theorem, look again at Figure 12.2. If property rights were vested in the producer of noise he would have no legal liability for any noise interference, and the pre-bargaining level of noise would be M_3. However, one would expect bargaining to take place between the affected parties, leading to the bargaining outcome M_2. If, on the other hand, people had the right to a noise-free environment, the musician would not be entitled to generate noise, and so the pre-bargaining pollu-

tion level would be M_1. However, the two parties still have the possibility of a mutually beneficial transaction. The neighbour allows the musician to produce M_2 without seeking redress through the courts. In return, the musician would compensate the neighbour by an amount up to the magnitude of the area **a** in Figure 12.2. You should convince yourself that such a deal would benefit both individuals.

The likelihood of such a bargain taking place is low unless enforceable property rights exist. Enforceability refers to the fact that the judicial system would impose penalties on one individual infringing another's property right. A bargain can be thought of as a contract whereby the holder of property rights agrees to waive any claim for damages resulting from the actions of the other party, in exchange for some compensation. If enforceable property rights do not exist, contractors could renege on contracts after compensations have been paid without fear of redress. The existence of property rights and of a legal system which guarantees the enforcement of contracts and of property rights appear to be necessary conditions for bargaining solutions.

Coase's results show that bargaining between affected parties may allow inefficient outcomes to be avoided without the need for any government intervention. Self-interested behaviour ensures that resources will be deployed efficiently, even where external effects take place. Secondly, bargaining leads to an efficient outcome irrespective of how property rights are initially distributed. If efficiency were the only thing that mattered, then this means that as long as property rights do exist, it is irrelevant how they are distributed. However, efficiency is not the only thing that matters, and so in general the initial distribution of property rights is relevant.

Limitations of bargaining solutions to environmental pollution problems

Bargaining is unlikely to take place if property rights do not exist. Two other conditions will also affect the probability of bargaining solutions taking place. First, the number of affected parties must be relatively small; if not, the costs and difficulties of bargaining may prevent the outcome being realised. Second, the affected parties should be identifiable. Once again, it is difficult to conceive of efficient bargains being conducted if it were not possible to identify and organise all parties affected by the activity.

Several factors limit the extent to which bargaining is likely to be a viable means of dealing with inefficiencies where the natural environment is concerned. The most important concerns the possibility of efficient bargaining in choices about the use of public goods. Externalities may be either private or public. A private externality occurs where the external effect in question is a private good. In our example the externality is private as, by assumption, the noise pollution spillover affects no third party. A public externality exists where the external effect is a public good. In this case, consumption of the externality by one person does not prevent another person also consuming it. For public goods, the free-rider problem and the incentive to misrepresent preferences (see Chapter 6 for details) lead one to suppose that bargaining will not yield efficient outcomes.

A second reason why bargaining solutions are of limited relevance to most environmental problems concerns the numbers of affected parties. Typically, environmental degradation affects many people. It is often difficult to identify all affected parties, and the costs of organising people to undertake a bargaining exercise can be enormous. If the number of affected individuals is large and the externality is public, the scope for efficient bargaining behaviour seems very restricted.

A third issue of interest is the possibility of intertemporal bargaining, including bargaining between current and future generations. Many environmental externalities cut across generations – our behaviour today imposes externalities on future persons.

While bargaining between affected individuals at one point in time seems feasible, it is difficult to imagine that this could happen between representatives of the present generation and those not yet living.

What does all this imply about the role for government? If one believes that bargaining is likely to result in efficiency gains, then government should aim to develop and sustain an institutional structure that maximises the scope for bargaining behaviour. Wherever practicable, property rights should be defined and allocated in a clearly defined manner. It may also be the case that government should take responsibility for environmental monitoring so as to identify pollution producers and recipients. Information from such monitoring exercises can then be made available to affected parties. Finally, access to the judicial system should be easy and cheap. If the legal system works to allow redress of grievances for damages caused by others, then these other parties will face a potential charge for any damages they cause. This may be sufficient in some situations for efficient outcomes to be achieved.

Legal redress of grievances

The role that may be played by the judicial system in helping to bring about efficient outcomes is implicit in our discussion of bargaining, so little more need be said about this. It is increasingly the case that emphasis is being placed on the development of judicial instruments as vehicles for pollution control. Most of these instruments are concerned, in one way or another, with establishing the legal liability of polluters for the damages that they generate. An interesting development is the process of establishing legal liability throughout the life cycle of a product, using the principle that producers are responsible for damage from 'cradle to grave'. It is important to note, however, that pollution targets sought by the EPA may not be equivalent to those we have described as 'efficient', and so may generate different outcomes from those achieved through bargaining.

Creation of enforceable property rights

Again, there is little more that need be said here, except that the creation of property rights is particularly important in two circumstances. Firstly, for economies in a state of transition to a market economy: in those economies, cultural and political practice involved mechanisms other than markets for allocating resources; these may have been effective at one time, but subsequently broke down in a process of socio-economic change. Secondly, and more generally, wherever property rights do not exist in environmental resources, the use of those resources is likely to be suboptimal. This came across strongly in our earlier examination of renewable resources. Developing appropriate and enforceable conditions of use offers the prospect of large efficiency gains under these circumstances.

Development of social responsibility

Educational and cultural socialisation measures can be valuable methods of helping to attain general environmental goals, although they are unlikely to be dependable in achieving specific targets. Their use may be appropriate in some circumstances. Government can encourage the education of individuals who may be affected by pollution, develop awareness of the environmental impacts of economic activity, and try to foster a business environment in which public opinion and market pressure elicit environmentally responsible behaviour. We leave it to the reader to assess the efficacy and desirability of these instruments.

Command and control instruments

We next look at a set of instruments that comprise quantitative and qualitative controls and regulations – often called command and control instruments. The controls may apply to the quantities of outputs produced (either the intended final output or the pollutant itself), to the quantities of inputs used, to the technology used in production processes, or to the location or timing of polluting activities. Our discussion of command and control instruments will be rather selective; details of where a more comprehensive coverage can be found will be given in the recommendations for further reading at the end of the chapter. Some examples of the use of command and control regulatory instruments are given in Box 12.1.

Instruments regulating the permissible quantity of emission

As pollution targets are often specified in terms of a total quantity of allowed emissions (or, equivalently, in terms of a quantity of required abatement), it follows that one instrument for implementing such a target is direct regulation of the quantity of pollution emitted by each potential source. This will necessitate the EPA adopting some criterion for apportioning the overall target among the individual sources. A permit or licence can then be allocated to each source, such that the aggregate target is met. Command and control instruments do not include the case where permits can be transferred by private bargains between different sources.

Successful operation of licence schemes is unlikely if polluters believe their actions are not observed, or if the penalties on polluters not meeting restrictions are low relative to the cost of abatement. Licence schemes will have to be supported, therefore, by effective pollution monitoring systems and by sufficiently harsh penalties for non-compliance.

The use of such regulations can be cost efficient, as it is possible in principle to choose emission standards for each polluter that result in the marginal cost of abatement being equal over all polluters. However, to do this, the control authority would need to know the abatement cost function for each firm. We explain this more formally in Appendix 12.1.

The EPA is very unlikely to have sufficient information to set standards for each polluter in this way. The costs of collecting informa-

Box 12.1 Command and control instruments and the United States Environmental Protection Agency

In this box, we shall look at some aspects of the United States regulatory approach to pollution control in the areas of emissions and effluent standards, and product bans. Our discussion follows that of a recent paper by Van Houtven and Cropper (1996) which, among other things, attempted to infer what value the United States Environmental Protection Agency (EPA) places on saving lives.

The EPA is responsible for issuing regulations to protect the public (and the natural environment) from unreasonable degrees of exposure to pollution. In issuing regulations and in setting standards, EPA must work within constraints set by the US Congress. These are briefly described for the set of regulatory areas studied by Van Houtven and Cropper in Table 12.3. It should be noted that the controls shown in the table are not representative of US environmental regulation in general as, rather unusually, two of the three categories considered require that a particular kind of balancing be carried out. Typically, quantitative regulations have focused mainly on the benefits of control.

In the discussions that follow, we consider only some specific areas of control; you should note that the coverage of the relevant legislation is much broader than these areas alone. Under the provisions of the TSCA, EPA issues bans on the use of asbestos in particular uses. As TSCA requires balancing, the EPA is required to consider the costs of regulation (in money terms) and the benefits of regulation (in terms of cancer cases avoided because of a ban). Of the 39 uses of asbestos it investigated, EPA was able to measure costs and benefits in 31 cases. Of these, 21 products were banned. Van Houtven and Cropper use data on the costs of regulation and the number of lives expected to be saved for each of the 39 cases to estimate the value of a statistical life that is implied by EPA decisions. By definition, if an action results in the expected level of deaths falling by one person over some relevant time period, that action has saved one statistical life.

Van Houtven and Cropper found that, on average, products were banned when the cost of saving one life was below $49 million (in 1989 US dollar prices). The EPA regulators appear, therefore, to value a life saved at $49 million. In other words, if that figure were used to put a money value on one life saved, a formal (economic) cost–benefit analysis would result in the same decisions as those made by the EPA.

FIFRA also requires that balancing be used by the EPA in determining whether particular uses of pesticides should be banned or restricted in their manner of application. Van Houtven and Cropper investigated 245 food crop applications of 19 pesticide active ingredients. Of these, 96 applications were banned after EPA Special Reviews. Van Houtven and Cropper estimated that the value of a fatal cancer avoided implied by EPA decisions was $51.51 million (in 1989 US dollar prices), a figure which is close to that for its asbestos regulations.

The two authors note that these values are considerably higher than the values which people seem to be willing to pay to reduce the risk of death. For example, one highly respected study (Viscusi, 1992, 1993) estimated the compensating wage differential required by workers to take on high-risk jobs. The wage differentials discovered imply a value of a statistical life of $5 million, just one tenth of that implied by EPA regulations.

Van Houtven and Cropper also investigated controls of toxic air pollutants – specifically benzene, arsenic, asbestos and mercury – under the provisions of the Clean Air Act. Prior to 1987, the implied value of a fatal cancer avoided was about $16 million. From Table 12.3 you can see that the Clean Air Act requires the EPA to only take account of the benefits of control in setting regulations over toxic air emissions. However, in 1987 a Court of Appeals ruling found that EPA has been (unlawfully) considering both benefits and costs in setting ambient standards. As a result, EPA tightened its standards (so that control was extended to cover emissions for which it previously felt that the cost-to-benefit ratio was too high to justify control). The implied value of a statistical life for EPA decisions after 1987 rose to $194 million.

Table 12.3 Factors to be considered by the United States EPA in setting standards and regulations.

Statute	Coverage	Factors to be considered in setting standards
Clean Air Act	Ambient air quality standards	Benefits of regulation but not costs
Clean Water Act	Effluent standards	Benefits and costs of regulation (but balancing not required)
Federal Insecticide, Fungicide, and Rodenticide Act (FIFRA)	Insecticides, fungicides, rodenticides and pesticides	Benefits and costs of regulation to be balanced
Toxic Substances Control Act (TSCA)	Toxic substances	Benefits and costs of regulation to be balanced

Box 12.1 continued

Our discussions show that the EPA is doing something similar to what we call in this chapter cost-effectiveness analysis. In deciding which products to ban, for example, it appears to be estimating the relative costs of each possible ban. Those with the lower costs are banned, those with higher costs are not banned. In this sense, the regulations can be called cost effective. However, even where 'balancing' is undertaken, the EPA is balancing its own assessment of the benefits of control against the actual costs of control. It is not equating the marginal cost and marginal benefit as revealed by the public, and so its controls are not economically efficient in the sense described in Chapter 11.

---

tion about abatement costs for each emitter could be prohibitive, and may outweigh the potential efficiency gains arising from intervention. An additional complication arises from information asymmetries and weak or perverse incentives to disclose information. The asymmetry arises from the fact that while firms may know their control cost functions, the regulator will not. Firms have strong incentives to withhold information, or worse, to provide misleading information. As a result, quantitative controls are likely to use some arbitrary method of distributing the abatement burden over firms. The controls will then not be cost efficient, as they will not attain a pollution reduction target at least cost. A second problem associated with command and control quantity restrictions is that they do not generate strong incentives to promote dynamic efficiency. We explain what this concept means later.

Instruments which impose minimum technology requirements

Another command and control approach to pollution control involves specifying required characteristics of production processes or capital equipment used. In other words, minimum technology requirements are imposed upon potential polluters. Examples of this approach have been variously known as 'best practicable means' (BPM), 'best available technology' (BAT) and 'best available technology not entailing excessive cost' (BATNEEC). Some further information on technology controls is given in Box 12.2.

In some variants of this approach, specific techniques are mandated, such as require-ments to use flue gas desulphurisation equipment in power generation, designation of minimum stack heights, the installation of catalytic converters in vehicle exhaust systems, and maximum permitted lead content in engine fuels. In other variants, production must employ the (technically) best technique available (sometimes subject to a reasonable cost qualification). The specific technique adopted is sometimes negotiated between the EPA and the regulated parties on an individual basis.

Required technology controls tend to somewhat blur the pollution target/pollution instrument distinction we have been drawing in this and the previous chapter. The target actually pursued tends to emerge jointly with the administration of the instrument. In other words, there is not an explicit definition of a target first, and then the pursuit of that predetermined target subsequently. Moreover, the manner in which the target is set may not require any comparison of the benefits and costs of the control programme. Emphasis is given almost exclusively to the costs of pollution reduction technologies, and in particular to what kind of cost premium is involved in the use of the technically best method as compared with its lower ranked alternatives.

These comments imply that the instrument tends not to be dependable, as the outcome is not known and cannot be calculated *a priori*. Much depends on the negotiation process taking place between the regulator and regulated parties. However, technology-based instruments can be very powerful in the sense of achieving large reductions in emis-

Box 12.2 Required technology controls

Regulations mandating the use of particular technologies are common forms of pollution control instrument in Europe, North America and the other OECD countries. In the UK, a criterion underlying required technology standards has been 'best practicable means'. The adjective *practicable* has never been given a precise legal definition, but the 1956 Clean Air Act stated that

> Practicable means reasonably practicable having regard, amongst other things, to local conditions and circumstances, to the financial implications and the current state of technology.

Despite an element of tautology in this statement, it can be interpreted as meaning that a practicable control technology should be technologically effective, subject to the constraint that it is not excessively costly. In recent years, the cost qualification has been given greater priority, and has been enshrined in the principle of BATNEEC: the best available technology not entailing excessive cost. This puts the instrument closer to the kind advocated by economists, as the 'excessive cost' condition implies a quasi cost–benefit calculation in the administration of the instrument.

However, while the cost of control is often measured by the regulator in money terms (for example, the additional money cost of one technique over another), the benefits are not usually measured in money terms; instead, benefits are seen in terms of reduced probabilities of death or serious damage to health. In this sense, although some balancing of costs against benefits does often take place, the approach being used is not 'cost–benefit analysis' in the economics sense of that term. Rather than using the public's estimate of benefits (in terms of willingness to pay) the regulator has to come to a view as to what cost is reasonable to save a life or reduce a health risk. Equivalent kinds of money-cost relative to health-benefit comparisons are also made in the US regulatory system.

The manner in which technology-based instruments have been implemented varies considerably between countries. In the UK, officials of the Inspectorate of Pollution negotiate controls with plant managers, but have the right, in the last instance, to require the adoption of certain control technologies. The United States Environmental Protection Agency administers a rather more uniform control programme; in 1990, Congress required EPA to establish technology-based standards for about 200 specific pollutants.

sions quickly, particularly when technological 'fixes' are available but not widely adopted. As shown in Box 12.2, the required use of specified pollution control technology has been the dominant instrument for environmental protection in most OECD economies. Technology controls have almost certainly resulted in huge reductions in pollution levels compared with what would be expected in their absence. However, they are usually not cost efficient. And as with all command and control approaches, the instrument does not intrinsically focus abatement effort on polluters that can abate at least cost. Technology regulation instruments also tend to be inflexible, and they do not generate strong incentives to promote dynamic efficiency.

Location

Pollution control objectives, in so far as they are concerned only with reducing human exposure to pollutants, could be met by moving affected persons to areas away from pollution sources. This is only relevant where the pollutant is not uniformly mixing, so that its effects are spatially differentiated. Implementing this *ex ante*, by zoning or planning decision, is relatively common. *Ex post* relocation decisions are more rare due to their draconian nature. There have been examples of people being removed from heavily contaminated areas, including movements away from irradiated sites such as Chernobyl, Times Beach (Missouri) and Love Canal (New York). However, it has been far more common to move pollution sources away from areas where people will be affected, or to use planning regulations to ensure separation. Planning controls and other forms of direct regulation directed at location have a large role to play in the control of pollution with localised impacts and for mobile source pollution. They are also used to prevent harmful spatial clustering of emission sources.

Location decisions of this kind will not be appropriate in many circumstances. Moving people away from a pollution source can not, for example, reduce impacts on ecosystems. Relocating (or planning the location of new) emission sources has wider applicability, but will be of no use in cases where pollution is uniformly mixing.

Economic incentive (quasi-market) instruments

Emissions taxes and pollution abatement subsidies

We begin with the simple case of uniformly mixed pollutants, for which the value of the damage created by an emission is independent of the location of its source. It is then shown later that the results also apply, with minor amendment, to non-uniformly mixing pollutants.

Taxes and subsidies operate through modification of relative prices. Taxation may be imposed either on the levels of particular inputs (such as coal), or on the levels of emissions. We concentrate on the latter case. Subsidies can be paid for pollution abatement. Taxes and subsidies exhibit a fundamental symmetry: the short-run incentive effects of an emissions tax and an abatement subsidy are essentially the same. References to tax schemes, therefore, also apply to abatement subsidy programmes. However, the long-run effects of subsidies may be different from those of taxes, given their different distributional consequences.

A tax on pollutant emissions has for long been the standard form of instrument advocated by economists to achieve a pollution target. It eliminates the wedge (created by pollution damage) between private and socially efficient prices; the tax brings private prices into line with social prices. When the target is to achieve an efficient level of pollution (in the sense explained in the previous chapter), the tax should be applied on each unit of pollution emitted at a rate equal to the monetary value of marginal damage at

the efficient level of pollution. The tax 'internalises the externality' by inducing the pollution generator to behave as if pollution costs entered its private cost functions. Decisions will then reflect all relevant costs, rather than just the producer's private costs, and so the profit-maximising pollution level will coincide with the socially efficient level.

Figure 12.3 illustrates this aspect of an emissions tax. Note that the diagram uses aggregate, economy-wide marginal benefit and marginal damage functions (not those of individuals or single firms). If firms behave without regard to the pollution they generate, output (and so emissions) will be produced to the point where no additional profit can be obtained. This is shown as $\hat{M}$, the uncontrolled level of emissions.

Now suppose an emissions tax was to be introduced, such that at each level of pollution, the tax rate is equal to the level of marginal damage at that pollution level. Given this, the post-tax marginal benefit schedule differs from its pre-tax counterpart by the value of marginal damage. Once the tax is operative, profit-maximising behaviour by firms leads to a pollution choice of M^*

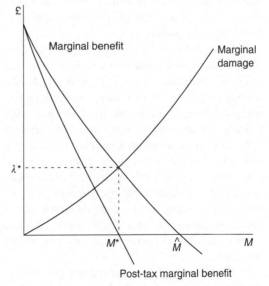

Figure 12.3 The effect of introducing an efficient emissions tax.

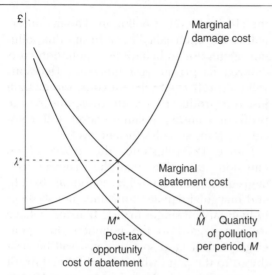

Figure 12.4 The effect of an emissions tax on marginal abatement cost.

(where the post tax marginal benefits of additional pollution are zero) rather than $\hat{M}$ as was the case before the tax. Note that at the efficient pollution level, the tax rate is equal to λ^*, the value of marginal external damage per unit of pollution at the efficient outcome. Bearing in mind our earlier comment about equivalence, it is clear that a subsidy at the rate λ^* on units of pollution abated would have an equal effect on emissions to a pollution tax at the rate λ^* on unabated units of pollution.

It is sometimes useful to view the problem in terms of abatement rather than the level of pollution, as in Figure 12.4. To change emphasis in this way, we replace the marginal benefit of pollution function with a marginal abatement cost function. (Recall from our discussions in Chapter 11 that the two are alternative ways of presenting the same information.) The marginal abatement cost function should be read from right to left – beginning from zero abatement at pollution level $\hat{M}$, marginal costs rise as, moving from right to left, abatement effort increases.

In the absence of an emissions tax (or an abatement subsidy), firms have no economic incentive to abate pollution. Profit-max-

imising behaviour implies that firms will undertake zero abatement, corresponding to the point $\hat{M}$. However, when an emissions tax is levied (or when an abatement subsidy is available) an incentive to abate exists, taking the form of either the avoidance of tax or the gain of subsidy. It will be profitable for firms to reduce pollution as long as their marginal abatement costs are less than the value of the tax rate per unit of pollution (or less than the subsidy per unit of emission abated). If the tax/subsidy is levied at the λ^* the pollution level M^* is attained.

We have argued that if the rate of subsidy were identical to the pollution tax rate, then the outcome in terms of levels of output and pollution would be the same under each scheme. This proposition is demonstrated more formally in Appendix 12.1. However, the distribution of gains and losses will usually differ, and this could affect the long-run level of pollution abatement under some circumstances. Some more discussion on this matter is given in Box 12.3.

Several points about pollution taxes are worth stressing, with similar comments also applying to abatement subsidies:

- For the tax to be cost efficient, the tax rate should be uniform over all polluters. That is, it should be applied at the same rate on all emitted units. A uniform tax rate implies that all abaters have the same cost at the margin, the requirement we saw earlier for a least-cost attainment of any pollution target.
- Uniformity of the tax rate applies only where the damage done by each unit of emissions is independent of time and place (that is, for uniformly mixed pollutants). Where pollution damage does depend on the location or timing of the emission, an efficient tax rate will no longer be uniform. We discuss this complication later.
- The tax we are referring to is levied on emissions, not on output. This encourages appropriate substitution effects to take place. Consider, two fuels currently selling

at a common price per unit of thermal energy, one generating a higher amount of pollutant per unit of produced energy than the other. For example, coal and natural gas may have similar prices per unit of energy, but in terms of CO_2 emissions, coal produces 1.8 times as much emission as gas per unit of produced energy. Suppose that a tax is applied on each fuel proportional to their relative emissions per unit of energy. The relative price of the more polluting fuel will then rise and so consumers will substitute towards the cleaner fuel. Further substitution effects will take place if relative prices of consumer goods alter in response to changes in energy prices. Substitution effects may also take place on the supply side as the pattern of exploration for new reserves changes in response to changing royalties.

Our discussion in this section so far has been focused largely on the case where the EPA wishes to attain the socially efficient level of emissions. We saw in the previous chapter that the EPA may not have sufficient information for this to be feasible. But even if it did have this information, the EPA may seek a different target, perhaps one based on health grounds alone. To attain any specific emissions target, knowledge of the aggregate (economy-wide) pollution abatement sche-

dule would be sufficient. Armed with this information, the EPA can calculate the required rate of tax as the marginal abatement cost at the target level of pollution. This tax instrument will attain the target at least total cost, and so would be cost efficient. Notice that the EPA does not need to know the abatement cost function of each firm to do this, only the aggregate abatement cost function, a far less demanding requirement for cost-efficiency than in the case of command and control instruments.

If the EPA knows neither marginal damage nor marginal abatement cost functions, it cannot identify the efficient pollution level, nor can it calculate what tax rate (or abatement subsidy) will deliver a specific pollution target. However, it could arbitrarily set a tax rate, confident in the knowledge that whatever level of abatement this generates would be attained at minimum feasible cost. Taxes and subsidies are, therefore, cost-efficient policy instruments, and could also, given sufficient information, achieve any chosen pollution level. This result is demonstrated formally in Appendix 12.1.

We illustrate these observations in Figure 12.5. Figure 12.5(a) shows a situation in which the EPA knows the marginal damage and abatement cost functions, and so can identify a tax rate, λ^*, which will yield the socially efficient level of pollution, M^* (or pollution abatement, $\hat{M} - M^*$). In Figure 12.5(b),

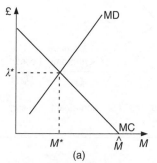
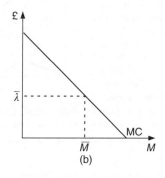
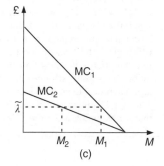

MD = marginal damages
MC = marginal abatement cost

Figure 12.5 The consequences of an emissions tax.

Box 12.3 Are pollution taxes and emissions abatement subsidies equivalent?

We have argued that an emission tax levied at the rate λ per unit of pollutant is equivalent to an abatement subsidy paid at the rate λ per unit of pollution abated. This statement needs some qualification. Let us clarify, first of all, the sense in which the two are equivalent. The claim made is that, for an industry of a given size, the two would result in an equal amount of emissions abatement. Thus, looking at Figure 12.4, a subsidy at the rate λ^* per unit of emission abatement and a tax at the rate λ^* per unit of emission will both reduce emissions from $\hat{M}$ to M^* for a single firm with a given capital structure. As the industry is simply the sum of all firms, if the number of firms remains constant and the capital structure of each firm is unchanged, then the effects of taxes and subsidies are identical.

However, the two instruments are not equivalent in all respects. One difference lies in their effects on income distribution. A firm gains additional income from an abatement subsidy, as it will undertake abatement only when the unit abatement subsidy exceeds its marginal abatement cost. A tax on the other hand results in a loss of income to the firm as it pays the tax on all its emissions. To make this comparison more precise, look at Figure 12.6, the functions in which reproduce those in Figure 12.4.

An emissions abatement subsidy will result in a payment to the firm equal to the areas $S_1 + S_2$, that is, λ^* multiplied by $(\hat{M} - M^*)$. However, by reducing pollution from $\hat{M}$ to M^* the firm loses S_2 in profit on final output. The net gain to the firm is equal, therefore, to the area S_1. An emission tax levied at the rate λ^* on emissions M^* will cost the firm $\lambda^* M^*$, that is, the sum of the areas S_3, S_4, S_5 and S_6. However, by reducing pollution from $\hat{M}$ to M^* the firm also loses profit on reduced output, the area S_2. So the income effects are entirely different.

Let us explore this difference a little further. Recall that the tax paid is equal in value to $\lambda^* M^*$, while the subsidy received is $\lambda^*(\hat{M} - M^*)$. But $\lambda^*(\hat{M} - M^*) = \lambda^*\hat{M} - \lambda^* M^*$. The second term on the right-hand side is the tax paid, and will depend on the amount of abatement undertaken. It is this second component which gives the firm an incentive to abate pollution. Recalling that λ is an outflow in a tax scheme and an inflow in a subsidy scheme, an outflow of $\lambda^* M^*$ (with a tax) is identical to an inflow of $-\lambda^* M^*$ (with a subsidy). The two incentive effects are identical, and it is this that forms the basis for the claim that the instruments

are equivalent. However, the subsidy differs from the tax by the presence of the additional term, $\lambda^*\hat{M}$, a fixed or lump sum payment, independent of the amount of abatement the firm actually undertakes. In the long-run such payments may alter industry profitability, and so alter the size of the industry itself. This lump sum payment component of the subsidy may destroy the equivalence between the two instruments in terms of their effects on pollution abatement.

We are thus faced with the possibility that a subsidy might enlarge the industry, partially or wholly offsetting the short-run pollution reduction. It is not possible to be more precise about the final outcome, as that depends on several other factors, including whether or not government introduces other fiscal changes to counteract the income effects we have just described. A general equilibrium analysis would be necessary to obtain clear results. This is beyond our scope in this text, so we just note that the equivalence asserted above is not valid in all cases.

Finally, note another aspect of an abatement subsidy scheme. As one component of the subsidy payment depends on the uncontrolled level of emissions (that is, the component $\lambda^*\hat{M}$), a firm has an incentive to misrepresent the uncontrolled level of emissions in order to obtain a favourable benchmark in terms of which the subsidy payments are calculated.

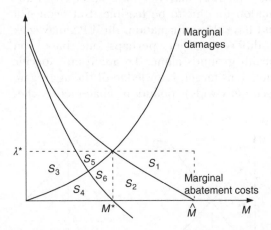

Figure 12.6 Emissions tax and abatement subsidy schemes: a comparison.

the EPA knows only the aggregate marginal abatement cost function; if it wished to restrict pollution to the level $\bar{M}$, it could do so by set-

ting the tax rate at $\bar{\lambda}$. In the third case, the control authority knows neither function. If it were to set a tax rate at the level $\tilde{\lambda}$ and the

Box 12.4 Pollution tax and abatement subsidies in practice

In OECD countries, the use of taxes and fees in environmental regulation has been growing since 1985. OECD (1995) identifies over 50 instances of fees or taxes in the areas of air, water and noise pollution, and waste disposal. Emissions charges are being used predominantly in Japan and a number of European countries. Effluent charges to control water pollution are used in France, Italy, Germany and the Netherlands. In some cases, the corresponding tax revenues are earmarked for purposes of environmental improvement. In the cases of Germany and Italy, charges are used in conjunction with effluent standards; those firms which meet or better the standards are taxed at a lower rate per unit of effluent than others.

France and Japan operate systems of air pollution emissions taxes. France has used charges as an incentive to install pollution abatement technology, with charges being repaid in the form of capital subsidies to firms adopting recommended control technologies. The Japanese system levies taxes in order to maintain a compensation fund for victims of air pollution; charge levels are dependent upon amounts of compensation paid out in previous years. Differential tax rates on leaded and unleaded petrol in the United Kingdom serve as an indirect charge on lead emissions, and Sweden has used differential charges and subsidies on cars and heavy vehicles to encourage the purchase of low pollution engines and the adoption of catalytic converters. Mention should also be made of the relatively high rates of tax on electricity and primary energy sources throughout Western Europe; while not being examples of pollution taxes as such, they do have similar incentive effects by encouraging energy conservation and enhancing energy efficiency.

The Commission of the European Community has for some time been studying the possibility of introducing a Europe-wide carbon tax to moderate greenhouse gas emissions, and to meet the EC objective of stabilising carbon dioxide emissions at the 1990 level by the year 2000. Initial plans were for the tax to be introduced in 1993 at the rate of $3 per barrel, and to be raised by $1 per year until it reached the level of $10 in 2000. Revenues would accrue to member states, to be used exclusively for environmental improvement. The Commission's plan has been rejected by the EC Council of Ministers, and is unlikely to be implemented in the near future. However, Finland, the Netherlands, Norway and Sweden all currently use a tax on the carbon content of fuels.

The USA makes very little use of emissions taxes or charges, the exceptions being a tax on chlorofluorocarbons introduced in 1989 to help in the phasing out of these chemicals, and fees on sewage and solid and hazardous waste at landfills (Goodstein, 1995). Households typically pay by the gallon for sewage disposal, and waste haulage firms pay by the ton for solid waste disposal. Unfortunately, from an efficiency perspective, these marginal disposal costs are not passed on to the initial producers of waste; household and business enterprises typically pay lump sum disposal charges. The United States has, though, made more extensive use of marketable emission permit instruments than European economies have (see Box 12.5).

Taxes or subsidies, where they have been used, have typically been set at low levels, with correspondingly low levels of impact, although the Netherlands, with relatively high rates, has shown large improvements in water quality. Sweden's use of differential taxes and subsidies, and the differential tax on unleaded petrol in the UK have been very effective in causing substitution in the intended directions. In some instances, the revenues from specific charges are earmarked for particular forms of environmental defensive or clean-up expenditure – one example is the use of taxes on new paint purchases in British Columbia to support reprocessing and safe disposal of used paint.

Sources: Tietenberg (1990), Goodstein (1995).

marginal cost of abatement cost function (unknown to the EPA) is actually MC_1 then the amount of pollution that would result is M_1. However, if the marginal abatement function were MC_2 then the amount of pollution that would result is M_2, and so more abatement takes place. In either case, the total abatement that occurs is achieved at least cost. Some information on practical experience with pollution taxes and abatement subsidies is given in Box 12.4.

Transferable (marketable) emissions permits

A marketable emission permits scheme for a uniformly mixing pollutant involves:

- A decision as to the total quantity of pollution that is to be allowed. The total amount of permits issued (measured in units of pollution) should be equal to that target level of pollution.
- A rule which states that no firm is allowed to emit pollution (of the designated type)

Box 12.5 Emissions permits in practice

The USA has had several years' experience with a variety of emissions permit trading programmes, and we review and assess the success of these programmes in this section. The material presented in this box draws heavily on Tietenberg (1990) and Goodstein (1995).

The nature of emissions permits in the USA is similar to that described in this chapter, but differs in some important details. American tradable permits operate in conjunction with more conventional standards or permit schemes. In essence they operate as follows. Suppose some particular pollutant is to be controlled. The United States Environmental Protection Agency (USEPA) establishes national standards in terms of ambient air quality, permissible pollutant concentrations in water systems and the like. To attain these standards controls are imposed on individual polluting sources, usually taking the form of required abatement technologies and upper limits on flows of pollutants. In all of this there is nothing novel – this is simply the conventional command and control (CAC) approach that has characterised pollution control in most countries in the twentieth century. The novelty arises in the next component of the programme.

If any polluter succeeds in reducing emissions by a greater amount than is required by the standard it must satisfy, it obtains 'emission reduction credits' (ERC) of that quantity. The firm which acquires these emission reduction credits can engage in trades, selling some or all of its ERC to other firms, which then obtain a legal entitlement to emit pollutants beyond the standard which the USEPA has imposed on them. Put another way, each firm is legally entitled to emit a quantity of pollutants up to the sum of its standard entitlement plus any ERC it has acquired. Each ERC is, thus, a transferable or marketable emissions permit. However, the number of permits being traded will be much less than we indicated in that earlier discussion. To explain this, suppose that the USEPA decided that no more than 100 million tons of SO_2 emissions will be permitted, and allocated permits to firms that added up to this total quantity. Suppose, also, that one set of firms chose to emit 25 million tons of SO_2 less than their allowed permits; they will then acquire ERC to the amount of 25 million tons, and that is the maximum amount of permits that can be traded on the market. In the alternative method of implementing the scheme that we outlined above, permits would be issued to the amount of 100 million tons.

The American ERC trading system has a number of other distinctive features:

- The *offset policy* allows existing firms to expand, or new firms to enter, areas in which emission

standards have not been met in the aggregate provided that they acquire sufficient quantities of ERC. In other words, growth can take place provided corresponding emissions reductions take place by existing firms within that area.
- The *bubble policy* treats an aggregate of firms as one polluting source (as if they were enclosed in a single bubble) and requires that the bubble as a whole meets a specified standard. If that is achieved, it does not matter whether an individual source within the bubble fails to meet the firm-specific standard imposed on it.
- *Emissions banking* allows firms to store ERC for subsequent use or sale to others.

The actual extent to which marketable pollution permit programmes have been used is limited, but has undergone considerable growth in recent years. It has been used to reduce the lead content in petrol, to control production and use of chlorofluorocarbon ozone-depleting substances, and in the 'Emissions Trading Program' for the control of volatile organic compounds, carbon monoxide, sulphur dioxide, particulates and nitrogen oxide. Details of the programmes which exist in the USA can be found in surveys by Cropper and Oates (1992), Tietenberg (1990), Hahn (1989, 1995), Hahn and Hester (1989a, 1989b), Opschoor and Vos (1989) and Goodstein (1995). The passage of the 1990 Amendments to the Clean Air Act has seen the United States introduce a major system of tradable permits to control sulphur emissions.

Most economists expect emissions trading to confer large efficiency gains relative to the use of command and control instruments alone. These gains arise from the reductions in overall abatement costs that trading permits; recall from our previous discussions that high cost abaters do less abatement and low cost abaters do more abatement when trading of permits or ERC is allowed. Tietenberg's assessment of the performance of the emissions permit trading schemes is

- The programme has unquestionably and substantially reduced the costs of complying with the Clean Air Act. Most estimates place the accumulated capital savings for all components of the programme at over $10 billion. This does not include the recurrent savings in operating costs. On the other hand the programme has not produced the magnitude of cost savings that was anticipated by its strongest proponents at its inception.
- The level of compliance with the basic provisions of the Clean Air Act has increased. The emissions trading programme increased the possible means for compliance and sources have responded accordingly.
- The vast majority of emissions trading transactions have involved large pollution sources.

Box 12.5 continued

- Though air quality has certainly improved for most of the covered pollutants, it is virtually impossible to say how much of the improvement can be attributed to the emissions trading programme.

Tietenberg, in Markandya and Richardson (1992),
pages 269–270

The Cropper and Oates survey confirms the view that the use of transferable permit programmes, and other market incentive schemes based on taxes or subsidies, has been very limited in scale, but they assess interest in and acceptability of market-based incentive instruments to be growing:

… effluent charges and marketable permit programs are few in number and often bear only a modest resemblance to the pure programs of economic incentives supported

by economists. … As we move into the 1990's, the general political and policy setting is one that is genuinely receptive to market approaches to solving our social problems. Not only in the United States but in other countries as well, the prevailing atmosphere is a conservative one with a strong predisposition towards the use of market incentives wherever possible, for the attainment of our social objectives.

Cropper and Oates (1992), pages 729–730

An important new development was initiated at Kyoto, Japan in 1997. The industrialised countries, in agreeing to a programme of greenhouse gas emissions limits, decided that the rights to emit pollutants could be traded between nations. This scheme, which has yet to be implemented, is discussed later in Chapter 13.

---

beyond the quantity of emission permits it possesses.

- A choice by the control authority over how the total quantity of emission permits is to be initially allocated between potential polluters.
- A guarantee that emission permits can be freely traded between firms at whichever price is agreed for that trade.

Transferable permit schemes differ from tax or subsidy schemes by working in terms of quantities rather than prices. But this feature is also true for command and control instruments such as quotas, licences and standards. What is the difference between these and a transferable permit scheme? The difference arises because of the transferability (also called tradability or marketability) of the permits in the latter case. In the case of command and control permits systems, these permits may not be transferred between firms. But they may be transferred under a marketable permit system. In effect, a marketable permit scheme creates a market in property rights: in this case the right to pollute. By creating property rights in access to the environment in this way, efficient resource use should follow.

Once the permits have been issued, firms – both those holding permits in sufficient number to cover their uncontrolled emission levels and those not holding sufficient for that purpose – will evaluate the marginal worth of permits to themselves. These valuations will differ over firms. At one extreme might be firms who have surplus permits: they hold permits to a greater amount than they intend to pollute anyway. At another extreme might be firms who have no permits and are desperate to get hold of some in order to remain in business. But more generally there will be firms who hold some permits but insufficient for the emissions that they would have chosen. Some of these firms will face very high abatement costs to bring down their pollution levels, and so will be willing to pay very high prices to purchase permits. Others might find that they could abate easily and cheaply, so that they are willing to pay only small sums to purchase permits. Indeed, if the price of permits were sufficiently high to exceed their marginal abatement costs, they would choose to sell rather than buy permits.

Against this background, a market will become established for transferable permits, and a single, equilibrium market price will emerge, say λ. Notice that trading does not alter the quantity of permits in existence, it merely redistributes that fixed amount between firms. Those that buy permits will tend to be firms with high abatement cost functions. Those that sell will be those with low abatement cost functions. However, in equilibrium marginal abatement costs will be equal over all firms. It is this property of the system which ensures that transferable marketable permits, like taxes and subsidies, achieve any given target at least-cost. Moreover, another equivalence arises. If the total quantity of permits issued is M^* and that quantity is identical to the level of pollution which will emerge from an emissions tax at the rate λ^* (or a subsidy scheme at the rate λ^*), then a marketable permit scheme will generate a market in which the equilibrium permit price is λ^*. In effect, the marketable permit system is an equivalent instrument to either pollution taxes or pollution abatement subsidies. We demonstrate this result algebraically in Appendix 12.1.

A diagrammatic treatment can also help in understanding the basic principle. Figure 12.7 shows the aggregate marginal abatement cost function for all polluting firms. The total number of permits (allowed pollution) is M^*. Given this quantity of permits, the market price for permits will be λ^*. Firms collectively are required to reduce pollution from $\hat{M}$ to M^* and so the real resource costs of the abate-

ment are given by the area of the shaded triangle to the right of M^*; that is, the sum of marginal abatement costs over the interval $\hat{M}$ to M^*. If firms must initially buy the permits from the government at the price λ^* then they will collectively face a further financial burden shown by the hatched area in the diagram. This will be a transfer of income from the business sector to the government, and so is not a real resource cost of abatement. When we discuss least-cost methods of abatement in this chapter, you should note that it is the real resource costs that are being minimised, not any transfer costs such as those just referred to.

To get further insight into the way that this instrument operates, consider the information shown in Table 12.4 that extends a numerical example we used earlier in the chapter. We suppose that a total permit allocation of 50 units of emission is selected. Suppose that the pollutant is emitted by just two firms, A and B, and that pollution abatement can only be undertaken by these firms. The EPA decides arbitrarily to allocate half to each firm, so A and B are allocated 25 permits each, allowing them to emit 25 units of the pollutant. We assume that in the absence of any control system, A would emit 40 units and B 50 units. Given the permit allocations, A must reduce pollution by 15 units and B by 25 units. It can be seen from Figure 12.8 (which reproduces exactly the abatement cost functions used previously in Figure 12.1) that A has marginal abatement costs of 45 and B marginal abatement costs of 125.

The fact that firm A has lower marginal abatement costs than firm B after the initial

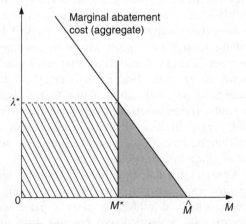

Figure 12.7 The determination of the market price of emissions permits.

Table 12.4 Pollution abatement data for firms A and B

	A	B	A + B
Uncontrolled emissions	40	50	90
Uncontrolled abatement	0	0	0
Efficient emissions	15	35	50
Efficient abatement	25	15	40
Initial permit allocation	25	25	50
Final permit allocation	15	35	50

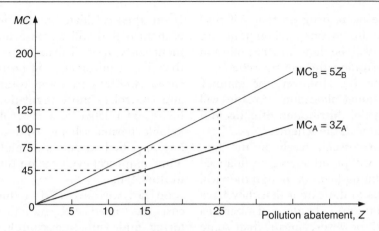

Figure 12.8 Efficient abatement with two firms and marketable permits.

permit allocation implies that the total abatement of 40 units of emission is not being achieved at least cost. Moreover, B places a much higher value on an incremental permit than does A (125 as compared with 40). Thus the two will find it mutually beneficial to trade with one another in permits. What will be the outcome of this trade? If the market behaved as if it were a competitive market, an equilibrium market price of 75 would emerge. At that price, firm B (the high-cost abater) would buy permits and A (the low cost abater) would sell permits. In fact, B would buy 10 permits from A at 75 each, because for each of those 10 permits, it would be paying less than it would cost the firm to abate the pollution instead. Conversely, A would sell 10 permits to B at 75 each, because for each of those 10 permits, it would be receiving more than it would cost the firm to abate the pollution instead.

Trading finishes at the point where A has 15 permits (10 less than its initial allocation) and B has 35 (10 more than its initial allocation). Marginal control costs are equalised across polluters, and the total cost of abating pollution by 40 units has thereby been minimised. The permit system will, therefore, have identical effects on output and pollution as an optimal tax or subsidy system, and will be identical in terms of its cost-effectiveness property. Some additional information on the complexities of marketable permit schemes that have been used in practice is given in Box 12.5.

Distributional aspects of marketable permit systems

As far as permit schemes are concerned, the distributional effects will depend primarily upon which method of initial permit allocation is chosen. An initial choice the control authority must make is whether to sell the permits, or allocate them at no charge. If the permits are sold, one way of doing so is through a competitive auction market. The equilibrium permit price in such a market will be determined by the aggregate marginal abatement cost at the level of abatement implied by the total number of issued permits.

Alternatively, the EPA may distribute the permits at no charge, and allow them to be subsequently traded in a free market. In a well-functioning competitive market, the market price that would emerge in this case would be identical to that which would be established if permits were sold at a competitive auction.

It is important to understand that the amount of abatement that takes place will depend only on the number of permits issued. Whether they are initially sold or given away freely, and who initially receives

them, will have no bearing on that – if permits to pollute up to one million tons are
available, that will be how much pollution
takes place (assuming the permit scheme is
enforced effectively). However, the manner
in which the initial allocation is made will
have effects on the distribution of gains and
losses associated with the scheme.

If permits are issued freely in the first
instance, there will be no aggregate financial
burden on polluting firms (although they will
experience costs to the extent that they have
to abate pollution). Trades of permits
between firms, however, mean that some
gain financially while others lose, even
though net transfers between firms are zero.
On the other hand, if the pollution control
agency decides to initially sell permits by
competitive auction, then there will be a net
transfer of income from polluters to the control agency equal to the total price paid for
the auctioned permits.

The fact that there are different net
income effects means that we must introduce
the same qualification we made earlier (in
comparing taxes with subsidies) about long-
run effects. An industry may contract in the
long run if permits must be initially purchased; this effect will not be present when
they are distributed at no charge.

**A comparison of the relative advantages of
command and control, emissions tax,
emission abatement subsidy and marketable
permit instruments**

Cost efficiency

We need add little to the remarks already
made about cost efficiency. To summarise, an
emissions tax, pollution abatement subsidy or
marketable permit system can achieve any
pollution target at least cost. A command and
control regulation instrument may, but will
not usually, be cost efficient. In order to be
cost-efficient, the EPA must know each polluter's marginal cost of abatement function.

It can then calculate an emission control for
each firm that will equalise marginal abatement costs over all firms. It is very unlikely
that this requirement will be met. The conclusion we draw from this is that a command
and control quantity regulation approach is
inefficient relative to a tax, subsidy or marketable permit scheme, and so will achieve
any specified target at a higher real cost.
Some empirical evidence on this is presented
in Box 12.6.

So far, we have said nothing about the
costs associated with monitoring, administering and enforcing compliance for each
instrument. These costs could be quite substantial, and if they are significantly different
between instruments, could affect which type
of instrument is the least cost one for
achieving a particular target. One reason for
the prevalence of minimum technology
requirements as a pollution control instrument may be that these costs are low relative
to those of instruments that try to regulate
pollution output levels.

Dependability of the control instrument

Dependability of an instrument depends very
much on how much information the EPA
possesses. For example, if the aggregate
abatement cost function is known with certainty, then the control authority can determine what emissions tax rate (or subsidy) is
needed to achieve any given level of abatement. Once that tax rate is introduced, abatement is attained at the desired level – the
instrument is completely dependable. A
similar result holds in this case for marketable permits; the control authority sets the
amount of permits issued, and trading on the
permits market will lead to a permit price
that can be perfectly predicted by the policy
maker. So knowledge of abatement costs
leads to dependability of the quantity of
emission abatement (and of the tax or permit
price) for both tax and permit systems.

However, where the abatement function is
not known with certainty, taxes and subsidies

Box 12.6 The costs of pollution abatement using command-and-control and market based instruments

A substantial literature now exists on the comparative costs of attaining pollution abatement targets using traditional quantity or technology regulations – what we call command and control (CAC) instruments – and so-called market instruments (particularly emissions taxes, abatement subsidies and marketable/transferable emissions permits). Much of this literature derives from experience in the USA with these two categories of instrument. Tietenberg (1990) provides an admirable account of recent evidence on these costs. Table 12.5 reproduces one of Tietenberg's tables, showing the ratio of costs under CAC approaches to the least-cost controls (using

market instruments) for air pollution control in the United States. We shall examine one of these studies – that by Krupnik (1986) – in more detail in Box 12.7.

Although they can be 'best' instruments in some circumstances, such direct controls are often extremely costly. Tietenberg (1984) finds that the CAC approach costs from twice to 22 times the least-cost alternative for given degrees of control. These ratios suggest that massive cost savings might be available if market instruments were to be used in place of CAC. In his 1990 paper, Tietenberg reports estimates that compliance with the US Clean Air Act through

Table 12.5 Empirical studies of air pollution control.

Study	Pollutants covered	Geographic area	CAC benchmark	Ratio of CAC cost to least cost
Atkinson and Lewis	Particulates	St Louis	SIP regulations	6.00[a]
Roach et al.	Sulphur dioxide	Four corners in Utah	SIP regulations Colorado, Arizona, and New Mexico	4.25
Hahn and Noll	Sulphates standards	Los Angeles	California emission	1.07
Krupnick	Nitrogen dioxide regulations	Baltimore	Proposed RACT	5.96[b]
Seskin et al.	Nitrogen dioxide regulations	Chicago	Proposed RACT	14.40[b]
McGartland	Particulates	Baltimore	SIP regulations	4.18
Spofford	Sulphur dioxide	Lower Delaware Valley	Uniform percentage regulations	1.78
	Particulates	Lower Delaware Valley	Uniform percentage regulations	22.0
Harrison	Airport noise	United States	Mandatory retrofit	1.72[c]
Maloney and Yandle	Hydrocarbons	All domestic DuPont plants	Uniform percentage reduction	4.15[d]
Palmer et al.	CFC emissions from non-aerosol applications	United States	Proposerd standards	1.96

Notes:
CAC = command and control, the traditional regulatory approach.
SIP = state implementation plan.
RACT = reasonably available control technologies, a set of standards imposed on existing sources in non-attainment areas.
[a] Based on a $40 \mu g/m^3$ at worst receptor.
[b] Based on a short-term, one-hour average of $250 \mu g/m^3$.
[c] Because it is a benefit–cost study instead of a cost-effectiveness study the Harrison comparison of the command-and-control approach with the least-cost allocation involves different benefit levels. Specifically, the benefit levels associated with the least-cost allocation are only 82% of those associated with the command-and-control allocation. To produce cost estimates based on more comparable benefits, as a first approximation the least-cost allocation was divided by 0.82 and the resulting number was compared with the command-and-control cost.
[d] Based on 85% reduction of emissions from all sources.

Source: Tietenberg (1990), Table 1.

Box 12.6 continued

market instruments has led to accumulated capital savings of over $10 billion. It should be pointed out, however, that most studies compare actual CAC costs with those theoretically expected under least-cost market-based instruments. In practice, one would not expect market instruments to operate at these theoretical minimum costs, and so the ratios we have quoted above overstate the cost savings that would be obtained in practice by switching from CAC techniques.

Three arguments underlie the tenet that market-based incentive approaches are likely to be more efficient than regulation and control. First, markets are effective in processing information; second, market instruments tend to result in pollution control being undertaken where that control is least costly in real terms; and third, market-based approaches generate dynamic gains through responses over time to their patterns of incentives.

However, stringent conditions are necessary for markets to guarantee efficient outcomes. Policy instrument choice takes place in a 'second-best' world, where results are much less clear. The absence of markets (including those for externalities and public goods), asymmetric information, moral hazard and other instances of market failure, all point to possible benefits of command and control based public intervention or to the inappropriateness of complete reliance on markets and market instruments. (See Fisher and Rothkopf (1989) for an excellent survey.)

We shall now consider a European example. Andreasson (1990) examines the costs of policies for reducing nitrate fertiliser use on the Swedish island of Gotland. This study is discussed at length in Hanley and Spash (1993), in a chapter devoted to analysing the costs and benefits of nitrate pollution control. Andreasson investigates three policies for achieving the Swedish government's upper limit of 30 milligrams per litre nitrates in drinking water. Model calculations suggest the need for a 50% reduction in nitrogenous fertiliser application to meet that target (scenario B). However, uncertainty exists about the rate at which nitrate leaches from manure and fertiliser, and it is possible that a more modest reduction in fertiliser application (14%) would be sufficient to achieve the target (scenario A).

The three policy instruments investigated by Andreasson are (non-tradable) quotas on fertiliser use, a tax on nitrogenous fertiliser, and a tradable permit system. Table 12.6 presents the real economic (resource) costs of achieving the pollution target under the two scenarios for each of the three policy instruments. In addition, Andreasson estimates the effects on farm incomes of the alternative policies; these farm income effects are also shown in Table 12.6.

These results are consistent with the conclusions suggested by our analysis in this chapter. Look first at the real economic costs (called resource costs in Table 12.6). As both taxes and tradable permits are fully efficient, their theoretical costs are identical. Costs under non-tradable quota controls are higher – here by about a third in scenario A and a half in scenario B. These higher costs arise from the fact that non-tradability means that marginal pollution control costs are not being equalised between different users of fertilisers. Second, the effects on farm incomes differ widely between the three policies. Taxes cause the largest loss of farm income under the lower reduction scenario, whereas quotas hit farm incomes most harshly when a high reduction is sought. Tradable permits are the least costly from the viewpoint of farmers in each case. This arises from the fact that Andreasson's simulations assume that the permits are initially allocated free of charge; if they were auctioned on a free market initially, losses to farm incomes would, of course, be higher than those indicated in the table.

Some additional references to studies which attempt to quantify the costs of attaining pollution standards using various instruments are given in the recommendations for further reading.

Table 12.6 Andreasson's real economic (resource) costs and effects on farm incomes.

Policy instrument	Resource costs (million kronor)		Farm income (% of total income)	
	Scenario A	Scenario B	Scenario A	Scenario B
Quotas	24.1	34.2	−10.0	−15.4
Tax	18.7	21.2	−13.9	−12.4
Tradable permits	18.7	21.2	−7.6	−9.0

Source: adapted from Hanley and Spash (1993), page 202.

and marketable permits differ. In the case of the tax instrument, the amount of abatement that results from any given tax rate will not be certainly known, as it will depend upon the unknown position of the abatement cost function. Marketable emission permits are always dependable in terms of abatement but where uncertainty exists about control costs the price of pollution permits cannot be predicted with certainty. The differing ways in which abatement cost uncertainty affects these two instruments are illustrated in Figure 12.9. In the upper half of the figure, a single abatement cost function is drawn, assumed to be known by the authority. Tax and permit regimes are identical in outcomes. Abatement cost uncertainty (shown in the lower half, with three different possible realisations of abatement costs) affects the amount of abatement under a tax system, while it affects the permit price under a marketable permits system.

Information requirements

Economic incentive instruments have a fundamental advantage over command-and-control instruments in this regard. In the absence of knowledge of individual firm abatement costs, command and control regulations cannot be cost effective except fortuitously. However, an emissions tax, subsidy or marketable permit scheme can achieve a predetermined pollution target at least total cost with knowledge only of the aggregate abatement cost schedule. Even if the EPA did not know that, use of any of these economic-incentive instruments would achieve some target at least cost.

Enforceability

As the enforceability of any control programme will depend very much on local circumstances and the details of the instrument used, there is little to be gained from trying

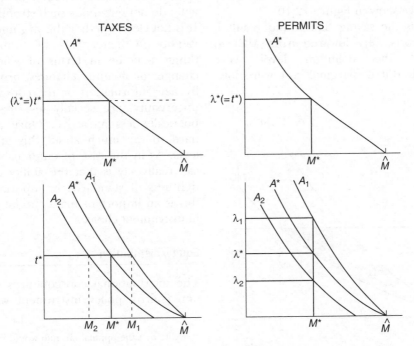

Figure 12.9 A comparison of taxes and marketable permits when control costs are uncertain.

to make general comments about this criterion. Suffice it to say that enforceability is important, and should be given high weight in the selection of instruments in practice.

Long-run effects

The long-run effects of an instrument depend mainly on two things: first, on the net income effects of the instrument, and so the effects on industry size (we have already covered this) and second, on the dynamic incentives generated by the instrument. We deal with this separately next.

Dynamic efficiency

An emissions tax (or abatement subsidy) will generate a dynamically efficient pattern of incentives on corporate (and consumer) behaviour. The key issue here is what incentives firms face in developing pollution-saving technology or developing new, environmentally cleaner products. Under a pollution tax scheme, these incentives are very strong, as we show in Figure 12.10.

Area Ω is the saving that would result if marginal costs were lowered from MC_1 to MC_2 and the pollution level were unchanged. But if marginal cost were low-

ered in this way, the firm's profit-maximising pollution abatement level would rise from Z_1^* to Z_2^*, and so an additional saving of Λ would accrue to the firm. The firm has an incentive to develop new technology to abate emission if the total costs of developing and applying the technology are less than the present value of the savings $\Omega + \Lambda$ accumulated over the life of the firm.[1]

The weaker dynamic incentives in regulatory systems are easy to understand. If a target is set in quantitative terms, then once that target has been met there is little or no further incentive on the polluter to reduce pollution. In a market-based scheme, such an incentive is always present as every unit of pollution reduction is rewarded by a tax saving.

Flexibility

It is sometimes argued that tax or subsidy schemes are inflexible as there is inherently strong resistance to changes in rates, while changes in permits (whether or not transferable) do not engender such strong resistance. It is not clear whether this argument has any validity. A better way of thinking about things may be in terms of whether price changes or quantity changes, brought about by new information or the consequences of uncertainty, are socially less desirable and politically less attractive. Once again, it is hard to say much about this at a general level. As in the case of enforceability, all we can really say is that the ability to vary the tightness of standards is important, and so this is an important matter to be considered in instrument choice.

Equity/distribution

The distributional consequences of a pollution control policy instrument will be very

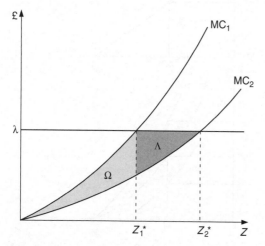

Figure 12.10 Dynamic incentives under pollution tax controls.

[1] Note that the optimal tax rate would change as new technology lowers control costs, so matters are a little more complicated.

important in determining which instruments are selected in practice. Different instruments for pollution control have different implications for the distribution of income within an economy. We have already examined the direct business financial gains and losses (which are, of course, exactly mirrored by offsetting government financial losses or gains). It is also necessary to think about the consequences for income and wealth distribution in society as a whole. For example, a pollution tax imposed upon fossil fuels will indirectly affect final consumers who purchase goods that have large energy input. Individuals for whom heating comprises a large proportion of their budget may well experience quite large falls in real income. Indeed, many kinds of 'green taxes' are likely to have regressive effects upon income distribution.

It is important to distinguish between income shifts that are redistributive and so do not correspond to any real resource gains and losses to the economy, and real income changes, which do imply real resource changes for the economy as a whole. The latter arise because pollution control does involve real costs. Of course, by having less pollution, there are benefits to be had as well, which in a well-designed pollution control programme should outweigh these real costs. Nevertheless, the beneficiaries and losers will not be the same individuals, and it is this that one is concerned with when discussing the equity or fairness of an instrument.

It should also be noted that emissions taxes have important implications for the relative competitiveness of national economies. Some analysts have advocated a switch from taxes on labour and capital to taxes on pollution to avoid excessive tax burdens, and schemes have been proposed to penalise nations that attempt to gain competitive advantage by not introducing emissions taxes. Good discussions of these issues are to be found in Bertram *et al.* (1989), Brown (1989), Grubb (1989a), Hansen (1990), Kosmo (1989) and Weizsacker (1989).

Note that even where a particular instrument has an adverse financial effect on one sector of the economy, it is open to the government to use compensating fiscal changes to offset those changes so that the distribution of income and wealth between individuals is not systematically changed. For example, the financial transfers implied by a pollution tax scheme could be compensated by lump sum payments to firms or by abatement subsidy payments. And income transfers from poorer groups facing higher energy bills, for example, could be compensated for by other fiscal changes.

The main point here is that additional tax revenues received by government could be distributed to groups adversely affected by the initial policy change. However, the difficulties in designing distributionally neutral packages are immense. Where compensation is paid to individuals or groups for whom the tax incidence is considered excessive, the form of compensation should be designed to not alter behaviour, otherwise the efficiency properties of the instrument will be adversely affected. This implies lump sum compensation should be used where possible. Neither can it be denied that compensation schemes of this form rarely happen in practice. But the point we wish to stress is that decision makers do have this option; whether they choose to exercise it is another matter.

Uncertainty

Quantitative emissions control, technology requirements and the standard-setting approach may be inadequate where uncertainties exist and new information is continually being obtained. Marketable permits, where control agencies have the flexibility to vary the stock of licences (as in the manner of open market operations for short-term debt), or pollution tax instruments where tax rates can be altered as new information becomes available, offer attractive alternatives (see also Barbier and Pearce, 1990).

A second important issue concerns the consequences of uncertainty for the efficiency losses that arise from the use of various instruments where wrong information is being used. We now examine this matter. In a situation of certainty, decision makers know the pollution abatement cost and pollution damage functions, and can therefore determine the efficient level of pollution abatement. In such circumstances, economic arguments of the kind used in the previous section suggest that market-based control instruments (taxes, subsidies and marketable permits) are in general the best means of achieving control targets.

However, where decision makers have uncertain knowledge of these functions, market instruments are no longer necessarily best. Under conditions of uncertainty, the government can overestimate or underestimate marginal abatement costs or benefits. Therefore, both a market-based instrument and a regulatory control system can lead to non-efficient amounts of pollution. One example of this is shown in Figure 12.11 for the case in which government underestimates the marginal costs of abatement.

Both types of instrument will result in an 'efficiency loss', in the sense that total net benefits are less than they could be if the efficient level of control had been implemented. Consider first a pollution tax instrument. Using its incorrect information, the government imposes a pollution tax at the rate λ_1 (as opposed to the value it should have been, λ_2). Firms will abate pollution as long as marginal abatement costs are below the tax, and so will emit M_1 units of pollution, a quantity in excess of the efficient level. The efficiency loss that corresponds to this is indicated by the area **bde**, the sum of the excess of marginal damage over marginal abatement costs for the excessive units of pollution.

Now consider the case of an emissions permit. Using its incorrect information, the government calculates its pollution target to be M_2, which is lower than the efficient level M^*. Put another way, incorrect information has led the government to impose too much abatement. In this case, the efficiency loss is indicated by the area **abc**, corresponding to the excess of marginal abatement costs over marginal damage for those excessive units of abatement.

What conclusions can we draw from this analysis? If the government makes mistakes in estimating one or both functions, the result will be an efficiency loss; abatement will be either too low or too high. To know which system gives the greater efficiency loss will require a comparison of the areas **abc** with **bde**. In general, we cannot say in advance which of these two will be greater. But at the very least, we can say that it is no longer true that market instruments are more efficient than quantitative regulations. They may be in some circumstances but not in others.

You can probably see that the relative sizes of the losses will depend upon the parameters of the respective marginal functions. To illustrate this point, look at Figure 12.12 in which the marginal benefit function is very 'flat' relative to the marginal damage function. As before, the government underestimates the true value of marginal abatement costs. In this case, the efficiency loss is less under a quantitative control (**abc**)

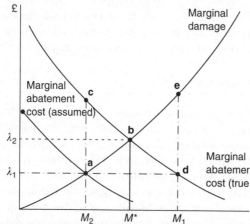

Area **abc** = efficiency loss under an 'incorrect' standard
Area **bde** = efficiency loss under an 'incorrect' emission tax

Figure 12.11 Uncertainty and the choice of pollution control instrument.

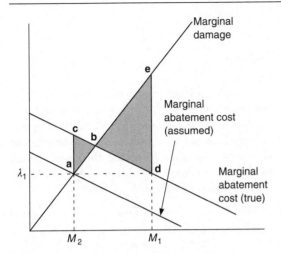

Figure 12.12 The efficiency loss arising when an error is made about the magnitude of abatement costs.

than under an emissions tax (**bde**). As Problem 5 shows, the opposite would be true if the marginal damage function had a slope lower in absolute value than the marginal abatement cost function.

We have looked at only two of the many possibilities here. Other possibilities arise when the marginal damage function is incorrectly estimated, or when mistakes are made with respect to both functions. Our conclusion must be that, once uncertainty is introduced into the analysis, it is not possible to claim superiority for one instrument in all circumstances.[2]

[2] The analysis in this section follows very closely that presented in Hartwick and Olewiler (1986). For further analysis of the design of policy under conditions of uncertainty, see page 422 in that reference. It is worth noting two further conclusions that Hartwick and Olewiler reach:

(1) When the government has imperfect information about the marginal abatement cost (MA) or marginal damage (MD) cost functions, it should use a quantity policy if MA is flatter than MD, and a tax if the reverse is true, if it wishes to minimise the efficiency losses arising from incorrect information.

(2) When the government is uncertain about the shape and location of both functions, a programme that combines a tax with a quantity control will minimise the expected losses arising from incorrect information (and will also minimise pollution control costs).

Pollution control where damages depend on location of the emissions

We now introduce a spatial dimension into our analysis. The previous discussion has worked on the premise that pollution targets have been specified in terms of emissions. This is appropriate when we are dealing with pure flow-damage pollutants. But what about the case where the pollutant is of the stock-damage variety? It turns out to be critical whether or not the pollutant is uniformly mixing.

Mixing of a pollutant refers to the extent to which physical processes cause the pollutant to be dispersed or spread out. A uniformly mixing pollutant becomes dispersed perfectly evenly; its spatial distribution is uniform. In this case, the location of the emission source is irrelevant as far as pollutant damages are concerned – all that matters is the total amount of those emissions. Individuals, buildings and ecosystems will experience the same amount of damage from an emission irrespective of where it is initially injected into the environment.

For a uniformly mixing stock-damage pollutant a target can be set either in terms of emissions (M) or in terms of pollutant concentrations (A), as there will be a one-to-one relationship between the two. Put another way, if the policy-maker's target is one specified in pollutant concentration, A^*, this can be translated into its implied emissions target, M^*.

However, where a stock-pollutant is not uniformly mixing, the location of emission sources matters because it determines the magnitude of the damage which results from a given quantity of emissions. There will not be a one-to-one relationship between emissions and concentration over all space. A given total value of M could lead to various values of A at different points in space, depending on where the emissions take place. In these circumstances, the design of good pollution control instruments becomes more complicated.

Non-uniform mixing is of great importance in practice as many types of pollution fall into this category, including ozone accumulation in the lower atmosphere, particulate pollutants from diesel engines and trace metal emissions. Some problems of water and ground pollution also fit this description too.

We saw earlier that one way in which the EPA may handle these issues is by controlling *ex ante* the location of polluters and people affected by pollution. But what should the EPA do when the location of polluters and people is already determined, and moving either is not a feasible option? The appropriate degree of control over emissions, or the appropriate tax or subsidy rate, will now not be uniform over all abaters. Those polluters whose emissions generate the most damage per unit of emission should be taxed more heavily (or controlled more tightly) than polluters whose damage per unit of emission is relatively low. And because location does matter, it will also not be appropriate for permits to be freely tradable on a one-to-one basis between firms.

Ambient pollution standards

Rather than viewing the environment as a single, homogeneous medium, it is now appropriate to think of the environment as a series of spatially distinct pollution 'reception' areas (or receptors, for short). Suppose that there are J distinct receptors, each being indexed by the subscript j (so $j = 1, 2, \ldots, J$) and N distinct pollution sources, each being indexed by the subscript i (so $i = 1, 2, \ldots, N$). A transfer coefficient, d_{ji} describes the impact on pollutant concentration from source i in receptor j.[3]

The total level (or concentration rate) of pollution at location j, A_j, will be the sum of the contributions to pollution at that location from all N emission sources. This can be written as

---

[3] Each coefficient d_{ji} will vary over time, depending on such things as climate and wind conditions. However, if we measure average values of these coefficients over some period of time, they can be regarded as constant coefficients for the purposes of our analysis.

$$A_j = \sum_{i=1}^{N} d_{ji} M_i \qquad (12.1)$$

where M_i denotes the total emissions from source i.

It might help to give a numerical example. Suppose there are $N = 3$ sources and $J = 2$ receptors. Then we can collect all six d_{ji} coefficients into a $J \times N$ matrix, $\mathbf{D}$. Denoting the vector of emissions from the three sources as $\mathbf{M}$ and the vector of ambient pollution levels in the two receptors as $\mathbf{A}$ we have

$$\mathbf{A} = \mathbf{DM} \qquad (12.2)$$

or

$$\begin{pmatrix} A_1 \\ A_2 \end{pmatrix} = \begin{bmatrix} d_{11} & d_{12} & d_{13} \\ d_{21} & d_{22} & d_{23} \end{bmatrix} \begin{pmatrix} M_1 \\ M_2 \\ M_3 \end{pmatrix} \qquad (12.3)$$

Thus we have

$$A_1 = d_{11}M_1 + d_{12}M_2 + d_{13}M_3 \qquad (12.4a)$$
$$A_2 = d_{21}M_1 + d_{22}M_2 + d_{23}M_3 \qquad (12.4b)$$

So knowledge of the $\mathbf{M}$ vector and the $\mathbf{D}$ matrix allow us to calculate ambient levels at each receptor area. If, for example, $\mathbf{D}$ and $\mathbf{M}$ are

$$\mathbf{D} = \begin{bmatrix} 0.4 & 0.6 & 0.8 \\ 0.5 & 0.3 & 0.2 \end{bmatrix} \mathbf{M} = \begin{pmatrix} 10 \\ 20 \\ 40 \end{pmatrix}$$

then $A_1 = 48$ and $A_2 = 17$.

Let A_j^* denote the EPA's target ambient pollutant concentration at receptor j. For simplicity we suppose that the target for each receptor area is the same, so that $A_j^* = A^*$ for all j. The overall goal of the EPA is that in no area should the pollutant concentration exceed A^*. That is

$$A_j = \sum_{i=1}^{N} d_{ji} M_i \leqslant A^* \qquad \text{for } j = 1, \ldots, J$$
$$(12.5)$$

If the EPA wishes to achieve this overall target at least cost, the solution (as we show in Appendix 12.1) requires that

$$\mathrm{MC}_i = \lambda_1^* d_{1i} + \lambda_2^* d_{2i} + \ldots + \lambda_J^* d_{Ji}$$
$$i = 1, 2, \ldots, N \qquad (12.6)$$

where MC_i denotes the marginal abatement cost of firm i. This may be compared with the condition

$$MC_i = \lambda^* \qquad i = 1, 2, \ldots, N$$

which was the solution for a uniformly mixing pollutant that we found earlier.

Equation 12.6 implies:

(1) There will be a separate shadow price λ_j^* for each receptor area.
(2) If an emissions tax (abatement subsidy) is the chosen instrument, the tax rate (abatement subsidy) that each firm pays will be equal to the sum, over all J receptor areas, of the product of the shadow price λ_j^* for the jth receptor area multiplied by a weighting factor d_{ji} which gives the contribution of the ith firm's emissions to ambient pollution levels in area j.

Therefore, even if all firms had the same marginal cost of abatement function, they would not do equal abatement (and neither would they pay the same rate of tax).

The least-cost solution can be obtained by any of the methods described earlier. However, as tax or subsidy instruments require that rates are unique to each pollution source, one of the attractive features of these instruments (that a single rate can be applied over all polluters) no longer applies. One would expect much less use to be made of pollution tax or subsidy instruments in the case of non-uniformly mixing air, water and ground pollution.

How would marketable permits work in this case? The system – known as an ambient marketable permits or spatially differentiated system – would operate as follows:

(1) For each receptor site, there will be a target ambient pollution concentration determined by the EPA. The EPA must then calculate how many emissions permits there can be that will allow firms to decrement (that is, worsen) ambient concentrations at that site. So for any site, the emissions 'arriving' there from all sources (and so the total permits to be issued) must be such that the target is met. This calculation must be done for each receptor site.
(2) These permits are issued to pollution sources, either by competitive auction or by free initial allocation ('grandfathering').
(3) A pollution source is prohibited from making an emission to any receptor site above the quantity of permits it holds for emissions to that site. Each firm will, therefore, be required to hold a portfolio of permits to worsen concentrations at specific receptor areas.
(4) A market for permits will emerge *for each receptor area*. Each polluting source will trade in many of these markets simultaneously. The results of these trades will determine a unique equilibrium price in each market.
(5) Permits for each receptor area are freely tradable on a one-to-one basis, but this does not apply to permits for different receptors.

How does this relate to Equation 12.6? The J shadow prices λ_j^* correspond to the equilibrium permit prices in each market. At the least-cost solution, a firm will equate the marginal cost of emissions abatement with the marginal cost of not abating the emission. The right-hand side of Equation 12.6 gives this latter cost, which is a weighted sum of these permit prices. The weights attached to the permit price for receptor j will be the impact that one unit of emissions has on pollutant concentration at site j. Thus the right-hand side gives the cost to the firm, in permit prices paid, for one unit of its emissions.

Clearly, the administration of an ideal least-cost marketable permit system is hugely demanding. Indeed, there are no actual examples of systems that match this ideal form. Existing permit systems are only approximations to the ideal type. The most important departure in practice is the absence of separate markets for permits for each receptor; this is replaced by the condition of separate markets only for each type of pollution generator.

The extent to which an ideal least-cost marketable permit scheme would attain ambient standards at lower cost than some alternative instruments has been analysed by several authors. We outline one of these studies (Krupnik, 1986) in Box 12.7. Krupnik's study also highlights another matter of considerable importance: abatement costs can rise very sharply as the desired targets are progressively tightened.

The severity of pollution control over time

Our dynamic analysis of stock-damage pollution in the previous chapter introduced an important temporal dimension. Targets will not necessarily be constant over time. In particular, if pollution stock levels rise over time and the marginal damage associated with additional units of emission becomes larger, an efficient control programme will require a progressive tightening of the pollution restrictions for as long as the stock level continues to increase and the marginal damage of emissions is rising. However, while targets may have to be tightened over time, this does not invalidate any of the analysis we have done in this chapter concerning pollution instruments. All it means is that the targets we have been taking as predetermined in this chapter will not necessarily be constant through time.

Mobile source pollution

Emissions from mobile sources, the main examples of which are land, air and sea vehicles, pose considerable problems in the design of appropriate policy instruments. Vehicle fuel combustion is the major source of three types of airborne pollutant – carbon monoxide, hydrocarbons (often in particulate form), and nitrogen oxides. It is also a sig-

nificant source of other harmful emissions, including lead and other trace metals, and carbon dioxide. The most acute damages tend to occur when atmospheric conditions lead to localised, temporary high concentrations of the pollutants, in the form, for example, of the smogs associated with Athens, London, Los Angeles, Mexico City and Tokyo.

The design of satisfactory policy instruments is more difficult for mobile than for stationary source pollutants. Among the reasons for this are the following characteristics of mobile source pollution.

(a) The extent of pollution damage depends upon the location of the emitting source. A particular quantity of nitrogen dioxide released in a heavily populated residential area, for example, will be more damaging than that quantity released in a thinly populated rural area. This is also true for many stationary-source pollutants. But the location effect has an additional dimension here: the origins of mobile source pollutants change. As the sources move, so the damages for which they are responsible change too. Pollution-charging systems for vehicle emissions require a tariff that is adjustable in quite subtle ways, a very difficult property to achieve. Similar comments apply to efficient quantitative regulation.

(b) Pollution damage depends upon the timing of the emission. Again, this is true not only for mobile-source pollution. But the highly localised nature of most important forms of mobile source pollution gives this a particular importance. Car exhaust emissions, for example, will be at their worst in situations of heavily congested traffic at particular times of the day. Damage is probably less acute for night rather than day travel, and so on. Again, this suggests that imagination will be required in the search for appropriate

Box 12.7 Costs of alternative policies for the control of nitrogen dioxide in Baltimore

Nitrogen dioxide (NO_2) is a good example of a non-uniformly mixing pollutant. Alan Krupnik's study investigates the cost of meeting alternative one-hour NO_2 standards in the Baltimore area of the United States. He compares a variety of control programmes applied to 200 large emission point sources in the area. He identified 404 separate receptor areas in the region. Krupnik considers three alternative standards applied for each receptor area: 250, 375 and $500\,\mu g/m^3$ control.

Simulation techniques are used to estimate total abatement costs for each of several different policy instruments. We deal with four of the cases here that Krupnik investigated:

- The least-cost instrument: a spatially-differentiated ambient pollution marketable permits scheme of the type discussed in the text.
- A type-specific fee: an effluent charge with charges differentiated by source-type (but not by receptor areas impacted)
- A uniform fee: an effluent charge not differentiated by source-type (nor location of impact)
- A hybrid instrument, labelled RACT/least-cost: a mixture of command and control and incentive instruments. The RACT part takes the form of a technology standard ('Reasonably Available Control Technology') which is imposed on all firms. For firms that fail to meet (weaker) national air quality standards, market incentives are used to induce further emissions reductions (the least-cost part).

The results of Krupnik's simulations (for two ambient targets) are shown in Table 12.7. Numbers not in parentheses refer to the stricter target of $250\,\mu g/m^3$, those in parentheses the weaker target of $500\,\mu g/m^3$. These targets were selected in view of the fact that uncontrolled emissions led to high ambient pollution levels of around 700–800 $\mu g/m^3$ at several receptor sites, and technology studies suggest that targets more strict than around 190 $\mu g/m^3$ are unobtainable given the presence of the existing point sources.

Comparing first the costs of attaining different targets, Krupnik notes that 'compliance costs rise steeply as the standard is tightened, regardless of the policy simulated. In the least-cost case, costs rise by a factor of 25 (from $66,000 to $1.633 million) when standards are halved (from 500 to $250\,\mu g/m^3$)'. The smaller proportionate increase in the hybrid case (RACT/least-cost) is due to the fact that the technology controls imposed by RACT give the firm little additional room for manoeuvre for further cost reductions when the standard is made stricter.

Notice that the emissions reduction is relatively small for the least-cost control compared with others. This happens because the target being sought is not a given total emissions reduction but a maximum ambient pollution standard over the whole area. Several of the instruments are inefficient (in abatement cost terms) because they operate in a more uniform manner than the spatially differentiated least-cost permit method. In so doing, the optimal distribution of abatement effort is not being applied, and excessive amounts of control are being adopted on many pollution sources.

For the type-specific fee, control costs are not much larger than the least-cost method (and are identical for the weaker control). A fee that distinguishes between different types of polluter does seem able to mimic fairly well a proper spatially differentiated permit (or tax) approach. This is reassuring, as type-specific fees are likely to be used in practice instead of least-cost ambient permit methods as a result of their much greater simplicity. In contrast, note that when a uniform fee is imposed to achieve the stricter ambient standard (and where uniformity means that no effort is made to relate the charge to impact of emissions on ambient levels at various places) control costs increase very dramatically. A uniform fee can result in the largest emission reduction, but without doing any better in terms of ambient standards, and at hugely additional cost. Note, finally, that a single market emissions permit system would have an identical effect to that of a uniform fee. Spatially differentiating permit markets offers huge cost savings in principle.

Table 12.7 Simulation results for the cost of meeting two ambient targets.

	Emissions reduction (%)		Abatement costs $US millions/year	
Least-cost (ambient permits)	32	(6)	1.663	(0.066)
Type-specific fee	34	(6)	1.719	(0.066)
RACT/least-cost	42	(36)	2.200	(1.521)
Uniform fee	73	(21)	14.423	(0.224)

Source: adapted from Krupnik (1986), tables II and III.

instruments. Both points (a) and (b) suggest that emission controls on vehicles at the point of manufacture – a very important component of policy in practice – are likely to be of little use in targeting effort efficiently.

(c) The monitoring, control and enforcement of regulations can be very difficult and costly because of the large numbers of individual pollution sources, and because of the mobility of the sources. Regulations stipulating minimum standards for exhaust emissions can easily be implemented for new vehicles, but less easily for existing vehicle stocks.

(d) It is the use of vehicles, not their production, which is the predominant source of pollution. A significant proportion of an economy's stock of vehicles is modernised or updated very infrequently. Hence there is an inertia effect or vintage effect – incentives or regulations designed to reduce environmental impacts of new vehicles have limited short-term effects. Users of cars, for example, can easily change the rate of use of their vehicles, but often cannot easily or cheaply introduce efficient technical substitutions.

Mobile source pollution policy in practice

In most countries, controls relating to mobile source pollution are predominantly confined to regulation at point of production, not use. These tend to take the form of mandatory technology standards, required capital equipment, or emissions standards required from engine units of given sizes. Such controls are imposed on the producer, and aim to achieve target levels of emissions per unit of distance driven. Examples include requirements to install catalytic converters, particulate emission standards for new diesel engines, requirements that engines be operable using unleaded fuel, or the more stringent regulations of environmental impact adopted in

California. A standards-based approach is the main component of control programmes in the United States and Europe. Economists tend to be sceptical of the impact that standards will have. They will certainly reduce the quantity of emissions per mile driven for given types of vehicle, but will only affect new sources; considerable time delays exist before such standards permeate the whole fleet. But most importantly, they fail to create the right incentives at the margin; such regulations will not affect user choices about total mileage driven, nor about its timing or location. A good summary of these drawbacks can be found in the eighteenth report of the Royal Commission on Environmental Pollution (1994).

The essence of the problem here is, once again, that when pollutants are not uniformly mixing, the use of uniform standards cannot be efficient. The control or incentive should bite more or less strongly in accordance with the extent of the damage. Moreover, standards or regulations applied at the point of manufacture do not generate incentives to improve technology. Indeed, they may even lead to perverse incentives, with manufacturers hiding potential technology improvements for fear of these becoming built into a tightened future standard. Not all is as bleak as this might suggest, however. If a control authority announces a programme of credible targets over time, where standards are progressively tightened in a planned manner, rational firms may try to anticipate these gradually tightening constraints. The programme may, therefore, generate appropriate dynamic incentives.

Regulations or other quantitative controls may be over use rather than build standard. Such instruments are becoming increasingly pervasive, and much discussion of car pollution is couched in terms of where and when cars should be permitted to travel and so on. Simple access restrictions (such as those on car use in some US National Parks, to city centres in several European countries, or those mooted for the English Lake District) may be necessary where congestion problems become intolerable, or where road traffic volume has risen to levels at which valuable environmental amenities are being destroyed.

Future policy options towards mobile source pollution

The preference of economists for price-based incentive policies carries over to mobile source pollution too. Obvious candidates are fuel taxes and congestion-related parking charges. The former partially takes account of spatial and temporal aspects, in so far as urban fuel use is higher than rural use, especially in busy periods. However, neither of these completely addresses the problems of spatial and temporal variation we described earlier. A number of schemes have been proposed that make use of modern electronic monitoring equipment. It is feasible (although perhaps not economically viable) to install in each vehicle a recording system that embodies the history of its movements. A flexible charging system could then extract appropriate payments from each user.

Instruments for conserving biodiversity

In earlier chapters, we investigated the causes and consequences of the decline in biological diversity. The Convention on Biological Diversity, one of three international environmental treaties signed at the UN Earth Summit in 1992, came into force in December 1993, and by 1995 had been ratified by over 130 countries. This calls for the conservation of biological diversity, the sustained use of its components and an equitable sharing of its benefits.

Which instruments might be used to reduce the rate at which biodiversity is being lost? In order to answer this question, it is worth recalling a distinction we made previously, between the proximate and the fundamental causes of loss of biodiversity. The instruments which economists recommend to conserve biodiversity are essentially concerned with the fundamental causes, and typically make use of the price system and market mechanisms to create appropriate patterns of incentives.

Following the framework adopted in OECD (1996), we can distinguish between four categories of incentives:

(1) Positive incentives: grants, subsidies, cost sharing agreements and the like, which create incentives to use resources in a conservationist manner.
(2) Disincentives: fees, tariffs, fines, legal liabilities and the like which penalise those whose behaviour directly or indirectly results in biodiversity decline.
(3) Indirect incentives: creation of property rights or markets where these were previously missing, or adoption of measures that improve the operation of markets.
(4) Removal of perverse incentives: such incentives often arise as unanticipated side effects of policies with different, and apparently independent, objectives. This implies the need for policy integration where the instruments used to attain particular targets have spillover effects on other objectives.

A listing of instruments for conserving biodiversity, classified according to these four incentive types, can be found in OECD (1996), and is reproduced in Table 12.8. A detailed description of each instrument can be found in the original reference.

Conclusions

We have discussed at some length the properties and relative advantages of various instruments that may be used to attain environmental policy targets. However, the reader may have noticed that our discussion of policy instruments in this chapter has taken place under the implicit assumption that some single authority has the ability to implement

Table 12.8 Instruments for the conservation of biodiversity.

Positive incentives	Disincentives	Indirect incentives	Removal of perverse incentives
Agricultural land set-aside (retirement schemes)	User fees	Individual transferable fishing quotas	Reduction and restructuring of agricultural support harmful to biodiversity
Public or grant-aided land purchase	Non-compliance fees	Tradable development rights	Agricultural conservation compliance measures
Wetland reserves	Fines for damages	Property-rights mechanisms	Reform of public forestry concession pricing, licence fees, reforestation fees and royalties
Covenants/conservation easements	Environmental liability	Species commercialisation	Full appraisal of forestry benefits
Cost-sharing/management agreements with payments for biodiversity maintenance	Performance bonds	Biodiversity prospecting deals	Discontinuation of below-cost timber sales
Species enhancement schemes	Habitat mitigation schemes	Forestry offsets	Reform of tax structures
Customary cultivation of biodiversity	Marine pollution liability	Air emission trading	Full-cost pricing for water services
International biodiversity transfers		Effluent discharge trading	Appraisal of biodiversity impacts in transport sector
Incentive payments for organic farming		Tradable water entitlements	Road pricing
Taxation and fiscal measures		Wetlands mitigation banking	Costing of biodiversity loss in energy investment appraisal
		Joint implementation Debt-for-nature swaps International franchise agreements Eco-labelling	

Source: adapted from OECD (1996), page 9.

and administer a control programme. But many pollution problems spill over national boundaries. Given that the world does not have a single government, how can policy targets and instruments be devised, introduced, administered and monitored for global or international pollution problems? This question is of great importance, but raises so many new problems that it warrants separate attention. We discuss these issues separately, therefore, in the following chapter.

Discussion questions

1 Consider a good whose production generates pollution damage. In what way will the effects of a tax on the output of the good differ from that of a tax on the pollutant emissions themselves? Which of the two is likely to be economically efficient?

2 Discuss the distributional implications of different possible methods by which marketable permits may be initially allocated.

3 Distinguish between private and public goods externalities. Discuss the likelihood of bargaining leading to an efficient allocation of resources in each case.

4 Use diagrams to contrast pollution tax instruments with marketable emission permit systems, paying particular attention to the distributional consequences of the two forms of instrument. (Assume a given, target level of pollution abatement, and

that permits are initially distributed through sale in a competitive market.)

5 Discuss the efficiency properties of a pollution tax where the tax revenues are earmarked in advance for the provision of subsidies for the installation of pollution abatement equipment.

6 Suppose that a municipal authority hires a firm to collect and dispose of household waste. The firm is paid a variable fee, proportional to the quantity of waste it collects, and is charged a fee per unit of waste disposed at a municipal waste landfill site. Households are not charged a variable fee for the amount of waste they leave for collection, instead paying an annual fixed charge. Comment on the economic efficiency of these arrangements and suggest how efficiency gains might be obtained.

Problems

1 The Coase Theorem claims that a unique and efficient allocation of resources would follow from rational bargaining, irrespective of how property rights were initially allocated. Demonstrate that the distribution of net gains between bargaining parties will, in general, depend upon the initial distribution of property rights.

2 Show that a pollution tax on emissions and a subsidy for each unit of pollution reduction would, if the rates of subsidy were identical to the pollution tax rate, lead to identical outcomes in terms of the levels of output and pollution for a given sized industry. Explain why the distribution of gains and losses will usually differ, and why the long-run level of pollution abatement may differ when the industry size may change.

3 In all discussions of pollution abatement costs in this chapter, the fixed costs of pollution abatement were implicitly taken

to be zero. Do any conclusions change if fixed costs are non-zero?

4 Demonstrate that in the simple special case of a uniformly mixing flow pollutant, in which the value of the damage created by the emission is independent of the location of the emission source or the time of the emission, the tax rate should be uniform over all polluters for the tax to be an efficient instrument (that is, it will be applied at the same rate per unit of pollution on all units of the pollutant).

5 Our discussion in this chapter has shown that if the control authority does not know the marginal damage function, it will not be able to identify the economically efficient level of pollution abatement, nor the efficient tax or subsidy level. Demonstrate that

(a) knowledge of the pollution abatement schedule alone means that it can calculate the required rate of tax to achieve any target level it wishes,

(b) if it knew neither the marginal damage nor the marginal abatement cost schedules, then it could arbitrarily set a tax rate, confident in the knowledge that whatever level of abatement this would generate would be attained at minimum feasible cost.

6 You are given the following information:

(a) A programme of air pollution control would reduce deaths from cancer from 1 in 8000 to 1 in 10 000 of the population.

(b) The cost of the programme is expected to lie in the interval £2 billion (£2000 million) to £3 billion annually.

(c) The size of the relevant population is 50 million persons.

(d) The 'statistical value' of a human life is agreed to lie in the interval £300 000 to £5 million.

If the only benefit from the programme is the reduced risk of death from cancer, can the adoption of the programme be justified using an economic efficiency criterion?

Further reading

Baumol and Oates (1988) is a classic source in the area of environmental regulation. The whole book is relevant but it is quite difficult and formal. Tietenberg (1992, chapters 14 to 20) provides an extensive and primarily descriptive coverage of specific types of pollution and the control techniques applied to each. Other good general accounts of pollution control policy are to be found in Fisher (1981, chapter 12), which discusses the work of Ronald Coase and the roles of wealth and bargaining power, Common (1996), Hartwick and Olewiler (1986) and Goodstein (1995). Fisher and Rothkopf (1989) consider the justification for public policy in terms of market failure.

OECD (1995) surveys the use of environmental taxes and other charges used for environmental protection in the OECD countries. Portney (1990) analyses air pollution policy in the USA, and Portney (1989) carefully assesses the US Clean Air Act. Crandall (1992) provides an interesting analysis of the relative inefficiency of a standards-based approach to fuel efficiency in the United States. Kolstad (1987) examines the efficiency losses associated with using undifferentiated taxes or other charges when economic efficiency requires that charges be differentiated across sources. Krupnik's (1986) paper on nitrogen dioxide control in Baltimore, discussed in Box 12.7, repays reading in the original.

Dales (1968) is the paper generally credited with having established the notion that marketable permits may be used for pollution control, and Montgomery (1972) derived the efficiency properties of marketable permits.

For a detailed analysis of issues concerning compensation in connection with distribution effects of tax changes, see Hartwick and Olewiler (1986, chapter 12). These authors also analyse the consequences of subsidies and taxes in the short run and the long run. The role and importance of non-convexities are discussed in Fisher (1981, page 177), Portes (1970) and Baumol and Oates (1988).

Discussion of the idea of a safe minimum standard of conservation can be found in Bishop (1978) and Randall and Farmer (1995). For analysis of the use of market-based pollution control instruments see Hahn (1984, 1989) Hahn and Hester (1989a,b), Opschoor and Vos (1989) and Tietenberg (1990, 1992). Jorgensen and Wilcoxen (1990a,b,c) analyse the impact of environmental regulation upon economic growth in the United States (but note that these papers are relatively difficult).

The 'Blueprint' series (see, for example, Pearce, 1991a) provides a clear and simple account of the new environmental economics policy stance, in a rather ideological style. Finally, a number of texts provide collections of papers, several of which are relevant to pollution control policy: these include Bromley (1995) and, at a more rigorous level, the three 'Handbooks' edited by Kneese and Sweeney (1985a,b, 1993).

Appendix 12.1   The least cost theorem and pollution control instruments

Suppose that there are N polluting firms, indexed $i = 1, \ldots, N$. Each firm faces a fixed output price and fixed input prices, and maximises profits by an appropriate choice of output level (Q_i) and emission level (M_i) . Emissions consist of a uniformly mixing pollutant, so that the source of the emission is irrelevant as far as the pollution damage is concerned.

Let $\hat{\Pi}_i$ be the maximised profit of the ith firm in the absence of any control over its emission level and in the absence of any charge for its emissions. This is its unconstrained maximum profit level. At this unconstrained profit maximum the firm's emission level is $\hat{M}_i$.

Let Π_i^* be the maximised profit of the ith firm when it is required to attain a level of emissions $M_i^* < \hat{M}_i$. This is its constrained maximum level of profits. To reduce emissions, some additional costs will have to be incurred or the firm's output level must change (or both). The constrained profit level will, therefore, be less than the unconstrained profit level. That is $\Pi_i^* < \hat{\Pi}_i$.

We next define the firm's abatement costs, C, as the difference between its unconstrained and constrained profits:

$$C_i = \hat{\Pi}_i - \Pi_i^*$$

Abatement costs will be a function of the severity of the emissions limit the firm faces; the lower is this limit, the greater will be the firm's abatement costs. Let us suppose that this abatement cost function is quadratic. That is

$$C_i = \alpha_i - \beta_i M_i^* + \delta_i M_i^{*2} \qquad (12.7)$$

We illustrate this abatement cost function in Figure 12.13. Note that the abatement cost function is defined only over part of the range of the quadratic function. Abatement costs are zero when the emission limit is set at $\hat{M}_i$, the level the firm would have itself chosen to emit in the absence of control. Abatement costs are maximised when $M_i^* = 0$, and so the firm is prohibited from producing any emissions.

Two things should be said about Equation 12.7. First, as each parameter is indexed by i, abatement costs are allowed to vary over firms. Second, the arguments that follow do

not depend on the abatement cost function being quadratic. We have chosen that functional form for expositional simplicity only.

The least cost theorem

We now consider the problem of the environmental protection agency (EPA) meeting some standard for total emissions (from all N firms) at the least cost. Let M^* denote the predetermined total emission target. In the expressions that follow, the M_i^* variables are to be interpreted as endogenous, the values for which are not predetermined but emerge from the optimising exercise being undertaken. The problem can be stated as

$$\text{Minimise } \sum_{i=1}^{N} C_i \text{ subject to } M^* = \sum_{i=1}^{N} M_i^*$$
$$(12.8)$$

The Lagrangian for this problem is

$$L = \sum_{i=1}^{N} C_i + \lambda \left(M^* - \sum_{i=1}^{N} M_i^* \right)$$

$$= \sum_{i=1}^{N} (\alpha_i - \beta_i M_i^* + \delta_i M_i^{*2})$$

$$+ \lambda \left(M^* - \sum_{i=1}^{N} M_i^* \right) \qquad (12.9)$$

The necessary conditions for a least-cost solution are

$$\frac{\partial L}{\partial M_i^*} = -\beta_i + 2\delta_i M_i^* - \lambda^* = 0$$
$$i = 1, 2, \ldots, N \qquad (12.10)$$

and

$$\frac{\partial L}{\partial \lambda} = M^* - \sum_{i=1}^{N} M_i^* = 0 \qquad (12.11)$$

Equations 12.10 and 12.11 give $N + 1$ equations in $N + 1$ unknowns. Solving these simultaneously gives each firm's emission limit, M_i^* (which now should be regarded as the *optimised* emissions limit for the firm), and the optimised shadow price of the pollution constraint (the Lagrange multiplier) λ^*.

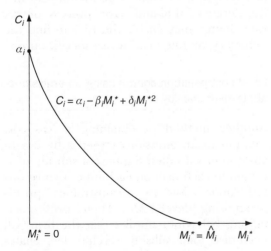

Figure 12.13 The firm's abatement cost function.

Equation 12.10 can be written as:

$$-\beta_i + 2\delta_i M_i^* = \lambda^* \qquad i = 1, 2, \ldots, N$$

The left-hand side of this equation, $-\beta_i + 2\delta_i M_i^*$ is the ith firm's marginal cost of abating pollution. This can be confirmed by differentiation of Equation 12.7. The right-hand side of the above equation, λ^*, is the shadow price of the emission constraint. A tightening of this constraint increases minimised total abatement costs.

Since λ^* is constant over all firms, we reach the conclusion that a least-cost pollution abatement programme requires that the marginal cost of abatement is equal over all firms.

Least-cost pollution control using quantitative regulation

If the EPA knew each firm's abatement cost function (that is, it knew C_i for $i = 1, \ldots, N$), then for any total emission standard it seeks, M^*, the system of Equations 12.10 and 12.11 could be solved for M_i^* for each firm. The EPA could then tell each firm how much it could emit. The total quantity of emissions would, from Equation 12.11, be reached exactly, and the target would, as the above theorem shows, be attained at least cost.

Least-cost pollution control using an emissions tax

As an alternative to setting quantitative emissions controls on each firm, an emission tax could be used. If the EPA knew each firm's abatement cost function, then for any total emission standard it seeks, M^*, the system of Equations 12.10 and 12.11 could be solved for the value of the shadow price of the pollution constraint, λ^*. Note that unlike M_i^*, this shadow price is constant for each firm. The EPA could then set a tax at a rate of t^* per unit emissions and charge each firm this tax on each unit of pollution it emitted. Profit-maximising behaviour would then lead each firm to produce M_i^* emissions, the least-cost solution.

To see why this should be so, note that in the absence of any quantity constraint on

emissions, profit-maximising behaviour in the face of an emissions tax implies that the firm will minimise the sum of its abatement costs and pollution tax costs. That is, the firm chooses M_i^* to minimise CT_i, the total of its abatement and tax costs:

$$CT_i = C_i + tM_i^* = \alpha_i - \beta_i M_i^* + \delta_i M_i^{*2} + t^* M_i^*$$

The necessary condition is

$$\frac{\partial CT_i}{\partial M_i^*} = -\beta_i + 2\delta_i M_i^* + t^* = 0 \qquad (12.12)$$
$$i = 1, 2, \ldots, N$$

Clearly, if t^* in Equations 12.12 is set equal to $-\lambda^*$ in Equations 12.10, the necessary conditions 12.10 and 12.12 are identical, and so the tax instrument achieves the total emissions target at least cost.

What role is there for a tax instrument where each firm's abatement cost functions are not known?

In general, the EPA will not know abatement costs. However, if an arbitrarily chosen tax rate, say $\bar{t}$, is selected, and each firm is charged that rate on each unit of emission, then *some* total quantity of emissions, say $\bar{M}$, will be realised at least cost. Of course, that amount $\bar{M}$ will in general be different from M^*. Only if $\bar{t} = t^*$ will $\bar{M}$ be identical to M^*. An iterative, trial-and-error process of tax rate change may enable the EPA to find the necessary tax rate to achieve a specific target.

Least-cost pollution control using an emissions-abatement subsidy

Another method of obtaining a least-cost solution to an emissions target is by use of abatement subsidies. Suppose a subsidy of s^* is paid to each firm on each unit of emissions reduction below its unconstrained profit-maximising level, $\hat{M}_i$. Then profit-maximising behaviour implies that the firm will maximise total subsidy receipts less abatement costs. That is, the firm maximises

$$CS_i = s(\hat{M}_i - M_i^*) - c_i = s(\hat{M}_i - M_i^*) \\ - (\alpha_i - \beta_i M_i^* + \delta_i M_i^{*2})$$

The necessary condition is

$$\frac{\partial S_i}{\partial M_i^*} = \beta_i - 2\delta_i M_i^* - s = 0 \qquad i = 1, 2, \ldots, N \tag{12.13}$$

which, after multiplying through by -1, is identical to Equation 12.12 if $s = t$. So once again, if s in Equation 12.13 is set equal to $-\lambda^*$ in Equation 12.10, the necessary conditions 12.10 and 12.13 are identical, and so the tax instrument achieves the total emissions target at least cost. Moreover, this result demonstrates that in terms of their effects on emissions, a tax rate of t per unit emissions is identical to a subsidy rate of s per unit of emissions abatement, provided $s = t$.

Least-cost pollution control using transferable emissions permits

Suppose that the EPA issues to each firm licenses permitting L_i^0 units of emissions. Firms are allowed to trade with one another in permits. The ith firm will trade in permits so as to minimise the sum of abatement costs and trade-acquired permits:

$$CL_i = C_i + P(L_i - L_i^0) = \alpha_i - \beta_i M_i \\ + \delta_i M_i^2 + P(L_i - L_i^0) \tag{12.14}$$

where P is the market price of one emission permit. Given that L_i is the quantity of emissions the firm will produce after trade we can write this as

$$CL_i = C_i + P(L_i - L_i^0) = \alpha_i - \beta_i L_i \\ + \delta_i L_i^2 + P(L_i - L_i^0) \tag{12.15}$$

The necessary condition for minimisation is

$$\frac{\partial CL_i}{\partial L_i} = -\beta_i + 2\delta_i L_i + P = 0 \qquad i = 1, 2, \ldots, N \tag{12.16}$$

which can be interpreted as the firm's demand function for permits.

If the EPA sets a total emissions target of M^* then M^* is the total supply of permits and

$$M^* = \sum_{i=1}^{N} L_i^0 = \sum_{i=1}^{N} L_i \tag{12.17}$$

Now compare Equations 12.16 and 12.17 with Equations 12.10 and 12.11. These are identical if $P = -\lambda^*$ (remembering that $L_i = M_i^*$). Moreover, comparison of Equation 12.16 with Equations 12.12 and 12.13 shows that $P = t = s$. So by an initial issue of permits (distributed in any way) equal to the emissions target, the EPA can realise the target at least cost. Moreover, it can do so without knowledge of individual firms' abatement cost functions.

Least-cost abatement for a non-uniformly mixing pollutant

The target of the EPA is now in terms of ambient pollution levels rather than emission flows. Specifically the EPA requires that

$$A_j = \sum_{i=1}^{N} d_{ji} M_i^* \leqslant A_j^* \qquad \text{for } j = 1, \ldots, J \tag{12.18}$$

The problem for the EPA is to attain this target at least cost. We deal with the case where the same ambient target is set for each receptor area. This problem can be stated as

$$\text{Minimise } \sum_{i=1}^{N} C_i \text{ subject to}$$

$$A_j = \sum_{i=1}^{N} d_{ji} M_i \leqslant A^* \text{ for } j = 1, \ldots, J \tag{12.19}$$

The Lagrangian for this problem is

$$L = \sum_{i=1}^{N} C_i + \lambda_1 \left(A^* - \sum_{i=1}^{N} d_{1i} M_i^* \right)$$

$$+ \ldots + \lambda_J \left(A^* - \sum_{i=1}^{N} d_{ji} M_i^* \right) \tag{12.20}$$

where $C_i = \alpha_i - \beta_i M_i^* + \delta_i M_i^{*2}$

The necessary conditions for a least cost solution are

$$\frac{\partial L}{\partial M_i^*} = -\beta_i + 2\delta_i M_i^* - \sum_{j=1}^{j=J} (\lambda_j^* d_{ji}) = 0$$

$$i = 1, 2, \ldots, N \tag{12.21}$$

and

$$\frac{\partial L}{\partial \lambda_j} = A^* - \sum_{i=1}^{N} d_{ji} M_i^* = 0 \text{ for } j = 1, \ldots, J$$

$$\tag{12.22}$$

Equation 12.21 can be written as

$$-\beta_i + 2\delta_i M_i^* = \sum_{j=1}^{j=J} (\lambda_j^* d_{ji}) \qquad i = 1, 2, \ldots, N$$

$$\tag{12.23}$$

which can be compared with the solution for the uniformly-mixing pollution case, Equation 12.10:

$$-\beta_i + 2\delta_i M_i^* = \lambda^* \qquad i = 1, 2, \ldots N$$

International environmental problems

But did thee feel the earth move?

Ernest Hemingway, *For Whom the Bell Tolls*, chapter 13

Introduction

In this chapter we investigate environmental problems in a framework which recognises that we live in a world of many sovereign states. There are two central themes running through our discussions. The first concerns the relationship between international trade and the environment, and the second concerns the transmission of pollution across national boundaries.

We begin by looking at the trade–environment relationship. A central tenet of economic theory is, and has for a long time been, that free trade can improve economic welfare. This belief explains the strength of attachment that many economists have to measures that liberalise international trade. However, there are conditions under which free trade will not be welfare enhancing. We explore one of these: free trade does not necessarily lead to welfare improvements when there are unresolved pollution problems within one or more countries, even where economies satisfy the 'ideal' requirements of perfect market economies in all other respects.

Trade between nations does not only involve the movement of ordinary goods and services; it can also affect the spatial location of pollution wastes. In particular, where countries differ in the degree to which environmentally damaging behaviour is regulated, trade and the international mobility of factors of production may lead countries with relatively weak environmental protection to become pollution dustbins, with important consequences for economic welfare. We

explore the mechanisms through which this may happen.

Our second central theme in this chapter concerns the consequences of cross-boundary pollution spillovers. Throughout our analysis of pollution in Chapters 11 and 12, an implicit assumption being made was that an emission has only domestic impacts. Pollution damages are borne entirely by residents of the nation in which the emissions occur, as are the costs of any control measures undertaken. In these circumstances, the principles we used in Chapters 11 and 12 to identify an efficient or optimal quantity of pollution and to design appropriate policy instruments are applicable in a straightforward manner. But matters are not so straightforward in a world of many sovereign states. In particular, the state of the environment in any country depends not only on its own behaviour but also on the behaviour of other countries.

To see how the environment can be affected by economic behaviour in other countries, consider those pollution flows that are transported over national boundaries by natural processes. Examples include oxides of nitrogen and sulphur, which can be moved over distances of several hundred miles. These precursors of acid rain are not uniformly mixing; their impacts tend to be focused in particular (but often quite large) areas clustered around the pollution source. Figure 13.1 shows the incremental sulphur dioxide concentrations attributable to a single oil combined cycle power station located near Stuttgart in Germany. Significant SO_2 depositions are felt over distances of up to 1000 miles and over most European states.

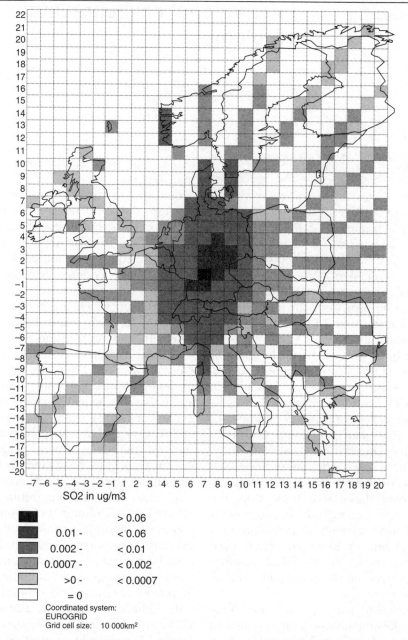

Figure 13.1 Incremental SO_2 concentrations from an oil combined cycle power station located in Lauffen, Germany.
Source: ExternE (1995), page 61.

Non-uniformly mixing pollutants of this kind could be described as regional pollutants, by virtue of this property of geographical clustering. Another class of pollutants has global impacts because the emissions enter the higher-level atmosphere and are eventually uniformly mixed. The impacts are not restricted to zones 'close' to points of emission as they are for regional pollutants. In this class are found the various greenhouse gases and those emissions that act to deplete stratospheric ozone.

Common to all regional and global pollution problems is the fact that the adverse impacts of the pollution are not borne entirely by citizens of any single nation. This adds major complications to the design and implementation of efficient and equitable control programmes. However, it still remains the case that the concepts of externalities and public goods provide powerful tools for the analysis of international pollution problems.

Our previous analyses of pollution, externalities and public goods have demonstrated that, in the absence of suitable regulatory mechanisms or incentives to alter behaviour, polluters are likely to regard environmental resources as free goods and pollute to levels that are economically inefficient. This remains true for global and regional pollutants. However, where significant proportions of the adverse impacts are felt in different political units from those where the emission occurs, or where significant proportions of the benefits of pollution control programmes accrue to those living in territories outside those in which the control is effected, the problems are greatly intensified. The likelihood that polluters will regard environmental media as free common property resources is increased, and the private incentives to control emissions will be weaker (and in some cases non-existent).

Of particular importance here is the structure of incentives facing governments. We assumed in Chapters 11 and 12 that government could, and often would, act to maximise the net social benefit of the community. But for the classes of pollutants we are examining in this chapter, the community of affected people is no longer identical with the citizens of an individual country. Look back again to Figure 13.1. Substantial amounts of sulphur dioxide precipitation from the Lauffen power station will fall as acid rain outside Germany. When the government is comparing the national costs and national

benefits of SO_2 abatement, those spillovers will not enter the calculations, with the result that it may effect less control than it would if the impacts of its emissions were felt entirely within its own boundaries.

So the existence of pollution spillovers may mean that an individual country has weak incentives to implement pollution control schemes unilaterally. Incentives may even act in a perverse direction. Not only may a country choose not to unilaterally undertake pollution control, it may find it individually rational not to participate in control programmes that others undertake. By not participating, it gets advantages from the control that others do but avoids the abatement costs that others incur and so gain a competitive advantage in international trade. In some instances, individual rationality may even lead a country to generate more pollution if others do less.

To illustrate our arguments, we shall examine three important cases of international environmental pollution: acid rain, ozone depletion and the so-called greenhouse effect. However, while it will be convenient to present our analysis largely in terms of international pollution problems, it is clear that environmental problems are not necessarily caused by pollution flows. Tropical deforestation, wilderness conversion and the loss of biological diversity, for example, are not principally caused by pollution flows. As you read through this chapter, ask yourself how the arguments being developed could be applied to non-pollution environmental problems (and also try to relate the analysis back to our studies of deforestation and biodiversity loss in earlier chapters). We shall also have more to say about the loss of natural wilderness areas in Chapter 15.

Trade and the environment

The proposition that free trade can improve economic welfare is one of the oldest, and

most widely accepted, principles of economics. It has played a part in shaping much
of the international political, economic and
institutional framework that has been built
up since 1945 (for example, single-market
areas such as the European Union, and
GATT, now known as the World Trade
Organization). Is the validity of this proposition affected by the existence of environmental pollution?

To examine this question, let us investigate
a simple 'world' of two countries, X and Y,
each of which produces two goods, A and B.[1]
Each country acts as a price-taker, regarding
the world price of a good as fixed and
beyond its control. It is generally thought
that free trade will bring positive net benefits
to both countries compared with a situation
where no trade is allowed. To see why, we
can examine the changes in consumers' surplus and producers' surplus that arise from
the introduction of trade.[2] Figure 13.2 portrays the demand and supply curves for good
A in each of the two countries. In the absence
of international trade, country X produces
and consumes the quantity A_X at price P_X;
country Y produces and consumes A_Y at
price P_Y.

The opening of free trade establishes a
common world price, P_W. As the world price
is below its pre-trade domestic price, X
becomes an importer of good A; Y becomes
an exporter of good A. Let us identify the
changes that take place in consumer and producer surpluses with respect to good A in the
two countries. For country X, in Figure
13.2(a), the opening of trade causes domestic
production to fall to A_{SX} while domestic consumption increases to A_{DX}. Imports make up
the shortfall of domestic production relative
to domestic consumption. Consumer surplus
– the area below the demand function but
above the price paid by consumers –

[1] The argument could be generalised to many
countries and many goods but for simplicity we shall not
do so.
[2] The concepts of consumers' and producers' surplus
were explained in Chapter 5.

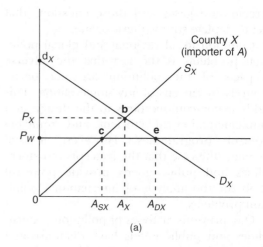

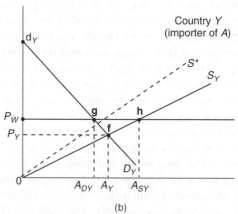

Figure 13.2   Trade and the environment.

increases from the area $P_X\mathbf{b}d_X$ to the area
$P_W\mathbf{e}d_X$. Producer surplus – the area above
the supply function but below the price
received by sellers – falls from $0\mathbf{b}P_X$ to $0\mathbf{c}P_W$.
The gain in consumer surplus is greater than
the loss of producer surplus by an amount
equal to the area **ceb**, and so the importing
country has a net gain in welfare from trade
in good A.

By inspection of the Figure 13.2(b), it can
be seen that the exporting country also
experiences a net welfare gain from the
opening of trade. With trade, domestic production of good A is A_{SY} while domestic consumption is A_{DY}. The surplus production is
exported to country X. Consumer surplus

associated with good A falls from the area $P_Y\mathbf{f}\mathbf{d}_Y$ to the area $P_W\mathbf{g}\mathbf{d}_Y$. Producer surplus increases from $0\mathbf{f}P_Y$ to $0\mathbf{h}P_W$. The gain in producer surplus is greater than the loss of consumer surplus by an amount equal to the area **fhg**, and so the exporter has a net gain in welfare from trade in good A.[3]

This is just one version of the familiar argument for free trade. However, it should be noted that the argument as it stands is only strictly valid if there are no 'distortions' present anywhere in the economies in question (that is, if all the conditions set out in Chapter 5 are satisfied). But does this argument for free trade carry over to a situation where production generates adverse environmental externalities? Suppose that producing good A generates an adverse externality that affects only the citizens of the producing country (that is, there is no international pollution spillover). For the importing country, we have already seen that the opening of trade reduces its domestic production of the good, and so the magnitude of the environmental externality will also fall there. Bringing external effects into the picture reinforces the argument for trade for this country.

But matters are not clear-cut for the country that becomes an exporter. Its increased volume of production raises external costs, which reduces the net gains from the opening of trade. The rise in pollution externalities may be larger than the previously explained net surplus gain, in which case the country will experience a net welfare loss. Further information is needed to derive an unambiguous conclusion about whether trade will benefit the exporting country (or indeed the two countries collectively). However, it is clear that the presence of production externalities weakens the case for free trade.

[3] Although it is not shown in Figure 13.2, equivalent conclusions must follow from examination of changes in welfare associated with trade in the other good (although the direction of trade flows would be reversed). So it does no harm to our analysis to focus on just one good.

Next suppose that the opening of an economy to international trade is accompanied by the introduction of some pollution control programme. Is it possible to be any more precise about the consequences of such a package? If, for example, a uniform tax rate were imposed on units of emission in the exporting country, the supply function would rotate anticlockwise to a position such as that shown by the function $0S^*$ in Figure 13.2(b). As compared with the trade-but-no-pollution-control situation, emissions will fall and so external costs will be reduced. However, producer surplus will also be smaller, as is evident from inspection of the figure. In general it is not possible to know whether the reduction in pollution externalities will be more or less than the fall in producer surplus, once again leaving the overall welfare effect ambiguous.

There is, however, one case where the outcome is not ambiguous. If the pollution control programme – whether it uses taxes, permits or other controls – is economically efficient then, as we demonstrated in Chapter 11, the gain in avoided pollution costs must exceed the fall in producer surplus – see particularly Figures 11.4 and 11.5 and the accompanying discussion. In this particular circumstance, therefore, we do have a clear result. Opening economies to international trade will result in net welfare gains provided that this is accompanied by the introduction of an economically efficient pollution control programme to internalise any pollution externality (provided that was the only distortion present).

As a matter of practice, however, one should note that the world is one in which distortions are pervasive, environmental pollution problems are rarely if ever fully internalised, and it is almost impossible to design fully efficient pollution control programmes. Whether free trade is a welfare maximising institutional framework is, therefore, a moot point. Now let us consider some other routes through which international trade may impact upon the environment. Runge (1995) discusses five ways in which this can happen, outlined in the following subsections.

Allocative efficiency effects (+)

Trade promotes allocative efficiency. The elimination of barriers to trade will tend, therefore, to result in efficiency gains. Runge cites, by way of example, the waste and inefficiency in the old Soviet bloc that arose partly because of its closure to international trade. Runge also claims (although rather more controversially) that the policy of self-sufficiency in agriculture within the European Union has contributed to substantial environmental damage. Note that these allocative efficiency gains are equivalent to the gains in consumer/producer surpluses described earlier in this chapter.

Scale effects (−)

The growth of international trade tends to increase the size of GDP per capita, and has a number of other scale increasing effects (such as on transportation and packaging). Ceteris paribus, the magnitudes of environmental impacts are positively related to the magnitude of economic throughput flows, and so to GDP (but see Chapter 2 and our discussion of the Environmental Kuznets Curve for some qualifications).

Composition of output effects (+)

Trade is typically associated with shifts in the relative sizes and sectoral composition of output.

Technology effects (+)

Trade tends to induce technological innovation.

Policy effects (?)

The growth of international trade induces policy reforms and responses.

Trade can affect the environment through each of these routes. Runge's assessment of the most likely direction of these impacts is indicated by the signs adjacent to the subheadings, where (+) denotes an expected beneficial impact and (−) an expected adverse impact. It is clear from inspection of the signs in this set of links that we must remain agnostic about even the direction of the overall impact.

However, there are some reasons why we might believe that trade could have a damaging overall effect. One we have already discussed. A second arises from the fact that the process of exchange of goods and services across national boundaries has as its counterpart the international movement of environmental 'bads'. Individual countries may, unwittingly or intentionally, 'export' pollution problems to others. In general, one would expect environmental bads to accumulate in those countries with the least environmental regulation (which will in general be the developing countries). So unless pollution policy were somehow coordinated so that the degree of regulation were uniform everywhere, one would expect to find that pollution will tend to accumulate in 'pollution havens' where regulation is the most weak.

Indeed, it may be that some countries deliberately choose to trade-off more environmental pollution for a better competitive position in terms of output and employment gained by lower environmental standards (see Esty, 1994). Also, the fear of losing international competitiveness by acting ahead of others in terms of environmental regulation may slow the adoption of stricter environmental controls. We return briefly to these issues in the final part of this chapter in discussing GATT (the General Agreement on Tariffs and Trade), now known as the World Trade Organization, or WTO for short.

If the effects we have described were merely redistributive, these arguments would be of limited consequence if our interest lies only in the total quantity of environmental degradation. But the effects are not only redistributive; they may also affect the total amount of degradation if the process of transfer entails environmental losses, dose–response functions are non-linear, or heavy concentrations of pollution exceed local carrying capacities.

A third reason for concern is that where environmental externalities spill across national boundaries, it is considerably more difficult to control environmental degradation, and to find appropriate instruments for doing so. In the absence of any international regulatory authority, international policy coordination is required. But as we show later, this is by no means easy to achieve.

The conclusion we draw is that the process of liberalising international trade (and possibly the growth of trade itself) may have adverse environmental consequences, and may increase the difficulty of controlling environmental degradation.

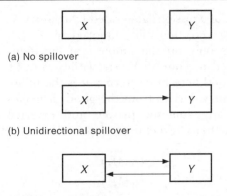

(a) No spillover

(b) Unidirectional spillover

(c) Reciprocal spillovers

Figure 13.3   Pollution flows over national boundaries.

Exploring behaviour when pollution spills over national boundaries

In this section, we try to deduce how countries might behave when the pollution generated within their economy spills over national boundaries. To keep things simple, we consider once again a world of only two countries; the results we obtain can easily be generalised to the many-country case. We also suppose that production in both countries generates a particular pollutant. Figure 13.3 presents a classification that will be useful in what follows.

In the first case, (a), there is no pollution spillover. Although each producer generates external effects on its own citizens, the zone of influence of each country's emissions is limited to its own territory. We call this the 'no spillover' case. It was the setting in which we investigated international trade in the previous section. Case (b) is that of a 'unidirectional spillover'. An asymmetry operates in this case: there is a one-way international pollution spillover. The emissions of one country – country X, let us suppose – affect citizens of the other country, but the emissions of the other country have no effect on the first. The third situation, case (c), is known as 'reciprocal spillovers'. Emissions in each country have adverse effects upon citizens in the other.

There are two ways in which economists investigate behaviour when a small number of players (in this case, countries) need to make choices in situations of strategic interdependence. One of these uses optimisation analysis to compare the likely outcomes of individualistic, non-cooperative behaviour with behaviour that is cooperative in the sense that the collective interest of the set of players as a whole is maximised. The second approach is through game-theory analysis. These will be explained and illustrated in the following two sections.

Non-cooperative and cooperative behaviour

To do optimisation analysis, it is necessary to specify one or more functions that are to be maximised. It seems sensible to assume that each country wishes to maximise some form of utility function. Using M to denote emissions and U to denote utility, we begin by describing the utility functions for each country. In the 'no spillovers' case, the utility enjoyed by X, U_X, depends only on the amount of emissions generated by country X, M_X. Likewise, the utility enjoyed by Y, U_Y, depends only on the amount of emissions generated by country Y, M_Y. Utility is to be understood here in net terms: it is the utility the country derives from the goods it makes net of any domestic private and external costs due to its own emissions. So we have

$$U_X = U_X(M_X)$$
$$U_Y = U_Y(M_Y)$$

Next consider the *unidirectional spillover* case. Specifically, Y's emissions only affect individuals in country Y, but X's emissions affect individuals in both countries. Then the utility functions are

$$U_X = U_X(M_X)$$
$$U_Y = U_Y(M_X, M_Y)$$

For the reciprocal spillover case, the utility in each country is affected by the emissions of both countries, so the utility functions are

$$U_X = U_X(M_X, M_Y)$$
$$U_Y = U_Y(M_X, M_Y)$$

Non-cooperative behaviour

Non-cooperative behaviour is sometimes called individualistic or isolated behaviour. Loosely speaking, it refers to the situation where each country does the best it can for itself, irrespective of the consequences this has on others. This description is a bit misleading because, as we will demonstrate, doing the 'best it can for itself' may necessitate some form of cooperation. A more precise way of defining this form of behaviour is as follows: each country sets the values of its instrument variables to maximise its own objective function, on the assumption that the values of other countries' instruments are given (fixed). In the examples we are considering each country has just one instrument: the choice of its own pollution level.

Box 13.1 shows the non-cooperative outcome for the no spillover, unidirectional spillover and reciprocal spillovers cases. The non-cooperative outcome is identical in all three cases; each country pollutes up to the point where it derives no additional utility from further emissions. The reason why the outcome is identical in each case is simple, and follows from the nature of non-cooperative behaviour itself: each country is ignoring the effect (if any) its emissions have on the other. So even in the two cases where there is a spillover effect, it will be ignored by decision makers and so does not influence their choices.

Cooperative behaviour

Even if countries are ultimately interested in their own well-being, non-cooperative behaviour does not necessarily secure the best outcomes available. It may be better to cooperate with other countries to seek joint improvements. For the problem with which we are concerned, cooperative behaviour consists of the two countries jointly choosing levels of emissions so as to maximise their collective well-being. The joint decision process may also involve negotiations about how the additional benefits from cooperation are to be distributed between the parties. Cooperative behaviour is equivalent to what would happen if the two countries were unified as a single country that behaved rationally.

In the no spillover case, actions in one country have no effect elsewhere, and so cooperation offers no additional benefits over individualistic behaviour. The collective interest is fully served by each country doing the best it can individually. It follows from this (and is confirmed in Box 13.1) that in the no spillover case the non-cooperative and cooperative outcomes are identical.

But this is not true in the other two cases. Consider first the unidirectional spillover. Cooperative behaviour entails choosing pollution levels in X and Y jointly to maximise the combined utility function $U = U_X + U_Y$. The

---

Box 13.1 Non-cooperative and cooperative outcomes to the three spillover cases

Case 1: No spillover

The utility functions for countries X and Y are:

$$U_X = U_X(M_X)$$
$$U_Y = U_Y(M_Y)$$

Non-cooperative solution

X chooses M_X so as to maximise U_X. The necessary condition for a maximum is

$$\frac{dU_X}{dM_X} = 0 \qquad (13.1)$$

Y chooses M_Y so as to maximise U_Y. The necessary condition for a maximum is

$$\frac{dU_Y}{dM_Y} = 0 \qquad (13.2)$$

Cooperative solution

The values of M_X and M_Y are jointly chosen so as to maximise the combined utility of the two countries, $U = U_X + U_Y$. The necessary conditions for a maximum are

$$\frac{\partial U}{\partial M_X} = 0 \Rightarrow \frac{dU_X}{dM_X} = 0 \qquad (13.3)$$

$$\frac{\partial U}{\partial M_Y} = 0 \Rightarrow \frac{dU_Y}{dM_Y} = 0 \qquad (13.4)$$

Case 2: Unidirectional spillover

The utility functions for countries X and Y are:

$$U_X = U_X(M_X)$$
$$U_Y = U_Y(M_X, M_Y)$$

Non-cooperative solution

As in the no spillover case, X chooses M_X so as to maximise U_X and Y chooses M_Y so as to maximise U_Y. The necessary conditions are Equations 13.1 and 13.2.

Cooperative solution

The values of M_X and M_Y are jointly chosen so as to maximise the combined utility of the two countries, $U = U_X + U_Y$. The necessary conditions for a maximum are

$$\frac{\partial U}{\partial M_X} = 0 \Rightarrow \frac{dU_X}{dM_X} + \frac{\delta U_Y}{\delta M_X} = 0 \qquad (13.5)$$

$$\frac{\partial U}{\partial M_Y} = 0 \Rightarrow \frac{\delta U_Y}{\delta M_Y} = 0 \qquad (13.6)$$

Note that Equation 13.5 implies that

$$\frac{dU_X}{dM_X} = -\frac{\delta U_Y}{\delta M_X} \qquad (13.7)$$

Case 3: Reciprocal spillovers

The utility functions for countries X and Y are

$$U_X = U_X(M_X, M_Y)$$
$$U_Y = U_Y(M_X, M_Y)$$

Non-cooperative solution

As in both previous cases, X chooses M_X so as to maximise U_X and Y chooses M_Y so as to maximise U_Y. The necessary conditions are again Equations 13.1 and 13.2.

Cooperative solution

The values of M_X and M_Y are jointly chosen so as to maximise the combined utility of the two countries, $U = U_X + U_Y$. The necessary conditions for a maximum are

$$\frac{\partial U}{\partial M_X} = 0 \Rightarrow \frac{\delta U_X}{\delta M_X} + \frac{\delta U_Y}{\delta M_X} = 0 \Rightarrow \frac{\delta U_X}{\delta M_X} = -\frac{\delta U_Y}{\delta M_X}$$
(13.8)

$$\frac{\partial U}{\partial M_Y} = 0 \Rightarrow \frac{\delta U_Y}{\delta M_Y} + \frac{\delta U_X}{\delta M_Y} = 0 \Rightarrow \frac{\delta U_Y}{\delta M_Y} = -\frac{\delta U_X}{\delta M_Y}$$
(13.9)

---

cooperative outcome does not require any change in the behaviour of Y as X is unaffected by Y's behaviour. But as U_Y depends on emissions in both X and Y, the optimisation process requires that X take into account the effect of its emissions not only upon itself but also on the other country. Specifically, the cooperative solution for X requires that

$$\frac{dU_X}{dM_X} = -\frac{\delta U_Y}{\delta M_X}$$

or, in alternative notation,

$$\mathrm{MU}_X^X = -\mathrm{MU}_X^Y$$

We represent this maximising condition in Figure 13.4. Note that MU_X^Y, the change in

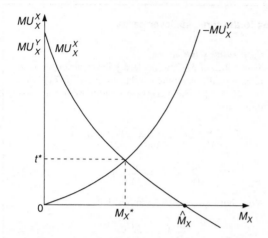

Figure 13.4 A unidirectional externality and its implications for pollutant emissions of the country generating the external effect.

Y's utility arising from a marginal increase in X's emissions, is negative. Multiplying it by minus one converts this magnitude into a positive quantity, as drawn in Figure 13.4. We have shown this marginal impact as rising in absolute value as the emission level of X becomes higher, but this is not necessarily true. However, different slopes for that function do not substantially alter the conclusions we shall reach. The emission level $\hat{M}_X$ can be thought of as the non-cooperative choice of emissions made by country X, choosing to ignore the external effect upon Y. In contrast, M_X^* is the cooperative choice. Note that at this emission level, the marginal utility X gains from an additional unit of emissions is equal to the (negative of) the marginal utility loss Y suffers from that additional unit. We could have described $-MU_X^Y$ as the marginal damage Y suffers from X's emissions, in which case you may recognise that this is just another example of a diagram we have used several times before. Indeed, it is identical in form to Figure 12.2, which represented the noise interference by a musician on his neighbour. This was also a unidirectional spillover, but between two individuals rather than two countries.

Much of the discussion surrounding that music example is also relevant here. What we called the 'efficient outcome' there is equivalent to M_X^* here. We also showed that side payments or compensation might be needed to bring about this efficient outcome. Those arguments generalise in a straightforward way to the case of international pollution, except that there may be no well-established property rights to the atmosphere so we might suspect that bargaining solutions would be rather difficult to achieve.

Finally, turning to the reciprocal spillover case, note that the cooperative outcome requires that both countries take account of their effects upon the other, and so two marginal conditions must be satisfied, each of which has a graphical interpretation of the type shown in Figure 13.4:

$$\frac{\delta U_X}{\delta M_X} = -\frac{\delta U_Y}{\delta M_X}$$

and

$$\frac{\delta U_Y}{\delta M_Y} = -\frac{\delta U_X}{\delta M_Y}$$

The cooperative solution we have described is fully efficient for the two countries when treated as a single entity. Indeed, if some supranational governmental body existed, acting to maximise total net benefits, and had sufficient authority to impose its decision, then the outcome would be a cooperative one such as we have described. It is also worth noting that if such a single supranational government chose to use a pollution tax as an instrument to bring about fully efficient abatement, our analysis can show how such a tax rate could be selected. For example, looking at Figure 13.4 again, the authority would impose a tax rate of t^* on each unit of pollution emitted by country X. This tax corresponds to the marginal pollution damage affecting other countries. Note that this tax would be additional to any tax on pollution that a national government might impose to deal with intra-national pollution damages.

Box 13.2 Cooperation and the greenhouse effect

When economists begin thinking a problem through, they often just use intuition to select some appropriate functions for analysis. The idea is to use some simple approximations as the basis for a first pass at the problem. Let us do this as a way of illustrating the possible benefits from cooperation over the greenhouse effect.

We can envisage international action – or the lack of it – concerning the greenhouse effect as a process of negotiation between two players: the developing countries (X, let's say) and the industrialised countries (Y).

We begin by choosing plausible functions to describe the costs and benefits of greenhouse gas (GHG) emissions for the two players. The total benefit functions are $B_X = 10M_X - M_X^2$ and $B_Y = 10M_Y - M_Y^2$. These are drawn in (a) of Figure 13.5. Three points are worth noting about these functions:

(a) For each group of countries, benefit is a quadratic function of its emissions. One way in which this would arise is if emissions are a constant multiple of goods output, and benefits are a quadratic function of goods output.

(b) The parameters of the benefit functions are identical for the two groups of countries. This would be true if the output–emissions ratio was the same for both, *and* the utility functions (linking goods to benefit) were identical. One might object that at present income levels the marginal benefit of goods (and so emissions) is higher in the poorer, developing countries.

(c) A quadratic function with a negative parameter on the second-order term in the function (that is, the variable which is squared) will eventually be negatively sloped. This does not make much sense. So strictly speaking, we wish to consider only the upward sloping part of the function. The solution will only make sense if it falls within that range.

The cost functions we use are $C_X = 4(M_X + M_Y)$ and $C_Y = 2(M_X + M_Y)$, as shown in Figure 13.5(b). There are two points of interest here:

(a) The costs to each player from greenhouse warming depend on the combined emissions from the two blocks of countries. This follows from the fact that greenhouse gas emissions are uniformly mixing pollutants.

(b) For any given value of $M_X + M_Y$ the damages are twice as high in group X. It seems plausible to claim that damages would be much higher in developing countries (although whether damages would be different if both regions were at the same level of development is a moot point).

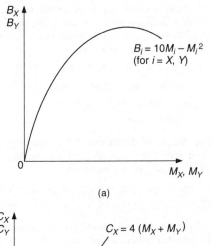

(a)

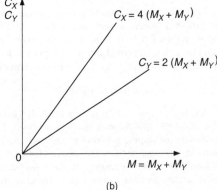

(b)

Figure 13.5 Benefits and costs in the greenhouse game.

Next, let us define 'utility' as benefits minus costs, so we have

$$U_X = 10M_X - M_X^2 - 4(M_X + M_Y) \quad (13.10)$$

$$U_Y = 10M_Y - M_Y^2 - 2(M_X + M_Y) \quad (13.11)$$

What we have called *non-cooperative* behaviour involves each block emitting up to the point where the marginal utility to itself of its own emissions is zero (see Equations 13.1 and 13.2). So we obtain the partial derivatives of U_X with respect to M_X and U_Y with respect to M_Y, set the resulting equations equal to zero, and solve for the individually maximising levels of emissions. This gives us:

$$\partial U_X/\partial M_X = 10 - 2M_X - 4 = 0 \Rightarrow M_X = 3 \quad (13.12)$$

$$\partial U_Y/\partial M_Y = 10 - 2M_Y - 2 = 0 \Rightarrow M_Y = 4 \quad (13.13)$$

with a world total emissions of 7 units.

Box 13.2 continued

Next, suppose that an international conference agrees that emissions are to be set at the collectively optimal (that is, cooperative) level. In other words, M_X and M_Y are chosen to maximise

$$U = U_X + U_Y = \{10M_X - M_X{}^2 - 4(M_X + M_Y)\}$$
$$+ \{10M_Y - M_Y{}^2 - 2(M_X + M_Y)\}$$
$$= 10M_X + 10M_Y - M_X{}^2 - M_Y{}^2$$
$$- 6(M_X + M_Y) \qquad (13.14)$$

Taking the partial derivatives of this collective utility function with respect to M_X and M_Y, setting these equal to zero and solving we obtain:

$$\partial U_X/\partial M_X = 10 - 2M_X - 6 = 0 \Rightarrow M_X = 2 \quad (13.15)$$
$$\partial U_Y/\partial M_Y = 10 - 2M_Y - 6 = 0 \Rightarrow M_Y = 2 \quad (13.16)$$

So cooperation involves each group cutting emissions, but by a larger amount in Y than in X. Total world emissions fall from 7 to 4. At this stage, you should check that you could interpret Equation 13.15 in terms of Figure 13.4. We can rewrite Equation 13.15 as

$$10 - 2M_X - 4 = 2$$

The left-hand side of this equality is simply $MU_X^X = \partial U_X/\partial M_X$ (for the non-cooperative case). This is the downward sloping function in Figure 13.4. The right-hand side is $-MU_X^Y = \partial U_Y/\partial M_X$. However, as this derivative is here constant at the value 2, the upward sloping function in the figure would need to be redrawn as a horizontal line in this case.

Let's return to the international conference. Suppose that negotiations break down. The developing countries say that they are too poor to cut emissions; indeed, they argue that the richer, industrialised countries should bear the burdens of reducing emissions, particularly given that they have been responsible for most of the emissions that have taken place so far.

Several possibilities then arise:

(1) With the breakdown of talks, both sides just revert to the previous non-cooperative position in which X emits 3 and Y emits 4.
(2) The industrialised countries are persuaded to act alone, partly because of the arguments just outlined, and partly in response to political pressure from their electorates. They agree to cut emissions to 2 units (the cooperative solution for that block of countries), irrespective of whatever the developing countries do. What happens to developing countries emissions in this case? The developing countries calculate their utility maximising emissions, given that M_Y is fixed at 2. That is, they choose M_X to maximise

$$U_X = 10M_X - M_X{}^2 - 4(M_X + 2)$$

which gives the solution $M_X = 3$. For the functions we have chosen in this hypothetical example, the result is that the developing countries choose the same emissions level as they would have in the non-cooperative situation. However, this outcome is simply a consequence of the functions we have selected. For some other functions, X's emissions would be higher than under no cooperation. It is even conceivable that emissions by X would rise by so much that total world emissions become higher than they would be under pure non-cooperation, in spite of the fact that one set of countries has made substantial emissions cuts. Hoel (1989) demonstrated this possibility.

(3) Another possibility is that the industrialised countries behave very altruistically. In particular, they agree to act so that whatever the developing countries emit, the industrialised countries will emit only as much as will make the world total 4, the cooperative optimum. Given such a commitment, how much would the developing countries produce? One's first intuition suggests that X would choose M_X to maximise

$$U_X = 10M_X - M_X{}^2$$

giving a solution of $M_X = 5$. The last term in the utility function 13.10 (representing GHG costs) does not appear in this expression because the coefficient on that term is, in effect, zero. Extra emissions by developing countries are compensated for by an equal sized reduction in industrialised country emissions. Developing countries incur no penalty for emitting more because the world total is unaffected.

But this intuition is not quite correct. If X emits 5 units then Y would have to emit -1 in order to attain world emissions of 4. But, of course, emissions cannot be negative. In fact, X has to solve the problem

$$\text{Max } U_X = 10M_X - M_X{}^2 - 4(M_X + M_Y)$$

subject to the constraint that Y's emissions are non-negative.[4] That is

$$M_Y = 4 - M_X \geqslant 0$$

The solution to this gives $M_X = 4$ and $M_Y = 0$. (This can be verified by solving the problem

---

[4] Strictly speaking, both countries must have non-negative emissions. But we have already deduced that this will be the case for X and so that constraint is redundant as it does not bind.

Box 13.2 continued

using the Lagrange multiplier technique for constrained optimisation, given that we know the constraint will bite and so can be written as $4 - M_X = 0$).

This solution – in which one country acts as a kind of cartel swing producer, adjusting its own output so that some given collective total is reached – is not feasible in the numerical example we have investigated. The reason for this is that the industrialised countries would end up with negative utility, as you can see by substituting $M_Y = 0$ in Equation 13.11. Nor does this kind of behaviour seem plausible in general. Whichever country acts as a swing producer of emissions stands to lose dramatically.

At the 1997 Kyoto conference (see the final section of this chapter for further details) the industrialised countries did agree to something similar to (2) above. They agreed to reduce emissions (although not by a huge amount) irrespective of what developing countries do. Until Kyoto, no such agreement had been forthcoming, partly because of fears of so-called carbon leaking. This is the name given to the process whereby cuts made in emissions by some countries fail to translate into effective global cuts because other countries increase their emissions in response. While there was no such carbon-leaking effect in our numerical example when Y acted alone, we have already noted that it could occur in some circumstances. Clearly the more likely it is thought to be, the harder it will be to achieve cuts in emissions by individual countries or groups of countries (which might be tempted to act alone in the hope of getting the ball rolling).

The numerical example we have studied investigated choices over the level of emissions. We could have set the problem up differently, beginning with functions describing the costs and benefits of emissions abatement, and then solving for abatement under various forms of behaviour. Problem 1 at the end of this chapter deals with a problem of this form, and we recommend you work through it now.

Game-theory analysis[5]

The second approach we use to examine pollution control behaviour in the face of international spillovers is game theory. This is particularly appropriate where the number of players is relatively small, and so the pollution control behaviour of each country is likely to be affected by issues of strategic choice. Game theory is used to analyse choices where the outcome of a decision by one player depends on the decisions of the other players, and where decisions of others are not known in advance. We shall present a simple introduction to some of the issues of game theory, and explain its relevance to the analysis of environmental issues. At the end of the chapter, you will find suggestions for further reading in game theory.

Game theory is clearly appropriate for our present concerns. Where a pollution problem involves reciprocal spillovers, expenditures by any one country on pollution abatement will give benefits not only to the country doing that abatement but to others as well. Similarly, if a country chooses to spend nothing on pollution control, it can obtain benefits if others do so. Moreover, there may be distinct advantages in not undertaking abatement spending when others do; the most obvious of these advantages is the enhanced competitiveness in international trade that a country may gain by avoiding higher costs associated with pollution abatement. This can be illustrated using Figure 13.2(b). The two supply functions indicated, S^* and S_Y, can be interpreted as those of two countries with differing pollution abatement costs, but with other costs being no different. Other things being equal, the ability of one country to export goods will be lower the greater is the size of abatement spending relative to that of the other country (note how the distance **gh** becomes smaller as the curve S_Y rotates anticlockwise about the point 0). One of the responsibilities of the World

[5] The games we shall consider here are played by countries. Another variant of game theory, explored in Chapter 15 but not here, is known as games against nature, which is concerned with choice by just one player under conditions of uncertainty.

Trade Organization is to 'police' the international trading system to prevent countries from gaining advantages over others in this way.

Again, we strip the analysis down to its barest essentials, looking at games between two players where each has two strategic options (choices) available. Emissions from sources in both X and Y cross their common national boundary and so affect domestic and foreign residents. This is an example of what we have previously called a reciprocal spillover. The countries are taken to be identical in terms of population size, income and pollution levels, pollution damages, and pollution abatement costs. Each country must choose whether or not to introduce a pollution abatement programme. We label a decision to introduce the programme as A (abatement) and to not undertake abatement as NA (no abatement). As there are two countries, each of which has two possible courses of action (or strategies), four joint outcomes are possible, as indicated in Figure 13.6.

The numbers in the cells of the matrix are the net benefits (or pay-off) that each country receives for each pair of strategies chosen by X and Y. We set net benefits for each country to zero where both countries do not abate pollution. Net benefits for each country for all other possible choice combinations are expressed relative to this baseline case. A

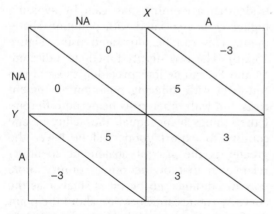

Figure 13.6 A two-player game with a dominant strategy.

number in an upper triangle describes a pay-off to X and a number in a lower triangle describes a pay-off to Y. For example, if X chooses abate and Y not abate the pay-offs are -3 to X and 5 to Y. Note that numbers in the matrix exhibit a symmetry property; we could reverse the notation of countries without altering any of the values in the matrix. This results from our simplifying assumption that the two countries are equivalent in all relevant respects.

Before attempting to identify the best strategy for each player, let us look at the *total* pay-off for the two countries in the four possible outcomes. For the base case where both countries choose the not abate strategy, summing individual country net benefits or pay-offs shows that total (world) pay-offs are zero. If both countries select the abate strategy, world net benefits are higher, at 6 units. The relative magnitude of these two pay-offs has been chosen to reflect an assumption we wish to make; namely that efficiency gains are possible to the world as a whole through pollution abatement. It seems plausible to assume also that if only one country abates, total net benefits to the world will be larger than under no abatement but smaller than where both abate. This assumption is satisfied by the numbers used in this pay-off matrix, as 2 units of net benefit are obtained in the world whenever one (but not both) abates.

How are the world outcomes distributed? If both countries abate, or if both do not abate, then the world net benefits are shared equally between the two countries. This seems reasonable given our assumption of equivalence of X and Y. However, assume that Y chooses to abate, while X does not abate. As you can see from the entries in the lower left cell, X gains but Y loses relative to the baseline case of no abatement. Why should this be so? It is easy to see why X gains; X incurs no additional abatement costs, but benefits from some of the pollution reduction arising from Y's abatement. Moreover, because Y will now have higher production costs (including abatement expenditure) but X will not, country X will gain a competitive advantage over Y, adding to X's net benefits even further. Country Y suffers for similar reasons: Y has incurred abatement costs, gains some but not all of the total world benefits of her abatement, and relative to X suffers a loss of competitive advantage. Identical results follow if the roles of X and Y are reversed in this argument. It is important to stress that these numbers are hypothetical, and have been chosen by the authors to illustrate an argument. Moreover, they are by no means the only numbers that are plausible.

The non-cooperative solution

Let us try to find the best strategy for each country on the two assumptions that, first, each behaves to maximise its own benefit, and second, no cooperation takes place between the two countries. We describe this as a non-cooperative game. First of all, we examine the pay-off matrix to see whether either player has a dominant strategy. A dominant strategy exists whenever one strategic option is best for one player irrespective of the choice made by the other. Look at the game from Y's point of view. If X chooses to not abate, Y's preferred choice is to not abate, as the pay-off of 0 from strategy NA is greater than the pay-off of -3 from A. If, conversely, X chooses strategy A, Y's preferred strategy is NA. Whatever X chooses to do, it is best for Y to not abate, and so not abating is Y's dominant strategy. You should confirm that the dominant strategy for X is also to not abate pollution. Game theory suggests that in the absence of cooperation, a player will play its dominant strategy if such a strategy exists. So, in our model, we predict that no abatement will take place.

What does this imply for the well-being of the two countries, and the state of the environment? First, the two countries act in a way that is less good for each of them than is feasible. With cooperation, the two countries could get pay-offs of 3 each rather than zero.

The non-cooperative solution to the game is inefficient relative to another possible outcome. In terms of the state of the environment, the non-cooperative solution is less good for the environment than the (cooperatively) efficient outcome – less pollution abatement is taking place than is efficient to do so. Why has this state of affairs come about? One answer is that it reflects the numbers we have chosen for the pay-offs; this is true, but does not really give us any insight into the nature of the 'problem'. To obtain an intuition for what is going on, look at the incentives facing player Y. If X does abate, there is a large benefit to Y from 'free-riding', letting X abate but not abating itself. In this way, country Y could obtain a net benefit of 5 units. Exactly the same argument applies, of course, to X. So there is a strong incentive operating on each player to attempt to obtain the benefits of free-riding on the other's pollution abatement. (We have already come across this incentive in our earlier discussion of the no spillover case, where one country had an incentive to gain a competitive advantage in international trade by adopting less strict environmental controls than others adopt.) The incentives to free ride reflect the fact that this is, in essence, a public goods situation. For global pollutants, pollution abatement is a global public good; once made available, no one can be excluded from consuming its benefits. Knowing what we do already about public goods, one may have predicted that pollution abatement will tend to be under-provided.

The example we have just looked at was one in which both players had a dominant strategy. But these do not always exist. Let us now look at the pay-offs in a second game in Figure 13.7. It is worth noting that the only difference in the pay-off matrices in Figures 13.6 and 13.7 is that in the latter, the pay-offs from both countries abating together are higher; indeed, the pay-offs to each exceed those obtained by one country free-riding. One might expect this would lead to the choice of both to abate, even in the absence

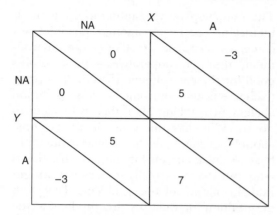

Figure 13.7 A two-player game without a dominant strategy.

of cooperation. This turns out to be possible but not certain. The first thing to note is that with this new pay-off matrix, neither country has a dominant strategy. In the absence of dominant strategies for each player, behaviour will depend upon the 'rules' that govern individual behaviour. One possibility is that each player may decide to pursue maximax behaviour. A maximax strategy is one that gives rise to the possibility of obtaining the best feasible outcome. The maximax strategies for X and Y are both to abate pollution; to see this, note that if Y chooses to abate, the best it could obtain is 7 units, whereas the best it could obtain by not abating is 5 units. Maximax yields an efficient outcome in this instance, but it is not the only plausible behavioural rule. Moreover, maximax strategies imply quite adventurous behaviour.

An alternative assumption one might make is that behaviour takes a maximin form. A maximin strategy is one that gives rise to the least bad possible outcome, which in this case would suggest that each country does not abate pollution. If Y abates, the worst outcome it could obtain would be -3, whereas if it chose to not abate, its worst possible outcome is 0. Since 0 is the least bad of these two outcomes, its maximin choice is to not abate. So maximin behaviour, often considered

plausible for risk-averse actors, yields an inefficient outcome. We discuss some other plausible behavioural rules in Chapter 15.

Cooperative solutions and the difficulties in arriving at them

Our arguments have shown that non-cooperative solutions to games can deliver inefficient outcomes. There are sometimes gains to be achieved through cooperative behaviour. In both of the examples we have investigated, the jointly efficient cooperative solution is achieved when the countries agree to abate pollution. Indeed, it is not difficult to deduce that each country can always do at least as well from cooperation and bargaining over the distribution of the benefits as it can from any form of non-cooperative behaviour – and very often it can do much better. Analysis of the Greenhouse Effect, acid rain pollution and ozone layer depletion all seem to suggest the possibility of substantial gains from cooperation.

Cooperation does sometimes occur, but it appears to take place to a lower extent than theoretical arguments suggest. Why do we not observe cooperative behaviour at all times when such gains are theoretically possible? Three points (among others) are pertinent here:

(1) Even where a single, sovereign decision-making unit exists, outcomes are not always fully efficient. Governments – and indeed all decision-making units – often fail to take advantage of potential efficiency gains.

(2) A supranational political institution with the authority and power to impose a cooperative solution does not yet exist.

(3) In the absence of a supranational political authority, cooperative outcomes will have to be arrived at by bargaining and negotiation. But as we saw in Chapter 12 bargaining solutions to externalities may be difficult to achieve when

- the number of affected parties is high;
- bargaining power is unevenly divided between actors;
- the expected gains and losses from cooperation differ widely;
- property rights are non-existent or not well defined;
- bargaining is about public goods;
- the costs of bargaining are large relative to the gains expected from cooperation.

With respect to the distribution of the potential net benefits of cooperation, for many types of pollution problem the costs of pollution damage are very unevenly distributed between nations. This also seems to be the case as regards the costs of pollution control. Furthermore, the degree of correlation across countries between control costs and damage costs appears to be very low; there is little, if any, tendency for countries with high damages to have high control costs, for example. This is likely to create difficulties when attempts are made to secure international agreements over pollution control.

To the list of potential difficulties we may add that bargaining is more difficult the greater is the degree of uncertainty about the magnitudes of the costs and benefits in aggregate and to individual parties. Each of the problems we investigate in this chapter is characterised by the existence of acute uncertainty about one or more of the causes, the effects, the value of damages, and the costs of control measures. In the case of the greenhouse effect, the costs of abatement efforts to slow down climate change are obvious and immediate, but the benefits of control are uncertain and will only accrue in the future. Scientists tell us that the possible consequences may be catastrophic for human populations, but cannot make reliable estimates of the probability of this or other outcomes. Decision making under risk and uncertainty is addressed specifically in Chapter 15. However, anticipating what we will conclude there, a more cautious form of

behaviour than would be selected under conditions of certainty may be warranted. Unfortunately, uncertainty is likely to increase the difficulty of arriving at internationally coordinated policy responses.

It should also be noted that cheating or reneging on agreements might sometimes confer large gains on individual cheaters, particularly if the cheating is not detectable, or if compliance to agreements is difficult to enforce. Free-riding can be advantageous to individual countries that succeed in avoiding penalties being imposed on them for non-compliance. All of this suggests that cooperation cannot be relied upon to prevail over individual countries acting non-cooperatively in ways which they perceive to be in their own interests. Non-cooperative outcomes can and do happen, even where it would be in the interest of all to behave cooperatively.

Acid rain pollution

Causes of acid rain pollution

The phenomenon of acid rain was first noticed in Scandinavia in the 1950s, when research related acidification of rivers and lakes to the previously unexplained death of freshwater fish. The physical processes underlying acid rain are well understood. Atmospheric stocks of sulphur dioxide and nitrous oxide accumulate primarily from fossil-fuelled power generation. Of secondary importance are emissions of unburned hydrocarbons and NO_X from vehicle exhausts. Stocks of potentially acidic material are transported in the higher levels of the atmosphere for distances of up to 600 miles.[6]

Acid rain occurs through two principal processes. In dry deposition, deposited parti-

[6] It is interesting to note that tall chimneys/emission stacks were introduced partly to reduce the ambient levels of pollution in the vicinity of the pollution sources. But a chimney does not eradicate a pollutant; it relocates it. Tall chimneys have been significant in disseminating pollutants over long distances.

culate matter is chemically transformed into acid through contact with surface water. Dry deposition is the most important mechanism of acidification in the south-western United States. By contrast, wet deposition is characterised by the formation of acidic substances, particularly sulphuric and nitric acids, in the atmosphere, which are subsequently deposited through rain or the movement of moist air.

Unpolluted rain precipitation is in itself mildly acidic. Acid rain itself refers to precipitation where the acidity level is unusually severe. Acidity is measured according to the pH scale, which is constructed so that a falling pH value is indicative of increasing acidity. The index is common logarithmic, with a change of one unit in the pH index corresponding to a tenfold change in the concentration of the acid in water. A pH measurement of 7 indicates neutrality; the substance in question lies on the border between being described as acidic and alkaline. Clean, unpolluted rainwater is mildly acidic with a pH value of between 5 and 6. Over much of north-west Europe, the current pH level of rainwater lies between 4 and 4.5. The lowest rainwater pH level recorded in Europe (obtained in Scotland) had a value of 2.4. Rainfall in the north-eastern United States currently has a typical pH of 4.4. In Wheeling, West Virginia, one rainstorm gave a pH value of 1.5; to obtain some idea of this level of acidity, note that car battery acid has a pH value of approximately 1.0.

Consequences of acid rain pollution

Major studies of the consequences of acid rain pollution in Europe have been conducted by the Commission of the European Communities (CEC, 1983) and the World Conservation Union (WCU, 1990). The National Acid Rain Precipitation Program began an important long-term study in the USA in 1980. These research programmes have identified the following consequences:

(1) Increased acidity of lakes. Water acidification results in aluminium being leached out of soils, with consequent water poisoning, and fish being starved of salt and oxygen. Damage of this form in the USA has been rated as modest by NAPAP (1990); 9% of lakes studied had pH < 5, at which few fish species can survive. Worst affected regions in the United States are the Adirondack Mountains in New York State, and Florida. Very severe damage has been recorded in Scandinavia. For example, in southern Norway lakes with a total area of 13 000 km^2 support no fish, and in another 20 000 km^2 fish stocks have been reduced by 50% (French, 1990). Similar evidence has been found in studies conducted in Germany, Scotland and Canada.

(2) Increased acidity of soils which reduces the number of plants that may be grown. However, current damage to crops is thought to be negligible in the USA (NAPAP, 1990) where no significant effects have been observed on crop growth, even at acidity levels ten times that currently prevailing in the eastern United States.

(3) Forest destruction due to calcium and potassium nutrient losses by leaching, and replacement by manganese and aluminium, both of which are harmful to root growth. Tree growth may also be affected by direct poisoning of leaves. Some reports have pointed to massive amounts of forest death in Europe, particularly in France, Germany, the Czech Republic, Slovakia and Sweden, with coniferous forests being the most heavily damaged. Although the majority of American forests appear healthy at present, some concern has been raised about effects on particular species (French, 1990).

(4) Acidification of domestic water supplies and sulphate pollution in general probably affects human health, but in

ways that are not yet fully identified. One study attributes up to 50 000 deaths per year in the United States to sulphate pollution (Office of Technology Assessment, 1984).

(5) Building and infrastructure erosion. Acid rain damages galvanised steel, bronze, limestone and other carbonate stone and carbonate-based paints, thus causing culturally important damage, such as that to the Acropolis and the Taj Mahal. Stained glass is badly eroded.

(6) Loss of visibility, caused by fine sulphate particles produced by airborne sulphuric acid. In the National Parks of the eastern USA this has caused an estimated 50–60% reduction in visibility.

Which countries are the principal polluters?

The precursors of acid rain are generated from stationary sources, such as coal-burning power plant, ore smelters and industrial boilers, and from mobile-source vehicle emissions. Acid rain deposition is principally associated with the heavily industrialised regions of Europe, China, the former Soviet Union and North America, where the most heavily polluted areas have levels of sulphur deposition ten times greater than the natural background rate (WR, 1992). Large-scale and systematic reciprocal cross-border acid rain pollution takes place between the countries of Central and Western Europe, and between the individual countries within those areas. Transfers of acid rain pollutants are also very extensive between the USA, Mexico and Canada. In terms of our earlier classification, this suggests that acid rain is a reciprocal spillover problem. However, meteorological patterns imply that many depositions are predominantly one-way, and so it is often better to view acid rain as a uni-directional spillover. For example, 70% of UK emissions are carried by prevailing winds to Germany, the Netherlands, Norway and Sweden. The heavily industrialised region of Silesia in southern Poland has significant adverse affects on neighbouring regions. And flows from the USA to Canada are considerably more important than the reverse flows.

Pollution control instruments

The principal control instruments available to an environmental protection agency are quantity-of-emissions regulation, requirements to install clean-up technology at the points of emission (such as sulphur scrubbing equipment), emissions charges and tradable permit schemes. The market-based instruments should induce substitution in the direction of using (more expensive) low sulphur coal or from coal to other primary fuels.

In the United States, the first substantial control programmes were launched after the passage of the 1970 Clean Air Act. This established a system of local ambient air quality standards, and conferred powers of enforcement on local governments through emission quantity regulations. The system proved to be rather disappointing in its overall effects. For example, the legislation led to taller emission stacks, which succeeded in attaining local ambient standards, but at the cost of largely passing on the problem to neighbouring areas.

Subsequent amendments to the legislation, resulting most recently in the 1990 Clean Air Act, look certain to have far stronger abatement effects. The Act requires nitrogen oxide emissions to be reduced by 2.5 million tonnes and sulphur dioxide to be reduced by over 50% to 10 million tonnes (relative to 1980 emission levels). Attainment of the 1990 Clean Air Act targets will be effected through a system of marketable permits in emissions of the precursors of acid rain. The programme's introduction is in two phases; in the first stage (in 1995) permits were issued for 110 large coal-burning utilities, followed later by permit issues for 2400 smaller generators. Permits, issued at no charge to generators, allow emissions of between 30% and

Box 13.3 Acid rain games in Europe

In a paper entitled 'Acid rain games in Europe', George Halkos and John Hutton (1993) demonstrated that acid rain causes greater environmental damage than would occur if countries act cooperatively. Using estimates of sulphur dioxide damage and abatement costs, Halkos and Hutton calculated the potential gains to some West European countries from cooperative SO_2 emissions control.

Halkos and Hutton commence by determining cost-efficient abatement cost functions for each country, which measure the cost of eliminating SO_2 emissions from the process of power generation. Abatement costs differ between countries as a result of country-specific factors such as the fuel mix used, the sulphur content of fuels, capacity utilisation and the scale installations. Figure 13.8 illustrates total abatement costs for one country, the United Kingdom. The 'staircase' shape of the abatement cost curve results from marginal cost increases as abatement rises; at higher abatement, polluters are forced to use more expensive control technologies. Note that the total abatement cost function provides information about the maximum level of pollution abatement that can be obtained for any given size of control budget. The second step in the exercise uses studies conducted by the Norwegian Meteorological Institute to construct a matrix of transfer coefficients, indicating what proportion of the total emissions from any particular country is eventually deposited in each of the 27 countries being studied.

Halkos and Hutton then proceed to estimate total SO_2 damage functions. First, they assume, on the basis of recent evidence, that the damage function is convex, rather than linear (see Chapter 11 for an explanation of convexity). It is not possible to estimate directly the parameters of the damage function, given the almost complete absence of relevant data. However, Halkos and Hutton assume that, for each country, national marginal abatement costs are equated with national marginal damage costs. To understand this, look at Figure 13.9. Halkos and Hutton assume that, when acting uncooperatively, each country considers the costs of pollution control (represented by NMAC) and the damages which it will avoid in its own country by doing that abatement (represented by the function labelled NMDC). A country will reduce pollution from the uncontrolled level, to the nationally efficient level, M^*. The cooperative solution is obtained when each country equates its national marginal abatement costs with the European (and not national) marginal damage function. By doing so, the outcome is identical to that which would be economically efficient if all Europe were a single country, and the European environmental protection agency equates European marginal costs and damages. This would yield M^{**} as the fully efficient pollution level or Z^{**} as the abatement. Notice that the cooperation result is a higher abatement level, Z^{**} than the non-cooperative solution, Z^*.

Returning to the main thread of our argument, it can be seen from Figure 13.9 that Halkos and Hutton are assuming that each country undertakes Z^* pollution abatement. The unobserved marginal damage can be calculated by noting that it is equal to the observable level of marginal abatement costs, C^* given that assumption. Using this information for each of the 27 countries studied, the parameters of a damage function can then be calibrated. Once this is done, the matrix of transfer coefficients can be used

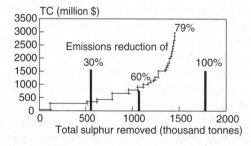

Figure 13.8 United Kingdom year 2000 total abatement cost curve.
Source: adapted from Halkos and Hutton (1993), page 5.

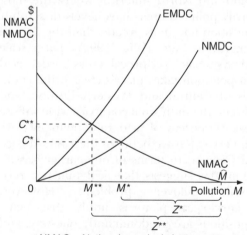

NMAC = National marginal abatement costs
NMDC = National marginal damage costs
EMDC = European marginal damage costs

Figure 13.9 Cooperative and non-cooperative outcomes in the presence of international pollution spillovers.

Box 13.3 continued

Table 13.1   Acid rain: gains from cooperative behaviour.

	Austria	Italy	FRG	UK	FRG	GDR
Percentages						
1992 Abatement	18.35	8.40	45.1	11.2	45.1	0.72
Privately efficient abatement (Z^*)	29.49	29.2	62.77	16.7	66.17	1.90
Socially efficient (Europe-wide) abatement (Z^{**})	35.4	35.5	62.41	24.81	63.46	25.24
Total costs of abatement and damage ($m 1985):						
Privately efficient abatement (Z^*)	233.9	720.68	1813.46	479.63	1991.00	84.15
		(954.58)		(2293.09)		(2075.15)
Socially efficient (Europe-wide) abatement (Z^{**})	215.51	729.27	1780.15	496.21	1843.50	156.20
		(944.78)		(2276.36)		(1999.70)
Total efficiency gain		[9.80]		[16.73]		[75.45]

Source: adapted from Halkos and Hutton (1993).

to calculate the total damage each country will experience for any level of SO_2 emissions by each of the 27 countries.

The final step in the analysis involves estimating the magnitudes of the gains that would be obtained from cooperative behaviour as compared with non-cooperative behaviour. Halkos and Hutton's results are presented in Table 13.1, for three pairs of countries. To understand the information given, let us read across the rows.

The first three rows of numbers refer to levels of abatement in percentages. In the '1992 Abatement' row we find percentage levels of abatements that the countries actually undertook in 1992; these show very marked variations. For example, in the GDR (the former East Germany), less than 1% of potential SO_2 emissions were actually abated in 1992; in the FRG (the former West Germany) the much greater priority given to environmental conservation led to over 45% abatement relative to the theoretical unconstrained level. Figures in the second row give the nationally efficient abatement percentages (corresponding to Z^* in Figure 13.9). In all cases, these exceed the 1992 abatement levels, implying that none of the five countries abated sulphur dioxide even to the level that would pay positive returns in terms of the own-country pollution reductions that would arise from abatement. The third row presents the socially efficient abatement levels, assuming that each of the pairs of countries shown in the table act in a cooperative manner. Socially efficient pollution abatement occurs when, for the two countries indicated, the sum of total abatement costs and total pollution costs for that pair of countries is minimised. In the case of the FRG and the GDR, cooperative efficiency actually required the

FRG to do a little less abatement than would be nationally optimal, while the GDR would have to do much more.

The lower part of the table shows the sum of total abatement and total damage costs for each country and for each pair of countries (in parentheses). Continuing to look at the case of the FRG and the GDR, note that the sum of costs is lower by 75.45 in the socially efficient case (Z^{**}) (costs = 1999.7) as compared with the privately efficient case (Z^*) (costs = 2075.15).

A scrutiny of the costs for individual countries brings out another aspect of this example. For West Germany, total abatement and damage costs fall by $147 million in moving to the cooperative solution, whereas for East Germany total costs rise by $72 million. For a cooperative solution to be possible it would be necessary for FRG to give a side-payment to GDR of at least $72 million (but less than $147 million), otherwise both parties would not benefit from the cooperation.

By way of contrast, the figures demonstrate that for the FRG/UK pair of countries, total costs would rise for the UK in the cooperation case. To induce the UK to undertake cooperation, side payments of at least £16.58 million annually by FRG to the UK would be required. It must be stressed that the 'total efficiency gains' referred to in the table are obtained by comparison of costs at Z^* and Z^{**}. However, the actual levels of current abatement are less in all cases than Z^*, and so the total net benefits in moving from 1992 abatement levels to the socially efficient levels would be greater (and probably substantially greater) than those indicated here.

Source: Halkos and Hutton (1993).

50% of 1985 pollution levels. Portney (1989) estimated the annual benefits to the USA to lie in the interval $2–$9 billion while control costs are predicted to be $4 billion.

The existence of a federal government in the USA facilitates the introduction of pollution control programmes; how easy has it been to abate the precursors of acid rain in Europe where no such unified sovereign governmental structure exists for all relevant areas? Some voluntary control was agreed in the 1980s by a number of European states, and the European Union has subsequently extended the coverage and severity of these controls in its member countries. In June 1988, EC Environment Ministers agreed to national reductions in emissions from large combustion plants. These and other agreements have met with some success, with SO_2 emissions falling by more than 20% between 1980 and 1989. At national levels, emission reductions have largely been implemented through command and control regulations, although some countries (including France and Sweden) have introduced emission taxes. The UK approach to sulphur emissions control has centred on mandatory abatement investments, including flue-gas desulphurisation technology. In the long term, larger-scale reductions in acid rain precursors in Europe will necessitate the use of either uniform emission taxes or tradable permit schemes. As yet, no European-wide example of either exists.

Stratospheric ozone depletion

Ozone is produced in the upper layers of the atmosphere by the action of ultraviolet light on oxygen molecules. The processes determining the concentrations of upper atmospheric ozone are complex and incompletely understood. What is known is that the ozone concentration is in a constant state of flux, resulting from the interaction of decay and creation processes. Several naturally occurring catalysts act to speed up natural rates of

decay; these catalysts include oxides of chlorine, nitrogen and hydrogen. There are large, naturally caused variations in these concentrations by time, spatial location and altitude. For example, normal dynamic fluctuations in ozone concentrations are as large as 30% from day to night, and 10% from day to day (Kemp, 1990).

During the early 1970s, scientific claims that ozone was being depleted in the stratosphere were first made. These original claims were not satisfactorily verified, but in the mid-1980s the discovery of the so-called hole in the ozone layer over Antarctica led the scientific community to conclude that serious reductions in ozone concentrations were taking place in certain parts of the atmosphere. The downward trend in ozone concentrations was attributed to inadvertent human interference with the chemistry of the atmosphere, related to the prevailing pattern of air pollution. Over the continent of Antarctica, the fall in concentration (relative to its 1975 level) was estimated to be in the interval 60–95%, depending upon the place of measurement (Everest, 1988).

Although much progress has been made towards understanding the chemistry of ozone depletion in the 10 years to 1994, we are still profoundly uncertain even as to the recent historical rates of depletion. Estimates of the actual rates of depletion experienced have been considerably lowered since the initial studies were published, and forecast depletion rates are now much less than early predictions. Current models forecast depletion to be no more than 5% on average over the next 50 years, as compared with initial predictions of depletions of up to 20%.

There are several ways in which human impacts on the ozone layer take place. Two of these – nuclear radiation and aircraft emissions – appear to have relatively little effect at present, but are potentially important. Evidence also implicates a number of other chemicals as ozone depleters, in particular nitrous oxide (associated with traffic and agricultural activity), carbon tetrachloride and chloroform. The dominant anthropogenic cause of ozone depletion appears to be the emission of CFC gases into the atmosphere. These substances act as catalysts to the decay of ozone, adding to the effects of the natural catalysts we mentioned earlier. Many forms of CFC exist and are being produced currently, two of them – CFC-11 and CFC-12 – being the dominant forms. The most important sources of CFC emissions by quantity are the production, use and disposal of aerosol propellants, cushioning foams, cleaning materials and refrigerative materials. In some cases, such as in aerosol uses, the release of the gas occurs at the time of manufacture or within a relatively short lapse of time after manufacture. In other cases, the release can occur at much later dates as items of hardware such as refrigerators and air conditioning units are scrapped. Estimates by Quinn (1986) suggest that CFCs have very high income elasticities of demand; if CFC gases are not subject to control, their use would rise very rapidly as world incomes increases.

What would be the effects of a continuing depletion of the atmospheric ozone layer? The consequences follow from the fact that ozone plays a natural, equilibrium-maintaining role in the stratosphere through

(a) absorption of ultraviolet (UV) radiation, and
(b) absorption of infrared (IR) radiation.

The absorption of IR radiation implies that CFC substances are greenhouse gases, contributing to global climate change. This aspect of ozone depletion is discussed in the following section. Here we focus on the role played by halons and chlorofluorocarbons (CFCs) in depleting the concentration of ozone in the upper atmosphere and leading to increased UV radiative flows. The ozone layer protects living organisms from receiving harmful UV radiation. It is now virtually certain that ozone depletion has increased the incidence of skin cancer among humans. Connor (1993) estimates that a 1%

depletion in ozone concentration would increase non-malignant skin cancers by more than 3%, but by rather less for malignant melanomas. The United States Environmental Protection Agency (EPA) has estimated that human-induced changes in the ozone layer will cause an additional 39 million contractions of skin cancer during the next century, leading to 800 000 additional deaths (Kemp, 1990).

Effects which may occur, but about which much doubt remains, include effects on human immune systems (including activation of the AIDS virus), radiation blindness and cataract formation, genetic damage to plants and animals, and losses to crops and other plant or animal damage. Of particular concern is the apparent damage to marine plankton growth; the importance of plankton in many food chains suggest that this may become a critical issue during the next century. Increased UV radiative flows are also likely to accelerate the degradation of polymer plastic materials.

Some indication of the likely magnitudes of the costs and benefits of control is given in a United States EPA 1989 study, the results of which are reported in Table 13.2. The estimates suggest that huge economic benefits would accrue from even very dramatic CFC control in the USA.

The north is currently far more important than the south in terms of the quantities of emissions of ozone depleting substances (WR, 1994). However, this seems set to change in the future as economies of the south undergo rapid economic growth, while those

Table 13.2 Costs and benefits of CFC control in the United States.

Level of control	Discounted benefits ($ billion)	Discounted costs ($ billion)
80% cut	3533	22
50% cut	3488	13
20% cut	3396	12
Freeze	3314	7

Source: adapted from *EPA* (1989).

in the north attempt to adhere to political commitments.

Action to date on abating emissions of ozone depleting substances

International action regarding ozone depletion has been coordinated by the United Nations Environment Programme (UNEP). The first steps towards international control measures were taken at the Vienna Convention in 1985, at which agreements were made for international cooperation in research, monitoring and the exchange of information. In September 1988, signatories to the Montreal Protocol (24 mainly industrialised countries) agreed to phased reductions in domestic consumption and production of ozone-depleting substances, and in particular to cease the production of chlorofluorocarbons (CFCs) by 1996. Developing countries could increase CFC production until 1999, after which it must be progressively reduced until it ends in 2010. The London Protocol, signed in July 1990 by 59 nations, agreed to a complete phasing out of halons and CFCs by the year 2000. In addition, controls were agreed on two other substances implicated in the depletion of ozone, carbon tetrachloride (to be eliminated by 2000) and methyl chloroform (by the year 2005). Financial support was made available to assist in the funding of projects to substitute from ozone-depleting substances in poorer counties.

International action to control the production and use of CFCs is widely regarded as the outstanding success of international environmental diplomacy. The agreements led to a rapid decline in global CFC emissions, although most of this was achieved in the developed countries (with the United States using a tradable permit scheme for domestic CFC usage).

More pessimistically, a continuing decline will depend upon the developing countries substituting away from CFCs as industrial output rises; at present CFC production is increasing very rapidly in these economies. In China, for example, government forecasts expect CFC emissions to increase from 48 000 metric tonnes in 1991 to 177 000 in 1999 in the absence of control, and to rise rapidly thereafter. China has indicated a willingness to gradually phase out the use of CFCs, but this is conditional upon similar action being taken elsewhere, technological transfers and financial assistance. As yet there is no sign that the rapid rate of growth of CFC and halon use in China is being halted. Even if target reductions are met on time, the ozone layer will not return to its normal state until the second half of the next century, before which ultraviolet levels are expected to rise by a further 10–15%, with a comparable increase in the incidence of skin cancers.

The greenhouse effect

Greenhouse gas emissions

Figure 13.10 provides us with a simple schema for thinking about the processes collectively known as the greenhouse effect. Economic activity gives rise to flows of greenhouse gas (GHG) emissions. The chemical and physical mechanisms by which the various greenhouse gases induce global climate change is now well understood and will not be repeated here. References to good accounts of these mechanisms are given at the end of the chapter. Greenhouse gases are examples *par excellence* of uniformly mixing pollutants; the geographical location of the pollution impacts is independent of the location of the emission source. Since all nations are emitters and each is affected by the emissions of all others, the greenhouse effect is an example of what we earlier called a reciprocal spillover.

The principal GHG – carbon dioxide – derives mainly from fossil-fuel use, but an important contribution is also made by defor-

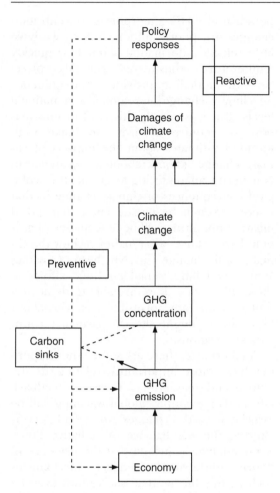

Figure 13.10 Modelling the greenhouse effect.

say with confidence is that global emissions will only remain near current levels under extremely optimistic (and most unlikely) assumptions. In contrast, were the world economy to grow rapidly and little change take place in energy production and consumption technologies, it is conceivable that emissions levels may be three times as high in 2010 as they were in 1990. Our ignorance about future emissions is one source of the uncertainty that surrounds the whole issue of global climate change.[7]

Stocks and flows: the relationship between emissions and concentrations

Although much of the debate about the greenhouse effect is couched in terms of emissions, it is important to appreciate that what ultimately determines global mean temperature is the concentration rate of greenhouse gases in the atmosphere, not the levels of GHG emissions. So any analysis of the greenhouse effect requires that we translate the predicted path through time of GHG emissions into the atmospheric concentrations of the gases that they imply.

The way in which emissions affect concentrations is apparently simple: emissions add to the stock and decay reduces the stock. This is exactly the kind of relationship that we looked at in our discussions of pollution flows and stocks in Chapter 11 (see, for example, Equation 11.25). But there are two nasty complications here. First, the rate of decay depends on the 'active' residence time of GHG molecules in the atmosphere. The expected lives of GHG molecules range from a few weeks for tropospheric ozone to 100 years or more for CFCs. Unfortunately, these

estation. Agricultural activity and the decomposition and disposal of waste are important emitters of methane, another GHG. Chlorofluorocarbon (CFC) emissions also act as potential global warming substances.

The extent to which global climate change will occur over the next century and beyond will depend upon GHG emissions levels. Forecasts over long-term horizons are very sensitive to the assumptions one makes, particularly about population and economic growth rates, and changes in fuel mix and energy efficiency. As a result, the range of predictions is huge, even for forecast horizons as short as the year 2010. What we can

[7] We use the term uncertainty to describe a particular form of imperfect foresight in which decision makers cannot attach probabilities to the possible outcomes of available choices. In some cases (radical uncertainty) it is not possible even to enumerate all the possible outcomes. The concept of uncertainty and its implications for decision making is explored in Chapter 15.

expected lives are probably unstable (and so difficult to predict), varying as the size of the stocks change and as the composition of different gases in the overall stock of GHGs alters.

The second complication arises from the operations of various 'sinks' that sequester carbon dioxide and other greenhouse gases. It is known, for example, that the oceans absorb some carbon dioxide. But it is not known how the capacity of oceans to absorb CO_2 will change as mean temperatures change or as GHG concentrations change. Once again, climate modelling is confronted by a fundamental ignorance (see Schneider, 1989, for further details).

Climate change models

Let us suppose that we are willing to stick our necks out and assume, for the sake of argument, some path that greenhouse gas concentrations will take over a relevant time horizon. The next step in modelling the greenhouse effect is to estimate the climatic changes that will occur in response to the assumed path of GHG concentrations over time. This is typically done through the use of global circulation models, which simulate atmospheric and oceanic dynamic processes.

From global circulation model simulations, a reasonably clear picture emerges of the equilibrium global mean temperature that would eventually arise if GHG concentrations were to stabilise at some particular level. In 1995 the Intergovernmental Panel on Climate Change (IPCC) reported model estimates of the effect on global average temperature of a doubling of the atmospheric concentration of carbon dioxide from its preindustrial level of 280 parts per million by volume (ppmv) ranging from 1.5 °C to 4.5 °C (Houghton et al., 1996; Houghton, 1997). The current concentration is approximately 360 ppmv.

But this kind of information, valuable as it is, is still very limited. First of all, the dynamics of the adjustment process of tem-perature to GHG atmospheric concentration changes are poorly understood, so we have little reliable information about how quickly temperature adjustments will take place. Second, modelling provides little guidance on climate change at regional and national levels. But it is exactly this kind of information we require in order to make well-founded estimates about the impacts of climate change. (Think about a researcher in Northern Canada trying to predict the ecological consequences of climate change in that region. Even if he or she knew that global mean temperature will be 5 °C higher, that is of little relevance; what matters is how the climate will change in Northern Canada.) While modelling is making huge efforts in these directions, all we are able to do at present is paint some plausible scenarios about how climate might alter in particular countries and regions.

Furthermore, there are some other imponderables, most importantly relating to the nature and magnitude of various feedback effects. For example, global warming will be associated with changes in cloud cover, altering the net balance of radiative flows. Some analyses conclude that the presence of poorly understood feedback mechanisms such as this means that one cannot even be sure of the direction of climate change, let alone its magnitude.

The impacts and costs of climate change

Given the pervasiveness of uncertainty in the science of the greenhouse effect, one may be tempted to conclude that there is little point in going any further until these uncertainties are much closer to being resolved. As we know so little about what is likely to happen, how can one obtain sensible impact estimates, and how could one derive meaningful policy prescriptions? Indeed, many commentators have taken a position close to this. However, several reasons (that we shall not examine here) point to the prudence of devoting some resources to estimating the impacts of a variety of plausible future climate scenarios; the information obtained from these exercises is valuable, and will become more valuable as uncertainties become resolved.

The physical, biological and ecological impacts of climate change include both beneficial and adverse changes. The variety of possible impacts is immense, and for many of these (particularly the ecological impacts) uncertainty is once again profound. A 1996 IPCC report predicted that by 2100 the sea level would have risen by 0.5 metres under central assumptions and in the absence of large-scale policy change. This alone could have catastrophic consequences for some parts of the world. Several inner continental areas would experience much increased probabilities of severe drought and soil degradation. Serious damage to people within developing countries is expected to operate through effects on farming. Those regions experiencing high population growth and/or decreasing soil fertility are likely to suffer the most. References to more extensive accounts of the possible impacts of climate change are given at the end of the chapter.

Once impacts have been estimated, one can then assign monetary values to some of these using the techniques we explore in the next chapter. There is now a very large literature in this area, part of which is referenced below. The general approach has been to estimate the damages that would arise from a doubling of atmospheric carbon dioxide concentrations (leading to an increase of between 1.5 and 4.0 °C mean temperature). These studies typically place damages in the range 1–1.5% of GDP per year for developed countries, and 2–9% for developing countries. However, there is no reason to believe that warming will stop within the range indicated above. It is quite possible that average temperatures will eventually increase by more than 10 °C, in which case damages would be considerably greater than those just indicated.

The damages arising from climate change will bear down very unequally between different regions of the world. The consensus is that there will be few, if any, 'big winners' but there will almost certainly be some very large losers (see Nordhaus, 1990a; Hansen, 1990). Nordhaus claims that developed countries experiencing a doubling of CO_2 concentrations within 100 years are unlikely to experience annual losses in excess of 1% of GNP. While he is unable to estimate a comparable figure for developing economies, he suggests that costs may be considerably higher there, and this is supported by the results of Hansen. On average, damage is expected to be inversely related to per capita income. Furthermore, those economies with the greatest incentive to cut emissions (or otherwise limit climate change) tend to have the poorest resource base to implement policies that adapt to climate change and minimise the most serious forms of damage.

Emission abatement costs

How much does it cost to undertake GHG emissions abatement? Obviously, the costs will depend on how much abatement takes place and how quickly it is implemented. It is perhaps surprising that there are very large differences in estimates of abatement costs across various studies, even when similar scenarios are being investigated.

The IPCC has surveyed much of the available evidence. In one report (IPCC, 1995b), it concluded from an examination of so-called 'bottom-up' studies that the cost of reducing emissions up to 20% below 1990 levels are negligible or even negative. (Bottom-up studies take a given energy production or energy use situation and identify cost-efficient emissions reductions that are available.) These studies suggest that in the longer term even larger cuts of up to 50% are available at no net cost.

Much of the explanation for these apparently costless opportunities arises from industrial and domestic energy efficiency and energy conservation programmes that have not been fully exploited. Energy savings schemes, it is argued, can quickly repay their initial costs in lower energy bills (see, for example, Keepin and Kats, 1988; ACE, 1989). If these results are trustworthy, they strongly imply the immediate adoption of moderate action to reduce GHG emissions and the desirability of gradually stepping-up the degree of control.

Economists tend to be rather sceptical about these 'free lunch' claims. After all, they beg an important question: if outputs could be generated at lower cost by alternative techniques or if profitable projects exist, why are these alternatives not already selected? There are in fact many plausible explanations (see Fisher and Rothkopf, 1989 for a good account). Explanations typically invoke information failures, quantity constraints in capital markets (for example, a local authority may have identified a profitable energy-saving scheme, but cash limits over capital spending may prevent the authority funding the project), and various other causes of market failure. However, the costs of eliminating apparent inefficiencies are often far from negligible, and may outweigh the original efficiency losses associated with the market failure.

There are also good reasons for believing that bottom-up studies give an over-optimistic picture of the costs of emissions abatement. When these are excluded from the sample of abatement cost studies being considered, the IPCC study we mentioned earlier concluded that the annual costs of holding carbon dioxide emissions at 1990 levels amount to about 1–2% of GDP in the OECD countries. There are also many opportunities for reducing the ratio of emissions to output at low cost in developing countries; however, given the high rates of output growth expected there, it will be considerably more costly for those countries to prevent emissions rising above 1990 levels.

Boero *et al.* (1991), in an excellent survey of the macroeconomic consequences of controlling greenhouse gases, identify several classes of abatement cost, and examine the relative merits of a number of alternative methods of estimating those costs. Abatement costs are classified into three types:

(a) possible GDP gains (negative costs) from correction of market failures: so-called 'no regret' policies;
(b) continuing costs in the form of losses from curtailed energy use or fuel substitution, consisting of foregone output or resource costs from energy-saving measures;
(c) transitional costs, due to disruption and premature scrapping of capital, and short-run labour immobility.

The first of these three classes – the so-called 'no regret' possibilities – which imply that some degree of GHG abatement is available at negative cost, have been discussed above. Class (c) (transitional) costs can be very important; few studies consider them explicitly. They will be minimised, though, by a gradual, phased introduction of abatement programmes.

Most empirical studies concentrate on category (b) costs. Several approaches can be identified in the attempts to measure these costs:

(1) *ad hoc* estimates of marginal costs per unit CO_2 saved for each abatement strategy considered in isolation;
(2) input–output models (see Chapter 16);
(3) the incorporation of a technical abatement module into a macroeconomic model, which measures abatement costs of alternative carbon emission scenarios in terms of foregone consumption possibilities;
(4) general equilibrium models, attempting to form a money measure of welfare costs such as the Hicksian equivalent or compensating variation (see Chapter 14 for an explanation of these concepts).

The *ad hoc* approach is exemplified by many of the pairwise comparisons of abatement strategies (e.g. Keepin and Kats, 1988 for nuclear power *vis-à-vis* energy efficiency; Hohmeyer (1988) for fossil versus renewable fuels), by the papers submitted by national governments to the IPCC Policy Panel (e.g. Department of Energy, 1989 for the UK), and by the McKinsey Report to the Ministerial Conference on Atmospheric Pollution and Climatic Change (McKinsey, 1989). These *ad hoc* studies attempt to find least-cost abatement techniques, but they do so without taking into account substitution possibilities and relative price effects. Their conclusions, therefore, have serious limitations.

Input–output models are discussed at length in Chapter 16, and we defer consideration of them until then. The third approach is exemplified by the work of Manne and Richels (1989, 1990), using a model which simulates CO_2–energy–economy interactions and which can be used to estimate the costs of carbon emissions limits. The model focuses on long-run energy–economy interactions, and permits a variety of assumptions to be made concerning elasticities of substitution (both between energy sources and between energy and other productive inputs) and rates of technological improvement. Manne and Richels examine the costs of emission limits under several scenarios, and demonstrate that the costs can be significantly reduced by adoption of the least-cost technologies.

The use of a computable general equilibrium (CGE) framework (see Chapter 16 for details) also permits a rich examination of policy options and yields conclusions about long-run cost savings. Most CGE models focus on static efficiency in the allocation of resources, with endogenous relative prices serving as the means by which efficient, equilibrium outcomes are achieved after carbon taxes (or other abatement instruments) are deployed.

Table 13.3 reports the main findings of the survey by Boero *et al*. The table is constructed so that increasingly stringent control is applied as one goes down the rows. The first column states the emissions change expected to be achieved in the final year of the projection (given in parentheses), expressed as a percentage of the emissions that would be expected in that final year under a 'do-nothing' or 'no intervention' scenario. The second column states the final emission change relative to the 'reference' year, shown in parentheses. This emission change in this second column is more unreliable than that in the first column, as it is dependent upon the assumption made regarding actual world growth rates over the simulation period. However, it is included because international GHG diplomacy is usually based upon changes relative to a base reference year (for example, international

Table 13.3 Estimates of GDP losses – main global models.

Emission change		Study	Loss of GDP per annum at end of projection period (relative to baseline) (%)
Relative to baseline (%)	Relative to reference year (%)		
−37 (2020)	+17 (1985)	Burniaux *et al*. (1991b)	1.8
−39 (2025)	0 (1988)	Edmonds and Barns (1990a)	1.8 – world cooperation
−39 (2025)	0 (1988)	Edmonds and Barns (1990a)	4.0 – OECD action only
−40 (2050)	+162 (1990)	Edmonds and Reilly (1985)	1.0
−50 (2100)	na	Nordhaus (1990b)	1.0
−50 (2030)	na	Whalley and Wigle (1990)	4.2 – global tax case
−51 (2025)	−20 (1988)	Edmonds and Barns (1990a)	2.3
−68 (2050)	+17 (1990)	Anderson and Bird (1990a)	2.8
−69 (2025)	−50 (1988)	Edmonds and Barns (1990a)	5.7
−75 (2100)	+16 (1990)	Manne and Richels (1990)	5.0
−88 (2075)	−67 (1990)	Mintzer (1987)	3.0 – slow build-up case

conferences have tended to set emissions targets relative to 1990 as the reference year).

After standardising the results as far as possible, Boero *et al.* conclude as follows.

> Abatement of 40 to 50 percent [relative to the baseline of what would have happened otherwise] might tentatively be expected to reduce long-run GDP by no more than 3 percent (a reduction in the growth rate of no more than one-tenth of one percent over thirty years followed by a resumption of normal growth).
>
> Boero *et al.* (1991), page 516

However, these cost estimates assume relatively slow adjustment in which no adjustment costs are incurred. Ingham and Ulph (1990) show that these costs are far from negligible, and would rise dramatically under rapid change.

Abatement targets

Given information about the costs and benefits of GHG abatement, one might be tempted to try to identify a globally optimal emissions abatement programme. Some academic research has been directed to this task. Nordhaus has explored optimal steady-state solutions, using 'plausible guesses' where hard information is absent. In a series of papers, he concluded that optimal control rates are in the range 9–20% of total global current CO_2 emissions (Nordhaus, 1982, 1989, 1990a).

In practice, insufficient information is available to set actual targets in this way, and political realities preclude the pursuit of optimal targets. Attempts to secure internationally coordinated reductions in greenhouse gas emissions have taken place largely through a series of international conventions organised under the auspices of the United Nations. On what basis have targets been set at recent international conferences? There appears to be a general presumption that emission levels are excessive, and that any modest reduction is bound to be desirable.

However, the willingness to incur costs in reducing GHG emissions has not matched this general belief in the desirability of abatement. The only realistic way forward at present seems to be to secure agreement to very modest emissions reductions in the near term (or, more precisely, reductions relative to forecast future trajectories) with some form of commitment to a programme of gradually tightening targets in the future. Given the widespread disparities in levels of economic development, it also seems to be inevitable that the major share of the abatement cost burden will have to be borne by the more affluent, industrialised economies. It is the manner in which the overall burden should be shared that constitutes the most difficult obstacle to significant emissions reductions.

Progress has been painfully slow. At the so-called Earth Summit in Rio de Janeiro, Brazil, in 1992, the Climate Change Convention required signatories to conduct national inventories of GHG emissions and to submit action plans for controlling emissions. The parties to that agreement were still unable to agree strict emissions limits at the Berlin summit in 1995, agreeing only on a procedure for negotiating such limits (to be concluded by 1997) and accepting in principle the need to reduce emissions below 1990 levels. Progress in securing agreement at Berlin was primarily hampered by the existence of marked differences of interest between various sub-groups within the nations present.

The Kyoto Protocol (1997) constitutes the first substantial agreement to set GHG emissions limits. The conference focused on five principal GHGs, and set the objective of cutting combined emissions of GHGs from developed countries by 5% from 1990 levels by the years 2008–2012. Moreover, it specifies the amount each industrialised nation must contribute towards the overall target (see Table 13.4). The Kyoto Protocol officially endorsed the principle of emissions trading, whereby countries in which emissions fall short of their allowed targets may

Table 13.4 National GHG emission targets set at Kyoto 1997.

Country	Kyoto target (percentage change from 1990 emissions)
Australia	+8
Bulgaria	−8
Canada	−6
Croatia	−5
Estonia	−8
European Union	−8
Hungary	−6
Iceland	+10
Japan	−6
Latvia	−8
Liechtenstein	−8
Lithuania	−8
Monaco	−8
New Zealand	0
Norway	+1
Poland	−6
Romania	−8
Russian Federation	0
Slovakia	−8
Slovenia	−8
Switzerland	−8
Ukraine	0
United States	−7

sell 'credits' to other nations, which can add these to their allowed targets. Details of the operations of the system have not yet been decided; first steps to doing so are to be taken at the 1998 negotiating session in Buenos Aires.

The Protocol did not set any binding commitments on developing countries. However, it did introduce the so-called 'Clean Development Mechanism' whereby developed nations can gain emissions credits for investing in projects that reduce emissions in developing countries.

It is interesting to note that we can, at least partially, interpret the Kyoto agreement in terms of the targets/instruments distinction introduced in our discussions of pollution in Chapters 11 and 12. We suggested there that a pollution control programme (at the single nation level) usually involves two steps: set an emissions target, then select one or more instruments to attain that target.

Kyoto did establish something like a global pollution target by requiring combined emissions of GHGs from developed countries to fall by 5% from 1990 levels by the years 2008–2012 (although this is not a truly global target as it was silent about emissions from developing countries). Moreover, as you have seen, the Protocol spells out national targets for each developed economy.

Although details of implementation have not yet been agreed, it seems likely that individual countries will be free to choose whatever instrument package they wish to attain their individual targets. Kyoto brings a new dimension into the picture by introducing something similar to a marketable permit scheme: countries will be allowed to trade pollution credits over national boundaries. So, for example, if Russia succeeds in polluting by less than the agreed target, the country can sell pollution credits to the USA, allowing that country to exceed its national target. One major advantage of this approach would be its potential to achieve the cost-efficiency property of tradable permit schemes: control will tend to be greatest in those countries that have the lowest abatement costs.

An interesting further possibility arises. Suppose that countries decide to use marketable permits within their own economies as instruments to attain their national targets. There are then tradable permit systems both within and between countries. These could be kept separate from one another. But there is nothing in principle to prevent the schemes being combined into one unified permit market in which trades are allowed without restriction: both governments and firms could be buyers and sellers of permits.

This variant is the most close to the pure textbook model of marketable permits: it guarantees that a single global permit price emerges, and so satisfies standard least-cost abatement conditions. However, it does not seem to be politically viable. A system of fully tradable permits exposes any national government to losing control over the amount of emissions (or abatement) that actually takes place within its own boundaries. Moreover, one would expect there to be huge uncertainty about what permit price will emerge from any given total amount of permits, at least until a considerable length of time has passed allowing reliable predictions to be made on the basis of previous experience (see Clunies Ross, 1990). It seems most unlikely that most countries would accept the perceived loss of national sovereignty or the exposure to price uncertainty that we have just described.

Distributional issues

We conclude our discussions of the greenhouse effect with a few observations about the consequences of concerted international action to reduce the rate of increase of greenhouse gas concentrations for the distributions of income and wealth across countries and between groups within countries.

The first thing to note is that bringing not only developed but also developing countries into the set of countries that are committed to significant GHG reductions will almost certainly require fairly large transfers of income to the poorer countries. This seems to be a necessary condition for the developing countries to participate in such programmes.

Secondly, although there is currently no head of steam behind the use of carbon (or other emission-based) taxes at an international level, it is interesting to think about what such a scheme might imply. The instrument could be operated in two ways. First, a common tax rate could be set for all countries, chosen so as to bring about whatever

was deemed to be the appropriate global emissions target. Notice that this implies that there cannot then be independent choices about national targets: what happens in any country will depend on how its producers and consumers react to the common world tax rate. Secondly, one might envisage there being both global and national targets. Then tax rates would have to differ between countries (and so the overall abatement effort would not be taking place at least cost).

A major problem with this second variant is that once tax rates are allowed to vary between nations, there are major implications for the relative competitiveness of economies (and we might expect countries to manoeuvre so as to get tax rates which give them a favourable position).

Whether or not the tax is uniform over countries, it would have substantial (and as yet largely unexplored) effects upon the international terms of trade. The magnitude of these changes would depend on the level of the tax, and on whether it is levied upon producers (thus acting like an export duty) or consumers (and so acting as an import tariff).

How large would (uniform) carbon taxes have to be in order to attain reasonable abatement targets? Calculations by Barrett (1990) shed some light on this issue. Barrett's estimates of the tax rates required on fossil fuels to reduce CO_2 emissions by 20% in the short term (within three years) and the long term (within ten years) are reproduced in Table 13.5

Boero *et al.*, in their 1991 survey, quote central tendency estimates of required tax rates from existing simulation work. In order

Table 13.5　Tax rates required to reduce carbon dioxide emissions by 20%.

	Short-run		Long-run	
	Tax rate (%)	Change in fuel demand (%)	Tax rate (%)	Change in fuel demand (%)
Gas	40	−4	14	+3
Coal	54	−9	19	+4
Oil	67	−11	24	−25

to achieve reductions (in long-run equilibrium) of CO_2 emissions by around 40% relative to their uncontrolled levels, a tax rate of between $100 and $300 per tonne of carbon would be required. However, carbon taxes to achieve such magnitudes of global CO_2 reduction, but imposed in OECD countries alone, either would be prohibitively expensive (Burniaux *et al.*, 1991b) or could not achieve the target (Edmonds and Barns, 1990a).

Taxes, either on carbon content or on pollutant emissions more generally, also have important implications for the tax structure within economies. Such taxes could be regressive in impact whether they are additional to or substitutes for existing taxes. Some evidence on this is reported in Pearson and Smith (1990), in which it is shown that a 15% VAT rate on domestic heating fuel (which was zero rated in the UK in 1990) would cut demand by 5.5% overall. However, the demand from the lowest decile would fall by 10% while that of the highest would fall by less than 2%, because of the relative impact of the charge. A dilemma is thus posed for tax schemes that aim to switch the base of tax from income to pollution-related expenditures. Although revenue neutrality may be achieved, other transfers would be required if distributional neutrality were sought. Symons *et al.* (1991) demonstrate that a 6.5p/kg carbon tax would be sufficient to meet a 20% CO_2 emissions reduction. However, this would have 'dramatic adverse distributional effects for low-income households' (page 20). The authors argue that it is possible to design a larger CO_2 tax (11–12p/kg, equivalent to a rate of $61.5 per tonne carbon) in conjunction with tax/benefit changes that maintains fiscal neutrality and largely avoids those adverse effects upon distribution. Common's results using input–output modelling (reported in Chapter 16), however, show that regressivity estimates are often biased upwards because only the direct, as opposed to the direct and indirect, effects are accounted for.

In addition to redistribution between household groups, there are likely to be substantial sectoral income shifts. Jorgensen and Wilcoxen (1990a,b,c) have employed macroeconomic modelling techniques to estimate the effects of environmental legislation on the US economy. The magnitude of potential impacts can be gauged from Jorgensen's estimate that a 20% drop in US carbon emissions would be associated with a 79% fall in US coal output. To the extent that sectoral production is geographically specialised (as it certainly is for primary fuel sources), sectoral impacts will have regionally specific distribution effects too.

Some analysts have advocated a compensating reduction in taxes on labour and capital to taxes on pollution to avoid excessive tax burdens. It is sometimes argued that such tax packages can yield 'double dividends' in the form of environmental improvements and general efficiency gains from eliminating known distortions of the existing tax structure. Good discussions of these issues are to be found in Grubb (1989a), Bertram *et al.* (1989), Weizsacker (1989), Weizsacker and Jesinghaus (1992), Weizsacker *et al.* (1997), Hansen (1990), Brown (1989) and Kosmo (1989).

International environmental cooperation

More than 170 international environmental treaties have been adopted to date. The past 15 years have seen increasing attention being paid to environmental issues in the conduct of international relations. This reflects a growing awareness that the issues of environmental protection, liberalisation of world trade, poverty and economic development, and North–South relationships are inextricably linked. From an examination of these agreements, it is possible to draw a number of tentative conclusions:

(1) International coordination of policy is easiest when an international political

institution exists with the authority and power to construct, administer and enforce a collective agreement.

(2) International coordination of policy is easier the smaller is the number of parties affected and the more similar they are culturally.

(3) International coordination of policy is easier the lower are the control costs of the intended programme.

(4) International coordination of policy is easier the higher are the benefits of the intended programme.

(5) International coordination of policy is easier the less is the uncertainty about costs and benefits of the intended programme.

(6) International coordination of policy is easier when it is relatively straightforward to achieve agreement about the appropriate international division of burdens of the intended programme.

To illustrate these lessons, let us look a little more closely at some international environmental agreements and their implementation. The first lesson is the most readily comprehensible one.

When private agents fail to achieve efficient outcomes through cooperation within one country, a sovereign authority exists which has the legitimacy and authority to use its regulatory or incentive powers to steer outcomes in the direction of economic efficiency. However, when sovereign nations acting in isolation fail to act cooperatively, there is as yet no equivalent global supranational authority to act in this coordinating role.

The growth and increasing authority of international political and economic organisations offers the prospect of creating vehicles for international coordination of behaviour. Those organisations which play important roles in environmental policy include the Committee on International Development Institutions on the Environment (CIDIE), the European Union, the Organization for Economic Cooperation and Development (OECD), the World Bank, various non-governmental organisations (NGOs), research institutions such as the World Resources Institute, as well as multilateral development banks. Of greatest actual and potential impact seem to be the various branches of the United Nations Organization.

The 1985 Helsinki Protocol, which bound 21 European states to a 30% reduction in sulphur dioxide emissions (in terms of 1980 base levels) by 1993, illustrates the advantages in securing agreements of a pre-existing international political institution (the European Union), cultural similarity and relatively small numbers of parties. Nevertheless, 13 countries in the geographically relevant area were not signatories to the Protocol. One of these, the United Kingdom, had very weak incentives to enter into voluntary regulation, with approximately 70% of its sulphur emissions being transported outside UK boundaries by the prevailing westerly winds, and receiving little acid rain deposition from other countries. Membership of the European Union has required the UK to reduce sulphur and nitrogen oxide emissions, even though the UK earlier had refused to accede to the Helsinki Protocol.

Until the collapse of communism in Eastern Europe, a particularly intractable problem had been reciprocal transfers of acid rain pollutants between the countries of Eastern and Western Europe. The scope for internationally negotiated reductions in sulphur and nitrogen emissions has increased with the demise of COMECON, and the prospects for membership of the European Union by a number of Central European states will further enhance the likelihood that mutually beneficial reductions in those pollutants occur.

Agreements to reduce emissions of the precursors of acid rain have also benefited from technological change (which has reduced abatement costs), high and well-understood pollution damages, and a reasonably high degree of similarity in the burdens that the agreements have imposed upon participating states (all of which correspond to lessons we mentioned above).

Where the conditions listed above are not favourable, agreements are most difficult to secure and implement. This is true above all for attempts to reduce emissions of greenhouse gases. It is not surprising that many countries have been reluctant to undertake substantial amounts of GHG reduction as the costs to many individual countries would be very high, the benefits are highly uncertain and very unevenly distributed, and the numbers of relevant parties is very large. While several of these features are also true for control of CFC emissions, it is noteworthy that control costs are very much lower and benefits more evenly spread. These factors possibly explain the relatively successful efforts on this front.

The main vehicle that has been used in attempts to reach cooperative solutions to regional and global environmental problems is that of the intergovernmental conference. The proactive role played by the UN system of international institutions has been one of the major successes of international diplomacy in the post-Cold War period. The adoption of a treaty through such a framework (particularly a treaty that is nonbinding) does not of itself imply that objectives and targets will be met. However, the moral, financial and political pressures that such treaties can bring to bear are very large. It is also noteworthy that the UN environmental strategy makes no attempt to treat issues of environmental protection and environmental sustainability in isolation from issues of economic development, particularly in the poorer nations. On the contrary, the whole thrust of the institutional structure established over recent years is towards a joint approach to the two objectives.

What arrangements have been made to monitor and enforce these treaties? Monitoring is the principal responsibility of a recently created (1993) institution, the UN Commission on Sustainable Development (CSD), which works in close collaboration with interested NGOs. In terms of enforcement, CSD has little direct power, having no budgetary or legal authority over national governments. Its major influence is expected to derive from the role it plays in organising information, and harnessing the influence of NGOs in the political processes of individual countries and regional organisations such as the European Union. Coordination and integration of policy between the work of the various UN agencies is promoted with the assistance of two other institutional mechanisms, the UN Administrative Committee on Coordination and the Inter-Agency Committee on Sustainable Development. Agenda 21 of the Rio Summit also recommended the strengthening of the other UN organs dealing with environmental and development issues, particularly the United Nations Environment Programme (UNEP) and the United Nations Development Programme (UNDP). A full account of the complex environmental/development structure of the UN, and an appraisal of its performance, is found in WR (1994, chapter 13).

Conclusions

We began this chapter by looking at some aspects of the trade–environment relationship. We observed that under conditions of free trade there would be a tendency for countries with relatively weak environmental regulation to experience relatively high levels of environmental degradation. Looked at in another way, it is clear that some countries may seek to enhance their international competitive advantage by allowing degradation of their own environments. This raises the question of whether it is appropriate for international institutions to seek the objective of completely free, unregulated trade in such circumstances. There are parallels here with the issue of exploitation of child or slave labour to gain trade advantages through low private costs of production. Many would argue that the usual presumption in favour of free trade should be suspended in those circumstances.

What is really at issue here is policy integration. GATT and its successor, the WTO, have been the principal international institutions responsible for liberalising world trade and policing trading arrangements. While GATT has always admitted some restrictions on free trade (such as giving a country the right to impose tariffs against a country 'dumping' its exports), these exceptions were intended to foster a climate in which trade restrictions would be penalised (and so free trade more effectively be promoted). Meanwhile, alternative institutional arrangements have been introduced to seek international cooperation in achieving international environmental targets, such as the conservation of biodiversity. There are clearly gains to be made by integrating policy objectives by ensuring that gains on one policy dimension are not partially or wholly offset by adverse side effects on others. Much of the recent debate about the operation of the WTO has been concerned with how the pursuit of environmental goals can be made consistent with its fundamental commitment to the liberalisation of trade.

Discussion questions

1 Discuss the proposition that marketable emissions permits are more appropriate than emissions taxes for controlling regional and global pollutants because of the much lower transfer costs associated with the former instrument.
2 Consider the following extracts from an article in the *Independent* newspaper (28 March 1995) by the economist Frances Cairncross:

> Work by William Cline, a scrupulous and scientifically literate American economist, suggests that the benefits of taking action do not overtake

the costs until about 2150. And Mr Cline sees global warming largely in terms of costs. Yet it is inconceivable that a change of such complexity will not bring gains ... as well as losses.

> Given the difficulties of doing something about climate change, should we try? Some measures are certainly worth taking because they make sense in their own right. ... Removing such [energy] subsidies would make the economy work more efficiently and benefit the environment, too.

> Indeed, wise governments should go further, and deliberately shift the tax burden away from earning and saving...towards energy consumption.

> Beyond that, governments should do little. The most rational course is to adapt to climate change, when it happens. ... Adaptation is especially appropriate for poor countries once they have taken all the low-cost and no-cost measures they can find. Given the scarcity of capital, it makes good sense for them to delay investing in expensive ways to curb carbon dioxide output. Future economic growth is likely to make them rich enough to offset those effects of climate change that cannot be prevented.

Provide a critical assessment of these arguments.
3 Compare and contrast the cost-effectiveness of
(a) a sulphur dioxide emission tax;
(b) a sulphur dioxide emission tax levied at the same rate as in (a), together with an arrangement by which emissions tax revenues are used to subsidise capital equipment designed to 'scrub' sulphur from industrial and power generation emissions.

Problems

1 The world consists of two countries, X which is poor and Y which is rich. The total benefits (B) and total costs (C) of emissions abatement (A) are given by the functions

$$B_X = 8(A_X + A_Y),\ B_Y = 5(A_X + A_Y),$$
$$C_X = 10 + 2A_X + 0.5A_X{}^2 \text{ and}$$
$$C_X = 10 + 2A_X + 0.5A_X{}^2$$

where the subscripts are used in the same way as in Box 13.2.

(a) Obtain the non-cooperative equilibrium levels of abatement for X and Y.

(b) Obtain the cooperative equilibrium levels of abatement for X and Y.

(c) Calculate the utility levels enjoyed by X and by Y in the non-cooperative and cooperative solutions. Does the cooperative solution deliver Pareto improvements for each country, or would one have to give a side-payment to the other to obtain Pareto improvements for each with cooperation?

(d) Obtain the privately optimising level of abatement for X, given that Y decides to emit at the level of emissions that Y would emit in the cooperative equilibrium.

(e) You should find that the answer to (d) is that X does the same amount of abatement that it would have done in the non-cooperative case. What property or properties of the cost and benefit function used in this example cause this particular result?

(f) Suppose that Y acts as a 'swing abater', doing whatever (non-negative) amount of abatement is required to make the combined world abatement equal to the combined total under a full cooperative solution. How much abatement is undertaken in the two countries?

Further reading

Trade

Anderson (1992a) provides a careful analysis of the benefits of free trade and associated conditions. Anderson (1992b) examines through a case study the environmental implications of increased world trade in agricultural products. Esty (1994) considers the argument that differing regulatory standards will lead to pollution havens. Runge (1995)

gives an excellent general account of trade–environment relationships. Cairncross (1992) and Porter (1990) suggest that environmental regulation may enhance rather than detract from national competitiveness by operating as a technology promoter. Mäler (1990) provides a very readable account of policy coordination issues using game theory.

Game theory

A good discussion of game theory, at an elementary level, is to be found in Varian (1987), chapters 27, 31 and 32. See also Mäler (1990). Barrett (1990) explores cooperative and non-cooperative outcomes for a range of types of spillover. Hoel (1989) demonstrates the worrying result that 'unselfish' unilateral action can result in outcomes that lead to greater levels of emission than in its absence. Dasgupta (1990) shows that cooperation need not require an outside agency to enforce agreements and that such cooperation could be sustained over time by means of norms of conduct. Victor *et al.* (1998) discuss the effectiveness of international commitments.

International coordination of policy and the use of tradable permits

Grubb (1989a) provides an excellent critical survey of the various initial allocation options for marketable permit systems to achieve internationally agreed pollution control targets. Other analyses are found in Hahn and Hester (1989b), Bertram *et al.* (1989) and Tietenberg (1984, 1990). These sources also discuss the distributional consequences of various alternative methods of allocating permits between countries. See also WR (1996), chapter 14.

Acid rain

The scientific basis is well described in Kemp (1990) and a definitive study is to be found in NAPAP (1990). A good analysis of the acid rain issue is to be found in Adams and Page (1985). Biannual editions of *World Resources* provide regular updates of the scientific evidence and economic assessments of the damages caused. Good economic analyses may be found in Feldman and Raufer (1982) and Tietenberg (1989). Two articles in the summer 1998 issue of the *Journal of Economic Perspectives* – Schmalensee *et al.* (1998) and Stavins (1998) – give authoritative appraisals of the United States SO_2 emissions trading programme.

Ozone depletion

Kemp (1990), WMO (1991) and French (1990) describe the scientific basis of ozone depletion. Biannual editions of *World Resources* provide regular updates. An excellent economic analysis is in Bailey (1982). See also Office of Air and Radiation (1995).

The greenhouse effect

A comprehensive general survey is given in Perman (1994). See also Cline (1992) and Nordhaus (1994). A more complete presentation of the 'scientific basis' for the greenhouse effect, written from the perspective of an economist, is given in Cline (1991). Schneider (1989) and Cline (1989, 1991) provide excellent accounts of the potential climate changes due to global warming. For information on the warming contribution of different GHGs, the reader should study Grubb (1989b), Nordhaus (1991a) and Lashof and Ahuja (1990). The most complete account is provided in the text by Houghton *et al.* (1990). Emissions forecasts are covered

in Reilly *et al.* (1987), IPCC (1992, 1994), International Energy Agency (1995), World Energy Council (1993) and in report DOE/EIA-0484 (95) from the Energy Information Administration (1995). Further information on damages is given in Nordhaus (1990a, 1990b), EPA (1988, 1989), IPCC (1995) and Hansen *et al.* (1988), Hansen (1990). Common (1989), Hansen (1990) and Nordhaus (1991a) discuss the uncertainties involved in damage estimation. Assessments of the economic costs of measures to reduce GHG emissions are provided in Department of Energy (1989) for the UK and in Nordhaus (1990a, 1990b) at the global level. Other studies include Barbier *et al.* (1990a) and Williams (1990a,b). For appropriate responses under uncertainty, see Barbier and Pearce (1990), Hansen (1990).

Control cost estimates are found in Manne and Richels (1989), IPCC (1995b), Nordhaus (1990b,1991a,b). Macroeconomic simulation models of abatement costs are presented in Barker (1990), Jorgensen and Wilcoxen (1990a,b,c), Anderson and Bird (1990a,b), Cline (1991), Edmonds and Barns (1990a,b), Edmonds and Reilly (1985), and Mintzer (1987). CGE simulations can be found in Whalley and Wigle (1989, 1990, 1991) and Burniaux *et al.* (1991a,b, 1992).

Tietenberg (1984, 1990) discusses the possible use of tradable emissions permits, and a persuasive argument that internationally tradable permits represent the best approach for international action towards the greenhouse effect is given in Grubb (1989a). For other analyses of policy instruments for controlling global pollutants, see Opschoor and Vos (1989) and Pearce (1991b).

CHAPTER 14

Valuing the environment

> If the environment is one of the world's bloodiest political battlefields, economics provides many of the weapons. Environmental lawsuits and regulatory debates would be starved of ammunition if economists did not lob their damage estimates into the fray. The trouble with these number wars is that the estimate's accuracy is often more akin to that of second-world-war bombers than precision-guided missiles.

The Economist, 3 December, 1994, page 106

Introduction

This chapter is about the way in which economists attach values to the unpriced services provided by the natural environment. 'Environmental valuation' is a very active and rapidly expanding field. It is also somewhat controversial. Many non-economists regard putting prices on environmental services as totally misconceived, if not wicked. While most economists accept the desirability of environmental valuation, there is disagreement over the prospects for actually doing it in a satisfactory way.

The original, and still the principal, motivation for environmental valuation was to enable environmental impacts to be included in cost–benefit analysis. Impacts can be favourable or unfavourable. Taking the latter first, suppose that there is proposed some development – a mine or a tourist resort – in a wilderness area. The argument for valuing the services provided by the wilderness area, which would be reduced, and perhaps totally lost, if the development goes ahead, is that only then can they be compared with the standard costs and benefits of the project so that a proper decision on it can be made. Introducing pollution control standards will have favourable impacts on the environment, but will involve abatement costs. As discussed in Chapter 11, efficiency in allocation requires that a standard be set such that marginal costs and benefits are equal. For this to be done, it is necessary to have a monetary measure of the variation of pollution reduction benefits with the level of reduction.

Environmental valuation for cost–benefit analysis has a history of some 30 years. In the past few years there have emerged two further sources of demand for environmental valuations. The first is the perceived need to take account of environmental damage in measuring economic performance, to be discussed in Chapter 17. Second, in the USA, since the late 1980s, economists' valuations of environmental damage are now admissible evidence in fixing the compensation to be paid by those the courts hold responsible for the damage.

The basic strategy for environmental valuation is the 'commodification' of the services that the natural environment provides. The services are used by households and firms, and are treated as arguments in utility and production functions, respectively. The standard theories for consumer and producer behaviour can then be used to derive methods for assigning values to environmental services. Most of the environmental valuation literature is about services which flow to households rather than firms, and we shall follow that emphasis in this chapter. We shall also focus mainly on a context which is the appraisal of a project with the potential to reduce the flow of environmental services from a wilderness area to households. The principles, and lessons from practice, that emerge in this context are of general applicability. By a 'household' here we mean an entity that takes and acts upon decisions about consumption. As in much of the economics literature, we shall also refer to such an entity as an 'individual' or as a 'consumer', depending on the context.

The chapter is organised as follows. The next section considers the way economists treat environmental services, and the classes of economic value that they ascribe to them. The third section deals with the utility theory that underpins standard environmental valuation techniques relating to services to households. In the fourth section of this chapter we discuss a range of valuation techniques, again focusing mainly on services to households. The fifth and final section reviews some of the criticism of environmental valuation as currently practised in economics and discusses some issues arising.

Dimensions of value

In Chapter 2 (see Figure 2.2 especially) we distinguished four categories of service that the natural environment provides for humans and their economic activities:

(a) inputs to production by firms, here to be referred to as R, for resources
(b) sinks for the assimilation of wastes generated in production and consumption, W
(c) amenity services to households, A
(d) life support services for firms and households, L

In order to introduce some of the basic ideas concerning environmental valuation we will first consider an old growth forest. In Table 14.1 we list, in the first column, ten potential 'outputs' from the forest area, and, in the second column, we assign each output to one or more of the above categories. The first point to be made is that this particular listing of outputs is somewhat arbitrary. The enumeration of forest outputs could be different. Some economists might choose, for example, to take flora and fauna together as 'biodiversity', as was the case in Box 6.7. A biologist would, no doubt, write the list in a quite different way. It is not a matter of right or wrong, but of fitness for purpose. The purpose in Table 14.1 is to provide a basis for discussing the way economists approach environmental valuation.

Note also that the identification of an output with a service category is also somewhat arbitrary in some cases, and that some outputs obviously entail more than one class of service. Harvested timber is unambiguously and uniquely an input to production, undertaken by firms, as indicated by the F in the third column. Table 14.1 has standing timber as, at least potentially, a source of amenity services via opportunities for recreation and aesthetic appreciation, provided to households as indicated by the H in the third column. One might wish to argue that standing trees also provide life support services by virtue of their role in ecosystem function. In Table 14.1 we have implicitly got standing timber in again as a subset of the output 'flora', and it is there that its life support services are accounted for. If minerals were extracted within the forest area, they would clearly be resource inputs. Flora and

Table 14.1 Forest outputs.

Output	Service	Users	Divisibility	Excludability	Marketed
Harvested timber	R	F	D	E	M
Standing timber	A	H	ND	NE	NM
Minerals	R	F	D	E	M
Flora	R, A, L	F, H	D, ND	E, NE	M, NM
Fauna	R, A, L	F, H	D, ND	E, NE	M, NM
Flood protection	L	F, H	ND	NE	NM
Water quality	W, A, R	F, H	D, ND	E, NE	NM
Soil protection	L, R	F	ND	NE	NM
Local climate	L	F, H	ND	NE	NM
Carbon fixation	W, L	F, H	ND	NE	NM

fauna get classified as R because they may be inputs to production, as, for example, in the cases of grazing and wild honey collection, which may both be commercial activities conducted by firms. In the old growth forest context, flora and fauna would more usually be thought of as contributing to recreational and aesthetic opportunities, A, and to ecosystem function and hence life support, L.

We leave it to the reader to consider the remaining output categories and their service classifications in Table 14.1. The third and fourth columns in Table 14.1 relate to the characteristics of divisibility and excludability introduced in Chapter 6 in the discussion of the differences between private and public goods (and bads), using D to indicate divisibility and ND for non-divisibility, and similarly for E and NE. The final column shows whether the output is marketed, M, or not, NM, and the entries follow from those in columns four and five. Again, in some cases here, there is some ambiguity given the broad 'output' classifications used. It should be noted that divisibility and excludability may be assessed in terms of current institutional arrangements or in terms of underlying physical characteristics. Harvested timber is clearly a private good, sold through markets. Given that we have classified standing timber as providing amenity services to households, we have marked it as non-divisible and non-excludable. However, there is no physical reason why a private, or public for that matter, forest owner should not construct a fence and so introduce excludability in regard to access for the enjoyment of the amenity services. Classification as non-divisible implies that there is no congestion. Clearly, if the level of recreational use is such that an additional recreationalist would reduce the amenity service level provided for existing recreationalists, then there is divisibility.

Environmental cost–benefit analysis

Now, suppose that the forest is wilderness. There is no timber harvesting, no mineral extraction, no harvesting of any of the flora and fauna. The forest wilderness is used for recreational purposes, and provides the other non-extractive outputs and associated services listed in Table 14.1. Next suppose that there is a proposal for some development project to occur in the area – a mine, a hydroelectric plant or timber harvesting, say. The question is whether the project should go ahead, in which case the environmental services that it supplies, as wilderness, to households will be reduced. We know, from Chapter 6, that the question of whether a project should go ahead or not is to be decided by cost–benefit analysis, and that in conducting such an analysis market failure should be corrected for – all of the impacts arising from going ahead with the project should be taken account of, irrespective of whether they have market prices attached to them. To emphasise that, in circumstances where a project involves environmental impacts that are not valued in markets, a proper cost–benefit analysis should take account of such impacts. Let us call it environmental cost–benefit analysis (ECBA).

From Chapter 6, we know that to do a cost–benefit analysis we calculate

$$NPV = \sum_t (B_t - C_t)/(1 + r)^t \qquad (14.1)$$

and that the project should go ahead if

$$NPV > 0 \qquad (14.2)$$

In ECBA benefits and costs are to include, respectively, the value of environmental improvement and of environmental deterioration consequent upon going ahead with the project. In fact, in discussing ECBA it is convenient for expositional purposes to keep ordinary benefits and costs separate from environmental benefits and costs. By 'ordinary' benefits and costs we mean the value of standard, non-environmental, outputs from and inputs to the project – such as, in the case of a mine, the extracted ore on the benefit side, and on the cost side inputs of labour, capital equipment, fuel and so on.

Let B_d be the discounted value of the

ordinary benefit stream over the project lifetime, and let C_d represent the discounted value of the ordinary cost stream over the project lifetime. Then

$$\text{NPV} = B_d - C_d - \text{EC} = \text{NPV}' - \text{EC} \quad (14.3)$$

where EC is the present value of the stream of the net value of the project's environmental impacts over the project's lifetime, and NPV' is what the project's NPV would be if environmental impacts were ignored. Note that in principle EC could be negative with $\text{NPV} > \text{NPV}'$. The net value of the environmental consequences of the project, could, that is, be such as to strengthen, rather than weaken, the case for the project. However, we shall assume that EC is positive. In fact, it will be convenient to make the stronger assumption that there are no desirable environmental consequences of going ahead with the project, that it causes only environmental damage. This assumption appears to sit well with development in a wilderness area, and is what is typically assumed about such development in the literature. Given this, EC stands for 'environmental cost'. It could also be taken to stand for 'external cost' as the unpriced environmental damages are externalities associated with the project.

Using Equation 14.3, the ECBA decision rule is that the project should go ahead if

$$\text{NPV}' = B_d - C_d > \text{EC} \quad (14.4)$$

The application of this criterion requires the identification and measurement of the impacts on the wilderness area, and then their valuation and aggregation to arrive at EC, which is a monetary measure of the environmental benefits of not going ahead with the project.

Assuming that the impacts involved are limited to those affecting households, and that these can be identified and measured, the basic strategy for valuation is to treat the environmental services impacted as arguments in household utility functions, as commodities. Then, as discussed in the next section, demand theory can be used to establish the

existence and nature of monetary measures of the impacts on utility. The implementation of this ECBA approach to social decision making then requires the estimation of the sizes of the appropriate monetary measures for affected households and their aggregation to obtain an estimate for EC. Techniques developed by economists for doing this are discussed in the fourth section. Here we can note that there are two basic approaches to the estimation of the monetary measures of impact for individuals, the indirect and the direct. Both derive from the fact that markets do not exist for the environmental services impacted by the project, due to non-excludability and/or non-divisibility. The 'indirect approach' involves recovering estimates from the observed behaviour of individuals in regard to marketed commodities; the 'direct approach' involves asking individuals questions relating to the affected environmental services.

Categories of environmental benefit

EC is the environmental cost of going ahead with the development project in the forest area. Equally, it can be seen as the environmental benefits arising from not going ahead with the project. We can divide EC into four classes of benefit potentially accruing to individuals:

(a) *use value* (UV) arises from the actual and/ or planned use of the service by an individual, for recreation for example;

(b) *existence value* (EV) arises from knowledge that the service exists and will continue to exist, independently of any actual or prospective use by the individual;

(c) *option value* (OV) relates to willingness to pay to guarantee the availability of the service for future use by the individual;

(d) *quasi-option value* (QOV) relates to willingness to pay to avoid an irreversible commitment to development now, given the expectation of future growth in knowledge relevant to the implications of development.

EC is the sum of these four sorts of value across all of the affected individuals:

$$EC = UV + EV + OV + QOV$$

Of course, for any particular project, and for some individuals, some, or all, of UV, EV, OV and QOV may be zero.

OV and QOV arise only where there is incomplete knowledge of future conditions, whereas UV and EV can exist where there is complete certainty about future conditions. Incomplete knowledge is, of course, the operative case. However, we shall in this chapter assume complete knowledge and consider just UV and EV, leaving discussion of OV and QOV to the next chapter, which deals explicitly with risk and uncertainty.

There is not in the literature a single standard categorisation, nor is terminology uniform. What we have called EC is sometimes known as 'total value' (TV), and it is stated that

$$TV = UV + NUV$$

or that

$$TV = UV + PUV$$

where NUV stands for non-use value and PUV for passive use value. Two categories of use value are sometimes distinguished – direct (DUV) and indirect (IUV). In this categorisation DUV is essentially UV as defined above, while IUV refers to the life support services role of the natural environment, which are 'indirectly used' by individuals (and by firms). In the first categorisation, the value attached to life support services is covered by EV.

The existence for an individual of EV is usually taken to imply some kind of altruism, and in the literature EV is itself sometimes subdivided on the basis of the object of the altruism. A 'philanthropic' motive relating to the provision of amenity services to human contemporaries is, for example, sometimes distinguished from a 'bequest' motive relating to amenity and life support services for future human generations. Again, a concern for the well-being of non-human entities is sometimes distinguished from a concern for the well-being of other humans, with the former referred to as 'intrinsic' value. However, in practice these distinctions are typically overlooked and the objective is simply to estimate total EV. It is also the case that most applications of the techniques developed to date seek to estimate total non-use value, rather than trying to estimate separately EV, OV and QOV. The point is that while there is a large literature distinguishing among the components of NUV, in practice the operative distinction is between UV, as direct use, and NUV. It is generally understood that whereas techniques based on indirect approaches can only be used to estimate use value, techniques based on direct approaches can be used to estimate both use and non-use values. The basis for this understanding is discussed in the next section, which deals with the extension of the theory of consumer behaviour to deal with 'commodities' that are environmental services.

The theory of environmental valuation

In this section we deal with the theoretical foundations for the techniques that economists have developed for environmental valuation in relation to services to households. The first step in that development is the assumption that environmental services, or indicators relating to environmental services, can be treated as arguments in well-behaved utility functions. This is an important first step as the conditions under which preferences can be represented by well-behaved utility functions are non-trivial, and, as we shall discuss in the final section of the chapter, some commentators argue that preferences over 'ordinary commodities' and 'environmental commodities' are unlikely, in many cases, to satisfy those conditions. For an account of the axiomatic basis for well-behaved utility functions the reader should consult a microeconomics text such as Kreps (1990), or Deaton and Muellbauer (1980) on the theory of consumer behaviour.

Here we follow the standard theory of environmental valuation in simply assuming the existence of the required utility functions. We then discuss the proper monetary measures of utility change, and the extent to which such measures are, in principle, observable, or can be approximated by measures which are observable. Finally here we discuss the conditions for the use of the indirect methods, and which define existence value. Appendix 14.1 covers much the same ground in a more general and formal way.

Price changes: equivalent and compensating variation

For the purpose of doing ECBA we require an estimate of EC. Given the assumption that the relevant environmental damages affect only consumers, what we require is a monetary measure of the utility changes experienced on account of the environmental damage done by the project. In Chapter 5 we discussed, in relation to the practice of partial equilibrium analysis, consumers' surplus, the area under the demand function minus actual expenditure (see Figure 5.6 especially). Given an individual's demand function, we could define individual consumer surplus in an exactly analogous way, and the consumers' surplus discussed in Chapter 5 would be the sum of the individual consumer surpluses. For an individual, the change in consumer surplus can be treated as a monetary measure of the individual's utility change when, for example, the price of some commodity falls. However, this is a valid measure of the utility change only under some restrictive assumptions. It would be required, for example, that the marginal utility of income is constant. Hicks (1941) developed a set of money measures of utility change which do not require such restrictive assumptions, and these are what we use, ideally, to estimate EC. As we shall see, in practice we frequently have to use consumer surplus, and one of the major concerns in the literature is the closeness of it to the proper,

Hicksian, measures. We shall use MCS to refer to consumer surplus, where the M is for Marshall, the nineteenth-century economist who popularised the use of consumers' surplus, the CS part, for welfare analysis.

To begin, we leave aside matters environmental. We wish to obtain a monetary measure of an individual's welfare change arising from a reduction in the price of some good C_1 from P_1' to P_1''. Define a second good, C_2, as the composite good which is all goods other than C_1, let the price of C_2 be unity, and suppose that the individual has a fixed money income, Y_0. The consumer's budget constraint, prior to the price fall, can then be written as:

$$P_1'C_1 + C_2 = Y_0 \qquad (14.5)$$

A utility maximising consumer will choose C_1 and C_2 so as to maximise $U = U(C_1, C_2)$ subject to this budget constraint. The solution is two consumption quantities, C_1' and C_2', and a maximised level of utility U_0, and is illustrated in Figure 14.1. We may interpret the vertical axis as being in units of money income. To see this, note from the budget constraint that if no expenditure took place on good 1 (so $C_1 = 0$), then C_2 is equal to the money income level Y_0.

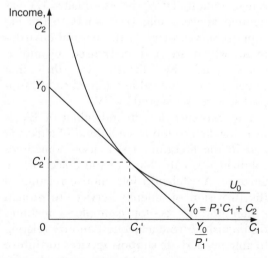

Figure 14.1 Utility maximisation subject to a budget constraint.

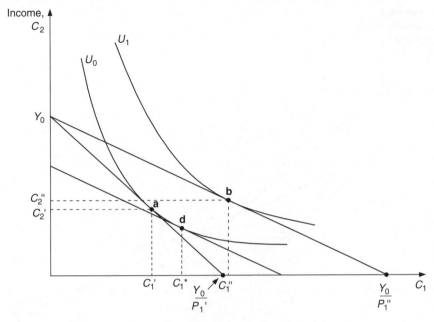

Figure 14.2 The income and substitution effects of a price reduction.

Now consider the consequence of the price fall of good C_1 from P_1' to P_1''. The budget constraint rotates anti-clockwise about the point Y_0 on the vertical axis to the new constraint

$$P_1''C_1 + C_2 = Y_0 \qquad (14.6)$$

as shown in Figure 14.2. Utility maximisation now implies consumption levels of C_1'' and C_2'', and a higher utility level, U_1. The increase in the consumption of C_1 from C_1' to C_1'' can be decomposed into a substitution effect, C_1' to C_1^*, and an income effect, C_1^* to C_1''.

There are two 'Hicksian' monetary measures of the utility change associated with a price change:

- The compensating variation (CV) is the change in income that would 'compensate' for the price change.
- The equivalent variation (EV), is the change in income that would be 'equivalent' to the proposed price change.

We will first examine CV and EV for a price fall for good C_1. The CV is the quantity of money income which, when taken from the

individual together with the price fall, leaves the individual at his or her initial level of utility. It is, therefore, the maximum amount that the individual would pay to have the price fall occur. The EV is the quantity of money income which, if given to the individual without the price fall, would give the same level of utility as he or she would have attained if the price fall had occurred. It is, therefore, the minimum compensation that the individual would accept in lieu of the price fall.

In Figure 14.3(a) the points labelled **a** and **b** denote the utility maximising consumption choices before and after the price fall. Begin at point **b**, at which the slope of the budget constraint is given by the final price, after the price fall. Keeping relative prices constant, reduce money income until the individual is constrained to have only the original level of utility, U_0, at the point marked **d**. The required income reduction is the amount $Y_0 - Y_1$, which is the compensating variation of the price fall. The CV measures, in units of money income, the utility change from U_0 to U_1, given that prices are fixed at their final level. The EV is given by amount $Y_2 - Y_0$ in

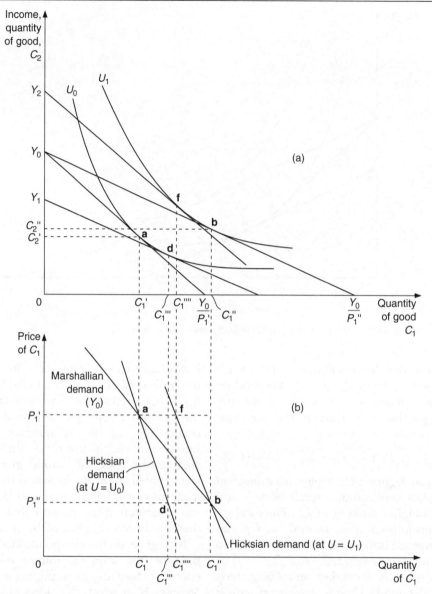

Figure 14.3 (a) The compensating variation of a price fall. (b) Hicksian and Marshallian demands.

Figure 14.3(a), leaving the individual at point **f**, and it measures, in units of money income, the utility change from U_0 to U_1, given that prices are fixed at their initial level. The two variations each measure the utility change from U_0 to U_1 in money-income units. They differ from one another because these changes are valued at different sets of prices and use different reference points.

An alternative geometrical interpretation for CV and EV is given in Figure 14.3(b), where two types of demand function are shown. We know that a price change will, in general, have both substitution and income effects. The Marshallian and Hicksian demand functions shown in Figure 14.3(b) differ in the way in which they deal with these two effects. The Marshallian demand function shows how the quantity of C_1 demanded varies with P_1, when the consumer's income and all other prices are held constant. It is the standard demand function from introductory microeconomics texts. A Hicksian demand function is the relationship between the quantity demanded of a particular good and the price of that good, holding all other prices and utility constant. It is constructed in such a way that compensation is made which eliminates the income effect of a price change. Movements along a Hicksian demand curve thus represent the pure substitution effect of a price change. Hicksian demand functions are sometimes referred to as 'compensated demand functions', and Marshallian as 'uncompensated'.

To derive the compensated demand function for our example, look again at the exercise we undertook in identifying the CV of a price fall, which we showed to be $Y_0 - Y_1$. Now consider the two points **a** and **d** in Figure 14.3(a). The move from **a** to **d** is the consequence of a fall in the price of the good, holding all other prices constant (in this case just the price of C_2) and holding utility constant (at U_0), and therefore represents the substitution effect of the fall in price of C_1. Points **a** and **d** constitute two points on the Hicksian demand curve for $U = U_0$, as shown in Figure 14.3(b). Note that a second Hicksian demand function can be obtained for the utility level $U = U_1$. The two combinations **b** and **f** constitute points on this Hicksian demand function.

We are now in a position to provide an alternative geometrical interpretation of CV and EV for a price fall. To do this, the Marshallian uncompensated demand curve and the two Hicksian compensated demands have been redrawn in Figure 14.4. CV is the area to the left of $H(U_0)$ and between the prices P_1' and P_1''. EV is the area to the left of $H(U_1)$ and between the prices P_1' and P_1''. Note that the area to the left of the Marshallian demand – the Marshallian consumer surplus, MCS, for the price change – is not exactly equal to either of the two Hicksian measures of utility change.

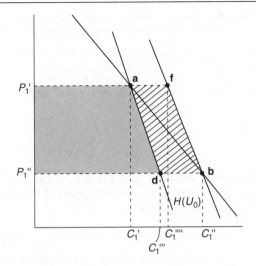

For a fall in the price of C_2:

$$CV = \int_{P_1''}^{P_1'} H(U_0) \, dP = \text{shaded area}$$

$$EV = \int_{P_1''}^{P_1'} H(U_1) \, dP = \text{shaded area} + \text{hatched area}$$

Figure 14.4 Compensating variation and equivalent variation.

Repeating the arguments that we have gone through for a price fall for a price increase leads to CV for a price increase as the minimum compensation that would leave an individual's utility unchanged, and EV as the maximum that the individual would be willing to pay to have the price increase not take place. Using WTP for willingness to pay and WTA for willingness to accept, Table 14.2 summarises the relationships between WTP/WTA and CV/EV.

From Figure 14.4 it is clear that for a price fall we have

$$CV < MCS < EV$$

which is the same as

$$WTP < MCS < WTA$$

For a price increase we get

$$CV > MCS > EV$$

Table 14.2   Monetary measures for price change effects.

	CV	EV
Price fall	WTP for the change occurring	WTA compensation for the change not occurring
Price rise	WTA compensation for the change occurring	WTP for the change not to occur

or

$$WTA > MCS > WTP$$

What this means is that, for the 'normal' sort of commodity for which Figures 14.3 and 14.4 are drawn, we have

$$WTP < MCS < WTA \qquad (14.7)$$

So, in principle, we can get at proper monetary measures of the utility effects of price changes for an individual if we can ascertain his or her WTP or WTA. If we cannot do that, but we know the individual's ordinary uncompensated (Marshallian) demand function, we can measure MCS, which we know is not a correct measure for either increases or decreases in price, though we also know that it lies between the two correct measures. Two questions arise. First, which of CV and EV should be used in any particular case? Second, if only MCS is feasible, how wrong will it be in relation to the correct measure?

Taking the second question first, the answer is 'not very much'. From the foregoing it should be apparent that the size of the error involved in using MCS will depend on the size of the income effect associated with a price change for the commodity of concern, as Hicksian demand functions correct for the income effect whereas Marshallian demand functions do not. It is generally understood, based on Willig (1976), that for most cases of practical concern the error involved in using MCS, with respect to either CV or EV, will be 5% or less. A special case is worth noting. When the income elasticity of demand for the good in question is zero, then the Hicksian demands become identical to the Marshallian demand function, and so EV = CV = MCS. The reason for this is that the income effect of the price change is zero.

The answer to the first question is that it depends on the circumstances and purposes of the analysis. If we think about it in terms of using WTP or WTA, it is really a question of whether we want to treat the status quo as a reference point to which the individual has some kind of entitlement, or not. We shall return to this question in the context of a discussion of monetary measures of changes in the consumption levels of environmental services, which is the subject of the next subsection. It will also come up again in our discussion of contingent valuation, a technique which seeks to directly ascertain WTP or WTA by asking individuals about them.

Quality changes: equivalent and compensating surplus

We now want to consider monetary measures for the utility change implications of changes in the quality or quantity of environmental services. To follow the preceding analysis, let us take C_1 as the environmental commodity, and change the notation from C_1 to E. We are assuming, then, that the individual has a well-behaved utility function $U = U(E, C_2)$. Changes in the level of E can refer to quantity changes or quality changes, depending on the particular environmental service involved. Both usages are encountered in the literature. It is important to be clear that analytically both usages refer to the same thing, changes in the level of E. Where there is reference to 'environmental quality', there is generally some quantitative measure involved, as with, for example, water quality. The measure may be ordinal rather than cardinal, and may be based on subjective evaluations.

Typically, as quality or quantity, E would be non-exclusive and non-divisible, so that

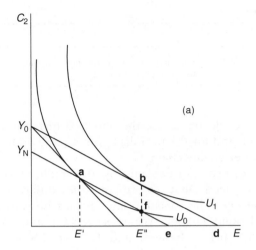

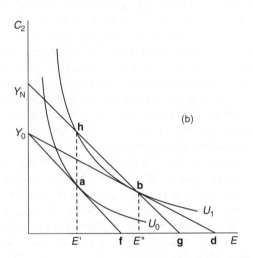

Figure 14.5 Equivalent and compensating surplus.

change, E increases from E' to E'' and the individual's utility increases. Increasing E with nothing else changing is equivalent to a reduction in the price of E. The slope of the budget line $Y_0\mathbf{d}$ gives the price ratio implicit in the quantity increase, tangential to an indifference curve for a higher level of utility, U_1, at $\mathbf{b}$. Now, draw $Y_N\mathbf{e}$ parallel to $Y_0\mathbf{d}$ and cutting the indifference curve for U_0 at $\mathbf{f}$ where the level of E is E''. This is not a point of tangency, reflecting the fact that the individual is constrained to experience E''. CS is $\mathbf{bf} = Y_0 - Y_N$, the amount of money that, if foregone by the individual with the policy change, would result in him or her experiencing the pre-change level of utility. Put another way, it is maximum willingness to pay for the environmental improvement – if the individual experienced E going from E' to E'' and paid an amount $Y_0 - Y_N$, he or she would remain at a constant level of utility U_0.

Now look at of Figure 14.5(b). Again, the increase in E means a move to $\mathbf{b}$ with the implicit new price ratio given by the slope of $Y_0\mathbf{d}$. Now draw $Y_N\mathbf{g}$ parallel to the original budget line $Y_0\mathbf{f}$ and passing through $\mathbf{b}$. It cuts the indifference curve for U_1 at $\mathbf{h}$. ES is $Y_N - Y_0 = \mathbf{ha}$. It is the amount of money that, at the original prices, would, if paid to the individual, move him or her to the same utility level as the environmental improvement would have done, given that the improvement does not, in fact, take place. Put another way, $\mathbf{ha}$ is the individual's minimum willingness to accept compensation for the prospective environmental improvement not happening.

If we consider a deterioration in the environment, a reduction in E, and examine CS and ES for that case, we find that CS is willingness to accept compensation for the lower E while ES is willingness to pay to avoid it. Table 14.3 summarises the situation in regard to monetary measures of the utility changes associated with changes in the quality/quantity of an environmental service, paralleling Table 14.2 for changes in the price of some commodity (which could be an

the individual cannot adjust his or her consumption level. For present purposes, we shall assume that E is a public good, something like water quality in a lake, say. There are two monetary measures of the utility change associated with a change in the level of E, compensating surplus (CS) and equivalent surplus (ES). They are shown, for the case of an improvement, or increase, from E' to E'' in Figure 14.5(a) and (b), respectively, where the mode of analysis is essentially the same as in the previous subsection.

In Figure 14.5(a), the individual is initially at a utility U_0. As a result of some policy

Table 14.3   Monetary measures for environmental quality changes.

	CS	ES
Improvement	WTP for the change occurring	WTA compensation for the change not occurring
Deterioration	WTA compensation for the change occurring	WTP for the change not to occur

environmental service that is not a public good).

In the case of Table 14.2 we made statements about the relative sizes of CV, EV and MCS. Until recently it was thought that similar statements could be made about CS, ES and MCS for a change in environmental quality. Since the publication of Bockstael and McConnell's paper (1993) it is realised that this is not the case – the results for CV, EV and MCS do not carry over to CS, ES and MCS. This means that for environmental quality changes it is not possible to use MCS as an approximation for the proper monetary measure of utility change.

Given that environmental quality is generally an unpriced public good, so that ordinary Marshallian demand functions cannot be estimated, the inability to say anything about MCS as an approximation to a proper measure would appear to be a non-problem. If MCS itself cannot be estimated, it might appear that it does not really matter that we do not know how it relates to CS and ES, so that the Bockstael and McConnell results are of little interest. However, their results are seen as important in relation to the indirect methods for environmental valuation, the theoretical basis for which we discuss next.

Weak complementarity

The basic idea behind the indirect methods of environmental valuation is to infer the monetary value of a change in the level of the environmental service of interest from observed market data on some ordinary commodity. If, for example, we observed an increase in the demand for fishing permits following an improvement in water quality,

we could try to use the observed increase in demand for the permits to put a value on the water quality change.

In order to explain how this might work, we need first to re-visit the difference between the variation and surplus measures of utility change. We associated CV and EV with price changes, and CS and ES with changes in quality or quantity. Reviewing the discussion, it will be seen that in the price change case the individual can adjust his or her consumption level for the commodity the price of which changes, whereas in the quality/quantity change case the consumption level for the environmental service is beyond the individual's control. In the latter case the change in the level of E is exogeneously imposed on the individual.

Consider an individual consuming N ordinary commodities, let C_1 be the quantity of daily fishing permits purchased, and let E be the level of water quality in the lake to which the permits relate. Then, we can write the compensated demand function for fishing days as:

$$C_1 = H_1(P_1, \ldots P_N, E, U_0) \quad (14.8)$$

A change in the level of E will shift this demand function for a given set of $P_1 \ldots P_N$, so that E is a parameter of the function, as illustrated in Figure 14.6. An improvement in water quality, an increase in E from E^0 to E^n, shifts the demand for fishing days so that at the constant permit price P_1^F, the individual's consumption increases from C_1' to C_1''. $P_1^C(E^0)$ is the price which would drive demand to zero – the 'choke price' – with E equal to E^0, and $P_1^C(E^n)$ is the price which would drive demand to zero for E equal to E^n.

Now, it follows from the analysis of Figure 14.4 that in Figure 14.6 the shaded area

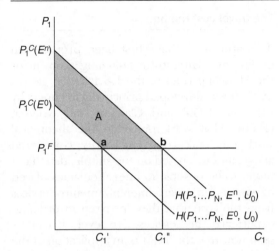

Figure 14.6 Environmental quality as a commodity demand function parameter.

$aP_1{}^C(E^0)P_1{}^C(E^n)b$, call it A, gives the CV change associated with the increased consumption of C_1 due to the parametric shift of the Hicksian demand function for C_1. For the purposes of environmental valuation, what is actually wanted is the CS associated with the environmental improvement that is the cause of the parametric shift in the compensated demand function for C_1. It has been established that the area A is exactly equal to the required CS if two conditions hold. The conditions are that C_1 is non-essential and that C_1 and E are weak complements:

- For an individual, C_1 is non-essential if it is possible to compensate him or her for the complete loss of C_1. In terms of the fishing example, suppose that an individual who has been using the lake is prohibited from doing so. Then C_1, days spent fishing at this lake, is a non-essential commodity for this individual if there is some income level that would enable his or her original level of utility to be regained after the prohibition.
- The complementarity between E and C_1 is weak if it is the case that for $C_1 = 0$, utility is not affected by variations in the level of E. In the example here, fishing and water quality are weak complements for an

individual if it is the case that given that the individual does not go fishing, perhaps because the price of a permit is above his or her choke price, then he or she does not care about variations in water quality in the lake.[1]

Now, given that all this is in terms of the unobservable Hicksian demand for C_1, the fact that, if non-essentialness and weak complementarity hold, the area A is exactly equal to the willingness to pay for the environmental improvement is not in itself of much use as A is inherently unknown. However, one could hope to determine a Marshallian, uncompensated, demand function for C_1 and thus derive the MCS associated with a change in E. We saw above that, for price changes, Willig established that MCS is close to CV. If this were also true for quantity changes, MCS could be used to give a close approximation to the CV associated with the change in the consumption of C_1, and hence to the CS monetary measure of the utility change arising from the improvement in environmental quality. Unfortunately, as we noted above, Bockstael and McConnell (1993) showed that the Willig results for variational measures do not, as was once thought, carry over to the surplus measures. Using an environmental quality induced change in MCS as an estimate of either CS or ES involves errors for which little is known about the potential size, or indeed the sign. Notwithstanding this, environmental economists continue to use indirect methods based on Marshallian demand functions, in the hope that the errors involved, with respect to the true surplus measures, are not too great.

We noted above that the contingent valuation method involves asking people about their willingness to pay (or accept), so that for some environmental improvement it could be used to directly get at CS, avoiding the problem outlined above. This direct method has not supplanted indirect methods

---

[1] These conditions are stated more formally in Appendix 14.1.

because it too has problems, as we will see below. There is one circumstance, however, where a direct method such as contingent valuation has to be used. In terms of the lake water quality example, suppose that the weak complementarity condition is violated such that for $C_1 = 0$ it is the case that the individual's utility is affected by variations in E. In this case, there is, as discussed above, existence value, which cannot be estimated by indirect methods since it leaves no behavioural traces in observed behaviour in relation to marketed commodities. Simply using some indirect method, such as travel cost, across many individuals to value a water quality improvement in the lake would result in a downward biased result to the extent that there were individuals for whom there was existence value. Note that since actual use of the lake by an individual for fishing, or anything else, is not necessary for that individual to have existence value in regard to it, the relevant population for estimating total value is not just those who actually use the lake. It may be very much larger.

Environmental valuation techniques

The literature on environmental valuation techniques is now very extensive, and we shall not be able to cover it all here. What this section does seek to do is to give a reasonably comprehensive account of the main features of two of the most widely used techniques, and to provide a brief introduction to the essential features of several other techniques. The first technique considered in some depth is the Travel Cost Method (TCM), which is an example of the indirect approach. The second is the Contingent Valuation Method (CVM), which is an example of the direct approach. We will consider some of the problems attending these techniques that have engaged economists. More fundamental questions about the economic approach to environmental valuation will be considered in the next, final, section of this chapter.

The travel cost method

This appears to have first been proposed in outline in a letter from Hotelling (known for the Hotelling rule) to the US Park Service in 1947. It was developed principally in papers by Clawson (1959) and Clawson and Knetsch (1966). That work preceded the theoretical work on weak complementarity considered above, and was based on the simple idea that it ought to be possible to infer the values placed by visitors on environmental amenity services from the costs that they incurred in order to experience the services. However, it can be seen now that the TCM is an application of the weak complementarity idea. The original TCM proposals related to national parks where entry was unpriced. In terms of Figure 14.6, in that context E is the amenity service that is enjoyed by a park visitor and C_1 is travel to the park. Then E and C_1 are complementary. The non-essentialness assumption is that there is some income level that would compensate for the closure of the park. The weak complementarity assumption is that if the individual does not visit the park, he or she does not care about the services that it provides.

We will fix ideas here by considering a situation where some project threatens the amenity services currently provided by a protected area, a national park say, for which there is no access fee. Those responsible for deciding whether the project should go ahead are going to use ECBA, and wish to know the environmental cost to compare with the net development benefit. For the purposes of exposition, we shall assume that if the project goes ahead the value of the recreational amenity services from the area in question will go to zero.

In practical terms the first basic assumption for the TCM is that visits to the park are determined by a trip, or visit, generating function

$$V_i = f(C_i, X_{1i}, X_{2i}, \ldots X_{Ni}) \qquad (14.9)$$

where V_i is visits from the ith origin or by the ith individual, C_i is the cost of a visit from origin i or by individual i, and the Xs are other relevant variables. The second basic assumption is that the cost of a visit comprises both travel costs T_i, varying with i, and admission price, P, constant across i, and that visitors treat travel costs and the price of admission as equivalent elements of the total cost of a visit. Visitors respond, that is, in exactly the same way to increases/decreases in total cost whether they are due to increases/decreases in travel cost or admission price, with $\partial V_i / \partial C_i < 0$. If we assume that the function $f(\cdot)$ is linear in costs, and suppress the role of other variables, this means that the trip generating equation to be estimated is

$$V_i = \alpha + \beta C_i + \varepsilon_i = \alpha + \beta(T_i + P) + \varepsilon_i$$
$$(14.10)$$

where ε_i is the stochastic component, or error term, assumed to be normally and independently distributed, with zero expectation. Travel and the recreational amenity services of the park are being assumed to be weak complements and it is assumed that travel and access costs are behaviourally equivalent. Note that the way that we have written Equation 14.10 means that β is assumed to be negative.

In the data for the case we are considering, P is zero.[2] However, given the second assumption here, α and β can be estimated from data on V_i and T_i and used to figure the effects on visits of hypothetical changes in P. Note that this could be useful for figuring the effects on visits of the introduction of access charging, as well as for figuring a monetary measure of the utility of the recreational amenity with free access. Note also that Equation 14.10 is a Marshallian, uncompensated, demand function for

visits. Given the assumption of zero expectation for the error term in Equation 14.10, if P varied the relationship between expected visits from origin i or by individual i and the price of access to the park would be

$$E[V_i] = \alpha + \beta P + T_i \qquad (14.11)$$

where $E[V_i]$ is the expectation operator. The relationship between $E[V_i]$ and P is shown diagrammatically in Figure 14.7 as the downward sloping straight line. There $E[V_i^*]$ is visits when the access price is zero, and P_i^* is the choke price that drives $E[V_i]$ to zero. Setting $E[V_i]$ equal to zero in Equation 14.11 and solving for the choke price gives

$$P_i^* = -(\alpha/\beta) - T_i \qquad (14.12)$$

and for P equal to zero:

$$E[V_i^*] = \alpha + \beta T_i \qquad (14.13)$$

Marshallian consumer surplus for origin/individual i at $P = 0$ is given by the area of the triangle $0E[V_i^*]P_i^*$ in Figure 14.7. The area of a triangle is half base times height, which in this case is 0.5 times $0E[V_i^*]$ times $0P_i^*$, which using Equations 14.12 and 14.13 gives

$$\text{MCS}_i = -(E[V_i^*])^2/(2\beta) \qquad (14.14)$$

Summing over i, total consumer surplus when $P = 0$ is

$$\text{MCS} = -(1/2\beta) \sum_i (E[V_i^*])^2 \qquad (14.15)$$

[2] Having P fixed, and the same for all i, at some non-zero value, say P', would not materially affect the account of the TCM that follows here. One would still estimate α and β from data on travel costs and visits, and use the results as discussed in connection with Figure 14.7. The only difference would be that in computing MCS_i one would subtract actual expenditure on access fees.

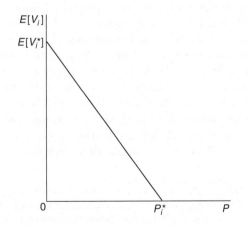

Figure 14.7 The linear trip generating function.

In some applications of the TCM, surplus for $P = 0$ is calculated across i using the actual observed visits for each origin/individual, as in:

$$\text{MCS} = -(1/2\beta) \sum_i V_i^2 \quad (14.16)$$

In either case, the crucial nature of the assumption that visits respond in the same way to changes in P as to variations in travel cost is apparent.[3] Given this assumption, the operational problem is to estimate α and β from data on V_i and T_i. This data is most usually obtained by surveying visitors to the site, in this case the park, though sometimes data is gathered on visitors and non-visitors by means of a usually postal survey of a sample of the population considered to be relevant as potential visitors. Survey respondents could be asked about their travel costs, but this is rare and typically travel costs are assigned to respondents by the analyst on the basis of distance travelled, which itself is usually estimated by the analyst by assigning respondents, on the basis of information supplied by them such as a postal or zip code, to a number of zones and measuring distance from the centre of each zone using a map. The regression is then, usually, of the number of visits per unit population from zone i on travel cost from zone i. For some sites and some surveys it is possible to have i index individuals, when the dependent variable is the number of visits in a period of time by individual i and the explanatory variable is travel costs per visit for individual i. Where the data is such that either approach could be followed, there is some dispute as to whether it is better to use the individual data or to average costs over individuals in given zones and regress total zonal visits per unit population on average zonal travel costs. Most TCM applications employ the

zonal average approach, often simply because of data limitations.

The MCS figure that is produced by the TCM as described here is the total MCS for the sample of visitors included in the survey. Unless the survey has been such that the sample is the population, there remains the question of how to go from this figure to the MCS figure to be used in ECBA. This can be quite complicated and the answer depends on the nature and timing of the survey in relation to the characteristics of the site concerned. One fairly standard procedure is to divide the MCS figure produced as described here by the total number of visits covered by the survey to get a figure for MCS per visit, which is then multiplied by the (usually estimated) number of visits per year to get a figure for MCS per year for use in the ECBA. In Willis and Garrod (1991) MCS per visit is estimated using both individual data on visits per year and zonal data on visits per unit population as dependent variables, with explanatory variables defined appropriately in each case. Across six forest sites in the UK MCS per visit ranged from £1.43 to £2.60 (average £2.03) using the zonal averaging approach, and from £0.06 to £0.96 (average £0.48) using individual data. The two methods did not even rank the sites in the same order. Clearly, given annual total visitor numbers of the order of one million, one could draw quite different conclusions as to the use value of one of these sites according to which of these approaches was used.

Some TCM problems

There are a number of other problems that can arise in the implementation of the TCM. Here we briefly discuss four of them. It should be noted that while we discuss each problem in isolation, they can, and do, occur simultaneously in particular TCM applications. References to fuller discussions of these problems, and of others, will be found in the further reading section at the end of the chapter.

---

[3] For an alternative account of the process by which total consumer surplus is calculated given estimates of the parameters of the trip generating equation see Common (1995) or Hanley and Spash (1993).

Functional form

In going from Equation 14.9 to Equation 14.10 we imposed linearity. There was no particular reason, apart from convenience, for doing this. The economic theory of constrained optimisation with weak complementarity does not imply any particular functional form for the trip generating equation. On *a priori* grounds, the trip generating equation could as well have been written as linear in logarithms:

$$\log(V_i) = \alpha + \beta \log(C_i) + \varepsilon_i \quad (14.17)$$

Given no *a priori* guidance, it is tempting to let the data decide, and, for example, to choose between the linear and linear logarithms specifications according to which fits the data better. The functional form chosen can have non-trivial implications for the result obtained. Hanley (1989) reports the results for MCS per visit for four different specifications of the trip generating equation fitted to travel cost and visit data, using the zonal averaging approach, for a forest site. The range is from £0.32 to £15.13. Many of the TCM applications reported in the literature do not provide this kind of sensitivity analysis, simply reporting an MCS result for the chosen functional form.

Estimation

In many of the early applications of the TCM the trip generating equation parameters are estimated by the method of ordinary least squares, but latterly it has been realised that there are a number of reasons why this may give rise to biased estimates of the parameters. The development of improved estimation techniques to deal with particular problems arising in different sorts of TCM application is now a very active area of research. If, for example, the data are collected from a survey of actual visitors to the site of interest, rather than from a sample of the population of potential visitors, then the dependent variable in the trip generating equation is constrained to be equal to or greater than one, where i indexes individuals

and the dependent variable is visits per period. In this case, a form of maximum likelihood estimation which takes account of the nature of the data generating system is superior to ordinary least squares. It needs to be noted that this is true so long as there are no other problems with the data and the analysis. If the 'wrong' functional form for the trip generating function is used, estimation using a method appropriate for censored and truncated data may produce more biased parameter estimates than estimation by ordinary least squares. Note carefully that we say 'may', not 'will', here. There is relatively little numerical guidance on these matters – we do not, that is, have much idea about how wrong parameter estimates will be under various circumstances.

Substitute sites

In going from Equation 14.9 to Equation 14.10 we suppressed the role of other variables in the trip generating function so as to focus on the key assumption of the equivalence of travel and access costs in the TCM. Clearly, one would not expect either visits by an individual or visits from a geographical area or zone to depend only on travel and access costs. Income, for example, could be expected to vary across i and to affect visitation rates. To the extent that relevant variables, such as income, are omitted from the trip generating equation that is estimated, the result will be biased estimation of α and β, and hence of MCS_i and MCS.[4] TCM researchers do now routinely collect in their surveys data on such matters as respondent

---

[4] A 'relevant' variable is one that does have a systematic effect on the dependent variable. Strictly, the statement in the text is true only if the omitted variable is not orthogonal to the variables included in the regression; that is, where the omitted relevant variable is totally uncorrelated with the included variables there is not a problem of biased estimation. However, such a situation would be unusual for a relevant variable, and is in any case hard to properly test for, so the standard working assumption is that omitted variables give rise to biased estimation. For further discussion see an econometrics text such as, Greene (1993).

income and include such variables in the estimated trip generating equation. A particular of the general class of omitted variables problem that has attracted a lot of attention in the TCM literature is the question of sites that are substitutes for the site of interest. In principle, the problem could be dealt with by estimating

$$V_{1i} = \alpha + \beta_1 C_{1i} + \sum_{j=2}^{j=J} \beta_j C_{ji} + \varepsilon_i \quad (14.18)$$

where j indexes sites, and site 1 is the site of interest. However, implementing this solution requires identifying substitute sites and collecting the relevant data for all so identified, and TCM applications generally do not deal adequately with the substitute sites issue.

Travel cost measurement

One might think that the question of measuring the travel costs on which the TCM relies so heavily would have received a lot of attention in the literature. With the exception of the time costs of travel, this has not, in fact, been the case.

The matter of including the time costs of travel in C_i in Equation 14.9 has been considered in the literature since the earliest interest in the TCM. The basic idea is that time spent travelling involves an opportunity cost, and should therefore be included in C_i at a unit price that reflects that opportunity cost. This idea has been formalised in the 'household production function' (HPF) formulation of the basis for the TCM. The HPF approach treats the recreational experience that is an argument in the utility function as a commodity produced by the household using inputs of other commodities – such as motor vehicles and fuel – and time. As in the standard approach, observed consumption levels are interpreted as the result of utility maximisation, but the HPF approach explicitly recognises two constraints, the standard income constraint together with a time constraint. Further, the two constraints are linked in so far as time spent producing recreational experience is not available for work to produce income. This leads naturally

to the idea that time spent travelling should be valued using the cost of not working.

There are a number of problems with this simple idea. Simply measuring time spent travelling is not always straightforward. The obvious thing to do, ask survey respondents about it, can lead to strange results, as can be seen in Table 14.4 in Box 14.1. If it is accepted that the cost of not working is the proper way to value time, the problem arises that this cost is going to vary widely over individuals and households. Again, experience suggests that survey responses on such things as wage rates can be unreliable unless great care is taken in survey design and administration. More fundamentally, a nontrivial proportion of visitors will not be in the labour force, and for those who are there is frequently no leisure/work choice to be made as weekly hours and annual holidays are fixed. Again, for some sites and some visitors it is intuitively plausible that time spent travelling would have positive utility as part of the total recreational experience, and should be assigned a negative cost. This has been confirmed empirically in some studies. Despite these difficulties, a number of TCM applications have included some measure of the value of time spent travelling in the definition of T_i, or included it as an additional variable to the money cost of travel. Results for MCS are sensitive to the valuation of time in either of these cases. Some TCM practitioners take the view that the whole matter is so fraught with difficulties of principle and practice that the best way to proceed is to ignore time cost and to treat the MCS based on solely monetary travel costs as a lower bound to some true but unknown MCS.

However, there are a number of problems that attend the measurement of those monetary costs themselves, which have not received much attention, nor been satisfactorily resolved, in the literature. Some examples follow. First, consider the matter of a visitor to a site who travels to it from a location where he or she is spending a vacation. Should site travel cost be assessed as just the expenditure

Box 14.1 The implications of alternative travel cost measurement conventions

A visitor survey was conducted at the Tidbinbilla nature reserve in 1994. The reserve is in the Australian Capital Territory (ACT), and the majority of visitors are residents of ACT and the nearby city of Queanbeyan in New South Wales. For these visitors there are no alternative sites that could be considered close substitutes for Tidbinbilla. The reserve is managed by the ACT Parks and Conservation Service. In 1994 there was no entry charge at Tidbinbilla and opportunities for on-site expenditure were restricted to a small information centre at the entrance selling a limited range of postcards and posters. A survey was completed by 800 visitors during two parts of the year, corresponding to peak and off-peak visitation periods, as determined from visitor number records kept by the ACT Parks and Conservation Service. Respondents were asked (among other things) to provide information on:

- their point of departure for the visit;
- their place of residence;
- their travel mode (there is no bus or rail route which serves Tidbinbilla; some respondents were cyclists);
- the make and model of their motor vehicle, if that mode was used;
- whether their trip from their point of departure involved visiting any other destinations;
- their number of visits to Tidbinbilla in the previous year;
- their perception of the one-way transport cost of this visit – respondents were asked Question 11: How much do you think the journey *to* Tidbinbilla has cost (i.e. one-way expenses incurred in getting here such as petrol and 'wear and tear' on the car)?
- their perception of the time taken for the one-way trip – respondents were asked Question 19: How long did the trip *here* take?

In order to avoid the problem of apportioning travel costs, responses where the trip involved destinations other than Tidbinbilla were removed from the data set. In order to minimise problems about discretionary travel-related expenditures, and to make for accurate distance measurement, responses where the place of residence was other than the ACT or Queanbeyan were also removed, as were the small number of responses from cyclists. Some respondents did not provide sufficient information to accurately identify the make and model of their motor vehicle, and these responses were not used. For the remaining 410 observations, distance was measured from a large-scale map as the distance from the centre of the respondent's ACT suburb, or Queanbeyan, to the entrance to the nature reserve. ACT suburbs are unambiguously identified and known to residents, and are small in area and population size (average 4000 residents). Hence, the measurement of distance travelled was less problematic than in many TCM applications.

An Australian motoring organisation, the NRMA, produces estimates of the costs per kilometre of using different makes and models of motor vehicle. For each vehicle type, the NRMA produces a figure for fuel cost per kilometre, here referred to as FCPK, and for total cost per kilometre, where the latter includes depreciation, maintenance and so on, and is referred to here as CPK. For each respondent, the perceived unit price of travel, ECPK, was calculated as the perceived one-way cost, the answer to Question 11, divided by the one-way distance. Also, for each respondent, average travel speed, SPEED, was calculated by dividing one-way distance by one-way time.

The first three columns of Table 14.4 report some descriptive statistics for this data set. Costs are in units which are Australian cents per kilometre: speed is kilometres per hour. Mean perceived cost, ECPK, lies between mean fuel cost and mean total vehicle cost per unit distance, but its range is greater than that for both FCPK and CPK. In regard to SPEED, note that from any origin considered in this data set the trip includes both urban and rural segments, and that the urban speed limit is, at most, 80 kph, while the rural is 100 kph.

Table 14.4 Tidbinbilla survey results.

	Mean	Minimum	Maximum	Estimated β
FCPK	8.84	5.00	14.00	−0.0072
CPK	49.02	21.00	92.00	−0.0011
ECPK	31.34	0.00	177.78	−0.0008
SPEED	63.92	10.33	168.00	

FCPK, fuel cost per kilometre; CPK, full cost per kilometre; ECPK, perceived price per kilometre.

The last column in Table 14.4 gives the estimated value for β, the coefficient on travel cost in the trip generating equation, obtained using each of these three measures of unit distance cost applied to distance travelled. The important point here is that the estimated coefficient on travel costs varies in orders of magnitude according to the way that variable is measured. Going from researcher assigned full costs, CPK, to researcher assigned fuel cost, FCPK, increases the absolute size of the estimated coefficient by a factor of 7. The ratio of the estimated coefficient using fuel costs, FCPK, to that using respondents' perceived costs, ECPK, is 9.

Source: Common *et al*. (1999)

incurred in getting to the site from the vacation location, or should some proportion of the expenses of getting to the vacation location from the normal place of residence be included? If the latter, how should the proportion be decided? Second, consider those who visit several sites during the course of a day trip from home. How should the total travel costs for the day be allocated over the sites visited? Third, there is the matter of discretionary expenses, such as meals consumed while travelling. For lengthy trips, eating along the way will be necessary, and it will generally involve greater expense than eating at home. In such cases, even if the nature of the addition to more straightforward travel costs, such as motor vehicle expenses, could be agreed, there could remain considerable difficulties in getting accurate information from survey respondents.

These examples should suffice to indicate that the measurement of travel costs involving actual monetary expenditure is something which involves judgement on the part of the TCM analyst. Different TCM analysts use different judgements and follow different conventions in measuring monetary travel costs. In Randall (1994) it is argued that for TCM the theoretically correct way to measure travel costs is according to the perceptions of those doing the travelling. This is rarely done. Most TCM applications involve, as described above, the TCM analyst calculating respondents travel cost using some convention together with information from the survey. Randall calls the results 'researcher assigned visitation cost estimates' and argues that when they are used:

> The resulting travel costs and welfare estimates remain artefacts of the travel cost accounting and specification conventions selected for imposition.
>
> Randall (1994), page 93

As a result, Randall claims that:

> the *best* that we can expect [from TCM applications that use researcher assigned visitation cost estimates] is ordinally measurable welfare estimates
>
> Randall (1994), page 95 (emphasis added)

Since the purpose of a TCM exercise is generally understood to be the production of cardinal monetary welfare measures, this is a fundamental criticism of TCM as usually practised to date, which would apply even if all TCM analysts used the same conventions for measuring travel costs, which they do not. Not all economists would agree that travel costs should, in principle, be assessed using survey respondent perceptions. However, if the argument for perceived costs is rejected, the question remains as to what convention should be followed in computing 'researcher assigned visitation cost estimates'. In Box 14.1 we report some results which give some sense of the potential magnitudes of error associated with different conventions.

The implications of adopting different conventions for measuring travel costs for the purpose of estimating consumers surplus for ECBA can be investigated using the computer-based technique of Monte Carlo analysis. This involves generating data in the computer according to known parameter values, and then using some procedure to estimate the parameters from the data so generated and stored in the computer. Comparison of the known values with the estimated values shows the errors involved.

In this case, data were generated using

$$V_i = 4 - 0.001T_i + \varepsilon_i: \ \varepsilon_i \sim N(0, \sigma_\varepsilon^2) \quad (14.19)$$

where

$$T_i = (20 + \mu_i)D_i: \ \mu_i \sim N(0, \sigma_\mu^2) \quad (14.20)$$

for $D_i = i$ for $i = 1, 2, \ldots 80$, where T_i is the perceived cost of a visit from location i, D_i is distance to the site from location i, and ε_i and μ_i are random variables. The Tidbinbilla study used 80 origins for visits. The parameter value of -0.001 for β is used in Equation 14.19 as it is an approximation to the value reported in Table 14.4 when using perceived travel costs, ECPK, and 4 for α comes about in the same way. The figure 20 for the expectation of perceived unit travel cost in Equation 14.20 comes from the entry for the mean of ECPK in Table 14.4, being adjusted so that when used in Equation 14.20 no negative values for V_i are generated. This use of, approximate, parameter values from previous empirical work in Monte Carlo experiments is sometimes known as 'bootstrapping'. It puts the results from the Monte Carlo analysis in a meaningful context.

The data on V_i generated in this way were used to estimate α and β by ordinary least squares together with travel cost data generated according to two rules:

$$C_i = 10D_i \tag{14.21}$$

$$C_i = 50D_i \tag{14.22}$$

The first of these mimics the situation where the TCM analyst computes travel costs using only the fuel costs of vehicle use – 10 is approximately the mean for FCPK in Table 14.4. The second mimics the use of the full costs of vehicle use – the mean for CPK in Table 14.4 is 49.02.

One Monte Carlo experiment involves 50 repetitions of:

(a) using Equations 14.19 and 14.20 to generate data on D_i and V_i, for given values for the variances of the random variables ε and μ, and to calculate total MCS;
(b) using the V_i data with C_i data from either Equation 14.21 or Equation 14.22 to estimate, by ordinary least squares, the intercept and slope coefficients of the trip generating equation which follow from using either the fuel or the full cost convention (note that given the way the data is generated in this experiment, ordinary least squares is an appropriate estimation method);
(c) using the results at (b) to calculate an estimate of MCS;
(d) averaging the results at (a), (b) and (c) across the 50 repetitions, and reporting the averages arising.

A number of such experiments were run for different values of the variances of the random variables ε and μ. However, one of the interesting results was that estimated coefficients of the trip generating equation and MCS were not very sensitive to the values for these variances. Hence here we report, in Table 14.5, only the results for the case where both variances were set at zero.

These results suggest that the TCM analyst's choice of convention for measuring travel costs may well have serious implications for the social decision making that the TCM as input to ECBA is supposed to inform. Consider the following. Suppose that the recreational site to which the results in Table 14.5 apply is the site for a project for which the net present value, leaving aside the impact on recreational value, is $B_d - C_d$, that going ahead with the project would mean that recreational benefits went to zero, and that non-use value was always zero. Let X represent the present value of the lost recreational benefits evaluated on the basis of perceived travel cost. Then, from the results above, evaluation using the full cost convention would give $2.5X$, while using the fuel cost convention would give $0.5X$, in round numbers. If, then, the proper basis for social decision making is recreationalists' perceived cost, four cases can be distinguished:

(a) $B_d - C_d < 0.5X$: the project should not go ahead, and this will be the decision whichever cost convention is used.
(b) $0.5X < B_d - C_d < X$: the project should not go ahead, but the decision will be to go ahead if the fuel cost convention is used, otherwise the decision will be correct.
(c) $X < B_d - C_d < 2.5X$: the project should go ahead, but the decision will go against the project if the full cost convention is used, otherwise the decision will be correct.

Table 14.5 Some Monte Carlo results.

	Slope Coefficient	MCS
FCPK	−0.002	\$208 000
ECPK	−0.001	\$416 000
CPK	−0.0004	\$1 040 000

(d) $B_d - C_d > 2.5X$: the project should go ahead, and this will be the decision whichever cost convention is used.

If it is taken that full cost is the proper basis for social decision making, then the cases are:

(e) $B_d - C_d < 0.5X$: the project should not go ahead, and this will be the decision whichever convention is used.

(f) $0.5X < B_d - C_d < X$: the project should not go ahead, but the decision will be to go ahead if the fuel cost convention is used, otherwise the decision will be correct.

(g) $X < B_d - C_d < 2.5X$: the project should not go ahead, which will be the decision only if the full cost convention is used.

(h) $B_d - C_d > 2.5X$: the project should go ahead, which will be the decision whichever convention is used.

The $ value of the band widths here depend on the value of X, which depends on the per trip consumers' surplus as estimated, the annual number of trips in the population, the length of time for which it is assumed that recreation benefit is lost, and the discount rate. Clearly, in some applications the bands could be wide, and, depending on the size of $B_d - C_d$, use of the incorrect cost convention could lead to large social losses.

Given the several problems attending the implementation of the TCM, one might wonder whether it is worth devoting scarce intellectual resources to it as currently practised, and what are the prospects for improving matters. Smith and Kaoru (1990) attempted an implied answer to the first question by looking directly at the question: are the MCS numbers produced in different TCM applications just random noise? To answer this question they conducted a meta-analysis which involved regressing MCS per visit from a large number of TCM studies on some of the characteristics of the studies, such as the type of recreation activity, whether the price of a substitute was included as an explanatory variable in the trip generating function, the functional

form for that equation, and the estimation method used. They found that 43% of the variation in MCS across the TCM applications could be explained in terms of the different characteristics of the studies, and concluded that the MCS results are not just random noise. This may be somewhat reassuring, but clearly means that there is a lot of variation, 57%, in the results that cannot be explained by the characteristics considered. It is of some interest that the convention adopted for measuring travel costs is not one of the characteristics considered by Smith and Kaoru.

If Randall's argument for perceived costs is accepted, then progress requires that all TCM surveys collect data on respondents' perceived travel costs. The range data for ECPK and SPEED in Table 14.4 in Box 14.1 might be taken as suggesting, consistently with other studies, that eliciting respondents' perceptions requires great care, and hence considerable expense, if it is to produce useful results. If the argument for perceived costs is not accepted, then comparability across TCM applications requires that all analysts adopt the same conventions for travel cost measurement. This seems unlikely to happen, and anyway leaves other problems noted above to be addressed. A more realistic hope might be that all TCM application results will include sensitivity analysis in respect of such matters as travel cost measurement conventions, functional forms for the trip generating equation, and estimation method.

It should be recalled, finally, that we have here been discussing the problems attending the use of the TCM for the estimation of MCS, whereas we know from the preceding section that this is not the correct welfare measure, and that, for quantity/quality changes, we do not know how it relates to the correct welfare measure.

Contingent valuation

The Contingent Valuation Method (CVM) is a direct method in that it involves asking a sample of the relevant population questions about their WTP or WTA. It is called 'contingent valuation' because the valuation is contingent on hypothetical scenario put to respondents. Its main use is to provide inputs to analyses of changes in the level of provision of public goods/bads, and especially of environmental 'commodities' which have the characteristics of non-excludability and non-divisibility. As compared with indirect methods it is seen by many economists as suffering from the problem that it asks hypothetical questions, whereas indirect methods exploit data on observed, actual, behaviour. On the other hand, the CVM has two advantages over indirect methods. First, it can deal with both use and non-use values, whereas the indirect methods cover only the former, and involve weak-complementarity assumptions. Second, in principle, and unlike the indirect methods, CVM answers to WTP or WTA questions go directly to the theoretically correct monetary measures of utility changes.

While the CVM can be used for both use and non-use values, its actual use has mainly been in regard to the latter. Particularly, most CVM applications have concerned existence, or passive-use, values. Given this, and the fact that indirect methods cannot address existence values, we shall discuss the CVM in the context of trying to ascertain existence values. This reflects the balance of the literature, and is where most of the debates and controversy are located.

We discussed the theoretically correct monetary measures of utility changes in the section headed 'The theory of environmental valuation'. Here we will confine our attention to changes in environmental quality indicators, in which case it is the surplus measures that are relevant, and Table 14.6 is a rearranged Table 14.3. If we can elicit the correct answer to an appropriate WTP/WTA question from an individual, the answer is the correct monetary measure sought for that individual. For either an improvement or a deterioration, the individual can be asked

Table 14.6 WTP and WTA for environmental quality changes.

	WTP	WTA compensation
Improvement	For the change to occur is CS	For the change not occurring is ES
Deterioration	For the change not to occur is ES	For the change occurring is CS

about WTP or WTA. Which is the correct question? From what they measure, CS or ES, and our previous discussion it is clear that the answer to this question is really a statement about the entitlements assumed. CS measures relate to the initial utility level and imply entitlements to the status quo. Thus, asking about WTP for an environmental improvement implies that the individual is entitled to the existing level, as does asking about WTA compensation for a deterioration. ES measures relate to the new level of utility. Asking about WTA compensation for a possible environmental improvement not actually occurring implies an entitlement to the higher level, while asking about WTP to avoid an environmental deterioration implies only an entitlement to the lower level.

The steps involved in applying the CVM can be stated as follows:

(1) Creating a survey instrument for the elicitation of individuals' WTP/WTA. This can be broken down into three distinct, but related, components:
  (a) designing the hypothetical scenario,
  (b) deciding whether to ask about WTP or WTA,
  (c) creating a scenario about the means of payment or compensation.
(2) Using the survey instrument with a sample of the population of interest.
(3) Analysing the responses to the survey. This can be seen as having two components:
  (a) using the sample data on WTP/WTA to estimate average WTP/WTA for the population,

(b) assessing the survey results so as to judge the accuracy of this estimate.
(4) Computing total WTP/WTA for the population of interest for use in an ECBA.
(5) Conducting sensitivity analysis.

An exhaustive discussion of each of these steps is well beyond the scope of this text. Here we simply comment on some of the more important aspects of CVM practice, and its evolution over time. Box 14.2 summarises a state-of-the-art application in the USA according to the steps enumerated above. References to fuller discussions of CVM practice will be found in the further reading section at the end of the chapter.

The survey

There appears now to be a fairly wide consensus about the form that the survey instrument should take, briefly summarised as follows. In regard to point (1)(a), it should posit some programme or policy intended to have clearly stated environmental impacts, either by way of improving matters (better air quality, say) or by way of preventing some deterioration (protecting biodiversity, say). Individuals should then, (1)(b), be asked about their WTP for such a programme or policy by means of, (1)(c), some kind of tax payment. The WTP question should take the form of specifying a sum of money and asking the respondent whether he or she would be willing to pay that sum. This type of WTP question requiring a yes/no answer is referred to as a 'dichotomous choice format' question. Note, especially given that it relates to a tax payment, that it is rather like being asked to cast a vote. The form of survey instrument described here is sometimes referred to as the 'referendum model' for CVM scenario structure. In some applications the respondent is asked to vote twice, with the amount offered at the second pass dependent on the first response, as in Box 14.2.

A number of potential 'biases' have been identified in the CVM literature, and survey design is seen as an exercise in reducing bias as much as possible. Two classes of problem are subsumed by the term 'bias' as used in the literature. The first concerns getting respondents to answer the question that would, if they answered honestly, elicit respondents' true WTP in regard to the policy issue that the exercise is intended to inform. The second concerns getting respondents to answer honestly. An example of 'bias' of the first class is where the environmental 'commodity' perceived as being of concern by the respondent differs from that intended by the CVM analyst. This is known as 'amenity mis-specification bias'. Dealing with this class of biases is mainly a matter of the design of the scenario presented, especially in terms of the background information to be given to respondents.

An example of 'bias' of the second class is where the respondent perceives what the analyst intends, but provides a response which is not his or her true WTP but is intended to influence the provision of the environmental 'commodity' and/or his or her level of payment for it. This is called 'strategic bias'. Suppose, for example, that the scenario concerns a programme to protect biodiversity by taking wilderness land into public ownership as a national park, and that respondents are asked what they would be willing to pay toward the cost of acquisition. A respondent who regards the cost collection part of the exercise as purely hypothetical and is desirous of having greater biodiversity protection might overstate his or her true WTP so as to increase the probability of the park coming into being, at no personal cost. On the other hand, a respondent, desiring the park, who thinks that he or she would have to pay the price stated as his or her WTP might understate his or her true WTP in the hope of free-riding on other respondents who honestly report higher WTP. Simply asking respondents to state what they would be willing to pay, as here, is known as 'open-ended bid elicitation' and was fairly common in early CVM applications. One of

Box 14.2 Using the CVM to estimate damages from the Exxon Valdez oil spill

In 1989 the Exxon Valdez ran into submerged rocks shortly after leaving the port of Valdez loaded with crude oil, and 11 million gallons of its cargo flowed from ruptured tanks into the waters of Prince William Sound on the coast of Alaska. This was the largest oil spill in US waters, and was widely regarded as a major environmental disaster, occurring as it did in a wilderness area of outstanding natural beauty. In anticipation of legal action against the ship's owners, the government of Alaska commissioned a team of economists to conduct a CVM study to estimate the damages from the oil spill as the lost existence, or passive use, value that the spill caused. In terms of the five steps in doing CVM work identified and discussed in the text, what the research team did can be summarised as follows.

(1) In designing the scenario and selecting a payment vehicle, the team's primary goal was to develop a survey instrument that would produce a valid and theoretically correct measure of the lost passive use values due to the natural resource injuries caused by the spill. This was seen as entailing:

(a) a scenario which fully described the spill's impacts and was intelligible to all potential respondents;
(b) a plausible payment vehicle;
(c) a scenario that would be seen by respondents as neutral as between the interests of the government, the oil company and environmentalists;
(d) a conservative approach to scenario construction, erring on the side of understating the environmental effects of the oil spill.

Requirement (a) was taken to imply the extensive use of maps, colour photographs and other visual aids, and extensive testing of alternative versions of the scenario and payment vehicle prior to the conduct of the survey itself. It also pointed to conducting the survey by means of face to face interviews of respondents. Given previous experience suggesting that respondents have difficulty with WTA questions, requirement (b) was taken to imply that the question asked should be a WTP question. Plausibility was also taken, in part on the basis of the testing of alternatives in focus groups and the like, to require that the payment vehicle should be a one-off tax payment. The focus group work also assisted in designing an instrument that would be seen as neutral. In regard to (d), where scenario construction necessitated choices between options for which neither theory nor survey research practice gave a strong ranking, the option was chosen which would, it was thought, if it had any effect, produce a lower WTP. Thus, for example, respondents were not shown pictures of oiled birds.

The development of the survey instrument used took place over a period of 18 months, and involved initially focus groups, followed by trial interviews and pilot surveys. The form that it finally took was as follows. After being asked about their views on various kinds of public goods and knowledge of the Exxon Valdez incident, respondents were presented with information about Prince William Sound, the port of Valdez, the spill and its environmental effects, and a programme to prevent damage from another spill. The programme would involve two coast guard vessels escorting each loaded tanker on its passage through Prince William Sound. These vessels would have two functions: first, reducing the likelihood of a grounding or collision, and second, should an accident occur, keeping the spill from spreading beyond the tanker. The interviewer then stated that the programme would be funded by a one-off tax on oil companies using the port of Valdez and that all households would also pay a one-off tax levy. Before asking about willingness to pay this tax, the interviewer presented material about the reasons why a respondent might not want to pay such a tax, so as to make it clear that a 'no' vote was socially acceptable.

The WTP question was whether the respondent would vote for the programme, given that the one-off household tax would be an amount x. The survey involved four different treatments in which the amount x varied as shown in Table 14.7 in the column headed A-15, which was the first WTP question number in the survey instrument. Depending on the answer to that question, a second WTP question was put to the interviewee. If the A-15 answer was 'yes', the respondent was asked whether he or she would vote for the programme if the tax cost were to be the higher amount shown in the column headed A-16. If the answer at A-15 was 'no', the interviewee was asked about voting given a tax cost at the lower amount shown in the column headed A-17.

Table 14.7 WTP question $s.

Treatment	A-15	A-16	A-17
A	10	30	5
B	30	60	10
C	60	120	30
D	120	250	60

After the WTP questions, the interviewer asked a number of debriefing type questions about the motives for the responses given, about attitudes and beliefs relevant to the scenario, and about the respondent's demographic and socio-economic characteristics.

Box 14.2 continued

(2) The survey was conducted using a stratified random sample of dwelling units in the USA. Approximately 1600 units were selected. Given the cost that producing and using foreign language versions of the survey instrument would have involved, non-English speaking households were dropped from the sample. Within the remaining households, one respondent was randomly selected. Respondents were randomly assigned to one of the four WTP treatments. The response rate, based on sample size after dropping non-English speaking households, was 75.2%.

(3) The second column of Table 14.8 gives the proportion of 'yes' responses to the first WTP question, A-15, across the four treatments. The next four columns give the proportions for response patterns over the two WTP questions that all respondents were asked. Thus, for example, in the third column 45.08% of respondents asked initially about $10 said 'yes' to it and to the $30 that they were subsequently asked about, while in the fifth column 11.67% of the respondents initially asked about $120 said 'no' to it but 'yes' to the $60 that they were subsequently asked about. For the 'Yes' answer to the first WTP question, and for the 'yes–yes' and 'no–no' patterns over the two questions, the entries in Table 14.8 look consistent with the basic idea that the probability of a 'yes' vote falls with the price tag attached. Note that the group answering 'No-No' may, as well as including respondents whose WTP lies between zero and the second $x put to them, include respondents who do not think that the escort ship plan would work or think that, as a matter of principle, the oil shippers should bear the whole cost.

Table 14.8 Response proportions.

Treatment	Yes	Yes–Yes	Yes–No	No–Yes	No–No
A ($10, 30, 5)	67.42	45.08	22.35	3.03	29.55
B ($30, 60, 10)	51.69	26.04	26.04	11.32	36.60
C ($60, 120, 30)	50.59	21.26	29.13	9.84	39.76
D ($120, 250, 60)	34.24	13.62	20.62	11.67	54.09

(3a) To use the response data to estimate a measure of average WTP, it is necessary to adopt some statistical model assumed to be generating the responses. In this study it was assumed that the underlying distribution of WTP is a Weibull distribution. Estimating the parameters of this distribution using maximum likelihood estimators and the response data gave an estimate of $30.30 (95% confidence interval $26.18–$35.08) for the median WTP and of $97.18 (95% confidence interval $85.82–$108.54) for mean WTP. In using the response data here, 'not sure' responses to either WTP question were treated as 'no' responses, consistent with the goal of producing a conservative estimate of average WTP.

(3b) A valuation function, using data on respondents' beliefs, attitudes and characteristics to construct explanatory variables for a regression with WTP as dependent variable, was estimated and the result was taken as demonstrating construct validity. It was found, for example, that a belief that in the absence of the escort ship programme the damage occurring in the future would be greater than in the Exxon Valdez case was positively associated with WTP, other things equal, while a belief that the damage would be less was negatively associated with WTP. Again, it was found that a respondent's self-identification as an environmentalist was positively associated with WTP, other things being equal, as was an expectation of a future visit to Alaska. WTP was found to be positively associated with income level.

(4) Taking the estimated median WTP of $30.30 as the relevant average and multiplying it by the number of English speaking households in the USA gives a total WTP for the escort ship programme of $2.75 billion. This was interpreted as representing an estimate of the lower bound on the correct, WTA-based, valuation of the passive use value lost as a result of the Exxon Valdez oil spill.

(5) Sensitivity analysis was conducted using the estimated valuation function. Thus, for example, the dummy variables representing beliefs about what the impact of a future spill would be in the absence of the escort vessels were all set to zero and the estimated function was then used to generate respondents' WTP. The intention here was to produce estimates of the WTP responses that would have arisen if all respondents had had the same belief in the efficacy of the escort vessel programme. The median of the individual WTP estimates so produced was $27, to be compared with $30.30 based on the actual responses. On the basis of several such experiments using the valuation function it was concluded that the result used at step (4) was reasonably robust.

Another type of sensitivity test involved re-running the survey. The survey described here was conducted in 1991. Two years later the same survey instrument was used again with a national sample, and 'almost identical' results were obtained.

Source: Carson *et al.* (1995)

the reasons why CVM practice has evolved from using the open-ended bid format to the dichotomous choice model, with taxation as the payment vehicle, described above has been the belief that the latter is less subject to strategic bias. Many CVM practitioners argue that with good survey instrument design strategic bias is not a major problem nowadays.

Good survey instrument design is now seen as involving extensive pre-testing, and the use of focus groups. These are small groups of individuals, up to a dozen or so, who are led by a facilitator through a loosely structured discussion of the issues raised by the scenario and payment vehicle. The purpose of this exercise is to avoid bias of the first kind noted above in regard to the scenario itself, and of the second kind in regard to the payment vehicle and related matters.

Getting responses

Given a survey instrument, there are three broad options for obtaining responses from the sample respondents. Conducting face to face interviews offers several advantages, notably a potentially high response rate and the potential for effective information provision, but is very expensive. Mail surveys are much cheaper, but get lower response rates and tend to restrict the amount of information that can be provided and the number of questions that can be asked. Telephone interviewing is cheap, but restricts the information that can be provided – graphics cannot be used, for example. Clearly, which of these methods is to be used will influence the details of survey instrument design. While the sample should be randomly selected from the population, possibly with some stratification, precisely how it is selected will clearly vary with how the survey is to be administered.

Averaging responses

In regard to reporting the average WTP across respondents, the options are the mean and the median. The median is less affected by 'outliers', which are a few very high WTP responses, and is generally found to be lower than the mean. Most CVM applications report both the mean and the median, but use the median for calculating total WTP. Where the survey follows the single pass referendum model, responses are analysed using logit analysis and logistic regression methods, and the median WTP is calculated as the sum of money which when used with the estimated regression parameters gives the probability of a 'yes' response as 0.5. For any given sum of money put to them in such a survey some respondents will say 'no' because they object to the question, rather than because the sum is greater than their WTP. It is now seen as important that the survey takes a form which enables such 'protest' responses to be distinguished from 'no' responses which do reflect the fact that the sum offered is greater than WTP. Where this is done, protest responses are usually ignored in calculating average WTP. Clearly, the treatment of outliers and protest responses can have significant implications for estimated median and, especially, mean WTP.

Evaluating responses

A standard procedure for assessing the results of a survey is to use the responses to estimate a 'valuation' or 'bid' function. Typically the survey would ask respondents about their demographic and socio-economic status, and about some of their attitudes, as well as simply asking them about WTP. The estimation of the valuation function takes the WTP response as the dependent variable in a regression with demographic, socio-economic and attitudinal indicators as explanatory variables. If the estimated parameters are consistent with economic theory and previous experience, this is taken as evidence that some confidence may be placed in all of the survey results, including estimated average WTP. If this is not the case, then the inference would be that the survey had not worked well. Thus, for example, theory and experience have respondents with higher incomes having, other things being equal, higher WTP, so that if the valuation function for a survey involved a regression coefficient on income which was negative and statistically significant, one would have little confidence in its average WTP result.

Total WTP

Given average WTP, total WTP is just that average times the size of the relevant population. A question which arises is: what is the relevant population? At one level the question is answered by the conduct of the CVM exercise in regard to sample selection. Thus, if the sample is randomly selected from the electoral rolls for a nation, then the population size is the nation's population. At another level, the question may be open and unresolved. If it is the existence value associated with a world famous wilderness area known for its biodiversity – the Amazon rainforest, say – that is at issue, it is not obvious that individuals with positive WTP will all be located within the boundaries of the nation where the area is located. But, for practical reasons, global surveys for environmental valuation are not undertaken. Another issue which can be numerically important is the question of on whose behalf respondents state WTP. Should respondents be understood to be stating what is strictly their own WTP, or WTP on behalf of the households that they belong to? Supposing that by good survey design the analyst can be sure that responses are of the first kind, there then remains the question of whether the arising average WTP should be multiplied by the population or by the number of adults in the population? Clearly, for any given average WTP, the answer to this question can make a large difference to calculated total WTP.

Sensitivity analysis

Sensitivity analysis can take several forms. The estimated valuation function can be used to figure how the average WTP is affected by variations in the demographic, socio-economic and attitudinal composition of respondents included in the sample used for calculating it. Average WTP can be recalculated following different procedures in relation to outliers and possible or actual protest responses. The survey can be repeated using a different sample, and possibly with minor variations to the scenario. The problem with the last approach to sensitivity analysis is that it is expensive. It will generally be useful to compare the total WTP estimated with the money sum to which the decision that the CVM is supposed to inform would be sensitive, as illustrated in Box 14.3.

Experience with the CVM

A bibliography of CVM 'studies and papers' (Carson *et al.*, 1995b) published at the beginning of 1995 contained 2131 entries. Even supposing that only 50% of the entries are reports of CVM applications, as opposed to theoretical exercises, and bearing in mind the growth in activity since 1995, this suggests a range of experience impossible to properly report here. What follows is, then, selective. We have chosen here to discuss four aspects of experience which have been seen as 'problems' for CVM. In the next subsection we consider some assessments of the CVM.

The size of total WTP

The first problem is the contention that the CVM produces results for total WTP which are implausibly large. Box 14.3 illustrates this with an Australian experience. As illustrated by the 'back of the envelope' calculations in the box, where existence values are involved so that the population is large even a small average WTP will give a very large total WTP. As to the implausibility of the $53 per year for the average, it can be noted that this is approximately equivalent to one small glass of beer per week at Australian prices. It is not obviously implausible that an average individual would say, if asked, that he or she was prepared to make that kind of sacrifice to preserve part of the national heritage.

Box 14.3 Mining at Coronation Hill?

In 1990 there emerged a proposal to develop a mine at Coronation Hill in the Kakadu national park, which is listed as a World Heritage Area. The Australian federal government referred the matter to a recently established advisory body, the Resource Assessment Commission, which undertook a very thorough exercise in environmental valuation using the CVM, implemented via a survey of a sample of the whole Australian population. This exercise produced a range of estimates for the median individual WTP to preserve Coronation Hill from the proposed development, the smallest of which was $53 per year, which implies a very large figure for total Australian WTP. If it is assumed, conservatively, that the $53 figure is WTP per household, and this annual WTP is converted to a present value capital sum in the same way as the commercial NPV for the mine was calculated, the EC to be compared with the mine NPV is, in round numbers, $1500 million.

The publication of this result gave rise to much comment, mainly critical, and some hilarity. It was pointed out that given the small size of the actual area directly affected, the implied per hectare value of Coronation Hill greatly exceeded real estate prices in Manhattan, whereas it was 'clapped out buffalo country' of little recreational or biological value. In fact, leaving aside environmental considerations and proceeding on a purely commercial basis gave the NPV for the mine as $80 million, so that the threshold per Australian household WTP required to reject the mining project was $5 per year, one-tenth of the low end of the range of estimated individual WTP on the part of Australians. Given that Kakadu is internationally famous for its geological formations, biodiversity and indigenous culture, a case could be made for extending the existence value relevant population, at least, to North America and Europe. On that basis, the size of WTP per Australian household required to block the project would be much smaller than $5.

In the event, the Australian federal government did not allow the mining project to go ahead. It is not clear that the CVM application actually played any part in that decision. What is clear is that even if the CVM result overestimated true Australian WTP by a factor of 10, it would still be the case that ECBA would reject the mining project even if the Australian population was taken to be the entire relevant population.

Source: Resource Assessment Commission (1991).

Price and scope sensitivity

The second and third problems – lack of price sensitivity and lack of sensitivity to the extent of the environmental 'commodity' – can be illustrated jointly in the context of another CVM application in Australia by the Resource Assessment Commission, the main features of which are reported in Box 14.4. The term 'preservation values' used there has the same meaning as our 'non-use values': a TCM exercise was jointly conducted to assess 'use values'. As noted above, where, as here, the single pass dichotomous choice model is used to elicit WTP, the results can be analysed using the logit model and logistic regression. The respondent is asked whether he or she is willing to pay X, and answers 'yes' or 'no'. For analysis, the response is treated as a binary variable taking the value 1 or 0. In this application a 'no' is given the value 1 and a 'yes' the value 0. In that case for the logit model

$$Pr(\text{no}) = e^{-z}/(1 + e^{-z}) \qquad (14.23)$$

so that with $Pr(\text{yes})$ equal to one minus $Pr(\text{no})$

$$Pr(\text{yes}) = 1/(1 + e^{-z}) \qquad (14.24)$$

where $z = f(x)$ is some linear function of the variables determining a yes or no response. If we define the 'odds' as

$$\text{Odds} = Pr(\text{yes})/Pr(\text{no})$$

from Equations (14.23) and (14.24) we get

$$\text{Odds} = e^z$$

so that

$$\ln(\text{Odds}) = z = f(x) \qquad (14.25)$$

A logistic regression package estimates the parameters of $f(x)$ from the data on individual respondents' yes/no answers and the values taken by the variables specified as arguments in $f(x)$ for individuals. In the case considered in Box 14.4 the arguments of $f(x)$ considered are the cost put to a respondent, X, income Y and age, A. With this notation

Box 14.4 The Resource Assessment Commission South-East Forest CV study

Management of the forests of the Australian states of New South Wales and Victoria has been the focus of considerable debate over many years, and in 1990 the Resource Assessment Commission was requested to conduct an Inquiry into forest management. One of several research projects undertaken as part of the 'Forest and Timber Inquiry' was a CV study directed at estimating 'preservation values' for the 'South-East forests'. While the major aim of the study was to collect information relevant to the preservation value of all the forest areas in south-eastern Australia that are on the Register of the National Estate, preservation values were estimated under three different scenarios; setting 100% of the National Estate forests aside for preservation, setting 50% aside, and setting 10% aside. The total sample of respondents comprised three sub-samples, each of which received a different scenario in terms of the area to be set aside for preservation.

Within each of these sub-samples, a further 11 sub-samples were employed to provide variation in the stated costs ($X) of preservation put to respondents, which ranged from $2 per year to $400 per year. A mail survey was employed which was administered by a consultancy firm. Reminder cards were sent out ten days after initial dispatch, and a further copy of the questionnaire was sent out ten days after this. The final valid response rate was slightly over 50%.

The questionnaire was pre-tested with focus groups. The final questionnaire, which began with a map of the region in question, was also designed to provide data for a travel cost study of recreation values. In addition to the CV relevant questions and general attitudinal and socio-economic questions, information was collected on recreation statistics such as expenses, activities undertaken, time spent at location and so forth.

The CV section of the questionnaire began by asking respondents to look at the map again. This was followed with:

> We are now going to ask you some questions about what you would like to see happen to the forests in the striped areas shown on the map.
>
> The Resource Assessment Commission is considering two options (A and B) for the future use of the forests in the striped areas of the map: we would like to know which of these options you prefer.

Respondents were then presented with concise summaries, in point form, of both of the options. Option A, referred to as 'Wood Production', was described as involving the setting aside of half of the area in question to grow trees for wood and each year a different 2% of the wood producing area would be logged, and then allowed to regrow until the next logging. The wood producing areas were described as having younger trees on average, they would cause habitat disturbance to some rare and endangered species: current job opportunities in the local region would be maintained as a result. Option B, referred to as 'Conservation Reserves', would set an area aside from wood production and consequently would have caused some job losses.

The remainder of the CV question was as follows:

> If you choose option B it could cost you $X each year. This is because:
>
> > –with less wood being available the prices of timber products you buy, such as house frames and paper, could rise; and government charges you pay could be increased to pay for the conservation of the areas.
>
> When you make your choice between Options A and B, keep in mind that there may also be other forests in Australia that you may wish to pay further money to have conserved. Which option do you prefer?

Response data was analysed using the Logit model. The logistic regression results for $z = f(x)$ for each preservation scenario are given in Table 14.9.

Table 14.9 Logistic regression results for three preservation scenarios.

	10% Preservation	50% Preservation	100% Preservation
Constant	−1.5227	0.1533	−1.1976
	(1.18)	(0.12)	(0.94)
$X	−0.0006	−0.0029*	−0.0017*
	(0.75)	(3.47)	(1.98)
Income	0.2942*	0.1325	0.2556*
(logarithm)	(2.47)	(1.01)	(2.13)
Age (years)	−0.0293*	−0.0234*	−0.0296*
	(4.15)	(3.40)	(4.22)
Median WTP	$200.00	$140.00	$43.50

*Indicates statistical significance at 5%, two-tailed test.
Source: adapted from Blamey *et al.* (1995).

we have

$$\ln (\text{Odds}) = \alpha + \beta_1 X + \beta_2 Y + \beta_3 A \quad (14.26)$$

where theory says that β_1 is negative and β_2 positive, so that the relative probability of a 'yes' decreases with increases in the 'price' asked of a respondent and increases with income. The results in Table 14.9 in Box 14.4 show the right signs.

However, and this is the second of the problems being illustrated, if we look at the estimated coefficients on X we see that for one preservation scenario the result is not significant at 5%, and that in all three cases the coefficients appear small. To see this consider the scenario where price sensitivity is the greatest, the 50% preservation scenario. There a coefficient of -0.0029 means that a $100 increase in X would reduce ln(Odds) by 0.29, that is, would reduce the relative probability of 'yes' by 1.3364, whereas a $1 increase in income would increase ln(Odds) by 0.1325, that is, increase the relative probability of a 'yes' by 1.1416. This lack of price sensitivity was in fact one of the reasons why the Resource Assessment Commission lacked confidence in the results of this CVM application.

Another reason for this lack of confidence is the illustration of the third problem that we are considering, which we described as a lack of sensitivity to the extent of the environmental 'commodity', and which has also been called 'scope insensitivity'. In one of the original papers calling attention to this problem it took the form that WTP for cleaning up the lakes in one region of the Canadian province of Ontario was 'strikingly similar' to that for cleaning up all the lakes in that province. In another CVM application it was found that WTP to prevent bird deaths did not differ significantly across scenarios in which the programme prevented 2000, 20 000 and 200 000 deaths. In the case of Box 14.4, the problem is even worse. Median WTP actually decreases as the area to be set aside for preservation increases.

The results in Box 14.4 are an illustration of two insensitivity problems that have appeared in a number of CVM applications. It is not the case that all CVM applications have produced results demonstrating these insensitivities. Carson (1995) reports results from over 30 CVM applications where the hypothesis of scope insensitivity can be tested, and is rejected, and argues that where there is scope insensitivity is a consequence of 'poor' survey design and administration.

Others take the view that, at least in some cases, these insensitivities reflect problems with the behavioural assumptions underlying the CVM. These positions are not necessarily mutually exclusive. It may be that while survey respondents have an inclination not to act as economists require, they can be induced to overcome that inclination by avoiding 'poor' survey design and administration. This raises questions which we return to in the final section of this chapter.

WTP or WTA?

The fourth problem to be briefly considered here concerns WTP and WTA results obtained in CVM applications. As noted in the section on the theory of environmental valuation, the CVM has an advantage over indirect methods in that it goes, in principle, directly to the correct monetary measures of utility change, rather than producing results for MCS. Given that where it is quality change that is at issue, the typical case in the environmental context, the approximation involved in using MCS is of unknown size, this is seen by many economists as an important advantage. However, the question remains as to whether to ask about WTP or WTA. Suppose that we are concerned with an ECBA of a proposed development in a wilderness area, so that the quality change at issue is a deterioration. Then, from Table 14.6 we see that we could try to elicit ES via a WTP question or CS via a WTA question. Which should we use?

In the early days of CVM application it was widely supposed that for a given scenario the result should not materially depend on which question was used. This belief persisted after it was recognised that the Willig (1976) result did not transfer from the CV/EV context (price changes) to the CS/ES context (quality changes). Randall and Stoll (1980) established that although the contexts differed, CS and ES would be close together for commodities for which expenditure was small in relation to income, so that WTP and WTA questions should produce similar results.

However, in CVM applications where both questions were asked, it was routinely found that WTA was much greater than WTP. In the first study to estimate both, for example, Hammack and Brown (1974) reported WTA four times larger than WTP for the same change. The apparent persistent mismatch between the predictions of utility theory and the CVM troubled economists working in the field. Acceptance of the theory implied that CVM practice was in some way deficient. However, similar results were emerging from experimental economics.

In 1986 a paper by Hanemann (1991) showed that it was the understanding of the predictions of the theory that was incorrect. He showed that utility theory actually predicts that for commodities where there are limited possibilities for substitution, WTA could be much larger than WTP. While this resolves the apparent contradiction between theory and evidence, it leads to another problem for using CVM as input to ECBA. If the theory says that WTA and WTP answers can be very different in circumstances likely to be typical in ECBA, then it matters which one is asked about. Given the observed size differences as between WTA and WTP results, which is used in an ECBA could make the difference between approving and rejecting a wilderness-threatening project. As noted earlier, the choice between CS and ES is really a decision about property rights. To ask about WTA and use CS is to take it that the status quo is the relevant reference point, so that individuals have an implicit property right in a public good which is an undisturbed wilderness, whereas to ask about WTP and use ES takes the situation with a damaged wilderness as the relevant reference point, and implies no such property rights. The policy implications arising are discussed in Knetsch (1990).

The general view appears to be that ECBA should in this kind of context proceed on the former basis, and properly use WTA questions. This is where the problem arises, as experience with CVM indicates that many individuals have difficulty with WTA questions. Where the WTA format has been used, there is a consistently high level of protest responses, with many individuals either refusing to accept any amount of compensation or accepting only indefinitely large amounts. In some cases the WTA format has produced protest response rates as high as 50% (Mitchell and Carson, 1989). This suggests that whatever the theoretical arguments for the WTA format, its use in practice is undesirable. Hence, there appears to be an emerging consensus that good CVM practice involves using the WTP format, and treating it as providing a lower bound for the more appropriate WTA result.

Assessing the CVM

Particularly where non-use values are at issue, the use of the CVM is, as we have previously noted, controversial. It is useful to distinguish two areas of debate. The first, which is mainly the subject matter of exchanges within the economics profession, takes the role of ECBA and the need for environmental valuation as given, but debates whether CVM can provide useful inputs to it. The second, although often focusing on CVM for non-use values, is actually about ECBA itself and the rationale for environmental valuation. This debate is largely, but not exclusively, conducted between economists and non-economists, and we defer consideration of it until the final section of the chapter.

Within economics, it is accepted that decisions should be made according to efficiency criteria, and that for this to happen information about individuals' preferences, as captured in such measures as CS and ES, is needed. Economists are generally much more comfortable with preference information revealed through actual behaviour than through answers to hypothetical questions. Given that, suspicion about CVM results persists because there is no way that they can be compared with what is known to be the truth to assess CVM performance. Assessing the validity and usefulness of CVM results is a matter of judgement based on evidence of various kinds from various sources. Drawing on work in psychology, where attempts are made to measure concepts like intelligence, it has been suggested that in coming to a judgement about the CVM it is useful to distinguish and consider three kinds of validity.

• Content validity concerns the extent to which all of the aspects of the concept are adequately covered. Assessing a particular CVM application for its content validity is a matter of forming a view about whether the scenario in all of its dimensions is likely to be conducive to the revelation of true WTP or WTA for the 'commodity' intended. Experience, in terms of protest responses and with focus groups, has led to content validity being considered more likely with a WTP format than with a WTA format.
• Construct validity concerns the degree to which the estimated CVM measure agrees with other measures as predicted by theory. Two particular forms have been distinguished in the literature. Convergent validity concerns agreement of the CVM result with a result for the same 'commodity' obtained by another method, such as the TCM, for example. Of course, such convergence does not definitively establish that the CVM result is correct: problems with the TCM were discussed above. Also, it should be noted that this assessment of convergent validity is only possible where it is use values that are at issue. Theoretical validity is assessed by considering the relationship between the CVM result and other variables that theory suggests are related to it in some particular way. An example of generating evidence on theoretical validity would be the use of the estimated valuation or bid function as described in Box 14.2, in which case the results were taken as establishing theoretical construct validity. Another

would be looking at scope sensitivity, as described in discussing Box 14.4, in which case the results were against theoretical construct validity.
• Criterion validity is assessed by comparing a CVM result with something, the criterion, that is definitely closer to what it is intended that the CVM measure than the CVM result itself. Clearly, the ideal criterion would be a market price data, but, equally clearly, such is not available – if it were nobody would be doing a CVM application. 'Simulated markets' have been used to consider criterion validity, and involve setting up experimental situations where individuals actually pay or get compensation.

Considering past experience in these terms, some economists have come to the judgement that it is worth continuing with CVM, especially in the non-use value context, on the grounds that where it has been done properly it has already produced useful results, and that where it has obviously failed what can be learned from analysing the likely causes of failure can improve future applications. We have discussed environmental valuation generally and CVM particularly in the context of ECBA. In the USA the courts have decided that CVM based evidence on non-use values may be admissible in determining the compensation payments to be made where actual damage has occurred. The sums of real money involved can be large – billions of dollars. This has sharpened the controversy. The US government agency responsible for setting the rules for the assessment of damages from oil spills, the National Oceanic and Atmospheric Administration (NOAA) of the US Department of Commerce convened a panel of experts, co-chaired by two Nobel laureates in economics (Arrow and Solow), to advise on the reliability of CVM for the role allowed it by the courts. The panel's report (US Department of Commerce, 1993) gave CVM for what it referred to as passive-use values a qualified endorsement. It states that

The Panel starts from the premise that passive-use loss – interim or permanent – is a meaningful component of the total damage resulting from environmental accidents.

and comments that

It has been argued in the literature and in comments addressed to the Panel that the results of CV studies are variable, sensitive to the details of the survey instrument used, and vulnerable to upward bias. These arguments are plausible. However, some antagonists of the CV approach go so far as to suggest that there can be no useful information content to CV results. The Panel is unpersuaded by these extreme arguments.

The Panel identified 'a number of stringent guidelines for the conduct of CV studies', concluding that

under those conditions ... CV studies convey useful information. We think it is fair to describe such information as reliable by the standards that seem to be implicit in similar contexts, like market analysis for new and innovative products and the assessment of other damages normally allowed in court proceedings.

and that

CV studies can produce estimates reliable enough to be the starting of a judicial process of damage assessment, including lost passive-use values.

The Panel's guidelines covered all aspects of the design and conduct of a CVM application. The Exxon Valdez exercise reported in Box 14.2 can be considered as exemplifying compliance with the guidelines. Particularly, the Panel recommended face to face interviewing, the use of the WTP question, and the 'use of a dichotomous question that asks respondents to vote for or against a particular level of taxation'. Discussing the problem of eliciting reliable 'CV estimates', the Panel stated that:

The simplest way to approach the problem is to consider the CV survey as essentially a self-contained referendum in which respondents vote on whether to tax themselves or not for a particular purpose.

Other economists are less optimistic about the prospects for CVM providing useful information on non-use values, whether for damage assessment in litigation or for use in

ECBA. There is a widespread view that it is necessarily the case that 'if you ask hypothetical questions you get hypothetical answers'. Peterson (1992) expressed the assessment, which he thought was shared by many, that

CV works where it is not needed (for example, to measure the value of private goods), but is flawed and useless for measuring those values for which it may be the only hope (for example, such extreme public goods as existence value or subsistence use of natural resources).

Such a judgement depends, as does that of the NOAA panel, on what is meant by 'works'. Recall that the original prospect for the CVM was the accurate estimation of the correct monetary measures of utility changes associated with environmental quality change – valuing environmental services – as required for input to ECBA. This is Peterson's criterion. The NOAA panel uses a different criterion. By 'works' it means the provision of 'useful information' about the taxes that people are willing to pay in connection with programmes intended to protect the environment, as in the Exxon Valdez case. We return to this distinction in the final section of the chapter.

Other techniques

For completeness, we now briefly review some other techniques for environmental valuation developed in recent decades. We do not go into any detail, merely sketching the basic nature of the techniques. In every case there are problems and issues similar in nature to those discussed above for the TCM and CVM, which have been more or less extensively canvassed and addressed in the literature. More information on the theoretical basis for and applications of these techniques can be found in the references provided in the further reading section at the end of the chapter.

Hedonic pricing

This is an indirect method, first proposed and used in the early 1970s, based on weak complementarity assumptions. As such, it is subject to the problems about the relationship between what can be estimated, an MCS monetary measure, and that which is required by the theory, a CS or ES monetary measure, that were discussed in the section on the theory of environmental valuation. There are also a number of problems attending the estimation of MCS itself. The basic approach can be indicated in the context of atmospheric pollution, where the hedonic pricing technique has been widely used. While clean air is not a traded good, it is an attribute which seems to influence residential property prices. Evidence from revealed preferences suggests that, other things being equal, a positive relationship exists between the prices that people are willing to pay for housing and the quality of ambient air standards. Examination of property prices might, therefore, enable one to impute the value of clean air.

Assume that data can be collected on housing rents (or house prices, from which rents can be imputed), air quality and a set of attributes which influence housing rents, such as house size, amenities, proximity to employment and neighbourhood characteristics. A representative sample of properties should be drawn, in such a way that properties in the sample are chosen from a variety of localities with differing levels of ambient air quality. Multiple regression analysis can then be used to estimate the relationship between rents and all of the attributes relevant to rents. That estimated relationship can then be used to figure the relationship between rent and air pollution, holding all the other determinants of rent constant. The estimated equation for the determination of rents is known as a 'hedonic price equation': the derived relationship between rent and pollution is often referred to as a 'rent-pollution function' or a 'rent gradient'. Box 14.5 presents one application for the purpose of estimating the value of air quality improvements in Los Angeles.

The hedonic travel cost method is a variant of the travel cost method which seeks to use data on the attributes of recreational sites together with data on visitation rates and travel costs to value site attributes. The basic idea can be illustrated by considering just two sites which are the same in all respects save that one has some attribute that the other does not. The valuation of that attribute would then be inferred from the difference in the relationship between visitation and travel costs between the two sites.

Choice modelling

What we have here called 'direct methods' are, for reasons which will be obvious from the discussion of the CVM, also known as 'stated preference methods'. A recent innovation in stated preference methods, choice modelling, has the same point of departure as hedonic pricing – the idea, originally formalised in Lancaster (1966), that a 'commodity' is most usefully treated as the embodiment of a bundle of attributes or characteristics, which are the things of real interest to consumers. In choice modelling individuals are asked to make a series of choices as between two or more resource use options. One of the options is the status quo, which is offered in every choice problem put to the individual. The levels of the attributes characterising the other options are varied across the choice problems. One option involves a monetary payment. The choices that individuals make are analysed using a multinomial logit model, and the values individuals assign to changes in environmental attributes are calculated by estimating the marginal rate of substitution between the monetary attribute and the environmental attributes of interest. Whereas the CVM provides an estimate of the value for just one option, choice modelling can, in principle, generate estimates of any option that can be constructed from the attributes and their levels represented in the choice sets put to individuals.

While there is quite a lot of experience with choice modelling in market research, where Lancaster's work has had considerable

Box 14.5 Valuing improvements in air quality in Los Angeles

Brookshire *et al.* (1982) took a sample of 634 sales of single family homes which occurred between January 1977 and March 1978 in the Los Angeles metropolitan area. Data on two air pollution variables – nitrogen dioxide (NO_2) and total suspended particulates (TSP) – that are collected regularly at air monitoring stations in the area were used in the study. The objective of the study was to estimate rent differentials associated with air quality improvements for various localities within Los Angeles.

Housing sale prices were assumed to be a function of four sets of variables, H, N, A, and Q, where

H = housing structure variables (living area, number of bathrooms, etc.)

N = neighbourhood variables (crime rate, school quality, population density etc.)

A = accessibility variables (distances to centres of employment, beaches etc.)

Q = air quality variables (total suspended particulate matter and NO_2)

Two hedonic price equations were estimated, one for each measure of pollution. Brookshire *et al.* searched through a variety of alternative functional forms for the hedonic equations, and those reported here are the ones that had the best statistical fit. In these two equations, note that the dependent variable is the natural logarithm of the home sale price (in 1978 US$1000). Thus a change of one unit in any one of the explanatory variables results in a proportionate change of the dollar house sale price, where the magnitude of that proportionate change is given by the estimated coefficient attached to the variable in question. However, in the cases where an explanatory variable also enters in log form, the associated coefficient gives the proportionate change in house sale price that results from a unit proportionate change in the explanatory variable; it is an elasticity.

So for example, if distance to the beach is increased by one unit (one unit is probably one mile, although the paper does not define units), then the home sale price will fall by 0.011 586 in proportionate terms (by 1.1586%), if all other variables are held constant. A unit proportionate increase in NO_2 concentration (a 100% increase, or a doubling) results, ceteris paribus, in a proportionate decrease in house prices of 0.224 07 (that is 22.407%).

In regard to the results in Table 14.10 note that

Table 14.10 Estimated hedonic rent gradient equations. Dependent variable = log(Home Sale Price, in $1000).

Independent variable	NO_2 equation		TSP equation	
Housing structure variables				
Sale date	.018591	(9.7577)	.018654	(9.7727)
Age	−.018171	(2.3385)	−.021411	(2.8147)
Living area	.00017568	(12.126)	.00017507	(12.069)
Bathrooms	.15602	(9.609)	.15703	(9.6636)
Pool	.058063	(4.6301)	.058397	(4.6518)
Fireplaces	.099577	(7.1705)	.099927	(7.1866)
Neighbourhood variables				
Log(crime)	−.08381	(1.5766)	−.10401	(1.9974)
School quality	.0019826	(3.9450)	.001771	(3.5769)
Ethnic composition (percentage white)	.027031	(4.3915)	.043472	(6.2583)
Housing density	−.000066926	(9.1277)	−.000067613	(9.2359)
Public safety expenditures	.00026192	(4.7602)	.00026143	(4.7418)
Accessibility variables				
Distance to beach	−.011586	(7.8321)	−.011612	(7.7822)
Distance to employment	−.28514	(14.786)	−.26232	(14.158)
Air pollution variables				
log (TSP)			−.22183	(3.8324)
log(NO_2)	−.22407	(4.0324)		
Constant	2.2325	(2.9296)	1.0527	(1.4537)
R^2	.89		.89	

Source: adapted from Brookshire, *et al.* (1982).
Figures in parentheses are *t*-statistic for the null hypothesis that the coefficient is zero.

Box 14.5 continued

(a) Approximately 90% of the variation in the home sale price is accounted for by variation in the explanatory variables of the models (see the R^2 statistics).

(b) All coefficients have the expected sign and, except for those on crime, all are statistically significant at the 1% level. Particularly, the pollution variables have their expected negative influence on sale price and are highly significant.

(c) With the exception only of ethnic composition, the estimated coefficients on variables are very similar across the two reported equations.

Brookshire *et al.* use this information to calculate the rent premium that would be implied if air quality were to improve, for identical homes in given localities. These rent premia differ from one locality to another, but the results indicate rent differentials from $15.44 to $45.92 per month (in 1978 prices) for an improvement from 'poor' to 'fair' air quality, and from $33.17 to $128.46 (in 1978 prices) for an improvement from 'fair' to 'good' air quality. In each case, the higher figures are associated with higher income communities.

---

impact, there is very little experience with it in the environmental valuation context. It is clear, however, that environmental choice modelling will face similar problems to the CVM in regard to survey design and administration. It is also the case that it shares with CVM, at least where existence value issues are concerned, the problem that there is no external data on the 'truth' against which to assess its performance.

Production function based techniques

In our discussion of environmental valuation we have thus far considered environmental services or indicators only as arguments in utility functions. As Table 14.1 makes clear, environmental conditions are of relevance to production, and this is not just a matter of resource inputs to production as usually understood. In Table 14.1 we have 'harvested timber' as a resource input service used exclusively by firms, but we also have, for example, 'local climate' as a life support service used by firms and households. We now consider several environmental valuation techniques based on environmental services or indicators as arguments in production functions.

We can represent the basis for these techniques as the production function

$$Q = f(L, K, E) \qquad (14.27)$$

where L and K have the usual meanings, and where E is some environmental indicator, and we have

$$\partial Q/\partial L > 0, \quad \partial Q/\partial K > 0, \quad \partial Q/\partial E > 0 \qquad (14.28)$$

To fix ideas, consider an example such as a river fishery where E is water quality.[5] Suppose that some policy to improve water quality is under consideration. If we knew the algebraic form of the production function and the parameter values, we could use that information to map some change in water quality, ΔE, into a change in harvest, ΔQ, for constant levels of L and K. If we could then convert ΔQ into a monetary measure we would have valued the environmental quality change as it affects production. Of course, if E was also an argument in utility functions, this would not be the end of the story – we would have to estimate the value of ΔE in consumption, as well as production, by one of the techniques already discussed.

As regards the effect on production, this is an outline description of what is often called the 'dose–response' valuation technique. It is tempting to think that to convert ΔQ to a monetary measure it is necessary only to multiply it by the unit price of Q, in this case caught fish, to get the change in revenue. This is, in fact, what many applications of the dose–response method do. It is, however, for

---

[5] Given our discussions of production functions in Chapter 2. Equations 14.27 and 14.28 are clearly gross oversimplifications, but they serve to make the point here.

ECBA purposes strictly incorrect. This is because it takes no account of changes in the opportunity cost of producing Q, and no account of the elasticity of the demand function. Ellis and Fisher (1987) show how this should, in general terms, be done using measures of changes in the sum of producer and consumer surplus, and give illustrative calculations for a case where E is wetland acreage and Q is the harvest of blue crabs.

Two closely related techniques that have been used for environmental valuation in relation to production are 'avoided cost' and 'averting expenditure'. Write the production function as

$$Q = f(L, K, E, A) \qquad (14.29)$$

where

$$\partial Q/\partial L > 0, \partial Q/\partial K > 0,$$
$$\partial Q/\partial E < 0, \partial Q/\partial A > 0 \qquad (14.30)$$

In this case increases in the environmental indicator E reduce output for given levels of input of L, Q and A, which is some 'averting' input. We are now considering, say, a factory for the production of computer components where clean air is important. E is ambient air quality where the factory is located, and A is inputs of air-filtration services. According to the averting expenditure approach, air quality deteriorations would be valued in terms of increases in expenditure on A. According to avoided cost approach, air quality improvements would be valued in terms of reduced expenditure on A.

The use of production functions for valuation is not confined to firms. The 'household production function' approach has households using purchased commodities with their own time and effort to produce some of the arguments that appear in its utility function. We have already noted that the TCM can be understood in this way.

Averting expenditure and avoided cost approaches to valuations for households can also be derived from a household production function formulation.

Environmental valuation, ethics and social choice

As noted at the beginning of this chapter the original, and still the principal, motivation for the work that economists have done on environmental valuation was to enable the natural environment to be accounted for in cost–benefit analysis. In working through the enormous literature on environmental valuation methodology that has appeared in the past few decades, it is easy to end up immersed in technical detail and losing sight of what it is all for. There can also be a tendency to overlook the relevance of some of the criticism of environmental valuation as practised by economists that has been made by non-economists, and by some economists. Much of that criticism is of ECBA, and the ethical foundations of welfare economics, rather than of environmental valuation *per se*, though often developed in the valuation context. In this section we provide a brief overview of some of the criticism and relate it to the problem of social decision making about projects, programmes and policies that affect the natural environment. Given the nature and breadth of the topic here, this section is necessarily something of a literature review.

'Ethics' are relevant in two ways here. First, ethics as the study of morally correct behaviour has been used to argue that ECBA is the wrong way for society to make decisions with environmental implications. This argument has focused particularly on decisions which have implications for those environmental services that economists treat as being covered by existence or non-use values, especially life support services. As we have seen, existence values are the domain of CVM. The second way in which ethics will concern us here is that it has been suggested that the ethical attitudes held by individuals will influence their responses about existence values in CVM surveys, with implications for the usefulness of the survey results in ECBA.

Ethical objections to ECBA

We discussed the ethical basis for standard welfare economics in Chapter 4. Here we can summarise by saying that welfare economics is based on a particular form of utilitarianism, which is 'consequentialist' and 'subjectivist' in nature. It is consequentialist in that actions are to be judged in terms of their consequences for human individuals. It is only human individuals that are of interest – only humans have 'moral standing'. It is subjectivist in that the measure of what is good for a human individual is that human individual's own assessment. The individual's assessment is to be ascertained from his or her preferences as revealed in behaviour. Further, it is assumed that individual preferences satisfy the conditions for the existence of 'well-behaved' utility functions. There are two classes of ethical objection to this way of proceeding.

The first accepts that only human individuals have moral standing but rejects consumer sovereignty, arguing that individual preferences are a poor guide to individual human interests. Following Penz (1986), four particular arguments can be distinguished:

(1) Individuals may be inadequately informed as to the consequences for themselves of the alternatives they face.
(2) Individuals may be insufficiently deliberative in assessing the consequences of alternative choices.
(3) Individuals may lack self-knowledge in the sense that they cannot properly relate the consequences of alternative choices to their preferences.
(4) Individuals' preferences may not reflect their true interests due to 'preference shaping' arising from socialisation processes and advertising.

These arguments are not restricted to the environmental context, but have been argued to have special force there: see, for examples, Vatn and Bromley (1995) and Norton (1994). The philosopher Sagoff (1988, 1994, 1998) particularly has argued against social choice on the basis of 'preference satisfaction', and for social choice by 'deliberative citizens' rather than 'consumers' in the environmental context. His point is that where serious environmental issues are involved, it is simply wrong to appeal to the self-interested preferences that might be acceptable as the criterion for deciding how much whisky as opposed to beer to produce. Sagoff argues that the correct way to make decisions with serious environmental implications is as the result of the deliberations of citizens, individuals whose views reflect their assessment of what is good for society.[6]

A second class of argument is that the scope of ethical concern should not be restricted to humans, that animals and plants (and in some versions non-living entities) should have 'moral standing': see, for examples, Naess (1972), Goodpaster (1978), Regan (1981) and Singer (1979, 1993). Booth (1994) argues that 'cost–benefit analysis cannot be legitimately applied where non-human natural entities are viewed as morally considerable' (page 241), and that the ethically correct principle for social decision making is that:

> Destruction of the natural environment shall not be undertaken unless absolutely necessary to maintain the real incomes of all human individuals at a level required for the living of a decent human life.
>
> Booth (1994), page 251

This clearly has affinities with the safe minimum standard idea, to be discussed in the next chapter, which is based upon a consequentialist theory restricted to human

---

[6] It should be noted that self-interest as assumed in economics does not exclude the possibility of altruism – other individuals' consumption could well be arguments in my utility function with positive derivatives (negative derivatives would imply envy). Sen (1977) distinguishes between this kind of altruism, which he calls 'sympathy', and altruism as 'commitment', which is where my concern for others is based on ethical principles and could involve my acting in their interests even though it reduces my own utility. Commitment would be a characteristic of Sagoff's 'citizens' but not of his 'consumers'.

interests, but which recognises the uncertainties that attend predicting the future costs of current environmental damage.

Sustainable development and environmental valuation

We considered sustainability and sustainable development in Chapters 2 and 3, and we will return to these matters in relation to valuation for environmental accounting in Chapter 17. Here we need to note that, as argued in Chapter 3, a commitment to sustainable development involves an ethical dimension. It involves the assertion that economic activity should observe sustainability constraints, and a statement containing 'should' involves ethics.

Common and Perrings (1992) show that observing sustainability constraints may involve overriding the outcomes that are consistent with consumer sovereignty. Individuals' preferences may be consistent with the requirements for sustainable development, but there is no guarantee that they will be even if it is assumed that individuals are well informed. It follows that market failure correction, which is what ECBA and environmental valuation seek to deliver, is not sufficient for sustainability. Supposing, that is, that CVM did elicit the true monetary measure of the utility changes that would follow from a decline in some environmental indicator, it does not follow that an ECBA on the project involved would produce an outcome consistent with sustainability. It may be, for example, that the project would lead to the extinction of some species of termite that plays a key role in ecosystem function, but that WTP for the preservation of the species is insufficient to stop the project.

There is another reason why the environmental valuations produced by standard methods would be rejected given an ethical commitment to sustainable development, even if it were believed that the methods 'worked' according to market failure correction standards. As articulated by the Brundtland Commission, sustainable development is about addressing current poverty and intratemporal inequality, as well as satisfying sustainability constraints. However, an important determinant of an individual's willingness to pay is his or her income – as we noted above, a positive association between reported WTP and income is taken to be required before a CVM survey is accepted as producing useful results. Environmental valuations by standard methods reflect the existing distribution of wealth and income, as do the market prices of ordinary produced commodities.

This last point can be illustrated with some results from a recent study (Costanza et al. 1997) which used the results from a number of exercises in environmental valuation – using the full range of methods discussed in this chapter – to value 17 ecosystem services from 17 biomes. The ultimate objective was to put a total value on ecosystem services across all biomes, with a view to promoting sustainable development by showing how important ecosystems are in relation to economic activity: see Chapter 17 for further discussion. Among the ecosystem services distinguished were recreation and food production. For the coral reefs biome the recreational value per hectare per annum is 3008 US$1984, while the food production value per hectare per annum is 220 US$1984. While the paper itself does not give the basis for the figures it reports, supplementary material giving methods and sources was made available through the journal that published the paper. From that material it is clear that what is driving the recreational value result are studies of the expenditure of affluent tourists from industrial nations, while food production is valued according to the market value of fish caught around the reefs.

Ethical attitudes and CVM responses

As discussed in the previous section, experience with the use of CVM to determine existence values has revealed several problems.

To recapitulate, those problems include:

- high incidence of protest responses
- high estimates of average WTP
- low sensitivity of yes/no responses to price variation (in dichotomous choice formats)
- low scope sensitivity
- large differences between WTP and WTA.

We now briefly review some contributions to the literature which treat these problems as arising from the fact that at least some of those who are subjects of CVM surveys are not behaving according to the theoretical model set out earlier in this chapter where a consumer maximises a single well-behaved utility function defined over commodities and environmental services.

Citizen responses

We noted above that Sagoff has argued that social choices involving important environmental impacts should be made by reference to citizens' deliberations rather than consumers' preferences. Sagoff has also advanced the hypothesis that many individuals will, in fact, be unable, or unwilling, to make trade-offs between ordinary commodities and important environmental services and attributes. The claim here is that, where existence values are at issue, responses are not typically on the basis of a single utility function with arguments that are both ordinary commodities and environmental services. Sagoff argues that there is a consumer self which deals with trade-offs between commodities, and a citizen self which deals with important environmental (and other) matters.

If some CVM responses do reflect citizen behaviour, then one could expect to find a lack of price sensitivity in them, where the dichotomous choice format is used, with respondents behaving as voters largely disregarding the price information contained in the question. For the CVM application reported in Box 14.4, Blamey *et al.* (1995) report results that support the Sagoff hypothesis: see also Blamey (1996). Blamey and

Common (1994) report results from some classroom experiments where the majority of subjects offered the choice, before being presented with any price information, between a political and a market-based approach to social decision making about preservation, opted for the former: see also Common *et al.* (1997). These subjects were, after committing to one or the other institutional setting, presented with a cost, which varied across subjects, and asked if they would be willing to meet it. Subjects opting for the political institutional framework were asked dichotomous choice questions regarding reallocations of government expenditure. The proportion answering 'yes' declined as the amount to be taken away from other government programmes increased. This suggests that individuals as citizens may be 'price' sensitive when they are asked questions that conform to their understanding of the proper context for dealing with the issues.

Lexicographic preferences

Cognitive psychologists have observed the use by individuals of non-compensatory, or conflict avoiding, strategies for choice. One form of non-compensatory decision rule is the lexicographic preference ordering, in which alternatives are compared on the most important dimension only, unless equal scores are obtained, in which case scores on the second most important dimension are considered, and so on until a decision is reached. If individuals have lexicographic preferences, well-behaved utility functions do not exist in the sense that indifference curves cannot be drawn.[7]

Edwards (1986) suggested that individuals' ethical attitudes could give rise to lexicographic preference orderings of ordinary commodities and environmental attributes, based on a moral commitment in favour of

---

[7] In technical terms the continuity condition for the existence of well-behaved utility functions is violated when preferences are lexicographic: see Deaton and Muellbauer (1980).

environmental protection. Edwards (1992) considered bounded lexicographic preferences where, for example, species preservation is always preferred to more income, so long as income is above some threshold level. Lexicographic preferences would imply a lack of price sensitivity, and could give rise to high estimates of average WTP for preservation. Spash and Hanley (1995) identified lexicographic preferences in a CVM study using open-ended questioning about WTP where respondents stated a zero WTP for the reason that biodiversity should be protected by law, and where respondents stated that animals/ecosystems/plants should be protected irrespective of the costs and refused to give a WTP amount. Common et al. (1997) conducted some experiments to investigate the possibility of lexicographic preferences with respect to environmental goods and obtained results consistent with lexicographic preferences for approximately a quarter of respondents.[8]

Responsibility considerations

Individuals are likely to think that treatment of problems is the responsibility of those who caused them in the first place, and/or those who most stand to benefit from their solution. Since most CVM questions imply that the respondent has some responsibility to help protect the environment, thereby justifying some sort of payment, the extent to which this aligns with the individual's own perception of responsibilities regarding the issue in question has an important influence on the likelihood of a yes response to a WTP question, and on

the likelihood of protest where the format allows it. Harris and Brown (1992) stress the important influence responsibility ascriptions may have on CV responses. Peterson et al. (1996) investigated the effects of different levels of moral responsibility on CV responses and concluded that:

> when in a role of agency for the public interest, people tend to use a different utility function than when in the role of individual consumer. When compared with shared responsibility, sole responsibility for choices among public circumstances tends to increase the relative value of public goods and services, with the effect being greatest for environmental goods.
>
> Peterson et al. (1996), page 156

An important question that arises is whether 'no' responses to the question 'would you be willing to pay $x?' that are motivated by denial of responsibility can be considered legitimate from a CBA standpoint. Denial of responsibility is likely to result in protest responses and outliers, which are not generally considered legitimate CVM responses for CBA. In fact, CVM surveys frequently have not investigated the basis for 'no' or 'yes' responses. If a proportion of 'no' responses are motivated by responsibility denial protest, and if it is accepted that such responses are not valid for CBA, then including such responses in the estimation of average WTP will produce results that are biased with respect to the desired outcome. Stevens et al. (1991) found that the majority of respondents would not pay any money for the existence of bald eagles or wild turkeys in New England, or for salmon restoration. In this study response motivations were investigated. In the case of bird preservation, 40% of zero WTP responses protested the payment vehicle used in the CVM question on responsibility grounds, stating that 'these species should be preserved but that the money should come from taxes or license fees'. Stevens et al. also report that: 'Twenty-five percent protested for ethical reasons, claiming that wildlife values should not be measured in dollar terms' (page 397).

---

[8] Ethical commitments are not the only possible source of lexicographic preference orderings. It appears consistent with work in psychology that they may alternatively reflect a rule of thumb strategy adopted to deal with information processing difficulties, or with uncertainty as to the consequences of choice. In the study reported in Common et al. (1997), an additional quarter of subjects reported preferences that were incomplete or intransitive. Faced with a dichotomous choice CVM question in a postal survey, individuals do not have the option of reporting such difficulties. They must answer yes or no, or not respond at all.

The purchase of moral satisfaction

A controversial paper by Kahneman and Knetsch (1992a) sought to explain scope insensitivity in CVM studies in terms of respondents using their participation in a CVM to get a 'warm inner glow' from the (hypothetical) purchase of moral satisfaction. According to Kahneman and Knetsch an important feature of the warm inner glow hypothesis is that the 'warm glow of moral satisfaction ... increases with the size of the contribution: for this unusual good, the expenditure is an essential aspect of consumption' (page 64). The hypothesis is claimed to explain scope insensitivity in that the 'moral satisfaction associated with contributions to an inclusive cause, extends with little loss to any subset of that cause'. This claim is disputed in a number of papers: see, for examples, Smith (1992) and Harrison (1992). Kahneman and Knetsch (1992b) is a response to some of the criticism that their work attracted. Subsequent contributions to this debate are Diamond *et al.* (1993), Plott (1993) and Kemp and Maxwell (1993). One of the issues raised in the debate is that the warm glow hypothesis proper has moral satisfaction attaching to actual donations to good causes, whereas responses to CVM questions do not entail actual expenditure.

Schkade and Payne (1993, 1994) used verbal protocol analysis to investigate the thought processes driving CVM responses, and found that 23% of respondents 'suggested a desire to signal concern for larger or more inclusive issues, [than those covered in the CVM question] such as preserving the environment or leaving the planet for their progeny'. They interpret this as support for the Kahneman and Knetsch hypothesis. Given our remarks above, it is not clear that it is, though it clearly is consistent with an influence from ethical attitudes to CVM responses for some individuals.

Expressive benefits and decisiveness discounting

We consider next a behavioural hypothesis for CVM respondents which has affinities with the Kahneman and Knetsch hypothesis, but is not subject to the difficulty that whereas the warm inner glow hypothesis proper relates to actual expenditure, CVM responses concern hypothetical expenditure. Public choice theory can be regarded as the application to politics of the methods and assumptions of economics. It seeks to explain voting behaviour in terms of the instrumental pursuit of self-interest – individuals vote for the candidate who promises to deliver what they want. However, in purely instrumental terms, it is difficult to see why any individual should incur the costs of voting given the low probability that his or her vote will be decisive. Brennan and Lomasky (1993) offer an explanation of voting in terms of, on the one hand, the benefits that individuals derive from the act of expressing what we have called ethical attitudes, and on the other the fact that whereas the instrumental benefits of voting are discounted by the low probability of being decisive, these expressive benefits are not so discounted.

Blamey (1998) argues that the Brennan and Lomasky argument applies to CVM responses, which are more like casting a vote than buying a commodity in relation to the likely salience of ethical attitudes and the decisiveness discounting of any instrumental personal benefits. This hypothesis can explain both a lack of price responsiveness and scope insensitivity type phenomena in CVM studies. Blamey also argues that this hypothesis about CVM responses can explain seemingly lexicographic preference revelation there.

WTP and WTA

In discussing experience with CVM in the previous section we noted that the large empirical discrepancies between WTP and WTA are not now regarded as necessarily discomforting for the standard theory of consumer behaviour. Here we note that there may be an alternative explanation in terms of ethical attitudes. Recall the Sagoff distinction between the citizen self and the consumer self. Requested to pay for environmental preservation as a consumer, the citizen will find the question inappropriate, but not wildly so. Asked to accept individual compensation for allowing damage to a collective asset such as the natural environment, and to say how much, the citizen will find the question wildly inappropriate. Consider an analogy. An individual might believe that poverty relief is properly a matter for the state, yet have few qualms about making a contribution, when asked, to a charity engaged in helping the poor. Now consider such an individual asked the question: how much would you need to be paid to compensate you for the abolition of all state-financed poverty relief? For many, but not all, such individuals there is likely to be a very large, but non-infinite, answer to such a question, some price at which the prospective consumer gain will compensate for the mental costs of acting against an ethical attitude.

'Best practice' CVM, deliberation and social choice

The reader will have noted that there is some overlap between the foregoing explanations for problems encountered in CVM applications. The important point here is that they all go outside of the standard assumptions set out earlier in this chapter about what an individual is doing when he or she responds to a CVM question. If it is accepted that at least some respondents have not been behaving according to the theory that is the basis for CVM, one can distinguish two sorts of response. The first would be to conclude that since the theory does not fit all respondents, CVM will not do what it is supposed to do and will therefore produce biased answers for use in ECBA, so that CVM and ECBA have to be abandoned as the means to inform social decisions that concern the environment in important ways. This, essentially, is the position adopted by the non-economist critics.

The alternative response would be to attribute the 'improper' behaviour of some respondents to poor CVM design and administration, taking the view that given good enough survey design and execution, all respondents could be induced to, in Sagoff's terminology, behave as consumers, to be scope sensitive and so on, so that a CVM would produce a result for the value of some environmental service suitable for input to an ECBA. Critics of ECBA on ethical grounds, such as Sagoff, would reject this response, even if they thought that it could be successful. It is the response that many economists working in the field have adopted.

In the section headed 'Assessing the CVM' we noted that a US panel of expert economists had reached the conclusion that, given that it satisfied 'certain conditions', a CVM would produce 'useful information'. In effect, that panel was specifying 'best practice' for CVM. It is tempting at this point to conclude that this 'best practice' was being promulgated as that which would be the result of the second response to CVM problems noted immediately above. Actually, reference back to our quotations from the panel's report indicates that this is not really the case. Recall that the panel concluded that 'useful information' resulted if best practice was followed, in which case the CVM was to be considered as 'essentially a self-contained referendum in which respondents vote on whether to tax themselves or not for a particular purpose'. Note that a 'particular purpose' cannot be an environmental service as such, and will, if it is to align properly with taxation, be some kind of government programme to protect, or improve, some aspect of the environment. We have, in pursuing the route of eliminating problems from CVM, gone from valuing the environment according to consumer preferences to obtaining useful information about voters' willingness to pay for environmental programmes. It is not clear that, operationally, this is all that far from Sagoff's position.

In fact, in his most recent paper on this subject Sagoff (1998) effectively moves toward the panel's operational position. In it he argues not for the abandonment of CVM but for its modification. His argument is that CVM can only take into account, as it should, individuals' 'principled views of the public interest, not private preferences about their own consumption' if it 'moves toward a deliberative, discursive, jury-like research method emphasising informed discussion leading toward a consensus'. Among Sagoff's arguments for the appropriateness of deliberation is that 'individuals do not come to CV surveys with predetermined preferences but must construct them'. This is effectively agreed in much of the available CVM design literature, and, as Sagoff notes, 'social learning' is also involved in the construction of preferences over ordinary, marketed, commodities.

If these arguments are accepted, there remains the problem of how, operationally, to incorporate deliberation into feasible methods for assessing and reporting the views of individuals to the institutions that actually take decisions about, or with implications for, serious environmental problems. Two models which could be the basis for progress in this direction are as follows.

Deliberative polling involves running an opinion poll then asking respondents to attend a meeting at which they will collectively consider the issues, by hearing and questioning expert witnesses and debating amongst themselves. At the end of this process, the participants are asked again to respond to the original survey instrument. As reported in Fishkin (1997) the results, in regard to the movement of opinion as between the first poll and that conducted after deliberation, are often striking. Of particular interest here are some of the results from three such exercises conducted in Texas. In Texas regulated public utilities are required to consult the public as part of their Integrated Resource Planning, and three chose to use deliberative polling to do this in regard to electricity supply planning. Respondents were asked to specify their first choice for the provision of additional power from four alternatives: renewable sources, fossil fuel sources, energy conservation, buying in electricity. As between the two polls respondents attended meetings at which they were provided with, *inter alia*, cost data on these four alternatives. In each case there was the same pattern of response variation as between the before and after polls. As first choice, renewable fell from 67% to 16%, 71% to 35%, and 67% to 28%, while conservation rose from 11% to 46%, 7% to 31%, and 16% to 50%. The cost data showed conservation to be less expensive than renewable sources.

An obvious problem with deliberative polling is that it is very costly. The idea is to poll a random sample of sufficient size to produce results up to the standard usual in opinion polling. This may mean hundreds of people, which makes the information provision and deliberative parts of the exercise expensive, especially where the population of interest covers a large geographical area. As practised to date, deliberative polling has usually involved opinions on somewhat broadbrush issues of interest to large media organisations. However, as exemplified by the example from Texas, the general strategy could, given funding, be applied to more narrowly defined decision problems, with respondents being required to consider resource constraints and their implications.

A citizens' jury exercise is less expensive than deliberative polling. In a report on experience with citizens' juries in the UK, Coote and Lenaghan (1997) describe what is involved as follows:

> Citizens' juries involve the public in their capacity as ordinary citizens with no special axe to grind. They are usually commissioned by an organisation which has power to act on their recommendations. Between 12 and 16 jurors are recruited, using a combination of random and stratified sampling, to be broadly representative of their community. Their task is to address an important question about policy or planning. They are brought together for four days, with a team of two moderators. They are fully briefed

about the background to the question, through written information and evidence from witnesses. Jurors scrutinise the information, cross-examine the witnesses and discuss different aspects of the question in small groups and plenary sessions. Their conclusions are compiled in a report that is returned to the jurors for their approval before being submitted to the commissioning authority. The jury's verdict need not be unanimous, nor is it binding. However, the commissioning authority is required to publicise the jury and its findings, to respond within a set time and either to follow its recommendations or to explain publicly why not.

Obviously the particulars described here are not immutable, and there could be considerable variation consistent with the underlying rationale. In the environmental context, for example, it would likely often prove necessary to provide access to appropriate modelling facilities. There is no reason why the jury cannot be required to observe appropriate resource constraints.

In regard to underlying rationale, Coote and Lenaghan put it as follows:

> Compared with other models, citizens' juries offer a unique combination of *information*, *time*, *scrutiny*, *deliberation* and *independence* [italics in the original]

Coote and Lenaghan report positively on the citizens' jury process. Of particular interest here, they judge that 'Jurors readily adopt a community perspective', that most 'accept that resources are finite and were willing to participate in decisions about priority setting', and that 'a substantial minority of jurors said they had changed their minds in the course of the session'. It should also be noted here that a number of the participating jurors expressed 'strong doubts about the jury's capacity to influence the commissioning authority'. Experience in using citizens' juries in relation to decisions concerning the natural environment is limited.

Discussion questions

1 Discuss the contention that contingent valuation is, in general, superior to all other techniques for valuing non-marketed goods or services as it is the only technique capable of incorporating non-use values as well as use values.

2 Discuss the contention that, where use values are at issue, contingent valuation is superior to indirect methods as it goes directly to the appropriate theoretical constructs for welfare analysis.

3 Should decisions about environmental policy be made on the basis of environmental cost–benefit analysis?

Problems

1 Suppose an individual has the following utility function, where U denotes total utility and Q the quantity of a good or service consumed in a given period of time:

$$U(Q) = \alpha Q + \frac{\beta}{2}Q^2$$

   (a) Obtain the individual's marginal utility function.
   Assume $\alpha = 10$ and $\beta = -1/2$, and that the individual's consumption rises from Q_1 to Q_2, where $Q_1 = 2$ and $Q_2 = 4$.
   (b) What is the individual's marginal utility at Q_1 and Q_2?
   (c) Show that total utility can be interpreted as an area under an appropriate marginal utility function, and use this result to obtain the increase in total utility when consumption rises from Q_1 to Q_2.

2 Suppose that an individual has the utility function

$$U = E^{0.25} + Y^{0.75}$$

where E is some index of environmental quality and Y is income. From an initial situation where $E = 1$ and $Y = 100$, calculate CS and ES for an increase in E to the level 0.5. (It may be useful to refer back to Table 14.3.)

3 With E as some index of environmental quality and C_1 and C_2 as two 'ordinary'

commodities, consider the following utility functions in regard to whether C_1 is non-essential and whether C_1 and E are weak complements:

(a) $U = E^\alpha + C_1{}^\beta + C_2{}^\delta$

(b) $U = E^\alpha C_1{}^\beta C_2{}^\delta$

(c) $U = E^\alpha C_1{}^\beta + C_2{}^\delta$

4 This problem works through an illustrative example for the widely used zonal average version of the TCM, and uses the alternative method for calculating total MCS from estimates of the parameters of the trip generating equation mentioned in footnote 3. With

> V for total visits from a zone
> Pop for the zone population
> D for distance in miles to the site from the zone centre

the basic data is:

Zone	V	Pop	D
1	15 000	2 000 000	10
2	48 000	8 000 000	15
3	11 250	2 500 000	20
4	45 000	15 000 000	25
5	34 000	22 660 000	30

Visits per thousand of population, v, are generated by

(a) $v = 10.5 - 0.3(C + P)$

where C is the average travel cost of a visit, given by

(b) $C = cD$

where c is the cost per mile, which is £1, and where P is the price of admission to the site, which is zero.

By setting $P = $ £5, £10, £15, £20, £25 and £30 use (a) to simulate visits from each zone at each of those admission prices. Plot the 'surrogate demand function', i.e. total visits from all zones against P, and work out the total MCS when P is zero.

Now suppose that the TCM analyst incorrectly figured that travel cost per mile was £1.2. Use the data on v and C which

would then eventuate to estimate by ordinary least squares the parameters of the trip generating equation which would replace (a), and proceeding as before work out total MCS. (*Note*: the data has been constructed so that the trip generating equation fits it without error, and the parameters are very easy to estimate using the standard formulae $\beta = \Sigma xy/\Sigma x^2$ and $\alpha = Y^* - \beta X^*$, where Y is the dependent variable and X is the explanatory variable, where X^* and Y^* are means, and where x and y are deviations from means.)

Further reading

Surveys of environmental valuation, with a practical orientation, are to be found in Winpenny (1991), Turner and Bateman (1990), Pearce and Markandya (1989), Johansson (1987) and Kneese (1984). Randall (1986) discusses categories of value attaching to environmental services. Hanley and Spash (1993) is about environmental cost–benefit analysis, and provides an overview of several of the valuation methods, as well as reporting case studies. Environmental valuation has generated a very large literature in the past three decades, and provided a substantial proportion of the articles in the most prestigious environmental economics journal, the *Journal of Environmental Economics and Management*: see also *Land Economics* and *Environmental and Resource Economics*. Bishop and Woodward (1995) provide an excellent account of the utility theory for environmental valuation, and Appendix 14.1 is based on their approach.

The travel cost method is examined and applied, for example, in Freeman (1979), Hanley (1989), Bockstael et al. (1987a,b) and Smith et al. (1983). A recent survey, concentrating mainly on theoretical developments, is Bockstael (1995).

Useful expositions and/or applications of contingent valuation are: Randall *et al.* (1974), Hanley (1988), Bishop and Heberlein

(1979), Schulze *et al.* (1981b), Bishop and Welsh (1992), Cummings *et al.* (1986) and Mitchell and Carson (1984). Mitchell and Carson (1989) is perhaps now the standard contingent valuation text, and includes an extensive review of applications. A useful recent review article is Bishop *et al.* (1995).

Discussions of the application of hedonic pricing are Freeman (1979), Hufschmidt *et al.* (1983) and Kneese (1984). The technique is surveyed in Nelson (1982). Interesting applications may also be found in Marin and Psacharopoulos (1982) and Willis and Garrod (1991a). A useful recent review article is Freeman (1995).

Choice modelling is a recent innovation which is described and compared with other stated preference methods in Boxall *et al.* (1996); see also Adamowicz *et al.* (1994).

There are a variety of methods that have been proposed as alternatives to ECBA which come under the general heading of multi-criteria analysis. They have in common that they seek to involve stakeholders in a process which involves stating preferences and making trade-offs, but which does not attempt to compare all attributes using a single metric such as money or utility. See Janssen (1992), Munda *et al.* (1994) and Van Pelt (1993).

Appendix 14.1 Demand theory and environmental valuation

We first state some standard results from consumer demand theory (see Deaton and Muellbauer, 1980 or Kreps, 1990) extended by the inclusion of environmental services as parametric arguments in the utility function, using the following notation:

$c = [C_1 \ldots C_N]$ is a vector of consumption levels for ordinary commodities
$p = [P_1 \ldots P_N]$ is the corresponding vector of prices
$e = [E_1 \ldots E_M]$ is a vector of levels of environmental quality indicators
Y is income

The Marshallian demand functions

$$C_i = C_i(p, Y, e) \qquad (14.31)$$

are obtained from the problem

$$\text{Max } U(c, e) \quad \text{subject to} \quad pc = Y \qquad (14.32)$$

while the Hicksian demand functions

$$C_i = H_i(p, U, e) \qquad (14.33)$$

can be obtained either from the cost minimisation dual to Equation 14.32

$$\text{Min } pc \text{ subject to} \quad U(c, e) = U \qquad (14.34)$$

or by differentiation of the cost function

$$M = M(p, U, e) \qquad (14.35)$$

which gives the minimum expenditure required to achieve some U level. The cost function is sometimes referred to as the expenditure function. The indirect utility function

$$U = V(p, Y, e) \qquad (14.36)$$

gives the maximum utility attainable, and is the inverse of the cost function.

Now, let

superscript o refer to the original situation prior to some policy intervention
superscript n refer to the new situation resulting from the policy intervention
superscript * to a vector symbol refer to that vector with one element missing

so that

$$U^o = V(P_i{}^o, p^*, Y, e) \qquad (14.37)$$

and

$$U^n = V(P_i{}^n, p^*, Y, e) \qquad (14.38)$$

respectively refer to maximum attainable utility in the original and new situations where the intervention takes the form of a change in the price of the commodity i.

Then, considering a change in the price of the ith commodity we have

$$\text{CV} = M(P_i{}^o, p^*, U^o, e) - M(P_i{}^n, p^*, U^o, e)$$
$$= -\int_{P_i{}^o}^{P_i{}^n} H_i(P_i, p^*, U^o, e) \mathrm{d}P_i \qquad (14.39)$$

and

$$EV = M(P_i^n, p^*, U^n, e) - M(P_i^o, p^*, U^n, e)$$

$$= \int_{P_i^o}^{P_i^n} H_i(P_i, p^*, U^n, e) dP_i \qquad (14.40)$$

while

$$MCS = \int_{P_i^o}^{P_i^n} C_i(P_i, p^*, Y, e) dP_i \qquad (14.41)$$

Considering a change in the level of the jth environmental quality indicator, the surplus measures are:

$$CS = M(p, U^o, E_j^R, e^*) - M(p, U^o, E_j^n, e^*) \qquad (14.42)$$

and

$$ES = M(p, U^n, E_j^R, e^*) - M(p, U^n, E_j^o, e^*) \qquad (14.43)$$

Expressing the variation and surplus measures in terms of cost functions makes apparent their relationship to willingness to pay and to accept, and hence the way that, in principle, a well-designed contingent valuation exercise would directly elicit these measures for individuals. The basis for the indirect approach can also be set out in these terms. Recall Figure 14.8 and the accompanying discussion of the example where an improvement in water quality increased the consumption of fishing days and the purchase of fishing permits, at a constant price. There we used C_1 for the commodity which is fishing days, and we will do that here. We will let the water quality indicator be E_1, and consider a policy intervention which improves E_1 from E_1^o to E_1^n. The shaded area A in Figure 14.8 is the change in CV associated with the increased consumption of C_1 which results from the shift in the demand function for C_1 caused by the improvement in water quality.

The change in the CV is given by:

$$\Delta CV = \int_{P_1^F}^{P_1^C(E_1^n)} H_1(P_1, p^*, U^o, E_1^n, e^*) dP_1$$

$$- \int_{P_1^F}^{P_1^C(E_1^o)} H_1(P_1, p^*, U^o, E_1^o, e^*) dP_1 \qquad (14.44)$$

Using Equation 14.39 and noting the minus sign on the right-hand side, we can substitute cost function differences for the integrals in Equation 14.44 so that

$$\begin{aligned} \Delta CV = {} & M(P_1^C(E_1^n), p^*, U^o, E_1^n, e^*) \\ & - M(P_1^F, p^*, U^o, E_1^n, e^*) \\ & + M(P_1^F, p^*, U^o, E_1^o, e^*) \\ & - M(P_1^C(E_1^o), p^*, U^o, E_1^o, e^*) \\ = {} & \{M(P_1^F, p^*, U^o, E_1^o, e^*) \\ & - M(P_1^F, p^*, U^o, E_1^n, e^*)\} \\ & + \{M(P_1^C(E_1^n), p^*, U^o, E_1^n, e^*) \\ & - M(P_1^C(E_1^o), p^*, U^o, E_1^o, e^*)\} \end{aligned} \qquad (14.45)$$

From Equation 14.42, the first term in braces in Equation 14.45 is just the CS associated with the environmental quality change from E_1^o to E_1^n, so that Equation 14.45 can be written

$$\begin{aligned} \Delta CV = CS + \{ & M(P_1^C(E_1^n), p^*, U^o, E_1^n, e^*) \\ & - M(P_1^C(E_1^o), p^*, U^o, E_1^o, e^*)\} \end{aligned}$$

and given two conditions to be discussed, the second right-hand side term here can be shown to be zero, so that

$$\Delta CV = CS \qquad (14.46)$$

The two conditions are those stated in the text of the chapter when discussing Figure 14.8. The non-essentialness condition can now be stated as the existence of some consumption bundle c_b^* with C_{1b} equal to zero such that:

$$U(C_{1a}, c_a^*, e) = U(0, c_b^*, e) \qquad (14.47)$$

where C_{1a} is any non-zero level for C_1. The weak complementarity condition is

$$\partial U(0, c^*, E_1, e^*)/\partial E_1 = 0 \qquad (14.48)$$

The proof that these conditions give Equation 14.46 is originally due to Mäler (1974): see also Bockstael and McConnell (1993).

CHAPTER 15

Irreversibility, risk and uncertainty

To know one's ignorance is the best part of knowledge

Lao Tzu, *The Tao*, no. 71

Introduction

Much of our analysis has assumed that the consequences of decisions are known with certainty and are reversible. However, many of our discussions have implied that these assumptions are not factually correct. Resource use decisions concern the future as well as the present, and we cannot know the future with certainty. Many such decisions have consequences that are irreversible. The ecological consequences of economic behaviour especially are frequently a matter of considerable ignorance, beyond the presumption of irreversible change. The assumption of certainty and reversibility in much of the literature is a simplifying device: it is convenient to assume away some real-world complexities in order to develop analytical insights. But simplifying things in this way is only appropriate when the thing being ignored does not have major consequences for the results of the analysis. It is important, therefore, to see what difference it makes to the analysis if it is assumed that the future is not known with certainty and may involve irreversible change.

The central objective of this chapter, then, is to consider how recognition of imperfect knowledge about the future and irreversibility affects resource and environmental economics. To orient our analysis, we shall consider the use of environmental cost–benefit analysis (ECBA) and particularly we shall make extensive use of the context often used to fix ideas in the previous chapter – the decision about whether to conserve a wilderness area or to allow it to be developed with the consequent loss of wilderness values. The insights developed in this context apply generally where there is incomplete knowledge and irreversibility.

The chapter is organised as follows. We begin, in the next section, by revisiting the basic idea of ECBA, using it to look at the implications of increasing relative prices for wilderness services and the irreversibility of their loss. In the third section of the chapter we distinguish two kinds of imperfect knowledge, risk and uncertainty, and discuss individual behaviour in a risky world, leaving decision making in the face of uncertainty for later consideration. We then consider, in the fourth and fifth sections, option value and quasi-option value, which were mentioned, but not explained, as components of total environmental value in the previous chapter. These arise when individual and social decisions have to be made in the face of risk. The next section draws on that discussion to consider ECBA which recognises risk. The penultimate section of the chapter discusses decision making in the face of uncertainty, and in the final section this analysis is used to consider the idea that, in the face of uncertainty combined with irreversibility, environmental policy should be cautious and adopt the safe minimum standard approach.

Wilderness development revisited

In the previous chapter we stated the ECBA criterion for going ahead with a development project in a wilderness area as

$$\text{NPV}' = B_d - C_d > \text{EC}$$

where NPV$'$ is what NPV would be if the environmental costs of development, EC, were to be, wrongly, ignored. That chapter was mainly about the means by which economists seek to derive a figure for EC. We saw that while there are a range of techniques that can be used, none is without problems, and that their use in ECBA is objected to by many non-economists. Now clearly, if $NPV' < 0$ then the project should not go ahead, independent of any consideration of the environmental damage that it might entail. A development of this observation, where NPV' has been assessed as some positive number, is to ask: how large would EC have to be in order, according to ECBA, for the project not to go ahead? The answer is obvious. The project should not go ahead if

$$EC \geqslant NPV' = B_d - C_d$$

so that

$$EC^* = NPV' = B_d - C_d \qquad (15.1)$$

defines a threshold value for EC. For $EC \geqslant EC^*$ the project should not go ahead.

This suggests that what we might call an 'inverse ECBA' could usefully precede, or at least accompany, attempts to properly quantify EC, which attempts typically involve non-trivial expenditure if they are done properly. Inverse ECBA simply means properly figuring NPV', and then asking what average WTP to prevent the environmental effects expected to follow from going ahead with the project would have to be to stop it; that is, calculating EC^*/N where N is the size of the relevant population of interested households. In some cases the result of this calculation will be such a small amount that it could be generally agreed, or at least widely agreed, that the project obviously should not go ahead. Even where this is not the case, and a serious attempt to estimate EC/N is undertaken, the value for EC^*/N will provide a useful benchmark against which to consider the result for EC/N. Clearly, given the problems surrounding environmental valuation techniques, estimating EC/N as, say, 10 times EC^*/N produces a very different decision situation from estimating EC/N as, say, 1.5 times EC^*/N. In the former case one might

be reasonably confident that the project should not go ahead; in the latter case much less so.

Given that for the present we are supposing that the consequences of the two alternatives – to go ahead with the project, or not to – are fully known, there are, from the previous chapter, two classes of value making up EC, use and existence values. For a given wilderness area where some development is proposed, the sizes of the populations taken to be relevant to EC might be quite different for use and existence value. Recall that existence value does not require actual or potential visitation. Thus, in regard to existence values, the whole population of the nation in which the wilderness is located is generally seen as the relevant population. Indeed, for wilderness areas that are internationally famous it could plausibly be argued that it is the global population that is the relevant population. Where N is large, the per capita existence value which will give EC greater than NPV' may be quite small. This was illustrated in Box 14.3.

The Krutilla–Fisher model

In Chapter 14, we gave, as Equation 14.3, the proper NPV for a project in a wilderness area:

$$NPV = B_d - C_d - EC = NPV' - EC$$

This NPV is the result of discounting and summing over time over the project's lifetime an annual net benefit stream which is

$$NB_t = B_{d,t} - C_{d,t} - EC_t \qquad (15.2)$$

where $B_{d,t}$, $C_{d,t}$ and EC_t are the annual, undiscounted, amounts for $t = 1, 2, \ldots, T$ and where T is the project lifetime, corresponding to the present values B_d, C_d and EC. We have already remarked that the environmental costs of going ahead with the project, the EC_t, are at the same time the environmental benefits of not proceeding with it. Instead of EC_t we could write $B(P)_t$ for the stream of environmental benefits of preservation.[1] If we also use $B(D)_t$ and $C(D)_t$ for the benefit and cost streams associated with development when environmental impacts are ignored, so that $B(D)_t - C(D)_t$ is what gets discounted to give NPV′, then Equation 15.2 can also be written as:

$$NB_t = B(D)_t - C(D)_t - B(P)_t \quad (15.3)$$

It will now be convenient to treat time as continuous, so that instead of

$$NPV = \sum_0^T \{B(D)_t - C(D)_t - B(P)_t\}/(1+r)^t$$

we use

$$NPV = \int_0^T \{B(D)_t - C(D)_t - B(P)_t\}e^{-rt}dt$$

which can be written:

$$NPV = \int_0^T \{B(D)_t - C(D)_t\}e^{-rt}dt$$
$$- \int_0^T B(P)_t\}e^{-rt}dt \quad (15.4)$$

Krutilla and Fisher (1975) introduced important and persuasive arguments as to why it should be assumed that the value of wilderness amenity services will, relative to the prices of the inputs to and outputs from development, be increasing over time. The arguments concern substitution possibilities, technical progress and the income elasticity of demand for wilderness services.

In the Krutilla–Fisher model the development option is seen as producing extracted intermediate outputs. It is typically the case that these intermediate outputs have relatively close substitutes. Moreover, the degree of substitutability tends to increase over time

---

[1] In some of the literature on wilderness development there would also be distinguished $C(P)$ for the costs of preservation, where such costs are those associated with, for example, managing the national park set up to realise preservation. Here we do not explicitly introduce such costs as this simplifies without any essential loss. Our $B(P)$ can be interpreted as preservation benefits net of any such costs. Clearly, such an interpretation does not substantially affect the plausibility of the assumptions about relative price movements to be introduced shortly.

as technical knowledge develops. If we consider hydroelectric power, for example, it is clear that this form of power has many close substitutes, such as power from fossil fuel and nuclear sources. Technological advances have increased these substitution possibilities in recent decades, and will almost certainly continue to do so in the foreseeable future. If fusion power were to become technically and commercially viable, very long-term substitution possibilities will have been opened up. Finally, one would expect that rising demand for the extractive outputs of the development use can be met at decreasing real costs over time, as energy production and conversion benefits from technological innovation.

This contrasts strongly with the case of wilderness preservation benefits. The substitution possibilities here are often effectively zero, and there is no reason to suppose that they will become greater due to technical progress. Second, it is plausible and consistent with the evidence that environmental amenity services, and especially those of wilderness areas, have a high income elasticity of demand. But, third, technological progress itself cannot augment the supply of such services.

With economic growth and technological change it is reasonable to assume a tendency for the relative value of amenity services from undeveloped environmental assets to increase. A simple way to introduce this into Equation 15.4 is to assume that preservation benefits grow at the rate a, while development benefits and costs are constant, so that

$$NPV = \int_0^T \{B - C\}e^{-rt}dt - \int_0^T \{Pe^{at}\}e^{-rt}dt$$
$$(15.5)$$

where B and C are the constant development benefit and cost flows, while Pe^{at} is the growing flow of preservation benefits. This can be written as

$$NPV = NPV' - \int_0^T Pe^{-(r-a)t}dt \quad (15.6)$$

Note here, first, that for $a > 0$, NPV will be less than for $a = 0$, for given NPV′. This means that for a given NPV', a development project is less likely to pass the intertemporal allocative efficiency test if the Krutilla–Fisher arguments are accepted and incorporated into ECBA. The second point to note is that if $a = r$ then, in effect preservation benefits are not discounted. If it were to be assumed that $a > r$, then those benefits would effectively get discounted at a negative rate, and the discounted stream for P_t would itself be growing over time.

Now, let us suppose that $T \to \infty$. There are two reasons for making this assumption. First, it means that we can use a standard mathematical result which greatly simplifies the analysis.[2] The result is that

$$\int_0^\infty xe^{-rt}\mathrm{d}t = x\int_0^\infty e^{-rt}\mathrm{d}t = x/r$$

where x is some constant. This result is actually quite a good approximation where T is of the order of 100. For $r = 0.05$, the present value of

x for 50 years is $0.9128(x/r)$
x for 75 years is $0.9742(x/r)$
x for 100 years is $0.9924(x/r)$
x for 125 years is $0.9978(x/r)$

and for T fixed, the approximation gets closer as r increases.

The second reason for having $T \to \infty$ is that in practice for wilderness development projects, T is appropriately taken to be a very large number. T is the project lifetime, which is defined not by the date at which the project ceases to serve the function for which it was undertaken, but the date at which the longest lived consequence of the project ceases. Thus, for example, if the project is a mine with an extraction life of 50 years, but where vegetation will take 200 years to recover after the closure of the mine, then T is 250.

Applying this result in Equation 15.6, it becomes:

$$\text{NPV} = \text{NPV}' - P/(r - a) \qquad (15.7)$$

[2] This result is proved in, for example, Chiang (1984): see page 464. The equivalent result in a discrete time context is established in chapter 8 of Common (1996).

Table 15.1 $P/(r - a)$ for $P = 1$.

a	For $r = 0.05$	For $r = 0.075$
0	20	13.33
0.01	25	15.39
0.02	33.33	18.18
0.03	50	22.22
0.04	100	28.57
0.05	∞	40
0.06		66.67
0.075		∞

Note that as a increases, so $P/(r - a)$ increases, so that for NPV' given, NPV decreases. This is illustrated in Table 15.1, which shows how the second term in Equation 15.7 varies with the value of a for $r = 0.05$ and $r = 0.075$, where $P = 1$. Note that the long-term rate of economic growth is generally taken to be around 2.5%, that is 0.025, and that it can be argued that this provides a plausible lower bound for the value that should be assumed for a. Note also that for $a > r$ the standard result used to go from Equation 15.6 to Equation 15.7 does not hold, because, as noted above, the discounted P_t are growing over time. For P at some value other than 1, the entries in Table 15.1 are the factors by which P, the current value of preservation benefits, would be multiplied to give the value of their loss forever.

Discount rate adjustment

Conservationists sometimes argue that when doing an ECBA of a project giving rise to long-lasting environmental damage, a lower discount rate should be used as this will give more weight to environmental costs far into the future, thus making it less likely that the project will get the go-ahead. This argument is not generally valid. We can consider what is involved by first writing Equation 15.5 as

$$\text{NPV} = \{B - C\}\int_0^T e^{-rt}\mathrm{d}t - P\int_0^T e^{-(r-a)t}\mathrm{d}t$$

or using D for net development benefits:

$$\text{NPV} = D\int_0^T e^{-rt}\mathrm{d}t - P\int_0^T e^{-(r-a)t}\mathrm{d}t$$

Using the standard result as an approximation for very large T, this is:

$$NPV = D/r - P/(r - a) \qquad (15.8)$$

Now, thus far in treating $D = (B - C)$ as constant over all t we have overlooked one feature of development projects, which is that they typically involve a short initial period with capital expenditure but no sales revenue – digging the mine or building the dam for the hydroelectric facility – followed by a long period with running costs and sales revenues. The stylised facts here can be captured by rewriting Equation 15.8 as

$$NPV = -X + D/r - P/(r - a) \qquad (15.9)$$

where X is the initial start-up cost, which does not get discounted.

Suppose that X is 1000, D is 75 and P is 12.5 in monetary units, say millions of pounds. Consider first a case where it is assumed that $a = 0$. Then

$$NPV = -X + (D - P)/r \qquad (15.10)$$

and for $r = 0.055$ NPV is 136.37, while for $r = 0.045$ NPV is 388.89. For these numbers, lowering the discount rate has increased the NPV. This is because reducing the discount rate affects both development net benefits and environmental costs in the same way. From Equation 15.10 it is clear that, for $(D - P)$ positive, reducing r will increase NPV. Of course, to the extent that both D and P are not everlasting, we are dealing here with an approximation. But for time horizons of 100 years or more, it will be a close approximation.

Now suppose that it is assumed that a in Equation 15.9 is 0.025. In this case, for $r = 0.055$ the NPV is -53.03, while for $r = 0.045$ the NPV is 41.67. Reducing the discount rate shifts the ECBA decision from rejection of the project to going ahead with it. Lowering r increases D/r by more than it increases $P/(r - a)$. The point here is not that reducing the interest rate for this kind of project will increase the NPV for any values for D and P and any initial r. From Equation 15.9 it is clear that this would not be the case.

The point is to provide an illustration of a counter-example to the proposition that reducing r will always work against projects with damaging and long-lasting environmental effects. That proposition is not generally true. While reducing r gives more weight to environmental damage very far into the future, it also gives more weight to net development benefits moderately far into the future, and far into the future if they continue that long.[3]

Irreversibility

Economic analysis usually assumes that resource allocation decisions are reversible. However, there is an implicit assumption in the foregoing that once development occurs, it is irreversible. If this were not so, when the project ceased to do what it was intended for – when the mine was exhausted or the dam at the end of its safe life – then it would be possible, at some cost, to restore the wilderness, and this should be reflected in an ECBA. At least on a timescale relevant to human decision making, the assumption that once lost, the benefits of wilderness preservation are lost forever, appears to be a reasonable approximation to the relevant stylised facts of wilderness development.

To introduce some of the implications of irreversibility, we will consider a wilderness area yielding flows of amenity services, to be denoted A. We will assume that A is a function of the proportion of the wilderness area preserved from, say, logging. As the size of the area where logging is permitted increases, A falls. We consider benefits and costs as a function of A. The benefits are the preservation benefits, in terms of use and non-use values as discussed in the previous chapter, and we assume that marginal benefits decline as A increases. Consistently with

---

[3] The analysis here is based on Porter (1982), where there is a more rigorous and extended discussion. See also chapter 8 of Common (1996) for a detailed numerical illustration of these points.

our previous treatment, we assume that the costs of preservation as such are zero. However, we assume that preservation does entail foregone development benefits, which we treat here as costs of preservation. We assume that marginal costs increase with the area set aside from logging, and hence increase with A.

These assumptions are shown in Figure 15.1(a), where there is also shown as A^* the level of amenity service flow that goes with allocative efficiency. Figure 15.1(b) shows the corresponding behaviour for benefits minus costs, that is, net benefit, NB. Net benefits attain a maximum at A^*. Figure 15.1(c) shows the corresponding behaviour for the derivative of net benefit, which is marginal net benefit, MNB, which is zero at the level of A for which NB attains a maximum, A^*. $MNB(A) = 0$ is an alternative way of stating the necessary condition for maximum NB. In what follows here it will be convenient to work with MNB. The downward sloping MNB function that we work with is a fairly generally appropriate assumption. The assumed linearity makes it possible, in Appendix 15.1, to do some simple algebra which supports the discussion in the text here.

We divide time into two periods, now and 'the future'. Now consider Figure 15.2, which, in (a), shows MNB_1 for period 1, now, and in (b) shows MNB_2 for period 2, 'the future'. Future net benefits are expressed in terms of their present value. As Figure 15.2 is drawn, even after discounting, period 2 MNB is greater than period 1 MNB for a given level of the service flow. Generally, this reflects the considerations advanced above in connection with the Krutilla–Fisher model concerning the relative prices of environmental amenity services and produced commodities. Particularly, in Figure 15.2 MNB_2 has the same slope as MNB_1 but a larger intercept.

Consider now the level of amenity service flow in each period that goes with current and intertemporal allocative efficiency if there is

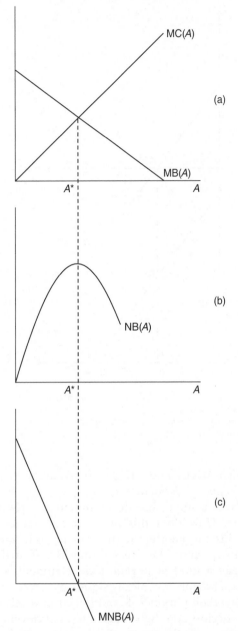

Figure 15.1 Alternative ways of identifying maximum net benefit.

no irreversibility. Given that we are dealing with period 2 in terms of appropriately discounted net benefit, in the absence of irreversibility, an efficient outcome would involve choosing a consumption level for environmental amenity services in each period for

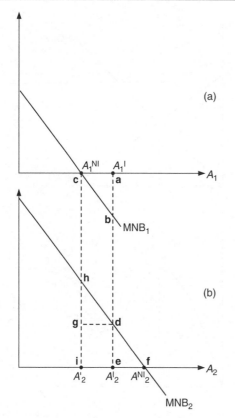

Figure 15.2 Irreversibility and development with the future known.

period 1 so as to secure benefits in period 2. The period 1 costs arise from selecting a level of A_1 above that where MNB_1 is equal to 0. The period 2 benefits resulting are due to a level of A_2 for which MNB_2 is nearer to 0 than at A_2'. For efficiency, costs and benefits must be equal at the margin. This is the case in Figure 15.2, where **ab**, MNB_1 at A_1^I, is equal to **de**, MNB_2 at A_2^I. Taking the irreversibility constraint into account leads to an outcome where MNB_1 and MNB_2 are equal but of opposite sign. Recall that MNB_2 refers to period 2 net benefits considered in present value terms in period 1.

As compared with a situation where development is reversible, irreversibility entails costs. In Figure 15.2 these costs are given by comparing A_1^{NI} with A_1^I and A_2^{NI} with A_2^I. In period 1 the cost is given by the area of the triangle **abc**, and in period 2 by the area of the triangle **def**. If there is irreversibility, ignoring it entails costs. Given irreversibility, the efficient outcome is A_1^I/A_2^I, but if irreversibility is ignored the actual outcome will be A_1^{NI}/A_2'. Ignoring irreversibility leads to a gain in period 1 given by the area of triangle **abc**, but to a loss in period 2 given by the area **edhi** in the diagram. The loss is greater than the gain, so that there is a net cost to ignoring irreversibility.

We have been assuming here that the future is known with certainty. In reality, when considering such matters as wilderness development, irreversibility is combined with imperfect future knowledge. We shall revisit this simple framework for considering the implications of irreversibility later in the chapter, taking account of imperfect knowledge of the future. In order to be able to do that we need an analysis of decision making given imperfect knowledge of the future, to which we now turn.

which MNB_1 and MNB_2 are equal to zero, A_1^{NI} and A_2^{NI}. Note that $A_2^{NI} > A_1^{NI}$.

Now assume that development is irreversible. How does this affect things? It constrains the choices in the two periods such that A_2 cannot be greater than A_1. If at the outset a level of period 1 development A_1^{NI} was chosen, myopically ignoring irreversibility, then period 2 A could be at most A_2'. If the decision on the period 1 level of development were taken in the light of the irreversibility constraint, the outcome would be A_1^I and A_2^I. As compared with the myopic decision making outcome, taking account of irreversibility means a higher level of A (less development) in period 1 and period 2.

Taking irreversibility into account means, as compared with the situation where irreversibility is ignored, incurring costs in

Individual decision making in the face of risk

In considering the implications of imperfect knowledge of the future, it is useful to distinguish between risk and uncertainty. Situations involving risk are those where the possible consequences of a decision can be completely enumerated, and probabilities assigned to each possibility. The possibilities are often referred to in the literature as 'states of the world' or 'states of nature', or just 'states'. Where the assignment of probabilities to all states is not possible, we are dealing with uncertainty. Two sorts of uncertainty can be distinguished. We mean by 'uncertainty' the situation where the possible consequences of a decision can be fully enumerated, but where the decision maker cannot assign probabilities. A more profound kind of uncertainty exists where the decision maker cannot enumerate all of the possible consequences of a decision – we call this radical uncertainty.

The distinction that we make between risk and uncertainty, originally due to Knight (1921), is not followed universally in the economics literature. Much modern usage conflates risk and uncertainty in Knight's sense under the general heading of uncertainty. So, for example, Freeman's definitive text on environmental valuation (Freeman, 1993) uses the term individual uncertainty to refer to:

> situations in which an individual is uncertain as to which of two or more alternative states of nature will be realised.

However, in the context of environmental and resource economics, where some decisions must be made in the face of what can only be properly described as ignorance, we feel that it is useful to continue with Knight's distinction.

The classic risk situations are gambling and insurance. In the former case, unless cheating is involved, probabilities can be assigned to outcomes on the basis of the known properties of the gamble – as with betting on the toss of a coin or the spin of a roulette wheel. In the latter case, probabilities are assigned on the basis of lots of past experience – as with life expectancies of individuals at different ages and in different circumstances, or with the incidence of accidents for motor vehicle drivers of different ages. In some gambling situations, such as horse racing, probabilities are also assigned on the basis of past 'form', albeit differently by different observers. Where there is no past 'form' and/or the underlying properties of the situation to be affected by the decision are not well understood, probabilities cannot be assigned by these means. This sort of situation is exemplified by the so-called 'greenhouse effect' in relation to prospective climate change, discussed in Chapter 13.

In many environmental decision contexts probabilities are derived from models of the processes of interest. In the case of urban air pollution, for example, for given levels of emissions from a given set of sources, ambient pollution levels at locations will vary with meteorological conditions. Physical models of the airshed can be used to simulate probabilities of different ambient levels at locations of interest: see the discussion of ambient pollution levels in Chapter 12. Again, models of nuclear reactors have been used to calculate the probabilities of various kinds of accident, there being little 'form' to go on, and experimentation to establish actual empirical knowledge being out of the question.

Where probabilities are assigned on the basis of form or knowledge, they are sometimes referred to as 'objective' probabilities. Some economists deal with situations where the assignment of objective probabilities is seen as impossible by treating the decision making problem as being dealt with by the assignment of 'subjective' probabilities. The idea is that the decision maker proceeds by assigning, on the basis of judgement, to each of the possible outcomes that he or she has identified a set of weights that satisfy the requirements for probabilities – basically they must comprise positive numbers that sum to unity. However, this assumes that the decision maker feels able to do this, and, more fundamentally, feels able to enumerate all possible outcomes. In our view, it is more appropriate to admit that there are environmental decision making problems, as exemplified by the greenhouse effect, which are not well characterised by these assumptions, and to consider uncertainty as distinct from risk. We defer discussion of decision making in the face of uncertainty until the final two sections of the chapter. Until then we proceed on the assumption that probabilities can somehow – possibly subjectively – be assigned to a complete enumeration of the outcomes considered possible.

The St Petersburg paradox

Consider the following potential gamble. A fair coin will be tossed. If it falls head up at the first toss, the gambler gets £1. If it falls head up at the second toss, the gambler gets £2, at the third toss £4, at the fourth £8 and so on. Tossing continues until the coin falls head up. How much would somebody be willing to pay for such a gamble? The answer might appear to be an infinite amount, because the expected monetary value of the gamble is infinite. The expected value is the sum of the probability weighted possible outcomes, which in this case is the infinite series

$$(0.5 \times 1) + (0.5^2 \times 2) + (0.5^3 \times 4)$$
$$+ (0.5^4 \times 8) + \ldots$$
$$= 0.5 + 0.5 + 0.5 + 0.5 + \ldots$$

which has an infinite sum. That anybody would be prepared to pay a very large amount of money for such a gamble violates everyday experience, and the example is known as the Bernoulli, or St Petersburg, paradox.[4]

The paradox can be resolved by assuming that individuals assess gambles in terms of expected utility, rather than expected monetary value, and that the utility function exhibits diminishing marginal utility. The relevant outcome is then the infinite series

$$0.5U(1) + 0.5^2U(2) + 0.5^3U(4) + 0.5^4U(8) + \ldots$$

---

[4] This paradox was posed by Bernoulli in the eighteenth century, and is sometimes known by his name. The origin of the name for the paradox used in the text lies in the Bernoulli family's long association with St Petersburg.

which has a finite sum, so long as there is some upper limit to U, which is what diminishing marginal utility implies. Diminishing marginal utility is a very natural assumption for economists. In economics, the basic approach to the analysis of individual behaviour in any kind of risky situation is to assume the maximisation of expected utility, and to assume diminishing marginal utility.

Basic concepts for risk analysis

The basic concepts used by economists here are expected value, expected utility, risk neutrality/aversion/preference, certainty equivalence and the cost of risk bearing. To develop these, consider an individual facing a gamble – though it could be any risky choice – where there are just two possible outcomes expressed in terms of the individual's income, Y_1 and Y_2. The probabilities associated with Y_1 and Y_2 are p_1 and p_2, where, by virtue of the fact that one of the outcomes must occur, $p_2 = (1 - p_1)$. Then, the expected value of the income outcome of the gamble is

$$E[Y] = p_1 Y_1 + (1 - p_1)Y_2 \qquad (15.11)$$

where $E[.]$ is the expected value operator. It says that we are referring to the expected value of whatever appears inside the square brackets. The term 'expectation' is sometimes used for 'expected value', so that Equation 15.11 would be said to give the expectation of the gamble. The expected utility of the gamble is:

$$E[U] = p_1 U(Y_1) + (1 - p_1)U(Y_2) \qquad (15.12)$$

If the utility function is given the algebraic form $U = Y^a$ where a is a positive fraction so that $dU/dY > 0$ and $d^2U/dY^2 < 0$, this is

$$E[U] = p_1 Y_1^a + (1 - p_1)Y_2^a \qquad (15.13)$$

The certainty equivalent to this gamble is the Y corresponding to its expected utility; that is, the result of solving

$$U(Y) = E[U]$$

for Y. For our case with $U(Y) = Y^a$ this is

$$Y^a = p_1 Y_1^a + (1 - p_1) Y_2^a \qquad (15.14)$$

to be solved for Y, given p_1, Y_1, Y_2 and a.

Now consider Figure 15.3 for this gamble. Y^{**} is the expected value of the gamble. The straight line **ACB** is the locus of expected value/expected utility combinations for a gamble with just two outcomes Y_1 and Y_2 as p_1 varies. If $p_1 = 1$, so that $p_2 = 0$ and Y_1 is certain, using Equations 15.11 and 15.12 we get point **A** with Y_1 and $U(Y_1)$. If $p_1 = 0$, we get **B** with Y_2 and $U(Y_2)$. If $p_1 = 0.5$, we get Y^{**} halfway between Y_1 and Y_2, $E[U]$ equal to the vertical distance Y^{**}**C**. To the left of **C** along **CA** $p_1 > 0.5$, to the right along **CB** $p_1 < 0.5$.

The utility function maps certain income into utility. If $Y^{**} = E[Y]$ were certain income, rather than the expected value of a gamble, the utility level corresponding would be that at point **E** on the $U(Y)$ curve, with $U(E[Y])$ corresponding. The horizontal line **C** to $E[U]$ cuts the $U(Y)$ curve at **D**, which corresponds to an income of Y^*. This is the certainty equivalent for this gamble, the solution for Y in Equation 15.14, as it is the certain level of income that yields the same utility as the expected utility of the gamble.

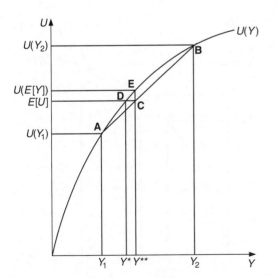

Figure 15.3 Risk aversion and the cost of risk bearing.

Y^* is, in Figure 15.3 and generally for $U = Y^a$ with $0 < a < 1$, less than Y^{**}. The certainty equivalent is less than the expected value of the gamble. Put another way, the utility of the certain payment of Y^{**} is greater than the utility of a gamble with expected value Y^{**}. If this individual were offered the sum of money Y^{**} or a free ticket to the gamble described here, he or she would not be indifferent but would prefer the sum of money over the actuarially equal gamble. We say that such an individual is 'risk averse'. If in $U = Y^a$, a took the value 1 then the graph for $U(Y)$ in Figure 15.3 would be a straight line with **ADEB** coinciding with **ACB**, and the individual would be indifferent between the money sum and the free ticket; in other words 'risk neutral'. If an individual had a utility function such that $dU/dY > 0$ and $d^2U/dY^2 > 0$, instead of $dU/dY > 0$ and $d^2U/dY^2 < 0$, then in a diagram like Figure 15.3 the arc **ADEC** would lie below the straight line **ACB** and the ticket to gamble would be preferred to the sum of money. Such an individual would be said to exhibit 'risk preference'.

Reflecting everyday experience, in economics it is assumed that the typical individual is risk averse, as depicted in Figure 15.3. For such individuals, taking a risk is costly in utility terms, which cost can be expressed in a monetary measure using the concepts developed here. The cost of risk bearing, CORB, is defined as the difference between the expected value of the gamble and its certainty equivalent:

$$\text{CORB} = Y^{**} - Y^* \qquad (15.15)$$

CORB is analogous to the measures of surplus and variation developed in the previous chapter, in that it is a monetary measure of a utility difference, which in this case would arise, for a risk averse individual, from being in a risky as opposed to an actuarially equivalent certain situation.

While we have here developed these concepts for the case of a gamble with just two outcomes, they are not restricted to such a context, which was adopted solely for expositional convenience. The number of possible outcomes does not have to be just two, nor do all possible outcomes have to have equal probabilities attached to them. The situation underlying the outcomes does not have to be a gamble as generally understood – it could, for example, be a choice about whether to insure or not, or climatic conditions affecting agricultural output.[5] Or, as discussed in the next section, the basic ideas can be used to consider the situation of individuals who do not know for sure what they will demand in the future, or what its availability will be.

Option price and option value

We now return to the context of a wilderness area for which some development is proposed and under consideration. The basic idea of option value was introduced by Weisbrod (1964) in considering a national park and the prospect of its closure. Park closure is equivalent, from the point of view of use value, to development driving the value of the wilderness area's amenity services to zero. We will adopt the particular Weisbrod context here. Weisbrod saw that as well as a loss to current visitors, closure would entail a loss to potential future visitors. He argued that the benefit of keeping the park open would be understated by just measuring current consumer surplus for visitors, and that there should be added to that a measure of the benefit of future availability. He called this additional component of preservation benefit 'option value'.

Weisbrod's definition of option value, and the claim that it was a preservation benefit additional to consumer surplus, led to some controversy. Eventually, Cichetti and Freeman (1971) established a set of definitions that proved generally acceptable, and appeared to support the basic thrust of Weis-

brod's position, at least in so far as individuals are risk averse. We now set out a simplified version of their analysis, using the concepts developed in the previous section.

Risky availability

Consider an individual and a national park wilderness area. In Figure 15.4, $U(A)$ is the level of utility that the individual attains for some given level of income, Y_A, if he or she wants to visit and the park is open. 'A' is for available. Using N for not available, $U(N)$ is the utility experienced if the individual wants to visit and the park has been closed. Given non-availability, how much would the individual be willing to pay for availability? The answer is the sum of money $Y_A - Y_N$, which would restore utility to the level $U(A)$.

Now, that question and the answer imply that the individual is either in a situation where access to the park is available, or in a situation where it is not. The idea of option value relates rather to a situation in which the individual does not know for sure whether future access will be available or not. Figure 15.4 deals with this situation along the lines set out for Figure 15.3 in relation to a gamble. Assign a probability of p_1 to the N

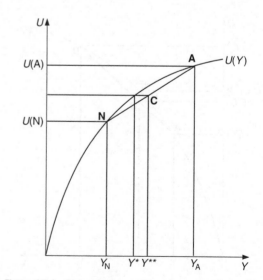

Figure 15.4   Risk aversion, option price and option value.

[5] Our treatment here of the economic analysis of individual behaviour in the face of risk has been neither rigorous nor comprehensive. For fuller accounts see, for example, Kreps (1990).

situation and $1 - p_1$ to the A situation. Then the straight line **NCA** in Figure 15.4 is the locus of U/Y combinations as p_1 varies – at N p_1 is 1, at A it is zero. As before, Y^{**} is the expected value of the outcome for some given p_1, and Y^* is the certainty equivalent.

The sum of money $Y_A - Y^{**}$ is the expected value of the individual's compensating surplus, $E[CS]$. For p_1 at 1, Y^{**} would coincide with Y_N, and willingness to pay for availability would be $Y_A - Y_N$. For $p_1 = 0$, Y^{**} would coincide with Y_A and CS would be zero. For situations where $0 < p_1 < 1$, the expected value of compensating surplus as willingness to pay is determined by the value for p_1. As Figure 15.4 is drawn, $p_1 = 0.5$ and Y^{**} is halfway between Y_N and Y_A.

The sum of money $Y_A - Y^*$, where Y^* is the certainty equivalent for this 'gamble' on availability, is what is known as 'option price', OP, the maximum amount that the individual would be willing to pay for an option which would guarantee access to an open park. As Figure 15.4 is drawn, $Y^{**} > Y^*$, so that OP is greater than $E[CS]$. Cicchetti and Freeman called the difference between OP and $E[CS]$ 'option value', OV, with

$$OP = E[CS] + OV \qquad (15.16)$$

with OV positive. From the previous section of this chapter we know that the way Figure 15.4 is drawn reflects the assumption of risk aversion. For a risk neutral individual the straight line **NCA** would coincide with the arc **NA**, so that Y^* and Y^{**} would coincide, and OV would be zero with OP = $E[CS]$. As Cicchetti and Freeman put it, 'Option value is a risk aversion premium' (page 536). Weisbrod's idea was, in this framework, that $E[CS]$ would understate the preservation benefits of keeping the park open, because risk averse individuals are willing to pay a premium to avoid risk.

Ex ante and ex post measurement

Our report of the Cicchetti and Freeman analysis, in the interest of getting at the basic idea,

was not entirely accurate. In particular, we treated risk as attaching to availability where the individual knows that he or she will want to visit in the future, whereas in the original formulation it (also) attaches to the individual's future preferences in an analysis of the policy decision as whether to allow development to close the park or keep it open. We now explore option value further in that context, distinguishing between *ex ante* and *ex post* perspectives.[6] The *ex ante* view is prior to outcomes being revealed; the *ex post* is after the event, when the outcomes are known.

We need now to introduce some additional notation. We will use s_k to denote one of S possible and mutually exclusive states of nature, $k = 1, 2 \ldots S$, and p_k for the corresponding probabilities. We will use δ_j for $j = 0$, 1 to denote one of the two possible environmental policy settings between which a decision is being made. Individuals are assumed to be able to rank, *ex post*, realised outcomes according to a utility function of the form $U(Y, \delta_j | s_k)$ where Y denotes the individual's income as before, and where the | means 'given that' so that $U(Y, \delta_j | s_k)$ is the utility for some Y and δ_j given that some particular s_k obtains. The | symbol can also be read as 'conditional on', so that $U(Y, \delta_j | s_k)$ is the utility associated with the Y and δ_j conditional on the state s_k.

Let δ_0 represent one policy setting and δ_1 represent the alternative. Then

$$U(Y, \delta_1 | s_k) > U(Y, \delta_0 | s_k) \qquad (15.17)$$

describes an *ex post* winner if δ_1 is adopted rather than δ_0, while

$$U(Y, \delta_1 | s_k) < U(Y, \delta_0 | s_k) \qquad (15.18)$$

represents a loser. In either case *ex post* compensating surplus is defined by:

$$U(Y - CS_k, \delta_1 | s_k) = U(Y, \delta_0 | s_k) \qquad (15.19)$$

Note that there is a k subscript on CS here – Equation 15.19 defines compensating surplus

[6] The discussion here largely follows that of Ready (1995).

given the kth state of nature. For a winner, CS_k is willingness to pay for the change of policy setting; for a loser CS_k is willingness to accept compensation. Of course, the fact that an individual is a winner under a policy setting in one state of nature does not mean that he or she will be a winner under that policy in other states of nature. The expected value of compensating surplus, or expected compensating surplus, denoted $E[CS]$ is the expectation of the compensated surpluses under each of the S possible states of nature:

$$E[CS] = \sum_{k=1}^{S} p_k CS_k \qquad (15.20)$$

We can illustrate this in the Weisbrod park closure context. There are just two possible states of nature – s_1, where the individual wants to visit the park, and s_2 where he or she does not. The respective probabilities are p_1 and $1 - p_1$. Let δ_1 be the policy setting where the park is open (wilderness preserved) and δ_0 be the park closed (development allowed to go ahead). Then the individual is an *ex post* winner if the park is open and

$$U(Y, \delta_1 | s_1) > U(Y, \delta_0 | s_1)$$

with

$$U(Y - CS_1, \delta_1 | s_1) = U(Y, \delta_0 | s_1)$$

defining CS_1, which would be WTP to have the park open. In this case CS_2 is zero because in the event that he or she does not want to visit the park, the individual will require no compensation for its closure. The individual is not a winner under δ_0, but neither is he or she a loser. Note that we are here assuming that the individual attaches no existence value to the park being open, to the wilderness remaining in an undeveloped state. In this case then,

$$\begin{aligned} E[CS] &= p_1 \cdot CS_1 + (1 - p_1) \cdot CS_2 \\ &= p_1 \cdot CS_1 + (1 - p_1) \cdot 0 \\ &= p_1 \cdot CS_1 \end{aligned}$$

Imagine the policy decision being taken repeatedly over time. Given that p_1 is the probability that the individual will suffer from a decision for closure, expected compensating surplus can be regarded as the average over many repetitions of his or her willingness to pay to avoid it.

Now consider matters *ex ante*, before the outcome is known, first in the general case. *Ex ante*, an individual's utility depends on the potential outcomes and their probabilities as assessed by that individual. If we use the ordinary utility function notation for *ex ante* utility,

$$U(Y, \delta_1) > U(Y, \delta_0) \qquad (15.21)$$

simply means that before the outcome is known the individual prefers δ_1 to δ_0, so that if policy setting δ_1 were to eventuate he or she would, *ex post*, be a winner. On the other hand

$$U(Y, \delta_1) < U(Y, \delta_0) \qquad (15.22)$$

says that *ex ante* the individual prefers δ_0 to δ_1, so that if policy setting δ_1 were to eventuate he or she would, *ex post*, be a loser. Given this,

$$U(Y - OP, \delta_1) = U(Y, \delta_0) \qquad (15.23)$$

defines OP as the option price for δ_1. For the 15.21 case OP would be WTP, *ex ante*, for δ_1 rather than δ_0, while for the 15.22 case OP would be WTA compensation to accept δ_1 rather than δ_0.

Ex ante, the individual's utility is a function of the potential outcomes and their associated probabilities, that is

$$U(Y, \delta) = \sum_{k=1}^{S} p_k U(Y, \delta | s_k) \qquad (15.24)$$

This says that *ex ante* the utility associated with a Y/δ pair is the expected value of the *ex post* utilities that would go with that pair under different states of nature. Substituting from Equation 15.24 into Equation 15.23 we get

$$\sum_{k=1}^{S} p_k U(Y - OP, \delta_1 | s_k) = \sum_{k=1}^{S} p_k U(Y, \delta_0 | s_k)$$

$$(15.25)$$

as defining OP for δ_1.

Consider the Weisbrod park policy decision again. We can define OP for the park staying open according to

$$U(Y - OP, \delta_1) = U(Y, \delta_0) \qquad (15.26)$$

or

$$p_1 U(Y - OP, \delta_1 \,|\, s_1) = p_1 U(Y, \delta_0 \,|\, s_1) \qquad (15.27)$$

Note that we do not find s_2 appearing in Equation 15.27 for the reason discussed above. Note also that instead of the δ notation, we could use here the A/N notation that we used when first considering the question of option value using Figure 15.5. Equations 15.26 and 15.27 could, that is, be written as

$$U(Y - OP, A) = U(Y, N) \qquad (15.28)$$

and

$$p_1 U(Y - OP, A \,|\, s_1) = p_1 U(Y, N \,|\, s_1) \qquad (15.29)$$

To make this more concrete, let us consider a simple numerical example. Suppose that what determines whether the individual wants to visit the park or not on a weekend is the weather. In fine weather the individual will definitely want to go, while in bad weather he or she will definitely not want to go. Suppose that the park is open for free and that the individual's WTP for entry on a fine weekend is £10, and that the probability of fine weather is 0.5. Then, the individual's $E[CS]$ is £5. Now suppose that he or she is told that the park might be closed next weekend, then offered a ticket guaranteeing him or her access. On an actuarial basis, with no risk aversion, the value of the ticket is £5 $= (0.5 \times £10) + (0.5 \times £0)$, $E[CS]$. If in order to avoid the risk of wanting to go to the park (fine weather) but not being able to (it is closed), the individual is WTP £6 for such a ticket, then OP = £6 and OV = £1.

According to this analysis, OV is not so much a separate category of preservation benefit as the difference between an *ex ante* measure, OP, and the expected value of an *ex post* measure, $E[CS]$. The question which arises is: which is the correct measure to use in ECBA? The consensus view emerging in

the literature is that an *ex ante* measure is the right one. Essentially the basis for this is the acceptance of consumer sovereignty. In actually taking decisions concerning 'ordinary commodities', consumers proceed on an *ex ante* basis, and the argument is that the best measure of an individual's own preferences and attitude to risk for policy analysis is his or her own *ex ante* utility function that informs decisions about 'ordinary commodities'.[7]

Unfortunately, OP cannot be estimated from data on observable behaviour. However, $E[CS]$ in some circumstances can be estimated from observable behaviour. In the Weisbrod park context, for example, and leaving aside the problems discussed in the previous chapter, one could use the TCM. If it were known that OV were positive, then from Equation 15.16 it would follow that OP was greater than $E[CS]$ and an estimate of $E[CS]$ based on observable behaviour could be treated as a lower bound for OP. However, while Figure 15.4 suggests that risk aversion necessarily implies a positive OV, recent analysis shows that even for a risk averse individual OV could in some circumstances be negative. Given this, $E[CS]$ would not necessarily represent a lower bound for OP.

In principle, this need not be a major problem, as instead of trying to get at OP via observed behaviour, one could use the CVM with an appropriate *ex ante* scenario to directly elicit OP as WTP/WTA. In practice, the design of 'an appropriate *ex ante* scenario' that is, one that effectively puts respondents in the intended hypothetical market and risk situation – is extremely difficult. We discussed some of the problems with the CVM where respondents are put in situations where outcomes are to be treated as certain in the previous chapter. These problems tend to be made worse when an effort to

---

[7] Ready (1995) argues for the use of *ex ante* OP from consideration of the properties of *ex ante* and *ex post* versions of compensation tests.

introduce risk into the scenario is undertaken, and there have been only a few CVM applications that have tried to elicit OP.

Risk and irreversibility

In the previous section we saw that, usually, for a risk averse individual option price is greater than expected compensating surplus by an amount which is option value. To the extent that social decision making adopts the principle of consumer sovereignty, and given that most individuals are risk averse, this leads to the conclusion that option price, rather than expected compensating surplus, should be used in ECBA. With respect to, for example, wilderness development, this suggests that the level that net development benefits have to attain to justify development is greater than would be the case in a world in which the future was certain. This conclusion is dependent on adopting a risk averse position. In this section we consider arguments that work in the same direction, but do not require risk aversion. Since we are not assuming risk aversion, we can, and do, work with expected values, sums of money, rather than expected utilities.

We begin by revisiting the discussion of the implications of irreversibility in the second section of the chapter. There, and see Figure 15.2 especially, we considered those implications in a world where the future was perfectly known. We are now in a position to adopt a more plausible assumption about knowledge of the future, namely that it is imperfect.

Irreversibility in a risky world

Figure 15.5(a) is the same as Figure 15.2(a), apart from the appearance of A_1^{IR}, to be explained. Figure 15.5(b) shows the same MNB function as in Figure 15.2(b), but here it is labelled MNB_2^2 instead of just MNB_2. The superscript 2 now appears because we also have MNB_2^1, which has the same inter-

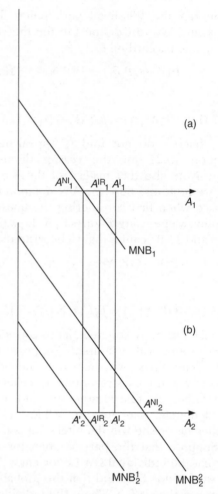

Figure 15.5 Irreversibility and development with imperfect future knowledge.

cept and slope as MNB_1 in Figure 15.5(a). We are now considering a situation where MNB as a function of A is known for period 1, but where the decision maker does not know for period 2 which of two MNB functions will eventuate, MNB_2^1, which is the same as MNB_1, or MNB_2^2, which has the same slope as MNB_1 but a larger intercept. While it is not known, when deciding on the level of period 1 development and hence the level of A_1, which of MNB_2^1 or MNB_2^2 will obtain in period 2, the decision maker can assign probabilities p to MNB_2^1 and $q = (1 - p)$ to MNB_2^2.

In Figure 15.5 A_1^{NI} is the same level of A_1 as A_1^{NI} in Figure 15.2, and both refer to the outcome of decision making which ignores irreversibility. Given irreversibility, A_2 must equal (strictly be no greater than) A_1, so A_1^{NI} the same in both figures implies A_2' the same in both. A_1^{I} and A_2^{I} in Figure 15.5 are also the same as in Figure 15.2, and refer to the outcome where there is irreversibility but no risk and it is known that the period 2 MNB function will be MNB_2^2, which is the same as MNB_2 in Figure 15.2. A_1^{IR} and A_2^{IR} are the outcomes for a decision making process that takes on board both irreversibility and risk, and adopts risk neutrality. In this case, adding imperfect future knowledge about MNB to irreversibility leads to lower levels of amenity – higher levels of development – than irreversibility alone, but which are higher – lower levels of development – than would have resulted if irreversibility were ignored.

This is established in Appendix 15.2. The results are reasonably intuitive. If irreversibility is ignored, then in the first period the level of A_1 can be chosen by setting MNB_1 equal to zero, and the fact that which of MNB_2^1 or MNB_2^2 will eventuate is unknown is irrelevant. Given that irreversibility is a fact, though ignored, the choice of the period 1 level of A immediately gives its period 2 level, and we get A_1^{NI} and A_2'. If the decision making process recognises irreversibility and assumes MNB_2^2, the situation is as discussed for Figure 15.2 and we get A_1^{I} and A_2^{I}. Where it also recognises that period 2 might involve MNB_2^2 or MNB_2^1, it uses the weighted average of these two alternatives, with weights that are the assigned probabilities, and ends up in an intermediate situation, A_1^{IR} and A_2^{IR}.

Quasi-option value

We now consider the implications of irreversibility in a world where there is imperfect knowledge of the future, but where more knowledge will become available after a deci-sion has been made. We again look at the matter of wilderness development. This is the context in which Arrow and Fisher (1974) introduced the concept of quasi-option value, and our treatment follows that of Arrow and Fisher quite closely. To sim-plify, we now consider a situation where development is 'all or nothing' in the sense that either development occurs and drives wilderness amenity benefits to zero, or devel-opment does not occur. This is like the deci-sion considered by Weisbrod – either the national park is permanently closed (to allow development) or it remains open.

The essential point that this special for-mulation makes clear is that where there is the prospect of improved information 'the expected benefits of an irreversible decision should be adjusted to reflect the loss of options it entails' (Arrow and Fisher, 1974, page 319). The adjustment is required even if the decision maker is risk neutral. The size of the adjustment is quasi-option value. While we discuss quasi-option value in an all or nothing development context, the basic idea carries over to situations where the wild-erness area can be partially developed – indeed, it carries over to any situation where one course of action is irreversible and where there will in the future be improved informa-tion about the future situation.

As before, time is divided into two periods, 1 being 'now' and 2 'the future'. The decision maker has complete knowledge of all relevant period 1 conditions. At the start of period 1, period 2 outcomes can be listed and prob-abilities attached to them. A decision involving irreversible consequences must be taken at the start of period 1. At the end of period 1, complete knowledge about period 2 will become available to the decision maker.

The decision to be taken at the start of period 1 is whether to permit development of a wilderness area. The options are shown in Table 15.2. As before, D is for develop-ment, P is for preservation, and period 2 costs and benefits are to be understood as discounted present values. R^i is the return

Table 15.2 Two period development/preservation options.

Option	Period 1	Period 2	Return
1	D	D	$R^1 = (B_{d1} - C_{d1}) + B_{d2}$
2	P	D	$R^2 = B_{p1} + (B_{d2} - C_{d2})$
3	P	P	$R^3 = B_{p1} + B_{p2}$
4	D	P	Is infeasible

associated with the ith option, B_{pt} is preservation benefits, B_{dt} is development benefits, C_{dt} is development costs, which are treated as arising only in the period in which the development project is undertaken, and as before we do not explicitly distinguish preservation costs. Option 1 involves initiating development at the start of period 1, and given irreversibility development in period 1 implies development in period 2. Hence, option 4, having the area developed in 1 but preserved in 2, is shown in Table 15.2 as infeasible. The operative alternatives to having the area in a developed state in both periods are option 2 – preservation then development at the start of period 2 – and option 3 – never develop.

Let us label the return to the decision taken at the start of period 1 to proceed immediately with development R^d, so that:

$$R^d = R^1 = (B_{d1} - C_{d1}) + B_{d2} \quad (15.30)$$

The return to the decision taken at the start of period 1 to preserve is either R^2 or R^3, depending on whether or not development is initiated at the start of period 2 given the information then available. If B_{p2} then is known to be bigger than $B_{d2} - C_{d2}$, the area will be preserved in period 2, giving R^3. If $B_{d2} - C_{d2}$ is then known to be bigger than B_{p2}, development will be undertaken at the start of period 2, giving R^2. We can express this as

$$R^p = B_{p1} + \text{Max}\{B_{p2}, (B_{d2} - C_{d2})\} \quad (15.31)$$

where R^p is the return to the period 1 decision for preservation, and the right hand side is to be read as B_{p1} plus whichever is the greater of B_{p2} and $(B_{d2} - C_{d2})$ – 'Max' is short for 'the largest of the terms appearing inside the braces'. Note that B_{p1} is common to both R^2 and R^3.

Now, suppose for the moment that the decision maker does have complete knowledge of the relevant future circumstances, that at the start of period 1 he or she knows all the B_{pt}, B_{dt} and C_{dt}. Then the decision maker also knows R^d and R^p, and the decision will be to go ahead with development immediately if $R^d > R^p$, which is if $R^d - R^p > 0$, which on substituting from Equations 15.30 and 15.31 is

$$\begin{aligned}(B_{d1} - C_{d1}) + B_{d2} - B_{p1} \\ - \text{Max}\{B_{p2}, (B_{d2} - C_{d2})\} > 0\end{aligned} \quad (15.32)$$

which can be written

$$N_1 + B_{d2} - \text{Max}\{B_{p2}, (B_{d2} - C_{d2})\} > 0 \quad (15.33)$$

where $N_1 = (B_{d1} - C_{d1}) - B_{p1}$. N_1 is, in other words, that which would actually be known to the decision maker at the start of period 1.

The other terms in the expression 15.33 could not, in fact, be known to the decision maker at the start of period 1, so 15.33 is not an operational decision rule. We are, however, assuming that the possible outcomes for B_{d2}, B_{p2} and $(B_{d2} - C_{d2})$ are known to the decision maker and that he or she can attach probabilities to the mutually exclusive outcomes. In that case, it is tempting to simply replace known outcomes in the expression 15.33 by the corresponding expectations, or expected values, and to write an operational decision rule as: go ahead with development at the start of period 1 if

$$\begin{aligned}N_1 + E[B_{d2}] - \text{Max}\{E[B_{p2}], \\ E[(B_{d2} - C_{d2})]\} > 0\end{aligned} \quad (15.34)$$

However, using this rule ignores the fact that more information will be available at the start of period 2. If the area is developed at the start of period 1 this information cannot be used, since the area will necessarily be in a developed state in period 2. If the area is not developed at the start of period 1, the new information could be used at the start of period 2 to decide between development and preservation then.

The proper decision rule is one that takes this on board, as the expression 15.34 does not. Now, of course, a decision has to be taken at the start of period 1, and the decision maker does not then have the information that will become available at the start of period 2. But, by assumption, the decision maker does at the start of period 1 know what the informational possibilities are and the probabilities to attach to outcomes in that respect. So, he or she could use the decision rule: go ahead with development at the start of period 1 if

$$N_1 + E[B_{d2}] - E[\text{Max}\{B_{p2}, (B_{d2} - C_{d2})\}] > 0 \tag{15.35}$$

Whereas in expression 15.34 the decision maker uses the maximum of the expected values of period 2 preservation benefits and net development benefits, in 15.35 he or she uses the expectation of the maximum of period 2 preservation benefits and net development benefits. The left-hand side of expression 15.35 will be larger than the left-hand side of 15.34, so that the former decision rule is a harder test for development to pass at the start of period 1. The difference between the left-hand sides of expressions 15.35 and 15.34 is quasi-option value. It is the amount by which a net development benefit assessment which simply replaces outcomes by their expectations should be reduced, given irreversibility, to reflect the payoff to keeping options open, by not developing, until more information about future conditions is available.

This analysis can be illustrated with a simple numerical example. Suppose that there are just two possible period 2 situations, A and B, differentiated only by what the preservation benefits for 'the future' will be learned to be. B_{d2} and C_{d2} are the same for A and B, and for both $(B_{d2} - C_{d2}) = 6$. For A, B_{p2} is 10: for B, B_{p2} is 5. At the beginning of period 1, A and B are seen as equiprobable so that $p^A = p^B = 0.5$. In this case, for 15.34 we have for the third term to the left of the $>$ sign

$$\text{Max}\{E[B_{p2}], E[(B_{d2} - C_{d2})]\}$$
$$= \text{Max}\{[(0.5 \times 10) + (0.5 \times 5)],$$
$$[(0.5 \times 6) + (0.5 \times 6)]\}$$
$$= \text{Max}\{7.5, 6\}$$
$$= 7.5$$

so the development will get the go-ahead if

$$N_1 + E[B_{d2}] - 7.5 > 0 \tag{15.36}$$

Now consider 15.35. We have two possible outcomes:

A where $B_{p2} > (B_{d2} - C_{d2})$, $B_{p2} = 10$, $p^A = 0.5$

B where $B_{p2} < (B_{d2} - C_{d2})$, $(B_{d2} - C_{d2}) = 6$, $p^B = 0.5$

Hence,

$$E[\text{Max}\{B_{p2}, (B_{d2} - C_{d2})\}]$$
$$= (0.5 \times 10) + (0.5 \times 6) = 8$$

and following this decision rule, development will get the go-ahead if

$$N_1 + E[B_{d2}] - 8 > 0 \tag{15.37}$$

Suppose $N_1 + E[B_{d2}] = 7.75$. Then, using 15.34/15.36 development would be decided on at the start of period 1, while using 15.35/15.37 the decision would be to preserve in period 1. The test based on 15.35 is harder to pass than the 15.34-based test. As compared with 15.34, 15.35 adds a premium to the value for $N_1 + E[B_{d2}]$ required to justify a decision for development at the start of period 1. That premium is quasi-option value, which in this example is $0.5 = 8 - 7.5$.

Positive quasi-option value is a general result. This is straightforward, and instructive, to establish where $E[B_{p2}] > E[(B_{d2} - C_{d2})]$, as in this numerical example.[8] Consider first 15.34 under that assumption, in which case it becomes

$$N_1 + E[B_{d2}] - E[B_{p2}] > 0 \tag{15.38}$$

Now consider $\text{Max}\{B_{p2}, (B_{d2} - C_{d2})\}$ from 15.35. This is either B_{p2} or a number larger

---

[8] The general result is established in Arrow and Fisher (1974). See also Fisher and Hanemann (1986).

than B_{p2}. So long as the possibility that $(B_{d2} - C_{d2}) > B_{p2}$ is entertained by the decision maker, $E[\text{Max}\{B_{p2}, (B_{d2} - C_{d2})\}]$ will be greater than $E[B_{p2}]$, and 15.35 which is

$$N_1 + E[B_{d2}] - E[\text{Max}\{B_{p2}, (B_{d2} - C_{d2})\}] > 0$$

will be a harder test to pass than 15.38, with

$$E[\text{Max}\{B_{p2}, (B_{d2} - C_{d2})\}] - E[B_{p2}] = \text{QOV}$$

where QOV is for quasi-option value.

The basic point about the existence of quasi-option value is that, where more knowledge about future conditions will become available after an irreversible decision has been made, even with risk neutrality, simply replacing random variables with their expectations and then optimising will lead to the wrong decision. Recall that in Figure 15.5 (and see also Appendix 15.2), we found that adding imperfect future knowledge to irreversibility led to a higher current level of development. We did not there incorporate any quasi-option value into the risk neutral, decision making procedure, because we did not assume that more information would become available at the end of period 1. In general the assumption of increased information in the future would be more appropriate than the contrary assumption, and social decision making should include quasi-option value. However, it is clear from the discussion here that in order to estimate quasi-option value it would be necessary to know, or to assume, a lot about possible outcomes, their current probabilities and the prospects for additional information in the future. In practice ECBA exercises rarely take any account of quasi-option value in any formal quantitative way.

Environmental cost–benefit analysis revisited

Let us briefly bring together some of the foregoing ideas in the following context. An area of completely undeveloped wilderness land is currently privately owned. A large mineral deposit has been discovered and the owner plans to open a mine. The government is considering purchasing the land and making it a national park so as to preserve the amenity and life support services that the area provides in its undeveloped state. If the mine went ahead there would be start-up costs with a present value of £20 million, to open the mine and construct the necessary infrastructure. Once operational the mine would yield net revenues of £6 million for 100 years, after which the ore body would be exhausted. Using the standard result for the present value of £x per annum forever as an approximation, at an interest rate of 5%, £6 million for 100 years has a present value of £120 million. Hence, we have NPV' for the mine equal to £100 million. This is the capitalised value of the area used for mining, the opportunity cost of the creation of a national park.

Consider first inverse ECBA. What is the minimum value of the environmental services yielded by the land in its undeveloped state that would justify stopping the mine and creating the park? We will assume that the only cost involved in the park option is the cost of acquiring the land. In that case, the answer is £100 million, in present value terms. If the relevant population were collectively willing to pay £100 million now, or more, the government would on standard allocative efficiency grounds be justified in buying the land to create a national park. The per capita test for going ahead with the park would be: is the average member of the population willing to pay a once off sum now of £$(100/N)$, where N is the population size in millions? For a population of 20 million, roughly the number of adults in the UK, this is a lump sum of £5. This can be converted to an equivalent annual payment for a given number of years.

Actually, if the arguments of Krutilla and Fisher about the relative prices of wilderness services and 'ordinary' commodities are accepted, this way of calculating the threshold value for the value of environmental services lost if the mine goes ahead is biased in favour of the mine. Equation 15.7 can be read as saying that for the mine

$$\text{NPV} = 0 \quad \text{if} \quad \text{NPV}' = P/(r - a)$$

where for the present example NPV' is £100 million and $r = 0.05$. Suppose that P, the initial value for preservation benefits is taken to be just £1 million per annum. What would a, the growth rate for the value of environmental services relative to ordinary commodities, then have to be to justify creating the park? Solving

$$100 = 1/(0.05 - a)$$

gives $a = 0.04$.

So, if it were known that the mine's NPV' were £100 million, that current population willingness to pay for the services of the area undeveloped was £1 million, that development would be irreversible in its impact on those services, and that their relative value would grow by 4% per annum or more, then the government would be justified in acquiring the land and creating the park. Of course, in fact things are not known in this way, and the question that arises is: how should ECBA take account of risk? It is tempting to answer that it is simply a matter of replacing known outcomes by their expected values. In that case, using continuous time notation for convenience, instead of calculating NPV according to Equation 15.4

$$\text{NPV} = \int_0^T \{B(D)_t - C(D)_t\}e^{-rt}\mathrm{d}t$$
$$- \int_0^T B(P)_t\}e^{-rt}\mathrm{d}t$$

we would use the probabilities for the various possibilities in regard to $B(D)$, $C(D)$ and $B(P)$ to calculate

$$E[\text{NPV}] = \int_0^T \{E[B(D)]_t - E[C(D)]_t\}e^{-rt}\mathrm{d}t$$
$$- \int_0^T E[B(P)]_t\}e^{-rt}\mathrm{d}t \qquad (15.39)$$

However, if individuals are risk averse and this is to be reflected in ECBA, this is incor-rect. Some allowance for risk aversion must be made. Then the proper test for the mining project, and for the creation of the park, is

$$\text{NPV}^* = \int_0^T \{E[B(D)]_t - E[C(D)]_t\}e^{-rt}\mathrm{d}t$$
$$- \int_0^T E[B(P)]_t\}e^{-rt} - \int_0^T \text{CORB}_t e^{-rt}$$
$$(15.40)$$

where CORB_t is the cost of risk bearing at time t. It is sometimes suggested that risk can be dealt with by using expected values and an increased rate of discount, as in

$$\text{NPV}^{**} = \int_0^T \{E[B(D)]_t - E[C(D)]_t\}e^{-(r+b)t}\mathrm{d}t$$
$$- \int_0^T E[B(P)]_t\}e^{-(r+b)t} \qquad (15.41)$$

where b is the 'risk premium' to be added to the standard discount rate. Apart from the problem of deciding on a proper value for b, this implies that the cost of risk bearing is decreasing exponentially over time. This can be seen by writing Equation 15.41 as

$$\text{NPV}^{**} = \int_0^T \{E[B(D)]_t - E[C(D)]_t\}$$
$$\{\text{CORB}e^{-bt}\}e^{-rt}\mathrm{d}t - \int_0^T \{E[B(P)]_t\}$$
$$\{\text{CORB}e^{-bt}\}e^{-rt}\mathrm{d}t$$

where CORB is some initial value for the cost of risk bearing, which thereafter declines at the rate b. While the assumption of an expo-nentially decreasing cost of risk may be appropriate in some cases, it clearly is not generally valid. The correct way to proceed is to estimate CORB_t over the life of the project and incorporate those estimates as in Equa-tion 15.40.

It has been argued (see Arrow and Lind, 1970) that when a project is undertaken by government on behalf of society as a whole, no allowances for risk need be made. The reasoning here is that when government undertakes risky projects, the risks are spread (or pooled or diversified) over many individuals. In aggregate, therefore, there is no risk attached to collectively undertaken investments, and no need to include estimates of $CORB_t$. This argument is not now accepted as being applicable in the context of projects that have environmental impacts. The reason for this is that environmental services are typically public goods – they are non-rival and non-excludable, so that the assumption of risk spreading does not hold.

The problem then remains of estimating $CORB_t$. As we have seen, this is now looked at under the 'option-value' rubric – in the ECBA context option-value is the cost of risk bearing. What this means is that, leaving aside existence values for the moment, an ECBA which does not simply ignore risk should use either Equation 15.40 with $E[B(P)]_t$ replaced by $E[CS]_t$ and $CORB_t$ replaced by OV_t, or, more directly, replace both $E[B(P)]_t$ and $CORB_t$ with OP_t, where CS is compensating surplus OV is option value, and OP is option price. It should use, that is, either

$$NPV^* = \int_0^T \{E[B(D)]_t - E[C(D)]_t\}e^{-rt}dt$$
$$- \int_0^T E[CS]_t e^{-rt} - \int_0^T OV_t e^{-rt} \quad (15.42)$$

or

$$NPV^* = \int_0^T \{E[B(D)]_t - E[C(D)]_t\}e^{-rt}dt$$
$$- \int_0^T OP_t e^{-rt} \quad (15.43)$$

In principle, as previously noted, OP could be obtained directly from suitable application of the CVM. In practice this is difficult. It is understood that in most cases OV will be positive, so that if Equation 15.42 is used with OV set at zero, NPV^* will be over-estimated. Of course, as discussed in the previous chapter, what actually gets estimated by, for example, the TCM is Marshallian consumer surplus, MCS, rather than the theoretically correct Hicksian measure. The

relationship between MCS and CS where it is quantity/quality change, rather than price change, that is at issue is, as discussed in the previous chapter, complex and they may diverge widely in unknown ways.

What all this means is that while at a theoretical level the proper way to do ECBA accounting for risk aversion is clear enough, the practical implementation of the procedures is difficult. In practice, an ECBA exercise of the kind we are considering here would use

$$NPV = \int_0^T \{B(D)_t - C(D)_t\}e^{-rt}dt$$
$$- \int_0^T B(P)_t\}e^{-rt}dt$$

where $B(P)$ would include estimated use and existence value for the relevant population, and then subject the central case result to sensitivity analysis. ECBA practitioners are aware of the importance of option value and quasi-option value, but find it hard to put numbers to these concepts. It is rather a matter of considering whether plausible variations to the central case numbers can produce a negative NPV, when some judgemental allowance is made for option and quasi-option value.

Decision theory: choices under uncertainty

In the third section of this chapter we made the distinction between risk and uncertainty. Thus far we have been considering individual and social decision making in circumstances of risk, that is where the decision maker proceeds on the assumption that he or she can enumerate all possible future states and assign probabilities to them. We now consider decision making in the face of uncertainty, where the decision maker enumerates all possible states relevant to the decision but cannot attach probabilities to those states. The approach that we adopt is called 'decision theory', which is a branch of the theory of games.

We focus on social decision making and treat what we shall call 'society' as one of the players of a game. The other 'player' is by convention called 'nature' and the games that we shall be considering are often called 'games against nature'. Society must select a move (or strategy) in ignorance about which state of nature will occur, and is unable to attach probabilities to states of nature. However, it is assumed that society can estimate its 'pay-off matrix'. The pay-off matrix is a statement of the alternative strategies open to society, the possible states of nature, and the pay-offs associated with each combination of strategy and state of nature. Table 15.3 is an example of a pay-off matrix constructed for the context that we considered in the previous section of the chapter – the decision as to whether to stop development in a wilderness area by making it a national park.

There are two strategies, A and B, and three possible states of nature C, D and E. The entries in Table 15.3 are millions of £s of NPV associated with the corresponding strategy/state of nature combination. If state C eventuates and the park exists, a large number of individuals choose to visit the park and enjoy its wilderness amenities, while if the mine is allowed to go ahead it turns out that it is a commercial failure. State E is the converse of this: if the park exists few individuals choose to visit it and the value attached to its existence by non-visitors is low, while the mine turns out to be very successful commercially. The state of nature D is intermediate between C and E: the mine is moderately successful if it goes ahead, as is the park if it does.

If C eventuates, society is richly rewarded *ex post* for adopting strategy A, receiving a pay-off of 120. In contrast, its returns to strategy B are very poor, obtaining a pay-off of just 5. The remaining four cells in the matrix show society's payoffs from A or B when the state of nature is either D or E. Note that the best of all possible outcomes is that given by the lower right cell, where society allows the mine to go ahead and it is commercially successful.

Which strategy, A or B, should the government acting on behalf of society select? Should it allow the mine to proceed or create a national park? Let us examine four of the decision rules that have been proposed for games against nature.

(1) *Maximin rule.* Government sets out the pay-off matrix and selects the strategy with the least bad worst outcome. The label 'maximin' signifies that the strategy that maximises the minimum possible outcome is selected. Inspection of the payoff matrix in Table 15.3 reveals A to be the maximin strategy. If B is selected, the worst possible outcome is 5, while if A is selected the worst outcome is 10.

While avoiding worst possible outcomes has some attraction, the maximin rule can easily lead to choices which seem to contradict common sense. This arises because the maximin rule ignores most of the information in the pay-off matrix. In particular, the pay-offs in best possible cases are ignored. Moreover, the maximin decision rule means that decisions are made entirely on the basis of the most adverse possibilities. If one strategy was only marginally better than a second in terms of its worst outcome, the first would be preferred no matter how much more preferable the second may be under all other states of nature.

(2) *Maximax rule.* In contrast to what may be regarded as the very cautious maximin strategy, the 'maximax' decision rule is very adventurous. Each available strategy is examined to identify its best outcome. The one selected is that with the best of

Table 15.3 A pay-off matrix.

	C	D	E
A Conserve the wilderness area as a national park	120	50	10
B Allow the mine to be developed	5	30	140

the best outcomes. This rule implies that government should adopt strategy B, as its best outcome is 140, in state E, whereas the best outcome from adopting A is 120, in state C.

The maximax rule suffers from a similar weakness to a maximin rule, as it ignores most of the information in the pay-off matrix. In this case, all pay-offs other than the best possible ones are ignored. Once again, the choices implied by this rule can fly in the face of common sense.

(3) *Minimax regret rule*. The essence of the 'minimax regret' rule is the avoidance of costly mistakes. To implement this rule, a regret matrix is derived from the payoff matrix. This is done by identifying for each state of nature the strategy with the largest pay-off and then expressing all the other pay-offs for that state of nature as deviations from the largest. The entries in the regret matrix are the difference between the actual pay-off for the strategy/state of nature combination and what the payoff would have been if the best strategy for the state of nature had been chosen. The regret matrix for our illustrative example is shown in Table 15.4.

Once the regret matrix has been calculated, government plays a minimax game using these regrets. Each row of the regret matrix is examined to identify the largest possible regret. The strategy with the lowest of the largest regrets is then chosen. The minimax regret rule leads to selection of B in this example, as its most costly mistake is 115 in state C, whereas for A the most costly mistake is 130 in state E.

(4) *Assignment of subjective probabilities.* According to 'the principle of insufficient reason', in the absence of any better information the decision maker should assign equal probabilities to the mutually exclusive outcomes, and adopt the strategy that then has the pay-off with the greatest expected value. For our example, this leads to selection of strategy A, which has an expected value of 60 whereas the expected value for B is $58\frac{1}{3}$.

The equal probabilities are just subjective probabilities. In some situations there may be information available which enables the assignation of unequal subjective probabilities. Unlike the previous decision rules, selecting the strategy with the largest expected value on the basis of subjective probabilities does consider all alternatives in the pay-off matrix.

It is clear from this brief exposition of decision theory that while it can provide insights into how decision makers might behave in the face of uncertainty, it cannot tell us which is the best way to make choices in an uncertain world. Indeed, the concept of rational behaviour is problematic in the face of uncertainty – there is no way of making decisions that can be unambiguously identified as doing the best for the decision maker in the relevant circumstances.

It may be that this is why many economists are uncomfortable with uncertainty, and prefer to deal with situations where the assignment of 'objective' probabilities is impossible by treating decision makers as assigning 'subjective' probabilities.

A safe minimum standard of conservation

In the third section of this chapter we defined as radical uncertainty a situation in which the decision maker is not able to list all of the possible outcomes. This is the context in which the idea of the 'safe minimum standard' was

Table 15.4 A regret matrix.

	C	D	E
A	0	0	130
B	115	20	0

originally formulated. To see what is involved, let us modify the illustrative example just considered. Let us confine the possibilities to state E, but suppose that it is known that the construction of the proposed mine will mean that a population of some plant will be destroyed, and that this population is thought to be the only one in existence. The mine proponents have undertaken to attempt the re-establishment of the plant in another location, and the cost of so doing is included in their project appraisal. It is unknown whether the attempt will be successful.

To consider the park/mine decision now, we can specify just two states of nature, F and U. F stands for 'favourable' and is where the relocation is successful, while U is for 'unfavourable', in which state of nature the relocation is unsuccessful. What pay-off should be assigned to having the mine go ahead if the state U eventuates? The problem is that not only is it impossible to assign probabilities to success and failure – it has never been tried before – but that it is also unknown whether any other populations of the plant species exist. In this case the state of nature U may imply extinction of the species. In this case, the regret matrix is then as shown in Table 15.5, where z is an unknown number. For state F the regrets in Table 15.5 are the same as in Table 15.4. For state U, the park option A would avoid the species extinction, whereas B could entail that extinction, which carries a large, but unknown, regret z.

In fact as Table 15.5 is constructed it is implicit, by virtue of the 0 entry for A/U, that although we have said that z is an unknown number, it is supposed large enough that A, stop the mine is the correct strategy in state U. But this presumption does not, following the minimax regret rule indicate which strategy to

adopt. One way to proceed would be to assume that although the cost of species extinction is unknown, it can be presumed large enough to make A the right strategy. It is exactly this presumption that underlies the idea of the safe minimum standard as originally put forward. As made by Bishop (1978) the argument for this presumption is as follows. Species extinction involves an irreversible reduction in the stock of potentially useful resources which is the existing portfolio of species. In a state of radical uncertainty there is no way of knowing how large the value to humans of any of the existing species might turn out to be in the future. Two kinds of ignorance are involved here. First, there is social ignorance about future preferences, needs and technologies. Second, there is scientific ignorance about the characteristics of existing species as they relate to future social possibilities and needs. The extinction of any species is, therefore, to be presumed to involve future costs that may be very large, even when discounted into present value terms. The argument here is essentially that the species that may become extinct may turn out to be one for which there is no substitute.

Applying the safe minimum standard for conservation (SMS) criterion as stated to projects which could entail species extinction would mean rejecting all such projects. All that is required for rejection is the possibility that going ahead with the project could involve species extinction. SMS is a very conservative rule. It means foregoing current gains, however large, in order to avoid future losses of unknown, but presumed very large, size. A modified SMS has been proposed according to which the strategy that ensures the survival of the species should be adopted, unless it entails unacceptably large costs. This is less conservative, but leaves it to be determined whether any given cost is 'unacceptably large'.

Renewable resource harvesting and SMS

Our discussion of renewable resource harvesting in Chapter 9 was based on the cri-

Table 15.5 A regret matrix for the possibility of species extinction.

	F	U
A	130	0
B	0	z

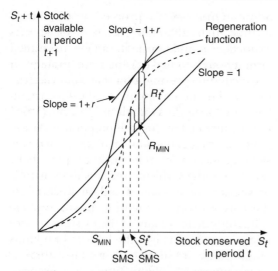

Figure 15.6 A safe minimum standard of conservation.

terion of economic efficiency. We saw there that the pursuit of an efficiency criterion is not sufficient to guarantee the survival of a renewable resource stock in perpetuity, particularly when resource prices are high, harvesting costs are low, discount rates are high, and uncertainty pervades the relevant functions. When such a stock is of high intrinsic value, so that we would be strongly averse to outcomes that involve the resource being driven to extinction, constraints on harvesting behaviour may be deemed appropriate.

Let us explore the concept of an SMS in this context by following the exposition in a recent paper by Randall and Farmer (1995). Suppose there is some renewable resource that grows over time in a particular way, illustrated by the curve labelled 'Regeneration function' in Figure 15.6. The function shows the resource stock level that will be available in period $t + 1$ for any level of stock that is conserved in period t. Resource stock levels are denoted by the letter S. Notice that the greater is the level of current stock conservation, the higher will be the stock level available in the next period.[9]

[9] The relationship is non-linear due to the characteristics of the resource stock–growth relationship for the renewable resource in question.

Randall and Farmer restrict their attention to sustainable resource use, interpreting sustainability to mean a sequence of states in which the resource stock does not decline over time. Therefore, only those levels of stock in period t corresponding to segments of the regeneration function that lie on or above the 45° line (labelled 'slope = 1') constitute sustainable stocks. The minimum sustainable level of stock conservation is labelled S_{MIN}.

The efficient level of stock conservation is S_t^*. To see this, construct a tangent to the regeneration function with a slope of $1 + r$, where r is a (consumption) social discount rate, and let h denote the rate of growth of the renewable resource. At any point on the regeneration function, a tangent to the function will have a slope of $1 + h$. For the particular stock level S_t^* we have

$$1 + r = 1 + h \ \text{ or } \ r = h$$

and so the rate of growth of the renewable resource, h, is equal to the social discount rate, r. This is an efficiency condition for steady-state renewable resource harvesting, as we have seen previously in Equation 9.16. Note also that at the efficient stock level, the amount of harvest that can be taken in perpetuity is R_t^*. By harvesting at this rate, the post-harvest stock in period $t + 1$ is equal to that in period t, thus satisfying the sustainability requirement.

Now suppose that the regeneration function is subject to random variation. For simplicity, assume that the worst possible outcome is indicated by the dotted regeneration function in Figure 15.6; at any current stock, the worst that can happen is that the available future stock falls short of the expected quantity by an amount equal to the vertical distance between the solid and dotted functions.

Now even in the worst outcome, if $\widetilde{SMS}$ is conserved in each period, the condition for perpetual sustainability of the stock will be maintained. We might regard $\widetilde{SMS}$ as a stock level that incorporates the safe minimum standard of conservation, reflecting the uncertainty due to random variability in the regeneration function. Put another way, whereas S_{MIN} is an appropriate minimum stock in the absence of uncertainty, $S\tilde{M}S$ takes account of uncertainty in a particular way.

In fact, $S\tilde{M}S$ is not what Randall and Farmer propose as a safe minimum standard of conservation. They argue that any sustainable path over time must involve some positive, non-declining level of resource harvesting and consumption in every period. Suppose that R_{MIN} is judged to be that minimum required level of resource consumption. Then Randall and Farmer's safe minimum standard of conservation is $S\hat{M}S$. If the stock in period t is kept from falling below this level then, even in the worst possible case, R_{MIN} can be harvested without interference with sustainability.

The SMS principle implies maintaining a renewable resource stock at or above some safe minimum level such as $S\hat{M}S$. In Figure 15.6, there is no conflict between the conservation and efficiency criteria. The safe minimum standard of conservation actually implies a lower target for the resource stock than that implied by economic efficiency. This will not always be true, however, and one can easily imagine circumstances where an SMS criterion implies more cautious behaviour than the economically efficient outcome.

Finally, what can be said about the qualification that the SMS should be pursued only where it does not entail excessive cost? Not surprisingly, it is difficult to make much headway here, as it is not clear how one might decide what constitutes excessive cost. Randall and Farmer suggest that no society can reasonably be expected to decimate itself. Therefore, if the SMS conflicted with the survival of human society, that would certainly entail excessive cost. But most people are likely to regard costs far less than this – such as extreme deprivation – as being excessive. Ultimately, the political process must generate views as to what constitutes excessive costs.

The SMS criterion can also be applied to pollution policy, where it would imply that threats to the survival of valuable resource systems from pollution flows are eliminated, provided that this does not entail excessive cost. Alternatively, one may view the SMS criterion here in terms of constraints – pollution policy should in general be determined using an efficiency criterion, but subject to the overriding constraint that an SMS is satisfied. This formulation of pollution policy recognises the importance of economic efficiency but accords it a lower priority than conservation when the two conflict, provided that the opportunity costs of conservation are not excessive. Again, we see that this compromise between efficiency and conservation criteria implies that 'correct' levels of pollution cannot be worked out analytically. Instead, judgements will need to be made about what constitutes excessive costs, and which resources are deemed sufficiently valuable for application of the SMS criterion.

Environmental performance bonds

The modified safe minimum standard approach to project appraisal says that a project with irreversible consequences which are unknown but could be serious should not be undertaken, unless the social costs of not undertaking the project are unacceptably high. A rather similar idea, the 'precautionary principle', is gaining widespread acceptance, at the governmental and intergovernmental levels, as a concept that should inform environmental policy. Thus, for example, Principle 15 of the June 1992 Rio Declaration is that:

> In order to protect the environment, the precautionary approach shall be widely applied by States according to their capabilities. Where there are threats of serious or irreversible damage, lack of full scientific certainty shall not be used as a reason for postponing cost-effective measures to prevent environmental degradation.[10]

[10] The Rio Declaration (United Nations 1993b) is a set of 27 short, non-binding statements of principle unanimously adopted at the United Nations Conference on Environment and Development that took place in Rio de Janeiro in June 1992.

Like the SMS, the precautionary principle can be taken as saying that there is a presumption against going ahead with projects that have serious irreversible environmental consequences, unless it can be shown that not to go ahead would involve unacceptable costs. The question which arises is whether there are any policy instruments that are consistent with this approach to irreversibility and uncertainty, which could constitute a feasible means for its implementation in such a way as to avoid an outcome that simply prohibits such projects.

Environmental performance bonds have recently been suggested as a response to the problem of devising a means of project appraisal which takes on board the ideas behind the SMS and the precautionary principle. The basic ideas involved can be discussed by considering some firm which wishes to undertake a project involving major technological innovation, so that there is no past experience according to which probabilities can be assigned to all possible outcomes. Indeed, in so far as genuine novelty is involved, there is radical uncertainty in that not all of the possible outcomes can be anticipated. An example of such a project would have been the construction of the first nuclear power plant.

We assume that there is in existence an Environmental Protection Agency (EPA), without permission from which the firm cannot go ahead with the project. The EPA takes independent expert advice on the project, and comes to a view about the worst conceivable environmental outcome of the project going ahead. Approval of the project is then conditional on the firm depositing with the EPA a bond of $x, where this is the estimate of the social cost of the worst conceivable outcome. The bond is fully or partially returned to the firm at the end of the project's lifetime, defined by the longest lasting conceived consequence of the project, not by the date at which it ceases to produce output, according to the damage actually occurring over the lifetime. Thus, if there is

no damage the firm gets back $x, plus some proportion of the interest. The withheld proportion of the interest is to cover EPA administration costs and to finance EPA research. If the damage actually occurring is $y, the firm gets back $x − $y, with appropriate interest adjustment. For $x equal to $y, the firm gets nothing back, forfeiting the full value of the bond. It is, of course, possible that $y will turn out to be greater than $x, in which case also the firm gets back $0.

The advantages claimed for such an instrument are in terms of the incentives it creates for the firm to undertake research to investigate environmental impact and means to reduce it, as well as in terms of stopping projects. Taking the latter point first, suppose that the EPA decides on $x as the size of the bond, and that the firm assesses lifetime project net returns to it as $(x − 1), and accepts that $x is the appropriate estimate of actual damage to arise. Then it will not wish to go ahead with the project. If, however, the firm took the view that actual damage would be $(x − 2) or less, it would wish to go ahead with the project. The firm has, then, an incentive to itself assess the damage that the project could cause, and to research means to reduce that damage. Further, if it does undertake the project it has an ongoing incentive to seek damage minimising methods of operation, so as to increase the eventual size of the sum returned to it, $x − $y. This incentive effect could be enhanced by having the size of the bond posted periodically adjustable. Thus, if the firm could at any point in time in the life of the project, on the basis of its research, convince the EPA that the worst conceivable lifetime damage was less than $x, the original bond could be returned and a new one for an amount less than $x be posted.

At the end of the project lifetime, the burden of proof as to the magnitude of actual damage would rest with the firm, not the EPA. The presumption would be, that is, that the bond was not returnable. It would be up to the firm to convince the EPA that actual damage was less than $x if it wished to get any of its money back. This would generate incentives for the firm to monitor damage in convincing ways, as well as to research means to minimise damage. In the event that damage up to the amount of the bond, $x, occurred, society, as represented by the EPA, would have received compensation. If damage in excess of $x had occurred, society would not receive full compensation. Recall that $x is to be set at the largest amount of damage seen as conceivable by the EPA at the outset, on the basis of expert advice. A socially responsible EPA would have an incentive to take a cautious view of the available evidence, implying a high figure for $x, so that society would not find itself uncompensated. This, it is argued, would coincide with the selfish motivations of EPA staff, since a higher $x would mean more funding available for EPA administration and research.

Environmental performance bonds are clearly an interesting idea for an addition to the range of instruments for environmental protection, given the pervasiveness of uncertainty and the need for research addressed to reducing it. In the form discussed here, they do not appear to be in use anywhere. Their usefulness would appear, as with other environmental policy instruments, to vary with particular circumstances, and clearly further consideration of the details of their possible implementation is warranted.

Discussion questions

1 In the context of a proposed hydroelectric development in a wilderness area, has the Krutilla–Fisher argument about the relative price movements that should be assumed in ECBA been affected by recent concerns about the implications for climate change of carbon dioxide emissions in fossil fuel combustion and about nuclear power stations?

2 Is the loss of a species of plant or animal necessarily of economic concern? Is this true for every species that currently exists? Do we now suffer as a consequence of earlier extinctions?

3 How could the value of an environmental performance bond be set?

4 Should the safe minimum standard approach be applied to setting standards for environment pollution? If so, how could it be done?

Problems

1 Solve Equation 15.9 for a with NPV set at 0 to get an expression for a^*, the value of a that makes the project marginal, in terms of r, X, P and D. Treat X, P and D as parameters and find $\partial a^*/\partial r$. What can be said about its sign? What is its sign for the values used in the chapter when discussing discount rate adjustment – $X = 1000$, $D = 75$ and $P = 12.5$? Confirm the answer by evaluating a^* for $r = 0.055$ and $r = 0.045$, and explain it.

2 Consider an individual for whom Y is initially £100 and $U(Y) = Y^a$, offered a bet on the toss of a fair coin at a price of £5. For each of the payouts A and B, calculate the expected value of the Y outcome, the individual's expected utility, certainty equivalent and cost of risk bearing, for a taking the values 0.9, 0.95, 0.99. 0.999 and 1.0. In situation A, the individual gets £15 if he or she calls the way the coin falls correctly, and nothing if he or she gets it wrong. In B, the payout on a correct call is £10. Note that A is actuarially a very good bet, while B is actuarially fair, and identify the circumstances in which the individual would take the bet. Note also that from Equation 15.14 the certainty equivalent is expected utility raised to the power $1/a$.

3 In Figure 15.2 with $MNB_1 = 10 - (A_1/2)$ and $MNB_2 = 20 - (A_2/2)$ known with certainty, find the levels of A_1 and A_2 (a) if there is no irreversibility, (b) if irreversibility applies but is ignored in decision making, and (c) if irreversibility is

taken into account. Hence calculate the cost of ignoring irreversibility. Suppose now that there is imperfect knowledge of the future, and a risk neutral decision maker aware of and taking into account irreversibility assigns equal probabilities to the mutually exclusive future states where $MNB_2 = 10 - (A_1/2)$ and $MNB_2 = 20 - (A_2/2)$. What will be the selected levels for A_1 and A_2?

4 The construction of a hydroelectric plant in a wilderness valley is under consideration. It is known that the valley contains an insect species found nowhere else, and the project includes relocating the insects. It is not known whether they can be successfully relocated. The pay-off matrix is

| | | State of nature | |
		F	U
Decision	P	+70	−20
	A	+20	+20

where F and U stand for favourable and unfavourable, P is the decision to go ahead with the hydroelectric plant, A is the decision to proceed instead with a coal fired plant, and the cell entries are NPV millions of £s. Favourable is the state of nature where species relocation is successful, unfavourable is where it is not. Ascertain the decisions following from adopting: (a) the principle of insufficient reason, (b) the maximin rule and (c) the maximax rule. Derive the regret matrix and ascertain the implications of the minimax regret rule, and compare the outcome with that arising from the safe minimum standard approach.

Further reading

A substantial literature now exists about pollution targets and instruments in a risky or uncertain world. References to some useful

reading in this area are given in Chapters 11 and 12. Of those mentioned there, a particularly useful source is chapter 13 from Baumol and Oates (1988) on controls versus taxes where the environment contains a stochastic component. See also Adar and Griffin (1976) for a discussion of taxes versus regulation where the EPA may make errors about the true marginal costs or benefits of abatement. You may also find it useful to follow up some of the references to the greenhouse effect in Chapter 13, given that this is an example par excellence of pollution in conditions of uncertainty. Risk and uncertainty also have a bearing, of course, on efficient and optimal resource depletion and harvesting. For reading on these matters, see Chapters 7 to 10. Dasgupta (1982) gives a good account of depletion under risk (chapter 4) and uncertainty with irreversibility (chapter 10).

The 1970s saw the publication of a number of books and papers concerning wilderness development. Many of these originated with the Washington DC organisation Resources for the Future, and involved the names Krutilla and Fisher. Particularly worth reading are Krutilla and Fisher (1975) and Krutilla (1967). Porter (1982) provides an overview and synthesis of much of this literature.

The economic analysis of individual decision making in the face of risk is covered in standard intermediate and advanced texts such as Deaton and Muellbauer (1980) or Kreps (1990).

Our treatment of option price and option value draws heavily on Ready (1995), which provides lots of references to the original literature, where important papers include Weisbrod (1964), Cicchetti and Freeman (1971), Bishop (1982), Freeman (1985), Plummer and Hartman (1986), Desvousges et al. (1987) and Boyle and Bishop (1987).

Arrow and Fisher (1974) introduced quasi-option value in the wilderness development context, on which see also Krutilla and Fisher (1975) and Fisher and Krutilla (1974). Fisher and Hanemann (1986) discuss quasi-option value in the context of pollution with irreversible consequences, and illustrate its estimation. Graham-Tomasi (1995) provides a generalisation of the setting and arguments originally proposed by Arrow and Fisher. Dixit and Pindyck (1994) consider project appraisal and show that an irreversible investment opportunity that need not be implemented immediately should only be undertaken now if its expected net present value exceeds the opportunity cost of keeping the investment option alive. The value of these options can be estimated using standard techniques for the valuation of call options developed in the financial markets literature.

Funtowicz and Ravertz (1991) consider uncertainty, as we define it, in the context of scientific knowledge about environmental problems, and argue that quality assurance requires the 'democratisation' of science. Faucheux and Froger (1995) consider decision making in the face of uncertainty in the context of policies for sustainable development. Dixit and Nalebuff (1991) is an excellent, and very easy to read, account of using game theory to make strategic choices in the context of uncertainty.

The safe minimum standard for conservation idea was originally proposed by Ciriacy-Wantrup (1968), and further developed by Bishop (1978). Barbier et al. (1994) review some contributions to the safe minimum standard and the precautionary principle in the context of biodiversity preservation; see also chapters 11, 12 and 13 in Heywood (1995). Perrings (1991) considers the theoretical content of the precautionary principle in relation to problems of uncertain environmental impact of large spatial and temporal dimension. Cameron and Aboucher (1991) give another useful discussion of the precautionary principle. As described in the text here, environmental performance bonds appear to have first been proposed by Perrings (1989), and are discussed further in Costanza and Perrings (1990): see Shogren et al. (1993) for a critique of the Costanza and Perrings proposals.

In the absence of irreversibility, the efficient levels of development would be chosen, so as to

$$\text{Maximise } F_1(A_1) + F_2(A_2)$$

where $F_1(A_1)$ and $F_2(A_2)$ are the net benefit functions. The necessary conditions are:

$$dF_1/dA_1 = 0$$
$$dF_2/dA_2 = 0 \qquad (15.44)$$

With the linear MNB functions shown in Figure 15.2, these conditions are

$$\alpha - \beta A_1 = 0$$
$$k\alpha - \beta A_2 = 0 \qquad (15.45)$$

where $k > 1$. Using the notation of Figure 15.2, solving Equation 15.45 gives:

$$A_1^{\text{NI}} = \alpha/\beta$$
$$A_2^{\text{NI}} = k(\alpha/\beta) = kA_1^{\text{NI}} \qquad (15.46)$$

If there is irreversibility but it is not taken account of in decision making, the result will be:

$$A_1' = A_1^{\text{NI}} = \alpha/\beta$$
$$A_2' = A_1' = \alpha/\beta \qquad (15.47)$$

With irreversibility taken into account in decision making, the problem is to

$$\text{Maximise } F_1(A_1) + F_2(A_2) \text{ subject to } A_1 = A_2$$

for which the Lagrangian

$$L = F_1(A_1) + F_2(A_2) + \lambda[A_1 - A_2]$$

gives the necessary conditions:

$$dlF_1/dA_1 + \lambda = 0$$
$$dF_2/dA_2 - \lambda = 0 \qquad (15.48)$$
$$A_1 - A_2 = 0$$

Substituting $\alpha - \beta A_1$ for dF_1/dA_1 and $k\alpha - \beta A_2$ for dF_2/dA_2 in Equation 15.48 and solving leads to:

$$A_1^I = A_2^I = (\alpha/\beta)\{(1+k)/2\} \qquad (15.49)$$

Comparing Equation 15.49 with 15.46 and 15.47 for $k > 1$ it is seen that

$$A_1^I > A_1^{NI} = A_1' \qquad (15.50)$$

and

$$A_2' < A_2^I < A_2^{NI} \qquad (15.51)$$

as shown in Figure 15.2.

Now consider the cost of irreversibility, when it is taken into account in decision making. As discussed in the text, this cost is the sum of the triangles **abc** and **def** in Figure 15.2. The area of **abc** is given by $0.5 \times \mathbf{ac} \times \mathbf{ab}$ where

$$\mathbf{ac} = A_1^I - A_1^{NI} = (\alpha/\beta)\{(1+k)/2\} - (\alpha/\beta)$$

$$= (\alpha/\beta)\{(k-1)/2\} \qquad (15.52)$$

and

$$\mathbf{ab} = \alpha - \beta A_1^I = \alpha - \beta(\alpha/\beta)\{(1+k)/2\}$$

$$= \{\alpha(1-k)/2\} \qquad (15.53)$$

so that:

$$\mathbf{abc} = \{\alpha^2(k-1)(1-k)\}/8\beta \qquad (15.54)$$

Proceeding in the same way, we get

$$\mathbf{ef} = A_2^{NI} - A_2^I = k(\alpha/\beta) - \{(1+k)/2\}(\alpha/\beta)$$

$$= (\alpha/\beta)\{(k-1)/2\} \qquad (15.55)$$

and

$$\mathbf{de} = k\alpha - \beta A_2^I = k\alpha - \beta(\alpha/\beta)\{(1+k)/2\}$$

$$= \alpha\{(k-1)/2\} \qquad (15.56)$$

so that:

$$\mathbf{def} = \{\alpha^2(k-1)(k-1)\}/8\beta \qquad (15.57)$$

Comparing Equations 15.53 and 15.56 we see that **ab** and **de** are equal, as stated in the text discussion of Figure 15.2, but of opposite sign. Equation 15.54 shows **abc** as negative, so to get the cost of irreversibility we use the absolute value; that is, 15.54 multiplied by -1, for **abc** plus **def**. This gives

$$|\mathbf{abc}| + \mathbf{def} = 2 \times \{\alpha^2(k-1)^2\}/8\beta$$

$$= \{\alpha^2(k-1)^2\}/4\beta \qquad (15.58)$$

for the cost of irreversibility.

Now consider the cost of ignoring irreversibility in decision making. This leads to A_1^{NI} instead of A_1^I, and to A_2' instead of A_2^I. As shown in Figure 15.2, in the first period there is a gain equal to the area of triangle **abc**, and in the second a loss equal to the area **edhi**. If **edhi** > **abc**, there is a net loss. Since **abc** and **def** have the same areas, this condition is **edhi** > **def**. Clearly, **edhi** is greater than **def** if **ie** = **ef**, which it is as **ie** = **ac** and by Equations 15.52 and 15.55 **ac** and **ef** are equal.

So there is a cost to ignoring irreversibility when it exists. For the linear MNB functions used in Figure 15.2, we can show that the cost of ignoring irreversibility is greater than the cost of irreversibility. The cost of ignoring irreversibility is area **edhi**, which is area **hgd** plus area **gdei**. Consider the latter first. We have

$$\mathbf{gdei} = \mathbf{de} \times \mathbf{ie} = \alpha\{(k-1)/2\} \times \mathbf{ie}$$

using Equation 15.56 for **de**. The distance **ie** is $A_2^I - A_2'$, so that using Equations 15.49 and 15.47

$$\mathbf{gdei} = \alpha\{(k-1)/2\} \times [(\alpha/\beta)\{(1+k)/2 - (\alpha/\beta)]$$

which on simplifying is:

$$\mathbf{gdei} = \{\alpha^2(k-1)^2\}/4\beta \qquad (15.59)$$

Comparing Equations 15.58 and 15.59 gives **gdei** equal to the cost of irreversibility. But the cost of ignoring irreversibility is **gdei** plus **hdg**, so the cost of ignoring irreversibility is greater than the cost of irreversibility.

Appendix 15.2 Irreversibility, development and risk

Consider first the case of a risk neutral decision maker where there is no irreversibility. With the two possible period 2 benefit functions as $F_2^1(A_2)$ and $F_2^2(A_2)$, where the respective probabilities are p and q with $q = 1 - p$, the decision maker's problem is to

$$\text{Maximise } F_1(A_1) + E[F_2(A_2)]$$

$$= F_1(A_1) + pF_2^1(A_2) + qF_2^2(A_2)$$

for which the necessary conditions are:

$$dF_1/dA_1 = 0$$
$$pdF_2^1/dA_2 + qdF_2^2/dA_2 = 0 \qquad (15.60)$$

For the linear MNB functions of Figure 15.5, we have

$$dF_1/dA_1 = \alpha - \beta A_1$$
$$dF_2^1/dA_2 = \alpha - \beta A_2 \qquad (15.61)$$
$$dF_2^2/dA_2 = k\alpha - \beta A_2$$

and substituting these into Equations 15.60 gives the necessary conditions as:

$$\alpha - \beta A_1 = 0 \qquad (15.62)$$

$$p(\alpha - \beta A_2) + q(k\alpha - \beta A_2) = 0 \qquad (15.63)$$

From Equation 15.62

$$A_1^{RNI} = \alpha/\beta \qquad (15.64)$$

and from Equation 15.63

$$A_2^{RNI} = (\alpha/\beta)(p + qk) \qquad (15.65)$$

give the period 1 and 2 levels of A, where the superscript RNI is for 'risk, no irreversibility'. The effect of the introduction of risk alone can be seen by comparing Equations 15.64 and 15.65 with Equation 15.46 from Appendix 15.1. There is no effect on the period 1 level of A. The size of the effect on the second period level depends on the sizes of p and q, but except for $p = 0$ it is the case that $A_2^{RNI} < A_2^{NI}$. This is because 15.65 can be rewritten, using $q = 1 - p$, as

$$A_2^{RNI} = k(\alpha/\beta) + p(\alpha/\beta)(1 - k)$$

where the second term is negative.

With irreversibility incorporated into the decision problem it becomes

Maximise $F_1(A_1) + E[F_2(A_2)]$

subject to $A_1 = A_2$

for which the Lagrangian is

$$L = F_1(A_1) + pF_2^1(A_2) + qF_2^2(A_2) + \lambda[A_1 - A_2]$$

giving as necessary conditions

$$dF_1/dA_1 + \lambda = 0$$
$$pdF_2^1/dA_2 + qdF_2^2/dA_2 - \lambda = 0 \qquad (15.66)$$
$$A_1 = A_2$$

Substituting for the derivatives in Equation 15.66 from 15.61 and solving leads to

$$A_1^{IR} = A_2^{IR} = \{\alpha(1 + p + qk)\}/2\beta \qquad (15.67)$$

where the superscript IR stands for 'irreversibility, risk'. In Appendix 15.1 the result for the case where there is irreversibility but perfect future knowledge was established as:

$$A_1^{I} = A_2^{I} = (\alpha/\beta)\{(1 + k)/2\} \qquad (15.68)$$

Consider the first period levels. A_1^{IR} is less than A_1^{I} if

$$\alpha(1 + p + qk)/2\beta < (\alpha/\beta)\{(1 + k)/2\} \qquad (15.69)$$

which using $q = 1 - p$ reduces to

$$p < pk$$

which follows from $k > 1$, for any $p > 0$. So, A_1^{IR} is less than A_1^{I}, as shown in Figure 15.5. The condition for $A_2^{IR} < A_2^{I}$, as shown in Figure 15.5, is also the expression 15.69, so that is also established for $k > 1, p > 0$.

Figure 15.5 also shows $A_1^{IR} > A_1^{NI}$ and $A_2^{IR} > A_2'$. From 15.56 in Appendix 15.1 and 15.67 the condition for $A_1^{IR} > A_1^{NI}$ is

$$\{\alpha(1 + p + qk)\}/2\beta > \alpha/\beta \qquad (15.70)$$

which, using $q = 1 - p$, reduces to

$$k > p(k - 1)$$

which is true for $k > 1$ and $0 < p < 1$. The condition for $A_2^{IR} > A_2'$ is also expression 15.70.

CHAPTER 16

Environmental input–output modelling

A model is simply an ordered set of assumptions about a complex system. ... The model we have constructed is, like every other model imperfect, oversimplified, and unfinished.

Meadows *et al.* (1972), page 20

Introduction

Appropriate environmental policy measures require a detailed understanding of the environmental impact of particular economic activities, and hence there is the need to model the relationships between the economy and the environment. For instance, which economic activities result in the emission of carbon dioxide gases, and by how much would particular economic activity levels have to be reduced to bring about a reduction of, say, 20% in CO_2 emissions? What level of 'carbon tax' would be necessary to bring about such a reduction? What would be the effects of such a tax on different types of household? For many policy purposes it is not enough to know simply the nature and direction of the changes that would be brought about by a particular measure (or by the failure to implement a measure): a quantitative estimate of the effects of the policy (or of its absence) is needed. It is for this purpose that models of interaction between the economy and the environment are constructed.

By using models to assess and compare the simulated quantitative effects of a range of feasible policy options, governments can hope to identify the 'best' (or least bad) policy or policy mix, avoid policy combinations that are inconsistent or that work in opposite directions, and achieve some kind of optimal trade-off between different, and potentially conflicting economic and environmental objectives[1].

Moreover, such simulation exercises underpin the formulation and implementation of proactive environmental policies, which attempt to anticipate or avoid undesirable outcomes by appropriate preventive measures. Although formal simulation modelling is not a precondition for proactive environmental policies, it can powerfully influence public attitudes and policy making, a recent example being predictions and simulations of the effects of greenhouse gases on global warming. In the absence of quantitative models of economy–environment interaction, policy is more likely to be reactive rather than proactive, which may be too late if environmental damage is irreversible (for example, species extinction).

A variety of model types have been used to examine economy–environment interactions: input–output models, computable general equilibrium models, and linear and non-linear programming (optimisation) models. This chapter is largely devoted to a discussion of environmental input–output (I/O) models and their application, which have been used quite extensively in environmental economics, particularly in studies related to energy and pollution. They are the basis for computable general equilibrium (CGE), models, which will also be discussed. It must be stressed that the availability and quality of data, both economic and environmental, are serious impediments to the development of all kinds of models of links between the economy and the environment.

[1] Of course, what is optimal to a government may not seem optimal to some interest groups, such as environmentalists, or the unemployed, or the political opposition, each of whom may, and most probably will, have different social welfare functions (or different perceptions of *the* Social Welfare function), and will attach different weights to particular economic and environmental outcomes.

Table 16.1 Input–output transactions table ($ million)

Sales to		Intermediate sectors			Final demand		Total output
		Agriculture	Manufacturing	Services	Households	Exports	
	Purchases from						
Intermediate sectors	Agriculture	0	400	0	500	100	1000
	Manufacturing	350	0	150	800	700	2000
	Services	100	200	0	300	0	600
Primary Inputs	Imports	250	600	50			
	Wages	200	500	300			
	Other value added	100	300	100			
	Total input	1000	2000	600			

The following section presents and explains the basic input–output model and its solution, while the next section shows how the basic model can be extended to incorporate economy–environment interactions, and includes examples of environmental input–output models and their application. These applications are concerned with the 'real' side of the economy, that is, with physical or constant value flows. We then show how the equations of the model can be reformulated to analyse the cost and price implications of environmental policies, such as pollution taxes, and how these results can be used to investigate the distributional implications of such policies. The last section of the chapter reviews the nature of CGE models and their application to environmental problems. The first appendix makes extensive use of matrix algebra to present a very general framework for environmental input–output analysis, while the second works through the algebra of the simple two-sector CGE model used in the final section of the chapter.

Input–output analysis

I/O models incorporate a number of simplifying assumptions which require a degree of caution in interpreting their results, but they are mathematically tractable and less demanding of data than many other multisectoral models. The basis for input–output modelling is the availability of suitable eco-nomic data, and we begin with a discussion of the accounting conventions according to which such data is made available.

Input–output accounting

The basis of the input–output system is the transactions table, which is essentially an extended version of the national accounts in which inter-industry transactions – that is, flows of goods and services between industries – are explicitly included and indeed form the centrepiece of the system of accounts. This contrasts with the conventional national accounts in which interindustry transactions are 'netted out', and the accounts record only the value added by each industry, and the value of sales to final buyers.

Table 16.1 is a hypothetical example of a transactions table, in which all production activities in the economy have been allocated to one of three sectors. Looking across any row of the table shows what the sector on the left sold to each sector at the top, e.g.

Agriculture sales =	(to)
0	(Agriculture)
+400	(Manufacturing)
+0	(Services)
+500	(Households)
+100	(Exports)
= 1000	(Total output)

Notice that sales are divided between those to intermediate sectors (agriculture, manufacturing and services) and to final demand (households and exports).[2]

The sum of intermediate and final sales for each sector is gross, or total, output. Again, for simplicity, we assume no government or investment expenditure, which normally would be included as additional components of final demand.

Looking down any column of the table shows what the sector listed at the top purchased from each sector on the left, for example

Manufacturing
purchases =   (from)
    400   (Agriculture)
    +0   (Manufacturing)
    +200   (Services)
    +600   (Imports)
    +500   (Wages)
    +300   (OVA)
    = 2000   (Total input)

Notice that purchases are divided between those from intermediate sectors (agriculture, manufacturing and services), and so-called 'primary input' purchases (imports, wages and other value added).

Like the national accounts, transactions tables are normally compiled on an annual basis. They are also typically expressed in value terms, in order to provide a standard unit of account across sectors, though in principle it would be possible to use sector-specific units of account (tonnes, metres, numbers, therms), or a combination of physical and monetary units.

A real transactions table will normally be larger than Table 16.1 because more sectors will be separately identified, but the interpretation of it will be the same. A recently-compiled input–output table for the UK, for example, contains 123 intermediate sectors, and the most recent table for the United States has 480 intermediate sectors. Tables of this size provide a highly detailed snapshot of the

structure of an economy in a particular year, and show the pervasive interdependence of sectors and agents.

Because of the accounting conventions adopted in the construction of an I/O transactions table, the following will always be true:

(1) For each industry: Total output ≡ Total input, that is, the sum of the elements in any row is equal to the sum of the elements in the corresponding column.
(2) For the table as a whole: Total intermediate sales ≡ Total intermediate purchases, and Total final demand ≡ Total primary input

Note the use here of the identity sign, ≡, reflecting the fact that these are accounting identities, which always hold in an I/O transactions table.

The standard national income accounts can be readily derived from the input–output accounts. For example, GDP can be derived from Table 16.1

(1) On the Income side as:

Wages $1000m
+OVA $500m
=GDP $1500m

or

(2) On the Expenditure side as:

Household expenditure $1600m
+Exports $800m
−Imports $900m
=GDP $1500m

Reading across rows the necessary equality of total output with the sum of its uses for each industry or sector can be written as a set of 'balance equations':

$$X_i \equiv \sum_j X_{ij} + Y_i \quad i = 1, \ldots, n \quad (16.1)$$

where

X_i = total output of industry i
X_{ij} = sales of commodity i to industry j
Y_i = sales of commodity i to final demand
n = the number of industries (3 in Table 16.1)

---

[2] As a further simplification, transactions between undertakings within the same sector (intra-industry transactions) have been netted out, so that the main diagonal of Table 16.1 has zeroes everywhere.

Input–output modelling

To go from accounting to analysis, the basic input–output modelling assumption is that

$$X_{ij} = a_{ij}X_j \qquad (16.2)$$

where a_{ij} is a constant. That is, it is assumed that intermediate inputs are constant proportions of the output of the purchasing industry. So for example if X_j represents the output of the steel industry (tonnes valued at constant prices) and X_{ij} records purchases of iron ore (tonnes valued at constant prices) by the steel industry, we are assuming that iron ore purchases are a constant fraction of the value of steel output (expressed in constant prices); if the output of steel doubles, inputs (purchases) of iron ore will double.

Substituting Equation 16.2 into 16.1 gives

$$X_i = \sum_j a_{ij}X_j + Y_i \quad i = 1,\ldots,n \quad (16.3)$$

as a system of n linear equations in $2n$ variables, the X_i and Y_i, and n^2 coefficients, the a_{ij}. If the Y_i – the final demand levels – are specified, there are n unknown X_i – the gross output levels – which can be solved for using the n equations. Given that the equations are linear, the solution can readily be accomplished using matrix algebra.[3] In matrix notation Equations 16.3 become

$$\mathbf{X} = \mathbf{AX} + \mathbf{Y}$$

which on rearrangement is

$$\mathbf{X} - \mathbf{AX} = \mathbf{Y} \qquad (16.4)$$

where $\mathbf{X}$ is an $n \times 1$ vector of gross outputs, X_i, $\mathbf{A}$ is an $n \times n$ matrix of intermediate input coefficients, a_{ij}, and $\mathbf{Y}$ is an $n \times 1$ vector of final demands, Y_i.

With $\mathbf{I}$ as an $n \times n$ identity matrix, Equation 16.4 can be written as

$$(\mathbf{I} - \mathbf{A})\mathbf{X} = \mathbf{Y}$$

[3] Readers who are unfamiliar with matrix algebra will find the essentials in one of the many texts on elementary mathematics for economists. The exposition in Chiang (1984) is particularly clear and is related to application in input–output analysis.

which has the solution

$$\mathbf{X} = (\mathbf{I} - \mathbf{A})^{-1}\mathbf{Y} \qquad (16.5)$$

where $(\mathbf{I} - \mathbf{A})^{-1}$ is the 'inverse' of $(\mathbf{I} - \mathbf{A})$. This solution can be written as

$$\mathbf{X} = \mathbf{LY} \qquad (16.6)$$

where $\mathbf{L} = (\mathbf{I} - \mathbf{A})^{-1}$, and the notation $\mathbf{L}$ used as this inverse is often referred to as the 'Leontief inverse' in recognition of the progenitor of input–output analysis, Wassily Leontief.

This is the basic input–output model. Its use involves a number of assumptions – notably Equation 16.2 and the constancy of the a_{ij} – which are clearly approximations to reality, but used judiciously input–output modelling can be a cost-effective and powerful tool in a number of applications. In the next section it is shown how the basic model can be extended to incorporate economy–environment interactions. Before doing that, it will be useful to consider further what it is that the basic model does, and to work through a numerical illustration of its application based on Table 16.1.

For a three-sector economy, the matrix Equation 16.6 can be written in ordinary algebra as the three equations

$$\begin{aligned} X_1 &= l_{11}Y_1 + l_{12}Y_2 + l_{13}Y_3 \\ X_2 &= l_{21}Y_1 + l_{22}Y_2 + l_{23}Y_3 \qquad (16.7) \\ X_3 &= l_{31}Y_1 + l_{32}Y_2 + l_{33}Y_3 \end{aligned}$$

where the l_{ij} are the elements of the Leontief inverse, $\mathbf{L}$. Each equation here gives the gross output of an industry as depending on the levels of final demand for each of the three commodities. The l_{ij} give the level of output in the ith industry to meet the direct and indirect requirements for a unit of final demand for commodity j. Thus, for example, the delivery of one unit of commodity 2 to final demand requires an output level l_{22} in industry 2. This level will meet both the direct requirement and the indirect requirement arising from the fact that commodity 2 is used in the production of commodities 1 and 3, which are used in the production of commodity 2. The actual gross output requirement for commodity 2, X_2, depends, in the same way, on the levels of delivery of all three commodities to final demand, as given by l_{21}, l_{22} and l_{23}, and similarly for X_1 and X_3.

From the data in Table 16.1, and using Equation 16.2, the elements of the matrix $\mathbf{A}$ are calculated as follows:

$a_{11} = 0$, $a_{12} = 400/2000 = 0.2000$, $a_{13} = 0$

$a_{21} = 350/1000 = 0.3500$, $a_{22} = 0$,

$a_{23} = 150/600 = 0.2500$

$a_{31} = 100/1000 = 0.1000$,

$a_{32} = 200/2000 = 0.1000$, $a_{33} = 0$

Hence,

$$\mathbf{A} = \begin{bmatrix} 0.0000 & 0.20000 & 0.0000 \\ 0.3500 & 0.0000 & 0.2500 \\ 0.1000 & 0.1000 & 0.0000 \end{bmatrix}$$

and

$$\mathbf{I} - \mathbf{A} = \begin{bmatrix} 1.0000 & -0.2000 & 0.0000 \\ -0.3500 & 1.0000 & -0.2500 \\ -0.1000 & -0.1000 & 1.0000 \end{bmatrix}$$

so that[4]

$$\mathbf{L} = (\mathbf{I} - \mathbf{A})^{-1} = \begin{bmatrix} 1.0833 & 0.2222 & 0.0556 \\ 0.4167 & 1.1111 & 0.2778 \\ 0.1500 & 0.1333 & 1.0333 \end{bmatrix}$$

Substituting into Equation 16.6 gives

$$\mathbf{X} = \begin{bmatrix} 1.0833 & 0.2222 & 0.0556 \\ 0.4167 & 1.1111 & 0.2778 \\ 0.1500 & 0.1333 & 1.0333 \end{bmatrix} \begin{bmatrix} Y_1 \\ Y_2 \\ Y_3 \end{bmatrix}$$

which is the same as:

$X_1 = 1.0833Y_1 + 0.2222Y_2 + 0.0556Y_3$

$X_2 = 0.4167Y_1 + 1.1111Y_2 + 0.2778Y_3$

$X_3 = 0.1500Y_1 + 0.1333Y_2 + 1.0333Y_3$

---

[4] While the inverse for a small matrix can be found using a calculating machine, using a method described in, for example, Chiang (1984), the calculation is tedious and prone to error. Even for small matrices, it is better to use the routine included in most spreadsheet packages for PCs.

If the Y_i here are replaced by the total final demand levels from Table 16.1 – $Y_1 = 600$ for agriculture, $Y_2 = 1500$ for manufacturing, $Y_3 = 300$ for services – this gives the gross output levels

Agriculture	$X_1 = 999.96$
Manufacturing	$X_2 = 2000.01$
Services	$X_3 = 599.94$

which are the same, allowing for inevitable small errors on account of rounding, as the total output levels shown in Table 16.1. This must be the case, given that the final demand levels are the same.

Now suppose that it is known that there will be an increase in the export demand for all commodities. What are the implications for gross output levels? Suppose that the new export demand levels are

Agriculture	200
Manufacturing	1000
Services	100

so that the new final demand levels are:

$$Y_1 = 700$$
$$Y_2 = 1800$$
$$Y_3 = 400$$

Using these with the elements of the Leontief inverse, as above, gives as the new gross output levels:

$X_1 = (1.0833 \times 700) + (0.2222 \times 1800)$
$\qquad + (0.0556 \times 400) = 1180.51$

$X_2 = (0.4167 \times 700) + (1.1111 \times 1800)$
$\qquad + (0.2778 \times 400) = 2402.79$

$X_3 = (0.1500 \times 700) + (0.1333 \times 1800)$
$\qquad + (0.0333 \times 400) = 758.26$

Note that for every industry the increase in gross output exceeds the increase in the final demand for the commodity that it produces. This is because commodities are used in the production of commodities. Input–output analysis is the investigation of the quantitative implications of such inter-industry relations.

Environmental input–output analysis

Proposals to extend input–output tables and models to include aspects of economy–environment links were first mooted in the late 1960s. The next 10–15 years saw a rapid development of environmental input–output models. Although there are some important differences between the models developed by different authors – so that for particular applications the choice of model is important – they all share a common basis of input–output methodology, including constant returns to scale production functions which permit no substitution between inputs (Leontief production functions), as described in the preceding section. A general input–output framework for economy–environment linkages is presented, using matrix algebra, in Appendix 16.1. Here we consider some particular, but useful and widely used, approaches to accounting and modelling.

Suppose that in addition to the data of Table 16.1 we also know that the use of oil by the three industries was

Agriculture	Manufacturing	Services
50	400	60

where the units are petajoules (PJ). A joule is a unit of measurement used in recording the use of energy in the economy (one joule is the energy conveyed by one watt of power for one second) and the prefix 'peta' stands for 10^{15}. With O_i for oil use by the ith industry, paralleling Equation 16.2, assume

$$O_i = r_i X_i \tag{16.8}$$

so that

$r_1 = 0.05$ for agriculture

$r_2 = 0.2$ for manufacturing

$r_3 = 0.1$ for services

These coefficients can be used to figure the implications for total oil use of changes in deliveries to final demand by applying them to the changes in the X_i associated with the change in final demand. Thus, for example,

in the previous section the following changes to final demand deliveries

$$\Delta Y_1 = 100 \quad \Delta Y_2 = 300 \quad \Delta Y_3 = 100$$

were found to imply

$$\Delta X_1 = 180.51 \quad \Delta X_2 = 402.79 \quad \Delta X_3 = 158.26$$

so that the oil use changes are

$$\Delta O_1 = 9.03 \quad \Delta O_2 = 80.56 \quad \Delta O_3 = 15.83$$

with an increase in total oil use from 510 to 615.42 PJ.

A similar approach can be used in regard to waste emissions. If the emissions levels of a particular kind, E_i, are known, then, paralleling Equation 16.8, assume

$$E_i = w_i X_i \tag{16.9}$$

and the implications of final demand changes for these emissions can be figured as just described for oil. Clearly, the same procedure can be followed for any number of particular kinds of emissions (or resource inputs), if the data is available.

In a recent study McNicoll and Blackmore (1993) calculated emissions coefficients for 12 pollutants for a (preliminary) 29-sector version of the 1989 input–output tables for Scotland. Coefficients were expressed in tonnes per £ million output, except radioactivity, which is measured in thousand becquerels. Applications of the model included a number of simulation studies, two of which involved assessing the impact on pollution emissions of (i) partial substitution by consumers of coal for gas, and (ii) partial substitution of road and air transport for rail transport. For SIM1 (coal for gas), final demand for coal was reduced by £30m, while that for gas was increased by £30m. For SIM2 (greater use of rail), final demand for road transport was reduced by £50m, and air transport by £20m, while final demand for rail transport was raised by £70m. In both cases aggregate final demand was kept unchanged in order to show the effects of different patterns of expenditure. Although the figures used are purely illustrative, the approach and discussion are suggestive of how environmental input–output models can be used to quantify and evaluate the effects of policies which influence the pattern, as well as the level, of economic activity. Especially in SIM2, for example, it is interesting that although rail travel is usually considered more environmentally friendly than road or air transport, the substitution suggests an increase in the output of certain pollutants.

Results of the simulations are summarised in Table 16.2. The left-hand columns record the estimated effects of the substitutions on sector outputs, compared with actual 1989 outputs. The right-hand columns show the estimated changes in emissions which would result from the substitutions. For SIM1, the

switch from coal to gas results in a fall in the output of all pollutants except solid radioactive waste. For SIM2, the switch from road/air to rail, the results are less clear cut; emissions of six pollutants decline, but six increase.

As well as permitting this kind of analysis, input–output methods can be used to account for resource use and/or pollution generation in terms of deliveries to final demand. Consider the case of resource, oil, use first. For the three industry case, using Equation 16.8 with Equation 16.7 gives

$$O_1 = r_1 X_1 = r_1 l_{11} Y_1 + r_1 l_{12} Y_2 + r_1 l_{13} Y_3$$
$$O_2 = r_2 X_2 = r_2 l_{21} Y_1 + r_2 l_{22} Y_2 + r_2 l_{23} Y_3$$
$$O_3 = r_3 X_3 = r_3 l_{31} Y_1 + r_3 l_{32} Y_2 + r_3 l_{33} Y_3$$

Table 16.2   SIM1 and SIM2 impacts on outputs and emissions

Sector	Δ Gross output[a]		Emission	Δ Emissions[b]	
	SIM1	SIM2		SIM1	SIM2
1	−0.04	+0.64	CO_2	−404.7	−287.7
2	−0.001	−0.04	CO_2(weight)	−110.4	−78.5
3	−0.02	+0.22	SO_2	−3.0	+0.11
4	−30.21	+0.08	Black smoke	−0.35	−0.06
5	−0.02	−0.02	NO_x	−0.88	−3.84
6	−0.73	−1.06	VOC	−0.14	−3.25
7	−0.27	+2.25	CO	−0.35	−21.16
8	+30.98	+0.60	Methane	−11.46	+0.09
9	−0.01	+0.17	Waste	−655.2	+24.26
10	−0.11	+0.07	Lead	−0.000005	−0.01
11	+0.03	+1.02	RA air	−0.001	+0.009
12	+0.004	+0.27	RA water	−0.00006	+0.0005
13	−0.09	+0.21	RA solid	0.0143	+0.121
14	−0.15	+0.14			
15	−0.009	+1.20			
16	−0.19	+2.13			
17	+0.02	+0.83			
18	+0.05	+0.97			
19	−0.08	+0.48			
20	+0.01	+1.65			
21	−0.42	+15.25			
22	+0.02	+70.29			
23	−0.04	−49.2			
24	+0.01	+0.21			
25	+0.09	−20.49			
26	+0.61	+2.80			
27	+2.64	+5.47			
28	−0.24	+2.89			
House	−5.84	+71.47			

Source: adapted from McNicoll and Blackmore (1993)

[a] Units are £ × 10^6.

[b] Units are tonnes × 10^3, except for RA.

and adding vertically gives

$$O_1 + O_2 + O_3 = (r_1 l_{11} + r_2 l_{21} + r_3 l_{31})Y_1$$
$$+ (r_1 l_{12} + r_2 l_{22} + r_3 l_{32})Y_2$$
$$+ (r_1 l_{13} + r_2 l_{23} + r_3 l_{33})Y_3$$

which can be written as

$$O_1 + O_2 + O_3 = i_1 Y_1 + i_2 Y_2 + i_3 Y_3 \qquad (16.10)$$

where $i_1 = r_1 l_{11} + r_2 l_{21} + r_3 l_{31}$ etc. The left-hand side of Equation 16.10 is total oil use. The right-hand side allocates that total as between final demand deliveries via the coefficients i. These coefficients give the oil intensities of final demand deliveries, oil use per unit, taking account of direct and indirect use. The coefficient i_1, for example, is the amount of oil use attributable to the delivery to final demand of one unit of agricultural output, when account is taken both of the direct use of oil in agriculture and of its indirect use via the use of inputs of manufacturing and services, the production of which uses oil inputs.

For the data on oil use given above with the data of Table 16.1, the oil intensities are

Agriculture	Manufacturing	Services
0.1525	0.2467	0.1617

which with final demand deliveries of

Agriculture	Manufacturing	Services
600	1500	300

gives total oil use, 510 PJ, allocated across final demand deliveries as

Agriculture	Manufacturing	Services
91.50	370.05	48.51

Note that as compared with the industry uses of oil from which the r_i were calculated, these numbers have more oil use attributed to agriculture and less to manufacturing and services. This reflects the fact that producing agricultural output uses oil indirectly when it uses inputs from manufacturing and services.

In matrix algebra, which would be the basis for doing the calculations where the number of sectors is realistically large, n, the foregoing is

$$O = RX = RLY = iY \qquad (16.11)$$

to define the intensities, where

O is total resource use (a scalar)

R is a $1 \times n$ vector of industry resource input coefficients

i is a $1 \times n$ vector of resource intensities for final demand deliveries

and **X**, **L** and **Y** are as previously defined. The resource uses attributable to final demand deliveries can be calculated as

$$O = R^*Y \qquad (16.11')$$

where

O is an $n \times 1$ vector of resource use levels

R* is an $n \times n$ matrix with the elements of **R** along the diagonal and 0s elsewhere.

With suitable changes of notation, all of this applies equally to calculation concerning waste emissions. Where there are several, m, resources, or types of emissions, being considered the vector **R** in Equation 16.11 becomes an $m \times n$ matrix, and with suitable dimensional adjustments elsewhere, the above carries through, and all the intensities for final demand deliveries can be calculated in one operation.

In the case of CO_2 emissions arising in fossil fuel combustion, it is not necessary to know the emissions levels for each industry, as these can be calculated using data on the fossil fuel inputs to each industry and a standard set of coefficients which give the amount of CO_2 released per unit of a particular fossil fuel burned:[5]

	Tonnes CO_2 per PJ
Natural gas	54 900
Oil	73 200
Black coal	104 100
Brown coal	112 700

In this case, fossil fuel intensities can be converted to CO_2 intensities by using these coef-

[5] Actually slightly different coefficient sets can be found in different sources: for an examination of the sensitivity of results to such variations see Common and Salma (1992a).

ficients and aggregating across the fuels. Table 16.3 gives results so obtained (Common and Salma 1992a) for Australia for 1986/7 for CO_2 intensities and levels for deliveries to final demand: the figures in parentheses are rankings. A CO_2 intensity is the quantity of CO_2 emitted per unit delivery to final demand. In the first column of Table 16.3 CO_2 units are thousands of tonnes, and final demand delivery units are millions of Australian dollars. The first point to note here is that deliveries of the output of the Agriculture, forestry and fishing sector to final demand are relatively CO_2, and fossil fuel, intensive, ranking sixth, and ahead of several manufacturing sectors. This counterintuitive result arises because the sector is a large indirect user of fossil fuels, with, parti-

cularly, large inputs of fertiliser, the production of which is fossil fuel intensive. It means that expansion of Australia's agricultural industry would, per unit, increase Australian CO_2 emissions by more than expansion of several manufacturing outputs. A second point worthy of noting explicitly is that while service sectors – such as Wholesale and retail, repairs, or Public administration, defence – rank low by intensity, they climb well up the ranking according to emissions levels, on account of their large size. The third point to be made here concerns electricity. It is frequently stated that for Australia – and the case is much the same in most other industrialised economies – electricity generation accounts for approximately 45% of CO_2 emissions associated with fossil fuel combus-

Table 16.3 CO_2 intensities and levels for final demand deliveries, Australia 1986/7.

Sector	CO_2 Intensity[a]	CO_2 Total[b]	Percentage of total
Agriculture, forestry, fishing, hunting	1.8007 (6)	13.836(8)	4.74
Mining	0.9854(11)	9.953(12)	3.41
Meat and milk products	1.0368(10)	8.515(13)	2.92
Food products	1.5325(8)	11.540(10)	4.00
Beverages and tobacco	0.9213(12)	3.399(20)	1.17
Textiles, clothing and footwear	0.5561(24)	3.062(21)	1.05
Wood, wood products, furniture	0.8771(14)	2.034(23)	0.70
Paper, products, printing, publishing	0.8707(15)	1.390(24)	0.48
Chemicals	1.2385(9)	2.579(22)	0.88
Petroleum and coal products	10.7272(2)	37.788(2)	12.95
Non-metallic mineral products	2.1980(5)	0.357(26)	0.12
Basic metals, products	4.4977(4)	20.25(4)	6.94
Fabricated metal products	1.7055(7)	3.484(19)	1.19
Transport equipment	0.7406(20)	4.706(17)	1.61
Machinery and equipment	0.8834(13)	5.296(16)	1.82
Miscellaneous manufacturing	0.7727(18)	1.012(25)	0.35
Electricity	15.2449(1)	43.747(1)	14.99
Gas	9.9663(3)	4.675(18)	1.60
Water	0.6680(22)	0.205(27)	0.07
Construction	0.7567(19)	28.111(3)	9.64
Wholesale and retail, repairs	0.4978(25)	18.225(5)	6.25
Transport, storage, communication	0.8157(17)	13.386(9)	4.58
Finance, property, business services	0.6242(23)	5.719(14)	1.96
Residential property	0.1992(27)	5.504(15)	1.89
Public administration, defence	0.8409(16)	14.352(7)	4.92
Community services	0.4437(26)	17.802(6)	6.10
Recreational, personal services	0.7205(21)	10.830(11)	3.71
Total		291.756	100.00

Source: adapted from Common and Salma (1992a)

[a] Tonnes $\times 10^3 (\$A \times 10^6)$
[b] Tonnes $\times 10^6$

tion. In Table 16.3, electricity accounts for only some 15% of total emissions. It is true that 45% of emissions are through the stacks of power stations. However, much of the electricity so generated is used as input to other productive activities, rather than consumed by households. The accounting in Table 16.3 attributes the emissions associated with electricity as an intermediate commodity to the sectors that use electricity in that way, and the CO_2 total for electricity relates solely to its use by final consumers. For many purposes, accounting for emissions in terms of final demand deliveries is more useful than accounting in terms of the location of fossil fuel combustion. It aligns, as the next section will show, with the impact of carbon taxation on relative prices.

The work from which Table 16.3 is taken also conducted some simulation experiments which illustrate the usefulness of input–output analysis in exploring the potential for alternative routes to the abatement of CO_2 emissions. Some examples are as follows. Cutting the final demand for electricity by 10% would reduce total emissions by 1.5%. Cutting the final demand for the output of the construction industry by 10% would reduce total emissions by 1.0%. This surprising result arises because, when indirect use is taken account of, construction is a relatively CO_2 intensive sector, and it is a large sector. If in the matrix of inter-industry coefficients, **A**, those for electricity inputs are all cut by 10%, then for the original set of final demands, total CO_2 emissions reduce by 4.4%. If, instead, the coefficients for basic metal inputs to all industries are cut by 10%, there is a 1.4% reduction in total emissions. Given that the basic metal industry is relatively energy and CO_2 intensive, conserving on inputs of its commodity is energy conserving and CO_2 abating. Materials conserving technical change is energy conserving, and CO_2 abating, because the extraction and processing of materials uses energy, which is currently predominantly based on fossil fuel use.

Costs and prices

In the preceding sections inputs and outputs were expressed in constant value terms for economic flows and in physical units for environmental extractions (resource inputs) and insertions (waste emissions). The accounting and analysis was concerned with the 'real' side of the economy, and with questions such as 'if final demand changes, what will happen to emissions?'. However, many of the most interesting and controversial issues in environmental economics involve questions of costs and prices. For instance, how would a carbon tax affect the prices facing households, and hence the cost of living?

These questions can be explored using the dual of the input–output model system outlined above. Analogous to Equation 16.1 based on the rows of the transactions table, we can write for the columns of that table

$$X_j \equiv \sum_i X_{ij} + M_j + W_j + \text{OVA}_j \qquad j = 1, \ldots, n$$
(16.12)

that is, the value of output of sector j covers the cost of purchases from other sectors $\sum_i X_{ij}$, plus the cost of imports used in the production of product M_j, plus labour costs, W_j, plus other value added, OVA_j, which includes profit and is essentially the balancing item in the accounting identity. To simplify the exposition, we aggregate imports, labour costs and other value added, so that

$$X_j \equiv \sum_i X_{ij} + V_j \qquad j = 1, \ldots, n \quad (16.13)$$

where V_j is primary input cost. We now assume as before that intermediate inputs are a fixed proportion of industry output, as in Equation 16.2. Substituting in Equation 16.13 this gives

$$X_j = \sum_i a_{ij} X_j + V_j \qquad j = 1, \ldots, n \quad (16.14)$$

Now, the inter-industry flows in the transactions table are expenditure flows, that is price times quantity. When we use the data to consider questions about the 'real' side of the economy, we are dealing with commodities where quantities are measured in units which are 'millions of dollars worth'. Such quantities have, in the accounts, prices which are unity. With P_j for the price of the jth commodity, Equation 16.14 can then be written

$$P_j X_j = \sum_i a_{ij} P_j X_j + V_j \qquad j = 1, \ldots, n$$

and dividing by X_j gives

$$P_j = \sum_i a_{ij} P_j + V_j/X_j \qquad j = 1, \ldots, n$$

or

$$P_j = \sum_i a_{ij} P_j + v_j \qquad j = 1, \ldots, n \qquad (16.15)$$

where v_j is primary input cost per unit output.

In matrix algebra Equation 16.15 is

$$\mathbf{P} = \mathbf{A}'\mathbf{P} + \mathbf{v} \qquad (16.16)$$

where $\mathbf{P}$ is an $n \times 1$ vector of prices, $\mathbf{A}'$ is the transpose of the $n \times n$ matrix of input–output coefficients, $\mathbf{A}$, and $\mathbf{v}$ is an $n \times 1$ vector of primary input cost coefficients.

From Equation 16.16

$$\mathbf{P} - \mathbf{A}'\mathbf{P} = \mathbf{v}$$

and with $\mathbf{I}$ as the identity matrix

$$(\mathbf{I} - \mathbf{A}')\mathbf{P} = \mathbf{v}$$

so that

$$\mathbf{P} = (\mathbf{I} - \mathbf{A}')^{-1}\mathbf{v}$$

This last result can be written more usefully as

$$\mathbf{P}' = \mathbf{v}'(\mathbf{I} - \mathbf{A})^{-1} = \mathbf{v}'\mathbf{L} \qquad (16.17)$$

where $\mathbf{P}'$ is a $1 \times n$ vector of prices (the transpose of $\mathbf{P}$), $\mathbf{v}'$ is a $1 \times n$ vector of primary input cost coefficients (the transpose of $\mathbf{v}$) and $\mathbf{L}$ is the $n \times n$ Leontief inverse matrix.

According to Equation 16.17, commodity prices can be calculated using the Leontief inverse and the primary input cost coefficients. This can be illustrated using data from the transactions table given in Table 16.1. The primary input cost coefficients are:

Agriculture	Manufacturing	Services
0.55	0.70	0.75

Using these in Equation 16.17 with the Leontief inverse

$$\mathbf{L} = \begin{bmatrix} 1.0833 & 0.222 & 0.0556 \\ 0.4167 & 1.1111 & 0.2778 \\ 0.1500 & 0.1333 & 1.0333 \end{bmatrix}$$

gives $P_1 = 1.00$, $P_2 = 1.00$ and $P_3 = 1.00$. For $n = 3$, Equation 16.14 is

$$X_1 = X_{11} + X_{21} + X_{31} + V_1$$
$$X_2 = X_{12} + X_{22} + X_{32} + V_2$$
$$X_3 = X_{13} + X_{23} + X_{33} + V_3$$

and following the steps above leads to Equations 16.15 as

$$P_1 = a_{11}P_1 + a_{21}P_1 + a_{31}P_1 + v_1$$
$$P_2 = a_{12}P_2 + a_{22}P_2 + a_{32}P_2 + v_2$$
$$P_3 = a_{13}P_3 + a_{23}P_3 + a_{33}P_3 + v_3$$

where on substituting for the a and v coefficients, it can readily be confirmed that $P_1 = P_2 = P_3 = 1$ is the solution.

Given that we already knew that all prices are unity in an input–output transactions table, Equation 16.17 does not appear very useful. In looking at the 'real' side of things, using the Leontief inverse calculated from the transactions table with the final demand given in the transactions table in Equation 16.6 would simply give the gross outputs reported in the transactions table. The usefulness of computing the Leontief inverse from the transactions table was in considering the implications for gross outputs, and flows to and from the environment, of different levels and patterns of final demand. Here, similarly, the point is that Equation 16.17 can be used to consider the commodity price implications of v coefficients other than those derived from the transactions table.

Suppose that for the hypothetical economy to which Table 16.1 refers, carbon taxation were under consideration. In the preceding section we gave data on the use of oil by each of the three sectors, and noted that the use of 1 PJ of oil meant the emission of 73.2×10^3 tonnes of CO_2. This means that the CO_2 emissions arising in each sector are, in kilotonnes = 10^3 tonnes:

Agriculture	Manufacturing	Services
3660	29280	4392

Suppose that the rate of carbon taxation under consideration is \$20 per tonne. From Equation 16.17 the change in prices for a change in the v coefficients is

$$\Delta \mathbf{P}' = \Delta \mathbf{v}' \mathbf{L} \qquad (16.18)$$

where $\Delta \mathbf{v}'$ is the transposed vector of changes in the primary input cost coefficients and $\Delta \mathbf{P}'$ is the transposed vector of consequent price changes. For the postulated rate of carbon taxation, using the figures above for emissions and the data from Table 16.1 gives

$$\Delta v_1 = 0.0067, \quad \Delta v_2 = 0.2265, \quad \Delta v_3 = 0.1277$$

for which Equation 16.18 with $\mathbf{L}$ as given above, yields

$$\Delta P_1 = 0.1208, \quad \Delta P_2 = 0.2702, \quad \Delta P_3 = 0.1277$$

Given that prior to the imposition of the carbon tax all the prices were unity, these are proportionate price increase; that is, the price of the commodity which is the output of the agricultural sector would increase by 12.08%. Note, for example, that whereas the manufacturing sector uses four times as much oil per unit gross output, and hence emits four times as much CO_2, as the agriculture sector, the ratio of price increases is smaller, 2.2. Using input–output analysis picks up the implications for pricing of the fact that the agriculture sector uses oil, so that delivering its output to final demand is responsible for CO_2 emissions, indirectly as well as directly.

It should also be noted that this analysis involves the assumption that the input–output coefficients, the a_{ij}, and the coefficients for oil inputs do not change in response to the imposition of a carbon tax. It involves the assumption, that is, that making oil inputs more expensive does not induce any substitution responses on the part of producers. In so far as any such responses would involve using less oil per unit output, and less of relatively oil intensive commodities as intermediate inputs, they would reduce the price increases consequent on the introduction of the carbon tax. The input–output

results can, that is, be regarded as setting upper bounds to the price increases that would actually occur. In so far as substitution responses take time to implement, it would be expected that those upper bounds would approximate the short-run impacts, rather than the long-run impacts.

Table 16.4 gives the results of calculations essentially the same as those described above using the same input–output data for Australia as was used for the results given in Table 16.3. The calculations differ in so far as there are several fuels, rather than just oil, used, and in so far as the Australian input–output data involves a distinction between the prices received by sellers and those paid by buyers, which reflects indirect taxation and the way in which the accounts treat distribution margins. It is because of the latter that the rankings in Table 16.4, shown in

Table 16.4 Price increases due to a carbon tax of A\$20 per tonne.

Sector	Percentage price increase
Agriculture, forestry, fishing, hunting	1.77(9)
Mining	1.69(12)
Meat and milk products	1.77(9)
Food products	1.46(16)
Beverages and tobacco	0.84(24)
Textiles, clothing and footwear	0.95(21)
Wood, wood products, furniture	1.31(15)
Paper, products, printing, publishing	1.12(20)
Chemicals	1.56(16)
Petroleum and coal products	9.97(4)
Non-metallic mineral products	1.89(8)
Basic metals, products	9.00(5)
Fabricated metal products	2.76(6)
Transport equipment	0.82(23)
Machinery and equipment	0.71(26)
Miscellaneous manufacturing	0.89(23)
Electricity	31.33(1)
Gas	21.41(2)
Water	1.34(18)
Construction	1.60(13)
Wholesale and retail, repairs	10.14(3)
Transport, storage, communication	2.28(7)
Finance, property, business services	1.21(19)
Residential property	0.42(27)
Public administration, defence	1.73(11)
Community services	0.93(21)
Recreational, personal services	1.62(13)

Source: adapted from Common and Salma 1992b.

parentheses, do not exactly match those shown in Table 16.3 for the CO_2 intensities of deliveries to final demand.

It is widely believed that carbon taxation would be regressive in its impact, would hurt the poor more than the rich. Input–output analysis of the impact on commodity prices can provide one input to a quantitative analysis of this question. The other necessary input is data on the expenditure patterns of households at different positions in the income distribution which is, or can be made, compatible with the input–output data in terms of its commodity classification. Where such data is available, the change in the cost of living for a household is given by

$$\Delta CPI_h = \sum_j \beta_{hj} \Delta P_j \qquad h = 1, \ldots, m \quad (16.19)$$

where CPI stands for Consumer Price Index, h indexes households, and β_{hj} is the budget share of commodity j for the hth household. Table 16.5 gives results for Australia, using the price changes from Table 16.4 here with data on Australian household expenditure patterns by expenditure decile.[6] In Table 16.5 H identifies the highest CPI effect, L the lowest. The presumption that carbon taxation would be regressive in its impact comes from the observation, generally valid for industrial economies, that lower income groups spend a larger proportion of their income on fuel then upper income groups. The third column in Table 16.5 shows the CPI impacts when j in Equation 16.19 indexes only the fuel commodities: electricity, gas, and petroleum and coal products. The second column shows the CPI impact when j indexes all 27 commodities, picking up the indirect as well as the direct price effects of carbon taxation. There is by the H/L ratio a regressive impact in both columns, but it is smaller in the second column. Just looking at direct fuel purchases

[6] The household expenditure data is for 1984, which was at the time that the study was done the most recent such data available by decile. For results using more recent household expenditure data, by quintile, see Common and Salma (1992b), which also gives a more detailed account of data and methods.

Table 16.5 CPI impacts of carbon taxation.

Decile	Accounting for direct and indirect impacts (%)	Accounting for only direct impacts (%)
1	2.89	1.53
2	3.00 H	1.66 H
3	2.97	1.60
4	2.85	1.44
5	2.88	1.45
6	2.77	1.35
7	2.80	1.31
8	2.77	1.28
9	2.67	1.16
10	2.62 L	1.10 L
All households	2.79	1.31
H/L ratio	1.15	1.51

Source: adapted from Common and Salma (1992b).

overstates the regressive impact of carbon taxation (and, equivalently, of higher fuel prices). Carbon dioxide taxation affects all commodity prices, roughly, in proportion to their carbon dioxide intensity. Thus, while the poor spend proportionately more on direct fuels purchases, the rich spend more on things, such as overseas travel, in which fuels are, directly and indirectly, used as inputs, and this reduces regressivity.

Two points need to be kept in mind when considering results such as those shown in Table 16.5. The first is that using Equation 16.19 involves the assumption that household expenditure patterns do not change in response to the changed relative prices induced by carbon taxation. The assumption of fixed budget shares for households is directly analogous to the assumption of fixed input–output coefficients in production, and has similar implications for the results of the analysis. Given changed relative prices following the introduction of carbon taxation, households would be expected to substitute commodities for which price had risen less for those for which it had risen more. Such behaviour would reduce the CPI impact of carbon taxation: results based on Equation 16.19 would, for each decile, represent an upper limit. The second point is that the impacts on households arising from carbon taxation

Table 16.6 Transactions table for the two-sector economy.

	Agriculture	Manufacturing	Consumption	Total output
Agriculture	0	1.3490	3.1615	4.5105
Manufacturing	1.1562	0	3.1615	4.3177
Wages	2.5157	1.4844		
Other value added	0.8386	1.4843		
Total input	4.5105	4.3177		

would not be confined to the expenditure side. There would also be income effects. As noted above, producers would also be expected to make substitution responses, which would have implications for employment opportunities and incomes. Also, carbon taxation would give rise to government revenue which could be used in a variety of ways, including increased welfare payments and/or lower income taxation for low income households, for example. If substitution responses, and discretion in the use of the tax receipts, are to be allowed for, analysing the full implications of the introduction of carbon taxation, and other environmental policies, is beyond the scope of input–output analysis. Such issues can, in principle, be investigated using the methods to be discussed in the following section.

Computable general equilibrium models

Environmental input–output models are undoubtedly useful for applied work in policy simulation, forecasting and structural analysis. They are transparent and computationally straightforward. However, they are seen by many economists as suffering from several serious deficiencies. Utility and profit maximising behaviour play no role in input–output models: there are no demand and supply equations and no capacity constraints. Concern with the rather limited behavioural basis of input–output models has led to a growing interest in applied, or computable, general equilibrium models. We will use the term 'computable general equilibrium' (CGE) models.

CGE models are essentially empirical versions of the Walrasian general equilibrium system and employ the theoretical (neo-classical) assumptions of that system, which, as remarked above, are absent from the input–output system. In general, CGE models cannot be solved algebraically, but thanks to recent increases in computing power, and the development of solution algorithms, they can be solved computationally. These developments have stimulated a rapid growth in applied CGE modelling, particularly on issues related to taxation, trade, structural adjustment and the environment.

An illustrative two-sector model

Here we will use constructed data for an imaginary economy and a simple CGE model of that economy to illustrate the essentials of CGE modelling in relation to environmental problems.[7]

Table 16.6 is the transactions table for a two-sector economy. This economy uses labour and oil as inputs to production, and in Table 16.6 'Other value added' refers to payments to the owners of oil deposits. The units of measurement are $\$ \times 10^6$ everywhere. The only component of final demand is consumption by the households which supply labour and own oil deposits – there is no foreign trade. The implication that households sell costlessly extracted oil to the producing sectors of the economy keeps what follows as simple as possible, while not affecting the essentials.

[7] For a good summary of recent work on CGE modelling and applications see Greenaway *et al.* (1993).

The prices of both produced commodities and of both primary inputs are known for the year to which Table 16.6 relates. Since, as we shall see, it is for present purposes only relative prices that matter, we set the price of labour at unity and express all other prices in terms of the 'wage rate' as numeraire. Then, the known prices are:

Agriculture	$P_1 = 2.4490$
Manufacturing	$P_2 = 3.1355$
Labour	$W = 1$
Oil	$P = 1.1620$

With these prices we can convert the transactions table into an input–output table expressed in physical units (Table 16.7). Take it that the units in Table 16.7 are: tonnes $\times 10^6$ for agriculture and manufacturing, person years for labour and PJs for oil. Table 16.7 has an additional row labelled emissions. Each PJ of oil used gives rise to 73.2×10^3 tonnes of CO_2, and in Table 16.7 emissions are reported in units of kilotonnes.

Suppose now that we want to consider policy in regard to CO_2 emissions. If we restrict ourselves to the assumptions of input–output modelling, we can, as discussed in the second section of this chapter, consider the implications of alternative final demand scenarios, and/or the implications of changes to the economy's technology, as reflected in the matrix **A**. We could also, as described in the previous section, consider the implications for commodity prices of the imposition of a carbon tax at various rates. Note that in the latter case, imposing a tax on emissions would not affect emissions levels.

The argument for CGE modelling is that by using the assumptions of general equilibrium theory, we can do more useful policy analysis, where agents respond to the policy intervention. Essentially, CGE modelling employs four sorts of assumption:

(1) Market clearing – all markets are in equilibrium
(2) Walras Law – all markets are connected
(3) Utility maximisation by households
(4) Profit maximisation by firms

Using assumptions (1) and (2) is a relatively straightforward matter of model specification. Using assumptions (3) and (4) requires additional assumptions and/or data.

In regard to (1), consider for example the commodity markets. The market clearing assumption there is that for each commodity, the amount produced is taken off the market by the sum of all the demands. Here, given intermediate uses of produced commodities, that is:

$$X_1 = X_{11} + X_{12} + C_1$$
$$X_2 = X_{21} + X_{22} + C_2$$

In regard to the use of intermediate goods in production, we will make the standard input–output modelling assumption, Equation 16.2. In that case, we have

$$X_1 = a_{11}X_1 + a_{12}X_2 + C_1$$
$$X_2 = a_{21}X_1 + a_{22}X_2 + C_2 \qquad (16.20)$$

In regard to (2), we know, for example, that for this simple economy

$$Y = W(L_1 + L_2) + P(R_1 + R_2) \qquad (16.21)$$

where Y is total household income, W is the wage rate, L_i is labour used in the ith sector, P is the price of oil and R_i is oil used in the ith sector.

Table 16.7 Physical data for the two-sector economy.

	Agriculture	Manufacturing	Consumption	Total output
Agriculture	0	0.5508	1.2909	1.8417
Manufacturing	0.3687	0	1.0083	1.3770
Labour	2.5157	1.4844		
Oil	0.7217	1.2774		
Emissions	52.8484	93.5057		

Together with demand equations for primary inputs and demand and supply equations for produced commodities, Equation 16.21 ties together the various markets in the economy.

The derivation of numerical demand and supply equations from the assumptions of utility and profit maximisation is less straightforward. Consider utility maximisation and household commodity demands. We will assume, as is typical in CGE modelling, that there is just one household. The general form of the commodity demand equations is then:

$$C_1 = C_1(Y, P_1, P_2)$$
$$C_2 = C_2(Y, P_1, P_2)$$
(16.22)

If it were the case that we had adequate time series data on this economy for C_1, C_2, Y, P_1 and P_2 we could use it to test alternative functional forms for these demand equations, and to estimate the parameters for the preferred functional form. In fact, this 'econometric' approach is generally not adopted in actual CGE modelling exercises, as there are not adequate time series data. The alternative, and widely used, approach is known as 'calibration'. This involves assuming some plausible functional form and setting its parameters so that the resulting equations are numerically consistent with the available data. Very often this 'benchmark' data is for a single year, as is the case with Table 16.6, the associated price data, and Table 16.7.

Let us assume, then, that the utility function for the household in this economy is

$$U = C_1^{\alpha} C_2^{\beta}$$
(16.23)

Maximising Equation 16.23 subject to the budget constraint

$$Y = P_1 C_1 + P_2 C_2$$

leads, as shown in Appendix 16.2, to the demand functions:

$$C_1 = [\alpha/(\alpha + \beta)P_1]Y$$
$$C_2 = [\beta/(\alpha + \beta)P_2]Y$$
(16.24)

Using the data for Y, P_1, P_2, C_1 and C_2, these can be written as

$$\alpha/(\alpha + \beta) = 0.5$$
$$\beta/(\alpha + \beta) = 0.5$$
(16.25)

which are two equations in two unknowns. Unfortunately, and not untypically, Equations 16.25 do not have a unique solution for the values of α and β. The solution to Equations 16.25 is $\alpha = \beta$. We need some more information. A typical approach in practice would be to 'import' a value for one of these parameters as estimated with some other data for a different economy. We shall simply impose the plausible value $\alpha = 0.5$.

As regards the other sources of demand for produced commodities, numerical parameterisation is straightforward, given that we are making the standard input–output assumptions about intermediate demands. From Table 16.7 we derive the matrix of physical, input–output coefficients as:

$$\mathbf{A} = \begin{bmatrix} 0 & 0.4 \\ 0.2 & 0 \end{bmatrix}$$

Now consider the production side of the model. We assume, as is typical in CGE practice, that each sector comprises a single firm, which behaves as a price-taker in its output market and the factor markets. We assume constant returns to scale and Cobb–Douglas production functions, with labour and oil as arguments. While the Cobb–Douglas assumption is adopted here mainly for simplicity, the first is generally used in actual CGE modelling, and has important consequences for model structure. As shown in Appendix 16.2, with constant returns to scale, profits are zero at all output levels and so there is no supply function. It is then necessary to construct the model such that firms produce to meet demand. As shown in Appendix 16.2, given the output level, the assumption of cost minimisation means that equations for factor demands per unit output can be derived. There remains the problem of fixing numerical values for the parameters of the production functions, and hence, the factor demand equations. The situation in regard to the production and factor demand side of the

---

Box 16.1 The illustrative CGE model specification and simulation results

Computable general equilibrium model specification

(1) $C_1 = Y/2P_1$

(2) $C_2 = Y/2P_2$

(3) $X_1 = 0.4X_2 + C_1$

(4) $X_2 = 0.2X_1 + C_2$

(5) $P_1 = 0.2P_2 + WU_{L1} + PU_{R1}$

(6) $P_2 = 0.4P_1 + WU_{L2} + PU_{R2}$

(7) $U_{L1} = [3(P/W)]^{0.25}$

(8) $L_1 = U_{L1}X_1$

(9) $U_{L2} = [P/W]^{0.5}$

(10) $L_2 = U_{L2}X_2$

(11) $U_{R1} = [0.33(W/P)]^{0.75}$

(12) $R_1 = U_{R1}X_1$

(13) $U_{R2} = [W/P]^{0.5}$

(14) $R_2 = U_{R2}X_2$

(15) $E = e_1R_1 + e_2R_2$

(16) $Y = W(L_1 + L_2) + P(R_1 + R_2)$

(17) $L_1 + L_2 = L^*$

(18) $R_1 + R_2 = R^*$

Computable general equilibrium model results

	Base case A	Base case B	50% emissions reduction	Reduction case as proportion of base case
W	1	5	1	1
P	1.1620	5.7751	2.3990	2.0645
P_1	2.4490	12.2410	3.0472	1.2443
P_2	3.1355	15.6702	4.3166	1.3767
X_1	1.8416	1.8421	1.4640	0.7950
X_2	1.3770	1.3770	1.0341	0.7510
L_1	2.5157	2.5164	2.3983	0.9533
L_2	1.4844	1.4836	1.6017	1.0790
R_1	0.7216	0.7226	0.3332	0.4618
R_2	1.2774	1.2780	0.6677	0.5227
R	2	2	1	0.5000
E_1	52.8484	52.8484	24.3902	0.4618
E_2	93.5057	93.5057	48.8756	0.5227
E	146.3541	146.3541	73.2658	0.5000
Y	6.324	31.615	6.3990	1.0119
C_1	1.2909	1.2912	1.0503	0.8136
C_2	1.0083	1.0087	0.7415	0.7354
U	1.1409	1.1412	0.8825	0.7735

economy is as discussed above for household demand equations. While econometric estimation is possible in principle, it is generally, though not always, precluded by the non-availability of the necessary data. Most usually, numerical parameter values are determined by importing some of them from other sources – or on grounds of 'plausibility' – and determining the remainder by calibration against the benchmark data set, here Table 16.7.

We shall not go into this any further here beyond saying that Box 16.1 lists the equations of our CGE model with numerical para-meter values which pass the calibration test – running the model listed there does, as shown in the lower part of the box, reproduce the data of Tables 16.6 and 16.7, and give the relative prices that go with that data. Equations (1) and (2) in the box are the household commodity demands, derived as discussed above. Equations (3) and (4) are the commodity balance equations using the values from the matrix **A** given above. Then we have a pair of simultaneous equations in P_1 and P_2. Given that U_{L1} and U_{R1}, for example, are respectively the use of labour and oil per unit output in sector 1, equations

(5) and (6) are the same as the pricing equations used in input–output analysis – see Equation 16.15 from the previous section – and go with zero profit in each line of production.

There follow eight equations relating to factor demands. Equations (7), (9), (11) and (13) give the quantity of factor input per unit output, and Equations (8), (10), (12) and (14) convert the results to factor demand levels using the corresponding output levels. The form of these equations is derived from cost minimisation, as described in Appendix 16.2. The numerical values appearing in Equations (7), (9), (11) and (13) in Box 16.1 go with the following numerical specifications for the production functions:

$$X_1 = L_1^{0.75} R_1^{0.25}$$
$$X_2 = L_2^{0.5} R_2^{0.5} \qquad (16.26)$$

Equation (15) gives the total of emissions as the sum of the emissions of CO_2 associated with oil combustion in each sector.

Equation (16) in Box 16.1 is Equation 16.21, giving total household income as arising from the sales of labour services and oil to both producing sectors. Finally, Equations (17) and (18) say that there is a fixed total amount of each factor, L^* and R^*, available to the economy, and that there is full employment of the available amount taking the two sectors together. These factor endowments are exogenous variables in this model. There are 18 endogenous variables: W, P, Y, E; and for $i = 1, 2$ U_{Li}, U_{Ri}, C_i, P_i, X_i, L_i and R_i.

The solution algorithm is based on the economic idea of price moving to clear excess demand/supply, exploits the fact that we are concerned only with relative prices, and is simplified by using Walras law.[8] It first takes in the numerical values for the parameters and the given total factor endowments L^* and R^*. In the light of the concern for relative prices, labour is selected as numeraire,

and W is set at some fixed value, which, given the discussion of the data above, is 1. Given an assumed, temporary, value for P the next step is to use Equations (7), (9), (11) and (13) from Box 16.1 to calculate the unit factor demands. These are used with the solution to the commodity pricing equations, Equations (5) and (6) (the nature of which solution was discussed in the previous section of the chapter), to derive commodity prices, and with an assumed, temporary, value for X_1 to find L_1 according to Equation (8) and R_1 according to Equation (12). L_2 is then calculated as $L^* - L_1$. X_2 can then be found from L_2 and the unit factor demand for labour in manufacturing, and given this value for X_2 the manufacturing demand for oil can be found using Equation (14). Given values for L_1, L_2, R_1 and R_2, Y can be calculated according to Equation (16), and hence household commodity demands from Equations (1) and (2).

At this point, the value of $R_1 + R_2$ is compared with that for R^*. If $R_1 + R_2$ is greater than R^*, the value of P is increased by a small amount, to reduce the excess demand for oil, and the calculation described in the previous paragraph repeated. If $R_1 + R_2$ is less than R^*, the value of P is reduced, to reduce the excess supply of oil, and the calculation described in the previous paragraph repeated. These iterations are repeated until a value for P is found for which, to some close approximation, $R_1 + R_2 = R^*$. At this point, the iteration process ceases. We know by virtue of the calculations as described that the oil market, the X_1 market, and the labour market are in equilibrium. And, by virtue of Walras law, we then know that the remaining market, for X_2, must also be in equilibrium. The computer program which implements the algorithm reports the values of all of the endogenous variables, and stops.

The results for base cases A and B are those that the model produces when L^* is set at 4 and R^* is set at 2, the total labour and oil use in Table 16.7, and when $e_i = 73.2$, as indicated by the data there. The input to the

[8] The algorithm is an adaptation of that listed in chapter 4 in Dinwiddy and Teale (1988).

two base case runs of the model differs only in the value given to W, 1 in A and 5 in B. The point of reporting results from these two runs is to illustrate that in a CGE model it is only relative prices that matter. Comparing the columns, we see, first, that for B the entries for W, P, P_1 and P_2 are all five times those for A, and, second, that all of the remaining entries, for the 'real' variables, are the same (leaving aside inevitable small differences due to the impact of the rule for stopping iterations in the algorithm). We also see that base case A reproduces the data on prices and quantities that we started with, the model calibrates.

The results in the third column arise when the model is run with base case A input, except that R^* is set at 1, 50% of the total amount of oil used in the original data set. Because emissions are linked to oil use by fixed coefficients, cutting total oil use by 50% will cut emissions by 50%. The results in the fourth column show those in the third as a proportion of those in the first. Looking at the results for the 50% emissions cut in comparison with base case A, we see first that P, the price of oil, increases by more than 100%. The prices of commodities 1 and 2 increase, with P_1 increasing less than P_2. Consistent with this, X_1, the total output of 1, falls by less than X_2. It is not the case that all factor inputs fall. Labour use in the production of commodity 1 goes down, but labour use in 2 goes up – recall that the model is structured so that there is always full employment of the labour available, so that in a two-sector model a reduction in labour input in one sector must be balanced by an increase in the other.

As a result of the reduced availability and hence higher price of oil, both producing sectors use less oil, and produce smaller amounts of emissions. Note, however, that it is not the case that R_1 and R_2, and E_1 and E_2, are reduced by equal amounts, of 50%. Oil use and emissions fall by more than 50% in the production of commodity 1, by less than 50% in the production of commodity 2. This is the efficient loading of total abatement

across sources discussed in Chapters 11 and 12, arising because the model mimics competitive firms responding to their relative cost structures.

Household consumption of both commodities falls, with that of the commodity, 1, the price of which rose least, falling least. National income, here the simple sum of household incomes which is equal to $P_1 C_1 + P_2 C_2$, increases because the rise in the price of oil more than compensates for the reduced quantity used, and the additional income is more than absorbed by the higher prices for C_1 and C_2. National income as reported in Box 16.1 is not corrected for the change in the general price level, and so misrepresents the welfare change, to the extent in this case of getting the sign for the direction of movement wrong. However, utility as a function of quantities consumed falls. In regard to this, it is important to note that the model has utility dependent only on commodity consumption levels. Emissions are not an argument in the utility function. This is typical of CGE models used for the analysis of the effects of programmes to reduce emissions or improve the environment. To the extent that people do derive benefit from reduced pollution, considering the utility change computed in a CGE model which does not allow for that benefit means that the reported utility change will be an underestimate. Again, the extent of this may be such that the direction of change is misrepresented – the unrecognised utility gain from reduced emissions could be larger than the utility loss due to reduced commodity consumption.

In this model the reduction in total oil use and emissions has to be simply imposed as action by a *deus ex machina*, and the impact is transmitted through a higher price for oil, which is received directly by the owners of oil deposits, who are the household sector. An actual study of the implications of prospective action on carbon dioxide emissions would be looking not at action by a *deus ex machina* but at some kind of change of policy by government. While it could be argued that a model without a government sector, like that considered above, gives some kind of first-cut feel for the implications of reducing emissions, it is clear that an interesting analysis of government policy requires that the government sector is explicitly represented in the model. Without a government sector, we would have to treat, for example, tradable emissions (or oil use) permits as equivalent to emissions (or oil) taxation, whereas the interesting questions are about how they compare. About the only interesting policy question that the above model could address is a comparison of an efficient policy – permits or tax – with an inefficient policy – making all sources cut in equal proportional amounts. Clearly, it is also the case that to be useful for policy analysis for a trading economy a CGE model would also need a trade sector. Extending the model in these ways makes it complex, and requires more data, or more assumptions about parameter values.

Rather than develop the illustrative model further in these directions, we now look briefly at results from two substantive exercises which serve to illustrate the sort of analysis that can be done when trade and government are explicitly represented in a CGE model.[9] Both exercises deal with aspects of greenhouse gas abatement. As discussed in Chapter 13, CGE models have been extensively used to analyse policy for the abatement of greenhouse gas emissions, focusing particularly on carbon dioxide emissions. A good recent survey is in the report of IPCC Working Group III published as Bruce et al. (1996).

The international distribution of abatement costs

Here we consider the modelling work of Whalley and Wigle (1991). In this model the

world is divided into six regional economies, as shown in Table 16.8. Two types of energy source are distinguished, the fossil fuel and other, non-carbon, sources such as nuclear power. These are substitutable for one another in production, and energy and other inputs are also substitutes in production. International trade involves fossil fuel energy but not non-fossil energy, and commodities produced using both energy sources. The entries in Table 16.8 are percentage changes in GDP. There is a cost where there is a minus sign, and a gain where there is a plus sign. Given that all fossil fuels are aggregated to a single composite 'fossil fuel', carbon taxation is actually achieved by taxing the fossil fuel commodity, it being assumed that the only way to reduce emissions is to reduce fuel use.

The results shown in Table 16.8 refer to three alternative routes to the achievement in the model of a global 50% reduction in emissions on what would otherwise have been the case. In options 1 and 2 each economy acts to cut its emissions by 50%. In 1 this is done by the imposition of the required rate of tax on the production of fossil fuels. In 2 it is the consumption of fossil fuels that is taxed. It should be noted that in terms of the discussion of alternative instruments for pollution abatement in Chapter 12, both of these are, at the global level, quantity control, or command and control, type instruments. Each economy is required to cut by 50%, so we are dealing, from the global perspective, with uniform emissions reductions across all

[9] Dinwiddy and Teale (1988) develop, in terms of the algebra and solution algorithms, an illustrative two-industry model to include government expenditure and taxation and foreign trade.

Table 16.8 Costs associated with alternative instruments for global emissions reductions.

Region	Option 1	Option 2	Option 3
EC	−4.0	−1.0	−3.8
North America	−4.3	−3.6	−9.8
Japan	−3.7	+0.5	−0.9
Other OECD	−2.3	−2.1	−4.4
Oil exporters	+4.5	−18.7	−13.0
Rest of world	−7.1	−6.8	1.8
World	**−4.4**	**−4.4**	**−4.2**

Source: adapted from Whalley and Wigle (1991).

sources. Each 'source' in this case is a regional economy, which uses taxation to achieve the emissions cutback required of it. Hence, at the global level standard theory would suggest that neither of these is an efficient way to achieve an overall 50% cut in emissions. This is shown in Table 16.8, where world costs are higher with both 1 and 2 than with option 3, which is the use of fossil fuel taxation at the same rate across all sources. In the model, the uniform global tax is levied and collected by an international agency. In this case it does not make any difference whether the tax is levied on production or consumption.

The results for the individual economies show how the distribution of costs varies with instrument choice. In options 1 and 2, tax revenues accrue to the individual economies, and are spent there. Option 1 then benefits carbon energy, i.e. fossil fuel, exporters at the expense of importers, especially the 'Rest of world'. Under option 1 GDP increases in the 'Oil exporters' economy. The 'Rest of world' economy includes the developing nations and the formerly centrally planned economies. It does slightly less badly where the 50% reductions in each economy are achieved by a fossil fuel consumption tax. In this case, the oil exporters suffer heavily, and Japan actually gains. With the tax levied on consumption, the costs to fossil fuel importers are reduced because the pre-tax world price of fossil fuel tax falls, due to reduced demand, and the tax revenues are recycled within the importing economies.

Under option 3 a uniform global tax is levied and collected by an international agency which disposes of the revenues by grants to each economy based on their population size. The per capita grant is the same throughout the world. In this case, not only do we have minimised cost to the global economy, but we also have a distributional impact that works to reduce inequity, by, generally, transferring funds to the 'Rest of world' economy, which comprises mainly developing economies. This economy actually gains

under option 3 when the joint effect of the tax and revenue distribution is considered. As is clear from the discussion in Chapter 13, equity is important here not only for itself, but also for the incentives for participation that arise. The large developing economies, such as India and China, would gain substantially under option 3. Note that a tradable permits regime could have effects similar to those shown for option 3, if the initial allocation of the permits was arranged so as to favour developing countries. This could be done by doing the initial allocation on the basis of equal per capita shares in the global total of emissions, which was the target, or equivalently in total global fossil fuel use. Each country would get an initial allocation equal to one per capita share times its population size.

Alternative uses of national carbon tax revenue

We now consider some CGE modelling results to illustrate the effects of different assumptions about the way in which any environmental tax revenue is used. Table 16.9 reports results for Australia obtained using a model called ORANI which includes a government sector and Australia's overseas trade. The columns refer to two different simulations of the ORANI model where Australia unilaterally introduces carbon taxation:

- S1: Carbon taxation is levied so as to raise revenue of A\$2 billion, which is used to reduce payroll taxation by the same amount. The tax rate involved is A\$7.40 per tonne of carbon dioxide.

Table 16.9 Effects of carbon taxation according to use of revenue.

	S1	S2
Real gross domestic product	0.07	−0.09
Consumer price index	−0.18	0.42
Budget balance[a]	−0.02	0.31
Employment	0.21	−0.04
CO_2 emissions	−3.9	−4.7

[a] As percentage of GDP.

Source: adapted from Common and Hamilton (1996).

- S2: Carbon taxation is levied so as to raise revenue of A$2 billion, which is used to reduce the government deficit by that amount.

The results shown for these two simulations in Table 16.9 are in terms of the percentage differences from the base case without carbon taxation.

In each of these simulations the standard CGE modelling practice is not followed in that the model is configured with money wage rates fixed, and the market clearing assumption in the labour market is dropped. This allows the model to examine the employment effects of alternative policies. It is regarded as a way of modelling the short-run effects of policy changes. ORANI modellers wishing to examine long run effects, where 'long-run' means enough time for complete adjustment, would set the model with flexible wage rates which would ensure market clearing in the labour market. This illustrates the point that CGE modelling results have to be understood in the light of the assumptions and intentions of the modellers. The same model can produce different results according to the way it is configured for a particular simulation.

The introduction of carbon taxation has an output and a substitution effect in the labour market. There is a reduction in the demand for labour on account of the contraction of economic activity due to fixed money wages and the trade effects of acting unilaterally. There is an increase in the demand for labour on account of the higher price of fossil fuel inputs relative to labour inputs. Where the carbon tax revenue is used to reduce payroll taxation, the non-wage costs to employers of using labour are reduced, thus reinforcing the substitution effect of the carbon tax itself.

This is seen in the comparison of the results for S1 and S2. Employment actually increases where payroll tax is cut in S1. Given the relative shares of labour and fossil fuel in expenditures on inputs, the switch from a tax on labour input to a tax on fossil fuel input leads to a reduction in the consumer price index. The overall impact gives an increase in real GDP. Where, in S2, the carbon tax revenue is used to reduce the budget deficit employment falls, as does GDP, and the consumer price index increases.

Benefits and costs of CGE modelling

As compared with I/O models, CGE models have the benefit that they incorporate behavioural responses on the part of producers and consumers to the price changes induced by policy actions. This entails costs. The structure of the behavioural sub-models reflects the assumptions of economic theory. To economists this is the natural and obvious way to proceed. However, many non-economists would argue that producers and consumers do not actually behave according to those assumptions, and there is quite a lot of evidence that can be cited in support of this view. Economists tend to respond to this line of argument, and the evidence, to the effect that either the evidence is flawed and/or that the critics are missing the point, which is that the standard assumptions, and CGE models, are not really about predicting short-run and ephemeral movements but about underlying long-run tendencies. Many non-economists, and some economists, are prone to overlook such caveats and regard CGE models as forecasting models. This appears to be less the case with I/O models, perhaps because their limitations are more readily apparent.

Going from I/O to CGE not only involves more assumptions, but also more data so that those assumptions, or their implications, can be quantified for incorporation into the model. As we have seen, the required data is frequently unavailable, so that the behavioural sub-models often use assumed parameter values that are plausible and consistent with a single benchmark data set for the variables included in the model. CGE model results are sensitive to changes in the parameter values used. Again, this is less of a problem to the extent that such models are seen as vehicles for gaining broad quantitative, or even purely qualitative, insights into policy questions, rather than forecasting models.

The use of CGE, and other economic models, in policy debate is often less fruitful than it might be due to a lack of awareness of the inherent limitations of the models themselves combining with a lack of awareness of the limits to the accuracy with which the variables that they track can actually be measured. National income can be measured in three ways, and the same result should arise whichever way it is done. In fact published official national income accounts always include as the 'residual error' the difference between the results of measurement according to two of the conventions. This residual error as a percentage of the measure regarded as most accurate varies over time, but typically is of the order of 0.5%, and goes as high as 1%. CGE model results for the national income cost of environmental policies should be looked at with this in mind. In Table 16.8, for example, we noted that the results for the world GDP costs of alternative instruments for a 50% reduction in global emissions did show, as theory predicts, that uniform taxation is the least-cost instrument. Note, however, that the difference between the least cost and the cost with the other instruments is just 0.2%. One might say, then, that while the model confirms the theory, it also suggests that the gain to going for the least-cost approach, rather than the alternatives considered, is quite small. It should be noted also that the model result is not anyway independent confirmation of the least-cost property of uniform taxation – the model incorporates the same assumptions as the standard theory, and could not produce a different result.

Similar considerations apply to the results in Table 16.9, and to those reported in Chapter 13. As regards the exercise reported on in Table 16.9, the real point is the demonstration that a standard economic model says that, in the short run at least, unilateral carbon taxation need not imply an increase

in unemployment and a reduction in national income if the revenue is used to reduce a distortionary tax. This is not a point that I/O modelling could make.

Discussion questions

1 Examine critically the basic assumptions of input–output models, in particular those related to the input–output (Leontief) production function and to factor supplies, and discuss the importance of these assumptions in affecting the validity and accuracy of environmental input–output applications.
2 In discussing the results in Table 16.8 it was asserted that with uniform global taxation, the result would be the same using either fossil fuel production or consumption as tax base. Why is this?

Problems

1 (a) Calculate import, wage and other value added coefficients from Table 16.1 analogous to the intermediate input coefficients a_{ij}. Check that for each industry, the sum of the intermediate and primary input coefficients is unity.
   (b) In the text we used coefficients derived from the data of Table 16.1 to find the gross output levels implied by new higher levels of export demand. Use those new gross output levels to derive a new transactions table, assuming constant input coefficients for both intermediate and primary inputs. Calculate the new level of GDP.
2 Suppose now we can add the following information about tonnes of waste emissions to the dataset of Table 16.1:

Industry of origin:

Agriculture	Manufacturing
4000	2500
Services	Total
150	6650

Calculate the change in the industry and total emissions levels that would be associated with an across-the-board increase of 20% in household expenditure.

3 The transactions table for a closed economy is:

	Agriculture	Manufacturing	Final demand
Agriculture	10	20	50
Manufacturing	20	50	80
Primary inputs	50	80	

The agriculture industry purchased 10 units of energy, the manufacturing sector 40 units.

(a) Calculate the energy intensities for deliveries to final demand by the agriculture and manufacturing industries.

(b) If the use of 1 unit of energy releases 3.5 units of CO_2, calculate total CO_2 emissions and allocate them to deliveries to final demand by the agriculture and manufacturing industries.

(c) Calculate what total CO_2 emissions would be for deliveries to final demand of 100 from agriculture and 240 from manufacturing.

4 Using the data of Table 16.1, and noting that $(I - A')^{-1} = [(I - A)^{-1}]'$, calculate the effect on prices of a 50% increase in the import costs in the agriculture sector, due to the imposition of a tax on fuel imports. Why is your calculation likely to overestimate the effects of this cost increase?

5 (a) Calculate the real income change that goes with the results given in Box 16.1 for a 50% reduction in emissions.

(b) If the utility function is assumed to have the form $C_1^{0.5} C_2^{0.5} E^{\delta}$, find the value of δ for which it would be true that utility did not fall with the 50% reduction in emissions.

Further reading

Our treatment of input–output analysis and its application to questions concerning nat-

ural resources and environmental pollution in the text is simplified though essentially valid. For a comprehensive guide to input–output analysis, including environmental and energy input–output models, see Miller and Blair (1985). Vaze (1998) presents environmental input–output accounts for the United Kingdom for 1993, and reports the results of simulations based upon them. Proops *et al.* (1993) is an extended account of the use of input–output methods to analyse CO_2 emissions and options for their abatement.

Xie (1996) is a good introduction to the use of CGE modelling to study environmental policy issues, and reports results for a Chinese application. Most CGE models are, like the illustrative model discussed in the text, comparative static models. This is a limitation, particularly in the context of a problem like that of thinking about policies for abating CO_2 emissions. The OECD has developed for this problem a dynamic CGE model, which is described and used in Nicoletti and Oliveira-Martins (1993) and Burniaux *et al.* (1994).

Appendix 16.1 A general framework for environmental input–output analysis

Figure 16.1 sets out schematically a general input–output system for analysing the interconnections between economic activity and the natural environment. The basis is the recognition that there are three types of linkage between the economy and the environment, which should properly be treated jointly. First, economic agents extract or exploit natural resources, including obvious forms of exploitation such as extraction of ores and minerals, fish harvesting and so on, but also in less obvious ways such as the 'consumption' of fresh air and landscape.

Second, the processing and consumption of these environmental resources yields residuals which are returned to the environment, and which may have undesirable economic, social or health effects, such as air

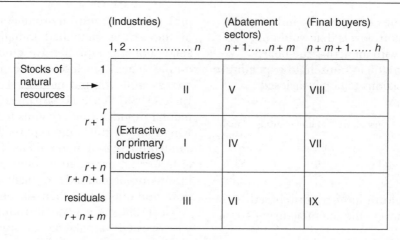

Figure 16.1 An extended input–output system.

pollution, soil degradation and loss of habitat. Attempts to eliminate, mitigate or compensate for these effects lead to the third type of economy–environment link, namely activities devoted to abatement or environmental renewal.

In Figure 16.1, the submatrices I and VII correspond to the conventional input–output table, I recording flows of goods and services between the n intermediate sectors of the economy, and VII recording deliveries to final buyers or users (private and government consumption, investment, exports). For simplicity, we assume here, as we did in the chapter itself, that each 'industry' produces a unique homogeneous 'commodity,' thus avoiding the need for a more complex system of accounts which links industries and commodities.

Submatrix II records the extraction or direct use of natural resources by industries, involving a reduction in the vector of stocks of natural resources. The cell ij of submatrix II records the amount or volume of resource i, measured in physical units, used or consumed by industry j during a particular time period, say one year. Thus if resource i is water and industry j is water supply, the entry in cell ij records the volume of water collected and processed by the water supply sector: subsequent sales or deliveries of water

to industry and households would appear in row $r + j$ of submatrices I and VII.

Following conventional input–output modelling practice, if we assume a constant proportional relation between inputs of resources and outputs of industries, we can derive a submatrix of resource input coefficients in which the typical coefficient r_{ij} indicates the amount of resource i (in physical units) required per unit of output (typically measured in value units) of industry j. Pursuing the example above, r_{ij} would record the number of gallons of water required per million dollars output of the water supply industry.

Many of the cells in submatrix II will be zero, since only a limited number of industries are engaged in the direct extraction or harvesting of natural resources. Processed natural resources will be classified as industrial products and distributed along the rows of submatrices I, IV and VII.

Submatrix III records residual wastes generated by each industry, there being a separate row for each type of residual: thus an entry in cell gk in III records the amount of residual g generated by industry k in the accounting period concerned. Again following standard input–output practice, if we assume a constant proportional relationship between industry output and residuals generation, we can derive a submatrix of waste coefficients in which the typical element w_{gk} indicates the amount of waste element g produced per million dollars output of industry k. Note that although the elements of submatrix III are outputs rather than inputs, they are treated here in an identical way to the input flows in submatrices II and I. Obvious examples of this type of waste production are pollutants generated by industrial production and distribution, considered in the text of the chapter.

Columns $n + 1$ to $n + m$ (submatrices IV, V and VI) represent residuals abatement or treatment activities. Note that although abatement activities are here accorded the status of separate industries, in practice such activities may be undertaken by and within the industries which are responsible for generating the residual concerned. For instance a firm which generates waste water may undertake water purification 'on site' before discharging the water back into the environment. In the accounting system here, the mainstream production and purification activities would be recorded separately. Note also that in this schema, certain abatement/treatment activities may operate at zero levels.

Like other industries, abatement industries purchase goods and services from other industries (submatrix IV), and may also absorb natural resources directly (submatrix V, though this submatrix could well be empty). Moreover, like other industries the abatement sectors may themselves generate residual wastes (submatrix VI).

The output of the abatement industries may be expressed in value terms, as are typically the other industries in the table, or in physical units, as the amount of residual treated or eliminated. In the latter case the input coefficients (submatrix IV) would measure (constant) dollar inputs per ton of residual treated or eliminated. Again, for these industries we assume the Leontief technology of fixed proportional input coefficients.

The final columns of the table record sales or deliveries to final buyers, typically household (private) consumption, government consumption, investment, changes in stocks, exports and (a negative column of) imports, but each of these categories may be further disaggregated. One possibility is to disaggregate the investment column to separately identify capital expenditures directed towards the renewal of natural resources, such as reafforestation, soil regeneration, fish stocks renewal, and so on. These activities then provide a link to the vector of stocks of natural resources at the beginning of the environment–economy–environment sequence in Figure 16.1, and are a step towards closure of the model system.

Submatrix VIII allows for the possibility of direct extraction or use of natural resources by final buyers (for example, fresh air, untreated water, fish caught for personal consumption, and so on), while submatrix IX includes residual wastes generated by households and other final buyers (CO_2, solid wastes, scrap, and so on).

More complex versions can be constructed, and alternative systems of accounting can be utilised, but the above schema captures the essential features of the environmental input–output system, from which a model can be constructed. Like the basic input–output model described in the chapter, the version presented below is an open, comparative static model in which final demands are exogenous (determined outside the model). There are no explicit capacity constraints on outputs, or limits to the supply of factors of production, which is equivalent to treating factor supplies as completely elastic at prevailing factor prices.[10]

To simplify the algebra, we assume in what follows that submatrices V and VIII are

[10] Other than natural resources, inputs of factors of production (labour and capital) are not shown in Figure 16.1, but the system could readily be extended to include them, in a manner similar to that used for natural resource flows.

empty. For the n 'conventional' input–output sectors the balance equations are

$$X_i - \sum_{j=1}^{n} a_{ij} X_j - \sum_{q=n+1}^{n+m} a_{iq} Z_q = F_i \qquad (16.27)$$

or

$$\mathbf{X} - \mathbf{A}_1 \mathbf{X} - \mathbf{A}_2 \mathbf{Z} = \mathbf{F} \qquad (16.28)$$

where $\mathbf{X}$ is the output vector for the conventional industries, $\mathbf{Z}$ is the output vector for the abatement industries (to be discussed below) and $\mathbf{F}$ is a vector of deliveries to final buyers. (For convenience we assume here that $\mathbf{F}$ is a vector.) The coefficients $a_{ij} \in \mathbf{A}_1$ and $a_{iq} \in \mathbf{A}_2$ are derived from the system of accounts in Figure 16.1 as

$$a_{ij} = X_{ij}/X_j \qquad (16.29)$$

where X_{ij} is purchases of commodity i to produce output X_j, and

$$a_{iq} = X_{iq}/Z_q \qquad (16.30)$$

where Z_q is the output of abatement sector q (or volume of residual q eliminated).

These assumptions of constant proportional input coefficients mirror those of the basic input–output model of the previous section, and reflect the properties of the Leontief production function, notably constant returns to scale and zero substitution between inputs, in contrast to the more usual neoclassical function used elsewhere in this book.

For the residuals submatrices (III, VI and IX), the production or generation of residuals can be written as

$$P_g = \sum_{j=1}^{n} w_{gj} X_j + \sum_{q=n+1}^{n+m} w_{gq} Z_q + w_{gF} \qquad (16.31)$$

where P_g is the amount of residual g generated by production, by abatement activities and by final demand.

In matrix form

$$\mathbf{P} = \mathbf{W}_1 \mathbf{X} + \mathbf{W}_2 \mathbf{Z} + \mathbf{W}_F \qquad (16.32)$$

Equation 16.32 measures gross production of residuals. The net production is gross production less the volume treated or elimi-

nated, which is the measured output of the abatement sector. How is this determined? For residual g, the net production (the volume of the residual returned to the environment) can be written

$$D_g = Z_g - P_g = Z_g - \sum w_{gj} X_j - \sum w_{gq} Z_q - w_{gF} \qquad (16.33)$$

where Z_g is the volume of residual g eliminated (the output of abatement sector g) and D_g is the net production of g (the volume not eliminated). Unless there is complete elimination, D_g will typically be negative, but its level may be amenable to control, and in ideal circumstances may be taken as a measure of the permitted level of net emission, waste or damage, where marginal damage and abatement costs are equal. By specifying this level as a negative final demand for the residual concerned, we have an equilibrium condition which enables us to determine the output of the abatement activity for that residual.

In matrix form,

$$\mathbf{Z} - \mathbf{W}_1 \mathbf{X} - \mathbf{W}_2 \mathbf{Z} = \mathbf{D} + \mathbf{W}_F \qquad (16.34)$$

We now write the complete model in the following partitioned from:

$$\begin{bmatrix} \mathbf{X} \\ \mathbf{Z} \end{bmatrix} - \begin{bmatrix} \mathbf{A}_1 & \mathbf{A}_2 \\ \mathbf{W}_1 & \mathbf{W}_2 \end{bmatrix} \begin{bmatrix} \mathbf{X} \\ \mathbf{Z} \end{bmatrix} = \begin{bmatrix} \mathbf{F} \\ \mathbf{D} + \mathbf{W}_F \end{bmatrix} \qquad (16.35)$$

$\mathbf{F}$ and $\mathbf{D}$ are the vectors of independent variables: $\mathbf{F}$ is final demand for the standard commodities, and $\mathbf{D}$ is tolerated or permitted emission, waste or damage levels. Once $\mathbf{F}$ and $\mathbf{D}$ are specified, we can solve for $\mathbf{X}$ (industry output levels) and $\mathbf{Z}$ (abatement levels):

$$\begin{bmatrix} \mathbf{X} \\ \mathbf{Z} \end{bmatrix} = \begin{bmatrix} \mathbf{I} - \mathbf{A}_1 & -\mathbf{A}_2 \\ -\mathbf{W}_1 & \mathbf{I} - \mathbf{W}_2 \end{bmatrix}^{-1} \begin{bmatrix} \mathbf{F} \\ \mathbf{D} + \mathbf{W}_F \end{bmatrix} \qquad (16.36)$$

Given the solution vector $[\mathbf{X}\ \mathbf{Z}]$, the level of natural resource consumption can be calculated as

$$\mathbf{N} = \mathbf{R}[\mathbf{X}\ \mathbf{Z}] \qquad (16.37)$$

where $\mathbf{R}$ is a matrix of natural resource input coefficients.

Although there have been numerous applications of environmental input–output models, none has attained the degree of detail and comprehensiveness of the model structure outlined above. Data problems have been severe, particularly in relation to the cost and production structures of abatement activities, but also in the definition and measurement of certain types of environmental degradation.

For this extended environmental input–output system, cost-price calculations can be introduced in a manner similar to that outlined in the third section of the chapter. In practice a range of approaches have been adopted, governed partly by data availability and partly by the particular form of model. For instance, cost-price equations for the abatement sectors (submatrices IV, V and VI of Figure 16.1) could be formulated so that the price of a unit of abatement is determined by its cost of production. In practice, abatement or elimination activity may be undertaken by and within the industry (or industries) which generates the pollution, and it may be difficult to identify the costs of the abatement activity.

If adequate data on abatement costs are available or can be collected, price equations can be formulated for the abatement sectors as

$$P_g = \sum a_{ij} P_i + v_g \qquad (16.38)$$

where P_g is the price or cost of eliminating one unit of pollutant g. How these equations are used in the extended model depends on the mechanism adopted for paying for abatement or elimination. If legislation obliges the polluter to pay, then polluting industries will buy abatement services from the abatement sectors, and the cost of these services will be included in the polluting industries' prices. The output price for industry j now becomes

$$P_j = \sum a_{ij} P_i + \sum a_{gj} P_g + v_j \qquad (16.39)$$

where a_{gj} is the quantity of abatement service g per unit of output which industry j is required to purchase, and P_g is the unit cost of abatement service g. The general solution to the extended price model then becomes

$$\mathbf{P} = (\mathbf{I} - \mathbf{A}')^{-1} \mathbf{v} \qquad (16.40)$$

where $\mathbf{P}$, $\mathbf{v}$ and $\mathbf{A}$ now include the abatement sectors. Alternatively, abatement/treatment may be financed through general taxation. In this case, polluting industry prices are unaffected (at least directly). Abatement services are provided by or purchased by government (central or local) and delivered to consumers as a public service (for example river purification, household waste collection, nuclear waste disposal).

Appendix 16.2 The algebra of the two-sector CGE model

The utility maximisation problem for the household is

Max $C_1{}^\alpha C_2{}^\beta$ subject to $Y = P_1 C_1 + P_2 C_2$

for which the Lagrangian is

$$L = C_1{}^\alpha C_2{}^\beta + \lambda[Y - P_1 C_1 - P_2 C_2]$$

giving the first order conditions:

$$\partial L/\partial C_1 = \alpha C_1{}^{\alpha-1} C_2{}^\beta - \lambda P_1 = 0 \qquad (16.41)$$

$$\partial L/\partial C_2 = \beta C_1{}^\alpha C_2{}^{\beta-1} - \lambda P_2 = 0 \qquad (16.42)$$

$$\partial L/\partial \lambda = Y - P_1 C_1 - P_2 C_2 = 0 \qquad (16.43)$$

Moving the terms in λ to the right-hand side in Equations 16.41 and 16.42 and then dividing the first equation by the second gives

$$(\alpha C_1{}^{\alpha-1} C_2{}^\beta)/(\beta C_1{}^\alpha C_2{}^{\beta-1}) = P_1/P_2$$

which can be solved for C_2 as

$$C_2 = (\beta P_1/\alpha P_2) C_1$$

which on substitution for C_2 in Equation 16.43 solves for

$$C_1 = [\alpha/(\alpha+\beta)P_1]Y \qquad (16.44)$$

Using Equation 16.44 to eliminate C_1 from the budget constraint and solving for C_2 yields

$$C_2 = [\beta/(\alpha+\beta)P_2]Y \qquad (16.45)$$

Equations 16.44 and 16.45 are Equations 16.25 in the text of the chapter.

Now consider the derivation of factor demands and the supply function for a profit maximising firm, where the production function is Cobb–Douglas in labour, L, and oil, R:

$$X = L^a R^b \qquad (16.46)$$

With W and P for the prices of labour and oil respectively, total cost is given by:

$$TC = WL + PR \qquad (16.47)$$

For cost minimisation, the Lagrangian is

$$L = WL + PR + \lambda[X - L^a R^b]$$

and the necessary conditions are

$$\partial L/\partial L = W - \lambda a L^{a-1} R^b = 0 \qquad (16.48)$$

$$\partial L/\partial R = P - \lambda b L^a R^{b-1} = 0 \qquad (16.49)$$

$$\partial L/\partial \lambda = X - L^a R^b = 0 \qquad (16.50)$$

Moving the terms in λ to the right-hand side in Equations 16.48 and 16.49 and dividing the first of the resulting equations by the second so as to eliminate λ, we get

$$W/P = (a/b)L^{-1}R$$

or

$$L/R = (a/b)PW^{-1} = (a/b)(P/W) \qquad (16.51)$$

which gives the ratio of factor use levels for cost minimisation as depending on the factor price ratio, and the parameters of the production function.

From Equation 16.50 we can write

$$L = (X/R^b)^{1/a}$$

and using this in Equation 16.51 to eliminate L, yields, after rearrangement

$$R = [(b/a)(W/P)]^{a/(a+b)} X^{1/(a+b)} \qquad (16.52)$$

for the firm's demand for oil as depending on factor prices and the level of output. Using Equation 16.50 again gives

$$R = (X/L^a)^{1/b}$$

which used in Equation 16.51 to eliminate R leads to

$$L = [(a/b)(P/W)]^{b/(a+b)} X^{1/(a+b)} \qquad (16.53)$$

for the firm's demand for labour.

Equations 16.52 and 16.53 are known as 'conditional factor demands', since they give demands conditional on the output level. To get, unconditional, factor demand equations we need to determine the profit maximising output level. With P_x for the price of output, profits are

$$\pi = P_X X - WL - PR$$

and substituting from the conditional factor demand equations, this is

$$\pi = P_X X - W[(a/b)(P/W)]^{b/(a+b)} X^{1/(a+b)}$$
$$\quad + P[(b/a)(W/P)]^{a/(a+b)} X^{1/(a+b)}$$

or

$$\pi = P_X X - Z X^{1/(a+b)} \qquad (16.54)$$

where

$$Z = W[(a/b)(P/W)]^{b/(a+b)} + P[(b/a)(W/P)]^{a/(a+b)} \qquad (16.55)$$

Taking the derivative of Equation 16.54 with respect to X and setting it equal to zero gives

$$P_X - [1/(a+b)]ZX^{1-\{1/(a+b)\}} = 0 \qquad (16.56)$$

as necessary for profit maximisation. Solving Equation 16.56 for X gives the profit maximising output level as:

$$X = [\{(a+b)P_X\}/Z]^{\{(a+b)/(a+b-1)\}} \qquad (16.57)$$

Equation 16.57 is a supply function giving profit maximising output as depending on the output price, P_X, and factor prices, P and W.

As in the chapter here, CGE models frequently employ the assumption of constant returns to scale in production. In this case, there is no supply function. For the Cobb–Douglas production function, constant returns to scale means $a + b = 1$, which means that the exponent of X in Equation 16.56 is zero. This means that the equation does not involve X and cannot be solved for it to give a supply function. For $a + b = 1$, Equation 16.56 becomes

$$P_X = Z$$

which, using Equation 16.55 with $a + b = 1$, is:

$$P_X = W[(a/b)(P/W)]^{(1-a)} + P[(b/a)(W/P)]^a \tag{16.58}$$

Now, using $a + b = 1$ in Equations 16.52 and 16.53 gives

$$R = [(\{1 - a\}/a)(W/P)]^a X$$

and

$$L = [(a/\{1 - a\})(P/W)]^{(1-a)} X$$

so that dividing by X,

$$U_R = R/X = [(\{1 - a\}/a)(W/P)]^a$$

and

$$U_L = L/X = [(a/\{1 - a\})(P/W)]^{(1-a)} \tag{16.60}$$

These two equations give the use of each factor per unit output as functions of the relative prices of the factors. If we knew the level of output X, we could use them to derive factor demands, by multiplying U_R and U_L by the output level.

On rearrangement, Equation 16.58 with $a + b = 1$ is

$$P_X = W^a P^{(1-a)}(a/\{1 - a\})^{(1-a)}$$
$$+ P^{(1-a)} W^a(\{1 - a\}/a)^a$$

so that it and Equations 16.59 and 16.60 mean that

$$P_X = WU_L + PU_R \tag{16.61}$$

which is the unit cost equation. It has the implication, well known from basic microeconomics, that for constant returns to scale in production, profits are zero at all levels of output. To see this, note that

$$WU_L + PU_R = W(L/X) + P(R/X)$$
$$= (WL + PR)/X$$

which is average cost, so that Equation 16.61 says that price equals average cost. Although demonstrated here for a Cobb–Douglas production function, this result holds for any constant returns to scale production function. With constant returns to scale, the firm produces to satisfy demand, using the factor input mix that follows from cost minimisation, and makes zero profit.

CHAPTER 17

Accounting for the environment

There is a dangerous asymmetry today in the way we measure, and hence, the way we think about, the value of natural resources. Man-made assets – buildings and equipment, for example – are valued as productive capital and are written off against the value of production as they depreciate. This practice recognizes that a consumption level maintained by drawing down the stock of capital exceeds the sustainable level of income. Natural resource assets are not so valued, and their loss entails no debit charge against current income that would account for the decrease in potential future production. A country could exhaust its mineral resources, cut down its forests, erode its soils, pollute its aquifers, and hunt its wildlife to extinction, but measured income would not be affected as these assets disappeared.

Repetto *et al.* (1989), page 4

Statisticians are trying to adjust measures of national wealth for pollution and depleted resources. This turns out to be all but impossible.

The Economist, 18 April 1998

Introduction

There is now a wide measure of agreement that the conventional system of national accounts, in most countries based upon the System of National Accounts (SNA) designed by the United Nations Statistical Division, is not adequate as a means of measuring or monitoring the impact of environmental changes on income or welfare. This is not surprising, as the development of national accounting (mainly in the 1940s and 1950s) took place in a period in which there was less concern about the impact of economic development on the environment. The conceptual basis and scope of the national accounts were governed by definitions of income and wealth which did not make any allowance for the depletion of natural resources or the costs of environmental damage such as pollution.

It is now widely appreciated that production and consumption activities have environmental effects which impose considerable costs, some of which will be borne by future generations. There is a perceived requirement for information that will permit economic activity to be so managed that it is sustainable.

This chapter is about emerging responses to that perception. The response that has most engaged economists is directed at modifications to national income accounting conventions such that what would get measured is sustainable income, which, as indicated in the quotation which heads this chapter, is not what currently gets measured. This is one area where there is a high level of agreement between environmental economists and environmental activists, most of whom also want to see changes to the national income accounting conventions. Many economists and environmentalists argue that such changes are essential for the pursuit of sustainability.

Criticism of current accounting conventions centres on three main issues: the absence of any allowance for the depletion of natural resources, the absence of any adjustment for degradation of environmental amenity, and the fact that activity to offset environmental damage is counted as part of income. The work done by economists on 'environmental accounting' – also sometimes referred to as 'natural resource accounting' or 'green accounting' – falls into two distinct, but related, parts. First, as discussed in the second part of this chapter, theoretical economists have used abstract models to consider how income should properly be measured, given the interdependence of the economy and the environment. Second, as discussed in the third part of this chapter, national income statisticians have developed proposals for the modification of the existing accounting conventions.

Not everybody who sees the need for information about environmental conditions is explicitly concerned about sustainability. There is a demand for biophysical data concerning the state of the environment which is independent of any interest in sustainable income. In any case, such data is a logical prerequisite to monetary data which can be used in economic accounts. Hence, in the next section we precede consideration of environmental accounting with a discussion of environmental indicators.

It will be seen that actually measuring sustainable income is extremely difficult. Indeed, some of the economists, and others, who have considered the problem in its practical as well as theoretical dimensions have come to the conclusion that it is impossible. Abandoning the goal of measuring sustainable income does not mean taking the view that it is impossible to provide information that could assist in the pursuit of sustainability. In the fourth section of this chapter we discuss 'sustainability indicators' of two kinds. First, there are economic indicators that are intended to signal whether some conditions for sustainability as conceived by economists are being met. Second, we review some proposals for using biophysical, and mixed socio-economic and biophysical, indicators to monitor performance in relation to broader sustainability criteria.

The chapter ends with some concluding remarks on environmental accounting and sustainability

Environmental indicators

Simply listing all of the features of the natural environment that are of direct concern to humans would take a long time, and providing information about such features and their behaviour over time would be expensive. But human interest in the natural environment extends beyond those things of direct concern. While there is much that is not known about the functioning of natural systems, we do know that the state of things of direct concern – soil quality, for example – depends on many things not of direct concern – soil microfauna, for example. Indeed, one of the reasons for generating and reporting data on the natural environment is to improve understanding of how the environment 'works' in relation to human interests, so that it can be better managed for human interests. So, a major problem in providing biophysical information is deciding what to report on. The term 'environmental indicators' is usually taken to refer to the provision of information by some public agency for the general public, rather than the generation of data for scientific research. This still leaves a very long list of potential indicators.

Agencies responsible for compiling and publishing data on environmental indicators have, therefore, to select from among potential indicators those that they will report. A long list runs the risk of information overload so that the public misses the overall picture and its important features, while a short list runs the risk that something important will be left out. Another selection criterion is the availability of data – indicators for which there are no data cannot be reported. Of course, it is always possible to decide to collect data where this was not previously done, but this entails spending money, so that decisions have to be made about costs and benefits across a range of potential, but currently unrecorded, indicators. Biophysical data on natural resources and the environment were first systematically collected and published in Norway in the mid-1970s. Since then, many other, mainly developed, countries have followed suit, and now publish environmental indicator data. Table 17.1 shows the key indicators selected by the Canadian environment ministry.

Table 17.1 Canada's preliminary environmental indicators, 1991.

Category	Issue	Indicator
Atmosphere	Climate change	Canadian energy-related emissions of carbon dioxide (CO_2)
		Atmospheric concentrations of CO_2
		Global air temperature
	Stratospheric ozone depletion	Canadian production and importation of ozone-depleting chemicals
		Stratospheric ozone levels
	Radiation exposure	Levels of radioactivity in the air
	Acid rain	Sulphur dioxide (SO_2) and nitrogen oxides (NO_x) emissions
	Outdoor urban air quality	Common air pollutants: nitrogen dioxides (NO_2) and carbon monoxide (CO) levels in urban air and emissions
		Common air pollutants: SO_2 and total suspended particulates (TSP) levels in urban air and emissions
		Ground level ozone concentrations
		Air toxics: lead concentrations in urban air
Water	Freshwater quality	Population served by treated water supply
		Municipal discharges to fresh water: BOD (biochemical oxygen demand), TSS (total suspended solids) and phosphorus
		Pulp and paper mill discharges to fresh water: TSS and BOD
		Discharges of regulated substances by petroleum refineries to water
		Concentration of phosphorus and nitrogen in water
		Maximum observed concentrations of pesticides in water: 2, 4-D-atrazine and lindane
	Toxic contaminants in the freshwater system	Contaminant levels in herring gull eggs in the Great Lakes Basin: PCBs (polychlorinated biphenyls) and system DDE (dichlorodiphenyldichloroethylene)
		Contaminant levels in Lake Trout, a sport fish from the Great Lakes Basin: PCBs and DDT (dichlorodiphenyltrichloroethane)
	Marine environmental quality	Municipal discharges to coastal waters: TSS and BOD
		Pulp and paper mill discharges to coastal waters: TSS and BOD
		Volume of significant marine spills
		Area closed to shellfish harvesting
		Contaminant levels in seabird eggs: PCBs
		Contaminant levels in seabird eggs: dioxins and furans
Biota (living organisms)	Biological diversity at risk	Wildlife species at risk
	State of wildlife	Levels of migratory game bird populations
Land	Protected areas	Land under protected status
	Urbanisation	Rural to urban land conversion
	Solid waste management	Municipal solid waste disposal trends
Natural economic resources	Forestry	Regeneration success versus total forest area harvested
	Agriculture	Changes in agricultural land use
		Amount of chemical fertiliser used and its associated nutrient content
		Agricultural pesticide application on cultivated land
	Fisheries	Total commercial fish catches in Canadian waters off the Atlantic coast
		Commercial fish harvest in the Great Lakes
	Water use	Total water withdrawal compared with growth in gross domestic product (GDP)
		Rates of water withdrawal and consumption by key economic sectors
		Rates of water recirculation by key industrial sectors
		Daily household water use per capita
	Energy	Total per capita primary energy use
		Emissions of CO_2 per unit of energy consumed
		Fossil fuel intensity of primary energy demand

Source: Environment Canada (1991), published in MacGillivray (1994).

Even where the list of indicators is relatively short, as in Table 17.1, comprehending the information provided can be difficult. One response to this is to use some framework, or model, to classify and organise the indicator data. The statistical office of the OECD has played a major role in the development of thinking about environmental indicators, and in OECD (1994a) it proposed a 'core' indicator list (40–50 items), and the 'pressure state response' model, shown in Figure 17.1, for their organisation. The idea is to report over time on indicators that signal the pressures that human activities are generating, on indicators that measure how the state of the environment is being affected by those pressures, and on indicators signalling how human activities are responding to changes in the state of the environment.

This model has found favour with a number of national environmental and statistical agencies in OECD member countries. Table 17.2 lists 46 indicators proposed for the UK in a recent report, where the indicators are characterised according to the OECD model. The selection of indicators was governed by the following criteria:

- a time series of the indicator should be available, including recent observations;
- the indicators should be sensitive to action by the UK authorities, and should allow the setting of meaningful targets for the monitoring of actions;
- the data should be uncontentious (as far as this is ever possible) and be from official or otherwise accessible sources;
- they should require little or no additional collection or processing;
- the indicator should have resonance with the intended audience; that is, be readily understood and be considered appropriate by that audience.

Comparing Tables 17.1 and 17.2 it is apparent that while the coverage of the 'Issue' and 'Theme' lists is similar, the indicator lists show greater differences.

The exercises reported on in Tables 17.1 and 17.2 are examples of what is called 'state of the environment reporting'. In such exercises, as illustrated in these examples, there is an emphasis on issues relating to environ-

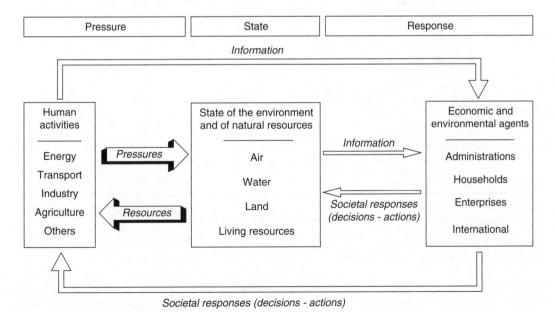

Figure 17.1   The OECD pressure state response model.
Source: OECD (1994a).

Table 17.2 Suggested environmental indicators for the UK.

Theme	Potential indicator idea	PSR[a]	Data[b]	Meaningful[c]	Resonant[d]
Biodiversity	1 Extinct species	S	✗	✓	?
	2 SSSI damage	S/P	✗	✓	?
	3 Farmland species index	S	✓a	✓	✓
	4 Declining species	S	✗	✓	✓
	5 Habitat status	S	✗	✓	✓
	6 Land under active conservation management	R	?	✓	✓
	7 Species Action Plans	R	✗	?	✗
Quality of life	8 Sustainable Economic Welfare	S	✓p	✓	✓
	9 Asthma cases reported by GPs	S	✓a	?✓	✓
Footprints abroad	10 Timber imports from sustainable sources	P	✓a	✓	✓
	11 Cotton imports from sustainable sources	P	?a	✓	✓
Atmosphere	12 CO_2 emissions	P	✓a	✓	✓
	13 NO_x emissions (from transport)	P	✓a	✓	✓
	14 SO_2 emissions	P	✓a	✓	✓
	15 Areas of SSSI at risk from acid rain	S	✗	?	?
	16 HCFC production	P	✗	✗	?
	17 Critical load exceedance	P/S	✗	✓	?
	18 Population exposed to poor air quality	S	?a	x	✓
	19 Other air quality measures	S	?	?	?
Land	20 Hedgerow loss	S/P	✓p	✓	✓
	21 Land use	S	?	?	?
	22 Tree health survey	S	✓a	?	✓
	23 Rates and types of new tree planting	S/R	?a	✗	✓
	24 Soil condition	S	✗	✗	?
Water	25 Nitrate in groundwater	S	✓a	✓	?
	26 Water consumption	P	✓a	✓	?
	27 Water pollution incidents	P	✓a	✗	✓
	28 Water quality measures	S	✓a	✓?	✓
Marine	29 Bathing beach standards	S	✓a	?	✓
	30 Coast watch litter	S/P	✓?a	?	✓
	31 Oiled seabirds	S	✓p	?	✓
	32 Fish stocks and catches	S/P	✓a	✓	✓
	33 Oil spill incidents	P	✓a	?	✓
	34 Eutrophication	P	✓a	✓	✗
Agriculture	35 Decline in farmland bird species	S	✓a	✓	✓
	36 Expenditure on agri-environment	P/R	✓a	?	✓
	37 Applications of fertiliser/pesticide per farmed hectare	P	✓a	✗	?
Energy	38 Energy consumption by fuel type	P	✓a	✓	✗
	39 Energy intensity of the economy	S?	✓a	✗?	✗
Industry	40 Special waste intensity	P	✓a	✗	✗
	41 Toxic releases	P	✗	✗	✓
	42 Contaminated land	S	✗	✗	✓?
Transport	43 Transport km by mode	P	✓a	✓	?
	44 Length of motorways/trunk road lanes	P	✓a	✓	?
	45 Journey length/time	P	✓p	✓	?
Waste	46 Toxic waste trade	P	✓a	✓?	✓

Source: MacGillivray (1994).

[a] P, = environmental pressures; S, = state of the environment; or R, = societal response to the situation.
[b] Is data available and reliable? a, Annual; p, periodic.
[c] Represents an important phenomenon.
[d] Likely to strike a chord with a public audience.

mental quality, as opposed to issues relating to natural resource use and availability. State of the Environment Reports are typically intended for an audience which is the con-

cerned general public, as indicated by the final criterion used in selecting the UK list of indicators. They report, again as illustrated in these two examples, mainly in biophysical units. While this approach avoids the problem of assigning monetary values to physical or qualitative flows which are not exchanged through a market, it makes it difficult, and some would argue impossible, to aggregate the effects of a number of environmental changes since there is no standard unit of measurement or agreed system of weights. In the next two sections we discuss, under the rubric of 'environmental accounting', work, mainly by economists, which is directed at using monetary valuation to capture in a smaller set of numbers the implications for human welfare of changes in the state of the natural environment. To date, this work has focused mainly on issues concerning the use of natural resources in production and the measurement of sustainable income, but many working in the area envisage that environmental quality issues can be handled in similar ways.

Environmental accounting: theory

In a lecture delivered at the Washington DC 'think tank' Resources for the Future in 1992 (Solow, 1992, 1993), the Nobel laureate economist Robert Solow suggested that 'an innovation in social accounting practice could contribute to more rational debate and perhaps more rational action in the economics of non-renewable resources and the approach to a sustainable economy'. We use the title of his lecture as the heading to the next sub section. In it he outlined the basis in economic theory for his view that proper national income accounting would promote sustainability. As we have noted, many environmentalists share this view, as do many economists. For the economists, the theory outlined by Solow is the basis for their views on this matter. In this section we shall consider that theory, and the modifications to current national income accounting conventions that it is taken to imply. We shall also make the important point that there appears to be some misunderstanding of the theory

and its implications for the ability of revised national income accounting conventions to promote sustainability. In the text here we shall try to tell the story in fairly intuitive terms. Appendices 17.1 and 17.2 tell the same story in mathematical terms. The theory to be considered here builds on the theory of natural resource use covered in Chapters 7, 8 and 9.

An almost practical step toward sustainability

We consider an economy that uses a non-renewable resource and man-made, reproducible, capital to produce output, which can be either consumed or added to the stock of capital. There is no technical progress. A sustainable path is one that involves constant utility forever. Given that there is just one commodity produced and consumed, and that utility depends only on consumption, constant utility is the same as constant consumption. We are going to consider the question: what kind of economic behaviour is necessary for sustainability in this sense? There is, of course, a prior question, which is: can such an economy be sustainable? Given that the stock of the resource is finite, it is obvious that the answer to this question depends, as discussed in Chapter 7, on the possibilities for substitution in production as between the resource and reproducible capital. If those possibilities are such that sustainability is infeasible – as they would be if the production function was $Q = K^{\alpha}R^{\beta}$, $\alpha + \beta = 1$ and $\beta > \alpha$ – then following the rules for economic behaviour that are the answer to the first question could not deliver sustainability. Those rules are necessary but not sufficient conditions for sustainability. We return to the question of feasibility at the end of this section.

As set out by Solow, the theory involves two 'key propositions'. The first is that 'properly defined net national product'

> measures the maximum current level of
> consumer satisfaction that can be
> sustained forever

and is therefore

> a measure of sustainable income given the state of the economy

The second proposition is that

> Properly defined and properly calculated, this year's net national product can always be regarded as this year's interest on society's total stock of capital

where the total stock of capital includes both reproducible capital and the resource stock. When these two propositions are put together, we get the rule for economic behaviour that gives sustainability. It is to maintain society's total stock of capital intact, by consuming only the interest on that capital. This implies adding to the stock of reproducible capital an amount equal to the depreciation of the resource stock – which is Hartwick's rule, discussed in Chapters 3 and 7 – where the depreciation of the resource stock is measured by the Hotelling rent arising in its extraction.

In his lecture, Solow was careful to state, several times, a caveat that attends these propositions as guides to policy in an actual economy. This is that the 'right prices' are used to value the capital stock and the resource stock. Note that without prices we could not add together the stocks of reproducible capital and the resource to get a figure for 'society's total wealth'. In order to be 'right', the prices must be, as Solow puts it, such that they 'make full allowance even for the distant future, and will even take account of how each future generation will take account of its future'. The theory ensures that the prices do this by working with a model in which there is a single representative agent with perfect future knowledge, who works out and follows a plan for consumption, investment and resource depletion on the basis of maximising the discounted sum of future utilities subject to the constraints imposed by the availability of the resource and the need to forego consumption in order to invest in reproducible capital. Such a model is set out in Appendix 17.1.

The justification for using such a model to think about these questions is that, given some very strong assumptions about agents' foresight and institutions, competitive markets would produce the same price behaviour. The model shows, for example, that the resource price is required to evolve according to Hotelling's rule, and, given strong assumptions, it can be shown that resource prices determined in competitive markets will follow the same rule. Solow is absolutely explicit about the relationship between actual market prices and the 'right prices' for guiding the economic behaviour that is necessary for sustainability:

> This story makes it obvious that everyday market prices can make no claim to embody that kind of foreknowledge. Least of all could the prices of natural resource products, which are famous for their volatility, have this property; but one could entertain legitimate doubts about other prices, too. The hope has to be that a careful attempt to average out speculative movements and to correct for the other imperfections I listed earlier would yield adjusted prices that might serve as a rough approximation to the theoretically correct ones. We act as if that were true in other contexts. The important hedge is not to claim too much.

Unfortunately, in their enthusiasm to use economic theory to promote sustainability, some economists do not explicitly qualify their contributions to policy analysis with 'the important hedge'.

There is, as set out in Appendix 17.1 and discussed below, a further 'hedge' of some importance, not made explicit in Solow's papers, and which tends to be glossed over in much of the literature. This is the fact that, even within the context of the representative agent model itself, the prices may not be 'right'. The 'right' prices are those which go with a constant consumption path. However, the representative agent will not necessarily choose a constant consumption path, unless constrained to do so. Hence, the prices ruling along the optimal path in such a model will not be the correct prices to use for the implementation of Hartwick's rule in pursuit of sustainability, unless it so happens that the representative agent's optimal path is one with constant consumption.

What has all this got to with environmental accounting? What is Solow's 'almost practical step'? It is the idea that if at a point in time we knew what sustainable income for the economy was we would know whether or not we were behaving in the interests of the future. Consumption in excess of sustainable income would indicate that we were not, while consumption equal to or less than sustainable income would indicate that we were. The step is 'almost practical' because of the need to use not currently observable market prices, but the 'right' prices.

A resource owner in a competitive economy

The idea that to behave sustainably involves keeping wealth intact by consuming just the interest income on that wealth has considerable intuitive appeal. We can make that appeal explicit by considering the situation of a resource owner in a competitive economy. Doing this will also serve to provide some insight into how the Hartwick rule works when it does, and some basis for a further discussion of the caveats noted above.

Consider, then, an individual who owns an oil deposit and sells extraction permits to a company in the oil production business. The individual pays the proceeds from permit sales into his or her bank account, from which is paid his or her her expenditure on consumption. Let us use here the following notation:

B is the size of the bank account, units £s
C is consumption expenditure, units £s
W is total wealth, units £s
R is the total of permit sales, units tonnes
X is the size of the remaining stock of mineral, units tonnes
h is the price of a permit, £s per tonne
V is the value of the mine, units £s
r is the interest rate, assumed constant over time

Let us also use $t-1$ to denote the first day of the relevant period of time, say a year, and t to denote the last day of the period. At $t-1$ the mine owner sells permits and banks the revenue. At t he or she writes a cheque on the bank account to pay for his or her consumption during the period. While this construction is somewhat special it serves to make what is going on clear. In this context, considering, as we shall, an infinite time horizon and the question of constant consumption by an individual forever is obviously rather strange. Individuals do not live forever. However, pretending that they do, or at least that they behave as if they do by treating their heirs as simple extensions of themselves, is not uncommon in economics, and does serve to generate some useful insights.

The behaviour over time of B is given by

$$B_t = (1+r)B_{t-1} + (1+r)h_{t-1}R_{t-1} - C_t \tag{17.1}$$

because B_{t-1} is the principal at the start of the year, to which is added, to earn interest over the year, the proceeds from permit sales at the start of the year. Equation 17.1 can be written as

$$B_t - B_{t-1} = rB_{t-1} + (1+r)h_{t-1}R_{t-1} - C_t \tag{17.2}$$

At t the value of the mine is given by the permit price at t multiplied by the amount of oil remaining, which is the amount remaining at the start of the period less the amount for which permits were sold at the start of the period. That is:

$$V_t = h_t(X_{t-1} - R_{t-1}) \tag{17.3}$$

The price of an extraction permit in a competitive economy will be the difference between the marginal cost of extraction and the price for which extracted oil sells; that is, the Hotelling rent. That is why we have used h here as the symbol for the price of an extraction permit. Again given a competitive economy, we know from Chapter 8 that Hotelling's rule governs the behaviour of rent, and hence the price of extraction permits, over time so that

$$h_t = (1+r)h_{t-1}$$

and substituting in Equation 17.3 gives

$$V_t = (1+r)h_{t-1}(X_{t-1} - R_{t-1})$$
$$= (1+r)(h_{t-1}X_{t-1} - h_{t-1}R_{t-1})$$

or

$$V_t = (1+r)(V_{t-1} - h_{t-1}R_{t-1}) \quad (17.4)$$

from which we get

$$V_t - V_{t-1} = rV_{t-1} - (1+r)h_{t-1}R_{t-1} \quad (17.5)$$

The individual's wealth is just the sum of the bank deposit and the value of the mine

$$W_t = B_t + V_t$$

so that the change in wealth over a period is:

$$W_t - W_{t-1} = (B_t - B_{t-1}) + (V_t - V_{t-1}) \quad (17.6)$$

Substituting in Equation 17.6 from Equations 17.2 and 17.5 gives

$$W_t - W_{t-1} = rB_{t-1} + (1+r)h_{t-1}R_{t-1}$$
$$- C_t + rV_{t-1} - (1+r)h_{t-1}R_{t-1}$$

or

$$W_t - W_{t-1} = rB_{t-1} + rV_{t-1} - C_t \quad (17.7)$$

which is

$$W_t - W_{t-1} = rW_{t-1} - C_t \quad (17.8)$$

Now, for constant wealth, $W_t - W_{t-1} = 0$, we get from Equation 17.8

$$C_t = rW_{t-1} \quad (17.9)$$

so that if a period's consumption is equal to the interest earned on total wealth at the start of the period, wealth will be the same at the end of the period as at the start. Further, Equation 17.9 holds for all t and $t-1$, for all periods, so that if we use the subscript 0 for the start of some initial period

$$C_t = rW_0 \quad (17.10)$$

will clearly be the maximum constant consumption level for all subsequent periods. Readers who are unconvinced that rW_0 is the largest possible constant consumption stream can convince themselves that this is the case by some numerical experiments. A numerical example on which such experiments could be based is given in Chapter 9 of Common (1996).

Given the result that the present value of x forever is x/r (see Chapter 15) the present value of the consumption stream rW_0 forever is

$$W^*_0 = W_0 \quad (17.11)$$

so that wealth as the current value of total assets and wealth as the present value of the largest future constant consumption level that is indefinitely sustainable are the same.

For this individual a period's income, Y, is given by the interest payment on the bank deposit plus the revenue from permit sales and the interest earned thereon:

$$Y_t = rB_{t-1} + (1+r)h_{t-1}R_{t-1} \quad (17.12)$$

Equation 17.7 for $W_t - W_{t-1} = 0$ gives

$$C_t = rB_{t-1} + rV_{t-1}$$

and if we define investment, I, as the difference between income and consumption we have

$$I_t = Y_t - C_t$$
$$= rB_{t-1} + (1+r)h_{t-1}R_{t-1} - rB_{t-1} - rV_{t-1}$$
$$= (1+r)h_{t-1}R_{t-1} - rV_{t-1} \quad (17.13)$$

From Equation 17.5, this can be written as

$$I_t = -(V_t - V_{t-1}) \quad (17.14)$$

which says that the individual is investing an amount equal to the depreciation of the mine. This is Hartwick's rule applied to this individual – investing in his or her reproducible capital, the bank account, in every period an amount equal to the depreciation of his or her resource stock, the oil deposit. The depreciation of the oil deposit is simply the reduction in its value over the period on account of the reduced size of the resource stock. Note that Equation 17.14 can also be read as saying that net investment – that is, investment less depreciation – is zero when wealth is maintained intact.

A widely used definition of 'sustainable income' is that it is the amount that can be consumed during a period without reducing wealth. Here it follows immediately from the preceding discussion that with $Y_{\text{sus},t}$ for the individual's sustainable income for the period starting on $t-1$ and ending on t is:

$$Y_{\text{sus},t} = rW_{t-1} \qquad (17.15)$$

Recall that Solow stated that properly measured net national product, or income, is both the interest on wealth and the level of consumption that can be maintained forever. Equation 17.15 gives sustainable income for the individual as the interest on wealth. We have already established in this context (Equation 17.9) that this is a level of consumption that can be maintained forever.

All of this is the basic result set out by Solow as discussed in the previous subsection – for sustainable consumption, maintain wealth intact by consuming just the interest on the constant wealth – but here it is shown to work for a non-renewable resource stock owning individual in a competitive economy with a constant interest rate rather than for an economy as a whole.[1] We look at the transferability of the result to an economy in the next subsection, but before doing that there are some further points to be made about the situation of an individual.

The first is to note the key role of the efficiency condition that the proportional rate of increase in rent is equal to the single ruling interest rate. If we have $h_t = (1+b)h_{t-1}$ rather than $h_t = (1+r)h_{t-1}$, then we cannot derive Equation 17.7.

We have shown that by consuming just the interest on wealth an individual resource stock owner achieves the highest sustainable level of consumption. We have not shown that such an individual would choose such a consumption pattern. In fact, an individual would do so only in special circumstances, as

we now show. There is a substantial and technically sophisticated literature on the choice of intertemporal consumption plans by individuals, but for our purposes a very simple formulation of the problem will suffice. We assume that the problem of choosing a consumption plan can be represented as

$$\text{Max} \int_0^\infty U(C_t) e^{-\rho t} \mathrm{d}t$$

$$\text{subject to } \mathrm{d}W/\mathrm{d}t = rW_t - C_t$$

where the notation is as before, but we have introduced the symbol ρ for the rate (assumed constant) at which the individual discounts future utility. For this problem, we get from the current value Hamiltonian necessary conditions which include

$$\partial H_t/\partial C_t = U_{Ct} - \lambda_t = 0$$

and

$$\mathrm{d}\lambda/\mathrm{d}t - \rho\lambda_t = -\partial Ht/\partial Wt = -\lambda_t r$$

where from the second condition we can write

$$\mathrm{d}\lambda/\mathrm{d}t = (\rho - r)\lambda_t$$

and we have, on standard assumptions about diminishing marginal utility

$$\rho = r \rightarrow \mathrm{d}\lambda/\mathrm{d}t = 0 \rightarrow OU_{Ct} \text{ constant,} \\ C_t \text{ constant}$$

$$\rho > r \rightarrow \mathrm{d}\lambda/\mathrm{d}t > 0 \rightarrow U_{Ct} \text{ increasing,} \\ C_t \text{ decreasing}$$

$$\rho < r \rightarrow \mathrm{d}\lambda/\mathrm{d}t < 0 \rightarrow OU_{Ct} \text{ decreasing,} \\ C_t \text{ increasing}$$

Thus, we see that the individual will choose constant consumption as his or her optimal plan only if his or her intertemporal utility discount rate is equal to the interest rate.

Suppose that our individual started out with C_t increasing and then for some reason decided at the start of period $T-1$ to T decided to switch to C_t constant. Given the foregoing it should be clear that the individual would thereafter be acting to consume the interest on the wealth at $T-1$ and maintaining that wealth intact and sustaining con-

---

[1] Note that if the interest rate r is not constant, sustainable consumption would not maintain wealth intact. Wealth would have to move in the opposite direction to any change in the interest rate, so that the product rW remains constant.

stant consumption forever, but that the wealth maintained intact would be less than the individual's initial wealth and the constant indefinitely sustainable consumption level would be lower than if such behaviour had been adopted at the outset. Again, the reader who wishes to confirm the above points can do so by simple numerical experimentation.

There is another point here that can also be confirmed in that way. We have not yet mentioned the eventual exhaustion of the oil deposit, and what happens when that occurs. In fact, in regard to consumption and wealth, nothing happens. By the time the oil is exhausted, given the behaviour from the outset that keeps wealth constant, the entire initial value of the oil stock will have been transferred to the bank deposit, and our individual can continue to have constant consumption forever, as the interest on the bank deposit, at the same level as initially.

Finally, we should note that, in order to establish a reference point for talking about economies as opposed to individuals, we have thus far ignored one area of opportunity open to an individual. We have assumed that the individual's consumption opportunities over time are given solely by the way he or she manages the asset portfolio, which comprises the bank account and the mine. In fact, an individual can borrow to alter his or her consumption path from that given by the asset portfolio, incurring debts for later repayment from the income stream that it generates. It can be shown that, given standard assumptions about competitive markets in loanable funds, the individual would manage his or her assets so as to maximise wealth, and then choose a consumption path reflecting his or her intertemporal preferences and the opportunities available by borrowing and repaying. There is, that is, a 'separation theorem' which shows that the problems of asset portfolio management and consumption planning can be treated sequentially – first maximise wealth ignoring intertemporal preferences, then arrange consumption over time subject to the constraint

arising from maximised wealth. We make this point to emphasise that our discussion here has been intended only as a means of providing some sense of economists' basic way of thinking about sustainability, rather than as a proper account of intertemporal consumption planning by an individual.[2]

Consumption, income and wealth for an economy

We now consider an economy which uses reproducible capital and a non-renewable resource to produce output, which can be either consumed or saved and added to the capital stock. The first point to be made is that there is an important distinction between an open economy, which trades with other economies, and a closed economy where there is no foreign trade. If we assume that an open economy is 'small', so that it takes world prices for traded goods as given, that there is complete freedom of international capital movements (with respect to which the economy is also 'small') and that all markets are competitive, then the situation for an open economy is essentially as set out above for an individual. We will return to this point in discussing two essential differences between a resource owning individual and a resource exploiting economy in relation to sustainability as constant consumption forever. Note that the global economy is a closed economy, and that the sustainability problem is really a global problem.

The first essential difference primarily concerns the feasibility of constant consumption forever. Equation 17.12 is the production function for the individual's income. It is linear, implying that the bank account and the oil deposit are perfect substitutes in the

[2] Most standard intermediate and advanced microeconomics texts provide an analysis of the individual intertemporal utility maximisation: see, for examples, Hirshleifer (1980) and Deaton and Muellbauer (1980). Chapter 16 in Hirshleifer (1980) discusses the separation theorem, on which see also chapter 6 of Common (1996).

production of income, and that the oil deposit is not essential in the production of income. As we noted above, for the individual mine owner exhaustion of the mine does not, if behaviour has previously been such as to maintain wealth intact, imply any reduction in wealth or sustainable consumption. In the economics literature on sustainability, it is not generally regarded as appropriate to assume for an economy that the resource is inessential in production. Note, however, that most of the literature is concerned with a closed economy. For a small open economy which can export the resource and invest in overseas assets the situation is essentially as for an individual and an income production function like Equation 17.12 would be appropriate. For a closed economy, it can be shown that even where the resource is essential, sustainability as constant consumption may be feasible. This is, as already noted, the case where the production function is

$$Q_t = K_t^{\alpha} R_t^{\beta} : \alpha + \beta = 1 \text{ and } \beta < \alpha \quad (17.16)$$

where K_t is the stock of reproducible capital and R_t is the resource use at time t.

The second essential difference concerns the behavioural rule that will give sustainability, if it is feasible. The point here is that whereas for an individual in a competitive economy, or for a small open economy in a competitive world economy, prices are exogenous and unaffected by the behaviour of the individual, or of a small open economy, for a closed economy prices are endogenous and depend upon the economy's behaviour. Also, for the individual analysed in the previous subsection, the marginal product of the bank account in producing income is constant, and equal to r, the single interest rate ruling throughout the economy. For a closed economy with Equation 17.16 as its production function, on the other hand, the behaviour of the marginal product of capital over time depends upon the time paths chosen for K_t and R_t, as does the marginal product of resource use. Analysing properly the full

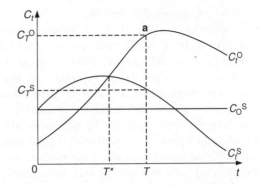

Figure 17.2 Optimal and sustainable consumption paths.

implications of the endogeneity of prices and rates of return on assets is difficult, and we will not attempt it here. Some analysis is provided in Appendix 17.1. We can, however, use Figure 17.2 to show some of the results.

In Figure 17.2 C^O_t is the optimal path for consumption from a representative agent model of a closed economy, where the discounted integral of the utility of consumption is maximised, subject to the constraints involving resource use and the allocation of output as between consumption and capital accumulation.[3] This is essentially the model considered in Chapter 7: see also Appendix 17.1. C^S_O is the constant consumption level that could be maintained forever if at the outset the agent went for the highest feasible level of constant consumption, rather than the optimal path C^O_t. C^S_t gives the time path under the optimal plan of the maximum level of consumption that would thereafter be indefinitely sustainable at each date. At T, for example, C^O_T is optimal consumption and C^S_T is the maximum constant level of consumption sustainable after T, given that the optimal plan is followed until T.

Now, the theory appealed to by Solow as discussed above has been interpreted as having the implication that if an economy had been following the optimal path and were at the point **a** on C^O_t the ruling prices and interest rate could be used with the stock of capital and of the resource to compute

[3] Figure 17.2 is based on figure 4 in Pezzey (1997).

wealth and sustainable income for which the corresponding future constant consumption level would be C^O_T. In fact, as Figure 17.2 shows, C^O_T would not be sustainable at T, given that C^O_t had been followed to that time. The maximum constant consumption level that could be indefinitely sustained forward from T, given that C^O_t had been followed until T, is C^S_T. Note that it is not being asserted that using prices and quantities from the optimal path will always overstate wealth, sustainable income and future constant consumption. To the left of T^* C^S_t is greater than C^O_t. The point is that, in general, using the prices and quantities that go with the optimal path will give incorrect signals regarding the level of sustainable income and constant future consumption as interest on wealth. To get the right signals at time T it would be necessary to use the prices and quantities that would hold at T on the path C^S_t. Note that both the efficiency condition (rent increasing proportionately at the rate of interest) and the Hartwick rule (zero total net investment) hold along C^S_O, given that the prices that go with that time path for consumption are used in stating them.

As we have already noted, in the case of an individual it is also true that the optimal consumption plan will, generally, not involve maximum constant consumption. And, to the extent that it does not, an individual who follows it initially will subsequently have stocks of assets that are different from those that would exist if the maximum constant consumption path had been followed. However, the prices and interest rate facing the individual, being independent of his or her behaviour, will not be affected. He or she could, should at some point he or she wished to follow a constant consumption path, use the ruling prices and interest rate to work out the maximum constant level of consumption possible, given the actual asset portfolio.

In discussing the case of the closed economy here we have been looking at a model economy tracking the optimal path, which is usually taken to being equivalent to

thinking about the path that a fully competitive perfect foresight economy would track. Of course, as emphasised by Solow, actual economies do not involve perfect foresight and competition. The model economy considered is special in a number of other ways also – it exploits just one non-renewable resource, there is no population growth and no technical progress. Models without such restrictions have been examined in the literature, and references are provided in the further reading section at the end of the chapter. We have focused here on this very simple model in order to highlight in it a point that applies generally – measuring sustainable income, and hence future constant consumption possibilities, requires using the prices that go with sustainability to measure total wealth. These are not, generally, the prices that obtain along the path that a competitive perfect foresight economy would track, and are not the prices that we observe in actual economies. These 'important hedges' are often overlooked, with the result that the prospects for actually measuring sustainable income for an actual economy are frequently oversold.

In saying this, it is implied that there is a sustainable income to be measured, that constant consumption forever is feasible. As we have noted, this is not assured. There is an extensive literature on feasibility conditions in the simple model considered here, and on extensions to encompass multiple resource inputs (renewable and non-renewable), population growth and technical progress. Again, we refer the reader to the further reading section, and move to considering the adjustments to standard measures of national income that this sort of economic theory, which we shall refer to as 'capital theory' in what follows, suggests are required.

Measuring national income

The simplest capital theory model used to address the question of the proper measurement of national income, or product, is a representative agent model of a closed economy where a single commodity is produced using just (non-depreciating) reproducible capital, which is accumulated by abstaining from consumption of the produced commodity. As shown in Appendix 17.2, the basic result derived is that the proper measure of national income is

$$\text{NDP}_t = C_t + I_t \qquad (17.17)$$

where NDP stands for Net Domestic Product, C for consumption and I for investment in reproducible capital. This 'proper measure of national income' is taken to be a measure of sustainable income, as that term was used in the previous subsections.

Theoretical arguments about how sustainable income should be measured are developed in terms of modifications to Equation 17.17 based on consideration of models that all have the same structure and nature except in regard to what is assumed about the way the economy relates to the environment in terms of arguments in the production and utility functions. A number of such models are presented in Appendix 17.2. Here we shall briefly review some of the results reported there.

For the model that is the basis for Figure 17.2, where production requires inputs of a single non-renewable resource as well as reproducible capital, and using EDP (environmentally adjusted domestic product) for sustainable income, the result is that

$$\text{EDP}_t = \text{NDP}_t - Q_{Rt}R_t = \text{NDP}_t - h_t R_t \qquad (17.18)$$

where Q_{Rt} is the marginal product of the resource in production, R_t is the amount used, and h_t is, as previously in this section, the Hotelling rent. In this model, resource extraction is costless, so that Hotelling rent is equal to marginal product. The second term on the right-hand side of Equation 17.18 is the depreciation of the resource stock. Two points need to be made here.

First, if we substitute Equation 17.17 into Equation 17.18 we get

$$\text{EDP}_t = C_t + I_t - h_t R_t$$

so that if total net investment is zero – investment in reproducible capital equals resource depreciation, the Hartwick rule – we have consumption equal to sustainable income, and, given the caveats of the previous subsection, constant wealth.

The second point concerns the interpretation of Hotelling rent times resource use as depreciation of the resource stock. Earlier, at Equation 17.5, we gave depreciation in the value of the mine as:

$$V_t - V_{t-1} = rV_{t-1} - (1+r)h_{t-1}R_{t-1}$$

Rearranging 17.5 we get depreciation as the change in the value of the mine as

$$V_t/(1+r) - V_{t-1} = h_{t-1}R_{t-1} \qquad (17.19)$$

where the right-hand side refers to the start of a period, so that the value of the mine at the end of the period, V_t, has to be discounted by $(1+r)$ on the left-hand side for comparability. In both discrete and continuous time, depreciation of the resource stock/mine is equal to Hotelling rent times the amount extracted.

In the model which is the basis for Figure 17.2 and for which Equation 17.18 is derived resource extraction is costless, and there is no exploration activity that can increase the size of the known resource stock. In a model economy where resource extraction involves cost, and new known reserves can be established at some cost, we find that

$$\text{EDP}_t = \text{NDP}_t - (Q_{Rt} - G_{Rt})(R_t - N_t)$$
$$= \text{NDP}_t - h_t(R_t - N_t) \qquad (17.20)$$

where Q_{Rt} is the marginal product of the resource, G_{Rt} is marginal extraction cost, and N_t is additions to the known stock as the result of exploration. Note that where extraction is costly, Hotelling rent is the difference between the marginal product of the resource and its marginal cost of extraction.

Suppose that a renewable resource rather than a non-renewable resource is used in production. Then we find that

$$\text{EDP}_t = \text{NDP}_t - (Q_{Rt} - G_{Rt})(R_t - F\{S_t\})$$
$$= \text{NDP}_t - h_t(R_t - F\{S_t\}) \qquad (17.21)$$

where G_{Rt} is the marginal cost of harvesting, and $F\{S_t\}$ is the growth function for the resource stock, where S_t is the stock size. Note that Equation 17.21 has exactly the same structure as Equation 17.20, with $F\{S_t\}$ playing the role in 17.21 that N_t plays in 17.20. Note also that for sustainable yield exploitation of the renewable resource, $R_t = F\{S_t\}$, there is no depreciation to account for, and $EDP_t = NDP_t$.

While some renewable resources are solely of economic interest as an input to production, some are also of direct interest to consumers. An example would be some tree species which is harvested and used in the production of commodities such as paper, and which as standing timber is a source of recreational services. In such a case we find that

$$EDP_t = NDP_t + (U_{St}/U_{Ct})S_t - h_t(R_t - F\{S_t\}) \tag{17.22}$$

where U_{St} is the marginal utility of standing trees and U_{Ct} is the marginal utility of produced commodity consumption. As compared with Equation 17.21 we now have an additional adjustment to make to net national income as conventionally measured. We have written this adjustment for the amenity value of standing timber valuing it using a ratio of marginal utilities because, typically, there will be no market price that we can observe for the amenity services of standing timber. If we want to measure sustainable income taking account of such amenity services, then we cannot rely on market prices. We could, in principle, think in terms of getting some kind of price to use with S_t from the methods discussed in Chapter 14, where we also discussed the problems that attend such methods.

More fundamentally, there is the question of whether there should be such an adjustment to NDP_t for any particular tree species. In the model which leads to Equation 17.22 it is assumed that standing timber yields services to consumers. In the model which leads to Equation 17.21 this assumption is

not made. The different prescriptions about adjustments to NDP_t arise from different models about how the economy relates to the environment. For any particular tree species we could, in principle, decide which is the appropriate model by using the methods of Chapter 14 to test for $U_S = 0$. While this is true, given many renewable resources which a priori could have direct utility it does imply a large research agenda for actually doing environmental accounting. In the absence of such empirical resolution, the prescriptions from capital theory for adjusting conventional income measurement to account for the environment are dependent on the assumptions embodied in the model.

As shown in Appendix 17.2, the point here also applies when we start to consider adjustments on account of the environmental deterioration due to emissions arising in production. What capital theory tells us about how to do environmental accounting and measure sustainable income depends on the model of economy–environment interdependence that is used. Given the current state of knowledge, there is no unique and generally agreed model. Given the uncertainty, as ignorance, that is central to the sustainability problem, it is unlikely that there will ever be such a model. It would, in any case, be a very complicated model, and unlikely to generate simple prescriptions for national income accounting purposes. While capital theory can provide some general insights, it cannot provide generally agreed definitive rules for practising national income accountants to follow. Further, the pricing caveats discussed in the context of the simplest model with production using a costlessly extracted non-renewable resource carry through to all the more complex models. And, as we shall see in the next section, even where the theory offers clear and unambiguous prescriptions over a limited area of the total problem, as with non-renewable resource depletion, implementation remains problematic.

Environmental accounting: practice[4]

In this section we consider environmental accounting from a perspective which is that of a national income statistician rather than an economic theorist. We begin with some observations on current national income accounting conventions, and their deficiencies in relation to matters environmental as argued by many commentators. We then look at proposals emanating from the United Nations for addressing such concerns. The second subsection of the chapter looks at the different ways in which non-renewable resource depreciation can be, and has been, measured in practice. The section finishes by looking at some unofficial attempts to produce a measure which better reflects a nation's economic progress, or the lack of it, when due account is taken of its environmental impacts.

Current national income accounting conventions actually produce a variety of measures relating to national income. The most widely used are Gross National Product (GNP) and Gross Domestic Product (GDP). The difference between GNP and GDP is not great for most economies, and its origins are not very relevant to our central concerns here. We shall conduct our discussion by referring to GDP.[5] The conventions now used for GDP measurement have their origin in the information requirements for management of the macroeconomy. For this purpose, what is needed is a measure of the total demand for the outputs of produced commodities. Given that GDP measures total demand, it also measures the output pro-

duced to meet that demand, and GDP has come to be seen as a measure of economic performance, or welfare. Indeed, for many commentators it has effectively become *the* performance/welfare indicator, notwithstanding that economists have long been aware of many ways in which it is a very poor performance/welfare indicator, even leaving aside environmental considerations.

GDP can be measured in three ways. First, GDP is the total output sold by firms measured by value added. In measuring national income, purchases of intermediate goods are netted out, as discussed in the previous chapter. Second, GDP is the sum of the incomes earned by persons in the economy. This is the most obvious rationale for calling GDP 'national income'. The sum of incomes is equal to the value of total output produced by firms by virtue of the convention that output is measured in terms of value added. Third, GDP is total expenditure by individuals on consumption plus expenditure by firms on items of capital equipment; that is, investment.

Given these conventions, each way of measuring GDP should produce the same numerical result. The value-added measure of firms' total output equals the incomes generated in firms equals total expenditure on non-intermediate goods. In practice, the three ways of measuring GDP do not produce the same numbers due to errors arising in the collection of data from the very large number of firms and individuals in an actual economy. To preserve the principle of the conventions, published national income accounts introduce a residual error term,

---

[4] Our discussion here is at the national level. National level accounts are compiled from data obtained from, among other sources, the accounts and records of corporations. Ultimately, successful national level environmental accounting will require changes to accounting practices at the level of companies. Gray (1994) provides a good critical account of research and debate on environmental accounting at that level.

[5] The national income accounting conventions are discussed in most macroeconomics texts. Beckerman (1980) provides a fuller discussion of the conventions than most such texts, and looks at the principles underlying them. Usher (1980) gives a very thorough discussion of the use of national income accounting data to measure economic growth, and contains an early discussion of adjustments for resource depletion and environmental deterioration. National statistical agencies publish detailed guides to the practices followed in their own accounts and publications: see also the United Nations publications cited in the further reading section at the end of this chapter.

and write the final output, expenditure and income numbers as the same after adding in that term. The expenditure measure of GDP is generally regarded as the most reliable. The size of the residual error term varies from year to year, but is often in excess of 0.5% of GDP. National income accounting is not an exact science.

It is universally agreed that, leaving aside environmental considerations, the proper measure of national income for purposes of monitoring national economic performance and welfare is Net Domestic Product (NDP). This is GDP less that part of it required to make good the depreciation of reproducible capital as it is used in production. In principle, depreciation for a period is measured as the reduction in the value of the economy's existing stock of capital equipment over that period, on account of its use in production. In fact, GDP is much more widely used than NDP. The reason for this is that it is very difficult to measure the depreciation of capital equipment accurately. National income statisticians prefer a number which is an accurate measure of an admittedly unsatisfactory concept to an inaccurate measure of a more satisfactory concept. This needs to be kept in mind when considering proposals for modifying national income measurement so as to account for the depreciation of environmental assets.

As noted in the introduction to this chapter, environmentally driven criticism of current accounting conventions focuses on three areas: depletion of natural resources, environmental degradation and defensive expenditure.

As regards natural resource depletion, the widely agreed principle is that stocks of natural resources such as oil and gas reserves, stocks of fish, and so on should be treated in the same way as stocks of man-made capital, so that a deduction should be made to allow for the depletion or consumption of these natural resources as they are used in production; that is, their depreciation. In this regard, there is a distinction between resources that

yield monetised flows (such as commercial forests, exploited oils and minerals, and so on) and those that yield non-monetised benefits (such as fresh air, lakes and oceans, and similar natural resources to which there are no exclusive property rights). In principle, the depreciation of the former ought to be observable in market data, while this will not be true of the latter. Where renewable resources are not traded in markets, or where they are exploited on an open-access basis, it is clearly going to be difficult to get firm data relating to depreciation. As well as the problem of valuation, there are often problems of physical measurement, given that there are no incentives for private measurement activity, as there are in the case of traded resources where exclusive property rights exist.

Degradation occurs when there is a decline in the quality of the natural environment, in particular of air, water and land quality. As with renewable and non-renewable resources, land, air and water can be viewed as assets, the degradation of which should be treated as depreciation and accounted for in the same way as depletion of reproducible capital. At the level of theory, there is no difference between this case and that of the depletion of natural resources. However, as a practical matter it is not always obvious how degradation should be defined and, even if satisfactorily defined, how it should be valued. An approach that has been suggested is to establish certain desirable quality standards, and then to measure degradation as the deviation from these quality levels. The value of the degradation can then be calculated as the cost of making good the degradation that has occurred or the cost of achieving the targeted quality standards. However, there is clearly the possibility of an arbitrary element in this since quality standards may be set which are higher than would occur in the 'natural' environment. It is unlikely that the quality standards established would be those which correspond to the efficient level of abatement; that is, where the marginal social cost of the pollution equals the marginal abatement cost.

If the use of the costs of achieving standards is considered inappropriate, alternative methods of valuing degradation must be sought. Willingness to pay (WTP) to avoid the degradation, or to make it good, has been proposed. The assessment of WTP in relation to the natural environment was considered in Chapter 14. Leaving aside the problems discussed there, from a national accounting standpoint there is the difficulty that WTP includes consumers' surplus whereas the standard components of the national accounts are valued using market prices.

Expenditures that are expressly designed to prevent degradation or to counteract the effects of degradation that has already taken place – so-called defensive expenditures – will be included in GDP as currently measured. Expenditure incurred by producers – for example, waste treatment by enterprises – will be reflected in product prices but not separately identifiable in the national accounts. Expenditure by households, government or non-profit-making institutions, or capital expenditure by enterprises, will be included on the expenditure side of GDP and should in principle be separately identifiable in the accounts currently produced. As noted, some commentators argue that such defensive expenditures should be deducted from GDP as now measured to arrive at a proper measure of national income. As a practical matter, quite apart from the difficulty of measuring defensive expenditure, it can be argued that there is no reason why defensive environmental expenditure should be treated differently from other forms of defensive expenditure, such as expenditure on armed forces, preventive medicine, policing and so on. A consistent approach to defensive expenditure would require major changes in the measurement of national income, beyond those required on environmental grounds. Some commentators argue that given the difficulties that such an approach would face, the construction of a measure of sustainable economic welfare should, rather than involve adjustments to national income, start somewhere else. We discuss some efforts of this nature in the final part of this section of the chapter.

The UNSTAT proposals: satellite accounting

The practical possibilities for environmental modifications to national income accounting conventions have been under active consideration by many individuals and institutions for a number of years. In the wake of the emergence of, and interest in, the idea of sustainable development, the United Nations Statistical Division (UNSTAT) has proposed draft guidelines for new national income accounting conventions, the System of integrated Environmental and Economic Accounting (SEEA). Here we provide an informal outline of the essentials of the guidelines: a more formal account is given in Appendix 17.3.

The essential idea is to measure the 'environmental cost' of economic activity in a period. Environmental cost (EC) is defined as the difference between the opening and closing value of the stock of environmental assets

$$EC_t \equiv \sum a_{it} v_{it} - \sum a_{it-1} v_{it-1} \qquad (17.23)$$

where the summation is over $i = 1, 2, \ldots, n$ assets, a_i represents the physical measure of the ith environmental asset, v_i the unit value assigned to the ith asset, and where $t-1$ refers to the start of the period and t to the end of the period. For the ith asset, $a_{it} v_{it} - a_{it-1} v_{it-1}$ is its depreciation over the period. EC_t is the change in the balance sheet value of all n environmental assets over the period, the depreciation of what is sometimes called 'natural capital'. In line with the discussion of the previous section, Environmentally Adjusted Net Domestic Product could then be defined as

$$EDP_t \equiv NDP_t - EC_t \equiv (GDP_t - D_{Mt}) - D_{Nt} \qquad (17.24)$$

where NDP stands for Net Domestic Product, D_M for the depreciation of man-made reproducible capital, and $D_N \equiv EC$ for the depreciation of natural capital.

The UNSTAT proposals do not envisage replacing the publication of the standard GDP/NDP accounts with the publication of EDP accounts. They do envisage complementing the standard accounts with balance sheets for natural capital, from which users of the accounts could work out EDP. This would leave intact the current conventions for the measurement of GDP and NDP, so that adoption of the proposal would mean that figures on these constructs would continue to be available on a consistent basis with past data. The balance sheets for environmental assets are, therefore, referred to as 'satellite accounts'. The potential, discussed below, for large year on year changes in estimates of the depreciation of non-renewable resources is another reason why most of those concerned with the production of national income accounts favour the satellite accounting approach, rather than producing only figures for environmentally adjusted national income. The idea is to publish each year conventional national income accounts accompanied by opening and closing balance sheet accounts for environmental assets.

In principle, the satellite accounts could cover all environmental assets relevant to production and consumption. This would require physical data and valuations for all relevant assets, and this is not now available even in those countries where the official statistical agencies have invested heavily in generating, collating and publishing environmental data. The problems are seen as especially acute with respect to valuation data for those assets not subject to market transactions. We shall see shortly, however, that even for mineral deposits subject to private property rights, there are quite serious problems about both physical data and valuation for depreciation. The UNSTAT proposals envisage that the range of assets which are used for the calculation of environmental cost be extended over time, starting with non-renewable resources and renewable resources involving market transactions.

As well as resource depletion and environmental degradation, we have noted that some commentators argue for the deduction of defensive environmental expenditures from the measure of NDP. The UNSTAT proposals do not involve treating defensive expenditures as an element of environmental cost for the adjustment of NDP to EDP, for two main reasons. First, as a practical matter, it is very difficult to definitively identify and measure such expenditures. Second, and more fundamentally, such subtraction might open the door to questioning the whole basis of measured national income as a welfare indicator. Leaving the natural environment aside, much of the expenditure counted in national income could be regarded as defensive – we eat and incur medical expenses to stay alive, we buy clothes to defend against the weather and social disapproval, and so on. The UNSTAT proposals do, however, involve identifying and separately reporting defensive environmental expenditures in the accounting system.

It must be emphasised that we have been discussing proposals and guidelines. No nation's official statistical office currently produces comprehensive satellite environmental accounts along with its standard national income accounts. Some have produced estimates of balance sheets for some natural resources, as exemplified by the data for Australia and the UK discussed in the next subsection, but these appear as special one-off publications, or are classified as 'preliminary estimates', rather than as routine elements of the national income accounting system. Some independent analysts have made attempts to produce measures of EDP. Two such efforts, for Indonesia and Australia, are discussed below.

Measuring the depreciation of non-renewable resources

A somewhat extended treatment of this particular of the practice of environmental accounting is justified because, given that non-renewable resources are generally subject to private property rights and traded in markets, they are, from the general class of environmental assets, the case where it is most straightforward to come up with numbers for depreciation. In fact, as we shall see, even in this case, obtaining a single 'correct' number for the depreciation of a particular resource is problematic, notwithstanding the availability of market data.

As we have seen, the theoretically correct measure of the depreciation of an economy's stock of a non-renewable resource is the total Hotelling rent (THR) arising in its extraction. With P for the price of the extracted resource, c for the marginal cost of extraction, R for the amount extracted, N for new discoveries, and D for the depreciation of the resource stock:

$$D = \text{THR} = (P - c)(R - N) \qquad (17.25)$$

Given standard assumptions for a fully competitive economy, we would have

$$\text{THR} = \text{CIV}$$

where CIV is the change in the value of the economy's stock of the non-renewable resource in question. In principle, and given the standard assumptions, D could be measured as either THR given by Equation 17.25 or as CIV, with the same result.

In practice, neither of these measures of D appears to have been used, nor are they proposed for use in the literature concerning how environmental accounts might actually be constructed. The most obvious problem with Equation 17.25 is that c, the marginal cost of extraction, is not observable in published, or readily available, data. As we shall see, there are other problems with using Equation 17.25 to measure D. If there existed competitive firms that were solely in the business of selling the rights to extract from the resource stock, which they owned, then stock market valuations of such firms could be used to measure CIV. Generally such firms do not exist, resource ownership and extraction being vertically integrated in mining firms. Stock market valuations of

mining firms are available, but these data confound the changes in other asset values with those of the mineral deposits owned, and reflect changes in overall stock market 'sentiment'. In any case, the minerals sector of an economy is rarely such that it can properly be characterised as 'competitive'.

There are three main methods that appear in the literature concerned with the practical implementation of environmental accounting.

Net price

This uses average cost, C, instead of marginal cost to compute rent, which is taken as the measure of depreciation, so that:

$$D = (P - C)(R - N) \qquad (17.26)$$

Note that for $c > C$, $(P - C) > (P - c)$ so that on this account there would arise an overestimation of THR using Equation 17.26. In many applications of the net price method, N is ignored. In what follows we shall refer to the net price method with new discoveries ignored as 'Net Price I', and to the use of Equation 17.26 with the N adjustment as 'Net Price II'. Given that actual accounts refer to periods of time, rather than to instants of time as in the theoretical literature, applications of Equation 17.26, with or without N, also vary as to the treatment of P and C in terms of dating. Clearly, each could be measured at the start or the end of the period, or as some average over the period. These three measures will only coincide if P and C are unchanging throughout the period, which in the case of P is uncommon.

Change in net present value

With 0 indicating the start of the accounting period and 1 its close, this method uses

$$D = \sum_{t=0}^{T_0} [(P_t - C_t)R_t/(1 + r)^t]$$
$$\qquad (17.27)$$
$$- \sum_{t=1}^{T_1} [(P_t - C_t)R_t/(1 + r)^t]$$

where T_0 and T_1 are deposit lifetimes, and r is the interest rate. Apart from the use of C

rather than c, this method can be seen as an alternative, to stock market valuations, method of measuring CIV. As actually used this method requires some specialising assumptions, as discussed below.

El Serafy's (user cost) rule

El Serafy is the name of the economist who proposed this method, which is intended to measure depreciation as 'user cost'. The rationale for and derivation of the rule is discussed in Appendix 17.4. According to the rule

$$D = R(P - C)/(1 + r)^{T+1} \quad (17.28)$$

where r is the interest rate, and T is the deposit lifetime assuming a constant rate of extraction.

Measurements of non-renewable resource depreciation for Australia and the United Kingdom

It is generally understood that the net price method is liable to produce large year on year fluctuations in estimated D, and this method is not recommended in the UNSTAT guidelines for environmental accounting. Those guidelines recommend the change in net present value method. The net price method is, however, quite widely used by analysts seeking a figure for D in respect of non-renewable resource stocks. It avoids the need for information/assumptions about mine lifetimes and interest rates, which arises with both of the other methods.

We now consider some results based on officially published data, measured by different methods for two countries. In the case of Australia the results for a wide range of non-renewable resources were added to estimate total depreciation for all mineral resources. In the case of the United Kingdom, attention was restricted to oil and natural gas.

The Australian Bureau of Statistics has produced preliminary balance sheet estimates for a range of assets including 'Subsoil assets'; that is, non-renewable mineral resources (ABS, 1995).[6] Table 3.3 of ABS (1995) gives for each of 33 minerals:

(1) The size of Economic Demonstrated Resources (EDR) at 30 June 1989, 1990, 1991 and 1992.
(2) The price of the extracted mineral at 30 June 1989, 1990, 1991 and 1992.
(3) The average cost of extraction at 30 June 1989, 1990, 1991 and 1992.
(4) Production of the mineral in the years ending 30 June 1989, 1990, 1991 and 1992.

From these data there is calculated for each of the 33 minerals, for each of four years, the NPV of the resource stock according to

$$PV_s = \sum_{t=1}^{T_s} [(P_t - C_t)R_t/(1 + r)^t]$$

where s refers to the balance sheet date (30 June 1989, 1990, 1991 and 1992) and T_S is the estimated stock lifetime at that date. Several specialising assumptions are made. First, R_t is set equal to R for all t where

$$R = 0.25(R_{88/9} + R_{89/90} + R_{90/1} + R_{91/2})$$

At each s the resource lifetime, T, is calculated as:

$$T_S = EDR_S/R$$

It is assumed that for all t, $(P_t - C_t) = (P_s - C_s)$. Using an interest rate of 7.5% the PV_S results are summed across minerals to give balance sheet valuations of Australia's 'subsoil assets' at 30 June 1989, 1990, 1991 and 1992.

The figures shown in Table 17.3 under 'ABS NPV change' are the differences between the closing and opening valuations for all Australian non-renewable resources, and are the results for the change in NPV method as described above.[7] The figures shown in Table 17.3 under 'El Serafy rule'

---

[6] For further information on the ABS data and details of the calculations for Table 17.3 here, see Common and Sanyal (1998).

[7] The ABS also did the calculations for interest rates of 5% and 10%. Their results illustrate the sensitivity of depreciation as measured by the change in NPV method to the interest rate used.

Table 17.3 Alternative estimates of minerals depreciation for Australia 1988/9 to 1991/2, AUS$ $\times 10^6$.

Year	El Serafy rule	Net price I	Net price II	ABS NPV change
1988/9	952	8511		
1989/90	1228	9872	−19 321	−6500
1990/1	1922	12023	−147 035	−19 900
1991/2	2328	13624	299 075	−9700

are calculated according to Equation 17.28 using the same P, C and T data from ABS (1995), and the same 7.5% interest rate. The 'Net price II' figures use the net price method, taking account of new discoveries, calculating rent as

$$(P_s - C_s)(R_s - N_s)$$

where P_s, C_s and R_s are taken direct from the ABS data, and N_s is inferred from $(EDR_s - EDR_{s-1})$ and R_s in that data. ABS (1995) notes a number of problems regarding the EDR data. Of particular concern are changes due to variation in P, technological change, and revisions of resource classification. The figures for 'Net price I' in Table 17.3 are the least affected by specialising assumptions and the problems attending the EDR data, being calculated as $(P_s - C_s)R_S$; in other words, ignoring new discoveries.

From a comparison of Equation 17.26, with N equal to zero, and Equation 17.28, it is clear that, for the same data, the 'Net price I' figure must always be larger than the 'El Serafy rule' figure. From Equation 17.26, assuming that N must be non-negative means that 'Net price II' must always be smaller than 'Net price I'. In Table 17.3, for 1989/90 and 1990/1 across all minerals new discoveries are positive and large enough to produce a negative figure for depreciation. However, for 1991/2 'Net price II' depreciation is much larger than 'Net price I' depreciation. This is primarily because of a reduction in the EDR figure for bauxite for 30 June 1992 by an amount which exceeds the previous year's production, 0.04 gigatonnes, by 3.96 gigatonnes, implying nega-

tive new discoveries. The pattern in the 'ABS NPV change' figures follows that for 'Net price II' with dampened swings, as would be expected given the method of calculation described above.

Which of these is the 'correct' way to measure depreciation? The capital theoretic approach could be taken to suggest 'Net price II', were it not for the fact that it uses average, rather than marginal, costs. Given marginal costs greater than average costs, one could argue, this measure should be taken as an upper bound on depreciation. However, given the problems about measuring 'new discoveries', the implications of this argument in practice can, as shown in Table 17.3, lead to negative figures for nonrenewable resource depletion. The change in NPV method, as implemented by ABS, also gives rise to negative depreciation for minerals, as shown in the final column of Table 17.3. A negative figure for depreciation means that the effect of accounting for the depletion of non-renewable resources would be, other things equal, to make sustainable national income larger than conventionally measured national income. Notice also that the 'Net price II' and 'ABS NPV change' results in Table 17.3 are more volatile than those for 'El Serafy rule' and 'Net price I'. Using either of the former to adjust conventionally measured national income would make the time series resulting highly volatile.

The point of reporting these results is not to criticise the work of the Australian Bureau of Statistics. It is, on the contrary, to demonstrate that even thorough work by a highly respected national statistical agency does not result in unambiguous measurement of the depreciation of non-renewable natural resources.

The results in Table 17.4 make the same point with data for the UK taken from a 1992 publication from the national statistical agency. In a subsequent publication, Vaze (1998), the same agency reports three sets of oil and gas depreciation estimates through to 1994. In addition to estimates according to

Table 17.4 Alternative estimates of depletion of the UK oil and natural gas reserves (£ m).

Year	User cost method 1	Depreciation method[a] 2	Ratio 2/1
1980	2600	6 600	2.54
1981	4200	9 400	2.24
1982	5300	10 700	2.02
1983	5200	12 400	2.39
1984	7700	15 400	2.00
1985	2900	14 200	4.90
1986	2800	4 500	1.61
1987	3400	5 100	1.50
1988	2000	2 000	1.00
1989	1700	1 800	1.06
1990	1600	2 200	1.38

[a] Based on the method proposed by Repetto *et al.* (1989), i.e. Net price II.
Source: adapted from CSO estimates from Bryant and Cook (1992).

Table 17.5 GDP and an EDP estimate for Indonesia 1971–1984.

Year	GDP	EDP	EDP/GDP
1971	1	1	1.20
1972	1.09	0.90	0.99
1973	1.22	0.97	0.96
1974	1.32	1.48	1.36
1975	1.38	0.98	0.85
1976	1.47	1.12	0.92
1977	1.60	1.08	0.81
1978	1.73	1.19	0.78
1979	1.83	1.19	0.78
1980	2.01	1.28	0.76
1981	2.17	1.48	0.82
1982	2.22	1.58	0.86
1983	2.32	1.49	0.78
1984	2.44	1.68	0.83

Source: based on Repetto *et al.* 1989.

the depreciation method (described as the net price method in the second publication) and the user cost method, estimates according to the present value method are reported. The estimates vary across methods to a similar extent to that shown in Table 17.3. It is stated that the agency's 'preferred approach is to use the net present value methodology' in an environmental satellite account.

Environmentally adjusted national income for Indonesia and Australia

The quotation from Repetto *et al.* (1989) which heads this chapter is from the introduction to a report in which a World Resources Institute team adjusted official national income measures for Indonesia by their estimates of the depreciation of three environmental assets – oil deposits, timber and soil. They proceeded by first constructing physical accounts, then applying unit values. In the case of oil opening stocks were valued at the current market price of the extracted oil less estimated average extraction cost. Closing stocks were computed by subtracting extraction during the year and adding new discoveries, and valued in the same way as the opening stocks using

the price ruling at the end of the period. This is an application of the Net price II method. The procedure followed with timber is the same except that it allows for estimated natural growth over the year. The physical data here is recognised as being less firmly based than in the case of oil. For soil erosion, estimated physical losses over the year were valued using estimates of the loss of agricultural output entailed.

Table 17.5 reports the results obtained by Repetto *et al.* in index number form, where EDP is GDP minus the depreciation of the three environmental assets considered. The average per annum growth rates are 7.1% for GDP and 4.1% for EDP. EDP grows more slowly than GDP over the period 1971–1984, and behaves more erratically. The fourth column shows the ratio of the EDP estimate to GDP. The erratic behaviour of the EDP series is principally due to the effect of changes in the price of extracted oil, and of new discoveries of oil. The EDP figures for 1973 and 1974 show the effects of the increase in the world price of oil. If EDP is understood as sustainable income, these figures show sustainable income increasing by 51% in one year, 1973 to 1974.

Young (1990) undertook a similar exercise for Australia, with the results shown in Table 17.6. Young treated all mineral resources in

Table 17.6 GDP and EDP estimates for Australia 1980–88.

Year	GDP	EDP_1	EDP_2	GDP/Pop	EDP_2/Pop
1980	1	1	1	1	1
1981	1.03	1.03	1.16	1.01	1.13
1982	1.07	1.07	1.14	1.03	1.10
1983	1.04	1.03	1.15	0.98	1.09
1984	1.09	1.09	1.04	1.00	0.96
1985	1.17	1.17	1.34	1.06	1.22
1986	1.22	1.22	1.62	1.08	1.44
1987	1.25	1.26	1.09	1.09	0.95
1988	1.31	1.32	1.52	1.12	1.30
Growth rate	3.4%	3.5%	5.4%	1.4%	3.3%

Source: based on Young (1990).

the way that Repetto *et al* treated just oil, and also followed them in considering from among the renewable resources only timber. However, Young's valuation of the depreciation of this asset is based only on an estimate of its implications for wildlife habitat loss. As regards soil degradation, Young used estimates of the value of agricultural productivity losses. Unlike Repetto *et al*, Young incorporates an estimate of the degradation of environmental assets by pollution. This is done by subtracting from GDP an estimate of expenditure by households and government to offset the effects of pollution. The problems associated with this way of measuring environmental degradation were noted above.

Young describes his calculations as 'back of the envelope', and claims to have been 'environmentally generous' in producing his figures. In Table 17.6, Young's results are reported in index number form for GDP, EDP_1 and EDP_2, where

$$EDP_1 = \text{GDP} - \text{depreciation on account of land degradation} - \text{depreciation on account of timber production} - \text{defensive expenditures}$$

and

$$EDP_2 = EDP_1 - \text{depreciation on account of mineral depletion}$$

'Pop' stands for population, and the last two columns give the index numbers for GDP per capita and EDP_2 per capita. Shown at the

bottom of each column is the average annual growth rate implied by the index numbers above.

Several points are worth noting. First, the behaviour of GDP and EDP_1 is quite similar. Second, as with the Repetto *et al.* figures, EDP_2 is quite erratic over time. This is, again, due to the effects of price changes and new discoveries. Third, the average growth rate for EDP_2 is actually substantially greater than that for GDP. The fourth point concerns the adjustment for population growth. Clearly, if we wish to give national income a welfare interpretation, it needs to be measured per capita. Official national statistical publications do not generally report on a per capita basis, and commentary is frequently based on those unadjusted figures. The Repetto *et al.* results in Table 17.5 are for Indonesia's total national income, not per capita national income. For Australia, Table 17.6 shows that adjusting for population growth reduces GDP growth by 2% per annum, whereas adjusting GDP for environmental depreciation actually increases national income growth. Fifth, on these figures, per capita sustainable income after allowing for environmental depreciation, is growing at 3.3% per annum.

It should be noted that Young, and Repetto *et al.*, do not subtract from GDP the depreciation of man-made capital. If this were done, it would reduce their EDP figures in terms of levels, but it is unlikely that it would much affect the growth rate results.

Measuring sustainable economic welfare

In recent years a number of economists interested in sustainability and welfare have taken the view that NDP is not the place from which to start the search for a satisfactory measurement.[8] Rather, they have constructed indices which start with personal

---

[8] For references to some of the precursors of the work discussed here see Daly and Cobb (1989).

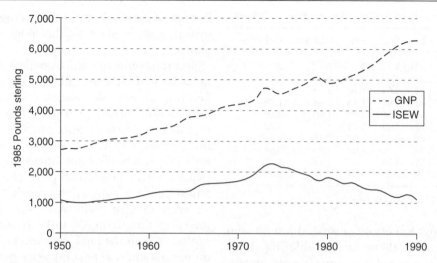

Figure 17.3 Index of sustainable economic welfare for the UK.
Source: Jackson and Marks (1994) – Index of Sustainable Economic Welfare.

consumption expenditure as recorded in the national income accounts and then make a series of adjustments to it which are intended to produce a better account of welfare which is sustainable. The result is usually called an 'index of sustainable economic welfare' (ISEW) or a 'genuine progress indicator' (GPI). Figure 17.3 shows the results obtained, in comparison with the movement of GNP, for the UK by Jackson and Marks (1994). In common with many ISEW/GPI results for industrialised economies, the main feature is that whereas national income grew more or less continually over recent decades, 'properly' measured sustainable welfare grew much more slowly overall, and actually went into decline starting around the mid-1970s: see, for examples, Daly and Cobb (1989) for the USA, Stockhammer *et al.* (1997) for Austria, and Hamilton (1997) for Australia.

The original ISEW was calculated for the USA by Daly and Cobb (1989), and we now briefly discuss their method and results. The definition that they use is

$$\text{ISEW} \equiv \{(C/D) + (E + F + G + H)$$
$$- (I + J + K + L + M + N + O + R$$
$$+ S + T + U) + (V + W)\}/\text{Pop}$$
$$(17.29)$$

where

C is personal consumption expenditure
D is an index of distributional inequality
E is an imputed value for extra-market labour services
F is an estimate of the flow of services from consumer durables
G is an estimate of the value of streets and highway services
H is an estimate of the value of publicly provided health and education services
I is expenditure on consumer durables
J is an estimate of private defensive spending on health and education
K is expenditure on advertising at the national level
L is an estimate of commuting cost
M is an estimate of the costs of urbanisation
N is an estimate of the costs of automobile accidents
O is an estimate of water pollution costs
P is an estimate of air pollution costs
Q is an estimate of noise pollution costs
R is an estimate of the costs of wetlands loss
S is an estimate of the costs of farmland loss
T is an estimate of the cost of non-renewable resource depletion

U is an estimate of the cost of long-term environmental damage

V is an estimate of net additions to the stock of reproducible capital

W is the change in net overseas indebtedness

Daly and Cobb (1989) report, in an appendix, the sources used and the estimation methods employed, and admit to the somewhat arbitrary assumptions that it was necessary to make in many cases. In effect, Equation 17.29 is a welfare function, which reflects the authors' judgements about the determinants of welfare, and what sustains them. Others may have different views about these matters. It should be noted, for example, that according to Equation 17.29, sustainable economic welfare increases when, other things constant, unpaid household labour increases. It should also be noted, on the other hand, that the value of leisure time does not appear as an argument in the welfare function. Many people would, one imagines, feel that their welfare had improved if they did less work around the house and worked shorter hours in paid employment. That said, it should also be noted that per capita national income takes no account of time spent in paid work, nor of unpaid work.

Table 17.7 gives the results from calculations using the data provided in the appendix to Daly and Cobb (1989), which illustrate the sensitivity of the ISEW to the removal of some of its components. The two columns of numbers show the effect of changing, by one year, the base year from which the average annual growth rates for GDP, ISEW and ISEW variants are measured. Note that the difference between the growth of per capita GDP and ISEW is reduced from 1.15% to 0.52%.

ISEW1 is ISEW without the adjustment for the distribution of income; that is, it is the result if the term *D* in Equation 17.29 is fixed at 1. The results for ISEW2, which is ISEW1 without the adjustment for unpaid extra market labour, shows that this adjustment has a major impact on the behaviour of ISEW. Without this adjustment, ISEW2 grows faster than GDP per capita whichever base year is used, and for the 1950 base ISEW2 grows by more than 1% faster. On the other hand, adding back in the adjustment for non-renewable resource depletion, to get ISEW3, makes little difference to the growth rate obtained for ISEW1. As the last row shows, the non-renewable resource depletion adjustment has an effect of essentially the same size as the adjustment for the costs of commuting, urbanisation and automobile accidents.

Other ISEW/GPI constructions make adjustments to personal consumption which, while generally similar in nature to those of Daly and Cobb, differ in detail on account of the judgements of the constructors and/or the availability of data. However, as noted above, they generally show similar patterns in relation to the behaviour of GDP per capita. What most ISEW/GPI constructions appear to have in common is an adjustment for unpaid labour, and we have noted for the case of the Daly and Cobb (1989) ISEW the large leverage that this exerts on the final result.

Sustainability indicators

From the preceding sections it is clear that it is difficult both in principle and in practice to measure sustainable income, or some alternative such as sustainable economic welfare. This has led to an interest in 'sustainability indicators' – measurements which, while not intended to capture the whole picture in a

Table 17.7 GDP and ISEW average annual growth rates for the USA.

	1950–1986	1951–1986
GDP	3.34	2.55
GDP per capita	2.02	1.52
ISEW	0.87	1.00
ISEW1	1.09	0.76
ISEW2 = ISEW1 − E	3.14	2.01
ISEW2 = ISEW1 + T	1.13	0.80
ISEW3 = ISEW1 + L + M + N	1.12	0.78

single number, are supposed to provide information useful to the pursuit of sustainability.

The Pearce–Atkinson indicator: measuring genuine saving

In the second section of this chapter we discussed the capital theoretic approach to sustainability and environmental accounting. The essential ideas from there suggest a necessary, but not sufficient, condition for sustainability with considerable intuitive appeal – that an economy's saving be sufficient to make good the depreciation of both its man-made and natural capital. Making good depreciation is an appealing guide to prudent asset management. This has led to an interest in an indicator which is intended to record whether an economy is satisfying this necessary condition for sustainability. We refer to this as the Pearce–Atkinson indicator. In Box 3.2 we reported some results of this indicator taken from Atkinson and Pearce (1993): similar results are reported by Pearce and Atkinson (1993, 1995). Here we work through the basis for the Pearce–Atkinson indicator, and we present some results for Australia.

With W for wealth, we can write

$$W_t - W_{t-1} = Y_t - C_t - D_t \qquad (17.30)$$

where Y is income, C is consumption and D is the depreciation of the asset portfolio. If we impose the condition that wealth is constant, this becomes

$$0 = Y_t - C_{\max,t} - D_t \qquad (17.31)$$

where $C_{\max,t}$ is the maximum level of consumption consistent with constant wealth. Rearranging Equation 17.31 we can write

$$C_{\max,t} = Y_t - D_t$$

and defining sustainable income as the maximum that can be consumed without reducing wealth, this gives

$$Y_{\text{sus},t} = Y_t - D_t \qquad (17.32)$$

where $Y_{\text{sus},t}$ stands for sustainable income. With $Y_t = C_t + S_t$, Equation 17.32 can be written as

$$Y_{\text{sus},t} - C_t = S_t - D_t$$

so that we have

$$C_t > Y_{\text{sus},t} \longleftrightarrow S_t - D_t < 0 \longleftrightarrow W_t - W_{t-1} < 0$$

$$C_t = Y_{\text{sus},t} \longleftrightarrow S_t - D_t = 0 \longleftrightarrow W_t - W_{t-1} = 0$$

$$C_t > Y_{\text{sus},t} \longleftrightarrow S_t - D_t > 0 \longleftrightarrow W_t - W_{t-1} > 0$$

$$(17.33)$$

If W_t comprises both man-made capital and natural capital, and we use D_{Mt} for the depreciation of the former and D_{Nt} for the depreciation of the latter, then

$$S_t \geqslant D_{Mt} + D_{Nt} \qquad (17.34)$$

is necessary for sustainability. An alternative way of stating this condition is as

$$GS_t = S_t - D_{Mt} - D_{Nt} \geqslant 0 \qquad (17.34')$$

where GS stands for 'genuine saving'. Pearce and Atkinson actually look at genuine saving as a proportion of national income, as shown in Box 3.2, but clearly if GS as defined by 17.34' is positive then so will GS divided by income be.

As we have seen, even where attention is restricted to the non-renewable resource component of natural capital, the measurement of D_N is problematic. As is well documented in the national income accounting literature, the measurement of D_M is also problematic. However, Pearce and Atkinson argue that looking at genuine saving is a useful, practical sustainability indicator in so far as it will, at relatively low cost, generate information about the attainment, or otherwise, of a minimal necessary condition for sustainability. If we find that genuine saving is positive, we certainly should not conclude that sustainability is assured, but if we find that it is negative then there are grounds for doubting that current behaviour is consistent with sustainability.

Table 17.8 gives some results for Australia, where only non-renewable resources are considered. As previously discussed, economists

Table 17.8 Saving and depreciation in Australia, 1979/80 to 1994/5.

Year	S $A\$ \times 10^6$	D_M $A\$ \times 10^6$	D_N $A\$ \times 10^6$	$S - D_M - D_N$ $A\$ \times 10^6$	D_N/D_M
1979/80	28 846	18 137	1845	8 684	0.102
1980/1	35 192	21 105	1665	12 422	0.079
1981/2	41 456	24 188	1743	15 525	0.072
1982/3	41 105	27 801	2099	11 205	0.076
1983/4	44 325	29 940	2937	11 448	0.098
1984/5	51 016	32 539	3064	15 413	0.094
1985/6	59 303	37 478	3417	18 408	0.091
1986/7	64 475	42 590	2726	19 159	0.064
1987/8	72 354	46 737	2658	22 959	0.057
1988/9	85 146	51 372	1332	32 442	0.026
1989/90	89 479	55 996	3010	30 473	0.054
1990/1	81 336	58 303	4956	18 077	0.085
1991/2	77 347	59 836	4311	13 200	0.072
1992/3	81 767	62 789	3893	15 085	0.062
1993/4	87 007	65 121	2743	19 143	0.042
1994/5	96 732	66 658	2057	28 017	0.031

Source: adapted from Common and Sanyal (1998).

take the view that the proper measure of depreciation of natural resources is the rent arising in a competitive economy. In the context of the Pearce–Atkinson indicator, a natural way to estimate the total rents actually arising in minerals extraction is via the national income accounts, as follows. For countries with well-developed national statistical services the published national income accounts give data for the Net Capital Stock (of reproducible, man-made, capital equipment), K, and Gross Operating Surplus, GOS, reported by industrial sectors. With N indicating the mining sector, the return on capital in sectors other than mining can be calculated as

$$g = \text{GOS}_{\text{non-N}}/K_{\text{non-N}}$$

which can be used to estimate a normal GOS in mining as

$$\text{EGOS}_N = gK_N$$

Mining rent is then given by the difference between the normal and actual GOS in the mining sector, and identifying rent with depreciation, we have:

$$D_N = \text{GOS}_N - \text{EGOS}_N$$

The results arising are shown in Table 17.8, together with data for S and D_M. There are

several points of interest. The first is that $\text{GS} = S - D_M - D_N$ is always positive, so that according to this indicator, we cannot say that Australia was behaving unsustainably over 1979/80 to 1994/5. Over this period, GS as measured in Table 17.8 varied between 3.4% and 9.8% of GDP. The second point to note is that D_M is very much larger than D_N, although Australia is, among developed countries, a country where minerals extraction is relatively high as a proportion of GDP. The size of D_N relative to D_M is falling over time in Table 17.8. In Table 17.3 we reported four different D_N estimates for Australia for some of the years shown in Table 17.8. The third point is then that we have here a fifth estimate for D_N, which is different from the other four. Comparing the two tables, it will be seen that the Table 17.8 estimate falls between the El Serafy rule and net price estimates from Table 17.3, and, like them, is much less volatile than the Net price II and NPV change estimates.

Pearce and Atkinson (1995) report results for their indicator for 18 countries, for 8 of which GS is negative. All of these 8 are developing countries. The exact coverage of, and method of calculation for, D_N by country is not reported. It appears that both vary across countries, and that for some 'natural capital' is broader than just mineral resources, which is the definition of 'natural capital' for the Australian results reported in Table 17.8. The World Bank has produced estimates for GS in which 'natural capital' includes renewable resources as well as minerals, and where D_N includes an estimate for damage arising on account of a country's emissions of greenhouse gases. In World Bank (1995) the depreciation of both mineral stocks and renewable resources is calculated as the quantity extracted/harvested multiplied by 50% of the price of the extracted/harvested resource. On this basis, GS for Australia averaged over 1989–91 is reported as between −1% and 1% of GNP. Australia, according to these results (see also World Bank, 1996), has a GS performance which is borderline in terms of satisfying the Pearce–Atkinson indicator condition for sustainability, among the worst of the developed countries, and worse than that of a number of developing countries. Again, we see that one can get substantially different results according to the conventions followed and estimates used.

The Proops–Atkinson indicator: accounting for international trade

Given international trade, one nation's inhabitants can depreciate natural capital in another nation. Thus, for example, Japan is frequently cited as a country which has high domestic saving and investment in man-made capital, and low natural capital depreciation domestically, but which is responsible for much natural capital depreciation overseas when it imports raw materials. The obverse case would be somewhere like Saudi Arabia, where natural capital depreciation is high on account of exported natural resource extraction. The Pearce–Atkinson indicator does not allow for such effects. Proops and Atkinson (1996) have proposed a method which modifies the indicator so as to allow for trade effects. The essential idea is to treat

each economy as a sector in the global economy, and to use the techniques of input–output modelling discussed in Chapter 16.

Consider 2 trading economies, 1 and 2. Let x_{12} be exports from 1 to 2, and x_{21} be exports from 2 to 1. Let y represent total output, and f represent final demand, comprising c for consumption and s for saving/investment. We can then write:

$$y_1 = x_{12} + c_1 + s_1 = x_{12} + f_1$$
$$y_2 = x_{21} + c_2 + s_2 = x_{21} + f_2$$ (17.35)

If we define coefficients $q_{12} = x_{12}/y_2$ and $q_{21} = x_{21}/y_1$, Equations 17.35 can be written as

$$y_1 = 0 + q_{12}y_2 + f_1$$
$$y_2 = q_{21}y_1 + 0 + f_2$$

which in matrix notation, using upper case letters for matrices and lower case for column vectors, is

$$\mathbf{y} = \mathbf{Qy} + \mathbf{f}$$

with the solution

$$\mathbf{y} = (\mathbf{I} - \mathbf{Q})^{-1}\mathbf{f} = \mathbf{Lf}$$ (17.36)

where $\mathbf{I}$ is the identity matrix.

Now, let

$$D_1 = D_{M1} + D_{N1} = d_{m1}y_1 + d_{n1}y_1 = z_1y_1$$
$$D_2 = D_{M2} + D_{N2} = d_{m2}y_2 + d_{n2}y_2 = z_2y_2$$

so that we can write for total global depreciation

$$D = z_1y_1 + z_2y_2$$

or, in matrix notation

$$D = \mathbf{z'y}$$ (17.37)

where $\mathbf{z'}$ is $[z_1 \ z_2]$. Substituting for $\mathbf{y}$ in Equation 17.37 from Equation 17.36 gives

$$D = \mathbf{z'Lf}$$

or

$$\mathbf{T} = \mathbf{ZLF}$$ (17.38)

where $\mathbf{Z}$ and $\mathbf{F}$ are matrices with the elements of $\mathbf{z}$ and $\mathbf{f}$ along the diagonals, and

Table 17.9 D^{IN} and D^{ATT} for Australia, US$ $\times 10^6$.

Year	D^{IN}	D^{ATT}
1984	23 110	24 214
1986	31 989	33 319
1988	39 069	40 647

Source: adapted from Common and Sanyal (1998).

zeroes elsewhere. For the two-country case, Equation 17.38 is:

$$\begin{bmatrix} t_{11} & t_{12} \\ t_{21} & t_{22} \end{bmatrix} = \begin{bmatrix} z_1 l_{11} f_1 & z_1 l_{12} f_2 \\ z_2 l_{21} f_1 & z_2 l_{22} f_2 \end{bmatrix}$$

In the matrix **T** the row elements give depreciation in a country arising by virtue of final demand in that and other countries, while column elements give depreciation in all countries by virtue of final demand in one country. So, row sums, $D_i{}^{IN}$, give depreciation in i, and column sums, $D_i{}^{ATT}$, give depreciation attributable to i. Thus, in the two-country case here $t_{11} + t_{12}$ is the depreciation of total capital actually taking place in country 1, while $t_{11} + t_{21}$ is the depreciation of capital in the global economy that is on account of, attributable to, final demand in country 1.

Table 17.9 gives the results arising for the world economy treated as two economies – Australia and the Rest of the World (ROW). For Australia, the depreciation of natural capital is calculated as described above for the results shown in Table 17.8. For ROW the data are those used in Proops and Atkinson (1996): for D_N they mainly derive their data from national income accounting data as described above for Table 17.8.[9] According to these results, the depreciation of man-made capital and non-renewable resources for which Australian residents are responsible is slightly greater than the depreciation which occurs in Australia. Given that Australia is a major exporter of minerals, and that such exports account for a large proportion of its total exports, these results might

[9] We are very grateful to John Proops for supplying this data, on which Table 17.10 here is also based.

seem surprising. However, as shown in Table 17.8, when estimated from national income accounts sources D_N is small in relation to D_M in Australia, and Australian imports involve both D_M and D_N overseas, where it is also generally the case that D_M is much larger than D_N.

However, the main point to be made here is that the differences between D^{IN} and D^{ATT} shown in Table 17.9 are small in relation to the differences between the differently based estimates of D_N in Tables 17.3 and 17.8. In Table 17.9 D^{ATT} exceeds D^{IN} by less than 5%, whereas, for one example, 'Net price I' in Table 17.3 exceeds the comparable figures in Table 17.8 by at least 140%.

A slight extension of the method of Proops and Atkinson allows for consideration of these issues on a per capita basis. Let **P** be the matrix with the reciprocals of population sizes along the diagonal and zeroes elsewhere. Then, for the two-country case,

$$\mathbf{A} = \mathbf{TP} = \mathbf{ZLFP} \qquad (17.39)$$

is

$$\begin{bmatrix} a_{11} & a_{12} \\ a_{21} & a_{22} \end{bmatrix} = \begin{bmatrix} z_1 l_{11}(f_1/p_1) & z_1 l_{12}(f_2/p_2) \\ z_2 l_{21}(f_1/p_1) & z_2 l_{22}(f_2/p_2) \end{bmatrix}$$

so that column sums from **A**, $d_i{}^{ATT}$, give depreciation in all countries attributable to per capita final demand in country i. And,

$$\mathbf{B} = \mathbf{PT} = \mathbf{PZLF} \qquad (17.40)$$

is

$$\begin{bmatrix} b_{11} & b_{12} \\ b_{21} & b_{22} \end{bmatrix} = \begin{bmatrix} (z_1/p_1)l_{11}f_1 & (z_1/p_1)l_{12}f_2 \\ (z_2/p_2)l_{21}f_1 & (z_2/p_2)l_{22}f_2 \end{bmatrix}$$

so that row sums from **B**, $d_i{}^{IN}$, give per capita depreciation in country i on account of global final demand. These depreciation measures can be compared with s_i, per capita saving in i.

The following interesting question can now be addressed: taking account of international trade, how does the average citizen of economy A compare with one of B in regard to contributions to the global difference between saving and the depreciation of total, man-made and natural, capital? This is an interesting question because, given trade, the sustainability question is really a global question – exhausting domestic natural resources is not a problem for a trading economy, provided that it has acquired other assets as it runs down its domestic resource stock, the income from which can replace its earnings from resource exportation. The problem really bites at the global level – the global economy is a closed economy which cannot import anything from anywhere. It is for this reason that most of the capital theory literature on sustainability, and the derived literature on accounting, deals with a closed economy.

To answer the question, we can calculate the elements of **A** and **B** above, and for each country use them to calculate the difference between its saving and its depreciation mea-

sured on the 'in' and 'attributable' basis. Some results are given in Table 17.10, where the entries are for the difference between $s_i - d_i$ for country i and $s - d$ for the global economy, where s is per capita saving and d is per capita depreciation. The upper part of the table refers to d_i calculated on the 'in' basis, the lower part to it calculated on the 'attributable' basis. Clearly, for the global economy it makes no difference which way d is measured, and so there is just one row for $s - d$ in the middle of the table.

The results in Table 17.10 use exactly the same data as Proops and Atkinson (1996) and therefore follow their categorisation of the global economy into 12 national and regional economies. There are several interesting points about these results that are

Table 17.10   Excesses of per capita saving over depreciation – difference from global excess.

| | $(s_i - d_i^{\text{IN}}) - (s - d)$
US$ | | | | |
	1980	1982	1984	1986	1988
Eastern Europe	−79	−58	70	78	35
USSR	55	−76	289	278	285
Western Europe	570	341	344	522	764
Canada	838	808	760	525	953
USA	153	−200	38	−429	−401
Japan	1278	1377	1557	2603	4066
Oceania	349	11	62	−109	113
Africa	−102	−68	−113	−140	−238
Latin America	124	79	5	−66	−42
Other America	−142	−68	−363	−311	−206
Middle East	−578	853	−1024	−1135	−978
Other Asia	−132	−38	−67	−70	−163
$s - d$	173	76	106	109	220

| | $(s_i - d_i^{\text{ATT}}) - (s - d)$
US$ | | | | |
	1980	1982	1984	1986	1988
Eastern Europe	−53	−35	97	84	57
USSR	47	−100	276	266	286
Western Europe	440	249	306	528	754
Canada	984	1002	1020	774	1186
USA	48	−271	−141	−613	579
Japan	1123	1265	1512	2673	4110
Oceania	318	−45	62	−114	172
Africa	−102	−79	−119	−146	−246
Latin America	103	70	16	−66	−35
Other America	−158	−76	−236	−252	−236
Middle East	238	−273	−708	−950	−779
Other Asia	−139	−44	−70	−72	−161

worth calling attention to. Note first that for the world as a whole, in each of the years distinguished, saving exceeded depreciation – genuine saving was positive. In noting this, we must also note that these data only cover the non-renewable resource component of natural capital. Overall, the picture in the upper part of the table is much the same as in the lower part – our appreciation of per capita national and regional contributions to the excess of global saving over depreciation is little affected by looking at things on an 'attributable' basis. Japan's per capita contribution is always greater than the global average, while that of Africa is always smaller. The situation for the USA is mixed, and in two years it does make a difference which way depreciation is measured. Note also that for the USA in every year except 1988, going from the 'in' to the 'attributable' basis for measuring depreciation reduces a positive entry or makes a negative one bigger.

Given our earlier discussion of the problems of measuring the depreciation of non-renewable resources, and our noting of the fact that measuring the depreciation of reproducible capital is itself difficult, these results should not be invested with too much significance at the level of detail. The point is rather that the methodology developed by Proops and Atkinson provides an interesting perspective on the global sustainability problem. It can be seen as complementary to looking at the way consumption levels, and patterns, vary as between countries, and the arising implications for resources use, as reported, for example, in UNDP (1998). In that context, it should be noted that the results as presented in Table 17.10 take no account of ability to save – Japan and the USA, for example, have much higher per capita income levels than, for example, Africa and Other Asia.

Biophysical and composite indicators

Pearce and Atkinson (1995) describe the inequality we state as 17.34 above as a 'weak sustainability rule'. This refers to a distinction that is made in some of the literature between 'weak' and 'strong' sustainability. The former refers to the view that the degree of substitutability between man-made capital and natural capital is such that the condition that genuine saving be positive is both necessary and sufficient, while the latter refers to the view that substitution possibilities are limited so that satisfying the condition will not, in itself, guarantee sustainability. Although this terminology is quite widely used, it is in many ways quite unhelpful. The distinction is between necessary and sufficient conditions for sustainability rather than between different kinds of sustainability. Based on the view that substitution possibilities are limited, many commentators argue that all we need to know to promote the pursuit of sustainability is not, and cannot be, captured solely in economic data and indicators. There is now a large literature on biophysical sustainability indicators, and here we can do no more than suggest something of its nature with some examples. We also give some examples of proposals for combining biophysical indicators with socio-economic indicators.

We have at various points throughout this book referred to the problem of biodiversity loss, which many see as a major threat to the sustainability of the global system. In terms of the distinction made above, the argument is that biodiversity is part of the life support services that the natural environment supplies (see the discussion accompanying Figure 2.2 in Chapter 2), and that reproducible capital can substitute for those services to a very limited extent. Several proximate causes of species extinction and biodiversity loss can be distinguished, but one way of looking at the matter is in terms of the appropriation of solar radiation. Ultimately, this is the basis for all life, and one effect of increasing human numbers and per capita consumption has been that the human species is appropriating to itself a larger share of the fixed solar budget. Vitousek *et al.* (1986) estimated human appropriation of net primary production, which is the amount of living tissue created from solar radiation by the process of photosynthesis. They provided low, intermediate and high estimates of the global percentage appropriated by humans as 3, 19 and 25. The basis of the different estimates is in conventions about what is counted as 'human appropriation'. In relation to their high estimate, they comment that

> An equivalent concentration of resources into one species and its satellites has probably not occurred since land plants first diversified

and they argue that even the lower estimate implies a threat to the sustainability of the global system.

Clearly the appropriation of the products of photosynthesis is an important biophysical sustainability indicator, but it does not appear to have received much attention as such in the literature. However, a closely related indicator, the 'ecological footprint', has evinced quite a lot of interest, and data on it for human societies at the local, regional and national levels has been produced, and work is ongoing. References are provided in Wackernagel and Rees (1997), where they provide a 'first approximation' definition as:

> the ecological footprint can be represented as the aggregate area of land and water in various ecological categories that is claimed by participants in the economy to produce all the resources they consume, and to absorb all the wastes they generate on a continuing basis, using prevailing technology.

They report that their own 'conservative estimates' show that the average person in an industrialised country today has an ecological footprint of '2–5 hectares of productive land to sustain his or her material consumption' whereas 'there are only 1.5 hectares per capita of ecologically productive land on Earth'.

In Chapter 3 we noted the set of biophysical indicators proposed by Schaeffer et al. (1988):

- changes in the number of native species
- changes in the standing crop of biomass

- changes in mineral micronutrient stocks
- changes in the mechanisms of and capacity for damping oscillations.

Azar et al. (1996) and Rennings and Wiggering (1997) are examples of arguments for the need for consideration in pursuit of sustainability of a set of indicators which includes both biophysical indicators of the type suggested by Schaeffer et al., and socioeconomic indicators. Both of these papers provide further references to the literature in this area, and make the point that there is a need for more basic biophysical information on the state of the environment. Ekins and Simon (1998) argue for the identification of 'sustainability gaps' as the difference between some biophysical indicator's current level and the level taken to be consistent with sustainability requirements. They also argue for a monetary value being placed on such a gap, but specifically argue against the use of such a valuation being used to adjust the measure of national income to produce a measure of sustainable income. The Ekins and Simon proposal bears a close affinity with approaches adopted in the Netherlands, on which they provide references: see also the case study on the Netherlands in Chapter 3.

As a global problem, the sustainability problem includes the problem of poverty in the developing world. UNDP publishes an annual report which since 1990 has included the results for the calculation of a Human Development Index (HDI) for each of some 170 countries: see UNDP (1998) for the latest set of results. The HDI has undergone some changes in the details of its construction over the years but has retained its essential features intact. The HDI itself is defined over three sub-indices which relate to per capita national income, longevity and education, and the definition is such that the value for a country's HDI score must lie between 0 and 1. While the HDI is open to criticism (see, for example, Sagar and Najam, 1998), it is a readily accessible source of data across a wide range of countries, on a reasonably consistent basis over a period of years, and should continue to be available in the future. Also, the annual publication gives the data from which the HDI and its sub-indices are calculated. Common (1995) reports results from the use of data for two of these sub-indices with a biophysical indicator to produce what is argued to be a low cost indicator of relevance to monitoring sustainable development. The indicator is longevity multiplied by annual per capita income, divided by greenhouse gas emissions per capita. It is argued that a country that improved its performance on this indicator could be said, as a first approximation, to be improving its performance against sustainable development criteria. The numerator is average lifetime income, and the denominator is the per capita contribution to a major global environmental problem. An increase in this ratio would indicate that more lifetime income was being generated per unit greenhouse gas emission.

Concluding remarks

Here we offer some remarks on where we think that we have got to, not just in this chapter but also in the course of the book as a whole. These remarks necessarily involve the authors' values and judgements, as well as technical economic considerations. The reader may come to different conclusions. Our purpose here is to offer our assessments for consideration, rather than to make pronouncements.

It will be clear that we do not see measuring sustainable national income as a practical step, or even an almost practical step, toward sustainability. Even if the capital theoretic characterisation of the sustainability problem is accepted, and leaving aside the question of feasibility, it is our judgement that the practical problems involved are unlikely ever to be satisfactorily resolved. As well as the difficulty of ascertaining the 'right

prices' for aggregation across quantities of reproducible and natural capital assets, there is the difficulty of measuring the quantities themselves.

It is not even clear that measuring sustainable national income is a particularly desirable thing to do in pursuit of sustainability. The problem involved is multi-faceted, complex and involves uncertainty. Dealing with it requires that these characteristics are recognised. Attempts to capture in a single number the answer to the question 'are we behaving sustainably?' tend to obscure the essential characteristics of the problem. And, one of those essential characteristics is that it is, at bottom, a global rather than a national problem.

It is clear that economic analysis can contribute much to the discussion of other, in our view, more practical steps than trying to measure sustainable income. We noted that the 'right prices' problem for that endeavour is something of a chicken and egg problem. If we are behaving as capital theory says we should for sustainability the right prices would be readily observable. If we are not, the prices that we do observe tell us little about how we should be behaving. However, while we may not know the 'right prices', so that computations of sustainable income are rather meaningless, we do in many cases have a good idea in which direction from current prices the right prices lie. In many contexts it is clear that using economic instruments – taxes, tradable permits and the like – would move actual prices paid by the users of environmental resources in the right direction. Making, for example, the use of fossil fuels more expensive would, we can be reasonably sure, do much for the amelioration of several of the environmental dimensions of the sustainability problem. In and of itself it could increase poverty, but that is a problem that can be addressed in other ways which economists are well equipped to advise on.

Of course, while economists can advise on dealing with the regressive impact of higher energy prices, this does not ensure that the appropriate measures will be put in place. That requires political action, as would the adoption of the fossil fuel price increasing measures in the first place. However good the analysis and the information, action will only occur if there is the political will for it. The hope is that good analysis and information will increase the political will to do 'the right thing'. It appears that for many, economist and non-economist, advocates of environmental accounting as the measurement of sustainable national income or some related concept, the real rationale for the activity is that it will produce results that affect the political climate. On this view, it does not really matter that the number produced is wrong or meaningless, so long as it moves perceptions in the 'right' direction. However, it is not clear that announcing in this way that economic performance is worse than had previously been thought, if that is the way the numbers do turn out, could be relied upon to have this effect.

On the other hand, we can be reasonably sure, on the basis of historical evidence, that actually changing prices does influence behaviour. It appears to us that, if the objective is to promote the cause of sustainability, it is much more important to move actual prices in the right direction than to get the right shadow prices for the computation of a number for sustainable income. To do this does require that decision makers and those who vote for them are well informed about the issues and the alternatives. Economists have an important role in providing some of this information, but there is an important role for other kinds of information, assessment and advice. Economists need to be honest about the quality of the information that they can provide, and the ethical basis for the advice that they offer. In saying this, we are not implying that economists are peculiar in this respect. All 'experts' contributing to public debate and deliberation on the many issues involved in the sustainability problem need to be circumspect about

the limits of, and basis for, their expertise. It is simply that this book is addressed to students doing an economics course.

Discussion questions

1 Five European countries have access to the water resources of the River Rhine, which are intensively used for commercial and industrial purposes. Discuss (a) methods of valuation of Rhine water quality degradation caused by human use, and (b) the allocation of these costs between the countries affected.

2 Discuss the arguments for and against the exclusion, or deduction, of defensive or preventive environmental expenditure from GDP. Identify other components of GDP which, it could be argued, should be excluded for identical or similar reasons.

3 Discuss the distinction between 'economic' and 'non-economic' environmental assets. Compile a short list of three or four specific non-economic environmental assets, and identify the costs and benefits associated with those assets, and how these might be valued for national accounts purposes.

4 There is lot more coal remaining than there is oil, in the world as a whole. The combustion of coal releases more CO_2, and other pollutants, per unit energy released, than is the case with oil. Which should have the higher shadow price for the purposes of environmental accounting.

5. Devise a checklist for the qualitative and quantitative information which a university should be asked to furnish as a basis for an environmental audit of its functional activities.

6.Given the valuation problems inherent in assessing many forms of environmental damage or degradation, is it better to concentrate efforts on developing a comprehensive system of physical environmental accounts, rather than attempt to incorporate environmental costs and benefits into the conventional system of national accounts?

Problems

1 A mineral resource is extracted and sold yielding £20m annual gross revenue to the owners. Purchases of goods and services used for extraction are £4m, labour costs are £2m and capital equipment is valued at £30m. The average rate of return on capital in the mineral extraction sector is 4.5%. At current extraction rates, reserves will be economically exhausted in 5 years. Assume a constant rate of extraction, a fixed extraction technology, and constant relative prices. Calculate a depletion rate for this mineral resource and hence the contribution of this extraction activity to gross and net national product, stating any necessary additional assumptions.

2 At the start of 1998 oil reserves in country X were 504×10^9 barrels. During 1998 country X produced 8×10^9 barrels, and there were no new discoveries of oil there. The world price of oil was constant at £3.125 per barrel throughout 1998, and the interest rate in X was also constant, at 5%. Total oil production costs in X, including a normal return on capital employed were £20×10^9.

   (a) Calculate the depreciation of country X's oil stock using
   (i) the net present value method,
   (ii) El Serafy's user cost rule.

   (b) Repeat (a) using an interest rate of 10%.

   (c) Repeat the calculation for a 5% interest rate, but with the world price of oil being £3.00 at the start of the year and £5.00 at the end of the year.

   (d) Comment on your results.

3 In the chapter we showed that the owner of an oil deposit in a fully competitive economy would keep his or her wealth constant and achieve the highest consistent level of constant consumption by following the Hartwick rule. Show that this would also be the case for the sole owner of a fishery, given sustainable yield harvesting. Show that it would also be the case for someone owning an oil deposit and a fishery.

Further reading

The capital theoretic literature which is relevant to environmental accounting is extensive and growing rapidly. We shall here just note some of the major original contributions, and some recent papers that themselves provide fuller references to the literature. Dasgupta and Heal (1974) was perhaps the first rigorous consideration of the optimal path for consumption in a representative agent single-commodity model, where the agent maximises the sum of discounted utility and production uses inputs of capital and a non-renewable resource. Solow (1974a) rigorously examined the feasibility of constant consumption forever in such a model, given various assumptions about substitutability in production, population growth and technical progress. Weitzman (1976) established the interpretation of net national product as sustainable income as the return on wealth, but did not explicitly consider natural resources. Hartwick (1977) showed that for an economy with a constant returns to scale Cobb–Douglas production function with capital and a non-renewable resource as arguments, zero net investment – investment in reproducible capital equal to resource depreciation – would give constant consumption. Hartwick's rule was generalised, in terms of the production conditions in which it held, in a number of subsequent papers by himself and others: see, for examples Hartwick (1978) and Dasgupta and Mitra (1983). Solow (1986) brought together the contributions of Weitzman and Hartwick, and set out the basic theory drawn upon in Solow (1992, 1993).

The literature on neo-classical growth theory, what we referred to as capital theory, in relation to sustainability was reviewed in Toman *et al.* (1995). Pezzey (1997) distinguishes several possible definitions of sustainability, emphasises that this is not the outcome in standard models where the integral of discounted future utility is maximised, and argues that adding a sustainability constraint to such models is not, as some economists have argued, a redundant exercise. Sustainability in small open economies is discussed in Asheim (1986) and Brekke (1997). Papers drawing on capital theory to derive propositions about the proper measurement of net national income as sustainable income, given the dependence of production and consumption on environmental inputs, include: Hartwick (1990), Mäler (1991), Dasgupta (1995) and Hamilton (1994). Faucheux *et al.* (1997) consider sustainability in the context of an overlapping generations model and argue that standard capital theory does not provide a satisfactory basis for environmental accounting. Weitzman (1997) looks at technical progress in relation to sustainability, and argues that on account of technical progress properly measured net national income will understate sustainable income.

The UNSTAT proposals for satellite accounting are set out in United Nations (1992, 1993a). Work on the UNSTAT proposals included the preparation of illustrative accounts for a hypothetical country, and of preliminary accounts for Mexico and Papua New Guinea, reported in chapters in Lutz (1993): see also Bartelmus (1994).

Appendix 17.1 National income, the return on wealth, Hartwick's rule and sustainable income

Jack Pezzey, Environment Department, University of York

In this appendix and the next we use the dot notation for derivatives with respect to time so as to reduce clutter in the exposition. For the same reason we omit the t subscript when referring to derivatives such as marginal uti-

lities and marginal products, writing, for example, U_C rather than U_{Ct} for $\partial U_t / \partial C_t$.

National income and the return on wealth

We begin here with the simplest optimal growth model where there is a single produced good which may be consumed or added to the stock of reproducible capital, which does not depreciate, and where the environment affects neither utility nor production. The problem to be considered is

$$\text{Max} \int_0^\infty U(C_t) e^{-\rho t} dt \text{ subject to } \dot{K}_t = Q(K_t) - C_t$$
$$(17.41a)$$

for which the current value Hamiltonian is

$$H_t = U(C_t) + w_t(Q\{K_t\} - C_t)$$

where the necessary conditions are

$$\partial H_t / \partial C_t = U_C - w_t = 0 \qquad (17.41b)$$

$$\dot{w}_t - \rho w_t = -\partial H_t / \partial K_t = -w_t Q_K \qquad (17.41c)$$

Replacing $Q(K_t) - C_t$ by $\dot{K}$, we can write the maximised value of the Hamiltonian as

$$H_t^* = U(C_t) + w_t \dot{K}_t$$

which by Equation 17.41b can also be written as

$$H_t^* = U(C_t) + U_C \dot{K}_t \qquad (17.41d)$$

where C_t and $\dot{K}_t$ are the *optimal* values for the maximisation problem (17.41a). We can interpret H_t^* as instantaneous national income measured in units which are utils. Observe that the right hand side of 17.41d is the current flow of utility plus the value of the change in the capital stock measured in units which reflect its contribution to future, maximised, utility.

This interpretation of H_t^* can be further supported by noting that if we linearise the utility function so that $U(C_t) = U_C C_t$, we can write Equation 17.41d as

$$H_t^* = U_C C_t + U_C \dot{K}_t$$

so that

$$H_t^* / U_C = C_t + I_t$$

where I_t for investment is $\dot{K}_t$.[10] Given the assumption that K does not depreciate, the right-hand side here is just the usual expression for net national income and if we use NDP for this, we have

$$\text{NDP}_t = H_t^*/U_C = C_t + I_t \quad (17.41\text{e})$$

Now introduce the use of a non-renewable natural resource into production, as in the simple exhaustible resource depletion problem considered in Chapter 7 (and see Appendix 7.2). We saw there that for

$$\text{Max} \int_0^\infty U(C_t)e^{-\rho t}dt \text{ subject to } \dot{S}_t = -R_t$$
$$\text{and} \quad \dot{K}_t = Q(K_t, R_t) - C_t$$

the current value Hamiltonian is

$$H_t = U(C_t) + P_t(-R_t) + w_t(Q\{K_t, R_t\} - C_t)$$

so that the necessary conditions are

$$\partial H_t/\partial C_t = U_C - w_t = 0 \quad (17.42\text{a})$$
$$\partial H_t/\partial R_t = -P_t + w_tQ_R = 0 \quad (17.42\text{b})$$
$$\dot{w}_t - \rho w_t = -\partial H_t/\partial K_t = -w_tQ_K \quad (17.42\text{c})$$
$$\dot{P}_t - \rho P_t = -\partial H_t/\partial S_t = 0 \quad (17.42\text{d})$$

These can respectively be written as

$$w_t = U_C \quad (17.42\text{e})$$
$$\dot{P}_t/P_t = \dot{w}_t/w_t + \dot{Q}_R/Q_R \quad (17.42\text{f})$$
$$Q_K = \rho - \dot{w}_t/w_t \quad (17.42\text{g})$$
$$\dot{P}_t/P_t = \rho \quad (17.42\text{h})$$

Note that Equation 17.42f comes from differentiating Equation 17.42b with respect to time, dividing both sides by P, and then substituting for P on the right-hand side from Equation 17.42b. For constant consumption, Equations 17.42g and 17.42a give, since U_C constant means $\dot{U}_C = 0$,

$$Q_K = \rho - \dot{U}_C/U_C = \rho \quad (17.42\text{i})$$

[10] Strictly speaking, linearising the utility function makes the Hamiltonian linear in consumption, and so gives rise to what are known as 'corner' or 'non-interior' solutions to the optimal control problem, for which equations like Equations 17.41b and 17.41c do not hold. However, in common with much of the relevant literature, we will overlook this technicality.

Finally, Equations 17.42g, 17.42f and 17.42h together give

$$\dot{Q}_R/Q_R = Q_K \quad (17.42\text{j})$$

as an alternative statement of the Hotelling rule which is used later.

However, our main interest here is in the Hamiltonian itself. Using the equations of motion, the maximised Hamiltonian can be written

$$H_t^* = U(C_t) + w_t\dot{K}_t + P_t\dot{S}_t \quad (17.42\text{k})$$

and proceeding to linearise the utility function as for the simple model above, this becomes

$$H_t^*/U_C = C_t + I_t + (P_t/w_t)\dot{S}_t$$

which by Equation 17.42b, and substituting for $\dot{S}_t$ from the equation of motion, can be written

$$H_t^*/U_C = C_t + I_t - Q_RR_t$$
$$= \text{NDP}_t - Q_RR_t \quad (17.42\text{l})$$
$$= \text{EDP}_t$$

where we still use NDP_t for national income as conventionally measured, and now introduce EDP_t to refer to national income as properly measured given the use of the natural resource in production. According to Equation 17.42l, EDP_t is NDP_t minus the rent Q_RR_t arising in the extraction of the resource, where that rent is the measure of the depreciation of the asset which is the resource stock. Depreciation is the amount extracted valued at the marginal product of the resource, which in this model with costless extraction is the unit rent.

We could write Equation 17.42l as

$$\text{EDP}_t = C_t + I_t - (P_t/w_t)R_t \quad (17.42\text{m})$$

where P_t/w_t is the relative (to the price of the numeraire commodity which is the consumption/capital good) price of the extracted resource, which in a model with costless extraction is the same as the price of the resource *in situ*. As we saw in Chapter 7, in a fully competitive economy the relative price of the resource would move over time as required by the necessary conditions for the maximisation of discounted utility. This is the basis for taking Equation 17.42m as a guide to how the conventional measure of national income should be adjusted to account for non-renewable resource depletion in an actual economy. The assumption is, that is, that actual economies should be treated as if they were fully competitive economies. Recall from Chapter 7 that the conditions characterising a fully competitive economy are strong.

Now, note that we have $H_t^* = H_t^*(K, S, w, P)$ and consider the differentiation of H_t^* with respect to time. We have

$$\dot{H}_t^* = (\partial H^*/\partial K)\,\dot{K}_t + (\partial H^*/\partial S)\,\dot{S}_t$$
$$+ (\partial H^*/\partial w)\,\dot{w}_t + (\partial H^*/\partial P)\,\dot{P}_t$$

Using Equation 17.42c for $(\partial H^*/\partial K)$, Equation 17.4d for $(\partial H^*/\partial S)$, and $\partial H^*/\partial w = \dot{K}_t$ and $\partial H^*/\partial P = \dot{S}_t$ from Equation 17.42k, we get

$$\dot{H}_t^* = \rho w_t \dot{K}_t + \rho P_t \dot{S}_t = \rho(w_t \dot{K}_t + P_t \dot{S}_t)$$
$$(17.42n)$$

From Equation 17.42l, using $\dot{U}_C = 0$ and Equation 17.42a,

$$(d/dt)\text{EDP}_t = \dot{H}_t^*/U_C = \dot{H}_t^*/w_t \quad (17.42o)$$

Combining Equations 17.42n, 17.42o and 17.42l then gives

$$(d/dt)\text{EDP}_t = \rho[\dot{K}_t + (P_t/w_t)\dot{S}_t]$$
$$= \rho(I_t - Q_R R_t)$$
$$= \rho(\text{EDP}_t - C_t) \quad (17.42p)$$

Using Equation 17.42i, the solution of this differential equation in EDP_t can be shown to be

$$\text{EDP}_t = \rho W_t = Q_K W_t \quad (17.42q)$$

where W_t is the economy's wealth at time t, as defined by the present discounted value of consumption from time t onwards:

$$W_t = \int_t^\infty C_\tau e^{\rho(\tau - t)}d\tau \quad (17.42r)$$

This is a rewritten version of a famous result due to Weitzman (1976). Since the marginal product of capital Q_K is the interest rate in a competitive economy, this is the basis for the interpretation of EDP_t, which is properly measured national income, as the 'return' (at the going rate of interest) on the economy's total stock of wealth. If, moreover, there are constant returns to scale in the economy's production function $Q(K_t, R_t)$, then wealth could be interpreted not just as the present discounted value of future consumption, but also as the value today in consumption units of the economy's productive assets:

$$W_t = K_t + Q_R S_t \quad (17.42s)$$

Hartwick's rule and sustainable income

There is a powerful appeal in the idea that income is the interest earned on wealth, and that consuming exactly one's income – no more and no less – should be sustainable forever. Is that what Equation 17.42q above is saying for an economy? That is, are there circumstances in which EDP is *sustainable* national income? The answer is 'yes', but only in a case of severely restricted practical value, which unfortunately is often misunderstood in the literature, creating much confusion on this topic. What can be said is the following. *If* optimal consumption happens to equal EDP *always*, and *if* constant consumption is physically feasible – note the 'if' and 'always' caveats – then both consumption and EDP will be constant forever; or in other words, sustainable. The proof of this is as follows. We start from the first 'if', by assuming

$$C_t = Q(K_t, R_t) - \dot{K}_t = \text{EDP}_t \quad (17.43a)$$

always, which from Equation 17.42l means that

$$\dot{K}_t = Q_R R_t \quad (17.43b)$$

always. The rule in Equation 17.43b, which says 'investment in reproducible capital is always equal to resource rents', is *Hartwick's rule* (after John Hartwick who discovered it in 1977, see Hartwick, 1977). Taking the time derivative of consumption from Equation 17.43a then gives

$$\dot{C}_t = Q_K \dot{K}_t + Q_R R_t - \ddot{K}_t$$
$$= Q_K \dot{K}_t + Q_R R_t - (\dot{Q}_R R_t + Q_R \dot{R}_t)$$

using Hartwick's rule. Note that without the 'always', we could not have taken and used the time derivative of $\dot{K} = Q_R R_t$ to substitute for $\ddot{K}$. Using Hotelling's rule written as Equation 17.42j then gives

$$\dot{C} = Q_K \dot{K}_t - Q_R Q_K R_t$$

which using Hartwick's rule again is

$$\dot{C} = 0$$

that is, constant consumption.

However, *there is no reason why optimal consumption should equal EDP*, and hence why Hartwick's rule (and hence constant consumption) should hold on an optimal path. Indeed, constant consumption may not even be feasible. In general, optimal consumption will rise or fall over time, and will be more or less than EDP at any point in time; and hence capital investment will be more or less than resource rents at any time.

However again, what happens if the economy is constrained to follow Hartwick's Rule? (We will not show how this constraint might be achieved, but one way would be to introduce a macroeconomically significant policy of tax incentives to invest more.) It turns out that consumption will indeed be constant, but the constraint policy will force the economy off the optimal path: Equation 17.41a will no longer be maximised. As a result, both prices and quantities on a constant consumption path will generally be different from their optimal values. Nevertheless, some sort of present value function, using a different utility discount factor (say $\lambda(t)$ instead of $e^{-\rho t}$ in Equation 17.41a) will still be maximised on the highest possible constant consumption path. ρ will be replaced throughout by $-\dot{\lambda}/\lambda$, but (as the reader can readily check) the form of Hotelling's rule as Equation 17.42j, used above in the proof of constant consumption, will be unchanged.

At any point in time, aggregate investment, defined as $\dot{K}_t - Q_R R_t$, is therefore an unreliable indicator of an economy's sustainability. The optimal path of an economy may be unsustainable at time t, and yet aggregate investment may be positive then. Or, if there is technical progress in production (which we have ignored above), it turns out that the economy can be sustainable at t even though aggregate investment is negative then. And the problem remains even if one tries to use the 'right' price, Q_R, that would apply on the constant consumption path, because the quantities of investment $\dot{K}_t$ and resource depletion R_t will still be wrong. Trying to use Hartwick's rule ('invest resource rents') as either a policy prescription to achieve sustainability, or as the basis for 'sustainability accounting', therefore faces a fundamental chicken-and-egg problem. The rule works only if sustainability, in the form of constant consumption, and hence both sustainability prices and quantities, have already been achieved! Moreover, achieving constant consumption when it is not the optimal path raises an awkward political question: which matters more, sustainability or optimality?

Another frequent misunderstanding in the literature is that keeping consumption constant means keeping wealth constant. The trouble is that wealth can be defined in different ways. If wealth is defined as the time integral of aggregate investment, then obviously it remains constant on a constant consumption path, thanks to Hartwick's rule. But if wealth is defined as earlier, as the present value of future consumption or the aggregate value of current assets, then wealth need not be constant. Indeed, in the best-known example of constant consumption with non-renewable resources discovered in 1974 by Robert Solow (Solow, 1974a), wealth must be *rising* forever to keep consumption constant. Intuitively, what is happening is that in the Cobb–Douglas production function Solow uses, $Q(K_t, R_t) = K_t^\alpha R_t^\beta$, the marginal product of capital investment Q_K is falling because an ever-rising stock of capital K_t has to be combined with an ever-shrinking resource flow R_t. So by Equation 17.42q, wealth W_t must be rising if the product $Q_K W_t = \text{EDP}_t = C_t$ is to be constant.

Appendix 17.2 Adjusting national income measurement to account for the environment

In this appendix we explore further the approach to national income measurement developed in Appendix 17.1, by applying it to models which capture other dimensions of the economy–environment interrelations that underlie an interest in environmental accounting. The caveats of Appendix 17.1 regarding the interpretation of the results as measures of sustainable income in the sense generally understood also apply here. We will, however, concentrate here on deriving the adjustments, rather than pursuing those issues in more general contexts.

Consider first a non-renewable resource using model economy, which is that of Appendix 17.1 modified such that resource extraction is costly and there is exploration activity. The optimisation problem is

$$\text{Max} \int_0^\infty U(C_t)e^{-\rho t}\mathrm{d}t \text{ subject to } \dot{S}_t = -R_t + N_t$$

and $\dot{K}_t = Q(K_t, R_t) - C_t - G(R_t, S_t) - F(N_t, S_t)$

where N_t is new discoveries brought about by exploration activity with the cost function $F(N_t, S_t)$, such that costs rise with the level of exploration activity, $F_N = \partial F_t / \partial N_t > 0$, and as the stock of resources is depleted, $F_S = \partial F_t / \partial S_t < 0$. The costs of extraction are given by $G(R_t, S_t)$, as in Appendix 8.3. For this problem the current value Hamiltonian is

$$H_t = U(C_t) + P_t(-R_t + N_t) + w_t(Q\{K_t, R_t\} - C_t - G\{R_t, S_t\} - F\{N_t, S_t\})$$

with necessary conditions which include

$$\partial H_t / \partial C_t = U_C - w_t = 0 \quad (17.44a)$$

$$\partial H_t / \partial R_t = -P_t + w_t Q_R - w_t G_R = 0 \quad (17.44b)$$

$$\partial H_t / \partial N_t = P_t - w_t F_N = 0 \quad (17.44c)$$

Note from Equations 17.44b and 17.44c that

$$P_t / w_t = Q_R - G_R = F_N$$

so that marginal discovery cost, F_N, is equal to marginal rent, $Q_R - G_R$.

The maximised Hamiltonian can be written as

$$H_t^* = U(C_t) + w_t \dot{K}_t + P_t \dot{S}_t$$

and using $U = U_C C$ and $U_C = w_t$ we can write

$$\text{EDP}_t = H_t^* / U_C = C_t + \dot{K}_t + (P_t / w_t)\dot{S}_t$$

which is

$$\begin{aligned} \text{EDP}_t &= C_t + I_t - (P_t / w_t)(R_t - N_t) \\ &= \text{NDP}_t - (Q_R - G_R)(R_t - N_t) \\ &= \text{NDP}_t - (Q_R - G_R)R_t + (Q_R - G_R)N_t \\ &= \text{NDP}_t - (Q_R - G_R)R_t + F_N N_t \end{aligned}$$

so that EDP_t for this economy is NDP_t less the depreciation of the non-renewable resource stock, which is the total Hotelling rent; that is, marginal rent multiplied by extraction net of new discoveries.

Now consider the use of renewable resources in production, so that the current value Hamiltonian is

$$\begin{aligned} H_t &= U(C_t) + P_t(F\{S_t\} - R_t) \\ &\quad + w_t(Q\{K_t, R_t\} - C_t - G\{R_t, S_t\}) \end{aligned}$$

where R_t is resource use again and $F(S_t)$ is the intrinsic growth function. In Chapter 9 we used $G(S_t)$ for this function, but here we retain $G(\cdot)$ for the cost function so as to make the results now to be derived readily comparable with those for the non-renewable resource model just considered. Note that harvest cost depends on the size of the harvest and the stock size. The necessary conditions here include

$$\partial H_t / \partial C_t = U_C - w_t = 0 \quad (17.45a)$$

$$\partial H_t / \partial R_t = -P_t + w_t Q_R - w_t G_R = 0 \quad (17.45b)$$

where Equation 17.45b implies

$$P_t = w_t(Q_R - G_R)$$

The maximised Hamiltonian can be again be written

$$H_t^* = U(C_t) + w_t \dot{K}_t + P_t \dot{S}_t$$

and, proceeding as previously, we get

$$EDP_t = C_t + I_t + (P_t/w_t)\dot{S}_t$$
$$= NDP_t - (Q_R - G_R)(R_t - F\{S_t\})$$
$$(17.45c)$$

which is the direct analogue to the result for a non-renewable resource. Here the marginal rent is multiplied by the harvest net of intrinsic growth. Note that if there is sustainable yield harvesting, $R_t = F(S_t)$ and no adjustment to NDP_t is required.

Suppose now that the renewable resource is not an input to the production of the consumption/capital good, but is an argument in the utility function. The production input case might be thought of as the way timber gets used, the utility function argument case as the way fish get used – whereas timber gets used to produce commodities for consumption, fish gets directly eaten. For this latter case,

$$H_t = U(C_t, R_t) + P_t(F\{S_t\} - R_t)$$
$$+ w_t(Q\{K_t\} - C_t - G\{R_t, S_t\})$$

with necessary conditions which include

$$\partial H_t/\partial C_t = U_C - w_t = 0 \qquad (17.46a)$$

$$\partial H_t/\partial R_t = U_R - P_t - w_t G_R = 0 \qquad (17.46b)$$

which imply

$$U_R/U_C = (P_t/w_t) + G_R \qquad (17.46c)$$

for the price of caught fish available for consumption; that is, the consumption price of fish is marginal rent plus marginal cost. Using $U(C_t, R_t) = U_C C_t + U_R R_t$ and proceeding as before

$$EDP_t = H_t^*/U_C = C_t + (U_R/U_C)R_t$$
$$+ \dot{K}_t + (P_t/w_t)\dot{S}_t$$
$$= (C_t + \{U_R/U_C\}R_t) + I_t$$
$$+ (P_t/w_t)(F\{s_t\} - R_t)$$

which by Equation 17.46c and using C_t^* for aggregate consumption is

$$EDP_t = C_t^* + I_t - (P_t/w_t)(R_t - F\{S_t\})$$
$$= NDP_t - (P_t/w_t)(R_t - F\{S_t\})$$
$$= NDP_t - (\{U_R/U_C\} - G_R)(R_t - F\{S_t\})$$
$$(17.46d)$$

This has the same structure as Equation 17.45c in that EDP_t is NDP_t less depreciation, but note that P_t/w_t, used to value the change in stock size, is different in this case.

A third plausible specification for a model of an economy exploiting renewable resources has the harvest as an input to production and the stock size as an argument in the utility function. Thus, for example, harvested timber is used in production, while standing timber is a source of aesthetic pleasure and recreation. In such a case, the Hamiltonian is

$$H_t = U(C_t, S_t) + P_t(F\{S_t\} - R_t)$$
$$+ w_t(Q\{K_t, R_t\} - C_t - G\{R_t, S_t\})$$

and the necessary conditions include

$$\partial H_t/\partial C_t = U_C - w_t = 0 \qquad (17.47a)$$

$$\partial H_t/\partial R_t = -P_t + w_t Q_R - w_t G_R = 0 \quad (17.47b)$$

where Equation 17.47b implies

$$P_t = w_t(Q_R - G_R) \qquad (17.47c)$$

Then using $U(C_t, S_t) = U_C C_t + U_S S_t$

$$H_t^*/U_t = C_t + (U_S/U_C)S_t + \dot{K}_t + (P_t/w_t)\dot{S}_t$$

and

$$EDP_t = NDP_t + (U_S/U_C)S_t$$
$$- (Q_R - G_R)(R_t - F\{S_t\})$$
$$(17.47d)$$

As compared with Equation 17.45c there is a structural difference here. As well as subtracting depreciation from NPD_t, it is now necessary to add the value of the stock of the renewable resource, where the valuation uses U_S/U_C. Note further that in this case, we would generally assume that there was no market in the consumption of the amenity services provided by the stock, so that this 'price' could not be revealed in fully competitive markets, but would have to be ascertained by the sorts of methods discussed in Chapter 14.

The point being made here in looking at these three renewable resource models is that what we think we have to do to go from NDP to EDP, in terms of the nature of the adjustments and the valuations used with them, depends on the model that is used to analyse the problem. Since reasonable people may reasonably disagree about the specification of the model that captures the stylised facts of the way economic activity uses environmental services, it follows that there is no single correct answer to the question of how to get from NDP to EDP. Also, the answer may imply the need for non-market valuation, even if we are prepared to assume fully competitive markets where markets operate. The same point arises if we consider the matter of pollution and arising environmental degradation.

To illustrate this consider the model from Chapter 11, which has an index of environmental quality affecting both utility and production, where that index is a function of the current flow of residuals and the accumulated stock, where the production function recognises the materials balance principle, and where clean-up is undertaken. The optimisation problem is

$$\text{Max} \int_0^\infty U(C_t, E\{R, A\}) e^{-\rho t}\, dt$$

$$\text{subject to}\quad \dot{S}_t = -R_t$$

$$\dot{K}_t = Q(K_t, R_t, E\{R_t, A_t\}) - C_t - G(R_t, S_t) - V_t$$

$$\dot{A}_t = M(R_t) - \alpha A_t - F(V_t)$$

Here $G(\cdot)$ is extraction cost, V_t is clean-up expenditure and $F(V_t)$ is the effect of that expenditure. The current value Hamiltonian is

$$H_t = U(C_t, E\{R_t, A_t\}) + P_t(-R_t)$$
$$+ w_t(Q\{K_t, R_t, E(R_t, A_t)\} - C_t$$
$$- G_t(R_t, S_t) - V_t) + \lambda_t(M\{R_t\}$$
$$- \alpha A_t - F\{V_t\})$$

with necessary conditions including

$$\partial H_t / \partial C_t = U_C - w_t = 0 \qquad (17.48\text{a})$$

$$\partial H_t / \partial R_t = U_E E_R - P_t + w_t Q_R$$
$$+ w_t Q_E E_R - w_t G_R + \lambda_t M_R = 0 \qquad (17.48\text{b})$$

$$\partial H_t / \partial V_t = -w_t - \lambda_t F_V = 0 \qquad (17.48\text{c})$$

From Equation 17.48c

$$\lambda_t / w_t = -1/F_V \qquad (17.48\text{d})$$

and using this and Equation 17.48a in Equation 17.48b gives

$$P_t / w_t = (U_E E_R / U_C) + Q_R + Q_E E_R$$
$$- G_R - (1/F_V) M_R$$
$$= (Q_R - G_R) + (\{U_E / U_C\} + Q_E) E_R$$
$$- (1/F_V) M_R$$
$$(17.48\text{e})$$

The maximised value of the Hamiltonian can be written

$$H_t^* = U(C_t, E\{R_t, A_t\}) + P_t \dot{S}_t + w_t \dot{K}_t + \lambda_t \dot{A}_t$$

and using $U(\cdot) = U_C C_t + U_E E_t$ and dividing by $U_C = w_t$

$$\text{EDP}_t = H_t^* / U_C$$
$$= C_t + (U_E / U_C) E_t + \dot{K}_t + (P_t / w_t) \dot{S}_t$$
$$+ (\lambda_t / w_t) \dot{A}_t$$

or

$$\text{EDP}_t = \text{NDP}_t + (U_E / U_C) E_t - (P_t / w_t) R_t$$
$$+ (\lambda_t / w_t)(M\{R_t\} - \alpha A_t - F\{V_t\})$$

which on substituting for P_t / w_t from Equation 17.48e and rearranging can be written as

$$\text{EDP}_t = \text{NDP}_t + (U_E / U_C) E_t - (Q_R - G_R) R_t$$
$$- (\{(U_E / U_C) + Q_E\} E_R - (1/E_V) M_R) R_t$$
$$- (1/F_V)(M\{R_t\} - \alpha A_t - F\{V_t\})$$
$$(17.48\text{f})$$

So, going from NDP to EDP now involves four adjustments. While the first two are easy to interpret (the second is just depreciation of the resource stock), an intuitive interpretation of the latter two is complicated. For our purposes there are two important points. The first is that implementing these adjustments would require non-market valuation. The second is that if the environmental quality does not affect utility, $U_E = 0$ so that the first adjustment in Equation 17.48f is not required and the third is modified. For any particular pollutant, whether $U_E = 0$ should be assumed or not is an empirical question, which would have to be decided by non-market valuation.

As another example of the dependency of the adjustment prescription on model specification, suppose that $M(R_t) = \beta R_t$ and E_t is a function only of A_t. Then the model might represent carbon dioxide emissions and the climate change problem, where gross emissions are a fixed proportion of the mass of fossil fuel, R, burned, and where it is only the concentration in the atmosphere that is relevant to climate change, which affects utility and production. In this case, clean-up can be thought of as tree planting. Then, with $E_R = 0$ Equation 17.48e becomes

$$P_t/w_t = Q_R - G_R - (\beta/F_V)$$

and Equation 17.48f becomes

$$\begin{aligned} \text{EDP}_t = \text{NDP}_t &+ (U_C/U_E)E_t - (Q_R - G_R)R_t \\ &+ (\alpha A_t)/F_V + F(V_t)/F_V \end{aligned}$$

$$(17.49)$$

which again illustrates the dependence of the necessary adjustments on model structure and assumptions.

Appendix 17.3 The UNSTAT proposals

The most recent version of the international System of National Accounts (SNA), published in 1993 by the United Nations Statistical Division (United Nations, 1993a), addresses for the first time the possible incorporation of environmental costs and assets in the SNA. However, the report does not recommend the integration of environmental accounts into the central or core SNA. Instead it proposes, for those countries interested in and capable of compiling environmental accounts, a system of satellite accounts. These take the standard SNA as a starting point, showing how they might be complemented or modified by the inclusion of stocks and flows arising from the interaction between the economy and the environment. The section of the report dealing with this is more of a review of the current state of the art, and a guide to national accounts practitioners who may wish to experiment

with environmental accounting, than it is a firm proposal for a particular design and methodology.

The discussion and presentation are closely modelled on the System of Environmental Economic Accounts (SEEA) proposed in the UN handbook *Integrated Environmental and Economic Accounting* (United Nations, 1992). The SEEA focuses on (i) accounting adequately for the depletion of scarce natural resources and (ii) measuring the costs of environmental degradation and its prevention. The basic structure of the SEEA and its links with the SNA is illustrated in Table 17.11, which can also be used to explain the derivation of the main aggregates of the satellite environmental accounts.

The shaded part of Table 17.11 covers the conventional SNA aggregates. Row i records opening assets, $K0_{p.ec}$ being the value of stocks of man-made (produced) capital, and $K0_{np.ec}$ the value of stocks of natural resources (oil and gas, cultivated forests, and so on) regarded as economic assets by the SNA.[11] Row ii records total supply, comprising domestic production (P) and imports (M).

Row iii shows how total supply is used. A proportion of supply is used in further production (Ci); the balance is either exported (X), consumed by households or government (C), or invested (Ig).

Column 1 shows the cost structure of domestic production P, comprising the cost of goods and services used in production (Ci), the cost of consumption of fixed (man-made) capital (CFC), and the balancing value-added, or net domestic product (NDP). Note that NDP + CFC = Gross Domestic Product. Consumption of fixed capital also appears as a negative item in Column 4; gross investment Ig less capital consumption CFC = net investment I.

Row v yields the familiar national accounts identity

$$\text{NDP} = (X - M) + C + I$$

[11] We retain the somewhat cumbersome notation used in the UN text, for ease of cross-reference.

Table 17.11   Basic structure of the SEEA.

		Production 1	Rest of world 2	Final consumption 3	Produced assets 4	Non-produced natural assets 5	Other non-produced natural assets 6
				Economic activities		**Economic assets**	**Environment**
Opening stock of assets	i					$K0_{p.ec}$	$K0_{np.ec}$
Supply	ii	P	M				
Economic uses	iii	Ci	X	C	Ig		
Consumption of fixed capital	iv	CFC			$-$ CFC		
Net domestic product	v	NDP	X $-$ M	C	I		
Use of non-produced natural assets	vi	Use $_{np}$				$-$ Use $_{np.ec}$	$-$ Use $_{np.env}$
Other accumulation of non-produced natural assets	vii					$I_{np.ec}$	$-I_{np.env}$
Environmentally adjusted aggregates in monetary environmental accounting	viii	EDP	X $-$ M	C	$A_{p.ec}$	$A_{np.ec}$	$-A_{np.env}$
Holding gains/losses	ix					$\text{Rev}_{p.ec}$	$\text{Rev}_{np.ec}$
Other changes in volume of assets	x					$\text{Vol}_{p.ec}$	$\text{Vol}_{np.ec}$
Closing stock of assets	xi					$K1_{p.ec}$	$K1_{np.ec}$

Source: United Nations (1993).

Rows ix and x include various adjustments to the stock of produced and non-produced assets, including adjustments to account for changes in prices of assets, destruction of assets due to natural disaster, and certain other changes which affect the level of stocks of assets. For produced economic assets, opening stocks $K0_{p.ec}$ plus net investment I, plus or minus adjustments $\text{Rev}_{p.ec}$ and $\text{Vol}_{p.ec}$, gives closing stocks $K1_{p.ec}$ (or opening stocks in the next accounting period). For non-produced economic assets, the entries $\text{Rev}_{np.ec}$ and $\text{Vol}_{np.ec}$ denote corresponding adjustments to opening stocks $K0_{np.ec}$, resulting in closing stocks $K1_{np.ec}$ The 'Other changes in volume of assets' $\text{Vol}_{np.ec}$ include changes in known economic reserves of natural assets.

The non-shaded part of the table shows how the system can be extended to incorporate other environmental accounts, which may be expressed in physical or monetary units, or both. Expressed in physical units, these additional flows can be viewed as sup-plementary to the SNA: expressed in monetary units, they could be used to obtain environmentally-adjusted measures of domestic product, as discussed in the chapter.

The additional column 6 covers natural capital not classified as economic (because their usage does not involve market or quasi-market transactions), such as air, uncultivated land, particular ecosystems, virgin forest, and most forms of surface water. The additional row vi records the use or consumption of non-produced natural assets, Use_{np} – that is, the depletion/degradation of natural capital, analogous to CFC for man-made capital. Use_{np} itself comprises $\text{Use}_{np.ec}$ – the depletion of economic natural assets such as subsoil minerals, commercially-exploited forests, and so on – and $\text{Use}_{np.env}$ – the degradation of other natural assets caused by human activities, such as air, water and soil pollution, extinction of species, and so on. These are entered as negative elements in columns 5 and 6, hence reducing the stocks of natural assets.

Row vii 'Other accumulation of non-produced natural assets' – records the transfer of assets from the non-economic to the economic category. For example, improved techniques of extraction have enhanced reserves of economically-recoverable oil; the quantity or value of the increase in reserves would appear as a positive entry in column 5, and as an equal but negative entry in column 6. By construction, the entries in this row will sum to zero.

The addition of rows vi and vii to the table will affect one of the entries in the SNA part of the table, namely 'other changes in the volume of (non-produced) assets', $Vol_{np.ec}$. In the SNA, this item includes changes in stocks of economic natural assets, whether through depletion/degradation, or the transfer of assets from the non-economic to the economic category. In the SEEA, these components of $Vol_{np.ec}$ will be recorded in rows vi and vii of column 5. If the entries in the additional rows and columns are expressed in physical units, this completes the table. The SNA monetary aggregates remain unchanged.

The environmental data supplement the monetary accounts by linking levels of economic activity with changes in the environment. However, if these environmental changes can be monetised, the conventional SNA aggregates can be modified to reflect the use of environmental assets.

Row viii records the modified data. In column 1, the consumption of natural capital (Use_{np}) is deducted from NDP (net domestic product) to give EDP – environmentally adjusted domestic product, which approaches the concept of sustainable income. Columns 2 and 3 remain unchanged. Columns 4–6 introduce the concept of net accumulation in place of net capital formation in the SNA. In fact, for produced assets, net accumulation is the same as net capital formation, so that $A_{p.ec} = I$. For non-produced economic assets, net accumulation is the sum of depletion/degradation $Use_{np.ec}$ (negative) and additions to economic reserves $I_{np.ec}$ (positive), hence $A_{np.ec}$ can be positive or negative. Net accu-

mulation of other non-produced natural assets ($A_{np.env}$) is always negative.

The accounting identity between net production and expenditure noted in the equation above now becomes

$$EDP = (X - M) + C + A_{p.ec} + (A_{np.ec} - A_{np.env})$$

Since $A_{p.ec} = I$, and $I_{np.ec}$ and $-I_{np.env}$ cancel out, the term inside the brackets is equal to $-Use_{np}$, which is also the difference between NDP and EDP, and hence the identity is maintained.

Presented as a satellite account, the SEEA has a number of obvious merits. It integrates environmental and economic accounts while maintaining continuity and consistency in time series of national accounts by retaining the conventional SNA definitions and aggregates. As satellite accounts, it is less important to attempt to achieve comprehensive coverage of environmental assets before compiling integrated accounts. For certain environmental assets, for example oil and gas, scarce subsoil minerals and commercial forestry, there are sufficient data on stocks, flows and market values to include them in a set of integrated accounts. However, as discussed in the text, even where such data are available it may be of doubtful value for the purposes of measuring sustainable income. In other cases, for example emissions of industrial pollutants, data on physical quantities may be adequate, but valuation may be difficult. As additional data become available, or acceptable methods of valuation are developed, the coverage of the satellite accounts can be extended.

The SEEA also proposes a more transparent treatment of expenditures on environmental protection (referred to in the preceding section as defensive expenditures), by proposing a finer breakdown of the ISIC codes which relate to environmental protection, and by transferring protective expenditures which are undertaken as ancillary activities from their industries of origin to the relevant subsector of environmental protection services. A possible subsectoral breakdown suggested in the SEEA is shown in

Table 17.12 Two-digit ISIC categories that identify environmental protection services.

Code	Category
37	Recycling
90	Sewage and refuse disposal, sanitation and similar activities
90.1[a]	Collection, transport, treatment and disposal of waste
90.2[a]	Collection and treatment of waste water
90.3[a]	Cleaning of exhaust gases
90.4[a]	Noise abatement
90.5[a]	Other environmental protection services n.e.c.
90.6[a]	Sanitation and similar services

Source: United Nations (1993).
[a] Proposed SEEA breakdown.

Table 17.12. Thus, for example, if a paper plant collects and treats waste water from its manufacturing process, the expenditures associated with that activity should be transferred from paper manufacturing to subsector 90.2 – collection and treatment of waste water. This would make it possible to identify more exactly the levels of expenditure on environmental protection (and, as some environmentalists have proposed, to adjust the measure of domestic product to exclude such defensive expenditures). However, as remarked in the previous section of this chapter, it is often difficult to separately identify these ancillary expenditures. For example, the cost of catalytic converters in vehicles is included in the vehicle price and it may not be feasible to separately identify the cost of the exhaust system, and more particularly the part of the vehicle running expenses attributable to exhaust gas cleaning. Nevertheless, environmental protection services, like other services, are growing in importance in relation to overall economic activity, and this in itself supports the case for a greater degree of detail in classification.

Appendix 17.4 El Serafy's method for the estimation of the depreciation of natural capital

The principle underlying El Serafy's rule for the calculation of a user cost measure of depreciation for a non-renewable resource is as follows. From the net receipts from sales a certain proportion is assumed to be set aside and invested at a constant rate of return in order to yield a constant level of income indefinitely. User cost is then defined as the difference between net receipts and that constant income, which is regarded as the true, or sustainable, income from resource depletion. Given some specialising assumptions, this principle leads to a very simple rule for calculating depreciation for non-renewable resources as user cost, and also the corresponding true income from resource extraction.

Assuming that receipts accrue at the end of the period, and using the same notation as in the text, the value of a resource deposit at the start of the period is given by:

$$V_0 = \{R_1(P_1 - C_1)/(1+r)\}$$
$$+ \{R_2(P_2 - C_2)/(1+r)^2\} + \ldots$$
$$+ \{R_T(P_T - C_T)/(1+r)^T\}$$
$$= \sum_{t=1}^{T} R_t(P_t - C_t)/(1+r)^t \quad (17.50)$$

If we use X for a constant perpetual income stream, the present value of that stream at the start of the period is given by:

$$W_0 = X/(1+r) + X/(1+r)^2$$
$$+ X/(1+r)^3 + \ldots$$
$$= \sum_{tt=1}^{\infty} X/(1+r)^t \quad (17.51)$$

Now assume $R_t = R$, $P_t = P$ and $C_t = C$ for all t, and use $N = R(P - C)$ for net receipts and $d = 1/(1+r)$ so that Equation 17.50 can be written as

$$V_0 = N[d + d^2 + \ldots + d^T] \quad (17.52)$$

and Equation 17.51 as

$$W_0 = X[d + d^2 + d^3 + \ldots] \quad (17.53)$$

where the term inside the brackets on the right-hand side of Equation 17.53 is an infinite series. Note that $d < 1$ for $r > 0$.

Multiplying both sides of Equation 17.52 by d gives

$$dV_0 = N[d^2 + d^3 + \ldots d^{T+1}] \qquad (17.54)$$

and subtracting Equation 17.54 from Equation 17.52 gives

$$V_0 - dV_0 = N[d - d^{T+1}]$$

so that

$$V_0 = N[d - d^{T+1}]/[1-d] \qquad (17.55)$$

Rewrite Equation 17.53 for a finite time horizon, n, as

$$W_0' = X[d + d^2 + \ldots d^n]$$

where n is some finite number, and proceeding as we did above we get

$$W_0' = X[d - d^{n+1}]/[1-d]$$

where letting $n \to \infty$ makes d^{n+1} vanish in the limit, so that we have

$$W_0 = \mathrm{Lim}\,(W_0') = dX/[1-d] \qquad (17.56)$$
$$n \to \infty$$

for the present value of the perpetual income stream.

Now, if this perpetual income stream is to be solely based on the ownership of the resource deposit, assuming a fully competitive economy, we must have $V_0 = W_0$; that is, the value of the mine at the start of the period must be equal to the present value of the perpetual income stream. Using Equations 17.55 and 17.56 this gives

$$N[d - d^{T+1}]/[1-d] = dX/[1-d]$$

which on collecting terms and substituting $1/(1+r)$ for d is

$$X = N[1 - \{1/(1+r)^{T+1}\}]$$

Table 17.13 User cost share of receipts from sales of non-renewable natural resources.

Lifetime of resource at current extraction rates (years)	Discount Rate (%)				
	1	3	5	7	10
1	98	94	91	87	83
5	94	84	75	67	56
10	90	72	58	48	35
25	78	46	28	17	8
50	60	28	8	3	1
100	37	14	2	0	0

Source: Adapted from El Serafy (1989).

or

$$N - X = N/(1+r)^{T+1}$$

where substituting for $N = R(P - C)$ we get

$$R(P - C) - X = R(P - C)/(1+r)^{T+1}$$

for user cost, so that for this measure of depreciation we have

$$D_N = R(P - C)/(1+r)^{T+1} \qquad (17.57)$$

as in the text of the chapter.

User cost/depreciation as a proportion of net receipts is

$$\{R(P - C) - X\}/\{R(P - C)\} = 1/(1+r)^{T+1}$$
$$(17.58)$$

and depends only on the lifetime of the resource stock and the interest rate. Sustainable or true income as a share of net receipts is simply one minus the share of user cost. Table 17.13 gives the user cost share for different values for resource lifetime and the interest rate. With low interest rates and short lifetimes, user cost is nearly 100% of net receipts (the income share is close to zero). With long lifetimes and high interest rates, nearly all net receipts count as income. For any given asset lifetime, notice the importance of the choice of interest rate.

Sources of environmental information on the internet

A huge volume of information of interest to the environmental economist can now be found on the internet. All of this can be read online, printed for future reference or saved to disk. Many sites offer extensive datasets, which can be retrieved as spreadsheet files. It is useful to have your web browser – typically a version of Internet Explorer or Netscape Navigator or Communicator – configured to automatically download such files into a spreadsheet program such as Excel. Many sites allow the reader to freely download extensive quantities of written material, including complete texts of books and journal articles. These are often written in pdf file format, which requires your computer to be configured to translate pdf files using the Acrobat reader.

To give the reader unfamiliar with this literature an introduction to what is available – and to give some new ideas to the experienced web searcher – we have constructed a set of web pages to accompany this book which provide, among other things, a structured set of online links. These will be regularly updated and extended. The internet address of the web site with these pages is:

> http://homepages.strath.ac.uk/~hbs96107/
> enviro7.html

However, in common with web addresses at many university servers, this address is likely to change at some time in the future. A link to the current address will be maintained on the higher education pages at the web site of Addison Wesley Longman, to be found at the address:

> http://awl-he.com

In the rest of this section, we will give you a flavour of what is available on the internet. This is far from comprehensive; a much larger sample of what is available can be found at our web site given above. It is also worth noting that many of these sites also con-tain a set of useful and relevant links. A little searching and experience will quickly give you an idea about which sites contain sets of links of most interest and relevance to you. All of the following, however, warrant trying at least once to find out what they offer.

In giving web addresses below, for notational brevity we omit the stem http://. This should precede all the addresses given below.

International organisations

Several international organisations maintain large web sites carrying huge amounts of information.

The United Nations Organization

The principal web site is at www.un.org/. Most environmental sites are indexed on the page entitled 'United Nations: Economic and Social Development', at www.un.org/esa/ You will find the following sites of UN orga-nisations particularly useful:

- United Nations Development Program (UNDP) at www.undp.org/
- United Nations Environment Program (UNEP) at www.unep.org/
- United Nations Conference on Trade and Development (UNCTAD) at www.unctad.org/
- United Nations Commission on Sustainable Development (UNSD) at www.un.org/esa/sustdev
- A large set of links to UN environmental programme sites is given at the page www.un.org/ecosocdev/topicse/ environe.htm

The UNDP site contains summaries of all editions of the *Human Development Report*, and current rankings of countries on the *Human Development Index* (and several other indices maintained by UNDP).

The World Bank

The homepage for the World Bank is at www.worldbank.org/. Of special interest are the organisation's World Development Indicators, at www.worldbank.org/wdi/wdi/wdi.htm

A large number of national and international research organisations also maintain extensive and very useful web sites.

The OECD

The starting point is either the OECD main site (www.oecd.org/), its list of activities (www.oecd.org/activities.htm) or its 'Environmental Issues' page at www.oecd.org/env/.

National environment agencies

The United States Environmental Protection Agency (EPA)

The EPA's site at www.epa.gov/ provides a wealth of information on pollution control costs, pollution damages, the use of economic incentives for pollution control, and pollution policy in general.

Ministries of the environment and national environmental protection agencies

These are listed and linked under a page at the UNEP web site, at the address www.unep.org/unep/newlink.htm. This listing is comprehensive for all those that have web sites, and is regularly updated as new sites are added.

Non-governmental organisations (NGOs) and environmental pressure groups

The World Resources Institute (WRI)

The full WRI publications catalogue is available at www.wri.org/. Summaries and press releases from many WRI publications, and complete versions of several recent versions of the biannual publication *World Resources*, are available online.

Resources for the Future (RFF)

The RFF site, at www.rff.org/, gives a large amount of top quality environmental and natural resources research output.

International Institute for Sustainable Development

This site at http://iisd1.iisd.ca, is useful for those interested in electronic mailing lists, as it provides a set of links to administrators of about 100 mailing lists concerned with sustainable development.

Academic sites maintained by individual academics or university departments

Many university economics departments or individual lecturers maintain web sites for their courses and for the wider academic community. One example is the site described as 'Ecological Economics and Sustainable Development' to be found at:

> http://csf.colorado.edu/ecolecon/
> related.html

Academic journals

Many journals, such as *Ecological Economics* and *Journal of Environmental Economics and Management*, now maintain a web site to accompany the journal.

Other sites of interest

Many other sites are difficult to classify but nevertheless contain much useful information. Some examples are:

> Trade and sustainable development:
>   http://greencross.unige.ch/greencross/
>   digiforum/tsdlinks.html
> Environment, ecology and sustainable
>   development:
>   http://www.clark.net/pub/global/eco.html
> ECONET:
>   http://www.econet.apc.org/econet/
>   en.issues.html

Much fuller lists are to be found on the text's web site.

E-mail: mailing lists and discussion groups

As stated earlier, the International Institute for Sustainable Development at http://iisd1.iisd.ca provides a set of links to administrators of about 100 mailing lists concerned with sustainable development, with brief information about how to subscribe.

References

ABS (1995) *National Balance Sheets for Australia: Issues and Experimental Estimates 1989 to 1992*. Australian Bureau of Statistics, Canberra.

ACE (1989) *Solving the Greenhouse Dilemma: A Strategy for the UK*. Association for the Conservation of Energy, 9 Sherlock Mews, London W1M 3RH, UK, June 1989.

Adamowicz, W., Louviere, J. and Williams, M. (1994) Combining revealed and stated preference methods for valuing environmental amenities. *Journal of Environmental Economics and Management* **26**, 271–292.

Adams, D.D. and Page, W.P. (1985) *Acid Deposition: Environmental, Economic and Policy Issues*. Plenum Press, New York.

Adar, Z. and Griffin, J.M. (1976) Uncertainty and the choice of pollution control instruments. *Journal of Environmental Economics and Management* **3**, 178–188.

Adelman, M.A. (1990) Mineral depletion, with special reference to petroleum. *Review of Economics and Statistics* **72**(1), 1–10.

Adelman, M.A. (1995) *The Genie out of the Bottle: World Oil Since 1970*. MIT Press, Cambridge, Massachusetts.

Adriaanse, A. (1993) *Environmental Policy Performance Indicators* (Sdu Uitgeverij).Uoninginnegracht, The Hague

Ahmad, Y., El Serafy, S. and Lutz, E. (eds) (1989) *Environmental Accounting for Sustainable Development: A UNDP–World Bank Symposium*. World Bank, Washington, DC.

Alexandratos, N. (ed.) (1995) *World Agriculture: Towards 2010, An FAO Study*. John Wiley & Sons, Chichester, and FAO, Rome.

Anderson, D. and Bird, C.D. (1990a) *The Carbon Accumulation Problem and Technical Progress*. University College, London and Balliol College, Oxford.

Anderson, D. and Bird, C.D. (1990b) *The Carbon Accumulation Problem and Technical Progress: A Simulation Study of the Costs*. University College, London and Balliol College, Oxford.

Anderson, F.J. (1985) *Natural Resources in Canada: Economic Theory and Policy*. Methuen, Agincourt, Ontario.

Anderson, F.J. (1991) *Natural Resources in Canada: Economic Theory and Policy*, 2nd edition. Nelson, Ontario.

Anderson, K. (1992a) The standard welfare economics of policies affecting trade and the environment, in Anderson, K. and Blackhurst, R. (eds) *The Greening of World Trade Issues*. Harvester Wheatsheaf, Hemel Hempstead.

Anderson, K. (1992b) Effects on the environment and welfare of liberalising world trade: the cases of coal and food, in Anderson, K. and Blackhurst, R. (eds) *The Greening of World Trade Issues*. Harvester Wheatsheaf, Hemel Hempstead.

Anderson, L.G. (ed.) (1977) *Economic Impacts of Extended Fisheries Jurisdiction*. Ann Arbor Science Publishers, Ann Arbor, Michigan.

Anderson, L.G. (1981) *Economic Analysis for Fisheries Management Plans*. Ann Arbor Science Publishers, Ann Arbor, Michigan.

Anderson, L.G. (1995) Privatising open access fisheries: individual transferable quotas, in Bromley, D.W. (ed.) *The Handbook of Environmental Economics*. Blackwell, Oxford.

Andreasson, I.-M. (1990) Costs for reducing farmer's use of nitrogen in Gotland, Sweden. *Ecological Economics* **2**(4), 287–300.

Arrow, K. and Fisher, A.C. (1974) Environmental preservation, uncertainty and irreversibility. *Quarterly Journal of Economics* **88**, 313–319.

Arrow, K. and Lind, R. (1970) Uncertainty and the evaluation of public investment decisions. *American Economic Review*, **60**, June.

Arrow, K., Bolin, B., Costanza, R., Dasgupta, P., Folke, C., Holling, C. S., Jansson, B-O., Levin, S., Mäler, K-G., Perrings, C. and Pimental, D. (1995) Economic growth, carrying capacity and the environment. *Science* **268**, 520–521.

Arrow, K.J., Cline, W.R., Mäler, K.-G., Munaasinghe, M., Squitieri, R., Stiglitz, J.E. (1996) Intertemporal equity, discounting and economic efficiency, in Bruce, J.P., Lee, H. and Haites, E.F. (eds) *Climate Change 1995: Economic and Social Dimensions of Climate Change*. Cambridge University Press, Cambridge.

Asheim, G. B. (1986) Hartwick's rule in open economies. *Canadian Journal of Economics* **19**, 395–402.

Atkinson, G. and Pearce D.W. (1993) Measuring sustainable development. *The Globe*, No. 13, June 1993, UK GER Office, Swindon.

Ayres, R.U. and Kneese, A.V. (1969) Production, consumption and externalities. *American Economic Review* **59**(3), 282–297.

Azar, C., Holmberg, J. and Lingren, K. (1996) Socio-ecological indicators for sustainability. *Ecological Economics* **18**, 89–112.

Bailey, M.J. (1982) Risks, costs and benefits of fluorocarbon regulations. *American Economic Review* **72**, 247–250.

Barbier, E.B. (1989a) *Economics, Natural Resources Scarcity and Development: Conventional and Alternative Views*. Earthscan, London.

Barbier, E.B. (1989b) The global greenhouse effect: economic impacts and policy considerations. *Natural Resources Forum* **13**(1).

Barbier, E.B. and Burgess, J.C. (1997) The economics of tropical forest land use options. *Land Economics* **73**(2), 174–195.

Barbier, E.B. and Markandya, A. (1990) The conditions for achieving environmentally sustainable development. *European Economic Review* **34**, 659–669.

Barbier, E.B. and Pearce, D.W. (1990) Thinking economically about climate change. *Energy Policy* **18**(1), 11–18.

Barbier, E.B., Burgess, J.C. and Pearce, D.W. (1990a) *Slowing Global Warming: Options for Greenhouse Gas Substitution*. London Environmental Economics Centre, London.

Barbier, E.B., Burgess, J.C., Swanson, T.M. and Pearce, D.W. (1990b) *Elephants, Economics and Ivory*. Earthscan, London.

Barbier, E.B., Burgess, J.C. and Folke, C. (1994) *Paradise Lost? The Ecological Economics of Biodiversity*. Earthscan, London.

Barker, T. (1990) *Review of Existing Models and Data in the United Kingdom for Environment–Economy Linkage*. Cambridge Econometrics, Department of Applied Economics, University of Cambridge, UK.

Barker, T. (1997) Taxing pollution instead of jobs: towards more employment without more inflation through fiscal reform in the UK, in O'Riordan, T. (ed.) (1997) *Ecotaxation*. Earthscan, London.

Barnett, H.J. (1979) Scarcity and growth revisited, in V. Kerry Smith (ed.) *Scarcity and Growth Reconsidered*. Johns Hopkins Press, Baltimore, Maryland.

Barnett, H.J. and Morse, C. (1963) *Scarcity and Growth: The Economics of Natural Resource Availability*. Johns Hopkins University Press, for Resources for the Future, Baltimore, Maryland.

Barney, G.O. (Study Director) (1980) *The Global 2000 Report to the President of the United States*, 3 vols. Pergamon Press, New York.

Barrett, S. (1990) *Pricing the Environment: The Economic and Environmental Consequences of a Carbon Tax*. Briefing Paper, London Business School, London.

Bartelmus, P. (1994) *Environment Growth and Development: The Concepts and Strategies of Sustainability*. Routledge, London.

Bartelmus, P., Stahmer, C. and van Tongeren, J. (1993) Integrated environmental and economic accounting – a framework for an SNA satellite system, in Lutz, E. (ed.) *Toward Improved Accounting for the Environment*. An UNSTAT–World Bank Symposium, The World Bank, Washington, DC.

Bator, F.M. (1957) The simple analytics of welfare maximisation. *American Economic Review* **47**, 22–59.

Baumol, W.J. (1977) *Economic Theory and Operations* Analysis, 4th edition. Prentice Hall, London.

Baumol, W.J. and Oates, W.E. (1971) The use of standards and prices for the protection of the environment. *Swedish Journal of Economics* **73**, 42–54.

Baumol, W.J. and Oates, W.E. (1979) *Economics, Environmental Policy and the Quality of Life*. Prentice Hall, Englewood Cliffs, New Jersey.

Baumol, W.J. and Oates, W.E. (1988) *The Theory of Environmental Policy: Externalities, Public Outlays and the Quality of Life*, 2nd edition. Prentice Hall, Englewood Cliffs, New Jersey.

Beauchamp, T.L. and Bowie, N.E. (1988) *Ethical Theory and Business*, 3rd edition. Prentice Hall, Englewood Cliffs, New Jersey.

Becker, G. (1960) An Economic Analysis of Fertility, in *Demographic and Economic Changes in Developed Countries*. Princeton University Press, Princeton, New Jersey, pp. 209–231.

Beckerman, W. (1972) Economists, scientists and environmental catastrophe. *Oxford Economic Papers* **24**, 237–244.

Beckerman, W. (1974) *In Defence of Economic Growth*. Jonathan Cape, London.

Beckerman, W. (1980) *Introduction to National Income Analysis*, 3rd edition. Weidenfeld and Nicholson, London.

Beckerman, W. (1992) Economic growth and the environment: whose growth? whose environment? *World Development* **20**, 481–496.

Beckerman, W. (1994) 'Sustainable development'. Is it a useful concept? *Environmental Values* **3**, 191–209.

Bell, F. and Leeworthy, V. (1990) Recreational demand by tourists for saltwater beach days. *Journal of Environmental Economics and Management* **18**(3), 189–205.

Benson, J. and Willis, K. (1991) *The Demand for Forests for Recreation*. University of Newcastle, Newcastle.

Bentham, J. (1789) *An Introduction to the Principles of Morals and Legislation*. L.J. LaFleur, New York, 1948.

Berck, P. (1979) The economics of timber: a renewable resource in the long run. *Bell Journal of Economics* **10**, 447–462.

Berck, P. (1995) Empirical consequences of the Hotelling principle, in Bromley, D.W. (ed.) *The Handbook of Environmental Economics*. Blackwell, Oxford.

Berck, P. and Roberts, M. (1996) Natural resource prices: will they ever turn up? *Journal of Environmental Economics and Management* **31**(1), 65–78.

Berndt, E. and Field, B. (eds) (1981) *Measuring and Modelling Natural Resource Substitution*. MIT Press, Cambridge, Massachusetts.

Bernstam, M.S. (1991) *The Wealth of Nations and the Environment*. Institute of Economic Affairs, London.

Bertram, I.G., Stephens, R.J. and Wallace, C.C. (1989) *The Relevance of Economic Instruments for Tackling the Greenhouse Effect*. Economics Department, Victoria University, New Zealand, Report to the New Zealand Ministry of the Environment.

Biancardi, C., Tiezzi, E. and Ulgiati, S. (1993) Complete recycling of matter in the frameworks of physics, biology and ecological economics. *Ecological Economics* **8**, 1–5.

Bishop, R.C. (1978) Endangered species and uncertainty: the economics of a safe minimum standard. *American Journal of Agricultural Economics* **60**, 10–18.

Bishop, R.C. (1982) Option value: an exposition and extension. *Land Economics* **58**, 1-1-5.

Bishop, R.C. and Heberlein, T.A. (1979) Measuring values of extramarket goods: are indirect measures biased? *American Journal of Agricultural Economics* **61**(5), 926–930.

Bishop, R.C. and Welsh, M.P. (1992) Existence value in benefit–cost analysis. *Land Economics* **68**, 405–417.

Bishop, R.C. and Woodward, R.T. (1995) Valuation of environmental quality under certainty, in Bromley, D.W. (ed.) *The Handbook of Environmental Economics*. Blackwell, Oxford.

Bishop, R.C., Champ, P.A. and Mullarkey, D.J. (1995) Contingent valuation, in Bromley, D.W. (ed.) *The Handbook of Environmental Economics*. Blackwell, Oxford.

Blamey, R.K. (1996) Citizens, consumers and contingent valuation: clarification and the expression of citizen values and issue-opinions, in Adamowicz, W.L., Boxall, P., Luckert, M.K., Phillips, W.E. and White, W.A. (eds) *Forestry, Economics and the Environment*. CAB International, Wallingford, pp. 103–133.

Blamey, R.K. (1998) Decisiveness, attitude expression and symbolic responses in contingent valuation surveys. *Journal of Economic Behavior and Organization* **34**, 577–601.

Blamey, R.K. and Common, M. (1994) Sustainability and the limits to pseudo market valuation, in van den Bergh, J.C.J.M. and van der Straaten, J. (eds) *Concepts and Methods for Sustainable Development: Critique and New Approaches*. Island Press, Washington, DC.

Blamey, R.K., Common, M. and Quiggin, J. (1995) Respondents to contingent valuation surveys: consumers or citizens? *Australian Journal of Agricultural Economics* **39**, 263–288.

Blaug, M. (1985) *Economic Theory in Retrospect*, 4th edition. Cambridge University Press, Cambridge.

Bockstael, N.E. (1995) Travel cost models, in Bromley, D.W. (ed.) *The Handbook of Environmental Economics*. Blackwell, Oxford.

Bockstael, N.E. and McConnell, K.E. (1993) Public goods as characteristics of non-market commodities. *Economic Journal* **103**, 1244.

Bockstael, N.E, Hanemann, W.M. and Strand, I.E. (1987a) *Measuring the Benefits of Water Quality Improvements using Recreational Demand Models*. Environmental Protection Agency Co-operative Agreement CR-811043-01-0.

Bockstael, N.E, Strand, I.E. and Hanemann, W.M. (1987b) Time and the recreational demand model. *American Journal of Agricultural Economics* **69**, 293–302.

Boero, G., Clarke, R. and Winters, L.A. (1991) *The Macroeconomic Consequences of Controlling Greenhouse Gases: A Survey*. UK Department of the Environment, Room A11, Romney House, 43 Marsham Street, London SW1P 3PY, UK (summary and full text available).

Böhm, P. and Russell C.C. (1985) Comparative analysis of alternative policy instruments, in Kneese, A.V. and Sweeney J.L. (eds) *Handbook of Natural Resource and Energy Economics*, vol. I. North-Holland, Amsterdam.

Booth, D.E. (1994) Ethics and the limits of environmental economics. *Ecological Economics* **9**, 241–252.

Boulding, K.E. (1966) The economics of the coming spaceship earth, in H. Jarrett (ed.) *Environmental Quality in a Growing Economy*. Resources for the Future/Johns Hopkins Press, Baltimore, Maryland, pp. 3–14.

Bowes, M.D. and Krutilla, J.V. (1985) Multiple use management of public forest lands, in Kneese, A.V. and Sweeney, J.L. (eds) *Handbook of Natural Resource and Energy Economics*, vol. II. North-Holland, Amsterdam.

Bowes, M.D. and Krutilla, J.V. (1989) *Multiple-Use Management: The Economics of Public Forestlands*. Resources for the Future, Washington, DC.

Bowler, P.J. (1992) *The Fontana History of the Environmental Sciences*. Fontana, London.

Boxall, P.C., Adamowicz, W., Swait, J, Williams, M. and Louviere, J. (1996) A comparison of stated preference methods for environmental valuation. *Ecological Economics* **18**, 243–253.

Boyle, K.J. and Bishop, R.C. (1987) Valuing wildlife in benefit–cost analysis: a case study involving endangered species. *Water Resources Research* **23**, 942–950.

Brekke, K.A. (1997) Hicksian income from resource extraction in an open economy. *Land Economics* **73**, 516–527.

Brennan, G. and Lomasky, L. (1993) *Democracy and Decision: The Pure Theory of Electoral Preference*. Cambridge University Press, Cambridge.

Bromley, D.W. (ed.) (1995) *The Handbook of Environmental Economics*. Blackwell, Oxford.

Brookshire, D.S, Thayer, M.A., Schulze, W.D. and D'Arge, R.C (1982) Valuing public goods: a comparison of survey and hedonic approaches. *American Economic Review* **71**, 165–177.

Brookshire, D., Eubanks, L. and Randall, A. (1983) Estimating option price and existence values for wildlife resources. *Land Economics* **59**(1), 1–15.

Brookshire, D., Thayer, M., Tschirhart, J. and Schulze, W. (1985) A test of the expected utility model: evidence from earthquake risks. *Journal of Political Economy* **93**(2), 369–389.

Broome, J. (1992) *Counting the Cost of Global Warming*. White Horse Press, Cambridge.

Browder, J.O. (ed.) (1988) *Fragile Lands of Latin America: Strategies for Sustainable Development*. Westfield Press, Boulder, Colorado.

Brown, G.M. and Field, B.C. (1978) Implications of alternative measures of natural resource scarcity. *Journal of Political Economy* **86**, 229–244.

Brown, G.M. and Field, B.C. (1979) The adequacy of measures for signalling natural resource scarcity, in V.K. Smith (ed.) *Scarcity and Growth Reconsidered*. Johns Hopkins University Press/Resources for the Future, Baltimore, Maryland.

Brown, G. and McGuire, C.B. (1967) A socially optimal pricing policy for a public water agency. *Water Resources Research* **3**, 33–44.

Brown I. (1989) Energy subsidies in the United States, in *Energy Pricing: Regulation Subsidies and Distortion*. Surrey Energy Economics Centre Discussion Paper No. 38, University of Surrey, UK, March 1989.

Brown, K. and Pearce, D.W. (1994) *The Causes of Tropical Deforestation*. University College of London (UCL) Press, London.

Brown, L.R. (1981) *Building a Sustainable Society*. W.W. Norton, New York.

Brown, L.R. and Kane, H. (1994) *Full House: Re-assessing the Earth's Population Carrying Capacity*. W.W. Norton, New York.

Bruce, J.P., Lee, H. and Haites, E.F. (1996) *Climate Change 1995: Economic and Social Dimensions of Climate Change*. Cambridge University Press, Cambridge.

Bryant, C. and Cook P. (1992) Environmental issues and the national accounts. *Economic Trends* No. 469, HMSO, London.

Burniaux, J-M., Martin, J.P., Nicoletti, G. and Martins, J.Q. (1991a) *GREEN – A Multi-Region Dynamic General Equilibrium Model for Quantifying the Costs of Curbing CO_2 Emissions: A Technical Manual*. OECD, Department of Economics and Statistics Working Paper No. 104, OECD/GD(91)119, Resource Allocation Division, OECD, June.

Burniaux, J-M., Martin, J.P., Nicoletti, G. and Martins, J.Q. (1991b) *The Costs of Policies to Reduce Global Emissions of CO_2: Initial Simulation Results with GREEN*. OECD, Department of Economics and Statistics Working Paper No. 103, OCDE/GD(91)115, Resource Allocation Division, OECD, June.

Burniaux, J-M., Martin, J.P., Nicoletti, G. and Martins, J.Q. (1992) The costs of international agreements to reduce CO_2 emissions, in *European Economy: The Economics of Limiting CO_2 Emissions*, Special Edition No. 1, Commission of the European Communities, Brussels.

Burniaux, J-M., Martin, J. P., Oliveira-Martins, J. and van der Mensbrugghe, D. (1994) Carbon abatement transfers and energy efficiency, in Goldin, I. and Winters, L. A. (eds) *The Economics of Sustainable Development*. Cambridge University Press, Cambridge.

Burrows, P. (1979) *The Economic Theory of Pollution Control*. Martin Robertson, Oxford.

Burrows, P. (1995) Nonconvexities and the Theory of External Costs, in Bromley D.W. (ed.) *The Handbook of Environmental Economics*. Blackwell, Oxford.

Business Week (1991) Saving the planet: environmentally advantaged technologies for economic growth. Special supplement, 30 December.

Cairncross, F. (1992) *Costing the Earth: The Challenge for Governments, the Opportunities for Business*. Harvard Business School, Boston, Massachusetts.

Calish, S., Fight, R.D. and Teeguarden, D.E. (1978) How do nontimber values affect Douglas-fir rotations? *Journal of Forestry* **76**, 217–221.

Cameron, J. and Aboucher, J. (1991) The precautionary principle: a fundamental principle of law and policy for the protection of the global environment. *Boston College International and Comparative Law Review* **14**, 1–27.

Carraro, C. and Siniscalco, D. (eds) (1993) *The European Carbon Tax: An Economic Assessment*. Kluwer, Dordrecht.

Carruthers, I. (1994) Going, going, gone! Tropical agriculture as we knew it. *Tropical Agriculture Newsletter* **13**(3), 1–5.

Carson, R.T. (1995) *Contingent Valuation Surveys and Tests of Insensitivity to Scope*. Mimeo, Department of Economics, University of California, San Diego.

Carson, R.T., Mitchell, R.C., Hanemann, M., Kopp, R.J., Presser, S. and Rudd, P.A. (1995) *Contingent Valuation and Lost Passive Use: Damages from the Exxon Valdez*. Department of Economics, University of California, San Diego, Discussion Paper 95-02, January 1995.

Carson, R.T., Wright, J., Carson, N., Alberni, A. and Flores, N. (1995b) *A Bibliography of Contingent Valuation Studies and Papers*. Natural Resource Damage Assessment Inc., La Jolla, California.

CEC (Commission of the European Communities) (1983) *Acid Rain: A Review of the Phenomenon in the EEC and Europe*. Graham and Trotman, London.

CGIAR (1994) (Consultative Group on International Agricultural Research Secretariat.) *Current CGIAR Research Efforts and their Expected Impact on Food, Agriculture, and National Development*. Draft paper, CGIAR, Washington, DC, March 1994.

Chiang, A.C. (1984) *Fundamental Methods of Mathematical Economics*, 3rd edition. McGraw-Hill, New York.

Chiang, A.C. (1992) *Elements of Dynamic Optimisation*. McGraw-Hill, New York.

Cicchetti, C.V. and Freeman, A.M. (1971) Option demand and consumer surplus, further comment. *Quarterly Journal of Economics* **85**, 528–539.

Cipolla, C.M. (1962) *The Economic History of World Population*. Penguin, Harmondsworth.

Ciriacy-Wantrup, S. von (1968) *Resource Conservation: Economics and Politics* 2nd Edition. University of California Press, Berkeley, California.

Clark, C.W. (1990) *Mathematical Bioeconomics: The Optimal Management of Renewable Resources*, 2nd edition. John Wiley & Sons, New York.

Clawson, M. (1959) *Methods of Measuring the Demand for and Value of Outdoor Recreation*. Reprint Number 10, Resources for the Future, Washington, DC.

Clawson, M. (1977) *Decision Making in Timber Production, Harvest, and Marketing*. Research Paper R-4, Resources for the Future, Washington, DC.

Clawson, M. and Knetsch, J. (1966) *Economics of Outdoor Recreation*. Johns Hopkins University Press, Baltimore, Maryland.

Cleveland, C.J. (1993) An exploration of alternative measures of resource scarcity: the case of petroleum resources. *Ecological Economics* **7**, 123–157.

Cline, W.R. (1989) *Political Economy of the Greenhouse Effect*. Mimeo, Institute for International Economics, Washington, USA.

Cline, W.R. (1991) Scientific basis for the greenhouse effect. *Economic Journal* **101**, 904–919.

Cline, W.R (1992) *The Economics of Global Warming*. Institute for International Economics, Washington, DC.

Clunies Ross, A. (1990) Transfers versus licenses as incentives to governments for environmental correctives. Paper submitted to the Development Studies Association Annual Conference 1990, University of Strathclyde, Department of Economics, 100 Cathedral Street, Glasgow, UK.

Coase, R. (1960) The problem of social cost. *Journal of Law and Economics* **3**, 1–44.

Cobbing, P. and Slee, W. (1993) A contingent valuation of the Mar Lodge Estate. *Journal of Environmental Planning and Management* **36**(1), 65–72

Cohen, M.A. (1986) The costs and benefits of oil spill prevention and enforcement. *Journal of Environmental Economics and Management* **13**, 167–188.

Cole, H.S.D., Freeman, C., Jahoda, M. and Pavitt, K.L.R. (eds) (1973) *Thinking about the Future: A Critique of the Limits to Growth*. Chatto and Windus, London, for Sussex University Press.

Common, M.S. (1985) The distributional implications of higher energy prices in the UK. *Applied Economics* **17**, 421–436.

Common, M.S. (1989) The choice of pollution control instruments: why is so little notice taken of economists' recommendations? *Environment and Planning A* **21**, 1297–1314.

Common, M. (1995) *Sustainability and Policy: Limits to Economics*. Cambridge University Press, Melbourne.

Common, M.S. (1996) *Environmental and Resource Economics: An Introduction*, 2nd Edition. Longman, Harlow.

Common, M.S. and Hamilton, C. (1996) The economic consequences of carbon taxation in Australia, in Bouma, W. J., Pearman, G.I. and Manning, M.R. (eds) *Greenhouse: Coping with Climate Change*. CSIRO Publishing, Collingwood.

Common, M.S. and McPherson, P. (1982) A note on energy requirements calculations using the 1968 and 1974 input output tables. *Energy Policy* **10**, 42–49.

Common, M.S. and Norton, T. W. (1992) Biodiversity: its conservation in Australia. *Ambio* **XXI**, 258–265.

Common, M.S. and Perrings, S.C. (1992) Towards an ecological economics of sustainability. *Ecological Economics* **6**(1), 7–34.

Common, M. and Salma, U. (1992) Accounting for Australian carbon dioxide emissions. *Economic Record* **68**, 31–42.

Common, M.S. and Salma, U. (1992a) Economic modelling and Australian carbon dioxide emissions. *Mathematics and Computers in Simulation* **33**, 581–596.

Common, M.S. and Salma, U. (1992b) *An Economic Analysis of Australian Carbon Dioxide Emissions and Energy Use: Report to the Energy Research and Development Corporation*. Centre for Resource and Environmental Studies, Australian National University Canberra.

Common, M. and Sanyal, K. (1998) Measuring the depreciation of Australia's non-renewable resources: a cautionary tale. *Ecological Economics* **26**, 23–30.

Common, M.S., Reid, I. and Blamey, R. (1997) Do existence values for cost benefit analysis exist? *Environmental and Resource Economics* **9**, 225–238.

Common, M.S., Stoeckl, N. and Bull, T. (1999) The travel cost method: an empirical investigation of Randall's difficulty. *Australian Journal of Agricultural Economics*, forthcoming.

Commoner, B. (1963) *Science and Survival*. Ballantine, New York.

Commoner, B. (1972) *The Closing Circle*. Jonathan Cape, London.

Connor, S. (1993) Ozone depletion linked in rise to harmful radiation. *The Independent*, 23 April.

Conrad, J.M. (1995) Bioeconomic models of the fishery, in Bromley, D.W. (ed.) *The Handbook of Environmental Economics*. Blackwell, Oxford.

Conrad, J.M. and Clark C.W. (1987) *Natural Resource Economics: Notes and Problems*. Cambridge University Press, Cambridge.

Conrad, J.M. and Olson, L.J. (1992) The economics of a stock pollutant: aldicarb on Long Island. *Environmental and Resource Economics* **2**, 245–258.

Conway, G.R. (1985) Agroecosystem analysis. *Agricultural Administration* **20**, 31–55.

Conway, G.R. (1992) Sustainability in agricultural development: trade-offs with productivity, stability and equitability. *Journal for Farming Systems Research and Extension*.

Coote, A. and Lenaghan, J. (1997) *Citizens' Juries: Theory and Practice*. Institute for Public Policy Research, London.

Costanza, R. (1989) What is ecological economics? *Ecological Economics* **1**, 1–17.

Costanza, R. (ed.) (1991) *Ecological Economics: The Science and Management of Sustainability*. Columbia University Press, New York.

Costanza, R. and Perrings, C. (1990) A flexible assurance bonding system for improved environmental management. *Ecological Economics* **2**, 57–75.

Costanza, R., Daly, H.E. and Bartholomew, J.A. (1991) Goals, agenda and policy recommendations for ecological economics, in Costanza, R. (ed.) *Ecological Economics*. Columbia University Press, New York.

Costanza, R., d'Arge, R., de Groot, R., Farber, S., Grasso, M., Hannon, B., Limburg, K., Naeem, S., O'Neill, R., Paruelo, J., Raskin, R., Sutton, P., van den Belt, M. (1997) The value of the world's ecosystem services and natural capital. *Nature* **387**, 253–260.

Crandall, R. (1992) Policy Watch: Corporate Average Fuel Economy Standards. *Journal of Economic Perspectives* **6**, Spring, 171–180.

Cropper, M.L. and Oates, W.E. (1992) Environmental economics: a survey. *Journal of Economic Literature* **XXX**, 675–740.

Crosson, P.R. and Brubaker, S. (1982) *Resource and Environmental Effects of US Agriculture*. Johns Hopkins University Press, for Resources for the Future, Baltimore, Maryland.

Cummings, R., Brookshire, D. and Schulze, W. (eds) (1986) *Valuing Environmental Goods: An Assessment of the Contingent Valuation Method*. Rowman and Allenheld, Lanham, Maryland.

Dales, J.H. (1968) *Pollution Property and Prices*. Toronto University Press, Toronto.

Daly, H.E. (1968) On economics as a life science. *Journal of Political Economy* **76**, 392–406.

Daly, H.E. (1973) The steady state economy: toward a political economy of biophysical equilibrium and moral growth, in Daly, H.E. (ed.) (1973) *Toward a Steady State Economy*. W.H. Freeman, San Francisco, California.

Daly, H.E. (1974) The economics of the steady state. *American Economic Review* **64**(2), 15–21.

Daly, H.E. (1977) *Steady State Economics*. W.H. Freeman, San Francisco, CA.

Daly, H.E. (1987) The economic growth debate: what some economists have learned but many have not. *Journal of Environmental Economics and Management* **14**(4).

Daly, H.E. and Cobb, J.B. (1989) *For the Common Good: Redirecting the Economy Toward Community, the Environment and a Sustainable Future*. Beacon Press, Boston, Massachusetts.

D'Arge, R.C. and Kogiku, K.C. (1972) Economic growth and the environment. *Review of Economic Studies* **40**, 61-78.

Dasgupta, P. (1982) *The Control of Resources*. Basil Blackwell, Oxford.

Dasgupta, P. (1990) The environment as a commodity. *Oxford Review of Economic Policy* **6**(1), 51–67.

Dasgupta, P. (1992) *The Population Problem*. Faculty of Economics and Politics, University of Cambridge, Cambridge.

Dasgupta, P. (1993) Natural resources in an age of substitutability, in Kneese, A.V. and Sweeney, J.L. (eds) *Handbook of Natural Resource and Energy Economics*, vol. 3. Elsevier, Amsterdam, ch. 23.

Dasgupta, P (1995) Optimal development and the idea of net national product, in Goldin, I. and Winters, L.A. (eds) *The Economics of Sustainable Development*. Cambridge University Press, Cambridge.

Dasgupta, P. and Heal, G.M. (1974) The optimal depletion of exhaustible resources. *Review of Economic Studies*, Symposium, May, pp. 3–28.

Dasgupta, P. and Heal, G.M. (1979) *Economic Theory and Exhaustible Resources*. Cambridge University Press, Cambridge.

Dasgupta, S. and Mitra, T. (1983) Intergenerational equity and efficient allocation of resources. *International Economic Review* **24**, 133–153.

Deaton, A. and Muellbauer, J. (1980) *Economics and Consumer Behaviour*. Cambridge University Press, Cambridge.

de Graaf, H.J., Musters, C.J.M. and ter Keurs, W.J. (1996) Sustainable development: looking for new strategies. *Ecological Economics* **16**, 205–216.

Department of Energy (1984) *Digest of United Kingdom Energy Statistics 1983*. HMSO, London.

Department of Energy (1989) *An Evaluation of Energy Related Greenhouse Gas Emissions and Measures to Ameliorate Them*. Energy Paper No. 58, January, HMSO, London.

Desvousges, W., Smith, V. and Fisher, A. (1987) Option price estimates for water quality improvements. *Journal of Environmental Economics and Management* **14**, 248–267.

Deverajan, S. and Fisher, A.C. (1980) Exploration and scarcity. *Journal of Political Economy* **90**, 1279–1290.

Deverajan, S. and Fisher, A.C. (1982) Measures of resource scarcity under uncertainty, in V. Kerry Smith and Krutilla, J.V. (eds) *Explorations in Natural Resource Economics*. Johns Hopkins University Press, for Resources for the Future, Baltimore, Maryland.

Diamond, P.A., Hausman, J.A., Leonard, G.K. and Denning, M.A. (1993) Does contingent valuation measure preferences? Experimental evidence, in J.A. Hausman (ed.) *Contingent Valuation: A Critical Assessment*. North-Holland, Amsterdam, pp. 31–85.

Dinwiddy, C.L. and Teale, F.J. (1988) *The Two-Sector General Equilibrium Model: A New Approach*. Philip Allan, Oxford.

Dixit, A.K. and Nalebuff, B. (1991) *Thinking Strategically*. W.W. Norton, New York.

Dixit, A.K. and Pindyck, R.S. (1994) *Investment under Uncertainty*. Princeton University Press, Princeton.

Dorfman, R. (1985) An economist's view of natural resource and environmental problems, in Repetto, R. (ed.) *The Global Possible*. Yale University Press, New Haven, Connecticut, ch. 4.

Dovers, S. (1994) Historical and current patterns of energy use, in Dovers, S. (ed.) *Sustainable Energy Systems: Pathways for Australian Energy Reform*. Cambridge University Press, Cambridge.

Durning, A.B. (1989) *Poverty and the Environment: Reversing the Downward Spiral*. Paper No. 92, Worldwatch Institute, Washington, DC.

Easterlin, R.A (1978) The economics and sociology of fertility: a synthesis, in Tilley, C. (ed.) *Historical Studies of Changing Fertility*. Princeton University Press, Princeton, New Jersey.

Easterlin, R.A. (ed.) (1980) *Population and Economic Change in Developing Countries*. University of Chicago Press, Chicago, Illinois.

Eckstein, O. (1958) *Water Resources Development: The Economics of Project Evaluation*. Harvard University Press, Cambridge, Massachusetts.

Edmonds, J. and Barns, D.W. (1990a) *Estimating the Marginal Cost of Reducing Global Fossil Fuel CO$_2$ Emissions*. PNL-SA-18361, Pacific Northwest Laboratory, Washington, DC.

Edmonds, J. and Barns, D.W. (1990b) *Factors Affecting the Long Term Cost of Global Fossil Fuel CO$_2$ Emissions Reductions*. Global Environmental Change Programme, Pacific Northwest Laboratory, Washington, DC.

Edmonds, J. and Reilly, J.M. (1985) *Global Energy: Assessing the Future*. Oxford University Press, New York.

Edwards, S.F. (1986) Ethical preferences and the assessment of existence values: does the neoclassical model fit? *Northeastern Journal of Agricultural Economics* 15, 145–159.

Edwards, S.F. (1992) Rethinking existence values. *Land Economics* 68, 120–122.

Ehrenfeld, D. (1988) Why put a value on biodiversity?, in E.O. Wilson (ed.) *Biodiversity*. National Academy of Science Press, Washington, DC, pp. 212–216.

Ehrlich, P.R. and Ehrlich, A.E. (1981) *Extinction: The Causes and Consequences of the Disappearance of Species*. Random House, New York.

Ehrlich, P.R. and Ehrlich, A.E. (1992) The value of biodiversity. *Ambio* XXI, 219–226.

Ekins, P. and Simon, S. (1998) Determining the sustainability gap – national accounting for environmental sustainability, in Vaze, P. (ed.) *UK Environmental Accounts 1998*. The Stationery Office, London.

Ellis, G. M. and Fisher, A. C. (1987) Valuing the environment as input. *Journal of Environmental Management* 25, 149–156.

El Serafy, S. (1989) The proper calculation of income from depletable natural resources, in Ahmad, Y.J., El Serafy, S. and Lutz, P. (eds) *Environmental Accounting for Sustainable Development*. World Bank, Washington, DC.

Energy Information Administration (1995) US Department of Energy. *International Energy Outlook, 1995*. Report No. DOE/EIA-0484 (95), US Printing Office, Washington, DC.

EPA (1988) *The Potential Effects of Global Climate Change on the United States*, edited by Smith, J.B. and Tirpak, D.A, 3 volumes. US Environmental Protection Agency, Washington, DC.

EPA (1989) *Policy Options for Stabilising Global Climate*. Draft Report to US Congress, edited by Lashof, J.A. and Tirpak, D.A., 2 volumes. US Environmental Protection Agency, Washington, DC.

EPA (1991) *Final Regulating Impact Analysis of National Primary Drinking Water Regulations for Lead and Copper*. US Office of Drinking Water, US Environmental Protection Agency, Washington, DC.

EPA (1993) *United States Environmental Protection Agency 33/50 Program: Third Progress Update*, EPA Report No 745-R-93-001. US Environmental Protection Agency, Washington, DC.

Esty, D.C. (1994) *Greening the GATT: Trade Environment and the Future*. Institute for International Economics, Washington, DC.

Everest, D. (1988) *The Greenhouse Effect, Issues for Policy Makers*. Joint Energy Programme, Royal Institute of International Affairs, London.

ExternE (1995) *Externalities of Energy*, vol. 4: *Oil and Gas*. EUR 16523 EN. Office for official publications of the European Communities.

FAO (1992) *Marine Fisheries and the Law of the Sea: A Decade of Change*. The Food and Agriculture Organisation of the United Nations, Rome.

FAO (1994) *The State of Food and Agriculture*. The Food and Agriculture Organisation of the United Nations, Rome.

FAO (1995) *Forest Resource Assessment 1990: Global Synthesis*. The Food and Agriculture Organisation of the United Nations, Rome.

Farmer, M.C. and Randall, A. (1997) Policies for sustainability: lessons from an overlapping generations model. *Land Economics* 73(4), 608–622.

Farrow, S. (1985) Testing the efficiency of extraction from a stock resource. *Journal of Political Economy* 93(3), 452–487.

Faucheux, S. and Froger, G. (1995) Decision making under environmental uncertainty. *Ecological Economics* 15, 29–42.

Faucheux, S., Muir, E. and O'Connor, M. (1997) Neoclassical natural capital theory and 'weak' indicators for sustainability. *Land Economics* 73, 528–552.

Feldman, S.L. and Raufer, R.K. (1982) *Emissions Trading and Acid Rain: Implementing a Market Approach to Pollution Control*. Rowman and Littlefield, New Jersey.

Fisher, A.C. (1979) Measurements of natural resource scarcity, in V. Kerry Smith (ed.) *Scarcity and Growth Reconsidered*. Johns Hopkins University Press, Baltimore, Maryland.

Fisher, A.C. (1981) *Resource and Environmental Economics*. Cambridge University Press, Cambridge.

Fisher, A.C. and Hanemann, W.M. (1986) Environmental damages and option values. *Natural Resources Modeling* 1, 111–124.

Fisher, A.C. and Hanemann, M. (1987) Quasi option-value: some misconceptions dispelled. *Journal of Environmental Economics and Management* 14, 183–190.

Fisher, A.C. and Krutilla, J.V. (1974) Valuing long run ecological consequences and irreversibilities. *Journal of Environmental Economics and Management* 1, 96–108.

Fisher, A.C. and Peterson, F. (1976) The environment in economics: a survey. *Journal of Economic Literature* 14, 1–33.

Fisher, A.C., and Rothkopf, M.H. (1989) Market failure and energy policy. *Energy Policy* 17(4), 397–406.

Fishkin, J.S. (1997) *Voice of the People*. Yale University Press, New Haven, Connecticut.

Forrester, J.W. (1971) *World Dynamics*. Wright-Allen Press, Cambridge, Massachusetts.

Forster, B.A. (1975) Optimal pollution control with a nonconstant exponential decay rate. *Journal of Environmental Economics and Management* 2(1), 1–6.

Freeman, A.M. (1979) *The Benefits of Environmental Improvement: Theory and Practice*. Johns Hopkins University Press, Baltimore, Maryland.

Freeman, A.M. (1985) Supply uncertainty, option price and option value. *Land Economics* **61**(2), 176–181.

Freeman, A.M. (1993) *The Measurement of Environmental and Resource Values*. Resources for the Future, Washington, DC.

Freeman, A.M. (1995) Hedonic pricing models, in Bromley, D.W. (ed.) *The Handbook of Environmental Economics*. Blackwell, Oxford.

French, H. (1990) Clearing the air, in Brown L.R. (ed.) *State of The World, 1990*. Norton, New York.

Frey, B.S., Schneider, F. and Pommerehne, W.W. (1985) Economists' opinions on environmental policy instruments: analysis of a survey. *Journal of Environmental Economics and Management*, **12**, 62–71.

Funtowicz, S.O. and Ravetz, J.R. (1991) A new scientific methodology for global environmental issues, in Costanza, R. (ed.) *Ecological Economics: The Science and Management of Sustainability*. Columbia University Press, New York.

Georgescu-Roegen, N. (1971) *The Entropy Law and the Economic Process*. Harvard University Press, Cambridge, Massachusetts.

Georgescu-Roegen, N. (1976) Energy and economic myths, in Georgescu-Roegen, N.E. *Energy and Economic Myths: Institutional and Analytical Economic Essays*. Pergamon Press, New York.

Georgescu-Roegen, N. (1979) Energy analysis and economic valuation. *Southern Economic Journal* **45**, 1023–1058.

Goldin, I. and Winters, L.A. (eds) (1995) *The Economics of Sustainable Development*. Cambridge University Press, Cambridge.

Goodpaster, K.E. (1978) On being morally considerable. *Journal of Philosophy* **75**, 168–176.

Goodstein, E.S. (1992) Saturday effects in tanker oil spills. *Journal of Environmental Economics and Management* **23**, 276–288.

Goodstein, E.S. (1995) *Economics and the Environment*. Prentice Hall, Englewood Cliffs, New Jersey.

Gordon, H.S. (1954) The economic theory of a common-property resource: the fishery. *Journal of Political Economy* **62**, 124–142.

Graham-Tomasi, T. (1995) Quasi-option value, in D.W. Bromley (ed.) *The Handbook of Environmental Economics*. Blackwell, Oxford.

Gray, L.C. (1914) Rent under the assumption of exhaustibility. *Quarterly Journal of Economics* **28**, 466–489.

Gray, R.H. (1994) Corporate reporting for sustainable development: accounting for sustainability in 2000 AD. *Environmental Values* **3**, 17–45.

Greenaway, D., Leybourne, S.J., Reed, G.V. and Whalley, J. (1993) *Applied General Equilibrium Modelling: Applications, Limitations and Future Development*. HMSO, London.

Greene, W.H. (1993) *Econometric Analysis*, 2nd edition. Macmillan, New York.

Groombridge, B. (ed.) (1992) *Global Biodiversity. Status of the Earth's Living Resources*. Chapman & Hall, London.

Grubb, M. (1989a) *The Greenhouse Effect: Negotiating Targets*. Royal Institute of International Affairs, London.

Grubb, M. (1989b) *On Coefficients for Determining Greenhouse Gas Emissions from Fossil Fuels*. IEA Expert Seminar on Technologies to Reduce Greenhouse Gas Emissions, Paris, March, IEA/OECD.

Hahn, R.W. (1984) Market power and transferable property rights. *Quarterly Journal of Economics* **99**, 763–765.

Hahn, R.W. (1989) Economic prescriptions for environmental problems: how the patient followed the doctor's orders. *The Journal of Economic Perspectives* **3**, 95–114.

Hahn, R.W. (1995) Economic prescriptions for environmental problems: lessons from the United States and continental Europe, in Eckersley, R. (ed.) *Markets, the State and the Environment*. Macmillan, Melbourne.

Hahn, R.W. and Hester, G.L. (1989a) Where did all the markets go? An analysis of the EPA's emission trading program. *Yale Journal of Regulation* **6**, 109–153.

Hahn, R.W. and Hester, G.L. (1989b) Marketable permits: lessons for theory and practice. *Ecology Law Quarterly* **16**, 361–406.

Halkos, G. and Hutton, J. (1993) *Acid Rain Games in Europe*. Discussion Papers in Economics No. 93/12, University of York, UK.

Hall, D.C. *et al.* (1989) Organic food and sustainable agriculture. *Contemporary Policy Issues*, 7, October.

Hall, D.C. and Hall, J.V. (1984) Concepts and measures of natural resource scarcity with a summary of recent trends. *Journal of Environmental Economics and Management* **11**, 363–379.

Halvorsen, R. and Smith, T.R. (1991) A test of the theory of exhaustible resources. *Quarterly Journal of Economics* **106**(1), 123–140.

Hamilton, C. (1997) *The Genuine Progress Indicator: A New Index of Changes in Well-being in Australia*. The Australia Institute, Canberra.

Hamilton, K. (1994) Green adjustments to GDP. *Resources Policy* **20**, 155–168.

Hamilton, K., Pearce, D.W., Atkinson, G., Gomez-Lobo, A. and Young, C. (1994) *The Policy Implications of Natural Resource and Environmental Accounting*. CSERGE Working Paper GEC 94–18. University College, London.

Hammack, J. and Brown, G. (1974) *Waterfowl and Wetlands: Towards Bioeconomic Analysis*. Johns Hopkins Press, Baltimore, Maryland.

Hanemann, M. (1991) Willingness to pay and willingness to accept: how much can they differ? *American Economic Review* **81**(3), 635–647.

Hanley, N. (1988) Using contingent valuation to value environmental improvements. *Applied Economics* **20**, 541–549.

Hanley, N. (1989b) *Problems in Valuing Environmental Improvements from Agricultural Policy Changes: The Case of Nitrate Pollution*. Discussion Paper No. 89/1, Economics Department, University of Stirling.

Hanley, N. (1989) Valuing rural recreation benefits: an empirical comparison of two approaches, *Journal of Agricultural Economics* **40**, 361–374.

Hanley, N. and Spash, C. (1993) *Cost–Benefit Analysis and the Environment*. Edward Elgar, Aldershot.

Hansen, J. (1990) *Greenhouse and Developing Countries*. Paper presented at the symposium Environment and Economics in the Developing Countries, Association of the Bar of the City of New York, 23 May.

Hansen, J. *et al.* (1988) Global climate changes as forecast by Goddard Institute for Space Studies three dimensional model. *Journal of Geophysical Research* **93**(D8), 9341–9364.

Harberger, A.C. (1971) Three basic postulates for applied welfare economics: an interpretative essay. *Journal of Economic Literature* **9**, 785–797.

Hardin, G. (1986) The tragedy of the commons. *Science* **162**, 1243–1248.

Hardin, G. (1993) *Living within Limits: Ecology, Economics and Population Taboos.* Oxford University Press, New York.

Hardin, G. and Baden, J. (1977) *Managing the Commons.* W.H. Freeman, San Francisco, California.

Harris, C.C. and Brown, G. (1992) Gain loss and personal responsibility: the role of motivation in resource valuation decision-making. *Ecological Economics* **5**, 73–92.

Harris, D.P. (1993) Mineral resource stocks and information. in Kneese, A.V. and Sweeney, J.L. (eds) *Handbook of Natural Resource and Energy Economics,* vol. 3, Elsevier, Amsterdam, ch. 21.

Harris, M. and Ross, E.B. (1987) *Death, Sex and Fertility: Population Regulation in Preindustrial and Developing Societies.* Columbia University Press, New York.

Harrison, G.W. (1992) Valuing public goods with the contingent valuation method: a critique of Kahneman and Knetsch. *Journal of Environmental Economics and Management* **23**, 248–257.

Harrod, R.F. (1948) *Towards a Dynamic Economy.* St Martins Press, London.

Hartman, R. (1976) The harvesting decision when a standing forest has value. *Economic Inquiry* **14**, 52–58.

Hartwick, J.M. (1977) Intergenerational equity and the investing of rents from exhaustible resources. *American Economic Review* **67**, 972–974.

Hartwick, J.M. (1978) Substitution among exhaustible resources and intergenerational equity. *Review of Economic Studies* **45**, 347–354.

Hartwick, J.M. (1990) Natural resource accounting and economic depreciation. *Journal of Public Economics* **43**, 291–304.

Hartwick, J.M. (1992) Deforestation and national accounting. *Environmental and Resource Economics* **2**, 513–521.

Hartwick, J.M. and Hageman, A.P. (1993) Economic depreciation of mineral stocks and the contribution of El Serafy, in Lutz, E. (ed.) *Toward Improved Accounting for the Environment: An UNSTAT-World Bank Symposium.* World Bank, Washington.

Hartwick, J.M. and Olewiler, N.D. (1986) *The Economics of Natural Resource Use.* Harper & Row, New York.

Hartwick, J.M. and Olewiler, N.D. (1998) *The Economics of Natural Resource Use,* 2nd edition. Harper & Row, New York.

Harvey, A.C. (1989) *Forecasting, Structural Time-Series Models and the Kalman Filter.* Cambridge University Press, Cambridge.

Hawksworth, D.L. (ed.) (1995) *Biodiversity: Measurement and Estimation.* Chapman & Hall, London.

Heal, G.M. (1981) Economics and resources, in Butlin, R. (ed.) *Economics of the Environment and Natural Resource Policy.* Westview Press, Boulder, Colorado.

Heijman, W. (1990) *Natural Resource Depletion and Market Forms.* Wageningen Economic Papers, Wageningen Agricultural University, The Netherlands.

Henderson, J.V. and Tugwell, M. (1979) Exploitation of the lobster fishery: some empirical results. *Journal of Environmental Economics and Management* **6**, 287–296.

Herfindahl, O.C. and Kneese, A.V. (1974) *Economic Theory of Natural Resources.* C.E. Merrill, Columbus, Ohio.

Heywood, V.H. (1995) *Global Biodiversity Assessment.* Cambridge University Press, for UNEP, Cambridge.

Hicks, J.R. (1939) *Value and Capital.* Oxford University Press, Oxford.

Hicks, J.R. (1941) The rehabilitation of consumers' surplus. *Review of Economic Studies* **8**, February, 108–116.

Hirsch, F. (1977) *Social Limits to Growth.* Routledge & Kegan Paul, London.

Hirschborn, J. (1991) Technological potential in pollution prevention. *Pollution Prevention* **1**(2), 21–24.

Hirshleifer, J. (1980) *Price Theory and Applications,* 2nd edition. Prentice Hall, London.

Hoel, M. (1989) *Global Environmental Problems: The Effects of Unilateral Action Taken by One Country.* Working Paper No. 11, Department of Economics, University of Oslo.

Hogan, W.H. and Manne, A.S. (1979) Energy–economy interactions: the fable of the elephant and the rabbit?, in Pindyck, R.S. (ed.) *Advances in the Economics of Energy and Resources,* vol. 1, JAI Press, Greenwich, Connecticut.

Hohmeyer, O. (1988) *Social Costs of Energy Consumption.* Springer, Heidelberg.

Holling, C.S. (1973) Resilience and stability of ecological systems. *Annual Review of Ecological Systems* **4**, 1–24.

Holling, C.S. (1986) The resilience of terrestrial ecosystems: local surprise and global change, in Clark, W.C. and Munn, R.E. (eds) *Sustainable Development in the Biosphere.* Cambridge University Press, Cambridge.

Hotelling, H. (1931) The economics of exhaustible resources. *Journal of Political Economy* **39**, 137–175.

Houghton, J.T. (1997) *Global Warming: The Complete Briefing,* 2nd edition. Cambridge University Press, Cambridge.

Houghton, J.T., Jenkins, G.J. and Ephrams, J.J. (1990) *Climate Change: the IPCC Scientific Assessment.* Cambridge University Press, Cambridge.

Houghton, J.T., Callander, B.A. and Varney, S.K. (eds) (1992) *Climate Change 1992: The Supplementary Report to the IPCC Scientific Assessment.* Cambridge University Press, Cambridge.

Houghton, J.T., Meira Filho, L.G., Callander, B.A., Harris, N., Katenberg, A. and Maskell, K. (1996) *Climate Change 1995: The Science of Climate Change.* Cambridge University Press, for the IPCC, Cambridge.

Hufschmidt, M.M. *et al.* (1983) *Environment, Natural Systems and Development: an Economic Valuation Guide.* Johns Hopkins University Press, Baltimore, Maryland.

Hume, D. (1739) A treatise on human nature, in *Hume's Moral and Political Philosophy* (1968), Hafner, New York.

Hume, D. (1751) An enquiry concerning the principle of morals, in *Hume's Moral and Political Philosophy* (1968), Hafner, New York.

Hunt, W.M. (1980) Are 'Mere things' morally considerable? *Environmental Ethics* **2**(1).

Huppert, D.H. (1990) *Managing Alaska's Groundfish Fisheries: History and Prospects.* University of Washington Institute for Marine Resources Working Paper, May.

IBRD (1992) *World Development Report 1992.* The World Bank, Oxford University Press, Oxford.

IEA (International Energy Agency) (1990) *Energy and The Environment: Policy Overview.* Organization for Economic Cooperation and Development, Paris.

IEA (International Energy Agency) (1995) *World Energy Outlook.* Organization for Economic Cooperation and Development, Paris.

Ingham, A. and Ulph, A. (1990) *Market-based Instruments for Reducing CO_2 Emissions – The Case of UK Manufacturing.* Discussion Paper in Economics and Econometrics, No. 9004, University of Southampton, UK, November.

International Union for Conservation of Nature and Natural

Resources (1980) *World Conservation Strategy*. IUCN/UNEP/WWF, Gland, Switzerland.

IPCC (1990) *Second Draft Reports of the Intergovernmental Panel On Climate Change (Climate, Impact and Policy Groups)*, April 1990. The report of the first group (Climate) has been published as: Houghton, R., Jenkins, G.J., and Ephraums, E (1990) *Climate Change: the IPCC Scientific Assessment*. Cambridge University Press, Cambridge.

IPCC (1992) *1992 Supplement: Scientific Assessment of Climate Change*. World Meteorological Organization/United Nations Environment Programme, Geneva.

IPCC (1994) *Radiative Forcing of Climate Change: The 1994 Report of the Scientific Assessment Working Group of IPCC*. World Meteorological Organization/United Nations Environment Programme, Geneva.

IPCC (1995) *IPCC Synthesis Report, July 29, 1995 draft*. World Meteorological Organization/United Nations Environment Programme, Geneva.

IPCC (1995b) A review of mitigation cost studies, in *IPCC Synthesis Report*. World Meteorological Organization/United Nations, Geneva, ch. 9.

IPCC (1995c) The social costs of climate change: greenhouse damage and the benefits of control. *Second Assessment Report, Working Group III, April 1995 Draft*. World Meteorological Organization/United Nations Environment Programme, Geneva, ch. 6.

Jackson, T. and Marks, N. (1994) *Measuring Sustainable Development – A Pilot Index: 1950–1990*. Stockholm Environment Institute, Stockholm, and New Economic Foundation, London.

Janssen, R. (1992) *Multiobjective Decision Support for Environmental Management*. Kluwer, Dordrecht.

Jansson, A.M., Hammer, M., Folke, C. and Costanza, R. (eds) (1994) *Investing in Natural Capital: The Ecological Economics Approach to Sustainability*. Island Press, Washington, DC.

Jeffries, M.J. (1997) *Biodiversity and Conservation*. Routledge, London

Jevons, W.S. (1865) *The Coal Question: An Inquiry Concerning the Progress of the Nation and the Probable Exhaustion of Our Coal Mines*, in Flux, A.W. (ed.) (revised 3rd edition (1965). A.M. Kelly, New York.

Jevons, W.S. (1871) *The Theory of Political Economy*, 1st edition. Macmillan, London.

Johansson, P.-O. (1987) *The Economic Theory and Measurement of Environmental Benefits*. Cambridge University Press, Cambridge.

Johansson, P. and Löfgren, K. (1985) *The Economics of Forestry and Natural Resources*. Basil Blackwell, Oxford.

Johnson, D.G. (1984) In Simon, J.L. and Kahn, H. (eds) *The Resourceful Earth*. Basil Blackwell, Oxford.

Johnson, M.G.M. (1989) *Leading Issues in Economic Development*, 5th edition. Oxford University Press, New York.

Johnson, R.W. and Brown, G.M. Jr (1976) *Cleaning up Europe's Waters: Economics, Management and Policies*. Praeger, New York.

Jorgensen, D. and Griliches, Z. (1967) The explanation of productivity change. *Review of Economics and Statistics* **34**, 250–282.

Jorgensen, D.W and Wilcoxen, P.J. (1990a) *The Costs of Controlling US Carbon Dioxide Emissions*. Paper presented at Workshop on Economic/Energy/Environmental Modelling for Climate Policy Analysis, Washington, DC, 22–23 October.

Jorgensen, D.W and Wilcoxen, P.J. (1990b) *Global Change, Energy Prices, and US Economic Growth*. Paper presented for the Energy Pricing Hearing, US Department of Energy, Washington, DC, 20 July.

Jorgensen, D.W and Wilcoxen, P.J. (1990c) Environmental regulation and US economic growth. *Rand Journal of Economics* **21**(2), 314–341.

Just, R.E., Hueth, D.L. and Schnitz, A. (1982) *Applied Welfare Economics and Public Policy*. Prentice Hall, Englewood Cliffs, New Jersey.

Kahneman, D. and Knetsch, J.L. (1992a) Valuing public goods: the purchase of moral satisfaction. *Journal of Environmental Economics and Management* **22**, 57–70.

Kahneman, D. and Knetsch, J.L. (1992b) Contingent valuation and the value of public goods: reply. *Journal of Environmental Economics and Management* **22**, 90–94.

Kamien, M.I. and Schwartz, N.L. (1991) *The Calculus of Variations and Optimal Control in Economics and Management*, 2nd edition. Elsevier, New York.

Kant, I. *Groundwork of the Metaphysic of Morals*, section II. Various translations and editions.

Keepin, B and Kats, G. (1988) Greenhouse warming: comparative analysis of nuclear and efficiency abatement strategies. *Energy Policy* **16**(6), 538–561.

Kemp, D.D. (1990) *Global Environmental Issues: A Climatological Approach*. Routledge, London.

Kemp, M.A. and Maxwell, C. (1993) Exploring a budget context for contingent valuation estimates, in J.A. Hausman (ed.) *Contingent Valuation: A Critical Assessment*. North-Holland, Amsterdam, pp. 218–265.

Keynes, J.M. (1936) *The General Theory of Employment, Interest and Money*. Macmillan, London.

Klassen, G.A.J. and Opschoor, J.B. (1991) Economics of sustainability or the sustainability of economics: different paradigms. *Ecological Economics* **4**, 93–115.

Kneese, A.V. (1984) *Measuring the Benefits of Clean Air and Water*. Resources for the Future, Washington, DC.

Kneese, A.V. and Bower, B.T. (1968) *Managing Water Quality: Economics Technology and Institutions*. Johns Hopkins University Press, Baltimore, Maryland.

Kneese, A.V. and Schulze, W.D. (1985) Ethics and environmental economics, in Kneese, A.V. and Sweeney, J.L. (eds) *Handbook of Natural Resource and Energy Economics*, vol. 1. Elsevier, Amsterdam, ch. 5.

Kneese, A.V. and Sweeney, J.L. (1985a) *Handbook of Natural Resource and Energy Economics*, vol. 1. Elsevier, Amsterdam.

Kneese, A.V. and Sweeney, J.L. (1985b) *Handbook of Natural Resource and Energy Economics*, vol. 2. Elsevier, Amsterdam.

Kneese, A.V. and Sweeney, J.L. (1993) *Handbook of Natural Resource and Energy Economics*, vol. 3, Elsevier, Amsterdam.

Kneese, A.V., Ayres, R.V. and D'Arge, R.C. (1970) *Economics and the Environment: A Materials Balance Approach*. Johns Hopkins University Press, Baltimore, Maryland.

Knetsch, J. (1990) Environmental policy implications of disparities between willingness to pay and compensation demanded. *Journal of Environmental Economics and Management* **18**, 227–237.

Knight, F.H. (1921) *Risk, Uncertainty and Profit*. Houghton Mifflin, New York.

Kolstad, C.D. (1987) Uniformity versus differentiation in regulating externalities. *Journal of Environmental Economics and Management* **14**, 386–399.

Kolstad, C.D. and Krautkraemer, J.A. (1993) Natural resource use and the environment, in Kneese, A.V. and Sweeney, J.L. (eds) *Handbook of Natural Resource and Energy Economics*, vol. 3. Elsevier, Amsterdam.

Kosmo, M. (1989) *Money to Burn? The High Price of Energy Subsidies*. World Resources Institute, Washington, DC.

Kramer, R.A. and Mercer, D.E. (1997) Valuing a global environmental good: US residents' willingness to pay to protect tropical rain forests. *Land Economics* 73(2), 196–210.

Krebs, C.J. (1972) *Ecology: The Experimental Analysis of Distribution and Abundance*. Harper & Row, New York.

Kreps, D.M. (1990) *A Course in Microeconomic Theory*. Harvester Wheatsheaf, New York.

Krupnick, A.J. (1986) Costs of alternative policies for the control of nitrogen dioxide in Baltimore, Maryland. *Journal of Environmental Economics and Management* 13, 189–197.

Krutilla, J.V. (1967) Conservation reconsidered. *American Economic Review* 54(4), 777–786.

Krutilla, J.V. and Fisher, A.C. (1975) *The Economics of Natural Environments: Studies in the Valuation of Commodity and Amenity Resources*. Johns Hopkins University Press, Baltimore, Maryland.

Kuznets, S. (1955) Economic growth and income inequality. *American Economic Review* 49,1–28.

Lancaster, K. (1966) A new approach to consumer theory. *Journal of Political Economy* 74, 132-157.

Lashof, D. and Ahuja, D.R. (1990) Relative contributions of greenhouse gas emissions to global warming. *Nature* 334, 529–531.

Layard, P.R.G. and Glaister, S. (eds) (1994) *Cost–Benefit Analysis*, 2nd edition. Cambridge University Press, Cambridge.

Layard, P.R.G. and Walters, A.A. (1978) *Microeconomic Theory*. McGraw-Hill, Maidenhead.

Leach, G. (1975) *Energy and Food Production*. International Institute for Environment and Development.

Lecomber, R. (1975) *Economic Growth versus the Environment*. Macmillan, London.

Lederberg, J., Shope, R.E. and Oaks, S.C. Jr. (1992) *Emerging Infections: Microbial Threats to Health in the United States*. National Academy Press. Washington, DC.

Lee, W.R. (1979) *European Demography and Economic Growth*. St Martins Press, New York.

Lele, S.M. (1991) Sustainable development: a critical review. *World Development* 19, 607–621

Leopold, A. (1970) A Sand County almanac, in *Essays on Conservation*. Round River, New York (first published 1949).

Leontief, W. (1966) *Input–Output Economics*. Oxford University Press, Oxford.

Leontief, W. (1970a) Environmental repercussions and the economic structure: an input–output approach. *Review of Economics and Statistics* 52, 262–277.

Leontief, W. (1970b) The dynamic inverse, in A.P. Carter and A. Brody (eds) *Contributions to Input–Output Analysis*. North-Holland, Amsterdam.

Leontief, W. and Ford, D. (1972) Air pollution and economic structure: empirical results of input output computations, in Brody, A. and Carter, A. (eds) *Input Output Techniques*. North-Holland, Amsterdam.

Leontief, W. *et al.* (1977) *The Future of the World Economy*. Oxford University Press, New York.

Lind, R. (ed.) (1982) *Discounting for Time and Risk in Energy Policy*. Johns Hopkins University Press, Baltimore, Maryland.

Locke, J. (1960) *Second Treatise on Civil Government*. Cambridge University Press, New York (Laslett edition).

Lovelock, J. (1989) *The Ages of Gaia: A Biography of Our Living Earth*. Oxford University Press, Oxford.

Ludwig, D., Hilborn, R. and Walters, C. (1993) Uncertainty, resource exploitation and conservation: lessons from history. *Science* 260, 17–18.

Lutz, E. (ed.) (1993) *Toward Improved Accounting for the Environment: An UNSTAT–World Bank Symposium*. World Bank, Washington, DC.

Maass, A., Hufschmidt, M., Dorfman, R., Thomas, H.A., Marglin, S. and Fair, G. (1962) *Design of Water Resource Systems*. Harvard University Press, Cambridge.

McCormick, J. (1989) *The Global Environmental Movement: Reclaiming Paradise*. Bellhaven.

MacGillivray, A. (1994) *Environmental Measures*. Environmental Challenge Group, London.

McInerney, J. (1976) The simple analytics of natural resource economics. *Journal of Agricultural Economics*, 27, 31–52.

McKinsey (1989) *Protecting the Global Environment*. McKinsey and Company, Report to Ministerial Conference on Atmospheric Pollution and Climatic Change, Noordwijk, The Netherlands, November.

McNeely, J.A. (1988) *Economics and Biological Diversity*. IUCN, Gland.

McNicoll, I.H. and Blackmore, D. (1993) *A Pilot Study on the Construction of a Scottish Environmental Input–Output System*. Report to Scottish Enterprise, Department of Economics, University of Strathclyde, Glasgow.

Mäler, K.-G. (1974) *Environmental Economics: A Theoretical Inquiry*. Johns Hopkins University Press, Baltimore, Maryland.

Mäler, K.-G. (1985) Welfare economics and the environment, in Kneese, A.V. and Sweeney, J.L. (eds) *Handbook of Natural Resource and Energy Economics*, vol. 1. Elsevier, Amsterdam, ch. 1.

Mäler, K-G. (1990) International environmental problems. *Oxford Review of Economic Policy* 6(1), 80–107.

Mäler, K.-G. (1991) National accounting and environmental resources. *Environmental and Resource Economics* 1, 1–15.

Malthus, T.R. (1798) *An Essay on the Principle of Population as it Affects the Future Improvement of Society*. Ward Lock, London. (Also available edited by Flew, A. (1970) Pelican.)

Manne, A.S. (1979) ETA macro, in R.S. Pindyck (ed.) *Advances in the Economics of Energy and Resources*, vol. 2. JAI Press, Greenwich, Connecticut.

Manne, A.S. and Richels, R.G. (1989) CO_2 *Emission Limits: An Economic Analysis for the USA*. Mimeo, Stanford University and Electric Power Research Institute, Paolo Alto, California, November 1989. (Also published in *The Energy Journal* 11(2), 51–74.)

Manne, A.S. and Richels, R.G. (1990) CO_2 emission limits: a global economic cost analysis. Paper presented at the workshop on Energy/CO_2 Data, International Institute for Applied System Analysis, Laxenburg, Austria, 22–23 January. Published in *The Energy Journal* (1991), 12(1).

Marglin, S. (1963) The social rate of discount and the optimal rate of investment. *Quarterly Journal of Economics* 77, 95–111.

Marin, A. and Psacharopoulos, G. (1982) The reward for risk in the labour market: evidence from the United Kingdom and a reconciliation with other studies. *Journal of Political Economy* **90**.

Markandya, A (1992) The value of the environment: a state of the art survey, in Markandya, A. and Richardson, J. (eds) *The Earthscan Reader in Environmental Economics*. Earthscan, London.

Markandya, A. and Richardson, J. (eds) (1992) *The Earthscan Reader in Environmental Economics*. Earthscan, London.

Marshall, A. (1890) *Principles of Economics*. Macmillan, London.

Martinez-Alier, J. (1987) *Ecological economics*. Basil Blackwell, Oxford.

Marx, K. (1960 edition) *Capital*, 3 volumes. Foreign Languages Publishing House, Moscow.

May, R.M. (1988) How many species are there on earth? *Science* **241**, 1441–1449.

Meadows, D.H., Meadows, D.L., Randers, J. and Behrens, W.W. (1972) *The Limits to Growth: A Report for The Club of Rome's Project on the Predicament of Mankind*. Earth Island, Universe Books, New York. (Also known as the Club of Rome Report.)

Meadows, D.H., Meadows, D.L. and Randers, J. (1992) *Beyond the Limits: Global Collapse or a Sustainable Future*. London, Earthscan.

Menger, K. (1950) *Principles of Economics*. Free Press, New York.

Mikesell, R (1977) *The Rate of Discount for Evaluating Public Projects*. American Enterprise for Public Policy Research, Washington, DC.

Mill, J.S. (1857) *Principles of Political Economy*. J.W. Parker and Son. (Sixth edition, 1865, Augustus M. Kelly, New York.)

Mill, J.S. (1863) *Utilitarianism*. Fontana Library, Collins, London.

Miller, M.H. and Upton, C.W. (1985) A test of the Hotelling valuation principle. *Journal of Political Economy* **93**(1), 1–25.

Miller, R.E. and Blair P.D. (1985) *Input–Output Analysis; Foundations and Extensions*. Prentice Hall, Englewood Cliffs, New Jersey.

Mills, E.S. (1978) *The Economics of Environmental Quality*. Norton, New York.

Mintzer, I.M. (1987) *A Matter of Degrees: The Potential for Controlling the Greenhouse Effect*. Research Report 5, World Resources Institute, Washington, DC.

Mishan, E.J. (1967) *The Costs of Economic Growth*. Staples Press, London.

Mishan, E.J. (1977) *The Economic Growth Debate: An Assessment*. George Allen and Unwin, London.

Mitchell, R. and Carson, R. (1984) *A Contingent Valuation Estimate of National Freshwater Benefits*. Technical Report to the United States Environmental Protection Agency. Resources for the Future, Washington, DC.

Mitchell, R. and Carson, R. (1989) *Using Surveys to Value Public Goods: The Contingent Valuation Method*. Resources for the Future, Washington, DC.

Montgomery, C.A. and Adams, D.M. (1995) Optimal timber management policies, in Bromley, D.W. (ed.) *The Handbook of Environmental Economics*. Blackwell, Oxford.

Montgomery, D.W. (1972) Markets in licences and efficient pollution control programs. *Journal of Economic Theory* **5**, 395–418.

Munda, G., Nijkamp, P. and Rietveld, P. (1994). Qualitative multicriteria evaluation for environmental management. *Ecological Economics*, **10**, 97–112.

Munro, G. (1981) The economics of fishing: an introduction, Butlin, J.A. (ed.) *The Economics of Environmental and Natural Resources Policy*. Westfield Press, Boulder, Colorado.

Munro, G. (1982) Fisheries, extended jurisdiction and the economics of common property resources. *Canadian Journal of Economics* **15**, 405–425.

Myers, N. (1979) *The Sinking Ark*. Pergamon Press, New York.

Naess, A. (1972) The shallow and the deep, long-range ecology movement. *Inquiry* **16**, 95–100.

NAPAP (1990) *National Acid Precipitation Assessment Program. 1989 Annual Report to the President and Congress*. Washington, DC.

Nelson, J.P. (1982) Highway noise and property values: a survey of recent evidence. *Journal of Transport Economics and Policy* **XIC**, 37–52.

Nicoletti, G. and Oliveira-Martins, J. (1993) Global effects of a European carbon tax, in Carraro, C. and Siniscalco, D. (eds) *The European Carbon Tax: An Economic Assessment*. Kluwer, Dordrecht.

Nordhaus, W.D. (1972) *World Dynamics: Measurement without Data*. Cowles Foundation Discussion Paper. Reprinted in *Economic Journal*, (1973) December, 1156–1183.

Nordhaus, W.D. (1973) The allocation of energy resources. *Brookings Papers on Economic Activity* **3**, 529–576.

Nordhaus, W.D. (1977) The demand for energy: an international perspective, in Nordhaus, W.D. (ed.) *International Studies in the Demand for Energy*. North Holland, Amsterdam.

Nordhaus, W. (1982) How fast should we graze the global commons? *American Economic Review*, *Papers and Proceedings* **72**, 242–246.

Nordhaus, W. (1989) *The Economics of the Greenhouse Effect*. Mimeo, Department of Economics, Yale University.

Nordhaus, W. (1990a) Greenhouse economics. *The Economist*, 7 July.

Nordhaus, W. (1990b) *An Intertemporal General Equilibrium Model of Economic Growth and Climate Change*. Yale University. Paper presented at Workshop on Economic/Energy/Environmental Modelling for Climate Policy Analysis, Washington, DC, 22–23 October.

Nordhaus, W. (1991a) To slow or not to slow: the economics of the greenhouse effect. *Economic Journal* **101**, 920–937.

Nordhaus, W. (1991b) The cost of slowing climate: a survey. *Energy Journal* **12**, 37–65.

Nordhaus, W.D. (1994) *Managing the Global Commons: The Economics of Climate Change*. MIT Press, Cambridge, Massachusetts.

Norgaard, R.B. (1975) Resource scarcity and new technology in US petroleum development. *Natural Resources Journal* **15**, 265–295.

Norgaard, R.B. (1984) Coevolutionary development potential. *Land Economics* **60**, 160–173.

Norgaard, R.B. (1988) The rise of the global economy and the loss of biological diversity, in E.O. Wilson (ed.) *Biodiversity*. National Academy of Science Press, Washington, DC.

Norton, B.G. (1994) Economists' preferences and the preferences of economists, *Environmental Values*, **3**, 311–332.

Nozick, R. (1974) *Anarchy, State and Utopia*. Johns Hopkins Press, Baltimore, Maryland.

O'Connor, M. (1993) Entropy structure and organisational change. *Ecological Economics* **8**, 95–122.

O'Connor, R. and Henry, E.W. (1975) *Input–Output Analysis and its Applications*. Charles Griffin and Co.

OECD (1975) *The Polluter Pays Principle: Definition Analysis Implementation*. OECD, Paris.

OECD (1989) *Economic Instruments for Environmental Protection*. OECD, Paris.

OECD (1994a) *Environmental Indicators: OECD Core Set*. OECD, Paris.

OECD (1994b) *Project and Policy Appraisal: Integrating Economics and Environment*. OECD, Paris.

OECD (1995) *Environmental Taxation in OECD Countries*. OECD, Paris.

OECD (1996) *Saving Biological Diversity*. OECD, Paris.

OECD (1996a) *Implementation Strategies for Environmental Taxes*. OECD, Paris.

OECD (1996b) *Subsidies and Environment: Exploring the Linkages*. OECD, Paris.

OECD (1997) *Energy Policies and Employment*. OECD, Paris.

OECD (1997b) *Environmental Taxes and Green Tax Reform*. OECD, Paris.

OECD (1998) *Improving the Environment through Reducing Subsidies*. Part I, *Summary and Policy Conclusions*. OECD, Paris.

Office of Air and Radiation, US Environmental Protection Agency (EPA) and the World Resources Institute (1995) *Protection of the Ozone Layer*. EPA Environmental Indicators, EPA 230-N-95-002, EPA, Washington, DC, June.

Office of Technology Assessment (1984) *Acid Rain and Transported Air Pollutants: Implications for Public Policy*. US GPO, Washington, DC.

Opschoor, J.B. and Vos, H.B. (1989) *The Application of Economic Instruments for Environmental Protection in OECD Member Countries*. OECD, Paris.

O'Riordan, T. (ed.) (1997) *Ecotaxation*. Earthscan, London.

Page, T. (1973) The non-renewable resources subsystem, in Cole, H.S.D., Freeman, C., Jahoda, M. and Pavitt, K.L.R. (eds) *Thinking About the Future: A Critique of the Limits to Growth*. Sussex University Press, London.

Page, T. (1977) *Conservation and Economic Efficiency: An Approach to Materials Policy*. Johns Hopkins University Press, Baltimore, Maryland.

Page, T. (1982) Intergenerational justice as opportunity, in MacLean, D. and Brown, P. (eds) *Energy and the Future*. Rowman and Littlefield, Ottowa.

Page, T. (1997) On the problem of achieving efficiency and equity, intergenerationally. *Land Economics* **73**(4), 580–596.

Panayotou, T. (1993) *Empirical Tests and Policy Analysis of Environmental Degradation at Different Stages of Economic Development*. Working Paper WP238, Technology and Employment Programme, International Labor Office, Geneva.

Pareto, V. (1897) *Cours d'Economie Politique*. Lausanne.

Payne, J.W., Bettman, J.R. and Johnson, E.J. (1992) Behavioural decision research: A constructive processing perspective. *Annual Review of Psychology* **43**, 87–131.

Pearce, D.W. (ed.) (1991a) *Blueprint 2: Greening the World Economy*. Earthscan, London.

Pearce, D.W. (1991b) The role of carbon taxes in adjusting to global warming. *Economic Journal* **101**, 938–948.

Pearce, D.W. (1994) Assessing the social rate of return from investment in temperate zone forestry, in Layard, R. and Glaister, S. (eds) *Cost–Benefit Analysis*, 2nd edition. Cambridge University Press, Cambridge, ch. 17.

Pearce, D.W. and Atkinson, G.D. (1993) Capital theory and the measurement of sustainable development: an indicator of 'weak' sustainability. *Ecological Economics* **8**, 103–108.

Pearce, D.W. and Atkinson, G. (1995) Measuring sustainable development, in Bromley, D.W. (ed.) *The Handbook of Environmental Economics*. Blackwell, Oxford.

Pearce, D.W. and Markandya, A. (1989) *Environmental Policy Benefits: Monetary Valuation*. OECD, Paris.

Pearce, D.W. and Moran, D. (1994) *The Economic Value of Biodiversity*. Earthscan, London.

Pearce, D.W. and Nash, C.A. (1981) *The Social Appraisal of Projects: A Text in Cost Benefit Analysis*. Macmillan, London.

Pearce, D.W. and Turner, R.K. (1990) *Economics of Natural Resources and the Environment*. Harvester Wheatsheaf, Hemel Hempstead.

Pearce, D.W., Markandya, A. and Barbier, E.B. (1989) *Blueprint for a Green Economy*. Earthscan, London.

Pearce, D.W., Barbier, E. and Markandya, A. (1990) *Sustainable Development: Economics and Environment in the Third World*. Edward Elgar, Aldershot.

Pearce, F. (1987) *Acid Rain*. Penguin, Harmondsworth.

Pearse, P.H. (1990) *Introduction to Forest Economics*. University of British Columbia Press, Vancouver.

Pearson, M. and Smith, S. (1990) Taxation and environmental policy: some initial evidence. *Institute of Fiscal Studies Commentary*, **19**.

Peet, J. (1992) *Energy and the Ecological Economics of Sustainability*. Island Press, Washington, DC.

Perlman, M. (1984) The role of population projections for the year 2000, in Simon, J.L. and Kahn, H. (eds) *The Resorceful Earth*. Basil Blackwell, Oxford.

Penz, C.P. (1986) *Consumer Sovereignty and Human Interests*. Cambridge University Press, Cambridge.

Perman, R. (1994) The economics of the greenhouse effect. *Journal of Economic Surveys* **8**(2), June.

Perrings, C. (1987) *Economy and Environment: A Theoretical Essay on the Interdependence of Economic and Environmental Systems*. Cambridge University Press, Cambridge.

Perrings, C. (1989) Environmental bonds and environmental research in innovative activities. *Ecological Economics* **1**, 95–115.

Perrings, C. (1991) Reserved rationality and the precautionary principle: technological change, time and uncertainty in environmental decision making, in Costanza, R. (ed.) *Ecological Economics: The Science and Management of Sustainability*. Columbia University Press, New York.

Perrings, C. (1995) Ecology, economics and ecological economics. *Ambio* **24**(1).

Perrings, C.A., Mäler, K.-G., Folke, C., Holling, C.S. and Jansson, B.-O. (1995) *Biodiversity Loss. Economic and Ecological Issues*. Cambridge University Press, Cambridge.

Peskin, H with Lutz, E. (1990) *A Survey of Resource and Environmental Accounting in Industrialised Countries*. Environmental Working Paper 37, World Bank, Washington, DC.

Peterson, F.M. and Fisher, A.C. (1977) The exploitation of extractive resources: a survey. *Economic Journal* **87**, 681–721.

Peterson, G.L. (1992) New horizons in economic valuation: integrating economics and psychology, in Lockwood, M. and DeLacey, T. (eds) *Valuing Natural Areas*, Johnstone

Centre of Parks Recreation and Heritage, Charles Stuart University, Albury.

Peterson, G.L., Brown, T.C., McCallum, D.W., Bell, P.A., Birjulin, A.A. and Clarke, A. (1996) Moral responsibility effects in valuation of WTA for public and private goods by the method of paired comparison, in Adamowicz, W.L., Boxall, P., Luckert, M.K., Phillips, E.E. and White, W.A. (eds) *Forestry Economics and the Environment*. CAB International, Wallingford.

Pezzey, J.C.V. (1992) Sustainability: an interdisciplinary guide. *Environmental Values* **1**, 321–362.

Pezzey, J.C.V. (1996) *An Analysis of Scientific and Economic Studies of Pollution Assimilation*. Working paper 1996/97, Centre for Resource and Environmental Studies, Australian National University, Canberra.

Pezzey, J. (1997) Sustainability constraints versus 'Optimality' versus intertemporal concern, and axioms versus data. *Land Economics* **73**(4), 448–466.

Pigou, A.C. (1920) *The Economics of Welfare*. Macmillan, London. (Fourth edition 1932.)

Pimental, D. *et al.* (1995) Environmental and economic costs of soil erosion and conservation benefits. *Science* **267** (5201), 1117–1122.

Pindyck, R.S. (1978) *The Structure of World Energy Demand*. MIT Press, Cambridge, Massachusetts.

Plott, C.R. (1993) Contingent valuation: a view of the conference and associated research, in J.A. Hausman (ed.) *Contingent Valuation: A Critical Assessment*. North-Holland, Amsterdam, pp. 468–478.

Plourde, C.G. (1972) A model of waste accumulation and disposal. *Canadian Journal of Economics* **5**, 199–225.

Plummer, M.L. and Hartman, R.C. (1986) Option value: a general approach. *Economic Inquiry* **24** (July), 455–471.

Pollock Shea, C. (1988) Shifting to renewable energy, in Starke, L. (ed) *State of the World 1988*. Worldwatch Institute, Washington, DC, pp. 62–82.

Porter, M. (1990) *The Competitive Advantage of Nations*. Free Press, New York.

Porter, R.C. (1982) The new approach to wilderness preservation through cost benefit analysis. *Journal of Environmental Economics and Management* **9**, 59–80.

Portes, R.D. (1970) The search for efficiency in the presence of externalities, in Streeten, P. (ed.) *Unfashionable Economics: Essays in Honour of Lord Balogh*. Weidenfeld and Nicholson, London, pp. 348–361.

Portney, P.R. (1989) Policy watch: economics and the Clean Air Act. *Journal of Economic Perspectives* **4**(4), 173–182.

Portney, P.R. (1990) Air pollution policy, in Portney, P. (ed.) *Public Policies for Environmental Protection*. Resources for the Future, Washington, DC.

Prell, M.A. (1996) Backstop technology and growth: doomsday or steady-state? *Journal of Environmental Economics and Management* **30**(2), 252–264.

Proops, J.L.R. and Atkinson, G. (1996) A practical sustainability criterion when there is international trade, in Fauchez, S., O'Connor, M. and van der Straaten, J. (eds) *Sustainable Development: Analysis and Public Policy*. Kluwer, Amsterdam.

Proops, J.L.R., Faber, M. and Wagenhals, G. (1993) *Reducing CO_2 Emissions: A Comparative Input–Output Study for Germany and the UK*. Springer-Verlag, Berlin.

Quinn, E.A. (1986) *Projected Use, Emission and Banks of Potential Ozone Depleting Substances*. Rand Corporation Report, No. 2282, EPA, Washington, DC.

Ramage, J. (1983) *Energy: A Guidebook*. Oxford University Press, Oxford.

Ramsey, F. (1928) A mathematical theory of savings. *Economic Journal*, **38**.

Randall, A. (1986), Human preferences, economics and the preservation of species, in Norton, B.G. (ed.) *The Preservation of Species.*: Princeton University Press, Princeton, New Jersey.

Randall, A. (1991) The value of biodiversity. *Ambio*, **20**, 64–68.

Randall, A. (1994) A difficulty with the travel cost method. *Land Economics* **70**, 88–96.

Randall, A. and Farmer, M.C. (1995) Benefits, costs, and the safe minimum standard of conservation, in D.W. Bromley (ed.) *The Handbook of Environmental Economics*. Blackwell, Oxford.

Randall, A. and Stoll, J.R. (1980) Consumer's surplus in commodity space. *American Economic Review* **70**, 449–455.

Randall, A., Ives, B. and Eastman, C. (1974) Bidding games for valuation or aesthetic environmental improvements. *Journal of Environmental Economics and Management* **1**, 132–149.

Rawls, J. (1971) *A Theory of Justice*. Oxford University Press, Cambridge, Massachusetts.

Ready, R.C. (1995) Environmental valuation under uncertainty, in Bromley, D.W. (ed.) *The Handbook of Environmental Economics*. Blackwell, Oxford.

Reaka-Kudla, M.L., Wilson, D.E. and Wilson, E.O. (eds) (1996) *Biodiversity II*. National Academy Press, Washington, DC.

Redclift, M. (1992) The meaning of sustainable development. *Geoforum* **23**(3), 395–403.

Regan, T. (1981) On the nature and possibility of an environmental ethic. *Environmental Ethics* **3**, 19–34.

Reilly, J.M., Edmonds, J.A., Gardner, R.H. and Brenkert, A.L. (1987) Uncertainty analysis of the IEA/ORAU CO_2 emissions model. *Energy Journal* **8**(3), 1–30.

Rennings, K. and Wiggering, H. (1997) Steps toward indicators of sustainable development: linking economic and ecological concepts. *Ecological Economics* **20**, 25–36.

Repetto, R. (ed.) (1985) *The Global Possible*. Yale University Press, New Haven, Connecticut.

Repetto, R. and Gillis, M. (1988) *Public Policies and the Misuse of Forest Resources*. Cambridge University Press, Cambridge.

Repetto, R., Wells, M., Beer, C. and Rossini, F. (1987) *Natural Resource Accounting for Indonesia*. World Resources Institute, Washington, DC.

Repetto, R., Magrath, W., Wells, M., Beer, C. and Rossini, F. (1989) *Wasting Assets: Natural Resources in the National Income Accounts*. World Resources Institute, Washington, DC.

Resource Assessment Commission (1991) *Kakadu Conservation Zone Inquiry: Final Report*. Australian Government Publishing Service, Canberra.

Rettig, R.B. (1995) Management regimes in ocean fisheries, in Bromley, D.W. (ed.) *The Handbook of Environmental Economics*. Blackwell, Oxford.

Ricardo, D. (1817) *Principles of Political Economy and Taxation*. Everyman, London (reprint, 1926).

Robbins, L. (1935) *An Essay on the Nature and Significance of Economic Science*. Macmillan, London.

Rose-Ackerman, S. (1973) Effluent charges: a critique. *Canadian Journal of Economics* **6**(4), 512–528.

Royal Commission on Environmental Pollution (1994) *Transport and the Environment*. Eighteenth Report, HMSO, London.

RSPB (1994) *Environmental Measures: Indicators for the UK Environment*. Royal Society for the Protection of Birds, Sandy, Bedfordshire.

Runge, C.F. (1995) Trade pollution and environmental protection, in Bromley, D.W. (ed.) *The Handbook of Environmental Economics*. Blackwell, Oxford.

Sagar, A.D. and Najam, A. (1998) The human development index: a critical review. *Ecological Economics* **25**, 249–264.

Sagoff, M. (1988) *The Economy of the Earth*. Cambridge University Press, Cambridge.

Sagoff, M. (1994) Should preferences count? *Land Economics* **70**, 127–144.

Sagoff, M. (1998) Aggregation and deliberation in valuing environmental public goods: a look beyond contingent pricing. *Ecological Economics* **24**, 213–230.

Sandler, T. (1993) Tropical deforestation: markets and market failure. *Land Economics* **69**, 225–233.

Sarokin, D. (1992) *Toxic Releases from Multinational Corporations*. The Public Data Project, Washington, DC.

Schaeffer, D.J., Herricks, E. and Kerster, H. (1988) Ecosystem health. I. Measuring ecosystem health. *Environmental Management* **12**(4), 445–455.

Schaeffer, M.D. (1957) Some consideration of population dynamics and economics in relation to the management of marine fisheries. *Journal of the Fisheries Research Board of Canada* **14**, 669–681.

Schkade, D.A. and Payne, J.W. (1993) Where do the numbers come from? How people respond to contingent valuation questions, in Hausman, J.A. (ed.) *Contingent Valuation: A Critical Assessment*. North-Holland, Amsterdam, pp. 271–293.

Schkade, D.A. and Payne, J.W. (1994) How people respond to contingent valuation questions: a verbal protocol analysis of willingness to pay for an environmental regulation. *Journal of Environmental Economics and Management* **26**, 88–109.

Schmalensee, R., Joskow, P.L., Ellerman, A.D., Montero, J.P. and Bailey, E.M. (1998) An interim evaluation of sulfur dioxide emission trading. *Journal of Economic Perspectives* **12**(3), 53–68.

Schmidheiny, S. (1992) *Changing Course: A Global Perspective on Development and the Environment*. MIT Press, Cambridge, Massachusetts.

Schneider, S.H. (1989) The greenhouse effect: science and policy. *Science* **243**, February, 771–781.

Schultz, W., D'Arge, R. and Brookshire, D. (1981b) Valuing environmental commodities: some recent experiments. *Land Economics* **57**, 151–172.

Schulze, W.D., Brookshire, D. and Saddler, T. (1981) The social rate of discount for nuclear waste storage. *Natural Resources Journal* **21**(4), 811–832.

Selden, T.M. and Song, D. (1992) *Environmental Quality and Development: Is There a Kuznets Curve for Air Pollution?* Department of Economics, Syracuse University, Syracuse, New York.

Sen, A.K. (1977) Rational fools: a critique of the behavioural foundations of economic theory. *Philosophy and Public Affairs* **16**, 317–344.

Sen, A.K. (1981) *Poverty and Famines: An Essay on Entitlement and Deprivation*. Clarendon Press, Oxford.

Sen, A. (1987) *On Ethics and Economics*. Blackwell, Oxford.

Seskin, E.P., Anderson, R. Jr and Reid, R.O. (1983) An empirical analysis of economic strategies for controlling air pollution. *Journal of Environmental Economics and Management* **10**, 112–124.

Shafik, N. and Bandyopadhyay, S. (1992) *Economic Growth and Environmental Quality: Time Series and Cross-Country Evidence*. Background Paper for the World Development Report 1992, The World Bank, Washington, DC.

Shogren, J.F., Herriges, J.A. and Govindasamy, R. (1993) Limits to environmental bonds. *Ecological Economics* **8**, 109–133.

Simon, J.L. (1981) *The Ultimate Resource*. Princeton University Press, Princeton, New Jersey.

Simon, J.L. and Kahn, H. (1984) *The Resourceful Earth*. Basil Blackwell, Oxford.

Simon, J.L. and Wildavsky, A. (1993) *Assessing the Empirical Basis of the 'Biodiversity Crisis'*. Competitive Enterprise Foundation, Washington, DC.

Singer, P. (1979) Not for humans only: the place of non-humans in environmental issues, in Goodpaster, K.E. and Sayes, K.M. (eds) *Ethics and Problems of the Twenty First Century*. University of Notre Dame Press, Notre Dame.

Singer, P. (1993) *Practical Ethics*, 2nd edition. Cambridge University Press, Cambridge.

Slade, M.E. (1982) Trends in natural-resource commodity prices: an analysis of the time domain. *Journal of Environmental Economics and Management* **9**, 122–137.

Smart, B. (1992) *Beyond Compliance: A New Industry View of the Environment*. World Resources Institute, Washington, DC.

Smith, A. (1776) The Wealth of Nations (1961 edition, edited by Cannan, E.). Methuen, London.

Smith, F.D.M., Daily, G.C. and Ehrlich, P.R. (1995) Human population dynamics and biodiversity loss, in Swanson, T.M. (ed.) *The Economics and Ecology of Biodiversity Decline*. Cambridge University Press, Cambridge.

Smith, S. (1993) Distributional implications of a European carbon tax, in Carraro, C. and Siniscalco, D. (eds) *The European Carbon Tax: An Economic Assessment*. Kluwer, Dordrecht.

Smith, V.L. (1972) Dynamics of waste accumulation versus recycling. *Quarterly Journal of Economics* **86**, 600–616.

Smith, V.K. (ed.) (1979) *Scarcity and Growth Reconsidered*. Johns Hopkins University Press, for Resources for the Future, Baltimore, Maryland.

Smith, V.K. (1992) Arbitrary values, good causes and premature verdicts. *Journal of Environmental Economics and Management* **22**, 71–89.

Smith, V.K. and Desvousges, W.H. (1986) *Measuring Water Quality Benefits*. Kluwer Nijhoff, Boston, Massachusetts.

Smith, V.K. and Kaoru, Y. (1990) Signals or noise? Explaining the variation in recreation benefit estimates. *American Journal of Agricultural Economics* **72**, 419–433.

Smith, V.K. and Krutilla, J.V. (1979) The economics of natural resource scarcity: an interpretive introduction, in Kerry Smith, V. (ed.) *Scarcity and Growth Reconsidered*. Johns Hopkins University Press, Baltimore, Maryland.

Smith, V.K., Desvousges, W.H. and McGivney, M.P. (1983) The opportunity cost of travel time in recreational demand models. *Land Economics* **59**, 259–278.

Solow, R.M. (1956) A contribution to the theory of economic growth. *Quarterly Journal of Economics* **70**, 65–94.

Solow, R.M. (1974a) Intergenerational equity and exhaustible resources. *Review of Economic Studies, Symposium*, May, 29–46.

Solow, R.M. (1974b) The economics of resources and the resources of economics. *American Economic Review* **64**, 1–14.

Solow, R. (1986) On the intergenerational allocation of natural resources. *Scandanavian Journal of Economics*, **88**(1), 141–149.

Solow, R.M. (1991) *Sustainability: An Economist's Perspective*. Paper presented at Woods Hole Oceanic Institution, Massachusetts, 14 June, and reprinted in Dorfman, R. and Dorfman, N. (eds) (1993) *Economics of the Environment: Selected Readings*, 3rd edition. W.W. Norton, New York.

Solow, R. (1992) *An Almost Practical Step Toward Sustainability*. Resources for the Future, Washington, DC.

Solow, R. (1993) An almost practical step toward sustainability. *Resources Policy*, September , 162–172.

>Spash, C.L. and Hanley, N.D. (1995) Preferences information and biodiversity preservation. *Ecological Economics* **12**, 191–208.

Spofford, W.O. Jr (1984) *Efficiency Properties of Alternative Source Control Policies for Meeting Ambient Air Quality Standards: An Empirical Application to the Lower Delaware Valley*. Discussion Paper D-118, November, Resources for the Future. Washington, DC.

Stavins, R.N. (1998) What can we learn from the grand policy experiment? Lessons from SO_2 allowance trading. *Journal of Economic Perspectives* **12**(3), 69–88.

Stebbing, A.R.D. (1992) Environmental capacity and the precautionary principle. *Marine Pollution Bulletin* **24**(6), 287–295.

Stern, D.I., Common, M.S. and Barbier, E.B. (1994) *Economic Growth and Environmental Degradation: A Critique of the Environmental Kuznets Curve*. Discussion Papers in Environmental Economics and Environmental Management, No. 9409, The University of York, August.

Stern, D.I., Common, M. and Barbier, E.B. (1996) Economic growth and environmental degradation: the environmental Kuznets curve and sustainable development. *World Development* **24**, 1151–1160.

Stevens, T.H., Echeverria, J., Glass, R.J., Hager, T. and More, T.A. (1991) Measuring the existence value of wildlife: what do CVM estimates really show? *Land Economics* **67**, 390–400.

Stiglitz, J.E. (1974) Growth with exhaustible resources: efficient and optimal growth paths. *Review of Economic Studies, Symposium* May, 139–152.

Stockhammer, E., Hochreiter, H., Obermayr, B. and Steiner, K. (1997) The index of sustainable economic welfare (ISEW) as an alternative to GDP in measuring economic welfare: the results of the Austrian (revised) ISEW calculation 1955–1992. *Ecological Economics* **21**, 19–34.

Stollery, K.R. (1983) Mineral depletion with cost as the extraction limit: a model applied to the behaviour of prices in the nickel industry. *Journal of Environmental Economics and Management* **10**, 151–165.

Streeten, P. (1987) *What Price Food? Agricultural Policies in Developing Countries*. St Martin's Press, New York.

Swallow, S.K. and Wear, D.N. (1993) Spatial interactions in multiple use forestry and substitution and wealth effects for the single stand. *Journal of Environmental Economics and Management* **25**, 103–120.

Swallow, S.K., Parks, P.J. and Wear, D.N. (1990) Policy-relevant nonconvexities in the production of multiple forest benefits. *Journal of Environmental Economics and Management* **19**, 264–280.

Swanson, T.M. (ed.) (1995a) *Intellectual Property Rights and Biodiversity Conservation*. Cambridge University Press, Cambridge.

Swanson, T.M. (ed.) (1995b) *The Economics and Ecology of Biodiversity Decline*. Cambridge University Press, Cambridge.

Symons, E.J., Proops, J. and Gay, P.W. (1991) Carbon taxes consumer demand and carbon dioxide emissions: a simulation analysis for the UK. *Fiscal Studies* **15**, 19–43.

Symons, E.J., Proops, J.L.R. and Gay, P.W. (1993) Carbon taxes, consumer demand and carbon dioxide emission: a simulation analysis for the UK. Mimeo, Department of Economics, University of Manchester, Manchester, UK.

Tahvonen, O. (1995) Dynamics of pollution control when damage is sensitive to the rate of pollution accumulation. *Environmental and Resource Economics* **5**, 9–27.

Tietenberg, T.H. (1980) Transferable discharge permits and the control of stationary source air pollution: a survey and synthesis. *Land Economics* **56**, 391–415.

Tietenberg, T.H. (1984) *Marketable Emission Permits in Theory and Practice*. Paper presented at the Conference, Economics of Energy and Environmental Problems, Yxtaholm, Sweden, 6–10 August.

Tietenberg, T.H. (1989) Acid rain reduction credits. *Challenge* 32, March/April.

Tietenberg, T.H. (1990) Economic instruments for environmental regulation. *Oxford Review of Economic Policy* **6**(1), 17–34.

Tietenberg, T. (1992) *Environmental and Natural Resource Economics*, 3rd edition. HarperCollins, New York.

Tietenberg, T.H. (1995) Transferable discharge permits and global warming, in Bromley, D.W. (ed.) *The Handbook of Environmental Economics*. Blackwell, Oxford.

Todaro, M.P. (1989) *Economic Development in the Third World*, 4th edition. Longman, New York.

Toman, M., Pezzey, J. and Krautkraemer, J. (1993) *Economic Theory and 'Sustainability'*. Department of Economics, University College London, Discussion Paper in Economics No. 93-15, August.

Toman, M.A., Pezzey, J. and Krautkraemer, J. (1995) Neoclassical economic growth theory and 'sustainability', in Bromley, D.W. (ed.) *The Handbook of Environmental Economics*. Blackwell. Oxford.

Turner, R.K. and Bateman, I. (1990) *A Critical Review of Monetary Assessment Methods and Techniques*. Environmental Appraisal Group, University of East Anglia.

UN (1989a) *World Population Prospects 1988*. Population Studies No. 106, United Nations Department of International Economic and Social Affairs, New York.

UN (1989b) *Levels and Trends of Contraceptive Use as Assessed in 1988*. Population Studies No. 110, United Nations Department of International Economic and Social Affairs, New York.

UN (1990) *Demographic Yearbook 1988*. United Nations Department of International Economic and Social Affairs, New York.

UN (1996) United Nations Population Division, *World Population Prospects 1950–2050* (The 1996 Revision), on diskette, United Nations, New York.

UN (1997) Critical Trends: Global Change and Sustainable Development United Nations, New York.

UNCTC (United Nations Centre for Transnational Corporations) (1992) *International Accounting*. UNCTC, New York.

UNDP (1990) United Nations Development Programme,

Human Development Report 1990. Oxford University Press, New York.

UNDP (1995) United Nations Development Programme, *Human Development Report 1995*. Oxford University Press, New York.

UNDP (1996) United Nations Development Programme, *Human Development Report 1996*. Oxford University Press, New York.

UNDP (1997) United Nations Development Programme, *Human Development Report 1997*. Oxford University Press, New York.

UNDP (1998) United Nations Development Programme, *Human Development Report 1998*. Oxford University Press, New York.

UNEP (1987) United Nations Environment Programme, *Environmental Data Report*, 1st edition 1987/88. Basil Blackwell, Oxford.

UNEP (1989) United Nations Environment Programme, *Environmental Data Report*, 2nd edition 1989/90. Basil Blackwell, Oxford.

UNEP (1991) United Nations Environment Programme, *Environmental Data Report*, 3rd edition. Basil Blackwell, Oxford.

UNEP (1995) *Global Biodiversity Assessment*. Cambridge University Press, Cambridge.

United Nations (1992) *Integrated Environmental and Economic Accounting*. United Nations, New York.

United Nations (1993a) *Systems of National Accounts 1993*. United Nations, New York.

United Nations (1993b) *Earth Summit: Agenda 21, the United Nations Programme of Action*. United Nations Department of Public Information, New York.

United Nations FAO (Food and Agriculture Organisation) (1979, 1981, 1985, 1989, 1994, 1995) *The State of Food and Agriculture*. Rome, Italy.

United Nations Population Fund (1995) *The State of World Population 1995*. UNFPA, New York.

US Department of Commerce National Oceanic and Atmospheric Administration (1993) *Natural Resource Damage Assessments under the Oil Pollution Act of 1990. Federal Register* **58**(10), 4601–4614.

Usher, D. (1980) *The Measurement of Economic Growth*. Blackwell, Oxford.

Van Pelt, M.J.F. (1993) Ecologically sustainable development and project appraisal in developing countries. *Ecological Economics* **7**, 19–42.

van den Bergh, J.C.J.M. and van der Straaten, J. (eds) (1994) *Concepts, Methods and Policy for Sustainable Development: Critique and New Approaches*. Island Press, Washington, DC.

Van Houtven, G. and Cropper, M.L. (1996) When is a life too costly to save? The evidence from US environmental regulations. *Journal of Environmental Economics and Management* **30**, 348–368.

Varian, H.R. (1987) *Intermediate Microeconomics*, 2nd edition. W.W. Norton, New York. (First edition, 1980.)

Vatn, A. and Bromley, D. (1995) Choices without prices without apologies, in Bromley, D.W. (ed.) *The Handbook of Environmental Economics*. Blackwell, Oxford.

Vaze, P. (1998) Environmental input–output tables for the United Kingdom, in Vaze, P. and Barron, J.B. (eds) *UK Environmental Accounts 1998*. The Stationery Office, London.

Vaze, P. (1998a). Environmental accounts – valuing the

depletion of oil and gas reserves, in Vaze, P. (ed.) *UK Environmental Accounts 1998*. The Stationery Office, London.

Vaze, P. (ed.) (1998b) *UK Environmental Accounts 1998*. The Stationery Office, London.

Victor, D.G., Rautsiala, K. and Skolnikoff, A. (eds) (1998) *The Implementation and Effectiveness of International Environmental Commitments*. MIT Press, Cambridge, Massachusetts.

Victor, P. (1972) *Pollution: Economy and Environment*. Toronto University Press, Toronto.

Vincent, J.R. (1992) The tropical timber trade and sustainable development. *Science* **256**, 19 June 1651–1655.

Vincent, J.R. and Blinkley, C.S. (1993) Efficient multiple-use forestry may require land-use specialisation. *Land Economics* **69**, 370–376.

Viscusi, W.K. (1992) *Fatal Tradeoffs. Public and Private Responsibilities for Risk*. Oxford University Press, Oxford.

Viscusi, W.K. (1993) The value of risks to life and health. *Journal of Economic Literature* **31**, 1912–1946.

Vitousek, P.M., Ehrlich, P.R., Ehrlich, A.H. and Matson, P.A. (1986) Human appropriation of the products of photosynthesis. *Bioscience* **36**, 368–373.

Wackernagel, M. and Rees, W.E. (1997) Perceptual and structural barriers to investing in natural capital: economics from an ecological footprint perspective. *Ecological Economics* **2**, 3–24.

Walras, L (1954) *Elements of Pure Economics*. Richard D. Irwin, Homewood, Illinois.

Warnock, G.J. (1971) *The Object of Morality*. Methuen, New York.

Watson, R.A. (1979) Self-consciousness and the rights of non-human animals. *Environmental Ethics* **1**(2), 99.

Watt, K.E.F. (1973) *Principles of Environmental Science*. McGraw-Hill, New York.

WCED (World Commission on Environment and Development) (1987) *Our Common Future*. Oxford University Press, Oxford, and United Nations, New York.

WCU (World Conservation Union) (1990) *Environmental Issues in Eastern Europe: Setting an Agenda*. The Royal Institute of Environmental Affairs, Energy and Environment Programme, London.

Weisbrod, B.A. (1964) Collective consumption services of individual consumption goods. *Quarterly Journal of Economics* **78**(3), 471–477.

Weitzman, M.L. (1976) On the welfare significance of national product in a dynamic economy. *Quarterly Journal of Economics* **90**, 156–162.

Weitzman, M.L. (1997) Sustainability and technical progress. *Scandanavian Journal of Economics* **99**, 1–13.

Weizsacker, E.U. (1989) *Global Warming and Environmental Taxes*. International Conference on Atmosphere, Climate and Man, Torino, Italy, January.

Weizsacker, E.U. and Jesinghaus, J. (1992) *Ecological Tax Reform: A Policy Proposal For Sustainable Development*. Zed Books, New Jersey.

Weizsacker, E.U., Lovins, A.B. and Lovins, L.H. (1997) *Factor Four: Doubling Wealth, Halving Resource Use*. Earthscan, London.

Whalley, J. and Wigle, R.M. (1989) *Cutting CO_2 Emissions: The Effect of Alternative Policy Approaches*. Paper presented at the NBER conference on AGE modelling, San Diego, California.

Whalley, J. and Wigle, R.M. (1990) *The International Incidence of Carbon Taxes*. Paper presented at conference on Economic Policy Responses to Global Warming, Rome, 4–6 October, October 1990 revision. National Bureau of Economic Research, Cambridge, MA; and Wilfrid Laurier University, Waterloo, Canada. Published in *Energy Journal* (1991) **11**(4).

Whalley, J. and Wigle, R. (1991) The international incidence of carbon taxes, in Dornbusch, R. and Poterba, J. (eds) *Economic Policy Responses to Global Warming*. MIT Press, Cambridge, Massachusetts.

WHO (1995) *The World Health Report 1995: Bridging the Gaps*. The United Nations World Health Organization (WHO), Geneva.

Wilen, J.E. (1985) Bioeconomics of renewable resource use, in Kneese, A.V. and Sweeney, J.L. (eds) *Handbook of Natural Resource and Energy Economics*, vol. 1, Elsevier, Amsterdam, ch. 2.

Williams, R.H. (1990a) Low-cost strategy for coping with CO_2 emission limits (a critique of CO_2 emission limits: an economic cost analysis for the USA by Alan Manne and Richard Richels), Centre for Energy and Environmental Studies, Princeton University, Princeton, USA. Published in *Energy Journal* (1990) **11**(4).

Williams, R.H. (1990b) *Will Constraining Fossil Fuel Carbon Dioxide Emissions Cost so Much?* Centre for Energy and Environmental Studies, Princeton University, Princeton, New Jersey.

Willig, R. D. (1976) Consumer's surplus without apology. *American Economic Review* **66**, 589–597.

Willis, K. and Garrod, G. (1991a) An individual travel cost method of evaluating forest recreation *Journal of Agricultural Economics* **42**, 33–42

Willis, K.G. and Garrod, G.D. (1991b) *The Hedonic Price Method and the Valuation of Countryside Characteristics*. ESRC Countryside Change Initiative Working Paper 14, University of Newcastle.

Wilson, E.O. (1980) Extract from article published in *Harvard Magazine*, January–February.

Wilson, E.O. (ed.) (1988) *BioDiversity*. National Academy of Science Press, Washington, DC.

Wilson, E.O. (1992) *The Diversity of Life*. Harvard University Press, Harvard, Massachusetts.

Winpenny (1991) *Policy appraisal and the Environment. A Guide for Government Departments*. HMSO, London.

Winter, I.A. (1992) The trade and welfare effects of greenhouse gas abatement: a survey of empirical estimates, in Anderson, K. and Blackhurst, R. (eds) *The Greening of World Trade Issues*. Harvester Wheatsheaf, New York.

WMO (World Meteorological Organisation and United Nations Environment Programme) (1991) *Scientific Assessment of Stratospheric Ozone, 1991*. Executive Summary, 22 October.

World Bank (1993) Mitchell, D.O. and Ingco, M.D. *The World Food Outlook*. World Bank, Washington, DC.

World Bank (1995) *Monitoring Environmental Progress: A Report on Work in Progress*. International Bank for Reconstruction and Development, Washington, DC.

World Bank (1996) *Monitoring Environmental Progress: Expanding the Measure of Wealth*. International Bank for Reconstruction and Development, Washington, DC.

World Commission on Environment and Development (Brundtland Commission) (1987) *Our Common Future*. Oxford University Press, Oxford.

World Energy Council (1993) *Energy for Tomorrow's World: The Realities, the Real Options, and the Agenda for Achievement*. Kogan Page, London, and St Martin's Press, New York.

WR (1990) *World Resources 1990–91*. World Resources Institute, Oxford University Press, Oxford.

WR (1992) *World Resources 1992–93*. World Resources Institute, Oxford University Press, Oxford.

WR (1994) *World Resources 1994–95*. World Resources Institute, Oxford University Press, Oxford.

WR (1996) *World Resources 1996–97*. World Resources Institute, Oxford University Press, New York.

WR (1998) *World Resources 1998–99*. World Resources Institute, Oxford University Press, New York.

WWF (1993) *The Right to Know: The Promise of Low-Cost Public Inventories of Toxic Chemicals*. World Wildlife Fund, Washington, DC.

Xie, J. (1996) *Environmental Policy Analysis: A General Equilibrium Approach*. Avebury, Aldershot.

Young, J.T. (1991) Is the entropy law relevant to the economics of natural resource scarcity? *Journal of Environmental Economics and Management* **21**(2), 169–179.

Young, M.D. (1990) Natural resource accounting, in Common, M.S. and Dovers, S. (eds) *Moving toward Global Sustainability: Policies and Implications for Australia*. Centre for Continuing Education, Australian National University, Canberra.

Young, M.D. (1992) *Sustainable Investment and Natural Resource Use: Equity, Environmental Integrity and Economic Efficiency*. United Nations Scientific and Cultural Organization, Paris.

Name Index

Subject Index